Russia in the Age of Catherine the Great

RUSSIA

in the Age of Catherine the Great

Isabel de Madariaga

New Haven and London
Yale University Press

To M. M.

Library of Congress Cataloging in Publication Data

De Madariaga, Isabel, 1919–
Russia in the age of Catherine the Great

Bibliography: p.
Includes index.
1. Russia – History – Catherine II, 1762–1796.
2. Catherine II, Empress of Russia, 1729–1796.
I. Title.
DK171.D45   947'.063   80-21993
ISBN 0-300-02515-7

Printed in the United States of America

10 9 8 7 6 5 4 3 2

Contents

CONTENTS

Part VIII   The Porte, Poland and the French Revolution

Part IX   Domestic Problems

Part X   The Declining Years

Maps

Preface

No full-scale history of the reign of Catherine II of Russia has appeared since A. Brückner, Professor of History at the University of Dorpat in Russian Estonia, published his *Katharina die Zweite* in Berlin in 1883.[1] The Russian historian, V.A. Bil'basov, embarked on what was to be a monumental history of her reign in several volumes at the end of the last century. Only the first volume was published in Russia in 1895 ; the work was then banned by the censorship, and eventually the first two volumes, dealing with Catherine's life as grand duchess and the first two years of her reign, were published in Russian in Berlin in 1900.[2]

Since then, most of the books which have been published belong to the biographical or *biographie romancée* variety. Yet considering the enormous significance of Catherine's long reign in the forward march of Russia towards the achievement of its national political and cultural aims, it is strange that her own role in the process should have been so neglected by historians, particularly since she was no *roi fainéant,* but a highly professional practitioner of the art of ruling.

Moreover, since Brückner's work appeared, not only has much new source material been published, but the craft of the historian has taken a new direction. Historians ask different questions, and attempt to grasp the long-term direction given to historical development by government policies. A whole school of Marxist historiography has arisen, within and without the USSR, which has opened up many new insights and given rise to many controversial judgments.

There need be no excuse, therefore, for embarking on an enterprise which has admittedly proved more lengthy and complex than when it was first light-heartedly undertaken some twelve years ago. A number of serious difficulties still face the historian of Catherinian Russia. Published primary sources are abundant, but very widely scattered in a number of historical journals and collections. More serious is the lack of up-to-date monographs on many aspects of her policy. There is no modern study of the implementation of the local government reform of 1775 to follow Got'ye's magisterial work on local administration in the period 1727–75.[3] In general, moreover, Soviet historians have tended to regard 1775 as a dividing line beyond which they do not go. Thus the distinguished historian S.M. Troitsky (whose early death is much to be lamented) covers only the middle of the eighteenth century, including the early part of Catherine's reign, both in his work on Russian financial policy, and in his study of the nobility.[4] Nineteenth-century Russian historians, and their twentieth-century Soviet, British and American counterparts, have been drawn to the study of the Russian élite, the noble class of *dvoryanstvo.* But too many antiquated notions have been perpetuated because no fresh archival research has been carried out on the way the new *soslovnyy* or 'estate' institutions actually functioned after 1775. There is not one single study of the working of a noble provincial or *uezd* assembly over a number of years. Similarly, in spite of the proliferation of Union Republican histories there is no systematic study of how local institutions actually worked. Much less attention, moreover, has been given to the urban estate as a whole, than to the nobility and not one monograph has been devoted to the implementation of the Charter to the Towns since Kizewetter's *Gorodovoye Polozheniye* appeared in 1909.[5] Russian local government still awaits its Sidney and Beatrice Webb.

Like many others working in Russian history, I am fully aware that the space devoted to particular aspects of Russian policy does not reflect their importance but the amount of material available. I have been compelled to write the kind of history which can be written (given the present state of research), not the history which ought to be written. Nevertheless the structure of the present work is on the whole the result of deliberate choice. In my view nearly all general histories of Russia are weighted in favour of social and economic history and devote far more space to the peasantry than do corresponding histories of England or France. It is true that the political history of these countries is far richer than that of Russia, but this is no reason why Russian political history should be disregarded in favour of massive chapters on the enserfed peasantry leading to an eschatological *dénouement* in 1861. I have, therefore, deliberately chosen to emphasize political history, including foreign policy and war, and administrative history, at the expense of economic history. I have also chosen to concentrate on Russia's European face (as distinct from the multi-ethnic empire still in formation) in which the only political class was the nobility and the ruling national group was composed of Great Russians, Ukrainians, and Baltic Germans. These groups made up the cadres of the Russian government and marked the political culture of Russia with their own – dissimilar – traditions.

For reasons of space I have also approached the cultural life of Russia very much from the angle of the court. The lively literary and artistic life of Russia in the second half of the eighteenth century would require as much space again as I have taken up here. Catherine herself played a vital role on this stage by providing material and moral encouragement to the process of assimilation of European culture – it was part of her conception of the duties of a ruler. It is from this perspective, therefore, that I have approached the cultural history of her reign.

To my mind, much modern Russian and Soviet historiography, both in general works and in specialized monographs and articles, suffers from too much interpretation mounted on too few facts. I have endeavoured to redress this balance by attempting to give a portrayal of 'wie es eigentlich gewesen war', by providing new facts and bringing together known ones within the covers of one book. I have refrained from reifying trends and institutions, and attributing intentions to inanimate bodies. I have also attempted to distinguish between the ruler's intentions – in so far as they can be accurately ascertained – and the sometimes unexpected results of a policy.

Other difficulties face the historian of Russia, notably the impossibility of finding exact translations in Western political and social terminology for the social and political institutions of Russia. I have translated the Russian *sosloviye* as 'estate', but the Russian 'estates' never acquired the corporate status and political weight of their Western counterparts. Just as complex is the word *samoderzhaviye* ('autocracy') which in the eighteenth century meant simply 'monarchy' or 'sovereignty'. I have kept the use of Russian terms to a minimum, but have provided a glossary of those which appear most frequently in an appendix. I also append a list of basic measurements of weight, distance and volume. Some confusion is caused by the fact that Russia had two capitals : St Petersburg and Moscow. I have tried to make clear to which I am referring. Finally, I have used old-style dating throughout (eleven days behind Western Europe), except in chapters on foreign policy and war where I have used double dates (Julian and Gregorian).

The chapter on the foundation of the Russian educational system by Catherine II is a modified version of an article which was first published in the *Slavonic and East European Review,* vol. 57, No 3, July 1979, and is reprinted with the permission of the Editorial Board. I must also thank the Royal Archives of Stockholm and the Archives des Affaires Etrangères at the Quai d'Orsay in Paris for permission to quote unpublished documents, and the Public Record Office for permission to quote from the diary of her visit to Russia kept by Gertrude Harris, the sister of Sir James.

Finally I owe a very great debt to many people in many libraries who have given me unstinting help. In particular I am greatly indebted to all the staff of the Library at the School of Slavonic and East European Studies, and specifically to Mrs H. Feuerstein and to Mrs J. Conolly, who has been invaluable in securing otherwise unobtainable works on inter-library loan and has also assisted by translating the occasional Polish text for me ; I could not have written this book without the rich collection of the London Library, and I record here my thanks to its Librarian and staff. And for years I have drawn on the magnificent collection of books, the helpful assistance of the staff and the inspiration of the beautiful reading room of the British Museum Library, as it was when I first began to work there.

In the course of writing this book I have had the opportunity to discuss various aspects of it with my colleagues at the School of Slavonic and East European Studies, in the Study Group on Eighteenth-Century Russia, and in various seminars, and have greatly benefited from their criticisms and suggestions. I must thank Professor Olga Crisp for many illuminating discussions on economic history. Dr A.G. Cross, Dr R. Bartlett, and Dr D. Budgen read a number of chapters and gave me valuable advice and assistance. Professor J. Łojek of the University of Warsaw read the chapters dealing with Poland and was most helpful even if I did not always agree with him. Professor D. Ransel read the whole manuscript and made many very constructive criticisms. Professor Franco Venturi kindly supplied me with his own edition of Cesare Beccaria's *magnum opus*.

Finally, I owe a great debt to Professor Ragnhild Hatton who went through the whole manuscript with an eagle eye and much improved its presentation in every way. If I have not always followed my distinguished mentors, the fault is mine. Mrs Judith Hicks did wonders with a messy manuscript, and Dr J. Hartley coped with the Index. I record my gratitude to them.

For years, whenever I saw my father, his first words were 'how is Catherine ?' It is a great grief to record that he did not live to see a work which he so warmly encouraged and in which he expressed so constant an interest.

Highgate, 1980

Isabel de Madariaga

Prologue

At eight o'clock in the morning of 26 June 1762 a travelling carriage drew up outside the barracks of the Izmailov regiment on the outskirts of St Petersburg. A guards officer descended and disappeared hastily inside. A few moments later, as a drummer alerted the soldiers, a woman of about thirty, dressed in dusty black, with her hair unpowdered, was handed down from the carriage and almost engulfed by a crowd of shouting, huzzaing soldiers. Shortly afterwards the crowd parted, and an elderly Orthodox priest advanced bearing aloft the cross. In loud tones, officers and men, led by their colonel, Count Kyrill Razumovsky, hetman of Little Russia,[1] swore allegiance to the newly proclaimed Empress Catherine, autocrat of all the Russias. By what strange combination of circumstances had this woman, born Sophia of Anhalt Zerbst, attained such eminence ?

The new empress was the daughter of a scion of an impoverished junior branch of the house of Anhalt, Prince Christian August, who had risen in the service of the King of Prussia, and had married in 1727, when he was thirty-seven, the sixteen-year-old Princess Johanna Elizabeth of Holstein-Gottorp, a marriage which connected him indirectly with two reigning houses in Europe. The House of Holstein-Gottorp had acquired, by geography and by marriage, a key position in the politics of the Baltic. In defence of their interests against Denmark, the dukes of Holstein-Gottorp had sought the alliance of Sweden. The mother of Charles xi was a princess of Holstein-Gottorp and his elder daughter Hedwig Sophia married Frederick ii, Duke of Holstein-Gottorp. The duke's younger brother Christian August was eventually elected Prince-Bishop of Lübeck Eutin, and it was his daughter, Johanna Elizabeth, who gave birth on 21 April/2 May 1729 to a princess, Sophia, in Stettin, where her husband the Prince of Anhalt Zerbst was stationed with his regiment.

Sophia, or Figchen as she was nicknamed, was very simply brought up. Her education was supervised mainly by a French Huguenot, Babette Cardel, who taught her the manners and graces of French society and introduced her to the pleasures of the best French classical literature of the time. In her childhood Sophia was evidently a bossy tomboy, indifferent to dolls, sewing and embroidery. In her memoirs she suggests that because she believed herself to be plain, she strove all the more to be witty.[2]

Sophia's mother, however, had access to a wider stage than Stettin provided. She had been brought up by her godmother, the dowager Duchess Elizabeth Sophia Maria of Brunswick Wolfenbüttel, who had arranged her marriage and paid her dowry. Johanna spent several months each year with her benefactress, and took her daughter with her. Sophia was introduced to one of the most brilliant courts of Germany, far outshining the Prussia of Frederick William I. Among her childhood acquaintances and playmates were Prince Louis of Brunswick, the future tutor to the Stadholder of the Netherlands; Prince Ferdinand of Brunswick, the future general in Prussian service ; and the future Queen Juliana Maria of Denmark. She also met Prince Henry of Prussia, and his sister, Princess Louise, the future Queen of Sweden, in Berlin. A contemporary account describes her at this time as 'well made, with a good figure and taller than average. She was not pretty, but her expression was agreeable ; her frank eyes and pleasing smile make her very attractive.'[3] But there was no reason as yet, either in Sophia's ancestry, which was not particularly distinguished, nor in her disposition and education, to suppose that she was singled out for a remarkable destiny. Her importance lay not in her character, but in her circumstances.

The year 1740 brought about a fundamental change in the dynastic position of the House of Holstein-Gottorp. At a time when his claims had met with but little support elsewhere, the reigning duke, Charles Frederick, had turned to Sweden's enemy, Russia, for assistance. Peter I had systematically used his nieces and his daughters to extend and consolidate Russian influence on the Baltic and in the Holy Roman Empire, and a marriage was arranged between his elder daughter Anna and the Duke of Holstein-Gottorp, which eventually took place in 1727. It was short-lived ; Anna Petrovna died of tuberculosis three months after the birth of her only son, Charles Peter, on 10/21 February 1728.

During the reigns of Peter II of Russia (1727–30) and of Anna Ivanovna (1730–40) the fortunes of the Duke of Holstein-Gottorp and of Peter I's grandson were in eclipse. Before her death in spring 1740, Anna Ivanovna proclaimed her great-nephew – known as Ivan Antonovich – son of her niece Anna Leopoldovna of Mecklenburg by her marriage to Anton Ulrich of Brunswick Lüneburg, as her heir. But Anna Ivanovna's elaborate planning came to nothing when Peter I's daughter Elizabeth Petrovna seized power in November 1740, sweeping away the baby emperor Ivan and his German family, who disappeared into captivity and exile. However Elizabeth too was faced with the problem of choosing a successor. She was then in her early thirties, but there was little likelihood of her marrying and giving birth to an heir. The many efforts to secure a good marriage for her had all failed in the past and she had sought consolation elsewhere during the years when she was held at arm's length by Anna Ivanovna. In all probability by the time she seized the throne the devout Elizabeth had been secretly married at a religious ceremony to Aleksey Razumovsky, the handsome Ukrainian peas-

and lad whose beautiful voice had brought him to the notice first of the Church hierarchy, then of the Grand Duchess Elizabeth herself. If such a marriage existed it could not be acknowledged publicly and Elizabeth, though not a Virgin Queen, followed the policy of her illustrious namesake in remaining officially single. She had favourites to whom she gave herself generously. There are occasional rumours that she had a number of children, but they have never been substantiated, and no child of hers was ever unofficially acknowledged.

Among Elizabeth's early suitors had been one of whom she preserved a most tender memory, who had died before the marriage could actually take place. This was Charles Augustus of Holstein-Gottorp, elder brother of Johanna Elizabeth, Sophia's mother. Sentiment thus drew Elizabeth doubly to the Holstein family. Her beloved sister Anna had married the reigning duke ; she herself had been betrothed to the duke's cousin. The choice as her heir of her nephew Charles Peter, reigning Duke of Holstein since the death of his father in 1739, was obvious. It was moreover politically advantageous for Russia to secure Charles Peter, in order to prevent the union of Holstein-Gottorp and Sweden which might occur if the boy were to be recognized as heir to the throne of Sweden. For Charles Peter was also the closest claimant to the Swedish throne, as the grandson of the elder sister of Charles XII, whose younger sister Ulrika Eleonora and her husband Frederick of Hesse, then reigning, were childless.

The accession of Elizabeth in Russia had been encouraged, indeed almost engineered, by France as part of a complicated policy aimed at breaking the alliance between Austria and Russia and throwing Russia back into Muscovite sloth at a time when France, in alliance with Prussia, was forcing Maria Theresa of Austria to fight for her inheritance. Sweden had played her part in the plot by invading Russia in 1740 in the hope of recovering some of the territory lost to Russia at the Peace of Nystadt of 1721. But the Swedes had been defeated by the Russian troops, and in the Peace of Abo in 1743, which put an end to the war, Elizabeth not only forced the Swedes to give up all plans to proclaim Charles Peter of Holstein as heir to the Swedish throne ; she imposed on them her own candidate, namely Adolf Frederick of Holstein-Gottorp, Prince-Bishop of Lübeck in succession to his father, and elder brother of Johanna Elizabeth.

The change in the fortunes of her house did not leave Johanna Elizabeth unaffected. A few years before, when Sophia and her second cousin, Charles Peter of Holstein, had met briefly at Eutin, court gossip had coupled their names. Once Charles Peter had been taken to Russia in 1743 and proclaimed grand duke, Sophia too began to believe that her fate was bound up with his : 'of all the suitors offered to me he was the most important.' Meanwhile Johanna Elizabeth used every opportunity to bring herself and her daughter to the notice of the Empress of Russia and made sure that portraits of Sophia were forwarded to the court.

But when Sophia was about fourteen her fate seemed about to take a very different direction. Her mother's younger brother, Georg-Ludwig, who was only twenty-four, fell in love with his niece. Georg-Ludwig sighed and groaned and finally declared his hopes of marrying the thunderstruck Sophia, who had envisaged no such *dénouement*. His wooing succeeded to the extent of securing the young girl's agreement to marry him provided her parents consented. Even reading between the lines of the heroine's own account of this episode, it seems that the lovesick Georg-Ludwig must have been – if only unintentionally – instrumental in arousing her adolescent sexuality. She herself describes the violence with which she 'galloped astride her pillows in bed' and the passion which she developed at this age for riding, which later in her life undoubtedly played a big part in her psychological and sensual make-up.[4]

Just at this time, however, Johanna's intrigues in Russia bore fruit. She was invited to pay a visit to the Russian court, together with her daughter, in January 1744. The object of such a visit was clear, though unstated : Sophia had been selected as the prospective bride for the Grand Duke Peter of Russia, and it would require a major blunder to break off the match once mother and daughter were actually on the spot. Yet at this moment Johanna hesitated, moved perhaps by affection for her younger brother ('mais mon frère Georges, que dira-t-il ?', she asked Sophia), perhaps by fear for her daughter's future in such an uncertain land.[5] According to the young Sophia herself, it was she who at this moment nerved both her parents to agree to the journey to Russia, arguing that her lovelorn uncle 'ne peut que souhaiter ma fortune et mon bonheur'.

It would be too simple to assume that Sophia's determination to pursue the Russian marriage already reflected her ambition to rule. She was after all only fourteen, and though she had been both flattered and excited by her uncle's interest in her, her heart does not seem to have been touched. Her first impressions of her second cousin Charles Peter of Holstein-Gottorp as a boy of ten had not been disagreeable, and Russia represented a greater position and a far wider stage than would be hers if she married a penniless younger son in her mother's family. Since marriage was the only respectable provision for a young woman of her social position it was natural to seek the best possible marriage – love might, or might not, come after.

The invitation to mother and daughter – Prince Christian August was not included – was the outcome of much thought and manoeuvring in Russia, where the marriage of Charles Peter, now the Grand Duke Peter Fyodorovich, was the object of incessant intrigue. The choice of his bride would provide an indication of the foreign policy Elizabeth's government would follow. Hence rumour spoke now of a French bride, now of a Saxon princess, now even of an English one.[6]

The Russian vice-chancellor, A.P. Bestuzhev Ryumin, who dominated foreign policy and sought to build up a coalition of Austria, Britain and the United Provinces, and Russia against Prussia and France, urged the claims of a Saxon princess. Frederick II countered by suggesting, through his envoy in Russia, the offspring of various German houses, including 'the young princess of Zerbst'.[7] Quite independently, Elizabeth had already selected Sophia of Anhalt

Zerbst. She was of the Holstein-Gottorp line, she was a Protestant, and she came from a minor German family which could put forward no extravagant claims and create no political complications.

Johanna set out with her daughter from Zerbst on 10 January 1744 NS for Berlin. Sophia took a fond farewell of the father she was never to see again. He in turn handed Johanna a long memorandum of guidance for his daughter, urging her to stay faithful to Lutheranism, to obey the empress in all things, to endeavour to please the grand duke, not to play cards for high stakes and not to interfere in matters of state.[8] Sophia was to disregard a good deal of this advice in due time.

In Berlin, Frederick II took the opportunity to inspect the young girl who was later to stand up to him with such tenacity, and to indoctrinate the mother with his own views of the Russian court, warning her against Bestuzhev and engaging her to act as an unofficial Prussian agent.[9]

The discomforts of travelling modestly and incognito as Countess Rheindorp and her daughter ceased abruptly when Johanna crossed the Russian border towards the end of January 1744, to be met with gun salutes, official escorts and, more important in the circumstances, presents of sable furs. Mother and daughter arrived in Moscow on 9/20 February, just in time for the birthday of the grand duke on the tenth of the month. Peter hastened to visit his bride, and then escorted both ladies to the empress's chamber. In her memoirs, Sophia describes the deep impression made upon her by the beauty and majesty of Elizabeth, who was then in her prime : tall, with an imposing figure, a beautiful complexion and lovely hair, radiant blue eyes and regular features marred only by the 'potato' nose common in Russian women. But Sophia says no word as yet about Peter.[10]

The young grand duke had been born under an unlucky star. He lost his mother as a three-month-old baby. He was handed over by his father, who died when Peter was eleven, to be educated by German pedants, under the overall authority of the marshal of the Holstein-Gottorp court, Count Otto Brummer, who approved of such sadistic practices as forcing the boy to kneel for hours on dried peas, starving him or even beating him, if he could not say his lessons. Never strong, the many illnesses of the grand duke constantly interrupted his education. His main interests in life were to become music – he genuinely loved it and may have played the violin really well – and military parades, at first with dolls, then with human beings. The tensions to which the boy was subjected during his early education made him 'impulsive, false, boastful and a liar'.[11] From a bullied, frightened boy Peter grew into an immature, even childish youth, happier playing at or with soldiers than with anything else ; though not without shrewdness, he was incapable of sustained mental application, and did not know the meaning of the word discretion. The pitiful product of lack of affection and unthinking brutality in those who surrounded him, he clung with the courage of desperation to the only attributes of his personality which seemed to be genuinely his in outlandish Russia : his Holstein-Gottorp heritage and Lutheranism. His compulsory and reluctant conversion to Orthodoxy had been punctuated by fierce arguments with his instructor, the distinguished theologian Simon Todorsky, abbot of the Ipat'yev monastery, and he found difficulty in mastering the Russian language.[12]

At first the young couple took to each other. They were both in their teens, and could form a united front as playmates against the adult world. Sophia showed both zeal and aptitude in learning the Russian language. Her instructor in the Orthodox religion was that same Simon Todorsky, whose Ukrainian pronunciation she took good care not to imitate. Abbot Simon had studied for four years in Halle, and he gave the impression to Princess Johanna of being to all intents and purposes a Lutheran. No wonder therefore that Sophia found it easy to accept the tenets of the Orthodox faith, though as she explained to her father, 'the external rites are quite different, but the Church here is bound to them by the uncouthness of the people'.[13]

Sophia's smooth progression to the status of grand duchess was interrupted first by a dangerous illness, during which she endeared herself to the empress by calling for an Orthodox priest instead of a Lutheran pastor ; and secondly by a political crisis provoked by the injudicious behaviour of her mother. Taking Frederick II's instructions seriously, Johanna Elizabeth had connected herself openly at court with the party plotting to overthrow the vice-chancellor, Bestuzhev Ryumin. In spring 1744, Bestuzhev counter-attacked ; he put before the Empress Elizabeth intercepts from letters quoting many incautious and critical statements by Johanna about the empress and her way of life, and describing her efforts to meddle in Russian politics on behalf of Prussia. Johanna Elizabeth suffered the sharp edge of the empress's tongue and emerged from their interview in tears. Nevertheless Elizabeth was too just to blame the daughter she liked for the sins of the mother she had begun to despise. Hence preparations for the wedding went ahead and the formal conversion of Sophia to Orthodoxy took place with great solemnity in Moscow on 28 June 1744. The young girl won all suffrages by her composed behaviour and the firm tones in which she made her declaration of faith in clearly enunciated Russian. From now on she became Catherine Alekseyevna, and when the next day she was formally betrothed to Peter, she was styled Grand Duchess and Imperial Highness, taking precedence of her mother. Catherine —as she will henceforth be known in these pages — was given her own court. Two of her three gentlemen of the bedchamber were to play a part later in her life : Zakhar Grigor'yevich Chernyshev, the future president of the College of War, and Alexander Mikhaylovich Golitsyn, the future field-marshal. Countess Maria Andreyevna Rumyantseva, a formidable lady who had once been the mistress of Peter the Great, and the mother of another future field-marshal, was placed in charge of her household.

It was now Peter's turn to place Catherine's future in jeopardy. He fell ill, first with pleurisy, then with chicken pox, in autumn 1744, and finally succumbed to small pox on 20 December, when the court had briefly stopped at an intermediate halt on its way back to St Petersburg from Moscow. Catherine was promptly whisked away, and Elizabeth rushed to her nephew's bedside and fearlessly took charge of him.

While Catherine waited anxiously for news of her fiancé, she met again briefly a man who on this occasion was to leave a permanent trace on her character and her career. A Swedish embassy arrived to announce the marriage of Catherine's uncle, Prince Adolf Frederick, heir to the throne of Sweden, to Louisa Ulrica, sister of Frederick II. Among its members was a certain Count H.A. Gyllenborg who had four years before been impressed by the intelligence of the young princess of Zerbst when he met her in Hamburg. He now took the opportunity to speak to Catherine as probably no one had ever spoken before. He dwelt on the need for self-discipline and self-knowledge in her precarious situation, and of nourishment for both the mind and the spirit. For him, Catherine drafted a 'Portrait of a fifteen-year-old philosopher' which has not survived ; he gave her a dozen pages of good advice which have not survived either. He advised her to read Plutarch, Tacitus, and Montesquieu's *Considérations sur les causes de la grandeur des Romains et de leur décadence* (published in 1734). Catherine promptly acted on his suggestions to the extent of ordering the catalogue of the library of the Academy of Sciences and its bookshop to be sent to her. The books, when they came, were above the head of a fifteen-year-old girl, and she put them by for the time being, but she turned to them later, and never forgot Gyllenborg's sound advice which in years to come stood her in good stead.[14]

When the grand duke recovered and returned to St Petersburg at the end of January 1745, he had become unrecognizable. Never handsome, he had grown tall and thin, his features had thickened, his face was still swollen and badly pockmarked, and his head, which had been shaved, was shrouded in a huge wig. 'Il était devenu affreux,' wrote Catherine in her memoirs, just at the time when Catherine herself was beginning to blossom. The change in her bridegroom overwhelmed the young girl, but she had advanced too far now to withdraw, and her policy had been laid down : 'Voici le raisonnement ou plutôt la conclusion que j'ai fait dès que j'ai vu que j'étais fixée en Russie et que je n'ai jamais perdu de vue un moment : (1) plaire au grand duc, (2) plaire à l'Impératrice, (3) plaire à la nation.'[15]

There was thus to be no turning back. The marriage of the grand duke and the grand duchess waited only on the empress's convenience. Elizabeth was determined to eclipse all previous weddings and had sent for the programmes of royal marriages in other countries. A special *ukaz* both authorized and encouraged the high court nobility to order new carriages and new clothes for themselves and their wives for the occasion.[16]

On 21 August 1745, the firing of guns at 5 a.m. heralded the beginning of the ceremonies, which outshone any previous Russian royal wedding. After the lengthy service, dinner, and a brief ball, Catherine was publicly put to bed by the empress between 9 and 10 p.m. There she waited alone for a couple of hours, until her lady-in-waiting informed her that Peter would join her when he had finished his supper.[17] When questioned the next morning on her marital experiences, Catherine had nothing to report. For ten days, ball followed ball, and masquerade followed masquerade ; there were fireworks and illuminations, fountains of wine and mountains of food, operas and comedies.

From Catherine's point of view, there was very little to celebrate. In the days before her marriage she had evidently been somewhat frightened at the idea of committing herself finally to a young man who had become physically repulsive to her, even though she still had a condescending affection for him. Hard though it is to believe, Catherine suggests that she was innocent of all sexual knowledge when she married. But she was not unawakened, and though she may have felt relieved, she was also humiliated by Peter's neglect of her, and his failure, night after night, to consummate the marriage. It is unlikely that Peter was equally innocent. Did he try, and fail to possess Catherine, and did this alienate him from her ? There can be no sure answer. But taking all the known evidence into account, it would seem that the seventeen-year-old bridegroom was as yet sexually unawakened. Sexual failure must have exacerbated the emotional tensions between two such different – indeed incompatible – characters, who were nevertheless compelled by court etiquette to share a bed.

Catherine's marriage was the signal for her mother's departure, and the young grand duchess now found herself at the age of fifteen quite alone, with no one to advise her. She got into debt, and as the months went by without any signs of an heir, she lost ground with the empress. A prank of the grand duke's (he bored peepholes in a door and spied on the empress entertaining her friends) led to the inauguration of a stricter regime for the 'young court'. A new mistress of the household was appointed, a second cousin of the empress's, twenty-four-year-old Maria Choglokova, who was selected as an example of wifely devotion and philoprogenitiveness. The instructions to Maria Choglokova and her husband were drafted by Bestuzhev Ryumin, now chancellor, and covered both personal and political behaviour. Catherine was forbidden in so many words to write letters to her family ; she could only sign her name to letters drafted for her in the College of Foreign Affairs. More humiliating still, Maria Choglokova was ordered to watch over Catherine's faithfulness to her husband, about which Elizabeth's suspicions had been aroused, as yet with no justification beyond a slight 'tendre' Catherine had felt for one of Peter's gentlemen-in-waiting. The grand duchess's society was restricted to those people only who were approved by Mme Choglokova, and no one was allowed to speak to her in a low voice or a whisper, or to give her any information about court intrigues or government policy. As soon as it was noticed that Catherine had taken a fancy to a maid of honour or even a chambermaid, she was promptly removed.

Amid the constant journeys from Moscow to St Petersburg, from Summer Palace to Winter Palace, from one country estate to another, Catherine learned to solace herself with riding and reading. She devised a special saddle which enabled her to switch unobserved from side saddle (all that the empress allowed) to riding astride. The more violent the exercise the happier she was. Some of her physical frustrations were perhaps worked off in this way.[18]

At the same time, she always had 'a book in her pocket'. Gyllenborg's good advice was now being followed. Over the years she read *The History of Germany* by Père Barre, Voltaire's *Essai sur les moeurs,* Baronius's *Annales Ecclesiastici, The History of Henri IV* by Hardouin de Beaumont de Péréfixe (Henri IV was always to remain a hero to Catherine), as well as the *Lettres* of Madame de Sévigné, and a number of French romances. Another author who may have exercised some influence on Catherine's moral values was Brantôme, whose *Les Vies des dames galantes* may have come into her hands with his other works.[19] She also set herself the task of reading through P. Bayle's *Dictionnaire historique et critique* which may have established the groundwork in her of an intolerant hatred of Catholic intolerance which her subsequent reading of the *Encyclopédie* only strengthened. Later on, she read the *Annals* of Tacitus, which also left their mark on her, as she was to admit. There was not so much republican virtue about Rome after all, and the Praetorian Guards made and unmade emperors. In the early 1750s she read for the first time Montesquieu's *Esprit des lois,* which was later to become her bedside book.[20]

As the years passed, the grand duke and the grand duchess drifted further apart. Forcing them to share a bed did not help matters much so long as the grand duke spent his time playing with dolls, or training a pack of dogs in the adjoining dressing room, while Catherine read Plato. Occasionally in Catherine's memoirs, there is a hint that her pride suffered bitterly at her husband's total indifference to her, particularly since a number of men attached to her court fell more or less passionately in love with her. Among them were the hetman of Little Russia, Kyrill Razumovsky,[21] Zakhar Chernyshev and A. Nikitich de Villebois, all of whom would reach high rank during her reign. Even before their marriage Peter had confided all his passing fancies to Catherine. Now she found such confidences both painful and humiliating, all the more when Peter came to bed drunk and sometimes even maltreated her.[22]

Portraits of Catherine at about this time show her to have had a slight, elegant figure. She had thick, curly, dark hair, and well-opened blue eyes. Her face was too long for beauty, with a high brow, a long nose and a long chin. But she had that more elusive quality, charm, which coupled with easy and unaffected manners, gaiety and wit, and an underlying streak of recklessness, heightened her attraction. Now, as throughout her life, she was adored by her servants. Compounded of passion and reason in very evenly balanced proportions, reason showed in Catherine's treatment of her dependants : she was considerate and tactful and regarded them as human beings. As a result even those set about her as spies were soon won over and became her devoted adherents, without any need for her to indulge in overt or covert bribery. Was there calculation in her attitude to her inferiors ? If there was, it was probably second nature to such a degree that Catherine herself was unaware of it. There was such a spontaneity about her attachments, friendships and opinions that it is hard to accept that they were the result of a perpetual system of deceit, as her detractors would have one believe. And, in spite of the constraints under which she lived, there was much gaiety in court life in which Catherine participated to the full – together with endless discomfort, thanks to the poor construction and even poorer furnishing of so many of the palaces occupied by Elizabeth's peripatetic court.

After nearly eight years of unconsummated marriage, in a court where love affairs were the order of the day, Catherine had become extremely vulnerable to the attentions of the first experienced seducer who could convince her that he loved her. She was twenty-three when he appeared, in the spring of 1752, in the person of Sergey Vasil'yevich Saltykov, one of two brothers who were chamberlains of the grand duke. Sergey was so handsome as to acquire the nickname 'le beau Serge' (a reputation not borne out by his portrait) ; he had the superficial *savoir-faire* of the man of the world, masking a cold and vain nature. Systematically he laid siege to Catherine's heart and, reading between the lines of her memoirs, he clearly attained his object.[23] The gossip about Catherine's affair finally reached the ears of the empress and had one good result. It led Maria Choglokova to explain to Elizabeth precisely why Catherine had no children. That she was not barren was already clear to Catherine, who secretly miscarried in December 1752 of a child by Saltykov. With or without the connivance of Elizabeth, Maria Choglokova and Sergey Saltykov now got together to solve the dual problem of the succession to the Russian throne and Saltykov's liaison with Catherine. On the one hand Maria Choglokova found a complaisant widow to initiate Peter in the mysteries of sexual life. On the other hand, she openly urged Catherine to pursue her love affair : 'I shall not be the one to put obstacles in your way,' she declared. Meanwhile Catherine herself decided to break out of her political isolation and held out an olive branch to Bestuzhev Ryumin, which was promptly seized by the chancellor, who now instructed all his creatures at Catherine's court to facilitate her relationship with Saltykov. In July 1753 Catherine suffered another and more serious miscarriage. By January 1754 she was pregnant again, and the long-desired son and heir to the throne of the Romanovs was born on 20 September 1754.

Was Paul Petrovich the son of the grand duke or of Sergey Saltykov ? Catherine leaves one in no doubt that she became Saltykov's mistress : in a passage which was omitted from the first edition of her memoirs published in 1907, Catherine, writing at a later date, explained her surrender : 'In spite of all the finest moral maxims buried in the mind, when emotion interferes, when feeling makes its appearance, one is already much further involved than one realizes. . . . Perhaps escape is the only solution . . . but how can one escape . . . in the atmosphere of a court ?'[24] But she says nothing, even by implication, of the consummation of her marriage with Peter. Indeed, even if the marriage was consummated, it is very probable that Peter was infertile. He is not known to have fathered any illegitimate children with his many subsequent mistresses. The evidence thus all points to the paternity of 'le beau Serge'. The only argument that has been put forward in favour of Peter's paternity is that the handsome Saltykov could scarcely have been the father of plain, pug-nosed Paul. But heredity moves in mysterious ways : Paul may have taken after his uncle, Peter Saltykov, who had 'deux grands yeux fixes, le nez camus et la bouche toujours entreouverte'.[25]

The birth of her son was an object lesson to the grand duchess on her total unimportance in the scheme of things. The baby was carried off at once by the empress, and the young mother, after a twelve-hour labour, was left unattended for four hours. The empress gave her a present of 100,000 rubles which she borrowed back a few days afterwards in order to reward the grand duke for his part in the proceedings. Sergey Saltykov was sent to Sweden to announce the birth of the heir, in order to remove him from Catherine. For some time already he had tried to evade her loving importunities, and he showed her that he was tired of her. On top of that, in the winter of 1754, Alexander Shuvalov had been appointed master of the grand ducal household. He was the head of the dreaded Secret Chancery, cousin of Elizabeth's new young favourite, Ivan Ivanovich Shuvalov, and an opponent of the man who had now become Catherine's friend and protector, the Chancellor A.P. Bestuzhev Ryumin.

Catherine was now twenty-five. She had stood up to a marriage which would have broken the spirit of anyone less resolute. She had learnt to pick her way unaided among the pitfalls of a court governed by an arbitrary, suspicious and at times violent ruler – Elizabeth. She had discovered the art of turning enemies and spies into friends and servants. She had lost her heart to a man who had soon ceased to love her – if he ever had – and had suffered despair and humiliation. She had become a mother, but every maternal feeling had been frustrated by Elizabeth's ruthless abduction of her son. She had matured and hardened, and if she was less important now that she had produced a son, she was also safer, and freer, as the mother of the heir. Her husband meanwhile entertained himself with drilling a detachment of troops he had imported from Holstein, and with his newly acquired mistress, Countess Elizabeth Vorontsova, niece of the vice-chancellor, Michael Larionovich Vorontsov.

It was now, in the summer of 1755, that Catherine embarked on her second great love affair, which soon became entangled in diplomatic intrigue. The new British envoy to the Russian court, Sir Charles Hanbury Williams, who presented his credentials in June 1755, had brought with him as his secretary of embassy the twenty-three-year-old Pole, Count Stanislas Augustus Poniatowski. The British envoy's mission was to prove a dismal failure. The young count was to achieve a signal success of a different kind.

There was nothing surprising in the love affair which developed between Stanislas and Catherine. Exceptionally gallant, charming, cultured, with beautiful manners, Stanislas knew England and had spent some time in Paris where he had frequented the salon of Madame Geoffrin whom he called 'Maman'. Falling in love with Catherine, he gave her for the first time in her life the experience of being genuinely loved by someone who could share her intellectual interests, tastes and pastimes, and at the same time treat her with both warmth and delicacy of feeling, with respectful adoration, passion and consideration for her position. Poniatowski is the only one of Catherine's lovers who has left a description of her, which conveys some of the magnetic enchantment of his mistress at this time : 'She was twenty-five years old and just risen from her first delivery. She had reached that time in life when any woman to whom beauty has been granted will be at her best. She had black hair, a radiant complexion and a high colour, large prominent and expressive blue eyes, long dark eyelashes, a pointed nose, a kissable mouth, perfect hands and arms, slender figure, tall rather than small ; she moved quickly yet with great nobility, and had an agreeable voice and a gay good-tempered laugh, moving with ease from the most madcap childish games to arithmetic tables, undaunted either by the labours involved or by the texts themselves.'[26]

In pursuit of her new love, Catherine took enormous risks. The underlying audacity of her character now came to the fore, as she acquired the habit of going out alone or escorted by a close friend at night, dressed in man's clothing. It was not from Peter, however, that she needed to conceal her new love, since the grand duke was only too happy after a supper at which he and Elizabeth Vorontsova, Catherine and Poniatowski were all present, to walk off with the words 'Ah ça mes enfants, vous n'avez plus besoin de moi'.[27]

As the clouds of war gathered in Europe in 1755, a convention was signed in September 1755 between Britain and Russia. The object was, in the case of Britain, to subsidize Russia to undertake the defence of Hanover against a possible Prussian attack – Prussia was still loosely allied to France. In the case of Russia, the object was to prepare for war on Prussia. The treaty represented the triumph of the pro-British, and anti-Prussian, anti-French, policy of Bestuzhev. The subsequent signature in January 1756 of the Convention of Westminster between Britain and Prussia, by which the two contracting parties guaranteed the security of their respective dominions, including Hanover, led to an uproar in the Russian capital, to the eventual destruction of Bestuzhev Ryumin's whole system and ultimately of his position. The first setback for the chancellor was the establishment in March 1756 of the so-called 'Conference', a council charged with the implementation of the anti-Prussian policy of Elizabeth, by all possible means. Bestuzhev was of course a member, but his power was diluted by the presence of his rivals the Shuvalovs and the Vice-Chancellor M.L. Vorontsov. The Convention of Westminster between Britain and Prussia was rapidly followed by the first Treaty of Versailles between France and Austria on 1 May 1756 and the so-called diplomatic revolution was now well under way. Anxious to forestall the formation of a coalition of France, Austria and Russia against him, Frederick II invaded Saxony in August 1756, and thus enabled that very coalition to take shape more rapidly.

For a while Bestuzhev Ryumin fought to maintain an impossible position, both pro-British and anti-Prussian at a time when these two powers were rapidly moving to an alliance, and Russia was negotiating with Austria with a view to attacking Prussia. In these circumstances his friendship with the young court acquired much greater significance for Bestuzhev. He and Hanbury Williams, each in his own way, facilitated Catherine's liaison with Poniatowski, so openly tolerated by the grand duke. Hanbury Williams too fell victim to the grand duchess's charm, just as she developed feelings of warm friendship for him. In the seventy letters she wrote to him and the eighty-seven letters he wrote to her, in the course of two years, there are many affectionate passages. 'I shall always love Catherine better than the Empress,' he wrote to her in August 1756, referring to his hopes of returning to Russia once she was on the throne.[28]

Catherine now served as a channel of communication between the British envoy and the chancellor, who was still working to hinder any Russian *rapprochement* with France following on the Franco-Austrian treaty, and struggling to defend himself against the intrigues of the pro-French party, composed of the vice-chancellor, Michael Vorontsov and his family, and the favourite, I.I. Shuvalov and his family. In the summer of 1756 Poniatowski was recalled by the Polish/Saxon government to Poland. Catherine put all possible pressure on Bestuzhev and Hanbury Williams (through whom her correspondence with her absent lover was conducted) to have him brought back to Russia. Hanbury Williams meanwhile indoctrinated her in the merits of the traditional alliance between England and Russia ('since the days of Ivan Basilowitz') and provided her with badly needed funds.[29] Times had changed since Bestuzhev had been the grand duchess's all-powerful enemy. It was now the chancellor, deprived of all support at court, who leant increasingly on Catherine. Hence he moved heaven and earth to obtain the return of Poniatowski, who re-appeared in the capital in December 1756, this time officially as envoy of the king of Poland (Augustus II of Saxony). He arrived soon after the birth of Catherine's daughter Anna Petrovna, who was generally assumed to be his. On this occasion too the empress took complete charge of the baby and Catherine did not see her daughter again for several weeks.

The accession of Russia to the Treaty of Versailles finally took place on 31 December 1756/11 January 1757 and was followed by a new treaty between Austria and Russia on 22 January/2 February 1757 setting out Russian war aims (the acquisition of Curland if East Prussia were ceded to the Poles).[30] Hanbury Williams had been too closely bound up with the negotiation of the Anglo-Russian treaty and with efforts to prevent a Russian *rapprochement* with France for him to continue as British envoy, once Russia was openly involved in war on the opposing side, and he was recalled to England in July 1757, much to Catherine's distress.

To what extent can Catherine's correspondence with him be regarded as treasonable ?[31] She was pursuing what had been Bestuzhev's policy (he too of course had long been in receipt of a British pension of 12,000 rubles per annum)[32] but it was no longer the policy of Elizabeth. The allegations of treasonable plottings concern Catherine's knowledge of Russian diplomatic and military dispositions and the extent to which this knowledge was passed on to Hanbury Williams and through Britain to Frederick II. Catherine was on friendly terms with General S.F. Apraksin, who had been appointed commander-in-chief of the Russian armies which were to act against Prussia. She undoubtedly endeavoured to persuade Apraksin, on Hanbury Williams's behalf, to oppose the arrival of a French envoy in Russia (diplomatic relations were about to be resumed after a twelve-year interval) and to delay the start of military operations. She also transmitted political and court gossip received from Apraksin and others to the British envoy, and documents which she received from Bestuzhev. Whether the documents or the information were important enough or reached Frederick in time for him to alter his plans is very difficult to assess. It was however the constant alarms, particularly in autumn 1756, about the Empress Elizabeth's health which led everyone, Hanbury Williams, Bestuzhev, Catherine, Apraksin, to calculate their conduct and plan for the future. All realized that the accession of the ardently Prussophile Peter would lead to a radical change in policy. Catherine may already have feared for her own person in the event of Elizabeth's death. At any rate Bestuzhev toyed with the idea that Catherine should be proclaimed joint ruler with Peter or that Peter should be passed over entirely and Catherine rule alone. He submitted to the grand duchess the draft of a manifesto proclaiming her co-ruler, and making himself all powerful as commander of all four guards regiments, and president of the three Colleges of War, Navy and Foreign Affairs. According to her memoirs, Catherine read this paper and returned it to the chancellor, thanking him for his kind thoughts but remarking that she did not think his plan easy to carry out.[33] There was probably more to it than that. It was being increasingly acknowledged both by Russians and by foreign envoys at the Russian court, that Peter was unfit to rule. The temptation for Catherine to become co-ruler, or regent for her son, must have been growing stronger but there are only occasional hints in Hanbury Williams's letters of what the future might be when Catherine 'sat on the throne'.[34] How to achieve such an object must however at this time have seemed beyond conjecture.

In May 1757 General Apraksin left for the front, and on 19/30 August the Russian forces defeated a Prussian army at the hard-fought battle of Gross Jägerndorf. Soon after, on 8/19 September, Elizabeth suffered a stroke just outside the parish church in Tsarskoye Selo. Her illness could not be concealed. Generals and officials hesitated whether to obey the setting or the rising sun. Apraksin, instead of pursuing his victory as everyone had expected, withdrew to Memel. At the time, even Catherine believed that he had withdrawn on receipt of the news of the empress's illness,[35] fearing that he might be disgraced by the new emperor, Peter. She may even have written to him and warned him of Elizabeth's illness – letters which Apraksin was wise enough to destroy. It appears, however, that Apraksin put the question of a withdrawal to Memel, because of Russian lack of supplies, to a council of war on 27 August, so that the retreat was decided on before the empress's stroke.[36] But the empress recovered ; and she was outraged to discover that policy had apparently been affected by doubts about her health. Apraksin was promptly recalled and threatened with a court martial. But his enemies were aiming at Bestuzhev Ryumin and indeed at the grand duchess. By mid-February 1758, the empress gave way to their pressure, and Bestuzhev was arrested, together with his wife and son, and all his papers were confiscated.

Since the chancellor was never formally charged, tried or convicted, it is impossible to tell exactly what the accusations against him were. But they certainly included attempts to alter the succession, and allowing the grand duchess to correspond with public figures, i.e. General Apraksin. Bestuzhev had succeeded in burning all compromising papers before his arrest, and he got word to Catherine to that effect. But a number of minor figures in his circle had been arrested and might incriminate Catherine. Moreover, there was no help to be had from Peter. Though he continued to worship the king of Prussia, and had himself publicly opposed the Russian *rapprochement* with France, and though he had tolerated Catherine's affair with Poniatowski and must have surmised that the little Anna was not his, he was now hastening to get back into Elizabeth's good graces by blackening Catherine's character.

In this most dangerous crisis she had to face, Catherine was totally isolated ; she did not even know what was going on until secret communications were established with Bestuzhev and others under arrest. Early in March 1758 a manifesto was issued, depriving Bestuzhev of his rank and position and announcing his forthcoming trial by a special commission. Still Catherine did not know whether she was implicated or not. In the circumstances, she took the risk of deliberately provoking an explosion which cleared the air between the empress and herself. Seizing her pen she wrote a careful appeal in Russian to the empress, begging, since she had had the misfortune to arouse Elizabeth's displeasure, to be sent home. In reply, Elizabeth promised to grant her a personal interview but nothing happened during the next six weeks, while every attempt was made to find evidence implicating Catherine in Bestuzhev's alleged treason. Her woman of the bedchamber, the confidante of her love affairs, was arrested ; Bestuzhev's papers were sifted again and again ; nothing was found but three letters, which had been among General Apraksin's papers, in which Catherine had warned the general that his conduct was being criticized and urged him to obey the empress's orders and continue to advance on the Prussian army.

The strain was beginning to tell on Catherine, but her good relations with the Orthodox Church now came to her help. One of her ladies-in-waiting was the niece of the empress's confessor. She arranged for her uncle to visit the grand duchess, and 'listen to her confession'. Whether Catherine told him everything is doubtful, but the good priest went straight to the empress and spoke to such effect that an interview was arranged for that same night, 13/24 April 1758. When

Catherine was ushered into the empress's presence, the latter was not alone. The grand duke was present as well as Alexander Shuvalov, head of the Secret Chancery and master of the grand ducal household. The favourite, I.I. Shuvalov, was hidden behind a screen.

Catherine has left her own description of the dramatic scene which followed : she fell on her knees, and begged through her tears to be sent home. Elizabeth reminded her of her children, but Catherine replied that they would be better off in the hands of the empress. Peter then launched into tirades against his wife, charging her with bad temper, which Elizabeth ignored, but she did question Catherine on the subject of her letters to Apraksin. Catherine swore again that they were totally innocent and disregarded all threats to torture Bestuzhev to make him confess their joint guilt. Finally Elizabeth, who had been pacing up and down the room in a state of uncertainty, seemed to be won over by Catherine. She dismissed the young couple, but sent a message to Catherine saying that she would see her again soon. Peter expressed the triumphant hope that Catherine would soon be repudiated so that he could marry his mistress, Elizabeth Vorontsova, and Catherine settled down to read the first volumes of the *Encyclopédie*.

The crucial interview between Elizabeth and Catherine took place on 23 May/4 June. Elizabeth challenged Catherine to answer all her questions, and interrogated her on her letters to Apraksin and on her relations with Peter. What did Catherine reply to this last question ? Here, alas, her memoirs break off. But Elizabeth must have known that Paul was not Peter's son. On a previous occasion when the Shuvalovs had hinted as much, Elizabeth had burst out : 'Hold your tongue you B. . . . I know what you mean, you want to insinuate he is a Bastard, but if he is he is not the first that has been in my family.'[37] Catherine succeeded at any rate in convincing Elizabeth that she was innocent of any treasonable intent or activities. In the course of 1758, Bestuzhev was exiled, Poniatowski was sent back to Poland for good and Catherine was more isolated than ever. She had lost her father in March 1747 ; her mother died in Paris, crippled with debt, in May 1760. The grand duchess's infant daughter Anna died in 1759 and though Catherine had only been allowed to see her children at long intervals, her loss was sincerely felt.

The Vorontsovs, and particularly their rivals the Shuvalovs, having overthrown their main enemy, Bestuzhev, could now afford to be generous to Catherine. They were far-sighted enough to realize that the wheel of fortune might one day place her in a position to do them substantial harm. Peter, meanwhile, with total lack of caution set about alienating the sympathies of most Russian officers and officials by his open championship of the king of Prussia and the unwise boasting in which he indulged of his secret contacts with Russia's enemies.

When therefore a distinguished Prussian prisoner of war, Count Schwerin, aide-de-camp to the king of Prussia, appeared in St Petersburg in 1760, he was welcomed and treated as an honoured guest by Peter. His Russian escort was a certain Grigory Grigor'yevich Orlov, captain of artillery, the second of five dare-devil brothers, who had made a name for himself by his courage and daring at the battle of Zorndorf, where he had been wounded. Handsome, reckless, lucky in love and in war, he was admitted to the young court where he fell in love with Catherine and she with him. It was now nearly two years since Poniatowski's departure. The atmosphere of amorous intrigue at court was not conducive to perpetual chastity, and moreover the gentleness and sameness of Poniatowski's manners may have begun to pall in Catherine's memory, when contrasted with the bold vigour of a Grigory Orlov.

Subconsciously Catherine may also have been moved by fear. She knew well that Elizabeth's death and Peter's accession might place her in grave danger. Peter had been heard to threaten to shut her up in a convent, and he had every reason to doubt his wife's fidelity. Grigory Orlov, popular with officers and men, backed up by his four brothers, could provide her with protection, and with a direct link with the Russian armed forces.[38] Precisely when the love affair between the two began is not known, but in the autumn of 1761 Catherine was again pregnant, and this time her pregnancy was carefully concealed.

As the year 1761 drew to a close all eyes were fixed on the fading Empress Elizabeth. Those who had driven Bestuzhev into exile and endangered Catherine now had to recognize that they might have more to gain from the grand duchess than from Peter, who made no secret of his intention to withdraw from the war against Prussia the moment he ascended the throne. What of Catherine herself? Was she thinking of a regency for her son Paul? Or had she already determined to try to seize the throne and rule in her own right?

Part I

The New Ruler and the New Government

1

Catherine's *Coup d'État*

On 25 December 1761, the Empress Elizabeth died. If Catherine had ever contemplated seizing power, her pregnancy now put it out of the question, and Peter acceded peacefully to the throne. The change of ruler made itself felt immediately in small things as in great. Peter had not the personal qualities to show up well in the transition period when mourning must be judiciously combined with rejoicing. His reign was to last barely six months. In at least four, if not five, major issues of policy, he succeeded in this brief time in alienating the governing élites of Russia. In addition the idiosyncrasies of his public and private behaviour were such as to lend credit to the most discreditable and improbable rumours, for instance the story that he had promised court ladies he would force them to divorce their husbands and marry their lovers – obviously a light-hearted joke.[1] Forcing elderly courtiers to play hopscotch while others endeavoured to fell them with a well-aimed knee in the behind was not likely to endear the emperor to his senior officials. Such behaviour aroused the contempt of the officers at court, as did the scenes of drunkenness in which these pastimes usually ended.[2]

Yet in some respects the policies enacted in Peter's reign and with his approval represented a continuation of the modernizing, westernizing trend associated with the Enlightenment. The penalties on religious dissidents, such as the Old Believers, were reduced, and their return to Russia facilitated. Controls over internal and external trade were eased. Above all the hated and feared Secret Chancery was abolished. This was the body devoted to the investigation of all crimes which came under the general heading of *lèse majesté,* treason, or sedition. The dread cry 'word and deed of the sovereign' (*slovo i delo gosudarevo*) had been enough to ensure that all those involved, accuser, accused and witnesses, would be arrested, tortured and, if they survived, probably exiled for ever. In a manifesto dated 21 February 1762, Peter III explained that this institution had been established by his ancestors because the *mores* of the Russian people were still barbarous. With time it had become less necessary, and unworthy people had come to take advantage of its existence to accuse people unjustly and to slander their superiors. In order to prevent injustice and cruelty in future, the

Secret Chancery was to be abolished, and pending cases were to be transferred to the Senate.

The abolition of the Secret Chancery did not entail the total disbandment of all security organs. Special secret departments were attached to the Senate in St Petersburg and Moscow to which the personnel of the old Secret Chancery was transferred. In future denunciations were to be made in writing (except in the case of illiterates) to the nearest military or civil office, and the victims of an accusation were not to be arrested until a full inquiry had been made. The accusers were to be held on bread and water for two days, to be sure that their denunciation was not merely frivolous.[3] Russian society was now to be protected against unjustified denunciations leading to arbitrary arrests and the indulgence of private vendettas.[4]

A second enactment was the manifesto on the freedom of the nobility, promulgated on 18 February 1762.[5] Little is known for certain of the prehistory of this manifesto, one of the most important milestones in the modernization of Russia.[6] On 17 January 1762, Peter III had attended a session of the Senate, at which he briefly announced his intentions with regard to noble service : in future nobles could serve as long as, and where, they wished, on condition that they volunteered for service in time of war.[7] On 18 February a very incomplete manifesto was promulgated. According to the jaundiced account of Prince M.M. Shcherbatov, it was written because Peter III on one occasion wished to conceal from his mistress his intention of spending the night elsewhere. He informed her that he intended working with one of his secretaries, D.V. Volkov. When the time came, he locked Volkov up, with instructions to produce 'an important ukaz by morning,' and went off on his own pursuits. The unfortunate Volkov, racking his brains for something to write about, remembered that Count Roman Vorontsov, the father of Peter's mistress Elizabeth, had frequently urged the emperor to 'do something' about freeing the nobility from service, and he produced the corresponding manifesto.[8]

Later research has not proved conclusively who was responsible for drafting the manifesto. As issued, it contained some slighting references to the state of barbarism previously prevailing in Russia, which had rendered compulsion necessary in order to force the nobility to serve the state. Now Russians had reached a degree of civilization which made it possible for the state to rely on their voluntary cooperation. Hence service was to be regulated in a new way. Serving nobles would be allowed to retire in time of peace, subject to their superiors' consent or to the emperor's consent in the case of senior officers. Nobles who had not reached officer's rank must serve twelve years before applying for retirement. Nobles might travel freely abroad, but must return when summoned on pain of confiscation of their estates. Wealthy nobles would be allowed to educate their children at home, but the state would continue to supervise the education of the children of poor nobles. The manifesto solemnly proclaimed that the freedom granted to the nobility was to be regarded as 'a perpetual and fundamental principle' (*pravilo*), binding on the ruler's heirs. Nobles were urged to respond to the imperial generosity by showing ever more zeal in service. Those who did not were to be despised and refused access to court.

Was the promulgation of the manifesto quite as accidental as Shcherbatov suggests ? Was it drafted by D. V. Volkov ? Was it a response to the pressure for improvement in the status of the nobility put forward by the Vorontsov group ? Or was it, as seems more likely, a compromise, prepared within the bureaucracy, probably by the procurator general, A.I. Glebov, a compromise which rejected the demands for economic and legal privileges such as the monopoly of the ownership of serfs and immunity from corporal punishment, put forward by the Vorontsovs, but accepted a degree of freedom from degrading compulsion, in the knowledge that the nobility would by and large serve in any case ?[9] Indeed, in the form in which it was enacted, the manifesto fits in well with a series of measures introduced under Peter III, designed to improve the quality of the bureaucracy and to create a corps of professional officials separate from the landed gentry, who would continue to provide officers for the armed services.[10]

If the abolition of the Secret Chancery and the manifesto of 26 February 1762 were measures likely to conciliate the nobility, in other respects the emperor seems to have set out deliberately to alienate important groups of his subjects. He had already created a bad impression on the higher clergy by his lack of respect for the Orthodox liturgy, and his open preference for Lutheran forms of worship. He was alleged to have told the Archbishop of Novgorod, Dmitry Sechenov, that all icons other than those portraying Jesus Christ should be removed from churches and that the clergy should shave and dress in the Western manner.[11] His tolerance towards the Old Believers met with little sympathy among the hierarchy. Priests in the capital were alienated by an order that private chapels in the houses of rich nobles and merchants should be shut down,[12] and parish priests, always closer to the peasantry and the soldiers, were outraged by the decision to include their sons and the sons of deacons among those liable to conscription in the armed forces.[13]

The last straw came when Peter revived, and actually began to carry out, the decision to secularize the lands of the Church, already reluctantly taken by the devout Elizabeth. The ukaz was issued on 21 March 1762.[14] The hasty and rough seizure of church property, often by army officers, led to an ukaz on 15 April 1762 forbidding them to enter and inventory the contents of monks' cells or the private houses of priests.[15] On 25 May 1762 the hierarchy formally protested against the policy of secularization.

The second important interest on which Peter launched a full-scale assault was the army. Russian participation in the Seven Years' War, the great victories of Gross Jägerndorf and Künersdorf, the lightning Russian raid on Berlin, and the occupation of East Prussia, had enormously increased the prestige of the army. A new generation of officers and men had proved a match for the far-famed Prussian troops and their brilliant military monarch, and they had emerged from the trial with increased self-confidence and a heightened sense of national self-esteem.

At the death of Elizabeth, in December 1761, Russian troops occupying East Prussia had only just received the surrender of the Prussian fortress of Kolberg, in Prussian Pomerania, which opened the way through Stettin to Berlin. A Russian corps under General Zakhar G. Chernyshev was acting with the Austrian army in Silesia. The victorious Russian generals were thunderstruck to hear that, on the pretext of announcing his accession, Peter III had sent one of his courtiers to reopen diplomatic relations with Prussia and prepare the way for peace talks. Negotiations for an armistice were begun at once in Pomerania, and General Chernyshev was ordered to leave the Austrian army and withdraw to the Vistula. On 12/23 February 1762, the Russian court issued a declaration to its allies that it intended to negotiate peace with Prussia and return all conquests.

Understandably delighted at the news from Russia, Frederick II appointed an envoy to St Petersburg, Count Goltz, who was authorized to cede East Prussia in perpetuity to Russia (against compensation), to guarantee Holstein against Danish aggression, and to promise neutrality in the event of a war between Russia and Denmark. It proved unnecessary to make such substantial concessions. Though the chancellor, Michael R. Vorontsov, attempted to make Peter see the need to discuss Russian policy with her allies, not only his views but his person was pushed aside.[16] Peter took the negotiations into his own hands, and the text of the peace treaty was actually drafted by the Prussian envoy.[17] It was signed on 24 April/5 May 1762, and it was evident from the text that Russian interests had been sacrificed by Peter to those of Holstein.[18] Russia was to return all her conquests from Prussia, while, in a treaty of alliance signed on the same day, Frederick bound himself to support Peter III's claims on Schleswig by force of arms if necessary. He also undertook to further the choice of Peter's uncle, Georg-Ludwig of Holstein-Gottorp, as Duke of Curland, a fief of the crown of Poland, which had once belonged to Duke Ernest Biron, the favourite of the Empress Anna of Russia, and which was now being claimed by Prince Charles of Saxony.

Peter at once launched rapid preparations for war with Denmark. A threatening note was despatched on 1 March 1762, demanding the return of Schleswig, and was followed up by an ultimatum on 24 May. Peter clearly envisaged that his new war with Denmark would involve him in the war between Prussia and Austria, but this time on the side of Prussia. Indeed even before the signature of the peace treaty with Prussia he had promised that Count Z. Chernyshev's corps would be transferred from the Austrian to the Prussian side.

Even those who wished to bring to an end the war with Prussia disapproved of the manner in which it was done, and of the price paid for peace. To all appearances Russian foreign policy was being directed by Frederick II, acting through his envoy, and indeed through the emperor himself. Most of the senior officials did their best to slow down Peter's impetuous determination to attack Denmark.

So, for quite different reasons, did Frederick II. Aware from his envoy's reports of the seething discontent in St Petersburg, Frederick urged the emperor not to leave his capital until after his coronation had sanctified and strengthened his authority, fearing that if he left Russia to command his troops in person, he would be deposed in his absence.[19] Undeterred, Peter pressed on, and on 21 May ordered General P.A. Rumyantsev, the hero of the siege of Kolberg, to start the occupation of Mecklenburg.

Meanwhile Peter had done his best to alienate the army he was to command. On his accession he had set up a military commission which in a short time completely remodelled the Russian establishment, drill, and uniforms on the Prussian style, much to the dismay of the guards regiments, attached to their Petrine uniforms. The Imperial Bodyguard, founded by the Empress Elizabeth, was disbanded, and the men dispersed to spread disaffection wherever they were sent. Moreover, though the sort of peace Peter had concluded outraged the pride of the officers, many were anxious to avail themselves of the permission to leave service granted by the manifesto of February 1762. The idea of a war against Denmark in the interests of Holstein was therefore highly unpopular. In addition, many high-ranking dignitaries in Russia held honorary military ranks. These now ceased to be honorary, and Peter derived much unseemly amusement from the spectacle of stout and elderly – or young and incompetent – generals like Kyrill Razumovsky, lieutenant-colonel of the Izmaylovsky Guards, puffing at the head of their troops on parade at crack of dawn.

Peter further undermined his status by the various moves he made to recast the central administration. He abolished the war cabinet of Elizabeth, the so-called 'Conference', and made a few changes of personnel, the long-term significance of which is difficult to assess since his reign was so short, but which seemed to represent the victory of the Vorontsov group over other court factions. His decision to lead the campaign against Denmark in person rendered it necessary to set up a body empowered to govern Russia in his absence. On 18 May 1762 he set up an informal Council, the composition of which indicates the people in whom Peter placed his trust. First in order of precedence he named his uncle, Georg-Ludwig of Holstein-Gottorp, who was also appointed colonel-in-chief of the Horseguards. Prince Augustus of Holstein-Beck was also named to the Council, and appointed governor-general of the capital, and commander-in-chief of all the troops in St Petersburg, Russian Finland and Estonia. The eighty-year-old Count B. Ch. Munich, recalled from Siberian exile by Peter, joined his fellow-Germans on the Russian Council.[20] Meanwhile, the powers of the Senate, the body charged with the coordination of all administration, were curbed, and the powers of the police increased and removed from the Senate's supervision.[21] So far, therefore, Peter had alienated the Church by attacking its economic interests and showing his open preference for a foreign form of worship. He had alienated the armed forces by a foreign policy which made a mockery of their great victories in war, and by a reorganization which injured national pride; and he had aroused discontent among senior officials by placing power in the hands of a small clique of advisers, drawn mainly from his family and mainly German. By itself, all this political clumsiness might not have been enough to topple him. But he made the mistake of threatening the one person capable of organizing a counter-attack, namely his wife.

It is impossible to say when and how the plot to remove Peter first took shape. That his situation was becoming precarious was clear to many,[22] and there were two possible candidates to the throne. One displaced emperor, Ivan VI, a mere baby when Elizabeth had seized the throne, had been immured in the fortress of Schlüsselburg for sixteen years, while his younger brothers were in exile in the far north. In March 1762 he was briefly brought to St Petersburg so that Peter III and a few others might see him. The unfortunate young man had been totally deprived of education, though he could apparently read and seemed to know who he was. Was he or was he not a born imbecile ? There is some argument among nineteenth-century Russian historians, but it is probable that his life had so warped the development of his faculties that, in no way abnormal at birth, he had been turned into an imbecile by human agency. At any rate it soon became generally known at court that he was quite unfit to rule.

The main candidate, logically enough, was the heir apparent, the seven-year-old Paul Petrovich. His situation had become precarious as a result of the tension between Peter III and Catherine. On his accession, Peter had not proclaimed Paul as his heir ; the formula for the oath of allegiance to the emperor pointedly excluded both Paul and his mother, and mentioned only 'such heir as he shall appoint'. As *tsarevich,* i.e. son of the tsar, but not as *naslednik* or heir, Paul was however included in the prayers offered for the imperial family in church, and Catherine was allocated an income of one million rubles (though she may not actually have received it). Rumour had it that Peter was preparing to repudiate Catherine in order to marry Elizabeth Vorontsova, and that he had also determined to disown Paul. He was reported to have disgraced Sergey Saltykov because the latter had refused to admit that he was the father of Paul, and thus provide Peter with grounds for divorcing his wife.[23] Since in accordance with the law of succession enacted by Peter the Great, the emperor was entitled to appoint his own heir, Paul's situation was clearly becoming vulnerable.

The respect Peter had once felt for Catherine had long turned into dislike, and she now had nothing but contempt for him. While he carelessly alienated opinion at court and in the capital, so she set about cultivating it. The new empress punctiliously carried out all the religious duties arising from the death of Elizabeth (Peter did not take part in the vigil by the body and disgraced himself by laughing and talking at the funeral). She behaved with dignity in the presence of foreign envoys and courtiers, bearing insults patiently and underlining forcefully the contrast between her intelligence and good manners and the graceless buffoonery of Peter.[24]

Catherine's position was particularly delicate since she was five months pregnant by Grigory Orlov at the death of Elizabeth. Royal pregnancies were not private affairs ; they were publicly proclaimed to all the courts of Europe at the first opportunity. The fact that Catherine had concealed her pregnancy from Elizabeth suggests that she was afraid that this time Peter would not acknowledge her child as his. There is certainly no evidence that Peter knew she was pregnant, and the wide mourning robes she wore, and the seclusion of her life during the first months of Peter's reign, helped to conceal her situation. On 10 April 1762 she was secretly delivered of a son, who grew up under the name Aleksey Grigor'yevich Bobrinsky, and was in later life generally recognized as her child, though never publicly acknowledged.[25] After her delivery, Catherine had greater freedom of action, and action seemed to become more necessary. Towards the end of April, at a banquet celebrating the signature of peace with Prussia, Peter, in the presence of the foreign envoys, shouted out *'dura'* (idiot) down the length of the table to his wife. Catherine burst into tears, but soon mastered herself. That same night Peter ordered his horror-struck adjutant to arrest the empress. The courtier rushed off to Peter's (and Catherine's) uncle, Georg-Ludwig of Holstein – that same uncle who had once hoped to marry her – who persuaded the emperor to rescind the order.

The threat to Catherine, and above all to the generally accepted heir, Paul, crystallized the attitudes of the increasing number of those who felt that a change must take place. Active supporters Peter had few. Even the chancellor, Michael Vorontsov, began to think of retiring to a country house in Tuscany.[26] But it is difficult to speak of a concerted plot to remove Peter until May or June. A number of separate conspiracies were developing among different people with different objects. One of the prime movers was Nikita Ivanovich Panin. Since he was to become Catherine's foreign minister during the first twenty years of her reign, his background and connections deserve attention. Born in 1718, he came from a minor service gentry family which rose in the eighteenth century through the marriage of Nikita's father to a niece of Peter the Great's favourite, Prince A.D. Menshikov. There were two sons and two daughters of the marriage. The daughters married into prominent families which had risen in the service of Peter I. Nikita and Peter Panin were well received at Elizabeth's court, where the empress is alleged to have had a passing fancy for Nikita. While Peter Panin made a career in the army, Nikita, after a period in the Imperial Bodyguard, was posted as minister to Denmark in 1747, and to Sweden in 1748, where he remained until 1760.[27]

In Sweden Panin had been able to observe at close quarters the operation of a political system in which the power of the Crown was severely limited by an aristocratic council and a diet representing the estates. He had played a very prominent part in the implementation of Russian foreign policy which was primarily directed at thwarting any attempt by the king of Sweden to restore absolutism which, in Russian eyes, might render Sweden more dangerous. He had a long experience of the manipulation of political parties and the use of large-scale bribery to achieve Russian objects in Sweden.

One advantage of Panin's long absence in Sweden was that he had been able to maintain his relations with all the court factions in St Petersburg while alienating none. Though appointed by the old chancellor, A.P. Bestuzhev Ryumin, he did not share his disgrace, and remained on friendly terms with Bestuzhev's rivals, the Vorontsovs. In the circumstances, his appointment by Elizabeth to the post of master of the household and tutor to the Grand Duke Paul in spring 1760 was not surprising. He was a cultured man of forty-two with a reputation for personal probity and no enemies.[28] He won the confidence, even the affection, of the young Paul, and by allowing Catherine freer access to her son than she had been given previously, he acquired her friendship and respect.

Panin had public and private motives for joining in a plot to dethrone Peter. The emperor provided an extreme example of the arbitrary and personal exercise of power which Panin had come to regard as harmful to Russia[29] and to the interests of the aristocratic service élite to which he belonged. He was equally opposed to Peter's foreign policy, not so much because of its pro-Prussian orientation but because he thoroughly disapproved of the campaign against Denmark.[30] Panin was an ambitious man, who knew his own worth, though he was not prepared to fight to the death for a principle. He realized that his own position as tutor to the grand duke would be worthless if Catherine were repudiated and Paul disinherited. But if Peter were removed and a regency were proclaimed, he would be in a position to influence government policy, even to play a prominent part in government.

The full details of Panin's participation in the conspiracy remain obscure. It seems that he was responsible for winning over General Prince M.N. Volkonsky, and possibly also the hetman, Kyrill Razumovsky, as well as the official, G.N. Teplov. All these hoped to proclaim the young Paul, with a regency council to advise his mother during the boy's minority. Princess Catherine Dashkova, the nineteen-year-old sister of Peter III's mistress, who harboured an extravagant hero-worship for Catherine, was also involved in the conspiracy, and according to her own later account, she too favoured a regency.[31]

But the prime movers in the plot, closest to Catherine herself and most active in winning the support of a sufficient number of officers and in preparing opinion among the troops, were the five Orlov brothers. Grigory, believing himself to be watched over by a suspicious Peter III, took little active part, though he tried to recruit one of the aide-de-camps to the chief of police, Baron N.A. Korf.[32] But he had been appointed treasurer of the artillery corps, and thus disposed of sums which enabled him to win a personal following among the rank and file soldiers. The grand master of the ordnance, in charge of the artillery corps, General A. de Villebois, was a member of Peter's Council of State. Unfortunately for Peter III, he had already decided to throw in his lot with Catherine, with whom, like Kyrill

Razumovsky, he had once been in love. The third Orlov, Aleksey, known as 'le balafré' from the scar which marred his good looks, was equally active and some forty guards officers were eventually recruited to the plot. The participants were however unaware of its ramifications, just as they were not agreed on its aims. Dashkova believed that she played a vital role in linking the plotters – but she was quite ignorant of the fact that Grigory Orlov was Catherine's lover.[33] The role of Baron Korf, the chief of police, is particularly obscure. He was close to Peter, but got into trouble with his unpredictable master towards the end of May, and began to sense the dangers of attaching himself too closely to a losing side. He started to cultivate the empress and call on her in her apartments, which may explain why, in spite of the openly seditious talk in the capital, the police did nothing to forestall the *coup d'état* they were undoubtedly expecting.[34]

In so far as the conspirators had reached any decision, they planned to arrest Peter when he left on the Danish campaign. He did indeed leave the capital on 12/23 June for the imperial summer palace at Oranienbaum nearby, while final arrangements were made for the troops to start their march. Catherine and Paul had remained in St Petersburg, but the empress departed for another summer palace at Peterhof on 17/28 June, leaving Paul in Panin's care in the capital. Probably the manifestos announcing her accession were secretly drawn up and printed at this time. On 19/30 June Catherine went to Oranienbaum to visit Peter. Still dressed in deep mourning, and looking sad and preoccupied, she attended a theatrical performance at which Peter played the violin. It was the last time she saw her husband.[35]

Meanwhile in St Petersburg imprudent talk had led to the arrest of one of the conspirators. Clearly the whole plot might be uncovered, and the leaders decided that Catherine should be brought back to the capital at once, and her accession should be proclaimed there, without waiting for the arrest of the emperor, who was still in Oranienbaum, with his own suite of courtiers, and incidentally the wives of many of the plotters.

Catherine has left her own description of the stirring events of that June day.[36] On 28 June/9 July she was aroused at dawn in Peterhof by Aleksey Orlov and set off at once for St Petersburg in a carriage he had brought. On the way she was met by Grigory Orlov, and under their escort she drove to the barracks of the Izmaylovsky regiment, where she was immediately proclaimed empress and sovereign of all the Russias by the triumphant Orlovs. A few calls from the officers for Paul and a regency were immediately silenced by the brothers. Then, escorted by the colonel, Kyrill Razumovsky, Catherine left for the Semyonovsky barracks, where the soldiers rushed forward to greet her. The next to join were the Preobrazhensky Guards, some of whose officers, loyal to Peter, had tried to restrain them and had been arrested for their pains.[37] 'Forgive us for coming last,' they cried, 'our officers detained us, and in our zeal we have arrested four of them. We want the same as our brothers.' The veterans of Elizabeth's *coup d'état* in 1740, the Imperial Bodyguard, which had been disbanded by Peter III, now joined the throng. Many soldiers had had time to dig out and don their old Russian uniforms and had discarded the hated Prussian uniforms introduced by Peter III. Then came the Horseguards, led by their colonel, Prince N.M. Volkonsky. Catherine now proceeded to the Kazan' cathedral, where the Church hierarchy proclaimed her sovereign, and her son Paul as heir to the throne. Shortly after, at the Winter Palace, the ceremony of swearing allegiance to the new ruler began. More regiments appeared before the palace, in some cases the men having arrested their officers. The Archbishop of Novgorod, Dmitry Sechenov, circulated among the troops administering the oath of allegiance, and the soldiers stationed themselves around and within the palace to 'guard' the empress 'they had made'.[38] The arrival of the young Paul, still in his nightshirt, was greeted with shouts of joy. News of the change of ruler was immediately sent to regiments in the neighbourhood and to the naval base in Kronstadt. Three regiments which had already started out for Narva on the first stage to Denmark turned round and marched back.

Though united by the desire to remove Peter, the conspirators were not united on how to replace him. But thanks to the promptitude of the Orlovs, Catherine had been proclaimed sole and sovereign ruler in her own right, and the partisans of a regency had missed their opportunity. Whatever his secret hopes might still be, Panin now devoted himself to ensuring the consolidation of Catherine's hold on the throne, and he ordered a strict watch to be kept on the gates of the capital to prevent news of the coup from reaching Peter III at Oranienbaum.

Meanwhile the new regime proceeded at once to rally the support of the groups which really mattered : the army, government officials and the Church. The plotters themselves were well placed to win over the soldiers with assurances that the Danish campaign would be called off, and the men evidently welcomed Catherine's accession with real rejoicing. The very limited degree of opposition in the army came from some of the officers, who may have taken seriously their oath of allegiance to Peter. No such scruple seemed to worry the Church hierarchy, which showed no hesitation whatever in administering the oath of allegiance to Catherine to those who had only six months previously sworn allegiance to Peter III. The first manifesto issued by the new government on 28 June 1762 showed its awareness of the most emotionally vulnerable points of popular opinion. It stressed that Catherine had taken power because of the danger to the Orthodox faith, and the insult to the Russian army implicit in the country's 'enslavement' to her worst enemy, namely Prussia, the policy attributed to Peter. As regards the high government officials, Catherine and her supporters were skilful enough to draw the Senate as an institution into cooperation in the measures required to consolidate her power. But the Senate was both strengthened and diluted by the addition of a number of Catherine's partisans, notably Nikita Panin himself, his brother-in-law, I.I. Neplyuyev, a much respected elder statesman, Kyrill Razumovsky, N.M. Volkonsky, and the police chief, Baron N.A. Korf.

Steps were immediately taken to forestall any counter-move by Peter III, who still lingered in Oranienbaum, in total ignorance that he had lost his throne. Orders were sent to the governor-general of Livonia to proclaim Catherine there, and in case Peter should attempt to take command of the troops already in Livonia, the governor-general was ordered to 'seize any opponent whatever his rank, alive or dead'.[39] General Peter Panin was ordered to take over command of the troops in Pomerania from General P.A. Rumyantsev, whose allegiance was as yet uncertain. Peter III himself was to be arrested and incarcerated in the fortress of Schlüsselburg.

On 29 June, Peter III paid a visit to Peterhof where Catherine was expected to provide an entertainment on the occasion of his name-day. When his party arrived they found the palace deserted ; Catherine's abandoned gala dress was the only sign of her presence. Thunderstruck, Peter wandered around in dismay. Three officials, including the chancellor, Count M.R. Vorontsov, volunteered to go to the capital to find out what was happening, and on arrival swore allegiance to Catherine. Almost alone the aged Count Münnich endeavoured to instil some resolution into his master, but when Peter's party, having boarded a ship, were refused permission to land at Kronstadt, which had already declared for Catherine, he lost his nerve completely. The fallen emperor drifted back disconsolately to Oranienbaum, surrounded by distraught courtiers, and the distracted wives and even children of some of the conspirators.[40]

Catherine now embarked on the most dramatic episode of the *coup d'état*. Dressed in a borrowed guards uniform, mounted on horseback, and escorted by Princess Dashkova, similarly attired, she rode out at the head of her troops to Oranienbaum, to arrest Peter. On the way she was met by the vice-chancellor, Prince A.M. Golitsyn, bearing a letter from Peter offering to negotiate. The letter was left unanswered, and the vice-chancellor swore allegiance to the new empress and joined her cavalcade. In a second letter Peter now abdicated the throne of Russia and asked merely to be allowed to leave for Holstein with his mistress. This letter too was not accepted, and eventually the vice-chancellor, Grigory Orlov and one of Peter's adherents, General M.L. Izmaylov, persuaded Peter to sign an unconditional abdication. He was then removed from Oranienbaum, with Elizabeth Vorontsova, and taken to Peterhof, where he was arrested and separated from his companion. Nikita Panin, who had now joined Catherine from the capital, personally selected a guard of three hundred for the deposed emperor, to 'protect' him against the irate common soldiers. 'Je compte pour un malheur de ma vie d'avoir été obligé de le voir,' he said some years later, of his painful final scene with the deposed emperor.[41] Given a choice of residence, Peter selected Ropsha, a country estate nearby, while accommodation was prepared for him in Schlüsselburg, which was to be his ultimate destination.[42]

The problem of what to do with Peter was indeed acute. Whether Catherine herself had reached the conclusion that his death was necessary to her security cannot be proved. But the implications of her position are unlikely to have escaped her, and they certainly did not escape the Orlov brothers, since Grigory could have no hope of marrying Catherine unless she were a widow. Aleksey Orlov was placed in command of the small detachment of troops in charge of Peter III at Ropsha, and in mysterious circumstances, allegedly in a drunken brawl, Peter was killed on 5/16 July 1762. The news reached Catherine in St Petersburg in an incoherent, scribbled note from Aleksey Orlov which accident has preserved :

Little Mother, most gracious lady, How can I explain or describe what happened. You will not believe your faithful servant but before God I speak the truth. . . . I am ready to go to death but I know not how this happened. We are ruined if you do not show mercy. Little Mother, he is no more. But it never occurred to anyone, how could anyone think of raising a hand against our sovereign lord. But sovereign Lady, the mischief is done. He started struggling with Prince Fyodor [Baryatynsky] at table. We had no time to separate them and he is no more. I don't remember what we did but all of us are guilty and worthy of punishment. Have mercy upon me if only for my brother's sake. I confess it all to you, and there is nothing to investigate. Forgive us, or order an end to be made quickly. Life is not worth living. We have angered you, and lost our souls forever.

This letter seems to suggest that Catherine had not issued any orders for the murder of her husband, however convenient his disappearance was for her. At any rate when her son Paul read it after his mother's death he was convinced that she was innocent of Peter's murder.[43] But she benefited from the crime and became an accessory after the fact. The actual murder was covered up, and a manifesto issued on 7/18 July declared that Peter had died of colic following an acute haemorrhoidal attack; Peter's unexpected death, stated the manifesto, was 'evidence of God's divine intent . . .' which had prepared Catherine's way to the throne.[44] None of the participants in Peter's murder was punished, but though Catherine's problem had been thus forcibly solved for her, she felt the stain on her character and on Russia in the eyes of Europe.[45]

Rewards were lavished on those who had helped Catherine to the throne. Nikita Panin, Kyrill Razumovsky and M.N. Volkonsky received life pensions of 5,000 r.p.a. Princess Dashkova reluctantly accepted 24,000 r. to pay her husband's debts, G.N. Teplov, probably the author of most of Catherine's manifestos, was awarded 20,000r., while Catherine's faithful valet, Vasily Shkurin, who cared for her son by Orlov, was ennobled and received one thousand serfs.[46] One other name deserves notice: that of an ensign in the Horseguards who, in Catherine's commendation, had shown discernment and zeal in her service : Grigory Aleksandrovich Potemkin was awarded 300 serfs and made a modest appearance on the stage he was to dominate so long.[47] In all, some 454 people were given promotions, decorations, estates, or monetary awards. The common people had already celebrated Catherine's accession in the traditional way by breaking into the taverns.[48]

On the other hand there were no proscriptions and no one was exiled. Elizabeth Vorontsova was quietly sent away to Moscow ; Peter's Holstein relatives and his Holstein troops were repatriated to Germany.[49] Most of Peter's high-ranking officials had gone over to Catherine in the course of her *coup d'état*. For the time being the chancellor, M.L. Vorontsov, the vice-chancellor, A.M. Golitsyn, and the president of the College of War, Prince N. Yu. Trubetskoy, remained at their posts, though Peter III's council of state was of course disbanded. The return to the capital of the old chancellor, A.P. Bestuzhev Ryumin, in July 1762, revived old hatreds and led to fierce if suppressed factional fighting around the new empress. Bestuzhev had not forgiven those who had caused his disgrace, notably the chancellor, Teplov, and D.V. Volkov. Catherine issued a manifesto exonerating Bestuzhev from all crimes and restoring his previous honours. But she did not give him back the chancellorship.[50]

Three different groups can be detected in the shifting factions around Catherine in these early days, united to some extent by kinship, to some extent by the support of similar policies. There were first those who had maintained a somewhat lukewarm loyalty to Peter until the end and who were now kept at a distance, such as D. V. Volkov, and A.P. Mel'gunov.[51] Secondly there was the group united by family ties and to some extent over programmes of internal reform or foreign policy (the two by no means always coincided) of which Nikita Panin was the mainspring. His brother, General Peter Panin, was appointed a senator on his return from the army, and their nephew by marriage, Prince N. V. Repnin, also gravitated eventually towards the family group. On a lower social level was the able and unscrupulous G.N. Teplov. The remains of the Vorontsov group also gravitated towards Panin. Many of Panin's circle, including Dashkova herself, had favoured the proclamation of a regency and they were thus united in opposing the ascendancy of the third group, namely the Orlov brothers.

The Orlovs were of course strong advocates of the undivided power of Catherine, and undoubtedly hoped that she would in due time marry Grigory. In the meantime the nature of their influence – arising from Catherine's personal attachment to Grigory – aroused the worst apprehensions of a revival of the favouritism which had marked Elizabeth's reign. Grigory, now general adjutant, gentleman of the bedchamber, and count, aroused the jealousy of conspirators dissatisfied with their rewards. Yet it was with the Orlovs that the old chancellor, Bestuzhev, now aligned himself, hoping with their help to return to power and revenge himself on those responsible for his fall.[52]

Catherine was fully aware that her own position on the throne was by no means secure, and decided to hasten her coronation, which would serve to strengthen her legitimacy, and to test the political climate in Moscow. The impressive ceremony took place on 22 September/3 October 1762 in the old capital. An endless round of public and private festivities distracted Muscovites from affairs of state. Nevertheless, Catherine's relations with Orlov crystallized the discontent of a group of young officers, two of whom had actually taken part in her *coup d'état,* and led them to talk of conspiring to dethrone her in favour of the ex-emperor Ivan Antonovich, with Nikita Panin or Ivan Shuvalov as regents. Early in October some fifteen arrests were made among officers and men. So seriously did Catherine take the alleged plot that she authorized the use of torture, but nothing emerged beyond confused recollections of drunken dinners. The Senate's verdict was issued on 21 October, and asked for the usual harsh penalties. It was followed on 24 October by a manifesto signed by Catherine, reducing the penalties on the two most guilty to loss of rank and noble status and exile to Kamchatka.[53]

But the groundswell of opposition remained. Meanwhile Grigory Orlov was pressing for a marriage, and it was believed that a precedent existed in the marriage thought to have taken place between Elizabeth Petrovna and Aleksey Razumovsky. In the winter of 1763, Bestuzhev started to canvas opinion in favour of petitioning the empress to marry again, since the legitimate heir, Grand Duke Paul, was known to be frail. A visit paid by Catherine to the Monastery of the Resurrection in Rostov in May 1763 started the rumour that she had gone there in order secretly to marry Orlov in a religious ceremony. Gossip flew around Moscow, and led to the arrest of a page of the bedchamber, F. Khitrovo, who had, it was alleged, said that Nikita Panin, Razumovsky, General Z. Chernyshev and a number of officers had joined to warn Catherine against the marriage proposed by Bestuzhev, and had urged her to marry one of the brothers of Ivan Antonovich instead. If she refused, the Orlovs were to be killed. The names of Princess Dashkova, and of the procurator general, A.I. Glebov, were also bandied about by Khitrovo.[54]

That the names of so many senior officials and officers should have been mentioned was enough to alarm Catherine. But under interrogation, Khitrovo now declared that he had joined in the plot in June 1762 believing that Catherine was to be proclaimed regent and not sole ruler, and that she herself had promised Panin that she intended to follow this course. He alleged that on the fateful day, Aleksey Orlov and two other guards officers had persuaded her to let herself be proclaimed sole ruler instead. The suggestion that she had ever agreed to be only a regent was much more dangerous to Catherine than rumours of a marriage, which in any case she knew now could never take place. Accordingly the whole affair was hushed up. Khitrovo, who came from a wealthy family, was banished to his estates, and the gossip in Moscow was clumsily repressed by the so-called 'Manifesto of Silence' issued on 4 June 1763, which forbade 'improper discussion and gossip on matters concerning the government'.[55]

The most serious shock was still to come. On 20 June 1764, Catherine departed for a tour of Livonia. On 9 July, in Riga, she received the news of a rising in Schlüsselburg, intended to free the ex-emperor Ivan Antonovich, which had ended in the latter's death. Under Elizabeth, orders had been issued by Alexander Shuvalov, then head of the Secret Chancery, that 'if the prisoner is disorderly or unruly or speaks in an improper manner' he was to be put in chains, and if that failed he could be whipped and beaten. Peter III had allowed Ivan Antonovich's keepers even greater latitude : on 1 January 1762 he instructed them in his own hand on no account to allow the prisoner to escape alive.[56] Moved out to make room for Peter himself, Ivan Antonovich was returned to Schlüsselburg after the death of the emperor, and some time on the return journey, in August 1762, Catherine saw and spoke to him.

It was now Nikita Panin who was entrusted with the arrangements for the security of Ivan, and he changed the guards and provided them with fresh instructions. Catherine's aim was to persuade the young man to opt for a monastic life (which would disqualify him as a candidate for the throne), and the infantry officers who guarded him were to use their best endeavours to incline him to this solution.[57] A supplementary instruction signed by Panin reinforced the orders given by Peter in his time : the guards were specifically allowed to put their prisoner to death if efforts to liberate him seemed likely to succeed.[58] Ivan thus remained in the hands of men anxious to end their solitary and irksome task, and ultimately authorized to kill him.

The rising on the night of 4/5 July 1764 was the product of a single mind, that of a young Ukrainian officer, V.Ya. Mirovich, whose family had sided with Mazeppa and Sweden during the Great Northern War of Peter I and had as a result lost all their estates. Brought up in poverty and resentment, the spectacle of sudden fortune descending on king-makers at Catherine's court aroused his hopes of acting the part of an Aleksey Orlov on behalf of Ivan, and achieving power and fortune at one stroke. He took only one fellow-officer into his confidence, who was drowned before the actual day of the rising. Mirovich's regiment was stationed on garrison duty in Schlüsselburg, though it was not in any way concerned with the special guard of the 'nameless prisoner'. But he had been able to discover his identity. In the middle of the night of 4/5 July Mirovich called upon a group of some thirty-eight totally unprepared soldiers and endeavoured to gain control of the fortress and access to the inner citadel where Ivan was held. The commandant of the fortress was stunned by a blow on the head, and Mirovich then proceeded to read to the soldiers the manifesto which he had prepared proclaiming Ivan tsar and written in his name:

Not long had Peter III possessed the throne when by the intrigues of his wife and by her hands he was given poison to drink, and by these means and by force the vain and spendthrift Catherine seized my hereditary throne. To the day of our accession she has sent out of my country on ships up to 25 million in gold and silver, wrought or in bar, to her brother the Roman General Field-marshal Frederick Augustus ; and moreover, her inborn weaknesses have led her to wish to take as her husband her subject Grigory Orlov, and not to return from her ill-intentioned and harmful journey [to Livonia], for which she will not be able to excuse herself at the last judgment.[59]

The manifesto reveals the essentially personal motives of Mirovich and the extent of his political capacities. It did not mean much to the soldiers, and after some aimless wandering, shots were exchanged with the inner garrison of sixteen men, and Mirovich brought up a cannon. This gave Ivan's two keepers their opportunity to free themselves from their burden, and they promptly despatched him with their swords. Meanwhile the inner garrison had ceased to oppose Mirovich, and when the latter rushed in to the citadel, seeking his emperor, it was to find him lying dead on the floor of his cell. Since the plot had now lost its object, Mirovich allowed himself to be arrested.

The commandant of Schlüsselburg reported the matter at once to Nikita Panin who was at Tsarskoye Selo, and who took steps to preserve order in the capital, to stifle the whole matter, and to begin an investigation. Catherine received his report in Riga, and in the midst of her horror and fear could not suppress an expression of thanks to providence for having allowed the affair to finish so well for her : 'La providence m'a donné un signe bien évident de sa grâce en tournant cette entreprise de la façon dont elle est finie.' But the implications did not escape her and in distant Riga it was more difficult to believe that the rising had been a desperate *coup de main* by one man rather than a widespread plot. It coincided moreover with a spate of flysheets and anonymous letters of a threatening description which had circulated in St Petersburg in spring 1764.[60]

Some fifty officers and men were arrested, and after a protracted investigation, a special court, composed of the Senate, the Synod, the presidents of the Colleges of Foreign Affairs, War and the Navy, and senior officials and officers, was set up on 17 August 1764. The manifesto setting up the court admitted in so many words that the life of Ivan Antonovich had been taken by his guards. But they were never placed on trial. The court was to inquire into and judge the seditious act carried out by Mirovich. Thus the guilt for Ivan's death was shifted from those who had actually killed him on to the man who had tried to free him.[61]

The presence of the procurator general, now Prince A.A. Vyazemsky,[62] on the court enabled Catherine to block demands that Mirovich should be tortured and to suppress any reference to Panin's secret orders authorizing Ivan's keepers to put him to death in the event of an attempt to free him. The existence of this instruction was kept a close secret, and the evil was attributed to the orders given by the Empress Elizabeth through A. Shuvalov. The verdict of the court was never in any doubt, and on 9 September sentence was pronounced. Mirovich was to be beheaded, his body exposed and finally burnt. Three corporals and three soldiers were condemned to run the gauntlet twelve and ten times respectively between one thousand men, and then to hard labour. Less drastic punishments were meted out to some of those accidentally involved, and fifteen men were acquitted. On 15 September 1764 the sentence on Mirovich was carried out in St Petersburg before a silent crowd which had not witnessed a public execution for twenty-two years.[63]

The execution of Mirovich for high treason could not cover up the fact, by now widely known, that Ivan had been killed by his guards. They were rewarded with promotion and seven thousand rubles ; their names are known but they disappear from history. From a public point of view the murder of Ivan, following on that of Peter, could not be worse. Catherine's supporters and the indifferent public might pretend, in the interests of political stability, that Peter III had died a natural death. But Ivan's death had not been necessary and was clearly murder. The immunity granted to his murderers led to rumours that the whole incident was a provocation engineered by the empress to remove a dangerous rival, and that Mirovich was merely her scapegoat.[64] Public opinion within Russia could be silenced, though the name of Ivan remained alive and was mentioned in several false manifestos and anonymous documents preserved in the Secret Department of the Senate. Abroad, it could not, and the prestige of Catherine suffered a serious blow, as evidenced by the spate of leaflets which appeared on the life and death of Peter III and Ivan respectively. Nevertheless Catherine's hold on the throne was now that much more secure. Those who had once favoured a regency for the young Paul, like Nikita Panin, were now too deeply committed to a regime which had begun to give a new and firmer direction to Russian government.

2

The Reform of the Central Government Institutions

When she seized the throne, Catherine had every intention of ruling as well as reigning. While she did not have a 'programme', she certainly had a sense of the general direction in which she wished to guide Russian government and society. The ukazy issued by Peter III were thus immediately examined and those most offensive to Russian feelings repealed.[1] But Catherine had no experience of government, and needed both information and advice. She solved two problems at the same time – the need to divide and control potential opposition, and the shortage of efficient collaborators – by establishing a number of commissions to study the most pressing problems of the country, commissions to which she appointed both government officials who had served Peter and her own supporters.

A commission composed of ecclesiastical and lay members was set up in August 1762 to re-examine Peter III's hasty secularization of Church lands.[2] A second commission was established in November 1762, composed of military experts and personal followers of Catherine's, to review the establishment of the armed forces. A commerce commission was set up in December 1763.[3] By early 1763 Catherine felt strong enough to dispense with the services of some of Elizabeth's old guard. The ex-favourite, Ivan Shuvalov, whom Catherine had never trusted, was allowed to travel abroad. Alexander Shuvalov retired with an award of two thousand serfs. The Grand Duke Paul became nominal head of the Admiralty College, while Ivan Chernyshev became vice-president, and his brother Zakhar Chernyshev became vice-president of the College of War – no president was appointed.

Having failed in his hope of placing the young Paul on the throne with a regency, Nikita Panin nevertheless thought it worth while to exploit the weakness of Catherine's position in order to attempt to limit the power of the ruler.[4] He contemplated three kinds of reform : first of all the reorganization of the administration along more functional lines ; secondly, the introduction into Russian political life of the concept of 'fundamental laws' as a guarantee against the arbitrariness of the regime and its attendant vice, favouritism ; and thirdly, he

38

seems to have hoped to achieve some kind of constitutional limitation on absolute power, to be exercised by the aristocracy.

The concept of fundamental laws was of course very vague and lacking in legal precision. In the European absolute monarchies, and among their noble supporters, fundamental laws had come to mean the recognition by the sovereign that certain customs and procedures had acquired the status of rights and obligations. The sovereign had the power to alter such procedures, but would not normally do so ; he would regard himself as bound to observe rules founded on precedent, natural law and Christian doctrine. Compared to other European states, Russia lacked fundamental laws, and resembled Montesquieu's despotism much more closely than his monarchy. For that very reason the ruler, the high nobility and the bureaucracy, all in different ways, felt the need to establish the permanent framework of an *état policé,* the eighteenth-century continental ideal of orderly government.

Some of these ideas are already reflected in the manifesto issued by Catherine on her accession, which was drawn up by Nikita Panin. The manifesto had accused Peter of treating supreme power not as a gift from God to be used for the benefit of the people, but as a casual acquisition, to be used for his own satisfaction ; of despising natural and civil law by disregarding the rights of his son to be proclaimed heir ; of disregarding the laws and the administration of justice, wasting the national revenue, embarking on an unnecessary war and placing Russian forces under foreign commanders, and finally of planning to eliminate his wife and son. With God's help, Catherine had responded to the general wish of all ranks to become her subjects, and the manifesto promised to defend Russia, preserve justice, eliminate unjust oppression and, above all, 'to enact such ordinances [*ustanovleniya*] that the government of my beloved country would function strongly within its borders in such a way that even in the future each government institution would have its proper limits and regulations for the proper observation of good order in everything.'[5]

Some time in summer 1762 Panin submitted to Catherine a plan to set up an imperial council as a permanent institution. In an introductory memorandum he delivered a damning indictment of the government of Catherine's predecessors. In his view, 'the principal, genuine and overall concern for the welfare of the state resided in the person of the sovereign. But the sovereign could not translate this concern into useful action except by sharing it out intelligently among a small number of persons specially selected for the purpose.'[6] Both the institutions and the persons who had in the past shared in this concern came in for Panin's criticism. The Senate was intended to be the supreme organ of administrative coordination ; but it had no power to make law, and was supposed to reach its decisions by basing itself on existing laws and regulations, however out of date they might be. In practice it stuck to the routine application of existing laws or business was held up indefinitely while it debated the need for new laws which it had not the power to issue. In doubtful cases, senators took the easy way of referring the matter to the sovereign, refraining from the more difficult task of attempting to iron out existing contradictions. Not one hour of the day, continued Panin, did these officials spend in studying the law in relation to the general welfare of the state and, relying on their subordinates for guidance, 'they arrived at their sessions like guests at a dinner, who knew neither the taste of the food, nor even the dishes to be served up to them'. In the same way the Colleges, or departments in charge of particular branches of the administration, acted only in accordance with the laws governing their own particular concerns and did not think in terms of the public welfare.

Panin also condemned the procuracy as inadequate. In theory, according to the regulations establishing this office in the reign of Peter the Great, the procurator general was supposed to provide precisely that coordination and general supervision which the Senate so signally failed to provide.[7] It was the link between the Senate and the sovereign, and was admittedly called the 'eye of the sovereign'. But the sovereign 'could not through one eye' survey all the changing administrative needs of the state. Hence the procurator general served merely as the one eye which saw to it that the Senate followed the proper procedures and applied existing laws.

The need for a supreme policy-making body had been felt in the past, argued Panin, and sometimes supplied. But Elizabeth's 'cabinet' had been only a private chancery, peopled by favourites and courtiers who acted secretly, ostensibly in the sovereign's name, accountable neither to the sovereign nor the public for their deeds. The sovereign would be blamed for its wrong-doing, but 'a person entrusted with the business of an institution which is secret and does not belong in any way to the government of the state, may consider that he is not subject to the judgment of the people, nor accountable to it, and therefore free from all obligation towards the sovereign and the state'. The 'Conference' set up by Elizabeth in 1757 to run the war effort, though an official body, did not escape Panin's strictures. The constitution of 'that monster' was inadequate, its personnel disastrous. 'It was neither properly established nor consistent – all was irresponsible. Favouritism ran riot, in pursuit of mere caprice.'

In making his recommendations to Catherine, Panin was on much more delicate ground than when he attacked the ramshackle government of Elizabeth. Nevertheless, he emphasized the need to guard against favouritism, and described his plan as one 'which establishes the form of the highest state institution for legislation from which, *as from* [my italics] a single sovereign and a single place, there will issue forth the monarch's own decision', thus protecting the 'sovereign power from its secret destroyers'. This highest legislative organ which Panin proposed to establish was to be a permanent council of six to eight members. At least four of the imperial councillors should be state secretaries representing the principal departments of state, namely war, the navy, foreign affairs and internal affairs. All matters falling outside the purview of the Senate itself were to be taken up by the council 'as if' by the empress personally. All

40

major legislative enactments, orders and regulations normally signed by the sovereign in person were to be countersigned by the state secretary and imperial councillor responsible for that particular branch of the administration. Nothing issuing from the imperial council would be valid however without the sovereign's signature.

Panin's plan did not provide for any collective action by the state councillors. The sovereign was merely sharing out the overall 'concern' for the national welfare among councillors with strictly departmental responsibilities. The council was to meet every day except Saturdays, Sundays and holidays, each secretary was to report on the affairs of his department and give his opinion, and the sovereign would make the final decision. Final coordination was thus concentrated as before in the ruler.

There has been considerable controversy around the ultimate object of Panin's plan for an imperial council.[8] Was he really hoping to use Catherine's lack of legitimacy to achieve a fundamental constitutional change in Russia ? Or was he only putting forward his plan for a Council because his only official position – senator and tutor to the grand duke – was weak, and a council of which he would undoubtedly be a member would provide him with an arena ? Foreign affairs, in which he had made his reputation, was in the hands of the chancellor, M.R. Vorontsov, and the vice-chancellor, A.M. Golitsyn. And though Panin was in fact very active in domestic affairs, he had no official appointment in this field. Or was Panin's plan merely a response to a request from Catherine for advice on the reform of the central government, as some historians have suggested ?

It is certainly possible that Catherine invited Panin to put before her some kind of plan for restructuring the central government, knowing that in the very first weeks of her reign it was essential to manoeuvre between the various factions at court. Rumours of a plan to set up a new kind of council were reported in dispatches from foreign envoys as early as July 1762.[9] The first mention in Russian sources occurs in the draft manifesto prepared by Catherine in August 1762 for the rehabilitation of Bestuzhev Ryumin, in which the old ex-chancellor is named as 'first member of the imperial council I propose to set up'.[10] On 29 August 1762, Teplov wrote to Panin expressing the hope that the role of the Orlov brothers would be decided by the imperial council.[11] Little is known of any other plans submitted to the empress, though a Soviet historian has suggested that the 'oligarchic party' (i.e. Panin and his friends) was so ill-prepared with plans as to allow the empress to seize the initiative and split the opponents of her sole power by inviting the various factions to submit different plans to her.[12]

Putting all the admittedly slender evidence together, it does seem that Panin, fearing that Catherine and Grigory Orlov would prove as fatal a combination to orderly government as Elizabeth and her favourites, did attempt to bring about constitutional changes in the central government of Russia. He stressed the importance of institutions as a safeguard against the arbitrary caprice of favourites, and he wished the functions and the powers of institutions to be precisely defined and formulated. Since he could not openly propose limitations on the sovereign's absolute power, he put forward institutional barriers against its misuse. By forcing all major policy decisions into one institutional channel the personal responsibility of the state secretary concerned would be emphasized, and the private influence of all-powerful favourites in the closet could be eliminated. With time the new procedures would acquire the status of 'fundamental laws'.

Panin's project also contained a feature new to the theory and practice of government in Russia, namely the dual accountability of the ruler's public servants both to the ruler and to the public. He did not define what he meant by 'public'. In all likelihood he confined it to the nobility in general, or possibly to the so-called *'generalitet'* (all ranks, military and civil, from major-general upwards).[13] His proposal implied the identification of a particular official with a particular policy in the eyes of the knowledgeable, and might therefore develop in officials a higher sense of responsibility for their actions. According to gossip among the foreign envoys, Panin would have liked to go much further towards establishing genuine political checks on the sovereign in the interests of the high service aristocracy. In the project submitted to Catherine he does not explain how imperial councillors were to be appointed, nor for how long. But according to what he told the French envoy, Baron de Breteuil, he intended that they should be appointed for life, and that they should only be removable, in case of misconduct, by a full assembly of the Senate.[14] The Senate would thus be raised to the role of arbiter between the empress and her council. Breteuil certainly understood at the time that Panin intended to limit Catherine's power, 'à peu près comme celle des rois de Suède'.[15] Later, Panin gave a more toned-down version to Breteuil of the advice he had given Catherine: he had not, he said, proposed to 'altérer son autorité despotique'. But he had advised her not to claim a power which she knew to be unjust. 'Le temps d'aveuglement et de soumission honteuse à l'homme était passé en Russie', and Catherine owed it to those who had raised her to the throne to take steps to ensure that they should no longer be liable to sudden and illegal arrests and punishments.[16]

There is no record of what Catherine herself thought of Panin's project for a council. But it is hard to believe that the empress, well read in contemporary European political literature, should not have seized on the danger to her absolute rule concealed in his plan. Her freedom to choose her public servants was to be severely curtailed in the interests of the group at present in a dominant position. She undoubtedly saw the parallel with Sweden, judging by a later reference to 'someone who, because he lived for a long time in this or that country, believed that everything should be established according to the system in that favourite country of his . . . . '[17] The empress was evidently under considerable pressure from Panin – judging by the latter's confidences to foreign envoys – and the extent of her hesitation is revealed by the fact that she actually signed the manifesto prepared by Panin, announcing the formation of the council, on 28 December 1762. But subsequently her signature was torn off and the manifesto was never promulgated. She certainly sounded opinion at court fairly widely. Most of the written comments which have survived do not deal with matters of substance, but one of her early supporters submitted a memorandum which may have influenced her. 'I do not know who drafted this plan,' he wrote,

but it seems to me that on the pretext of defending the monarchy, in a subtle way it inclines towards an aristocratic form of government. The influential people, appointed by law to a council of state . . . can easily turn into co-rulers. . . . The Russian sovereign must have unlimited power. An imperial council brings the subject too close to the sovereign and the subject may begin to harbour hopes of sharing power with the sovereign.[18]

Catherine herself never wavered in the conviction that absolutism was the only form of government suitable for Russia and suitable for her.[19] In this, she was encouraged by the Orlovs, and by Bestuzhev Ryumin, who had pinned his hopes to the favourite and still hankered after the restoration of his previous dominant position. At most the Orlovs would agree to a purely advisory council such as had existed in Elizabeth's day, a solution which Panin utterly rejected.[20] By the beginning of February 1763 it was clear that there was to be no council. Catherine had concluded that Panin represented a minority opinion which she could disregard, and that the divisions among the magnates left her plenty of room to manoeuvre. But since she was always conciliatory, she appointed all those who would have been members of the council to a commission set up on 11 February 1763 to examine Peter III's manifesto on the freedom of the nobility, a law which to the dismay of many of the nobles she had not yet confirmed. She thus sidetracked and postponed the projected council of state, while giving its intended members an opportunity to influence policy-making in an area vital to the interests of the noble estate.[21] Two months later, on 17 April 1763, this same commission was entrusted with the totally unrelated subject of studying the reform of the Senate.[22] It thus began to take on the complexion of an advisory council, such as the Orlovs and Bestuzhev had proposed, though it remained a purely *ad hoc* body.

At no stage in these early days was the Senate considered as a possible alternative to the projected council. But its reorganization had been contemplated in Panin's plan, in order to make it a more effective body in the administrative field, subordinated to the new council. For a brief period, after Catherine's seizure of power, the Senate had recovered some of its earlier political significance. Catherine had associated it closely with herself, since she required institutional support during the crucial days when Peter III was still at large. It was through the Senate that orders were issued to the Russian troops abroad, and it was to the care of the Senate that Catherine had confided the young Paul when she rode off at the head of her troops to secure the person of Peter III. The sittings of the Senate were moved to the Summer Palace where it was easier for Catherine to attend them, which she did about twice a week until she left for her coronation in Moscow.[23] In addition she appointed Fyodor Orlov, younger brother of

Grigory, 'to be constantly in attendance in the Senate', in order to have her own private channel of information and control over its proceedings.[24]

In Panin's plan, legislation would have been confined to the future imperial council while the Senate should have been concerned with the administration ; he had proposed to divide it into six departments, composed of four or five members, with specific administrative and judicial functions. The departments were to reach their decision by unanimity, but the general assembly of the Senate, which was to discuss issues requiring fresh legislation or a change in existing laws, should decide by a majority vote. Panin also proposed that a right to make 'representations' 'concerning even our own commands if their implementation touches upon or negatively affects the laws of the state or the welfare of our people', granted by Peter I to the Senate, should be restored.[25]

No records have been published of the debates in the commission on the reform of the Senate. It is evident however that both in the Senate and in the commission there was considerable discussion on matters of principle, namely the rights of the nobility as such, their participation in central and local government, and the rights which the Senate should enjoy. To what extent the Senate itself was concerned with its own reorganization we do not know. That Catherine was dissatisfied with its performance is attested by an exceptionally outspoken ukaz of hers of 6 June 1763, which, in milder language, recalls some of Peter I's instructions to his quarrelsome subordinates. 'I cannot say that you are lacking in patriotic concern for my welfare and the general welfare,' wrote Catherine, 'but I am sorry to say that things are not moving towards their appointed end as successfully as one would wish.' The cause of this delay, Catherine pointed out, was the existence of 'internal disagreements, enmity and hatred' leading to the formation of parties seeking to hurt each other, and to behaviour unworthy of sensible, respectable people desirous of doing good. However mild and patient the sovereign, such lack of harmony must move him to anger. Senators criticized each other's decisions simply because they had not taken them themselves. In any case, Catherine added, not everyone was equally talented, and it was up to all to exercise moderation and to pursue the common good without obstinacy and with common sense.[26]

Catherine's rebuke, read in conjunction with the instruction she drafted early in 1764 to the newly appointed procurator general, A.A. Vyazemsky, reflects the existence within the Senate of factions divided on the issue of bureaucratic centralization as against aristocratic participation in the formulation of policy. 'In the Senate you will find two parties,' she wrote to Vyazemsky, 'but the sensible policy from my point of view requires me to pay no attention to them, in order not to give them more consistency . . . so I merely watch them with an unsleeping eye and employ people in this or that affair according to their capacity. Each of these parties will now try to get you on their side. In the one you will find honest people, if of limited intelligence. In the other I think more long-range plans are harboured, but I am not sure that they are always useful.' Catherine warned Vyazemsky to pay no heed to either party, but to listen to all and behave impartially.[27]

Catherine's view of the proper function of the Senate is expressed in her instruction to Vyazemsky. 'The Senate has been established for the carrying out of laws prescribed to it. But it has often issued laws itself, granted ranks, honours, money and lands, in one word . . . almost everything. Having once exceeded its limits the Senate now still finds it difficult to adapt itself to the new order within which it should confine itself.' The new order which Catherine had devised for the Senate was made public in an ukaz of 15 December 1763.[28]

The available evidence does not help to determine on whose advice she acted and by whom she was mainly influenced. It is possible that the then procurator general, A.I. Glebov, supported her in a programme designed to limit the power of the Senate, since any rise in its power might be at the expense of the procurator general. For Catherine's reform of the Senate involved a reduction of its legislative initiative and a complete functional reorganization. This was to some extent modelled on the plan put forward by Panin, though with substantial changes in the functional division. The Senate was divided into six departments, of which the first was by far the most important, since it was charged with all 'state and political affairs'. This incuded the Colleges of Commerce, Mining, Manufacturing ; the various financial institutions ; the Noble and Merchant Banks, the Salt Office, the Coinage and Currency Offices, supervision over the *magistraty* or town councils, the Chancery of Confiscations, and the College of Foreign Affairs, where it impinged on internal matters. The first department also dealt with frontiers, and the illicit trade in spirits. Finally it controlled the Herald's Office (in charge of the registration of the nobility), the Holy Synod, the Secret Department or security organ, and the Legislative Commission or Commission for the Drafting of a New Code, inherited from Elizabethan days.

The second department was concerned mainly with matters arising in the judicial field or with judicial implications: it dealt with the College of Justice, the *Sudnyy prikaz* or judicial office, the Land Survey[29] (which gave rise to complex legal problems), the Votchina College or College of Landed Estates, and the Petitions Office, i.e. the office to which petitions to the empress were to be submitted. The second department also dealt with prisoners and convicts. The third department was placed in charge of territories governed by their own laws, such as Livonia and Estonia, Narva, Vyborg and the Ukraine. It also dealt with a number of miscellaneous matters of internal policy such as education (the University of Moscow, the Academy of Sciences, the College of Medicine), communications, public buildings, the preservation of public order and decency. The fourth department supervised the armed forces and the foreign settlements in New Serbia in the south. The fifth and sixth departments were to be located in Moscow and duplicated the functions of the first and second departments respectively.[30] In the long run, only the first and second departments acquired any real importance. The presidents of the Colleges of War, Navy and Foreign Affairs had direct access to the empress without going through the Senate, as did the chief of police.[31]

The Senate's activities thus fell into two broad categories : general administrative duties, and general judicial duties. A department was entitled to issue an ukaz if a decision had been reached unanimously, and was authorized by an existing law. If the department could not reach a decision, or if a new law was needed, the matter had to be referred to a full session of the Senate. And if the Senate failed to reach a unanimous decision, or decided that a new law was necessary, it reported accordingly to the empress.

This was a considerable departure from Panin's plan for the reform of the Senate, in which senators could decide matters referred to a full assembly by departments by majority vote. Catherine evidently realized the danger of losing the vital power of deciding between factions in that body.[32] But though senators were entitled to issue ukazy, when in agreement, Catherine in later years complained that they tended to refer too many matters to her decision. If there was a clear law, then the Senate *must* reach a decision. 'And thus', she wrote in January 1771, 'I have wasted an entire morning of which every minute is precious to me, on an affair which can be decided according to the law without me. I am sending it back to the Senate for them to finish the matter without me.'[33]

The Senate's significance was even further reduced by Catherine's policy in relation to the procuracy.[34] According to Petrine tradition, the procurator general was the guardian of legality in the proceedings of the Senate and, through the network of procurators, in central and local administration. He was also the link between the sovereign and the Senate, which reported to the empress through him and received her orders through him. Finally, the procurator general was also the head of the chancery of the Senate and ultimately the master of its agenda. But Catherine immeasurably strengthened his position by appointing him also to head the important and wide-ranging First Department of the Senate. *Oberprokurory,* belonging to the same service as the *General Prokuror,* and reporting to him, were appointed to the other departments, and were supposed to bring to his attention any issues on which the senators in that department could not agree. All problems requiring interpretation or revision of the law were referred to the procurator general, who would call a full assembly of the Senate, and if no agreement was reached, would then refer the matter to the empress for decision. The procurator general thus, by virtue of his role as intermediary between the ruler and the senate, head of its chancery, and head of the largest single department within it, acquired an ascendancy over the Senate which deprived the latter of institutional independence. Both its administrative and its judicial functions were subject to his scrutiny as watchdog over the interpretation and application of the law. The effect of Catherine's changes in the structure of the central government was thus heavily in favour of strengthening the 'personal' as against the collegiate system, while rationalizing the division of functions.

There is no doubt that the empress's decision to drop the plan for a council, and the nature of the reform of the Senate, represented a setback for Panin and a weakening of his position in the struggle for influence at court. For the time being the star of Bestuzhev Ryumin was in the ascendant, particularly at the time – spring 1763 – when he was trying to pave the way for Catherine to marry Grigory Orlov. Panin suffered not only because of his known objections to the marriage, but because his name was mentioned by the dissatisfied guards officers who had plotted or merely talked against Catherine.[35] Moreover factional divisions also extended to foreign affairs. Bestuzhev favoured the old alignment with Britain and Austria, while Panin pressed for acceptance of the new Prussian orientation given to Russian foreign policy by Peter III.[36]

In these tense circumstances the foreign envoys were at a loss to know who was really in charge of the government, and with whom to discuss issues of foreign policy. M.L. Vorontsov was still chancellor in name, and the vice-chancellor saw the foreign envoys – protocol forbade Panin to receive them. But Catherine discussed dispatches with both Panin and Bestuzhev, who were now at daggers drawn. It was Panin who was entrusted in August 1763 with negotiating a treaty of alliance with Prussia, but the definitive outcome of the factional struggle at court did not take place until October 1763, as a result of the unexpected death of Augustus III of Saxony Poland. Faced with the need for decisive action, Catherine called a meeting of her advisers on 6 October.[37] A few days later, Nikita Panin was appointed senior member of the College of Foreign Affairs. Vorontsov had already gone abroad, and Bestuzhev retired to his estates in semi-disgrace. Panin had seemingly won a resounding victory, and from now until 1781 he remained to all intents and purposes the minister for foreign affairs.

The question however arises whether this was what Panin really wanted. Had he not hoped to be first minister, in charge of internal affairs in Catherine's first months ? According to Breteuil, 'il ne rêve que commerce et administration intérieure'.[38] In Catherine's first draft list of members of the council to be, Panin is noted as secretary of state for internal affairs.[39] Most of his work was concerned with domestic policy, including security. Was Catherine perhaps achieving a brilliant coup in October 1763 by dismissing Bestuzhev and relegating Panin to an area which gave great scope to his talents, but where he could do her little harm ? To foreign envoys foreign affairs came first ; they were politics par excellence. But the senior member of the College of Foreign Affairs had limited patronage and no armed force at his disposal. Catherine may have thought it too dangerous to allow a man with the sort of ideas Panin was known to have to build up a network of power and patronage in the far more sensitive area of domestic policy. Such an interpretation is confirmed by her appointments to the armed forces. Peter Panin was passed over as acting head of the College of War in favour of Zakhar Chernyshev (who had once been in love with her), while Ivan Chernyshev was given the navy. Six months later, Catherine was to choose her own man for the key post of procurator general.[40]

3

Local Administration
and the Procuracy

Russian local administration did not escape Catherine's early reforming zeal. The basic territorial unit in the system, which had been refashioned in 1727, was the *guberniya* of which there were fourteen, subdivided in turn into provinces which were subdivided into *uezdy* or districts. The governor of a guberniya, appointed by and responsible to the Senate, combined administrative, judicial, financial and military functions. The whole system was strictly hierarchical ; a town *voyevoda* or commandant in a uezd was responsible to the provincial voyevoda, who in turn was responsible to the governor. Governors and voyevodas were under the orders of the individual Colleges or departments in the capital, and they could be punished, usually by fines, for failure to carry them out successfully.

In the financial sphere governors were responsible for collecting a whole array of miscellaneous dues and taxes and despatching the sums collected under convoy to the guberniya chancery or to the institutions for whose upkeep they were allocated. The most important was the poll-tax, collected by military officers, the proceeds of which were sent straight to the corresponding military units. One of the major problems of local administration was coping with the mounting arrears in all forms of taxation. Methods were primitive : soldiers were used to arrest debtors or the officials elected as tax collectors, such as hundredmen and village elders ; soldiers were billeted on defaulters and seized their goods. Not only peasants were rounded up, but members of the town councils (*magistraty*) were held in chains, and even landowners were arrested.

The general administrative duties laid on the governors and their subordinate voyevodas were even more varied, with both a civil and a military character. First of all they were responsible for the recruit levy. Failure to deliver the required number of recruits subjected them to severe penalties. They were ultimately responsible also for levying horses, forage, food supplies and magazines, ammunition, all this under the direction of the College of War. A vestige of old Muscovy was the duty in frontier provinces to maintain direct relations with foreign lands, which remained of great importance on the southern borders of Russia, on the frontiers with Turkey, the Crimea, Persia, Georgia, and in the east, on the frontier with China. In addition, the governors of Smolensk and Novgorod had the particularly difficult task of preventing the flight of Russian peasants over the borders into Poland, securing their recovery, and preventing Russian landowners from taking matters into their own hands and violating the Polish frontier.

The maintenance of public order was both the most important and the most difficult task laid on the local administration. The governors and voyevodas had at their disposal small military detachments which provided sentries for guard duties, convoys for cash or convicts, or patrols which could be used to squeeze arrears of taxes out of the population. Brigandage was endemic in both the towns and the countryside and sometimes reached astonishing dimensions. Landowners, village priests and peasants all suffered from their depredations, though more often than not the peasant would shelter the brigand, and the brigand would refrain from robbing the peasant. Robber bands were mainly composed of runaway serfs, deserters from the army, escaped convicts ; sometimes even members of the noble estate organized their peasants into bands and robbed their neighbours.

The authorities often had to call on special military detachments to 'clean up' a whole area, detachments which acted independently of the authorities, under the command of the 'chief thief-catcher' (*syshchyk*). A strict watch was kept through the elected village elders to make sure that no brigands were hidden or sheltered in villages, indeed that no unauthorized person was there at all. In the same way the authorities strove to ensure that every individual was inscribed in his proper status, and stayed there. The so-called 'free wanderers' (*vol'no gulyashchiye lyudi*) were perpetually hunted down, but the desire to escape the burdens of poll-tax, military service and serfdom ensured that their ranks were always refilled, and it was from among them that the bands of brigands were mainly recruited.

The instrument by which the population was kept in its place was the internal passport ; the townsman received his passport from the town councils or magistraty ; the peasants could receive passports from their communes, or if serfs from their owners for journeys of not more than thirty versts. For greater distances passports had to be obtained from the local authorities at the cost of four kopeks.

There was of course no national police force, though police offices (*kontory*) existed in the two capitals and twenty-three of the chief towns. Their functions were varied and ill defined, but comprised supervision of public and private decency, public hygiene, medical services, fire prevention (a real problem in Russian towns built mainly of wood), the control of epidemics and the supervision of bears kept in private yards (it was forbidden to keep bears in the two capitals). The police did not exist everywhere, and the coercive power of the state in the domestic field was still exercised by means of military rather than civil force.

Other functions of the local authorities in the administrative sphere included the proclamation of laws and ukazy, and the administration of the oath of allegiance on the accession of a sovereign ; the repression of illegal distilling (a universal practice, carried out by nobles, peasants, village priests, retired soldiers) ; the maintenance (but not as yet the improvement) of roads and bridges, and the organization of the compulsory labour services needed therefor ; the renting and distribution of unsettled state lands, the development of colonization in the east and south, and the care of state forests. In the field of public education, the local authorities were concerned only with the education of chancery servants and soldiers' children in the garrison schools. Because of its importance to the state as a whole, they were expected to report regularly on the state of the harvest.

The local authorities were also in charge of the execution of sentences, the upkeep of prisons, and the detention and maintenance of prisoners, whether convicted or under investigation. Prisons played little part in the Russian mid-eighteenth-century penal system. The idea that the state should spend its already scarce funds on the maintenance of criminals in idleness was too novel. In the Code of 1649 some forty offences carried prison sentences, usually with corporal punishment as well (sacrilege, inadequate fire prevention, theft, murder of children, etc.). But the main deterrent was corporal punishment, mutilation, or the death penalty. In Peter I's legislation, prison played an even smaller part. His Military Code, which together with the Code of 1649 provided the legal basis for sentences, was barbaric in its severity.[1]

By the mid-eighteenth century, both the Code of 1649 and the Military Code were felt to be out of date in more cultured circles, at any rate for such circles themselves, if not for others. As the century advanced penalties suitable for a poor society, death, corporal punishment, branding and multilation, were gradually replaced by new penalties suitable to a wealthier and more sophisticated society : dishonour or deprivation of liberty, which hit the noble, fines which hit the wealthy – the poor of course remained subject to the only punishments it was thought they could really feel. Nevertheless, though corporal punishment was beginning to die out as applied to the nobles, and the death penalty was *de facto* if not *de jure* abolished, prison remained a relatively rare form of punishment.

Monasteries frequently served as places of detention for both male and female convicted offenders, and the regime was often extremely harsh, with small, damp, unheated and unlit cells, poor food and brutal treatment.[2] Some urban prisons existed in the chief towns and fortresses, but the bulk of the inhabitants consisted of people awaiting investigation, or runaways. The state made little provision for the upkeep of prisoners, which could range from one to three kopeks a day. Hence it was common in Russian provincial towns to see a procession of prisoners, some in chains, wending their way under escort and begging for alms in the streets. In these prisons no distinctions were made between old and young, sick and healthy, men and women, hardened criminals and first offenders. Wealthier families could make the stay of their relatives more comfortable and the allowance made by the state also took into account the social rank of the prisoner.

Forced labour in addition to corporal punishment was usually the lot of the poorer classes of the population in cases of serious crime. They would be sent to the mines at Nerchinsk, the naval establishments in Kronstadt and St Petersburg, or Roggerwick in Livonia. According to A.A. Bolotov, there were in 1755 some one thousand convicts in Rogervik, including nobles, merchants, priests, peasants, foreigners, Tartars, etc., who were employed in building a mole. The better-off prisoners could pay for better accommodation, and if the commander of the prison felt inclined could be excused hard labour.[3]

In eighteenth-century Russia there was no clear distinction between administrative and judicial functions in local administration. In terms of the general law of the land, no distinction was made between the various estates, and the extent of the jurisdiction of the local authorities over them. In practice however whole categories of the population escaped the jurisdiction of the local authorities. The nobles, in other than civil lawsuits, came under the jurisdiction of the institutions in which they served (College of War, of the Navy, the various civil colleges, etc.) or under the College of Justice for criminal offences, and they were tried according to the corresponding legal codes, i.e. the Military or Naval Codes if in the armed forces.

The relationship of the local authorities with the clerical estate was complex and the extent of their jurisdiction limited. In principle members of the clerical estate came under the jurisdiction of the ecclesiastical authorities but in practice much depended on rank ; whereas a church dignitary, or an abbot, would be respected by governors and voyevodas, the local village priest or local church servants were often arrested with impunity, particularly if there was any suspicion of connivance with peasant disorders. But the Church authorities called on the civil authorities for legal support in such important matters as combatting heresy and sacrilege, preventing proselytizing activities of other faiths and the conversion of infidels to Orthodoxy. This task was particularly important in those guberniyi containing large Tartar populations, e.g. Kazan'. The civil authorities dealt with the Old Believers, and it was their function to attempt to prevent the acts of collective self-immolation by fire which occasionally occurred among the more extreme groups. In addition the civil authorities, both at the request of the ecclesiastical authorities and on their own initiative, prosecuted those of all classes who failed to attend confession and communion, and to appear regularly at church, those guilty of adultery and evil living, etc.

Yet another social category came under its own code, though its members were tried by the local authorities for civil and criminal offences : these were the employees of government offices and the chancery servants (clerks, scribes etc.). The general principle was that the higher the social and service rank, the lighter the punishment. Cases of serious corruption, embezzlement, assault, bribery, etc., in the higher ranks were usually dealt with by the College of Justice and the

Senate, and before 1744, some notorious cases even ended in the death penalty for a voyevoda. The higher levels of the bureaucracy despised and looked down on the chancery clerks and such offences as laziness, lateness, incorrect copying, drunkenness, bribe-taking, were summarily dealt with on the spot by beatings, whippings, and locking up the offenders in fetters.

The nature of Russian society required the local authorities to superintend and organize the fulfilment of their obligations to the state by the various social estates. Thus governors and voyevodas played a big part in the service life and in the property relations of the nobility. In this respect they acted as the local agents of the Heraldmaster's Office, the College of War, and the Votchina or Estate College. The Heraldmaster's Office supplied the governor with a more or less accurate list of the nobles in his guberniya. The governor kept an eye on nobles retired from service, or on leave, and saw to it that they rejoined their services when summoned. The task of forcing reluctant nobles serving in the administration or the army to appear in their offices or rejoin their units was part of the daily life of the local authorities. Youths who had reached the age to enter service and were malingering on their estates had to be hunted out ; the sick had to be verified, the hidden had to be found. Any serving or retired officer might be summoned to the capital and it was the governor's duty to see that he went. If he fell ill on the way, the voyevoda of the district he was in had to be notified, and certify his illness. (It may be added that such verification was not carried out by doctors but by fellow-officers or government servants.) In addition the governor had to superintend the proper education of young nobles, and arrange their periodic appearance before him so that he could test their achievements.

In the field of property the local authorities acted as the agents of the Votchina College in maintaining records of sales of settled land (i.e. land with serfs) and inheritance – a survival from the days of the service tenure of the *pomest'ye* or estate. They also registered sales of serfs without land (in increasing numbers), personal loans and agreements. They had to keep records of the movements of serfs allowed to go elsewhere on passports, of the emancipation of serfs, and of the voluntary enserfment of free people (a phenomenon recorded up to 1775 when it was forbidden), and return runaway serfs to their owners. In relation to the serfs, the local authorities acted both as agents of the central government and of the landowners.

How well equipped was this local administration to carry out such a multitude of tasks in sparsely populated areas with poor communications ? To begin with the service was clearly divided between the *chinovniki,* namely those in the higher ranks, with a *chin,* or rank in the Table of Ranks and the chancery servants or *prikaznyye lyudi*, without a *chin*.[4] The upper levels were almost exclusively staffed by members of the noble estate, though these by no means formed a corps of loyal bureaucrats, but were sharply divided between upper and lower ranks, greater and lesser families. There was a clear distinction between those who were appointed – mainly governors – because their services were known and appreciated by the court, and those who were merely chosen from the lists of serving nobles held by the Heraldmaster's Office, and who could never aim higher than provincial voyevoda or governor's deputy, and who in any case until 1762 had to serve where they were sent, willy-nilly, unless they were well-connected enough to have some attention paid to their wishes.[5] If the governors were usually high-ranking and wealthy army officers who regarded a governorship as a stage in their career, the voyevodas were of much more modest means. Of 185 voyevodas in 1745, 70 per cent owned fewer than one hundred serfs ; two voyevodas owned none, two owned between one and two thousand.[6] In order to prevent abuse of power, governors and voyevodas were not allowed to own or purchase estates in the areas they ruled over – a measure which served to increase their dependence on the state and sever their links with local society.

The connecting link between the governors and the lower ranks without *chin* in the chanceries was the secretary. Since Peter I's reign this post was reserved for the nobility ; appointments had to be approved by the Senate and the Heraldmaster's Office.[7] The importance of the secretaryship is clear since the office coincided in the Table of Ranks precisely with that degree which would grant hereditary nobility to a non-noble. In fact the local authorities frequently appointed to the post, and evidently non-nobles were promoted often enough to cause disquiet, particularly in a period of noble ascendancy. Access from the lower ranks of the chancery service to the higher ranks with a *chin* was however by no means easy, and the two levels of government service in local administration were kept apart.

Members of the chancery service were drawn from a variety of social categories but ended up by forming an 'estate' of their own.[8] Since they did not pay the poll-tax, every effort was made to eliminate from among them those who were inscribed on the poll-tax registers, such as townspeople or merchants. In 1744 all such poll-tax payers were formally excluded from the 'estate' of the chancery servants,[9] and in 1752 the measure was extended to Cossacks. On the other hand attempts were made to prevent those who could genuinely be identified as belonging to the estate of the 'bureaucracy' from escaping into other occupations. An ukaz of 1755 in fact enjoined that in future 'children of chancery servants who were not nobles were not to be allotted to any service other than chancery service under pain of a fine'.[10] Runaway clerks were sought out, punished, and brought back in the same way as runaway serfs.[11] In spite of these measures the chancery servants continued to include recruits from a variety of social origins apart from the descendants of the Muscovite civil servants, such as soldiers' children, priests' children, the children of church servants – in fact all those who by reason of their origin or by chance had acquired somewhat more of an education than their fellows.

In general members of this 'estate' were economically closer to townspeople, and suffered from some of the same burdens, such as the obligation to billet troops and officers. But psychologically they identified themselves as much as

53

possible with nobles, and demanded to be accorded the same privileges such as the ownership of settled land. Government policy aimed at delimiting the estate as such both from the nobility above and the taxable common people below, by prohibiting on the one hand the ownership of serfs and settled land in 1754, and rendering promotion above the rank of secretary more difficult, but maintaining the personal immunity from taxation on the other. The dependence of the chancery servants on the state thus became complete.

The economies introduced in 1726–7 had drastically reduced the establishments of both central and local government. The most nefarious aspect of this policy was the reduction in the number of salaried posts as distinct from unsalaried ones. Salaries were now to be paid only to secretaries and to those *chinovniki* and clerks who had been in salaried posts before 1700. This return to the habits of the seventeenth century meant in practice that large numbers of chancery servants had to live off the perquisites of their posts.[12] Thus of 209 chinovniki employed in local administration in 1738, only 26 were in receipt of a salary, a situation which accounts in great measure for the bribery, embezzlement of state property and corruption typical of local government. Moreover even where the establishment provided for salaried posts there was no uniformity in the salaries paid for the same post in different guberniyi, and no regularity in their payment.[13]

The economy drive affected the salaries of the upper ranks of the chinovniki much less. As members of the noble estate they were in a better position to defend themselves.[14] However they lived under the threat of large fines or even confiscation of their estates if they failed in any of the tasks placed upon them, or even if they absented themselves from their posts without permission.

If there was no uniformity in salaries, there was also no uniformity in the number of staff allocated to the various government offices. These numbers (or the numbers of those who received salaries) had last been laid down in 1732. Moscow had the largest guberniya chancery, composed of 128 chancery servants, Astrakhan had only 22. Moreover, every office had a miscellaneous number of chancery servants 'not on the establishment' who lived off what they could squeeze out of the public. The variety in size makes it impossible to give a figure of the numbers actually employed but the ideal as the Senate envisaged it in 1755 was 30 chancery servants in a guberniya chancery, 15 in a provincial chancery and 10 in a voyevoda's chancery.[15] Even though the establishments had been so thoroughly cut in 1726–7, it remained difficult to find enough qualified people to fill all posts, hence the continued possibility for members of other estates, even peasants, to creep into the service, and the constant drive to 'attach' members of the chancery families to the service.

The chanceries were housed in old, crumbling wooden buildings, sometimes in stone buildings in the bigger cities. In the course of the eighteenth century rules were laid down for the building of new offices, diverging from the old Muscovite tradition and reflecting the gradual westernization of domestic architecture which could also be seen in noble country dwellings. Work started early, at 6 a.m. or 8 a.m. according to the time of year, and lasted until 5 p.m., an improvement on Muscovite custom which usually insisted on a ten- or twelve-hour day.

Neither from the point of view of the government nor from that of society was the local administration satisfactory, and shortly after Catherine's accession, on 23 July 1762, the Senate was charged with the duty of examining the establishments (*shtaty*) in the civilian administration. The ex-procurator general, P. Ya. Shakhovskoy, was specifically entrusted with the preparation of a more wideranging report on local government. Shakhovskoy, an elderly man who remembered Peter I's experiments with elected noble officials, went in fact much further, and prepared a project which amounted to a considerable remodelling of the provincial administration. He provided for the election of representatives of the nobles and the merchants as *tovarishchi* or assistants to a governor-general (also a new post). To be called *zemskiye sovetniki* or land councillors, these nobles were to take part in all matters handled in the governor-general's chancery. Representatives of the merchants were only to concern themselves with 'merchant affairs' ; they were to receive no salary, but the local merchant community was expected to compensate them for their efforts. Shakhovskoy also proposed the election by the nobility of a commissar in each uezd, disposing of a small force and acting under the orders of the governor-general.

In spite of the approval of the Senate, in February 1763, Shakhovskoy's plan met with considerable opposition, and was ultimately shelved. The evidence available makes it unfortunately almost impossible to trace the alignment of opinions at court. However, certain tentative deductions can be drawn. The Senate had approved a plan which preserved its own status and powers undiluted, precisely at the time when Catherine was concerning herself with reducing its significance. Secondly, Catherine was evidently attracted by the idea of reinforcing the network of procurators throughout the country, as the direct instrument of the ruler – a policy which was put forward by the then procurator general, A.I. Glebov, with whom she was in frequent consultation. Finally, the implications of Shakhovskoy's plan – the large place allotted to elected representatives of the nobility – may well have gone beyond what she considered safe or sensible. She was more concerned with improving the existing system and keeping it under her close control, than with allowing it to slip out of her hands. Thus the new *shtaty*, approved on 15 December 1763, reflect Catherine's rejection of the 'representative' principle in favour of the maintenance and improvement of the bureaucratic principle in local administration.[16]

For the first time, in Catherine's reform of 1763, uniformity was introduced into the civil establishments at guberniya level, with the appointment of a governor assisted by two vice-governors (*tovarishchi*). At town and uezd level, the voyevoda was now given a permanently appointed assistant, and was placed in complete charge of administration, justice and tax-collecting – thus eliminating the previously existing 'officer in charge of collecting the poll-tax'. At each level, the numbers of officials, their duties, rank and salaries were defined, the *chin* of each post was established and the salary was related to the post, not the *chin*.[17] Pensions were introduced for those with thirty-five years' service.[18] Whereas in Peter I's time those who failed to live up to his exacting standards were threatened with awful penalties (exile, the knut, mutilation, the galleys), the new shtaty endeavoured to increase the self-respect and improve the self-image of the government servant by using more civilized terminology in letters of appointment,[19] and providing salaries 'not only to judges (*sud'i*) but even for the lowest copyist such that no one would dare to take bribes'.[20] Not only were salaries restored, they were in many cases nearly doubled. The total number of employees in the civil administration rose to 16,504, and the amount spent on local government in 1764 came to 2,310,594 rubles, about ten per cent of the national expenditure.[21]

A mere increase in salaries, security and status was however quite insufficient to correct the inherent vices of Russian officialdom. Most of the personnel remained the same; even the new salaries were regarded as insufficient,[22] and it proved difficult to change the age-old habit of living off the people subordinate to a particular local authority. As in the field of justice, so in the administration, the concept of service to an abstract state, or even of service to the public, on a fixed standard, was still too alien to the bulk of society at all levels for a reform of this nature to alter the whole spirit of local administration. The Russian civil servant served himself, his relatives and his friends. Nevertheless an intensive drive against abuses was begun at this time, affecting both high and low, from the procurator general himself, A.I. Glebov, to governors and deputy governors. The years 1762–5 saw the largest number of prosecutions for bribery of the half century.[23]

In a fresh instruction issued on 21 April 1764 Catherine raised the status of governors and altered their relationship to the central government. Whereas previously a governor had been invested with enormous powers over his subordinate area, but had been himself merely the tool of the central government, he was now told to regard himself as 'a person trusted by the sovereign, the head, master and real trustee of the guberniya placed in his care', under the direction of the empress and the Senate. The Petrine ideal of the responsible official whose duty it was to use his own initiative in preserving order and promoting the public welfare (e.g. the provision of hospitals and schools), was revived and coupled with the concept of the governor as a specially trusted servant of the Crown. All the agencies of local administration were now concentrated under his authority with the exception of the procurators. At the same time governors were authorized to correspond directly with the empress, not only through the Senate, thus raising their own status at the expense of the Senate, as well as ensuring that Catherine herself should maintain direct control of these extremely important agents of the Crown in the provinces. The Colleges too lost all power to punish governors even on judicial matters.[24] A special instruction was issued on 12 January 1765 to the governors of the two capital cities, St Petersburg and Moscow. It had always been recognized that their situation was somewhat different. They were closer to the central government, hence problems could be referred to the ruler more easily for a quick decision. Moreover, some of the functions carried out by governors in a guberniya were carried out by agencies of the central government in the capitals, hence the range of activity of the governors was somewhat narrower.[25]

The final touch to the 'little reform' of the 1760s was given by the strengthening of the role of the procuracy.

All the procurators were directly subordinated to the procurator general, who thus controlled a network of his own throughout the country, parallel to the local administration. The rank of the procurators attached to the courts had been defined by Peter I as equivalent to that of lieutenant-colonel with a corresponding salary of 400 r.p.a. The new network of guberniya procurators which replaced them after 1732 suffered from the economy drive ; they kept their rank but their salaries were cut to some 232r. 80k. per annum, a mere quarter of the salary of a governor, and at least 20 per cent less than the salaries of voyevodas.

The duties of the procurator were mainly passive. He was to sit at his own table in the office of the local governor and listen to the proceedings. These could be very varied since the governor could turn from a criminal prosecution to a decision about tax collecting, or the billetting of troops, without leaving his seat. The procurator kept a journal in which on one side he recorded the law, on the other the decision taken. Should he wish to protest against a decision on the grounds that it was against the law, he could do so verbally to the governor, or in writing to the senior procurator of the College within the range of which the issue fell ; the governor in turn reported the matter to the Senate, and the final decision would be taken there. The senior procurators in the central government institutions were also subordinated to the procurator general, but were not hierarchically superior to the guberniya procurators who came directly under the latter's orders.

The relationship of the procurators with other institutions was in many respects ill-defined. They had no executive power, and could only report abuses. But their relationship with the local government officials was vitiated by several factors. One was their low rank and salary, already noted. Procurators rarely had the courage to denounce the misdeeds of governors, since it was dangerous for a mere captain or major (acting lieutenant-colonel as a procurator) to denounce a lieutenant-general, his senior in a service to which he might return. The second factor which militated against the effective operation of the procuracy was the interchangeability of personnel between it and the local government administration. No particular qualifications were required for this essentially judicial post (or indeed for *any* post in the Russian bureaucracy) and a man could be a procurator one day, a voyevoda the next.

Finally the procuracy suffered from the changing nature of the tasks imposed upon it. Since they were there, it was naturally tempting to use the procurators increasingly to supervise the carrying out of administrative duties by the local administration, instead of confining them to judicial matters. The task of 'advocate of the interests of the state' was interpreted as involving the 'instigation' of action designed to protect these interests (the word *instigovat'* is used in the original Russian to describe this function) frequently neglected by local officials in their own private interests. Catherine now considerably increased the numbers and the powers of the procuracy in local administration, and when she dismissed the procurator general A.I.Glebov for embezzlement in 1764 she chose for this important post a man of thirty-seven who was to remain her faithful servant almost to his death in 1792. Prince A.A. Vyazemsky was prompt and efficient in the conduct of business, sober, hard-working and practical. He proved a loyal instrument of Catherine's will, never attempting to increase his power at her expense, though he may not have hesitated to do so at the expense of others. He had already carried out a special mission of pacification and inquiry into a revolt of the assigned peasants attached to industries in the Urals, and though he had shown the usual 'firmness' in repressing the rising, he had also shown some understanding of the grievances of the people. Without being formally appointed, he had then been placed in charge of the Secret Department in the Senate with Nikita Panin, and in that position he had supervised the activities of the special commission set up to try Mirovich.[26] On his appointment to the post of procurator general in February 1764, Catherine drew up an instruction for him in her own hand which is one of the most important documents illustrating her conception of statecraft. The Senate, in her view, owing to the negligence of some of her predecessors, had exceeded its bounds and had come to oppress other government organs ; in particular the organs of local administration had lost all initiative as a result of their subordination to the Senate. In contrast to those who hankered after foreign models, Catherine – echoing Montesquieu – stressed that 'everywhere internal arrangements are made in accordance with the customs of the nation'. The new procurator was to keep away from and above the factions in the Senate, to be responsible to the empress alone, and to rely on her alone for support. In a concluding paragraph she summed up her own views on government and on the nature of the relationship she hoped to see established between herself and Vyazemsky :

You must know with whom you will have to deal. . . . You will find that I have no other view than the greatest welfare and glory of the fatherland, and I wish for nothing but the happiness of my subjects, of whatever order they may be. All my thoughts are directed only to the preservation of external and internal peace, satisfaction and tranquillity. I am very fond of the truth, and you may tell me the truth fearlessly and argue with me without any danger if it leads to good results in affairs. I hear that you are regarded as an honest man by all ; I hope to show you by experience that people with such qualities do well at court. And I may add that I require no flattery from you, but only honest behaviour and firmness in affairs.[27]

Procurators were now attached to voyevodas at provincial level, thus trebling the actual number employed, which rose from 15–16 to 50–60. Their importance lay in the fact that they were the only local agents who were not under the control of the governor. After the appointment of Vyazemsky, and with the support of the central government, the guberniya procurators began to act more energetically and to interpret their functions more widely. They dared to put forward complaints against their superiors in rank more often than in the past, and attempted to keep an eye on the legality of the proceedings in all local offices. They were entrusted with some specific functions, notably the implementation of a secret ukaz of 1763 which enjoined that in criminal cases, where the use of torture was sanctioned by law, it should not be applied without a special report to the governor, who in turn was to consult the Senate.[28] As the procurators gradually turned more and more into the agents of the procurator general in his *de facto* capacity of minister of the interior, so they were entrusted with the task of reporting on a variety of special problems, ranging from the state of the harvest to the numbers of peasants on money or labour dues, or the number of distilleries, etc. They were also encouraged to 'instigate' on a much wider front, notably in the field of welfare, and to make suggestions to the centre on their own initiative.

The procurator general thus had his own subordinates strategically placed in every department of the Senate at the centre and at guberniya and provincial level in the country at large. In addition, however, he controlled appointments both to his own service and to the civilian service as a whole. Though no special training of any kind was required for any post, an effort was made in the 1760s to improve the quality of the personnel at all levels in central and local administration. Appointments to the more senior posts were made by the Senate and ratified by the empress. But the service records of the nobility were kept by the herald-master, whose office came under the procurator general. He could thus supervise the choice of personnel for the more important provincial appointments.

One of the difficulties which faced Vyazemsky was that most of the procurators, including the new ones appointed in the 1760s, were army officers of middle rank (lieutenants, majors, one colonel). They were thus lower in army rank than the governors and voyevodas whose activities they were supposed to supervise. Deference to a superior *chin* was reinforced by the habit of military discipline, and as Governor Sievers of Novgorod pointed out: 'the spirit of the military . . . which knows only orders and obedience, is different from civil service, in which both laws and reason establish equality among its members.'[29] Aware of the awkwardness inherent in the fact that a procurator one day might revert to being the direct subordinate of a governor the next, Vyazemsky attempted to achieve a greater separation of personnel between the local administration and the procuracy. By 1771 he had ensured that procurators should also dispose of their own clerical staff which should no longer be interchangeable with that of the local government offices. The effort to create two quite separate networks, the one composed of governors and their staffs, the other composed of procurators and their staffs, did not work out in practice, since there were always some exceptions to the rule. Nevertheless, it can be said that the procuracy represented the first genuine attempt in Russia at creating a functionally separate service within the civil administration, with its own selected personnel.

The general shortage of qualified people was however also reflected in the newly organized procuracy. Though dead wood was cleared out in the 1760s (only three existing guberniya procurators were confirmed in their posts, two were promoted, and the rest were removed), and salaries were doubled,[30] many procurators failed to live up to the standards required, took bribes, became involved in brawls, and abused their powers. There were constant disputes between governors and procurators, who sometimes erred by excess of zeal, and sometimes suffered from overbearing governors. Again, the extent of the procurators' right to intervene in the affairs of the urban administrative and judicial organs, the 'magistraty' and 'ratushi', was unclear.[31]

To sum up, the first changes in the structure and spirit of the government in Russia undertaken by the new regime all tended to the strengthening of the direct personal control of the sovereign over the institutions of central and local government and their personnel. At a time when Catherine might have been expected to woo the nobility in order to consolidate her precarious hold on the throne, no concession whatsoever was made to noble ambitions. No outright attack was made on the vested interests of the high aristocracy. But by playing off the partisans of the imperial council against the partisans of the Senate Catherine succeeded in killing the one, and downgrading the other. Meanwhile the procuracy, under Catherine's obedient servant, Vyazemsky, with his subordinate network of procurators, served increasingly as the *oko gosudarevo,* the 'eye of the sovereign' and the effective instrument of her policy and her power.

4

The Baltic Provinces
and Little Russia

In June 1764 Catherine embarked on the first of many journeys within the Russian Empire, namely a tour of Estonia and Livonia, which had been planned since the previous summer. She understood the value of a personal appearance to consolidate her authority. At the same time she was convinced of the necessity of drawing together the various parts of the empire living under their own laws. Her policy was outlined in February 1764 in her instruction to A.A. Vyazemsky, on his appointment as procurator general:

Little Russia, Livonia and Finland[1] are provinces governed according to privileges which have been confirmed ; to destroy them by revoking them all suddenly would be unseemly – but to call them alien and to treat them as such would be more than a mistake, it would be really stupid. These provinces, as well as Smolensk,[2] should, in the gentlest manner, be brought to the point when they become Russian and stop looking like wolves to the woods. The approach to this is very simple if sensible people are appointed to rule in these provinces ; when there is no longer a hetman in Little Russia we must strive to make the name and memory of hetman disappear and let no one be appointed to that post.[3]

When Livonia and Estonia were conquered and incorporated in the Russian Empire in 1710 their charters and privileges had been confirmed by Peter I. Lutheranism was the state religion, and the provinces maintained their own *Landtage* (which all nobles could attend in person) and an elaborate system of standing committees and commissions, as well as their own judicial institutions from which appeal lay in the last instance to the Senate in St Petersburg. The Russian Crown was also a large landowner and normally leased out its farms or *myzy*.

At the beginning of each reign the charters of Livonian privileges were dug out of the archives and presented to the new sovereign for confirmation, and a deputy of the Livonian nobility, Karl Schoultz von Ascheraden, attended Catherine's coronation in Moscow for this purpose. The empress duly confirmed the Livonian privileges in December 1762, but it was a purely tactical move on her part : 'Il faut cependant en confidence que je vous dise', she wrote to the grand master of the ordnance, A. de Villebois (himself an Estonian noble), 'qu'en honneur ni moi ni personne ne sais ce que je confirmerai, si cela est utile au pais, si ce sont des moeurs ou des coutumes ou des loix, mais j'ai cru que le repos d'une province entière étoit préférable à tout le reste.'[4]

It is probable that this incident contributed to arouse Catherine's interest in Livonia. The discussions in the commission on the manifesto granting freedom to the nobility[5] may also have attracted her attention to Livonian practice. She began to show an unhealthy curiosity about the *matricula* or register of nobles. How many were matriculated ? And when ? And why ? Then, in March 1764, Catherine attempted to include fifteen officers, mainly Germans and Swedes of bourgeois origin, in the register of the Livonian and Estonian gentry, on the grounds that they had reached the rank conferring nobility in the Table of Ranks. The empress's ukaz met with a storm of protest in Livonia, but it was nevertheless put into effect though the reference to the Table of Ranks was deleted from the final text. It was too much of a challenge as yet to the corporate rights of the Livonian gentry to claim that the Table of Ranks could ennoble in Livonia. A straightforward ennoblement by the Crown was less offensive.

The shortage of landed estates with which to reward her supporters in the *coup d'état* led Catherine as early as July 1762 to inquire into the availability of Crown farms in Livonia. How many were leased, and how many vacant ? In October she prohibited the renewal of twelve-year leases when they expired, until fresh arrangements were made.[6]

Catherine left St Petersburg on 24 June 1764, and spent roughly a month on a journey which the Estonian and Livonian gentry deliberately turned into a triumphal progress. She was welcomed in Reval by the population, the town council and the assembled nobles, and spent a few days there before proceeding to Riga. It proved unncessary to prepare special accommodation for the imperial party since the Livonian nobility made it a point of honour to entertain the empress in their comfortable manor houses. The welcome accorded to Catherine by the nobles and the common people served to convince her that 'les Livoniens commencent à avoir des influences de leurs conquerants'.[7] She in turn took great care to appear always as a Russian empress and not a German princess on the Russian throne. Official speeches were made in Russian, and the empress ostentatiously attended Orthodox religious ceremonies in Reval and Riga.[8]

Catherine found much to admire in Livonia but she was determined to undermine the autonomy of the non-Russian provinces, and to increase the revenue Russia obtained from Estonia and Livonia. The easiest point of attack in these areas was the problem of the peasantry, for a number of reasons. In the first place the 1760s were the period of Catherine's most personal and active interest in the question of serfdom, both in terms of the development of agriculture in the interests of the national economy, and in terms of the peasant as a human being. Most of her private remarks and jottings on the status of the serfs belong to this period.[9] Moreover it was in the Livonian context that her interest had first been aroused in the possibility of practical action.

A certain Lutheran pastor, Johann Georg Eisen, originally from Franconia but settled in Livonia, had been brought to the attention of Peter III during the latter's brief reign. Eisen was known to concern himself with problems of agriculture ; he believed that allowing the peasantry to own some land would enrich the state, the landowners and the peasants. Peter III invited him to St Petersburg to examine the possibility of establishing colonies of German peasants in Livonia, from which some twenty German regiments might eventually be recruited for service in the Russian army. When Peter died, Eisen returned to Livonia. But he had not only been interested in the military importance of a free peasantry ; he had actively preached in favour of the abolition of serfdom in Livonia. His ideas were known in a limited circle of enlightened officials around the empress, including Grigory Orlov, and he was invited to come back to Russia and formally introduced to Catherine by Aleksey Orlov in October 1763.[10] At her request he prepared an account of the peasantry in Livonia which was subsequently published in the *Sammlung russischer Geschichte,* a historical journal published in German in St Petersburg by G. Müller, evidently with Catherine's consent, and with the addition of a comparison between the condition of the Livonian peasantry and the Russian serfs weighted in favour of the latter.[11]

Since Catherine at this time was undoubtedly interested in projects of agrarian reform, including the regulation of serfdom, Eisen's memorandum gave her the pretext she needed to attack where resistance would be weakest. It was much easier for her to test the strength of the opposition to the regulation of master-serf relations in Livonia than in Russia, where she could not as yet afford to alienate noble support. An assault on Livonian privilege, even in the domain of serfdom, would not arouse the apprehensions of the rank and file Russian nobility, and might even find some support among Russian high officials. Even in Livonia there were nobles on whom it had dawned that the formal regulation of the relationship between landowner and serf was a small price to pay for the preservation of political autonomy, provided such regulation was carried out and administered by the Livonians themselves. Among the most prominent of them was that same Karl Schoultz von Ascheraden, who had secured the confirmation of Livonian privileges in December 1762.

The Livonian landowning system had been inherited from the period of Swedish rule. In law, only a noble inscribed in the matricula was allowed to own land. But leasing or pledging land to non-nobles (*Landsassen*) was allowed, and was indeed encouraged by the nobles as a means of obtaining credit. Leases were usually for six or twelve years, but they could be for as long as ninety-nine years, amounting thus to a concealed sale ; sub-leasing was also very common. As a result a host of administrators intervened between the landowner and his serfs – and were paid, or paid themselves, out of the profits of the estate. The obligations of the serfs had been laid down under Swedish rule in the so-called *Wakkenbuche,* or *Wackenbücher,* known in Russian as *'bakenbukhi',* which calculated these obligations in relation to the amount of land cultivated.

There was no poll-tax (or recruit levy) in Livonia, but a tax was levied on peasant land, though not on noble land. But revenue from this tax had been steadily declining (from 135,000 albertine thalers in 1740 to 105,000 thalers in 1759) as a result of the expansion of allodial noble-owned land at the expense of state-owned peasant land. Such a loss of revenue at a time when Russia was scraping the barrel to pay for the Seven Years' War led the government to order a *reviziya,* or re-allocation of the tax burden per haken of land, in 1756–60. This *reviziya* gave Catherine the opportunity to regulate relationships on Crown lands, both with a view to raising revenue and to improving the situation of the peasantry. The obvious place to begin was the island of Esel, where the Crown owned more than half the land. Here a modest programme of agrarian reform was planned in 1765, involving the registration of the labour and other dues of the peasants. Leaseholders were to be threatened with the loss of their leases if they failed to conform to their terms. There were also plans to draft new forms of contract for leases of Crown farms in Estonia and Livonia, which would insist on the observance of the norms of services laid down in the old *bakenbukhi.* [12] Much of the inspiration for the attempts at agrarian reform in these years can be traced directly to the influence of Pastor Eisen. [13] But whether Catherine had determined to interfere in the relationship between landowners and serfs in Estonia and Livonia before she visited the provinces, or whether the spectacle of agrarian poverty which met her eyes there inspired her to act is a matter for debate. [14]

The Russian assault began at the Landtag summoned for the second half of January 1765. Governor George Browne [15] laid before the assembled nobles a number of propositions agreed upon behind the scenes with Catherine, many of which dealt directly or indirectly with the peasantry. The most important was the third which demanded that the peasants should be guaranteed the right of ownership in all their moveable property; the right to trade freely in agricultural produce ; the regulation of labour services ; the definition of the judicial rights of landowners, and the recognition of the serf's right to complain against his master. The moral appeal to improve the conditions of the serfs ('whose plight had been brought to the attention of the throne') was reinforced by the hint of a proposal to increase the tax burden per haken. [16]

Whether by secret agreement with Catherine, or on his own initiative, Schoultz von Ascheraden now laid before the Landtag the Peasant Code (*Bauernrecht*) he had drafted and applied in two of his own estates. It corresponded very closely with Browne's 'Propositions', so much so that many of the Livonian nobles thought that he had drafted them. Schoultz thought that his code showed what an individual noble could do on his own land, and hoped that his example might be followed. He defended his code before the Landtag with arguments drawn from the moral arsenal of the Enlightenment. He attacked unlimited serfdom as barbarous and uneconomic, and stressed the possibility that if the Livonians did not act for themselves, the Russian government might act for them, which represented a greater danger to their autonomy. His warnings were disregarded by the majority of the Landtag. If the peasants were miserable, this could be blamed on excessive Russian taxation, and on the exactions of the Landsassen, who fleeced the peasantry. (The nobles had frequently found it necessary to introduce provisions for the protection of their serfs into leases, since leaseholders had no compunction about ravaging the estate in the interest of immediate profit, particularly in the case of short-term leases.) But though the nobles assembled in the Landtag rejected Browne's propositions at first, sheltering behind Catherine's confirmation of Livonian privileges in 1762, they could not stand up against a formal request from the empress, put to the Landtag by the governor. A compromise solution was reached, and a resolution composed of fifteen points was finally approved and published in Livonia as the 'Patent of 12 April 1765' in German, with abridged versions in Estonian and Lettish.

The 'Patent' followed Schoultz's code, with some divergences. Peasants were guaranteed the ownership of moveable property. Money dues were not to be raised. Labour dues were to be left to the discretion of landowners, who however had to publish the norms by 1 August 1765, calculated according to the amount of land cultivated. In addition the peasant was granted access to the lower courts (*Ordnungsgericht*), and could complain against ill-treatment by the landowners, or undue labour services, thus extending to serfs a right already enjoyed by the Crown peasants. There were however limitations. If a peasant complained against his master without just ground he could be whipped with 'ten pairs of birches before the church' for a first offence, and be sent to hard labour for a year for a third offence. Moreover, since the members of the *Ordnungsgericht* were nobles, the chances of obtaining justice were weighted against the peasants. But the possibility of appeal was there, and Governor Browne often enough reversed the decisions of the lower courts to arouse the indignation of the gentry, who complained that he was bringing their elected courts into discredit.

A more serious drawback from the peasant point of view was the failure to enforce the registration of the labour dues. It was taken for granted that they had been laid down on each estate and that in the absence of peasant complaint, they were being observed. Few nobles followed Schoultz's policy of drafting their own peasant codes, for their own estates, which could at least to some extent fill the gap left by the absence of national legislation. The fact that the extent of the labour dues was left largely to the discretion of the landowners, and that no measures were taken to enforce their registration, led both contemporaries and subsequent historians to regard the 'Patent' of 1765 as without significance for the peasant. Moreover it did nothing to improve the economic situation of the serf. Neither the populist historians of the nineteenth century, nor Soviet scholars, can admit that an improvement, however slight, in the legal rights of the peasantry, without any corresponding improvement in their economic situation, can lead to a lightening of the peasants' burden. Yet the fact that the peasant now had a legal right to his immoveable property, and access to the courts of the land, might increase his self-respect if it did not raise his standard of living. More research on the actual operation of the Patent is necessary before a final verdict can be passed.[17] Catherine at least believed that a reform on the lines of Schoultz's peasant code would improve the situation of the Livonian peasantry, and that the Patent would be implemented.[18]

The Ukraine was the name given in the eighteenth century to a vast area extending on both banks of the Dniepr, from around Starodub in the north to the borders of the khanate of Crimea in the south, partly in Poland, partly in Russia. In Russian Ukraine, there were two distinct areas which had been incorporated into Russia in different ways. Slobodska Ukraine, centring around Khar'kov, had been gradually settled in the seventeenth century by fugitives from Polish Ukraine, which then extended over both banks of the Dniepr, and by refugees from the civil wars which raged there until 1686. It had always been exclusively under Muscovite sovereignty, and was governed by Russian appointed voyevodas and governors. Left Bank Ukraine, or Little Russia as it was generally known in the eighteenth century, had placed itself under Russian suzerainty in 1654, under the leadership of the Cossack hetman, Bogdan Khmel'nitsky, and had been finally ceded to Russia by Poland in 1686. (Right Bank Ukraine remained under Polish rule until the second partition of Poland in 1792.)[19] The total population of Left Bank Ukraine (i.e. Little Russia and Slobodska Ukraine, but excluding the city of Kiev) in 1762 was 1,342,221, of which 96.84 per cent were peasants and 52.69 per cent landlords' peasants ; 28,184 (2.10 per cent) were townsmen, and there were a further 14,284 'non-taxable' population, i.e. officers, officials, clerics, etc.[20]

Beyond the borders of these more settled lands were the lands of the Cossack Hosts, namely the Zaporozhian Host, based on an island in the Dniepr ; the Don Cossacks ; and the Yaik Cossacks, who were not part of the Ukraine.

The administration of Little Russia was organized on Cossack lines. The office of hetman had been allowed to lapse in 1734, since a hetman could easily become a focus for Little Russian separatism. But it was restored in 1750, largely as a result of pressure by the Ukrainian 'gentry' who found a spokesman in Aleksey Razumovsky, lover and presumed morganatic husband of the Empress Elizabeth and himself of Ukrainian Cossack origin.[21] The man selected for the post was Aleksey's younger brother, Kyrill, then aged twenty-two. It was first necessary to organize the young man's election by the Cossack *starshina,* the collective noun which designated the colonels and senior officers of the regiments. The actual investiture took place on 13 March 1751, when the regalia of the hetmanate were handed over to the new hetman, and the privileges and franchises of Little Russia were solemnly confirmed by Elizabeth. Supervision over Little Russian affairs was transferred from the Senate to the College of Foreign Affairs, thus emphasizing the separate status of Little Russia.

For administrative purposes Little Russia was divided into *polki* or regiments, mixed territorial and military units. Each *polk* was subdivided into 'hundreds', with its own elected officials, colonels, secretaries, hundredmen, etc. Within each territorial unit specific lands were allotted to the maintenance of the regimental offices (*rangovyye zemli*) in addition to lands which belonged to the host as a whole (*voyskovyye maetnosti*). The landowning class in the Ukraine also included non-Cossack Little Russian landowners who had survived through all regimes, and Great Russian landowners to whom large estates had been donated from the days of Peter the Great onwards.[22] The interests of the Cossack starshina and of the Ukrainian gentry merged in the political field. Both were concerned to achieve equal status with the Russian *dvoryanstvo* or nobility. They pressed for the former by constant petitions to the Russian government. And the starshina systematically turned 'service' lands into hereditary estates with the connivance of the various hetmans, forcibly buying up or otherwise seizing Cossack and peasant lands. By the second quarter of the eighteenth century lands held on hereditary tenure predominated over other types of landholding.[23]

Having transformed themselves from military servitors maintained by the produce of regimental lands to economic exploiters of their own lands, the Cossack landowners inevitably attempted to shackle the peasantry, legally and economically. A number of *universaly* (decrees issued by the hetman) limited or prohibited the freedom of movement of the peasants from one village to another even within a polk. The rank and file Cossacks also suffered from their declining status. Some were hardly distinguishable from peasants, and found themselves in bondage to a clerical or secular landowner through debt or legal trickery. The wealthier Cossacks were separately recorded in 1735 as the so-called 'elected', and were freed from any obligations but their military duties ; their poorer brethren bore the same burdens as the peasantry but in less degree, in exchange for providing the 'elected' with supplies for their campaigns.

Apart from labour dues to the landowners, ranging from two to four days a week, peasants paid dues in kind and in cash for the maintenance of a number of foot and horse regiments, for the regimental and hundred administration, for the hetman, for the Church. They did not pay the poll-tax, nor were they subjected to the recruit levy. Escape lay in flight to the Cossack Hosts on the Don or the Dniepr, or in joining the Cossack regiments maintained in Little Russia or Slobodska Ukraine, or in hiring themselves out as landless labourers, *podsosedki,* to wealthier Cossacks, or other landowners, in which case taxes weighed less heavily on them, but they ran the risk of losing their freedom.

The cities and towns of Little Russia were self-governing enclaves which elected their own administrative and judicial organs in accordance with the charters issued to them of old by the Polish Lithuanian Commonwealth, the so-called Magdeburg Laws. Craftsmen in the cities were organized into guilds, often called *bratstva* or brotherhoods, some of which could become very powerful within the city. Smaller cities however often fell into dependence on the colonel of a local polk.

The Russian Code of 1649 was not applied in Little Russia which was governed by the Lithuanian Statute, in its various versions, of which the texts existed in Latin and Polish. A commission of Ukrainian jurists attempted in the 1730s to produce a 'Code of the Rights of the Little Russian People', compiled from the Magdeburg Laws, and the 1566 and 1588 versions of the Lithuanian Statute which were strongly influenced by contemporary Polish noble attitudes. Completed in 1743, the code was never promulgated, since in principle the Russian government did not favour any moves tending to underline the separate status of the Ukraine. Nevertheless, though not promulgated, the principles expressed in the code, now more clearly formulated, were regarded by the Little Russian gentry as the genuine expression of national law, and were *de facto* adopted as the basis for the administrative reforms undertaken particularly in the judicial field during Kyrill Razumovsky's hetmanship.

Razumovsky introduced into his Little Russian capital in Glukhov, a copy of the court of St Petersburg, and lived like a great magnate surrounded by courtiers. This tended to strengthen both the aspirations of the Ukrainian gentry to aristocratic status, and their consciousness of a separate Ukrainian nationhood. Razumovsky was also lavish in his distribution of Cossack lands in hereditary possession to landowners. A decree of 1760 prohibited peasants from leaving an estate without the permission of the landowner, and prohibited landowners from settling peasants on their land without the written consent of their previous landowner. The predominance of the gentry was further consolidated by the reform of the judicial system in 1763. The multiplicity of courts, with conflicting jurisdictions, had led to great abuses. They were now reconstructed, within the framework of the Lithuanian Statute ; assessors were elected by the regiments to the high or general court ; a series of land and civil courts were introduced, composed of judges elected by the gentry, and the regiment courts were renamed 'city courts'.[24]

With the restoration of the hetmanate in 1751, the administration of the Zaporozhian Cossack Host was placed under the hetman, who was charged with the difficult task of controlling their tendency to raid into Turkish and Tartar territory. The Zaporozhian Host formed a unique community. Their lands extended in a wide and ill-defined arc on the left and right banks of the Dniepr, 'below the rapids'. More anarchic than the Don Cossacks, more numerous than the Yaik Cossacks, they were ideally placed to intrigue with Turkey, Poland and Russia, to seek refuge in one country from the oppression of the other, to harbour fugitives from them all. The Host had been dispersed in the reign of Peter the Great, when the hetman Mazeppa sided with Charles XII of Sweden and was defeated at Poltava in 1709. But it was reformed and in 1734 it returned to its original allegiance to the Russian Crown, while geographically it settled in lands which in law belonged to the Ottoman Empire. Their unique territorial base led the Zaporozhians to make certain assumptions about their past and present rights to specific lands which no one but themselves accepted. They ceased to consider themselves as a military confraternity with a small headquarters, and began to think of themselves as an embryonic state with territorial claims. They even adopted the by no means original practice of producing false charters, allegedly signed by the king of Poland, Stephen Bathory, or by Bogdan Khmel'nitsky, granting them their lands.[25]

Numbers are difficult to assess, but the Zaporozhian population in the 1760s has been estimated at some eighteen to twenty-two thousand adult males, divided into two unequal groups : the larger, the Cossacks proper, and the smaller, the so-called *pospolity*. Essentially a military organization, the centre was a fortified island in the rapids of the Dniepr, the 'Sech', in which were the administrative offices of the community as well as their military headquarters, barracks for the permanent garrison of the Sech, a school and a church, magazines and store-houses. The poorer unmarried Cossacks, the *seroma*, lived in these barracks. For administrative purposes, the Sech was divided into eight districts (*palanki*), centred on settlements (*slobody*) in which resided the local administration under a colonel (*polkovnik*), and the garrison. The population of the *slobody*, both Cossacks and *pospolity*, elected their leaders or *atamany*, who were responsible to the colonel. He in turn was responsible directly to the Cossack administration in the Sech, the '*kosh*,' or general staff. This general staff was elected by the Cossacks at general assemblies or *rady*, which met once a year in January. It was composed of the *ataman* or leader, a chancellor (*pisar*), judges, treasurers, aides-de-camp (*esaul*) and standard bearers. Thanks however to the social and military organization of the Cossacks, it was possible for the wealthier oligarchy, the starshina, to manipulate these elections in order to maintain themselves in power.

The obligations of the Cossacks to the state were military : in war they took part in campaigns, in peace-time they guarded the frontier with the Tartars and the Ottoman Empire. They were bound to provide their own clothing, arms, horses and supplies. In return they received salaries in cash and kind from the government, which were mostly monopolized by the powerful members of the starshina. They also enjoyed full rights over the lands assigned to the Sech, which were allotted to the various regiments. Here too the starshina succeeded in obtaining for themselves privileges in the use and distribution of land and the exploitation of fisheries and forests, as well as in the extensive trade in agricultural produce. This oligarchy also drew on the funds of the regiments, raised by means of taxes on the non-Cossack population and of various excises. They exploited the labour of the poorer or landless Cossacks and often hired them to take over their military duties.

As the frontier with the Tartars became more secure, Cossacks turned to agriculture as well as cattle breeding. Market gardening, orchards, and corn growing flourished so that the community which in the 1730s had been corn importing, became in the 1770s an exporter of corn.

The pospolity were on a quite different footing ; they were in a sense the 'subjects' of the Cossacks. They had no military obligations, but were heavily burdened with labour dues (transport by land and water). Their right to the use of 'military land' was limited, they were not allowed to settle on individual farms (*khutory*) but only in villages or settlements. Even within this lowly group there were differences between the *tyaglyye* who had enough land and stock to farm on their own, and the *peshiye* who had nothing but their *khata* (hut) or not even that. Further down the social scale came the *polususedki,* who owned not even a *khata,* and lived on other people's land.

As the Cossack starshina became more and more concerned with maintaining and developing its economic wealth, so it came to identify its interests more closely with those of the Russian government, and united to suppress the occasional revolts among the poorer Cossacks. These poor Cossacks had one outlet, the so-called *haydamachestvo,* or brigandage by bands who made a living by pillaging Polish Ukraine, or attacking wealthier Cossacks in the Zaporozhian lands.

Nevertheless, compared to areas under direct Russian administration, the Zaporozhian Cossack world remained an island of freedom. The starshina was not yet a closed hereditary group ; a new man could make his way up the scale if he were enterprising and lucky ; a fugitive peasant could still find a refuge in the Sech. Cossack traditions of freedom and equality still survived and were kept alive in popular ballads and folklore.

The Don Cossack Host had suffered a similar evolution – indeed the starshina of the Don Cossacks was even more permeated by the ideology of the Russian noble landowner than in the Zaporozhian Host. The presence of Russian landowners who had introduced their own serfs on estates close to Cossack lands encouraged the aspirations of the starshina to the achievement of similar privileges. Stepan Yefremov, who succeeded his father as *ataman* or leader of the Don Cossacks in 1753, owned over five hundred serfs. Here too improved security led to the development of agriculture and trade, and hence to greater stratification according to wealth. Revolts among the Don Cossacks were less frequent than among the Zaporozhians. They were also more quickly dealt with. In 1754 the Russian government began to grant Russian military rank to especially favoured members of the Don Cossack starshina, and treating Don Cossack officials as salaried government servants. Many of them rose in the Table of Ranks to Russian noble rank, which enabled them to acquire serfs. At the same time the status of the rank and file Cossack declined. The wealthier were registered as Cossacks, subject to compulsory military service, but freed from personal taxation. The poorer Cossacks, and incoming fugitive peasants, were no longer regarded as Cossacks, but were subjected to the poll-tax. The Don Cossacks were thus well on the way to becoming a privileged military elite at the disposal of the government for the maintenance of internal order.[26]

The Yaik Cossacks were the poorest of the Cossack Hosts. They were still actively involved in the defence of Russia against Kazakh raids, and their lands were unsuitable to agriculture. Registered Cossacks numbered about four thousand, but if all under age and retired Cossacks were called upon, a host of twelve thousand could be raised. In addition there was a large population of Kazakh, Kalmuck and Tartar fugitives, some of whom were incorporated in unregistered Cossack units, with some degree of autonomy. Life on the Yaik was primitive, and service harsh.[27]

The situation in Little Russia was unsatisfactory for Catherine who had little sympathy with the untidy remnants of military feudalism and foreign rule which still survived there. On her accession she had confirmed the charters of those Ukrainian cities, including Kiev, which enjoyed Magdeburg rights, and the hetman, Kyrill Razumovsky, continued in office. But in formulating her policy Catherine was influenced by senior Russian officials, above all by G.N. Teplov, who had been the hetman's right-hand man in the government of Little Russia for fourteen years and was now her secretary.

Teplov, in a long memorandum to the empress, probably submitted in June 1763, summarized the harmful consequences of the existing lax Russian control of Little Russia in the social, economic and judicial fields. By implication, he suggested that Razumovsky had allowed himself to become the tool of the Cossack starshina in the conversion of Cossack land into private hereditary estates. The result was that the wealthier Cossacks bought themselves out of their service duties, while the poorer Cossacks became peasants, paying a kopek or two in taxes, and were exempt from military service. The judiciary connived at this state of affairs by registering false bills of sale of Cossack land, and allowing the enserfment of poor or landless Cossacks.

From the economic standpoint, Teplov stressed the decline in agricultural productivity arising from peasant mobility. Free movement had been limited in 1760 but the rich landowner could still lure peasants with the promise of favourable terms : he would 'set up his great wooden cross' on empty land, with a placard setting out the number of years during which no labour or money dues would be demanded, and peasants would flock to settle round the cross. When the period of grace expired, they would move on with their families elsewhere, seeking a new 'cross'. As a result the rich landowner became richer, the poor landowner became poorer, and the peasants themselves wandered from estate to estate without settling anywhere, paid no taxes and became drunken, lazy and destitute, starving in a fertile land.

The form of government did not escape Teplov's criticisms. In principle, landowners were not to concern themselves with Cossack settlements, which were to be ruled by their elected hundredmen, and subordinated to the colonels of the regiments. In practice, the 'election' of a hundredman was rigged by the Cossack elders, and there was no proper delimitation of the lands held by Cossacks, peasants, towns, villages, hamlets, etc., as a result of which disputes were settled by violence, even murder. Above all, Teplov rejected out of hand any suggestion that Little Russia was a separate land, united to Russia by a dynastic union expressed in treaties. Little Russia, he argued, had been 'Russian from ancient times', and belonged under Catherine's suzerainty.[28]

Catherine's policy certainly shows that she did not feel bound to respect the existing territorial boundaries of Little Russia. The first encroachment on Little Russian lands occurred in June 1764 with the setting up of a new guberniya or province of New Russia, incorporating two districts, New Serbia and Slavyano-serbia, originally areas of Serb military settlement, parts of Slobodska Ukraine, and lands belonging to four Little Russian polki, comprising some forty thousand inhabitants. The hetman was not informed in advance of the transfer of Little Russian territories to the guberniya of New Russia, and complained to the Senate on the grounds that the population in the amputated Little Russian regiments would be unable to meet their taxes.[29]

Undoubtedly aware of the trend of Catherine's policy, Kyrill Razumovsky attempted in the autumn of 1763 to capitalize on the ferment in Little Russia to strengthen his own position. At the general assembly of the starshina which took place in Glukhov on 6 October 1763 a petition to the empress was drafted setting out a wide-ranging programme of autonomy for Little Russia. In exchange for his support for this programme Razumovsky obtained the backing of many of the starshina for his proposal that the hetmanate should be made hereditary in the Razumovsky family.[30] It was a daring gamble, since there was no hereditary tradition in Little Russia, and support proved patchy. The religious hierarchy was unsympathetic, as were most of the highest ranking Cossack officers, but the colonels of regiments and other lower-rank officials signified their support, by signing a petition in the hetman's favour. The petition was forwarded to St Petersburg,[31] though it was not formally submitted to the empress. But she knew of its existence, and it sealed the fate of the hetmanate.

Meanwhile steps were taken to break down the legal separation between Little Russia and Russia proper. Little Russians, settled outside the borders of the Ukraine, were now allowed to register as members of the merchant class or of the townspeople, if they had married into these social groups. This of course made them liable to the poll-tax and the recruit levy.[32] An ukaz was also issued on 10 December 1763 clarifying the situation with regard to peasant mobility. It confirmed the right of the Little Russian peasant to move from place to place provided he had the permission of his existing landowner to leave. The preamble to the ukaz stated that its object was to induce the peasants to settle permanently in one place because of the harm done to the economy by constant movement, as Teplov had pointed out. If the peasants felt that their right to move was guaranteed by law, they would not wish to wander from place to place, settling nowhere permanently and sinking into poverty.[33]

But the principal problem remained : how to remove Kyrill Razumovsky from the hetmanate ? From a purely personal point of view it was difficult for Catherine to proceed against the hetman. He had been in love with her in her early years at court ; he had been one of the leaders of the conspiracy which had placed her on the throne. He was president of the commission to revise army establishments set up in 1763, and his name had appeared on the list of proposed councillors of state in 1762–3. He was a member of the commission on the freedom of the nobility. He was also commander-in-chief of the Cossack Hosts. Gossip among the foreign diplomats suggested that Grigory Orlov was pressing the empress to relieve Razumovsky and appoint him to lead the Cossacks in his stead. 'L'impératrice s'assure de cette manière à tout évènement des cosaques . . . en mettant à leur tête un homme tout devoué à ses interêts et à ses ordres.'[34]

The atmosphere grew increasingly embittered. Razumovsky was forbidden the palace, and Catherine indulged in some petty persecution of his wife. But her policy was fully supported – if not inspired – by the highest government officials, who had scant sympathy with Little Russian aspirations for autonomy, or with their form of government, and relative immunity from taxation.[35] Finally, at a personal interview in February or early March 1764 with the empress, Razumovsky was brought to the point of 'asking to be relieved of such a difficult and dangerous post'.[36] Further progress was then held up by Catherine's journey to Livonia and Estonia, and by the Mirovich affair, which aroused considerable feeling against the Ukraine at court. Meanwhile, on the recommendation of the College of Foreign Affairs, the body in charge of Little Russia, it was decided to abolish the hetmanate and replace it by a College under a Russian governor-general.[37]

The Little Russian College was duly set up on 10 November 1764, with four Russian members and four Little Russian members, under the presidency of General Count P.A. Rumyantsev, who was granted supreme military and civil power and placed in command of the Cossacks of the Zaporozhian Host. In selecting Rumyantsev for this post Catherine showed considerable skill. He was a popular and successful commander in the Seven Years' War, and his mother was not averse to hinting at the possible paternity of Peter the Great.[38] Rumyantsev had bitterly resented his supersession by Peter Panin as commander of the Russian troops in East Prussia at the time of Catherine's *coup d'état*. He had lingered in Germany and had even contemplated entering Prussian service.[39] He was summoned back to Russia by Catherine in a letter typical of her relationship with her public servants :

I think it essential to explain myself to you . . . you judge of me according to past standards of behaviour, when the personality counted for more than the qualities and the services of a man, and you believe that your past favour [with Peter III] will now be held against you. . . . But let me say, you do not know me well. Return here if your health permits. You will be received with the distinction which your rank and your services to the country warrant.[40]

On his return to Russia, Rumyantsev was appointed to the commission on army establishments, but was not otherwise employed. He had spent part of his childhood in Little Russia and was well-disposed towards its people. By appointing him therefore, Catherine showed not only her skill at conciliating potentially hostile public figures, and her determination not to waste her more talented public servants ; she also removed Rumyantsev from court and gave him a task which might make or break him.[41]

The instructions drafted for Rumyantsev followed closely the memorandum prepared for her by Teplov. The empress criticized the incredible confusion of civilian and military government, the endless delays and injustices in the courts, the arbitrary enactment of temporary privileges as permanent, the harmful effects of peasant mobility, the ingrained laziness of the inhabitants, and their hatred of Russia. Everyone knew the natural wealth of Little Russia. But everyone knew that, particularly under the last hetman, Russia derived no revenue from it, indeed she disbursed some 48,000 rubles annually. Rumyantsev was instructed to take steps to survey the population and the resources of the area and to have proper maps prepared. And, since the government could not count on any fixed revenue as long as the peasants moved from place to place, he was to use all convenient means 'to convince the people that such movement should be stopped completely'. Catherine expressed the hope that both the landowners and the peasants could be brought to recognize the disadvantages of the free movement of the peasants. Instability could not of course benefit the landowners. But, wrote Catherine,

the peasants, feeding their hopes only on dreams of freedom, don't understand that their labours on the land in permanent settlements are infinitely more profitable for themselves and their descendants ; nor do they understand that if they were to settle, they would not lose their freedom, as we see from the example of peasants in many European states, where, though they are neither serfs nor in bondage, yet for their own benefit, they remain settled in one place.[42]

This paragraph in the secret instruction to Rumyantsev is especially relevant to the interpretation of Catherine's attitude to serfdom. Taking the ukaz and the instruction to Rumyantsev at their face value, it would seem that the primary motive in controlling the freedom of movement of the peasantry was to improve the economy, and increase the revenue obtainable from taxation by the state. On the other hand, both the ukaz and the instruction can be regarded as acceptance by the government, and Catherine, of noble pressure to extend serfdom in Little Russia in the interests of their class – since serfdom had in fact followed the limitation of peasant movement in Russia proper. Analysis of motives in this case cannot be conclusive, since it must take into account many imponderables. It may be worth pointing out that though the ukaz of 1763 was public, the instruction to Rumyantsev, in which Catherine points to the existence in Europe of permanent settlement without loss of freedom, was secret, and therefore probably reflects more closely her own opinion.[43] She was well aware of the distinction between bondage to a person and bondage to the soil, and she regarded the latter as less onerous. It is more than likely therefore that at this stage she was concerned, in the interests of the national revenue and the national economy, with controlling the labour and not the persons of the Little Russian peasants.

Rumyantsev was also ordered to be particularly vigilant in ecclesiastical matters. The secularization of Church lands had not been extended to the Ukraine,[44] and Catherine particularly warned Rumyantsev to forestall ecclesiastical efforts to extend the spiritual power into the secular field. She pointed out that candidates for ecclesiastical posts, trained in Polish and Ukrainian seminaries 'according to the corrupt principles of the Roman clergy, were infected by an insatiable lust for power, the harmful consequences of which have filled past European history'. He was therefore to acquaint himself with the powers, wealth and resources of the Church, and to put forward right-thinking candidates for promotion. Supervision of the judiciary, the promotion of industry, development of communications also fell within his field. Finally he was to devote special care to the delicate political problem of eradicating Little Russian hatred of Russia which had been fostered by the starshina among the common people in order to preserve their own lawless rule. He was to keep a discreet watch over the starshina and by adopting a just, disinterested and mild behaviour, the empress hoped that he would lead the discontented to appreciate the advantages bestowed upon them by their deliverance from the oppression 'of many small tyrants'.

The hetman received a princely 'golden handshake'. He retained his annual salary of 50,000 r., as well as 10,000 r.p.a, from the Little Russian revenues ; he was granted the town of Gadyach, several other dependencies and his palace in Baturin. In 1765 he travelled abroad, but returned to Russia in 1767. The dispute over the hetmanate left no lasting trace on Razumovsky's relations with Catherine, and the Cossack starshina accepted the abolition of the hetmanate without a murmur.

The abolition of the hetmanate was essentially a political operation, designed to break down the territorial and psychological separatism of Little Russia by the extension of Russian authority and the introduction of Russian institutions – even if for the time being these were only partially superimposed over existing Ukrainian institutions. Not only Little Russia, but other lands belonging to the Ukraine by settlement and tradition, such as Slobodska Ukraine and New Russia, were affected. The Russian government successfully asserted its right to reorganize the government and the territorial distribution of lands between these three areas and prepared the way for the eventual division of the lands into separate gubernii, incorporated directly into the Russian state. The purely military aspects of the reform should not however be overlooked. The southern frontier of Russia was consolidated by increasing the number of settlers, both civilian and military, and its defence was improved by the formation of permanent Cossack pike and hussar regiments, officered in the Russian manner.

Part II

The Estates

5

The Nobility

Bondage, in one form or another, extended all the way through Russian society : the individual was bound to serve a person or the state ; he was bound to a particular community which he could not leave without the permission of the corresponding authority ; and he was bound by a system of collective responsibility to the other members of the community he belonged to, a system known in Russian as *krugovaya poruka*. The essential link between these forms of bondage was the financial and military needs of the state, which could not be met otherwise in view of the primitive nature of the administrative apparatus, the relatively undeveloped economy, and the prevailing political climate. Russia had thus become a society in which activity did not depend on the free initiative of the individual but on the permission of the government. Everyone was assigned to a particular legal category or status (*sosloviye* or *sostoyaniye,* most conveniently translated by 'estate') and could only carry out the activities proper to that estate, or enjoy its privileges. Thus, more than any other contemporary society, it could be summed up as one in which all that was not specifically authorized was forbidden, and only that could be done which was specifically authorized. It was also a society in which physical mobility from place to place and from estate to estate was hampered at every turn. The one exception to this rule of physical immobility was the estate of the *dvoryanstvo,* or nobility.[1]

The reforms of Peter I had both clarified and simplified Muscovite social structure and rendered it more rigid by providing a legal foundation for it. It was he who introduced the practice of granting the title of count or baron, which was borne by all the children of the holder in accordance with Muscovite custom, and he founded the first Russian order of chivalry, the Order of St Andrew, in 1700.[2] The final organization of the nobility – as it is convenient to call it – came with the introduction of the Table of Ranks in 1722. The Table laid down fourteen ranks or *chiny* (originally corresponding to actual functions) in the military and naval spheres, and a parallel ladder of 'court' or civil ranks. A non-noble entrant in the service acquired hereditary nobility with the fourteenth rank (the lowest commissioned rank) in the armed forces (for himself and his children born *after* he reached that rank) and with the eighth rank in the civil service. But the social status conferred by the Table of Ranks on official occasions did not supersede the status conferred by society on birth. A noble with no rank was still a noble, with all the other attendant privileges of that estate. On the other hand automatic promotion into the ranks of the nobility tended to depress the value of nobility of birth, since precedence on official occasions and in church services was graded according to *chin,* and the order of precedence laid down for public occasions easily crept into private social gatherings. Thus the average Russian noble came to regard his degree as linked essentially to his rank in state service rather than to what he might think of as his rank in society. An offence would be resented as aimed at a public person, not a private one ; the concept of personal honour and private standards of behaviour was weakened in favour of esteem accorded to public position. Nevertheless, two different conceptions of nobility, fundamentally incompatible with each other, survived within the Petrine estate. The noble by birth fought, often within the same breast, with the noble by service rank.

The Table of Ranks, modified in subsequent reigns, also laid down the external privileges of *chin* as distinct from social rank in terms of title. The number of horses, the type of carriage, the livery to be worn by servants were all carefully defined. Under Elizabeth for instance the wearing of lace was limited to the top five classes, and those with no *chin* were not allowed to wear velvet at all. Occupation of the wrong place in church could lead to a fine of two months' pay.

The life of a noble was regulated from a tender age. The revised rules, introduced in 1736, laid down that at the age of seven, then at the age of twelve, all boys were to present themselves to the local governor, or to the proper quarters in the two capitals. After a test of literacy at sixteen (at which any who failed were faced with service as a common soldier, or worse still as a common sailor) they were finally allotted to serve at the age of twenty. Such a rigid system was bound in fact to fail. There was widespread evasion, in spite of the heavy fines. Under Elizabeth wealthy and well placed nobles adopted the practice of enrolling their children when infants as privates in the guards regiments, and securing promotion for them on 'length of service'. The future Field-Marshal Rumyantsev was six years old when he was enlisted.

The estate of the nobility did not form a homogeneous class. Estimated to number some fifty thousand adult males in mid-eighteenth century, the range of wealth varied enormously. The normal method of assessment was by ownership of serfs ('souls') and figures for 1762 show the following spread :

Number of serfs	*Percentage of landowners in 1762*
Less than 20	51
21–100	31
101–500	15
501–1000	2
Over 1000	1

Thus in mid-century 82 per cent of the nobles owned fewer than one hundred serfs.[3]

The actual income derived by the nobles from their estates also varied greatly. *gap whi the gentry* It was estimated at 2·5 rubles per male serf in the 1770s, hence the money income of 62 per cent of the nobility was below 100 r.p.a. The vast majority of the nobility were poor or even very poor. Many nobles in Novgorod guberniya ploughed their own land and had almost no serfs.[4] The serfs lived under the same roof as their masters, and the estate produced just enough for their common subsistence. Those who owned fewer than twenty were not subject to the recruit levy. In Tver' guberniya there were whole villages where nobles who owned no serfs cultivated the land themselves.[5] There could thus be little in common between them and the great magnates like the Sheremet'yevs, the Shuvalovs, the Razumovskys, the Vorontsovs, who owned thousands of serfs, and spent fortunes on every kind of luxury that the eighteenth century could devise. Tapestries, fine porcelain and mirrors, paintings, bought or commissioned, and carpets decorated the palaces and great houses on estates which more often than not had been gifts from the sovereign to the present owners or their immediate ancestors. Fabulous sums were spent on carriages and above all clothes and jewellery, by men as well as women.[6] In contrast the provincial gentry lived perhaps in a little 'nest' or group of houses in a village of which they each owned a small share. Distrusting stone houses as bad for the health, their dwellings were often little more than wooden huts, with two low dark rooms ; walls and ceilings had no form of decoration other than the inevitable icons. Furniture consisted of wooden benches and tables, perhaps a few chairs. Instead of the delicacies prepared by French chefs, their table was supplied by the produce of their estate, and by the hunting and fishing which was one of their principal occupations. Bear-baiting, parlour games, and lawsuits with their neighbours over their lands provided their main entertainment.[7]

Clearly these different social groups in the estate of the nobility conceived of *education* the interests of the estate as a whole in differing ways. Owing to Peter I's enforcement of the service principle, the problem of education had come to be a central one in the life of the noble. Indeed the importance attached in Russia to education as a necessary concomitant of nobility is striking and reflects the fact that the more self-conscious assessment of the role and duties of the noble in society came to the fore in Russia at a time when the Enlightenment had stressed education as the key to human progress. The nobility reacted in different ways. There was much resentment in the more conservative circles at the compulsory education required by the Table of Ranks, particularly among young sprigs running wild in the countryside and possibly just learning their letters if there was a parish school, run by a semi-literate priest. On the other hand there was also a demand for more educational facilities for the poorer nobles who could not afford the services of a private tutor (a species which abounded in Russia and ranged from a retired non-commissioned officer to a fraudulent French hairdresser or valet).[8] In mid-century illiteracy was still widespread among the provincial nobility.[9] Hence there was strong pressure for a state-subsidized educational system, which would enable the noble to qualify for the service to which he was bound.

In so far as these facilities existed, notably the Cadet Corps and Moscow University, founded in 1731 and 1755 respectively, they were not easily accessible to the poorest provincial nobility. But the Cadet Corps did play an important role in developing noble self-consciousness, based on European traditions of the social role of the nobility. It provided an education less purely technical and more humanistic than its name might imply. Its object was not merely to train students in necessary skills, but to mould character and develop qualities of leadership. It endeavoured to instil norms of behaviour based on 'noblesse oblige' and underlined the concept that only the noble by birth had the capacity to see the whole, while others, moved by necessity, saw only their immediate needs. Thus the noble had a right to power, but a duty to perfect himself and to lead the society of which he was the highest cultural exponent. By 1759 the Cadet Corps in St Petersburg published its own journal (*Prazdnoye vremya,* 'Idle Time') and its library was well stocked with foreign works. Moscow University served to propagate the same outlook in the second capital.[10]

State service was of course the normal way in which these ideals could be put into practice by those who held them. And for the many who did not, government service was nevertheless the only way to supplement a meagre income (except for those nobles who were too poor to serve at all). What came to be regarded as unworthy and oppressive was the compulsory nature of the service and of the necessary education. In this respect the trend of opinion among the lower nobles converged with that of the wealthy and the magnates, who wanted the prestige, privilege and power of the noble estate as a whole to be raised up and guaranteed against the arbitrary caprice of the ruler. The higher nobility and court magnates suffered less – except in their personal dignity – from compulsory service, since official positions at court or in the government were amply rewarded with salaries, grants of land and opportunities of enriching oneself at state expense. But they were anxious to assert the principle of personal freedom, freedom from arrest without just cause and due legal process, immunity from torture and corporal punishment and the right to travel. By mid-century there had also grown up a strong desire to limit entry to the estate of the nobility by reducing the opportunities for promotion which the Table of Ranks provided. The fact that nobility was granted bureaucratically and automatically with a rise in *chin,* instead of being the personal grant of the monarch to an individual in reward for his services, devalued the estate in the eyes of the aristocratically minded. Admittedly, there were very few high officials of non-noble origin : only 18 out of 145 in the top five ranks in the Table of Ranks in 1755. But in ranks 6–8 inclusive, 130 out of 562 were of non-noble birth, and in ranks 9–14 inclusive, of 1,344 officials, 881 were personal nobles i.e. of non-noble origin. At the same date, 83·38 per cent of the officers in the armed forces were hereditary nobles, and 16·62 per cent were promoted from the ranks – mainly from 'soldiers' children'. Comparison with the status of the French, Swedish or Polish nobility led the Russian nobles to covet similar privileges. Travelling through Poland in the early 1760s, the young Alexander Vorontsov 'n'avait pu imaginer rien de plus sage et de plus heureux pour lui et pour le pays que d'être un grand seigneur tel qu'il y en avait alors en Pologne, avec les mêmes droits et les mêmes privilèges'.[11]

Among the ukazy issued by Peter III which Catherine had to confirm or repeal was the manifesto granting freedom from service to the nobility. What evidence there is of her own view of the manifesto suggests that she did not approve of it in the form in which it had been issued. She may have feared that it would lead to an immediate outflow of qualified manpower just when she was increasing the numbers employed in the bureaucracy. She may also have objected to it on the grounds that the connecting link between legal privilege and public service seemed to have been broken. In a series of personal notes dating from the 1760s, Catherine went very thoroughly into the various categories of nobles which existed throughout Europe. Her general conclusion was that nobility was a status conferred by the head of the state in reward for service.[12]

Catherine's failure to confirm the manifesto at once led to some murmuring in the capital. Some, as the French envoy shrewdly pointed out, preferred that she should not confirm the manifesto, since such a confirmation implied that their freedom was in fact a matter of imperial grant.[13] But the murmurings continued and finally forced Catherine to take action.[14] On 11 February 1763 she set up a commission to examine the freedom of the nobility, composed of those same people whose names had been thought of for the abortive imperial council.[15]

The terms of reference of the commission were typical of Catherine's cautious approach to major issues at the beginning of her reign. On the one hand they implied that Peter III's manifesto had not gone far enough in establishing noble freedom on a sound basis – a view which Catherine appeared to endorse when she presided at the opening session of the commission.[16] On the other hand they stressed the need to give legal expression to Catherine's belief in the connection between nobility and service. By reopening discussion of the substance of the manifesto Catherine was in a position to postpone immediate confirmation, and she could ensure that the state's need for service could be met in any new draft.

Nothing is known of discussion within the commission, but drafts of two submissions have survived. Bestuzhev Ryumin submitted his proposals on 20 February 1763. Nikita Panin's views are known only from his comments on Bestuzhev Ryumin's draft. In both cases the triangular relationship of promotion (including ennoblement), service, and ownership of land and serfs was crucial. Bestuzhev Ryumin proposed that ennoblement should not be the automatic consequence of promotion in the Table of Ranks but should only be granted by the Crown. Only nobles who had served should be entitled to acquire settled estates (he is not clear on inheritance). And non-noble officials and officers who were promoted in the

Table of Ranks but not ennobled could enjoy the salary and all the privileges of rank except landownership. The adoption of such a policy might well have led to the formation of a professional 'official' class of non-nobles, while fusing the existing nobility into a closed caste of serf-owners, who would, if Bestuzhev Ryumin had his way, enjoy absolute control of their serfs, a prominent position in local administration and some local corporate organization.[17]

Panin treated the link between nobility, service and serf-owning quite differently. He emphasized that Peter I himself had ranked civil service lower than military. He proposed therefore that non-nobles who had reached noble rank in active military service, or the eighth (noble) rank in civil service, should keep their noble rank. But in future the right to buy settled land, and other legal and economic privileges normally attached to nobility should be divorced from noble rank and be attached to service rank with or without nobility. From the seventh rank upwards non-nobles could petition the sovereign to be granted hereditary nobility.[18]

The main burden of Panin's comments was thus : all should be encouraged to serve, and the reward for service should be the right at a given level in the Table of Ranks to buy serf villages. This reward should be granted equally to non-nobles and to nobles and should be divorced from the grant of nobility by the sovereign. Automatic ennoblement would be abolished. In support of his proposal, Panin argued that the state so far had paid no attention to the balance between the need to spur the nobles on to serve the state, and the general needs of the national economy. By forbidding nobles who had not served to buy settled land, and enabling non-nobles, who had served, to buy such land while remaining non-noble, he was killing several birds with one stone. The numbers of the nobility would not increase so fast, and they would remain, as Panin wished, a relatively closed élite, high in status and public esteem, receiving their patent of nobility from the sovereign in person. But the nobles would be encouraged to serve, since only service would entitle them to buy serf villages. On the other hand the non-nobles would also be encouraged to serve by the prospect of the ownership of settled land, which was the main material benefit they previously derived from promotion to noble rank. There is evidently in Panin's observations an effort to bring the Russian social structure closer to that of non-serf-owning Europe, where ownership of land was not the monopoly of a particular class. Unlike Bestuzhev therefore, Panin was prepared to see the nobility sharing its most exclusive privilege, serf-ownership, with non-nobles. The result of his policy would have been the creation of two ladders of promotion in government service, one military and mainly noble, one civil, reaching nobility only at the very top – a pattern which might lead to a much freer and more flexible social structure, and may reflect the views of a man who knew Western European nobility by personal experience and not merely by hearsay.[19]

On 5 March 1763, Chancellor Vorontsov's 'Points for the discussion of the freedom of the nobility' were discussed by the commission. Michael Vorontsov did not reject service but thought its duration should be stated ; he suggested that special privileges should be accorded to the old nobility as distinct from the new-comers, and particularly to the titled nobility 'as is done in other countries'. He proposed that specific honours should be conferred on members of the first class in the Table of Ranks on retirement, such as a special residential quarter, guards, salutes, and correspondingly lower awards to members of the third, fourth and fifth classes. More interestingly, he proposed that following the example of other countries (notably France), titles should be attached to landed estates which should be turned into principalities, counties, baronies and *seigneuries (gospo-darstva)*. A principality should comprise between four and five thousand serfs, a county between two and three thousand, the title of the estate should be added to the family title, and the estate should be preserved against fragmentation.[20]

Michael Vorontsov's project raised issues far wider than those which the commission had been established to discuss, notably the whole problem of defining nobility. The abolition of compulsory service inevitably raised the question of how to define rank in society. What, in future, would be the social rank of some-one who had never served ? Vorontsov's solution was that since the Table of Ranks could not apply to non-serving nobles, precedence in society should be granted according to ancestry and title. In the Russian context this was a revolu-tionary proposal, since if accepted it would have broken the stranglehold of the Table of Ranks on Russian society and might have led to the development of a genuine aristocracy, independent of the ruler. Typically however, the commis-sion refused even to discuss the matter raised by Vorontsov, on the grounds that it did not come within its terms of reference, which were to improve Peter III's manifesto on the freedom of the nobility. As for the vexed question of who was to be accounted a noble, the commission decided to keep to the rule laid down by Peter I in 1724. When the College of War had asked the emperor for guidance, whether to consider someone a noble on grounds of property (one hundred home-steads or more) or on grounds of class in the Table of Ranks, Peter had briefly replied : 'A noble is he who is useful.'[21]

The recommendations finally put forward by the commission on 18 March 1763 to the empress do dimly reflect a striving towards the establishment of two distinct social hierarchies – a separation of rank in society from rank in the state's hierarchy. This would imply some diminution of the power of the state over soci-ety, since it would no longer be the exclusive dispenser of rank and status.

But the commission's recommendations are also of fundamental importance to an understanding of the Russian nobility's conception of itself, and underline the essential difference between it and the *noblesse* of other European states. To begin with, the compulsory service enforced by Peter the Great was recognized as having been necessary in view of the state of backwardness and ignorance of the nobility in his time. The freedom from compulsory service which the nobility now felt itself entitled to claim was justified by the greater degree of education, which by following the example of other countries, the Russian nobility had acquired. In a key sentence, the commission stated that it had laid down such rights for the nobility as would combine their freedom with zeal in the civil and military service of the state, which would be inspired by no other consideration than the sense of honour inculcated by education, and would require no limitation on their freedom.[22]

The strong emphasis on the importance of education in the whole preamble reflects the Petrine ethos rather than the European consciousness of aristocratic honour, though it purports to describe the practice of the Livonian and to some extent the Swedish and Danish nobility. The excellent education for service allegedly given to sprigs of the nobility in these countries is outlined in detail as well as the advantages and principles to be derived therefrom.

But throughout the preamble, the commission, in spite of its reliance on foreign models, never once based the demand for freedom on the concept of the inborn honour of the nobility. The dependence of the nobility on recognition of its services by the Crown was explicitly assumed, in contrast to the Western European conception of a nobility in which the sense of honour was inborn and not inculcated by education, and in which service was a matter of choice by those who often considered themselves above the monarch, and with rights which did not derive from him, but from a much older law. The commission showed a pragmatic and utilitarian approach to personal benefits and accepted that the nobility was not entitled to freedom from service as of right, but because 'the education of the Russian nobility had now reached such a level that there was no need for them to be compelled to serve'.[23]

Without daring to attack the fundamental problem of the nature of nobility and its relation to the state, the commission did however attempt to assert the rights of birth as against those of service rank, and in so doing to separate the three elements which Peter I had indissolubly linked together : nobility, service and the Table of Ranks. In article 1 of its projected code the Russian nobility was defined as consisting of all those who were descended from nobles or who had been ennobled by the monarch, and had received diplomas and coats of arms. Article 2, and particularly the explanation appended to it, made the attempt to separate rank in society from rank in service. Points 11 and 15 of the Table of Ranks, it was stated in the explanation, provided that officers of non-noble origin were to be regarded as equal to nobles by descent, but 'the commission understands that this refers only to the esteem in which their rank is to be held, and does not entitle them to participate in the rights of the nobility . . .'. Their reason for thinking so was that non-nobles could be promoted to officer's rank by a number of institutions (the Senate, the Colleges, army commanders), whereas ennoblement could only be conferred personally by a crowned head. The commission therefore endorsed the views of Bestuzhev, Vorontsov and Panin, to the effect that such promoted officers should content themselves with their rank and salary, but should be granted the right to petition the sovereign for ennoblement, in order not to discourage them from zealous service.

However, if article 2 put rank in society above rank in service, article 3 firmly returned to the traditional pattern. 'A noble, with no *chin* in the Table of Ranks,' it ran, 'and who enjoys only the status of nobility, must give place to the lowest state servant of officer rank.' In the explanatory paragraph, it was pointed out that this article was intended to spur the noble to service ; moreover, 'it was only just that those who served should be honoured above those who did not'.[24]

The commission had burked the issue of establishing precedence in society based on titles (as proposed by Michael Vorontsov). Hence its recommendations amounted to separating rank in society, which it accepted as being based on *chin* in the Table of Ranks, from noble rights acquired only by personal grant from the monarch. What were these rights ? As put forward in the commission's recommendations, they were, first and foremost, the exclusive right to own settled estates, i.e. serfs (article 2). The remaining rights which the nobility felt itself entitled to were : the right to travel abroad (nothing prepared the noble better for service, commented Catherine sharply, than 'milling around Parisian theatres and brothels'), enter foreign service, or emigrate for good ; legal privileges, i.e. no arrest without trial, no corporal punishment, no confiscation of property except for debt ; and the right to establish entails.[25] The nobility thus demanded both exclusiveness and restricted entry but contented itself with a limited degree of social precedence in exchange for narrowly conceived personal immunities, legal, and above all economic, privileges.

The commission submitted its report to Catherine with the suggestion that some of its proposals should be incorporated in a statute on the nobility ; other points, of a more temporary nature, could be added to existing military law and to the new civil code still to be produced. Catherine sat upon the report until 11 October 1763, when she returned it to the commission with the proposal that it should set about drafting the corresponding laws and manifesto. But the commission now revealed a total lack of initiative by simply returning the ball to Catherine's court with the remark that its members could not proceed further unless they knew which of the rights they had put forward the empress accepted and which she rejected. Their plan, they declared, was linked by a continuous thread and should the empress subsequently decide to modify their project their work would have been done in vain. It is not surprising that Catherine felt strong enough to brave noble discontent and allowed the whole problem to fade quietly away, leaving Peter III's manifesto unconfirmed for the time being, even though it was in practice acted upon in cases referred to the Senate.[26]

The discussions surrounding the Manifesto of 1762, and the report of the commission set up by Catherine show that the nobility was by no means united in what it expected from the throne. Broadly one can distinguish three trends of opinion : the wealthy court magnates (whether of the *new* or the *old* nobility), who had been influenced by Western models, were more concerned with social status and legal immunities accorded to rank ; they wished rank in society to be independent of rank in service ; their proposals implied the setting up of two parallel social scales, the one based on birth, the other based on service – reflecting perhaps the situation existing in France, where the *noblesse d'épée* and the *noblesse de robe* started from separate backgrounds but met and intermarried at the top. There is some – though not much – evidence that they were less concerned with economic privileges – largely because they were usually very wealthy already. The recommendations of the commission reflect the views of this group, namely the governing élite of the country, who would enter service as a matter of course, be quickly promoted and amply rewarded, and who wanted to protect themselves from a too catastrophic fall from favour. A second group of nobles saw the problem with the eyes of the state rather than of the 'estate'. Socially they might come from the same milieu as the first – wealthy new or old court magnates – but they were more concerned with the state's right to exact service from the nobility, and the need for this service nobility to be firmly under state control, to depend on the state for its social status and economic well-being. Finally, the general run of the minor nobility viewed the problem almost entirely from the point of view of their economic needs and were prepared to give up social status, and freedom, in exchange for the guarantee of their monopoly of settled labour and service posts. None of these attitudes was new in the Russian context ; precedents can be found in the sixteenth and the seventeenth centuries. What earlier Russian history also shows however is that the first trend, the demand for social status based exclusively on rank in society, had always been viewed askance by the government (in the person of the principal government servants or bureaucrats) and by the run of the mill nobles. It had therefore as little chance of succeeding in 1763 as in earlier – or later – times. Nevertheless, it is arguable that the failure to separate the bureaucracy from the nobility by creating two scales of social rank prevented the formation of a genuine nobility just as it prevented the formation of a genuine bureaucracy.

Though Catherine did not formally confirm Peter III's manifesto, it had introduced some changes into the life of the Russian nobility. The drift back to the countryside had begun before 1762, but the manifesto made it possible for considerable numbers of nobles in the prime of life to retire from service and return to their estates. Though the report of the commission in 1763 did not touch on this issue at all, the provincial nobility were already beginning to take a more active interest in local administration and to criticize its inadequacies.[27] In a positive sense also, nobles who had served in the armies operating beyond the Russian frontiers brought back new ideas, new experiences and a vision of a more comfortable and cultured way of life. For the noble boor, 1762 meant that he could sink back into the traditional village sloth ; but for many, retiring now at a younger age than their parents, life in the provinces had to be made more bearable by the building of better houses, the acquisition of books and furniture, the development of a more civilized way of life. Closer and more constant contact with the local administration would also lead to demands for its improvement.

What, finally, was the significance of the manifesto in the social history of

Russia ? This question has given rise to considerable discussion among Russian historians. When the manifesto was first promulgated, it was acclaimed by the nobility, some of whom voted to erect a golden statue to Peter III. Subsequently, historians such as for instance V.O. Klyuchevsky,[28] have argued that contemporaries misunderstood the significance of the manifesto, which in his view merely abolished the compulsory length of service, not the fact of service. Surely however the feelings of contemporaries must be given due weight ; if they felt that the manifesto introduced an important change in their status, then it must have done so. And indeed, *pace* Klyuchevsky, the manifesto did open the way to the creation of a totally new class in Russia, what one might call 'private man' as distinct from service man, society as distinct from and opposed to the state. Until 1762 there was no such person in Russia as an independent gentleman, living on his estate, cultivating his mind or his turnips, participating as much or as little as he wished in public affairs, secure and self-confident. The manifesto made it possible for a young man of twenty-five or thirty to resign from the service and devote himself to travel, literature or the arts. If he was prepared to do without the precedence conferred by service rank, he need not serve at all. Moreover it is impossible to measure in precise terms the psychological impact on the nobility of their new freedom. Historians have not tired of pointing out that in spite of the manifesto, the nobility continued to serve. But there is a great difference between being compelled to serve and choosing to serve. In this respect the Russian noble was at last on a par with the gentry and nobility of other countries. If his social status in Russia still depended on his *chin,* his social status abroad depended more on title, wealth and even personality. The Russian noble was no longer 'enserfed' to the state.[29] Though the manifesto was issued in the reign of Peter III, and was not formally confirmed by Catherine in the 1760s, it is in her reign that its social consequences were almost immediately felt, particularly in the field of cultural development. Without exaggerating the numbers involved, it is evident that the literary and artistic interests of the latter half of the eighteenth century flourished because of the new freedom and self respect of the nobility.

6

The Towns, the Peasants
and the Land

As in the case of the nobility, the structure of the urban estate and of the peasantry had been rendered more rigid by the transformation of Russian society effected by Peter I. The number of townspeople cannot be stated precisely since in addition to registered town dwellers or *grazhdane*, there was a floating unregistered population composed of nobles, officials, clergy, serfs and state peasants with passports, vagrants, convicts and sometimes exiles. The towns varied enormously in size. At mid-century 44·5 per cent had fewer than 500 inhabitants ; Moscow, with about 400,000 and St Petersburg with about 200,000, were the two capitals. In the 1780s, Riga, Astrakhan' and Kronstadt had over 30,000 inhabitants.[1] However, the urban estate itself, i.e. the registered urban taxpayers, was very much smaller than these figures suggest.

In the 1740s Moscow had a total of 13,458 registered urban taxpayers, St Petersburg only 3,471, Kazan', 3014. The third census, in the 1760s, gave the registered urban population at 258,532 male souls, or 3 per cent of the whole taxable population of Russia.[2]

Whether a settlement was legally a town or not depended not on its size but on the state.[3] There were towns on the 'establishment' (*shtatnyy*) and towns which were not (*zashtatnyy,* or supernumerary). In addition there were *slobody* or suburbs which had grown up outside the boundaries of an existing legally recognized town, sometimes as much as thirty or forty versts away, as a result of economic development on private or state-owned land. They were looked at askance by registered town-dwellers since their inhabitants escaped town taxes and state services, and were therefore in a better position to compete with registered town-dwellers. Similar to the *slobody* were the *pripisnyye* towns, 'townlets' attached to a more important centre. Some of the unrecognized towns had grown up on private or monastic land, though there were in general few seigneurial or monastic towns in Russia.[4]

The registered town-dwellers formed the urban estate, membership of which was hereditary. They were further divided into three guilds, and a number of craft unions below which came the common people (*podlyye lyudi*). The division into guilds reflected differences of wealth, not differences of occupation – as in Muscovy. Members of the first guild disposed of a capital between 100 and 500 r. ; in the second guild were merchants with a capital between 50 and 100 r. The third guild comprised *kuptsy* whose capital might range from 10 to 50 r. In 1766 of the 8,733 kuptsy or merchants in Moscow, 992 belonged to the first guild, 3,491 to the second and 4,250 to the third. Of these last 80 per cent did not live by trade. A kupets might well remain registered as a member of a guild which in no way reflected either his occupation or the amount of capital he disposed of. Below the kuptsy came the surpisingly small number of craftsmen formed into craft unions or *tsekhi*. The craft unions did not carry out the functions of professional training, maintenance of standards and limitation of competition of the Western guilds ; they served the purpose of organizing their members into bodies on which the state could lay taxes and from which it could exact services.[5] The administration of the urban estate was entrusted to magistraty, or ratushi in smaller towns, elected councils with judicial and administrative functions, named after the German model from which Peter I drew his inspiration. The magistraty acted as courts for disputes involving members of the merchant estate ; they also allocated taxes, and arranged for the performance of the various services required by the state. They were subordinated throughout the country to the *Glavnyy Magistrat* or Chief Magistracy, in St Petersburg, which ranked as one of the Colleges under the Senate, but they were also supervised by the local voyevodas.

The magistraty were in a sense the tip of the iceberg of urban life, the link between the government and the community of registered citizens as a whole. The assembly of townspeople or *posadskiy skhod* (occasionally also described as *mirskiy skhod*) consisted of all the registered taxpayers ; attendance was compulsory and exemption difficult to achieve. As with all Russian assemblies there were few fixed rules, and no quorum. The assembly elected the members of the magistrat or ratusha, discussed the allocation of normal or special state taxes, as well as the town taxes, and the fulfilment of police requirements including billeting. The *skhod* also elected its own *starosta,* the executive head of the assembly. He presided over the assembly and acted as the connecting link between the magistrat and the people, transmitting the instructions of the magistrat, and representing the assembly to it. He was thus in the unenviable position of being responsible both to those above him and to those below him. The assembly itself was not composed of people present in their individual capacities. It was the sum of a number of different self-administering units, suburbs and wards, guilds and craft unions, each of which in turn had its own assembly, elders and starosta.[6]

The magistraty and the courts made heavy demands on manpower. But in addition the townspeople acted as the government's (or the town's) agents in the collection of taxes and customs dues, and the sale of certain commodities such as salt, gunpowder, tobacco, pitch, tar and liquor, etc. At least twenty-nine different unpaid services of this kind were carried out, ranging from the sale of stamped paper to collecting the taxes on salt. In 46 towns, in the 1760s, more than a hundred people were engaged in these and other administrative services ; Yaroslavl had a registered population of 7,255 in 1745 of which 361 were engaged in government services. Moscow probably had approximately 550 such agents, out of a registered population of 13,673 ; Tambov with 430 registered town-dwellers had 38 agents of this kind.[7]

The town-dweller was subject to the recruit levy, paid the poll-tax at a higher rate than the peasant, 1 r. 24, and was bound to his town and to his fellows by the system of collective guarantees, to ensure that he did not escape his share of the taxes and other burdens. Entitled to trade beyond the limits of his district (uezd), the kupets needed a passport to do so which he could only obtain if he had paid urban and state taxes in advance for the whole period of his absence from his home town, and which would be issued to him by a body – the magistrat – composed of his business rivals. Since the poll-tax was allocated among the merchants according to their capacity to pay, the community was very reluctant to allow a rich merchant to leave it.[8]

Lack of mobility between estates in Russia tended to limit urban growth. The transfer of permanent residence from one town to another could only be finally registered on receipt of certificates that all taxes and dues had been paid in the previous residence. An urban dweller in a town in which he was not registered was liable to be regarded as a fugitive from his own town, and haled back by force as a deserter. It was even more difficult for a state peasant to change his status. To be registered as a town-dweller he had to acquire immoveable property in the town and to prove his capacity to keep himself while paying both town taxes, and his share of the village taxes in the village where he was registered, until the next census, when the transfer from one estate to another would be entered in the poll-tax register – a process which could take between ten and fifteen years.

This tidy picture of a society firmly clamped into its various estates must be modified to take account of the fact that life was stronger than law. Many who were registered as kuptsy or merchants made a living by agriculture.[9] And some of the peasant families (sometimes of serf origin, registered as kuptsy with the permission of their owners) created veritable dynasties of traders and entrepreneurs. In the 1750s some 10 per cent of the kuptsy who owned textile firms were of peasant origin.[10] One Savva Yakovlev, a peasant from Ostashkov born in 1712, made his fortune by contracting with the government for food supplies for the court. He was ennobled in 1758, embarked on a fresh career as an entrepreneur and ended up a millionaire.[11]

The nature of Russian bondage entailed a strict definition of the economic activities which each estate was entitled to pursue and the elimination of unfair competition. When making contracts with the state, the individual kupets had to produce guarantees of his financial standing from the merchant community (the collective responsibility of society to the state) and personal guarantees of his standing to the merchant society (the individual's responsibility to the community). Hence the emphasis on the capital at the individual's disposal, and the reduction of the element of competition. The most extreme formulation of this totally uncapitalistic attitude can be found in a provision in the draft of a code for the rights of the merchants, produced by a legislative commission in 1761. It proposed that the merchant guilds should each elect members of good standing to allocate the taxes according to ability to pay ; every two years the kuptsy were to *verstat'* (equalize) their wealth so that there should always be some 'levelling distribution between the poor and the rich to reduce the offensiveness of wealth'.[12]

The uncompetitive nature of the economy rendered particularly fierce the struggle to prevent unfair competition. The growth of a new class of entrepreneurs, registered as kuptsy but in fact industrialists, cut across the traditional classification of occupations. The industrialists came under the jurisdiction of the Colleges of Mining and of Manufactures, not of the Glavnyy Magistrat, and they had been freed, as part of Peter I's great drive towards industrialization, from many of the taxes and service burdens which fell upon the merchants. Hence retail sale of their production in cities amounted to unfair competition. So too was the unfettered economic activity of the unregistered town-dwellers, the floating population of peasants and hired workers. These unregistered migrant traders who evaded the town taxes presented the real challenge of private enterprise to the regulated life of the kupets community.

In one respect, and one only, was the town a territorial unit: it owned land (*vygonnyye zemli*) which belonged to the whole town. In primitive conditions of transport and agricultural production, local production of raw materials and market gardening were a necessary part of any urban settlement, and indeed usually took place within its borders. But land for pasture and timber was also a necessity. Towns were not allowed to own settled land (i.e. serfs), and town-dwellers were in theory conditional holders of their plots, though in fact land was bought, sold and bequeathed.[13]

The peasantry : the serfs

The peasants suffered more than any other class in Russia from servitude. They were divided into two categories : serfs, or peasants in bondage to private owners, the Church, or the court, and state peasants with whom the various borderline categories of surviving military land tenures (one-homestead-men or *odnodvortsy*, soldier farmers, or *pakhotnyye soldaty*, etc.) are usually counted. In the third census of 1762–4, the peasant population numbered 9,978,113 (excluding the Baltic provinces) of which 5,611,531 (56·24 per cent of the peasants) were serfs of landowners, 1,061,639 (10·02 per cent) were Church peasants, 524,275 (4·95 per cent) were court peasants, and 2,780,868 (26·25 per cent) were state peasants.

There was a considerable difference in law as well as in fact between the status of the privately-owned serf, the Church peasant and the court peasant. Though in law the serf was not a slave, many aspects of the relationship between the serf and his master on the one hand and the serf and the state on the other were ill defined. The serfs paid taxes to the state, were liable to military conscription, and billeting. It is frequently stated that since the accession of Elizabeth in 1741 they had ceased to take the oath of allegiance to the ruler, implying that they were no longer the ruler's direct subjects. This view is based on a misreading of the relevant ukaz which excused *all* peasants working in the fields from attending church to swear fealty.[14]

The legal status of the serf's moveable property (cattle, stock, tools, furniture, cash) depended on the whim of his landowner. He was not allowed to acquire immoveable property in his own name (shop, dwelling, workshop in a town), nor could he borrow money, or undertake to fulfil state or private contracts without his master's consent. He needed permission and a passport to leave his village, to register as a merchant in a town, to volunteer for the army, or to enter a monastery.

All these disabilities were the result of laws passed by successive Russian governments, sometimes for state purposes, sometimes under the influence of the landowning class, for whom the control of labour was economically of more importance than the control of land, sometimes to prevent peasant indebtedness from rebounding on their masters. But the state scarcely entered into the regulation of personal relationships between lords and serfs, and left a wide discretion to landowners in the exercise of police powers over the serfs. The Code of 1649, and subsequent eighteenth-century legislation, failed to specify the nature and even the extent of the jurisdiction of the lord over his serfs. The only limitation was that the lord was not supposed to inflict the death penalty or to kill a serf – though no penalty was laid down if a serf died as a result of punishment.[15] In theory landlords had jurisdiction in all petty offences committed by their serfs against other serfs or peasants (theft, brawls, drunkenness and disorder), but not in major crimes such as murder or brigandage, which were dealt with by the state courts. But no distinction was made by landowners between offences against the laws of the state, and 'private' offences, such as failure to carry out the economic obligations imposed by the owner, refusal to work, or malingering, laziness, lying, etc. In theory too, owners were not supposed to compel serfs to marriage, but in practice they could both compel marriage or refuse their consent to it.

Where the state had left a vacuum, the individual stepped in. Owners of large estates, where the population constituted a real community, frequently legislated for their own private domains, and drew up their own codes, strongly influenced by the Petrine forms of administrative regulation. The codes laid down the punishments for brawling, theft and drunkenness, and for malingering, refusal to work or to obey orders, or to attend church. Codes of this kind were common on large estates where their application would be left to the steward in conjunction with the elected village elders or the commune itself, which thus participated in varying degrees in the process and enabled the private relationships between peasants to be decided on the basis of customary law.

The code prepared in 1751 by the future Field-Marshal Rumyantsev for his estate illustrates this curious combination of economic exploitation and legal administration. His manual covered the cultivation of the soil, the care of cattle, sheep and geese and the keeping of accounts. Chapter 10, under the heading 'on punishments', covered problems of discipline. Three articles dealt with offences against religion ; failure to attend services without good reason or unseemly behaviour in church incurred fines, of ten and two kopeks respectively, which were paid to the church (the alternative if the culprit had no money was twenty-four hours chained in a cell). An offence against a serf belonging to another owner involved a beating 'until the other owner was satisfied'. Corporal punishment and confiscation of property was the usual penalty for theft, and laziness was fined.[16]

If the serf peasant was almost defenceless against his lord, the domestic serf was even worse off. Landowners had the right to move families from estate to estate and to move individuals from the land into domestic service as stableboys, coachmen, lackeys, valets, chambermaids, nursemaids, etc. These domestic serfs were little better than slaves at the mercy of their masters, and even worse, of their mistresses. The domestic serf could in addition suffer from the fact that, educated by one master for a skilled or confidential post and treated as a friend, he might, when his master died, find himself relegated by the heir to inferior or uncongenial work, or even sold off. The morals of a noble household being no better than they were anywhere else, serf children could often be the half-brothers or half-sisters of their young master, and yet completely in his power – a situation scarcely conducive to family harmony. Young and pretty serf girls were particularly vulnerable since they suffered from both the lust of the master and the jealousy of the mistress.

Freedom in such a situation was both difficult to conceive of, and difficult to achieve. Most serf peasants thought of freedom not in terms of the law or of freedom to choose a way of life, but as freedom from dependence on a landowner. Becoming a state peasant was therefore their main aim. Those to whom personal freedom meant everything fled to the Cossacks or to Sweden or Poland or even Turkey. A domestic serf could be freed in the will of his owner[17] – and many were – or he could purchase his freedom. There was no fixed price for purchasing one's freedom, and the price would be agreed in relation to what the serf could pay, rather than in terms of the normal market value of serf labour. Purchasing freedom does not seem to have occurred frequently until the end of the eighteenth century, when the growth of serf-owned industry provided both the incentive and the necessary funds on a large scale. The legal status of freed serfs who remained peasants is obscure. A freed serf peasant was an anomaly in a village and did not fit into its economic structure. Nor could a whole serf village be freed with land. The serf conscripted into the army also became free, together with his wife and the children born of the marriage after conscription ; but few peasants welcomed the idea of being torn from their villages for ever and forced into the army.

The noble landowner had certain responsibilities towards the serfs, and certain obligations towards the state in respect of his serfs. He was enjoined to provide for the welfare of his peasants, to care for them in hard times, and not to allow them 'to wander about the world'. He was responsible to the state for the poll-tax payable by his peasants, and if they were in arrears the state could exact the payment from him or punish him. Under the Empress Anna the arrest of a land-owner for arrears of poll-tax was not infrequent, and the practice was legalized by an ukaz of Peter III which laid the burden of collecting the tax and the responsibilities for arrears on the landowners.[18]

Privately owned estates were exploited by means of *obrok*, money dues, or *barshchina,* labour service, or both together. The obrok in the 1760s averaged 2 r. per male soul per annum, rising to 2·50 in the 1770s. Landlords tended to abide by what was customary ; but far larger dues could be exacted when serfs were themselves acting as entrepreneurs in industry (as in textiles) or in the processing of forest products. Obrok was levied on peasants who took over the cultivation of the landlord's demesne, on peasants employed in non-agricultural work on the estate, and on peasants who sought work away from the estate in transport, construction, or industry. Labour services customarily averaged three days a week, working on the landlord's demesne, leaving three days for work on the peasants' private plot. Again this would not normally be increased, though it was perfectly possible for the landlord to demand five or six days a week, or to put a number of peasants on labour dues in industrial enterprises, such as distilling. Dues in kind, mainly food supplies, but including woven cloth or yarn, were also demanded in both types of exploitation.

In the 1760s, it was the current opinion among informed Russian officials that the general trend in estate management was away from barshchina and towards a more general application of obrok. It does indeed appear to be the case, judging by the many reports from governors and other data,[19] that landlords in less fertile areas, anxious to increase their own revenues, were willing to allow the peasants to leave the villages and seek work in the towns, leaving the land uncultivated.

The trend towards obrok did not meet with the approval of the empress[20] and her officials. They feared that it would encourage peasant *otkhodnichestvo* or departure from the village to seek more rewarding and better rewarded work off the land, and hence to a decline in agriculture and a rise in the price of corn, particularly in the northern and central gubernii of Russia. Contemporary accounts, and subsequent studies, suggest that landowners saw advantages in both forms of exploitation, depending on the nature and fertility of the soil, the distance separating the estate from one or other of the capital cities, the ratio of land and labour, ease of communications and the extent to which the estate was incorporated in the general market system. Obrok was useful where peasants were expected to leave the village and seek employment in the winter months, but where, as around Moscow, both agriculture and industrial activity in the estates were organized with an eye to the Moscow market, barshchina was common, reaching 70 per cent of the serfs in Moscow uezd itself, 88 per cent in Dmitrovsky uezd.[21]

There seems also to be little evidence to support the traditional nineteenth-century view that the larger estates belonging to the magnates were more likely to be on obrok, the smaller on barshchina. The choice of method of exploitation seems in all cases to have been governed by purely economic criteria with a view to maximizing profits.[22] Broadly speaking, barshchina played a bigger role where agriculture was the main source of income, obrok where industry acquired economic importance. From a different perspective, the Soviet economic historian Rubinstein has argued that obrok favoured the commercial development of the peasant economy, while barshchina favoured the commercial development of the landlord economy, which was however, in the long run, destructive of the productive forces.[23]

The Church peasants

The largest single category of peasants in bondage to an institution was composed of the Church peasants. They fell into different groups according to whether they were attached to a monastery, a cathedral or a city church, or even in some rare cases a village *pop,* or priest, or whether they were specifically assigned for the upkeep of the various ranks in the ecclesiastical hierarchy.

Church peasants formed a large part of the population in Northern European Russia, particularly in the gubernii of Novgorod, Archangel, Nizhniy Novgorod and Moscow, a distribution which reflects the earlier geographic spread of monasteries into relatively uninhabited areas of the country. Monasteries were in general large landowners ; some 70 per cent owned more than 100 male serfs, 16 per cent owned from 30 to 100 and 13·4 per cent fewer than 30. The Troitsko Sergeyevsky monastery near Moscow, with its dependencies, owned more than 106,000 and was the largest single landowner in the whole country.[24] At the other end of the scale however were the smaller holdings attached to cathedrals or parish churches (50 cathedrals and 516 parish churches owned a total of 31,535 male serfs, on an average 56 serfs).

The rights of the Church over its peasants were not so extensive as those of the private owner over his serfs. The Church could not sell serfs either with or without land, nor could it emancipate them or take over the moveable property of a serf. It could not interfere with marriages, though it could demand a marriage fee if the serf wished to marry outside the estate. On the other hand peasants could be compelled to become private servants of the ecclesiastical hierarchy or of Church servants.

If the legal situation of the Church peasants was more secure than that of the private serfs, the exploitation of their labour seems to have been exceptionally heavy. They were burdened with a large number of dues in kind (corn, hay, mushrooms, fats, meat, honey) and in labour (brickmaking, building and repair work, milling, distilling, ice-collecting and guard duties), sometimes with, sometimes without money dues as well. The larger monasteries and estates established a regular bureaucracy in charge of the economic exploitation and the judicial administration of the domain. Apart from organizing the actual work on the estate, the functions of the stewards (often monks) included the collection of the poll-tax, the organization of the recruit levy, the collection of dues payable to the monastery, the administration of justice, and supervision of morals – all of which provided plenty of opportunity for extortion. The jurisdiction of the stewards extended only to minor offences (which were to be judged in accordance with the Code of 1649). Criminal offences were dealt with by the voyevoda's chancellery and the state organs of local administration and justice.

The court peasants

The court peasants, or *dvortsovyye krest'yane*, peasants belonging to the patrimony of the Crown, or to the ruler as an individual, as distinct from the state, formed the next largest group. On these private estates of the Crown, the sovereign stood in relation to the land and the peasants as any other landowner. Efforts were made to preserve the compactness and viability of estates, which were sometimes so large as to cover an entire administrative unit (*uezd, volost'*, etc.). The best lands had been kept in the ruler's hands, and indeed at the end of the eighteenth century, the best lands of central Russia still remained in imperial possession. The court peasants fell into several different categories which were functional rather than legal, since peasants could be freely transferred from one to another.[25] These categories comprised the *gosudarevyye* or sovereign's peasants, allotted as private estates for life to members of the imperial family of which there were few since the imperial family was very small. Then there were the fowlers and hawkers, remnants from the great days of the Muscovite chase, and the stable peasants attached to the imperial stables and horsebreeding establishments.

The administration of the court estates, the Main Court Chancery, had been set up by Peter I in 1724 in St Petersburg with a subsidiary office in Moscow. Members of the imperial family had direct control over the estates allotted to them, which were run by their own *votchinaya kantselariya* (estate chancellery), but all court estates remained under the ultimate authority of the Main Court Chancery. Governors and voyevodas were ordered not to interfere in questions concerning court peasants, and their jurisdiction even in criminal cases was limited in that they could act only with the consent of the Main Court Chancery. Thus the court estates constituted an *imperium in imperio* which escaped the normal processes of government even more than the votchina of the small landowner.

The Main Court Chancery had its own special bureaucracy to run the whole complex of estates, ranging from generals, titled courtiers, and state councillors who occupied the top posts of salaries from 4,500 r.p.a. to 2,500 r.p.a. to copy clerks at a humble 15 r.p.a. and craftsmen (goldsmiths, silversmiths, cooks, candlemakers, coopers, gardeners) with salaries of 4 to 10 r.p.a. It was in fact cheaper to employ people who had risen from the court peasantry for many duties ('it is possible to pay these servants less and to exact more from them'). Hence from the 1730s the practice grew up of educating and training the children of court peasants (and children of Church servants and clerks) in geodesy, architecture, veterinary science, etc. Schools were set up, mainly attached to the chancery of the stables, and the number of pupils slowly increased. There was even a special school of icon painting. The children were given an allowance of 6 r.p.a., plus 3 kopeks a day for subsistence, uniform and shoes. They were exempt from the poll-tax which was to be paid for them out of the revenues of the Chancery.[26] In the 1760s there were at least eight such schools in different parts of the country in which some 200 children were being educated. In a modest way they served to spread education in a limited circle of peasants who were thus prepared for a variety of technical employments, and some of whom emerged as professionally qualified.

As a landowner the sovereign had the same rights over his peasants as any other landowner, and the peasant suffered from the same limitations on his personal freedom and economic activity. Codes, both for economic activity and judicial administration, were drawn up at fairly regular intervals by the Main Court Chancery.[27] Efforts were made by the centre to reduce bribery and corruption and the ill-treatment and exploitation of the peasantry, probably with little result.

The administrators of the individual estate or villages (upraviteli), socially a very mixed group ranging from army officers to promoted peasants, were responsible for organizing the exploitation of the estates, the assessment of the poll tax and the organization of the recruit levy. In common with the Church peasants, the court peasants were at first forbidden to buy serfs as substitutes for the recruit levy, but this prohibition was lifted in 1757, in connection with the outbreak of the Seven Years' War. The court peasants were also allowed to hand over vagrants, landless labourers and unprofitable characters to the army in advance of their quota, though an effort was made to ensure strict supervision by the administrators in order to prevent abuses by the village elders or the wealthier peasants.[28]

The revenue which this vast complex of estates and economic enterprises produced is difficult to calculate for lack of adequate data and above all bookkeeping. The income in money rose steadily to an annual average of 347,606 in 1755–61 and 427,703 in 1762–5. A considerable amount was also collected in kind (corn, rye, butter, honey, sheep, chickens, geese, wood, etc.). The peasants also paid a special tax destined for the upkeep of the court (kantselyarskiy sbor), the income from which in 1755 amounted to 128,564 r., and a number of miscellaneous ad hoc impositions, including of course the poll-tax.[29]

The state peasants

The state or treasury peasants (*gosudarsvtennyye* or *kazennyye krest'yane*) emerged as a specific group at the beginning of the eighteenth century. They were to be found mainly in northeast Russia and in Siberia, along the old military lines in the south, and in Left Bank Ukraine, and New Russia. When Peter I introduced the poll-tax, which was to bear on all the non-noble population, he decreed that since private serfs and Church peasants paid labour or money dues to their owners in addition to the poll-tax, so the free peasants, i.e. those who had no lord but His Imperial Majesty, should, in addition to the poll-tax of 70 kopeks, pay a tax or obrok of 40 kopeks. This attempt to equalize the financial burden borne by the peasants, by levying an additional rent on the state peasants, led to the extension to these peasants of bondage to the state, parallel to the bondage of the serf to the private owner. It was a re-assertion of the state's power, as ultimate owner of all land, to exact the same kind of payment from the peasant as the landowner exacted from the serf. The state peasants and the land they occupied belonged to the ruler in his public capacity, and the state proceeded to extend its control over their legal freedom, their personal lives and their economic activity. The judicial and administrative relationship was developed not in terms of the ruler and his subjects with whom relationships were primarily legal and political, but in terms of the state as owner of peasants, tied to a sector of the economy on whom the revenue of the state largely depended.

The formal definition of a state peasant thus became 'a free rural dweller settled on state land and paying money or labour dues to the state' (or to the person who rented the land from the state, *arendator*). In law he was in a much better position than the serf. He had a civil personality and could be summoned to join in public business. The weakness in his legal status was that he could be personally conscripted by the state to work in a factory or a mine or on public works, and he could as a member of a village community be 'assigned' to carry out the auxiliary labour required in industry. On the other hand the state peasant who had obtained permission to leave his commune could settle in a town as an unregistered townsman, and practise a trade or a craft, and eventually join the 'estate' of the townsmen or the merchants and sever his connection with the countryside.

Apart from the poll-tax the state peasants paid dues in labour, kind or cash (or all three) according to the circumstances and the locality. The annual money *obrok* of 40 kopeks rose steadily throughout the eighteenth century, consciously following the practice of private landlords. It reached 55 kopeks in 1745 and one ruble in 1760. Labour dues tended to decline, but service obligations were heavy in terms of road- and bridge-mending, building (forts, magazines, local offices), the billeting of troops and travelling officials (both exacting and experts at extortion), escorting convicts, serving as forest guards, and providing transport for people and goods. There were in addition local cash dues, intended for the building and maintenance of roads and barracks (*zemskiye povinnosti*), which were allocated every three years among the inhabitants of a guberniya, and communal taxes (*mirskiye sbory*) for the expenses of administering the commune. The state peasants were also subject to the recruit levy and paid taxes on marriage outside their commune.

There were however many aspects of the legal and economic life of the state peasants which escape classification. Different practices prevailed in different parts of the vast country, and old privileges had sometimes survived in unexpected ways. State peasants as a community could buy individual serfs or even serf villages, though the main object was usually the purchase of substitutes for the army. They enjoyed varying degrees of freedom in the administration of their affairs, and came under the jurisdiction of the voyevoda and the ordinary courts in criminal or civil matters.

Usually grouped with the state peasants were the *odnodvortsy* or one-home-stead-men, and other small landowners, or retired soldiers settled on the land, remnants of the Muscovite military land tenures.[30] In 1762 there were some 510,000 odnodvortsy, who were bound to a fifteen-year term of service in the land militia, of which in 1764 there were ten regiments totalling 21,812 men. The odnodvortsy were subjected to a special recruit levy (supposedly one man in fifty, often one man in twenty-five). The land they cultivated theoretically belonged to the state, though in practice, like the dvoryane, they bought and sold both service land and patrimonial land together (thus leading to endless litigation). The laws of Peter I had swept them into the category of poll-tax payers, and had also re-asserted state ownership of their lands by exacting the money due of 40 kopeks, equal to that paid by the state peasants. Nevertheless the odnodvortsy held on grimly to certain privileges. They were free in the sense that the state could not donate them to private landowners, or send them to work in industry, and they had the right to own serfs (though relatively few were wealthy enough to do so). Though the state did not recognize them as nobles, they clung to this status, particularly after mid-century, when various ukazy limited the right to own serfs to those who could prove nobility. Until then, many landowners had freely classed themselves as odnodvortsy without worrying about noble status.[31] In practice the life of most odnodvortsy differed little from that of state peasants since they were also compelled to provide food and fodder for the militia regiments, and were liable to be called on to work on the construction of forts, etc. Nevertheless they presented an anomaly within the formally tidy framework of Russian society in that they claimed to be noble, were entitled to own serfs and yet paid the poll-tax, and were liable for military service; and at the same time they were unique in escaping one of the forms of bondage typical of Russian society, namely the bondage of members of a group to each other. The odnodvortsy were not affected by the system of collective guarantee; each man was responsible only for his own obligations to the state; if one defaulted, the others were not liable to make up for him, since there was no community on which the collective obligations could be made to weigh.[32]

The commune

A common feature of all types of peasant villages was the existence of some form of more or less independent commune (*obshchina* or *mir*). The origins of the commune are still much debated but most recent Soviet scholarship suggests that by the eighteenth century it had become an institution of peasant self-government favoured by landowners because it organized the delivery of their 'feudal' income ; favoured by the state because it organized the delivery of taxes and recruits ; and favoured by the peasants themselves because it enabled them to maintain – even against the landowner – a degree of autonomy based on customary law. The commune not only regulated the economic exploitation of the estate, and the relationship between the peasants and the landowner, but also the private relationships of peasants with each other. A sphere of activity thus survived in which peasant attitudes towards economic and personal morality and social justice could find expression.

According to its size, the peasant community elected a number of elders (*starosty*), tenth men (*desyatskiye*) etc, who exercised authority in the commune, together with the village assembly or *mirskiy skhod*. They organized agricultural work, rented vacant land, or even land with serfs, collected the communal taxes, settled disputes over land or money between peasants, punished the drunk and disorderly, or dissolute women, took care of orphans or illegitimate children, acted on the commune's behalf in discussions with owners or administrators and were the channel through which the latter issued their orders, whether of a judicial or an economic nature. The larger the basic village unit, the better organized and more developed these peasant institutions. On really large estates the elected officials could be assisted by clerks to keep the records.

Inevitably these elected posts, which carried great influence in the village, tended to be monopolized by the wealthier or more reliable peasants, thus reflecting the economic stratification which was already taking place. It suited the authorities, whether state or private, to attract to the 'official' side those who had shown the capacity to enrich themselves by their labour, just as it suited the wealthier peasants to make use of their 'official' position to pass on common burdens to the poorer peasants. The system of collective guarantee (*krugovaya poruka*) which operated in the villages as elsewhere reinforced this trend, since it was in the interests of the richer peasants to see that all fulfilled their obligations to the state. Otherwise the wealthy would have to pay for the poor. Their interests thus often drove them to the side of the authorities rather than to that of their poorer brethren.

The village assembly, or *skhod,* was composed of all the adult males in the village or community. It was these village assemblies, which operated by means of an agreed consensus of opinion, not by majority voting, which sometimes appointed duly recognized deputies and drew up petitions setting out their grievances, to be put before the local or central authorities or even the empresses themselves. The village assemblies also joined with the elected elders in two important functions, which were closely related : the allocation of the poll-tax and the redistribution of land.

In theory the poll-tax was paid by every male peasant listed in the census. However the censuses were taken at irregular intervals, and usually spread over a number of years. Thus at any given moment there were always inaccuracies owing to unrecorded births and deaths. A global figure of the tax due was set by the authorities for the village, based on the last census figures and not the real numbers, and the village was responsible for the payment of the tax of the dead until they were deleted from the records. In practice they achieved their own rough justice by means of a system which reduced the poll-tax to a fiction, since it ceased to be a tax on the individual but became a tax adjusted to a taxable unit, the *tyaglo*. '*Tyaglo*' has so many meanings as to be virtually untranslatable ; it covers both tax liability and tax-paying capacity. Normally it came to be applied to a labour unit composed of man and wife. A peasant household could comprise more than one tyaglo unit, according to the number of couples, and of single men and women in it. Unmarried women were sometimes exempt, and younger children were sometimes counted as a half or quarter unit. The amount of land and stock held was also taken into account by the commune in assessing the number of tyaglo units in a homestead. There was no uniformity about the system which varied according to what was customary in different areas. There was also no general rule as to the age at which a young man would be incorporated in a tyaglo unit, a decision which might be taken either by the administrator or by the village elders or by the assembly. The lowest age seems to have been 14 years, and the upper limit 65, after which in theory the peasant ceased to share in the burden of taxation.[33] Once the tyaglo units were established, the global figure for the poll-tax was divided among them, thus to some extent placing the burden on those physically best able to bear it, and lightening the load on e.g. widows with young children or old people.

The origin of the practice of redistribution of land is much debated ; it certainly existed already in the eighteenth century among serfs, court peasants and Church peasants in central Russia and less uniformly among state peasants. It was much less frequent in northeast Russia and unnecessary in Siberia. At fixed intervals, the commune carried out a reallocation among the tyaglo units, thus ensuring a fair share of good quality land, pasture and meadow land or land near the village, or access to water, etc., to all the units. The land was thus divided up into a multiplicity of small strips, but the cultivation was done in common.

The practice of redistributing the land corresponded to the interests of the landowner, the state and the peasant, hence perhaps its strength, and the pressure to introduce it where it did not exist.[34] From the state's point of view, if the peasants' tax-paying capacity was to be preserved, he had to be provided with a sufficiency of land to enable him to produce enough for himself and his family, and a surplus in kind or labour for payment of taxes to the state or dues to the owner.

The landowner's point of view coincided with that of the state, with which he shared in varying proportions the surplus value of the peasant's production. From the peasant's point of view, redistribution of the land furnished him with the means to pay his taxes to the state and his dues to the owner, and to provide for the changing needs of a family. Moreover, the equalization of landholdings responded to the peasant's sense of social justice by reducing the opportunities for a permanent differentiation of wealth in the village. The equalization of burdens was met with the demand for an equalization of resources. The complications which this system could give rise to when a village was split by inheritance or sale between various owners were considerable, for the commune still held in theory to the indivisibility of the communal land, though ownership might be vested in quite different people.[35]

The industrial labour force

Viewed from the strictly juridical point of view, the industrial labour force must be regarded as part of the peasantry, since it was drawn from the peasant class and in many cases returned to it. Broadly speaking, the industrial labour force in Russia fell into two groups, 'servile' and 'free' ; but the nature of the servitude and the nature of the freedom require some qualification. The servile labour force was composed of the *possessionnyye* serfs who belonged to an enterprise, not to the owner of the enterprise ; of assigned (*pripisnyye*) state peasants attached to an enterprise, for a shorter or longer period, but who remained state peasants ; and of serfs belonging to private landlords, employed by those landlords in industrial enterprises on their own lands. The servile labour force was supplemented by free labour which had been 'accidentally' enserfed by being registered to an enterprise in the census of 1736 ; and by convicts, vagrants with no visible means of livelihood, illegitimate children, runaway serfs, Old Believers and the flotsam and jetsam of society, which in accordance with Russian administrative practice must be firmly anchored to some definite place and social category.

Industrial bondage had its origins in Peter I's determination to develop the industrial base necessary to maintain Russia's great power status. In 1721 he had authorized members of the merchant class to buy serfs for employment in industry, provided these were removed from the land and attached permanently to the industrial enterprise itself. An ukaz of 1752 regulated the number of homesteads which could be bought for each blast furnace, or loom, etc.[36]

The wages paid to the industrial serf had been laid down by Peter I in 1724 and they did not change much during the first half of the century. The most detailed information dates from 1737. Then, in the state-owned metallurgical works, master craftsmen were to be paid 30–36 r.p.a., junior masters, 18–24 r.p.a., apprentices and unskilled labour, 10–15 r.p.a. In 1766 a locksmith received 30 r.p.a., a blacksmith 18 r.p.a., a turner 16 r.p.a., and apprentices 12 r.p.a. Master craftsmen in blast furnaces received 36 r.p.a., junior masters 24 r.p.a., unskilled labour 16 r.p.a. and apprentices 15 r.p.a.[37] From this sum the industrial worker paid the poll-tax of 70 kopeks in cash ; he did not have to pay a further obrok to the state like the state peasant. The wages paid to industrial workers do not compare unfavourably with the salaries received by clerks and copy-clerks in the lower ranks of the bureaucracy. Moreover, in some areas, notably the Urals, the industrial serf was able to supplement his wage by exploiting the produce of the surrounding land and forest, and the labour of his female dependants (male children were trained up for work in the industry). Where no land was available and the worker lived in barracks on the site, he could hire himself out for other jobs, such as transport, woodcutting, etc. Bearing in mind the great variety imposed by geographical location and the fertility of the soil, it is probable that the material standard of living of a worker in the Urals was higher than that of the industrial worker in many Western countries.[38]

In law the industrial serf was in some respects privileged. He could not be sold separately from the enterprise, freed, or transferred from one enterprise to another. He could not be sent to the army in exchange for a recruit quittance ; his widow and daughters could marry outside the enterprise without asking permission or paying an exit fee.[39] He had the right to complain of ill-treatment by the management through established channels, an important right even if the complaints went unheeded.

In common with noble owners and state administrators of agricultural estates, industrial managements enjoyed wide jurisdictional powers over the industrial serfs, and offences against the law were not distinguished from offences against the economic regulations of the industry. The managements had the power to inflict corporal punishment and fines. Nevertheless their jurisdiction was subject to some state control, owing to one of the peculiar features of the organization of Russian industry as established by Peter I. The whole complex of industry and manufacturing, other than that owned by nobles employing their own serfs on their estates, came under the central authority of the two Colleges of Mining and Manufacturing respectively, and was not under the jurisdiction of the organs of local government, the governors and voyevodas and the town tribunals or magistraty. Major disputes between management and labour were referred to these two central bodies, and sentences passed locally, e.g. to hard labour, had to be confirmed by them. The greater state control over the possessional serfs reflected the underlying economic fact that they had originally represented a state subsidy to industry in terms of labour.

Life for the industrial worker was hard. Hours of work were rarely regulated (according to the Code of 1649, work was to cease three hours before sundown on Saturdays) and seem to have averaged twelve to thirteen hours with breaks for meals ; female and child labour was also unregulated (child labour was used very widely in textiles),[40] wages were often delayed and workers were compelled to buy necessaries from the enterprises and easily got into debt. The industrial workers however were well aware that their status in law was better than that of a private serf : 'They are not our lords, and we are not their serfs' was how they put it.

While the industrial serf provided the nucleus of a skilled hereditary labour force, a much larger number of unskilled workers was needed to provide all the ancillary services (transport, construction, woodcutting, charcoal burning, food production). The demand was met by 'assigning' villages of state peasants to particular enterprises, the so-called *pripisnyye* peasants. In 1762 assigned peasants numbered 99,330 male souls attached to state factories and 43,187 assigned to privately owned enterprises. The assigned peasant was in theory supposed to work off the poll-tax and the obrok he owed to the state by working for the enterprise and then return to his village. This amount did not in fact represent the extent of his personal obligation, since the village was 'assigned' as a village, and those peasants who actually worked in the enterprise had to work off the total obrok and poll-tax due from the community, including those who had remained behind.[41] The peasant was however often kept for a longer period, for which he was to be paid a wage, which could be relatively high, owing to the shortage of labour. According to the tariff of 1724, which remained in operation until 1768, a peasant with a horse received 10 kopeks a day (i.e., a rate of $31 \cdot 20$ r.p.a. counting six days' work a week) ; a peasant without a horse received 5 kopeks a day.

The assigned peasants remained members of their village community. Owing to the vast distances of Russia, they often had to travel anything up to 300 to 500 versts to reach the enterprise to which they were assigned, and then after fulfilling their obligation, return to their villages – journeys which might well take a couple of months each way. While working in the enterprise the assigned peasants came under the jurisdiction of the management in the same way as the industrial serfs. Otherwise, as state peasants, assigned peasants came under the jurisdiction of the local government offices. The peasant assigned to a state enterprise was on the whole better off than the peasant assigned to a privately-owned enterprise. Labour was more lavishly supplied, and the profit motive played a smaller part in a state enterprise. In both cases however the assigned peasants reacted violently against the long separation from their families and their villages.

The extent of the use of free hired labour in industry in mid-eighteenth century is difficult to assess. The word free in this context does not refer to the personal status of the individual worker, who might be a serf, a state or a Church peasant, but to the relation between the worker and the enterprise, which was based on contract. In the 1750s the trend in the Ural metallurgical industries had been towards the increasing use of free hired labour, and a reduction in the use of assigned peasants, who were beginning to prove uneconomic.[42]

From the 1750s onwards, non-noble manufacturers often failed to make use of the right to buy serf villages for industry, and preferred to make use of hired labour. For many types of manufacturing industry the purchase of serf villages

106

was both wasteful and inconvenient. The owner had to invest capital in acquiring land and unemployable dependants, and a sufficient number of people had to be employed on the land to produce food supplies. Moreover manufacturing industries were often situated near or in towns where hired labour was easier to find.[43] Thus the proportion of hired labour in the total industrial labour force grew rapidly. By the mid 1760s some 26 per cent employed only servile labour ; most factories employed a mixed labour force. The different wage rates of the possessional serfs, the free hired labour and the 'permanently' assigned peasants led to constant ill-feeling and discontent. Worst off were the workers employed in a factory or workshop on a privately owned estate where the owner used his own serfs. Here there was no control by any state organ and no channel of complaint against the owner, who could organize the work as he wished. Peasants could be brigaded into gangs, supplied with food and clothing and no more, and lodged in barracks. The owner naturally had the same powers over their private and working lives as he had over his serfs working the land.

The land

Fundamental to the relationship between the nobility, the townspeople and the peasantry in the economic field was the problem of land. The right to own land outright, as a *votchina*, patrimonial or allodial estate, had originally existed in Russia, though it was eventually limited to princes, boyars and military servitors. Ivan IV, however, had introduced in the sixteenth century the principle that 'all land must serve'. Boyars now had to serve because they owned land, while military servitors, the *pomeshchiki* or future nobles, were allotted land for which service was exacted. While patrimonial land had in the past been cultivated by a variety of forms of labour, ranging from free tenants to temporary or permanent bondsmen or even slaves, *pomest'ye* or service land was cultivated by peasants bound to the soil. In the course of the seventeenth century the two forms of land tenure and the two forms of labour merged in fact if not in law. The pomest'ye was regarded as a hereditary property like a patrimonial estate and was sold, mortgaged or bequeathed as though it were patrimonial land. It came to be treated as private property on which peasants received their allotment not from the state but from the landlord.[44]

But in the seventeenth century service land had not been allotted only to military servitors; estates were also granted to officials and clerks in the various government offices as the main component of their salaries.[45] When, in 1714, Peter I finally legalized the fusion of the votchina with the pomest'ye (the patrimonial estate with the service estate), sweeping both together into the category of a patrimonial estate as regards the nature of the property rights of the landowner, he ceased also to grant land in service tenure, and replaced such grants with salaries (often paid after great delays). But many non-noble officials, clerks, lower rank military men, and church officials, were left in enjoyment of an estate with serfs, once a pomest'ye, now de facto a votchina, to the outright ownership of which they were not entitled according to the Code of 1649. This situation escaped notice at first, but the introduction of the poll-tax in 1721, and the recruit levy for non-nobles, drew attention to the anomaly, since the owner of a votchina, as a noble, was not liable to pay a personal tax such as the poll-tax. Thus the service pomest'ye, it was now argued, could only be owned by a born (or promoted) noble.[46]

The principle that 'the land must serve', coupled with the increasingly tight adscription of the peasant to the soil, served as a brake on the development of a free market in land. A further impediment arose from the fact that even when the land was ultimately owned by an individual, it was collectively used. The pressure of this collective use, together with the collective guarantee for the fulfilment of obligations such as the poll-tax, the recruit levy and labour services, and the compulsory attachment of a peasant to a community, made it impossible for a class of individual peasant farmers to develop, like the *laboureurs* of France or the yeomen of England, based on a free market in land. A landowner who emancipated a serf could not grant him land in individual tenure even if he so wished, since the ex-serf was compelled to belong to some kind of collective community in order to fulfil his other obligations to the state. As a result the conception of privately owned and exploited land survived only in very small groups such as the odnodvortsy and farmer soldiers, and a market in land existed only on a very small scale, usually hidden behind a series of legal fictions.

There was no absolute shortage of land but the chaotic condition of Russian land law led to ruthless and even armed struggles over land. Pitched battles occurred between landowners who organized their own serfs for the struggle, and raided the harvests or the cattle of their neighbours. Landgrabbing was a universal phenomenon : pomeshchiki seized land from each other, from the odnodvortsy, from the towns and the state peasants, from anyone whose title was the slightest bit dubious, and from the state. The state no longer knew the extent of the settled or unsettled land it controlled, let alone the area of vacant lands (*pustoshi*), forests, frontier zones (*zaseki*), or the huge territories in the Volga basin and beyond. Nor was there clear evidence of what settled lands had been ceded and on what terms, to industrial entrepreneurs, factory-owners, merchants, etc. There were even serf villages with no recorded owners. Increasing noble pressure for a monopoly of all forms of ownership of settled land culminated in a law of 1746 which prohibited the acquisition of settled land by all those who paid the poll-tax except kuptsy who were still allowed to buy serf villages for industry.[47] The emphasis was still however on 'buy', not 'own'.

The government's response to rural lawlessness was to embark on a fresh cadastral survey of lands and land ownership. The practice of describing, measuring and listing state land had been important in Muscovy, since the state needed to know the extent of the land available for pomest'ye grants, the extent of the pomestiya actually granted, the amount of service obtained, and the validity of the pomeshchik's title. When Peter I ceased to use the pomest'ye and replaced it with a salary from public funds in 1714, the connection between land tenure and service disappeared ; the government no longer concerned itself with the scrupulous maintenance of records of land tenure, estates changed hands or were inherited and the registers of land ownership ceased to have any relationship with reality. The last land survey had taken place in 1684. By mid-eighteenth century boundaries were forgotten, had been moved or had disappeared, and the frequent lawsuits between owners only too often ended in violence.

Thus, finally, in 1754 an ukaz ordering a general land survey was issued. The survey was to delimit existing privately owned and state land and to verify title to the land (a policy reverting to the old need to verify title to a pomest'ye). All non-nobles, even if they had acquired settled land legally, were now forced to sell it within six months. Whole groups of serf-owners fell under the ban, such as descendants of Muscovite chancery clerks and officials (*prikaznyye lyudi*) and lower rank military servitors (*boyarskiye deti*) as well as the odd cleric, personal noble or merchant who had managed to cling on to his land. On the other hand nobles who could not prove their title to state lands which they had seized would be forced to disgorge them. As a result the survey proceeded very slowly and in eleven years only 359 *dachi,* or blocs of land, comprising 57,319 desyatinas had been surveyed.[48]

The existing chaos was brought forcibly to Catherine's attention with the secularization of Church lands in 1764, when it proved extremely difficult to determine the boundaries of the plots to be allotted for the maintenance of churches and monasteries.[49] In accordance with her usual practice the problem was referred to a commission on 20 February 1765 and led to the promulgation of a new manifesto on the land survey on 19 September 1765. Fresh principles were proclaimed distinguishing clearly between the measurement and description of the land and its produce, and the confirmation of rights of ownership. Government surveyors would deal with the former ; disputes over boundaries would be referred to special land survey courts, and problems of disputed title were to go before the Votchina College.

The survey did not, as one might expect, delimit individual estates. It measured, described, and allotted land to individual villages, whether serf, state peasant or odnodvortsy, just as it measured and allocated land to towns, churches and cathedrals. If the whole village was owned by one person, then the allotment of land and the title coincided. But if the village was divided into a number of estates owned by different people, then the delimitation of the actual estates was to be done by agreement between the owners, or by the surveyors at the expense of the owners. The importance of labour as distinct from land is reflected in the fact that where vacant land was available, and existing allotments to villages were vague, eight desyatinas of land were to be allotted per male soul. Thus the basic principle was not the property rights of an individual landowner, but the establishment of the amount and the boundaries of the land which belonged to a given village, whether it had one or several owners or belonged to the state. The prohibition of the ownership of land in a personal capacity by those who paid the poll-tax was confirmed, though lands could be allotted to them on a collective basis, i.e. to a village.

The significance of the land survey lies not only in the greater order it introduced into the Russian countryside by the elimination of disputes. It also led to a considerable enlargement of the sown area in Russia. Vacant land within existing land allocations was now allotted to villages, and large areas of land in the underpopulated areas were sold at one ruble per desyatina ; while land which had been illegally seized or occupied was sold for three times that sum. Huge areas were distributed, usually in grants of several hundred desyatinas. As a result the Russian landowning class, and the peasantry in general, were launched on to the path of systematic intensification of agricultural production which marked the last quarter of the eighteenth century.[50]

Inaugurated on 13 June 1766 by parties of surveyors starting out from the gates of Moscow, by 1796 more than 165,000 blocs comprising about 144 million desyatinas of land in 22 guberniya had been surveyed. The survey continued under Paul and, on the principles laid down in 1776, most of European Russia had been covered by the 1840s.

Illegal ownership continued but, precisely because it was concealed under various legal devices, its extent is difficult to gauge.[51] Merchant owners seem to have been more common in northeast Russia where nobles were few. Merchants acquired land either by outright purchase, or as a result of peasant indebtedness to them, or even by lease from the state or from landowners. Peasants on these lands were reduced to the status of sharecroppers (*polovniki*) and continued to work for their new masters.[52] Merchant land ownership often meant that the kupets, though registered in a town, left his proper activities to occupy himself exclusively with large-scale agricultural enterprises of a commercial kind : production of grain for the market, hay and cattle raising. Wherever in fact there was land available, few nobles, and the possibility of employing non-Russian labour (e.g. Saratov on the Volga), merchants tended to explore the possibilities of the commercial exploitation of agriculture.

More widespread still than merchant land-holding was the purchase or renting of land by serf or state peasants. Wealthy serfs rented or bought land from their own landowner or from neighbouring serf or state villages, and bought serfs to work it – all in the name of their landowner. The purchases of serf industrial entrepreneurs were particularly large, e.g. the Grachev dynasty in the Sheremet'yev estate of Ivanovo who bought 1,144 desyatinas and 244 male serfs of their own.[53]

7

The Orthodox Church

The Church, at any rate in the capital, had helped to smooth Catherine's way to power, and one of the most pressing problems on her accession was to repair the damage done by Peter III's rough handling of clerical susceptibilities.[1]

In its time the Church and the hierarchy had suffered from Peter I's drastic remodelling of Russian institutions. He was much less concerned with the spiritual salvation of his people than with their moral and material welfare. Disregarding therefore the Church's concern with problems of the next world, Peter I bent it to serve his purpose in this world, namely the education of honest and reliable servants of the state.

Peter I's policy was bound to lead to a cultural shock from which Russia never perhaps recovered. In Muscovy the Church had provided the one force which united all social groups, from the top to the bottom of the pyramid, in a common faith, with a common ritual, common public and private festivals. With the introduction of Western secular ideas, the different classes lived at a different tempo, according to how much or how little of the new ways they adopted, and the unifying principle was gravely weakened. In 1720 the new 'Spiritual Regulations' drafted by the Metropolitan Feofan Prokopovich, the main theorist of Petrine absolutism, were forced upon a reluctant hierarchy and in 1721 the Spiritual College was established, to replace the Patriarchy (in abeyance since 1700) as the government of the Church. Later renamed the Holy Synod, the new institution was composed of eleven or twelve members, not necessarily bishops, under a president. In 1722 a member of the procuracy was appointed to the Synod, representing the extension of the power of the bureaucracy into the sphere of Church government. As a result the bishops lost the power of participating ex-officio in the conciliar government of the Church.[2] The collegiate principle which Peter I had applied to the secular sphere was extended to the Church, in an institution created by and subordinate to the tsar, and theoretically of equal status with the Senate.

The Synod was charged with supervising Church administration and exercised jurisdiction over the clergy and many fields of social activity, including religious

111

censorship (it was forbidden to paint icons of the Trinity with three faces and four eyes), the investigation of heresies, and miracles, and the defence of members of the clerical estate brought before civil courts.[3] As regards the secular population, clerical jurisdiction was mainly concerned with births, marriages, deaths, and wills and testaments. Certain offences against religion came before church courts such as witchcraft, sacrilege and the failure to confess and commune at least once a year – a measure introduced in order to force the sectarian Old Believers into the open. Priests were also charged with enforcing church attendance on twenty-eight festivals in the years at vespers, liturgy and matins.

In 1700 there were, in addition to the patriarchal see, twenty-one dioceses, which were very uneven in size and rarely coincided with secular administrative divisions. In mid-century the patriarchal see was broken up into the four bishoprics of Moscow, Kostroma, Pereyaslavl' Zalessky and Tambov. The title of metropolitan did not go with any particular diocese, but was personal to the incumbent. The powers of the bishops were considerable : they supervised matters of faith and morals, the conduct of church services, the selection and appointment of parish priests, and they defended the interests of the clerical estate against the bureaucracy. On the other hand they ruled despotically over the subordinate clergy. Priests and church servants were subjected to severe corporal punishment by ecclesiastical courts. One archbishop exacted a personal oath of loyalty to himself, and as late as 1773, archbishops were forbidden to issue ukazy raising people to the rank of officers, i.e. promoting laymen to the rank of noble.[4] The arbitrary, even brutal, manner in which bishops exercised their power was bound to lead to a low moral standard among the parish priests, who could only hope for promotion by pandering to their superiors.

The clerical estate was divided into the black or monastic clergy and the white or parish clergy, who had to be married before they were ordained. Bishops were drawn from the black clergy ; the white clergy could rise no higher than the rank of archpriest. The white clergy in the eighteenth century was gradually being transformed into a closed estate, difficult to leave, almost impossible to join. Priests enjoyed one great advantage : they did not pay the poll-tax nor were they subject to the recruit levy. Candidates for the priesthood were put forward by the parishioners when a vacancy arose, and after a short period of instruction were ordained by the bishop. It was in the state's interest to make sure that a vacancy really existed and that a poll-tax payer should not be appointed to it. On the other hand it was in the priestly families' interest to ensure that their sons, or sons-in-law, should be appointed to parishes so that they should not drop back into the mass of poll-tax payers. The interests of the state and of the priests worked therefore to limit entry into the priesthood from outside.[5] But, inevitably with a married priesthood, there were far more priests' sons than parishes they could fill. The state responded by conscripting superfluous priests' sons and churchmen and their sons at intervals, either into the tax-paying population, or under Anna, in 1736, straight into the army. In the conscriptions of the 1740s and 1750s members of the clerical estate who delayed choosing a status in the poll-tax paying population might find themselves enserfed to the nobility.

Peter I had also laid down the 'establishment' for parishes. A community of 100–150 households was entitled to one priest ; 200–250 households were entitled to two, and 250–300 to three priests and a corresponding number of 'churchmen' or nonordained auxiliaries (sextons, sacristans, deacons, etc.). By 1764 the clerical estate (priests, deacons and church servants on the establishment but excluding their dependants) numbered 67,111 to serve 15,761 churches and a small number of private chapels.[6]

If the cultural level of the priesthood was low, so was their standard of living. The principal sources of income were the payments of the faithful for the rites of the church, *treby*, voluntary gifts, and produce from the land attached to the parish church, which the priest was often forced to cultivate himself.

As Western habits and culture spread among the gentry, the gulf separating the priest and the noble grew wider. The priest was never the social equal of the landowner ; he regarded him as *barin* or master, as would any peasant. Where serfdom predominated, the priest's status was inevitably affected by the landowner's attitude to his serfs, and his dependence on the landowner was almost equal to theirs. The adverse effects of this dependence on the quality of the spiritual and moral leadership of the Church had been noted in Russia from the beginning of the eighteenth century. The more enlightened had seen that the priesthood needed an assured livelihood, which would free them from the back-breaking toil on the land, and from their dependence on payments for services rendered by the peasantry. But nothing was in fact done to raise their social status and strengthen their moral authority.

Barely a week after her accession, on 3 July 1762, Catherine ordered the Senate to examine the policy to be followed to the Church. The hierarchy, sensing the new empress's hesitation, hastened to bring pressure to bear on individuals and institutions for the return of their lands. Archbishop Ambrosius of Moscow complained that Peter III's soldiers had actually fished in ecclesiastical fishponds, while Archbishop Arseniy of Rostov described plaintively to the ex-chancellor Bestuzhev Ryumin the seizure of his barnyard fowl.

The Senate's first proposal on 16 July 1762 was to return the estates to the Church, but to raise the tax levied on the Church peasants by one ruble per soul, 50 kopeks for the Church, 50 for charitable purposes. The peasants however should be allowed to elect their own administration. While the hierarchy expressed satisfaction at the first half of the proposal, they rejected the proposed division of the revenue.

A split now began to emerge within the hierarchy, which reflected the cultural background of the archbishops. The Great Russians, led by Dmitry Sechenov of Novgorod, accepted without difficulty the idea of giving up the burden of administering agricultural estates and becoming paid servants of the state on the same footing as the army or the bureaucracy. The Little Russian bishops, imbued with Polish conceptions of honour, often from landowning families themselves, identified the defence of their financial autonomy with the defence of the freedom of the Church.[7]

The Archbishop of Novgorod was a man after Catherine's own heart : he is 'ni persecuteur ni fanatique', wrote Catherine to Voltaire. 'Il abhorre la proposition des deux puissances' (the equality of Church and state).[8] He also had solid reasons, in the shape of one thousand serfs granted to him personally for his support of Catherine's accession to power, to work with the empress. He now proposed the setting up of a mixed religious and secular commission on Church lands to examine whether 50 k. per soul would provide sufficient revenue for the Church. In the meantime Catherine signed a manifesto on 12 August 1762 returning the Church lands temporarily to ecclesiastical administration.[9]

In the first few weeks of her reign Catherine had to pick her way carefully, which probably explains her decision. Clearly she could not alienate the hierarchy – particularly her supporters among them. There is little evidence of the division of opinion in government circles, though Bestuzhev Ryumin seems to have favoured the hierarchy, and Nikita Panin, closer to the traditions of the Enlightenment, favoured state administration of Church property.[10] From the point of view of the Church, Catherine's manifesto of 12 August 1762 contained a few ominous hints for the future. It hinted at the desirability of freeing the Church from the burden of worldly cares, and remarked that it was unfortunate that in the past the state had had to instruct the Church on how to behave to its peasants. Though she had no wish to acquire Church lands, continued Catherine, nevertheless it was her responsibility to lay down the laws for the best use of Church lands, for the glory of God and the welfare of the fatherland.

The Commission on Church Lands was set up on 29 November 1762. It was composed of the Metropolitan of Novgorod, Dmitry Sechenov, the Archbishop of St Petersburg, Gavriil Kremenetsky, and the Bishop of Pereyaslavl' Zalesskiy, Silvester Starogodsky (a not very courageous opponent of secularization) ; the secular members were Count I.L. Vorontsov, Prince B.A. Kurakin, Prince S. Gagarin, the Procurator of the Holy Synod, Prince A.S. Kozlovky, and most important, the driving spirit in this as in so many fields at this time, G.N. Teplov. The instruction given to the commission echoed the didactic tone so often used by Peter I. The empress observed (probably in the words of Teplov) that the word of God was the foundation of national well-being, but unfortunately the simple people were far from knowing it. Indeed many priests were 'unenlightened', uneducated, and a bad example to the people. The purpose of the vast immovable wealth of the Church was to maintain the Church hierarchy in moderate but respectable comfort, as well as to provide for schools and the care of the needy. It was now proposed that the commission should revise the 'establishments' of the bishoprics, monasteries and cathedrals, etc. Its terms of reference were extremely wide. It was to produce an up-to-date register of lands and souls owned by the Church, analyse the economic resources available, and propose methods for their economic development without burdening the peasants. Having assessed the revenues from each see, the commission was to submit proposals for the establishment of each bishopric, monastery or cathedral church in accordance with its rank and dignity.

The failure of the Church to develop activities in the field of education was duly pointed out in paragraph 7 of the instruction, in which the commission was invited to make proposals for setting up seminaries in each see, providing a wide general education as well as theological training, using both secular and religious teachers, and with adequate libraries, since teaching without reading was not enough to achieve enlightenment. Monasteries were also urged to set up small primary schools from which promising children could graduate to the Church schools. Children should be carefully selected, since it was better to teach a few well than for many to learn nothing. The commission was also urged to make proposals for the creation of almshouses for the old, injured or needy. Church funds should be devoted in the first place to the dignified upkeep of the Church, to education and to welfare. If any funds were left over they could be assigned to the creation of an Order of Knighthood, with pensions attached. The instruction also pointed out that it would be necessary to set up a central administrative body to receive the revenue and to administer the estates – which implies that the decision had already been taken to secularize the lands of the Church.[11]

Early in 1763 the fiercest opponent of secularization, the Ukrainian-born Metropolitan Arseniy of Rostov and richest of all the metropolitans, disposing of 16,340 souls, was moved to action. In his view the Church had been granted its property by the faithful not for secular but for spiritual purposes, and it had passed straight from the apostles to the archbishops. On the first Sunday in Lent the Church traditionally pronounced anathemas against those who had lapsed from the faith. Arseniy took the opportunity to add a few, of his own composition, against those who contested the Church's right to its estates.

On 6 March 1763, Arseniy forwarded to the Holy Synod a formidable denunciation of the whole policy of secularization. He reminded the Synod that Catherine had promised on her accession to protect the Orthodox religion, and hinted at the discrepancy between promise and performance. He protested violently against *shtaty* or 'establishments' for the Church. Even Moslems, he wrote, did not treat their priesthood thus. He declaimed against the suggestion that the priesthood should deal in philosophy, theology, mathematics, astronomy, when their Christian duty was to preach the word of God. Where had bishops ever 'set up academies' ? It was for the state to do so, and it was the state's duty to care for disabled soldiers. Arseniy was thus claiming the right of the Church both to spiritual and material independence of the state, and he pinpointed the crucial issue : bishops would no longer be the shepherds of their people, but 'hired servants' accountable for every crust of bread.[12]

Arseniy seems to have failed completely to understand the strength of the forces aligned against him. He still hoped that on the occasion of a proposed visit by Catherine to Rostov, where the bones of St Dmitry the Miracle Worker were to be placed in a new shrine, he would be able to influence the empress personally. Yet secularization had been the ultimate aim of the state since the days of Peter I, and the forces in its favour were strong. The run-of-the-mill nobility hoped for access to more land and labour ; the enlightened nobility and high government servants were too deeply secular in outlook to have any sympathy whatsoever with Arseniy's vision of the Church as an *imperium in imperio ;* and, finally, financial stringency was such that the state could not dispense with the extensive revenues of the Church. Nevertheless Arseniy's protest against the transfer of the priesthood from the status of landowners to that of paid servants of the state was grounded on one of the economic facts of life in eighteenth-century Russia. In a second denunciation addressed to the Holy Synod, on 15 March 1763, he made the point : 'This is not England – where people can live and make do with money alone. . . . It will be necessary to beg and pray the peasants to work for double, treble pay. The bishops will be dependent on the peasants . . . the magnificence of the Church will be gone for ever.'[13] The habit of living on a money income alone scarcely existed in Russia, where salaried labour was rare, where a large proportion of an individual's income was in kind, not in cash, and where in any case coin was in short supply.

Arseniy had not spared his colleagues in the Holy Synod, 'who sat like dumb dogs without barking', and had alienated the most influential of them, Dmitry of Novgorod. Undoubtedly as the result of pressures behind the scenes, the Synod decided on 13 March that his first denunciation (the second had not yet been received) constituted *lèse majesté* and contained incorrect interpretations of the Scriptures. On the next day Catherine signed an ukaz in which she committed Arseniy for trial by the Synod. The offending bishop was swept into a carriage in Rostov under guard and brought to a monastery in Moscow. Catherine's personal vindictiveness towards Arseniy has often been commented upon. Its source lay not merely in the offensive terms used in the denunciations he had submitted to the Synod. Arseniy continued to express himself incautiously in other ways. Catherine was present at his interrogation, together with the procurator general, then A.I. Glebov, Grigory Orlov, and S. Sheshkovsky, the head of the secret department of the Senate. Accounts of the interview suggest that Arseniy touched on the delicate question of her right to the throne, possibly even on the disappearance of Peter III. Catherine herself noted four years later that Arseniy had said : 'Our present sovereign is not native, and is not firm in the faith, she should not have taken the throne which should have gone to Ivan Antonovich.' No wonder Catherine covered her ears and shrieked 'stop his mouth'.[14]

The trial of Arseniy began on 1 April 1763. The Metropolitan of Rostov denied that he had intentionally committed *lèse majesté*, but the issue was a foregone conclusion. He was found guilty and sentenced to the loss of his ecclesiastical rank and to confinement in a distant monastery where he was not to be allowed writing materials. Having achieved victory in the Synod, Catherine had now to impress public opinion in Moscow with the rightness of the verdict. At a public ceremony in the Kremlin, Arseniy, in full robes, in the presence of the Synod and other Church dignitaries, was solemnly disgraced. According to tradition, as his ecclesiastical garments were removed, one by one, he reproached his fellow metropolitans, foretelling their own disastrous ends : Dmitry of Novgorod 'would be strangled by his own tongue' (he died of a stroke four years later) ; Gedeon of Pskov 'would never see his bishopric again' (he died on the return journey) ; Ambrosius of Moscow 'would be cut down like an ox' (he was murdered during the plague riots in Moscow in 1771).

The subsequent fate of Arseniy deserves a brief mention. He was sentenced to do hard labour in the monastery grounds three days a week. But he was allowed to take his personal servants with him, and was granted 50 kopeks a day for his expenses ; he had considerable freedom and was treated with respect. Nevertheless, he continued to rail against secularization ('the Turks make grants to their mosques, here it is like Sodom and Gomorrah') ; he spoke incautiously about the empress's right to the throne, declared that she ought to marry Ivan Antonovich rather than Grigory Orlov, and after the murder of Ivan Antonovich, regarded two of the latter's younger brothers as the legitimate heirs to the throne in the event of the death of the Grand Duke Paul. Following on a denunciation, the charges against Arseniy were again investigated, this time by the procurator general, Vyazemsky. By a simple ukaz, Catherine, in December 1767, ordered him to be deprived of the status and garb of a monk, renamed Andrew the Liar, and transferred to a cell in the fort of Reval where his guards would not be Russian speaking, and would not even know his real name. At first allowed reasonable supplies of food and clothing, unsubstantiated nineteenth-century rumours allege that after a further investigation in 1771, he was held even more strictly, walled up in a cell, his food handed in through a hole in the wall. He died on 28 February 1772, with the reputation of a saint and a miracle worker.[15]

By failing to defend Arseniy, the Church hierarchy had cut the ground from under their feet, and could no longer oppose the imperial policy of secularization. The mounting peasant disorder on ecclesiastical estates led to the decision to re-establish a College in May 1763 to administer the Church lands without waiting for the commission to produce its recommendations.[16]

Finally, on 26 February 1764, a manifesto was issued which secularized Church lands, and laid down the future establishments of the Church and the monasteries.[17] The twenty-six bishoprics were divided into three categories and endowed accordingly. The first comprised only Novgorod, St Petersburg, and Moscow, which were allotted 11,031, 15,000 and 7,510 r.p.a. respectively. The eight sees in the second group were granted 5,500 r.p.a. and fifteen in the third 4,232 r.p.a. Some sees benefited from the more uniform allocation of resources, e.g. Tver', which rose from 1,200 to 5,500 r.p.a. and Ustyug which rose from 926 to 4,232.[18] Cathedrals and churches together had owned only 35,003 souls at the latest census, and the allocation of 50 r.p.a. (or 115 r.p.a. where there were two) was sufficient compensation for the loss of such peasants as they possessed. The total annual income allocated to bishoprics and cathedral churches was 149,586 r. 65 k. p.a.

Monasteries and convents were similarly divided into three categories. Some were so small and poor that they were simply closed or turned into parish churches. Of the total of 572 monasteries only 161 survived. Four received special treatment : the great Troitsko Sergeyevsky monastery was allotted 10,070 r.p.a. ; the St Alexander Nevsky in St Petersburg, 15,000 r.p.a. ; the Sofia Monastery in Novgorod 11,031 and the Episcopal Monastery in Moscow 7,510. Fifteen monasteries came into the first class with 2,017 r.p.a. ; 41 in the second with 1,311 and 100 in the third with 806 r.p.a. Only sixty-seven out of 219 convents survived. They too were placed in three categories. Four, in the first, received from 1,009 to 1,506 r.p.a. ; 18 in the second received 475 r.p.a. and 45 in the third 375 r.p.a.[19] The establishment of the Holy Synod was also revised, with salaries ranging from 2,000 r.p.a. for the senior bishop to 600 for an archpriest. The total sum allotted for this ecclesiastical bureaucracy was initially 25,082 r.p.a.

The manifesto also provided allotments of land of 30, 9 and 8 desyatinas according to category for churches, monasteries, etc., for pasture, cultivation and fisheries, but without serf labour. The monasteries were freed from the obligation of providing almshouses for ex-officers and soldiers (since the priesthood did not know how to keep order among ex-service men, and were too unworldly to be in charge of soldiers, stated the manifesto). But each diocese had to maintain an almshouse for the needy of other ranks, providing 50, 30 or 25 places according to its category. This was estimated to provide 705 places in the 26 dioceses which, at the cost of 5 r.p.a. each would be a charge of 3,825 r.p.a. on the new College of Economy's revenue.

The total income made available to the state from Church lands amounted to some 1,366,299 r.p.a. From this sum, the state paid to the Church about 462,868 r.p.a. in the years 1764–8. Over the years, state income from the church peasants rose steadily, reaching 3,648,000 r. in 1784. The state grant to the Church also rose to 540,000 r.p.a. in 1782, 710,000 in 1792 and 820,000 in 1796.[20] A further 115,000 r.p.a. was allotted to the almshouses for retired officers and soldiers and funds were made available to seminaries. The state had thus made a very good bargain at the expense of the Church ; clearly a free gift of 300,000 r.p.a., as the Archbishop of Tver' had proposed in order to ward off secularization, was of little advantage. For the time being secularization was introduced only in Great Russia, and was not extended to Little Russia and Slobodska Ukraine. Their turn was to come later.[21]

Catherine used two further means to consolidate her victory over the hierarchy. First, she gradually reduced the number of Little Russian bishops in favour of more reliable Great Russians, and secondly she used the procuracy to extend her control of religious life through the Synod. The colourless Prince A.S. Kozlovsky was replaced as oberprokuror of the Synod in June 1763 by General

I.I. Melissino, a deeply anti-clerical Freemason. Shortly afterwards Catherine appointed Grigory Potemkin to act as a deputy for the oberprokuror, and gave him a personal instruction authorizing him to report directly to her – evidence of her continuing interest in the young guards officer.[22] Temperamentally Potemkin was well suited to work in this atmosphere, since he had many friends in ecclesiastical circles, and combined throughout his life an interest in Western culture with a deep Orthodox piety.

In the new balance she had created between Church and state Catherine was careful to conceal the iron hand of state control in a velvet glove. The Synod could report to her without going through the oberprokuror, and Church dignitaries were treated in private and in public with respect.[23] In her correspondence with foreigners Catherine did occasionally describe herself as the head of the Russian Church, but she made no claim to incorporate this title into her official nomenclature.

The secularization of Church lands, and the ensuing legislation, affected the parish priest in a number of ways. To begin with, in the 1760s a number of taxes on the priests were abolished now that the bishops had a fixed income. But the income of the urban or rural parish priest still remained low and insecure. Rural parishes were allotted 33 desyatinas of land (30 arable, 3 pasture) in 1765 but it was often very difficult to secure the full amount of land from the landowners or the peasant villages. In cities and towns where land could not be allocated, a state 'subsidy' was provided of 65 r.p.a. for a priest, 18 r.p.a. for a Church servant and 10 r.p.a. for the church itself.[24]

The scale of charges for the various rites performed by parish priests was laid down in 1765. It was intended to be the maximum which priests could demand from poor peasants, and in cities priests usually charged considerably more. Fees ranged from 3 kopeks for a baptism, 10 kopeks for a funeral or a wedding in the country, but in Moscow a baptism might well cost 25–50 kopeks and a wedding from one to two rubles.[25] The average income of a parish priest is difficult to assess, since it included not only fees but the produce of the land allotted to the parish church and gifts in kind. Priests could supplement their income by various other activities such as teaching village children. One village priest who has left a diary for the years 1775–6 did book binding. His money income (including 10 r.p.a. for parish land cultivated for him by peasants) totalled 40 r.p.a., and he received about 21 r.p.a. in kind. His expenses were about 60 r.p.a. and in his diary he is careful to enter the meals – and particularly the drinks – he consumed at the expense of others since they materially affected his standard of living.[26] The death of a wife could be a fatal blow, since widowers were not allowed to officiate, nor could they remarry. The position of a priest too old to fulfil his duties and of the dependants of a deceased priest remained very difficult unless a relative could be speedily inducted.

This economic uncertainty contributed to preserve the closed nature of the priestly caste since only by holding on to the parish for a member of one's own family could the livelihood of numerous dependants be secured. There was also little incentive for superfluous clerics to move into another estate since this meant paying the poll-tax (and being subjected to the recruit levy), and there were proportionately few openings in the bureaucracy. Only those who had done well in the seminaries could hope to advance in the secular professions such as teaching in schools or universities, medicine, the arts, or even the world of business. Under Catherine the government enforced more strictly and more efficiently the ban on entry into the priesthood from the tax-paying population, since there were too many, not too few, candidates. Indeed the policy of conscription into other estates was carried out even more drastically by Catherine than by her predecessors. In 1769 she ordered the conscription of 25 per cent of all youths and 50 per cent of supernumerary churchmen and netted nearly 9,000 men for the armed forces. A second conscription in 1783–4 removed all supernumerary churchmen, and all uneducated youths over fifteen ; 32,000 were caught, but they were not this time sent to the army but allowed to choose a new 'status'. Most of them entered the bureaucracy or the urban estate. None was enserfed or became a soldier.[27] But the problem of surplus population in the clerical estate remained, and the only attempt to solve it in the eighteenth century was by periodical conscriptions.

The years after 1764 brought some improvement however in the legal and social position of the white priesthood. This reflected the increasing concern shown by the hierarchy at the gap in status between the nobility and the clerical estate. Hence while the more enlightened bishops took steps to improve the selection of parish priests and modernize their education, a parallel move was made to protect them from arbitrary justice and above all from the indignities of corporal punishment. An ukaz of 7 June 1767 prohibited bishops' courts from sentencing priests to corporal punishment, and the prohibition was extended to deacons in 1771.[28] Unfrocked priests were treated by secular courts in the same way as all commoners. In 1791 a small pension fund was set up from the profits of the Synod press.[29]

Among officials and courtiers, both those who survived from previous reigns and those appointed by Catherine, there was strong support for the policy of secularization, a support which was not primarily motivated by the desire to acquire Church lands. Impervious to the world of purely spiritual values, Catherine and those closest to her at this time were essentially deists. The arguments put forward by Arseniy, and some of the Little Russians in the hierarchy who sympathized with him, in defence of the wealth of the Church, were the least likely to appeal to those who believed that the only function of the Church was educational and social. Under the new system the Church could no longer claim to own property 'by divine right'. Its property rights were those which the state allowed it to have and the service principle had now been extended to Church lands too. The Church was the last to surrender on this issue and it is not surprising that the final flicker of resistance should have come from a bishop educated in the Polish rather than the Russian tradition. It was also unfortunate that some of the defenders of Church wealth (including Arseniy) had a very bad reputation for arrogance towards and ill-treatment of their subordinates.[30]

From a moral point of view the Church benefited from ceasing to be the owner of human souls, and the second half of the eighteenth century saw a genuine effort to raise the standards of the priesthood, improve their social status, develop better education in the seminaries, force the priests to improve their appearance by wearing clothing fitted to their calling (e.g. shoes and cassocks) and trimming their beards, and reduce drunkenness, their besetting vice.[31] Of the spiritual quality of the priesthood, it is harder to speak. The hierarchy was not untouched by the rationalism of the Enlightenment, and attempted to purge village life of its colourful superstitions, myths and false miracles. Metropolitan Platon of Moscow, probably the most distinguished ecclesiastical figure in late-eighteenth-century Russia, did a great deal to regulate Church life and impose a more dignified pattern upon it. Yet it is likely that genuine religious fervour was to be found rather in the continuing current of medieval hesychastic mysticism, and in the schismatic sects.

Hesychasm, the search for direct knowledge of God through silent personal prayer, which came to Russia from Mount Athos, had dominated Russian monasticism in the fourteenth and fifteenth centuries. It re-emerged in monasteries in the eighteenth century, in reaction to the increasingly secular culture introduced by Peter I. Its earliest exponent in the eighteenth century was a monk, Paisy Velichkovsky, of Ukrainian origin, who translated into Russian the collection of Greek mystical literature attributed to St Antony, under the name of the *Philokalia*.[32] Paisy's influence led to a revival of hesychasm and to the foundation of a number of hermitages, mainly in Moldavia, and south Russia, in which the ascetic life of constant prayer was practised. More influential outside the Church and the monasteries was St Tikhon Zadonsky, an educated man, who left the Church hierarchy (he had been bishop of Novgorod) for the monastic life.[33] Of an entirely different type was the strange Ukrainian philosopher/poet/wanderer, Grigory Skovoroda. He rejected not only the secular culture of the court but also the official Orthodox religion – he was the product of the Kievan Academy, and himself taught in a number of seminaries. But he turned his back on organized religion in his personal search for God, and was closer to the various sects of schismatics.[34]

The importance of the schismatics cannot be overestimated. Usually called Old Believers, or Old Ritualists, because they rejected the liturgical reforms introduced by Patriarch Nikon in the 1650s and 1660s, they had been severely persecuted in seventeenth-century Russia. They soon developed into two groups, those with priests and the priestless, according to whether they accepted priests ordained in the Orthodox Church, in spite of the Nikonian aberrations, or rejected priests altogether.

The Old Believers struck roots in Little Russia, among the Cossacks, in Astrakhan', on the Don and the Yaik and in Siberia ; the priestless predominated in the north and northeast, e.g., in the well-known Vyg community. They all rejected Peter I's reforms, the census (the mark of the beast in the Apocalypse), the recruit levy and the poll-tax, shaving and Western clothes. Sensing their political opposition Peter I reacted by imposing double taxation, double fines for failure to attend services, fines for marrying outside a church. Old Believers were not allowed to act as officials, or to give evidence in courts. This was an improvement on torture and the stake, but many communities, particularly among the priestless, reacted by burning themselves alive in considerable numbers.

Already under Peter III, there was some improvement in their lot. Among his first ukazy was one inviting Old Believers to return to Russia from Poland and promising them a quiet life ; more important almost was the appointment of a senator to act as guardian of a group attached to the Isetsk foundries, to see that they were not persecuted. Catherine's policy followed on the same lines. Before the Pugachev revolt the Old Believers seemed to present no political threat to her and she took steps to stop persecution and renewed the offer of amnesty to all who returned from abroad. In 1769 the right to give evidence in court was restored to them.[35]

Apart from the major priestless communities, a number of extremist sects came into the open in the more tolerant religious climate of the late eighteenth century. Some may represent a response to Western Protestant influence, spreading from the German colonies in the south, though the tradition of reverting directly to the Scriptures may even go back to the Bogomilism of early Bulgaria. Notable among them were the Dukhobors, or wrestlers with the spirit, and the Molokane or milk-drinkers (who drank milk on fast days, a practice rejected by Orthodoxy). They extended to the state their attitude to organized religion and rejected the tsar and his government and institutions, and as a result were intermittently persecuted in Catherine's later years. Even more difficult for the state to assimilate were the *khlysty* or flagellants, also descended from early Bogomilism. They too believed in the individual reincarnation of Christ (khlysty is a pun on Christ), mortification of the flesh, and ecstatic trances. Out of the khlysty came the *skoptsy* who added the practice of castration to the usual austerities of the khlysty. Their founder, a serf, by name Selivanov, having passed himself off as Peter III, was sentenced to exile in Siberia. In an ukaz of 2 July 1772 Catherine ordered the arrest of the originators who were to be sentenced to the knut and to work in Nerchinsk, while the preachers were to be sent to hard labour in Riga. The most appalling mutilations were inflicted on men and women by the followers of this strange doctrine, who increased to over 100,000 in the eighteenth century.[36]

8

Industrial and Agrarian Unrest : Repression and Reform in the 1760s

The early years of Catherine's reign were marked by continuing peasant disturbances. According to her own account, written in 1769, at her accession 49,000 assigned peasants and as many as 150,000 church peasants were in open revolt ; even serfs had ceased to obey, 'and it was necessary to pacify them all'.[1] Catherine in these years was extremely concerned to improve the lot of the peasantry. She consequently embarked on a policy which combined repression of disorder with some attempts at reform. Most serious from the government's point of view was the unrest in the mines and foundries of the Urals, and a few weeks after her accession Catherine raised the matter in the Senate and called for a report on the situation of the assigned peasants.[2]

The conscription of labour might have been necessary in the early stages of Russian industrialization but by the middle of the eighteenth century it was one among several methods of recruiting labour, and many highly placed officials opposed it for both social and economic reasons.[3] Moreover the number of peasants assigned to private enterprises had increased as the result of the massive transfer of state enterprises to private owners in the reign of Elizabeth – and disturbances occurred more frequently in these private establishments. Thus, in its recommenation to Catherine in the autumn of 1762, the Senate pronounced itself in favour of a new form of lease of enterprises on the understanding that assigned peasants should be withdrawn completely from the labour force.[4]

This was clearly too much of an upheaval and would take too much time to implement. Order must first be restored, and in December 1762, Catherine commissioned Prince A.A. Vyazemsky, the future procurator general, to pacify the whole area of the Urals and to conduct a wide-ranging investigation into the grievances of the assigned peasants. He was authorized to arrest non-serf managers, and to remove and punish serf managers : 'In a word do everything you think proper for the satisfaction of the peasants ; but take suitable precautions so that the peasants should not imagine that their managers will be afraid of them in the future . . . if you find managers guilty of great inhumanity, you may punish them publicly ; but if someone has exacted more work than is right you may

123

punish him secretly, thus you will not give the common people grounds to lose their proper dutifulness.' In addition Vyazemsky was to look into the question of replacing assigned peasants by hired workers, 'in order if possible to avert such disturbances in future and to make work more stable and profitable'.[5]

In the course of 1763 and 1764, Vyazemsky toured the various industrial enterprises in the Urals, arresting and punishing ringleaders in the various disorders with the usual lavish accompaniment of corporal punishment and sentences to hard labour. But he took very seriously the second part of his task, namely the investigation of the grievances of the assigned peasants, and the punishment of managers guilty of cruelty or extortion. In some cases he meted out justice on the spot. In other cases the evidence provided by the peasants was not regarded as sufficient, and they were punished for having complained. But some managers were removed, some overdue wages were paid.

Vyazemsky was recalled to St Petersburg in January 1764, when Catherine appointed him procurator general, and replaced by General A.I. Bibikov. But before he left he had pinpointed a number of abuses which led him to draft a set of regulations for the work of assigned peasants in foundries and mines. In an ukaz of 9 April 1763 the empress endorsed these regulations as a model to be followed generally in industry. Their main provisions were : that peasants should be assigned to a particular establishment and should not be sent from one to the other except in case of dire necessity, and in that case should be paid for the journey (at the rate of 5k. a day on foot and 10k. with a horse in summer, and 4k. per day and 6k. with a horse in winter). Groups were to be organized in teams of one hundred, each to work three months of the year, thus enabling the teams to take it in turn to spend the summer months in the village. Managers were forbidden to demand more work than was required to pay off the poll-tax, levied on the group and its male dependants as a whole, bound together under the collective guarantee. The peasant was now to pay his own poll-tax directly to the state – this meant that the management had to pay him his full wage without deduction. Secondly, the teams of one hundred were to elect their own headman, elders and scribes who were to have jurisdiction in all minor disputes among the peasants, referring if necessary to the full group or team. The team elders were charged with punishing ('whip mercilessly') those guilty of incitement to revolt. The teams were also to keep written records of wages received and work demanded. If the management withheld pay, or otherwise oppressed the peasants, the teams were to elect deputies and petition the nearest government office, but they were not to indulge in direct action. Thus in three important fields, the payment of the poll-tax, the organization of work, and jurisdiction over minor offences, the control of the management was weakened and the self-administration of the assigned peasants strengthened.

What remains uncertain is the extent to which these regulations, which undoubtedly represented an improvement in the conditions of the assigned peasants, were actually applied. Vyazemsky himself was not quite systematic in following them in the later stages of his tour, notably with regard to the jurisdiction of the factory managements. Nevertheless, the regulations were eventually adopted in state-owned industries, and government offices tended thereafter to apply them in the event of disputes between labour and management being referred to them by private owners. In the words of Portal, 'tout en remettant pour l'essentiel les choses dans l'ordre ancien, le passage de Viazemski dans l'Oural a marqué le début d'une amélioration du sort des paysans inscrits.'[6]

Experience of the disturbances among the assigned peasants did however strengthen the government's resolution not to assign any more peasants in future to industrial enterprises, though those who were already assigned continued to be so.[7] At the same time, since the noble owners of foundries and mines had totally failed to pay the instalments due to the state on their acquisitions, the state now began to recover them in payment of debts owed to the treasury.[8] Even so, there were outbreaks of unrest from time to time, and in July 1765 Catherine set up a special commisson 'to consider all matters concerned with mining', and to seek 'means for the improvement of the foundries, bearing in mind the easing of the people's burdens and their peace of mind, as well as the national welfare and the need to bring the factories within the law'. The commission was also to examine whether industry should be in state or private hands, and if private, should these hands be non-noble ? It was to remain a secret body to prevent rumours from circulating among the assigned peasants that they were going to be freed from work in industry.[9] The commission did at one stage make recommendations for an increase in the wages of the assigned peasants, but otherwise it does not seem to have had any impact on policy. In these circumstances, unrest continued to simmer just under the surface until it finally exploded in the Pugachev revolt in 1773.[10]

In one field at least it proved possible for Catherine to take action which radically altered the status of a substantial group of the peasantry, namely the transfer of the Church peasants to the status of state peasants in all but name. The administration of the Church and monastic estates had been returned to their previous owners in August 1762, when Catherine was still hesitating to proceed against the wishes of many prominent archbishops. But the changing status of the Church peasants, bandied to and fro between state and Church, led to renewed unrest. The peasants accused the Church authorities of concealing a manifesto signed by the empress granting them the Church lands, and rejected the ukaz of 12 August 1762 : 'Tear it up and spit on it !'[11] The extent of peasant unrest led the government to re-establish the College of Economy in May 1763 ;[12] for the time being a certain amount of land was to be allotted to bishoprics and monasteries for the upkeep of their establishments, which was to be administered directly by them with full rights of justice and economic exploitation. The College of Economy was to supervise all the estates, and to administer the remaining lands directly. But peasant unrest continued. Petitioners approaching the empress in person were as usual severely punished[13] and petitions submitted to the new College of Economy fared not much better.

The repeal of Peter's ukaz on secularization had been a tactical withdrawal on

Catherine's part, at a time when she could not afford to alienate the clergy. But secularization was the logical outcome of her own attitude, both to the relationship of Church and state, and to the problem of serfdom. She could reduce the independence of the Church and subordinate it economically to the state, and at the same time transfer a sizable number of peasants from the status of serfs to that of state peasants. The constant peasant unrest facilitated her policy.[14]

The manifesto secularizing the Church lands was issued on 26 February 1764. All settled lands belonging to the Church and to monasteries in Great Russia and Siberia were now transferred to the College of Economy, and the peasants were placed on an obrok of 1·50r. per annum, payable in addition to the poll-tax of 70k.[15] Nearly one million male serfs thus changed their status overnight and were known for a number of years as 'economic peasants'.[16] They were freed from Church levies, taxes in kind, labour dues, and direct personal relationships with ecclesiastical stewards and administrators, who no longer exercised any jurisdiction over them. The land previously owned by churches and monasteries or attached to bishoprics, was almost entirely allotted to the peasants who cultivated it. The amount of land was of course not uniform throughout the country since much depended on the size of the estate and on the number of souls, and the balance between arable land, meadow land and wood land varied considerably. Thus in the guberniya of St Petersburg, the averge allotment per soul consisted of 2·7 desyatinas of arable, 0·6 desyatinas of pasture, and 21·7 desyatinas of woodland ; in Novgorod guberniya peasants received 5 desyatinas of arable, 1 desyatina of pasture and 19·5 desyatinas of woodland. In more densely cultivated and inhabited areas such as Pskov or Smolensk, the amount of arable was slightly smaller, 3·9 or 4·4 desyatinas per soul, and the allotment of woodland was small, 5·5 desyatinas in Pskov, 2·2 in Smolensk, and the total allotment was of course much smaller. On the whole the allotments and the proportion between the different types of land corresponded fairly closely to the amounts of land available to serfs for their cultivation and use on estates in the same areas, exploited by means of obrok. Lands more than 20 versts away from a village or settlement were not allotted but were rented out to villages of 'economic' or other peasants at a low rent – and sometimes to others.

The secularization of Church lands threw up a number of problems which were gradually tackled. Superfluous Church servants, not provided for on the new Church establishments which accompanied the act of secularization, were counted as peasants and attached to communes which had to provide them with land. Some effort had also to be made to equalize allotments between neighbouring settlements and villages, and where land was in short supply a policy of voluntary resettlement was adopted. Within the village, land was distributed for cultivation on the basis of the *tyaglo* unit, i.e. the unit of labour, and not by souls, a policy which fitted in with the customs of the peasants, and tended to equalize the burdens in the commune. A special administration, to replace the church and monastic administration, was established by an ukaz of 13 August 1764[17] to supervise the economic exploitation and organization of the estates belonging to the College of Economy, and to act as the spokesman for the peasants in dealings with other government institutions and the courts.

In the opinion of V.I. Semevsky, the secularization of Church lands carried out in 1764 'was a great and beneficent reform for the peasants', based on 'sensible principles'. That the peasants were on the whole satisfied is proved in his view by the almost total decline of unrest among them ; later research however suggests that unrest continued in the form of seizures of noble land and even brigandage.[18] But some of the nobility showed dissatisfaction, and even alarm. The solution found for the ecclesiastical estates led many to fear some kind of state intervention between them and their serfs. And in any case, most of the run-of-the-mill nobility believed that the Church's estates should be used to swell the landholdings of the nobility, not of the state. Using the argument that since secularization the economic peasants, who were now on obrok, neglected agriculture and left large tracts of land uncultivated, various projects were put forward by members of the nobility to improve agricultural productivity by transferring these lands, either outright or by leases, to noble control. Catherine and her government resisted all such pressures. Indeed Catherine was clearly determined to maintain intact the total number of 'economic' peasants. They were very rarely used as a source from which grants to private owners could be made.[19]

It was far more difficult for the government to deal with the unrest among serfs on privately owned estates. It is also difficult to gauge its extent since much depends on the criteria used for defining a revolt, which can range from a major riot requiring to be put down by soldiers to a band of peasants setting fire to a hayrick. Peasant unrest normally took one or more of three forms : revolt against the landowner, flight, and brigandage.

The number of known serf revolts in the years 1762–9 have been given as 36 by one historian, and 73 by another.[20] The worst year was 1767, with 27 risings, and the largest total of murders of landowners by their serfs.[21] An incomplete list for the years 1764–9 in Moscow guberniya alone notes the murder of 21 landowners, 9 noblewomen, and 5 attempted murders.[22] The extent of the evil was such that Nikita Panin even pressed Catherine to restore the death penalty in Russia for the murder of landowners by serfs and the Senate drafted a law which made no difference between the offence of murdering a noble and failing to defend a noble against a murderer. Catherine protested forcibly to the procurator general against such a law. If whole villages were to be destroyed to avenge one landowner, she wrote, there would be a general revolt. The position of the serfs was so critical that only peace and humane institutions could forestall a general movement to throw off 'an unbearable yoke' ; if 'we do not agree', added Catherine, 'to reduce cruelty and moderate a situation intolerable for human beings, then they themselves will take things in hand'.[23]

Serious rioting on noble estates usually led to the calling in of troops, and occasionally to pitched battles between soldiers and peasants armed with staves and stones. Peasant resistance can be gauged by the fact that on one occasion they wounded an officer and kept 64 soldiers prisoner for three days. In May 1767, the serfs on estates belonging to the Olsuf'ev brothers, one of whom was secretary to the empress, took the opportunity of Catherine's progress along the Volga to petition her directly. Rejecting her admonitions to return to work, they collected a sum of money to send a representative to Moscow with their complaints. An infantry regiment soon put paid to their efforts ; some 130 were arrested and a number sentenced to the knut.[24]

The frequency with which troops had to be called out to repress rural rioting led to a regularization of the procedure, designed to weigh even more heavily on the serfs. An ukaz issued on 11 July 1763 ordered that all the costs of a military expedition to restore order on an estate should be recovered from the peasants themselves – who were thus to pay for the maintenance of the detachment, for the arms used against them, and the knuts with which they were flogged.[25] The College of War then issued regulations for the use of these punitive expeditions : the soldiers were instructed to start by attempting conciliation. Only afterwards could they proceed to fire blank shots, or shoot in the air, and set fire to haystacks or straw ; they were only to fire with intent to wound if attacked.[26] A detailed study of Russian peasant revolts is required to establish whether these optimistic instructions were followed.

Flight had always been the Russian peasant's principal defence against oppression. Internal flight, in large family groups, had declined somewhat in the 1750s and 1760s, because as government control and noble settlement advanced, it was more difficult for a family to conceal itself. Lands to which serfs had previously fled like Simbirsk and Penza became lands from which they fled to the lower Volga and beyond.[27] But with the decline of internal movement, secret flitting over the border into Sweden and Poland increased, and assumed very serious proportions in the war years 1757–63.[28] Up to 100 families, totalling some 500 people, fled from Novgorod into Poland in spring 1763. In 1767 another fifty families fled from St Petersburg guberniya. In 1767 the local nobles estimated that there were some 50,000 fugitive serfs from Smolensk in Poland. While the authorities, in the interests of settling the vast empty spaces in South Russia and Siberia, turned a blind eye to the presence of runaways in these areas, and implemented in a very lax way the various ukazy directing landowners, industries and Cossack communities not to harbour fugitives, they could not be indifferent to a loss of population by flight abroad.

Charged in 1763 with an investigation into the causes of peasant flight, General Peter Panin pointed to a number of reasons, including religious oppression of the Old Believers, abuse of the recruit levy by landowners, ill-treatment of the recruits themselves, the unlimited power of landowners over their serfs and the fact that landowners over the Polish border were less exacting, and that salt and liquor were both cheaper there. To remedy the situation, Panin proposed the secret regulation of landlord/serf economic relations, the replacement of the recruit levy in frontier areas by a tax of 100 r. per recruit, money which would be used to enlist volunteers, and guarantees that fugitives who returned would not be given back to their owners but bought by the state and settled elsewhere. Only the latter recommendation was put into effect.[29]

Peter III had already issued manifestos urging fugitives to return to Russia within a period of years, and the same policy was pursued by Catherine, while force was also used to recover deserters. In August 1763 Russian detachments crossed into Poland and recovered 2,000 serfs who were returned to their owners.[30] But a manifesto signed on 13 May 1763 offered fugitives who had left before 1762 an amnesty, permission to settle on state lands, and six years' immunity from taxes and labour dues. Owners of fugitive serfs who returned on these terms would be given recruit quittances.[31]

In 1766 the government endeavoured to remedy one of the main causes of flight among peasants – all peasants – namely the practice of buying serfs, to be sent to the army as recruits, by prohibiting the sale of adult male serfs for three months before a recruit levy.[32] The prohibition continued in force throughout Catherine's reign, but it did not need much ingenuity to find ways round it. The Senate attempted to put a stop to this in 1768, by prohibiting the acceptance of 'free' (or 'voluntary') recruits from peasant communities, but the practice continued.[33]

Brigandage was also endemic in the vast unpoliced expanses of Russia. The definition of what constitutes brigandage, and what can be regarded as legitimate class war, has exercised Soviet historians. In the terminology of the time, *bunt* or revolt was directed by serfs against their own landowners. Brigandage or *razboy* was carried out by bands of miscellaneous origin, attacking landowners, merchants, and officials indiscriminately. In Soviet interpretation, the peasant who joined a band of brigands might be a robber in the first place, but he would then move on to exact revenge for the grievances of his fellows, and would become an avenger of the wrongs of the people. The borderline between *bunt* and *razboy* was in any case very fine, since serfs occasionally attacked their own master 'under the guise of brigands' in order to conceal their participation.[34] There were however many who followed this way of life for choice, including *déclassé* nobles. The Volga area seems to have been particularly plagued owing to the large number of fugitive peasants, the vicinity of Cossack settlements with their tradition of lawlessness and freedom, and the absence of administrative or military government personnel. The 1760s saw an increasing number of bands operating in Nizhniy Novgorod, Voronezh and Kazan'. In Simbirsk, in 1768, more than thirty estates were destroyed, and landowners, their families and serf stewards murdered. One band grew from thirty-one to over seventy members, with four cannon.[35] Notable were the so-called 'brave youths of the franchise of the lower lands' (*ponizovaya vol'nitsa*), operating in the Lower Volga area, and the band of ataman Ivanov, composed of some hundred fugitive peasants and deserters, operating between the Don and the Volga.

The Ukraine produced its own special brand of brigandage or class war, known as *haydamachestvo*. The *haydamaki* emerged from the poorer bachelor members of the Zaporozhian Cossack Host, and their hired servants or peasants. Bands, rising sometimes to 150–200 people, formed and dispersed rapidly to their various hideouts. *Haydamachestvo* knew no frontiers and operated indiscriminately against Russian landowners or merchants, and wealthy Cossacks, and under the name *koliivshchina,* in Right Bank Ukraine, where the brigands attacked Polish landowners and officials, and Catholic priests. The bands extended their operations to the borders of Polish crown territory and attacked Turks and Tartars to the south. Members of defeated bands fled back into Russia, making their way to the world of the Cossacks into which they merged, and some of their leaders, notably the Cossack Dudarenko, later became prominent in Pugachev's following.[36]

The disorder prevailing in the countryside led the government to issue a number of ukazy, most of which were of an *ad hoc* nature, designed to cope with specific cases, though some of them had wider implications. Only a week after her accession, Catherine had repeated almost word for word an ukaz issued by Peter III on 19 June 1762, assuring landowners that the state would maintain them in peaceful ownership of their estates, and enjoining the serfs to obey their masters.[37] In 1765, the College of the Navy was empowered to receive and employ serfs sentenced by their masters to hard labour for unruliness, for such periods as their masters should lay down.[38] In common with other subjects of the empress, belonging to any estate, peasants were forbidden to petition the empress personally, but had to go through the recognized channels. The procedure was laid down in 1765 in an ukaz which specified in considerable detail the various punishments to be inflicted on the various social classes of both sexes for attempting to approach the empress in person. The penalties were carefully graduated according to whether it was a first, second, third or even fourth offence, and according to the social status and *chin,* or rank, of the offender. Thus the penalty for a third offence for all townspeople, peasants and serfs was a public whipping and perpetual exile to the mines of Nerchinsk. Owners of serfs sentenced in this way would receive a recruit quittance.[39]

But the right of serfs to petition the authorities and to denounce their masters was limited by a much older law, the Code of 1649. In Chapter II, article 13, serfs were specifically threatened with the knut if they denounced their masters, except in cases involving sedition or treason.[40] This prohibition was restated in an ukaz of 22 August 1767 which was promulgated as the result of serious rioting on a number of estates in which the peasants had presented petitions to the empress. Catherine forwarded the petitions to the Senate, urging that steps should be taken to reduce peasant discontent. The Senate thereupon proposed to issue an ukaz prohibiting serfs from complaining against their masters except on those matters authorized by the Code of 1649 and other later ukazy, until a new law should be drafted by the Legislative Commission which had just begun its sittings.[41] In the case of the particular riots which had given rise to the petitions, the Senate ordered the peasants involved to be punished. But it also recommended that the landowners concerned who had undoubtedly overburdened their serfs should be 'privately admonished' to behave with greater humanity. Four magnates were appointed to deliver these secret admonitions, including Peter Panin who was charged to speak to his cousin General Leont'yev. His success can be estimated by the fact that Leont'yev was murdered by his serfs two years later.[42] The ukaz promulgated on 22 August 1767 introduced nothing new into the relations between master and serf, though it increased the penalty for petitioning, by adding hard labour in the mines of Nerchinsk. And since no new law ever emerged from the Legislative Commission, it remained in force, at any rate until 1775, and possibly after.[43]

The intensification of peasant unrest in the years 1762–7 has often been attributed to specific policies pursued by Catherine at this time designed to increase the powers of landowners over their serfs in order to keep the support of the class which had placed her on the throne. There are serious drawbacks to this interpretation. First of all, one of the policies which seemed to increase the landowners' powers, namely the right to send serfs to settlement in Siberia for unruly behaviour, was adopted in December 1760, in the reign of Elizabeth, in order to speed up the influx of Russian settlers into these empty lands.[44] Moreover this particular law authorized all social groups, including merchants, state peasants, and Church peasants, to banish unreliable members of their communities to settlement in Siberia, in exchange for a recruit quittance. How widely this power was used other than by the landowners is not known. But there is no doubt that it was used by merchants, and long after other groups had been deprived of it in the nineteenth century, peasants continued to exile peasants to Siberia.[45]

Secondly, it has been argued that peasant disturbances occurred because Catherine transformed large numbers of state peasants into serfs by donating them to her supporters and favourites in these same years, in order to strengthen her position. The number and source of the settled estates Catherine donated in the first ten years of her reign is known: 18,725 souls were given away at once in 1762 to those who had participated in the plot to make her empress, and another 48,000 were given away in the ten years to 1772. Of these, the bulk were court peasants, and 5,097 were in Livonia or Little Russia. In many cases estates were specially purchased, but no state peasants were turned into serfs. Indeed, the British envoy, George Macartney, noted at the time that peasants of the Crown 'are looked upon as inalienably annexed to the crown' ; court peasants could be given away, 'but the present empress indeed has been much more sparing in this respect than her predecessors'.[46]

However several other factors may have contributed to the undoubted ferment among the peasants. The first, chronologically, was the manifesto of 1762 freeing the nobility from service to the state. The impact of the manifesto on the serfs has been variously interpreted by historians. According to Rubinstein too much importance should not be attached to the influence of a law, at the expense of the class war. Portal notes that in the Urals it led the peasants to expect their own liberation, particularly since the further purchase of serfs for industry was prohibited at the same time.[47] The peasantry undoubtedly knew of the manifesto, and it was not beyond their intelligence to discern that the equilibrium between peasant servitude to the noble, and noble servitude to the state had been broken, and had created an 'unjust' situation which must be remedied. The government reacted by issuing an ukaz on 19 June 1762, which was repeated again word for word on 4 July, after Catherine's accession, warning peasants not to be misled by 'lying rumours', presumably rumours of their impending freedom.[48] A fake ukaz, allegedly issued by the empress on 30 October 1763, illustrates some of these peasant attitudes: 'The time has come to uproot extortion, since I much desire to live in peace ; but, however, our nobility do much neglect the law of God and the law of the state, and in that they do great harm to the state.' The fake ukaz then recalled that the nobility had been granted their lands by previous rulers, but they had forgotten this and were no longer willing to serve the state. In the days of Peter the Great they had been kept in order, but now 'all law has been chased from the land . . .'. 'The Russian people had been orphaned.'[49]

Equally unsettling for the bulk of the serfs was the secularization of the Church peasants, which must have aroused their hopes of being taken over 'by the sovereign'. And barely three years later came the news of the summoning of the Legislative Commission, to which the serfs were not sending deputies, though they lived cheek by jowl with the state peasants who were. The ukaz of 22 August 1767, which prohibited complaints against landowners specifically warned against ill-intentioned people 'who spread stories about changes in the laws'. The point of view of the serfs has been enshrined in the so-called 'Serf's Lament' :

> The master can kill the serf like a gelding,
> But a serf's denunciation will not be believed.
> Unjust officials have drawn up an ukaz
> To knut us tyrannically for such denunciations.
> They are changing the laws now to their own advantage
> But they are not electing serfs as deputies. . . .
>
> They don't want to serve the tsar
> As long as they can squeeze the last drop from us. . . .[50]

Finally, it is possible that rumours of Catherine's intervention between landowners and peasants in Livonia, as expressed in the Patent of April 1765, and of various other experiments in new forms of land tenure, circulated fairly widely, perhaps in a distorted form, and again contributed to unsettle peasant mood and opinion, and convey the impression that something was in the air.

Catherine had been able to put into effect specific policies designed to improve the lot of the assigned peasants and the Church peasants with the full support of many high officials. But the relationship between the Russian landowner and the serf had to be approached far more discreetly. Before her accession educated society showed no signs of even conceiving of the abolition of serfdom: '[abolition] does not concord with our monarchical form of government and it would be dangerous to touch the deep-rooted principle of bondage,' wrote the eighteenth-century historian N.I. Tatishchev.[51] In contrast, Catherine, while still grand duchess, had noted down a means of abolishing serfdom which she thought might take about a hundred years, namely that every time an estate changed hands by sale, the serfs should become free ; since nearly all estates would change hands once in a hundred years, 'voilà le peuple libre'.[52] And it was Catherine who now, in a variety of ways, brought the issue before the embryonic Russian public opinion.

At first Catherine did not go beyond the regulation within serfdom of relations between landowner, serf and land, and the reform movement originated with her most intimate friends, namely Grigory and Aleksey Orlov, who had first brought Pastor Eisen to her notice. Eisen was invited to prepare a plan to introduce 'peasant ownership of land' in the estate of Ropsha, scene of the murder of Peter III, which now, by a grim irony, belonged to the Orlov brothers, and in two other estates in which he was to replace serfdom by 'colonies'. Eisen was to prepare leases which would turn the peasants into tenants. He worked for eighteen months but was dismissed for unknown reasons in 1766, shortly before the summoning of the Legislative Assembly. It is possible that the empress, sensing opposition to her plans, took the easy way of postponing the question by handing it over to the Legislative Assembly.

The same principles were however taken up, with Catherine's approval, by Governor J. Sievers of Novgorod, in a large court estate at Korostina, near the city. Sievers began with a land survey in order to determine the peasants' obligations, and he prepared leases which would enable the state to control relations between the tenant/landlord and the peasant. It is evident that these enlightened officials regarded the leasing of estates as a step in the right direction, away from serfdom, since the landlords' rights over peasant labour would be restricted by the lease, and the peasant would have legally enforceable rights. Hence Sievers proposed extending the system of renting out estates to the Church lands. He saw in such a policy the means of providing for an enlarged officer corps, while safeguarding the position of the serfs, since the tenant could be given notice if he did not observe the conditions of the lease. Catherine was sufficiently persuaded of the merits of his proposal to put it before the College of Economy, in charge of the Church lands, but it was turned down, for reasons which have not been explained.[53]

A variant on Sievers's plan was introduced by Catherine's secretary I.P. Yelagin on the same court estate in Novgorod guberniya. Yelagin proposed instituting hereditary leases, registering the obligations of the court peasants, on estates which should then be rented to nobles. But he also proposed abolishing the commune, and setting up farming units of equal size based on tyaglo units of four workers, whether related or not. Yelagin's proposals met with the strongest resistance from the peasants.

Prince Dmitry Aleksandrovich Golitsyn, friend of Helvetius and Diderot, Russian envoy to Paris and The Hague, was both more naive and more original. He believed in the economic advantages of peasant ownership of land, and proposed that Catherine should set an example by granting the court peasants full ownership of the land, on the assumption that her lead would be voluntarily followed by the noble serf-owners. This suggestion called forth a tart comment from Catherine : 'It is doubtful that example will be enough to move our compatriots. . . . Not many will wish to sacrifice substantial advantages to the noble feelings of a patriotic heart.' More unusual was Golitsyn's proposal to establish a peripatetic tribunal entitled to hear complaints against officials and landowners.[54]

The whole question of serfdom was given far wider publicity as a result of an essay competition launched by the Free Economic Society in 1766 at the secret instigation of Catherine herself. The society had been founded in 1765 by a group of fifteen enlightened nobles, mostly large landowners, inspired by the increasing interest in the national economy encouraged by the *Encyclopédie* and the physiocrats. It was the first secular independent cultural institution in Russia, and it lasted until the Bolshevik Revolution in 1917.[55] It published its own transactions (*Trudy*), which disseminated information on all kinds of agricultural improvements, and it attempted to run model farms, and organize essay competitions on various aspects of rural life. Though independent of the government, the society benefited from Catherine's moral – and material – support and its membership was by no means confined to the nobility. The theme of the competition was : 'What is most useful for society – that the peasant should own the land or only moveable property, and how far should his rights over the one or the other extend ?'

It was obvious that this question opened the door to a discussion of peasant freedom. So much so that the poet and dramatist A.P. Sumarokov dashed off a sharp letter of protest to the society : 'A canary is better off without a cage and a dog without a chain ; but the one will fly away, the other will bite people ; thus the one is necessary for the sake of the peasant, the other for the sake of the noble.'[56] The members of the society were so well aware of the explosive nature of the topic that the essays submitted were circulated among them in a locked dispatch case of which only members had the key. Some 160 entries were sent in, of which 129 came from Germans, 7 from Russians, the remainder from other parts of Europe (including entries by Voltaire and Marmontel).

Of the seven Russian entries, one (No. 88), by S. Aleksandrov, stressed in modest language the right to the hereditary usufruct of land dear to the peasant's heart; No. 99, written without punctuation or grammar (perhaps by a farmer soldier?), demanded the right to the ownership of moveable property, and an extension of the right of usufruct; both these entries were rather simple expressions of a directly peasant point of view, not essays in the strict sense of the term. Neither conceived of absolute ownership of the land by the peasantry, or of the abolition of serfdom. No. 71, possibly written by a *raznochinets,* went further : the author founded the peasant's right to personal freedom and the ownership of moveable and immoveable property in natural law. All men were born free and should enjoy the same civic rights ; society was founded for the protection of property, and if that principle were breached, society was doomed. The most interesting of the Russian entries was by a certain A. Ya. Polenov, a translator in the Academy of Sciences. His analysis was bold and outspoken, and the remedies he proposed were marked by a common-sense appreciation of Russian realities. He did not demand the immediate and outright abolition of serfdom, but the legal regulation of dues and duties (limited to one day a week); legal protection for the hereditary use of land ; the prohibition of the sale of individual peasants or of peasants without land ; measures of social welfare, such as schools and medical care, and the establishment of special courts to judge peasant grievances against landowners or the administration.

Though recognized by some of the members of the selection committee as the best and most substantial entry, others saw in it 'many exaggerated expressions unsuitable and improper in present circumstances'. Hence the author was invited to expurgate his essay, in which case his entry would be included in the second class, with all awards except publication.[57]

The prize was awarded on 9 April 1766 to a doctor of laws of Aachen, Beardé de l'Abbaye. His essay, while not related to Russian reality as that of Polenov in its description of the state of the peasantry, nevertheless stressed in purest physiocratic terms the importance of the peasant as the foundation of national prosperity. The poorest peasant, proclaimed the author, was more necessary for the state than the useless, uncultured and avaricious magnate. The peasant must be personally free, and must be entitled to own land and moveable property. The progressive emancipation of the serfs should be achieved without government intervention, on the initiative of the owners, who could at the same time set the price high. Peasant personal moveable property should be the reward of increased productivity, to be followed eventually by ownership of land; personal emancipation should come as the final reward for increasing the landlord's revenues.

The second prize was awarded to the entry by the French physiocrat Graslin, who wrote as an economist, not a politician, or a moralist. In his view, for one member of society to 'own' the labour of another was a breach of the basic foundations of social organization. Hence serf-owners and landowners were parasites who weakened society both politically and economically.

Many members of the Free Economic Society seemed to have felt that the language even of Beardé de l'Abbaye was too outspoken to be published at a time of peasant unrest. The empress raised no objection to publication, and left it to the members of the society to decide. Here the final vote was twelve in favour of publication and sixteen against. But the twelve in favour included those closest to the empress such as two of the Orlovs, R. Vorontsov, Count A.S. Stroganov, Count I. Chernyshev, Count Sievers, G.N. Teplov ; in view of which the society finally decided that 'these Russian gentlemen occupying high positions in the Russian state' were in a better position to judge in a matter which was more political than economic. Hence the verdict of the liberal but weightier minority carried the day, and Beardé de l'Abbaye's essay was published in Russian in St Petersburg in 1768, together with the French and German originals of three others.

The importance of this episode should not be underestimated. Beardé de l'Abbaye's description of the condition of the peasantry – if somewhat abstract – was couched in the same language, with the same overtones, the same insistence on the horror and the immorality of bondage which characterized other entries such as that of Polenov. The very fact that his essay was published in Russian during the sessions of the Legislative Commission when the peasant problem aroused great feeling, was therefore a formal indictment, authorized on high, of the inhumanity of the system as such. But not one of the entries, except that of Polenov, was geared to Russian realities. There was a good deal of discussion on the importance of a free agriculture for national prosperity – there was very little discussion of the economics of emancipation and its political consequences.

Yet these problems would have to be faced by any government attempting to act. For the moment the problem was posed in abstract terms. Two trends emerged, neither of which had much following among the nobility at large. The first, based on the Russian tradition, was represented by Polenov. It urged state regulation of the existing system, with a clear assertion that the serf was the subject of the state, not the slave of the landowner. The respective claims of the state and the landowner on the serf's labour should be defined, and the serf should have access to state courts for the redress of grievances against the landowner. The second trend derived from the humanitarian and economic theories of the Enlightenment. Though unrelated to Russian realities, it opened men's minds to new ideas – and indeed it led eventually to the development of a counter-movement – a completely new school of defenders of serfdom, an institution which had never needed defending before.

It is worth noting that the questions of communal ownership, communal labour, redistribution of land, and communal responsibility for taxes were simply not touched upon by these abstract theorists of the reform of serfdom. As a result they have at times been harshly criticized by nineteenth-century supporters of the commune. Yet, within the political climate of their age, more concerned with the demand for individual human rights in the struggle for freedom against despotism, than with economic and social rights, their viewpoint is explicable, generous and humane. They thought of the peasant as an individual, or at most a family, whose personal dignity could be enhanced by freedom and whose personal security could be enhanced by property. But they did not scratch the surface of the whole complex problem of the place of the serf in a system in which every taxpayer was bound to a place and was assessed as part of a taxable unit, not as an individual.

Part III

The National Dialogue

9

The Legislative Commission
of 1767

Having surmounted the first crises of her reign, Catherine embarked in the mid-1760s on a major, highly personal political experiment. On 14 December 1766, she issued a manifesto inviting all the free 'estates' of the realm and the central government offices to send deputies to the capital, empowered to explain the needs and problems of their communities, and to take part in the preparation of a new code of laws.[1]

Since the days of Peter the Great the government had been well aware of the need to bring the Code of 1649[2] up to date, and a number of 'Legislative Commissions' had been set up in the eighteenth century, composed of a small number of mainly noble bureaucrats and non-noble experts, ranging from university professors to members of the merchant community.[3] But Catherine's manifesto of December 1766 immediately made it clear that she had something different in mind. Past commissions had been small committees meeting in private, and only when the spade work had been done were deputies of the various estates summoned in small numbers to comment separately on the relevant portions of a draft code. But the elected assembly Catherine was now calling together was to be much larger than any of its eighteenth-century predecessors, and the elected deputies themselves were to take part in drafting the code.

The manifesto explained that representation would be accorded to government institutions, and to social groups not already represented by a government institution or by landowners. Thus the Senate, the Synod, the Colleges, and such chanceries as the Senate should decide (not however those connected with local administration), should be represented by an elected deputy, not necessarily their head. As regards the 'estates', the basic electoral unit was territorial: the nobles were to select one deputy for each district (*uezd* in Russia, *polk* in the Ukraine, *kreis* in Livonia) regardless of the number of nobles in the district ; each registered town was to send one deputy, regardless of the number of inhabitants ; and the odnodvortsy, and other categories of free soldier farmers, and the state peasants and tribute-paying peasants were to send one deputy for each province. The settled tribes, whether Christian or pagan, were to send one deputy for each tribe in each provence, and finally, the Cossack Hosts were to send 'the appropriate number of deputies as decided upon by their commanding authorities'.[4] In contrast with the practice in the Assemblies of the Land in the seventeenth century (*Zemskiye Sobory*), the clerical estate was not represented as an estate in Catherine's Legislative Commission but as a branch of the government, by a deputy elected by the Holy Synod.

Attendance as a deputy at a Legislative Commission had been regarded in the eighteenth century as merely one more form of service exacted from an overburdened nobility, to be evaded if possible.[5] Catherine endeavoured to turn it into a privilege to be sought by attaching a number of prerogatives to the status of deputy. In the first place deputies were to be paid a salary, ranging from 400r.p.a. for nobles and 122r.p.a. for town deputies to 37r.p.a. for others. They were to be immune from the death penalty, corporal punishment and torture for life.[6] Their property was protected from confiscation except in the case of debt, and anyone assaulting a deputy would incur a double penalty. Finally deputies were to be issued with a special badge of office which was to be returned to the state on their death. Nobles were entitled to incorporate this badge in their coats of arms so that 'their descendants may know that they took part in this great affair'.[7]

There was nothing of the modern representative body or parliament in Catherine's Legislative Commission, which was essentially an *ancien régime* institution. Moreover the Manifesto of 14 December 1766 left many of the implications of calling such an assembly in doubt. To begin with, the very use of the words elections and electors perpetuates a misunderstanding about the nature of political representation in Russian assemblies of the land or legislative commissions. 'The Russian word for elections, ''vybory'', literally means choices or selections.'[8] This observation on Soviet elections today is even more true of the process of selecting a deputy to the Legislative Commission in the eighteenth century. A deputy was to be *chosen* or *selected,* according to the Manifesto of 14 December 1766. There were no candidates ; all those qualified to choose a deputy could also be chosen. On the great day, all those present were to approach a central table in a reputable house, and as each name was called out, they were to place a ball in one of two boxes, marked 'chosen' or 'not chosen'. The man for whom most balls were cast into the box marked 'chosen' (to which postal votes were also added) was selected to be the deputy. Catherine herself, it must be added, had no intention of allowing the role of a deputy to evolve into that of a Member of Parliament, and nipped all such attempts in the bud. A sharply worded ukaz of 1773 stated that deputies were not to set themselves up as 'defenders of the people', nor were they to act as spokesmen, pursuing matters in government offices on behalf of local people.[9] Moreover, since a deputy who wished to resign could simply hand over his mandate to someone of his own choice, without consulting those who had elected him, he was clearly in no way regarded as responsible to his electors. In the same way, since nothing depended on a vote in the assembly, the fact that numbers could fluctuate was irrelevant.

Deputies sometimes resigned or were expelled without being replaced, and governors and voyevodas, if they happened to be in the capital, would attend the assembly *ex officio*.[10]

Thus the Legislative Commission was not intended to represent 'the people', let alone 'the will of the people'. It was purely consultative, and in the strict sense it was not 'legislative' at all. Hence the presence of deputies from government departments need cause no surprise. They were assumed to be familiar with problems of administration, with the needs of those sections of society with which they were concerned, and with the law. The government departments produced their own *nakazy* or instructions, which should not be identified with any particular centrally formulated government policy, but with the professional experience of the department concerned.[11]

A glance at some of the elections illustrates the haphazard attitude of the government and the total inadequacy of the electoral procedure devised. Nobles were entitled to participate in selecting a deputy in all districts in which they owned land, and if they could not attend in person, for reasons of health or because they were serving, they could send their vote by post. Women owning estates in their own name were not admitted to the electoral meetings but could vote by post. The first stage in electing a noble deputy was the election of a local 'marshal' of the nobility, to hold office for two years, under the auspices of the local governor. The governor then retired from the proceedings, and the marshal appointed the day and the place for the elections. After the deputy had been chosen, the assembled nobles appointed a committee of five to draft an instruction or nakaz, which was then signed by all of them. The deputy then departed for Moscow, where his credentials were submitted to the Heraldmaster's Office in the Senate for approval, whereupon he could start drawing his salary and receive his insignia. The marshal of the nobility remained behind in the district, and was to keep himself at the disposal of the government. At this time the function of the marshal was not defined, but the election of a permanent leader of the nobles in each district represented the dawn of their corporate organization.[12]

The fairly simple procedure outlined above immediately ran into difficulties. According to the electoral rules, if there were fewer than fifteen resident nobles in a district, they were free to choose whether to send a deputy or not; no minimum number of electors was specified. Catherine herself listed some fifteen districts which she expected to be unrepresented. In fact there were many more. In Zvenigorod district there were eighty landowners ; only two were resident and they refused to attend the election meeting on the grounds that they were ill. In Kashira district, of 711 landowners, only 38 attended the electoral meeting, but 323 postal votes were received.[13]

Catherine expected 173 districts to elect noble deputies, out of a total of 300 in the Russian Empire.[14] Many districts of course had no noble landowners, for instance in Siberia. On the evidence available, it is difficult to pronounce on the degree of favour or hostility with which the nobility viewed the Legislative Commission in general and elections in particular. Many nobles possessed estates in more than one district, and may not have bothered to use their postal vote if they were participating in elections where they habitually resided. Noble owners of small estates on active military and civil service had neither the time nor the means to make the long journey home. The attitude of the nobility was probably to a great extent influenced by distance from the two capital cities. The nobility in the distant, less cultured provinces still conceived of a summons to the capital as some form of state service, to be evaded if at all possible. Governor Sievers of Novgorod reported that in his guberniya the manifesto had been received with rejoicing, but one noble ('ein edles oder vielmehr ein unedles Thier') had protested, on the grounds that since 1762 the nobility had been freed from service.[15] In districts where high court officials or magnates held estates, the nobility tended to elect them. Three of the Orlov brothers were elected, the two Chernyshevs, Peter Panin (for the city of Moscow). It is probable that Catherine put pressure on her friends to visit the districts in which they held estates, where their standing would ensure their election. But there is no evidence of any manipulation of the election by the central government with a 'party' political purpose in view. Indeed since the government had no precise idea how many deputies would be elected, it was impossible, let alone unnecessary, to organize a government 'party'.[16]

Very little is known about the drafting of the 'instructions' to the deputies. There was no bar to the expression of general political views, and any grievance could be touched upon, whether local, or national. Only demands for redress of individual grievances were excluded. It often however proved difficult to weld local opinion together and to wean the electors from the habit of 'petitioning', (chelobit'ye), the traditional form of placing grievances before the ruler. Some of the instructions were laconic to a degree. The nakaz of the noble deputy of Murom stated briefly that Murom had no needs, suffered from no oppression and required no new laws.[17] In very few cases did the nobility rise to the formulations of their views in abstract political terms. This can be explained by the low cultural level, even illiteracy, still typical of the provincial noble over forty or fifty years of age, whether in service or not. In one case a son signed the nakaz for his father, 'who is illiterate and cannot sign his name'. In Arzamas, one man signed for eight others 'who could not write themselves'.[18]

Catherine's electoral procedure led to even more difficulties in the urban elections since it ignored the deep divisions between the social groups in the towns altogether, in favour of the simpler approach of granting the vote to all householders. It is now generally accepted by historians that Catherine was consciously endeavouring to develop the town as a territorial unit and to weld its population together into one single estate.[19] But the merchants or kuptsy were not accustomed to any form of cooperation with the ordinary town-dwellers on terms of equality, and did not accept as citizens those who played no part in the economic life of the town, like minor officials. Local authorities too had in the past been accustomed to deal primarily with the kuptsy, and it is evident that they were often bewildered by the new approach which ran counter to all their past experience.

The electoral rules were of little help since they left undefined the concepts of 'householder', 'resident', and 'town'. Was a state peasant who owned a hut and a stall to vote with the townspeople, or with the state peasants of the province? Did the grown son of a kupets who lived with his father have a vote? Were householders in urban suburbs some forty to sixty versts from the town entitled to vote, and if so where? Some of these questions were taken to the Senate and even to the empress, but rulings were by no means always observed. The confusion surrounding the electoral procedure served often to frustrate the aim of achieving the collective representation of all the social groups resident in one township by a single deputy. The kuptsy, long accustomed to dominate urban life, endeavoured to exclude other groups, and to monopolize the election of the deputy for their own estate. In one case members of the service class below officer rank who were householders were excluded. In another, kuptsy succeeded in excluding two noble householders and all the townspeople who did not belong to the *kupechestvo* or merchant estate. The Senate quashed both these elections and ordered new ones. But in most cases where irregularities occurred neither the voyevoda, nor the excluded electors, protested, so that in the end, of 209 urban deputies, 83 were elected exclusively by members of the merchant estate. The social group most widely excluded from the urban elections were the clergy, who were noted as taking part in only 13 out of 209 elections.[20]

As in the case of the nobility, the elections began with the choice of a town chief (*gorodskaya golova*) who then took over the direction of proceedings. He was elected for two years, and he was to act as the representative of the householders and 'all inhabitants of the town' should the government wish to consult them. The town chief thus incarnated the new corporate principle in regard to the urban class, and it is evident that he was to act on behalf of all social groups: merchants, townspeople, clerics, chancery servants, etc. If the town was very large, elections could take place in two stages. The householders in each quarter (*chast'*) into which the town was divided would meet first and elect up to a hundred representatives who would then take part in the final selection of a deputy.

In the two capitals the nobility took an active part in the elections and overwhelmed the merchant estate to the extent that in St Petersburg in the first round many nobles were elected; it was the chief of police who suggested that it might be advisable to elect a few merchants instead of very busy magnates. But when the second round of the elections took place, the urban population of the capital chose as their deputy none other than Aleksey Orlov. It was again the chief of police who urged that the inhabitants of Moscow should elect a few merchants in the first round. But in the end they too chose to be represented by a noble, Prince A.M. Golitsyn, and elected the procurator general, Prince A.A. Vyazemsky, as town chief. As in the case of the nobility, it is evident that not all those entitled to take part in the elections did so ; in St Petersburg, for instance, only 450 electors out of 3,000–3,500 householders took part ; in Moscow the proportion was even smaller : 878 out of 10,000–12,000 householders.[21] The low response of a potentially fairly large electorate may indicate bewilderment, indifference, distrust, or simply ignorance and illiteracy ; or it may reflect the efforts of the town oligarchy to prevent the town-dwellers from taking part in the proceedings.

So little were the townspeople accustomed to the territorial as distinct from the 'estate' principle, that in some cases where they could not agree on common interests, they elected more than one deputy. Astrakhan' and Saratov sent five deputies, Kazan' sent one for the Russian population and one for the Tartars. How many of these deputies were actually admitted to sit in the Legislative Commission is not clear, though in the records at least three spokesmen appear for the town of Astrakhan'.[22]

The preparation of the town nakazy or instructions also presented difficulties. The merchant class as such had a long tradition of drafting petitions, couched in stereotyped form, and addressed to the central college concerned with their estate, namely the Glavnyy Magistrat. Moreover the local town councils were accustomed to communicating with each other on such occasions, exchanging information, and combining to work out collective petitions submitted by a number of towns. But their petitions had been designed mainly to shift tax and service burdens from their shoulders to those of other social groups. They were thus essentially *soslovnyye* or 'estate' in character, expressing the interests of the élite among the tax-paying members of a township. But the nakaz to the town deputy was supposed to be all-inclusive, to consider the needs and requirements of the town as a unit. Such harmony was very difficult to achieve, and where agreement could not be reached more than one deputy was elected and each was supplied with his own nakaz. On the whole, the town nakazy did little more than reflect local problems and issues ; many of them were merely lists of grievances, sometimes contradictory, yet tacked together by the five-man drafting committees. Few showed the capacity to distinguish between general principles and national needs, and issues of local maladministration.[23]

Members of the clerical estate were enabled to exercise some influence behind the scenes, by contributing to the drafting of the town nakazy. Some of these nakazy simply included demands of interest to the clergy ; in other cases the nakazy were actually signed by clerics. In Uglich, the very first demand in the nakaz came from the white clergy, and the nakaz was signed by at least 22 priests, deacons and subdeacons. The town deputy of Uglich was a chancery servant in the religious administration, who was very active in the proceedings of the Legislative Commission, and can almost be regarded as a supplementary deputy of the Church.[24]

The haphazard nature of the elections in the towns confirms the impression already produced by the elections of noble deputies in the districts, that the government had no very precise idea of the number of deputies which these two social groups would send to the commission. The irregularities in the elections, the failure to decide in advance which units (*slobody, pristani, posady*) were to be allowed to send deputies, the permission not to send any deputies at all if the town was too small or too poor, the acceptance of a number of deputies for a town, which theoretically was only supposed to elect one deputy and finally the fact that towns could elect a deputy who was a noble,[25] all go to show that the social balance of the whole assembly was thought of in very general terms. In the same way, it is unlikely that the government had a very precise idea of the number of deputies who would be elected by the remaining Russian groups, the state peasants, the odnodvortsy and other free militia groups.

The electoral procedure in the case of the peasants involved three stages. They were not invited to draft nakazy for their deputies, but *chelobit'ye* (petitions) – a word of course much more familiar to them – nor was it mentioned in the relevant section of the manifesto that deputies were being summoned to draft a code of laws. In their case the procedure was as follows : the manifesto was to be read on three consecutive Sundays in the churches of every village or settlement, and a day was to be set aside thereafter for the election of a district elector in each village or settlement. All those who owned a house and land in the settlement were entitled to vote. The village electors then handed the district elector a written statement of their 'needs and requirements'. On an appointed day, the various district electors chose a provincial elector who took part in the selection of the deputy for the province, and provided him with a full power to act on their behalf, and with 'their humble petitions and representations' on their needs and requirements, as well as the petitions prepared at village and district level. In the case of the odnodvortsy and the peasants no provision was made for committees to be established to draft instructions or nakazy ; the deputies were simply supplied with the uncoordinated petitions of villages, districts and provinces, and this may account for the extremely large number of peasant petitions which were submitted to the Legislative Commission, over a thousand, many of which still remain unpublished.[26]

The peasants were in any case even less able than the nobles and the townsmen to formulate their grievances in abstract terms, and they limited themselves to recounting particular local burdens and problems. In this respect their petitions are an invaluable source for local social history, though one must bear in mind that they tended to emphasize the evils of their situation. Almost entirely illiterate, they were probably helped by the village priest, or some sympathetic chancery clerk, to put their demands in writing. They were also very vulnerable to local pressure by the nobility or government officials and it was hard for them to be frank in their complaints against the local administration if their petitions were actually drawn up in these same offices. It is a tribute to the toughness of the Russian peasant that the various groups of state peasants elected mainly peasants to represent them – when the assembly was finally dispersed in 1768, only one peasant mandate had been transferred to a noble. The odnodvortsy, when the Commission was dispersed, had three noble deputies. Among peasant deputies elected there were several 'assigned' peasants, though no 'possessional' peasants (who were 'represented' by the Colleges of Mines and Manufacturers respectively and thus were not entitled to take part in the elections).

Until 1761 the areas of the Russian empire living under their own laws, i.e. the Baltic Provinces, Little Russia, and the non-Russian tribes, had not been invited to send deputies to Legislative Commissions.[27] However, Catherine believed in unifying the empire under the same institutions and the present opportunity of welding the outlying provinces together seemed too good to be missed. Thus, in the manifesto as published it was made clear that all parts of the empire were expected to participate in elections.

Unfortunately the electoral procedure was designed with even less regard for the political attitudes and the social complexity of the non-Russian provinces than for those of the Great Russian provinces. The Livonians and Estonians were divided over two issues : whether to participate in elections to the Legislative Assembly at all, thus recognizing the right of an all-Russian assembly to draft laws for them ; and who was to be regarded as a noble and thus entitled to vote. The first question did not lead to serious problems. Many of those who were dissatisfied with the existing system of local privileges (some nobles, some of the town population) were willing to make use of the opportunity to press their views, and with the backing of the Russian-appointed governor-general, there was no way to prevent the elections. The social problem proved – as so often – more difficult to solve than the political one.

The Baltic nobles, whose names were recorded in the register or *matricula,* attesting the antiquity of their families, refused to recognize the right of the non-noble landowners to take part in the elections, on the grounds that though landowners (and indeed serf-owners), they were not real nobles. In Estonia the nobles entrusted the post of marshal of the nobility to the head of the noble order, F.J. von Ulrich, without any elections ; he in turn nominated four candidates from each *kreis* in Estonia ; the deputies were elected from among these nominated candidates, and included Ulrich himself, on condition that his brother should then act as marshal of the nobility. The Russian Senate promptly quashed the elections and ordered them to be held afresh. The governor, Prince Peter of Holstein-Beck, proceeded to justify himself on the grounds of local custom, and received a stern rebuke. He was told that the manifesto made the procedure perfectly clear, and since it had been translated into many foreign languages, he could not claim not to have understood it ; he was also informed that he should not have allowed the Estonian nobles to act according to their private customs when the general law was clearly laid down, nor should he put forward frivolous objections such as the lack of a house large enough for the Estonian nobility to assemble in – the nobility of St Petersburg and Moscow had regarded it as an honour to lend their houses for elections.[28]

The pretensions of the Baltic nobles met indeed with little sympathy from

Catherine, who did not accept their claim that they, not she, decided who was a noble. 'Russia has no noble register (*matricula*) and the same electoral law applies everywhere.'[29] Nevertheless it proved impossible to get the nobles and the non-noble landowners to agree either on a deputy or on his instructions. It would of course have been extremely awkward for the deputy to produce contradictory instructions, and in the end the empress, observing that the four districts of Livonia had in fact elected only two deputies, proposed that the non-nobles should send and instruct a deputy of their own.[30]

The Livonian towns showed no enthusiasm for electing a deputy, and only four were eventually represented in the Assembly, Riga, Dorpat, Wenden and Pernau. The Livonian peasants sent no deputies since they were regarded as serfs. The survival of some free peasants of Swedish descent, mainly on the islands, was overlooked, but four deputies of the free peasantry in Russian Finland (Vyborg guberniya) sat in the meeting for nearly nine months before their presence was queried. Since under Swedish law they had been free, Catherine endorsed their right to attend the Commission.[31] In the event, Livonia was represented by six nobles and four town deputies.

In Little Russia the nobility elected a deputy for each polk or *povet* (the equivalent of a district). The towns elected a deputy, as in Russia proper, and the Cossacks and free peasants elected a deputy for each polk. Old Believers in the hetmanate were allowed one deputy. The semi-free peasants (*pospolity*) of Yekaterininskaya province and of Yelizavetgrad province succeeded also in electing deputies. The elections caused the governor-general, P.A. Rumyantsev, much trouble. Basically the same attitudes were reflected in Little Russia as in Livonia, namely doubt as to whether to take part in an all-Russian assembly at all; disputes about the social standing of the various individual electors; and conflicts over the content of the instructions. Rumyantsev launched the election in Little Russia with a circular, inviting the Ukrainians to remember that the laws of a nation must be devised in the interests of all its parts – a clear hint against putting forward any demands for autonomy,[32] which failed of its purpose, judging by his subsequent reports. 'Many here have acquired a taste for independence to the point that every state law or decree is regarded by them as an interference with their laws and privileges; they all exclaim: "why should we go there?"' 'Others', added Rumyantsev in a later report, 'are so blinded by the love of their little country that they think they – as wise and learned men – have been summoned only to advise on drafting laws for the Great Russians. . . .'[33]

The call to elect deputies inevitably revived the discussion of Little Russia's ancient liberties, and the demand to restore the hetmanate. In Nezhin and Baturin a spokesman of extreme views was chosen in a somewhat disorderly election, which Rumyantsev was unable to contest. He appealed to the Senate which quashed the election and ordered the arrest and trial in civil and military courts of those who had disregarded the electoral instructions and disobeyed the governor-general.[34]

Other elements in the population might share the desire for Little Russian autonomy, yet resent the pretensions of the gentry. These social tensions were reflected in the elections which took place in the towns, since, unlike in Russia proper, many members of the gentry lived and owned land in the townships, and were thus entitled to take part in the election of a town deputy. But the gentry despised the townspeople, and often refused to sit with them or take part in elections with them. It proved almost impossible to conciliate the interests of Cossack officers, administrators with some kind of military rank, merchants and townspeople. On the other hand, nowhere was the status of noble less clearly defined than in Little Russia. Not one assembly of the gentry, wrote Rumyantsev to Catherine, took place without recriminations and accusations that even the most noble was descended from some tradesman or Jew, and that many had changed their names. Indeed the problem, as Rumyantsev put it, was that the Ukrainians had rendered the word 'gentry' meaningless : 'Any runaway peasant who marries a Cossack girl' they accept as a noble, 'and that same noble or Cossack, sometimes by a court order, and sometimes without, and more often than not illegally they turn into a peasant. . . .'[35] Sometimes the nobles boycotted the elections, as in Priluki ; sometimes, as in Pogara, they left things to the townspeople, and only when the instruction had been drawn up and the deputy elected, did they complain to the governor-general that the elected town chief had ignored the gentry and allowed ignorant townspeople to draft the instruction. In Lubny, the gentry prevented the townspeople from incorporating criticisms of the Cossack officers and officials into their instruction. In Starodub one deputy was elected but he was provided with two instructions, one from the gentry, and one from the merchants. The deputy for Nezhin was supplied with no fewer than four instructions : one from the gentry, one from the townspeople, one from the Great Russian merchants and one from the Greek merchant community or brotherhood. All in all, the Little Russian gentry took the opportunity to put forward their claims to autonomy, and their grievances against Russia, and Rumyantsev, in turn, acted in a high-handed manner in suppressing nakazy he disapproved of or quashing unsuitable elections.[36]

In accordance with the electoral manifesto, Rumyantsev arranged for each Ukrainian polk to elect a Cossack deputy, and these elections seem to have caused little trouble. The Zaporozhian Sech was allowed two deputies on the grounds that it was much more numerous than any other polk. However, the elections in Kremenchug and Vlasovka, though perhaps untypical, reflect some of the problems in the sphere of the common people among the Cossacks. Probably because the commander of the polk did not allow the rank and file to draw up their own instruction for a deputy, the latter declared that they would elect their own deputy. Adjourning to the steppe, they proceeded to elect a certain Denisov and gave him an instruction. Denisov duly appeared in Moscow, took his seat in the Commission and even took part in discussions. He wrote back to his electors, inviting them to inform him of local needs, and declared that he was in her Imperial Majesty's good graces, in spite of the fact that some evil-minded people had tried to prevent him from being admitted as a deputy. But the local governor caught up with him, and demanded his arrest on the grounds that he was elected 'incognito, without the knowledge of the administration', and that his letters were stirring up trouble locally. Denisov was arrested, and sent back under escort, but escaped on the road, and disappears from recorded history.[37]

There was also trouble at the elections among the free settled peasants (*voyskovyye obyvateli*) in Slobodska Ukraine. Prokop Guk, who had been elected peasant deputy, took his duties so seriously that he ordered the local land surveyor to stop his activities until he returned from the Commission in Moscow. He collected some sixty rubles from twenty-two local villages on the promise that he would exercise pressure on the survey office in favour of the peasants. Denounced, probably by a local landowner, who feared that Guk might 'spread some peasant poison even in the Commission', he was arrested, deprived of his status (and of the money), and whipped, and new elections were ordered.[38]

The clergy do not seem to have influenced the instructions of the towns as in some Russian elections. On the other hand, when the Synod drafted its instruction for its deputy to the Commission, the Little Russian hierarchy was consulted, and used the opportunity, notably in Kiev, to submit a number of nakazy pressing for the continuance of the Church's property rights and its spiritual and judicial autonomy. Some of these demands were appended to the instruction from the Synod.[39]

The admission of deputies from the non-Russian tribes to the assembly was a tribute to the enlightenment of the empress. Most of the deputies elected (if elections took place at all) did not know Russian ; many of them belonged to the ruling groups of Tartars, Bashkirs, Cheremiss, Chuvash, etc. The governor of Siberia described the situation to his brother, the chief of police, Nicolas Chicherin :

Two princelings have turned up here, who received their titles from Godunov – Obdorsky and Kunovatsky, from Berezovo, who are wandering to the Artic Ocean, along the Ob'. They have come because of the manifesto, but they bring no instruction, no reference to needs, nothing. They only asked me, does the empress go about in the streets, and when I replied that she was graciously pleased to do so, they fell on their knees, and begged me to send them on. . . . You will find my two princelings are like little wild beasts, strange in their looks and clothing. . . .

The special position of the deputies from the non-Russian tribes was fully recognized in Moscow. The government appointed three 'guardians' to look after them, namely Prince S. Vyazemsky, A.V. Olsuf'yev, and G.A. Potemkin, who thus began to show his interest in the exotic peoples of Russia. The procurator general ordered German and Russian – and Samoyed – garments to be prepared for them at state expense.[40]

The assembly which finally resulted from this somewhat haphazard electoral procedure was composed of: 29 deputies of government institutions ; 142 deputies of the district assemblies of the nobility ; 22 deputies from the Ukrainian gentry and officer class ; 42 deputies of the odnodvortsy ; 29 deputies of the different groups of free peasantry ; 44 deputies of the Cossacks (Siberian, Yaik, Volga and Don) ; 209 deputies from the towns ; 54 deputies from the non-Russian tribes. The social composition of the assembly, regardless of whom the deputy represented was : nobles, 205 ; merchants, 167 ; odnodvortsy, 42 ; peasants, 29 ; Cossacks, 44 ; industrialists, 7 ; chancery clerks, etc., 19 ; tribesmen, 54.[41]

The elections undoubtedly served to arouse the lethargic Russian countryside. It was the first attempt in imperial Russia to associate the people more widely with the government. Some, like the sardonic and sceptical Andrey Bolotov, believed that there would be a lot of noise and a lot of expense, with nothing to show for it. Others threw themselves into the fray with enthusiasm, celebrating the occasion with salvoes of gunfire, banquets and fireworks. While the elections were taking place in spring 1767, Catherine undertook a journey of inspection in the Volga provinces. In many places, the local nobility, already assembled in the towns for the elections, was presented to the empress, and organized suitable festivities. Catherine visited Tver', Yaroslavl', Nizhiny Novgorod and Kazan'. 'Me voilà en Asie,' she wrote gleefully to Voltaire on 29 May 1767. 'Il y a dans cette ville vingt peuples divers, qui ne se ressemblent point du tout. Il faut pourtant leur faire un habit qui leur soit propre à tous. Ils peuvent se bien trouver des principes généraux, mais les détails ?' Catherine was now fully aware of the tremendous variety of her empire. She set about establishing 'les principes généraux' in the 'Great Instruction' she wrote for the Legislative Commission.[42]

10

The Great Instruction

In the manifesto of 14 December 1766, calling the Legislative Commission into existence, Catherine had referred to her intention of providing an 'Instruction' or *Nakaz* for the deputies.[1] The first part of this document was published in Moscow on 30 July 1767, and is one of the most remarkable political treatises ever compiled and published by a reigning sovereign in modern times. It was composed of 526 articles, grouped into twenty chapters. Two further chapters, dealing with the police and the economy, were published separately in the course of 1768. Translations of the Russian text into French and German appeared almost at once in St Petersburg, and a semi-official English translation was published in London in 1768.[2]

Catherine has left no known record of what induced her to write her Instruction, on which she started work around January 1765,[3] nor is it known whether she thought of the Instruction and the Legislative Commission together from the first or joined the two ideas at a later stage. According to her own account written in the 1790s, 'for two years I read and wrote, and for eighteen months I consulted no one, but was guided solely by my heart and reason . . .'[4] Much confusion was caused at the time because the Nakaz and the Legislative Commission were often taken to be a code of laws and a parliament – a confusion which continues to this day. But the Nakaz was not a code of laws but a compendium of the general principles on which good government and an orderly society should be based, culled from the best eighteenth-century authors.

When she forwarded a copy of the German translation to Frederick II of Prussia, Catherine explained two of her difficulties :

Je dois prévenir V.M. de deux choses,' she wrote, 'l'une qu'elle trouvera differens endroits qui lui paraitront peut être singuliers, je la prie de se souvenir que j'ai du m'accomoder souvent au présent et cependant ne point fermer le chemin à un avenir plus favorable. L'autre que la langue russe est beaucoup plus energique et plus riche en expressions que l'allemand et en inversions que le français . . . on a souvent été obligé de paraphraser ce qui avait été dit avec un seul mot en russe. . . .[5]

Catherine touches here on two of the issues which have bedevilled the analysis of the political content of her Nakaz and have led to the blanket charge that she perverted the theories of Montesquieu in order to conceal the iron hand of absolutism under the velvet glove of monarchy.[6] But her letter to Frederick suggests that she was well aware of the discrepancy between Russia as she knew it and an ideal polity. This did not stop her from projecting before the élite of Russian society the image of what Russia ought to be. Her remarks on the Russian language spring however from patriotism rather than from experience of expressing political concepts in Russian. However rich the language in ordinary speech, Russian had not yet evolved a precise terminology for the language of politics. One has only to compare the various translations of Catherine's Instruction into other languages, and note the difficulties faced by translators in finding exact equivalents. To take but two examples: the word *samoderzhavnyy,* for which 'autocratic' is used in the twentieth century, was the Russian word for 'sovereign' in the eighteenth century. Similarly the word *gosudarstvennyy,* 'of the state', was often chosen to translate the French *politique,* and was evidently used in the sense of that which pertains to the sphere of government in general, and not specifically as in modern Russian, in the sense of that which pertains to the state.

These semantic difficulties acquire particular importance for two reasons: first, the interpretation of Catherine's political 'doctrine' has hinged a great deal on her use of words ; secondly, because she borrowed so widely from other writers it is essential to understand precisely what she thought she was borrowing. A careful comparison reveals that out of a total of 526 articles in Part I of the Instruction, 294 were taken from Montesquieu's *Esprit des Lois,* and 108 from Cesare Beccaria's *Delle delitte e delle pene* ; and that Catherine drew also on the *Encyclopédie,* on the *Institutions Politiques* of Baron Bielfeld, on the works of J.H. Gottlob von Justi in the chapter dealing with cities, townsmen and trade, and on F. Quesnay's *Le Droit Naturel* in dealing with the economy.[7]

The speed with which Catherine seized on ideas relevant to her purpose was striking. The French translation of Beccaria's book appeared only in 1765. Catherine rejected the theory of society based on the social contract, on which Beccaria founded his views on penal law ; but many of the Italian jurist's formulations could be accepted by those who were revolted by the savagery of contemporary punishments and the inhuman use of torture. Catherine was attracted by the humanitarian and utilitarian aspects of Beccaria's thought and took steps to invite him to Russia, but he preferred to stay in Milan.[8] Similarly, Bielfeld sent her the first volume of his *Institutions Politiques* which appeared in 1762 and on which she based her Chapter XXI on the police. She wrote to thank him in April 1765, and doubtless on her initiative a Russian translation of the first volume of his work appeared in 1768.[9] She was also one of the first to make use of the ideas of Adam Smith. One of Smith's Russian disciples, S.E. Desnitsky, submitted memoranda on the form of government and on the organization of public finance to the empress in 1768. In Desnitsky's text there were clear traces of the influence of Adam Smith. Catherine in turn, in Chapter XXII of her Instruction published in April 1768, incorporated almost *verbatim* some of Desnitsky's propositons, based on the lectures of Adam Smith.[10]

The first three chapters of Catherine's Nakaz constitute an 'inquiry into the natural situation' of Russia, in accordance with the doctrine of Montesquieu who is directly quoted in article 5 : 'For those Laws have the greatest Conformity with Nature whose particular Regulations are best adapted to the situation and circumstances of the People for Whom they are instituted.'[11] Chapter I starts with a clarion call : 'Russia is an European state' (article 6), thus sweeping away the traditional Russian Orthodox isolation and laying the ground-work for Catherine's further propositon, that Russia is a monarchy in Montesquieu's sense of the word.[12]

The ensuing chapters are both an attempt to define the Russian government as Catherine believed it to be, and as she thought it ought to be if it were to be a legitimate monarchy, i.e. a monarchy ruled according to fundamental laws – hence the many inconsistencies. The first hurdle passed by Catherine was Montesquieu's statement that in the nature of things a large empire must be a despotism.[13] Anxious to evade this appellation, Catherine altered Montesquieu's formula, and in article 10 proclaimed that 'the extent of the Dominion requires an absolute power to be vested in the person who rules over it'. Thereafter, and throughout the Instruction, Catherine applies to her vast empire those definitions which Montesquieu had applied to monarchies. She assumes the existence of fundamental laws, though Russia lacked the one which Montesquieu considered to be most fundamental of all, namely a law of succession. An undated and unfinished draft illustrates the specific difficulties for Catherine of drawing up a law of succession which should at the same time legalize her own seizure of the throne. 'The first principal law of this sovereign realm', she wrote, 'is the stability of the throne and a fixed succession.' Further, she jotted down : 'the imperial throne can never be vacant' ; 'on my death my son will inherit' ; 'after my son, if his son is already 21 years old, then this eldest son will inherit ; if he is less than 21 years old, then his mother should be concerned, and let her reign for the rest of her life ; for a minority of the sovereign would be dangerous for the empire ; if there is no male heir then let the eldest daughter. . . .'[14] The suggestion that in a minority the mother of the emperor should reign for the rest of her life clearly referred to Catherine's own case.

A true monarchy, according to Montesquieu, required 'intermediary and dependent' bodies (i.e. estates or corporations with legal prerogatives) through which power flowed. The most natural intermediary body was the nobility.[15] For Catherine however, the intermediary powers, or channels through which power flowed, were courts or tribunals[16] set up by the government, not social estates such as the nobility, the towns or the clergy with all the weight of their traditional rights and hereditary prerogatives. Catherine undoubtedly deviated here from Montesquieu's analysis by locating the restraints on power not in social institutions but in legal institutions, which were at the same time the 'depository of the laws'. The reluctance to accept Montesquieu's view of the role of the nobility may reflect Catherine's own lack of sympathy for any increase of their power as an organized corporate group *vis-à-vis* the Crown. But it may also reflect her acceptance of Russian reality : the total dependence of the Russian nobility on the Crown and the lack of any institutions by which they could bring any corporate pressure to bear on the ruler. On the other hand when Catherine argued that the depository of the laws should be a tribunal like the Russian Senate, she is correctly interpreting Montesquieu, since the French *parlements,* of which he is evidently thinking, (though he does not mention them by name) are just such royal courts of law.[17] The Russian Senate was the only institution which since the days of Peter I had maintained a certain continuity and consistency in the coordination of legislation. There was however no real parallel between the well established 'droit de remontrance' of the French *parlements,* their right to postpone the registration of a royal edict, and the very modest right 'to make representations' of the Russian Senate. The former was a public act, which could only be overruled by another public act, a royal *lit de justice ;* the latter was a private communication from his advisers to the tsar.

Nevertheless the definition of the right to make representations as given by Catherine in article 21 introduced into Russia a number of new and perhaps startling conceptions. In the first place the right to make representations against a new law on the grounds that it is 'unconstitutional', or 'contraire au Code des Lois'[18] implies that there is such a thing as a constitution or a code binding on the sovereign. The article goes on to state that such laws, which permit 'representations' also on the grounds that new edicts are obscure and impracticable 'constitute the firm and immoveable basis of every state'. Catherine reverts to the subject of fundamental laws in Chapter XIX, in which she proposes to divide law (*le droit*) into three kinds : Laws (*Lois, zakony*) ; 'momentary regulations which depend upon circumstances' (*reglemens, uchrezhdeniya vremenyya*) and 'injunctions' (*ordonnances, ukazy*). The 'Laws' should comprise 'fundamental institutions' (*dispositions, ustanovleniya*) 'which ought never to be altered and the number of such cannot be great'.[19] Here therefore Catherine again endorsed the theory that absolute power should be exercised within certain fixed and established limits. The fundamental laws, though few in number, are permanent, exist independently of the reigning sovereign, and provide the framework within which he must operate. Power is limited, if only by the existence of laws which the sovereign regards as binding. The area within which the arbitrary will of the ruler can act is limited by distinguishing between the ruler and the state. This concept was not entirely new in Russia, but it had never before been clothed in the dignified language of the *philosophes* nor publicly proclaimed from the throne.

Nowhere in the Nakaz does Catherine discuss the process of legislation, representative assemblies or the theory of the separation of powers. The separation of powers was not in any case relevant. Montesquieu discusses it primarily in the context of the particular type of monarchy which has liberty as its main object, namely the English monarchy. But he recognizes that in other monarchies, 'les trois pouvoirs n'y sont point distribués et fondés sur le modèle de la constitution dont nous avons parlé. Ils ont chacun une distribution particulière selon laquelle ils approchent plus ou moins de la liberté politique ; et s'ils n'en approchaient pas, la monarchie dégènererait en despotisme.'[20] Catherine paid tribute to the principle of the separation of powers at least by reserving to the sovereign the sole right to issue penal legislation (article 148), but arguing in article 149 that he 'ought to abstain from sitting as *Judge himself*. . . . Therefore he ought to appoint *other Persons,* who should judge according to the laws.'[21] The judges, continues Catherine, should have no right to interpret the laws – a right which is reserved to the legislator – but should only apply them, and she puts forward a principle novel to Russia, yet of fundamental importance ; 'Nothing is so dangerous as this general Axiom : *the Spirit of the Law ought to be considered and not the letter.* This can mean nothing else but to break down the Fence, which opposes the Torrent of popular Opinions' (article 153).[22] If judges could interpret the law 'we should see the *same* Crimes punished *differently* at *different* Times by the *very same* court . . . if they will not listen to the invariable Voice of the fixed established Laws, but follow the deceitful Inconstancy of their own arbitrary Interpretations'. In Catherine's view, the harm done by sticking to the letter of the law was less than the flood of abuses which following the spirit could give rise to. In the essentially unlegalistic climate of Russia, where justice was venal and arbitrary, her championship of the letter of the law was unusual, and it is doubtful if it met with much understanding.

In the chapters on crime and punishment, Catherine put forward views never proclaimed before from the throne in Russia – or indeed anywhere else. Basing herself on Montesquieu and Beccaria, she declared that no citizen should be punished until he had been proved guilty in a court of law ; this implied a distinction between taking a man into custody during investigation, and imprisonment as a punishment. It also implied the condemnation of torture : 'for this Reason, *That the Innocent ought not to be tortured ;* and in the Eyes of the Law, every Person is Innocent whose crime is not yet *proved*' (article 194). For purely humanitarian reasons, Catherine condemned punishments which maimed the human body and proclaimed that 'The Usage of torture is contrary to all the Dictates of Nature and Reason ; even Mankind itself cries out against it, and demands loudly the total Abolition of it' (article 123). In general Catherine took her stand in favour of correction and prevention, rather than retribution ; the punishment ought to be designed to fit the crime. She even argued against capital punishment in times of peace and stability. Crimes against property, she stated, should be punished by deprivation of property, but she was realistic enough to recognize that those guilty of crimes against property were usually those who had none.[23]

Following Montesquieu, rather than Beccaria,[24] Catherine admitted that in 'Governments where a Distinction of Persons is introduced, there must likewise be a personal Pre-eminence, established by the Laws', namely 'to be judged before one of the Courts of Judicature preferably to any other' (article 110) ; and paraphrasing Montesquieu, she adds in article 127, 'It is likewise just that some of the Judges should be of the same Rank of Citizenship as the Defendant : that is his Equals ; that he might not think himself fallen into the Hands of such People as would violently overrule the Affair to his Prejudice. . . .'[25]

Indeed Catherine accepts as a matter of course the division of society into orders or estates, and deals separately with each one. Nobility is defined as an 'Appellation of *Honour*' (articles 360–68) and can be acquired both by military and by civil virtue ; it is not regarded as 'innate'. Admission to the middling rank of people was conditioned by *'Good Manners and Incitements to Industry'*, and was open to those who were 'neither *Gentlemen* nor *Husbandmen*' but were employed in crafts and commerce or had been educated in schools and colleges, and 'also the Children of People belonging to the Law'. They enjoyed 'a State of Liberty without intermixing either with the *Nobility* or the *Husbandmen*', (articles 377–82). In the lower ranks, occupation determined residence : 'The Husbandmen who cultivate the Lands to produce Food for People in every Rank of Life, live in Country Towns and Villages. That is their lot' (article 358) ; 'The Burghers who employ their Time in mechanick Trades, Commerce, Arts and Sciences, *inhabit the cities'* (article 359). The privileges of citizens extended to those who owned a house and property in the city, and paid the appropriate taxes. Those who did not 'give this *common Pledge'* were not entitled to the privileges of citizens (articles 394–5).

In Chapter XI of the Nakaz Catherine deals with the sensitive problems of serfdom and slavery. The issue is introduced by the general statement that 'a Society of Citizens . . . requires a certain fixed order : there ought to be *some to govern*, and *others to obey'*, which leads to the conclusion, 'and this is the Origin of every Kind of Subjection'. Yet governments should 'shun all Occasions of Reducing People to a State of Slavery' and should only do so in the interests of the state and on rare occasions (articles 250–3). Two more articles refer indirectly to serfdom : 'A great Number of Slaves ought not to be infranchised all at once nor by a general Law' ; and 'a Law may be productive of public Benefit which gives some *private* Property to a Slave' (articles 260–1).[26]

In Chapter V, Catherine puts forward her views on equality and liberty : 'The Equality of the Citizens consists in this : that they should all be subject to the same Laws' ; and this equality needed to be supported by institutions which would prevent the wealthy from abusing their functions as magistrates for their own ends (article 34). There is no suggestion of social equality, and indeed her statement does not necessarily condemn inequality of punishment for the same offence, since the law can specify both the offence and the punishment, graded according to status. The definitions of political liberty are lifted straight from

Montesquieu : 'La liberté est le droit de faire tout ce que les lois permettent. . . .'[27] Liberty is therefore not a natural right, but a number of rights conferred by society, by means of laws, which however should be adapted to the 'general Sense of a nation', and ought not to forbid anything unless it 'may be prejudicial either to every individual in particular, or to the whole Community in general' (articles 57 and 41).

Among other startling innovations in the context of Russian society Catherine argued the need to prepare public opinion for legislation (article 58), and recognized the existence of spheres of human activity which did not 'come under the Cognizance of the Laws' (article 63), a point of some importance in Russia where few things were 'indifferent in their Nature' and unregulated by the state. Her attitude to censorship was liberal and she recommended religious toleration and caution in dealing with witchcraft and heresy (articles 493–7).[28]

Finally, in articles 501–22, Catherine poses the problem : How can we know when a state approaches its fall and final dissolution ? 'The Corruption of every Government generally begins by the *Corruption of its fundamental Principles,*' states article 503, and Catherine goes on to develop the view that governments decay when the idea of the state 'ingrafted in the Minds of the People by the Law, which may be termed the Equality prescribed *by the Laws',* is undermined ; and even more when the idea of equality takes root in the people and grows 'to *such* a Pitch of Licentiousness, that every one *aims* at being *equal* to him, who is ordained by the Laws *to rule over him'*. Such a situation leads to government by fear, and the predominance of private over public interest. The value of these articles in the Russian context is that they put before the readers the view that governments are not static but in a continuous state of flux ; and that the art of statecraft consists in constant delicate adjustments of the equilibrium between government and society.

Some six months later, in February 1768, Catherine issued as a supplement to the Instruction a further Chapter XXI, 'Of good order, otherwise termed the police'. As Catherine explains (articles 529–30), everything appertains to the police 'which conduces to the Preservation of good Order in a Society'. The police, in this sense, was not merely the body concerned with security and the prevention and detection of crime, as in the modern sense ; it was also charged with a multiplicity of functions which are today divided among different public bodies. It carried out its functions by compelling the public 'to live in the Society, according to the *established Rules*' (article 534). It was a corrective, rather than a punitive institution, and since 'the Objects of the police are *Affairs* which may happen at every hour, and are generally Matters of little Consequence . . . therefore judicial Formalities are here quite unnecessary' (article 535). However, 'where the Limits of the Power of the *Police* end, there the Power of *civil* Jurisdiction begins' (article 562). Thus the police could arrest a criminal, 'but *it* recommends the *decision* of the Business to that Court of Judicature which his Case properly belongs to' (article 563). The police ought not 'to inflict severe Punishments on the Delinquents . . . its Punishments should consist in *Corrections, Amercements*', and such penalties 'as bring shame and infamy' (article 564).

A final chapter, no. XXII of the Instruction, was published in April 1768 and dealt with the management of public finance and taxation. Broad principles of humanity were proclaimed in article 573, which stated that whether he be a sovereign or a ploughman, a merchant or an idler, yet 'every *individual* of *all these* is still but a Man', with the same necessities. Catherine then listed the needs of the state, ranging from defence, public order, public utility (cities, roads, schools, hospitals, etc.) and finally the 'Affluence and Magnificence' which should surround the throne . . . 'from which flow Rewards, Encouragements and Bounties'. She then turned to revenue, and in the first place to taxation, analysing the objects on which governments consider that taxes could be laid, and putting before the Commission for discussion a number of questions on the reasons why revenue from taxation did not come up to expectations. She discussed the economy of the state, considering its greatest source of wealth to be first population, then agriculture, which was the foundation of commerce. Further articles discussed different forms of wealth, and the chapter ended on the optimistic note 'that the *Sum total* of the Expenses might not, if possible, *exceed* the *revenue*' (article 653) and 'that the Accounts should always be regularly kept . . .' (article 654).

The work involved in compiling the Instruction was considerable, and was undertaken by Catherine herself with the assistance mainly of one of her secretaries, G. Kozitsky. All the materials used in the Instruction were chosen by her and written out in her own hand, and Kozitsky's task was to translate the results of her labours into Russian and other languages. From June 1765 onwards, she began to show portions of the Instruction to selected confidants.[29] Grigory Orlov 'rated my work very high', wrote Catherine later, but Count Nikita Panin exclaimed: 'Ce sont des maximes à renverser des murailles.'[30] At some stage Catherine ordered the procurator general to read the draft Nakaz to the Senate, since changes could still be made.[31] She herself 'summoned several persons of different ways of thinking . . . to hear the Instruction. Every part of it evoked division. I let them erase what they pleased and they struck out more than half of what I had written.'[32]

A comparison of the various drafts shows that Catherine, whether because she changed her mind, or because of the criticism of others, cut down very considerably the analysis *à la* Montesquieu of the Russian government (including the problem of succession), and expanded the sections dealing with jurisprudence and penal law, probably under the immediate impact of her reading of Beccaria. The chapter which suffered the severest cuts was the one ultimately published as Chapter XI, dealing with serfdom. Following Montesquieu closely, Catherine had, in her unpublished drafts, distinguished between bondage to the soil and personal bondage. It was a great abuse, when bondage was both personal and to the soil. Whatever the type of slavery, she had added, the civil laws must prevent the abuse of slavery, at the same time as they guarded against the dangers arising therefrom. All people should be granted by law food and clothing corresponding to their estate, and the laws should establish that serfs should be cared for in illness and old age. One of the omitted articles dealt with the means of 'creating new citizens', i.e. reducing the number of serfs. Copying almost word for word from Montesquieu,[33] Catherine proposed that serfs should be allowed to accumulate sufficient property to buy their freedom, or that servitude should be limited to six years. She introduced a modification of her own however in the middle of Montesquieu's paragraph: 'One can also establish that once a serf has been freed, he should never be enserfed again. The state would also benefit from this since it would lead to a gradual increase in the number of *meshchane* [common people] in small towns.'[34] The civil laws should also, she suggested, define precisely how much the serfs should pay for their enfranchisement. As regards the rights of landowners Catherine, again following her master, stated that landowners in the exercise of their punitive powers should act as judges, not as owners, and she refers to the practice in Russian Finland, where the peasants elected a number among themselves to form a court, by which the severity of landowners or their stewards could be mitigated. In a different draft of this controversial chapter Catherine also quoted with approval the recent Livonian legislation which, as she understood it, enabled the peasants to acquire moveable goods; fixed the norms of money or labour dues and regulated the landowners' powers of punisment.[35]

It is evident that these propositions represented Catherine's personal views on serfdom, since she would not otherwise have troubled to copy them out and include them in her draft. Unfortunately almost nothing is known of the pressures brought to bear on her to tone down her remarks on this sensitive subject. She may have met with opposition in her own immediate circle; or she may have been warned of the danger of alienating the nobility by putting forward such propositions in public. Some of the surviving comments on the draft Nakaz indicate the climate of opinion Catherine was attempting to mould.

The dramatist A.P. Sumarokov probably reflects the attitude of the conservative nobility. He objected to the special privileges accorded to deputies to the Legislative Commission, such as immunity for life from corporal punishment. Catherine commented in the margin: 'this work requires much encouragement of the spirit.' He also objected to the principle of majority voting. 'The majority of votes does not confirm the truth. Truth is confirmed by profound reason and impartiality.' To this Catherine commented: 'The majority does not confirm the truth, but only indicates the wishes of the majority.' Though Sumarokov agreed that in principle freedom was better than unfreedom, for both Crown and people, yet anarchy (*svoyevol'stvo*) was worse than unfreedom. In his comments on Chapter XI of the Instruction Sumarokov objected to the suggestion that the law should prescribe the supply of food and clothing to serfs, since it was in any case already provided. Similarly, he objected to any judicial interposition between lords and serfs, and roundly opposed the emancipation of the peasantry (though he did agree that human beings should not be sold like cattle). If the peasantry were freed the poor nobles would have neither cook, nor coachman, nor lackey. They would make endless concessions in order to keep their labour ; their trained cooks and hairdressers would run away to better paid jobs, and there would be constant disturbances requiring military force to put them down. Whereas at present landowners lived quietly on their estates, wrote Sumarokov, 'and have their throats cut from time to time,' commented Catherine. It was known that lords loved their serfs and were loved by them, Sumarokov concluded, and in any case the common people had not as yet any noble feelings, 'and cannot have in present circumstances', added Catherine.[36]

Both the nature of the Legislative Commission as an institution and the political content of Catherine's Instruction have given rise to considerable argument among historians, since the kind of promises implied in the former inevitably affect their judgment of Catherine's performance throughout her reign. The interpretation of the most influential scholar of this period, Georg Sacke, a disciple of M.N. Pokrovsky, has found an echo in Soviet and non-Soviet historiography, and must be briefly summarized here. In Sacke's view, Catherine felt her position to be extremely unstable in the early 1760s, and she was particularly perturbed by the alleged efforts of an 'aristocratic party', led by Nikita Panin, to limit her absolute power. She had successfully countered Panin's first effort in this direction, his plan for an imperial council. But feeling the need to strengthen her position further, she decided to overcome her distaste for a representative assembly, and to summon deputies from the various estates and social groups, in the hope of achieving two objects : the neutralization of 'aristocratic' opposition to absolutism by swamping it with a display of lower noble and urban support ; and the consolidation of her position by endowing it with an aura of legitimacy and national consent.[37] Sacke further bolsters his theory by postulating that Catherine so managed the composition of the Legislative Commission as to ensure a majority of deputies from the towns, and he emphasizes that the political tenor of the Instruction drafted by Catherine was designed to defend absolutism as the system of government in Russia. He also argues that during its existence, the activities of the Commission were stage managed (and its record doctored) in order to produce the desired result. Underlying this interpretation lies Sacke's assumption that Russian economic development had reached a stage in which an alliance between the Crown, the bourgeoisie, and the minor nobility against the aristocracy was bound to happen.

It is certainly true that Catherine was much attracted by the idea of increasing the number and the weight of the third estate in Russia – the words *'tret'yy rod'* were on every lip at the time.[38] But the trading, craft and professional groups in Russia did not yet form a homogeneous class, were numerically still only a very small proportion of the whole population, and were economically backward. To suggest that the capitalist form of production had already developed sufficiently in Russia for the state to begin consciously to act as the agent of the bourgeoisie is, even for a Marxist, to anticipate developments by more than a hundred years.

More convincing in this respect are the conclusions of another Marxist historian, namely Ya.Zutis, who portrays Catherine as choosing between two contradictory trends which had developed within the nobility. All landowners, he assumes, were interested in increasing their income ; but whereas the bulk of the conservative minor nobility could conceive of increased production only by means of more compulsory labour and more complete control over the life and the property of the peasantry, the more enlightened (and usually wealthier) nobles believed that productivity could be increased by granting more incentives to the peasantry, such as allowing them to own moveable property.[39] Zutis's thesis that there existed a group of nobles near the Court whose approach to the peasant problem was relatively more liberal than that of the run-of-the-mill nobles is to some extent borne out by Catherine's Livonian policy, and the early projects of the Orlovs and Pastor Eisen.[40] Sacke interprets Nikita Panin's exclamation on the Nakaz : 'ce sont des maximes à renverser des murailles', as expressing his horror at Catherine's outspoken defence of absolutism. It is much more likely however that they reflect Panin's fear that Catherine's ideas in the field of serfdom, and in the field of penal law and social relationships, might well lead to public disturbances in a country as unaccustomed as was Russia to such liberal views.

Even if Sacke's roundabout interpretation of Catherine's intentions must be discarded, the problem still remains : why did she call a Legislative Commission of this kind ? Again, we have very little evidence stemming from herself, and no records of discussions with her advisers. The most convincing explanation, on reflection, may be that Catherine and her supporters were well aware of the precariousness of her tenure of the throne. Some of the magnates had been alienated by her evasion of a regency ; others had supported Peter III and were not reconciled to her rule ; the ascendancy of the Orlovs and the fear that favouritism in the Elizabethan manner would revive aroused jealousy and ill-feeling. Moreover Catherine had not openly confirmed Peter III's manifesto on the freedom of the nobility, thus rendering the rank and file nobility uneasy. Even more alarming for the gentry was the gossip around the court to the effect that the empress intended to limit the authority of the serf-owners over their serfs and to regulate the extent of the latter's obligations to their owners. There was both dissatisfaction and bewilderment, penetratingly outlined in a French diplomatic analysis of 1767 :

La noblesse désire avec impatience que le souverain relâche les chaînes qui gènent sa liberté. Il [the sovereign] paroit y être résolu ; mais en accordant cette faveur à la noblesse, il voudroit adoucir en même temps l'esclavage des paysans. Car il sent que si ces deux classes de la nation ne marchent pas d'un pas égal vers la liberté, l'industrie nationale qui est concentrée dans la classe du peuple restera toujours sans activité tandis que le repos intérieur qui résulte de la soumission uniforme de tous les sujets risquerait d'être troublée. Le noble seul libre pourroit devenir trop indépendant. Le paysan esclave resteroit sans émulation et sans talens.

La noblesse a montré jusqu'ici peut-être plus d'opposition au changement projetté dans l'Etat des paysans que d'impatience pour alléger le sien. Le gouvernement sera obligé d'employer beaucoup d'adresse pour vaincre cette opposition.[41]

If this French analysis is correct, Catherine may well have thought that a public and resounding endorsement of the legitimacy of her rule would strengthen her position. An assembly composed of such conflicting social groups could, with skilful management, be harnessed to her political purposes. At the same time she would be seen to be fulfilling the pledge given in the manifesto proclaiming her *coup d'état,* of devoting herself to the improvement of the machinery of government. Moreover, by allowing some public expression of the various grievances harboured by the different social groups, she provided at the same time a safety valve for discontent, and an opportunity for the forces of society to feel that they were participating in the political life of the country. She could also try out the subject of serfdom before a wider audience. That Catherine dared to summon such an assembly reflects both her self-confidence and her fine judgment of the risks involved as against the benefits to be derived. None of Catherine's legitimate successors on the throne of the Romanovs dared to summon such an assembly again until forced to by revolution in 1906.[42]

In analysing Catherine's motives, the influence of the Enlightenment must not be underestimated. Still a novice in the art of government, and of governing Russia in particular, and as yet only lightly touched by the blight of practical experience, Catherine, as is evident from her Instruction, still held very theoretical notions on the importance of good laws. Moreover, what better way was there of demonstrating that Russia was not a 'despotism', but a genuine monarchy, than by this display of public consultation between government and society ? And what better object could such a consultation have than the establishment of rational laws ?

The study of the Legislative Commission of 1767, its role as Catherine conceived it, and its nature as an institution, has been greatly obscured by the assumptions both of contemporaries and of subsequent historians which reflect the preoccupations of their own time. Foreign contemporary observers read into the assembly the politics and the intellectual trends of their respective countries. British observers, the diplomats Macartney, Shirley and Cathcart, judged it as a House of Commons which failed to come up to their standards of organization and procedure, with Catherine acting the role of a Newcastle or a George III, and filling the assembly with her own party.[43] French diplomatic observers saw the Legislative Commission against the background of French political life, in which the struggle between the *parlements* and the Crown, which was to culminate in 1770 with the abolition of the *parlements,* was at its height. They read into the

Russian scene motives analogous to those of the French *parlementaires* and aristocratic frondeurs against royal absolutism. On the other hand, because Russian weakness suited French foreign policy, these diplomats were on the watch for any signs of hostility to Catherine, any weakness in her position. They stressed the dissatisfaction of the nobles with the rewards they had received in 1762, and remarked upon their freedom of speech. They dwelt on the desire of the nobles not included in the Orlov circle to limit the power of the ruler, with the ultimate object of creating a regime resembling that of Poland – a consummation devoutly desired by France and which coloured French interpretations.[44]

How widely known was Catherine's Instruction, at the time, and later? In 1767 instructions were issued to send copies to some fifty-seven government offices throughout Russia, where the Nakaz was to be regularly read on Saturday mornings ('when they have nothing else to do') to senior government officials, but was to be kept away from clerks and the lower ranks.[45] Nevertheless, it seems in later years to have circulated fairly widely since it was both advertised, and sold in bookshops. P. Kakhovskoy, one of the Decembrists sentenced to death in 1826, described in a letter to Nicolas I on the eve of his execution, with what emotion he had attended meetings of peasant communes and listened in these little republics to the simple eloquence of the Russian peasant. Here, he added, 'for the first time I heard extracts from the Nakaz of the Great Catherine'.[46]

11

The Great Debate

The unprecedented nature of the assembly called together by Catherine entailed the most careful attention to its management and procedure. The assembly was to open in Moscow and by the end of July 1767 a sufficient number of deputies (460) had assembled for proceedings to begin. In a ceremony which may have been modelled on the opening of parliamentary sessions in England, the empress, in imperial robes and wearing the 'small crown', drove in an impressive carriage procession to the Kremlin where a solemn religious service was held in the Cathedral of the Dormition. As befitted the principles of tolerance preached by Catherine, deputies from non-Christian tribes were allowed to remain outside during the service. The empress then proceeded to the Assembly Hall where the deputies were presented to her. A speech from the throne was read on her behalf by the vice-chancellor, Prince A.M. Golitsyn, who also presented to the assembly Catherine's Nakaz and two further important documents : the Rules of Procedure of the Commission and an Instruction to the procurator general.[1]

In accordance with the prescriptions in the Rules of Procedure, the deputies sat in groups on benches according to the guberniya they came from as listed in the nomenclature of the imperial title. The nobility were placed in front, with an empty stool before them available for the governor of the guberniya, should he attend. Behind them sat the townspeople, and behind them the peasant deputies. Cossack deputies were placed behind the nobles, but in front of the townspeople, in the gubernii to which their regiments belonged.[2] Voting was not by curiae but by heads. The role of the marshal, or speaker, was of such importance that his election could not be left to chance. Hence a complicated procedure was laid down by which the deputies and the procurator general respectively elected or nominated candidates and the empress made the final choice. Far from taking the opportunity to select spokesmen of a 'frondeur' trend, the deputies sheepishly chose two of the Orlov brothers, in an evident desire to please Catherine. Fourth on their list was General A.I. Bibikov, who had all along been the empress's choice for the post. He was put forward by the procurator general as his candidate, and was in due course appointed marshal.[3]

Between them, the marshal and the procurator general were charged with organizing the work of the Commission. While compilations of existing laws on a variety of different topics, or setting out the rights of the social 'estates', were to be read aloud and debated in the full assembly, interspersed with regular readings of portions of Catherine's Nakaz, the main work of analysis, coordination, and drafting was to be referred to a number of sub-commissions. These sub-commissions were also composed by the mixed process of election by the assembly, nomination by the procurator general, and final selection by the empress. Three of the sub-commissions were established at once : an editing commission, entrusted with polishing the style of documents ; a sub-commission for the analysis of the instructions of deputies, charged with coordinating the various demands put forward in the nakazy and forwarding them to the relevant sub-commissions ; and a directing commission which included the marshal and the procurator general *ex-officio,* and was charged with directing the activity of the Commission, the organization of its secretariat, the provision of specialized legal advice [4] and the keeping of records. Andrey P. Shuvalov, son of the Elizabethan statesman and a connoisseur of Western culture, was appointed director of the journals. A number of nobles, among them the future publisher, N. Novikov, were stationed about the hall where the Assembly met and instructed to note as accurately as possible what was said, by whom, whether coldly or with heat, who disputed with whom, who changed his mind, etc. Catherine's instructions show that she attached great importance to the protocols of the Commission. They were submitted to her every day, and read aloud at the beginning of each session, so that 'future times' would have 'a faithful record of this great event, and be able to judge of the cast of mind of this century'.[5] Whereas the proportion of high government officials in the full Commission was not high, the composition of the sub-commissions reflected a predominance of the nobility over other classes of society, and was remarkable for the number of high government officials, and Baltic nobles trained in jurisprudence.[6] The full assembly acted as a general debating arena. Its conclusions were to be forwarded to the corresponding sub-commissions not as 'instructions', but as 'observations' (*remarki*). The sub-commissions were to produce drafts of laws which were then to be discussed with the corresponding government departments, Colleges and chanceries, before returning to the directing commission.

Rules of behaviour were also prescribed : deputies were not to interrupt each other's speeches under pain of a fine of up to 10 rubles. Swords were not to be worn in the assembly. Brawling between deputies was to be punished by fines, and even exclusion from the assembly. In the hierarchical Russian society the scene in which the noble deputy of Oboyan, M. Glazov, was forced to apologize to the assembly and to pay a fine of 5 rubles for his outrageous personal attacks on a deputy of the odnodvortsy, must have been remarkable.[7] Submissions in writing by illiterate deputies had to be signed by those who had written for them. Deputies were also clearly instructed to concern themselves only with drafting a new code of laws. In no circumstances were they to try to enlarge the scope of their functions, to turn themselves into permanent spokesmen for their communities.[8]

Before embarking on its main task, the Commission proceeded to record its gratitude to the empress who had called it into being. At the the third session the newly elected marshal delivered a fulsome speech proclaiming the services of Catherine to her motherland (Russia) and expressing the hope that the deputies would live up to her expectations. But Catherine gracefully declined a proposal that she should accept the title 'Catherine the Great, All Wise Mother of the Fatherland'. The incident however was not without its importance, and the offer may well have been engineered behind the scenes with Catherine's concurrence. For there is no doubt that the formal offer of a title of this kind by an assembly of deputies of all the free estates of the land considerably strengthened the legitimacy of Catherine's position on the throne. No idea of a regency could possibly be entertained thereafter, and the accession of Paul when he came of age was fended off.[9]

The first seven sessions of the full assembly were taken up with the reading of Catherine's Instruction, the Rules of Procedure and elections to the various sub-commissions. A hitch now occurred in the proceedings. A 'Codification Commission' had been entrusted with the task of digesting the existing laws, so that extracts could be read to the assembly. It had started work in January 1767, but though the copyists had slaved from 5 A.M. to 10 P.M. they had been unable to complete their task in time for the opening of the Commission on 31 July 1767. Thus the following 14 sessions had to find something else to do, and occupied themselves by reading from some of the nakazy submitted by the deputies, though in principle these nakazy were not to be read out in the full sessions, but processed first in the sub-commissions. Accident led the Commission to start with a number of nakazy from state peasants and non-Russian tribes and farmer soldiers. They were to be the only nakazy ever read out in the assembly.[10]

By the twenty-first session, on 11 September, the Codification Commission had completed its work, and the full assembly settled down to listen to and discuss first the existing laws on the rights of the nobility, and then of the merchant estate,[11] followed by the laws governing the rights of the Baltic nobility.[12]

Meanwhile Catherine had decided that the Commission should be transferred to St Petersburg when she herself returned to the northern capital from Moscow. This gave rise to some administrative problems because of the number of deputies who were also officials. As early as 11 August, Catherine had issued instructions that deputies who were also government officials should take part in meetings of the general assembly only twice a week.[13] Rumours of a move to St Petersburg were circulating as early as September,[14] and the Commission was formally notified on 20 November that sessions would be prorogued on 14 December and that it would re-open in St Petersburg on 18 February 1768.[15] Officials employed in Moscow, and in some other provincial posts, were ordered to remain in Moscow or to return to their posts ; some 35 deputies were affected by this instruction and ceased to attend.[16]

When the Commission re-opened in St Petersburg in February 1768, it continued with the reading and debating of the existing laws on justice and judicial procedure. The trouble with the laws on 'justice' was that the Codification Commission had neither the time, nor the competence to order them in any systematic manner. As a result ukazy dealing with specific cases were jumbled together with statutes of wider significance, and problems of judicial procedure and the organization of the courts were interspersed with penal laws, many of which had lapsed. The 'opinions' of the deputies submitted in the debates in the assembly referred sometimes to the laws read in that session, sometimes to those read in earlier sessions, and the lengthy discussions devoted to justice, one of the most vital spheres of government, were particularly shapeless, only occasionally rising to matters of general principles.

Possibly dismayed by the rambling nature of this discussion, on 8 April 1768 Catherine issued a further instruction on general principles of legislation and on the procedure to be followed in the Commission. She now attempted to divide legislation into two broad areas of what she termed private and public law, and at the same time she recommended the setting up of more sub-commissions to deal with particular branches of legislation.[17] Elections to these sub-commissions took place gradually throughout April, May and June 1768, interspersed with the discussion of the laws on justice.

By the beginning of July 1768 a draft law on the rights of the nobility had at last been produced and was laid before the full Commission. At this point the deficiencies in its procedure made themselves felt. No copy of the draft was circulated to the deputies, and they refused to be pushed into immediate approval of each article as it was read aloud. They demanded an interval of a week to familiarize themselves with it – a request granted by Bibikov, probably at Catherine's insistence.[18] Catherine now issued a fresh instruction to the marshal designed to clarify procedure and to ensure that all points of view should be heard and even voted on, without allowing the discussion to get bogged down or to venture into criticism of the fundamental principles underlying the draft.[19]

In spite of Bibikov's attempts to keep discussion to one article at a time, 'opinions' tended to range over a wide field, and culminated in some thoroughgoing criticism of the whole draft law by representatives of the Baltic nobility. The specific interest of these sessions, extending from 10 July to 29 September 1768, is that, faced for the first time with a concrete draft on their rights and status, the deputies consolidated themselves into groups expressive of specific interests – 'aristocratic', lower nobility, urban or regional, and indicated their allegiances by 'adhering' to the opinions expressed by one or other of their spokesmen. The assembly therefore began to acquire some of the complexion of a genuine political institution. Nevertheless, in spite of Catherine's latest instruction on procedure, no decision was reached on the rights of nobles. Though three days were set aside for a debate on the draft as a whole, none of those responsible for drafting it appeared in the full assembly to speak for it. It was left to the deputy for the nobility of Kozlov, G. Korob'in, to appear as the defender of most of the articles, occasionally aided by the deputy for Kopor'e, the favourite G. Orlov, against attacks led mainly by Prince M. Shcherbatov, and the deputy for the town of Dorpat, Ya. I. Ursinus. No vote was taken, and finally on 6 October the Commission agreed to return the draft project, together with its comments and the record of the discussion to the directing sub-commission.

The Commission then turned to the reading and discussion of existing laws on landed property, a subject closely related to the rights of the nobility, since many crucial issues, such as the right to own settled land, the possibility of freeing serfs, the freedom of testamentary disposition, and the property rights of women, fell under this heading. Merely reading these laws occupied most of the time until the middle of December. There were very few speeches and little discussion. The proceedings were briefly interrupted when a deputation from the assembly presented its congratulations to the empress on her successful inoculation against smallpox in October 1768. The shadow of war with the Porte was beginning to loom over the assembly, and at the 195th session, on 18 December 1768, the marshal announced the empress's decision to prorogue the full Legislative Commission in view of the number of deputies who had already left, or who would have to return to their military or civil duties.[20] The sub-commissions were however to continue in being and the ukaz proroguing the Commission indicated that it would be recalled when the sub-commissions had finished their work. The last session of the full assembly – the 203rd – took place on 12 January 1769.

The work of the sub-commissions in the ensuing years was intermittent and some met but seldom, but a number of draft codes on the rights of the various estates were eventually produced. A joint session of the sub-commissions was called only once, on 8 June 1770, in order to fill some vacancies. By September 1771 even the directing sub-commission had ceased to meet.[21] At intervals, in 1772 and 1773, ukazy to the procurator general indicated that the empress still intended to recall the full assembly,[22] possibly after the conclusion of the Russo-Turkish war. But the Legislative Commission was never convened again.

Since the summoning and the dispersal of the Legislative Commission play such an important part in the assessment of Catherine's personality and policy, some attention must be paid to the various explanations which have been put forward for its prorogation at this point. According to M.T. Belyavsky, the discussions, particularly on the question of serfdom, had proved so heated, and the spokesmen for the serfs so effective, that Catherine, who had no sympathy with any moves designed to improve the lot of the serfs, seized the opportunity of the outbreak of the Turkish war to close down a potentially dangerous arena of debate.[23] G. Sacke maintains that Catherine, having achieved her main purpose, namely the consolidation of her hold on the throne, and the crushing of an alleged 'aristocratic party', lost interest in the legislative function of the Commission, and did her best gradually to weaken and destroy it. He rejects the argument that the Commission was prorogued to enable deputies to take up their military duties on the grounds that in his assessment only thirty-eight deputies did in fact go to the army.[24] He also argues that the debate on serfdom which had erupted in the assembly was dangerous for Catherine. In his view, Catherine had deliberately contrived a bourgeois/peasant majority in the Commission. But she could not allow this majority to give full rein to its anti-noble views, since the open alienation of the nobility might even lead to a new palace revolution. It was easier for her to carry out her anti-noble policy without the Commission.[25]

Again, it has been argued, by Sacke among others, that Catherine viewed with alarm the growth of political consciousness in various social groups, and the evidence of their conflicts with each other. The polarization of views in the Commission, and particularly the systematic adherence of particular deputies to the views defended by particular spokesmen, seemed to indicate a growth of consciousness of potential political power, and Catherine feared the growing antagonism between government and nobility on the one hand, and between the different estates on the other.[26] Belyavsky, however, stresses the opposition manifested in the assembly, and particularly among the opponents of unrestricted serfdom, to the government as such.[27] Again other historians such as V. Sergeyevich suggest that the empress had been disillusioned by the incapacity shown by the deputies, and their inability to live up to the enlightened maxims of her Nakaz.[28]

But the official explanation, namely that in time of war the noble – and urban – deputies were required for other duties carries more weight.[29] There were 92 serving officers among the 160 deputies of the nobility, and the 54 Cossack deputies would be required for active service. Moreover the energies of the empress and of the most important government servants would inevitably be absorbed in the mobilization of the country's civil and military resources for war.

Though when it was prorogued the Commission had not completed the draft of a single law, the discussions and the various documents submitted to the full assembly, or subsequently prepared in the sub-commissions, provide valuable evidence both on the policies of the government and on the attitudes of society. Three types of material must be considered : first, the instructions which the deputies brought with them ; secondly, the discussions on the laws read out in the assembly ; and thirdly the drafts produced by the sub-commissions and the ensuing debates.

The instructions were all drafted before the Commission opened in Moscow ; they thus reflect local opinion, *before* the deputies had been submitted to the invigorating ideas expressed in Catherine's Nakaz. They are very informative on local history since they contain a mass of detail on local conditions, and particularly local grievances, but they are rarely illuminating as regards political attitudes. The discussions arising on the laws and on the draft project for the rights of the nobility already show the influence of Catherine's Nakaz which provided many deputies with new ideas, or new formulations for existing ideas. Deputies with a broader horizon could and did quote frequently from the Nakaz in defence of a liberal policy, whether in the field of trade, noble or urban rights, personal freedom or even serfdom. With the authority of the empress behind them, they were able to put forward more daring propositions than appear in the local nakazy. Finally the drafts produced in the sub-commissions – inadequate and abstract as they are – reflect the views of high government officials as well as of ordinary deputies, since officials of the Senate and Colleges were consulted before the drafts were finalized, and the projects were passed through the directing sub-commission for its approval.

Disregarding chronology, it will be convenient to analyse the opinions expressed in the assembly and in the various documents in terms of a number of important issues which arose. Most prominent because of the social importance and the political weight of the group involved, was the definition of the status and the rights of the nobility and the role of the Table of Ranks. Many of the noble nakazy specifically rejected the ennoblement apparently automatically linked with promotion in the Table of Ranks. Some demanded either the strict demarcation between the nobility of birth and the 'promoted' noble, or the total rejection of ennoblement except by personal grant from the monarch. The nobles of Pustorzhevo asked for some external sign to distinguish the ancient nobles from the non-nobles, such as the use in Western Europe of 'von, de, Don'. The nobles' desire for a legal definition of their status is explained in great part by their growing awareness of the gulf separating them from their Western counterparts, and their consciousness of the insecurity of their social status. In general the attack on automatic ennoblement by the Table of Ranks came from centres of the old nobility, while areas where nobility was dubious such as New Russia and Little Russia were anxious to maintain ennoblement by promotion. These attitudes emerged very clearly in the course of the debates on the existing laws, and on the project for a code of rights of the nobility.

The draft code of rights of the nobility deserves some attention, since it had been commented on by the Heraldmaster's office and the directing sub-commission and probably approved by the empress herself.[30] The sub-commission which produced the draft had not confined itself to the study of the nakazy from noble deputies, but had also examined the laws concerning the nobility of Livonia and Little Russia, the rights of the English, German and French aristocracies, and even, on 13 November 1767, 'read the Great Charter given by the English King John to his subjects'.[31] However, the definition of nobility stumped this sub-commission too and it came up with a paraphrase of article 360 of Catherine's Nakaz : 'Nobility is a title of honour, distinguishing those who bear it from others.' Nobles derived their status from descent, or by grant from the monarch, and though, according to the sub-commission's draft, virtue and services 'could raise people to the rank of nobility', the directing sub-commission amended this to read 'only the monarch can however actually raise to this rank', thus eliminating automatic promotion by the Senate or field commanders (who could promote up to the rank of captain, which carried hereditary nobility). The draft also proclaimed that all nobles were personally free, and could choose to serve or not as they pleased ; it put forward other claims, e.g. freedom from corporal punishment and personal taxation, already *de facto* enjoyed by the nobility. Their economic rights were specificed, and many articles were devoted to testamentary arrangements, and the rights of noblewomen. But the project accepted that social precedence derived from rank in service, not rank in society. Thus titles, whether traditional (prince) or new (count) would not grant precedence, and a noble in service would always take precedence over a non-serving noble, thus ensuring the priority of service rank over title. The draft did not take up the many noble requests to register separately the different categories of nobles in Russia, though it did propose that a 'matricula' or register of the nobility should be kept in each uezd, thus bowing to noble pressure to limit the efforts of non-nobles to smuggle themselves in through the many back doors opened by corruption.

Discussion ranged widely on the question of the origin of nobility. Even the most blue-blooded noble, argued some deputies, had at one time been promoted or raised to that rank because of his services to the monarch. 'With us, military honours are granted to rank, not to nobility, when on guard duty. Which title will be considered most honourable, that of an officer or that of a noble without service ?' exclaimed the deputy of the Terek (Caucasus) Cossacks, N. Mironov.[32] A strictly rational analysis was put forward by N. Motonis, deputy of the nobility of the Mirgorod and Poltava regiments in the Ukraine. It was original in that Motonis stressed that virtue and service to the state were at the origin of nobility, and both could be manifested not only in war but in peace. If perpetual war prevailed the contract binding together the different estates which constituted society was broken and in the ensuing chaos 'many could become nobles'. Peace however was better for the welfare of the state as a whole and ultimately even for the military. 'The sovereign, as a father, loved all his subjects equally' and rewarded them according to their virtue and services. This had always been Russian practice, and the Table of Ranks had introduced no new principle. In the sovereign's eyes, no one was *podlyy,* base, except those who broke the law and lacked public conscience. Logically, concluded Motonis, the Commission ought to study how many nobles there were, and how many were necessary for state service. If there were not enough then the Table of Ranks should be preserved – if there were too many then the Legislative Commission should propose limiting promotion and ensuring that those who rose to a *chin* entitling them to nobility should content themselves with the material privileges corresponding to their *chin* without seeking to be ennobled.

Motonis's analysis is interesting, not only for its utilitarian bias, but because it seems to accept a state of affairs where rank in society could be divorced from rank in service, while at the same time rejecting the aristocratic pretensions of Prince Shcherbatov who deeply resented the suggestion that the Russian dvoryane had ever been base-born, and pointed to their descent from Ryurik and other grand princes. The discussions in the Commission suggest in fact that Russian social structure was under attack from two opposite directions. On the one hand, the champions of an aristocratic polity, making use of Montesquieu's definition of a moderate monarchy, demanded freedom from service, recognition of social rank independently of service rank, participation in local administration as the natural consequence of their social status, and occasionally even some share in political power or at least some constitutional channels through which their voice could reach the throne. On the other hand, other speakers, coloured more by the ideas of the Encyclopedists, adopted a far more rationalist egalitarian attitude to the noble estate, within which all were equal. From Montesquieu they derived the concept of virtue, and though it would be anachronistic to regard them as exponents of 'bourgeois' values, nevertheless they did propose that Russia should jump straight from the service-bound state to a meritocracy, without passing through the phase of aristocratic preponderance to be found in e.g. England, Sweden or even France. Yakov Kozel'sky, for instance, the deputy of the Dnieper pike regiment in Slobodska Ukraine, relying on Chapter XV of Catherine's Nakaz, which gave priority to virtue and service over birth as the origin of nobility, warned that if nobles were allowed to inflate their pretensions, based on social status alone, they would end by despising both civil and military service to the state.[33] Between these two extremes there remained the defenders of the *status quo,* i.e. the bondage of all to the service of the state, and automatic promotion in the Table of Ranks.

The rights of the Livonian and Little Russian nobles aroused some controversy. Having once agreed to participate in the Legislative Commission, their deputies took the opportunity to stress their specific and independent rights, and to demand their fresh confirmation by Catherine. While the Livonian and Estonian nobles rejected the concept of the Table of Ranks, alien to their tradition, the Little Russian nobles on the contrary demanded to be granted the same rights and status as their Great Russian brethren, and supported the system of automatic promotion.

The claims of the Baltic nobility were viewed with suspicion by the Russian lower nobility, resentful of privileges they did not share, and had no hope of sharing. Making use of the article in Catherine's Nakaz, which stated that citizens should all be subjected to the same law, they rejected the special rights incorporated in the capitulations signed with Peter I after the conquest of Livonia. 'The laws for the Livonian knights granted in the fifteenth and sixteenth centuries by the grace of God and Pope Nicholas' were no longer relevant in the view of Lev Shishkov, deputy from Novosil'skiy uezd, and more than twelve deputies supported him.[34] Some of the speakers made the point that the special privileges of the Baltic nobles (including their immunity from the poll-tax and the recruit levy) weighed heavily on the rest of Russian society : the conquerors were thus worse off than the conquered. It was strange moreover that parts of the Russian Empire should be ruled by foreign laws.[35]

The campaign of the minority groups was undoubtedly concerted between the Baltic and Little Russian nobles. Both sheltered under article 43 of the draft code for the nobility, which stated that the privileges enumerated therein were enjoyed by all Russian nobles. V. Zolotnitsky of the Kiev regiment proposed that this article should be extended to specify that the Baltic and Little Russian nobles were to remain under their own laws ; if the Legislative Commission had the right to propose new privileges for the Russian nobles, it must certainly have the right to propose the confirmation of existing ones for non-Russian nobles. G. Poletika of Lubny rejected the whole draft code as inapplicable to the Little Russian nobles who enjoyed many additional privileges. He argued that the government of Little Russia, below the supreme power, depended on the nobility ; the nobility had the right to establish, repeal and amend laws, and request the sovereign's confirmation of them ; together with administrative officials they had the right to decide on taxes ; and they had the right to elect civil and military officials who had to be Little Russian nobles, etc.[36] This bold assertion of the full range of Little Russian claims to autonomy was met with evident sympathy by the Baltic nobles who put forward their claims in similar terms, using the same peg, namely article 43 of the draft code. Baron G.F. Löwenwolde even proposed that the project for the Russian nobles should include some of the corporate rights already enjoyed by Livonian nobles, such as a new clause to the effect that a governor should be unable to take any action, not previously authorized by law, without consulting with the elected representatives of the nobility and obtaining their agreement. At this point Marshal Bibikov put a stop to further discussion. He refused to accept the 'opinions' submitted by the Baltic deputies, on the grounds that according to the rules of procedure the Legislative Commision was to draft a Code of Laws, but not to intervene in constitutional[37] matters. The question of confirming the privileges of the Baltic, Little Russian and Smolensk[38] nobilities was a matter for the sovereign alone, and could not be incorporated in a law on the status of the nobility. This move in all probability stemmed from the empress who viewed the Baltic and Little Russian claims to autonomy with scant sympathy.

One of the most striking confrontations between the old and the new Russia, Muscovy and the West, occurred over the concept of freedom. The discussion arose around two articles in the draft code for the nobility. The first (Chapter II, article 1), stated: 'All nobles are free'. The second (Chapter II, article 2) stated that the nobility was free to choose to serve in any branch of government service or not at all. Several deputies objected to the statement that the noble was free. The Cossack deputy F. Antsyferov argued that only the sovereign ruler was free since he was not accountable for his actions to anyone on earth, whereas the nobility was accountable not only to the ruler but to the law in matters of service and duty. 'And when someone is under the law, that one cannot be called free,' he added.[39] The deputy from the nobility of Belgorod, Ivan Vyrodov, also argued that only the sovereign was free. Only in the field of his domestic economy was the noble totally free. Otherwise his freedom was limited since he was under an obligation to serve his country. If it were left to the nobles to decide whether to serve or not, the country would be defenceless, for 'freedom does not defend a fatherland'. G. Korob'in, the deputy of the nobility of Kozlov, replied, paraphrasing Catherine's Nakaz (and of course Montesquieu), that a free man could do all that was not prohibited by the laws. He could choose not to take service ; but this did not imply that he would not defend the fatherland when called upon ; there was a difference between compulsory service and spontaneous defence of one's country. The disputants agreed in the end to differ, since, as Korob'in put it, they had 'different conceptions of freedom'.[40] The view that any legal definition of noble freedom was *ipso facto* a limitation on the power of the sovereign was shared by members of the non-noble classes who had no wish to see the emergence of a class superior to themselves and free from bondage to the state. 'We should remember that we are to draft a new code of laws – to bind the people, not the sovereign,' said Vasily Tambovstsev of the Yaik Cossacks.[41]

The question of serfdom was discussed only incidentally, in the course of debates on the rights of other classes to own serfs, on the problem of fugitives, on taxation, etc. The nakazy of the nobility stressed, if they mentioned the subject, the claim to the exclusive right to own serf labour, and to complete freedom in dealing with the serf population, both from an economic and from a judicial point of view. At least two nakazy demanded that the new class of 'economic peasants' should be sold to the nobility.

The attitude towards ownership of serfs reflects however an economic problem that went deeper than social status and privileges, namely the difficulty in a primitive landed economy of mobilizing the wealth of the country for the purposes of the state. The point is well illustrated in the discussion on the Table of Ranks. M. Davydov, deputy of the Yeletsk odnodvortsy, pointed out that government employees with a *chin* in the Table of Ranks but below the rank of noble, and who were therefore not allowed to own estates, could live on their salaries while they worked ; but what happened if they were too old or ill to work, and were dismissed ? They had to beg their bread. Hence they should either be allowed to buy estates (with serfs), or be given a pension. V. Vedeneyev, of the Tambov odnodvortsy, opposed the granting of estates, but urged that these employees should be entitled to a pension after a number of years of service. M. Glazov, quoting article 145 of Catherine's Instruction ('if you wish to prevent crime, strive for the spread of enlightenment'), argued that to protect the state from having to pay out large sums in pensions, it would be better never to promote non-nobles to any rank in the Table of Ranks. The economic straitjacket confining land, labour and social classes rendered the birth-pangs of a professional salaried bureaucracy difficult indeed.[42]

Serfdom was again discussed when the laws dealing with the recovery of fugitive serfs were being read aloud. The noble nakazy had argued that serf flight was
provoked mainly by the state, i.e. by heavy state taxes, the recruit levy, burdens
in kind or labour, and the excise on liquor and salt. In the debate others blamed
serf flight on the laziness and drunkenness of the peasantry and their innate incapacity.[43] At this point G. Korob'in again intervened. He argued that the principal
cause of serf flight was the exactions of the landowners and their control over the
serfs' property. He proposed, quoting article 261 of Catherine's Nakaz ('the law
may establish something useful for the personal property of serfs'), that the right
of the serf to some property should be established by law, and that the sum paid
to the landowner in cash or kind should be moderate and also fixed by law. He
did not propose limiting the landowner's administrative power over his serfs, but
only his power over the serfs' property.[44] Korob'in's speech launched a heated
discussion on the relationship between landowners and serfs, in which he was
supported by some five speakers, and attacked by many more. M. Glazov, the
deputy from Oboyan, angrily stressed that Korob'in had not been elected by the
nobles of Kozlov – was he a landowner there ? Had he indeed ever been there ?
Was he following the nakaz given to him ?[45] Korob'in defended himself by
pointing out that when there was a divergence between the noble nakazy and
Catherine's Nakaz, surely loyal subjects should abide by the latter.[46] The most
cogent attack on Korob'in's views came from Prince M. Shcherbatov who stated
that it was unnecessary to pass laws providing for serf ownership of moveable
property since they owned it anyhow in terms of something much more powerful
than the law, namely custom and mutual profit. As for immoveable property,
since the land belonged to the nobles, where could it come from ? He was
surprised however that Korob'in did not touch on the landowner's jurisdiction
over his serfs. For if the body was in someone's power, so was the property. A
landowner with the power to punish his serfs arbitrarily could also take away
their property. Should the peasants in such case have recourse to the courts ?
God forbid, for they would spend their time rejecting the landowners' legitimate
demands. One should beware, he argued, of breaking the chain linking the peasant with the landowner, by limiting the latter's power. Such a break would create
the situation which the empress warned against in her Nakaz (articles 502, 503
and 504), when the foundations of the state are shaken, when the spirit of equality takes such hold that people would no longer obey those set by the law above
them. The only way to prevent abuses was to empower local officials and local
noble assemblies to report cases of ill-treatment to the government with a view to
appointing trustees.[47]

In many ways the most modern voice was that of Yakov Kozel'sky, the deputy
of the Dniepr pike regiment in Slobodska Ukraine. He proposed that in all
parts of Russia the land should be divided among individual peasant owners in
hereditary usufruct; that, by obrok or barshchina according to climate, location
and fertility, the peasant household should work two days a week for the state,
two days a week for the landowner and two days a week for themselves, resting

on Sundays. According to his assessment the value of the work done for the land-owner would amount to some 10 rubles a year (including women's work), and the tax to the state could be calculated to amount to an equivalent sum per house-hold. Peasants should dispose entirely of their moveable and immoveable prop-erty, which should be hereditary, though without the permission of the land-owner they should neither sell nor mortgage their immoveable property. He also proposed setting up something in the nature of a Ministry of Agriculture, which should collect information from landowners and others and supervise cultivation. Landowners would continue to administer estates but their relationship with the peasants would be much improved. Landowners who demanded unlimited pow-ers over their serfs were asking for more than they were entitled to, since even the supreme sovereign power did not demand more than specified services except in time of war. To the reproach that peasants were lazy and drunk, Kozel'sky gave the humane reply: 'The peasant has his feelings. . . . He knows that all he owns belongs to his landowner . . . how can he be good and virtuous, when he is deprived of all means of being so . . . he drinks not from laziness but from downheartedness . . . the hardest worker becomes careless if he is constantly oppressed and owns nothing. . . .' Kozel'sky was the only speaker to touch on the question of individual ownership of land by the peasantry, which of course would have involved the breakup of the commune, and the creation of a class of free tenant farmers or smallholders. He was way ahead of his time, and he did not spell out the implications of his proposals.[48]

The most wide-ranging discussion of serfdom arose however in the context of three articles in Chapter II of the draft law for the nobility. Article 13 stated : 'Nobles if they so wish may transform the rights of ownership over serf estates into rights of ownership over free estates. But they cannot transform free estates into serf estates.' Article 14 read : 'Nobles may dispose by will to other nobles of free estates, in conditions laid down by law, but they cannot dispose of serf es-tates in this way'. Article 17 stated that nobles could free their serfs individ-ually.[49] The directing sub-commission however removed discussion of articles 14 and 17 by pointing out that they belonged to the sphere of competence of other sub-commissions.

Article 13 however completely bewildered the deputies. The drafting was so slovenly that the actual meaning of the clause was obscure. There was in fact no such thing as a 'free estate' in Russia ; how could the nobles transform serf es-tates into free estates ? The 'freedom' granted to the nobles seemed moreover to be one way : a noble could emancipate a serf estate but not enserf a free one. Amid the general confusion Shcherbatov again intervened. 'It is a great right, to grant someone freedom.' Freedom might resound in one's heart, but the condi-tions of the country must also be considered. The article seemed to suggest that nobles would have the right to give certain rights to peasant villages, which could not be taken back again. What good could come of this right, and what harm, he asked ? Sensing that the only right which mattered in this context was the right to freedom, Shcherbatov stressed eloquently the damage to the Russian state if the serfs were freed : no landowner would devote such care to free peasants as to his serfs and whence could serfs become enlightened if not through their masters ? A. Protasov, the noble deputy of Gorokhovets, somewhat inconsistently argued that in other sovereign absolute states where the peasants were free, their freedom was more apparent than real in view of the burdens they bore. But if free estates were introduced into Russia, the serfs would become discontented. Moreover free peasants could not be forced to work like serfs.[50]

Once again Grigory Korob'in spoke up in defence of article 13 of the draft. In answer to Shcherbatov, he declared that the word 'freedom' was not harmful. 'I could prove this to you elsewhere, if I could speak to you quietly,' he added, whereupon the marshal, Bibikov, intervened to say that he could speak openly, since there should be no secret views. Korob'in thereupon repeated his support for granting nobles the right to create 'free estates'.[51] L. Tatishchev of the nobility of Izium went even further. The empress wanted the peasants to be free, he declared. Bibikov again intervened. The question at issue was not whether the peasants should be free but whether the nobles should have the right to create free villages. The empress's wishes should not be brought into the discussion, since if she had decided on something, there was no room for further argument on the subject. Nothing daunted, Tatishchev replied that the empress wanted to imbue her people with the spirit of freedom, and that such a spirit would do no harm to agriculture since landowners would have subjects and not slaves. He advanced the example of England, but was again interrupted by the marshal who pointed out that the deputies were discussing Russian and not English laws.[52]

The discussion around article 13 is of considerable importance for the interpretation of Catherine's attitude towards serfdom. It is noteworthy that Korob'in, one of the most outspoken critics of serfdom, spoke in the full session of the Commission as the defender of a number of clauses in the draft law on the rights of the nobles, occasionally assisted by Grigory Orlov. No member of the sub-commission responsible for the draft, nor of the directing sub-commission, explained or defended any of its clauses in the assembly. Was Korob'in put up to do so by the sub-commission or the directing sub-commission ? Some historians have even suggested that he was Catherine's mouthpiece and that she introduced him into the assembly.[53] If this is so, then his views on serfdom can have come as no surprise to her, and certainly his remarks in the assembly coincided with her own opinions as expressed in many of her private papers and in the excised portions of the Nakaz. In the words of one of the leading Russian historians of the Legislative Commission, the liberal views of Korob'in and others represented not 'opposition to Her Majesty' but 'Her Majesty's Opposition'.[54] Belyavsky, committed to the view that Catherine was the tool of the nobility, and never concerned herself with the welfare of the serfs, has argued that Korob'in and Tatishchev were both forced by Catherine to lay down their mandates as deputies because of their outspoken criticism of serfdom. More recent research by Soviet scholars has disproved Belyavsky's assumption in the case of Korob'in.[55] What no one has commented on in this context is the fact that the proposal to create 'free estates', to enable the nobles to emancipate not merely individuals but whole settlements, emanated from a committee of high nobles, and that the cautious comments of the directing sub-commission on the question of the sale of serfs and the extent of the landlords' power over their serfs also emanated from a committee containing some of Catherine's closest collaborators, notably A.A. Vyazemsky. In the Russian context, the proposal to create 'free estates' was far more revolutionary than it might seem to be at first sight. Though the two sub-commissions concerned failed completely to explain in detail what the legal status of such free estates would be or whether the peasants would continue to be bound to the soil, it is evident that the proposal involved creating a new class of subjects of the Russian crown, neither state peasants, nor odnodvortsy (since the land would belong to a private owner), but personally free and bound only by some kind of contractual obligation to the landowner. Article 13 therefore must be seen as a *ballon d'essai,* launched with imperial approval, with the intention of precipitating precisely the kind of discussion which took place, in order to test opinion. Evidently the discussion could not go so far as to alienate noble opinion from the throne, and thus no official spokesman was appointed to defend Article 13. But if the empress wished to avoid discussion of serfdom in the assembly these controversial clauses need never have been included in the draft law.[56]

Another clause affecting serfs caused an incident in the assembly. Article 31 of the draft law for the nobility stated that 'the denunciation by, or the evidence of a serf against his owner shall not be acted upon'. A. Aleynikov, the deputy for the Cossacks of the Novokopersky fort, who on the whole systematically spoke for or supported opinions in favour of alleviating the burdens of the peasantry, proposed briefly that this clause should be replaced by the words 'the denunciation and the evidence of a serf against his master shall be taken into account'. The daily journals of the assembly suggest that Aleynikov's bold move led to a certain disarray. They read : 'After which, and after a certain interval, the Marshal declared that no one else wished to speak on that article and the next article was read.' Reading between the lines one senses the uproar, hidden behind the neutral words 'after a certain interval'.[57] Aleynikov, about whom little is known, spoke also in defence of the rights of newly christened pagans, quoting from Catherine's Nakaz to bolster his argument that such people should be educated and introduced to Orthodoxy for the glory of God, rather than enslaved.

There is no evidence that a digest of the laws concerning the free peasantry had been prepared and was to be read aloud to the deputies. The peasants were the objects of laws specifying the rights of other estates, not the subjects of laws on their own rights. Well over a thousand nakazy[58] were submitted by the various peasant deputies, and they were collated and digested by the relevant sub-commission. A summary of 170 'points' was prepared, and presumably forwarded to the sub-commission on the different estates, charged with drawing up the code of rights of the third estate.[59] The twenty-nine Russian peasant deputies did not play a large part in the debates except for the indefatigable autodidact, I.A. Chuprov, deputy of the peasantry from Archangel who intervened fifteen times, equalling the total of all the other peasant speeches. Some peasant deputies revealed a deplorable lack of class consciousness by transferring their mandates to members of other estates, including nobles.[60] Only one peasant deputy and two odnod-vortsy were elected to sub-commissions.[61]

The nakazy of the peasants are an invaluable source for the social history of Russia, but they need to be used with some discrimination. Allowance must be made for the fact that they are specifically lists of grievances written by unsophisticated people, couched in the terminology of the 'petition'. Once they were offered the chance of laying their needs before the distant empress, every past abuse, present burden and future fear was jumbled together in a desperate protest against their condition. But it would be a mistake to accept these nakazy as descriptions, accurate to the last detail, of peasant life. They reflect a memory and a mentality, the peasant view of the totality of their lives and of their relation with the other classes of society and within the state. They present a cumulative picture of all the harshest aspects of what was indeed a harsh life – but this does not necessarily render them immune from the critical study to which any historical document should be subjected.

The grievances of the state peasants fall into a fairly standard pattern. They complained about heavy taxation, owing to the long interval between censuses and the obligation to pay the poll-tax on behalf of minors, the sick and the old. In addition they were burdened with heavy labour services by the kuptsy in connection with the salt and vodka monopolies (as porters, guards, inspectors, etc.) which took them away from agricultural work, and since they could be fined for failure to fulfil these duties they got further into debt. The rates of pay for the labour services exacted from them by the state for building and road repairs were too low.

The peasants also complained of the social and legal limitations on their economic activity: the merchants placed obstacles in the way of their carrying on retail trade in their produce in the towns; they were no longer allowed by law to bind themselves by promissory notes or to enter into contracts for supplies; there were state limitations on the exploitation of woods and fisheries and on the right of the peasants to clear unused land or to sell, pledge, buy or bequeath cultivated land. As regards the administration, the peasants complained of their inability to secure justice from the courts. If dvoryane and merchants encroached on their lands or abused their persons, they were defenceless. They suffered from the low esteem in which they were held. Frequent requests were made to elect their own peasant officials and to remove the appointed administrators.

The nakazy of the assigned peasants suggest that the reforms introduced by A.A. Vyazemsky in 1764 had either failed in their object, or had not yet been implemented.[62] They suffered particularly from the arbitrariness of the poll-tax assessment. The assigned peasants of Voznesensk had to pay off the poll-tax for 1,000 male souls, when, since 1754, they numbered only 500. In the village of Esaul, 220 fit men worked off the tax for 671 souls. Among the Siberian assigned peasants, the nakazy stressed the fear of future assignment to industry, rather than present suffering.[63] In general the assigned peasants' nakazy stressed their wish to remain peasants (*byt'v krest'yanstve*).

To sum up, in many cases the peasant nakazy reflect the belief that if the existing laws were properly applied their situation would improve. They showed a constant awareness of the glaring illegality with which the peasants were treated (forced levies, labour dues, physical violence, military brutality, particularly towards their women), and their inability to obtain justice. They accepted the division of society into estates and demanded that members of other estates (merchants, townspeople, ecclesiastics) should not be allowed to own land unless they shared the burdens imposed on the peasantry. They demanded recognition of their maturity and ability to bind themselves by contract and to expand their commercial activities. In the strictly economic field they demanded freedom from labour services, and for the assigned peasants the replacement of assigned labour by hired labour, or at the very least a more realistic assessment of the poll-tax payable, less work, payment on the same scale as the hired worker, and for time spent in travel.

Much less is known about the state of mind of the possessional serfs, the permanent labour force hereditarily attached to the factory and not to the factory-owner. In theory the College of Mines and the College of Manufactures represented them at the Legislative Commission. The instruction of the College of Mines merely asked (in article 14) for guidance on the relationship between mine-owners and the owners of labour. Typically, however, the College of Mines put forward policies for the benefit of the employees of the state mining bureaucracy rather than for the labour force in the mines. It proposed that the mining service should be placed on the same footing as the corps of artillery and engineers; it requested a salary commensurate with the hard life, which involved constant travel, and since 'members of the service became decrepit' sooner than in other services, it requested the award of landed estates 'so that their trembling nerves might be soothed and find comfort'.[64] The nakazy of the possessional serfs tended to stress the general hardship of their lives, and to put forward demands more typical of a professional social group than of peasants. They wanted higher wages, shorter hours, less tax, and payment on holidays and Sundays from private owners as they received in state-owned enterprises.[65]

The nakaz of the College of Manufactures did however raise questions of principle: it welcomed the policy endorsed by Catherine in 1762 of prohibiting the purchase of serfs by factory-owners and it noted that the assignment of people as skilled workers to factories increased the numbers of people in bondage, 'whereas skilled workers should go to swell the numbers of those living happily in towns, knowing no slavery other than that of obedience to the laws'.[66]

The problems of the state peasantry were only discussed incidentally in the debates in the commission in connection with the rights of other estates. The problems of the assigned peasants were discussed only twice – once at the very beginning of its sessions, when the nakaz from the peasants assigned to the Demidov works was read, and the peasants' demand for better conditions was met with some sympathy by the deputies; and later on 26 November 1768 when the peasant deputy for Kungur described in detail the deplorable situation of the assigned peasants in the course of a debate on the rights of the merchant class.[67]

Many noble nakazy objected to the purchase of serf estates by members of the merchant class for industry and preferred them to rely on hired labour. The most extreme statement of this position came from N.B. Tolmachev, deputy of the Liubim nobility, who demanded an inquiry into the position of serfs ascribed to factories. If the goods produced by these factories were cheaper for the state than those produced by hired labour, all was well. But if the state had to pay the same price, then it would be better to free these serfs, since according to article 253 of Catherine's Nakaz people should not be enserfed except in cases of extreme emergency, and then not for individual profit, but because of the needs of the state.[68]

The odnodvortsy were represented in the Legislative Commission by 42 deputies, some of whom were very vocal.[69] They submitted over 200 nakazy of which more than 130 remain unpublished.[70] Socially half way between the nobility and the state peasants, the odnodvortsy clamoured to be assimilated to the nobility as regards rights and privileges ; they complained of the burden of military service, of the additional services required of them, and of delays in promotion to commissioned rank. Above all, however the odnodvortsy complained of the ruthless way in which neighbouring landowners encroached on their lands, sometimes using bands of their armed serfs to expel the odnodvorets owner. Landowners were accused of kidnapping the daughters of odnodvortsy, marrying them off to their serfs, and thus enserfing them. The nakazy did not hesitate to name great magnates as well as minor landowners who had between them reduced the land available to the odnodvortsy, and forced them into the position of renting back their own lands. In spite of laws prohibiting the alienation of their land, the odnodvortsy complained of their inability to secure justice from the local administration, and stressed the way in which the General Land Survey was being used by landowners to reduce their landholdings still further.[71]

In the course of the debates in the full assembly, some of the odnodvortsy revealed a considerable degree of maturity. They were almost unanimous in demanding self-government as a separate social 'estate', through their own elected 'hundredmen' and 'tenthmen', and the setting up of elected courts with oral procedure to deal with minor civil cases. They did not hesitate to underline the fact that the small landowners suffered as much as they did themselves from the depredations of the wealthier and more powerful landowners. A. Maslov, the deputy of the odnodvortsy of Belgorod province, for instance, put forward the idea that a special college with local branches should be established for the administration of all peasants, including serfs. Such a college should be charged with organizing the recruit levy, collecting the poll-tax, and collecting dues owed by serfs to their landowners. The poll-tax revenue would be sent 'where the government directs' ; the dues paid by the serfs to the college would be paid over to the landowners. All disputes between serfs, or peasants and serfs, would be dealt with in courts dependent on this college, which would also decide cases where serfs had been compelled to do something illegal by their owners. At present, as Maslov put it, if a peasant refuses to act against the law when ordered to do so by his master, his master beats him ; and if he obeys his master, then he is beaten in the courts. If his project were accepted, Maslov continued, the peasant would be dealt with by law, in accordance with article 244 of Catherine's Nakaz, 'let the people fear the law and only the law'.[72]

The Legislative Commission was prorogued before the sub-commission on the different estates had produced draft projects of the rights of any social group other than the nobles. But the drafts which were later prepared, and which were submitted for comment to various government bodies, are of considerable interest, since not only do they reveal the trend of thought in the higher ranges of government and society at the time but they served to some extent as sources for subsequent general or partial legislation. A special sub-commission was formed, under the guidance of the commission on the different estates, to draft the laws concerning the third estate and the Cossacks. The members of this sub-commission were guided in their labours by a special plan issued by Catherine on 8 April 1768, which casts an interesting light on her understanding of the link between serfdom and the national economy. 'These people [the Third Estate]', wrote Catherine, 'are valuable sons of their country, but one cannot ignore the fact that they are sometimes overburdened.' She proposed that the subcommission should study the conditions of the peasants, bearing in mind that

in view of their different status in the vast areas of Russia, when the needs of the state or private utility do not enable the tillers of the soil to be everywhere free or unfree, because of the danger that the land might remain uncultivated because of their flight, is it not possible to seek means by which, so to speak, they could be firmly attached to the soil . . . in a manner which benefits equally the owner and the cultivator [and] . . . which could insensibly introduce some improvement in the status of the lower sorts of people and cut short evils which oppress these useful members of society.

Thus, when faced with giving public guidance to a group actually engaged in drafting laws, Catherine accepted the necessity of adscription to the soil even if relations between serf and master were better regulated.[73]

Catherine had never intended that the Legislative Commission should concern itself with what could be termed constitutional matters, i.e. the form of government in Russia, and indeed it showed no inclination whatsoever to do so. The powers of the ruler were taken for granted. But if the principles of the central government were never touched upon, the deficiencies of the local administration of the country were discussed both in the nakazy and in the debates and provided Catherine with much necessary information when, at the end of the war with the Porte, she was able to turn to internal reform again.

Part I V

Foreign Policy : Poland
and the Ottoman Empire

12

Foreign Policy : from Peace to War

In common with most contemporary rulers, Catherine believed the conduct of foreign policy to be the true *métier de roi,* and from the beginning of her reign she left her advisers in no doubt that she intended to take the decisions herself. One of the most urgent tasks which faced her on her accession was to disentangle Russia from the disastrous foreign policy of Peter III. Uncertain with whom they were to deal, the College of Foreign Affairs on 2/13 July 1762 forwarded a series of questions directly to the empress requesting her guidance on a number of urgent issues. Catherine's replies revealed her firm grasp of essentials, and her determination to be fully informed and to see all dispatches herself.[1]

Any illusion that the overthrow of Peter III would lead Russia to re-enter the war on the side of Austria was at once dispelled. Catherine needed peace to consolidate her hold on the throne, and the Russian treasury was exhausted.[2] The Russian forces operating with Prussia were at once recalled, and on 29 June / 10 July 1762, Catherine notified all the courts of her intention to maintain peace with all powers. To Frederick II she confirmed on 1/12 July that she would abide by the peace treaty signed with him by Peter III, but she refused to ratify the treaty of alliance.[3] The consequence however for Russia of withdrawing from the war was that she was excluded from the peace negotiations between Austria and Prussia.

Catherine's solution for one of the minor problems inherited from Peter III provides some indication of the future direction of her foreign policy, and of the high-handed manner of its execution. Duke Ernst Johann of Curland, the Biron who had been the favourite of Empress Anna, had been exiled to Siberia in 1741, when he was regent for the infant emperor Ivan VI. In 1758, his overlord, Augustus III of Saxony Poland, attempted to transfer the duchy to his son, Prince Charles, with the full support of Elizabeth of Russia. But one of Peter III's first moves was to withdraw all support for a Saxon, and therefore anti-Prussian, claimant to the duchy. He recalled Biron from exile, and pressed him to abdicate in favour of Georg-Ludwig of Holstein-Gottorp. Barely was Catherine on the throne when Russian policy changed again. In accordance with the opinion she had long ago expressed as grand duchess,[4] that Curland should either be returned to its legitimate ruler or be absorbed by Russia, Catherine ordered the Russian envoy in Mittau to support Biron's restoration. Biron was after all totally dependent on Russia, and on 4 August 1762 he signed an agreement binding himself to protect the Orthodox faith in Mittau, to favour Russian merchants, to have no dealings with enemies of Russia, to allow Russian troops free passage, and Russian ships free use of his harbours, and to be attentive to Russian requests for the leasing of estates.[5] By April 1763, Russia had forced Prince Charles out of Curland, and though it continued to be a Polish fief, it had become to all intents and purposes a Russian protectorate.

After this initial success, which seems to have been supported by all Catherine's advisers (Bestuzhev Ryumin and Biron were old colleagues), control of the orientation of Russian foreign policy became the object of a bitter court struggle. Catherine's two main counsellors, neither of whom was at the time a member of the College of Foreign Affairs, were the ex-chancellor Bestuzhev, and Nikita Panin. Bestuzhev had aged ; he was out of touch as a result of his four years' exile, and he drank too much. On his return to the capital he had found the author of his disgrace, the chancellor M.L. Vorontsov, still in office, even if he did not enjoy the empress's confidence. Both Bestuzhev and Vorontsov favoured alliance with Austria, combined with Britain in the case of Bestuzhev, with France in the case of Vorontsov. Panin, who had spent eight years fighting French influence in Sweden, regarded the Bourbon dynasty as essentially hostile to Russia, and hoped to build up a counterpoise to the Franco-Austrian hegemony on land. Catherine herself, judging by what she frequently wrote, preferred not to commit herself to any particular pattern of alliances and to pursue a purely opportunistic policy.[6]

The issue over which rivalry between the factions at court came to a head was the future of Poland. The health of Augustus III was declining, and in the event of his death, the alternatives were a Saxon candidate, the likely choice of Austria and France, and a *piast* or native Pole, the choice in his time of Peter III,[7] and of Catherine who had already in August 1762 decided on the man, namely her ex-lover, Stanislas Poniatowski: 'J'envoie incessament le comte Keyserling ambassadeur en Pologne pour vous faire Roy . . . ,' she wrote to him on 2/13 August 1762.[8] Thus Poniatowski, who had hoped to become prince consort in Russia, was consoled with the prospect of becoming king in Poland.

Imposing a king of her choice on Poland was not a policy Catherine thought she could carry out without the support of another power. Austria and France would support the Saxon house, and France might well urge the Ottoman Porte to declare war on Russia if she were deeply committed in Poland. The only powers Russia could approach in the dangerous isolation she had been left in by Peter III's arbitrary foreign policy, were Britain and Prussia. Britain and Russia had not been at war with each other during the Seven Years' War, and when a new British envoy, the Earl of Buckinghamshire, was appointed in August 1762, he was instructed to broach the subject of the renewal of the Anglo-Russian treaty of alliance of 1742, which had long since lapsed, as had the treaty of commerce of 1734. As early as the autumn of 1762, feelers were put out by Russia to test British willingness to support Russian policy in Poland, but there was no desire on either side to embark on formal negotiations until peace had been restored in Europe.[9]

The alternative to Britain was Prussia. Frederick II had already shown his readiness to accept a native Polish candidate for the throne of Poland in his treaty of alliance with Peter III, and he was extremely anxious to secure the Russian alliance. Early in January 1763, before peace between Austria and Prussia had been finally concluded, Augustus III of Poland fell dangerously ill. At a specially convened 'conference' of her advisers on 4/15 February Bestuzhev again pressed Catherine to decide in favour of a Saxon candidate, and an Austrian alliance. But he was overruled, and it was decided to support Stanislas Poniatowski.[10]

The Peace of Hubertusburg between Prussia and Austria was signed on 4/15 February 1763 and Frederick II immediately opened negotiations for an alliance with Russia. Augustus III however recovered from his illness, and the crisis was postponed for the time being, while the struggle at the Russian court between Bestuzhev and Panin reached new depths. Whether the real struggle was over positions or policies is hard to disentangle. But the horizon became somewhat clearer once the question of Catherine's marriage to Grigory Orlov was shelved. In mid-August 1763, M.L. Vorontsov left at last for a prolonged stay abroad, still keeping the title of chancellor. Then, quite unexpectedly, on 24 September/5 October, Augustus III died. At a special conference on 6/17 October Bestuzhev made a last vain effort to win Catherine over to his views. He failed and the broad lines of Russian policy were laid down : a native Pole was to be supported ; troops were to be stationed along the Polish border in readiness to act if required, and Prince N.V. Repnin, Panin's nephew by marriage, was to be sent as special envoy to assist the zealous, if elderly and ailing Count Keyserling, Russian envoy in Warsaw. It was also at this meeting that Count Zakhar Chernyshev, now vice-president of the College of War, put forward a plan for the modification of the Russo-Polish frontier in the strategic interests of Russia, and indicated the territories he thought Russia should annexe – territories which coincided closely with what Russia eventually acquired in the first partition of Poland.[11]

In the last week of October, Nikita Panin was formally appointed senior member of the College of Foreign Affairs, and took charge of Russian foreign policy. But he was not granted the coveted title and rank of chancellor, then or later.[12] Catherine had most skilfully succeeded in extricating herself from Bestuzhev's importunities and in eliminating Vorontsov, without giving to Panin the same degree of authority.

The timetable for the Polish elections had been laid down in November 1763 : dietines were to meet in February 1764 to elect representatives to the Convocation Diet, which would meet on 26 April. Within Poland, Poniatowski could count on the support of a pro-Russian party, led by his mother's family, the Czartoryskis, which hoped to be allowed to introduce reforms into the anarchic Polish constitution with Russian agreement (though they also at times toyed with the idea of pushing the candidacy of young Prince Adam Czartoryski). Panin now used the intervening time to win over other courts to support Russian policy in Poland, or at least to neutralize their hostility.

The new elector of Saxony had meanwhile been pressing his claims to Poland and attempting to secure the support of Austria, Prussia and France. But the hopes of the Saxon house suffered a serious blow when the elector died suddenly of smallpox on 17 December 1763, leaving a thirteen-year-old heir. The Saxon candidature passed to a younger son of Augustus III, Prince Xavier, but the Saxon court proved unable to mobilize any support for him. Even Austria showed no signs of going beyond diplomatic support[13] while French policy had not recovered from the twin disasters of Louis XV's secret diplomacy and defeat in the Seven Years' War. Officially France committed herself only to supporting a totally free election, i.e. one in which non-Polish candidates could be considered, and the maintenance of the territorial integrity of Poland. Behind the scenes, Choiseul Praslin attempted to arouse the Porte against Russia. In these circumstances the Russian negotiations for a treaty of alliance with Britain came to life again. Even before the death of Augustus, a Russian draft treaty had been produced which contained certain significant departures from the Treaty of 1742. Russia now required British subsidies to support her policy in Poland, and cooperation in Sweden. But in view of the possibility of armed Turkish opposition to Catherine's Polish policy, British assistance to Russia in the event of a war with the Porte was not excluded from the treaty. The draft was rejected out of hand in London in September 1763, but after the death of Augustus, Panin reduced his demands. He gave up the 'Turkey clause' in exchange for a subsidy of 500,000 rubles in Poland. Again however the Russian terms were rejected in England, on the now standard grounds that Parliament would not pay subsidies in peacetime.[14] Panin now fell back on Prussia, with whom Russia had been negotiating all along in a leisurely way.

The possibility that Catherine might achieve her objects in Poland even without a treaty with Prussia induced Frederick to press ever more strongly for the conclusion of an alliance between the two powers, while at the same time he fell in with Catherine's demands for joint action in Poland.[15] The visit of an envoy from the Ottoman Porte, who arrived in Berlin in November 1763, enabled him to increase the pressure on Russia. The parsimonious king provided the envoy and his suite of seventy people with lavish entertainment, while discussions of a treaty of alliance between the two powers were carried on. The spectre of an alliance between Prussia and the Ottoman Porte persuaded Catherine of the need to conclude the agreement with Frederick ; negotiations began again seriously in January 1764, and the treaty was signed on 31 March/11 April 1764. Ostensibly

a defensive alliance, the two powers guaranteed each other's European possessions (including ducal Holstein in the case of Russia) ; in the event of attack by a
third power, they undertook to provide 10,000 infantry and 2,000 cavalry. There
were four secret articles : the first provided that in the event of an attack by the
Porte on Russia, or by another power beyond the Weser on Prussian possessions,
military assistance could be replaced by a subsidy of 400,000 rubles ; secondly
the contracting parties agreed to observe the existing balance of political parties
in Sweden, and in the event of danger to the Swedish form of government, to
concert their measures ; thirdly, the King of Prussia guaranteed ducal Holstein to
the Grand Duke Paul ; and fourthly the contracting parties agreed not to allow
any changes in the Polish constitution, and to forestall any attempt to make such
changes by force of arms if need be. The treaty was to last for eight years. A separate convention bound Frederick to support the election of Stanislas Poniatowski to the Polish throne, and a later declaration of 12/23 April 1764 asserted
the intention of the two allies to protect the 'dissidents', i.e. adherents of the Orthodox and Protestant confessions in Poland.[16]

When news of the negotiations between Prussia and Russia became public, it
became obvious to the Poles that only another piast could be put forward as an
anti-Russian candidate. He emerged in the person of the elderly Crown hetman,
Jan Branicki, who commanded the corps of 1,200 Polish troops allowed to the
king. Both the pro-Russian Czartoryskis and the anti-Russian Branicki faction
used violence to influence voting in the dietines, and the Czartoryskis appealed to
Russia to send troops to assist them. Branicki and his supporters, who included
many members of the great Polish families, notably Prince K. Radziwill, protested on 30 March/10 April against the Russian violation of Polish territory. But
on 9/20 April, twenty-six Polish magnates put their names to a letter thanking the
empress for sending her troops to defend their liberties ; they included two
bishops, four Czartoryskis, and of course Stanislas Poniatowski.[17]

By the end of April the deputies were flocking to Warsaw, which had all the
appearance of a city divided into two armed camps. Radziwill and Branicki had
over three thousand troops ; the Czartoryskis could call on the Russians encamped nearby. The efforts of Branicki's party to protest at the holding of the
Diet in the presence of foreign troops were ignored, and he failed in his attempt
to break up the Convocation Diet on 26 April/7 May. Whereupon the Crown hetman left Warsaw, with the intention of proclaiming a Confederation elsewhere.
Russian troops under Prince Dashkov pursued Branicki and Radziwill and defeated their forces in a number of skirmishes on Polish soil. Radziwill escaped
into Hungary, where he was eventually joined by Branicki, who was now deprived of his post of Crown hetman by the victorious Czartoryskis. The election
Diet was called for 16/27 August, and on 26 August/6 September, Stanislas
Poniatowski was elected king – as Stanislas Augustus – in what he described as
the quietest election Poland had ever known.[18] Catherine congratulated Nikita
Panin 'on the king we have made' and on his faultless conduct of the whole

operation. Yet seeing that there were no foreign candidates, and that no foreign court was intervening in the election, the introduction of over 14,000 Russian troops into Poland seems an almost unnecessary display of force. At the outset visible rewards for Russia were few : the Coronation Diet recognized the Russian imperial title. The King of Poland received a present of 100,000 ducats from Catherine to help him to set up house, and he sent her a case of truffles.[19] Far more dangerous for Russia in the long run, however, was the introduction of Prussia, by treaty, into what had come to be regarded as an exclusively Russian preserve, namely the internal government of Poland.

Even during the negotiations with Prussia Catherine and Panin had hoped not to be forced to choose between Austria and Prussia to the extent of cutting their Austrian connections. But with the signature of the Russo-Prussian treaty, Russia found herself committed to one of the German powers. Neither Catherine nor Panin favoured a passive foreign policy, and hence, from 1764, Panin began to develop his so-called 'Northern system', destined to preserve peace in the North.[20] In its widest extent the Northern system was conceived of as a counterbalance to the Southern and Catholic alliance between the Bourbon powers and the Hapsburgs. The nucleus of the new system was to be the treaty with Prussia, and Panin hoped to extend it to include Denmark and Britain as active partners and Sweden, Poland and Saxony as passive powers. With the aid of Prussia, Britain and Denmark, Panin planned to keep factions favourable to Russia in power in Sweden and Poland. In these circumstances of *de facto* Russian hegemony in the Baltic, the peace of the North could be guaranteed. Such a system, as its many opponents within Russia did not fail to point out, was of no assistance to Russia against its principal enemy, the Ottoman Porte. But alliance with Austria was out of the question so long as her ally France was opposing Russian policy in those very areas – Sweden, Poland and the Porte – of most importance to Russian security.

In Panin's view, genuine cooperation between Russia and Denmark could not be achieved as long as the duchy of Holstein remained an issue between the two powers. On the death of Peter III, Catherine had parried the efforts of the king of Denmark to exercise the regency in the duchy on behalf of her son, and had sent Georg-Ludwig of Holstein-Gottorp to take charge in Kiel. In a memorandum to Catherine, Panin now stressed that though in the past Peter the Great had done his utmost to secure for his house a voice in the affairs of the Holy Roman Empire, Russia was now a great power and no longer needed to acquire influence by such means. He proposed therefore to accept earlier Danish offers to exchange ducal Holstein for the counties of Oldenburg and Delmenhorst, to be held by a junior branch of the house of Holstein-Gottorp. Catherine concurred with his views ; she may also have been moved by the thought that her own position would be safer if her son were deprived of an independent power base over which she would have no control once he came of age.[21]

As a first step, a defensive alliance between Russia and Denmark was concluded on 28 February/11 March 1765. The contracting parties guaranteed each other's possessions, and bound themselves to assist each other in the event of attack, though such assistance might take the form of a subsidy in the event of a Turkish attack on Russia. The exchange treaty was signed on 11/22 April 1767, but the actual exchange was not to take place until the grand duke reached his majority. In the meantime Denmark was inevitably committed to a pro-Russian policy.[22]

Panin was less successful in his negotiations with Britain. For one thing, he received no encouragement from Frederick II who had no wish to share his ally, Russia, with anyone else. And secondly Britain was passing through a phase of splendid isolation which led her to refuse to make any concessions to Russian needs when her own were not directly involved. Meanwhile Panin was determined to achieve the treaty of alliance only on Russia's terms, and a treaty of commerce on more equal terms than those which had been embodied in the Treaty of 1734. In spring 1764, the Earl of Buckinghamshire was recalled, and replaced by George Macartney who arrived in December 1764.

As with the treaty of alliance, Britain had hoped for renewal of the treaty of commerce without any modification if no improvements could be obtained. But what Russia had granted in 1734 no longer suited the confident, indeed arrogant Russia of 1765. 'Strengthened as they are by the alliance of Denmark and Prussia, proud of having imposed a monarch upon Poland . . . I am persuaded that we shall every day find them less moderate in their pretensions,' wrote Macartney on 5/16 November 1765.[23] The principal modifications which Russia now proposed to the Treaty of 1734 were to article 4 which allowed English merchants to pay the same export dues as Russian merchants. This equality of treatment was omitted from the Russian draft. In addition, in a new article 4, Russia now reserved to herself the right to make such internal regulations as she thought fit in order to promote Russian navigation, and the draft actually introduced the words : 'en réciprocité de l'Acte de Navigation de la Grande Bretagne.'[24] Sensing perhaps that Macartney could be driven (he was only twenty-seven) Panin put increasing pressure on him to sign the treaty by threatening a total rupture of negotiations, leaving British trade unprotected, should he refuse. Without referring the final text to London, Macartney signed on 4/15 August 1765, possibly urged on by the British merchants in the capital who may have felt that some privileges were better than none. But though Macartney had secured most of the British demands, including payment of dues in Russian currency, he was promptly and sharply rebuked, and ordered to inform Panin that Britain could not ratify the treaty as it stood. Britain could not allow Russia unilaterally to modify her trade regulations. Worse still was the explicit mention of the Navigation Act. Even if Russia had the shipping to benefit from such a clause, wrote the British Secretary of State, Macartney was 'establishing a precedent by introducing that act by name (hitherto always avoided) and which in future treaties other nations may claim, who may be in a situation to make use of it, greatly to the disadvantage of this country'.[25]

After a good deal of somewhat acrimonious argument with Panin, Macartney finally succeeded in obtaining the removal of the offending reference to the Navigation Act and a minor amendment to the new article 4. Again, under the threat of the annulment of existing British commercial privileges, Macartney took the risk of signing on 20 June/1 July 1765 and this time he was not disavowed.[26] But still no progress was made with a treaty of alliance. The main obstacle now was the Turkish *casus foederis* which Britain would not grant. While Russia, having secured its inclusion in the treaties with Prussia and Denmark, was determined not to admit its exclusion from the treaty with Britain.[27]

There was one new factor in the conduct of foreign policy in St Petersburg which foreign courts took some time to appreciate : bribery no longer affected policy. In the past, Bestuzhev had been on the British payroll. M.L. Vorontsov may at one time have taken money from France, but Buckinghamshire's attempts to bribe him were so clumsy that the British government had to apologize to the chancellor. Macartney was alleged to have spent 150,000r. from the secret funds, though it was nearer 10,000r. He secured information, but no influence on policy. Even Frederick II had thought at one time of trying to buy Nikita Panin himself with the princely sum of 200,000 thalers. But Panin was not to be bribed, nor was Catherine. Money could still buy information at the Russian court ; it might even speed up matters here and there if the recipient was highly placed enough, but it could do no more.[28]

Even though no Anglo-Russian treaty was concluded, cooperation with Britain formed part of Panin's 'Northern system', and nowhere was this more clearly demonstrated than in Sweden. The pro-French Hat party had been responsible for Sweden's participation in the Seven Years' War, but the defection of Peter III and Russia had left Sweden open to an attack by Prussia and a hasty separate peace, restoring the *status quo ante*, had been patched up by the good offices of Queen Louisa Ulrica of Sweden, the sister of Frederick II. Peter III had also in his brief reign reversed the traditional Russian policy of limiting royal power in Sweden. When the College of Foreign Affairs submitted its request for guidance to Catherine on 2/13 July 1762, she promptly went back on his policy and scribbled briefly : 'Limit the form of government, support the party opposed to the one at present in power.'[29]

Implicit in this instruction was a more far-reaching change of policy. Catherine, undoubtedly advised by the expert on Sweden, Nikita Panin, considered that the changes introduced into the Swedish Constitution of 1720, particularly during the crisis of 1756, had gone too far in weakening the Crown, and allowing one party, in this case the anti-Russian Hats, to acquire so much influence in the Council as to be able to act effectively in pursuit of a policy. It was now in Russian interests to maintain a balance between Crown, Council and estates, thus ensuring Swedish passivity. The Russian envoy, I.A. Osterman, was instructed to work for the preservation of this equilibrium, as expressed in the Constitution of 1720, while strengthening Russian influence in the opposition party, the Caps.[30]

France meanwhile attempted to secure her hold on the Hat party by promising in summer 1764 a subsidy of 1.5 million livres p.a. until 1768, or even 1772. Direct relations between Britain and Sweden had been broken off in 1757, but a British envoy, Sir John Goodricke, was readmitted in spring 1764. He and Osterman cooperated closely in the pursuit of their respective policies : breaking the Franco-Swedish alliance in the case of Britain ; securing the victory of the Cap party and constitutional revision in the case of Russia. Both were well equipped with funds to provide 'pensions' for the well intentioned, and an open table during sessions of the Diet.[31] Goodricke also thoughtfully supplied Osterman with intercepts of the French correspondence between Stockholm and Paris and Stockholm and St Petersburg, thus providing Russia with valuable information on French secret contacts with the court party of Queen Louisa Ulrica.[32]

All Swedish parties were anxious to avoid summoning a Diet but it was rendered necessary by the acute financial crisis in Sweden and a Riksdag was thus finally convened for January 1765. A combination of bribery by the foreign envoys, subsidized party organization and a genuine desire for change led to an overwhelming victory for the Cap party. Catherine could now hope to put through the policies with which Russia was mainly concerned, and Panin could hope to regard Sweden as attached to his 'Northern system'. In April 1765, the betrothal of Crown Prince Gustavus of Sweden to a Danish princess was announced, shortly after the conclusion of the treaty between Russia and Denmark in March 1765. In the field of constitutional reform, by summer 1766, the combined pressure of Russia, Britain and the Caps had secured acceptance of a provision by which in future any amendment to the constitution would require the consent of all four estates at two consecutive meetings of the Diet. In this way Panin fondly hoped to have ruled out the restoration of absolutism in Sweden. Finally the conclusion of a treaty of friendship between Britain and Sweden on 25 January/5 February 1766 destroyed the Franco-Swedish alliance.[33]

The conduct of Russian diplomacy in Stockholm in these years was closely concerted with both Denmark and Britain, though the three powers had slightly different objects in view. To this extent their activity illustrates the 'Northern system' in action. But Frederick II brushed aside all attempts to draw Prussia into a wider system of alliances, and placed strict limits on his intervention in internal Swedish affairs in support of Russian policy. He wanted to be dragged into no adventures, and he wanted no alliance with Britain. Meanwhile Russian relations with France were marked by increasing coldness. Desultory negotiations for a commercial treaty had been carried on in 1764, but France was not prepared to support the infant French trade in Russia, and regarded the negotiations as a diversion, intended to slow down Anglo-Russian understanding.[34] Moreover any hope of concluding a treaty was jeopardized by the French refusal to recognize the Russian imperial title, without the formality of a *reversale* (a Russian declaration that acceptance of the title by France created no precedent and implied no change in the etiquette among courts). Catherine's tenure of the throne was not sufficiently secure for her to accept any kind of humiliation, and when a new

French envoy, de Bausset, arrived in spring 1764, she refused to receive him because the word 'imperial' was not included in his credentials. The French argument that the noun 'majesty' could not be qualified by *any* adjective in the French language cut no ice with the College of Foreign Affairs, and eventually envoys were replaced by chargés d'affaires in both courts.[35]

Considering the situation she had inherited, Catherine had succeeded by 1766 in building up Russia's position in Europe to an unprecedented degree. She had recovered from the isolation brought about by Peter ; she was bound by treaties of alliance with one strong military power, Prussia, and one naval power, Denmark. She had achieved her objects in Sweden ; Britain remained bound to her by commercial ties which imposed no obligations on Russia. She had given a king of her choice to Poland. Overconfidence now led Catherine to overplay her hand.

The imposition of a king on Poland was not the only channel Russia could use in order to extend her control over the political life of her neighbour. The existence of a large number of adherents of the Orthodox Church within the boundaries of the Polish-Lithuanian Commonwealth provided her with an excellent base for the formation of a party of her own, though only few had any social standing. Their principal spokesman at the Russian court was Bishop Koniski of Polish Belorussia. He was the only foreign Orthodox bishop to attend Catherine's coronation, and on that occasion, speaking in the 'name of the empress's subjects', he had hailed Catherine's accession as heralding the restoration of the true faith in Russia, and had appealed to the empress in biblical language of great eloquence to extend her protection to the faithful suffering under Polish persecution.[36] Non-Catholics, whether Orthodox or Protestant, had been deprived of political rights in Poland, and the Orthodox suffered in addition from considerable pressure to join the Uniat Church, i.e. the Church which used Orthodox ritual but accepted the supremacy of the Pope. Persecution of the Orthodox community by the Catholics in Poland gave Catherine just the opportunity she needed to appear as the champion of the Orthodox faith – outside the borders of Russia – at a time when state control was being extended over the Orthodox Church within the borders of the empire.

Catherine had raised the question of the rights of the 'dissidents', as they were called, at the time of the summoning of the Convocation Diet in April 1764 ; in July 1764, Russia and Prussia presented a joint declaration demanding that the deliberately unspecified rights, liberties and privileges of the dissidents should be restored to them. But the Coronation Diet of 22 November/3 December 1764 showed little inclination to admit of any improvements in their situation. From the Polish point of view the danger of making any concession was clearly put in a letter destined to be shown to Catherine : 'Si la Russie s'obstine à introduire les dissidents dans la législation, ce sont (ne fussent-ils que dix ou douze) autant de chefs toujours légalement existants d'un parti qui ne peut regarder l'état et le gouvernement de Pologne que comme un adversaire, contre lequel ils doivent

nécessairement et perpetuellement chercher l'appui au dehors.'[37] This was however precisely what Catherine hoped to achieve.

Nevertheless in the autumn of 1764 Panin, and possibly Catherine too, were
willing to consider moderate reform in Poland, designed to render it more 'gov-
ernable'. And Stanislas Augustus hoped to strike some sort of a bargain : majority voting in the dietines and abolition of the 'liberum veto'[38] – in exchange for
an improvement in the status and rights of the dissidents. Panin realized that majority voting in Poland would be no obstacle to the intervention of foreign powers
in her government, just as in Sweden. But Frederick II dismissed any such suggestion out of hand. Stanislas Augustus could be trusted ; but his successors might
prove dangerous. Thus Prussia was already limiting Catherine's freedom of action in Poland.

The Convocation Diet of April 1764 was, according to the Polish constitution,
a General Confederation of the estates, at which decisions could be taken by majority vote instead of by unanimity. It had therefore been in a position during the
interregnum between the death of Augustus III and the election of Stanislas to
approve certain reforms designed to centralize control of finances and of the
armed forces. The Coronation Diet of 22 November/3 December 1764 endorsed
these plans, and decided to maintain the General Confederation in being. It was
thus possible for the time being for a decision in a national Diet to be taken by a
simple majority.

A new Diet was called for September/October 1766. The Russian envoy,
Prince N.V. Repnin, was given instructions to press for the full range of concessions to the dissidents and was authorized to encourage them to form a confederation if necessary and ask for Russian protection.[39] Repnin was also authorized
to use the funds at his disposal to 'influence' the king and the Czartoryskis, and
to bribe deputies at the Diet. The instructions to Repnin were accompanied by the
text of a declaration on the dissidents which he was to make, for which Catherine
hoped to get the support of the Protestant powers, namely Prussia, Denmark and
Britain.[40] The declaration stressed the benefits Russia had already conferred on
Poland in assisting in the free election of a native king, and went on to demand
full freedom of religion for all dissidents, who should not be required to pay dues
to the official Catholic Church, and should come under the jurisdiction of secular
courts only. The original constitution of the republic, where all religions were
equally represented in the government, should be restored. Panin fully realized
that the Russian programme could only be put through the Diet if it was confederated, i.e. if decisions need not be unanimous. If the liberum veto could be
used, Russian demands would undoubtedly be rejected. Hence Repnin was also
instructed to keep the General Confederation in being.[41]

Within Poland, three trends of opinion had emerged. The king, and those close
to him, wished for constitutional changes to strengthen the government, and
were willing to grant political rights to the dissidents, though they were aware
that in the present state of Polish public opinion such a policy would not be

tolerated by the Catholic majority. A second group approved of constitutional change, while opposing religious toleration, let alone political rights for the dissidents. Finally the diehards were equally opposed to constitutional change and to toleration in religion. On the eve of the opening of the Diet, Repnin made a fresh effort, together with his British, Danish and Prussian colleagues, to press the case for granting political rights to the dissidents, but even the king refused to consider admitting them to the legislature or to administrative positions. Knowing that Russian aims could only be achieved by force, Repnin sent for the detachment of Russian troops which had been placed at his disposal, and ordered his men on 24 September/4 October to occupy the lands of the bishops of Cracow and Vilna.[42]

When the Diet opened two days later, the diehards, who were the largest party, not surprisingly found a leader in Bishop Sołtyk of Cracow. He at once demanded maintenance of the *status quo,* and the abolition of the General Confederation. Meanwhile the Czartoryskis succeeded in putting through the Confederated Diet the reform programme which had originally been agreed by the Convocation Diet in April 1764. Catherine was outraged that the reform party should have achieved the approval of their own policies, i.e. constitutional reform, before ensuring that her own demands for political rights for the dissidents were approved. She berated the king and the Czartoryskis, who had abused her goodwill in the attempt to secure their own power without conceding anything to Russia. Repnin was now ordered to proceed with the rupture of the General Confederation, allying himself with the enemies of the Czartoryskis, in the knowledge that 'Poland had not one neighbour who would not prefer to see her government composed entirely of dissidents rather than to allow her to be dependent in the matter of taxes, revenue and the increase of the armed forces on some forty or fifty creatures of the Czartoryskis . . . who can always obtain a majority of the votes in the Diet.'[43]

Catherine's *volte face* regarding the General Confederation met with Frederick II's full approval. He had repeatedly demanded that Russia should not allow majority voting to be introduced into the ordinary Diets of Poland, and was deeply suspicious of Russian willingness to allow a measure of reform in Poland.[44] Thus, early in November Russia and Prussia submitted declarations to the diet demanding the abolition of the General Confederation set up by the Convocation Diet, and insisting that the liberum veto should remain in force for all financial and military matters in ordinary Diets – i.e. the revocation of the Czartoryski reforms. At the same time the two powers read out the declarations in favour of the dissidents, which were eventually supported by Denmark and Britain.[45]

Knowing that they could secure political reform only by supporting the Russian programme for the dissidents, the Czartoryskis dropped the reform programme. On 11/22 November 1766, a proposal that in no circumstances could taxes or the armed forces be augmented without the unanimous consent of the full diet was carried by majority vote, without discussion. The Czartoryskis were silent ; the king was heartbroken.[46] But on 13/24 November the diehards achieved total victory in the matter of the dissidents : a law reaffirming all the previous laws dealing with the dissidents and spelling out their disabilities was passed by unanimous vote. Russian policy had killed reform, but it had defeated its own aims in the process.

Repnin drew the moral for the Russian court. From Warsaw, he was much more aware of the strength of the feelings aroused. He did not believe that the king or the Czartoryskis *could* put through Catherine's programme for the dissidents, however much they might have wished to. The proof of this, in his view, was the fact that they had abandoned their demand for majority voting, which was much dearer to their hearts, in order not to alienate Russia ; but to give way on political rights for dissidents spelt political death.[47] There was indeed in Catherine's whole attitude to the problem of the dissidents an insensitiveness which goes beyond mere diplomatic arrogance or clumsiness. She had been brought up by a devoutly Lutheran father, but religion sat lightly on her and she had accepted Orthodoxy with ease. She had no personal experience whatsoever of the Catholic Church or of a Catholic country and her ideas on Catholicism were derived from Voltaire, Raynal and the *Encyclopédie*. Not only was she ignorant of the profound imprint left by Catholic culture wherever it had prevailed, she was unable in herself to experience the power of religious belief. The Catholic fanaticism of the Polish noble backwoodsman was unintelligible to the daughter of the Enlightenment, who had incidentally, in her treatment of Archbishop Arseniy Matseyevich, showed equal incomprehension of Orthodox fantacism.

Moreover Catherine had no experience of a political system in which the ecclesiastical hierarchy formed part of the government – as in England and Poland. Repnin had tried hard to convince the Poles that though the spiritual rights of the dissidents could properly be discussed with the bishops, their civil rights were no concern of the spiritual estate. The Poles, he said, 'refused to understand him'. When the question of defining the status of the dissidents at the Diet was referred to a Council of Bishops Catherine's immediate reaction was to protest that it was improper for matters which had been put by foreign powers to the Diet and the king to be referred for decision to a body of ecclesiastics. It was 'un manque d'égards dont toute l'Europe sera étonnée. . . .' The status of the dissidents, she argued, should be regulated by legislative process and not by a decree of mere bishops who had no legislative power of their own.

Catherine's knowledge of Church–state relations in general was very superficial. She dated the disabilities of English Catholics from the gunpowder plot ; of the disabilities of the English dissenters which rendered the British declaration in support of the Polish dissidents somewhat ironical, she seems to have been ignorant. As for the Polish bishops, 'il faudrait tacher d'acheter quelques evêques ; ils sont accoutumés à aimer les ducats,' she commented.[48] Panin too had never served in a Catholic country and showed all the *furor theologicus* of the

Enlightenment. His attitude to religious belief emerges clearly in a dispatch to Repnin, which he wrote in a moment of leisure. He explained that Russia had no intention of allowing the spread of Protestantism in Poland. The Protestant religion, as Panin put it, by 'limiting superstition and the power of the priesthood, might, if it spread in Poland, arouse the Poles from their uncouthness . . . and by freeing them from it', might bring about the kind of reforms likely to prejudice Russian interests. Russia need have no such fears, Panin added, about their fellow Orthodox : but if their number were to increase and their status were to become secure, they would cease to require Russian protection. So there was to be no encouragement for conversions from Catholicism to Orthodoxy. Moreover, if the Orthodox were both secure and free in Poland, it would encourage the Russians to flee over the border into Poland. As regards the Uniats, the very name should not be mentioned. They were renegades from the true faith who could not be respected since they had not even become true Catholics, and they were mainly responsible for the persecution of the Orthodox.[49]

Thus far Russia had been prepared to negotiate on the Polish constitution provided she obtained concessions on the status of the dissidents. The news that the Diet had refused any concessions was greeted with incredulity in St Petersburg, and Russia fell back on force. Repnin was instructed to press for the convocation of an extraordinary Diet, and secretly to organize confederations of the dissidents whose emergence into the open would be timed to coincide with the entry of Russian troops into Poland in winter 1767. He was also to recruit the support of those opposed to constitutional reform by stressing that the Russian invasion was taking place as a consequence of the reform plans put forward at the previous Diet.[50]

On 31 January/11 February 1767 Repnin was given his final instructions. The Russian-sponsored dissident confederations were to be proclaimed on 26 February/9 March under Russian armed protection. As soon as news of the confederation reached Warsaw, Repnin was to present a declaration calling for the summoning of an extraordinary Diet. If the king and his supporters used force against the dissidents, Russian troops were to protect them. If the king remained quietly in Warsaw, Repnin was to assure him of the Russian desire to enter into negotiations with the Commonwealth in order once and for all to eliminate the differences between the two countries.[51]

Repnin meanwhile had been organizing the opponents of the king and by early 1767 dissident confederations were formed in Sluck for the Orthodox of Lithuania, and in Thorn for the Protestants in Poland, under the protection of Russian bayonets. Catholic anti-royal confederations also sprang up and petitioned Catherine to guarantee the unreformed Polish constitution. Many Catholics joined these confederations in the hope of getting rid of the king, who was associated with constitutional reform. But Catherine had no intention of removing Stanislas or allowing him to be removed. Repnin was instructed to reassure the king that he, personally, would be protected against the Catholic confederations. Thus, coerced by Repnin, the Catholic confederates were forced to drop their opposition to the king and to agree to the summoning of an extraordinary Diet which was called for 24 September/5 October 1767.

Catherine and Panin had now realized that equal political rights for the dissidents could not be achieved. Hence Repnin was told to reduce somewhat the range of Russian demands at the extraordinary Diet : first of all he should induce the Poles to request a Russian guarantee of their constitution and their territorial integrity, thus placing their political freedom in Russian hands. Secondly Repnin was to secure the restoration of the dissidents to such a degree of equality with the Catholics as might be achieved without actual 'unpleasantness.' Catherine would agree to the exclusion of the dissidents from the highest ministerial and military posts, but not from the legislature (i.e the Diet and the Senate).[52]

The dietines for the elections to the extraordinary Diet had been summoned for 13/24 August 1767 and Repnin was active in using threats, bribes, influence and Russian troops to ensure that they elected the right kind of deputies to the Diet, committed to support the Russian programme. All was not going well. The signatories of the Catholic confederations had begun to realize that Repnin was deceiving them into agreeing to grant rights to the dissidents in exchange for the maintenance of the unreformed Polish constitution. Some of the more ardent Catholics, led by the intransigent and outspoken Bishop Sołtyk, fiercely rejected any such concessions. Questions were raised about the presence of Russian troops in Poland ; there were scenes of violence at some of the dietines. What had appeared to be a well organized and controlled group prepared to act on Russia's behalf was coming to grief on the one issue which neither Catherine nor Panin, nor evidently Repnin, understood – religion.

To encourage right thinking, Repnin moved the Russian troops to the outskirts of Warsaw, and a detachment of Cossacks camped in his own garden, in mid-September. This time the Diet would be able to reach decisions by a simple majority, since it was meeting under the aegis of a confederation. But its final resolutions would have to be approved by an ordinary Diet. On the very day it was due to meet, 24 September/5 October the Papal nuncio summoned the leaders of the Catholic confederations to defend their faith.[53] The majority were strongly moved by this appeal ; the minority, including the king, the primate, the marshals of the confederation and a number of deputies, were helpless. Repnin now descended upon the Diet and amid scenes of increasing violence warned the deputies that he would use force. He hoped to guide the debate towards two decisions : first, the appointment of a commission of plenipotentiaries to negotiate the status of the dissidents and a treaty of alliance with Russia by which Russia would guarantee the Polish constitution ; and secondly the adjournment of the Diet. But the Diet simply would not do what it was told. All Repnin's efforts were in vain and he resorted to coercion. Some of the most outspoken leaders, including Bishop Sołtyk, were arrested in mid-October, and packed off to Russia. Stanislas Augustus, who had throughout manoeuvred between the various factions, accepting endless humiliations from Repnin – and from Catherine – in the hope of saving his throne and some of his reform programme from the wreck, worked to calm spirits, which in any case under the shock of Repnin's forceful tactics now sobered down. The plenipotentiaries were appointed, and the Diet agreed on 8/19 October 1767 to adjourn to February 1768. In the ensuing interval, Repnin and the Polish plenipotentiaries agreed on the definition of the civil and political rights of the dissidents. All nobles, whether dissident or Catholic, should have equal rights, but the king must be a Catholic and Catholicism was admitted by Russia to be the religion of state. Repnin was evidently not inhuman ; the scenes he had lived through, the gap between words and deeds in the Russian position, seemed to have made some mark on him. He made an almost eloquent plea to Panin for some consideration to be given to the position of the king, and for some improvement in the form of government. If Russia wanted to re-introduce the unlimited liberum veto, she could do it, wrote Repnin ; but, he warned, 'this will not only reduce our influence here, it will destroy it ; it will leave a wound in the heart of all sensible and honourable people . . . and these are the only people on whom we may rely.' Catherine, on reading this, noted in the margin : 'Nikita Ivanovich, you may prepare a reply in the terms we have discussed ; as long as we have the means of using the liberum veto when we need to, there is no reason why we should not allow our neighbours some other system which is indifferent to us, which we may even be able to turn to our own ends.'[54]

It was thus with Russian permission that some constitutional reforms voted by the Convocation Diet were allowed to survive, such as decisions in current economic matters by simple majority. But the rule of unanimity was preserved for all questions of taxation and the armed forces, and the king's request to be allowed to set up a permanent council to sit between sessions of the Diet was rejected. Both the political and the religious documents were incorporated in a treaty between Russia and Poland, which was approved by the extraordinary Diet almost without protest, when it renewed its sessions on 13/24 February 1768. The treaty spelled out in so many words that in response to the request of the Polish Commonwealth, the empress of Russia extended her solemn guarantee for all time to the constitution, form of government, freedoms, and laws of Poland. Other articles defined the rights of the dissidents as agreed between the plenipotentiaries and Repnin, listing specifically the various civil and military offices which were now opened to non-Catholics. A further article provided that both contracting parties guaranteed the territorial integrity of each other's possessions. A separate agreement specified which were the 'matters of state' subject to the liberum veto. Having fulfilled their function the General Confederation and the extraordinary Diet were dissolved.[55]

The presence of such a large number of Russian troops in Poland had in the meantime created a good deal of anxiety in neighbouring countries. Frederick II had all along viewed Russian intervention in Poland with a jaundiced eye, and he insisted on the conclusion of a special convention with Russia in April 1767, which committed him only to diplomatic support of Russia's efforts on behalf of the dissidents. Should Austria attack Russia, he would however come to Russia's aid and Russia promised him in that case a suitable indemnity.[56] It was with great relief therefore that he heard of the conclusion of the agreement between Russia and Poland, particularly the provision for maintaining the liberum veto.

Meanwhile, since Russia had achieved a political predominance in the republic which rendered a military presence unnecessary, orders were given to the Russian troops to begin evacuating the country. Yet what appeared to be the moment of Russian triumph was the moment which showed up their real failure : the assault on the deeply held faith and on the cherished liberties of the Poles had driven the country to open revolt. Without waiting for the total evacuation of Poland by Russian troops, a conspiracy which had been maturing for some time among magnates opposed to the concessions to the dissidents, and opposed above all to the dictation of Russia, came into the open as a confederation proclaimed in the small fort of Bar in Podolia. The manifesto issued by the confederation rejected the decisions of the extraordinary Diet in February 1768 as having been made under duress. Their programme, insofar as it was ever agreed, constituted an outright challenge to Russia, since its members were united in their anti-Russian attitude if in nothing else.

As a number of Polish provinces joined the confederation, Repnin halted the Russian evacuation of Poland, and called for more troops. But Poland was in the grip of a crisis which could not be easily put down ; guerrilla warfare, looting and raiding provided a means of livelihood to many a poor noble. The first confederate forces could not stand up to the disciplined Russians, and were dispersed by June 1768. But new confederations sprang up, indistinguishable at times from brigands. The fighting was marked on both sides by great cruelty. The disorder was such that no revenue reached the king, and there was no possibility of calling the Diet for October 1768 as usual, since only some thirty deputies were able to reach the capital.

It was however Orthodox religious fanaticism – though no Russian statesman admitted the fact – which led to war. Ever since Catherine had first stood forth as the protector of the dissidents, religious ferment had developed in Polish Right Bank Ukraine, where the gentry was Polish and Catholic and the peasantry Ukrainian Orthodox or Uniat. The religious settlement approved by the Diet at the end of February 1768 filled the hearts of the Uniats with dismay since they had every reason to believe that the Orthodox would now turn against them and revenge themselves for previous Catholic oppression. Religious fanaticism was the spark which set fire to the always inflammable Ukraine, and Cossacks, lower nobles and peasants rose against Catholics, Uniates, nobles and Jews, in a wave of *haydamachestvo*.[57] In July 1768, a band of Orthodox Cossack *haydamaki* crossed into Turkish territory, in pursuit of Polish confederates, attacked the town of Balta, a dependency of the khan of Crimea, and set about massacring the Jews.

Unfortunately the Russian envoy to the Porte had already assured the Turks that Russian troops would be withdrawn from Poland after the conclusion of the Diet in February 1768. Now, however there were more Russian troops than ever in Poland, and as Russian operations against the confederates inevitably concentrated in areas closer and closer to the Turkish border, Turkish apprehension grew. The Russian demand to occupy the great Polish fort at Kamenets Podol'sk, on the southernmost border, near the Dniestr, would threaten Turkish security ; news of the Cossack assault on Balta outraged the Turks and the khan of Crimea, and the Porte made ever more pressing demands on the Russian envoy for the total Russian evacuation of Polish Podolia.

Catherine's difficulty gave France her opportunity. The Duc de Choiseul had replaced his cousin Choiseul Praslin in 1766 as foreign minister. He had to accept the fact that France's famous eastern barrier was in ruins. France had been worsted without a fight in Poland, and after a struggle in Sweden. There remained only the Porte. The Polish confederates were too weak and disorganized to be supported openly, but the Turks might pull the French chestnuts out of the fire. France still believed that a few military reverses would be enough to sweep Catherine off the throne.[58] Mounting discontent in Turkey, supported by 3 million French livres, outweighed all the assurances of the Russian envoy, with 70,000 rubles, that Russia would evacuate Poland as soon as the confederates had been put down. At the end of August the pacific Grand Vizir was replaced by a more warlike one, and at the beginning of October the Porte issued an ultimatum to Russia demanding the evacuation of Poland, the withdrawal of the Russian guarantee of the Polish constitution, and of Russian protection for the dissidents. When the Russian envoy rejected the ultimatum, he was promptly locked up in the fort of the Seven Towers, the Turkish equivalent of a declaration of war.[59] Russian policy had now brought civil war to Poland and war to Russia. 'Bon Dieu, que ne s'est on borné à faire un roi de Pologne,' wailed Frederick II.[60]

13

The First Turkish War

The Turkish declaration of war forced Catherine to re-assess the priorities to be given to her various projects. The Legislative Commission was prorogued, and plans for administrative reform postponed. The outbreak of war also awoke Catherine to the need for some permanent advisory body to coordinate military and political policy. She consulted Nikita Panin on its composition, and found, possibly to her surprise, that he strongly objected to the establishment of such a body, which he thought would only serve to delay decisions. The empress would do much better to call *ad hoc* conferences of her advisers as she had done on previous occasions. However, if she insisted on setting up a permanent Council, then he proposed that the members should include the favourite Grigory Orlov, the vice-president of the College of War, Count Z. Chernyshev, A.A. Vyazemsky, himself, and the vice-chancellor, and finally Kyrill Razumovsky, who was thought abroad to be close to Catherine and whose presence in the Council would strengthen confidence in the unity of the government.[1]

Nikita Panin's objections to the setting up of a formal council did not arise merely from his fear that it would prove to be Elizabeth's Conference writ large,[2] the kind of body with ill-defined powers which interfered everywhere and allowed favourites to exercise an unjustified influence. He realized full well that it represented a criticism of his foreign policy, which had led Russia into war. It was on his advice that the Prussian alliance had been made the cornerstone of Russian foreign policy, and he was the architect, with Catherine, of the campaign in favour of the dissidents in Poland. A Council was thus a personal defeat, a reduction in the extent of his influence. In November and December 1768 ten meetings of an *ad hoc* conference bringing together all those Panin had suggested to the empress as members of a possible Council, as well as Field-Marshal A.M. Golitsyn, and Generals P.I. Panin and M.N. Volkonsky, took place, all of which were attended by Catherine. During this period Panin fought to keep his influence. On 14/25 November Grigory Orlov challenged him over the origins of the war. The non-committal wording of the protocols cannot conceal the fact that Panin was forced to defend his policy in Poland, and the steps he was now taking to restore order there : 'And on all that has been described above, there were various political arguments,' noted the protocols.[3] The first battle arose over the appointment of a commander-in-chief of the Russian forces operating against Turkey. There were two obvious candidates, General P.A. Rumyantsev, then president of the Little Russian College, and General P.I. Panin. A compromise candidate was found in Field-Marshal A.M. Golitsyn, senior to them both, and by no means decrepit since he was under fifty. Evidently Nikita Panin had opposed Rumyantsev in the interests of his brother Peter, and Grigory Orlov, who since 1764 had been grand master of the ordnance, favoured the field-marshal in order to keep out Peter Panin. Nikita Panin then made a bid to be considered as 'first minister', in overall charge of policy, including military operations, but he was opposed by Z. Chernyshev, who successfully asserted his right to report directly to the empress.[4]

Finally on 22 January 1769 an ukaz announced the establishment for the duration of the war of a 'Council attached to the Court', charged with coordinating policy in all fields concerned with the war, including peace negotiations, and which would deal directly with individual colleges. The membership was the same as that of the autumn conferences, except for Field-Marshal Golitsyn, and General Volkonsky, who had been called away on military duties. The new Council was an informal body, its composition was not laid down, there were no ex-officio members. Some people attended when they were in the capital, then went away on special duties, and attended when they returned. It had less power than Elizabeth's Conference, since it could not issue ukazy. It was in fact exactly what Catherine needed: a body in which political rivals could fight it out and neutralize each other, and from which she could draw the best advice available to her at the time. She was also skilful enough to make the Council share the responsibility for decisions with her, when these were in fact made on its advice. In a note put before the Council by her on 8/19 December 1768, she wrote as follows :

I intend to carry out all the measures proposed with great firmness, since I take them to be measures which you, moved by zeal, fervour and devotion to me and to your country, have unanimously advised me to take in this important matter; hence, if any one still has any doubts, let him say so without loss of time.[5]

Even before the Council was formally established, Russian war aims had been discussed : they included securing free navigation for Russian ships on the Black Sea, prohibited by the Treaty of Belgrade of 1739,[6] and 'secure' frontiers with Poland. By contemporary standards the Russian army was an extremely efficient fighting force. Many of its supporting services were no lower in standard than those of other armies, though the Russians were more in the habit of living off the country they were quartered in. Many foreign officers were recruited, but the Russians did not make a practice of hiring foreign mercenary troops. Excluding special light and militia units and Cossacks, the total force fit for service in 1767 numbered 186,869, comprising 149,303 infantry and 37,566 cavalry. In addition there were some 92,000 men on garrison duty.[7] Immediate steps were taken to raise more troops. A recruit levy of one in 300 was decreed on 8/19 October 1768, which raised only 19,500 out of an estimated 33,000. On 14/25 November a second levy was ordered raising the total recruited in 1768 to 50,747.[8]

In any Russian war with Turkey, the Turks started with certain advantages. First of all they controlled the Crimea, which gave them a point of entry from which they could fan out into the Russian mainland. Secondly, they controlled the Black Sea, which enabled them to reinforce and supply their troops at any point along the coast, and gave them the choice of the main theatre of operations. Thirdly, their main armies would be operating much nearer their bases, while the Russian forces would have to march long distances and to transport supplies. In this particular war, moreover, it was important for the Russians to prevent any military junction between the Turks and the Polish confederates.

The Russian forces were therefore to be divided into two armies: the first, of some 80,000 men, under Field-Marshal A.M. Golitsyn, was to concentrate around Kiev, and thence march into Polish Podolia. Its objective was the occupation of the Polish fort of Kamenets Podol'sk, before advancing on the major Turkish fort commanding the Dniestr, Khotin. The second army, of some 40,000 men under General P.A. Rumyantsev, was to concentrate in New Russia, manning the line from Yekaterinoslav to Bakhmut, with a view to operations against the Crimea; it would also cover the rear of the first army and protect its communications.[9]

The Turks were theoretically able to put some 600,000 men in the field, without counting their Tartar auxiliaries, though it is unlikely that this figure was ever reached. Their armies were divided into three: the main corps of some 400,000 was to advance through Khotin to Kamenets Podol'sk and join up with the Polish confederates. A second corps was to act with the Crimean cavalry and invade the Ukraine. The third corps was to operate in the Northern Caucasus, with Astrakhan' as its ultimate objective.

During the winter of 1769 there were only minor skirmishes between the Russians and parties of Tartar cavalry. In spring Golitsyn occupied Kamenets Podol'sk, but failed before Khotin. On 13/24 August 1768, the Council decided to recall him and place the First Army under Rumyantsev ; Peter Panin was now appointed to the Second Army. Meanwhile Golitsyn seized Khotin on 10/21 September, and a fortnight later occupied Jassy. In a gay letter Catherine informed the ex-marshal of the Legislative Commission, General Bibikov, 'the new Princess of Moldavia greets you'.[10] A Russian corps now pushed as far as Bucharest, where a local magnate, Prince Cantacuzene, imprisoned the Turkish appointed hospodar and went over to the Russians. Azov and Taganrog were taken and the building of a flotilla on the Sea of Azov was put in hand at once. But by the time Rumyantsev took over command of the First Army in September the Russian lines were dangerously exposed to attack from the great Turkish fort of Bender on the lower Dniestr. It was too late for further campaigning, and the army went into winter quarters on Polish territory between the Dniestr and the Bug.

For 1770, the Council decided that the Second Army under Peter Panin should be given the main task of capturing Bender, while Rumyantsev acted in an auxiliary capacity, but events worked out differently. In order to keep his hold on Moldavia and Walachia, Rumyantsev decided to seek out and destroy the main Turkish army of some 22,000 Turks and 50,000 Tartars, encamped on the south side of the river Pruth. With a force totalling some 37,000 he crossed the Pruth on 17/28 June 1769 and attacked the Turkish right flank. Lieutenant-General G.A. Potemkin, with the reserves, was detailed to cross the Pruth some three miles further downstream and take the Turks in the rear. The operation was completely successful, and the Turkish army broke up in a panic.[11] Anxious not to lose momentum, Rumyantsev continued down the Pruth, where around 21 June/2 July, he came up with a force of 80,000 Turks and Crimean Tartars, encamped on the left bank at the junction with the river Larga, awaiting the arrival of the main Turkish army under the Grand Vizir. Still with his small force of 37,000 men, Rumyantsev attacked and routed the enemy on 7/18 July 1770.

Meanwhile Peter Panin, who had been delayed by an outbreak of plague in Moldavia, arrived at last before Bender on 17/28 July and settled down to a siege. The Turkish Grand Vizir determined to prevent any junction between the forces of Rumyantsev and the army under Peter Panin. Crossing to the northern shore of the Danube, he advanced up the Pruth to Lake Kagul, where the Turkish forces fleeing from the battle of Larga joined him. Rumyantsev did not wait to be attacked, however, and with only 25,000 of his men, he set upon the huge Turkish force of some 150,000 on 21 July/1 August and after a fierce battle, routed the Turkish army completely. His victory opened up the whole territory between the Danube and the Dniestr to the Russians. By 26 July Izmail had fallen ; on 10 August Kilia was taken, on 28 August Akkerman. On 16 September Bender was taken by storm by Panin, and on 10 November Brailov fell to Rumyantsev, who wound up his campaign and withdrew to winter quarters near Jassy. The news of his great victory at Kagul was greeted with joy in the capital, where a Te Deum was held amid the salute of guns, and Catherine raised her successful general to the rank of field-marshal.[12]

The year 1770 was indeed to be the *annus mirabilis* for Russia, for it also saw the triumph of the first Russian naval expedition to the Mediterranean. The idea of sending the Russian navy to fight the Turks in their own waters had first been mooted by Grigory Orlov in the Council in November 1768. It was a project after Catherine's own heart, and the man to carry it out was already on the spot : Aleksey Orlov, who was convalescing from an illness in Italy. He had no experience whatever of naval warfare, and had probably never been on board a warship. But Catherine's faith in 'Alekhan' was unbounded, and on 29 January 1769 he was notified of the impending naval expedition, and was ordered to maintain contacts with Russian envoys at other courts, and to cultivate the Orthodox populations of the Ottoman Empire.[13]

Meanwhile preparations went ahead to bring the Russian fleet into a seaworthy condition. The name which above all springs to mind in this context is that of the man who in Russia was known as Samuel Karlovich Grieg, a Scotsman who joined the Russian navy in 1764, and was to prove its leading foreign commander and adviser until his death in action in 1788.[14] It was necessary to recruit seamen in Russia and Livonia, officers, mainly from Britain, and to arrange for Russian ships to be allowed to stop and refit in friendly ports on the way from the Baltic to the Mediterranean.

The secret of the Russian intention could not be kept for long. Catherine herself was bursting with glee at the thought of the 'noise' she was going to make in Europe. To Ivan Chernyshev, the vice-president of the Admiralty College, whom she appointed ambassador in London in order to negotiate facilities for the Russian fleet, she wrote on 14/25 December in typical good spirits :

et voilà qu' on a reveillé le chat qui dormoit, et voilà que la chatte va courir sur les souris, et voilà que vous allés voir ce que vous verrés, et voilà qu'on parlera de nous, et voilà qu'on ne s'attendoit pas à tout le tintamare que nous ferons, et voilà que les turcs seront battus et voilà que les françois seront partout traités comme les Corses les traitent, et voilà bien du verbiage, adieu Monsieur.[15]

The appearance of a Russian fleet in the North Sea, the Channel, and the Mediterranean, was such a challenge to the traditional balance of maritime power that it required extensive diplomatic preparation. By the end of May 1769 the French chargé d'affaires was already reporting to Choiseul that a Russian squadron was fitting out in Kronstadt which was intended to be used in the Adriatic and the Aegean to rouse the Orthodox against the Turks.[16] In July 1769 Chernyshev was instructed to communicate Russian plans in confidence to the British government, and to ask, in view of the friendship between the two courts, for a friendly reception for Russian ships in British harbours, and for all assistance (upon payment) compatible with British neutrality in the Russo-Turkish conflict. It was also essential to avoid incidents with ships of unfriendly powers such as France on the high seas. Panin therefore declared the empress's intention not to interfere with the shipping of any Christian power in the Mediterranean, and evaded the ticklish issue of being forced to dip the flag first to British ships of the Royal Navy by secretly ordering Russian admirals to lower their flags before entering the Channel, in which case they would merely make a gunfire salute.[17]

First Denmark, then Britain, Portugal and the British bases in the Mediterranean, notably Gibraltar and Menorca, provided the most obvious friendly ports for the Russian fleet. But special agents were appointed in other ports, such as Venice, Malta and Leghorn. British assistance was amply forthcoming at first since Russia was regarded as an anti-French power, and France was freely regarded as having egged the Turks on to declare war. Thus the first Russian squadron to sail, under Admiral Spiridov, with eleven ships of the line and a number of smaller vessels, put into Hull in October 1769 with over 800 on the sicklist. Peasants taken off the land and pushed into the navy could not stand the food, the overcrowded and airless conditions and the sea. Only those who came from Archangel, reported Chernyshev, who visited the fleets in Hull and in Portsmouth, proved themselves to be real sailors.[18] The British Admiralty provided much-needed assistance in the way of masts and rigging and facilities for payment, and towards the end of October Spiridov, who had now been joined by Grieg, was able to set sail, and reached Port Mahon in Menorca in mid-December.

On his arrival at Port Mahon, Spiridov received his orders to place himself at the disposal of Aleksey Orlov in order to provide naval support for the latter's plans to arouse the Montenegrins and the Greeks. A certain Major-General Yuri V. Dolgorukiy had already been dispatched in the autumn of 1768 to begin a propaganda campaign in Montenegro. There was an element of high comedy however about his mission. He found, on his arrival, that one Stepan Maly (Stephen the Little), allegedly an Italian named Bandini who had lived in Russia and then fled from a criminal charge, had proclaimed himself to be the Emperor of Russia Peter III, and was ruling in Cetinje. Meanwhile the Venetian Republic became alarmed at the signs of unrest along the Adriatic coast encouraged by the Russian incitement to revolt. Venice feared both the arrival of the Russian fleet in its Adriatic ports and Turkish reprisals, and the Venetian Senate finally issued a declaration of neutrality, refusing to admit the warships of any nation to its harbours. When it proved impossible for the Russian fleet to support him in Montenegro, Dolgorukiy's efforts petered out. Having at first arrested the local 'Peter III', he now released him, gave him a Russian officer's uniform and left him to rule his Montenegrins.[19] Russian political activity henceforward was concentrated in the Morea.

Aleksey Orlov hoped that the Greek native population could be roused to throw off the Turkish yoke, and create a diversion serious enough to force the Turks to withdraw troops from the Russian front. But the Russians grossly underestimated the difficulty of organizing a scattered, untrained, largely leaderless population, whose language moreover they did not even speak. The greatest reliance was placed on the Greek Mainiotes in the Peloponnese, known for their warlike qualities. A number of landings were effected, but it soon became evident that the joint Russian Greek forces were not strong enough to defeat the Turks in the interior, not even to hold a port effectively.[20] Inevitably the Russians began to entertain a very poor opinion of the Greeks. The people were 'flatterers, deceitful, unstable, bold and cowardly, eager for money and booty . . . they profess their faith only with their lips and have no trace in their hearts of Christian virtue', wrote Aleksey Orlov. Having failed in his main objective, Orlov decided to abandon Navarino which had been successfully besieged and taken on 10/21 April 1770, and the fleet sailed on 26 May/6 June. It was soon reinforced by a fresh squadron from Russia, under the Englishman, John Elphinstone, who had joined Russian service as a rear-admiral. His presence led to some undignified squabbling for precedence between the English and the Russian senior admirals which had to be put down by Aleksey Orlov.

For the next month, the Russian fleet chased the Turkish Aegean fleet in and out of the Greek islands, until on 24 June/5 July, the Turkish commander finally decided to accept battle in the channel between Chios and the Anatolian coast, near the fort of Chesme. The Turks had sixteen ships of the line, six frigates and some smaller ships. The Russians had nine ships of the line, three frigates, and some smaller vessels. But the Turks had six ships of eighty to ninety guns to the Russians' one, the *Svyatoslav*, on which Elphinstone flew his flag. Spiridov was with Fyodor Orlov on the *Yevstafiy*, and Aleksey Orlov with Captain Greig on the *Tri ierarkha*. The battle began at 11 a.m. and in the midst of the cannonade, the burning mast of the Turkish flagship fell on to the deck of the *Yevstafiy* and blew up the powder magazine. The ship exploded and sank almost immediately, but Spiridov and Fyodor Orlov were rescued. It was ultimately poor Turkish manoeuvring rather than Russian gunfire which threw the Turkish line into disorder and led the fleet to withdraw in a panic to the harbour of Chesme. At the ensuing Russian council of war, it was decided to attempt to set fire to the Turkish fleet in the harbour. The attack took place in the night of 25/26 June and was totally successful. Flames spread from ship to ship as the fireboats did their job under cover of the Russian gunfire. By the next day the whole Turkish fleet had been destroyed with the loss of some 11,000 men.[21]

The battle of Chesme ranks with Lepanto and Trafalgar as a naval battle which marked the course of history and created a national myth. It was greeted with indescribable joy in St Petersburg. A Te Deum was sung in honour of the victory, and tribute was paid where it was due, to Peter the Great, in a special memorial service.[22] Rewards were showered on every man in the fleet by the euphoric empress and Aleksey Orlov was allowed to add 'Chesmensky' (of Chesme) to his name.[23]

The subsequent activity of the Russian fleet did not live up to the expectations raised by the victory at Chesme. Efforts to blockade the Dardanelles and to conquer Lemnos failed and Orlov decided to make Paros and the port of Auza his main base. The Russians could count on a friendly reception in the Greek islands since the defeat of the Turkish fleet, and the inhabitants of many of them even took an oath of loyalty to the empress. Meanwhile a third Russian squadron arrived from the Baltic, this time commanded by the Danish-born Admiral Arf. Leaving Spiridov in overall command of the Russian forces, Aleksey Orlov departed in November 1770 to spend the winter in Leghorn.

During a lightning visit he paid to Russia in March 1771, he advised abandoning the attempt to use the Greeks against the Turks, 'because of their innate tendency to slavery and their frivolous character', and henceforward the fleet was ordered to concentrate on blockading the Dardanelles, and cutting Turkish communications with the islands. Orlov was also authorized to undertake direct peace negotiations with the Turks should occasion arise.[24]

The campaign of 1771 was less dramatic than that of 1770. Further recruit levies were decreed, of one man in 150 in September 1769, another one in 150 in 1770, and the highest of all, one man in 100 in 1771.[25] The strategy for the new campaign was discussed in the Council in November 1770. The minutes of the meeting are drawn up very discreetly, but they do not conceal that Grigory Orlov was thinking in terms of a descent on Constantinople. For the time being however the main thrust of the Russian land attack was to be directed against the Crimean khanate.[26] In Moldavia and Walachia the Turks refused battle, and Rumyantsev with his 45,000 Russians could do little against the 120,000 Turks. Both sides suffered from the poor harvest, and from the outbreak of plague which was sweeping across southern and eastern Europe. The summer passed in minor operations, though in October 1771 a major Russian assault was successfully launched against the Turkish forts at the mouth of the Danube which were captured together with quantities of guns and supplies.

Peter Panin, in command of the Second Army, had been placed in charge of complex negotiations with the Tartar Hordes, and had achieved an agreement with the Nogay Tartars by which they finally consented to move from their lands between the Danube and the Dniestr, and were resettled in the Kuban. General Panin had also been instructed to negotiate with the khan of Crimea with a view to detaching him from the Ottoman Empire and setting up the Crimea as an independent khanate. In the autumn of 1770, however, he threw up his command in a huff and asked leave to retire from government service completely. He had been bitterly offended because his victory at Bender had been outshone in Catherine's eyes by Rumyantsev's victories in the Danubian Principalities and Orlov's at Chesme, and he felt that he had not been sufficiently rewarded.[27] Catherine, who had never liked him, allowed him to go, and Prince Vasily M. Dolgorukiy took over his command and was instructed to proceed with the occupation of the Crimean peninsula, promising to restore its former independence from the Porte. The Russian occupation began on 3/14 June 1771 and by mid-July those Crimeans who had not gone over to the Russians had capitulated. The khan, Selim Girey, escaped and fled to the Turks.

A new political structure had now to be devised for the Crimea and the terms of its cooperation with Russia worked out. A new khan, Salip Girey, was elected, and his younger brother, Shahin Girey, was sent to St Petersburg to negotiate a treaty. There difficulties arose over the extent of the khan's authority over other Tartar Hordes such as the Nogays, and over the Russian demands to establish garrisons in Kerch, Yenikale, Kinburn and Kaffa. Control of the Straits of Kerch would enable the Russian flotilla, which Admiral Senyavin had been busily building in the Sea of Azov, to break out into the Black Sea at last. Negotiations with the Tartar leaders (who were themselves not united and under constant Ottoman pressure) culminated in the Treaty of Karazubazar in November 1772. It recognized the independence of the Crimea, proclaimed eternal friendship and alliance between Russia and the Crimea and allowed the Russians to maintain garrisons in all the ports they had asked for except Kaffa.[28] If the campaign of 1771 on land and sea was not so spectacular as that of 1770, yet the occupation of the Crimea provided Catherine with a substantial bargaining counter in any negotiations for peace.

Peace was indeed beginning to seem desirable. As the summer of 1771 wore on not only was Catherine faced with increasing anxieties in the field of foreign policy, where Frederick II was proving an exacting ally, and Austria an unpredictable potential enemy,[29] but in Russia itself the strain of the war began to be felt. To finance it, taxation had to be increased : the obrok payable by all taxpayers except serfs, in addition to the poll-tax, was raised to 2 rubles as from July 1769, though the blow was softened for the assigned peasants in industry by slightly increased scales of pay.[30] Taxes and the recruit levy weighed heavily on the population, and it is against this background of increasing social tension that the great plague riots of autumn 1771 in Moscow must be seen.

Plague had been rife in southern Russia and European Turkey since 1769, and even led the government to cease the recruit levy for a time after 1771.[31] By August 1771 it had spread to Moscow where between 400 and 500 deaths were taking place daily. Panic hit the city; nobles left for the countryside, factories and workshops closed down, and the population of workers, and peasants without money, food or work, was left to shift for itself in a city abandoned by its upper class, and from which even the governor, General P.S. Saltykov, had departed. Archbishop Ambrosius of Moscow attempted to reduce infection by preventing the formation of crowds, and removed a miracle-working icon, in which the people had much faith, from one of the gates of Moscow. His well-meant attempt provoked a riot on 16/27 September 1771. The crowd broke into the monastery in which he was sheltering, dragged him out and cut him down – just as Archbishop Arseniy Matseyevich had once prophesied.[32] The mob then rampaged through the city, and unrest began to spread to the countryside. The riot was put down by troops and nearly 300 people were arrested.

Catherine reacted by appointing a new governor, General P. Yeropkin, to replace Saltykov, and sent the favourite, Grigory Orlov, to control the epidemic and restore order. Orlov, given for perhaps the first time in his life a chance to show what he could do, proved efficient and humane. He promised serfs who volunteered to work in hospitals their freedom, opened orphanages, distributed food and money, and reopened the public baths, which had been closed as a measure of quarantine – a closure which had contributed to the riots. More than 3,000 old houses were burnt, 6,000 were disinfected, work was provided. In two and a half months Orlov spent over 95,000 rubles, of which 16,000 went on clothing and 17,000 on food. Deaths, which had risen to over 21,000 in September, dropped to 17,561 in October, 5,255 in November and 805 in December – either because of Orlov's measures or, more probably, because of the onset of the colder weather. The total number of deaths in Moscow was estimated at between 75,000 and 100,000, reaching nearly 200,000 if Moscow district is taken into account.[33]

14

The Impact of the War on
Russian Foreign Policy

With the Turkish declaration of war, Russia at once became more vulnerable in the field of foreign policy. As in Poland, so in Sweden the Russian intervention in the struggle between the Hats and the Caps had left much ill-feeling and Russian influence had to be maintained by lavish distributions of pensions to the leaders of the Cap party in the Council. Meanwhile events in Poland provided a vivid example of what might be in store for Sweden : 'From Poland, always the same news : anarchy and corruption ; the same fate awaits us if we do not soon take strong measures,' noted Crown Prince Gustavus in his diary in November 1767.[1]

A change in French policy was to provide him with the help he needed. Choiseul had definitely decided, when he resumed office in April 1766, to stake everything on strengthening the Swedish Crown against the Hat and Cap parties. The task was not easy for if one thing united the two parties it was the resolve not to allow the restoration of royal absolutism, or even of the unadulterated constitution of 1720, in Sweden. But France benefited from the fact that, having once supplied Osterman with 26,000 rubles in March 1768, Panin left him almost without instructions while he concentrated on Polish affairs and the defence of his own position at court.[2] Osterman had to fight not only against the Hats ; he found himself engaged in a social war with the queen as leader of the court party, now supported by France. The queen, reported Osterman, had only to hear that he had organized a reception or a dinner to choose the same evening for one of her own.

To achieve their aims, the calling of a Diet was essential. The conspirators forced the issue by means of a ploy with an extraordinarily contemporary ring : in December 1768, the king threatened to go on strike, that is to say he threatened to abdicate, which would render a Diet necessary. When the Council delayed its reply, Crown Prince Gustavus visited all the government Colleges and the armed forces ; all refused to carry on government business until the Council gave in, which it finally did on 9/20 December. A Diet was then summoned.

Meanwhile in Denmark the vagaries of Christian VII, unbalanced, though not as yet insane, required constant Russian vigilance. The ascendancy acquired by his physician, Johann Friedrich Struensee, was already marked, and the king showed every inclination to break away from Denmark's present orientation toward Britain and Russia. Nevertheless, the outbreak of the Russo-Turkish war in October 1768, and more particularly Adolf Frederick's coup in Sweden in December, brought the two powers closer together. Both felt that their security depended on the weakness of Sweden implicit in the existing constitution. Bernstorff, the Danish foreign minister, had frequently hinted at the desirability of a *pacte de famille* between Denmark and Russia ('the House of Oldenburg rules from the Elbe to China'). On hearing the news from Sweden, Panin showed himself more willing to meet Bernstorff's wishes, particularly in view of the need to concert military operations in the event of war following on a constitutional coup in Sweden. Should war ensue, Panin was willing to agree to, and to guarantee, Danish acquisitions at the expense of Sweden.

Bernstorff was equally alarmed at the course of events in Sweden, and he began to mobilize Danish forces in February 1769. This brought Choiseul on the scene with a warning against attacking Sweden, which was echoed by Spain. French threats merely drove Bernstorff further into Russian arms, and he pressed on with negotiations for a new treaty between the two powers, proposing that by the following May both powers should have ten ships of the line and 20,000 men available for operations. Denmark proposed using half her troops for a landing in Schonen, and keeping half on the border between Norway and Sweden. But in order to give consistence to the new alliance, Bernstorff also wanted the immediate implementation of the Holstein-Oldenburg exchange treaty of 1767.[3] From his point of view there were two reasons for urgency : in the first place, should Catherine be overthrown, and her son succeed her, he might well repudiate the exchange treaty on his majority. But Paul might also die, and in that case the heir to the duchy was the king of Sweden, unless Adolf Frederick could be forced to implement an earlier undertaking to cede his rights to the king of Denmark in exchange for Oldenburg.

Catherine would not however consent to the immediate exchange. She was determined that Paul himself must be a consenting party to the cession of his duchy, and that negotiations should be completed by him on his majority. And she knew full well that as long as the exchange had not been carried out, and Bernstorff remained in power, Denmark was tied to her apron strings. She refused therefore Bernstorff's proposals for a *pacte de famille,* but agreed to regard Holstein as already in the power of Denmark and to guarantee it against all other powers.[4]

Meanwhile elections for the Swedish Diet were carried on to the accompaniment of an ever greater shower of gold. France, by mid-February, had expended 750,000 livres ; the Russians, by April, over 930,000.[5] In all Osterman asked his court for 205,250 rubles.[6] When the Diet finally met on 19 April 1769 in the small town of Norköping, it was evident that the Hats had won a sweeping victory. But they were not united. The king might have helped them but this did not mean that they were willing to help him. The division in their ranks enabled Os-terman, supported by his Danish and British allies, to continue to fight against any change in the existing constitution, and against a renewal of treaty relations with France (which France had no intention of renewing *unless* the power of the Crown were strengthened). When the Diet was at last dissolved in January 1770, in spite of the vast sums of money spent by all the foreign powers involved, all that had really been achieved was the payment of the debts of the king and queen.[7]

While the political struggle continued in Sweden from April 1769 to the end of the year, negotiations between Denmark and Russia for a new treaty of alliance dragged on. Both powers mobilized their fleets and their land forces ; but Den-mark could not be certain whether Russian naval preparations were directed against Sweden, or were really, as turned out to be the case, aimed at the Porte. And Russian troop movements on the Finnish border were modest enough to lead Bernstorff to fear that Russia might leave Denmark to bear the brunt of land war-fare at the last moment.[8]

Both powers attempted to induce Frederick II to commit himself to playing an active part in the defence of the Swedish constitution. But Frederick would not be drawn. At the outbreak of the Russo-Turkish war he had offered his good of-fices to the Porte (as had George III). But when Catherine was approached, she brushed aside all such offers as premature, at least until Russia should have achieved a resounding victory. The news of Adolf Frederick's coup in December 1768 briefly brought to life the negotiations for an Anglo-Russian alliance which had languished since the recall of Macartney in 1766. Russia was now willing to give up the Turkish *casus foederis* in exchange for substantial subsidies to com-bat French policy in Sweden. But Chernyshev in London always received the same reply : Parliament would not agree to grant subsidies in peace-time, and the existing government could not do, in office, what it had combatted in opposi-tion.[9]

All the more important was it therefore to secure the cooperation of Prussia. But Frederick used the opportunity to press for a renewal of the Russo-Prussian treaty. It was only due to expire in 1772, but he wanted it to outlast the favour of Nikita Panin. Catherine was in no hurry to renew the treaty ahead of time, since she was still obliged to take into account the division in the Russian court be-tween a pro-Prussian and a pro-Austrian party which had emerged into the open with the outbreak of war. But events in Sweden, and the calling of the extraordi-nary Swedish diet for April 1769, led her to lend a more willing ear to Prussian demands. Frederick made clear however that he was not prepared to follow Rus-sian policy in Sweden ; he would agree to renew his guarantee of the Swedish constitution in general terms, but he was not willing to accept that any slight modification should be a *casus foederis* of his alliance with Russia.[10]

He had other reasons too, in summer 1769, for making Russia wait. He was about to meet the Emperor Joseph at Neisse in August 1769, and he expected this sudden rapprochement between Prussia and Austria to render Russia more amenable to his wishes. 'Il faut la [cette negotiation] trainer car je suis curieux de savoir ce que me dira l'empereur,' he wrote in August 1769. . . . 'Si l'empereur ne dit rien d'intéressant, il sera toujours temps de conclure notre traité avec les russes.'[11] What did emerge from the meeting between the two rulers at the end of August was a secret agreement between them to keep the peace in Germany in the event of war between Britain and the Bourbon powers, or any other war. This effective neutralization of Germany removed one of Frederick's major anxieties, particularly since he believed that France had secretly agreed to it.[12] But he continued to press for the renewal of the Russo-Prussian treaty, and as he had anticipated, his brief flirtation with Austria at Neisse rendered Russia more amenable. The treaty was finally signed on 12/23 October 1769 ; agreement was reached on the extent of Prussian guarantees of the Swedish constitution, by enumerating those specific changes which would be considered as an overthrow of the fundamental laws of Sweden. A Swedish attack on Russia, or the restoration of absolutism in Sweden (la souveraineté) were to be regarded as the *casus foederis* of the treaty. In such case Frederick engaged himself to make a diversion in Swedish Pomerania, where he could hope to make some acquisitions.[13]

Meanwhile Bernstorff had been pressing for the conclusion of the treaty between Denmark and Russia. The Bourbon powers continued to use threatening language, and he wanted to strengthen his links with Russia in the event of a war with Sweden which seemed at times throughout the summer almost inevitable. The treaty was finally signed on 2/13 December 1769. A secret article provided that any alteration of the Swedish constitution should constitute the *casus foederis* of the treaty. In the event of war, Denmark could make acquisitions on her Norwegian border, Russia in Finland. Both powers were to prepare land and sea forces for a campaign in spring 1770.[14]

There was to be no campaign. The threat of war with Sweden declined after the dispersal of the extraordinary Diet in January 1770. In the autumn of 1770, Crown Prince Gustavus left Sweden on a visit to Western Europe and France. Russia had all the more reason to feel relief at the easing of tension in the North, since affairs in Denmark were now taking a very unsatisfactory turn. The influence of Struensee over King Christian VII culminated in the dismissal of Bernstorff in September 1770. Denmark now moved away for a while from the pro-Russian policies which he had pursued in the interests of the final settlement of the Holstein question.

Hard on the heels of the fall of Bernstorff came a further blow : the unexpected death of King Adolf Frederick of Sweden on 1/12 February 1771. Gustavus had only just arrived, incognito, in Paris, on 4 February 1771, as a crown prince. He left on 14/25 March, still incognito but as a king who had already negotiated with France the resumption of French subsidies and who had been promised financial and diplomatic support during the forthcoming Diet. Though Choiseul had been dismissed in 1770, his successor continued the policy of strengthening the Swedish Crown at the expense of the parties.

Meanwhile the outbreak of war had forced Russia to make some effort at reaching an accommodation in Poland which might enable her to remove her troops from the country. Prince N.V. Repnin was recalled and allowed to join the army fighting against the Turks. He was replaced by Prince N.M. Volkonsky. But the instructions given to Volkonsky on 31 March/11 April 1769 indicated little change in Russian policy. He was to support the existing government, to confirm the Russian guarantee of the territory and constitution of the republic as laid down in the Diet of February 1768 ; he was to keep the king on the throne and prevent the Poles from joining the Turks. He was given some discretion in the matter of the dissidents : though he was to admit no formal alteration of their status, he was allowed to turn a blind eye to such changes as they themselves might propose, in order to secure the return of internal peace. But he need not hesitate to threaten the Poles with the danger of religious war : 'Not only Russia was interested in the dissidents, but all Protestant powers and if the Catholic powers meddle, then a war disastrous for all Christendom will follow, during which Catholicism may be completely exterminated in Poland.'[15] Volkonsky proved no more successful than Repnin in Poland. It was clear that the Polish confederates would wait until military operations in the Russo-Turkish war swung the balance to one side or the other.

The unruliness of the confederates, and their frequent incursions over the borders of Prussia and Austria had already led the latter to throw a military cordon around the county of Zips in Poland in February 1769, ostensibly to protect Hungary from confederate raids. In July 1770 the cordon was extended almost to Cracow, on the additional pretext of enforcing quarantine against the plague which was beginning to spread.[16] When the Polish court protested to Austria against this occupation, Kaunitz now challenged Poland to prove her title to these lands. The new understanding reached between Prussia and Austria at Neisse evidently led Frederick to wink at this Austrian occupation, which served him as a pretext to extend a military cordon of his own to Marienwerder on the Vistula, on the pretext of protecting his communications with Polish Prussia, and also as a quarantine measure.[17]

Always anxious to bring the war to an end and to prevent his Russian ally from achieving too much, Frederick II allowed the rapprochement which had taken place between Joseph II and himself to go a stage further, at a second meeting between the two rulers at Neustadt in September 1770. 'Mon petit voyage en Moravie fera des impressions plus pacifiques sur l'impératrice de Russie que toutes les troupes et toutes les revues du monde,' he wrote to his brother Prince Henry on 6/17 June 1770.[18] Catherine had meanwhile continued to evade all proposals for a mediation, but while urging massive preparations for a campaign in 1771, she had authorized Field-Marshal Rumyantsev in August 1770 to discuss peace terms directly with the Turks but only after the release of the Russian envoy from the Seven Towers.[19]

Prince Kaunitz had accompanied Joseph II to Neustadt and it was to the Austrian chancellor that Frederick expounded at length his desire to see peace restored between Russia and the Porte, and his conviction that Austria did not wish to see Russia make too many gains. Kaunitz agreed that Austria could not accept the total humiliation of the Porte, and that Russia should not be allowed to keep too many of her conquests.[20] While Prussia and Austria were thus uniting to deprive Russia of the fruits of her victories, news reached Frederick and Joseph at Neustadt that the Porte had made a formal request for the mediation of the two powers. Kaunitz asked Frederick, Russia's ally, to take the initiative in forwarding the request to Catherine and the two concerted their approach to Russia.[21]

The Turkish request for a joint Prussian and Austrian mediation was conveyed to Catherine in September 1770 by Frederick. The empress still much preferred to negotiate directly with the Porte through Rumyantsev, and instructions were hastily sent to him to attempt to open talks with the Grand Vizir on the spot.[22] The Prussian overture was for the time being refused on the grounds that it would be insulting to Britain who had offered her good offices at the beginning of the war, to leave her out of a mediation. Meanwhile Russian peace terms were redefined at a meeting of the Council on 16/27 September 1770. They were now to include the retention of Azov and Taganrog ; free commercial navigation on the Black Sea ; an amnesty for all Turkish subjects who had taken the Russian side in the war ; the retention of an island in the Archipelago if one were captured ; the independence of those Tartars who should have thrown off the yoke of the Porte (a reference to the proposed Russian occupation of the Crimea), and finally the occupation of the Danubian Principalities for long enough for Russia to compensate herself from their revenue for the costs of the war. But this indemnity could be waived in favour of the greater good of securing the independence of the Principalities from the Porte.[23]

When the Turks rejected Rumyantsev's offer of direct talks, and insisted that peace could only be treated through the mediation of Austria and Prussia, the Russian peace terms were put to Frederick in confidence. He greeted them with horror : 'Les cornes me sont venues à la tête,' he wrote to Prince Henry on 3 January 1771. 'Jamais je ne puis me charger de les proposer ni aux Turcs ni aux Autrichiens . . . vous pouvez regarder cette pièce comme une déclaration de guerre . . . on se moque de nous.' He would not, he declared, go to war with Austria in order to procure such gains for Russia. To the Austrian ambassador in Berlin Frederick was equally outspoken : the Russian peace terms were 'exhorbitantes, intolérables'. Having thus warned his fellow mediator that he would not support the Russian peace terms, Frederick now wrote to Catherine to persuade her that Austria would never accept them. The empress must content herself with Azov, free navigation on the Black Sea and some territorial adjustments in the Caucasus.[24]

Needless to say Catherine was extremely unlikely to do anything of the kind. She had scarcely expected to find in Frederick the advocate of the Turks, she remarked, and moreover it was peace with Turkey, not peace with Austria which was under consideration. 'Let us hold fast, and not a step back, and everything will work out ; but if they see that we are chasing peace, we will get a bad peace,' she added.[25] Catherine wrote again to Frederick, on 19/30 January 1771, defending her peace terms, and threw cold water on the so-called 'équilibre d'Orient', a phrase which was beginning to be used and which she suspected had been invented by France. 'Qui a pu jamais apprécier que cette balance soit juste, lorque les frontières de la domination turque s'estendent au Niester, et qu'elle soit renversée, lorsque ces même frontières se trouvent restreintes au Danube?' Thus Catherine held to what she thought her armies had conquered for her.[26]

Frederick's anxiety about Austria's reaction to the Russian peace terms, particularly the independence of the Danubian Principalities, had in it an element of genuine fear that Austria might be driven to take up arms in defence of the Porte. Though he hoped that the understanding reached at Neisse in 1769 would secure him from attack, he was nevertheless extremely anxious to end the whole war, which was costing him a lot in the subsidies he was bound by treaty to pay to Russia. But there was another side to his performance, namely the hope that Prussia could in some way benefit from the war. He had long contemplated the acquisition of Polish territory in order to bring together his scattered domains. As far back as February 1769, he had asked his envoy in Russia, Solms, to discuss with Panin a plan for the partition of Poland. He attributed the plan to a certain Count Lynar,[27] though it was in fact his own. Austria could have the county of Zips and part of Galicia ; Prussia could have Polish Prussia, Warmia and a right of protection over Danzig, and Russia whatever suited her. Both Prussia and Austria would then join Russia against the Turks. At the time, winter 1769, Panin showed no interest in the proposal when sounded by Solms, though Russia too had long contemplated 'frontier adjustments' with Poland.[28]

Not content with testing the ground in Russia, Frederick did the same with Austria, in a conversation with the Austrian envoy in Berlin in May 1770 : he proposed that Austria should help herself to Parma and Plasencia, 'avec quelque-chose de l'état de Venise', to which Nugent had suggested to Prussia in exchange a neat 'arrondissement' at the expense of Poland.[29] But one of the principal advocates of Prussian expansion in Poland was Prince Henry of Prussia, who paid a protracted visit to Russia in September 1770. In December 1770, or early January 1771, there was some lighthearted and cynical banter at court. Catherine referred to the Austrian occupation of the county of Sandec in Poland in December 1770, and exclaimed : 'Mais pourquoi tout le monde ne prendrait-il pas aussi ?' to which Zakhar Chernyshev then added : 'il faut après tout que chacun ait quelquechose.'[30] In a long report to Frederick, Solms expanded on the subject. According to the gossip at the Russian court, he wrote, in January 1771, since Austria had justified her seizures in Poland on the grounds that these territories had belonged of old to the Crown of Hungary, Russia and Prussia should search their archives, and would surely find good legal claims on the bishopric of War-mia and on Polish Livonia respectively. Russia might even take the territory up to the Dvina, and then draw a line down to the Dniepr.

. . . ce serait au moins quelquechose qu'on pourrait appeler un dédommagement pour six ans de guerre en Pologne et contre les Turcs, et qu'on aurait aussi procuré à un bon allié comme V.M. un dédommagement pour les frais et les dépenses qu'elle avait eues à cause de l'alliance, et qu'au reste l'enlèvement de ces provinces à la Pologne ne rendroit pas son roi moins puissant ou moins consideré qu'il devait l'être.[31]

Thus it appeared that opinion at the Russian court favoured making Poland pay for the Russian occupation and for Prussian subsidies to Russia.

Prince Henry returned to Berlin in February 1771, convinced that Russia would not oppose Prussian acquisitions in Poland as compensation for her own gains at the expense of Turkey. Whether he now persuaded his brother to adopt his plans, or whether Frederick now saw his own secretly harboured plans matur-ing is irrelevant. The king went ahead with persuading Russia to give him 'oint-ment for the burn' as he put it in a letter to Solms on 20 February 1771.[32] Panin too at last admitted openly to Solms the connection between Russian acquisitions from the Porte and Prussian compensation at the expense of Poland. In a crucial conversation with Solms in mid-February 1771, the Russian minister agreed that Russia would not prolong the war merely for the sake of making more acquisi-tions at the expense of the Porte. He referred specifically to the Crimea, which had not yet been occupied by Russia. But Russia would require compensation for what she had refrained from acquiring : '. . . en renonçant ainsi à l'espérance d'obtenir les avantages en question, il fallait songer à procurer à la Russie un autre dédommagement,' said Panin to Solms, and the latter understood that such compensation would be found in Poland.[33] Frederick had no objection to this solution which opened the way for him. And since Austria had already helped herself, he wrote, 'je ne pourrai pas me dispenser non plus de me procurer de la même façon, quelque petite partie de la Pologne, ne fut-ce qu'en guise d'équiva-lent de mes subsides . . .'[34] The king went ahead therefore with the preparation of his 'legal claims' on what he thought he could get away with at the time, namely Pomerellia,[35] which he prepared to occupy on the grounds that he had to extend his cordon against the plague, just as the Austrians had done. Thus al-ready a legally dubious dynastic claim was to be put forward to disguise the out-right demand for compensation which would preserve the balance of power be-tween Russia and her ally Prussia.

The relative passivity with which Austria had watched Russian victories gave way early in 1771 to genuine alarm at their extent and at the nature of the Russian peace terms. By February 1771, Austria began to arm, and troops were stationed in Hungary. Highly secret negotiations were begun with the Porte with a view to Austria entering the war on the Turkish side, in order to restrain Russia. Panin, pressed by Prussia to agree to compensation in Poland, attempted to discover the grounds on which Austria justified the annexation of Zips, but Kaunitz fobbed him off with assurances that the territories had merely been temporarily occupied, and their future was subject to amicable discussion with Poland.[36]

The lightning visit of Aleksey Orlov to St Petersburg in March 1771 led to a change of emphasis in the Russian peace terms. Orlov's advice to give up the demand for an island in the Archipelago on the grounds that it would be too expensive to defend was accepted. But there was a divergence of views between Catherine and her advisers on the Danubian Principalities. Catherine wished to achieve their independence, rather than an idemnity for their return to the Porte. In the end however, presumably on the advice of Panin and Orlov, it was decided to ask for a huge indemnity of 25 million rubles, paid in one year, for their return to the Ottoman Empire.[37] Unofficially these terms were communicated by Aleksey Orlov to Kaunitz on his return journey through Vienna to Italy. The Austrian chancellor regarded them as excessive,[38] and continued with his negotiations with the Turks. Panin's hints to the Austrian envoy that Austria too might find some compensation for Russian gains were not taken up. In vain he urged that dynastic or other grounds could always be found, and assured the Austrian envoy, Lobkowitz, 'qu'il n'y avait aucun état qui n'eut des prétentions sur son voisin et qui ne put produire des titres quand l'occasion se présentait de les faire valoir'.[39]

Meanwhile the joint efforts of Prussia and Austria as potential mediators had at last secured the release of the Russian resident, A.M. Obreskov, from the Seven Towers. Catherine could no longer delay accepting Austrian and Prussian mediation and again the Council met in May 1771 to consider Russian peace terms. For the first time its members were informed of the negotiations with Prussia over Poland, which seemed to offer a solution for the problem of the Danubian Principalities if, in accordance with Catherine's wishes, they were not to be restored to the Porte. Panin explained that since Frederick II had decided to follow Austria's example and annex certain territories in Poland, Russia would lay claim to Polish Livonia in order to establish the Russo-Polish frontier along a waterway. Moldavia and Walachia would be transferred to Poland in compensation.[40]

The Russian peace terms, including the plan to compensate Poland with the Danubian Principalities for the loss of Polish Livonia, were communicated to Lobkowitz on 18/29 May, and on the following day Panin discussed with Solms, with 'a map on the table', exactly what Frederick proposed to take in Poland. The Russian peace terms which were also communicated to Frederick now seemed to him 'quite moderate' – indeed he thought the idea of compensating Poland with the Principalities a very good one, or at any rate this was the impression he sought to give in Vienna.[41]

In no circumstances however would Austria agree to the handing over of Moldavia and Walachia to Poland[42] or to the weakening of the Ottoman Empire such a loss implied. It was better for Austria to throw in her lot with the Turks against

Russia, and on 25 June/6 July 1771 a treaty was signed between the two powers by which the Porte agreed to pay 20,000 purses of 500 piastres to Austria, and to cede parts of Walachia to her, if Austria, either by her mediation or by force of arms, secured the return of all Russian conquests to Turkey and a guarantee of the political independence and territorial integrity of Poland.[43]

The joint mediation by Prussia and Austria between the belligerents now faded away for a while. There was clearly no chance of persuading Frederick, sure now of his share of Poland, to join Austria in pressing moderation on Russia.[44] Austria meanwhile attempted to get Russia to content herself with the acquisition of the Kabardas in the Caucasus, free navigation in the Black Sea and an indemnity, and declared her intention of returning the counties annexed from Poland if Russia would guarantee the integrity of the Republic.[45] Tension mounted in the autumn, and Russia now urged Frederick to commit himself to come to her assistance with 20,000 troops if Austria attempted to send her forces into Poland or into the Turkish provinces occupied by Russia.[46]

The strong nerves which Catherine was invariably to show in foreign relations were now revealed. The Council on 22 August/2 September decided to call the Austrian bluff. It was unlikely, they decided, that Austria really meant war ; she was trying by a show of force to make Russia alter her policy. The answer was clearly a corresponding show of force which would have the additional advantage of stiffening Frederick's resolve to stand by his ally. It was decided to send reinforcements to Poland, and to embark again on negotiations for an alliance with Britain, without the Turkish *casus foederis,* in case France should come to the aid of Austria.[47]

But the Russo-Prussian negotiations had in the meantime come up against an obstacle : in exchange for Prussian assistance to Russia against possible Austrian intervention in Poland and the Principalities, Frederick raised his price. He wanted Danzig,[48] and he continued to press Russia to give up the demand for Moldavia and Walachia, believing that though Austria might allow Russia to keep the Crimea, she would go to war for the Principalities.[49] On the other hand Austria was aware that since the fall of Choiseul in December 1770 she could not count on French assistance. Could Austria take on Russia with no alliance other than that of Turkey ? Catherine too began to reconsider her terms. Secure now of the Crimea, which had been successfully occupied in the summer of 1771, the Council agreed on 24 October/5 November 1771 to return the Principalities to the Porte but to demand in exchange Ochakov and Kinburn, the forts which controlled the estuary of the Dniepr on the Black Sea.[50] This resolution was confirmed at a meeting of the Council on 22 November/2 December at which rumours that Austria would come to the aid of the Turks were first reported.[51] At the same time Catherine, under the severe financial pressure of the war, and in view of the plague and the riots in Moscow, agreed to the renewal of peace talks with the Turks in the autumn.[52]

Once Russia had agreed to restore the Principalities to the Porte it became possible for Austria to decide whether to ratify the treaty of 25 June/6 July 1771 with the Porte and fight Russia in order to maintain the integrity of Poland, acquiring her compensation from the Porte ; or, seeing that the main Austrian demand had been granted, to drop the Turks, and seek compensation without a fight either in Poland or elsewhere, for what would no longer be acquired from the Turks. Maria Theresa hoped for small territorial cessions but Joseph hoped that Austria might receive Glatz and part of Silesia, while Frederick took more of Poland.[53]

Meanwhile Russia had discovered the details of the secret Austrian treaty with the Porte of 25 June 1771. The threat of Austrian participation in the war on the Turkish side led Panin to come further into the open with the Austrian envoy in St Petersburg, to admit that if Russia gave up the Principalities she would seek compensation in Poland, and to invite Austria to compensate herself in Poland too, rather than in Turkey. '. . . il n'est point d'état qui n'ait toujours des droits ouverts vis à vis de ses voisins . . . de même qu'il n'en est aucun qui ne soit pénetré du besoin de l'équilibre de puissance.' Austria was now frankly invited by Panin to join Russia and Prussia in maintaining this balance of power.[54]

While Kaunitz, Maria Theresa and Joseph hesitated whether to seek compensation in Turkey, in Prussia or in Poland, Frederick pressed for the conclusion of his secret convention with Russia. He wanted it to be concluded before Russia made peace with the Porte, fearing that if Russia was once free of the Turkish war, she could no longer be driven to partition Poland for his benefit. Partition must come before peace, while the Russians naturally preferred peace before partition. A bargain was struck when Frederick on 23 December/4 January 1772, gave up the demand for the cession of Danzig which Russia had systematically refused.

By the end of January Kaunitz had succeeded in cooling Joseph II's warlike ardour, and in persuading Maria Theresa that Austria must not be excluded from the mediation between Russia and the Porte, and must take her share of Poland. It remained to persuade the Turks that they would get as much by Austrian support in peace negotiations with Russia as they would have acquired by Austrian armed intervention, and the Austrian internuncio at the Porte, Thugut, was instructed to cooperate with his Prussian opposite number.

Thereafter events moved quickly. News of the Austrian surrender reached Russia on 1/12 February 1772.[55] It hastened the signature of the Russo-Prussian convention, which took place on 6/17 February 1772, though it was antedated to 4/15 January in order to avoid giving the impression that it had been signed only when the Austrians were about to join in. A preliminary agreement was reached between the three courts on 7/18 March 1772. Kaunitz now dragged out the negotiations in order to obtain as much as possible, thus lending substance to Frederick II's cruel words about Maria Theresa : 'Elle pleure, mais elle prend toujours.' The convention between the three powers was signed on 5 August 1772.[56] It remained to force it on the unwilling victim.

15

From the Partition of Poland to the Peace of Kuchuk Kainardzhi

Having decided against military intervention in the Russo-Turkish war, Austria informed the Porte in May 1772 that the secret treaty of 6 July 1771 would not be ratified. The Porte nevertheless agreed that should it recover both the Danubian Principalities and the Crimea at the peace, Austria would be given the stipulated price of her good offices, namely Little Walachia, and would not be asked to repay the three million piastres she had already received under the treaty.[1]

Meanwhile direct negotiations for a truce began between Rumyantsev and the Turkish commander in April 1772. His efforts were supported in Constantinople by the Prussian and Austrian envoys in their capacity as mediators. The truce was signed on 19/30 May 1772[2] and was extended to the Mediterranean on 20/31 July. It did not prevent Russia from continuing to build up a flotilla on the Danube and a fleet in the sea of Azov.

The plenipotentiaries were to meet at Fokshany in Moldavia, which was to be regarded as Russian territory, and the Russians would act as hosts.[3] A.M. Obreskov, the Russian resident who had been freed from the Seven Towers early in 1771, and who had lived in the Ottoman Empire some thirty-four years, was appointed one of the Russian plenipotentiaries. The chief plenipotentiary however was Grigory Orlov. The reasons for his appointment can only be surmised. He had no diplomatic experience whatsoever, but he may have longed to distinguish himself in a war in which his brother so far had won all the laurels. It has been suggested that Catherine appointed him to counteract Panin's influence on the negotiations, since Obreskov was regarded as a 'Panin' man. Obreskov corresponded directly with Panin during the negotiations and was often highly critical of Orlov.[4] The Turkish plenipotentiaries were Osman Efendi, a previous Reis-Efendi, and Yassinizade, who was to defend Moslem spiritual interests. Accompanied by the Prussian envoy Zegelin, and the Austrian internuncio Thugut, the Turkish plenipotentiaries arrived on the Danube on 8/19 July 1772 with a suite of some 500 followers and negotiations began on 27 July/8 August.

Early in January a cloud was removed from the Russian horizon : a court plot succeeded in overthrowing Struensee in Denmark. Until his trial and execution were over in April 1772, Denmark played a passive part in international affairs, but after a while, with the appointment of Andreas Petrus Bernstorff to office in 1773, Danish policy reverted to its normal channels. But news of the beginning of Russo-Turkish peace negotiations galvanized Gustavus III of Sweden into action. The success of the Danish *coup d'état,* which brought Denmark again into the Russian sphere, and even more, news of the impending partition of Poland, nerved him to act before Russian forces might be freed by a peace to turn against him. On 8/19 August 1772 the leaders of the estates in the diet were arrested and the constitution of Sweden suspended. Through Hanoverian intercepts, both Britain and Russia had had warning of Gustavus's intention, and Osterman had been supplied with a further 50,000 rubles to organize opposition to the king. But the money and the instructions, despatched on 13/24 August 1772, arrived too late. Russian policy, the work of Panin in the 1750s and of Osterman in the 1760s, was in ruins.

From Catherine's point of view, Gustavus's coup was particularly ill-timed. Though a prolongation of the armistice with the Turks until 10/21 September had been agreed upon, negotiations in Fokshany had ground to a halt over the Russian demand for the total independence of the Crimean khanate, and Turkish insistence on maintaining at least a spiritual suzerainty. With the possibility that Gustavus's coup in the North might be followed by war, it was essential to keep the Turkish negotiations going, and prevent the resumption of hostilities in the South. Instructions were sent to the Russian envoys at Fokshany to leave the question of Crimean independence. But they arrived too late.[5] On 17/28 August, Orlov delivered what amounted to an ultimatum to the Turks, who broke off all further talks, and were recalled. Orlov himself, without waiting for further orders, left Fokshany on 23 August/3 September,[6] for St Petersburg, where in his absence a major revolution had taken place : his ten-year reign as favourite was over.[7]

Catherine was thus faced at the same time with a personal and a political crisis. She nerved herself to order Grigory Orlov to remain in quarantine at an estate outside the capital, on the pretext that he had arrived from plague-ridden Moldavia, while a new favourite, A.S. Vasil'chikov, was installed. In such a situation the star of Nikita Panin was in the ascendant, and he set about repairing the damage done by Grigory Orlov at Fokshany. Orders were immediately sent to Rumyantsev to communicate directly with the Turkish Grand Vizir and to inform him that he was authorized to renew the peace talks. At the same time he was to prepare for a renewal of the war. Russian policy in the event of a Swedish attack was agreed at a meeting of the Council of 1/12 September 1772 : the Principalities were to be laid waste, and their inhabitants evacuated to Russia. The army would withdraw behind the Dniepr and concentrate on holding the Crimea.[8]

Turkey too needed peace and on 7/18 September Osman Efendi had himself approached Rumyantsev for a prolongation of the truce. Ignorant as yet of Gustavus III's *coup d'état,* Rumyantsev would not grant more than forty days' prolongation on his own initiative, until 20/31 October, but he also reported to St Petersburg the Turkish desire to resume peace talks, this time in Bucharest. Hence Panin's new instructions of 1/12 September proved very welcome to him. The threat of war with Sweden had led Panin to accept that the Crimeans should be allowed to elect a khan who would subsequently receive his 'investiture' from the sultan. In exchange the Russians asked for the cession of Kerch and Yenikale by the Porte and were prepared to give up the claim to Ochakov and Kinburn if they could keep Bender.[9] There was no question now of a mediation, let alone even of the presence of Thugut and Zegelin who had played little part in Fokshany. The two sides eventually agreed to prolong the truce until 9/20 March 1773. But the Russian position at Bucharest was undermined by the news of Gustavus's *coup d'état* which had by now reached the Turks. They refused to give way over the independence of the Crimea and free navigation in the Black Sea or to confirm the cession of Kerch and Yenikale by the Crimeans in the Treaty of Karazubazar.[10]

Once again the Council considered the peace terms to be offered to the Turks. Once again Catherine herself intervened decisively. In a note she put before the Council at its session of 3/14 January 1773 she declared roundly :

On no account do I wish that the Turks should dictate to me what ships I may or may not have on the Black Sea. The Turks are beaten, it is not for them to lay down the law to us. . . . As for Kerch and Yenikale, we have not received them from the Turks, we have conquered them from the Tartars, and the Tartars have ceded them to us by treaty. What need have we of Turkish consent ? It would be better to consign this article of the treaty to silence and not put it forward any more.

Should the Turks ask Obreskov about these articles, he was to reply that he had no instructions. He could also tell the Turks, Catherine had jotted down, 'that when the armistice runs out on 9 (20) March, I shall not renew it'.[11]

Nevertheless the Council did succeed, on the same day, in persuading Catherine that limitations on the free navigation on the Black Sea, i.e., the exclusion of warships, was a price worth paying in order to prevent any Turkish naval threat to the Crimea – particularly, as the minutes of the Council pointed out, since merchant ships could easily be converted into warships. Instructions to Obreskov in this new sense were accordingly drafted.[12] But the Turks were proving more stubborn, since the Porte was in hourly expectation of a Swedish diversion – a diversion which never came. During the autumn of 1772 and the winter of 1773, war in the Baltic was in the balance. Gustavus mobilized with the dual intention of extending his frontier towards Norway and preventing Denmark and Russia from attacking him. Russia regarrisoned her Finnish border, fearing that France would mastermind (and pay for) a Swedish attack on Russia in order to take the pressure off Turkey in the South. Denmark mobilized to defend Russia in accordance with her treaty obligations and to ward off a Swedish attack. Frederick II did not mobilize, but his fear of war led him to scold his nephew, the king of Sweden, in the sort of language which led Gustavus to assume that Prussia too was prepared to join the league of his enemies : Frederick was after all bound by treaty with Russia to defend the constitution of 1720, and his reward was to be in Swedish Pomerania. War was avoided in the autumn of 1772 by the moderation of Denmark, who refused to be provoked by Swedish mobilization, and England, who refused to be drawn into the Russian policy of issuing threatening declarations. But Russia seemed merely to be postponing revenge until the spring, when naval campaigns in the Baltic could take place, and the four courts, England, Prussia, Russia and Denmark could compel Sweden by a joint show of force to abandon constitutional experiments.[13] Yet in the event, the anxious consultations between the courts in Europe had less to do with restraining Gustavus's warlike ardour than the renewal of the peace talks in Bucharest.

Meanwhile the partitioning powers had turned to the task of enforcing it on Poland. Volkonsky had been unable to achieve anything in the shifting sands of Poland, where the civil war between the king, the Russians and the confederates continued. He was replaced in 1771 by Caspar von Saldern and since he was not a soldier, General A.I. Bibikov was given command of the Russian troops. Highly critical of his predecessor's policy which, he averred, had alienated the king and the reliable friends of Russia, Saldern proceeded to discover for himself that Russia had no friends, whether reliable or not. Appeals to the confederates to lay down their arms went unheeded, and Saldern, who detested, and was detested by, the Poles and found his post more and more unrewarding, begged to be recalled.

By the summer of 1772, Russian troops had crushed the confederate ones ; on 4/15 August 1772, Saldern was replaced by Count Stackelberg, who on 7/18 September, together with the Prussian envoy Benoit, handed the joint declaration announcing the partition to the Poles. Catherine had to overcome a little obstacle which did not affect her partners : she had guaranteed the integrity of the territory of the Polish Lithuanian Commonwealth in the treaty of March 1768 which she had forced on the Poles. She now had to find valid arguments for going back on her guarantee. These were soon found. The Russian declaration argued that the internal disorders in Poland arising from the spirit of discord which dominated part of the nation had repercussions on the neighbouring states which they could not suffer. Hence the three neighbouring powers had joined to take steps to restore public order and good government in Poland in accordance with her ancient constitution. But having united to prevent the dissolution of Poland, they might not in future always be so successful ; hence they had decided to put forward now the various claims they justifiably had to parts of Polish territory and they summoned the Poles to accept the situation and attend a diet at which their political salvation could be worked out.[14] Stanislas Augustus was called upon by Catherine in December 1772 to summon a Diet no later than 1/12 February 1773 at which the justice of the partition should be recognized by the Poles themselves, and a plan of pacification agreed. Final arrangements between the three courts and Poland should be completed by the end of March 1773.[15]

It proved impossible to abide by the timetable proposed by Catherine, but a Diet was summoned for 8/19 April 1773. The plan to be followed by the three courts was worked out in detail : corrected in Catherine's own hand it was divided into two sections dealing with preparations for the Diet, and the policy to be followed at the Diet. A common fund of some 45,000 ducats was to be set up to bribe deputies at the dietines. It was also foreseen that the Diet would have to be confederated (i.e., with majority voting) since a free Diet would never ratify the partitions. Once a confederated Diet had been arranged, the envoys of the three powers would secure its consent to the cessions to their respective rulers, and would proceed to the constitutional settlement of Poland ('la fixation de l'état de la république').

Here Catherine's proposals were more restrictive than in 1768. 'Le gouvernement de la Pologne sera à perpetuité un gouvernement républicain,' she stated. The crown was to be elective, but among native Poles. In order to achieve a proper balance between the Crown, the Senate, and the noble order, the power of the Crown was to be still further reduced. The liberum veto was to be preserved in full. The relatives of the king (and the queen) were to be excluded from senior posts ; the king was not to command any troops of the republic, other than a small personal guard of foreigners. The dissidents were to be allowed 'voluntarily' and in the interests of peace to climb down from the demand to sit in the Privy Council and the Senate in exchange for the abolition of the death penalty for apostasy from the Catholic religion. A proposal to eliminate the Radziwills, Czartoryskis, Potockis and Mniszechs from Polish public life was struck out by Catherine on the grounds that she hated 'personal persecution.'[16]

It proved more difficult than the partitioning powers had supposed to get a Diet elected since the deputies in the dietines refused to be browbeaten ; some dietines did not meet at all, others refused to elect a deputy. But a reduced Diet did finally meet on 8/19 April 1773. Efforts to force through a confederation were met with a prolonged filibuster, but were finally successful. Even the truncated Diet proved reluctant to name the delegation whose task was to negotiate with the partitioning powers both Polish recognition of the partition, and a new constitution for the republic. The troops of the three powers were again deployed against the Diet in mid-May, and only after it was prorogued on 6/17 May was a delegation appointed by agreement between the king and the confederated deputies. The motion to accept the partition was put to the Diet when it was recalled in September 1773, and was met with silence and a few muttered 'agreed'. On 30 September without a vote the marshal of the Diet declared that the treaties between Poland and the partitioning powers had been accepted.[17] Behind the scenes, many had already made terms with the Russians, in order to secure the desequestration of their estates, or payment for what had been requisitioned, or other favourable terms.

Only by March 1775, were the details of the political settlement worked out in accordance with the plan put forward by Catherine. The liberum veto was maintained, but some effort was made to restore the royal revenue. In a separate Acte of 4/15 March 1775, Russia and Poland defined the new constitution including the political rights of the dissidents, which were more limited than those Catherine had pressed for in 1767, and Russia solemnly guaranteed the Polish constitution as now laid down.[18]

No court was prepared to act on behalf of Poland, nor was public opinion much moved by her fate – in public. Since Austria was a participant, France could not protest. Britain was mainly concerned that Danzig should remain a free port ; Poland was merely an outpost of French influence, of little weight in the scales when Britain was intermittently counting on a Russian alliance. Moreover the confederate Poles had been portrayed in the English press as fanatical Catholics anxious to exterminate all Protestants and Orthodox. Edmund Burke at least saw the danger : 'Poland was but a breakfast . . . where will they dine ?' he exclaimed.[19] Most of the *philosophes,* however, including Voltaire, approved, or did not disapprove, of the partition, largely because Poland represented in the age of the Enlightenment an even more fanatical Catholicism than that of Spain. Diderot himself was too deeply committed to Catherine to make any public protest regarding what he described in private as 'une offense à l'espèce humaine'.[20]

By April 1773, when the Polish Diet adjourned, the Russo-Turkish talks in Bucharest had again ground to a halt, in view of the possibility of a Swedish attack on Russia which would relieve the pressure on the Porte. Indeed a secret treaty had been concluded between France and Sweden in February 1773, and in Russia it was believed that it had been followed by a treaty between Sweden and the Porte.[21] While Russia immediately adopted a more conciliatory tone to Sweden, and assured the Swedes in April 1773 that she had no intention of attacking them, Britain warned France against any attempt to assist either Sweden or Turkey by sea.[22] The immediate danger in the Baltic had again been conjured for the time being. In the circumstances it was not surprising that Panin should take up again, though in a new form, the negotiations for an alliance with Britain. He proposed this time, in April 1773, that Denmark should take the place previously occupied by Sweden in Britain's northern policy: Britain should now take over the defence of Denmark against Sweden (and France). Once a British alliance with Denmark had been achieved, a treaty with Russia would soon follow.[23] These proposals were completely useless to Britain, whose main concern in Europe was still the defence of Hanover. Meanwhile, Catherine would not give up the Turkish *casus foederis* without a substantial *quid pro quo,* and Britain would not accept a subsidy to Denmark as the foundation of a treaty with Russia, nor would she guarantee Russian 'usurpations' in Poland.[24] British support for

Russia was now by no means so whole-hearted as it had been in 1769. Distrust of France had led Britain in the summer of 1770, again in March 1772 and finally in April 1773 to force France to abandon any effort to interfere with Russian naval activity in the Mediterranean. But since 1771 she was more reluctant to assist the Russian fleet, and hoped to confine her future maritime activity to the Black Sea, by opposing Russian annexation of an island in the Aegean.[25]

Catherine had not waited for the peace talks with the Turks to be broken off before discussing the Russian plan of campaign for 1773. On 18 February/1 March the Council decided that a sudden attack should be launched on the main Turkish army south of the Danube.[26] Rumyantsev was not at all happy about the plan; the land south of the Danube was thickly dotted with Turkish forts, and St Petersburg seemed unperturbed by the total absence of maps of the area.[27] After a number of raids across the river, the main army crossed the Danube between 6/17 June and 11/22 June. But a determined Russian assault on Silistria was beaten off, and realizing that his army was dangerously exposed, Rumyantsev withdrew to the left bank of the river at the beginning of July. In a series of dis-culpatory letters to the disappointed empress Rumyantsev argued the impossi-bility of maintaining the much reduced Russian army south of the Danube while forts such as Silistria with large garrisons threatened his communications. A glance at a map shows even the uninitiated that his caution was justified. Finally Rumyantsev complained to Panin, and to Catherine herself, of neglect, inatten-tion to his recommendations and requests for reinforcements, and the intrigues of his enemies against him.[28]

Rumyantsev's reports were discussed at a meeting of the Council on 15/26 July 1773. Russia had evidently suffered a reverse in the eyes of Turkey and of Europe. Fortunately the Turkish army was not in a fit state to mount an offensive. Rumyantsev had spoken of the need to double or triple his forces. This was clearly impossible but some regiments were moved to the southern front from Poland. Catherine's first care was to soothe the ruffled feathers of her most brilliant military commander. In a long letter of 18/29 July 1773 she openly expressed her disappointment at his withdrawal across the Danube, since it was bound to delay peace. But, Catherine assured Rumyantsev, 'I am not accustomed to judge people who have distinguished themselves so much above others by their qualities, their services, and their rank, except by their actions and their zeal'. Turning to his specific requests, Catherine reminded Rumyantsev how small the contingent had been which had won such a great victory at Kagul in 1770. This victory had confirmed her in the belief that an army relied not on numbers but on the qualities of leadership of the commander and the obedience and bravery of the soldier. She accepted Rumyantsev's description of the total unsuitability of the terrain south of the Danube for war. She could not double or triple his army but was sending him reinforcements from Poland. She realized that nothing more could be done in the course of the present campaigning sea-son : 'In this, as in everything I leave you a free hand,' she wrote, 'now, as before, it is up to you to deliver such blows at the enemy as you think you are able to. You cannot wish me to have more confidence in you. . . .'[29] The letter is very typical of Catherine's manner of handling her senior servants. Whether Rumyantsev feared for his position, or whether, as happened in the case of other Russians (including Peter I), he suffered from that sudden utter and complete collapse of self-confidence when faced with a task seemingly too great for him, it is difficult to tell. But the carping complaints in his letters to Panin suggest that he was trying to justify his own failure to achieve a resounding victory to himself as well as to the empress.

The failure of the campaign of 1773 led to an early consideration of the aims and objectives of the campaign of 1774. A fresh recruit levy of one in 100 was ordered in August 1773, the sixth, since 1767, which produced 74,739 men. A total of some 323,360 men had thus been called up in five years.[30] It was hoped to raise Rumyantsev's army to 116,000, in which case he would be strong enough to operate south of the Danube.[31]

Rumyantsev forwarded his own plan of campaign for 1774 to St Petersburg on 28 November/9 December 1773. It did not differ much from what he had proposed to do in 1773. The ultimate objective would be the headquarters of the Turkish vizir in Shumla ; but he would first have to seize the main Turkish forts south of the Danube, namely Silistria, Rushchuk and Varna. Moreover there were no bridges across the Danube, no cattle for transports and no roads. To protect his left flank he recommended that the Azov flotilla and the army in the Crimea should attack Ochakov.[32] Final instructions approving his plans were sent to Rumyantsev on 17/28 January 1774,[33] but they were almost immediately overtaken by news which opened up fresh possibilities, namely the death of Sultan Mustapha III and the accession of his brother, Abdul Hamid. Would the new sultan incline for peace or war ? Rumyantsev was again given powers to negotiate peace directly with the Grand Vizir, should opportunity offer.

Since the failure of the campaign of 1773, Russia had in fact lowered her terms again. The Austro-Prussian mediation had petered out completely, but Frederick II was still anxious to bring the war to an end, and his envoy in Constantinople, Zegelin, had continued to act as an unofficial intermediary between Russia and the Porte after the failure of the talks at Bucharest. Zegelin reported in November 1773 that the Turks might agree to cede Kinburn, if Russia gave up the demand for Kerch and Yenikale. But, as Grigory Orlov, who by this time had resumed some of his political functions, pointed out at a meeting of the Council, though Kinburn served to hold Ochakov in check, it was not a port, and was thus a poor substitute for Kerch and Yenikale, which in addition controlled the straits between the sea of Azov and the Black Sea. Catherine finally agreed that Zegelin could convey to the Turks that Russia would give up Kerch and Yenikale in exchange for Kinburn, Ochakov, and the strip of coast between the Dniepr and the Bug. But she would not give up the independence of the Crimea, 'if the war lasted for another ten years'.[34]

It soon became clear however that the Grand Vizir, though anxious for peace in order to return to Constantinople to consolidate his position in a new reign, was not authorized to do more than pick up where the talks at Bucharest had left off in March 1773. In the meantime, the changed atmosphere in the South, which put the peace negotiations into the hands of the military commanders on the spot, and away from the interference of the Prussian and Austrian envoys to the Porte, fell in entirely with Catherine's wishes. In spite of a good deal of disagreement over the final peace terms which is reflected in the protocols of the Council,[35] Rumyantsev was given fresh instructions on 10/21 April 1774. Ten articles already agreed at Bucharest were to be maintained. Rumyantsev was authorized to state that Russia would ask only for commercial navigation on the Black Sea, and would leave Kerch and Yenikale in the hands of the Crimean Tartars if the Porte would remove all Turkish garrisons from the Crimea and ceded Taman, the Kuban' and all the land between the Bug and the Dniepr, as well as Ochakov and Kinburn.[36] These terms seemed generous to Catherine who was returning all her other conquests : the Principalities, Bessarabia, and some twenty islands in the Archipelago.

The Grand Vizir rejected these terms when Rumyantsev proposed them. The Russian returned to the charge, dropping the demand for Kerch and Yenikale to remain Crimean, but asking for Kinburn, Ochakov, and Gadzhibey. This last fort was mentioned now for the first time in negotiations, and was included by Rumyantsev on his own initiative as the only really suitable harbour between the Bug and the Dniestr. The time was not yet for its acquisition by Russia, but Rumyantsev had already seen the possibilities of what was to become Odessa. Again the Grand Vizir refused to cede any territory other than Azov. There was nothing in the military or the diplomatic situation to force the Porte to greater concessions than she had been prepared for in 1772. French pressure not to give way may have played its part. The Pugachev revolt, which was raging throughout Bashkiria, probably played a bigger one.

Military operations were therefore resumed and the main Russian army under Rumyantsev himself was ferried across the Danube on 9/20 June 1774. His policy was to cut the Turkish forts from each other, without wasting time in formal sieges, while attempting to draw the Turks into a pitched battle. The advance guard, under Generals Kamensky and Suvorov, had already crossed in April, and on the same day, 9/20 June, they came unexpectedly on the main Turkish army near Kozludzhi, routed it, and captured the Turkish camp. The defeat at Kozludzhi broke the back of Turkish resistance. The headquarters of the Grand Vizir were cut off from the main Turkish forts, and Russian detachments even swept south of Shumla into the Balkan mountains. On 20 June/1 July, the Turkish leader asked for a truce. But this time Rumyantsev was not to be caught : there was to be no truce and no congress. Let the Grand Vizir send envoys to his camp to 'conclude', not to 'negotiate'.[37] The field-marshal himself moved to the village of Kuchuk Kainardzhi where the Turkish envoys arrived on 5/16 July.

Rumyantsev gave them five days in which to conclude the peace. Moreover he now reverted to the maximum Russian demands and insisted on the cession of Kerch and Yenikale as well as Kinburn and the coast between the Bug and the Dniepr, but gave up Ochakov. The clause on shipping in the Black Sea, as agreed, excluded warships, but as Rumyantsev pointed out to Catherine, there was no limit on the number of guns a merchant ship could carry and no prohibition on the construction of a battle fleet.[38] Russia would return her conquests but would receive an indemnity of 4.5 million rubles. For five days the Turks fought a losing diplomatic battle, and on 10/21 July peace was finally signed. It was, as Rumyantsev wrote to Catherine, a peace achieved without ministerial formalities, and *manu militari*.[39]

It was indeed a glorious peace for Russia. Not only was it welcome because of Russia's parlous domestic position, but because Rumyantsev had secured far more than Russia could have expected.[40] Catherine was the first to acknowledge it. Rumyantsev, by now ill with malaria, was relieved by Prince Repnin, in command of the Russian forces. The grateful empress prepared a hero's welcome for him in Moscow in 1775, when Russian internal peace had been restored, and conferred on him the title 'Zadunaysky' or 'beyond the Danube' to commemorate his exploits. Not since the days of Svyatoslav in the tenth century had Russian forces been seen across the river.

While Russia had achieved a resounding victory in the South, and incorporated some substantial concessions in the treaty of Kuchuk Kainardzhi, she had paid a price for these successes in the Baltic and Poland. Gustavus's coup was a serious blow to Russian prestige in the North but Catherine had to swallow her vexation and make the best of it.

More serious, because of its long-term implications, was the partition of Poland. It is evident that the Russian court was very divided on the issue. Some, for instance Grigory Orlov, would allow Prussia to be compensated in Poland if this was the only way for Russia to keep her conquests at the expense of Turkey.[41] Panin, according to all the evidence, clung to the original idea of the 'Northern system', in which a Russian-dominated Poland played its part.[42] Unfortunately we have very little direct evidence of the development of opinion and the course of events. The foreign envoys reported what they were told, which was not necessarily the truth, or what they surmised, which was not necessarily accurate. The discussions are not even reflected in the protocols of the Council, where the subject was mentioned for the first time in May 1771.

There have been many attempts to assess the responsibilities for the first partition of Poland. When Catherine dropped her 'why don't we help ourselves' was she seriously considering partition ? Or was she thinking of frontier adjustments along the line of the Austrian occupation of Zips ? Did Prince Henry seize upon a piece of light-hearted if cruel banter, and drive it home for all it was worth ? We do not know what happened during the critical two months of December 1770 and January 1771.[43]

It does seem however that in those months there were no pressing military reasons why Russia should give way to Prussian pressure for compensation at the expense of Poland. Austria, it is true, had begun to express anxiety about Russian victories, but the secret Austro-Turkish treaty was still six months away. At this time it was really Frederick, anxious to get 'ointment for the burn', who stressed the Austrian threat to Russia, and the 'outrageous' Russian peace terms to Austria. The question really hinges on what would Russia have preferred : the 'independence' of Moldavia Walachia (and what Catherine meant by independence is clear from her policy to the Polish dissidents), or Russian annexation of Polish Livonia ? It was Austrian armament and her utter refusal to accept anything less than the return of the Principalities to the Porte, which eventually enabled Frederick to persuade Russia to give up the demand for the independence of the Principalities in exchange for Polish territory. Austria was then faced with the choice : she would be compensated by the Porte if she ratified the treaty of alliance, and intervened victoriously in the war with Russia on the Turkish side. She could be compensated by both Poland *and* the Porte, without shedding a drop of blood, if she left the Turks in the lurch and joined Prussia and Russia. Having acquired her share of Poland in autumn 1773, Austria duly received from the Porte the cession of Bukovina as the price for the return of the Principalities by Russia to the Ottoman Empire.[44] In effect Catherine found her freedom of action in Poland reduced, and her relations with Prussia bedevilled by Frederick's constant nagging. The territories Russia acquired could, in the long run, be assimilated. The manner of their acquisition, the obligation to share with two other predatory powers, permanently weakened Russia's western barrier.

Part V

The Internal Crisis
of 1773–4

16

The Revolt of the Cossacks
and the Peasant War

The great revolt of 1773–5 must be seen against the background of the increasing tension in the Cossack Hosts, as the 'regulating' power of the Russian state was inexorably extended over them. It was triggered off by the emergence of a potential leader, the Don Cossack deserter, Emelyan Pugachev, after five years of war, plague, rising prices and increasingly heavy service burdens and recruit levies. The substance of much Cossack discontent had already emerged from the instructions and the speeches of their deputies in the Legislative Commission, as well as from the constant unrest of the late 1760s and the 1770s. All the Hosts suffered from friction between the upper ranks in the hierarchy and the rank and file, between rich and poor, between those who could buy themselves out of service and those who had to serve, and from the exactions of the Russian government and the individual ambitions of Cossack leaders. In 1768, as a result of a mutiny among the Zaporozhian Cossacks, their leader, Peter Kalnyshevsky, called on Russian troops to defend the starshina. Soon he was himself threatening to seek the protection of the Porte if the grievances of the Host were not remedied by the Russian government.[1]

On the Don, the ambitions of ataman Yefremov kept the Host in a turmoil. He had participated in Catherine's *coup d'état* and been amply rewarded.[2] But since the outbreak of war he had been intriguing with the Kuban' Tartars in the Ottoman Empire, and seeking to increase his own authority in the Host at the expense of that of the government. When the authorities attempted to arrest him in November 1772, the Cossacks rioted and killed several regular officers. Yefremov was eventually arrested and tried for treasonable relations with the Kuban' Tartars. He was sentenced to exile in Livonia, while peace was restored in the Host.[3]

More serious ultimately were the disturbances in the Yaik Host, where the tensions between the starshina and the rank and file split the community into two factions, the 'obedient' and the 'disobedient'. In 1769 several hundred of the latter mutinied, refusing to serve in a distant outpost. Government troops under General Traubenberg crushed the mutiny, handing down the usual harsh sentences. When a deputation to St Petersburg got nowhere with an appeal against the sentences, fresh disturbances broke out in January 1773, in which Traubenberg was killed. More troops were sent under General Freyman to restore order. Arriving in June 1773, Freyman reorganized the administration of the Host, strengthening government control over appointments, and set up a special commission to try the ringleaders of the 1773 revolt. Again there were many condemnations to the knut, hard labour, etc., and the 2,461 ordinary Cossacks implicated in the revolt were ordered to pay a collective fine of 20,000 rubles. The sentences were carried out in Yaitsk itself, in July 1773. As a result, the Host was like a powder keg, needing only a spark to set it ablaze.[4]

In such a situation rumours that another tsar was alive who might give legitimacy to the claims of the discontented were bound to fall on fertile soil. Throughout the seventeenth and eighteenth centuries Russians had pinned their hopes of escape from oppression on the existence somewhere of a true tsar deprived of his throne by the machinations of the boyars. The instability of the succession in the eighteenth century led to the emergence of a number of pretenders claiming to be Peter II (1727-30), or the young Ivan VI, or even Aleksey Petrovich, the son of Peter the Great. How far did these pretenders believe that they were who they claimed to be ? How far did their followers believe in them ? It seems probable that they all lived in a world of simultaneous belief and disbelief – believing in order to justify themselves, in order not to sin against the divinely appointed tsar from whom alone an improvement in their lot could be expected ; and disbelieving the moment they came up against the harsh reality of arrest and brutal punishment. Rarely did the common people ask for any proof of the identity of a pretender, beyond inspecting him to see if his body bore the 'marks of tsardom'. The fact that rumours always centred around those who had never reigned or reigned only briefly, or who had died young, who were thus unknown and mysterious and full of promise of better times, places the whole phenomenon of 'pretenderism' in the world of folklore, myth, ballad and heroic poetry, in which the imagination of the humiliated and oppressed has ever found refuge. It is worth noting that no one ever claimed to be Peter the Great, or that he was not dead.[5]

Peter III's short reign made him an obvious candidate for 'pretenderism' and rumours that he was still alive had spread in St Petersburg almost immediately after his death. In 1763 a soldier was denounced for declaring that he was alive ; when asked how he knew, he replied : 'Don't you know that the Bishop of Rostov [Arseniy Matseyevich] has been defrocked because he falsely buried Peter III ?' – a classical example of the way political events are turned into myths. In the same year a rumour was current in Orenburg that Peter III had taken refuge with the Yaik Cossack Host.[6] Other pretenders came and went (ten all told between 1764 and 1772) of whom F.I. Bogomolov, a fugitive serf, was probably the most important in crystallizing Cossack hopes. With Cossack support he had put himself forward in March 1772 as 'Peter III'. He was arrested in December, and died on the way to Siberia. But rumours about him spread so widely that the government ordered special publicity to be given in the Don Cossack Host and on the Volga to the arrest and punishment of a so-called tsar. As a result belief in the survival of Peter III became even more widespread among the Cossacks.

Only a few weeks after the carrying out of the sentences on the Yaik Cossacks in July 1773, a new and more formidable 'Peter III' appeared on the scene. Emelyan Pugachev was born around 1742 in a rank and file Don Cossack family. He served in the Seven Years' War, and again in the war against the Porte in 1768, in which he earned promotion to the rank of *khorunzhiy,* the lowest Cossack officer rank. In 1771 he deserted, wandering south to Taganrog, where he had relatives, then to the Cossack community on the Terek river. After further peregrinations from Old Believer settlement to Old Believer settlement, he took advantage of one of the many amnesties proclaimed by the Russian government for returning fugitives and reappeared in the Don Host, ostensibly as a native of Poland. Given a passport in August 1772, he started again on his wanderings, staying with Old Believers, and frequently posing as a wealthy merchant. In November he turned up in Yaitsk, and was again lodged by an Old Believer. It was only five months since the mutiny in the Host; the sentences were still to come.

At this stage, Pugachev put himself forward as a wealthy merchant, 'with more than 200,000 rubles abroad, let alone merchandise to the tune of 70,000 rubles'. He offered to lead the discontented Cossacks out of Russia to the Kuban' in the Crimean khanate ; he would give twelve rubles to any Cossack who would follow him, and assured his hearers that the 'Turkish pasha' would welcome them. For the first time here, in Yaitsk, Pugachev claimed to be Peter III. The circumstances in which he did so remained mysterious in view of the conflicting evidence given later by Pugachev himself and his partisans, anxious to disculpate themselves. According to Pugachev's account he told his host that he was the Emperor Peter III, who had been miraculously saved from death and and had afterwards wandered in Egypt, Constantinople and Poland.

There is no doubt that Pugachev found the mood among the Yaik Cossacks encouraging. What remains uncertain is what he himself was planning at that stage to do. Undoubtedly he had long lived in a world of fantasy. While still in the army, he had bragged that his 'trusty' sword had been given to him by his 'godfather Peter the Great'. The report of the claim of Bogomolov to be Peter III and of his arrest may have given him precisely the stimulus he needed to pretend that he himself was the tsar. On the other hand the idea may have emerged first among the Yaik Cossacks and been suggested to him. The assumption that Pugachev invented the idea himself is popular in Soviet historiography, since it strengthens one of its fundamental assumptions, namely that Pugachev was consciously planning a nation-wide revolt against serfdom, and decided to assume the character of Peter III as a vital strategic move in his campaign. The evidence for such a far-reaching plan is however somewhat slender. The accounts of his followers speak of Pugachev as planning to lead them over the border into Turkey. They too may have been falsifying their evidence in order to minimize their guilt in the eyes of the Russian government. Yet departure into other lands was more consonant with Cossack tradition than a frontal assault on the Russian state. Pugachev's words show him to be essentially concerned with the crisis in the Cossack way of life caused by the pressure of the Russian state, not with the woes of the peasantry as a whole.

Pugachev stayed only a week on this, his first visit to the Yaik Host, and returning to the Don, he was soon afterwards arrested as a deserter. He was taken to Kazan' early in January 1773, and admitted under interrogation that he had urged the Yaik Cossacks to flight, but made no mention of his claim to be Peter III. He succeeded in escaping in May 1773, and was on the run again until August 1773, when he reappeared once more in Yaitsk. Here, in the bath, Pugachev showed his hosts the 'marks of tsardom', in this case the scars of scrofula on his chest – a curious inversion of the traditional attributes of the divinely appointed king. From now on, the report that the merchant Pugachev was in reality Peter III began to be widely believed in the Host, which, it will be remembered, was still smarting under the sentences inflicted on the mutineers in July 1773. Visiting Cossacks explained their grievances to 'Peter III' : Russian officials wanted to introduce new 'establishments', new formations, while the Cossacks wanted to serve as of old, as 'in the days of Peter I and according to their charters'. Together with a small group of bold spirits among the Cossacks, and a few Tartars, Pugachev now devised the programme by means of which he would secure recognition as Peter III by the Yaik Host. He promised to guarantee the old, free way of life, which could be summed up as free access to the fisheries of the Yaik, free use of land and appurtenances, tax-free access to pasturage, free salt, and to each Cossack twelve rubles per annum, and twelve 'chetverti' of corn.[7]

These particular Cossacks were fully aware that Peter III was in fact the runaway Don Cossack, Pugachev. They must be regarded as leading spirits in planning the revolt, aware of the necessity, if it was to spread, of assuming the mantle of legitimacy. Indeed, in the existing state of seething discontent they clearly welcomed the arrival of a resolute man, prepared to take over the role. The circle in the secret of Pugachev's true identity grew larger, comprising both Cossacks with simple Cossack aims, and such figures as the fugitive ex-leader of the Yaik 'disobedient' faction, I. Ul'yanov, who hoped that Pugachev would 'seize the state' and that he, Ul'yanov, 'would become a great man'.[8] It may also be true that Pugachev's claim to be tsar was the more easily accepted precisely because he was a simple Cossack – an easily identifiable father of his people, not a man separated from his followers by an unbridgeable cultural gulf. Hence the mixture of familiarity and respect with which he was treated may not have been part of a plot, but a genuine effort to live in the real and the false worlds at one and the same time.[9]

The actual rising was planned for the opening of the winter fishing season. Meanwhile Pugachev's supporters found him suitable raiment – a crimson kaftan and a velvet cap – and a secretary, Ivan Pochitalin, since he was illiterate.[10] But outside events precipitated matters. The commandant of Yaitsk heard rumours of the presence of a pretender, and sent out patrols to arrest him. The conspirators decided to act at once. Pugachev's first manifesto was hastily drafted, and on the morning of 17 September 1773 it was read out at the *khutor* of a wealthy Cossack family a hundred versts from Yaitsk, to some 60–100 assembled Cossacks who were joined by a number of Kalmucks and Tartars. In the name of 'amparator Petr Fadaravich', Pugachev's subjects were forgiven all previous crimes towards him, and the Cossack programme was put before them, namely 'the freedom of the rivers from their sources to their mouths, and the land and the growth thereon and payment in money, and lead and powder and supplies of corn'.

Pugachev moved at once on Yaitsk, and by the next day, when he stopped before the fort, his forces numbered 300. They carried the Cossack standards of the revolt of 1772 aloft on pikes, with the Old Believer Cross sewn on to them. The commandant in Yaitsk had over a thousand troops but he knew that he could not rely on the Cossacks, many of whom went over at once to Pugachev. Others were seized and hanged by the rebels as an example. But a rebel assault on the fort was beaten off on 19 September, and Pugachev realized that he could not stand up to the gunfire of regular troops. He moved away along the river Yaik, mopping up the smaller forts as he went. Everywhere the Cossacks and the soldiers went over to the rebels or were shot. Cossack and army officers as well as some priests were hanged. One Cossack officer who went over to Pugachev was the ex-deputy to the Legislative Commission, T. Padurov.

The choice of the next target reflects the essentially Cossack priorities of the rebel movement at this stage. Pugachev could have turned towards the Samara line and the interior. He chose instead to advance on Orenburg, the military administrative centre which had dominated the Yaik since its foundation in 1735. He arrived before the city on 5 October 1773 with over 3,000 men and 20–30 guns but was not strong enough to take it by storm. He settled down therefore to besiege Orenburg, making his headquarters in Berda, some 5 versts away.

Meanwhile news of the appearance of a new 'Peter III' on the Yaik at last reached St Petersburg on 15 October 1773. It seemed from a distance to be but a minor, local affray, a continuation of the rebellion of 1772. The government was well aware that the guberniya of Orenburg, which comprised most of Bashkiria, was thinly settled and lightly garrisoned. In the vast neighbouring guberniya of Kazan', there were only eighty permanent officials for two and a half million inhabitants. But Catherine was straining every nerve to mount a fresh offensive against the Turks, and seasoned troops could not be spared. Hence a small punitive expedition was dispatched under General Kar, from Kazan', together with two other detachments from Simbirsk and Siberia. But Kar's force was defeated early in November, and he himself departed for the capital to report.[11] A week later Pugachev's forces defeated the government detachment coming from Simbirsk (and hanged the colonel). Flushed with victory, indeed, drunk with it in the strict sense of the word, Pugachev allowed the third column with 2,400 men and 22 guns to slip into Orenburg, thus enabling its resolute governor, Reinsdorp, to concentrate on sitting out a siege which was to last six months. In Yaitsk too the commandant shut himself up in the citadel and prepared to defend it, leaving the rest of the town to the rebels.

The defeat of the imperial punitive expeditions opened the way for the extension of the revolt into Bashkiria, where Zarubin Chika, one of Pugachev's ablest lieutenants, laid siege to Ufa at the end of November, while another of his followers, Ilya Arapov, briefly occupied Samara (where he was greeted with church bells and prayers were said for Peter III) at the end of December 1773.

Meanwhile the very success of the initial revolt gave rise to problems of organization and supply which could no longer be dealt with by the small group of intimates who had provided the leadership in the first phase of the rising. Hence, on 6 November 1773, in Pugachev's headquarters in Berda, the main governmental organ of the rebels was founded : the 'College of War'. Its name was borrowed from the existing central governmental institution because the College of War was the body most familiar to the Cossacks. Moreover the establishment of such a body strengthened the illusion of a revolt led by the tsar, who was at the same time able to erect a barrier between himself and his followers – necessary for the effective organization of the revolt, but tending to reduce the element of egalitarianism which had characterized its earlier stages.[12]

The principal official or *sud*, 'judge', of the College in accordance with normal Russian terminology, was a prosperous member of the Yaik starshina, Andrey Vitoshnov. Ivan Pochitalin, who had drafted Pugachev's manifestos, was appointed *dumnyy d'yak* (*duma* clerk or clerk of the council), reviving a Muscovite title which had lapsed since the reforms of Peter the Great. The rebel College of War also recruited a number of literate clerks and one of the few hereditary nobles to go over to the rebels, M.A. Shvanvich, conducted its correspondence in German and French. Two leading Tartars, Idyr Baymekov, and his son Baltay, conducted the correspondence and wrote manifestos in 'Arabic, Persian, Turkic and Tartar'. The functions of the College were both civil and military : it dealt with the reception of the volunteers who flocked to join Pugachev, usually armed only with farming tools or pikes, and with their organization into military formations based on the Cossack model. Once a volunteer was accepted into the force he was recognized as a Cossack to distinguish him from the 'soldiers' who fought for Catherine. From the moment that Pugachev settled down in his headquarters at Berda, outside Orenburg, the rebel movement was faced with the problem of recruitment. Sizable bodies of rebels came to operate at some distance from Berda, around Ufa, and as far as Yekaterinburg and Chelyabinsk. The need to extend the area of operations, or to prepare for defence against government troops, soon led the rebel leaders to borrow a weapon from the tsarist ar-

moury, namely conscription. Orders were issued to the local population to produce recruits at the rate of 'one man for three households' or even 'one man per
household'.[13] In January 1774 a rebel ukaz ordered 'to take people into the service of the Lord Peter Fyodorovich against their will, and destroy those who refuse and take away their property'.[14] Taking the oath to 'Peter III' served as a formal declaration of allegiance, and all who came before the pretender or were
captured were thus forced to declare themselves. There was scant choice, since
the penalty was immediate and usually painful death for those who refused.

The rebel College of War also had to cope with the problems of supply of mu-
nitions, food and forage. This brought it into relationship with the civil population in areas controlled by Pugachev's forces, or where his adherents had killed
their previous officials and elected new ones. In the first flush of the revolt some
local landowners, their wives, children and household serfs, as well as local officials, church servants, etc., had been killed, often with terrifying barbarity.[15]
The rebel College of War attempted to exercise some control in this field by
'ukazy' which reserved judgment to headquarters. It was also the final instance in
the quarrels which inevitably broke out between Cossacks and Bashkirs on the
one hand, and the civil population on the other.

'Tsarist illusions' were maintained in the rebel camp by a device which illustrates the psychological tensions within the leadership. Pugachev set up his own
court, also modelled on that of Catherine. A number of his closest collaborators
adopted the names and titles of magnates at Catherine's court. M. Shigayev, one
of the original group, who acted as treasurer for the copper money (Pugachev
kept the silver himself) and *de facto* as Pugachev's deputy, called himself Count
Vorontsov. Ovchinikov, one of the most outstanding and faithful military
leaders, called himself Count Panin, another leader became Count Orlov, and
Zarubin Chika, the boldest of them all, called himself Field-Marshal Count Chernyshev, after the vice-president of the College of War in St Petersburg. In February 1774 Pugachev, who had abandoned his wife and children on the Don, 'married' the daughter of a Yaik Cossack, Yustina Kuznetsova. She was treated as
'Her Imperial Majesty' and Cossack women were appointed her Maids of Honour (*freyliny*). However, Pugachev's marriage weakened his position. All knew
that 'Peter III' had a wife, Catherine, who had seized his throne. It was to win
this throne from his usurping wife that the common people had joined his force.
Moreover a real tsar would not marry the daughter of a common Cossack. Selfish
personal motives tore through the veil of illusion.

Again in the interests of authenticity, but reflecting the only conception of the
legitimate source of power which the Cossack world could grasp, 'Peter III'
issued 'ukazy', drafted as far as possible in Russian eighteenth-century of-
ficialese. Some were even printed, since only printed ukazy were legal in Russia,
and sealed with a variety of seals. Among the most picturesque is one Pugachev
used in August 1774, which bears the inscription 'Peter III by the grace of God
emperor of the "corown" (*karuna*)', surrounding the portrait of a man in a wig,

with a moustache, and dressed in armour, with the broad ribbon of an order across his breast – resembling if anything an imaginary portrait of Peter the Great. Other leaders used seals with the arms of noble families, of factories, even of a distillery.

It is very difficult to assess what degree of authority Pugachev himself exercised in the inner circle of those who knew his real identity. In public he was treated with deference. In private the leaders sat and feasted together. Those who had risen to the top at first tried to prevent others from approaching Pugachev and acquiring influence with him. 'My street is but narrow,' he exclaimed one day to a boon companion. He was not always able to save those he wished to save, and frequently found himself faced with *faits accomplis*.[16] Though the leaders may have hoped to introduce some discipline in the rebel camp, it remained, according to contemporaries, a dissolute rabble. Prayers were said daily for the emperor, 'Peter III' and for his wife, Catherine, until Pugachev married Yustina.[17] But the camp was full of the wives and daughters of officers, who had been captured and distributed as booty among the rebels ; executions took place at any moment, the surrounding ravines were full of unburied corpses, drunken feasting was common.

From the very beginning of the rising, in September 1773, Pugachev had directed his appeals to the non-Russian peoples of the vast area between the Volga, the Yaik, and Western Siberia. Among his very first supporters in September 1773, there were 20 Tartars and 20 Kalmucks out of a total of 80 men, and his first manifesto was specifically directed also to them. It included an amnesty for all those who had fought long and hard against the Russian state in the Bashkir wars of the 1740s.[18] A number of manifestos were issued in October 1773, promising the Bashkirs their traditional way of life : the freedom of lands, water and woods, their faith and their laws, food, clothing, salaries, powder and shot, and also their 'bodies', presumably a promise not to enslave them, and the right to 'be like wild animals of the steppe', or to a free nomadic life. But in contrast with the appeals directed to his Russian followers, Pugachev's manifestos were addressed not to the underdogs of Bashkiria, urging them to rise against their chiefs, but to the Bashkir tribal leaders, urging them to throw off the oppression of the Russian state.

By October 1773, Pugachev had been joined by at least a thousand Bashkirs under the leadership of Kinzya Arslanov who was to be with him to the very end. Almost at once the Bashkirs turned on one of the most hated signs of the Russian presence in their land : the foundries. By the end of the year some 44 foundries and mines were in rebel hands, providing Pugachev with substantial supplies of guns, ammunition and the possibility of making more. The industrial enterprises did not however always go over at once to the rebels. Pugachev's manifestos had not specifically referred to the problems of the assigned peasants or the factory serfs. The assigned peasants were sometimes used by the rebels to keep the industries working. The industrial serfs, who had become more closely identified with factory life, sometimes defended their enterprise against Bashkir efforts to destroy it.[19]

By the beginning of January 1774, a mixed force of some 2,000 Tartars, factory serfs, farmer soldiers, and assigned peasants, commanded by the young Bashkir leader, Salavat Yulyayev, and I. Kuznetsov, launched an attack on the copper foundries of the Urals. Kungur and Yekaterinburg defended themselves, but Chelyabinsk was briefly occupied. The rebels then moved on the great Dalmatov monastery, which had had a very bad reputation in the days when the Church owned serfs. The monastery was surrounded by high walls, and possessed sixteen guns of various calibres ; the defence consisted of monks and church officials and unreliable peasants. But the monastery was relieved on 14 March by government forces which defeated the rebel army in the neighbourhood.[20]

Government forces were indeed at last on the move. The news of the defeat of Kar's detachment in October 1773, coupled with the reports from the governor of Orenburg, aroused Catherine in November to the seriousness of the situation. On 29 November 1773, General A.I. Bibikov, the ex-marshal of the Legislative Commission, was appointed to put down the rising, with full powers over military, civil and ecclesiastical authorities, 'on the basis of existing military and civil laws'.[21] Bibikov was also to set up a commission of inquiry into the origins and the course of the revolt, which eventually became known as the Kazan' Secret Commission.

Making Kazan' his headquarters, Bibikov, who arrived on 26 December, took immediate steps to re-assert the government's authority and to restore morale. The nobles were persuaded to form a number of volunteer corps, arming their own peasants. The empress followed suit, and as a 'landowner of Kazan'', she ordered a levy to be made among court peasants and sent officers to command them.[22] The Church hierarchy took an active part in distributing government manifestos and exposing the imposture of Pugachev.[23] By the end of January the major part of the troops which had been placed at Bibikov's disposal had arrived, and various detachments were sent out to clear the rebel bands operating between Kazan' and Ufa.

Meanwhile Ufa had been loosely under siege since mid-November 1773. Almost the whole of the non-Russian population of the province took part in the rising,[24] but the voyevoda and the civil population as well as the commander of the regular forces kept their nerve and proceeded to organize an effective defence. On 24 January 1774 a strong attack was mounted by Zarubin Chika with 12,000 men, but it was beaten off. The rebels now settled down to a blockade, and during February and March 1774 military operations languished, while Zarubin Chika conducted frequent negotiations for a surrender with the defenders of Ufa. Meanwhile government troops were advancing under Lieutenant-Colonel Mikhel'son, a veteran of the Seven Years' War, and quarrels broke out within the rebel leadership. On 23–4 March Zarubin Chika, with between seven and ten thousand men, was defeated in a fierce battle with Mikhel'son's professional soldiers. The siege of Ufa was lifted ; Zarubin and Ul'yanov were seized by Cossacks and handed over to Mikhel'son.[25]

There still remained Orenburg, under siege for nearly six months, and the commandant of Yaitsk was still shut up in its citadel. In both places the shortage of food, fodder and fuel was acute throughout the winter months. To relieve them both, large forces were being concentrated in the area of Buguruslan and Bugulma, under the overall command of General P.M. Golitsyn, for a drive against Pugachev himself. The rebel leader decided to make a stand at Tatishchevo, which commanded the junction of the roads to Orenburg and to Yaitsk, and brought up some 9,000 men and 36 guns. Golitsyn had 6,500 soldiers and 22–25 guns. The decisive battle took place on 22 March, and after a fierce artillery duel Golitsyn's regulars broke the rebels' resistance. Once again, rebel forces had proved unable to stand up to smaller units of trained soldiers, but there were heavy casualties on both sides : Golitsyn lost 140 killed and over 500 wounded ; the rebels 1,315 killed, a further 1,180 cut down in the pursuit, and nearly 4,000 prisoners. Pugachev and a few other leaders galloped off to Berda.

The defeat at Tatishchevo precipitated a crisis among the rebels. The hard core of the Yaik Cossacks – the force closest to Pugachev – replaced the peasants and soldiers on guard duty at Berda. At the same time some of them began to load up their belongings on transports, arousing the suspicions of the non-Cossack masses. With government forces approaching, it was clear that only those owning horses would be able to get away. The peasants would have to be left to look after themselves. But in abandoning the poorly armed *muzhiki* to their fate, the Cossacks were consciously or unconsciously revealing the fundamental contempt of the warrior for the tillers of the soil : 'for the common people are not fighters, the common people are just sheep.'[26] At the same time many of the Cossacks began to think of saving their own skins. A plot to seize Pugachev and surrender him was foiled just in time. Tension within Berda grew worse, and on 23 March Pugachev abandoned his headquarters with 2,000 men and 10 guns. On the same day Golitsyn's advance guard entered Berda, which broke up in an orgy of looting, drunkenness and panic. Remnants of Pugachev's escaping force were hunted down and captured, including most of the leaders of the 'College of War', and the secretary, Pochitalin. The siege of Orenburg was over. On 16 April, the garrison of Yaitsk, almost starving by now, was relieved, and a fortnight later, the fort of Gur'yev, at the mouth of the Yaik on the Caspian Sea, was cleared of rebels. The architect of victory did not live to consolidate it. Bibikov, who had directed the troop movements, fell ill of a fever, and died on 7 April, to Catherine's great distress.[27] His military command devolved upon Lieutenant-General Prince F.F. Shcherbatov.

The Secret Commission set up by Bibikov in Kazan' had meanwhile been pursuing its investigation into the origins of the revolt : how Pugachev came to call himself 'Peter III'. Was there any foreign influence at work, French or Turkish ?

What was the extent of participation by disgruntled nobles and Old Believers ? The Secret Commission, or Bibikov alone, was empowered to pass and execute death sentences, though in the case of nobles and officials it was normal to refer them to the empress for confirmation. In the first weeks of its activities, the Kazan' Secret Commission was sparing in its use of the death penalty. One serf was hanged for murdering his mistress, and a few Tartar soldiers were hanged for taking part in the revolt.[28] Others were sentenced to the usual variety of corporal punishments, many of those only marginally involved were released after renewing their oath of allegiance to the empress. The Secret Commission undoubtedly used the classic method of extorting confessions, namely the knut, in spite of Catherine's efforts to reduce the use of torture. 'I don't doubt you will keep to my rules,' wrote Catherine to Bibikov, on 15 January 1774, 'though at times severity will be necessary.' 'Please order the Secret Commission to be cautious in deciding what punishments to inflict : in my opinion soldiers X and Y were flogged though innocent. Also what need is there to flog during investigations ? For twelve years the Secret Expedition under my own eyes has not flogged a single person under interrogation, and every single affair has been properly sorted out, and even more came out than we needed to know,' she wrote again on 15 March.[29] But Catherine confirmed the death sentences, particularly on officers who had failed in their duty, though she left the actual execution to Bibikov's discretion, and some of them got off with running the gauntlet (usually up to six times, in Catherine's reign), and garrison service as a private.

As the government forces defeated the various rebel bands the number of prisoners increased so much that Kazan' could no longer hold them. In many cases officers commanding the relieving forces meted out punishment on the spot, sending only the ringleaders to Kazan', and granting certificates of pardon to the rest.[30] With the death of Bibikov, the Secret Commission found itself without a master, with 169 prisoners in Kazan', over 4,000 in Orenburg, and many others in different centres. In the belief that the back of the revolt was broken, Catherine on 16 April 1774 appointed General F.F. Shcherbatov to take over from Bibikov, but without his wide powers, and confirmed the arrangement the latter had already made to set up a branch of the Secret Commission in Orenburg. Both Secret Commissions were placed for the time being under the authority of the respective local governors.

But the government had rested too quickly on its laurels: Pugachev was still at large. Abandoning all hope of making for the Kuban', or even Persia, Pugachev, with a following of some 5,000 poorly armed Bashkirs, and a leavening of factory serfs and Cossacks, advanced from foundry to foundry in a wide arc through Bashkiria. Some of the Bashkir leaders were already beginning to make their peace with the government and assist the patrols of regular soldiers.[31] But others, like Salavat Yulyayev, continued the struggle, whether in the interests of Pugachev or their own remains uncertain. Lieutenant-Colonel Mikhel'son, in overall command of the government detachments in the area, chased Pugachev from foundry to foundry, but the thaw which had set in in earnest rendered operations difficult for both sides. After forty days of almost continuous pursuit, Mikhel'-son's forces were so exhausted that he withdrew to Ufa to rest and recoup. The whole of Bashkiria was in an uproar, and even the town of Ufa trembled again for its safety. No one knew where Pugachev was, and where he would strike next. Bypassing Ufa, he had in fact gone north, and appeared before the fort of Osa on 18 June 1774. After a three-day siege, the fort surrendered to 'Peter III' who was greeted with military and imperial honours. The next step was to cross the Kama and make for Kazan'. Factory serfs and peasants flocked from Perm' guberniya to join the rebels, together with many more Bashkirs. Pausing to burn down the Izhevsk and Votkin foundries where, in spite of the efforts of the defenders, Pugachev was welcomed by the peasants and factory serfs with bells and icons, the rebel army, with nothing behind it, and nothing in front, advanced on defenceless Kazan'.

Kazan' was a city of some 11,000 inhabitants, many of whom were Tartars. It was mainly built of wood; even the kremlin, or fort, was wooden. General von Brandt, the ailing governor, had already been aware of his danger, and on 24 June he wrote urgently to the commander-in-chief in the whole area, Prince F.F. Shcherbatov, demanding reinforcements, and sent couriers in all directions, notably to Mikhel'son. Shcherbatov stayed where he was – in Orenburg – until 5 July. But Mikhel'son pressed forward in an effort to cross the Kama and intercept Pugachev. He hoped to reach Kazan' by 8 or 9 July but was delayed by the need to ford a number of rivers, and had only just crossed the Kama on 3 July – well behind Pugachev, who on 11 July appeared with some 20,000 men before the city. On 12 July a three-pronged rebel attack overwhelmed the improvised defence of the city, and the government forces fled back to the citadel, and barricaded themselves in. An orgy of looting and destruction followed, lasting from 6 a.m. to midnight ; according to a contemporary, 'those in German dress and without a beard were killed', women in 'German dress' were seized and taken to Pugachev's camp. All government prisoners were freed, among them Pugachev's first and only real wife and his children, who were taken to his camp, where their presence caused the pretender a certain embarrassment. They were introduced as the wife and children of his old friend the Don Cossack, Emelyan Pugachev, and lodged together with the women who formed his harem. The city was set on fire at nine different points, and the rabble roamed the streets, looting, drinking, raping, until the smoke drove them off. Of 2,873 houses in the city, 2,063 were destroyed by fire.[32]

On the evening of 11 July, Mikhel'son was only 65 versts from Kazan'. Having rested his horses for three hours, he started at 1 a.m. on 12 July on a forced march to the city, from which rising columns of smoke could soon be discerned. At the village of Tsaitsyn, Mikhel'son heard that Pugachev awaited him with some 12,000 men. With his exhausted force of only 800, Mikhel'son launched a fierce attack against the rebel centre, which broke in disorder after a five-hour battle. But Mikhel'son's forces were too worn out to pursue the rebels.

On 13 July 1774, Mikhel'son entered Kazan' and began at once to mop up the parties of rebel looters. But he was not yet done with Pugachev. With a smaller force the rebel leader returned to the charge the next day, and was again beaten by the government forces. Undaunted, Pugachev moved some twenty versts away, regrouped and refilled his ranks, and returned with what was no longer an army, but a mob of some 15,000. Mikhel'son went out to meet him on the same field where they had first met outside the city. Pugachev's forces now fought with the courage of despair, but after a four-hour battle they were completely routed, with the loss of 2,000 killed and wounded and 5,000 prisoners. Some 10,000 captives of both sexes held in Pugachev's camp were now freed.

Where would Pugachev go next ? An advance on Nizhniy Novgorod would carry the revolt into the heartland of serf-owning Russia. The governor-general of Moscow, now Prince N.M. Volkonsky, began to plan the defence of the city and the surrounding countryside. In a number of smaller towns the local gentry and townspeople met and decided to raise troops locally to meet the challenge. But it never came ; Pugachev had turned south. Did he ever really plan to march on Moscow ? It was frequently spoken of among his closest intimates. Pugachev was reported to have said : 'If I can take Orenburg and Yaitsk, then I will go with just the cavalry to Kazan' and after taking it I will march on Moscow and Petersburg, send the empress to a convent, and pay the boyars back in kind.'[33] This does not have the ring of a well-thought out plan of campaign. But 'marching on Moscow' was a necessary psychological element in the process of legitimizing Pugachev's role as 'Peter III' who had been forced by wicked dvoryane to wander in strange lands for years and was now returning to recover his throne. However, when faced with probable defeat, Pugachev did what one might expect : he made for home, to the ground he knew well, the land of the Don Cossacks.[34]

The decision to march south led to a change of emphasis in Pugachev's manifestos, related to the nature of the area in which he was now operating. He was cut off from Bashkiria (though the revolt continued to rumble there) and to a great extent he was also cut off from the support of the factory workers. He was now entering an area very largely peopled by small landowners with under twenty serfs,[35] though there were also some very large estates. By contemporary standards the peasants were relatively prosperous, but it was mainly a subsistence economy, with very little cultivation for sale or for local marketing. It was however overwhelmingly an area of barshchina cultivation though some of the larger estates were on obrok.[36] The towns too were mainly overgrown agricultural settlements providing no market for the countryside, since the town-dwellers grew their own food. Thinly settled, the whole region was the refuge of many bold spirits, runaway peasants, Old Believers, and there was also a population of some 1–2 per cent of Little Russians and non-Christian native tribes.

The manifestos issued by Pugachev, and carried from village to village by his emissaries, now specifically called on the serfs to rise against their masters, to overthrow the whole system of serfdom and to take over the land. The new Peter III appealed to Old Believers by granting 'the old cross and prayers, heads and beards' ; he granted them liberty, 'and to be forever Cossacks', free from the poll-tax and the recruit levy, and from the taxes and money dues imposed by evil landowners and corrupt judges. He urged the peasants to seize those who had previously been nobles and oppressors of the peasants, and to execute and hang them and treat them in the same unchristian fashion as they had treated the peasants.[37] With or without benefit of Pugachev's manifestos, or Pugachev's presence, serf risings now spread from village to village. Sometimes small groups of Cossacks appeared in a village and encouraged the peasants to rise against their landowners ; elsewhere peasants rose on their own initiative, stimulated by rumour and the bush telegraph. Larger groups of peasants sometimes roamed far afield, recruiting and destroying as they went, sufficiently strong even to give a good account of themselves in pitched battles with government troops. If the rising took place within measurable distance of Pugachev's main forces, the peasants brought the gentry and officials with them to his headquarters, to be 'sentenced' by the 'emperor' himself. Elsewhere vengeance was immediately wreaked on the landowners – men, women and children – and on officials, stewards, priests, contractors. Significantly, it was mainly the owners of small estates who were murdered, where personal contact was close, and barshchina common.[38]

Meanwhile Pugachev's own forces were advancing from town to town, leaving a trail of destruction. On 23 July he arrived in Alatyr and was met with solemn oaths of loyalty, church services and processions. Here he filled up his ranks, both with volunteers, and with conscripts 'among those fit for service'. The same performance was repeated on 26 July in Saransk, where Pugachev dined in the house of the voyevoda's widow and then hanged her.[39] The primitiveness of the area, and of the people taking part on both sides in this social war, led to increasing ruthlessness. Before the revolt, armed conflicts between rival dvoryane leading their serf followers had not been unknown, and the authority of the civil administration over the 'gentry' was but slender. Major Mellin, in charge of one of the government detachments, was horrified to hear reports 'which I refuse to believe', that, profiting from the general disorder, some nobles were fighting each other and destroying each other's estates and hanging their enemies.[40] On the other hand the spectacle of nobles hanged in droves, with heads, hands and feet cut off, roused the forces of order to equally savage repressions.

On 1 August a group of Cossacks proclaimed in the marketplace in Penza that 'Peter III' was on his way, and if he were not welcomed with bread and salt, all in the city down to the last baby would be put to the sword. Pugachev was duly welcomed, the treasury was looted and 200 men were forcibly recruited. Knowing that government forces were hard on his heels, Pugachev and his motley force made for Saratov on the Volga. The numbers in his 'army' cannot be estimated exactly ; contemporary accounts range from eight hundred to several thousand. But it was no longer a fighting force. Volga boatmen and fugitive serfs provided a core of tough fighters, but they were untrained. The peasants who flocked to volunteer as often faded away. The hard core of some 300–400 Yaik Cossacks was also much reduced, and not all were now loyal to 'Peter III.'

On the other hand the 'towns' which Pugachev had so far seized with such ease were towns only in name. Saratov was another matter. It was one of the most important urban centres on the Lower Volga, the administrative capital of the foreign colonists. There were a few small factories in the neighbourhood (hats, stockings and rope). The population numbered some 7,000 including about 1,000 kuptsy. But the town had suffered a serious fire in May 1774, which had laid it waste and its fortifications were negligible, though the garrison numbered 780 men.

Divided counsels among the defenders (in which the poet Derzhavin played a somewhat inglorious part) contributed directly to the fall of the town on 6 August. Pugachev camped outside Saratov for three days. Solemn oaths of loyalty to 'Peter III' were sworn, and church services were held in honour of the emperor, his heir, 'Paul', and his 'wife' Yustinya. Twenty-four landowners and twenty-one chancery clerks were hanged and the massacre of men and women of all ranks continued. Half-drunk priests administered oaths of loyalty to those fit for service. The state depots of corn, liquor and money were broken open and the contents looted. Even after Pugachev's main host had moved away, some twenty-nine armed bands roamed the neighbourhood, looting, killing and destroying.

As Pugachev raced southwards towards Tsaritsyn, he made constant efforts to win the Don Cossacks to his cause. But from the beginning of the revolt the government had been aware of this particular danger and had taken steps to ward it off. In October 1773, orders were issued to watch out for any sign of dissaffection in the Host, and to seize and burn all Pugachev's manifestos. Countermanifestos were issued by the War Chancery of the Don Cossacks, warning them against the pretender Pugachev. It was only, however, when Pugachev was actually in the area between the Volga and the Don that the danger became acute. He issued a manifesto on 13 August 1774, specially directed to the Don Cossacks, stressing that Peter III had been acknowledged by nearly the whole of Russia and that he had promised the Cossacks 'freedom, the cross, prayers, heads and beards of our ancestors, and that now the Cossacks were blinded and misled by the wiles of the cursed race of nobles, who not content with Russia want to turn the native Cossack Host into peasants, and destroy the Cossack people'. Thus once again Pugachev proclaimed the utopia of the Cossack Old Believers. But it was in vain. A reward of 20,000 rubles had been promised for the capture of Pugachev, and the Don Cossacks mostly remained loyal. In all likelihood they were held back from joining the rebels by two factors : the signature of the treaty of Kuchuk Kainardzhi on 14 July 1774[41] and the end of the war with the Porte would release troops which could be used to repress the revolt ; and reluctance to join an evidently losing side.[42] Thus, though a few wavered at times, and joined Pugachev, elsewhere Don Cossacks were used against the rebel forces. The Cossacks of the Lower Don were in any case well aware that Pugachev was Pugachev and not Peter III.

Still in the hope of arousing his fellow-Cossacks, Pugachev issued a further manifesto, one of the most revealing of the general objects of the movement : 'the Christian law of the old tradition of our holy fathers has been completely destroyed, and instead of it, a new law, of evil intent, and German habits have been introduced into Russia, and the most disgusting shaving of the beard, and other outrages against the Christian faith and cross.'[43] Here again Pugachev declared that he had been deprived of his throne because he wanted to bring about freedom in Russia (*uchinit' vo vsey Rossii vol'nost'*) and that he had already been accepted as ruler in Kazan', Orenburg and among the Kalmucks and the Bashkirs.

Finally, on 21 August, Pugachev appeared before Tsaritsyn. The commandant had already taken steps to defend the town, by summoning Don Cossack regiments, and he was expecting reinforcements from the Second Army in the South. Encamped before Tsaritsyn, Pugachev went forward to parley with a group of Don Cossacks who came forward to meet him, and was publicly recognized. From that moment, disbelief spread among the Don Cossacks, and also among Pugachev's close followers. Cracks began to appear in their faith in the pretender ; the world of suspended belief in which so many lived began to collapse about their ears, and thoughts for their own safety came to the fore.[44]

After a five-hour artillery duel with the garrison of Tsaritsyn, Pugachev withdrew down the river, pausing to ravage the German Herrenhut colony at Sarepta. The next day, his convoy of barges loaded with treasure and noble and other prisoners was seized by the commandant of Tsaritsyn. On the same day, Colonel Mikhel'son, who had been pursuing Pugachev as fast as he could, arrived in the city. Stopping only to leave his sick and rest his horses, and taking with him the Don Cossacks in the garrison, he started off again on 23 August, and two days later the final encounter took place. Pugachev had some 10,000 men, though more than half were unarmed peasants. Dividing his force into three, and taking command of the centre, Mikhel'son broke the centre of Pugachev's army, in spite of heavy gunfire. The defeat became a rout. Pugachev, with some thirty followers, managed to cross the Volga, taking his wife – the real one – with him.

Where was Pugachev to go now ? Reinforced by some 200 Yaik Cossacks who had managed to rejoin him, and accompanied by Kinzya Arslanov and a few more intimates, Pugachev now abandoned the idea he had put forward before the final battle, of going to Persia through Turkestan, 'where there were khans friendly to him'. He proposed instead to go either to the Zaporozhian Sech, or to Siberia, or beyond the Caspian to arouse the 'Hordes' (Tartars). The Yaik Cossacks refused to go to all these 'foreign lands' (counting the Zaporozhians as foreign), and insisted on returning to the Yaik, where after all they had left their homes and families. According to the evidence given to the investigating Secret Commission by Ivan Tvorogov, who had joined the revolt at the very beginning, in October 1773, he had, just before the attack on Saratov, discovered that Pugachev was an impostor. He and a Yaik Cossack, also one of the original conspirators, now acted as the moving spirits in a plot to save themselves by seizing Pugachev and delivering him to the authorities. A number of other Cossacks were won over to the plot, and persuaded Pugachev to agree to march into the Kalmuck steppe, towards Uzen', and Lake El'ton. On the way, the Cossacks seized the horses of the non-Cossacks in the company, thus forcing them to drop behind. Kinzya Arslanov was allowed to continue with them since otherwise Pugachev's suspicions would be aroused. His wife and son Trofimov also continued with the fugitives. Beyond Uzen', the conspirators seized and disarmed Pugachev ; he made one desperate bid for freedom, but was finally bound. 'How dare you raise your hands on your emperor ? You will not achieve anything. If I do not punish you, I have still an heir, Paul Petrovich,' exclaimed 'Peter III', but the imposture was over. Hearing that 'a just judge' was now in charge in Yaitsk, the Cossacks determined to deliver their prisoner to him. So, on 15 September 1774, the revolt ended where it had begun, on the Yaik.[45]

17

The Court Crisis of 1773–4
and the Restoration
of Order

While Catherine's armies were winning glorious victories over the Turks, and her generals negotiating triumphant peace treaties, she was herself facing the most serious challenge to her domestic authority, passing through a major crisis in her emotional and political life, and fending off a major threat to her position from her only real rival, her son.

Though Paul was an ever-present menace to Catherine's power, he was also her only justification for having ever acquired any. There was little likelihood, as long as Paul was not of age, of a plot to place him on the throne, since this would only give power to a regent, most probably Nikita Panin. On the other hand, should Paul die, and he was delicate, then the succession to the throne would be wide open ; Catherine might find it difficult to summon enough support for her rule.[1]

Paul's death would also spell the end of Nikita Panin's power. Catherine and Panin were thus united in their determination to preserve the grand duke's health. For these same political reasons, the empress agreed to leave Paul in Panin's hands ; many years later she explained to her secretary, A.S. Khrapovitsky : 'At first I was not free, and then for political reasons I did not take him [Paul] from Panin. All thought that if he was not with Panin he would perish.'[2]

Catherine's remark hints at a further complication : the existence of her son by Grigory Orlov. He had not been, and could not be, acknowledged. But his existence was widely known, and Orlov's enemies feared that he might be brought forward as heir to the throne should Paul die. The fact that Paul, who was very popular in St Petersburg and above all in Moscow, was her rival for power, was bound to poison the relations between mother and son, particularly as Paul grew old enough to be aware of his position.

The education of the grand duke was carefully supervised. It comprised languages, history, geography, mathematics, the graces (drawing, dancing, fencing, music) ; he was taught physics and astronomy by F.I. Aepinus, later a distinguished scientist in Russia,[3] and religion by Archimandrite Platon, the future metropolitan, one of the most enlightened churchmen of Russia. Simeon Poroshin, a graduate of the Cadet Corps, young, well-educated and kind, taught him science and mathematics. Poroshin's diary, covering the years 1766–8, gives a picture of the daily life of the young prince. It was Panin's practice to invite senators, generals, senior officials, to dine at the grand duke's table. The conversation dealt with court intrigues, both amorous and political, and extended to criticism of Catherine's policies and of the individuals who carried them out, coupled with unbounded admiration for Frederick II. What Panin said to his pupil about the *coup d'état* of June 1762 we do not know. But he certainly succeeded in clearing himself in Paul's eyes of all guilt by association with the plot which had led to the murder of the grand duke's father, and the usurpation of the throne by his mother. He may well have informed the grand duke that he, Panin, had intended to proclaim the boy emperor with a regency, and had been foiled by his mother's supporters. Paul's relations with the favorite Grigory Orlov were ambiguous. By eighteenth-century standards there was nothing particularly outrageous in the long-standing liaison – it was to last nearly twelve years – between Catherine and Grigory Orlov. But Orlov was not able to evade his share of the guilt for Peter III's overthrow. At first he tried to conciliate Paul, but as the boy grew older and more hostile, the favourite became more negligent. At some stage Paul must have heard of the existence of his step-brother, Aleksey Bobrinsky. How this affected him is unknown, but in later life, as emperor, he was on friendly terms with him.

In summer 1771 Paul suffered from a serious illness. Both Catherine and Panin watched anxiously over the boy, and rumours spread again that in the event of his death Bobrinsky would be proclaimed heir. The absence of a proper law of succession meant that there was no precedent for deciding when Paul should come of age, but it would be difficult to postpone his majority much beyond his eighteenth birthday in September 1772. This was above all the moment when Catherine would have to guard against any movement to place him on the throne. At the same time Paul's delicate health rendered the question of his marriage urgent in order to settle the succession. To make sure that he would be capable of producing an heir, he was encouraged in a liaison with an accommodating widow, by whom he had a son in 1772, who was known as Simeon Velikiy. Brought up by Catherine in her own rooms (as distinct from Bobrinsky), he subsequently entered first the Russian, then the British Navy, and died in 1794 in the West Indies.[4]

As early as 1768 Catherine had arranged for the Danish envoy in St Petersburg, von der Asseburg, to inspect the available German princesses to find a suitable bride for Paul. The most favoured, Sophia of Württemberg, was too young, and the choice of Catherine, and incidentally of Frederick II, fell on one of the daughters of the Landgraf of Hesse Darmstadt – that military martinet whose troops were on hire to all comers – whose eldest daughter had married Frederick II's nephew and heir. The question of Paul's majority was now postponed until his marriage, and the Landgräfin and her daughters were invited to pay a visit to Russia in 1773.

The precariousness of Catherine's title to the throne explains in great part her dependence on the Orlov brothers in general and on Grigory in particular. She loved him, and she relied on them to guard her against the specific dangers which beset a woman on the throne, rendered all the more acute in the case of an usurper. She needed men bound to her by the closest ties, whose fate was joined to hers, to establish and maintain links with the armed forces. Grigory was appointed grand master of the Ordnance in 1763, Aleksey was lieutenant colonel of the Preobrazhensky Guards. The eldest brother, Ivan, played little part in public life, but all five were closely united, acting together in defence of their position, and indeed owning much of their property in common. They may not have been popular, but they were reliable. Grigory remains, in spite of his prominent post, a somewhat shadowy figure. He was interested in literature, he invited Rousseau – in vain – to settle in Russia, he sponsored the plans of Pastor Eisen for the reform of serfdom.[5] He was evidently a liberal-minded, and according to many accounts, a kind-hearted man. He and Aleksey were reputed to speak no French, only German. Gossip credited Catherine with anything from two to five children (in addition to Bobrinsky) by Orlov, allegedly being brought up by one of her ladies-in-waiting, Anna S. Protasova, who was a cousin of the Orlovs. It is difficult to substantiate this story. Protasova certainly brought up two girls called Alekseyeva, who may have been daughters of Orlov, but not necessarily by Catherine. They were never publicly recognized, and in later years were not treated by Paul with the same intimacy he showed to Bobrinsky.[6] At any rate, with or without children, Catherine was bound to Orlov by many ties of affection and shared undertakings, and her trust in him was absolute.

That her apprehensions were justified is proved by a number of outbursts of discontent in the guards regiments in the late 1760s and early 1770s. Among officers, the main complaint was that Catherine favoured the serfs. Stones had been thrown at the palace in Moscow, during the sessions of the Legislative Commission, when the question of improving the conditions of the serfs had been raised, wrote Catherine in later years.[7] At the beginning of the war, in 1768, a captain in the Horseguards had complained that 'now they are going to take away our estates completely, when they give freedom to the peasants, what shall we live on ?' The name of the grand duke cropped up, and high hopes were pinned on the year 1769 : 'As soon as Venus has finished her transit [the great scientific event of the year], God will do something ; she can't be transiting in vain.' Other officers were caught criticizing an alleged 'new law giving freedom to the serfs'. Denounced, the plotters, if they may be so called, were sentenced to loss of rank, hard labour and exile to settlement in Siberia.

The guards officers, alarmed by what they had understood of the debates in the Legislative Commission, feared that the empress was neglecting the interests of the nobility. The private soldiers rebelled in spring 1772 against the cruelty and injustice of their officers. The plot came to a head as a result of the departure of Grigory Orlov for Fokshany for the peace negotiations with the Turks, in June 1772. A number of non-commissioned officers and soldiers of the Preobrazhensky Guards Regiment believed that he had gone 'to the army to persuade them to swear allegiance to him' and that he intended to make himself 'Prince of Moldavia and Emperor'. Better therefore to forestall him, proclaim Paul emperor, and shut up Catherine in a convent. If Paul refused to be proclaimed, he should be killed and the people should choose a new tsar, if not one of the guardsmen, then for instance, Prince M.M. Shcherbatov. Between thirty and one hundred guardsmen were mentioned as having taken part in the plot.[8] Catherine appeared at first to be much shaken, and according to one report she withdrew to Finland with her intimates, Kyrill Razumovsky, Ivan Chernyshev and Grigory Potemkin, to confer on measures to purge the guards regiments.[9] The plotters were eventually convicted and sentenced to astonishingly mild penalties, since most of them were under age.

It was in this atmosphere of tension, surrounding Paul's imminent majority, that Catherine was faced with a major crisis in her personal life. Soon after Grigory Orlov's departure for Fokshany, some kind friend enlightened her on the extent of his many infidelities.[10] She may already have wearied of him, and this was perhaps the last straw. At any rate she took advantage of his absence and replaced him by a new lover, A.S. Vasil'chikov, who was appointed gentleman in-waiting to the empress on 1/12 August 1772. Racing back at full speed to the capital, Orlov was stopped outside by imperial order, while on 30 August/10 September Vasil'chikov was formally appointed adjutant general to the empress and moved into the apartments formerly occupied by Orlov in the palace.

Catherine had dismissed Orlov for personal reasons, but his failure at Fokshany and his unauthorized return to the capital aroused her anger on purely political grounds as well. She was also clearly frightened of what he might do. Her private life became at once a matter for the whole court, and united many of Orlov's enemies in support of the new favourite. Nikita Panin's influence seemed again to be all-powerful, as he steered Catherine's love life into calmer waters, fended off Swedish attacks, and finalized plans for the partition of Poland. But Zakhar Chernyshev, though no friend of the Orlovs, feared that he might be edged out of the College of War in favour of General Peter Panin, and hence he secretly supported the fallen favourite, while his brother Ivan was the intermediary through whom Catherine negotiated his final withdrawal with Grigory Orlov. The fallen favourite was treated with the greatest generosity in small things as in great. He was allowed to accept the title of Prince of the Holy Roman Empire conferred upon him by the Emperor Francis in 1763 and hitherto not used. He was granted a pension of 150,000 rubles and a present of 100,000 rubles to set up house in the so-called Marble Palace, then under construction. The estates he owned jointly with Aleksey were increased from 4,000 to 10,000 serfs, and he was given two silver table services (one for everyday, one for best !).[11] Infinitely more touching than this shower of gold and silver were Catherine's careful instructions to the director of the posts to see that gazettes which mentioned his disgrace should be kept from him.[12] Since Catherine wanted to avoid a personal interview, Grigory Orlov reappeared only briefly at court on Christmas Eve 1772, and spent the winter in Reval.

With Orlov's dismissal, the factional struggles at court reached a new intensity, and became more dangerous in so far as they centred around Paul, who had now come of age as regards Holstein. It is almost impossible, in the welter of gossip and evidence, to disentangle the various intrigues. Caspar von Saldern, who returned to the capital in summer 1772 after his disastrous mission in Poland, now played a prominent part. He had easy access to the grand duke at this time since he was charged with the final negotiations for the transfer of the Duchy of Holstein to Denmark. It was he who, with Panin, sat up with the young man throughout the whole of one night to persuade him into signing away his heritage forever.[13]

In the winter of 1773, while Orlov was still in Reval, Saldern proposed to Panin that now that the grand duke had reached his majority, his mother should be forced to share power with him as emperor and co-ruler (with the recent example of Joseph II in mind). Saldern offered himself to direct the plot, but the pusillanimous Panin refused to follow him (or the honourable Panin was outraged by such treasonable proposals, runs another version). Saldern had then tried to win Paul himself over, and the young man had been sufficiently dazzled by the prospect of power to commit himself to paper and allegedly to promise to follow Saldern. As Panin explained to Count Solms, Saldern 's'était jété sur le Grand Duc, a qui . . . il avait tenu des propos si indécents contre sa mère, contre la nation russe en general et contre lui [Panin] en particulier, que ce jeune prince n'avait plus su à quoi il en était . . .'. Paul was induced at this time to distrust all those who surrounded him. But Panin, having noted Paul's reserve, had succeeded in winning his confidence. Paul had confessed the whole to him : . . . 'depuis ce temps ce prince avait reconnu le méchant caractère de Saldern et avait cessé de le voir et de lui parler.'[14] Either to protect Paul, or to protect himself, Panin did not however at this stage denounce Saldern's treasonable behaviour.

Consolation now lay in store for Paul. The Landgräfin of Hesse Darmstadt and her three daughters arrived in St Petersburg in great state and at Russian expense, at the end of June 1773. It did not take long for Paul to decide, as everyone expected, that he preferred the second daughter, Princess Wilhelmina, who on 15/26 August 1773 was received into the Orthodox Church as Natalia Alekseyevna (what Frederick II called her 'natalization').[15] As in the case of Catherine herself, the mother of the bride was indifferent to the change of religion ; the bride was 'sufficiently enlightened' to find that there was very little difference between Orthodoxy and Lutheranism, and it was the father who objected – from a distance and too late.

Not long before the wedding the final touches were put to the cession of Holstein to Denmark which was concluded at Tsarskoye Selo on 1/12 June. On 14/25 July, Paul formally ceded the counties of Oldenburg and Delmenhorst, which he had received in exchange, to Frederick Augustus, coadjutor of Lübeck, representing the junior Holstein-Gottorp line, and brother of his maternal grandmother, Johanna. On 12 August 1773, there followed the definitive Russian treaty of alliance with Denmark.[16]

Faced with Paul's impending wedding, Nikita Panin now waged a losing battle to keep his influence over the grand duke. With the loss of his post as tutor, he would be deprived of his main base at court, which entitled him to live in the palace. On his marriage Paul would become more independent of his mother. Catherine wished him to become more independent of Panin as well, particularly since she discovered that her minister was trying to acquire an ascendancy over the future grand duchess also.[17] She used Saldern, and probably others, to persuade Panin to content himself with his position in the College of Foreign Affairs and abandon his control of the grand ducal household.[18]

Panin had been riding high on the crest of the wave in autumn 1772 when he helped the empress to break with Orlov. But the ex-favourite had returned to the capital in May 1773, and had been readmitted to the Council in June.[19] He and his supporters were only too willing to turn the tables now on Nikita Panin, and help Catherine to break his hold on the grand duke. By September the battle was raging furiously, with Vyazemsky, the Chernyshevs, and the Orlovs, all of whom had reappeared in the capital, ranged on one side, Kyrill Razumovsky neutral, and the vice-chancellor, A.M. Golitsyn, as well as Field-Marshal A.M. Golitsyn and Vasil'chikov supporting Panin.[20] Meanwhile Panin had been threatening to retire altogether if he were separated from the grand duke : 'ce serait le séparer de son seul appui et . . . il quitterait alors tout le reste pour se retirer entièrement.'[21] In the event Catherine found an elegant if expensive solution to her problems : Panin ceased to be tutor, a post which now lapsed, and vacated his rooms in the palace. He was raised to the first rank in the Table of Ranks, equivalent to a field-marshal (according to some accounts he *refused* the title of chancellor), and continued in charge of foreign affairs, with a pension of 30,000 r.p.a., a salary of 14,000 r.p.a. and the gift of an estate of 9,000 souls in ex-Polish territory. Catherine also wrote him a letter thanking him for his care of her son.[22] To even things out, Zakhar Chernyshev was promoted to field-marshal and to be president of the College of War,

The wedding of the young couple took place on 29 September/10 October, followed by ten days of festivities, balls, theatrical performances, masquerades for the nobility and the merchants, and fireworks for the common people.[23] No separate court was established for the grand ducal couple, but General N.I. Saltykov was appointed to run their small household.[24]

A few days before the grand duke's wedding, Pugachev had raised the standard of revolt on the Yaik. Though at the time Catherine felt no particular alarm, she knew already that she was faced with a further campaign against the Turks.

By December the extent of the rising in the southeast was becoming clearer. How precisely these events influenced her personal drama can only be guessed. But early in January 1774 Lieutenant-General Grigory Aleksandrovich Potemkin arrived in the capital from the Danubian front. The great romance of Catherine's life was about to begin.

Potemkin came from a minor but ancient gentry family near Smolensk. His date of birth is variously given as 1736, 1739 or 1742; it was probably 1739.[25] Brought up in Moscow, he showed a remarkable gift for languages, and learnt French, German, Latin and Greek. He was also interested in theology and acquired an extensive knowledge of Church Slavonic and Russian ecclesiastical literature. According to some accounts of his life, he spent some time in a monastery in the early 1760s. His career at Moscow University already gives an indication of the unevenness which was to characterize his life : he won a gold medal one year, and was expelled for laziness the next. Enrolled in the Horse Guards as a private in 1755, Potemkin was promoted *in absentia* in the usual way, and by 1760 had achieved the rank of corporal ; he then joined the *jeunesse dorée* of the capital. He had been rewarded with promotion, peasants and the rank of kammerjunker for his participation in the *coup d'état* of June 1762.[26] In recognition perhaps of his contacts with the priesthood, Catherine appointed him assistant procurator of the Holy Synod in 1763. In 1767, Potemkin attended the empress in Moscow for the sessions of the Legislative Commission and was made one of the guardians and official spokesmen of the deputies of the non-Russian peoples – another reflection of his exotic interests. He became a member of the civil and ecclesiastical sub-commission of the commission.

It is probable that during these years Potemkin, who as a kammerjunker had access to court, fairly frequently came to the empress's notice. There are endless stories about him and his relations with the Orlovs, who are even charged with attacking him in a cowardly manner (two Orlovs against one Potemkin) and with responsibility for the loss of an eye which was to disfigure an allegedly otherwise handsome countenance. He was a remarkable mimic, and so the story runs, enchanted Catherine by mimicking her strong German accent to her face. She liked him, and he had let it be known that he was in love with her.

On the outbreak of the war with the Porte Potemkin volunteered for active service.[27] His promotion was rapid, and by 1773 he had risen to the rank of lieutenant general. Successful engagements conducted by him were twice mentioned in the Council.[28] His high rank, and possibly the knowledge that he belonged to the inner circle at court, enabled Potemkin to obtain leave of absence from the front to visit the capital during the winter lull in the fighting, and he is known to have been there in the winter of 1770–1 and in 1771–2.[29]

Did Catherine send for Potemkin in December 1773 because she had already learnt to love him and wished to replace the negligible Vasil'chikov ? Or did Potemkin rush in and lay siege to a heart which had been bruised by Orlov, and found no comfort in Vasil'chikov ? The order of events in the winter of 1774 cannot be exactly established. All existing reconstructions are based on one single letter from Catherine to Potemkin of 16/27 December 1773 which is the only one from this period to have been published and which on the surface at least conveys no invitation.[30] But Potemkin arrived in the capital in January ; by the end of February 1774, evidently by arrangement, he requested Catherine to appoint him personal adjutant general – a rank which was known to be worn by the current favourite. The unfortunate Vasil'chikov was dismissed with a generous pension.[31]

The appointment of Potemkin as adjutant general to the empress was the first external sign of a new regime. It was followed by his appointment to command the Preobrazhensky Guards Regiment (which had previously belonged to Aleksey Orlov) and in May 1774 to the Council.[32] The foreign diplomats, as well as Russian high officials, were immediately aware that a new scene had opened. 'His figure is gigantic and disproportioned, and his countenance very far from engaging,' wrote Sir Robert Gunning on 4/15 March 1774,[33] but he could not as yet interpret what the change would mean. Frederick II wrote off crossly to his brother, asking for information about this 'général Patukin ou Tapuquin' who, he feared, might prove 'préjudiciable au bien des affaires'.[34]

Cautiously feeling his way at first, Potemkin seemed to side with Panin against the Orlovs and the Chernyshevs. Little by little it became clear that he was no nondescript Vasil'chikov, and that his ascendancy spelled the end of the regime of the Orlovs, and indeed of Zakhar Chernyshev as well. The Potemkin 'clan' would now descend upon the capital and its members would benefit from imperial generosity. Their presence would extend the new favourite's network of supporters, and open up new avenues of patronage to new clientèles. Moreover, as distinct from Panin, and even from Grigory Orlov, who had seen no service since the Seven Years' War, Potemkin had all the authority of an active soldier with a distinguished military career. His first target however was Zakhar Chernyshev, who had lost ground as a consequence of the Pugachev revolt, which had been attributed by his enemies to his poor handling of the Cossacks. The battle between Chernyshev and Potemkin was short and fierce, but by the end of July, the former had been edged out of the College of War, and Potemkin took over with the rank of vice-president.[35] Aleksey Orlov[36] departed to resume his command of the Mediterranean fleet, and after a violent altercation with Catherine, Grigory Orlov left for a prolonged foreign trip. Meanwhile Potemkin's cousin, General P.S. Potemkin, was appointed in June to head the Secret Commission which was still functioning in Kazan' in order to investigate the origins of the Pugachev revolt. Having eliminated the Orlovs and Zakhar Chernyshev, Potemkin was going to be faced with the Panins in July 1774.

The news of the sacking of Kazan' by Pugachev was received in St Petersburg on 21 July, and was greeted with appalled dismay, particularly since the latest report from Rumyantsev showed that though peace was near, it had not yet been concluded. At a meeting of the Council on 21 July, it was decided to send reinforcements to Moscow at once, and to appoint a 'distinguished person' to take charge of putting down the revolt with the same full powers General Bibikov had once enjoyed.[37] Catherine herself heatedly declared her intention of going to Moscow in order by her presence to restore confidence. Her councillors were stunned into silence at first, but finally succeeded in persuading her that she would only underline the seriousness of the revolt by going to Moscow.[38] The Council decided to wait for further news from Rumyantsev, in ignorance of the fact that the peace had been signed two days before the sacking of Kazan'.

Meanwhile the question remained of appointing the 'distinguished person' to take charge of military operations against the rebels. Nikita Panin forced the issue, by proposing to go himself, and answering for the willingness of his brother, Peter Panin, then in Moscow, to go. On 22 July, Catherine agreed reluctantly to appoint Peter Panin, but before his appointment could be confirmed news of the long awaited peace at last reached St Petersburg on 23 July. A great burden was lifted from Catherine's shoulders and the government could now concentrate its seasoned troops and its best generals on the repression of internal disorder.

Between them Nikita and Peter Panin had forced Catherine's hand, and she was committed to the appointment of a man she deeply distrusted to a position of great power.[39] Peter Panin demanded complete authority over all the military detachments putting down the revolt, and over all the inhabitants and officials in the areas affected with power of life and death over all but those in the highest ranks. He wished to choose his own staff, and to be placed in command of all army corps, excluding the First Army (Rumyantsev's), the Second Army (in the Crimea) and the forces in Poland.[40]

Catherine's reaction to these vast claims was only to be expected: 'You see my friend', she wrote to Potemkin, 'from the enclosed pieces that Count Panin wants to make his brother the ruler with unlimited powers in the best part of the empire . . . and sous entendu there are other things: If I sign this not only will Prince Volkonsky [the governor-general and commander-in-chief in Moscow] be offended and made to look silly, but I myself will be totally unguarded – from fear of Pugachev above all other mortals, I will be seen publicly to be raising and praising a man who is a first-class liar and who has personally offended me.'[41]

With Potemkin at her elbow, Catherine felt strong enough to resist the pressures put upon her by the Panins, which in any case were reduced not only by news of the peace with the Porte, but also by news of the victories of Mikhel'son over Pugachev outside Kazan' and the recovery of the city. The care taken to pare down Peter Panin's powers is evident from the many drafts of the instructions which were finally sent to him. He was only given command of the forces already engaged in repressing the revolt, and authority over the governors and officials in Kazan', Orenburg and Nizhniy Novgorod. A separate rescript ordered all spiritual, military and civilian authorities to obey General Panin's orders 'in matters concerning his dual object', i.e. putting down the revolt and restoring order. The empress stressed that she expected Panin to preserve the laws intact in the use of his powers. Nor was he given the general of his choice, namely Prince N.V. Repnin ; General A.S. Suvorov was instead detailed to assist him.[42] To a suggestion by Vyazemsky that to prevent 'collisions' P.S. Potemkin's Secret Commission in Kazan' should be placed under P.I. Panin, Catherine noted briefly in the margin : 'No, because it is under me.'[43] By the summer of 1774 Catherine, supported by Potemkin, had thus manoeuvred fairly successfully between the court factions, and had freed herself from emotional and political dependence on the Orlov brothers while at the same time putting the Panins and the Chernyshevs at a distance. Nevertheless, she had been forced to accept the services of Peter Panin, largely as a result of the panic caused by the rebel destruction of Kazan'.

Paradoxically enough Peter Panin was appointed to a post almost commensurate with his ambitions at a time when political, rather than military, talents were required of an order he did not possess. He combined the qualities of a military martinet, who believed that Russia should be ruled by a man,[44] with a high conception of aristocratic political and social rights, which rendered it beneath him to control his temper. A stickler for military etiquette, he could nevertheless appear in the anteroom of his headquarters in a wide grey satin nightgown and a large French nightcap tied up with pink ribbons.[45] Panin received his instructions on 2 August 1774 in Moscow, and decided to stay in the capital until he knew in which direction Pugachev was heading. In his view an outright defeat of Pugachev's wandering horde was less necessary at that moment than guarding Moscow against the infiltration of small bands which might inflame the lower orders.

In the event, neither Panin nor Suvorov[46] was concerned in the capture of Pugachev. But when the rebel leader was handed over by the Cossacks who had betrayed him to the authorities in Yaitsk, the various generals in the field hastened to claim the credit for his capture and fought for control of his person. Meanwhile, General P.S. Potemkin, who had been confirmed by Catherine as head of the Secret Commission in Kazan', had been pitchforked in July into taking command of the city and defending it against Pugachev. But he had been forced to assume a more active role on the death of the governor, von Brandt, on 3 August, and was busy clearing out rebel bands and restoring order in the countryside. Most of the 10,000 prisoners taken in the battles outside Kazan' were released with 15 kopeks travel money, though some of the major rebels were tried and executed on the spot. In all the Kazan' Commission dealt with 9,164 people of whom 38 were executed, and 8,342 were released without further punishment.[47]

The division of authority which Catherine had been so careful to maintain between Peter Panin and Paul Potemkin soon led to considerable friction between the two hot-tempered and arrogant men, who were not unaffected by the factional struggle in the capital between their respective relatives and patrons, Nikita Panin and Grigory Potemkin. Paul Potemkin was charged with investigating the origins of the revolt ; Peter Panin's duty was to mop up rebel bands and re-store order. But in the course of his punitive expeditions, many important pris-oners fell into Panin's hands whom he did not hand over to Potemkin for inter-rogation.[48] The crisis became acute when Panin refused to allow Potemkin access to Pugachev himself, or even to see reports of what the rebel leader had said. It was clearly impossible to allow the Secret Commission in Kazan' to con-tinue in being, now that Peter Panin controlled the prisoners ; Catherine solved the problem by setting up a Special Commission of the Secret Department of the Senate[49] in Moscow, under Prince Volkonsky, assisted by Sheshkovsky, to prepare the trial of the leading rebels. To this commission she appointed Paul Po-temkin and allowed the work of the Kazan' Commission, with its sub-commis-sions in Orenburg and Yaitsk, to be wound up.[50]

In the first few months of the revolt, until April 1774, severe sentences had been passed on the rebels as a deterrent. After the relief of Orenburg, when Pugachev disappeared into Bashkiria, the vast majority of Pugachev's followers taken prisoner were simply released with a safe conduct on repenting of their misdeeds.[51] But when the revolt entered its last desperate phase, with Puga-chev's descent of the Volga, when the largest number of noble men, women and children met their deaths, the government responded by fierce and prompt repri-sals. On 24 August 1774, Peter Panin issued a general proclamation threatening all those who had taken part in the revolt, murderers, and leaders of rebel bands with death by quartering, after due and proper Christian preparation. In every village, gallows, gibbets and wheels were to be erected, under which sentences were to be carried out.[52] In a letter to Catherine Panin explained that rumours were circulating that he, the brother of the tutor to the Grand Duke Paul, was ad-vancing to welcome Pugachev with bread and salt. The only way to scotch such rumours was to threaten measures of particular severity. But they were intended only to terrorize and he would never carry them out, knowing that he had no au-thority.[53] Nevertheless, at Panin's request, the death penalty was restored in those villages in which punitive detachments were operating.

Panin showed himself particularly harsh towards renegade nobles and of-ficials, and above all priests.[54] He did not hesitate to execute those who had par-ticipated in the revolt. Rough justice was meted out on the spot in towns and villages. Army units descended on the countryside, and on the evidence of sur-viving landowners, peasants were 'whipped under the gallows',[55] or suffered the more severe penalty of the knut and the cutting off of an ear. According to Panin's own computation, 324 rebels were executed while he remained the supreme ruler over Kazan' and the Volga ; 399 suffered the knut and the loss of an ear, and some 7,000 others suffered some form of corporal punishment. On his orders, corpses were left to rot on the gallows in the towns and villages of the Volga area, until the voyevoda of Saratov protested in January 1775 at the danger to public health.[56]

On 4 November 1774, Pugachev himself arrived in Moscow, confined in an iron cage, placed on a cart, and drawn through streets crowded with people who viewed the fallen leader either with joy or with dismay. Catherine, in a letter to the governor-general, Prince Volkonsky, had urged, 'For God's sake refrain from all questioning under torture, which always obscures the truth', and actual physical torture of Pugachev, and his lieutenants, does not seem to have been used.[57] A special court, composed of high-ranking officials and members of the Holy Synod, was set up to try the accused. Its verdict was not in doubt, but behind the scenes Catherine again attempted to mitigate the almost inevitable barbarity of the sentences. 'Please help to induce in them [the court] all moderation both in the number and in the kind of executions,' she wrote to Volkonsky on 1 January 1775, and to the procurator general, Vyazemsky, who had arrived in Moscow to keep an eye on proceedings on her behalf, she expressed herself even more trenchantly : 'As regards executions, there must be no painful ones, and not more than three or four people.'[58] It was not easy however to swim against the current of vindictiveness which held sway among the Moscow nobility and which had been reinforced by the arrival of Peter Panin in the second capital. It was his turn to feel disgruntled since he was not a member of the special commission in Moscow, and P.S. Potemkin was.[59]

The special court met on 30 December ; when Pugachev was brought before it, much weakened by long confinement, he fell on his knees, admitted that he was the Don Cossack Emelyan Pugachev, and declared himself repentant before God, the all-merciful empress, and all Christian people.[60] The court's verdict was not in doubt, and its sentences were drawn up by reference to Solomon, Matthew, Mark and Moses, the Code of 1649, the Military Statute of 1716, and the Naval Statute of 1720. A difficulty arose over Padurov, who had been a deputy to the Legislative Commission, and according to the Manifesto of 14 December 1766, could not be sentenced to death. A way round was found by deciding that immunity from the death penalty applied only to deputies who had taken part in the drafting of projects in the sub-commissions.[61] In the event the court sentenced Pugachev and one other to be quartered, and three more to be hanged. Zarubin Chika was sentenced to be beheaded in Ufa, and twenty-one were sentenced to various forms of corporal punishment and hard labour.

Meanwhile Vyazemsky had been fulfilling the empress's orders, and making a secret arrangement with the chief of police in Moscow that Pugachev should be beheaded *before* the rest of the grisly sentence was carried out. The convicted received the last rites of the Church, except for Perfil'yev, firm in the Old Belief, who rejected the service of a Nikonian priest. On 10 January 1775, in the presence of an enormous crowd, the last strange episode took place. To the rage of many of the spectators, the executioner seemed to have bungled his job : Pugachev had first been beheaded. An official nearby rounded on the executioner and exclaimed : 'You son of a bitch, what have you done ?' – thus convincing the crowd that the executioner was either inexperienced or had been bribed by Pugachev's supporters.[62] Contemporaries assumed that the unfortunate man had been severely punished for his mistake.[63] But he had merely been carrying out the empress's secret orders.[64]

The remaining sentences were immediately carried out, and the following day the scaffold and all the remains were removed and burnt. Catherine was anxious to wipe out all traces of the episode as soon as possible. Of the 832 prisoners held by the Secret Expedition in Moscow 605 were released without any form of punishment and the remainder were sentenced to hard labour or exile, with or without corporal punishment.[65] The two wives and three children of Pugachev were incarcerated in the fort of Kexholm in Russian Finland ; they were given fifteen kopeks a day for maintenance and could move about freely within the walls.[66] The Cossacks who had handed over Pugachev were pardoned, but were not allowed to return to Yaitsk. The house which had belonged to Pugachev in the Zimoveyskaya stanitsa on the Don was destroyed, and the settlement was re-named Potemkinskaya after the rising star.

The bulk of the Bashkir forces had returned to their homeland after the defeat of the rebels outside Kazan', and carried on the struggle there in order to destroy the encroachments of Russian industry. By the autumn however the Bashkir leadership was very divided. After the capture of Pugachev, more Russian troops had been released for repression in Bashkiria, and moreover the main unifying factor behind the revolt, 'Peter III', was no more. By mid-November only six of the well-known Bashkir leaders still held out ; Salavat Yulyayev was finally captured with a few faithful followers on 24 November. The captured Bashkir leaders suffered the most severe penalties, the knut, clipping of nostrils, branding, and hard labour in Rogervik, where they still survived in 1797.[67]

While sparks of revolt continued to blaze up and be snuffed out, the process of winding up the repressive measures was hurried on. As soon as Catherine heard that Pugachev had been executed, she started for Moscow, where she arrived on 25 January 1775. An imposing entry had been devised with triumphal arches and scenes representing the victory of Russian arms over external and internal foes, and portraying allegorically Catherine's concern with law and justice. The stage was now set for the final act : an amnesty which would put an end to 'all cases arising from the late troubles'.[68] On 17 March 1775 a manifesto was promulgated which proclaimed an amnesty for all offences committed during the Pugachev revolt, 'since affairs of this kind are beyond the bounds of that social order for which the laws and their functioning have been established'. All those sentenced to death either as a result of the rebellion or for other causes were to have the sentence commuted to hard labour ; those sentenced to corporal punishment were to have this part of the sentence commuted and were to be sent to settlement in Siberia instead. State prosecutions which had lasted for more than ten years were to be dropped, and all offences more than ten years old were to be consigned to oblivion. Deserters from the army and fugitive state peasants and townspeople would be pardoned if they gave themselves up or returned home within a year.[69]

Three provisions in the manifesto marked a further development of Catherine's social policy : article 16 allowed anyone to set up a workshop or practise a craft without asking for state permission – a great advance in the liberalization of Russian domestic industry. Article 47 remodelled the structure of the town-dwellers and removed some of them from the category of poll-tax payers ; and finally Catherine took the opportunity to translate into law an idea which she had first mooted when she was drafting her Great Instruction : [70] article 46 declared that a serf who had once been freed by his master could register in whatever social status he chose, as a state peasant, a kupets, or a town-dweller, and pay the corresponding taxes. [71] Article 46 was explained and expanded in an even more important ukaz on 6 April 1775 which laid down that even if freed serfs wished it, once they had been freed they could never be enserfed again. Landowners were made responsible for the poll-tax of freed serfs until the following census. [72]

Though Catherine did her best to consign the revolt to oblivion, the human and material losses caused by the Pugachevshchina were severe. Figures are bound to be only approximate, but the rebels were estimated to have killed 1,572 nobles (including wives and children), 237 clerics, and 1,037 officers and officials. These figures leave out of account household serfs, peasants and townspeople who fell foul of rebel bands ; in Kazan' for instance, 50 nobles were killed, but 49 kuptsy and 42 peasants and household serfs also lost their lives. [73] Government casualties were estimated at 600 killed and 1,000 wounded. Casualties among Pugachev's forces were infinitely higher : some 20,000 killed in the actual fighting, to which must be added those executed by Peter Panin, and uncounted Bashkirs and members of other Tartar tribes. [74]

There was also considerable damage to property, private, public, and ecclesiastical. Noble women and girls freed by government troops were often quite destitute, their menfolk killed and their estates destroyed. The empress had authorized Peter Panin to assist families rendered penniless by the revolt, and he distributed nearly 100,000 rubles to some 1,038 families. [75] More long-term help was provided on Panin's suggestion by means of loans through the Nobles' Bank of which branches were opened in Orenburg, Kazan' and Nizhniy Novgorod. [76] Church property was also frequently wrecked ; the plate was stolen, or broken up and shared out, and Old Believers among the Yaik Cossacks put out the eyes of icons. [77] The industries of the Urals were not however irreparably damaged by the revolt, though the material losses, including lost production, were estimated at 5,536,193 rubles. [78] Peter Panin had been given powers to get the local administration going again, recruiting new staff to replace those who had been killed or who had disgraced themselves. Extraordinary measures were taken to ward off famine in the areas affected by the revolt, where in many cases the peasants had simply ceased to till the soil. Finally, by August 1775, having, as he put it, restored order and tranquillity, and brought back the people to their obedience, Panin was relieved of his special commission and received a warm letter of thanks from the empress. [79] Their correspondence reveals that they did not see eye to eye, and Panin now withdrew again to sulk majestically in Moscow for the rest of his life.

From the start of the uprising Catherine had been very concerned to discover whether Turkey or France was implicated, whether there was any trace of a conspiracy involving her own subjects, and finally what had induced Pugachev to assume the mantle of Peter III, and what were his connections with the Old Belief. The extensive investigations conducted by the Secret Commissions of Kazan' and Orenburg convinced her that conspiracy played no part – either foreign or domestic. It was more difficult to reach a verdict on the causes of the revolt and on the origin of the imposture. In the long run, the various investigators agreed that the revolt had originated as a result of internal disputes within the Yaik Cossack Host. Nowhere else could Pugachev have acquired the following necessary to start the revolt, and he won his support by promising to restore the Old Belief and Cossack institutions.

In attempting from the present-day standpoint to analyse this greatest of the internal Russian revolts, the historian is hampered by the traditional description of the Pugachevshchina as a 'peasant war'. For it was only in the last phase, after the defeat outside Kazan', that it turned into a veritable *jacquerie*. It was not regarded as a peasant war at the time. Indeed Paul Potemkin and Prince Volkonsky, in a report forwarded to Catherine, had concluded that 'Pugachev's extirpation of the gentry had not been his own conscious policy but a chance result of the rebels' frenzied rage and of serfs complaining against their masters'.[80]

The real motive force in sparking off the revolt, the drive behind its initial success, seems, in retrospect, to have been the rejection by the Yaik Cossack community of the advancing Petrine state, their refusal to provide the services it required in the form in which it required them. The prevalence of Old Belief among them confirms their traditionalist attitude, rooted in the Muscovite state and its practices. The Yaik Cossacks were the furthest Host from the centre and the least integrated. Like all Cossack Hosts, they had a strong sense of being an élite. The potential loss of this status, the advance of *regulyarstvo* (i.e. incorporation into the regular army) is what they rose against, in a movement whose psychological roots have much in common with those of the *strel'tsy* or musketeers who rose against Peter I at the end of the seventeenth century. In Pugachev's manifestos directed to the Yaik Cossacks, not only were specific Cossack grievances redressed and specific demands granted (i.e. pardon for the revolt of 1772); the Cossacks were promised that they would be *the* privileged élite of the future. 'You and your descendants will be . . . the first before the great Sovereign.'[81] Throughout the rising the political conceptions of Pugachev and his followers (if one may use the word political of something so vague and formless) never went beyond a society organized on Cossack lines in which the Cossacks would be a ruling élite. As I. Ya. Pochitalin put it, '[Pugachev's] intention was to make of everyone, whatever his estate, a Cossack'.[82] But this Cossack world would turn its back on modernization and all the evils which flowed from it. 'If God gives me power over the state, I will order everyone to hold by the Old Belief, to wear Russian clothes, I will forbid shaving of the beard, and all will have their hair cut in Cossack fashion.'[83] This Muscovite psychology explains the attacks on foreigners in Kazan', and some of the appalling cruelty towards officers and officers' wives dressed in their Western clothes. 'Our little father the Tsar did not love Germans [foreigners].'[84]

The first non-Cossack adherents of the revolt were moved by similar feelings : the rejection of the Petrine state. The assigned peasants rose against a way of life which tore them from their traditional occupation to serve the mechanical monsters demanded by the regular army. But the backward-looking nature of the movement's inspiration explains the ambivalent attitude of the factory serfs to the rebels. Whereas the assigned peasants, still linked to the land, found in rebel promises an answer to their prayers, the factory serfs had begun to develop a professional pride, however hard their lives, and their links with the villages had been totally severed. There was no room for them in a Cossack Utopia. The destruction of the factories would deprive them of their livelihood, such as it was, and though many joined the rebellion, many tried to prevent the destruction of the factories in the later stages of the revolt. As for the Bashkirs, they rose in defence of their freedom and their lands. They made common cause with Pugachev at first, but they deserted him after Kazan' to continue to fight their own battle – and one is entitled to doubt whether their frequently difficult cooperation with 'Peter III' would have continued had he been more successful. The Russian state – any Russian state – was their ultimate enemy.

The attitude of the enserfed peasantry is much simpler to explain. Belief in Peter III was easily fostered by such reports as that on his accession he had issued an ukaz enacting that peasants 'should no longer be in the possession of the nobles'. This was why the nobles had deprived him of his throne. Now, after eleven years, 'he had recovered himself' and had again proclaimed the freedom of the peasants.[85] In different manifestos, or verbal pronouncements, the peasants were promised freedom from taxes for two years, seven years, ten years, for ever ; freedom from the recruit levy ; freedom to seize the landowners' property. They were urged to kill the landowners, they were promised that 'he who kills a landowner and destroys his house will be given a wage – 100 rubles ; he who kills ten landowners and destroys their houses will be given 1,000 rubles and a general's rank'.[86]

Yet deep though the peasant hatred for serfdom was, current Soviet historiography in general does not bring out one of the features characterizing much of the evidence given to the investigating commissions.[87] This is the fact that the peasants 'waited'[88] for the arrival of rebel forces in their neighbourhood, for an ukaz from 'Peter III' or for the actual presence in their village of a group of Cossacks (usually described as Yaik Cossacks) before they rose. And even then, they were not given much choice : 'Look, *muzhiki*, on no account work for the landowner, or pay him any dues ; and if in the future we should find that you work for the landowner, we shall cut you down.'[89] It is only too easy to assume that *all* the serfs rose against *all* their masters. Some serfs, particularly household serfs, and stewards, lost their lives in defence of their masters. Wealthy peasants, whether serfs or not, were frequently attacked or killed.[90] It was a war in which those who 'are not with me are against me', and Pugachev's forces did not hesitate to execute deserters, conscript peasants, or to take hostages from among them – and many peasants quietly slipped back home when they had a chance while others sat on the fence and hoped that the upheaval would pass them by.

The history of the Pugachev revolt remains to be written, in spite of the enormous literature on the subject. It has, so far, mainly been approached in the Soviet Union from preconceived positions, which attribute more conscious political views and a more sophisticated programme to a heroic leadership than they actually harboured ; and a more 'progressive' role in the Marxist scheme than a non-Marxist would ever accept, since by no stretch of the imagination can a Cossack Utopia be regarded as bourgeois even though property relationships and the exploitation of land largely escaped the legal stranglehold of serfdom. In the result the heights and the depths to which the movement could rise or fall have been left out of account, the savage poetry, the depths of beastliness, the drunken orgies, the mental confusion, the courage, the hopes and the despair. For the Cossacks, Pugachev was the 'tsar of our hopes', (*nadezha gosudar*); Pugachev appealed to them thus : 'Now, my children, my bright falcons, see, don't abandon me ; now I am a dove-coloured eagle. . . . raise the wings of the dove-coloured eagle, and I will look after you. . . .'[91] As Padurov put it in his testimony to the Secret Commission : though he knew that Pugachev was not Peter III, 'I was afraid to leave him, I was bound to him as by an invisible force, as by enchantment – how this happened I don't know'.[92]

To what extent can it be said that the Pugachev revolt shook the foundations of Catherine's regime ? Though there is agreement on the geographical area affected by the revolt in its various stages, the numbers of people involved are variously estimated.[93] Evidently, in the course of the one year which the revolt lasted, a large number of people were caught up in it, willingly or unwillingly, as active participants, passive followers or victims. But in spite of the fact that such a large proportion of the Russian army was engaged in the Turkish war, Pugachev was never able to attack the centre, as distinct from the periphery of Russia. The successful sacking of Kazan' in July 1774 should not mislead one. No modern small town would be able to defend itself against the whirlwind approach of 20,000 attackers from within the state.[94] But Pugachev's motley forces could not stand up against professional troops, and his defeat outside Kazan' by Mikhel'son coincided with the signature of the peace with Turkey and was achieved before troops could be moved away from the Turkish front. From then on the revolt became a *jacquerie* pure and simple, spreading in eddying waves along both sides of the Volga, but sparked off by the knowledge that 'Peter III' was near at hand. Whatever the fears of the nobility in the two capitals, whatever the rumbling murmurs in the street and the countryside, no one actually rose. They were 'waiting' for Peter III to arrive. One cannot therefore measure the extent of the actual danger by the extent of the panic of the gentry or the security precautions of the government. The further Pugachev went from his Cossack base on the Yaik, the smaller the chance of success. Indeed it may well be argued that if there were no large-scale revolts after the crushing of Pugachev's rising, it was because the opportunity was then taken to tame the Cossacks for good and bind them closely to the purposes of the Russian state.[95]

Part VI

The Reforming Decade

18

The Reform of Local Administration in 1775

The Pugachev revolt underlined in a dramatic way the deficiencies of Russian local administration which had already been so graphically described in the noble nakazy to the Legislative Commission and in the debates.[1] The peace of Kuchuk Kainardzhi released Catherine's mental energies from the task of prosecuting the war, and already in August 1774 she wrote to Jacob Sievers, the governor of Novgorod, warning him that she was planning a reform of the local administration.[2] There was a good deal of material available for her to draw upon. As long ago as October 1764, she had ordered governors of guberniya to consider the redelimitation of the uezdy in their guberniya in such a way that they should contain approximately 30,000 inhabitants,[3] thus equalizing the revenue to be derived from taxation. Governors were asked to propose centrally situated uezd towns so that inhabitants with business there could reach them without difficulty, and ordered to provide maps and lists of the towns in their guberniya, since all projects of local government reform had come up against the total lack of accurate information about the number and limits of existing uezdy.

The reports, proposals and comments which were sent in by the various governors were collated by the Senate, and submitted to the empress on 11 January 1768, after the opening of the Legislative Commission. Not content with replying to the ukaz of October 1764, many governors had also underlined the difficulties they met with, and four of them submitted a joint note to the empress in February 1768, in which they urged the need for more money, more staff and more power. They proposed that governors on tour should be able to dispense summary justice, without going through the written procedure of the normal judicial system. They wished to appoint their own staffs and to extend their control over them by being granted the right to promote to higher *chiny* – a right so far carefully preserved to the Senate except in the military field. They also demanded the right to call on nobles living in the provinces to carry out specific services as and when required – thus cutting right across the freedom from service of the dvoryane.[4]

The problem of local administration had been referred by the Legislative Commission to a sub-commission, clumsily entitled 'On the Structure of the State in matters of public law', which was established around 16–22 April 1768.[5] This sub-commission disposed of extracts from previous legislation on local administration ; of the nakazy from local government institutions and from the deputies, and of the Senate's report of 11 January 1768 to the empress.[6] In addition Catherine herself supplied the sub-commission with three 'lessons' (*uroki*) which are of considerable importance in illustrating the trend of her thoughts. The first lesson, dated 29 April 1768, echoes Catherine's mentor, Montesquieu. The object of the sub-commission, stated Catherine to the deputies, was to study the 'intermediate subordinate powers dependent on the supreme power, and forming the substance of government', and the 'division into parts of the whole of society for the better observation of good order'. Since nothing could be achieved without a clear picture of the existing situation, the sub-commission was invited to produce a report on the existing territorial division and analysis of the structure, powers and hierarchy of local institutions. The second lesson, dated 20 May 1768, invited the sub-commission to examine the principles of a new territorial division of local administration. In the third lesson, of 26 May, Catherine took for granted the functional separation between the administration and the judiciary. She invited the sub-commission to consider the number of government offices required, their functions, their division into separate departments, their hierarchical relationship with each other and with the central government ; the sub-commission was to define the duties of proposed offices and officials, and to provide a list of the establishment and proposed salaries of each office.[7]

The sub-commission started its labours in April 1768, drawing also on the work of two other sub-commissions, that on justice and that on public order, and continued to labour until October 1771 when it petered out. Its work was badly organized and haphazard, but it must be recognized that its task was Herculean. In attempting to describe the existing structure of local government, it discovered that in the maps procured from the Senate, 'the limits of many guberniya were not indicated or incorrectly indicated, the limits of provinces and uezdy were not indicated at all'. Two gubernii, Novorossiysk (New Russia) and Slobodska Ukraine, were not marked on the maps (they were too new). The whereabouts of the town of Kadue caused trouble since it did not figure on the maps either ; but the problem was eventually solved by the receipt of 'private information' as to its whereabouts.[8]

No complete plan emerged – as far as is known – from these sessions, but the general pinciples on which the sub-commission was basing its work can be deduced, namely : the complete restructuring of local administration, not merely the improvement of what existed ; the separation of functions, judicial, administrative and financial ; the setting up of a completely new 'police' of public order, and a new division of the administrative units of the country based on a principle of equalization. It was also now that the need to associate elected members of society – primarily of course the nobility – with local government was finally ac-

278

cepted. The views of the empress, her principal government servants, the members of the sub-commission, the deputies, all coincided both on the need for fundamental reform, and on the broad principles which such reform should follow.[9]

When the sub-commission ceased to meet in autumn 1771, Russia was in the throes of the war with Turkey. The outbreak of the Pugachev revolt in September 1773 further dangerously strained the resources of the empire. But in spite of the lack of any formal progress in the remodelling of local administration, scattered legislation throughout the years 1768–74 suggests that the idea had not been dropped. A feature of the election manifesto of December 1766 must be recalled here, namely the election by the local dvoryanstvo of a 'marshal' of the nobility in the uezd, and of a 'town chief' by the urban population. Originally elected for two years, further ukazy of 1768 and 1771 ordered fresh elections to be held.[10] But apart from keeping themselves in readiness to act as the channel of communication between the government and the local nobility or township as a body, they had no specific functions. Possibly the most significant evidence of the trend in government thinking was the organization of local administration in 1773 in the two new gubernii, Mogilev and Pskov, formed from the lands seized from Poland in the first partition, and neighbouring Russian lands. After he had been edged out of the College of War by Potemkin, General Z. Chernyshev was appointed governor-general of the two gubernii which were subdivided into four provinces under voyevody. The new institutions set up for these gubernii represent a transitional phase in the process of reforming Russian local administration.[11]

The complete remodelling of local administration may also have been postponed to 1775 for a reason connected with Catherine's own temperament : there is no doubt that in the years 1766 onwards she placed great faith in the Legislative Commission as the source of all major enactments to take place in the future. There are frequent references in her own jottings to problems which she does not want to decide on until the Commission should have had its say. In addition she evidently preferred large-scale reform to piecemeal tinkering – in accordance with her rationalist outlook, and the 'enlightened' approach to government. But the Pugachev revolt convinced her that local government reform was urgently needed.

From the government's point of view, the success of Pugachev's motley forces could be ascribed to the 'weakness, laziness, negligence, idleness, disputes, disagreements, corruption and injustice' of local officials[12] and 'the weak conduct of both military and civil leaders'.[13]

As soon as Catherine reached Moscow in January 1775, she went to work with a will. She disposed in turn of all the materials which had been available to the sub-commission, and of materials produced by or submitted to the Senate.[14] The governor of Kazan', Prince P.S. Meshchersky, had also submitted in November 1774 a plan for local reform of his vast guberniya in which he proposed functional separation (administration, finance and justice) ; the subdivision of the guberniya into smaller units, and the division of the uezdy into 'kommissariats' in which a kommissar would be 'elected or chosen in some appropriate manner'. In the case of Kazan' Catherine authorized the governor to implement his plans immediately.[15] The governor of Moscow, Volkonsky, had submitted a more wide-ranging plan to the empress. He advocated a large measure of decentralization of the central government offices, a reduction in the size of the gubernii and the appointment at the lowest level of 'land courts' responsible for the supervision of local order, with a kommissar elected by the local nobility as the executive agent.[16] In addition Catherine could draw on memoranda on the legal systems of Livonia, Estonia and Russian Finland.[17]

The reform project went through about six drafts, many of which were written out by Catherine herself or under her direction ; over six hundred worksheets in her own hand survive.[18] She consulted the procurator general, A.A. Vyazemsky, the secretaries, P.V. Zavadovsky and A.A. Bezborodko, and N. Engel'gardt, the governor of Vyborg. But her closest collaborator was Count Yacov Sievers, who had already advised her in 1764 when the instructions to the governors were remodelled.[19] Sievers came from a family settled in the Baltic provinces with whose institutions he was familiar. More relevant, at the moment, he had lived for seven years – 1748–55 – in England and knew and admired its political institutions.[20] Catherine herself was at this time avidly reading W. Blackstone's *Commentaries on the Laws of England* (in a French translation), which had replaced *L'Esprit des Lois* as her bedside book, and as she wrote to Grimm, 'she was unwinding the thread in her own way'.[21] This may also have led her to draw upon the Scottish-trained jurist, S. Desnitsky, though concrete evidence of his cooperation is lacking.[22]

Two laws, one issued in December 1774, the other in March 1775, must also be taken into account when attempting to analyse Catherine's internal policy. The first of these is an 'Instruction to Hundredsmen' of 19 December 1774[23] which provided for the election in each village every December of 'hundredmen', 'fiftyiethmen' and 'tenthmen' to carry out a whole list of police functions. These rural officials were to take the oath of loyalty, and to carry out duties such as enforcing church attendance, guarding against heresy and witchcraft, preventing crimes such as theft and brigandage, countering spies and rumourmongers, epidemics, etc. The peasant officials were also to see to it that transfers of peasants from estate to estate should be notified to the local chancery and that no more should be collected in dues from the peasants than was allowed. They were to superintend the preservation of game and timber, and finally to report on 'monsters and curious beasts and birds'. The hundredman was to know his instruction thoroughly, hence it must be read to him by a priest or other literate person once a week.

This ukaz presents many interesting features. In the first place it refers specifically both to state peasants and to serfs of private owners – indeed the ukaz states in so many words that when the hundredman is fulfilling his official duties, he is not to be called on to do other work either by an administrator (*upravitel'*) or by a landowner (*pomeshchik*), both of whom are on the contrary enjoined to assist him. The state is thus asserting its right to intervene between the landowner and the serf, by specifying the form which the administration of all villages is to take, and by requiring the serf hundredman to take the oath of loyalty to the sovereign. Yet the ukaz seems totally to disregard the realities of serf life. Some of the functions laid on the hundredmen such as sanitary and medical supervision he had no means of fulfilling ; and how could he ensure that the transfer of serfs was registered at the local government chancellery ? Moreover at the end of his period of office a hundredman would revert to his status as a serf, and be totally at the mercy of his landlord. In the circumstances he could scarcely be expected to act up to what the 'Instruction' required of him. Nevertheless, unrealistic though it was, the ukaz seems to indicate an intention of regularizing the lowest level of administration, the smallest unit, the village, before turning to the larger units.[24]

The second relevant enactment was included in the manifesto issued on 17 March 1775 on the occasion of the end of the war with the Porte. Article 46 enacted a restructuring of the town population obviously intended to modernize it in view of the forthcoming reform. The status of kupets or merchant was now reserved to all those town-dwellers with a capital of 500 r. or more. All others were to be meshchane or common people. Access to the status of kupets was to be purely a matter of money : if a meshchanin accumulated enough capital he could apply to become a kupets ; if a kupets lost his fortune he dropped to the status of meshchanin. The kuptsy were to continue to be divided into three guilds and were to be freed from the poll-tax, instead of which they were to pay a tax of one per cent of their declared capital per annum – which was expected to yield a higher return.[25] They were also freed from the recruit levy and allowed to make a payment instead.[26]

From the point of view of the projected reform of local administration however, the significance of this apparently minor measure was the replacement of the division of the town population into legal 'estates' by a straightforward stratification according to wealth, i.e., it represented the application of a new principle of social stratification to the urban population, a principle which would reflect existing economic realities and purge the estate of the kuptsy of those who still legally belonged to the estate but were in fact small tradesmen, craftsmen, hired labourers or tillers of the soil. The result of this shake-out of the whole class of the kuptsy was to reduce their number in 1775 to some 27,000, out of a total of between 221,573 and 222,767 registered merchants. Over 194,000 therefore did not possess – or declared that they did not possess – the minimum capital of 500 r. required.[27]

To give it its full title, the Statute for the Administration of the Gubernii of the Russian Empire was presented to the Council on 2 November and without further discussion it was promulgated on 5 November 1775. It established the basic structure of Russian local administration and of the judicial system which lasted until the reforms of 1864, and the basic territorial division which lasted until the October Revolution. The existing gubernii were to be redivided into units of from 300,000 to 400,000 inhabitants, which in turn were to be subdivided into uezdy of between 20,000 and 30,000 inhabitants. The old intermediate unit, the province, was eliminated. A governor was to be appointed in each guberniya, and two gubernii formed a 'namestnichestvo' and were placed under a *namestnik,* lord lieutenant or governor-general, who also acted as governor of one of them. The new Statute provided for a clear separation of administration, finance and justice, for the establishment of separate judicial organs for each estate, with elected participation by members of that estate, and for a degree of social participation in the management of welfare and education in each estate.

At the head of the pyramid was the governor or governor-general or head of the executive, who was charged with the supervision of the proper functioning of all organs of local administration, responsibility for the public good, the redressing of injustices and watching over the interests of the injured and oppressed. It was specifically underlined that he was not a judge and had no judicial functions.[28] He was entitled to correspond directly with the empress and had a seat in the Senate when he came to the capital. The governor-general or the governor was assisted by a deputy governor, in charge of financial matters, and a board of local government composed of the above, and two appointed councillors, which was to form the collegial board from which orders were issued. The new judicial organs were placed under this collegial board : at the top were a criminal court and a civil court, all members of which were appointed, from which appeal lay to the Senate. Cases affecting all estates came before these two courts. Below them, the judicial system was divided into separate branches for each 'estate', composed of the higher land court and the uezd court for the nobles ; in the former, the judge was appointed but assisted by assessors elected by the nobles ; in the latter the judge and the assessors were all elected.

The parallel system for the townspeople comprised the guberniya magistrat, and the town magistrat ; in the former the two judges were appointed and the six assessors elected, in the latter the two judges and the four assessors were elected by the townspeople. In small towns a *ratusha* of one *burgmistr* and two assessors was elected. In addition the 'verbal courts' (courts with entirely oral procedure) (*slovesnyye sudy*), elected by town-dwellers survived in the various town districts for cases involving very small sums of money.[29] Where the free population reached 30 per cent of the total, the Statute allowed the establishment of lower summary courts (*nizhnyaya rasprava*) (for 10,000 to 30,000 inhabitants) and a higher summary court (*verkhnyaya rasprava*) (where one or more lower summary courts were set up) for the odnodvortsy, state, court, economic and assigned peasants. The judges were appointed, from people with a *chin,* but the ten and eight assessors respectively were to be elected by the peasants under the jurisdiction of these courts, from among themselves, or from the nobility, people with a *chin,* learned men, or raznochintsy.[30]

Strictly within the judicial field, the Statute attempted to introduce an entirely new principle in Russian jurisprudence, namely the 'courts of equity', to which all classes had access. The judge of the equity court was appointed and was to be assisted by two assessors elected by the nobles, the townspeople and the free peasants respectively, in cases concerning the corresponding estate. The origins of this innovation have been discussed in Russian historical literature. Grigor'yev, the historian of the reforms of 1775, suggests that the main model was the English court of equity, and that S.E. Desnitsky might have written this chapter in the statute. More recent research suggests that the immediate source of Catherine's new courts of equity was the great *Encyclopédie* rather than Blackstone. Among her drafts and papers, extracts from the entries *Equité, Droit* and *Habeas Corpus* have been found, which commended the English Chancery Court.[31] Catherine welded together in her equity courts some of the ideas underlying the English court of equity, and some of the principles of habeas corpus.

The functions of the judge of the equity courts, as set out in Chapter XXVI, para 397 of the Statute, were to dispense justice according to the laws, but also to safeguard personal security. In judging civil cases brought before him he was to act as an arbiter, whose judgment was binding on the parties who had sought his verdict. Those who had been under arrest for more than three days without being informed of the charge against them could appeal to him. He could order the prisoner to be produced before him and release him on bail unless he were charged with *lèse majesté,* treason, murder, theft or brigandage. Severe fines of up to 300 rubles could be incurred by those who disregarded his orders.[32] The range of cases to which the Russian form of habeas corpus would apply was much smaller than in England but the very idea that a man should be released on bail was a totally new one in Russia.

The judiciary and the administrative functions were however re-united at the lowest level in the countryside. A lower land court was established in each uezd, presided over by a *zemskiy ispravnik* or land commissar, assisted by two assessors, elected by the nobility of the uezd. The lower land court was charged with policing the countryside, and with the execution of the orders of the board of local government and the decisions of the higher courts. The land commissar, as its president and executive agent, was entrusted with a large variety of functions, ranging from public order, relations with the military over billeting, epidemics, fugitive serfs, roads, bridges, fires, forests, beggars, etc. He was not entitled to impose fines or punishments on his own authority, this being reserved to the lower land court.[33] The relationship between the land commissars and the hundredmen to be elected by the villages is nowhere mentioned in the Statute. Yet there is evidence that in some way they were connected in Catherine's plans.

'V.M.I. ne daigneroit-elle pas jetter un coup d'oeil sur le projet du Procureur General pour les uezdnyye smotriteli [uezd inspectors – the original name of the land commissars] que j'ai revu avec lui – les oukases qui établissent dans les paroisses les sotskiya [hundred men] et leurs fonctions – on en tireroit peut-être quelquechose pour le nizhniy zemskiy sud [lower land courts],' wrote Sievers to the empress.[34] In one of Catherine's earlier drafts it was suggested that where all villages were owned by nobles, the land commissar should be elected by the nobility ; where they were state property, he should be appointed, and the villages should elect an assessor to the court. In the Statute it was merely stated that in uezdy where there were no or few noble estates, the land commissar should be appointed from among those with a *chin,* which did not necessarily mean a noble since the post was only in the ninth *chin.* But no indication was given of how the gap was to be bridged between the village *sotskiye* and the land commissar.

If the police in the countryside was mainly in the hands of the nobility, in the towns it was subordinated to the bureaucracy. The need for an official to be in charge of public order in the towns had been pointed out to Catherine by Sievers. 'Si vous feres cet homme la trop grand il se heurtera continuellement avec les "sudi" [judges] et s'il sera trop petit il n'aura aucune considération,' commented Catherine. In the event she introduced the *gorodnichi,* or 'provost', in each uezd town, whose functions were described in precisely the same terms as those of the land commissar.[35] Like the land commissar, the provost was not a judge. Unlike the land commissar, he was in command of small detachments of armed guards. He was strictly enjoined not to leave his post when the city was in danger (a reflection on the behaviour of officials during the Pugachev revolt). He was appointed by the Senate and was granted the eighth *chin,* i.e. he would be a noble or promoted to noble rank on appointment. His authority extended over all the inhabitants of the town, whether kuptsy, meshchane or simple town-dwellers. Though it is not stated in the Statute, he could presumably also arrest a noble.

To complete this sketch of the judicial structure the role of the procurators must be mentioned. Procurators were appointed to the guberniya board of local government, to the guberniya magistrat, the higher land court, and the higher summary court. They were to be the guardians of the legality of the action taken by the boards of administration and the courts ; they were to see that the different institutions did not encroach on each other's field of activity and to supervise the manner in which laws and orders were carried out – involving the conduct of members of the bureaucracy. The guberniya procurator reported illegalities not only to the governor or *namestnik* of the guberniya, but also to the procurator general at the centre. He was also specifically charged with the welfare of those under arrest or in prison. Thus, though the guberniya procurator was subordinated to the governor the procuracy continued to function as a separate network throughout the country, responsible to and reporting to the procurator general.

The financial functions of local administration were entrusted to a new body, the treasury chamber (*kazennaya palata*) which was described as a local branch of the central Revenue College (*Kammer Kollegiya*) and of the central Auditing College (*Revizion Kollegiya*). Headed by the deputy governor, assisted by a director of finance and a collegial board, the treasury chamber was placed in charge of the census, local income and expenditure, collection of taxes, checking accounts, the salt monopoly and the farming of liquor taxes, the maintenance of state buildings. It had no judicial powers, and could only prosecute defaulters in the courts through the agency of the financial pleader (*stryapchii*).[36]

A further innovation of the Statute was the setting up, under the board of local government, of a board of social welfare (*prikaz obshchestvennogo prizreniya*) composed of the governor, two assessors from the higher land court (nobles), two assessors from the guberniya magistrat (merchants) and two assessors from the higher summary court (free peasants), if there was one. The board was granted a capital sum of 15,000 r. in each guberniya and charged with the establishment and supervision of schools, hospitals, almshouses and houses of correction. The Statute enjoined the boards to set up primary schools in all towns and in large villages where there was a higher summary court. Attendance was to be voluntary, and the poor could attend for nothing. The Statute briefly touched on the curriculum (the three Rs and religion) but went into considerable detail on matters of hygiene, such as keeping the windows open all day in summer and for some time in winter. The teachers were forbidden to use corporal punishment.

Hospitals were also to be set up, near but outside major towns, and down-river from them. Male and female patients should be kept separate, and so should those suffering from infectious diseases.[37] Considerable emphasis was laid on cleanliness and fresh air, and separate accommodation for the incurably ill and lunatics was advised. Workhouses were to be established for the poor but fit, and houses of correction were to be established specifically for those of both sexes who fell into evil ways, such as disobedience to their parents, extravagance and debt, a dishonourable life, 'serfs who were lazy and wandered about, people who did not want to work for their food', and women of evil life. Such people could be sentenced for a time or for ever to incarceration either by the board of local government, by the courts, or at the request of parents to the board of social welfare, and at the request of a landowner or a master. In the last three cases, parents, landowners or masters were to provide maintenance, otherwise the house of correction would refuse admittance. As usual with Catherine, the Statute laid down in detail the way inmates were to be treated – they were to be made to work, in strong buildings, well guarded, and supplied with baths. Those who refused to work could be punished with up to three strokes with rods, or bread and water for three days or not more than a week in a dark cell.[38]

It remains now to describe two offices which were taken over in the Statute from the Manifesto of 14 December 1766, setting out the electoral procedure for the Legislative Commission, namely the marshal of the nobility and the town chief. Nowhere in the Statute were their functions defined. The marshal of the nobility in each uezd was to be elected every three years. He organized the elections of the noble assessors and officials of the various courts, though this is not stated. The noble assembly which elected the various officials met every three years and was granted the right, most unusual in Russia, of submitting collective as distinct from individual petitions to the empress. The marshal was also to be the chairman of a body, best translated as the noble board of guardians (*Opeka*), subordinated to the higher land court, which was charged with watching over the interests of noble widows and children, and orphans. Elected every three years, the town chief presided over a similar institution, the town orphans court, which depended on the town magistrat, and looked after widows and orphans of the urban classes.

A further innovation, already hinted at in Catherine's Great Instruction,[39] was incorporated in the Statute, namely the right to make representations to the Senate on new laws, conferred on the governor in joint session with the three higher courts, namely the criminal court, the civil court and the treasury chamber. Such representations had to be unanimous. However, that this was no 'droit de remontrance' in the French manner was made clear by the injunction that should the law be confirmed by the supreme power after such representations, it was to be applied without further ado.

How far did this new network of institutions respond to the demands put forward by the different estates at the Legislative Assembly ? As regards the nobility it undoubtedly met the need to multiply the organs of local administration and bring them nearer to the localities, as well as the demand to participate in the institutions of local administration and to control the policing of the countryside. In areas where serfdom predominated, the land commissar was in a position to consolidate the authority of the landowners over their serfs ; in areas where there were few or no noble estates, little is known of his role.[40] It must however be stressed that though many of the nakazy submitted by the nobles to the Legislative Commission demanded a closer association of the nobility with local administration, in practice, the nobility was proving very reluctant to accept appointments in the local bureaucracy. The Statute, by establishing a new hierarchy of administrative posts in the provinces, most of them salaried, rendered local service more attractive and more lucrative than it had been before.[41] The service principle was thus re-introduced into the provinces in a more civilized and flexible way. If the demand to elect the voyevoda was not fulfilled, and the senior posts in local administration were filled by appointment, not election, the noble assemblies did elect the various assessors. But in the last resort it was the government which paid the salaries – the piper could call the tune.

In the towns, much of the pre-existing system of courts elected by members of the merchant estate survived : only the registered town-dwellers, the kuptsy and the meshchane took part in the election of judges and assessors. But the town chief presented an anomaly, since he was elected by the whole of 'urban' society (all householders). However some of the demands made by deputies of the towns in the Legislative Assembly were met : the limited period of service (three years) in elective offices ; raising the status of the magistraty to the level of the corresponding noble courts ; granting *chin* and salaries to elected urban officials, thus compensating them for losses arising from absence from their businesses, and protecting them from abuse by their social superiors. The Statute however did not free town-dwellers of whatever rank from burdens in kind such as the billeting of troops. But in the end, service for the townspeople became less of a compulsory burden and more of a lucrative place than in the past.[42]

Catherine had originally intended to introduce the Statute first in a new guberniya of Tver' (to be carved out of the guberniya of Novgorod), under the direction of Sievers himself. But the members of the Council urged that, in view of the parlous state of the country after the Pugachevshchina, the reform should be implemented everywhere as soon as possible.[43] It was in fact a major operation spread over many years, involving complex questions such as the location of new guberniya capitals and new uezd towns, the provision of suitable buildings, the winding up of existing cases, the division and transfer of archives to the new institutions, the recruitment of personnel, by appointment and by election. As the new institutions were established, gaps in the Statute were gradually revealed. Other more practical problems arose, such as shortage of personnel or the difficulty in finding suitable settlements to be raised to the status of uezd towns.

Between 1775 and 1785 the existing twenty-five gubernii were redivided into forty-one ; the forty-second, Taurida, was established after the annexation of the Crimea, in 1787. By Catherine's death in 1796, Russia was divided into fifty gubernii, including those formed out of the annexed portions of Poland. The 169 uezdy of 1775 had grown to 493.[44]

The introduction of the reform was carefully prepared and carried out, with the active participation of the Senate, and under Catherine's own constant personal supervision. She had appointed specially chosen and trustworthy servants of hers as governors-general ; they were given a specific instruction on how to proceed, modelled on that issued to Count Sievers. The first task was the territorial delimitation of the new gubernii and uezdy. The choice of guberniya capitals seems to have provided relatively little difficulty, but the selection of uezd towns was much more complicated, since if the settlement selected was inhabited mainly by state peasants, their status would have to be changed, and if – as occasionally happened – it belonged to a private landowner, the serf population would have to be bought out. This procedure enabled peasants and serfs to become 'townspeople' (*posadskiye lyudi*) at the stroke of a pen, without paying the double tax as members of both estates, normally payable until the next census, by peasants desiring to register as townsmen.[45] The peasants by no means always welcomed their forcible transformation into townspeople, but the proportionately small urban population of Russia simply did not provide a basis for the large number of towns provided for in the Statute. In the promoted court village of Balashov

(Saratov guberniya), of eighty-seven families only nineteen consented to become meshchane.[46]

The difficulty of finding suitable uezd towns is illustrated by the case of Smolensk, one of the first of the new guberniya to be set up, as a 'model'. Eight new towns had to be formed to complete the twelve needed. Of these the town of Sychevka had nine kuptsy and 112 meshchane ; El'nya had 3 kuptsy and 175 meshchane ; Kasplya had 3 kuptsy and 64 meshchane, and Ruposovo had no kuptsy and 40 meshchane. These towns would find it impossible to staff the elective posts in the local administration, particularly as, in the case of Sychevka and Ruposovo, practically all the kuptsy were illiterate. The governor proposed allowing the inhabitants to elect nobles to the urban magistrat ; even this did not work, since it turned out that Ruposovo was too isolated and Sychevka was composed half of court peasants and half of serfs belonging to A.I. Naryshkin. In 1778 the 133 serfs (male) belonging to Naryshkin, with their lands, were bought out for 15,000 rubles.

In delimiting the uezdy the numerical principle of some 20,000 to 30,000 inhabitants was held to. Where possible, existing economic, geographic and ethnic unity was taken into account, but these were not primary considerations. The presence of a sufficient number of nobles in a given uezd to staff the institutions required was a factor,[47] and efforts were made to select new towns from state, court or economic peasants' settlements to avoid the necessity of spending money on buying out landowners. In a number of gubernii economic factors were undoubtedly taken into account – reflecting perhaps the approach of a specific governor-general – notably in Smolensk, Yaroslavl', the new Moscow guberniya. In the central-industrial region of Russia, of 35 new towns founded, a third were already towns in the economic sense of the word ; a third were settlements with considerable potential for growth, and a third had an inadequate economic basis, and were destined to lag or even to be demoted in the future. In the whole of this area there were after the reform 114 towns instead of the previous 75. Of these only eight were eventually reduced to the status of 'towns not on the establishment' (i.e. *zashtatnyye*), that is to say towns not capitals of an uezd.

In the central black earth area, the existing administrative division was particularly out of date. The reform did not in the event increase the total number of towns – 23 were abolished and 25 were created – but it brought administration and economic potential into greater harmony, as well as extending and consolidating the effectiveness of the local government.

In the Volga area, Nizhniy Novgorod was the obvious capital of a guberniya composed of thirteen uezdy ; but nine new uezd towns had to be founded. Even the settlement of Makar'evo, where the great annual fair took place, counted only 246 male souls at the time of the reform. The vast guberniya of Kazan' presented special problems, since the population was very unevenly distributed. In Kazan' uezd proper there were 312,216 inhabitants, in Simbirsk, 188,358, whereas there were outlying uezdy with only ten to thirteen thousand. Great difficulty was experienced in finding settlements suitable to be raised to the status of towns, over and above those which already had an economic life of their own. On the Lower Volga a number of basically agricultural settlements of court peasants or free farming soldiers were raised to the status of towns, even if the inhabitants did not change their way of life or their occupations.

In the Ural region, so recently ravaged by the Pugachev revolt, particular attention was paid to strengthening the administration, with little regard to economic potential. A notable exception however was the foundation of a new town, Perm', as the capital of the governor-generalship of that name. Chosen for its geographical situation near the junction of the river Kama and the Chusova, it was an important centre of convergence of a number of trade routes, and its growth soon justified the choice. Orenburg was passed over in favour of Ufa as a guberniya capital, with the aim of extending government control over the territory largely inhabited by Bashkirs recently involved in the revolt. The closer control exercised by the government in the area of the Urals is reflected by the fact that the number of towns increased from 19 to 41, though most of them were administrative rather than economic centres. In the northeast, the two principal towns, Archangel and Vologda, became gubernii capitals, and with great difficulty 10 new towns were added to the existing 11, since the area was vast and thinly inhabited. Siberia was divided into three new guberniya, Tobol'sk, Kolyvan and Irkutsk. Tobol'sk and Irkutsk were old established trading centres, but the majority of the new towns established in accordance with the Statute of 1775 were fortified posts with but little connection with the local economic life. As a result of the reform there was a total of 499 registered towns in 1787 but, some 50 of the new towns were deregistered by the end of the century, having failed to strike roots as urban settlements.

Leaving aside the demands of the townspeople for specific administrative or social privileges, only some of which were met in 1775, the Statute of 1775 undoubtedly had a considerable impact on the structure of urban Russia. Just as the manifesto of 17 March 1775, with its frank adoption of the principle of stratification by wealth in the urban community had led to a general shaking out of the merchant estate and to a closer correspondence between financial and legal status, so the Statute of November 1775 led to a shaking out of the urban structure, the demotion of administrative or military settlements which had ceased to correspond to any real needs.[48] On the other hand, where economic conditions were favourable, the multiplication of institutions of local government enlivened urban life, helped to create a wider and more varied market, and contributed to provincial economic and cultural development.[49]

This last aspect of the local government reform seems by no means to have been ignored by the government. New stone buildings were built, old ones refurbished ; the governors-general were given special allowances for furniture and plate. The new institutions were inaugurated with considerable pomp and ceremony. Local nobles flocked in to the guberniya town, and after solemn religious services, elections to the various posts took place. The governors gave balls and masquerades, there were operatic performances and fireworks. In Polotsk, religious services took place simultaneously in the Orthodox, Catholic and Uniat churches and in the Jewish synagogues outside the walls.[50] The opening of the new institutions in Kazan' was distinguished by a remarkable programme of music and poetry in Greek, Latin, Tartar, German, Kalmuck, Votian, Mordvin, Chuvash and Cheremis, as well as of course Russian. The participants were then all invited to dine with the metropolitan.[51] The governors-general sometimes however pocketed the funds allocated to furnishing the new offices adequately, judging by the experience of the poet Derzhavin, when he was appointed governor of Olonets in 1784, and had to provide the furniture out of his own pocket.[52]

The new Statute led to a considerable increase in the numbers of officials and in the cost of local administration. In 1773 the total number of officials employed in central and local administration was 16,500.[53] In 1774, before the reform, 12,712 were employed in local administration alone ; this had risen to an estimated 22,000 by 1781, and an estimated 27,000 by 1796.[54] Of this total more than a third were elected officials, in receipt of a salary. The cost of local administration rose from 1,712,465 r.p.a. in 1774 to 5,618,957 in 1785 and to 10,921,388 by 1796.[55]

How well did the new local administration work? There is unfortunately little direct evidence based on the study of the records of courts or government offices. An official account of a journey of inspection carried out by the empress in 1780 through the gubernii of St Petersburg, Pskov, Polotsk, Mogilev, Smolensk and Novgorod provides some information. Officials in her suite were instructed to inquire in each of the gubernii she visited to what extent the provisions of the Statute of 1775 had been carried out, and to report to her. In particular they were to inquire into the backlog of undecided civil and criminal cases and the number of convicts ; to examine the functioning of the boards of social welfare, to study the local economy and to receive representations from the marshals of the nobility and the town chiefs on local needs.

The reports submitted suggest that the courts were working well in terms of the number of cases decided. The backlog of undecided cases does not seem excessive – 230 in Pskov, 284 in Novgorod ; in Porkhov, an uezd town of some 30,000 inhabitants, only 43. The number of convicts ranged from 64 in Novgorod and 19 in Pskov to 1–7 in smaller uezd towns. In Smolensk and Polotsk, the court of equity was singled out for particular praise. In Smolensk it had dealt with 18 criminal cases and settled 700 civil cases since it had been set up.[56] This figure suggests however that the equity court was being used in a manner not foreseen in the Statute and that people were having recourse to it because its procedure was speedier than that of the ordinary 'estate' courts. Unfortunately very little is known about the workings of the equity courts and the extent to which criminal cases were referred to them.[57] The boards of social welfare were also, according to the reports, taking their responsibilities seriously, founding new schools or maintaining pre-existing ones. Mogilev had 32 schools with 850 pupils, Pskov had six, for 300 nobles and 130 townspeople, Smolensk 12, with 359 pupils, Novgorod ten all told with over a thousand pupils. Almshouses also existed in most uezdy, ranging from 42 in Mogilev guberniya to 8 in Novgorod.

The empress's tour of inspection must have encouraged further development, since it was accompanied by the distribution of additional grants for schools, almshouses, the building of stone houses by townspeople, etc. But though the early achievements of the new local administration may have seemed satisfactory on paper, the quality of the administration, and particularly of the justice dispensed, may not have changed very much. The judge of the court of equity in Ufa for instance boasted that in 12 years he had not dealt with 12 cases, and his servant chased the Chuvash and Mordvin petitioners from his door. How could a simple judge deal with cases of magic? As Vinsky, the memoirist of Ufa, remarked sardonically, there were cases when whole villages were convicted of witchcraft – some as witches, and others, by their own admission, as bewitched.[58] As usual in eighteenth-century Russia the problem was in great part one of lack of suitable personnel. Aware of this, Catherine had endeavoured to take over into the new administration only the best officials from the previous one. But many of the previous governors were taken into the new service, and lower down the scale, the new service was almost entirely staffed from members of the old. Human beings formed the bridge which spanned the gulf between the old institutions and the new, and they brought with them the old habits which flourished in a new soil. But quite apart from the inevitable legacy of past corrupt practices and chicanery, even some of the new, specially appointed men who enjoyed the confidence of the empress showed themselves totally unable to understand the new principles of legality which she was trying to introduce ; indeed even the empress herself, in the long run, allowed the strict barriers between justice and administration to become confused, and failed always to enforce the principles she had endeavoured to lay down.[59]

19

The Reforms of the 1780s

The Statute of 1775 by no means exhausted Catherine's reforming zeal. Its gradual implementation revealed the existence of inconsistencies and loopholes on which her guidance was required, and it was inevitably the starting-point for many of the later reforms, designed to fill gaps in social or administrative organization, or to follow through some of the consequences of the decentralization of government. Thus the Police Ordinance of 1782 supplemented the Statute by providing the legal and constitutional framework for the maintenance of public order in the towns, while the Charters to the Nobility and the Towns in 1785 organized the noble and urban estates and laid down the institutions of urban self-government which were to last until the reforms of Alexander II.

When he abolished the Secret Chancery in February 1762 Peter III had enormously increased the power and position of the chief of police of St Petersburg, placing him in charge of police chiefs throughout the empire.[1] This great concentration of power was broken up by Catherine, who returned the police function to local governors and voyevodas in 1764.[2] The security department remained under Catherine as Peter III had left it, namely a department of the Senate under the procurator general, reporting directly to the empress herself.

Catherine had published her own views on the subject of the police in the First Supplement to her Nakaz, in 1768.[3] The sources she drew on are easily identifiable. She is known to have been acquainted with the classic work of Nicolas de la Mare, *Traité de Police*, published in Paris in 1713, from which she drew the list of the functions of the police quoted in the Supplement to the Nakaz.[4] De la Mare himself was but the French exponent of a theory and a practice already extensively developed in seventeenth-century German cameralist thought, and further expounded in the eighteenth century by such writers on *Polizeiwissenschaft* as Justi and Sonnenfels.[5]

The word 'police' in this context did not refer to a body of men, but to a function, namely the rational organization of social and economic activities in the interests of the state and hence of the people. The police was therefore not merely a repressive or coercive organ, designed to impose a deathly public tranquillity,

292

but a creative institution, the eighteenth-century tool of social engineering. As de la Mare put it : 'La Police . . . est . . . la science de gouverner les hommes et de les faire du bien, la manière de les rendre autant qu'il est possible, ce qu'ils doivent être pour l'intérêt général de la société.'[6]

Catherine had established the post of town provost (*gorodnichi*) in the Statute of 1775, and placed him in charge of the police functions in the towns. He was not a judge, but was to supervise public order and decency, and carry out the decisions of the board of local administration and the law courts. She may have been urged to proceed with more wide-ranging legislation by her meeting with Joseph II in 1780. Joseph was a great believer in the regulation of the minutest details of public life, in keeping the mechanism of the state moving like clockwork. He may have been the channel through which Catherine received a copy of the memorandum for Maria Theresa on the police of Paris prepared by J.B. Le Maire for the French minister Sartine on which she drew extensively.[7] At any rate two years after their interview, the Police Ordinance was promulgated on 8 April 1782.[8] It is an inordinately long document, composed of 274 articles. But it does not deal only with the organization and powers of the police in cities ; it represents also an attempt to codify the law governing civil and criminal offences in general, both those falling under the jurisdiction of the police and those of a more serious nature falling under the jurisdiction of the law courts. Thus a large number of specific offences were defined (smuggling, selling contaminated foodstuffs, duelling, seizure of another man's land, unauthorized public gathering, etc.) and specific penalties were laid down (not including corporal punishment, which is never mentioned).

The actual organization of the police was based on the division of towns into quarters (*chasti*) of 200 – 700 households, subdivided into wards (*kvartali*) of 50–100 households. The town provost (in the eighth chin), appointed by the Senate, was to preside over a board (*uprava*), assisted by two appointed commissioners, one for civil and one for criminal affairs (in the ninth rank), and two councillors elected by the local magistrat. The town provost would thus be a noble, or would be promoted to noble rank on appointment. The police board was placed directly under the board of local administration presided over by the governor. Commissioners were appointed to the quarters and in the wards inspectors and constables were elected every three years. The actual number of police was very small, but the town provost commanded military units which could be used for guard duties and for law enforcement. The numbers varied from some 30 in uezd towns to 100 or so in guberniya capitals.[9]

To guide them, the police boards received a typically Catherinian instruction or nakaz. It began with a didactic section, entitled 'The Mirror of the Police' divided into moral rules, social duties of the general public, and rules for the proper conduct of the police. The moral rules include such *obiter dicta* as 'Do not unto others what you would not wish to be done unto you'; 'Help each other, lead the blind, feed the poor, give water to the thirsty'; 'Have compassion on him who drowns, and hold out a helping hand to him who stumbles.' This section was followed by a restatement of the Christian duties of husbands and wives and fathers and children ; in the third section the police were enjoined to be loyal and zealous, to show common sense and good will and not to take bribes, since bribes 'darken the eyes, corrupt the mind and the heart and seal the lips'.[10]

Subsequent articles set out the responsibilities of the police in detail, and the procedure to be followed. The police were to supervise all public assemblies and entertainments ; they were to enforce sumptuary laws, inspect buildings and public baths (strictly enforcing the separation of sexes), organize firefighting services, and street lighting, superintend trade and street trading ; they were also to look after foreigners or those from other towns, and watch over the activities of the *'makler'* or labour broker who ran a compulsory employment office for servants and workers ; and of course they were to deal with crime. Each quarter was supposed to set up a free school but the police were given no specific powers over schools.[11]

The police were empowered to deal summarily with minor offences such as opening eating-houses before the end of the Sunday morning religious services ('fine him the equivalent of the daily sustenance of a poor man, and keep him under guard until he pays') by means of fines and short periods of arrest, or detention in houses of correction. In all other cases and in all offences involving sums of more than 20 rubles, the matters had to be referred to the courts to be dealt with according to the law. It is nowhere stated that the police had the power of sentencing to corporal punishment, though they would have to carry out such sentences on behalf of the courts. The fines are mostly calculated in terms of one or more day's keep in a house of correction. Drunks were treated leniently – 24 hours on bread and water. More ingenious is the punishment devised for men and women over 7 years of age who had penetrated into the bath-houses of the opposite sex. They were to be fined half a day's keep in a house of correction, and could work it off by heating the bath-water in the bath-house.[12]

The urban summary courts (*slovesnyy sud*) with oral procedure were remodelled and given a clearer direction. A court was to be set up in each quarter of the city composed of one or more justices and a number of assessors. All members were to be elected by the quarter, and approved by the provost. The court dealt only with civil matters, each case was to be cleared up in a day, and the whole procedure was to be oral. Appeal lay to the town magistrat court. Here too the police do not seem to have had any powers, other than approving the composition of the courts.[13]

The police were in no sense a security or political agency in the modern sense of the term. But the town-dwellers were ordered to report to the constable the arrival and departure of any visitors, and the registers of the labour brokers were to contain full personal details of all applicants and be open to the police.[14] The police were also later – in 1783 – charged with the duty of passing for publication books produced on private printing presses.[15]

How did this elaborate ordinance work in fact ? Unfortunately, though most Russian historians take for granted that it did not work, and that it was merely an additional tool for the political control of a resentful population, we have absolutely no detailed studies to go upon.[16] Human nature being what it is, one is entitled to assume that the ordinance was more often honoured in the breach than the observance. All one can state is that it produced an institutional framework and laid down the rules within which certain habits and activities could develop, and that it probably somewhat increased the security of the major cities and towns. Even if the network of inspectors and constables only provided for the routine settlement of minor disputes and misdemeanours by offering a certain venue for a plaintiff to turn to, it would already begin to organize Russian urban life into more defined patterns.

However, the Police Ordinance was only the first stage in a far more elaborate programme of social and administrative modernization. It was followed in 1785 by the promulgation of two Charters, one to the nobility, the second to the towns. Both Charters dealt with the organization of the social estates, but the Charter to the Towns in addition laid down an elaborate system of urban administration.

Catherine's concept of local government in the provinces and administration in the towns required the cooperation of the *sosloviya* or estates of the country in order to make it work. But to secure this cooperation she had in the first place to create and give legal form to corporate institutions of the nobility and the towns, institutions which the estates had never succeeded in developing for themselves. It is not that Catherine's thought was conservative, but rather that she was influenced by existing models elsewhere (and notably by Montesquieu's support for a society of estates) and accepted without demur that, given the shortage of trained cadres in Russia, the government could not govern by bureaucracy alone.

It was therefore necessary for Catherine to define the personal rights of the nobles and the collective rights of the noble estate. At the same time the role of the nobility in local administration, as laid down in the Statute of 1775, had to be clarified. It soon became clear that governors trained in an authoritarian tradition found it very difficult to understand the degree of autonomy Catherine was proposing to grant to the noble estate. The nature of the problem is illustrated by her replies to a list of questions submitted to her by Governor Yacov Sievers in October 1778, replies which were published as a decree of general application in November 1778. In answer to Sievers's questions Catherine stressed the independent role of the marshal of the nobility and the noble assembly. Though it was for the governor to summon a meeting of the assembly, he was not allowed to attend its sessions or to be present at elections for local office. The marshal, not the governor, was to administer the oath of allegiance to elected noble officials and to preside at the election of his successor. The corporate rights of the noble assemblies were already adumbrated : they could meet after the elections to discuss local needs, and they could select deputies to lay these before the empress. The assemblies were also allowed to levy voluntary taxes. In reply to

Sievers's question whether each session should follow exactly the same procedure as on the first introduction of the new institutions, Catherine gave the typical reply : 'Read out the duties of each post at each session, but one sprinkling of holy water is sufficient.'[17] The gradual maturing of her policy in the 1780s is illustrated by a decree enabling officials to keep their pensions while serving in salaried elective posts, and by decrees forbidding governors to dismiss elected officials or fill vacant posts by appointment. The noble assemblies were given complete freedom before the Charter of 1785 was promulgated, to decide in what manner elections should be conducted, and in particular on the age and property qualifications of noble electors.[18]

Issued on 21 April 1785, together with the Charter to the Towns, in order to celebrate Catherine's birthday, the Charter to the Nobility confirmed the previously existing civil rights of the nobility, and defined a number of new ones. It also laid down the legal framework for the exercise of corporate rights of the noble estate. Among personal rights, the Charter confirmed the immunity of the noble from loss of rank, estate, honour or life without trial by his equals. Nobility was defined as hereditary ; a woman marrying a non-noble did not lose her rank, but she could not confer it on her children. Noble rank could be forfeited on conviction of such crimes as breach of oath, treason, robbery, etc. Nobles were immune from corporal punishment, and nobles serving in non-commissioned ranks in the armed forces were to be punished as officers. So far the Charter was enacting in law for the first time what had in fact been practised since mid-eighteenth century. It then went on to confirm rights granted in the Manifesto of 1762, such as freedom from service, and the right to travel and to enter service abroad. Next the Charter confirmed or enacted a number of property rights, such as the exclusive right to buy 'villages', to establish manufactures and industrial enterprises on their estates, to sell wholesale their produce or manufactured goods, to establish fairs, to buy houses in towns and set up craft workshops (though if they wanted to make use of town rights nobles had to obey town laws), to the free exploitation of the growth above ground (including forests), or the riches of the subsoil in their estates.[19] Finally, the noble was declared free from personal taxation and his house on his estate was freed from billeting obligations.

The corporate rights of the nobles made the guberniya the basic unit of their organization. They were allowed to form an assembly, to meet every three years when summoned by the governor. Their public business was to choose candidates for the various elective posts in local administration, their choice to be confirmed by the governor. No one was to be elected who did not have an income of at least one hundred rubles from land or who had not reached the age of twenty-five. The guberniya noble assembly was entitled to make representations to the governor regarding local needs, and its right to make representations to the Senate, or to the empress herself, through deputies, was confirmed, provided that such representations involved no breach of the law. It was also authorized to acquire a house, to keep archives and a seal, to appoint a secretary, and to set up a fund by means of voluntary contributions. The nobility as a whole was not to be held responsible for the crime of an individual noble, nor was the assembly to appear before a court, except through its 'pleader' (*stryapchiy*). All nobles registered in the guberniya who had reached their majority could sit in the assembly but nobles who had not served at all, or had not reached commissioned rank in service, could neither vote nor be chosen to fill elective posts.

The main function of the assembly however was to keep the register of the nobility based in the particular guberniya. Deputies were to be elected in each uezd who together with the guberniya marshal would draw up and keep up to date the local register. The Charter specified the principles to be applied. The nobles were to be divided into six groups : in the first were those ennobled by personal grant of Catherine or other crowned heads, together with those whose nobility stretched back at least a hundred years ; in the second were those who had risen to noble rank in the armed forces (fourteenth rank in the Table of Ranks) ; in the third were those who had reached nobility in the eighth rank, in the civil service ; the fourth group covered foreign nobles. The fifth included all those with titles of prince, count or baron, and finally, in the sixth group were those whose undisputed nobility was lost in the mists of antiquity. In a final section the Charter proceeded to lay down the proofs of nobility which should be produced by those nobles who wished to be registered. These numbered fifteen (in addition to seventeenth-century laws on *mestnichestvo*) and included such obvious proofs as diplomas or patents. But at least six involved proof of the ownership of settled land, a clear indication of what had become the main attribute of nobility by 1785. Evidence that a man's ancestors had lived nobly, or had been in service which carried noble rank, if attested by twelve reputable witnesses, was also regarded as proof of nobility.

Though, in common with most Russian eighteenth-century enactments, the Charter suffers from occasional slovenly drafting, it was nevertheless a much more coherent document than the Manifesto of 1762, and the definition of corporate rights and duties was related to the corresponding paragraphs of the Statute on Local Administration. The Russian nobility was now, in a law enacted 'for all time', placed on a footing of equality at any rate as regards personal status and rights, with the European nobility. Inevitably the Charter's place in the history of the relations between the Russian Crown and the nobles has been interpreted in various ways. Some have seen it as the first step towards the introduction of civil rights in Russia, which might subsequently be extended downwards to the rest of society. Others see in it the consolidation of privilege in the hands of the few at the expense of the serf population. Still others see in it the government's loss of control over the noble estate, to which the right to decide on who was a noble had now been ceded, a loss which was paralleled by its loss of control over the bureaucracy, when the right of automatic promotion in the civil service was seemingly granted in 1764 and 1767.[20]

The personal rights clearly responded to some, though not all, of the demands put forward in the nakazy of 1767, and the project of 1768. Where the project however had firmly asserted that nobles in service took precedence over nobles who had not served or were not in service, the Charter, while confirming that nobility could be achieved by promotion in the Table of Ranks, left open the question of precedence. In practice, at official functions, precedence continued to depend not on title, wealth or ancestry but on service rank. But court magnates of new or old family, and great wealth, usually also belonged in the first four ranks of the Table of Ranks, and were less affected by its gradations. Catherine however now pandered to the caste consciousness of the nobility by introducing the division into six categories, of which the last two were clearly socially more exclusive than the first four.[21] Moreover the second and third groups, by segregating nobles promoted from the ranks in the military and the civil branches from the older nobility by descent or by personal grant of the monarch, were inevitably regarded as 'second-class' nobles. The provisions for promotion of personal nobles to the status of hereditary nobles further confirmed this inferior type of nobility.[22] The distinction introduced here responded to the ancestral nobles' desire to be in some way differentiated from the influx of promoted nobles, which was particularly noticeable after the extension of Russian noble rights to Little Russian and Ukrainian nobles and Cossack officers in 1781.[23] It is also clear that active participation in the noble assemblies was reserved to the relatively limited number of nobles who owned enough settled land to produce 100 r.p.a. (at least 25 serfs), excluding from elective posts the increasing number of landless nobles, or owners of estates of fewer than 20 serfs (estimated at 59 per cent of the nobility in 1777).[24]

If the Crown did not lose control of the noble estate, what price did it pay in terms of delivering the privately owned serf more completely into the land-owners' power ? It is a commonplace of Russian historiography that the Charter confirmed the nobility's exclusive right to the ownership of settled land and 'exempted them [the serfs], as property from the protection of the law, . . . consigning them to the arbitrary despotism of the serf owner'.[25] It must be noted that if the Charter introduced any changes in these fields, it was by omission rather than commission. The serfs are nowhere explicitly mentioned ; and implicitly only in article 26 which states : 'the right of nobles to buy [serf] villages is confirmed.'

Did Catherine ever intend to include the regulation of relationships between landowners and serfs in the Charter to the Nobility ? This question cannot be answered on the evidence available. There is an unsubstantiated report that she had drafted a plan by which all serfs born after 1785 should be free.[26] More relevant is the fact that among the materials prepared for her to draw upon when drafting the Charter to the Nobility was a series of questions based on the project for the rights of the nobility prepared by the sub-commission on the different estates of the Legislative Commission.[27] Four of these questions dealt with serfdom ; they are : May the right of landownership over serf villages be transformed into ownership over free villages ? Can free villages be transformed into serf villages ? Can serfs be freed ? In what respect is a denunciation, or evidence, by a serf against his master invalid ?[28] The Charter passes over all these questions in silence. Catherine may have abandoned the subject because it was too delicate. Or she may have thought that a Charter setting out the rights of the nobility was the wrong place to deal with the status and obligations of serfs. The sub-commission on the third estate of the Legislative Commission, in its draft project of the laws for the third estate, had included serfs together with state peasants as members of that estate. On the other hand it had stated in so many words that serfs of the nobles were 'entirely in their power'.[29] No draft charter for the serfs has so far been found among Catherine's papers and published. But she spent much time and a good deal of ink in preparing a draft charter for the state peasants, closely modelled on the Charters to the Nobility and the Towns. It granted corporate rights to peasant 'societies' (including the right to put forward collective petitions) ; a large measure of autonomy through elected officials, trial by their equals, security of property, a register of village-dwellers, divided into six categories like the nobles (of which the category of very wealthy rural dwellers would be immune from corporal punishment). The charter was never promulgated, possibly because of the outbreak of the second Turkish war and the French Revolution, possibly because Catherine realized that any charter to the state peasants would lead to dangerous unrest among the serfs, possibly because the magnitude of the peasant problem was too much for her.[30] Yet, contrary to the general assumption, the Charter to the Nobles did not increase the nobles' power over their serfs. It simply left the existing situation unchanged.

The Charter to the Towns is a far more wide-ranging document than the Charter to the Nobility, and deals with three separate matters : first, the individual and collective rights of the urban estate : secondly, the regulations for craft guilds ; and thirdly, the organization of urban self-government. Here again Catherine made extensive use of the materials digested for, or prepared by the sub-commissions of the Legislative Commission as well as of the urban laws of the Baltic provinces, Magdeburg Law (in use in some Little Russian cities), the Lithuanian Statutes, the Swedish Guild Ordinance of 1669, the Prussian *Handwerksordnung* of 1733 and the rules for East Prussia issued by Frederick II in 1774. The resulting charter was very much Catherine's own handiwork (several drafts in her own hand and with her marginal comments have survived) ; and this may explain some of the terminological inconsistencies which have been pointed out by its critics.[31]

A further source which Catherine was certainly acquainted with was a 'Plan for the privileges and duties of the merchant and townspeople's estate' drawn up by the Senate between 1775 and 1778. The plan summarized many of the requests put forward by the townspeople in 1767, particularly for the monopoly of wholesale trade in general and retail trade in towns. Greater concessions were made to class consciousness in that the plan proposed allowing kuptsy of the first guild to be received at court and to wear swords. Those with a capital of over 80,000 r. were to be regarded as 'equal' to the eighth rank in the Table of Ranks ; a kupets who carried on foreign trade with a turnover of more than 50,000 rubles for five years was to be regarded as equal to the seventh rank.[32]

As though to underline the basically corporate nature of the structure envisaged, the Charter was issued to the towns, not to the town-dwellers, and begins by setting out the rights and privileges of towns as such : no taxes were to be imposed on towns by any person in authority or by the Senate, without the confirmation of the sovereign ; a new resident in the town must sign a declaration that he agrees to abide by its civil laws and accept the consequent burdens ; a noble owning property in the town, even if he himself lived in it, was subject to all town taxes, and was only free from personal taxes and services. The town, not the citizens, was authorized to set up schools, mills, inns, etc. The Charter then turned to the corporate rights of town-dwellers, starting with the right to form a 'town society' – the equivalent of the noble assembly. The town society's rights followed very closely those granted to the noble assemblies : the right to elect officials to the various posts established in the Statute of 1775 ; the right to address collective requests to the governor (but not to the Senate or the empress) on local needs ; the duty to listen, and reply properly, to proposals from governors ; the right to a house for meetings, to archives, a secretary and a seal, and to levy voluntary contributions. The town society was also not responsible in law for the actions of its members.

The town society was composed of all registered citizens of the town, but there was a property and age qualification limiting active participation : no one could be elected to a post who had capital providing an income of less than fifty rubles a year (half that required for a noble) or who was younger than twenty-five, at any rate in the larger towns. An exception was made for small towns with only a small number of wealthy merchants. A young man of under twenty-five with no capital could attend meetings of the town society, but had no voice and no vote.

Again, with an evident aim of achieving symmetry with the noble estate, the citizens were to keep a register of residents, drawn up by elected elders and deputies of the cities ; all those in the city who owned a house or other building or land, who were inscribed in a merchant guild or a craft guild, or who were engaged in activities suitable to townspeople were to be entered in the register. Like the noble genealogical records, the town register was divided into six categories. These were first owners of houses or immoveable property in the town ; secondly members of the three merchant guilds, who had to dispose of capital ranging from 10,000 to 50,000 r. ; 5,000 to 10,000 r. and 1,000 to 5,000 r. respectively. The third category comprised registered craftsmen, the fourth, foreigners and citizens of other towns. The fifth comprised 'distinguished citizens', i.e. those who had been elected more than once to official posts ; graduates of universities or other educational establishments ; artists including architects, painters, sculptors, composers, with publicly recognized qualifications ; 'capitalists' of all kinds, disposing of capital over 50,000 r. ; bankers, disposing of sums between 100,000 and 200,000 r. ; wholesalers, and shipowners dealing in exports. Finally the sixth category comprised all those born or settled in the town who did not enter into any of the other groups. Nobles owning houses or other buildings were also to be entered in the register. Again as with the nobles, town-dwellers had to provide acceptable evidence of their right to be registered, and 26 different forms of proof are duly listed.

Turning to the personal rights of town-dwellers, the model is again the Charter to the Nobility. The Charter to the Towns defines a town-dweller as belonging to the second or middle estate. Article 80 of the Charter states somewhat clumsily : 'Town dwellers of the middle estate or ''meshchane'' are called thus as a result of their zeal and good conduct, which has enabled them to acquire a distinguished status.' Meshchane conferred their status on their wives and children ; they could not be deprived of their property, life or good name without trial, which should take place before their equals. They would lose their status for the same crimes as nobles, and they could set up workshops of all kinds, for all crafts, without asking permission. Elaborate rules were laid down to punish those who insulted the honour of the meshchane, their wives and above all their daughters. Thus far the Charter dealt with rights common to members of all categories of meshchane, but unlike the nobles – who were all in law regarded as equal – the different categories of townspeople were granted additional special rights : members of merchant guilds could buy themselves (or their families) out of the recruit levy and labour services, and were not to be conscripted to work in the Salt Office or various other government offices. Members of the first guild were allowed to drive in a carriage and pair ; members of the second guild could ride in a barouche and pair. Members of the third guild were not to ride in carriages at all, and winter or summer were not to harness more than one horse to any conveyance. 'Distinguished citizens' were even more handsomely treated and could drive in a carriage and four. Together with members of the first and second guilds, they were immune from corporal punishment, and in the third generation they could petition to be raised to the nobility. They were allowed to own houses and gardens outside the city. Members of the first and second guilds, distinguished citizens and foreigners, were allowed to have factories and manufactories. Membership of a particular category in the towns was entirely a matter of financial status, except in the case of distinguished citizens and foreigners.

The section of the Charter establishing the new institutions of urban self-government had little in common with the project of the rights of the middle estate of 1768 and the Charter to the Nobility. To begin with, urban government now moved away entirely from the concept of 'estates' or 'sosloviya' within the town. The urban 'society' may have been divided into social categories, but all registered citizens were equally entitled to participate, the only limitation being a property qualification in order to elect or to be elected. In this, as in other aspects of the Charter, Catherine seems to have found her model in the city organization of German towns. The very concept of a *vsesoslovnoye* urban society, embracing all the estates, goes back in Germany to earliest times, when all owners of a plot of land in the city, including nobles, belonged to the *Bürgerschaft*, though not necessarily to the *Bürgerstand*.

Basically, the urban institutions fell into three separate levels : urban society as a whole ; an elected duma and an elected executive organ. The town duma was composed of representatives of the six categories of registered town-dwellers (a clear reflection of the German practice of providing for the representation of the corporations), separately elected every three years by the whole urban society. The town duma then elected a six-man duma (one man for each category), of which the town chief (*gorodskaya golova*), provision for whose election had been made as long ago as 1767, was president. It was the duty of the town duma to promote the welfare of the town and the citizens by facilitating trade, supervising magazines, storehouses, warehouses, etc. It must preserve the peace with neighbouring towns, and promote public order within it, though it should not encroach on the functions of the police or of the law courts. It should endeavour to increase the revenue of the town, particularly in connection with the expenses of the board of public welfare. It had no judicial functions of any kind. Those who were dissatisfied with the activity of the six-man duma or the town duma could appeal to the guberniya magistrat court.

A large part of the Charter was devoted to the regulation of the so-called craft guilds or *tsekhi*. This was more of a novelty in Russia, where craft guilds of the medieval Western European type had never developed. Peter I had recognized their utility and had endeavoured to organize Russian craftsmen into some sort of guild structure, but they continued to be very *ad hoc* affairs.[33] Catherine followed Peter's example in drawing on foreign sources for her craft guild regulations. She was not an unconditional admirer of guild organization ; she regarded it as useful in the early stages of economic development, in order to introduce crafts and promote quality. But in the long run, she regarded guilds as monopolistic organizations hampering free economic activity.[34] This explains therefore why her guild regulations concentrate primarily on the social organization of craft workers in towns, and the maintenance of standards of quality and honesty. The regulations provided that each branch of production should elect its own officials, and no one could practise that trade or craft without being accepted as a member of the craft guild on the basis of an examination of his work. But the guilds could neither set the price nor limit the quantity produced. The elected officials in each craft guild formed part of the town duma, and in turn they elected a chief or head of the craft guilds who sat in the six-man duma, thus providing for a direct elected link between the craft workers and the executive in the town. The regulations go into the usual elaborate details beloved of Catherine for every kind of situation. Notably, it is prescribed (article 103) that craftsmen are to work six days a week, and must not work on Sundays or on the twelve prescribed religious festivals.[35]

It is extremely difficult to assess on present evidence how effectively the corporate institutions of nobles and towns operated, as well as the police ordinance and the institutions of urban autonomy. No studies of how any one of these institutions functioned in a particular locality are available in the West ; the studies dealing with class institutions throughout the country are very general and many are out of date.[36] Moreover, barely eleven years after the promulgation of the two Charters, Catherine was dead, and many of her policies were reversed or irremediably distorted by her son Paul and by Alexander I. Though the first generation of Catherine's specially chosen governors may have raised the prestige of provincial service, there is no doubt that, particularly after the outbreak of war in 1787, the higher and more cultured nobility tended to seek for promotion and prospects in the armed forces or the capital rather than in the provinces. Nevertheless, by 1796, 4,053 nobles had been drawn into elective service in the provinces.[37] A contemporary remarked that in different political circumstances the guberniya noble assemblies might have proved to be the seedbed of revolution (thinking perhaps of the assemblies of notables in France). But after their initial success in Catherine's reign, as far as can be judged on our present evidence, the assemblies, faced with the hostility of Paul I and the indifference of Alexander I, confined themselves mainly to the regulation of the noble estate, and made but little use of their other powers, though they survived until 1917.

For different reasons, the institutions of urban self-government also proved unable to develop a great deal of independence. In the course of the years 1785–8, they seem to have been introduced piecemeal into most towns. But there was frequently considerable difficulty in setting up the full array except in the two capitals, among other reasons because there was a shortage of suitable inhabitants in the towns. The Charter had weighted active representation in favour of those with property – immoveable property and a minimum capital of at least 1,000 r., producing an income of 50 r.p.a.[38] Even in urbanized Livonia, only Riga had enough registered townspeople to fill all the elective posts, and a more limited and simplified plan was adopted by the Senate on 12 October 1787, which may have served as a model for smaller towns throughout Russia.

The Charter also failed to iron out many inconsistencies. Could a registered town-dweller belong to more than one category of residents ? And could he vote in more than one ? What was the relationship between the 'town society', the town duma, and the six-man duma ? Was the six-man duma accountable to the town duma ? And the town duma to the town society ? More complicated still were the relations between the six-man duma and the guberniya magistrat which still preserved some administrative responsibilities, as a result of which there was a good deal of overlapping.

However the main weakness of the six-man duma was its inability to stand up to the governor and the local government board. Many governors were quite unable to wean themselves from the tradition of issuing orders to the urban estate and calling on its members for services. Even Catherine occasionally diverged from her stated object of securing the personal immunity from service of the urban authorities. In the field of finance the six-man duma was strictly subordinated to the governor. When the local income was adequate, as for instance in Moscow, the governor did not hesitate to order the six-man duma to disburse 4,968 rubles in 1787 to the board of social welfare, to set up the remaining 14 junior schools prescribed for the city, or even to claim 5,000 rubles for a police force and 300 rubles for a military band.[39] In the smaller towns throughout Russia the expense of the urban institutions was all the more burdensome. In the long run, the old traditional estate of the merchants and the craftsmen dominated the new urban institutions as they had the old.

It has also been argued that the appointment of the town provost as head of the police by the Senate delivered urban life into the power of the nobility as a class. The town provost, as local chief of police, commanded a small detachment of troops. Logically enough he was an officer, and hence a noble. However he was lower in rank than the first and second presidents of the guberniya magistrat, and would have to deal with the relatively more mature population of the towns. The appointed town provost represents not the victory of the nobility over the towns, but the consolidation of bureaucratic administration under the Crown.[40]

The wide-ranging reform of urban and provincial administration had inevitable repercussions on the structure of the central government. The Council which Catherine had set up in January 1769 to advise her during the war had continued in being after the peace, and indeed lasted until Catherine's death. It discussed foreign and domestic policy, finance, military operations. Judging by the protocols, discussion was extremely frank and free, even in the presence of the empress. But the Council had no powers of its own ; its members could advise the empress on policy, but many of Catherine's major reforms did not come before it at all. Its main purpose was to bring together the very highest officials of the state to ensure some coordination of policy at the top.

The multiplication of government agencies in the provinces led to the disbanding of a number of colleges in 1786. The College of Justice served no useful purpose now that appeals lay from the guberniya criminal or civil courts to the Senate. In the same way the Votchina or Estate College had lost its *raison d'être* since records of landownership were now to be kept in the guberniya capitals, and the College of Economy became superfluous since the 'economic' peasants were merged with the state peasants and administered by the guberniya treasury chambers. The Glavnyy Magistrat, or central College for the urban estate, was abolished in 1782 ; the College of Manufactures in 1779, of Mining in 1784. The College of Commerce was only finally abolished in 1796.[41] This wholesale removal of the central government institutions has been variously judged by Russian historians.[42] Some suggest that it was the result of a well-thought-out programme of decentralization coupled with reconcentration into very few hands – such as the presidents of the three major Colleges of War, Admiralty and Foreign Affairs, and the procurator general – of the coordination of internal administration under the Senate. It is true that the Statute of 1775 did not bring about a genuine decentralization of Russian government. It was on the contrary a multiplication of the number of agencies in the localities ; but these agencies were no longer accountable to a variety of central government offices. They were all put under the authority of the local governor or governor-general, and he alone was responsible to the Senate and to the empress. The power of the governor was thus enormously increased, and theoretically at least the central government was in more direct control of local administration than previously. This explains the reasoning behind the elimination of the central Colleges. On the other hand the haphazard way in which the central institutions were closed down led in the judgment of some contemporaries to a lack of administrative coherence at the centre which was only remedied when Paul I restored some of the Colleges after Catherine's death.

In the absence of any detailed studies of the functioning of the central administration in the last fifteen years of Catherine's reign, the question must be left undecided. But there is no doubt that during these years there was a proliferation of *ad hoc* commissions and offices to fill gaps as they arose. The resulting picture suggests that the impact of provincial decentralization on the central government had not been carefully thought out in advance. On the positive side however, a systematic effort was made to improve the financial administration. Catherine inherited the system set up by Peter I of three different colleges : the *Kammer Kollegiya* or College of Revenue charged with supervising and coordinating income ; the *Stats Kontora,* or Office of Expenditure, and the *Revizion Kollegiya,* or College of Audit. None of the Colleges was coping with its task, and though Catherine reorganized the College of Audit in 1763 and doubled its personnel, it could do nothing so long as the figures it operated with were inaccurate.

The procurator general was charged with bringing order out of this chaos, and began in 1771 by ordering all government departments to provide accurate reports of income and expenditure. After the Statute of 1775 was promulgated, officials were at once assigned to the treasury chambers and charged with the local collection of the poll-tax, the dues from the state, economic and court peasants, and the income from leases on economic activity. The treasury chambers became the local offices of the central financial Colleges, and were charged with forwarding to a new Bureau of State Revenue in the Senate records of all receipts and disbursements in the guberniya. Little by little, by centralizing all information in the hands of one official, Vyazemsky, it became possible to draw up a complete record of income and expenditure for three sample years, 1769, 1773, and 1776–7. In 1780, the Bureau of State Revenue was divided into four departments under a treasurer (Vyazemsky himself). These four departments dealt with income, expenditure, audit, and arrears (or corruption). Finally, in 1787, for the first time a budget was presented to the empress, and became henceforward an annual feature.[43] Once financial administration had been concentrated within the first department of the Senate, the financial Colleges became superfluous and were dispensed with.[44] Both pre-revolutionary and Soviet historians have admitted that financial administration was improved under Catherine. Many of the procedures laid down at this time remained in use until the 1860s.[45]

Was Catherine concerned to restructure the form of government itself ? In unpublished drafts dating from the 1770s and 1780s she set out a plan for an Imperial Council selected by the ruler, in addition to the Senate, and for a totally new institution, the *Glavnaya Raspravnaya Palata* or High Chamber of Justice.[46] The Chamber, in Catherine's sketch, was to be composed of three departments, one concerned with criminal justice, one acting as a high court of equity, and a third with legislative functions. All three departments would be composed of appointed presidents and councillors and elected assessors drawn from representatives of the nobility, the townspeople and the free peasantry, in each guberniya. One representative of each estate would be elected every three years in each guberniya providing therefore a total of some 150 representatives available to act as assessors in matters concerning their respective estates. The Chamber was to be subordinated to the Senate. In Catherine's various drafts, the functions of the Chamber vary, but the first department undoubtedly had legislative functions (though not powers). It could initiate legislation, and all laws had to be considered by it, the decision being forwarded to the Senate and thence to the ruler. It was also charged with scrutinizing new legislation to ensure that it was in harmony with existing laws.

Catherine's plans for a recasting of the central political institutions of Russia reflect an essentially eclectic approach. One may see in her Chamber some features of the English Parliament as a High Court of Justice ; there are also reminiscences of the French *Parlements* with their right of remonstrance ; there are perhaps echoes of the Austrian *Reichsrat* of 1760 (as Raeff suggests) with its elected membership. There may even be reminiscences of the projects of the reformers in 1730 and of the *Zemskiye Sobory* of the seventeenth century. At any rate it is clear that as late as the 1780s Catherine could still devote much time and energy to meditating on profound political changes, and that she still envisaged the participation of elected representatives in an advisory capacity in judicial and legislative institutions. In the boldness of her vision (she was after all writing before the French Revolution) she was more imaginative and far-sighted than any subsequent ruler of Russia.[47]

Not unconnected with these far-reaching plans were Catherine's projects for the reorganization of the Senate, on which she proposed to work in 1787 and 1788. It was indeed her chosen occupation for her leisure moments during her journey to the Crimea in 1787. The Senate had certainly continued to maintain its role as the principal coordinator of administration, particularly since it was from his base in the first department that the procurator general, A.A. Vyazemsky, operated as *de facto* minister of the interior. Her secretary Khrapovitsky was ordered to bring with him on her journey her own Nakaz, her notes on Blackstone's *Commentaries* and the drafts of the Senate reform.[48]

Not much is known about Catherine's plans, except that she was proposing to divide the Senate afresh into four departments, the first to supervise administration, the second to act as a court of appeal in criminal cases, the third as a court of appeal for civil cases and the fourth to supervise matters concerning the economy.[49] Catherine hoped to have her reform ready for a manifesto on 28 June 1787 (the twenty-fifth anniversary of her accession), but the day was marked by other graces. The manifesto seems to have been ready by October 1787, but probably because of the war, the reform was dropped. Towards the end of March 1788, Khrapovitsky noted Catherine's words briefly in his diary : 'It is not the right time now for reforms.'[50] Nevertheless at intervals she still pondered the question of reforming the Senate. She was clearly working towards the idea of setting up a kind of supreme court, above the Senate, and composed of the Senate, the Synod, the first four ranks of the Empire, and the presidents of the Colleges and law courts. In Catherine's drafts, its composition was precise, and she wrote out details of its procedure.[51] Unfortunately its main purpose, the kind of cases which were to go before it, remains unclear. However, the papers which have survived show that the empress was never satisfied with her reforms and continued to read, ponder and draft almost until the end of her reign.

20

The Integration of Little Russia and Livonia into the Russian Empire

Appointed president of the Little Russian College in 1764, P.A. Rumyantsev's activity had been somewhat intermittent, since he was absent on military duties between 1768 and 1775. Briefed by the ubiquitous Teplov, Rumyantsev had produced a programme of reform in May 1764 which included a Crown resumption of state lands ; the introduction of salaries for officials in lieu of land grants (i.e. phasing out the remnants of the *pomest'ye* system in its Ukrainian variant) ; educational and judicial reforms and the secularization of Church lands. Anxious not to alienate the Ukrainians unduly, Catherine referred most of Rumyantsev's proposals to commissions for study, though she approved the establishment of a postal service which served to link Little Russia more effectively with the rest of the empire.

Little Russia, which was not subject to the poll-tax, contributed less in revenue to the Russian treasury than what it cost. But its people suffered particularly heavily from the billeting of troops and from the deliveries in kind which had to be supplied to the armed forces, since it was on the route both to the Polish and to the Tartar frontiers. In a thinly populated area two out of three households might have troops billeted on them. To relieve the burden on the population and to achieve a more regular income, Rumyantsev introduced a new tax of one ruble per household levied on all but nobles, officers and clerics. It proved difficult to collect the tax and arrears mounted up. Even so the income more than exceeded military requirements and the surplus could be devoted to the general administration of the province.[1] The mounting arrears,[2] which were attributed to the mobility of the peasantry, led to the introduction in 1770 of a law ordering the return of 'runaway peasants' (*beglyye*) to their masters, so that they could be made to pay their taxes.[3] The Muscovite pattern leading to peasant adscription to the land was beginning to be repeated.

A further major step put in hand by Rumyantsev in 1765 with the object of modernizing and centralizing the administration of Little Russia was a general census of the inhabitants, in far more detail than the usual *revizii*. Rumyantsev endeavoured to explain that the census was in the interests of the population – a statement which was met with widespread disbelief. Even noble landowners refused to supply information, and slept in different places every night. The census proceeded on its leisurely way until it was closed down in February 1769, as a result of the outbreak of war. Unfortunately, the records were stored in the archives in such condition that by 1778 when Rumyantsev remembered their existence, some documents had rotted away ; they were never used in the eighteenth century, and have proved a happy, if somewhat elusive, hunting ground for nineteenth-century scholars.[4]

In the short time at his disposal Rumyantsev also tried to improve the administration and discipline of the Cossack forces. Though he made few concessions to Ukrainian autonomist sensibilities he did take seriously the task of reducing the animosity between Ukrainians and Great Russians by recruiting the Ukrainian élite into Russian service and granting its members rank and promotion. The chink in the armour of the Little Russian *shlyakhetstvo* (as they called themselves and were called on the Polish pattern) was their passionate desire to be given the same status in the Russian Empire as the Russian dvoryane. In 1761 they had been refused admission to the Noble Cadet Corps, on the grounds that there were no nobles in Little Russia – a decision reversed by Rumyantsev in 1767, when the Smol'nyy Convent for girls was also opened to Little Russian 'noble' girls.[5]

The Legislative Commission of 1767 provided the Little Russian nobility with the opportunity to press for the resurrection or the confirmation of a variety of their traditional political and legal rights as well as for the maintenance of their own cultural traditions, as for instance the demand for the establishment of a university in Little Russia.[6] The only means of extending equality to the Little Russian gentry, since ancestry and title alone could not grant them rank, was to extend the Table of Ranks to the Little Russian and Cossack hierarchy. From the Russian point of view there were two difficulties about the Little Russian shlyakhetstvo. The first was the inadequate definition of who was and who was not a noble. Little Russians themselves argued that nobility derived from diplomas issued by the king of Poland ; charters of the tsars of Russia ; *de facto* ownership of land with peasants over several generations ; status of nobility in the country of origin (be it Poland, Walachia, Lithuania, etc.) ; and membership of the Cossack starshina. But in addition all Cossacks could attempt to prove themselves noble, in accordance with the Lithuanian Statute which accepted as evidence of nobility the testimony of twelve nobles to that effect. The white clergy also claimed noble status in Little Russia. Unfortunately actual documentary evidence of any or all of the above conditions was only too frequently lacking, hence in part the disregard in which the Little Russian shlyakhetstvo was held. Rumyantsev reported that many people simply changed their surnames to that of an existing noble family, 'a step which was both forbidden and unforgivable'.

The second question, namely the actual extent of the rights of the Little Russian nobility, was even more complex, since on paper these rights derived from the various versions of the Lithuanian Statute (1588, etc.) on to which were grafted clauses in the treaty of Pereyaslavl' of 1654 between hetman Bogdan Khmel'nitsky of the Ukraine and Tsar Aleksey, and the various ordinances of Peter I and his successors, which unilaterally overrode many of these theoretical rights. Thus, on paper, Little Russian noble status could only be conferred for outstanding valour by the sovereign, in agreement with the Senate, during a session of the Diet, i.e., by the king of Poland. Military service too was at the orders of the Diet. Some Little Russians even took the extreme view that Little Russian nobles enjoyed the same rights as Polish nobles and were therefore entitled to elect their ruler. A noble could be executed in various horrible ways but he could not be tortured, nor was he subjected to the Russian forms of degrading corporal punishment. His family was not answerable for his crimes, he had to be judged by his peers, his estate and his peasants were free from taxes and duties in kind and he had complete property rights over his land and what was below it and complete freedom to dispose of it.[7]

Rumyantsev himself was in favour of introducing the Table of Ranks into the Ukraine. Since the practice of granting lands in service tenure to officials had been abolished in the 1760s he considered that it was only right that 'class ranks' (klassnyye chiny) in the Table of Ranks should be granted together with salaries. Moreover such a procedure would foster Little Russian attachment to Russia.[8]

The final attack on the specifically Ukrainian institutions and on the remnants of Ukrainian autonomy was launched when Catherine decided in May 1779 to introduce the Statute of Local Administration of 1775 into Little Russia. Rumyantsev, who had already been engaged in the remodelling of the guberniya of Kursk and Khar'kov, was left in overall command, and a member of a distinguished Ukrainian family, General A.S. Miloradovich, was appointed to assist him. The hetmanate was divided into three gubernii, Kiev, Chernigov, and Novgorod Seversk, with a total disregard for historical links or economic sense. The concept of 'Little Russia' was to disappear, and to be replaced by that of three gubernii directly under the Crown, and with no particular constitutional link with each other, even if they were all placed under one lord lieutenant. The new gubernii were solemnly inaugurated in January 1782.

The Statute implied a thorough remodelling not only of the administrative and judicial institutions of Little Russia, but also of its social structure, military organization, ecclesiastical hierarchy and property, and its finances. In a memorandum to Catherine, Rumyantsev pointed out some of the difficulties of applying the Statute, designed for Russia, to the more complex society of the Ukraine. In the first place, clerics, townspeople and Cossacks traditionally elected many officials who, in the Statute of 1775, were to be elected only by nobles. Moreover Cossacks in the hetmanate appeared before the same courts as the nobility. The towns too in Little Russia could own lands from which they derived their income. Catherine in a reply dated 26 October 1781 showed again her determination to impose complete institutional uniformity throughout the empire: town and Cossack lands were to be taken over by the new treasury boards in each guberniya which would be responsible for financial matters ; Cossacks were to come under the jurisdiction of the higher and lower summary courts, that is to say their status was equated with that of the state peasants.[9] From 1782, the old titles and ranks of office based on the Lithuanian Statute, Magdeburg Law, or Little Russian custom were not to be used but to be replaced by those of the Statute of Local Administration.[10]

The staffing of the various elective institutions brought to a head the problem of defining who was a noble in Little Russia. To assist him in separating the sheep from the goats, Catherine forwarded to Rumyantsev in 1781 a first draft of what was to become the Charter to the Nobility, which laid down proofs of nobility for Russians, but provided little guidance through the thickets of the various enactments by which Little Russian nobility could be claimed.[11] According to Catherine's draft, it was the local assemblies of the nobility which had to pronounce on the validity of claims to noble status. Both existing and aspiring nobles flooded these assemblies with an enormous variety of alleged proofs of nobility, *chin,* or genealogical tables. Many arranged with Polish Jews to buy Polish patents of nobility which secured recognition in Russia. The word went around that there had been only 10,000 nobles when the Poles were chased out of Little Russia (in 1686) – and now there were 100,000. The most reliable estimate brings this figure nearer to 30,000 in the 1780s.[12]

It was generally recognized that the census of 1782 had been carried out in a very slapdash way, and moreover the happy-go-lucky Little Russians had at the time been unaware of the fact that if they allowed themselves to be registered in a particular place in 1782, they might, in 1783, be condemned to live in that place and in that status permanently. Hence the flood of claims for registration as nobles which descended on the assemblies of the nobility from 1782 onwards. On the whole these bodies seem to have been generous with recognition – with or without a *douceur.* Rumyantsev, who had struck roots in Little Russia, had become a popular and respected figure, who now favoured the Ukrainian nobility, and was not above sympathizing even with some of the autonomists' views.[13] As a result he proved generous in approving claims for change of status.

Possibly because some of those whose claims to noble status were accepted were at the time serfs, Little Russian nobles were by no means unanimously in favour of the easy-going attitude of the noble assemblies. It may have been the echo of these disputes which caused the Senate in an ukaz of 14 June 1789 to demand a full report on those whose claims to nobility had been accepted but who had not yet been removed from the register of poll-tax payers.[14]

The request came after the departure of Rumyantsev from his position as governor-general, in order to command one of the armies on the Turkish front after the outbreak of war in 1787. His replacement, General Krechetnikov, threw himself with gusto into the task of depressing Little Russian pretensions. It was only too easy, since by 1790 the three Little Russian gubernii had approved the claims of 22,702 people on the poll-tax rolls to noble status, thus depriving the state of 22,702 tax payers.[15] The Senate thereupon ordered the assemblies to do their work all over again, with more speed and more accuracy.

Krechetnikov, delighted that Rumyantsev's work had been criticized, now put the screws on the noble assemblies. Under the impulsion of the new governor-general, the assemblies completed their work in record time, and by 1795, only 12,597 claimants were recognized as undoubted nobles, i.e. fewer than half the number registered before 1791. It is typical of the absence of any sense of law in Russia that the noble assemblies in Chernigov guberniya acted on the ukazy of the Senate of 1789 and 1791, while Kiev and Novgorod Seversk acted on article 36 of the Charter to the Nobility. Ukrainian protests lasted until a reasonably generous settlement was made by Nicholas I in 1835.[16]

The Statute of 1775 also completely undermined the separate military organization of Little Russia, namely the Cossack Host. Little by little, under Rumyantsev's aegis, ten regular regiments of carabineers were established, with a six-year term of service and a deliberately high turnover. They formed part of the regular Russian army, but retained the names and the territorial connections of the old Cossack 'polki'. This distinction between the free Cossack soldier and the conscripted peasant soldier began, however, to disappear in 1786, when Cossacks were transferred to an ordinary dragoon regiment, and it suffered even more with the extension of the recruit levy to the previously exempt Little Russia in 1789, during the second Turkish war. From then on, the Little Russian Cossacks were conscripted like any other poll-tax payers, and could be incorporated into any regiment anywhere, for twenty-five years. The carabineer regiments were finally abolished by Paul I, and though Little Russian Cossack units were formed from time to time, during military emergencies, they were shortlived. Little Russian Cossackdom ceased to exist as a way of life.[17]

The Ukrainian Church had escaped secularization in 1764. But Catherine viewed with particular disfavour any idea of a separate Little Russian hierarchy, and the attempt of the Kievan metropolitan, Arseniy Mogilyansky, to use the title 'Metropolitan of Kiev and Little Russia' had been rejected by the Holy Synod. The extension of the Statute of 1775 to Little Russia gave Catherine the opportunity to recast the boundaries of the Ukrainian bishoprics in 1785 to make them coincide with those of gubernii.[18] The next stage was the secularization of the lands of the Church, which followed the Russian pattern. In an ukaz directed to the Synod which barely conceals the *Volteryanstvo* never far from the surface in Catherine, the empress explained that : 'Having succeeded with the help of God in reorganizing the bishoprics and monasteries in the greater part of Russia, on such a foundation as corresponded with the original principles of an honourable Christian Church and with the public welfare,' she now proposed to extend these benefits to Little Russia, and to 'relieve' clerics and monks of the task of administering their peasants, a task which did not become their cloth, particularly since it entailed constant litigation.[19] The Church peasants were to be regarded as state peasants, under the jurisdiction of the director of economy, and pay a poll-tax of 70 kopeks, an obrok of 1 r.p.a. plus 2 kopeks for administration. Superfluous houses and convents could be used for social purposes. The metropolitan of Kiev was given the same status – and income – as the metropolitan of Moscow, and the other bishoprics and the monasteries were graded according to category. A grant of 8,000 r.p.a. was made to the Kievan Academy from the Church funds, and the boards of social welfare were to take over some of the hermitages and use them for primary schools.[20]

The question of ownership of land by churchmen in their private capacity posed a problem in Little Russia which had not existed in Russia proper. Not only were there priests who genuinely belonged to noble families. It was also believed by many that the priesthood as such conferred nobility, as was argued at length by one claimant, who adduced as evidence not only the Old and New Testaments but also Peter I's naval code.[21] But in Russia it was considered that a noble, on becoming a priest, ceased to belong to the estate of the nobility and was transferred to that of the clergy. Under Rumyantsev, who was on the whole well disposed to Ukrainians, no pressure was put on clerics to dispose of their estates. Krechetnikov suffered from no such inhibitions, and the consequent uproar led the Senate in 1792 to postpone the question until a decision had been reached on the criteria for nobility. The numbers involved were not large.[22] The most far-reaching change of all in the long run was the introduction of the poll-tax into Little Russia with the ultimate consequence of depriving the peasantry of their remaining freedom of movement. The ukaz of 1770[23] had already pointed the way. The poll-tax itself was introduced into Little Russia in an ukaz designed to bring about uniformity in the levying of taxes throughout the empire by putting the gubernii of Little Russia, Slobodska Ukraine, the Baltic provinces and Finland, and the newly acquired Polish provinces, on the same footing as the rest of Russia. The word 'serfdom' does not of course occur in the ukaz, which simply states that the previous tax of one ruble in Little Russia is to be replaced by taxes of 1 per cent of their capital for the kuptsy, 1 r. 20 on townspeople, and 70 k. on peasants, state peasants, Church peasants and privately owned serfs. Peasants under state administration were to pay the usual additional obrok of one ruble per annum. Cossacks were to pay a tax of 1 r. 20 instead of the previously arbitrarily levied taxes. In order to facilitate collection, the ukaz added (article 8) that inhabitants of the gubernii of Kiev, Chernigov and Novgorod Seversk were to remain in the place and status in which they had been registered at the last census (unless they had left before the issuing of the present ukaz). Anyone who departed after the ukaz had been issued should be dealt with in accordance with the law.[24] Article 11 of the ukaz extended these provisions to Slobodska Ukraine and the gubernii of Kursk, Khar'kov and Voronezh. It was not necessary to extend the provision fastening the taxable inhabitants to their places of residence to Livonia, Finland and Belorussia since the peasantry were already bound to the soil there.

The ukaz of 1783 was the final stage in the gradual whittling down of peasant mobility in Little Russia which had steadily been taking place since the middle of the century. It deprived the peasant of the right to negotiate his departure from one landowner in order to move to another. It did not increase the total number of peasants already bound to some extent to the soil but it changed the nature of the existing bondage both in relation to the state and to the private landowner. To what extent did the ukaz introduce the full range of Russian serfdom? Could the Little Russian peasant be bought and sold, separated from the land and transferred from estate to estate? This is a subject needing further study.[25]

The prospect of imminent bondage to the soil and the place of residence for those who were not peasants increased the rush for patents of nobility, or at least for some sort of claim to the status of a Cossack. Cossacks who had drifted into the peasantry tried to get out again; peasants tried to transfer to Cossack status. Raznochintsy smuggled themselves into the nobility. The peasants reacted in their usual way : violence, and flight. They do not seem to have had any particular feeling for Little Russian institutions as such; but bondage to the soil led to petitions and protests (occasionally successful). In the years 1781–2 some 35,000 peasants fled from Kiev and Chernigov and went to Southern Ukraine and the Don – almost 5 per cent of the peasant population of the two gubernii.[26]

At the same time as the poll-tax was introduced, a whole lot of anomalies in Ukrainian life were straightened out in order to force the province to conform to the Russian pattern. Cities and towns which owned land lost the administration of these lands to the 'director of economy', charged under the Statute of 1775 with the administration of state lands (though the revenue was to be paid to them). A new onslaught was now made, first on nobles who owned land in cities and secondly on the ownership of land by kuptsy and meshchane, which in the Ukraine, where this had not involved the ownership of labour, was quite frequent. Now that ownership of land had become ownership of labour, the government intervened and ordered all such peasants or servants to be removed and registered as free in the corresponding status, since no law had ever allowed townspeople to own noble land.[27] From now on the clear division between nobles and townspeople prevalent (in law) in Great Russia was to be the rule in Little Russia too.

The turn of the cities came with the promulgation of the Charter to the Towns in April 1785. By January 1786 the urban institutions of Little Russia had been reorganized, magistraty and ratushi set up, and the population of the towns divided into the six categories listed in the Charter. The police was introduced in accordance with the Police Ordinance of 1782, and all Cossack institutions were phased out. Courts were to dispense justice in civil matters in accordance with the Lithuanian Statute or Magdeburg Law, though Cossacks were still judged by Peter I's military code.

Whether the reform was worthwhile in the Ukraine remains a very debatable question. From the point of view of the landowner, who had been pressing for full adscription of the peasant to the soil for a long time, no doubt it was. The undisputed nobles lost the remaining vestiges of the traditional autonomous structure, which in any case had never worked well, and acquired the right to elect marshals and form district and guberniya assemblies as well as to elect their own representatives to a number of local administrative bodies – a right which many had already previously enjoyed. In 1781–3, when the new institutions were set up, their personal rights were actually greater, under the Lithuanian Statute, than those of the Great Russians, which were 'raised' to the Little Russian level only with the Charter of 1785, which was of course applied in Little Russia in that year as well.

For the Cossack and the peasant, the 'reform' and above all the poll-tax, with its corollary of adscription to the soil, was the end of the age of freedom. Russian government officials saw it as necessary for the development of civil society. But the peasant/Cossack lost the mobility which had been his pride. The tragedy of 1783, and Catherine's part in it, was enshrined in popular Ukrainian song. In his memoirs, S.A. Tuchkov gives an idyllic picture of the prosperity and abundance in Little Russia in the 1760s, and of the gay lilting tunes sung to the gusli instead of the sad and melancholy Russian songs. But, 'in one moment the whole of Little Russia fell into great sadness' with the 'reforms' of the 1780s. The Cossacks detested the poll-tax ('soul' tax in Russian) : 'Does our soul belong not to God but to the Tsar? Let him have only the body.' Many committed suicide, he wrote, others fled over the borders into Poland, Moldavia and Turkey. Tuchkov, who left Little Russia in 1783 at the age of sixteen cannot himself have seen the consequences of the policies he criticized, but, writing much later, he sensed the rejection of Russia and Russians which arose among the common people, though not the bulk of the nobility, in the 1780s.[28]

For integration into Russia had been achieved on terms favourable on the whole to the Little Rusian noble and officer class. An increasing number of salaried positions were opened to them in Little Russian and Ukrainian administration, and the highly placed Ukrainian colony in the capital led by such figures as A.A. Bezborodko and P.V. Zavadovsky provided openings in government service for friends, relatives and clients. But an undercurrent of nostalgia for the restoration of Little Russian and Cossack liberties remained, of which the spokesman was the dramatist Vasily Kapnist, who was the marshal of the nobility in Kiev, and of which the most complete written expression was the anonymous *Istoriya Rusov* which circulated at the beginning of the nineteenth century. Vasily Kapnist may indeed have held secrets talks in Berlin in 1791, during the Russo-Turkish war, to inquire whether in the event of the outbreak of war between Russia and Prussia, the Ukrainian autonomists could count on Prussian support if they attempted to break away from Russia. Kapnist's mission remained completely unknown at the time, and the cooperation between Russia and Prussia in the second partition of Poland put paid to any hopes he might have harboured.[29]

The fact that Catherine had borrowed extensively from Livonian and Estonian practices in drafting the Statute of 1775 did not imply that she accepted their re- tention of a separate status. As early as February 1777 she had considered the idea of introducing the Statute of 1775 into Livonia.[30] The privileges of Livonia, which had been confirmed by Catherine, without, it will be remembered, any very precise knowledge as yet of what she was confirming,[31] had an impressive pedigree going back to the Privilege of Sigismund Augustus in 1561 ; other charters had been granted by the Swedish kings, guaranteeing the rights of the *Landratskollegium* or corporation of the Livonian nobility; then there were the capitulations with Peter I of 1710 and 1712, and later enactments which had been confirmed by successive Russian governments.[32] It was therefore incumbent on Catherine to proceed cautiously, in forcing her Statute on the Baltic provinces, since she was dealing with a society well prepared with arguments drawn from history and law to defend its entrenched positions, and her own authority was limited in this area by treaty obligations. She strove therefore to manoeuvre the barons by a process of persuasion and threats to petition themselves for the in- troduction of the Statute in order to forestall and invalidate any attempt by Sweden to intervene in defence of Livonian rights on the grounds that the peace treaties of Nystadt (1721) and Åbo (1743) had been violated.

There were two chinks in the Livonian armour, against which Catherine directed her attack. The first was the administration of justice ;[33] the second was the ownership and exploitation of land. The attack on the quality of the Livonian courts arose as a result of the provision of the Patent of 1765, which permitted serfs to complain of ill-treatment by their masters to the lowest court, the *Ordnungsgericht;* but there was no guarantee that they would receive justice. In 1777 Governor-General Browne reminded landowners of this provision of the Patent, and also of the fact that landowners were supposed to register the extent of the peasants' obligations on their estates – a provision more honoured in the breach than the observance. But by far the worst case of partial justice oc- curred in 1776–7 when Count Yacov Sievers asked for the prosecution of a cer- tain Major von Klodt and his wife, to whom he had rented one of his estates, on the grounds that they had tortured a ten-year-old serf girl belonging to him to death over a period of several months. The High Court condemned the couple to life imprisonment but the Riga High Court reduced the sentence to public church repentance and six years' imprisonment. But the Senate in 1779 rejected the ver- dict and declared the members of the Livonian high court to be unworthy of their office. Catherine did nothing about the particular case (the Klodt couple had died in prison in the meantime) but 'The High Court and Livonian privileges were both sentenced to death'.[34]

On the land front, it was the estates held originally as fiefs in Livonia, Estonia and Esel, which interested the Russian government. It argued that the condi- tions laid down in Swedish times were still valid. These stated that feudal tenure had to be renewed with each reign and that there could be no transactions involv- ing land without the overlord's consent.[35] In the course of the eighteenth century, not only had land held on feudal tenure been quietly absorbed into allodial estates under the indifferent eyes of benevolent empresses, but much state-owned, taxable peasant land leased to landowners had also been swallowed up by noble owners, leading to a loss of revenue for the government. A new census of land was postponed until after the Turkish war, in exchange for a substantial tax offering on the part of the provinces, but in 1774 the proposal cropped up again. A new plan for the taking of a census was devised and land surveyors were instructed to 'rescue' taxable peasant land for the state. It was of course greeted with dismay by the landowners, who opposed any effort to delimit peasant and noble land, and in the event Catherine drew back from the principles expressed in the plan at that time.

The Livonian addiction to lengthy lawsuits over land played into Catherine's hands by further convincing her of the superiority of one of the features of the Statute of 1775, namely the limit of two years after the sale of an estate, after which legal claims could no longer be entertained.[36] The opening shot in Catherine's campaign was therefore an ukaz of 14 February 1777, forbidding the sale, gift or mortgaging of lands on feudal tenure — an ukaz which sent a shudder of horror through the province. The Livonian nobles responded by petitioning the empress in summer 1779 to recognize all land in Livonia as allodial, in the same way as the Empress Anna had finally recognized the assimilation of the Russian pomest'ye or service land and the votchina or patrimonial estate in 1731.

Meantime, Catherine, through Governor Browne, prepared the way for the introduction of the Statute of 1775. A memorandum was drafted, ostensibly by Browne, in all probability carefully composed by Catherine and Vyazemsky, setting out the advantages of the new system for Livonia. The Russian 'plan' was put forward as in no way prejudicing existing Livonian rights and privileges ; on the contrary, Livonians would receive wider and more stable rights under the Statute. The law courts would have to be reorganized to conform to the new division between civil and criminal justice, and to the system of election of assessors from the various estates. The Justice College for Livonian, Estonian and Finnish affairs in St Petersburg would be abolished, and replaced by high criminal and civil courts in Riga, with appeal to the governor-general and the Senate. But Livonian, not Russian law would be applied. The Russian memorandum was communicated in confidence in August 1779 to selected Livonian nobles, who met Browne again in October and submitted their observations.[37]

Two of them, Karl Schoultz von Ascheraden and Friedrich Rheinhold von Berg, now set out the full range of rights and privileges which mattered to Livonians, notably the establishment of the Lutheran religion ; the use of German in the courts ; the 'indigenat' (the exceptions were the governor-general who could be Russian or a foreigner, and in whose chancery Russians could be employed) ; the maintenance of the *Landesstaat* and the *Landtag,* with its twelve *Landräte,* the marshal and the secretary, and their agreed salaries ; unlimited property rights over both allodial and feudal (*Lehn*) land which could both be freely exchanged or sold (a view contested by the Russian government in connection with feudal lands) ; immunity from taxation of noble land (though not of peasant land where it survived) ; the preservation of customary German law, statutes and procedure in the courts. Among the innovations which they specifically criticized were the powers attributed to the governor-general to supervise the functioning of judicial institutions in general, and to intervene administratively in the relations between landowners and serfs. There could be no objections to the form of the board of administration which was modelled on the Livonian in any case ; but the nobles objected strongly to the presence of an elected Russian assessor proposed in the Memorandum. But their principal objections were directed at the purely Russian institution of the procuracy, independent of the local judiciary and subordinated ultimately to the Russian procurator general in the capital. The existing local system of fiscals was quite sufficient in their view for Livonian needs. The installation of the board of social welfare presented no problem, though it was regarded as superfluous. The equity court was also welcomed as a useful innovation, but the division of the courts into civil and criminal sections was rejected on the grounds that there was almost no crime among the barons. District assemblies of the nobility were also rejected as superfluous, since the Livonian nobility constituted one single corporation and its *Landtage* were quite adequate for the election of the necessary officials. There were however, in their view, too many officials and above all too many law courts for the nobility to use and to man. Some of the courts established for Russia such as the lower summary courts were in any case unnecessary since there were very few peasants who were not serfs.[38]

The generally negative response of the nobility to the Statute of 1775 converted even the Governor, General Browne, to a degree of opposition to Catherine's policy, which among other things would involve an increase in government expenditure of 70,000 rubles.[39] He had also received confidential memoranda from deputies of the high court, and of the city council. Basically, the Livonians of the privileged classes saw no particular improvements in the Statute of 1775 and felt no need to change institutions evolved over the centuries for the sake of uniformity. If Governor Browne did not hurry to forward the Livonians' reply to Catherine's Memorandum, he did indicate that he himself was in favour of the transformation of feudal land into allodial land, and urged the nobles to send deputies to St Petersburg to present their case. Caspar Heinrich von Rosenkampf for Livonia, and Gustav Rheinhold von Ulrich (that same Ulrich who had assisted Catherine with information in 1775) for Estonia were chosen as deputies and submitted their petition to Catherine on 7 November 1779. Almost at once the nature of the bargain Catherine was going to drive became clear : she would view the request to merge feudal and allodial land favourably if the Livonians proved accommodating over the Statute of 1775.[40] In the meantime, the Senate decreed in autumn 1781 that the census should take place every twenty years in the Baltic as elsewhere in Russia, and that 'souls', not 'haken' as heretofore should be counted.[41]

Much depended now on Browne, who paid a visit to the capital in June 1782. A.R. Vorontsov, the president of the College of Commerce, who was taking an increasing interest in Livonian matters, was charged with persuading him to bring over the Livonian nobles to the Russian point of view, with a promise that he would be offered the governor-generalship.[42]

In the meantime Livonian prestige suffered a serious blow when von Rosenkampf towards the end of 1781 fled St Petersburg having embezzled over 35,000 rubles. Arrested in Riga, he was transferred to St Petersburg then back to Riga where he was prosecuted for forgery. That such a man should have been an elected *Landrat* for Livonia, and deputy for the province to deal with Catherine, gave the Russians an excellent handle to consider Livonian institutions as inferior to the Russian Statute of 1775.[43] The decision to go ahead in both the Baltic provinces was taken in early summer 1782.

While urging the Estonian nobles – who were throughout treated more leniently – to take steps to 'invite' Catherine to introduce the Statute, Browne, on his return from St Petersburg in June, convened a meeting of the noble assembly in Riga for 23 June 1782, to discuss, in his own absence, a letter setting out Catherine's decision, assuring the nobles that the empress intended to secure their rights, and inviting the nobles to submit to him a list of those conditions which should be observed in introducing the reform in order to ensure the preservation of their privileges.[44] The Livonians replied on 7 July with a formidable repetition of all their privileges going back to the fifteenth century, as listed in October 1779 by Schoultz von Ascheraden and Rheinhold von Berg. The Regulations of the Landtag of 1765, guaranteeing the right of the serfs to moveable property and laying down norms for their labour, were also regarded as one of the 'privileges' to be maintained. Instead of the courts proposed by the Statute of 1775 it was suggested that disputes between peasants and landowners should be referred to the *Ordnungsgericht* (as previously) and appeals should go to special commissions composed of the Landrat and two deputies of the nobility. All judges except those of the lowest courts should have higher education or long experience, and hence they opposed their election every three years. The assessment and collection of taxes was to be carried out as before and noble land and economic activity were to be free of tax.[45]

Meanwhile the Estonian gentry too prepared their reply, listing privileges going back to 1321, and specifying eighteen points on which the Statute departed from the Estonian constitution. They objected to the composition of the courts, the introduction of the procuracy, denied the need for higher and lower peasant courts since there were no free peasants (which was not in fact the case) and dwelt on Catherine's promise, as late as 24 January 1775, to exclude Estonia from any such reform.[46] Browne forwarded these somewhat unpromising replies to St Petersburg, hoping that A.R. Vorontsov would act as his intermediary with Catherine. But in the capital Vorontsov, together with Bezborodko, Vyazemsky and Dahl, was committed to the implementation of the reform. He refused to put before the empress documents which he alleged would give her a poor opinion of the Baltic provinces. As Dahl wrote to Browne, Catherine would not negotiate with the provinces ; she had 'climbed mountains', she would not therefore find it difficult to 'climb hills', and Dahl concluded with some evidently officially inspired hints at the possibility of Browne's retirement (he was after all 84 !). Finally on 3 December 1782, an ukaz briefly stated that Browne had been ordered to proceed with the division of Livonia and Estonia into uezdy (or *Kreise*) to pave the way for the reform.[47]

The ukaz of December 1782 came as a thunderbolt to the barons. 'Our happy constitution, the legacy of our ancestors, is coming to an end,' wrote one of them. 'Delenda est Carthago, the word has gone forth.'[48] But there still remained room for manoeuvre over the modalities of the introduction of the Statute of 1775, in negotiations with Browne, who remained basically loyal to the imperial promise of 1778 that Livonian rights would not be sacrificed. The process of harmonizing the institutions of Livonia and Estonia with the Statute was eased by the fact that the Statute was itself so extensively modelled on Livonian and Estonian originals. Even more helpful however was the one major concession to baronial wishes granted by Catherine in spring 1783, once she was certain of having her own way. Two ukazy of great significance in the assimilation of the Baltic provinces to Russia were issued on 3 May 1783. The first finally abolished the distinction between feudal tenure and allodial property or land.[49] The Baltic barons thus received what they had long clamoured for, not as a specific grant to themselves but as part of their assimilation into Russia. But to their horror, the assimilation was carried further with the introduction into the provinces of the poll-tax in an ukaz of the same day.[50] The unilateral alteration of the whole basis of taxation of land and of urban dwellers aroused the Livonians to the full awareness of their helplessness in the face of Russian absolutism.[51] There was no mechanism by which they could protest against government policy.

The next blow came with an ukaz of 3 July 1783 ordering Browne to proceed with the division of Livonia into eight districts, and Estonia into five, and with the election by the nobles and the townspeople of the various officials needed to staff the new or reformed institutions, using the electoral procedures laid down in Catherine's manifesto of 14 December 1766 for the summoning of the Legislative Commission.[52] No notice was taken of the endless efforts at 'harmonization' which had been going on since the previous December. The local Landtage were never consulted. Nothing could more clearly prove Catherine's determination to achieve uniformity throughout the empire than her utter refusal to allow Livonian penal law to take precedence over the penal clauses of the Statute ; her rejection of the traditional right of Livonian judges to accept fees from litigants, and her refusal to allow a different nomenclature for the courts, and above all her insistence on the right of procurators to report directly to the procurator general in St Petersburg without passing through the governor-general. 'It was our duty', wrote Catherine to Browne on 15 April 1784, putting an end to the argument, 'to introduce uniformity into the internal administration of our Empire', and she expressed her pleasure at finding that other provinces which had previously had their own laws (Little Russia and Belorussia) had accepted the reform as an improvement on previous conditions.[53]

The new institutions were formally inaugurated on 29 October 1783 in Riga, on 10 December in Reval. A further indication of 'russification' was the precedence given at the ceremonies to Orthodox religious services.[54] The usual festivities accompanied what for some of the traditionalists represented the end of constitutional freedom, and the introduction of despotism, for others the opportunity to find salaried employment in government service.

For the gentry the merging of feudal with allodial land rendered their property secure ; the introduction of the poll-tax did away with the fears aroused by the earlier Russian proposal of 1774 to seek out and take back originally peasant land and tax it. Moreover the landowner could try to recover the cost of the poll-tax by intensifying the labour dues. For the peasant however, who paid part of the 70 kopeks in kind, the low tariff at which corn and hay was assessed increased his burdens, and there was much serious rioting in 1783–4. The Senate did in fact increase the tariff somewhat in early 1784. The main disadvantage of the poll-tax was the effect it had on mobility. The Livonian serf had always been attached to the land. But the free peasants or craftsmen, even the town-dwellers below the level of the registered merchants, who were now divided into guilds in accordance with the Russian pattern, found themselves attached to their dwelling-place by the census. Landowners and town councils had now to issue passports to those who wished to earn a living elsewhere. The process had to be regulated ; landowners would otherwise ask for the poll-tax to be paid for twenty years in advance before allowing a free craftsman to move from the village where he was registered. Elaborate rules – and tariffs – were devised to register permits and passports with the courts, but inevitably the power of landowners over dwellers on their land increased as a result. The town magistracy too complained about the poll-tax on the grounds that it ran counter to their privileges and that certain lands belonging to the towns had always been regarded as free from tax. Their protests were ignored.

If the poll-tax, and particularly the fact that normally it was collected and assessed and paid by the landowner (though the serf could pay it himself), enormously increased the power of the landowner over the peasants, in one respect at least, the introduction of the Statute of 1775 favoured the peasants' position. In the first place the provisions of the Patent of 1765 were maintained and repeatedly confirmed and the pressure on landowners to register the norms of the labour dues exacted led to a considerable increase in registrations.[55] More important however was the preservation of the right of the peasant, given in 1765, to complain against ill-treatment by his landlord to the lower land court. Under pressure from the Russian government, moreover, the higher and lower summary courts for free peasants were set up (*verkhnyaya* and *nizhnyaya rasprava*), and on 4 September 1784, in a personal rescript to governor-general Browne, Catherine ordered him to see to the election of the assessors to those courts, who should not be *chinovniki*, but 'village-dwellers'. To sum up, the 'reform' worsened the economic position of the peasant in some respects, but it increased his legal power to defend himself against injustice and exploitation. Not only did the free peasants have access now to the courts ; even the enserfed peasants found their status improved by the emergence of 'peasant assessors' in the lower land courts, who appear often to have been serfs, and who saw to it that the complaints of their fellows against ill-treatment, excessive labour dues or injustice in the collection of the poll-tax did not go unheard.[56]

The next stage in reducing the Livonian polity to the Russian model was the promulgation of the Charter to the Nobility in 1785. Most of the personal and property rights granted in the Charter presented no problem in Livonia, since they were to a great extent drawn from the same sources as the Livonian rights.[57] But the section of the Charter dealing with the corporate rights of the nobility led to an immediate confrontation between the Livonian nobles and the Russian state. The Livonian constitution provided for regular meetings of the Landtag, or Diet, which had the right to initiate discussion of new laws and regulations, and to comment on, and in theory even reject, government taxes. Only nobles on the 'matricula' or register could participate in the Landtag, and they formed a corporation, represented by twelve *Landräte* with the rank of major-general, who advised the governor. Deputies of the districts or *Kreise* met regularly in local conventions, and the nobles maintained their own treasury and could raise voluntary contributions on their own 'estate'.

The provisions of the Charter to the Nobility totally altered the legal foundation both of the government of the Livonian Province – the Landtag would disappear – and of the noble corporation. The balance of power between central government and provincial institutions would be radically changed in favour of the former ; the composition and powers of the noble estate would be altered to the disadvantage of the matriculated nobility.

The weakness of the Livonian nobility lay in the existence in the province of the *Landsassen,* who in the Russian context would undoubtedly be accepted as 'dvoryane', since they were landowners and had usually served as Russian officers, but who in Livonia were not accepted as nobles and therefore had no rights of representation in the Livonian constitution. Their existence had already caused confusion in the elections to the Legislative Commission in 1766, and Catherine had finally ordered them to elect their own separate deputy.[58] The Charter offered them entry into the noble corporation and the right to be elected to posts in local administration hitherto reserved for matriculated nobles. The Landsassen now complained to the Senate in St Petersburg that they were not being consulted about the Charter. A Senate ukaz promptly followed on 22

November 1785 ordering the Livonian nobles to proceed with the preparation of genealogical books on the Russian model, to replace the matricula. This the council of the Landräte refused to do, on the grounds that admission to the 'matricula' was a matter reserved to the Landtag as a whole. On 29 November 1785 they submitted a long memorial to the governor-general, pointing out the differences between the Russian Charter of 1785 and their own rights, stressing the constitutional functions of the Landtag and the Landräte and pointing out that the right to be elected to or to vote for candidates for public office in Livonia did not, as in Russia, depend on a property and a service qualification, but belonged by birth to every matriculated noble. It was for the Landtag to decide whether to accept newcomers into the noble corporation and not the Heraldmaster's office as in Russia. For this reason the nobles could not accept the division of their estate into six classes as provided in articles 76–82 of the Charter. The Livonian nobles, including those with Russian titles, constituted one single class, entry into which was based more on birth than on service, as in Germany.[59] Though they were grateful for access to the special facilities for nobles provided in Russia (loans from the Nobles Bank, entry into the guards regiments and special educational establishments), these benefits did not lead them to merge into the Russian nobility. In the most courteous manner, the nobles concluded that the Charter was all very well for the Russian nobility, but it did not suit them.[60]

The governor-general to whom the memorial was addressed replied on 8 December that uniformity in the organization of government demanded uniformity in the organization of the social estates. Let the nobles accept the Charter gracefully, and discrepancies could be ironed out at the next Landtag. The nobles nevertheless determined to continue the struggle ; a convention of the noble deputies met on 29 January 1786, and a fresh analysis of the constitutional divergencies was prepared setting out the familiar arguments, and signed on 9 February. Baron Igelstrom was sent to present the memorial in St Petersburg but Catherine, supported by Vyazemsky, had no intention of allowing any deviation from her own model. All the petitions were referred to the first department of the Senate (under Vyazemsky), which at last, on 7 August 1786, issued an ukaz to Governor-General Browne of unheard of severity. The vacillations of the governor-general and his administration were blamed for the delay in implementing the Charter. 'A minority of the nobility, which does not appreciate the advantages offered to it, but clings to traditional habits and deep-rooted opinions has advanced unfounded objections, while the remaining nobles [i.e. the Landsassen], as the Senate well knows, are hoping wholeheartedly for the rapid implementation of laws from which they hope to benefit.' The duty of government offices was to implement the laws ; the administration in the provinces had allowed itself to indulge in requests for explanations which no other guberniya had demanded. 'The dispositions of the rulers should at all times be accepted with respect and obeyed without demur, particularly when the Sovereign had endowed the nobility and towns with such . . . privileges. . . .' Browne was ordered to implement the Charters without further delay.[61]

The Landrat College was thereupon ordered to proceed with preparing the genealogical book, and elections were to take place on 1 October. In August the final blow fell. An ukaz dated 14 August 1786 simply abolished the institutions of the Landräte, the Landtag and the Landrat College in Livonia and Estonia. As the Senate explained, these bodies had been set up of old because the different parts of the administration were not properly ordered. Now these offices were no longer necessary, since rights and privileges were protected by the laws of the land and by the institutions 'established by our sovereign power'. The nobles had now been given the right to elect marshals and deputies to compile the genealogical records, and the right to petition the governor, the Senate, and the empress herself concerning their needs. No further elections were therefore to take place to these various traditional bodies and the lands and treasure belonging to them were to be taken over by the treasury boards for other purposes. Landräte who had no other *chin* could be given the fourth rank as 'effective state councillors'.[62] On 26 August the Landräte resigned their offices. The Charter to the Towns was implemented in the same highhanded manner – the protests of the city of Riga being totally ignored. In the words of the German historian of this episode, Bienemann, 'what a century had slowly built up and 150 years had kept in being, was wiped out in 10 days – there was something here of the magnitude of a Tamerlane or a St Just.'[63]

The abrogation of the Livonian constitution has been variously interpreted by historians, according to their national viewpoint and their ideological preconceptions. Bienemann echoes the views and feelings of the Livonian German nobility, unhappy at having to be united in a common social group with the Landsassen, 'promoted officers and bureaucrats, without traditions or manners and who were not even important by reason of their numbers, since they amounted to only one eleventh of the total number of nobles'.[64] On the other hand Zutis sees in the opening up of the narrow German noble oligarchy, and the suppression of their *Stände* organs, the triumph of the absolutist state, which was 'clearing the way for economic, social, and political progress'. In his view, German historians admit the progressive nature of Russian policy, but justify the opposition of the Baltic nobles on the grounds of the need to maintain German influence in the area.[65] The 'reform' of the Livonian nobility was carried through with a thoroughness and a brutality typical of Joseph II. Uniformity was in any case desirable ; but above all no autonomous political rights should be allowed to challenge the central government. Livonian social structure played into Catherine's hands. She had the support of the Landsassen and of the poorer landless nobles for whom jobs would now be available ; they had complained to the Senate of the fact that the nobles excluded them from all political activity, though they owned 20 per cent of the land – 'Even state peasants', they argued, 'were allowed to elect their own magistrates.'[66] She also had the support of the Russian nobility, who now saw the possibility of access to Livonian lands and influence, and of the Russian high officials who were at one with her in their approval of uniformity and centralization.[67]

Part VII

Court Politics

Court and Culture

From the beginning of her reign Catherine was fully aware of the importance of a well run court as a means of moulding public opinion at home and influencing it abroad. Soon after her accession she put a stop to the disorder which had prevailed under Peter III, who had treated the court as a cross between a barracks and a tavern. Regulations were drafted setting out the various court ranks, and palace housekeeping – though criticized for its parsimony – improved to the extent that Catherine's ladies-in-waiting no longer starved as they had done in Peter's time.[1]

The court was not merely the private dwelling-place of the ruler. It was the centre from which the cultural life of the country radiated as far as its light could penetrate. Catherine followed on the tradition of Elizabeth in promoting the theatre, but she gave a much more vigorous impulse to Russian intellectual life by her patronage of literary activity, translations and journalism.

The court theatre and opera were not open to the general public on a commercial basis. But access was more widespread than this might imply : 'all ranks of the table of ranks (both sexes) and non-commissioned officers in the guards were admitted without pay in the 1760s,' the poet Derzhavin recorded ;[2] while in the 1770s I.I. Dmitriyev noted that though seats in boxes and stalls were distributed free according to rank, people of any class were admitted to the upper gallery unless they were in livery.[3] Plays were put on both in Russian and in French.[4]

The Russian theatre was at first directed by, and frequently performed the plays of, the leading Russian dramatist of the time, A.P. Sumarokov. He came from an old boyar family and was the first noble to make letters his profession, and the first Russian to publish his own periodical, *Trudolyubivaya pchela* ('The Busy Bee') in 1759. Sumarokov's tragedies belonged, particularly in his earlier years, to the high classical style, following the rules of Boileau. But in his comedies, tales and poetry, he looked beyond classicism, extending his interests to Voltaire and Shakespeare. He was also the first Russian author to bring peasants onto the stage.

In January 1766 one of Catherine's personal friends, her secretary I.P. Yelagin, was appointed Director of Spectacles and Music at court. He had already acted as an unofficial Maecenas to a number of young Russian playwrights, the most prominent of whom were V.I. Lukin and D.I. Fonvizin. Lukin was particularly influential in preaching the need to adapt foreign models to a Russian background, by transposing plots and characters and satirizing the actual defects of Russian society. Battle between Sumarokov and Lukin was engaged on personal as well as on dramatic grounds (Lukin was of non-noble birth). The polemics between playwrights were fought out in their plays in which they mercilessly lampooned or caricatured each other. Their satire extended to their personal enemies, whether relatives or officials, and actors in the know ensured that the audience should see the point by 'imitating the mannerisms, way of speaking and dress of the originals'.[5]

Denis Ivanovich Fonvizin was to prove the most outstanding dramatist of Catherinian Russia. Of Livonian origin, he was educated at Moscow University and began his service career as a translator in the College of Foreign Affairs. He was seconded to Yelagin's office in 1763, and after publishing a number of translations, he embarked on his major original play, *Brigadir,* between 1766 and 1769. It was a satire on the gallomania prevalent in Russian noble circles, but it was also remarkable for the range of Russian portraits, some allegedly drawn from life. It proved an outstanding example of the theatre with a social purpose, satirizing vices, praising where praise was due and ensuring the ultimate triumph of virtue. The play was read to Catherine in 1769 with such success that the author was invited to repeat the reading to the Grand Duke Paul, and was brought to the notice of Nikita Panin. Fonvizin was then promoted to be the latter's secretary in the College of Foreign Affairs, thus inaugurating long years of close personal friendship and political fellow-feeling between the playwright and the minister.[6]

Catherine herself tried her hand at writing satirical plays, four of which appeared in 1772. They dealt with such topics as superstition, laziness, ignorance and arranged marriages between young people. Other writers satirized corruption in the bureaucracy and the judiciary, usually stressing that an enlightened empress had taken steps to eradicate it. A more humane attitude to the peasantry emerged, as when N. Nikolev, in *Rozana i Lyubim,* showed that a peasant could love and could be as magnanimous as a tsar. Ya. B. Knyazhnin, in the libretto for the Russian comic opera *Neschast'ye ot karety* ('Misfortune from a Carriage', 1779) came close to condemning a system which allowed a couple of francophile enthusiasts to break up the marriage plans of two serf servants in order to have enough money to buy a French carriage. Generally speaking, cruel or callous landowners were satirized as unworthy of their high estate, but the institution of serfdom was not discussed – let alone condemned – as such.

It was in comic opera that the theme of the peasantry found its most constant expression. Starting in 1772 with *Anyuta,* by the non-noble writer, M.I. Popov, in which, though the peasant girl Anyuta is eventually revealed as the daughter of a noble, there is considerable emphasis on the language of the people and the hard life of the peasant, the high point was reached with A.A. Ablesimov's

Mel'nik, koldun, obmanshchik i svat ('The Miller, Wizard, Quack and Match-maker', 1779) a peasant love story couched in popular language. The use of folk-song in these comic operas gave them a uniquely Russian flavour.[7]

Musical performances of various kinds were well established at court and in Russian society. A court orchestra and a court choir had been lavishly patronized by the music-loving Razumovskys under Elizabeth. Peter III had played the violin, and during his brief reign he had encouraged amateur performances of chamber music at court, in which he was joined by such performers as G.N. Teplov.[8] Catherine in contrast was not musical – indeed she appears to have been tone deaf – but music formed a necessary part of the radiance of a court. Hence opera seria, sometimes in Russian, continued to be performed at court, alternating at first with Italian opera buffa, and after 1764 with French light opera.[9]

What remained specific to Russian culture was the reliance on vocal music. The court choir and the boys' choir sang Russian church music at church services and Russian popular songs at court, and gave concert performances of choral symphonies and concertos by such young Russian composers as M.S. Bere-zovsky and D.S. Bortnyansky. The Italian composer Galuppi arrived in St Petersburg in 1765 as director of the court orchestra and turned it into a veritable forcing-house of vocal and orchestral talent.[10] Like his predecessor, Aleksey Razumovsky, Grigory Orlov seems to have enjoyed Russian popular songs. The Russian court journal describes one evening at court as follows : 'after dinner HIM graciously returned to her inner apartments, and the gentlemen in the card room themselves sang songs, to the accompaniment of various wines ; then the court singers and servants . . . and on the orders of Count G.G. Orlov, the n.c.o.s and soldiers of the guard at Tsarskoye Selo, sang gay songs in another room.'[11]

Love of music, and skill in performance, spread throughout the upper classes as a result of court patronage and of the education given in government establishments. But it was by no means confined to court circles. There were so-called *vol'nyye,* private or free theatres, which staged popular comedies, and maintained a number of performers on a variety of musical instruments. Such theatres also encouraged the singing of popular songs and performed popular dramas handed down in manuscript form.[12] These new, more mixed, audiences paved the way for the appreciation of bourgeois comedy, peasant themes and folk-song.

Two further sources went to swell the stream of Russian music. One was the numerous, and growing, number of serf performers of various instruments. Many nobles had their own orchestras which performed at the balls and dances which played the largest part in Muscovite social life of the *haut ton.* In addition the army provided its own peculiar brand of music, the unique Russian horn orchestras, in which each performer played on a horn with only one single note.[13]

The 1760s can scarcely be regarded as a golden age in Russian literature. The giant of the Elizabethan age, Lomonosov, died in 1765, and none of his followers inherited his genius. Yet the advent of a new ruler, Catherine's own marked interest in letters, and the vast programme of translations she sponsored, gave a tremendous impetus to the literary life of the capital and encouraged a whole crop of new writers of noble and non-noble origin to experiment with new forms of novels, tales, poetry and journalism.

From her accession, Catherine had encouraged the translation of foreign literary, scientific and philosophical works into Russian. Indeed, she gave the example herself. On the occasion of a journey by barge to Kazan' in spring 1767, the empress and her immediate entourage entertained themselves by translating Marmontel's *Bélisaire,* which had only just been published in January 1767, and promptly condemned by the Sorbonne. The various chapters were distributed among Catherine's courtiers, and she reserved the chapter on the duties of a monarch to herself. Marmontel, speaking to Justinian through Belisarius, argued in favour of government according to the laws, and warned that arbitrary government was bound to lead to tyranny. The same group of courtiers had also tried their hand at translating a selection of articles from the *Encyclopédie,* which was published in three volumes by Moscow University Press in 1767.

On 4/15 November 1768, Catherine founded a Society for the Translation of Foreign Books into Russian, which she endowed with two thousand rubles to start with. Through G. Kozitsky, her literary secretary, she kept in touch with the activities of this Society, which functioned until the establishment of the Russian Academy of Letters in 1783. It sponsored a very wide programme of translations, from the *Iliad* to *Gulliver's Travels,* from the latest French comedy to *Robinson Crusoe.* In the 1760s and 1770s for instance, all Rousseau's works except the *Social Contract* appeared in Russian translation.[14]

The bulk of the books published in Russia continued to be works of devotion in Old Church Slavonic, though the old alphabet was also used for secular works.[15] But of the books published in the secular script, the overwhelming majority were translations, undertaken in many cases by those who would later make their own name as writers, such as Fonvizin or Radishchev. Novikov, who had early realized that publication must be followed up by distribution and sale, set up a short-lived company in the 1770s to market translations produced by the Society for the Translation of Foreign Books. It was still an uphill task since provincial demand was very slight, and the efforts of V.G. Orlov, the director of the Academy of Sciences, to market the publications of the Academy in the provinces met with total failure.[16]

A central figure of the literary scene was M. Kheraskov. First as director, then as curator of Moscow University, he published two journals in the early 1760s, *Poleznoye Uveseleniye,* ('Useful Entertainment') and *Svobodnyye Chasy* ('Leisure Hours'), in which his own literary productions and those of a group of young poets and writers centring around the university were published. Throughout his long life, Kheraskov wrote in many genres, including a vast epic on Ivan IV's conquest of Kazan', the *Rossiada,* modelled on Voltaire's *Henriade ;* plays, lyric poems, triumphal odes, flowed from his pen. Both in the theatre and in poetry he is important as a transitional figure between classical and bourgeois drama, or *comédie larmoyante,* and between classical and sentimental poetry. His personal influence – his house in Moscow was the nearest thing to a literary salon in Russia – was just as important.

None of the poets of the 1760s could rival Lomonosov. V. Petrov was of humble origin, and attracted attention with an ode on the occasion of a 'carrousel', a form of tournament much in vogue with Catherine in the 1760s. In April 1769, he was promoted to the post of translator in Catherine's secretariat, and he continued to the end of her reign to celebrate important events in solemn odes.[17] His capacity to turn out poems on demand earned him the title of Catherine's pocket poet.

The novel in the 1760s began to rival poetry in popularity and the flood of translations sponsored by Catherine paved the way for the development of the Russian original novel. F. Emin published seven novels in as many years, two of which developed the type of didactic philosophical and political novel typical of the Enlightenment and aimed at a readership which went well beyond the nobility to the third estate. His best known work, 'The Letters of Ernest and Dovrara' is modelled on *La Nouvelle Héloïse* and foreshadows Russian sentimentalism. Kheraskov too wrote long classical novels, deeply imbued with Enlightenment ideas under which the initiated could detect the deeper stream of masonic occult symbolism.[18] In a different vein was *Prigozhaya povarikha,* or the tale of a dissolute woman, by M. Chulkov, a kind of Russian Moll Flanders. Chulkov is also remembered for his *Peresmeshnik,* a collection of tales of all times and places which went through several editions, and for his monumental collection of Russian popular and Cossack songs. In the same more popular genre was *Van'ka Kain,* a tale by M. Komarev, which harks back to seventeenth-century Russian popular fiction.

Sumarokov's periodical, *Trudolyubivaya pchela,* had been followed by other more or less short-lived journals between 1762 and 1764. Then there was a lull, broken early in 1769 by the announcement of the forthcoming appearance of the first Russian weekly, *Vsyakaya vsyachina* ('All Sorts of Things'), edited by the empress's secretary, G. Kozitsky. His role as editor was sufficient to indicate to those in the know that Catherine had a close personal interest in the journal, though its extent was not fully realized. No satisfactory explanation has been offered for her sudden interest in the publication of a journal at that time. She may have wished to continue, 'by other means', the opinion-forming function of the Legislative Commission. Or she may have been moved by the desire to set down the canons and limits within which satire should flourish in Russia, since the backbiting, the bitterly personalized satire in the Russian drama was exceeding the bounds of propriety. 'All Sorts of Things' was modelled on the English *Spectator,*[19] and the anonymous editor appeared in the character of 'Babushka' or 'Granny'. In the first number, 'Granny' coyly expressed the hope that her example would be followed : 'I see the future,' she declared. 'I see the endless posterity of "All Sorts of Things". I see that it will be followed by legitimate and illegitimate children.' By January 1769, 'This and That' had already appeared, followed by 'Neither This nor That', 'Miscellany', 'The Drone' and 'The Infernal Post, or correspondence between a lame devil and a crooked devil'.[20] The best known of them, for the quality of the contents, and of the editing, was *Truten'* or 'The Drone', edited by N.I. Novikov.

N.I. Novikov (1743–1820) came of an old service gentry family comfortably off without being rich (the family owned three hundred serfs). He was educated at Moscow University where he coincided in time with D.I. Fonvizin and G.A. Potemkin.[21] He afterwards entered the Izmailovsky Guards Regiment, where he was serving at the time of Catherine's accession, and was selected to act as a report writer in the Legislative Commission of 1767–8. Promoted to the rank of lieutenant, Novikov was transferred on the outbreak of war to an infantry regiment. Then, for reasons which have never been explained, the twenty-five-year-old Novikov, a serving officer, was allowed to retire from the army in wartime and devote himself to literary pursuits.[22]

Novikov's journal, 'The Drone', probably took its title from Sumarokov's 'The Busy Bee', but it also hinted at 'The Drone's' affiliation with *The Spectator, The Idler, The Tatler,* and the sophisticated use of an editorial 'persona' to give unity to the viewpoint of the periodical.[23] Indeed the fact that all the Russian periodicals borrowed extensively from English models has now been established, notably the definition of the 'proper limits' of satire which appeared in 'All Sorts of Things'. According to *The Tatler* and *The Spectator,* satire should be directed at vice in general and not at identifiable persons. In Russian this became *satira na porok* as distinct from *satira na litso.* 'All Sorts of Things' several times reverted to the definition of acceptable satire, and adopted *The Spectator*'s criticism of wounding personal attacks.

The debate on the limits of satire was not new in Russia, and it was taken up afresh by the periodicals of the 1760s with particular gusto. While 'All Sorts of Things' held to the view that satire should be directed at vice in general, Novikov in 'The Drone' was prepared to go further and allow personal criticism, provided that the person was not named. The debate between the two was carried on by means of fictitious characters : Novikov mocked middle-aged ladies who could not write Russian properly, while 'Granny' accused the Drone of such a jaundiced attitude to humanity that he wished to 'knut' them for every little thing.

However, such polemics were by no means confined to 'All Sorts of Things' and 'The Drone'. All the journals indulged in sharp polemics with each other, and with the grandmother of them all, as well as in satire against highly placed people, princes and boyars, wicked landowners and contractors who grew fat on the 'bloody sweat' of the peasants. They too directed a great deal of light-hearted banter against a 'feeble' and 'forgetful' grandmother.[24]

It has become a commonplace of Soviet scholarship that the debate on satire between Novikov and Catherine, together with Novikov's attacks on serfdom in 'The Drone' led Catherine to close his journal. There is however no evidence that 'The Drone' was closed by government action.[25] 'All Sorts of Things' lasted for only one year, as originally intended; but all the other journals gradually closed down, and none lasted much over a year. The main difficulty was the small size of the reading public. It could not absorb eight new periodicals in one year, and the novelty soon wore off. Novikov himself realized this and berated his fickle readers for abandoning him in a satirical farewell in which he threatened to punish them by never writing another line.[26] That it was financial difficulties rather than censorship or government pressure which closed down the journals is suggested by two things: the first is that five of the journals were printed throughout on the press of the Academy of Sciences (including 'Miscellany' and 'The Drone') ; and a reprint of 'Miscellany' (one of the most outspoken) in book form appeared in 1771. And secondly, when 'The Drone' closed down, arrangements had already been made by Novikov to start a second journal, *Pustomelya* ('The Tatler') to be printed also on the Academy press.

Throughout the 1770s Novikov continued with his publishing ventures. 'The Tatler,' of which two issues appeared, continued the literary polemics with other writers and the outspoken attacks on the Russian bureaucracy. That such attacks in no way jeopardized Novikov's career is indicated by the fact that he returned at this time to service as a translator in the College of Foreign Affairs and that, with Catherine's benevolent patronage, he launched on what was to prove one of his major contributions to Russian culture, namely the collection and publication of historical documents, under the title 'Ancient Russian Library'. He was given the run of the Empress's library and was supplied with documents from official archives. In April 1772, he again announced his intention to publish a satirical journal, and put himself, if in a veiled way, under imperial patronage.[27] Catherine is said to have contributed to 'The Painter' (*Zhivopisets*), which nevertheless of all Novikov's journals published the most biting indictments of serfdom and of backward, boorish, uncultured nobles, as well as a 'letter' from 'a debauched maiden already in her forties, proud of the fact that no one now can tell her "to live with and love one man only" '. 'The Painter' ceased publication after fifty-two rather unpunctual issues, and it is again alleged in Soviet historiography that it was forced to close down by the difficulties placed in Novikov's path. This seems unlikely since he republished 'The Painter' in book form in 1775 and took the opportunity to sharpen even further some of his remarks.[28] Moreover he continued to publish the 'Ancient Russian Library' after 'The Painter' closed down, and launched yet another periodical, 'The Bag' (*Koshelyok*) of which only two issues appeared. Both these publications reflected Novikov's anxiety to counter foreign criticisms of Russia and the worship of false foreign fashions and. idols by Russians. A new, nationalist note crept into his writings, and he began to reaffirm the value of Russian traditions and ceremonial. His programme was not that of a radical politician. He was essentially a *moraliste,* anxious to put before the Russian public a portrait of an ideal noble, rather than to overthrow a class. It is difficult to see in him at this stage a resolute defiance of all that Catherine stood for, and the assumption of a deep-rooted antagonism between the empress and the writer rests far less on contemporary facts than on a reading back into these years of the tragic conflict of the 1790s.

By the use of much ingenuity, it has been possible for Soviet scholars to detect in comedies and tragedies, odes and epics, hints of an opposition to Catherine which she was supposedly too dim-witted to appreciate, otherwise she would have censored them.[29] This interpretation derives from an extremely narrow approach to the intellectual climate of Russia in the 1760s and 1770s, as though 'progressive' writers could think of only one thing : opposition to the empress. But in this exceptionally free period writers of various kinds were allowed to express daring thoughts on quite a number of themes which were only concerned with the Russian government in a very indirect way. Thus when the young Radishchev published in 1773 his translation of Abbé S.B. de Mably's *Observations sur l'Histoire de la Grèce* (printed on a government press) he could with impunity supply in the footnotes his own view of absolutism as 'the condition most repugnant to human nature'.

What kind of censorship existed at this time in Russia ? One must distinguish between the control of imported literature and the control of locally published works. The principles concerning the former were laid down by Catherine in an ukaz of 6/17 September 1763 which pointed out that since bookshops were not supervised undesirable books were being sold such as 'Rousseau's Emile, Memoirs of Peter III, Jewish Letters in the French Language' and others. It was the Memoirs of Peter III which particularly drew Catherine's attention, and she now ordered that booksellers should be instructed to submit lists of the books they proposed to import to the Academy of Sciences or the University of Moscow, which should delete books 'contrary to religion, good manners and ourselves'.[30] Hence, the power to censor was lodged not in the police, but in 'intellectual' government agencies, and it applied only to imported works. In the 1760s Catherine had personally intervened on one or two occasions to ban or to permit a work, and in general at this time there was considerable freedom, both in the spoken and the written word.[31]

The theoretical principles of freedom of expression had been discussed publicly for the first time in Russia in the Nakaz of Catherine II, and had been illustrated in practice in the debates of the Legislative Commission. In the Nakaz, freedom of expression was negatively defined in that Catherine did not positively proclaim it as a right ; she distinguished between *lèse majesté* and permissible criticism but pointed out that words should not be punished in the same way as deeds and stressed the need for freedom of the creative mind : 'How then can so capital a crime as High Treason be made of words and punished as the very action itself ?' (Article 482) while in relation to written matter caution must be used 'representing to ourselves, that Danger of debasing the human Mind by Restraint and Oppression ; which can be productive of nothing but Ignorance and must *cramp* and *depress* the *rising Efforts* of Genius, and destroy the *very Will* for writing' (Article 484).

There was in Russia at that time however no government office primarily concerned with censorship. Individual governors might report on seditious talk or broadsheets ; religious authorities kept an eye on works and words contrary to public morality and the faith. As far as work published in Russia was concerned, the matter was considerably simplified by the fact that all the existing printing presses belonged to institutions dependent on the government (the Cadet Corps, the Academy of Sciences, the Senate, the Synod, the University of Moscow, etc.). When the first private press was authorized in 1771 for the printing of works in languages other than Russian, the relevant ukaz forbade the printing of material against the Christian religion, common decency or the government.[32] The owner of the press was to submit all the material he proposed to print to the Academy of Sciences in advance.[33]

Since most of the journals were printed on the presses of the Academy of Sciences, it was the Academy which was supposed to examine manuscripts presented for publication. But it seems that this precaution had been allowed to lapse in the first half of 1769 ; as a result the identity of the editors of some of the journals remains unknown to this day. But an outspoken attack on the Church published in 'Miscellany' led to an order from the Director of the Academy that in future manuscripts were to be examined before being printed. A specific supervisor, the academician S.K. Kotel'nikov was allotted to 'The Drone' in January 1770. Nothing is known of how these censors worked, nor is anything known about Catherine's interventions if there were any.[34]

Apart from her patronage of letters within Russia, Catherine performed a signal service for Russian cultural life by developing and strengthening its ties with the intellectual life of Western Europe, both by putting Russia on the European map, and by initiating direct contacts with some of the best minds of the European Enlightenment. Her first step was to invite d'Alembert in autumn 1762 to take charge of the education of Grand Duke Paul. D'Alembert refused : 'Je suis trop sujet aux hémorrhoïdes et elles sont trop sérieuses dans ce pays là,' he wrote to Voltaire, alluding to the alleged cause of Peter III's death. Moreover, apart from his reluctance to leave his Paris friends, d'Alembert was the pensioner of the King of Prussia (with whom he spent most of the summer of 1763) and he could not easily desert one patron for another. The correspondence with Catherine continued, mainly prompted by d'Alembert, until 1767, but it never attained that spontaneity which characterized the empress's relations with Voltaire or Grimm. Catherine was certainly piqued at d'Alembert's refusal of her offer, as her letters show ; did she perhaps hear of his coarse allusion to the death of Peter III ? At any rate, when in 1772 d'Alembert allowed himself to be used in order to plead for the liberation of a number of French officers who had been captured while fighting for the confederate forces in Poland, he received a very dusty answer, which put an end to all communication between the two.[35]

Direct relations with Voltaire were launched much more successfully. Voltaire had long been interested in Russia. The first part of his history of Peter the Great was published in 1760 ; the second appeared in 1763, and he sent a few presentation copies for the empress to her secretary, the Genevese Pictet.[36] Through Pictet, Catherine had already been able to provide Voltaire with a 'reliable' account of her accession, but he was unforthcoming at first, uncertain how long her rule would last. In August 1762 Catherine informed Voltaire indirectly that she was willing to allow the Encyclopedists to transfer the printing and publication of their great work to Riga, in view of the difficulties they had been meeting in France. Since his quarrel with Frederick II in 1753, Voltaire had been left without his own particular philosopher king, and intellectual knight errantry may have made him all the more willing to become the *cavalier servant* of an empress, still young and reputedly handsome.[37] When Catherine thanked Voltaire for his *Histoire de Pierre le Grand,* direct correspondence between them was launched, and it continued until Voltaire's death in 1778. It was a correspondence which thrived on distance, on the fact that the two never met. Indeed Catherine took good care, later in her life, to warn Voltaire against coming to Russia. Tell him that 'Cateau n'est bonne qu'à être vue de loin', she wrote to Grimm in March 1778.[38] Apart from their value to each other as a mutual admiration society, Voltaire was very useful to Catherine in proclaiming her views and her victories over their common foes : the Catholic Church, clericalism, barbarism, fanaticism and the Turks – not as Moslems but as the destroyers of classical Greece. In common with other anti-Catholic *philosophes,* Voltaire praised the Russian invasion of Poland designed, as he put it, to impose toleration by armed force, and to be victorious 'over both the Holy Father and the Mufti'. He even wrote up and published the Russian version of religious dissension in Poland on Catherine's behalf,[39] and when the time came he welcomed the partition of 'ce gateau de roi', Catholic Poland. Voltaire's adulation for 'Our Lady of Saint Petersburg'[40] and the callousness implicit in much of the light-hearted banter over the fighting in Poland and Turkey do not show him at his best. Diderot, who owed Catherine more, was also more discreet.

In spite of many obstacles Diderot had been able to continue printing the *Encyclopédie* in France. But his personal financial difficulties brought him again to the notice of Catherine, and enabled her to bring off a veritable coup. Needing money to provide – in the distant future – a dowry for his daughter, then aged six, Diderot had decided to sacrifice his library. When Catherine heard that it was for sale, she purchased it for the sum he had asked, but her generosity did not stop there : she left him the use of his library for life and paid him a pension of a thousand livres per annum in a lump sum in advance as her librarian. Diderot was rendered speechless at first by this princely treatment but, warm and expansive by nature, he soon led the chorus of praise for the Semiramis of the North.[41] He threw himself into the task of recruiting talent for Catherine, advising visiting Russians, and in one case rendered her a real service, by persuading Claude de Rulhière, who had been secretary of the French embassy at the time of Catherine's *coup d'état*, not to publish his *Anecdotes* in which Catherine's part in the death of Peter III was clearly hinted at.

It was through Diderot that the French sculptor Falconet was persuaded to go to Russia and undertake the monument to Peter I which has been immortalized in Pushkin's Bronze Horseman. He was less successful with his next candidate for service in Russia, Mercier de la Rivière. The latter had served as intendant in Martinique and was the author of *De l'ordre naturel et essential des sociétés politiques*, which was read in manuscript by Diderot, and aroused his immediate and boundless enthusiasm. On Diderot's recommendation Catherine ordered Panin to begin negotiations with the Frenchman to attract him to Russian service. But from the beginning there were misunderstandings between the empress and the *philosophe*. Catherine had seen in Mercier a man whose work was persecuted in France, and who wished to enter Russian service and settle in Russia. Mercier de la Rivière intended to honour the empress with his advice for a couple of years and then return to his country. In January 1768 Catherine had several interviews with Mercier and evidently found him wanting. She had no intention of taking into her confidential councils a Frenchman who was likely to return to his country and reveal her inmost secrets to her political enemies within two years. In turn Mercier de la Rivière was disappointed to discover that he was not to be a leading minister, but merely one of several legal advisers to the procurator general for the work of codification of the Legislative Commission. Mercier's arrogance and his tactlessness in expressing an unvarnished opinion of Russia in a letter to Raynal,[42] which probably passed through Catherine's *cabinet noir*, alienated Russian opinion, and Mercier returned to France, the richer by 100,000 rubles.[43]

Mercier de la Rivière's visit was in any case inopportune, since Catherine was particularly incensed with Choiseul at the time, owing to the publication of the *Voyage en Sibérie . . . contenant les moeurs, les usages russes*, etc., (with romanticized engravings by Le Prince) by the abbé Chappe d'Auteroche in Paris. A member of the French Academy and an astronomer, Chappe d'Auteroche arrived in St Petersburg in 1761 on his way to Siberia to observe the transit of Venus in that year. He was given a generous welcome by the Russians, and stayed in Tobol'sk for a few months. His book was published in 1768, and could not have appeared at a worse time for Catherine, when she had just embarked on a war with Turkey. She naturally suspected the hand of her enemy Choiseul for Chappe d'Auteroche had not only described Russia as a barbarous country, he also spoke derisively of its military power. To the Frenchman, Russia was a country sunk in sloth and ignorance ; its people were slaves living in grinding poverty, borne down by the yoke of serfdom : 'Personne n'ose penser en

Russie ; l'ame, avilie et abrutie en perd jusqu'à la faculté . . . Le souffle empoisonné du despote s'étend sur tous les arts, sur toutes les manufactures et pénètre dans tous les ateliers. L'on y voit les artistes enchainés à leur établi. . . . La seule volonté [de Catherine] suffit pour disposer de la vie et des biens de ses sujets : on ne parait devant elle que prosterné. . . .' Having condemned the Russian government, Chappe went on to lambast the Russian people in terms which explain Catherine's wrath : 'On conclut aisément . . . que les russes doivent avoir un suc nerveux grossier, sans jeu et sans activité, plus propre à former des tempéraments vigoureux que des hommes de génie . . .' Possibly she was also outraged to read that on the accession of Peter III, 'L'impératrice sa femme vient se prosterner à ses pieds, et frappant du front contre la terre elle lui rend ses hommages comme sa première esclave. . . .'[44]

The *Voyage en Sibérie* was not well received in Paris.[45] But it provoked Catherine into her longest, if not her most successful, venture into authorship. Her reply, entitled *Antidote,* had an even worse press.[46] It is a tedious and long-winded work written in a niggling manner, taking up and refuting all Chappe's alleged malicious mistakes. Nevertheless it is of some interest in that it indicates what Catherine believed to be the truth about Russia, past and present, not merely what she wished others to believe. The work is imbued with genuine nationalistic indignation :

Il n'y a point de nation, de laquelle l'on ait debité plus de faussetés, d'absurdités, d'impertinences, que de la Russe. Cependant si l'on voulait . . . les comparer avec un coup d'oeil philosophique à ce que nous voyons du reste du genre humain l'on verroit qu'elle est à peu pres de niveau avec toutes les autres nations de l'Europe. . . . Les allemands . . . cherchoient des Allemands dans les Russes ; ne les trouvant point, ils on pris de l'humeur ; tout étoit mal ; les Russes avoient grand tort d'être Russes chez eux.[47]

In one respect at least moreover, Catherine was able to turn the *philosophes'* arguments against them when she rejected the 'odious' title of 'despot' which Chappe constantly applied to the ruler of Russia. In what way was she more despotic than the King of France ? If France had her *parlements* with their right of remonstrance (which could be overruled by the king), Russia had her Senate with its right of representation. If France had – and still had – the Bastille and the *lettres de cachet,* the Russian Secret Chancery had been abolished. Even the existence of France's fundamental laws remained a matter of dispute. Finally the author of the *Antidote* could point triumphantly to the fact that the Great Instruction of the Empress of Russia had been banned in France, and that the Sorbonne had condemned *Bélisaire,* which the empress and her courtiers had translated.

Catherine's attitude to Rousseau was ambivalent. When she banned *Emile* in 1763 she had probably not yet read it since it had only just been published in France. The prohibition may have emanated from the Holy Synod since the *Confessions* of the Savoyard vicar were no more to the taste of the Russian hierarchy than of the French. Grigory Orlov in 1765 invited Rousseau to settle in Russia – an invitation which cannot have been extended without Catherine's knowledge. Most of his works were translated into Russian, but *Du Contrat Social* was interpreted as anti-Russian by Catherine,[48] and she did not, so she declared in 1770, like Rousseau's ideas on education.[49] Meanwhile Diderot had been screwing up his courage to embark on that journey to Russia which everyone felt he owed to Catherine, and and he finally arrived in St Petersburg in October 1773. In some respects, he timed his visit badly, since Russia was still in the throes of the Turkish war and the Pugachev revolt was already a faint cloud on the horizon. But his journey had not been unwelcome to the French government which hoped to make use of his reputation to achieve a *rapprochement* between France and Russia.[50]

It was easy for Catherine to snub Diderot's reluctant efforts at diplomacy, without harming their relationship. The tale of their friendship is well known : Diderot was received by Catherine in private some three afternoons a week. At first their conversations ranged widely, and both spoke very freely. But, according to Catherine's later account, the time came when she considered that Diderot's plans for reform were more fitted for the study than for real life : '. . . vous ne travaillez que sur le papier, qui souffre tout,' said the empress to the *philosophe*, '. . . tandis que moi, pauvre impératrice, je travaille sur la peau humaine qui est bien autrement irritable et chatouilleuse.'[51] Diderot's own letters confirm that by December 1773, the first fine rapture of their intercourse had worn off. His own increasing ill health, his loneliness in an alien court, the intrigues of hostile Russians (those who opposed him because he was French, and those who opposed him because he was a *philosophe*), all contributed to Diderot's growing nostalgia and longing to return home. He saw almost nothing of Russia but the capital. But he did see a great deal of Catherine.

In any circumstances the long sessions in the autumn of 1773 between Catherine and Diderot must be accounted remarkable. Even if he did not slap her on the thigh in his enthusiasm,[52] their regular afternoon meetings were completely informal. Catherine would sit on the imperial sofa, sometimes with a piece of needlework in her hands, and her guest would take his place in a comfortable armchair opposite her. The cordiality of his reception encouraged Diderot's hope that he had at last found a ruler willing to be educated in the principles of the Enlightenment, and to apply them to her government. Moreover, in common with many of his contemporaries, he believed that it was easier to reform Russia than France, since Russia was new, a blank page on which history had as yet written nothing, a country without structures or institutions.

With some idea of the topics likely to be discussed, Diderot usually prepared shorter or longer notes, which he read to the empress, and which they subsequently argued about. These papers have survived, and illustrate the quite remarkable freedom of expression, written and verbal, which characterized their dialogue. Diderot put before Catherine his views on education, toleration, the process of legislation, divorce (which he favoured), gaming (which he opposed). He begged her to provide Russia with a law of succession ; to keep the Legislative Commission in being, as the 'depository of the laws' in Russia, and the guarantee that the people had given their consent to what had been enacted. He urged Catherine to introduce the study of anatomy in girls' schools, in order to make them better 'wives and mothers, protected by innocence instead of ignorance against the wiles of seducers.[53]

It has frequently been suggested that because Catherine did not adopt any or all of the ideas of Diderot, her admiration for the Enlightenment was sheer hypocrisy designed to influence public opinion abroad in her favour while she continued to act as she pleased at home. What is far more rarely – if ever – pointed out is that Diderot's ideas do not constitute a practical programme for Russia as it actually was in the mid-1770s or for any country at any time. A *philosophe* was not necessarily a practical politician or administrator – Diderot certainly was not. Many of his ideas sounded attractive in theory but bore no relation to any reality. Noble, generous, idealistic in many respects, they represent a frame of mind rather than a political programme.

Diderot left Russia on 4 March 1774 ; parting gifts were exchanged, and Catherine paid for his travel expenses and provided him with a specially constructed carriage in which he could lie down.[54] At The Hague, he stayed with the Russian envoy, D.A. Golitsyn, and while there he arranged for the publication in French of the Statutes on Education and the regulations for the Russian Foundling Hospital which had been drafted by I.I. Betskoy for Catherine.[55] It was also at this time that he wrote his 'Considerations sur le Nakaz', or comments on Catherine's Great Instruction.[56] These were forwarded to Catherine after Diderot's death in 1784, and she found them and read them some time in 1785. By then Diderot's criticisms evidently touched her on the raw. 'Cette pièce est un vrai babil dans lequel on ne trouve ni connaissance de choses, ni prudence, ni prévoyance ; . . . La critique est aisée, mais l'art est difficile,' she added, particularly for a *philosophe* who in his own life 'était d'une prudence à vivre sous tutelle'.[57]

While Diderot lived, Catherine continued to maintain a cordial interest in him, but it was in Friedrich Melchior Grimm that she found a life-long literary friend. The son of a Lutheran dignitary, he was born in Regensburg in 1723, and had moved to Paris in the hope of making his fortune. Through his patron, the heir of the Duke of Saxe Gotha, then on a visit to France, Grimm soon made his way into the salons, and became the intimate friend of Diderot and of Rousseau. From 1754, Grimm took over and developed the *Correspondance Littéraire*, a literary newsletter, originally started by the abbé Raynal. It was an extremely exclusive fortnightly report from Paris on books, poetry, the theatre, painting and sculpture. The fifteen or so subscribers, crowned heads, or princes of the Holy Roman Empire, received their copies through their embassies in Paris, which enabled Grimm to express himself fairly freely. Catherine was an early subscriber but her personal acquaintance with Grimm began when he escorted the young Landgraf of Hesse Darmstadt to St Petersburg, for the wedding of his sister Wilhelmina with Grand Duke Paul in September 1773.

Not, like Diderot, an enthusiastic and impractical hothead, Grimm may have appealed to Catherine by his sound German common sense, combined with wit and an unsuspected charm. From September 1773 to April 1774, he was frequently received in private tête-à-tête by Catherine and enjoyed the same kind of treatment as Diderot. He refused however to enter Russian service, and remain in St Petersburg, but when he left regular correspondence was established between the two, which continued without interruption until Catherine's last letter, dated a month before her death. Grimm paid a second visit to St Petersburg in 1776 (in time for the second marriage of Grand Duke Paul) and returned to Paris as Catherine's official agent, with a salary of 2,000 rubles per annum, in charge of her artistic and intellectual errands, and of confidential private undertakings (as for instance the supervision of her son by Grigory Orlov, Aleksey Bobrinsky, who was sowing a substantial crop of wild oats).

In a strange way, Grimm acted as a safety valve for Catherine – her whipping-boy (*souffre douleur*) as she always called him. To him, and to him only, among her correspondents, she wrote with the freedom she might have used to a brother or an uncle, while he never overstepped the bounds which marked him as her 'servant'. It was to Grimm that she could speak with boundless enthusiasm of her lovers, and pour out her grief when one of them – A.D. Lanskoy – died in 1784.

Closer contact with the thought of France and Germany and the flood of translations into Russian did not as yet lead to the production of original works of political significance by Russians. All the more remarkable therefore were the *Filozoficheskiye predlozheniya* ('Philosophical Propositions') of Ya. P. Kozel'sky, published on the Senate Press in 1768.[58] It can scarcely be called an original work, since it consists mainly of a series of numbered propositions on law, philosophy, politics, etc., which are drawn from contemporary eighteenth-century authors (notably as Kozel'sky himself admits, from Rousseau, Montesquieu, Helvetius, and an anonymous author who turns out to be Shaftesbury as remodelled by Diderot).[59] Kozel'sky does not discuss the form of government of Russia, but in general terms he accepts the social contract between ruler and ruled and he expresses a preference for republican forms of government, notably the Dutch Republic ('which in its simplicity and moderation considers itself and is considered as the happiest people in Europe').[60] He disapproved of great inequality of wealth, which allowed the rich to oppress the poor and fostered subservience in the latter (No. 415) ; he proposed an eight-hour day for work, leaving eight hours for enjoyment and eight for sleep (No. 426) and he believed in lightening the burden on the common people as the only means of civilizing them. He took his stand therefore on the principle : free the people if you want them to be enlightened, rather than on the more usual principle : when they are enlightened the people will deserve to be free. No organized system emerges from Kozel'sky's 'Propositions', but he was clearly a rationalist republican, and the total absence of any reference to religion as a source of morality, indeed to religion in any context, is remarkable.

If Kozel'sky drew his inspiration from French and German political theorists, his contemporary S.E. Desnitsky was primarily inspired by English and Scottish thinkers. Desnitsky had been sent to study in Glasgow University in 1761 and had heard the lectures of John Millar and Adam Smith.[61] On his return to Russia Desnitsky was appointed to lecture in Roman law in its application to Russian law at the University of Moscow,[62] and in 1773 he was appointed to the chair of Russian law (he was incidentally the first professor of law to lecture in Russian, not German or Latin). Both in Desnitsky's published works (a series of public addresses at the university), which dealt with a wide range of problems of jurisprudence and history of law, and in the 'Project for the Establishment of a Legislative, Judicial and Executive Power' in the Russian Empire which he submitted to Catherine in February 1768, the influence of English thought, notably that of Blackstone's *Commentaries on the Laws of England,* and of English practice is fundamental. The Project was not published until 1905, but Desnitsky's work at the university, and his free translation of Blackstone's *Commentaries* into Russian in the 1780s undoubtedly influenced the development of Russian knowledge of jurisprudence.

22

Favouritism

The appointment of G.A. Potemkin as adjutant general to the empress in winter 1774 not only marked a new phase in the political history of her reign. It opened a new and exciting page in Catherine's private life. A passionate love affair blazed out between the two of which many most human tokens have survived. Potemkin was extremely jealous of Catherine's past affairs and the letter she wrote to him, to justify herself, is a moving exposition of her own emotional pilgrimage. It is loving and humble, and shows her not as the Messalina of the North but as a woman who longed to love and be loved. 'Had it been my fate to have a husband whom I could love,' she wrote, 'I would never have changed towards him.' She explained the circumstances which had driven her first to Sergey Saltykov and then to Poniatowski. She had loved them and they had been taken away. She would never have dismissed Orlov had he not been unfaithful to her. Only in the case of Vasil'chikov, wrote Catherine, had she felt unhappy and ashamed. And so, she had sent for the 'hero' in the hope that his feelings for her were what she had been told they were.[1]

A further document illustrates the kind of quarrels that flared up between them and how they were settled :

In Potemkin's hand:

Let me at least say this, my love,
which will I hope end our dispute
Don't be surprised if I am
disturbed by our love.
Not only have you showered
good deeds on me, you have placed
me in your heart. I want to be
there alone, and above everyone else
because no one has ever loved you
so much; and as I have been made by
your hands, I want my peace to be the

In Catherine's hand:

I allow it
The sooner the better
Don't be disturbed

So have you on me
You are there, firmly
and strongly and will
remain there
I see it and believe it
In my heart I shall
be happy to do so

work of your hands, that you should be happy in being good to me; that you should find rest from the great labours arising from your high station in thinking of my comfort	*It will be my greatest pleasure* *Of course.*
Amen	*Give rest to our thoughts, and let our feelings act freely they are most tender, they will find the best way.* *End of quarrel* *Amen* [2]

Catherine's letters to Potemkin, many of which have survived because he carried them about in his pocket, are an extraordinary mixture of passionate and tender notes to her 'Muscovite', 'Pugachev of the Yaik' (of all things !), 'golden tiger', 'cossack', 'giaour' and straight business communications.[3] To some extent these letters bear out the supposition that Catherine and Potemkin were secretly married at a religious ceremony. In her letters she often calls him her husband, as in the following *billet :* 'mon mari m'a dit tantôt : "Where shall I go ? Where shall I put myself ?'' Mon cher et bien aimé époux, venez chez moi, vous serez reçu à bras ouverts.'[4] But perhaps because of its very intensity the physical passion of Catherine and Potemkin did not last, even though they continued in a somewhat unusual way to behave like a married couple for the rest of their lives, united by profound affection and absolute trust.

If one may speculate on the reasons why they ceased to be lovers, it seems that discord may have arisen, as Catherine once wrote to Potemkin, 'from power, not from love'. On the other hand there were frequent quarrels between them, nearly always arising from his jealousy or unkindness. 'My darling, are you not ashamed to have said what you did : he who will replace me will not survive me ! How can you try to keep a heart in bondage by fear ?' runs one of Catherine's letters to her stormy lover. On another occasion the empress of all the Russias turned sadly away from Potemkin's door, because his valet was with him.[5] No one can tell whether the initiative for the break came from her side or from his. Potemkin may have realized that he ran the risk of losing the substance – power – for the shadow – love – if he continued to weary Catherine with constant jealous outbursts. Catherine may have thought that Potemkin loved the empress more than the woman. Or she may have wearied of his embraces and hoped that she could keep the friend – possibly husband – if she left him the power and sought sexual satisfaction elsewhere, allowing him too to give full rein to the instincts of a pasha. The main actors in this domestic drama have left no records of their dialogue. But by the winter of 1776, gossip was rife at the Russian court, and Potemkin was thought by many to be 'on the way out'.

Catherine had already chosen her next lover. When Rumyantsev had arrived in Moscow in June 1775, to celebrate the end of the war with the Porte, he brought with him two young Ukrainians who were to make brilliant careers at court, P. V. Zavadovsky and A.A. Bezborodko. Both were well-educated and had served in Rumyantsev's chancery during the peace negotiations. There they laid the foundations of a life-long friendship with Simon R. Vorontsov. When Catherine asked Rumyantsev to recommend two young officials to her, he put forward the names of his two protégés. Zavadovsky was appointed secretary to the empress to receive petitions, and Bezborodko her secretary for her literary activity, to replace G. Kozitsky who had committed suicide. Zavadovsky was reputedly a very handsome man (in contrast to Bezborodko who was almost repulsive), and Catherine was not impervious to masculine good looks. The replacement of Potemkin by Zavadovsky was carried out with a discretion absent from Catherine's later affairs. He was mentioned by the English envoy, Gunning, in January, by the Frenchman Corberon in February 1776. In March, Potemkin was authorized to use the title of prince, conferred on him by the Holy Roman Emperor, a dignity which had accompanied Grigory Orlov's dismissal from favour.

The crisis in Catherine's relations with Potemkin coincided with a tragedy in the life of the Grand Duke Paul. For a while, in 1773, Catherine had arranged that her son should visit her several times a week to discuss policy. She envisaged this as a kind of tuition in statecraft (and Catherine prided herself throughout her life upon her ability to teach this subject), not as participation in government. She knew that if Paul were given an inch, circumstances would give him an ell. Should he be admitted to the Council, he might willy-nilly become the leader of an 'opposition party' for, when all was said and done, Catherine, in relation to Paul, was head of a 'governing party'. Her supporters were bound to oppose the grand duke in whom they would see the avenger of the murdered Peter III. Paul's popularity in the country did him a disservice in this respect ; the use made of his name by some of the plotters against Catherine in the 1760s and 1770s and above all by Pugachev, killed any hope of allowing him an active role in government.

Moreover closer contact with her son convinced Catherine that in their ideas and their temperaments they were poles apart. At the age of eighteen Paul was scarcely likely to have original views. It did not need much penetration to detect, in a memorandum he submitted to his mother, the influence of the two Panin brothers. Peace, wrote Paul, was the first requirement after the exhaustion of war. Russia should give up any offensive policy, withdraw behind fortified frontiers, manned by troops recruited from a hereditary caste of soldiers' children (a foretaste of Alexander I's military colonies) ; the most severe hierarchical subordination and discipline should be imposed as the only way of eliminating the existing inefficiency, corruption, and caprice.[6] Such a programme already hinted at Paul's faith in the militarization of society so alien to his mother's method of government. Meanwhile the young man found comfort in the joys of a happy marriage. His grand duchess, Natalia Alekseyevna, was seemingly all he could wish ; but she was not all that Catherine wished. She got into debt, which was to be expected ; but she also proved 'difficult'. She failed to learn Russian and she dabbled in politics. However she fulfilled her first obligation to the state and was expecting to be delivered in April 1776. Her labour was long and fruitless, and after five days she died. Her death unleashed a scandal of major dimensions. The opening of her private papers revealed the extent of her intimacy with one of Paul's closest friends, Aleksey Kirilovich Razumovsky, a son of the ex-het-man's.[7] According to court gossip, Natalia had been his mistress, the child was his. The gossip is to some extent substantiated by the fact that Catherine had at least once warned Paul about his wife's indiscretions ; and by the fact that Aleksey Razumovsky was ordered to leave the capital the day after the funeral and was subsequently appointed envoy to Naples and departed without being allowed to see the grand duke again.[8]

The autopsy performed on the grand duchess revealed that owing to a physical defect, she was unable to give birth to living children. This official version was at the time disbelieved in favour of an alternative one which stated that since an heir to the throne was essential, and the grand duchess would probably not be able to have further children, she had been deliberately allowed to die.[9] Catherine certainly took her daughter-in-law's death calmly ; on the day she died she jotted down a memorandum on the steps to be taken to procure the bride she had all along really wanted for her son, namely Princess Sophia Dorothea of Württemberg, who had been too young at the time of Paul's first marriage.[10]

Matters were rendered easier by the presence in St Petersburg of Prince Henry of Prussia on a second visit to Russia. Since the chosen bride was his great-niece, and the bonds between Russia and Prussia would thus again be strengthened by matrimony, Prince Henry set to work to remove all obstacles. Agreement was soon reached between the parties, and it was arranged that the young people should meet in Berlin. Foreign travel was just what Paul needed to comfort him, not so much for the loss of his wife as for the stinging humiliation of his betrayal, and he departed towards the end of June, accompanied by Prince Henry and escorted by a galaxy of Russian notables. Gossip at court now reverted to the topic of the imminent fall of Potemkin from favour. Some thought that Grigory Orlov would recover his old place, and that his brother Aleksey would be given the College of War. Meanwhile, evidently by arrangement with Catherine, Potemkin left on a journey of inspection through the guberniya of Novgorod on 23 June/4 July, pursued by affectionate letters from the empress, and received everywhere with triumphal arches.[11] Catherine turned a deaf ear to Aleksey Orlov's demands that she should dismiss Potemkin ; she was equally deaf to Potemkin's request for the dismissal of Zavadovsky.[12] Rumour was piled on rumour, but within a month Potemkin was back in his rooms in the palace.

In Berlin meanwhile, Frederick spared no expense in the effort to win over the grand duke. Money was poured out on parades, receptions, triumphal arches, and Paul's head was somewhat turned by attentions to which he was not accustomed at home. The young couple took an immediate liking to each other ; not only was Sophia Dorothea young and healthy, she was also beautiful and good-natured. Anxious to hurry on the wedding, Paul returned to Russia at the end of August 1776, followed a few days later by his fiancée. Catherine too was enchanted with her future daughter-in-law, who was quickly convinced by an enlightened Lutheran pastor and an enlightened Orthodox priest that there was little difference between Lutheranism and Orthodoxy. The wedding took place on 26 September/7 October 1776, with the same ceremonial and public rejoicings which had accompanied Paul's first marriage. What is more, the new Grand Duchess Maria Fyodorovna set about fulfilling her duty to the dynasty with commendable promptitude. Her first son, the future Alexander I, was born on 12/23 December 1777. The changed scene at court was completed when Zavadovsky officially became favourite in November 1776.

But though Potemkin ceased to be Catherine's lover in winter 1776, he continued to play a crucial part in her private, and public, life, until the day of his death in 1791. In the 1770s, while he was still climbing up the ladder of fortune, he was distinguished by a lively intelligence, quick understanding, unusual memory, ambition, audacity, and willingness to defend what he thought right. Such at least was the verdict of his nephew [13] and it is supported by other contemporary accounts. In these years, Potemkin could still abide by certain rules of courtesy to the empress and to other courtiers, and had not yet become the spoilt child of fortune. As his ascendancy was more firmly established, and as he grew older, he indulged in eccentricities of behaviour which shocked both domestic and foreign opinion. He would receive the foreign envoys lolling on his bed, clad in a fur robe and slippers and no more. The French envoy, the Comte de Ségur, describes how, having been treated in this way, he invited Potemkin to dinner, with other guests who were forewarned, and received the favourite in precisely the same garb. Potemkin, typically, was not offended ; but he took the hint and subsequently either received Ségur fully dressed, or at least apologized for his informality. He continued however to wander through the palace to visit the empress clad in his dressing-gown or in his uniform cloak, with a pink bandanna round his head. [14]

Able and original, with a great capacity for going intuitively to the essence of things, Potemkin was also devout, even superstitious, and passionately interested in Church history ; his attention could always be aroused by the topic of the schism between the Greek and Latin Churches, the Councils of Nicaea or Florence. [15] In this respect he provided a valuable counterpoise to the Voltairean court, since his personal relationships with the hierarchy and the humble priesthood – of all faiths – served to bridge the gap between the westernized state and the common people. Indeed of all Catherine's lovers and public servants, Potemkin was undoubtedly the most Russian, the least affected by the chill rationalism of the West. He was cast rather in the antique Russian heroic mould, a *bogatyr* or hero, as was Aleksey Orlov. In his achievements as in his failures, he was slightly larger than life. He could change in a moment from the slovenly layabed, bellowing out his orders, to the exquisitely dressed courtier ; arrogance turned into easy affability, laziness became bustling energy, gaiety and good humour became deadly spleen. Of his capacity to charm when he felt so inclined contemporaries provide eloquent evidence. As Sir James Harris wrote of him, 'he discovered a mixture of wit, levity, learning and humour I never met in the same man'.[16] Women certainly found him attractive judging by his many successes.[17] A patron of the arts, literature and particularly music, Potemkin's extravagances in the field of clothing, jewelry, the table, carriages, horses, palaces and gardens, became legendary. He was in the unique position of disposing of all the resources needed to conjure into existence every image presented to him by his imagination, every whim of his capricious nature. As a result he was frequently overwhelmed by satiety, and lapsed into total prostration. The one pleasure he was deprived of, he once complained, was the pleasure of having to wait for something he had asked for.[18] At the same time he was distinguished by a Puckish sense of humour, great generosity to friends and to the needy, coupled with meanness about paying debts to tradesmen and craftsmen. His total absence of vindictiveness made his ascendancy somewhat less unbearable.

The probability of Potemkin's secret marriage to Catherine is confirmed by the self-confidence with which he acted, and the manner in which he was treated to all intents and purposes as a consort, with public honours and private privileges. With the assumption of the title of prince of the Holy Roman Empire in 1776, Potemkin became known throughout the land as *svyatleyshiy,* His Serene Highness. When he left the capital in 1786 to visit his southern territories, he was received everywhere with as much ceremonial as the heir to the throne.[19] Their long and frequent correspondence, for even when they were under the same roof Catherine and Potemkin usually exchanged notes more than once a day, is marked by a mixture of business and personal matters ; it switches from Catherine's inquiries about Potemkin's health to questions of high policy, from Russian to French, from the formal 'you' to the familiar 'thou'. Potemkin wrote to his *matushka gosudarynya* ('little mother, sovereign lady') and Catherine to her *knyazyushka* ('princeling').

Meanwhile Potemkin's many love affairs with ladies of the court, above all with his five nieces, caused public scandal but did not offend Catherine. Indeed Potemkin's eldest niece Alexandra remained one of Catherine's closest friends. Neither Potemkin's affairs nor Catherine's 'pupils' weakened the extraordinary domestic link between these two. Yet it must not be assumed that Potemkin had it all his own way. Catherine could and did disapprove of his plans, and often rejected his suggestions. While they were still lovers, Potemkin sulked and raged and created scenes of jealousy ; once he was certain of his power, he learnt to be more flexible and accommodating, both with Catherine herself and with others. After a time, wrote the Prussian envoy Goertz, even those who hated him most learnt to live with him, on the principle that if he were toppled, he might be replaced by someone even worse.[20]

It was in Catherine's nature to be recklessly generous to her lovers, but even her generosity could not satisfy Potemkin's vast needs. Though he used public and private funds indiscriminately for public and private purposes, he always needed more. Catherine lavished on him porcelain dinner services, silver plate, jewels, several estates including one of some 1,000 square miles and 14,000 serfs in Belorussia, and hundreds of thousands of rubles to pay his debts.[21] Potemkin himself was constantly buying and selling his properties, and took an active interest in the exploitation of their natural resources. He owned glass and porcelain factories, and his estates in Belorussia developed into a thriving industrial complex supplying naval stores to Kherson.[22]

Potemkin's avidity was not merely the consequence of his ostentation. There was a hidden method behind his accumulation of wealth, which arose from the danger implicit in his own position. He could rely on the empress, but he knew (and undoubtedly so did Catherine) that with her death he might be exposed to disgrace, if not exile and the total loss of his fortune at the hands of Paul. Relations between Grigory Orlov and the grand duke had always been strained. With Potemkin, Paul was on even worse terms, because, thanks to the influence of Nikita Panin, Paul remained wedded to the Russo-Prussian alliance which Potemkin was out to undermine.

The vulnerability of his position (whether married to Catherine or not) led Potemkin to toy from the beginning of his favour with the idea of finding for himself a secure base outside the borders of Russia. At first he had thought of Curland and in May 1776 Catherine had instructed her envoy in Warsaw, Count Stackelberg, to begin the long process by which Poland might agree to remove the existing Duke Peter of the Biron family, in favour of her ex-lover.[23] The plan came to nothing and next Poland, then Moldavia and Walachia attracted the prince. Potemkin's constant buying and selling of estates indicates the areas to which his interests were directed. In 1775 he acquired the Polish 'indigenat', which entitled him to be regarded as naturalized in Poland. At one time it was rumoured that he hoped to make a principality for himself in Crimea. Later, it was believed that Catherine intended to make him King of Greece.[24] The most substantial of these rumours, one which is actually confirmed by Potemkin's own actions, was the plan to create a base for himself in Poland. As early as the spring of 1781, at the time of the signature of the secret Austro-Russian treaty, Potemkin was already reported to be heaping up ready money by selling estates, horses and jewels, with a view to placing his assets outside Russia.[25] In the autumn, Cobenzl reported to Joseph that the prince had made large purchases of land in Poland.[26]

As vice-president of the College of War and a member of the Council, Potemkin played a large part in the formulation of foreign policy. He shared Catherine's enthusiasm for the 'Greek project' and was the prime mover in the *rapprochement* with Austria in 1781. Inevitably he clashed with Nikita Panin in a battle for personal and political influence. Nikita Panin clung to his own Prussian-oriented 'Northern system' in part because it was supported by the Grand Duke Paul, with whose interests and possible future reign Panin had increasingly identified himself. Quarrels over foreign policy between the two men reached unheard of depths of acrimony in 1780.[27]

These quarrels had their repercussions in Catherine's relations with her son. After attempting, briefly, to win over Paul in 1774, Potemkin gave up. He ceased to attend the grand ducal receptions at Pavlovsk, the delightful palace Catherine had given Paul for his own use, and treated Paul with the same careless arrogance he used towards all except those he wished to charm.

Increasingly in the late 1770s, the 'young court' had begun to pose difficulties for Catherine. Paul's second marriage was a happy one. Probably genuinely fond of her husband, the grand duchess treated him with respect, and brought out his best qualities in the domestic circle. By providing him with a sphere in which he was undoubted master, his happy private life gave greater depth and harmony to the suspicious and unstable Paul. Nevertheless, his relations with his mother did not improve. He, above all, suffered from the presence of his mother's favourites. The vast sums bestowed by Catherine on them, particularly on Potemkin, must have further underlined to the perpetually indebted Paul the difference in their situations. Ever resentful of his exclusion from power, he suffered too from Catherine's complete disregard of his every proposal for the public weal. Moreover Paul's admiration of Frederick II made him into such a bitter opponent of his mother's foreign policy, as to carry him to the verge of sedition.

Possibly in order to convince Paul of the value of an Austrian alliance, Catherine early in 1781 indirectly suggested to the grand ducal couple that they should set out on a European tour, which would take in Vienna, Italy, Montbeliard, Paris and Dresden but which pointedly excluded Prussia, to the great disappointment of Paul. When the grand duke, suspicious as ever of his mother's designs, discovered that the plan originated with her, he acquired the conviction that she intended to exclude him from the succession and prevent his return to Russia.[28] His departure, on which, however, Catherine appeared determined, was fixed for mid-September 1781. The tension between mother and son was further heightened by the dismissal of Nikita Panin from the College of Foreign Affairs in September 1781.[29] The dismissed minister made one last-ditch attempt to persuade Paul and the grand duchess not to leave Russia, but they were finally bundled into their carriage on 1 October 1781.[30] On his journey abroad, Paul was to be escorted by a suite appointed by his mother ; he felt himself to be surrounded by spies and it was only after much pleading that he was allowed the company of his childhood friend and constant companion, A.B. Kurakin (great-nephew and ward of Nikita Panin). Inevitably Potemkin and the pro-Austrian party at court planned to take the slightest advantage of any carelessness on Paul's part and to watch his correspondence with his friends in Russia.[31] During the grand duke's stay in Vienna Joseph II informed him of the signature of a secret Austro-Russian treaty in May/June 1781. Paul accepted the news with apparent calm, but his real feelings were expressed in an outburst in Florence to Leopold of Tuscany in which he accused Potemkin, A.R. Vorontsov, Bezborodko, and those responsible for the Austro-Russian treaty of accepting Austrian gold ; 'Je les ferai ausruthen et je les casserai et chasserai, . . .' he declared.[32]

What Paul's enemies expected duly happened. P.A. Bibikov, a young officer (son of the marshal of the Legislative Commission) was imprudent enough to write from Russia in April 1782 by official courier to A.B. Kurakin. The letter was of course intercepted ; it proved to contain aspersions on Catherine's policy and on Potemkin ('le borgne'), as well as hopes for the future, and expressions of Bibikov's determination to prove, by deeds, his attachment to the grand duke.[33] Bibikov was arrested and interrogated at length about letters which the courier was allegedly also carrying from Panin and others but nothing further was found. He was exiled without trial to Astrakhan', where he died soon after of a fever, and A.B. Kurakin, on his return to Russia, was sent to live on his family estates for the rest of Catherine's reign, though he was later allowed to visit Paul every two years. He had been one of the channels through which Paul had communicated with the Prussian envoy, which may explain the severity with which he was treated.[34]

The flattering welcome accorded everywhere to the Comte and Comtesse du Nord (an incognito which annoyed Gustavus III since it seemed to lay claim to the whole of the North for Russia) served to increase Paul's sense of his own importance and made his return to Russia and insignificance all the harder to bear. The grand duchess was met merely with an order prohibiting the adoption of the fashionable high head-dress for women which put paid to her hopes of introducing French fashions into Russia – procured at great expense from the famous Mademoiselle Bertin. 'The hair is not to exceed the height of 2 inches and a half, and the whole of the regulation (wise and judicious for more than one reason) tends to reduce the ornaments of the private person to a natural and decent standard,' as Sir James Harris put it.[35] On his arrival, Paul found that his 'party', in so far as he had ever had one, had been decimated in his absence. At the College of Foreign Affairs he no longer had any friends – even Denis I. Fonvizin had resigned in spring 1782. Peter Panin lived permanently in Moscow ; Nikita Panin, whose health had collapsed after Paul's departure, continued gravely ill. Paul visited the fallen minister on his return, then failed for some time either to call or even to enquire. Had he been led to fear Catherine's displeasure by the letters of Peter Panin, complaining of the 'terrible examples' of repressions directed against 'whole legions of sons for only opposing despotism' ?[36] But at least Paul and his wife were present at the deathbed of the man who had in fact been the grand duke's friend and protector for twenty-three years.[37]

Before his death, which took place in April 1783, Nikita Panin allegedly dictated to Denis Fonvizin his political testament, the remarkable document entitled *A Discourse on Fundamental Laws of State*. This discourse may represent Panin's views, but more recent scholarship attributes it to Fonvizin. The author argues that just as God is almighty because he can do nothing but good, and has therefore 'instituted principles of everlasting truth, unalterable by Himself . . . which he himself cannot transgress without ceasing to be God', so the enlightened ruler institutes permanent laws which he cannot infringe without ceasing to be a worthy sovereign.[38] A ruler cannot be worthy unless he accepts the necessity of safeguarding freedom and property by means of fundamental laws, adapted 'to the physical situation of the state and the moral temper of his nation'. After what is in effect an apologia for enlightened absolutism, founded on a society divided into estates, each with its privileges, Fonvizin, in an impassioned passage, describes a country in which the succession is at the mercy of bestial hordes in taverns, no estates possess established privileges, there is no code of laws, men own other men ; a state which is not despotic, since it has courts of law ; not monarchic, since it has no fundamental laws ; not aristocratic since it is administered by a soulless machine and not democratic since the common people bear 'the yoke of cruel slavery'.

There is a suggestion in the *Discourse* that an enlightened monarch will begin his rule by issuing fundamental laws to heal the country of the evils brought upon it by absolute rule (though Fonvizin warns of the danger of a sudden and unprepared grant of privileges such as European nations have long enjoyed). The enlightened monarch, it was assumed, was to be Paul I, since Fonvizin's *Discourse* was in all probability written as the introduction to a manifesto to be issued by Paul on his accession, drafted by Peter Panin. More in sorrow than in anger, Panin, in the draft manifesto, in a sentence of twenty-seven printed lines, described the suffering of the heir, forced to watch the corruption and abuses of the government. The fundamental laws he then proposed in no way limited the power of the ruler, in the formal sense, but provided for the laying down of certain permanent procedures to deal with administration, taxation, justice, and civil rights. The rights of landowners over their serfs and the duties of serfs to landowners were to be defined. In the event, it is doubtful whether Fonvizin's *Discourse* or Peter Panin's constitutional draft reached the grand duke's hands.[39]

If anything could serve to exacerbate even further relations between Paul and Potemkin, it was the latter's policy as president of the College of War. Paul envied above all others the role of supreme war lord which Frederick II had so effectively played. But he was forced merely to watch, while Potemkin reformed the Russian army. The prince's influence in this field is harder for the nonspecialist to assess. Many of his innovations were strongly criticized by his contemporaries, but they not infrequently had their own axes to grind. He was accused of placing too much emphasis on light cavalry and particularly on Cossack forces.[40] Others complained of the indiscipline encouraged allegedly by Potemkin's desire to win popularity among the common soldiers.[41] He certainly won their affection by redesigning their uniforms. In a memorandum to Catherine Potemkin argued that the mistake of the foreign officers in the Russian army had been to equate *regulyarstvo* (i.e. discipline, what the Cossacks so desperately feared) with 'pigtails, hats, pocket flaps, and facings. . . .' 'Was it a soldier's business', he asked, 'to curl and powder and braid his hair ? They have no valets, what do they want curls for ? What is better, just to wash and comb his hair, or to weigh himself down with powder, grease, flour, curlpins, braids ? A soldier's toilette should be : up and ready !'[42] He also abolished tight uniforms and gaiters and replaced them with loose tunics, loose breeches falling over short boots, loose cloaks, and round felt caps with a leather visor against the sun.[43]

The prince also attempted to humanize the treatment of soldiers by officers, and the treatment of officers themselves in the military regulations,[44] and he showed concern for supplies and medical services.[45] His common sense and humane approach left its mark on the soldiers. One of Potemkin's one time aides-de-camp once asked an old grenadier whom the soldiers had liked better, Potemkin or Rumyantsev. The answer is most revealing of the quality of the two men : 'He [Potemkin] was our father, he made service lighter, he fulfilled our wants, we were his spoilt children. We'll never have such a commander again.' But of Rumyantsev the old grenadier said 'though life was hard, service was gay . . . he inspired us with a special sense of courage'.[46]

To Paul, Potemkin's uniforms and training methods were anathema. On the death of Grigory Orlov in 1783, the estate of Gatchina which Catherine had once given to her lover was now granted to her son. Paul withdrew to the country and proceeded to build up what he regarded as a model army and a model village. He conscripted (as admiral-in-chief) a number of sailors and engaged a Prussian drill master ('He will be to me what Lefort was to Peter the Great'). By 1788 Paul's private army consisted of five companies clothed in tightly buttoned uniforms, huge boots, wigs and all the paraphernalia of the Frederician army, and drilled to exhaustion. The village of Gatchina itself lived under the benevolent but tyrannical eye of its new master.[47]

By withdrawing to Gatchina, Paul to some extent shielded himself from the spectacle of his mother's court and the glaring procession of her favourites. Zavadovsky's ascendancy did not last long. Potemkin was still jealous enough to nip in the bud any effort to rival him as a public figure. Zavadovsky was not a boy, and judging by his subsequent career he must have sought to be more than a kept man. Maybe the touch of narrow-minded pedantry and mean-mindedness he was to reveal later in life bored Catherine. At any rate by the summer of 1777 he was given six months' leave, a pension of 5,000 r.p.a., 80,000 rubles, 1,800 serfs in Little Russia and 2,000 in Poland and plate to the value of 81,500 rubles. He withdrew from court life for a while but in 1780 he was appointed to the rank of privy councillor and in 1781 director of the State Bank (which was founded largely on a plan put forward by him). Subsequently he was actively involved in

Catherine's educational projects. Zavadovsky was the only one of Catherine's lovers (other than Potemkin) to make a career in public service after his favour ceased. Politically he gravitated towards his early friends, Bezborodko and the Vorontsovs, to form the nucleus of a group of efficient bureaucrats opposed to the unpredictable and arbitrary Potemkin.[48]

With the dismissal of Zavadovsky the procession of Catherine's favourites acquired an outrageous character. The empress imposed her lovers on the Russian court by making of favouritism an institution. The current favourite was appointed to the post of adjutant to the empress, given high army rank and apartments conveniently situated near hers in the various palaces. From then on, he accompanied the empress everywhere, attended her in the evening at court receptions, played cards with her, and withdrew with her. As the empress grew older, the favourites became younger and the disparity in age became more striking.

Simon Zorich, who followed Zavadovsky for a year, was thirty-two. Of Serbian origin he was distinguished by great courage in the field and had been a prisoner of war in Turkey for five years. In May 1777 he was adjutant to Potemkin, and by June his name was already being mentioned as the next favourite. Very handsome, he was of limited intelligence and little culture ; by February 1778 he was on the way out and in May, he was dismissed and withdrew to an estate in Belorussia, Shklov, where he lived in immense style. His only claim to fame was the foundation in Shklov of a cadet school for nobles which became the nucleus of the future Moscow Army Cadet School. He was a compulsive gambler and ended his days in disgrace under Paul for embezzling army funds.[49]

Zorich was replaced by I.N. Rimsky Korsakov, then twenty-four, whose tenure of the position was very brief since he was discovered in the throes of an affair with the Countess Bruce, Catherine's principal lady-in-waiting and for long one of her closest friends. The whole court gossiped about the countess's passion for Korsakov, long before the empress was aware of his infidelity.[50] In her letters to Grimm Catherine raves about Korsakov's beauty ; he was so handsome, that he was 'l'écueil des peintres, le désespoir des sculpteurs'. By October 1779 Korsakov was on his way to Moscow, where he was joined not by Countess Bruce, who went back to her husband, the governor-general of Moscow, Yacov Bruce, but by the wife of one of Catherine's great magnates, Count A.S. Stroganov.[51]

For some six months Catherine marked time, but in spring 1780 a new favourite was appointed. A.D. Lanskoy, then aged twenty-two (Catherine was fifty-one), had served in the Horse Guards and had been for some months aide-de-camp to Potemkin. Catherine may have noticed him earlier, but at any rate not until Easter 1780 was he officially installed in the apartments which had been vacated by Korsakov. Catherine seems to have inspired real devotion in Lanskoy. His education had been modest (he came from a good but provincial and impoverished family) but he was genuinely interested in learning and in painting and architecture. Catherine found him 'kind, gay, honest and full of gentleness', so much so that according to contemporary gossip, when her eye wandered in spring 1781 towards a rival, and Lanskoy was heartbroken at the thought of leaving her, she relented, and their relationship was resumed with greater mutual attachment than ever. Some of Lanskoy's relatives benefited by his position, and his sisters, married to modest nobles, were appointed ladies of the bedchamber. He took no part in political life, and refused to act as a channel to the empress. It was generally agreed that he did more good than harm. But Catherine was again unlucky. Having established a relationship which seemed to be lasting, death intervened. Gossip attributed Lanskoy's death to the use of aphrodisiacs ; but the medical evidence suggests that it was diphtheria which swept him off in six days on 25 June 1784. Catherine was heartbroken : 'je suis plongée dans la douleur la plus vive et mon bonheur n'est plus,' she wrote to Baron Grimm on 2/13 July.[52] Bezborodko sent at once for Potemkin, then in his southern guberniya, and by 10/21 July he was at Catherine's side. He comforted the empress by 'howling' with her – indeed, according to the Austrian envoy Cobenzl, in moments of real distress for Catherine Potemkin reverted to his role of husband.[53] Catherine could not bear Tsarskoye Selo without Lanskoy and did not return there that summer, nor did she appear again in public until September. In the capital she also refused to return to her apartments in the Winter Palace and stayed in the adjoining Hermitage until February 1785. Her grief was deeply felt and sincere, and she was still writing to Grimm about the virtues of Lanskoy on the anniversary of his death.[54] One virtue Lanskoy certainly had : he was not interested. On his death he bequeathed the vast fortune he had made as favourite to the empress. It was Catherine who then distributed it among his relatives.

Catherine's next venture was unsuccessful and lasted but a few months, A.P. Yermolov was thirty and was also serving as aide de camp to Potemkin. He seems to have been a perfect cypher, and he made the mistake of allowing himself to be used by Potemkin's enemies to criticize the prince to the empress. He was promptly dismissed in July 1786.[55]

After Yermolov came Alexander Dmitriyev Mamonov, aged twenty-six. Distantly related to Potemkin, he was of course handsome, but also well educated, fluent in French and Italian, fond of music, lively and interested in public affairs. He was the most cultured and intelligent of Catherine's younger lovers and he acquired a good deal of influence at court. Catherine was anxious to educate him for public as well as private office and to advance his career, but after a while relations between the two became strained, as Mamonov attempted to evade his engagements and showed signs of finding his life with Catherine burdensome. The growing tension is reflected in the laconic entries in his diary made by Catherine's secretary A.V. Khrapovitsky : 'tears' ; or 'after dinner Potemkin made peace'. His favour lasted until June 1789.[56]

The stories about Catherine's love life are legion; its drama has been inflated to the extent that it arouses more interest than her statecraft. It is as well therefore to stress that there is no evidence of any kind to support the more colourful tales, such as the alleged tests of virility carried out by Catherine's ladies-in-waiting, Countess Bruce, or Anna Protasova (the 'éprouveuse' of Byron's Don Juan), or the alleged vetting for venereal disease carried out by Dr J. Roggerson. There is also no evidence that Potemkin chose Catherine's lovers for her, a story probably based on the fact that three of them had been his aides-de-camp, and that Catherine was more likely to notice young men who were about the court. As for the tales of multiple orgies in Catherine's declining years, they can be dismissed as inventions.[57] Nothing at all is known for certain about the intimacies of Catherine's sexual life, and one can only speculate. But much is known about her emotional life. Not that she paraded it in public ; she was reserved, indeed prudish, particularly in her later years. Ségur tells the story of his attempt to amuse the empress with a slightly *risqué* joke, when riding in her sledge on their travels in 1787. The empress was not amused and turned the subject.[58] She found Beaumarchais's *Le Mariage de Figaro* objectionable because, unlike in Molière's plays, obscenity and *double entendre* were dragged in for effect.[59] In public Catherine's favourites were treated as particularly high officials of the court, travelling with her in her carriage and attending her at all times. The prominence given to immature young men, the patience with which Catherine listened to them or even gave in to them, was commented upon adversely by the more stuffy of her guests, such as Joseph II, who felt the injury to his imperial dignity in waiting on the caprices of a Dmitriyev Mamonov.[60] But in public all was conducted with decorum.

It is in her letters to Grimm and to Potemkin, that Catherine allows full vent to her feelings. To Grimm she poured out her hopes, she described her activities, the way she educated her young men for statecraft. Her affection for 'Pyrrhus, king of Epirus' (Rimsky Korsakov), 'Red Coat' (Mamonov), or 'The Black One' (Zubov), is in every line she writes about them. All her geese were swans – never were there such wonderful young men. Her remarks on the death of Lanskoy suggest a further dimension of her relationships. She saw Lanskoy as a permanency : 'J'espérai qu'il deviendrait l'appui de ma vieillesse . . . c'était un jeune homme que j'élevai. . . .'[61]

If one surveys the known story of Catherine and her lovers, it is possible to detect a pattern which explains some at least of her vagaries. Her own emotional and sexual life had been submitted to a number of very severe strains : married at fourteen to a husband who remained impotent or indifferent for more than eight years ; urged to produce an heir by a lover of her choice ; frustrated in her maternal feelings first of all by the physical deprivation of her children inflicted on her by Elizabeth, then by the political fact of life that her son Paul was her most dangerous rival and her son by Orlov, Bobrinsky, could not be acknowledged, it is not surprising if Catherine began to suffer from certain emotional deformations. But the most serious strain in all probability was the fact that she could not 'hold' her lovers. True, Poniatowski had genuinely loved her and had continued to do so, but he had been removed. Saltykov and Orlov had both been unfaithful, and even Potemkin, the one 'great love', had broken away. This may have been the ultimate psychological shock. Until that moment (except in the case of Vasil'chikov) Catherine had been wooed like any other woman by men who loved her or merely wished to seduce her. From now on, she did the choosing, and she seems to have divided her emotional life into two categories : Potemkin was the friend, colleague, partner, the confidant whom she trusted utterly, in spite of their quarrels, the one person with whom all pretences could be dropped, probably her husband, possibly intermittently her lover, a man whose love for her continued though he no longer desired her. On the other hand there were the young lovers who satisfied her sexually but at the same time allowed her to give vent to her maternal instincts, to her deep passion for 'educating' (so clearly expressed in her Nakaz and in many of her legislative projects as well as in her relations with her grandchildren). For Catherine sought more than handsome animals in her lovers. Those who showed a genuine interest in her intellectual or artistic pursuits or a positive attitude to matters of government were assured of a lasting relationship.

There is no doubt that the magnificent Prince of Tauris, the title granted by Catherine to Potemkin in 1787, threw all his rivals at the Russian court into the shade. It has also been argued that he deliberately surrounded Catherine with his own creatures, eliminating the old nobility, and also that he championed the interests of the medium and lower nobility (from which he sprang) who supported the autocracy against the so-called 'aristocratic constitutionalists', such as N.I. Panin, or the Vorontsovs. These propositions are very difficult to substantiate. There was certainly between 1777 and 1785–6 a considerable change in the high personnel at the Russian court. Many prominent figures retired or died in these years, notably Nikita Panin in April 1783, who was followed by his brother Peter in 1789. Grigory Orlov went mad in the autumn of 1782. To the surprise of her courtiers and of the British envoy, Catherine behaved to her former lover with a humanity rare in those days in the treatment of lunatics. Though he occasionally burst out into obscure references to repentance for past ill deeds, Catherine 'absolutely forbids any harsh methods to be employed, rejects all ideas of confinement or discipline . . . and . . . admits him at all hours and in all dresses'.[62] Orlov died in 1783, and was always remembered by Catherine with affection, admiration and gratitude.[63] Field-Marshal A.M. Golitsyn, governor of St Petersburg, died in 1783 ; Field-Marshal Z.G. Chernyshev, governor of Moscow, in 1784. Between 1779 and 1789, nineteen senators died, as compared with eight who died between 1762 and 1779.[64]

More to the point, what criteria can be used to define an 'old' noble ? In eighteenth-century Russia, there were very 'old' nobles who were too poor and too insignificant to play any part in politics. Basically an 'old' noble was a man who thought and behaved like an 'old' noble, and who succeeded on grounds of rank or wealth or both in being accepted into the magic circle of self-defined aristocratic magnates. But these great magnates, in the eighteenth century, were mostly 'new' families, who had come to the fore because they were related to the wives of tsars, like the Naryshkins and the Skavronskys ; or through favouritism, like the Vorontsovs, the Shuvalovs, the Razumovskys, the Orlovs ; or through service, like the Chernyshevs, Rumyantsev and the Panins.[65] A careful study of the incumbents of the most important posts in Catherine's imperial and local administration, in the court, the army, the navy, and the foreign service shows that on the whole, and particularly at the highest level, the turnover of public servants was small.

Of all Catherine's high officials Zakhar Chernyshev was the one who suffered most, since Potemkin wanted, and got, his post. But otherwise many of Potemkin's alleged enemies showed remarkable powers of survival : A.A. Vyazemsky remained procurator general and member of the Council until 1792 ; Ivan G. Chernyshev, appointed vice-president of the Admiralty in 1768 (the Grand Duke Paul was president), remained in office, and a member of the Council, until Catherine's death. A.R. Vorontsov was president of the College of Commerce from 1773 to 1793 (when he voluntarily retired, after Potemkin's death). Moreover, when the Council was reformed with an influx of new blood in 1787, the new members included A.R. Vorontsov, General N.I. Saltykov, Count V.P. Musin Pushkin and A.P. Shuvalov. The parvenus on the council were A.A. Bezborodko and P.V. Zavadovsky, scarcely creatures of Potemkin. So in other posts at court the names of old or accepted families were constantly to be found, often for many years at a stretch. Moreover, if after 1775 many of the great magnates of the early part of Catherine's reign were absent from court, it was in great part due to the enormous demands on highly skilled, able manpower to staff the new institutions created by the Statute of 1775. Catherine made use of every capable man available in positions of great responsibility and enormous authority. Leading generals like Rumyantsev, Z. Chernyshev, N.V. Repnin, and Potemkin himself, were appointed to sensitive frontier guberniyas, or combined the posts of governor and commander-in-chief in one or other of the capital cities. Here too, where possible, Catherine seems to have preferred to leave a governor for some time : as for instance that remarkable Irishman, General George Browne, who entered Russian service in 1730, was appointed governor of Livonia in 1762 and of Livonia and Estonia in 1775, and died at the ripe age of ninety-four in office, in 1792. Again, shortage of qualified personnel imposed a certain amount of movement. It is however impossible to detect in these changes any deliberate elimination of Potemkin's enemies. The magnates who sulked in Moscow were in the first place Aleksey Orlov, and P.I. Panin, who were not old nobles ; Catherine's ex-lovers (Rimsky Korsakov, Dmitriyev Mamonov, who belonged to old families !) and in the 1780s the circle of intellectual *frondeurs* who sought refuge from the aridity of the Petersburg enlightenment in the joys of Freemasonry.

23

The Viceroy of the South

First as governor-general of New Russia, a post to which he was appointed on 31 March 1774, then in 1775 as governor-general of the newly formed gubernii of Azov and New Russia,[1] and in 1785 of the guberniya of Yekaterinoslav and the district of Tauris (Crimea), Potemkin became *de facto* viceroy of Southern Russia and indisputable ruler from the Bug to the Caspian.

The first problem which faced Potemkin in his new role was the reorganization of the Cossack Hosts in order to forestall any future outbreak similar to the disastrous Pugachevshchina, and the first of the Cossack Hosts to be brought to heel were inevitably the Yaik Cossacks. Those who were not deported were placed under a trusted ataman appointed by the government. Regular troops were stationed in the area, and the town and the river were renamed Ural'sk and Ural. The Volga Host was also broken up and most of the Cossacks transferred to the Terek line and to the Caucasus.[2]

The Don Cossacks presented a more serious problem. They had fought well against the Turks, and they had not followed Pugachev. But the tendency to separatism which had been briefly manifested in 1772 might presage danger to the state. Potemkin therefore drafted a new Statute for the Don Cossacks, drawing on the projects which had been prepared in the sub-commissions of the Legislative Commission. The new Statute was promulgated in a manifesto on 15 February 1775. It divided the administration of the Cossack Host into a military and a civil branch. The former was left to the Cossack hierarchy, who thus continued to organize their military contribution to the defence of Russia in the traditional way. The civil branch, covering justice and taxation, was placed in the hands of elected and appointed officials under the ultimate authority of the civilian institutions of the guberniya. The Cossacks thus ceased to be a self-governing autonomous community. Their capital, Cherkassk, and their lands, were included in the guberniya of Azov.[3]

The assimilation of the Don Cossacks to the Russian state was furthered by partial Russia acceptance of the starshina's demand to be considered on a par with the Russian dvoryanstvo. The manifesto of February 1775 laid down that commanders of regiments (polki) should be considered as having attained officer's rank, and hence hereditary nobility. But lower Cossack officer ranks did not qualify for nobility, and commanders of polki were below majors in the Russian army.[4]

There remained the Zaporozhian Host. Its performance in the Russo-Turkish war had been praised in a special proclamation issued by its new commander-in-chief, G.A. Potemkin himself, on 21 June 1774. But the treaty of Kuchuk Kainardzhi spelled the end of the Zaporozhian Host. They were always trouble-makers, encroaching on the lands of New Russia or Slobodska Ukraine in a manner indistinguishable from brigandage. After the peace treaty with the Porte, the Host put forward a claim to the lands between the Bug and the Dniepr ceded by the Turks,[5] thus confirming the impression that it regarded itself as an *imperium in imperio* with a definite territorial basis.[6] But from the Russian point of view, once the Crimea was independent, the Zaporozhian Host had ceased to perform the function of a frontier defence force against potential Turkish aggression. The Russian government was much more interested in the exploitation of this rich land by colonization and settlement, protected by stable civilian government.

The solution put forward by Potemkin was the destruction of the Zaporozhian *kosh* and the dispersal of the Host. His policy was approved by Catherine and by the Council, and on 6 June 1775 a detachment of the regular army appeared before the Zaporozhian headquarters on the Dnieper and summoned the Cossacks to surrender. The three thousand Cossacks present at the time gave in without a blow. The last hetman, P. Kal'nyshevsky, and other members of the starshina, were arrested and interned in monastery prisons. Kal'nyshevsky, a wealthy man by any standards, and already eighty-two years old, was conveyed in state to the Solovetsky monastery in the White Sea, followed by six cartloads of his goods. He was allowed one ruble a day for maintenance. Freed in 1801, he continued to live in the monastery and died there at the age of 110.[7]

The destruction of the Zaporozhian Host was proclaimed in a manifesto of 3 August 1775. All their pretensions to an independent existence, let alone to a territorial status, were dismissed out of hand. So was the 'brotherhood' itself, which was condemned as 'a political assemblage . . . opposed to the intentions of the Creator, who blesses the multiplication of mankind', a reference to the allegation that the Host lived without women, and would soon have died out had it not accepted into its ranks fugitives of all races and creeds. The manifesto listed the crimes with which the Zaporozhians were charged, notably the demand for the lands ceded by the Turks 'as always having belonged to them'; the kidnapping of up to 8,000 inhabitants of New Russia ; the seizure of lands, the granting of asylum to fugitives, indeed the hiring of peasants in order to have agricultural labour at their disposal – in which they had been so successful that they now had 'up to 50,000' peasants working for them. It was clear, went on the manifesto, that their development of agriculture was intended to reduce their dependence on the Russian throne, and that they were intending to set up a completely independent area (*oblast'*) under their own 'wild' government. Moreover direct Russian trade with the Porte, for which the way was now open, could not flourish if it remained at the mercy of 'the pernicious mob of Cossacks'. That 'political monstrosity' the Sech, therefore, would cease to exist, its name would be wiped out and the territory would be incorporated in the guberniya of New Russia.[8]

Potemkin had attempted in 1774–5 to procure information on land and population, but a proper survey proved quite impossible in such a vast and thinly populated area, where most of the land was collective pasture, and no one had ever bothered to delimit it for permanent occupation. Since only a small number of the starshina were arrested, most of the officials and the rank and file Cossacks kept their lands ; some registered as kuptsy or meshchane. Others remained on the land though their title to it was at times uncertain and they ran the risk of being registered, i.e. enserfed, to a new owner. For vast tracts of seemingly uninhabited lands were distributed to favourites, high government officials (up to 100,000 desyatinas to A.A. Vyazemsky, or to Potemkin himself). Those who refused the terms offered by Potemkin in 1775 fled over the border into Turkey, where, at the request of the Russian government, they were to be kept south of the Danube, though many in fact settled in Turkish territory on the north of the Bug. Surviving remnants of the Zaporozhian Host were reformed by Potemkin during the second Turkish war into a Russian 'Black Sea' Cossack fighting force.[9]

Potemkin had also inherited the policy of encouraging immigration and settlement in the empty lands of the south from his predecessor in favour, Grigory Orlov. The doctrine that the power of the state depended on the size of its population was popular in mid-eighteenth century, and plans to settle foreign colonists had been pursued with varying success in Prussia, Austria and Spain. Catherine herself naturally took up the fashionable idea. Even as grand duchess she had criticized any interference with polygamy, since many wives led to many children. Soon after her accession the Senate was ordered to admit into Russia all foreigners wishing to settle there except Jews, and the many amnesties appealing to fugitives to return to Russia from Poland, Sweden or Turkey were inspired by the same policy. A manifesto inviting foreigners to settle in Russia was issued in December 1762, but it left so many loose ends that largely on the urging of Catherine herself a more precise policy was formulated.[10]

On 22 July 1764, a chancery for the protection of foreigners was set up, under Grigory Orlov, equal in status to a College, and charged with the implementation of a programme of foreign settlement.[11] On the same day a manifesto was issued, which was to form the groundwork for Russian immigration policy for the next forty years, the 'civil constitution' of the immigrants. Foreigners wishing to settle in the Russian Empire were allowed to choose residence and occupation.

On taking an oath of 'fidelity and subjection', they were granted the free exercise of their religion and the right to build churches 'with steeples for bells', in villages. They were forbidden to proselytize except among Moslems. Settlers would be free of taxes for thirty years as peasants, and for shorter periods if they became townsmen. They would not be required to furnish recruits or to billet troops. The sum of 200,000 r.p.a. was allocated to the chancery to assist its work.[12]

Since many Western European nations banned the publication of the Russian manifesto, or forbade their subjects to emigrate, 'recruitment' was mainly successful in the states of western and southern Germany and in the free cities of the Holy Roman Empire. It was carried out by professional recruiters, who were paid either with a cash bonus or a land grant.

The first foreign settlements suffered from the teething troubles common to all such enterprises. The recruiting agents proved unscrupulous and dishonest, the settlers were untrained in agricultural labour, the areas of settlement were often as yet undecided when the immigrants began to arrive. But over the years, the German colonies on the right bank of the Volga were built up, of which the Herrenhut colony at Sarepta became the best known. The colonies suffered in 1774 from the ravages of the Pugachev revolt ; several hundred joined the rebels, though others, notably the Herrenhuters, did not. But Sarepta itself was plundered and temporarily ruined.[13] These disasters led to a major reconsideration of the colonies, and the settlers unfit for farming were weeded out. With time, the 25,000 original immigrants grew into the three million Volga Germans who were later deported by Stalin, and from one of whom Lenin's mother was descended.

Apart from settlements organized by state recruiting agents foreign colonies were also established by direct negotiation by Russian landowners under special procedures either on land leased from the state or on their own land.[14]

A somewhat different approach was adopted in 1764 to the colonization of the area of New Russia, a long sausage-shaped wedge of territory extending from the Bug to the Donets, which at the time formed the southern frontier of Russia bordering on Zaporozhian territory. Here a special attempt was made to recruit both civilian and military settlers. Settlers were given generous grants of land, amounting to 26 desyatinas, or 30 if there was no timber. Landowners and recruiting agents were allocated up to a maximum of 48 plots on condition that they recruited civilian or military settlers ; they were also granted a *chin* in the Table of Ranks – a major's rank for 300 military settlers, a captaincy for 150 ; a mere 30 entitled one to become a sergeant. Entrepreneurs, merchants and craftsmen were also encouraged to settle and offered subsidies, while settlers were freed from payment of taxes for a number of years. An elaborate programme of education and welfare was devised on paper – nothing is known about its implementation. The colonization of New Russia developed rapidly as a result of this policy in the period 1764–74. In one province alone, the male population rose from 32,571 in 1764 to 62,299 in 1774.[15]

362

When Potemkin became governor of New Russia and Azov in 1775 he adopted and adapted the 1764 plan of settlement for the colonization of the territories annexed at the peace of Kuchuk Kainardzhi and the lands of the Zaporozhian Cossacks. In the course of the following twenty-five years the plan continued to provide the framework for the settlement of the south, though a number of modifications were introduced, reducing the number of settlers a landowner had to provide, lengthening the period of recruitment, easing the payment of taxes. Allotments of land were larger than in New Russia since so much land was available. The urgent need to provide labour led Potemkin to offer particularly favourable terms to the peasants, safeguarding their personal freedom and guaranteeing them against enserfment. Serfs who escaped to Poland and then turned up as settlers in the new lands, deserters, fugitives from religious persecution or criminals were offered an amnesty and favourable terms, and Potemkin refused to return to their landowners serfs who had taken refuge with the Zaporozhian Host in the days of its prime. Craftsmen were bought or conscripted, convicts were sent from other provinces to work off their sentences.[16]

Foreigners also flocked to the area, not so much in specific colonies like the Volga Germans, but as refugees, mainly from the Ottoman Empire. Among them were Moldavians, Walachians, Bulgars, Greeks and orthodox Poles, who all had the advantage of a common religion, as well as Polish Jews.[17] The result of this intensive drive to populate the new lands was a social structure differing in fundamental respects from that of old Great Russia. There was everywhere a military presence. The bulk of the nobility in the area were serving officers, but variety was added by the presence of promoted 'recruiters' or large-scale entrepreneurs like the merchant M.L. Faleyev, who by 1779 held the rank of major. After the annexation of the Crimea, in the period 1783–7, land was distributed even more briskly. Many hundreds of desyatinas were given to merchants, industrialists, townspeople, priests, officials, as well as thousands to powerful nobles and army officers. In the Great Atlas of the Governor Generalship, drawn up at Potemkin's bidding, all landowners, whatever their social origin, were simply described as *pomeshchiki,* the word used to describe the noble landowner. Most of the peasants were free, and relationships in the economic field were based upon free market forces and not upon non-economic compulsion. The free market economy of the New Russian and the Cossack lands was extended over the whole area, and coupled with the fertile soil and the good river communications, undoubtedly contributed to the speed of its development.[18]

Urban development also proceeded apace. Taganrog and Azov were strengthened after 1774 and immediate steps were taken to enlarge Kerch and Yenikale after the peace of Kuchuk Kainardzhi. Kherson was founded in 1778,[19] Mariupol in 1782, to provide a home for the Christian population evacuated from the Crimea in 1778. Kherson was located on the estuary of the Dniepr, some 70 versts from the open sea, in order to protect it from the Turkish guns in Ochakov. As a result, it proved necessary to transship goods at a deep-water harbour nearer the mouth of the estuary, and the ships built in the Kherson dockyards had to be floated down the river on 'camels'.[20] However defective Kherson may have been as a harbour, within two years Potemkin's enterprising factotum, Faleyev, had founded the Black Sea Company and embarked on trade in the Black Sea.[21] The keel of a 60-gun warship was laid down in May 1779 ; in May 1781 work began on two more.[22] Pressure to take all possible advantage of the new opportunities for trade with the Ottoman Empire and through the straits into the Mediterranean was building up, not so much because of the need to export as for political reasons.[23]

The next major development in Russian colonization supervised by Potemkin occurred as a result of the annexation of the Crimea in 1783. The Tartar khanate showed all the marks of a country impoverished by a combination of war, civil war, plague and the emigration of a large group, the Christians. The remaining population, according to the reports collected by the new Russian governor, numbered approximately 53,600 males.[24]

The manifesto proclaiming the annexation had promised the Tartars the free exercise of their religion and the maintenance of their property rights.[25] The Tartars were to take an oath of allegiance to the empress, according to their own creed, and those who did not wish to do so were free to depart with their moveable property. The Crimea was temporarily administered by a governor, appointed by Potemkin,[26] assisted by a Crimean government board (*krymskoye zemskoye pravleniye*) composed of Tartar notables. Basically, the Russians left administration and justice to the traditional Tartar bodies, but took over finance and taxation. The Tartar officials were paid a salary of 300 rubles, which was roughly the same as the salary paid to their Russian opposite numbers in the Volga region.

The reorganization of local administration in accordance with the Act of 1775 in the Kazan' and Volga regions, with their large Tartar populations, had coincided with the annexation of the Crimea. Catherine drew on her experience of these areas in setting up the new Crimean government but also drew on Crimean experience in finalizing arrangements for the Volga area and Kazan'. The administration of the Crimea was modelled on that which had finally been introduced in the Volga area, in line with Catherine's general policy of uniformity. An ukaz of 2 February 1784 proclaimed the whole Tartar khanate, except the Kuban', to be a new region (*oblast'*) of Tauris until such time as its population and institutions qualified it for the status of a guberniya. The oblast' was divided into seven districts (uezdy) within which the institutions provided by the Statute of 1775 were to be set up, staffed by Tartar notables to whom Russian ranks would be give.[27] To complete the assimilation of the Tartar administration to the Russian pattern, the social structure was also adapted : an ukaz of 2 February 1784 had granted to all Kazan' Tartar *mirzas* (heads of landowning families) the status of Russian nobles.[28] This was extended in May to all Crimean Tartar *mirzas,* who were now entitled to own land and Moslem, but not Christian, serfs.[29]

The Tartars were not subject to the recruit levy, but a small volunteer force was set up, paid for out of the revenues of the peninsula, which served as a channel for the promotion of young Tartar nobles.[30] The peasantry was assimilated to the Russian state peasantry.

Catherine and Potemkin both believed in religious toleration, and their policy signified the abandonment of the previous intensive and often brutal policy of conversion.[31] Islam and its priesthood were taken into the Russian administration to perform there the same functions carried out by the Orthodox Church and its priests in Russia proper. Thus the previous mufti was reappointed by Potemkin, paid by the Russian state, and placed in charge of all mosques and schools, as well as of the *kadis* or Moslem judges, whose sphere was now limited to the spiritual one.[32]

The population drain from the Crimea was not halted by Russian annexation and many Tartar landowners continued to emigrate to Moslem lands. The landowners who remained encouraged the Russians, who were only too willing, to place obstacles in the way of the emigration of the Tartar peasantry, who usually did not sell their property but simply departed with their flocks and herds. As a result of the exodus, and the confiscation of the lands of the khan, there was an enormous amount of vacant land available, some of which was at once distributed under Potemkin's direction. By 1787, some 148,000 desyatinas had been given away, occasionally in large grants to high officials and favourites, more often in smaller grants to officials and officers, including Tartars, Greeks, and Ukrainians as well as Russians.[33] Land was also allocated to non-nobles for the establishment of a variety of manufacturing enterprises, or the processing of agricultural products. Potemkin also sold land, but there was so much that sales were rare.

Efforts were made by Potemkin to attract badly needed labour to the peninsula. Russian pomeshchiki could of course bring their serfs, but seem to have done so rarely. By 1793 there were still only 226 registered Russian serfs of both sexes in the Crimea.[34] The main sources of Russian settlers were the state or court peasants, ex-soldiers, and Potemkin made a particular effort to attract Old Believers. Housing, working cattle and implements were to be prepared for these settlers. Special measures were taken to correct the imbalance in favour of men; 4,425 wives of recruits to Potemkin's regiments were sent for to join their husbands. Recruiting agents were given 5 rubles for each marriageable girl brought to Tauris, who was married off to a settler on arrival.[35] Every encouragement was given by the Russian government to immigrants of Orthodox faith from the Ottoman Empire and from Poland ; and Potemkin turned his blind eye to the presence of fugitive serfs, who had occasionally made a detour through Polish territory. By 1800 it is estimated that some 35,000 non-Moslems had settled in the Crimea.[36]

Urban development in the peninsula and its hinterland was also a matter of immediate concern to the government. In 1775, in the whole area of the Zaporozhian Cossacks, there were no towns, and to the south of their lands only one,

Rostov, before the Crimean border. The situation in the Crimea was somewhat different. Urban centres already existed, though many had suffered seriously in the previous troubled years. Peace and the opening up of trade contributed to the revival of towns such as Simferopol, which had been reduced to a mere huddle of bricks. The little village of Akhtiar was chosen as the site of a new port and grew quickly into the naval base of Sebastopol. Sebastopol, Feodosia and Kherson were declared free ports, through which trade with the Porte now developed, taking advantage of the Russian practice of allowing the use of the Russian flag by ships of other nations to break the Turkish prohibition on navigation in the Black Sea by all but Russian and Ottoman ships.[37] A further fillip to urban development and embellishment and the improvement of roads was the news that the empress in person proposed to pay a visit to her new acquisition.

It must be recognized that, on paper at least, the Russian conquerors attempted to make the bitter pill of annexation as palatable as possible to the Tartar population of the Crimea. But there were problems of adjustment and adaptation. Emigration into Ottoman territory continued and indeed increased during the second Russo-Turkish war of 1787–91, encouraged by Moslem religious leaders, and it turned into a massive exodus in the ensuing years. According to one high local Russian official, by 1812, two thirds of the Tartar population had abandoned the peninsula.[38] Inevitably the Russian landowners, given their traditional serf-owning mentality, and the Russian officials, given their traditional inability to conceive of any human being, particularly a peasant, as free, or to consider land as the private property of a peasant and not of the Crown, attempted to reduce the personal and property rights of the Tartar peasantry. To the credit of the Crown be it noted that when the question of Tartar rights reached the capital in 1796, it was decided in favour of the Tartar peasants whose freedom and property rights were preserved.[39]

Emigration from the peninsula was a form of silent protest against a new and alien way of life imposed on the Moslem Tartar world. The Tartar magnates who remained, though given large grants of land, were not necessarily loyal to Russia, and there was frequent tension between them and the Russian officials. In accordance with the Russian policy of assimilation, and eventual uniformity, a new Tartar nobility was created by the granting of rank in the Table of Ranks, and the extension of dvoryanstvo status to the *mirzas*. Even so, they were not numerous enough to staff the institutions of local administration provided for by the Statute of 1775; and, in any case, the Russian government thought it advisable to dilute the Tartar element and introduce other racial and religious groups such as Greeks, Jews and Armenians, into these bodies.

The annexation of the Crimea inevitably rebounded on the hinterland where the population ceased to be a frontier force. In 1783 the Statute of 1775 was extended to the two gubernii of New Russia and Azov though they were still well below the population requirements. The capital of the new *namestnichestvo* was the city of Yekaterinoslav, first founded in 1778 on the banks of the Samara, but moved in 1784 to a healthier situation on the Dniepr.[40]

It is at the plans for the construction of Yekaterinoslav that the mockery of nineteenth-century historians, who had never heard of centralized town planning, has been directed. In accordance with the systematic approach to town planning which Catherine had embarked on as early as 1763, its design was carefully laid out.[41] The broad main street of the city (though not the buildings) exists to this day under the name of Karl Marx Prospekt in Dniepropetrovsk.[42] The original plans provided for a university, a theatre, a musical academy, a cathedral to rival St Paul without the Walls, official buildings, an Exchange, shops, almshouses, a separate quarter for factories, etc. Most of these grandiose plans were abandoned after the outbreak of the second Turkish war, and Kremenchug remained the *de facto* capital of the guberniya until 1789. Nevertheless, Potemkin concerned himself from the beginning with the cultural development of his territory. Schools were founded in Kherson and a secondary school for girls in Kremenchug. Potemkin's mobile printing press served to develop local printing presses in Greek, Latin, French and Russian, which published the usual Western classics, or theological and devotional works.[43] In the whole area of the Yekaterinoslav governor-generalship, the rural working population (i.e. excluding officials and the military) numbered 351,507 male souls by 1784, of which only 4,139 were serfs, though there were 14,480 settlers on privately owned land. The total male population was estimated at 724,678 in 1787 and 819,731 in 1793.[44] Potemkin continued to welcome settlers from many lands : Swedes, Corsicans, Germans, and to the immense disgust of the Russian ambassador in London, he was even willing to accept English convicts.[45]

The existence of a territory in which serfdom was minimal and landownership was not limited to the nobility, which was moreover governed by her favourite, presented Catherine with the opportunity of trying out some of her ideas on the organization of the free peasantry which were enacted in a special instruction issued in December 1787. This instruction provided for a substantial degree of peasant self-government by means of elected officials for the administration of justice, and the allocation and collection of taxes. The hundredmen and tenthmen were to exercise supervision over the economic activity of the villages, deal with welfare, and try to prevent peasant flight.[46] However harsh the life, however inefficient the plans for colonization, for the state peasants life in the new territories clearly provided opportunities for enrichment and a taste of freedom long absent from old Russia. Their position in the south was more secure moreover than that of peasants working by contract on privately owned land, who had to wage a running battle against the landowners' efforts to enserf them by the simple process of registering them during a census. Many peasants complained to the government offices ; unfortunately the final results of their complaints are not known.[47]

It remains to this day extremely difficult to assess how successful Potemkin was in the development of his vast domains. Both contemporary and subsequent critics have stressed the enormous gap between intent and achievement, the wildly ambitious plans and the modest results, the element of illusion or even of ' "play", in Huyzinga's sense of the word', in Potemkin's passion for display and magnificence.[48] Potemkin planned and directed to a great extent from a distance, but he kept an extremely close watch over the minutest detail by correspondence and the ultimate decision rested with him. He had the great advantage of combining in one person the supreme military authority throughout the Empire, and the supreme civil authority in his own governor-generalship. This enabled him to lay down direct channels of command, and avoid friction between competing jurisdictions. His government was essentially organized on military lines and, as a result, suffered from the failure to relate the cost of an operation to its result. To Potemkin, cost was almost irrelevant, since he was barely accountable even to the empress for the vast sums he spent.[49] Undoubtedly he was at times deceived by his subordinates ; no doubt he himself was aware of the failure to implement many of his plans. Nevertheless the carping criticisms of the time should be placed in their context : they were often the outcome of enmity, or envy. No German, and very rarely a Frenchman, ever admitted that the Russians could achieve anything, let alone be efficient. It is most instructive to contrast the sour remarks of Joseph II on Kherson ('the fort is built of sand and would collapse even at a salute') and on the fleet ('built of green timber, worm-eaten')[50] with the comments of the South American, Francisco de Miranda, whose standards were perhaps less high and who had no axe to grind. Of Kherson, where he arrived in November 1786, Miranda complained of the bitter cold and the deep mud. But he praised the layout of the fortifications, though he too remarked that the building materials were poor. As for the ships, neither the timber nor the workmanship could be improved upon. Built in the English manner (and if Miranda can be accused of bias it is in favour of England), they seemed to him better than either French or Spanish ships.[51]

Indeed Potemkin spared no effort to develop Russia's Black Sea fleet, first in Kherson, then in Sebastopol. The first warship to be laid down in Kherson, in 1778, was to be named the *Glory of Catherine*. Catherine, ever prudent, suggested that such high-sounding names might be difficult to live up to, and should be avoided : 'Il vaut mieux être, que paraître et ne pas être,' she wrote to Potemkin on 13/24 June 1783.[52] An experienced naval officer, N.S. Mordvinov, trained in Britain, was placed in command of the shipyards in Kherson and the construction of the Black Sea fleet was pushed on apace.

There were territories on the borders of the Russian Empire which were beyond the reach of the empress's reforming zeal, but the foundations for future Russian penetration in the two Kabardas and the Caucasian kingdoms were laid in her reign. The decision to annex the Kabardas was taken during the first Russo-Turkish war,[53] and their actual cession was confirmed in the treaty of

Karazubazar of 1 November 1772 with the khan of Crimea. It was subsequently reluctantly accepted by the Porte in article 21 of the Treaty of Kuchuk Kainardzhi in 1774.[54] No systematic efforts were made to assert Russian control of the area until 1793, when the provisions of the Statute of Local Administration of 1775 were introduced, with but scant relevance. The problem of assimilating the Kabardas remained unsolved in the eighteenth century.[55]

Russian relations with the Caucasian kingdoms were complex and tenuous, and left a great deal to the discretion (or indiscretion) of local commanders. (So little was known about the area that when an emissary of King Solomon of Imeretia asked to be received in St Petersburg in 1768, Catherine called for maps, and found that according to some of them Tiflis was on the Black Sea, according to others, on the Caspian.) King Heraclius of Georgia had succeeded in welding together a number of disparate elements to found a mountain kingdom, and he hoped to increase his Georgian power base with Russian protection. During the first Turkish war a Russian force was sent to fight with the Georgians against the Turks. In 1771 King Heraclius offered to place himself under Russian suzerainty, but the Georgian offer was not taken up at the time. All the Georgians obtained was the inclusion in article 23 of the peace of Kuchuk Kainardzhi of a complete amnesty for Georgians who had fought against the Turks, and the abandonment of the Turkish levy of Christian slaves. Turkish suzerainty was explicitly recognized, and Russia agreed not to interfere in the affairs of the Caucasian mountain kingdoms.

Nevertheless, in the 1770s, Potemkin began to prepare the ground for future expansion. The Cossack line along the border was strengthened with the foundation of a number of forts at Yekateringrad, Georgievsk and Stavropol, and Russian state peasants began to colonize the Kuban'. The next step was the building of the fort of Vladikavkaz – an ominous name : 'master of the Caucasus' – which was connected by a line of blockhouses with Mozdok on the Terek. A new access road to Georgia was built in 1782, avoiding the mountains, and 'opening up the whole of Turkey'.[56] Heraclius continued to press for a Russian protectorate, and achieved his aims by threatening to approach Joseph II instead. The treaty of Georgievsk was signed on 24 July 1783. Russia guaranteed the territorial integrity of Georgia and the existing dynasty, while Georgia promised to aid Russia whenever required and agreed to conduct her foreign relations only through Russia. Georgian rulers would in future receive their investiture from Russia, and Georgian nobles were given the status of Russian nobles. Potemkin's cousin, General Paul S. Potemkin, was sent as the first Russian envoy and the proclamation of Russian suzerainty was read aloud in Tiflis on 24 January 1784.[57]

For political and private reasons Catherine's proposal to visit the Crimea had been postponed more than once, but it was finally fixed for early 1787. It was a tribute to the empress's status in Europe that she had constrained Joseph II to embark, most reluctantly, on a second visit to Russia, and he was appointed to meet her in Kherson in June. King Stanislas of Poland also waited on her pleasure, though in this case the initiative came from him. He had projects of his own he wished to discuss with leading Russian officials, and on 9/20 March 1787 he received Potemkin, together with the Russian ambassador to Poland, Stackelberg, the Polish crown hetman, Fr. Xavier Branicki (Potemkin's nephew by marriage) and other clients of the prince in Chwostow. Conversation was not confined to Potemkin's plans to found a musical conservatoire, in the Venetian style, under the direction of Sarti, in Yekaterinoslav. The prince wore his Polish orders, and the uniform of the nobles of Bratslav ; he allowed the Russian ambassador to hint to the King of Poland that he hoped to secure the agreement of the next Diet to the setting up of a kind of feudal principality for himself in the vast Polish estate of Smiła which he had recently acquired. Stanislas in turn hinted at his hopes for a defensive alliance with Russia which would enable him to put forward certain internal reforms by means of a confederated Diet.[58] Arrangements for the meeting between Catherine and Stanislas were now agreed on.

At last, on 7/18 January 1787, Catherine embarked on the great journey. Escorted by the envoys of Britain, France and Austria (at her invitation) and by the leading officials of the court, the empress travelled with her suite in 14 carriages, 124 sledges and 40 supplementary vehicles ; 560 horses waited at each post station. In the depths of winter the procession of sledges flew over the snow. The travellers were wrapped in bearskins and wore beaver bonnets so that the intense cold did not affect them. The road was excellent and illuminated on both sides by large bonfires of pine, cypress and birch. By day there was nothing to be seen but the broad expanse of snow criss-crossed by the tracks of numberless sledges transporting people and goods ; at sunset (about 3 p.m.) the snowy plain was traversed by the fiery avenue along which the imperial cortège advanced. Outside each town the people waited to welcome the empress. At various stops, Catherine received the assembled nobles under their marshals, the town provosts and the officials of the magistraty. Special largesse was handed out here and there, to towns which had suffered from fire, to educational establishments, almshouses, etc. Some of the great magnates took the opportunity to entertain the empress and her suite in their own homes. But the foreign envoys in other places had to content themselves with lodgings in the house of some rich kupets or even, at times, with sharing a peasant's *izba* with his stove, his wife and his children.

Catherine did not relax from her routine. Rising at 6 a.m. she worked with her ministers ; then she breakfasted, received the foreign envoys, and the whole procession started off at 9 a.m. Dinner was at 2 p.m. at some convenient pavillion or private house. The journey continued until 7 p.m. The empress then descended at her specially prepared dwelling, spent a few moments tidying her dress, joined the envoys and chatted until 9 p.m. when, since she never supped, she withdrew to work until 11 o'clock.

Such a day, during which she was never alone, but always spending herself in entertaining one or other of her distinguished travelling companions, must have been exhausting – and indeed, arrived at Smolensk on 12/23 January 1787,

Catherine decided to stop for three days. However, as the French envoy, Ségur, remarked, the endless audiences, receptions, balls for the local nobility, and lengthy church services ('We Latins take things more easily in the search for our salvation'), must have been even more exhausting. Finally, on 29 January/9 February Catherine arrived in Kiev where she was received by the governor-general, Field-Marshal Rumyantsev, and by Potemkin. In Kiev, where Catherine stayed nearly three months, some of the underlying tensions between Potemkin and other high officials came to the surface. Rumyantsev, now definitely hostile to Potemkin, since he felt himself relegated to his Little Russian governor-generalship, took the opportunity to carp and criticize. Potemkin lodged away from the court, in the Pecherskaya Lavra, where he received Poles, Georgians, Tartars, Jews, and all the more colourful peoples of the Empire in his own court.[59] Finally, on 22 April/3 May Catherine and her suite at last embarked on seven specially prepared galleys which were to take them down the Dniepr, followed by 80 ships and 3,000 troops. They were richly appointed, with silk hangings, elegant sitting rooms and comfortable divans. Each galley was provided with its own small orchestra. The select company of ten ambassadors and high officials foregathered every day at 1 p.m. on the empress's galley for dinner, though she also entertained a larger company on a second galley specially devised to seat up to sixty guests.

On both banks of the Dniepr, the procession was greeted by crowds of spectators, peasants, Cossacks, townspeople. Towns, villages, country houses and peasant huts were gaily decorated with wreaths of flowers or triumphal arches.[60] Potemkin had carefully calculated the various halting places to make sure the galleys drew up before a village or some picturesque old settlement. Huge herds dotted the vast fields, according to Ségur; large numbers of peasants flocked on the banks, and boats full of young people crowded round the galleys.[61] It was this spectacle which gave rise to the malicious witticism that the villages were made of cardboard, the ships and guns in Sebastopol merely painted, the whole spectacle an illusion prepared by a master conjuror. The phrase 'Potemkin villages' has ever since been applied to unreal achievements. The Prince de Ligne, one of Catherine's guests, mentioned the remark at the time already as a groundless quip; though he recognized that there were limitations on what the empress could inspect for herself, that there were unfinished towns and houses, and that the empress was shown only the fairest side of her southern provinces, he nevertheless confirmed that much had indeed been achieved.[62]

The Comte de Ségur was also impressed with what had been accomplished in so short a time, though he too noted the signs of hasty planning and execution.[63] More conclusive than any of these comments is the description given by Kyrill Razumovsky (no friend of Potemkin's) in 1782, in the course of a journey to Kherson: 'my sight was constantly occupied with the pleasant surprise since on that steppe, so frighteningly empty, where not so long ago there was scarcely an *izba* . . . particularly on the road from Kremenchug to Kherson, I found many settlements, some 20 or 25, not more than 30 versts apart with a good water supply. . . . As for Kherson, it is so agreeable that I have acquired a building plot.'[64] Certainly villages and towns were decorated, repaired or painted for Catherine's visit – such preparations for a royal tour are not unknown today.[65] But only one diarist went on record at the time with a description of the deliberate concealment of the people's poverty from the eyes of the empress. It is again Miranda who remarks that in Tula, in the guberniya of that name, far away from Potemkin's lands, at the end of the city two rows of boards had been set up on either side of the street for at least one verst, so that the sovereign should not see the poor huts of the inhabitants . . . the best houses were painted, others were artificial and nothing appeared to be what it was. Otherwise, Miranda noted that the people of Tula dressed better and seemed more prosperous than elsewhere.[66]

On 25 April/6 May, the empress arrived off Kaniev, on Polish territory, where King Stanislas Augustus was waiting *incognito* to call on her in her galley. The meeting between the ex-lovers – the first since they had parted more than twenty-five years before – took place under the lynx eyes of a crowd of watching courtiers. Cold, majestic greetings were exchanged, then Catherine and Stanislas withdrew for half an hour. When they rejoined the company, they showed slight signs of sadness and embarrassment. The entertainments on the imperial galley were as usual lavish, but Catherine refused to go ashore in Poland and attend a ball given by Stanislas for the Russian visitors and the attendant Polish nobility.

Stanislas had pressed his plans for an alliance with Russia and a confederated Diet on the Russian officials who had paid their respects to him while the empress was at Kiev. But he had received no answer as yet though Potemkin assured him that the empress would listen sympathetically to his views. Catherine, however, was not inclined to plunge into Polish affairs on Potemkin's behalf ; still less was she willing to assist Stanislas in a programme designed to strengthen the Polish government and the Polish armed forces. Potemkin meanwhile pursued a double policy, now assuring Stanislas of Russian good will, now secretly egging on the anti-royalist faction in Poland, to which his clients, Branicki and Potocki, belonged.

Catherine's refusal to linger in Kaniev may have been caused by the awkwardness of the interview with a man she had once loved, and to whom she had behaved subsequently with such cruelty. She put forward various excuses : she was tired, she found ceremonial clothing too hot and heavy, 'the Emperor [Joseph] would be kept waiting . . .'. Stanislas could not conceal his mortification at Catherine's refusal to be persuaded and Potemkin, who feared for his Polish projects, was furious with Catherine, and sulked visibly.[67]

The next major halt was Kremenchug, the *de facto* capital of Potemkin's own territories, where Catherine received deputations from a number of Tartar tribes and entertained the nobility and townspeople to dinner. A few days later, hearing that the emperor, who had already arrived in Kherson, had set out to meet her in Novyy Haydak, Catherine left her galley, and with a small escort, hastened to meet Joseph on land. So hasty was her departure that no arrangements had been made for feeding the illustrious guest, and the cooking eventually devolved on Potemkin, much to the emperor's disgust.

On 12/23 May the emperor and the empress made their solemn entry into Kherson. At the time of the imperial visit, nine years after its foundation, the city possessed more than 1,200 stone buildings and a population of over 24,000 military and naval personnel, over 4,000 convicts, and approximately 20,000 officials, kuptsy and craftsmen.[68] During her stay in Kherson, Catherine as usual entertained the first six classes to dinner, received the kuptsy and common people, who were allowed to kiss her hand,[69] and distributed 3,000 rubles to the Church, and one ruble to each serving soldier and sailor (totalling 24,560). She also visited the dockyard to watch the launching of warships and a frigate built in Kherson. A new 80-gun warship – of which the keel was laid in Kherson – was named *St Joseph*.

On 17/28 May the empress and her guest left for the Crimea ; on 22 May/2 June they dined at Inkerman, in full view of the harbour of Sebastopol, where 15 warships and frigates were anchored together with 16 bombketches. As Catherine approached the fleet in the harbour the ships were dressed overall, the sails were unfurled, guns fired and the sailors cheered. Joseph was certainly impressed. After visiting Bakhchisaray, Simferopol and Karazubazar, Joseph and Catherine parted at Berislav, he to return to deal with incipient revolt in the Austrian Netherlands, Catherine to continue her triumphant tour, which took her by a different route (passing through Poltava, where Potemkin had arranged a re-enactment of the famous battle) to Moscow, where her grandchildren awaited her, and on to Tsarskoye Selo where she arrived on 11/22 July 1787.

The tour had been a triumph indeed, above all for Potemkin. Catherine glowed with pleasure at the prospect of proving wrong all those who had whispered that the Crimea was worthless, that the vast sums of money entrusted to the prince had been embezzled for his own purposes. All doubtless would not bear the scrutiny of too close an accountant, but the results were there for the emperor and the three foreign envoys to see. The Turks too drew their own conclusions. In August they declared war.

Part VIII

The Porte, Poland and the French Revolution

24

Between the Wars : Foreign Policy in the 1780s

The treaty of Kuchuk Kainardzhi of June 1774 marked a much-needed breathing space for Russia who required time to exploit her newly won territories, and her newly won commercial concessions. But the implementation of the provisions of the treaty was hampered by the unwillingness of the Turks to accept the losses inflicted on them, and by the evident instability of the arrangements made regarding the Crimea. The Porte from the start demanded the revision of the treaty ; but ratified it in January 1775, under pressure of disturbances on its frontier with Persia. Russia received the first instalment of the indemnity ; Kinburn was handed over to the Russian troops. But the Porte, though giving way in most fields, and even accepting to cede Bukovina to Austria in the hope of securing Austrian diplomatic support against Russia, continued to put obstacles in the way of Russian Black Sea trade and Russian policy in the Crimea.

Though Russian-Crimean relations had been settled by the Treaty of Karazubazar in 1772, the khan, Sahip Girey, in late 1773 had abruptly switched sides and imprisoned the Russian resident, Veselitsky. Thus when the Treaty of Kuchuk Kainardzhi was signed, guaranteeing the independence of the Crimea, the ruler of that independent state was in open conflict with Russia. But the fate of the Crimea was decided by quarrels within the Girey family. Sahip Girey was overthrown in December 1774 by Devlet Girey, who tried to win the support of the Russians by releasing Veselitsky and received a somewhat unenthusiastic investiture from the Porte. For the time being Catherine also recognized Devlet Girey though she had her own candidate for the khanate available in the wings, namely Shagin Girey, then living in Poltava. Russia began to prepare for an invasion of the Crimea in March 1776, and in November General Prozorovsky seized the fort of Perekop. The risk of extending the conflict was taken into account, but the Porte was involved in preparations for war in the East, neither Austria nor Prussia was likely to move, and France's attention had already been engaged by the prospect of the impending Anglo-American struggle.[1]

The Russian invasion of the Crimea was explained in a manifesto which proclaimed the Russian intention to safeguard the liberties of the Crimeans, and the independence of the peninsula as agreed in the treaty of Karazubazar.[2] The Russian commander made good use of the divisions among Crimeans, many of whom now abandoned Devlet in favour of Russia's protégé, Shagin Girey. By April 1777 Shagin Girey had been elected khan of Crimea, and Devlet departed, unsupported by the Porte, for Constantinople where he died a few years later.

The Russian government, having secured a 'genuinely independent' khan of Crimea, left Shagin Girey to govern very much as he pleased. Shagin Girey saw himself as a westernizing reformer ; as a result by October 1777 a revolt against him had broken out, which was only finally put down in February 1778, after fierce and cruel fighting, in which Russian troops took part.[3] Ottoman efforts to enthrone a rival khan proved fruitless, and since neither side wanted war, the diplomats took over for a time.

But while Russia and the Porte were squabbling over the Crimea, events in the New World were shaking the major European powers out of their traditional orbits. Catherine had watched with close attention the growing tension between Britain and America, and in the summer of 1775 she had rejected somewhat sharply a British request for the loan of 20,000 Russian troops.[4] She was more directly concerned with the niggling disagreements which had arisen with Prussia over the delimitation of the exact boundaries of the Prussian portion of Poland, and in particular over the Prussian attempt to control the trade of Danzig, if not the city itself. Frederick II's determination to squeeze the maximum out of Poland, which Catherine was now more prepared to protect than to partition, turned the Prussian alliance into a burden from which Russia had not much to gain.[5] It was in the hope of recovering Catherine's full friendship that Prince Henry of Prussia had set out on his second visit to St Petersburg in April 1776. A bargain of sorts was eventually struck : Frederick gave way over the Prussian-Polish border and Danzig in exchange for an immediate renewal of the Russo-Prussian treaty which was only due to expire in 1780. The border convention between the partitioning powers was signed in Warsaw on 22 August 1776[6] and the treaty between Russia and Prussia was renewed for a further eight years on 20/31 March 1777.[7] From the Russian point of view an active policy vis-à-vis the Porte became safer, in the knowledge that Frederick II would use his influence to prevent the outbreak of war.

It was however in Germany that the next crisis arose, and it was Frederick II who benefited from the treaty. On 30 December 1777, the Elector of Bavaria unexpectedly died. Joseph II seized the opportunity to attempt to carry out one of his pet schemes of aggrandisement, namely the acquisition of parts of Bavaria. He forced the Elector Palatine, heir to Bavaria, to cede the coveted territories to him in a convention of 3 January 1778. But any increase in Hapsburg power was dangerous for Prussia in Frederick's view, and he at once appealed to Russia for the support he was entitled to under the treaty in the event of war with Austria. At the same time he invited Russian mediation in the conflict, and took steps to defuse Russo-Turkish tension and thus free Russia to support him.

France was at the same time, and for a different reason, urging peace upon the Porte. Negotiations for the recognition of the infant United States culminated in the treaties of alliance and commerce of 6 February 1778. With these treaties, France committed herself to war with Britain and peace on the continent. Hence not only were Joseph II's demands for succour against Prussia, under the terms of the Austro-French treaty of 1756, rejected by France, but the French ambassador was instructed to press the Porte to incline the Turks towards conciliation with Russia.[8] While France was thus damping down Turkish military ardour, her ally Austria was secretly egging the Turks on, in the hope that should war break out in the Empire over the Bavarian succession, Prussia's ally Russia would be diverted by the Porte. At the other end of Europe, Russia's alliance was being sought by Britain with naval reinforcements in mind, in view of the inevitable war with France. There were thus three sources of possible armed conflict in Europe : the Russo-Turkish tension, the confrontation between Prussia and Austria in the Holy Roman Empire and the Anglo-French duel which was about to be resumed. Could these three conflicts be kept apart ?

It was clear that neither Russia nor France wished to be drawn into a war in Germany. For once their interests concurred, and it was thus not surprising that they should reach at least a temporary understanding. Catherine's response to Frederick's demands for armed help or subsidies was cool, and in March 1778 she proposed putting the Bavarian dispute before the Reichstag and seeking a legalistic solution.[9] Yet Russian reluctance to assist Frederick was concealed from Austria in the hope of restraining her while the Turks continued to threaten the Crimea. But a sizable Turkish naval expedition in August 1778 was a failure. Russian guns and Russian warships, whose presence contravened the provisions of the treaty of Kuchuk Kainardzhi, prevented a landing, and on the return of the fleet from this last attempt to rescue Crimean independence, the war party at the Porte had to give way to those who favoured negotiations, and accept a French offer of mediation with Russia.[10]

Meanwhile in June 1778 France and Britain drifted into war and in July Frederick II declared war on Austria. Britain continued to seek Russia's alliance, and was listened to with more cordiality now that war had actually broken out : but the old obstacle to a closer union between the two powers remained : Russia refused to give up the Turkish *casus foederis,* particularly now that she was on the verge of a Turkish war.

Military operations between Prussia and Austria on the Bohemian border were at first conducted in so half-hearted a way as to earn the conflict its nickname of 'the Potato War'. Talks behind the scenes finally broke down at the end of August 1778, and Frederick once more appealed to his ally for support. But in July 1778, France had already offered her mediation in the Austro-Prussian conflict, and at the same time as Frederick demanded Russian assistance he informed Vergennes, the French foreign minister, of his willingness to accept French mediation provided his ally Russia was associated with it. Circumstances were now playing into Catherine's hands. The Porte's acceptance of the French offer of mediation suggested that there was no longer so much to fear on the southern frontier. The French offer of mediation to Prussia suggested that Austrian belligerence was not being supported by France. Catherine could therefore take the risk of making a strong demonstration in Prussia's favour, while at the same time urging Austria to negotiate with her enemy. While an auxiliary corps was at last offered to Prussia, provided Prussia paid its expenses, Catherine sent a strongly worded declaration to Vienna on 22 September/3 October 1778 which crossed a courier from Vienna announcing Austrian willingness to accept a joint Franco-Russian mediation in the conflict. Thus largely thanks to French initiative two of the potential centres of war were defused at roughly the same time, leaving France, as Vergennes had planned, free to concentrate on the war with Britain in America.

Saint-Priest, the French ambassador in Constantinople, succeeded rapidly in bringing the two sides to agree, and a Russo-Turkish convention was signed at Ainalikawak on 10 March 1779. The independence of the Crimea was solemnly confirmed, and the Turks accepted Shagin Girey as khan of Crimea ; while the Russians agreed to certain refinements in the procedure for the religious investiture of Crimean khans, and accepted that the appointment of *kadis* or judges belonged to the sphere of spiritual, i.e. Turkish, authority and not to the secular or Crimean authority.[11] On these terms Russia agreed to evacuate the peninsula.

Before reaching this agreement Russia had taken a step which was to be a major factor in undermining the stability of the Crimean khanate : the evacuation of its Christian population. The plan had originated in 1777–8 out of the probably well founded fear that the the Christian population might be subjected to Moslem reprisals after the withdrawal of the Russian troops. But the advantages of recruiting a large body of Christian settlers for the south Russian territories soon overlaid this original idea, and fear for the safety of the Crimean Christians became a mere pretext. The Christians in the Crimea had played a part not unlike that of Jewish communities in western Europe : they enjoyed the special protection of the ruler as his most reliable taxpayers. Not only were they the most economically advanced section of society, they were also the main support of the 'westernizing' policies of Shagin Girey, who at once protested to Catherine against the plan to remove them. In spite of his objections the exodus began from July 1778 onwards, protected by Russian troops. By September a total of 31,098 Christians had abandoned their homes in Crimea, many no doubt reluctantly and under pressure, for an uncertain future in the guberniya of Azov.[12] The new colonists were granted generous amounts of territory and a considerable degree of civil and religious autonomy within the framework of Russian laws.[13]

Parallel with the negotiations for Russian peace with the Porte, negotiations for the pacification of Germany had begun in March 1779 in Teschen, and peace was signed on 13 May 1779. By terms of the treaty, Austria annexed a small portion of Bavaria, the Innviertel, and agreed to support Frederick's claim to the

Margraviates of Anspach and Bayreuth on the extinction of the then ruling family.

From the Russian point of view the joint mediation with France in the Bavarian conflict was an outstanding success. It served to extend Russian influence right into the heart of the Holy Roman Empire ; though without a territorial base there, Russia could now claim to replace the influence previously exercised by Sweden. She would henceforward be able to pursue her political objectives directly in the Empire, without having to 'go through' Prussia.[14] Moreover, by becoming a guarantor of the peace of Westphalia, the renewal of which was included in the peace of Teschen, Russia could claim the right to pronounce on the interpretation of these treaties and their implementation in the Holy Roman Empire.[15] The mediation thus brought Russian influence into the centre of Europe, and at the same time the process of collaborating in the pacification of Germany helped to create an understanding between France and Russia. Russia emerged strengthened from both the potential conflicts in which she had been involved. She had not given Frederick the support he had hoped for, but had interpreted the Russo-Prussian treaty to suit herself, and Joseph had learned that he could do nothing without a Russian alliance. For the time being there continued to be a genuine convergence of interests between France and Russia in maintaining peace in Europe.

Meanwhile Britain had been brought, by the threat of Spanish intervention in the war with France, to renew her offer of alliance to Russia in October 1778 and to abandon most reluctantly the 'Turkey clause', to the extent of offering Russia a subsidy but no more, in the event of a Russo-Turkish war, in exchange for the use of part of the Russian navy in her present war with France.[16] The success of the parallel negotiations with the Porte and in Germany enabled the Russians to refuse these offers in December 1778. And their satisfactory progress at the same time introduced two new elements into Nikita Panin's policy, namely an attempt to secure a Russian mediation in the conflict between Britain and France, and the setting up of Russia as the defender of neutral trade against the depredations of the belligerents, particularly Britain.

When he rejected Britain's overtures for an alliance in December 1778, not only did Panin refer to Russian hopes of bringing about peace between Britain and France ; he also – and for the first time – protested at Britain's policy of detaining all neutral ships bound for France,[17] and condemning any cargoes destined for France as enemy property. Only the Dutch who could claim, by virtue of their treaty of 1674 with England, the benefit of the principle of 'free ships free goods' (i.e. the right to trade with enemy countries except in contraband of war – which did not however include naval stores), were paid for the cargoes condemned in Britain. Faced with neutral protestations, Lord Suffolk, Secretary of State for the North, issued a declaration on 10 November 1778 restating the British position : neutral ships would be detained, naval stores would be condemned as contraband, and enemy property would be condemned ; cargoes of naval stores captured before that date would be purchased. French policy, initially even more severe than that of Britain towards the neutrals, had been modified in July 1778 by Vergennes in view of the needs of the French navy and of his desire to consolidate French leadership of the neutral powers against Britain.[18]

The Russians were moved by a number of factors in the defence of neutral trade, such as the desire to free Russian foreign trade from its dependence on the British merchant navy ; and the urge to make use of the heightened demand for Russian goods, primarily naval stores, during a maritime war. The pretext came easily to hand since articles 10 and 11 of the Anglo-Russian commerical treaty of 1766 stated that the flag covered the goods and did not specify that naval stores were contraband. Hence, Russian ships were in the Russian view permitted to carry naval stores to the enemies of Britain without impediment.[19] Russia's merchant navy however was far too small for her to be able to make much use of her privileged position. But the export of Russian naval stores to all the belligerents would be increased if other powers, notably the Dutch, could secure from Britain the recognition of their right to trade in naval stores, and if access to Russian ports could be rendered secure against the depredations of privateers.

The appearance in Russian waters of an American privateer, in August 1778, led Catherine to take up with her ally Denmark the organization of a naval patrol to protect their coasts in spring 1779. French pressure behind the scenes on Denmark, Sweden and the United Provinces combined to induce the Danish foreign minister Count A.P. Bernstorff to put forward in September 1778 a more wideranging plan for the promulgation of certain principles to be enforced by the naval patrols of the contracting powers. These principles include the claim to 'free ships free goods', and they defined contraband in such a way as to allow Denmark to trade in naval stores. Sweden too promptly put forward a proposal for cooperation with the fleets of Denmark and Russia.

For the time being the Danish plan went further than Russia wished to go. She had no need to protect ships trading on the high seas, but only the access to her coasts ; and action with a pro-French Sweden might prove dangerous. Hence Russia limited herself to making strong verbal representations to Great Britain in December 1778. In February 1779 Catherine rejected proposals for a convention with the other two Baltic powers but declared her intention to act on her own and arm a small squadron to protect access to her coasts.[20] But the limited Russian action proved as unpopular with France as with Britain, and neither power felt inclined to accept the offer of Russian good offices which Panin pressed on Britain in December 1778 and on France in May 1779. The intervention of Spain in the war, in June 1779, altered the whole picture and rendered Russian maritime assistance far more urgent for Britain than her offers of mediation.

The presence of the Bourbon fleets in the Channel in the summer of 1779 induced the British government to make further efforts to secure Russian naval assistance, this time in exchange for the Turkish *casus foederis* incorporated in a formal alliance, though Britain would be happier with a Russian mediation backed by the threat of force. Yet again Catherine turned down in January 1780 a proposal which she saw clearly was bound to lead her into war, and shortly afterwards she embarked on a policy which was to cement her neutrality and extend Russian influence even more widely in Europe.

Already in the course of 1779 Russia had complained to Britain about the British detention of Russian cargoes intended for France on board Dutch ships, and about the detention of Russian-registered ships. When early in 1780 a Russian ship was detained by Spain Catherine was in a position to launch a policy which would not appear to be overtly anti-British, though it was largely aimed at preventing British interference with Danish, Dutch and Swedish shipping. Thus in mid-February 1780 Catherine solemnly proclaimed the principles which should govern the rights of neutral trade and neutral ships at sea, and proposed forming a league of neutrals composed of Russia, Denmark, the United Provinces and Sweden in the first place, to defend these principles.[21]

The next step was to negotiate a number of conventions by which the neutrals would agree to arm their fleets in defence of the maritime principles. A convention was signed with Denmark on 9 July 1780, and Denmark issued her own declaration to the belligerents defining contraband in accordance with article 2 of the Anglo-Danish treaty of 1670. But at that same time Bernstorff was negotiating secretly with Britain to give up the right to trade in naval stores in exchange for a certain right to export foodstuffs to France and Spain. The Swedish declaration was issued on 21 July and the convention with Russia was signed on 1 August 1780, and in September Denmark and Sweden acceded to the Russian-Swedish and Russian-Danish conventions respectively.[22]

Negotiations with the Dutch took longer. The States General appointed plenipotentiaries to negotiate in St Petersburg who only arrived in September 1780. Meanwhile a shift took place in Russian foreign policy which had been preparing for some time but which now began to be perceptible thanks to the initiative of Joseph II.

The emperor had, since the war of the Bavarian succession, realized that his ambitions could not be achieved without detaching Russia from the Prussian alliance. He therefore proposed to Catherine in January 1780 that he should visit her on the occasion of a tour that she was to undertake in the spring in the provinces acquired from Poland. It was a proposal which set the seal on the high position Russia had acquired in European politics under Catherine's rule, and she hastened to accept.[23] While neither ruler envisaged any formal links between their two states, and indeed Catherine had no wish to be drawn into Joseph's German adventures, yet under Potemkin's inspiration her imagination was beginning to turn towards the realization of the so-called 'Greek project', namely the overthrow of the Ottoman Empire and the liberation of Constantinople.[24] In anticipation Catherine's second grandson had been given a Greek name – Constantine – and a Greek nurse, to prepare him for his future role.

It would be an exaggeration to suggest that this was a concrete, well-thought-out policy but it was more than a mere gambit in the relations between Russia and Austria. It was an aim, a direction, a dream, but one for which Austrian, not Prussian, cooperation would be necessary.[25] The new orientation of Catherine's policy became the object of bitter contention at the Russian court. Nikita Panin, seeing in the 'Greek project' the end of the Prussian alliance to which he attached great political importance, and on which he pinned his own hopes of power and office in the future, fought against the new, pro-Austrian orientation championed by Potemkin with every open and underhand weapon he could command. But the visit of Joseph II, who, under the name of Count Falckenstein, met the empress in Mogilev at the end of May 1780, was an outstanding success largely, it must be said, because both parties were determined that it should be. To restore the balance Frederick II sent his nephew and heir ('le gros Gu' as Catherine unkindly called him) in September 1780. The empress found his visit wearisome,[26] but this counted much less than the decision she had now reached to work for a *rapprochement* with Austria, and to allow the Prussian alliance to fade away.

The accession of the Dutch to the Neutral League constituted the only serious challenge the League might present to Britain's maritime supplies since the United Provinces had the tonnage to carry Russian exports of naval stores to France and Spain, and a navy capable of defending their merchant ships. Britain preferred an open breach to a hidden enemy, and she broke off relations with the Dutch on a trumped-up issue and by 20 December the war at sea began. Two weeks later, on 4 January 1781, in St Petersburg, the Dutch plenipotentiaries signed the treaty with Russia acceding to the Armed Neutrality, unaware that they were no longer neutrals. At the same time as Britain took on a fresh enemy, however, she opened up a double diplomatic manoeuvre : on the one hand she pressed for the joint mediation by Austria and Russia in her conflict with France ; on the other hand she made a final attempt in winter 1781 to induce Russia to take part in the war as Britain's ally in exchange for the cession of Minorca to Russia.

However tempting the prize ('the bride is too beautiful . . . they are seeking to deceive me,' as Catherine put it), the empress was aware of the danger of being lured into war by the offer of an acquisition which she could only hope to hold with British permission. Moreover, having erected the structure of the Neutral League, she had more to gain by maintaining her neutrality and extending her influence in Europe by mediating between the belligerents. Indeed she had already, before Britain's offer of Minorca reached her, accepted the British-inspired offer forwarded to her in January 1781 by Joseph II to mediate jointly with him in the conflict between Britain and France.

Mediation also rescued the empress from the embarrassing situation in which she found herself as a result of Britain's breach with the Dutch. On the outbreak of war with Britain the United Provinces had appealed for the armed assistance of their co-signatories in the Neutral League. Russia had no intention of embroiling herself in war on behalf of Dutch trade, and it was possible to evade her treaty obligations on the technicality that war had broken out before the Dutch had signed the treaty. In mid-February Catherine offered her formal mediation to reconcile Britain and the Dutch, a mediation which excluded her co-signatories of the Neutral League, and Austria.[27]

Meanwhile, with the death of Maria Theresa in November 1780, negotiations for an alliance between Russia and Austria had begun. It was typical of the inflated conception of Russia's prestige which her recent diplomatic successes had engendered in Catherine that she brought the negotiations almost to a standstill by insisting that Joseph II should grant Russia the 'alternative' i.e. that he should give up the traditional right of the Holy Roman Emperor to sign first on both copies of a treaty. From November to May no progress was made, but finally Catherine proposed a solution which Joseph's pride could swallow, namely that the treaty should take the form of the secret exchange of two autograph letters setting out the obligations each side undertook to the other. In view of the publicity which had surrounded the negotiations, and the dispute over the alternative, it was officially given out that they had been broken off. Meanwhile both Joseph and Catherine wrote out the engagements they were making to each other in their own august hands and Catherine seems thoroughly to have enjoyed deceiving all the assembled diplomats.[28]

The treaty provided for the mutual defence of the territories of the signatories, including the acquisitions in Poland in 1772, but excluding Russia's Asiatic possessions and Austria's Italian lands. In the event of an attack on the Austrian Netherlands, Russian assistance would take the form of a subsidy. Both powers undertook to maintain the existing Polish constitution and to defend Polish territorial integrity. In separate letters existing treaties between the signatories and the Porte were unilaterally guaranteed ; should the Porte fail to carry out its treaty obligations, or declare war on either party the other was bound to come to its assistance within three months.[29] For Russia, the treaty provided the basis for a forward policy in the South. Though it rendered the Russo-Prussian treaty, which had not yet expired, *de facto* null and void, Catherine could still be fairly certain that Prussia would not attack her in the event of a war between the two new allies and the Porte, but would be more tempted to turn against Austria.

While the dispute over the alternative lasted, no progress could be made with a joint mediation by Austria and Russia between Britain and France since the mediating powers could not put their names to a document. Barely was the ink dry on letters exchanged between the two rulers when the mediation came to life. Meanwhile Catherine had been pressing on with the formation of the Neutral League ; even if the Dutch were no longer neutrals there were other powers which could be induced to join. The actual maritime principles, namely 'free ships free goods', enunciated by the empress, had been accepted in April 1780 with enthusiasm by France, more ungraciously by Spain. In the course of 1782 and 1783, Portugal and the kingdom of the Two Sicilies were induced to sign.[30] More damaging ultimately to the British war effort was the accession of Austria and Prussia. Both rulers spoke only sarcastically of what they regarded as Catherine's pet project. But Frederick clutched at any straw which could strengthen his ties with Russia – and the Prussian accession, which took place in May 1781, just when Catherine was writing out her undertakings to Joseph II, naturally served to induce Joseph to respond favourably to Catherine's invitation to join, and Austria acceded in October 1781. Russian exports benefitted from their accession because Dutch ships now transferred in large numbers to the Prussian or Austrian Netherlands flag and thus could claim the right to trade in Russian goods with France and Spain.[31]

The success from Catherine's point of view of her maritime policy, which had extended her diplomatic links as far as Portugal and which had placed her in a seemingly dominant position in Europe as a joint mediator in the Anglo-French conflict, led her to take up the formulation of a naval code for the Russian merchant marine, the systematic extension of the network of Russian consuls throughout Europe and the conclusion of a number of commercial treaties.[32] In addition Russian fleets, which had confined themselves to limited patrols in Northern waters in 1779, now appeared in strength in the Mediterranean again on the pretext of defending Russian merchant ships against French or Spanish privateers.

The Austro-Russian treaty, representing as it did a fundamental shift in the orientation of Russian foreign policy away from the 'Northern system', had serious repercussions at the Russian court as well. Nikita Panin had always been identified with the Prussian alliance ; he had at first opposed the formation of the Neutral League, but when he realized that it represented a genuinely neutral stance which would be to Britain's disadvantage, he supported it wholeheartedly. He had been driven into a strongly anti-British attitude by the British envoy Sir James Harris who, despairing of obtaining Russian armed assistance from the foreign secretary, had attached himself to Prince Potemkin and endeavoured to procure the removal of Panin. In the battle for influence over Catherine, British interests played but a secondary part. It was a struggle between Panin and his 'Northern system' (supported by the grand duke) and Potemkin and the Austrian orientation of Russian foreign policy. Inevitably, given the acrimoniousness of the relations between the two men, Panin foresaw disgrace and the loss of power. He played no part in the negotiations with Austria, which were conducted by Potemkin and Bezborodko ; indeed he declared outright that 'he could not soil his hand' by putting his name to such a treaty, and demanded permission to retire to the country. Catherine in turn was growing impatient with Panin's evident thwarting of her wishes, and when he returned from the country, in September 1781, he was ordered to hand over the business of the College of Foreign Affairs to the vice-chancellor, Count I.A. Osterman, while A.A. Bezborodko, a member of the College, became Catherine's principal adviser in foreign affairs.

The dismissal of Nikita Panin marked the end of an era in Russian foreign policy. Even though the existence, let alone the terms, of the Austro-Russian treaty of May 1781 remained a secret, it was clear that Austria and Russia were now cooperating in foreign policy as they had not done before, and equally clear that the Prussian alliance was dead.[33] Frederick II drew the inevitable conclusions, and started trying to mend his fences elsewhere.

During 1782 all powers marked time. The fall of Yorktown in December 1781 led by March 1782 to the resignation of the North government and the coming to power of the Whigs in Britain. The policy of the new Secretary of State for Foreign Affairs, Charles James Fox, included the improvement of British relations with Russia. In pursuit of this aim, Fox gave up British insistence on the exclusion of the principle 'free ships free goods' from the negotiation of a peace treaty with the Dutch and Catherine smiled on Britain again. Secret peace talks began in May 1782 between France and Britain, but neither side was as yet prepared to admit defeat, though both parties were anxious to evade the interfering good offices of the imperial mediators. Fox made one further effort to secure the alliance of Russia in June 1782, and was prepared to accept Russia's maritime principles as the price of this alliance.[34] By now, however, Catherine had other fish to fry.

In the winter of 1780–1, revolt broke out again in the Crimean khanate and culminated in May 1782 with the flight of Shagin Girey to the Russian port of Kerch. A rival khan, Bahadir Girey, was elected and prepared to approach the Porte for recognition and aid. In spite of the provisions of the treaty of Ainalikawak, by which the Porte had bound itself to recognize Shagin Girey for life, the Turks desired to recognize the new khan. Catherine was faced with the choice between restoring Shagin Girey once more or liquidating the Crimean problem for good. For the time being Potemkin was merely ordered on 3/14 August 1782 to march into the Crimea and restore Shagin Girey to his throne. Meanwhile the empress proceeded to test out the reaction of Joseph II to a possible war with the Porte. No mention was made of any Russian acquisitions in the Crimea, but Catherine proposed in a long letter of 10/21 September to Joseph the conclusion of an additional convention between Russia and Austria setting out the acquisitions each side might make : Russian acquisitions were limited to Ochakov, the coast between the Bug and the Dniestr, and 'an island or two' in the Greek Archipelago. This seemed modest enough, but Catherine also proposed the setting up of a kingdom formed from Moldavia, Walachia and Bessarabia, to remain for ever independent of both Russia and Austria (the unspoken assumption was that this would be Potemkin's kingdom of Dacia).

In expounding her policy, Catherine undertook a *tour d'horizon* analysing the attitudes of the other powers : Poland was under control, Denmark was a loyal ally, Sweden would only move if encouraged – and subsidized – and it was to be Joseph's task to discourage France from offering these subsidies. Prussia was the main possible obstacle, but the king was old and would not move unless supported by France or Britain ; Joseph could restrain France, Russia would restrain Britain. And in any case Russia and Austria together were strong enough to oppose Prussia effectively. Should the forces of the two powers be successful in delivering Europe from the Turk, she hoped Joseph would assist her in setting her grandson Constantine on the throne of Constantinople.[35] Joseph's response to these vast plans was deliberately unrealistic. He wanted Khotin (to protect the Bukovina), part of Walachia, and the towns of Belgrade, Orsova and Vidin. From Belgrade a straight line to the sea would mark his southern border in the Gulf of the Drina. Venice would cede Istria and Dalmatia, but receive Morea, Cyprus and Crete, and Constantine could have his empire, and Potemkin his kingdom of Dacia. All this however, Joseph pointed out, could not be achieved merely by trusting that Frederick II was too old to act. Without French participation and guarantees against Prussia, he would not move. Therefore France must be allowed to share in the spoils, possibly in Egypt, and Venice must be compensated.[36]

Meanwhile Joseph was supporting Russian diplomatic pressure in Constantinople, to persuade the Porte to cease opposing Shagin Girey's rule in the Crimean peninsula[37] and the Tartar khan was restored to his throne by Russian arms in October 1782. But Potemkin was now busy promoting a pro-Russian movement in the peninsula and pressing on Catherine the advantages of annexation, or at least of the acquisition of the port of Akhtiar, a policy also supported by Bezborodko. Aware of the audacity of her plan, and of the serious risk of war, Catherine issued a rescript to Potemkin on 14/25 December 1782 which authorized him to annex the peninsula but only in certain circumstances and on certain conditions : for instance the death of Shagin Girey, or a revolt against him, or the Porte's refusal to agree to other Russian demands, or if Shagin Girey refused to cede Akhtiar.[38]

But faced with the combined Austrian and Russian pressure, the Turks gave way, thus cutting the ground from under Russian feet, as Joseph did not hesitate to point out.[39] For the time being the more ambitious 'Greek project' had to be abandoned. But in March Potemkin returned to St Petersburg and threw his influence into the scales in favour of outright annexation.[40] A trumped-up excuse was found – an alleged incursion by the Porte in Taman' – and on 8 April 1783, Catherine signed the manifesto proclaiming her intention of annexing the Crimea. She justified the decision on the grounds that Russia had already spent twelve million rubles in defending the khanate's independence, and that the Porte had destroyed the mutual treaty obligations between Russia and Turkey by its attack on Taman'. The manifesto undertook to respect the persons and property of the Tartars, to grant them the free exercise of their religion, and to extend to them the rights enjoyed by Russians.[41]

On the same day Catherine signed a second rescript to Potemkin dealing with military preparations in the event of the outbreak of war with the Porte.[42] From a diplomatic point of view it was essential to strike at once – indeed the ideal moment might already have escaped her. For on 20 January 1783, the preliminaries of peace between France and Britain had been signed (without the participation of the two imperial mediators). The two powers would thus begin to recover their freedom of action and would be in a better position to oppose Russian plans. In communicating to Joseph II her intention to settle the Crimean problem once and for all, Catherine did not call on him for military assistance, confident that Russian armies would, as before, be a match for the Turks.[43] 'I rely on my ally,' she wrote to Potemkin, 'as little as I fear French thunder, or to put it better, summer lightning.' But, 'when the cake is baked, all will become hungry'.[44] Potemkin set about occupying the Crimea in a leisurely way. He left St Petersburg at the beginning of April 1783, pursued by a series of letters from Catherine, in which she urged her temperamental minister to write more often and to date his letters. Still waiting for news that Crimea had been occupied, Catherine heard in May 1783 that Gustavus III who was proposing to visit Finland in June had accepted a pressing invitation to meet her.[45]

Gustavus III still hoped to conquer Norway for the Swedish Crown, since there was but scant possibility of recovering the lands lost to Russia at Nystadt in 1721. News in April 1783 of the Russian intention to annex the Crimea however revived his hopes, since war between Russia and Turkey might follow and engage Russia's full attention. He anticipated that Catherine would agree to abandon Denmark if Sweden abandoned the Turks, and banked on a Russo-Turkish war, or an agreement with Russia, or both. If he could secure neither, his plans to launch an attack on Denmark in the summer of 1784 would have to be dropped. Catherine was fully awake to Gustavus's ambitions ; but a personal interview between the two sovereigns at that particular time might serve to convince the Turks that they could not count on Swedish assistance in the event of war with Russia. Originally fixed for May, the interview was postponed when Gustavus fell from his horse and broke his arm. 'Pardi mon ami,' wrote Catherine derisively to Potemkin, 'voilà un héros bien maladroit, que de tomber comme cela devant ses troupes.'[46]

The meeting with Gustavus III finally took place on 18/29 June in Fridrikshamm, in Russian Finland, and lasted three days. Gustavus emerged disappointed : to his plans for war with Denmark, Catherine opposed projects for an alliance of Russia, Denmark and Sweden against the Bourbon powers.[47] Meanwhile the interview had served her purpose of warning off the Turks. Early in July Potemkin advanced into the Crimea ; for five weeks Catherine had remained without news from him ; she had expected the annexation of the Crimea to be proclaimed in mid-May, she wrote to him in despair on 15/26 July, and 'I know no more of what is happening than the Pope of Rome'. A sharp edge was given to her anxiety by the epidemic of plague in Constantinople which had already spread to the Crimea.[48] Finally on 20/31 July, she received the long-awaited report that the Crimeans and the two Nogay hordes had taken the oath of allegiance to Russia.[49] It remained to induce the Turks to take the Russian *coup de main* lying down.

By an ironical turn of fate, a few days earlier, Catherine had received the text of the commercial treaty with the Porte, which the new and skilful Russian envoy in Constantinople, Yakov Bulgakov, had successfully negotiated. Catherine had welcomed a commercial treaty when the Turks proposed it, but rejected a parallel proposal for an offensive and defensive alliance between Russia and the Porte, sensing in it a *zamashka* (trick) aimed against 'Constantine II'.[50] Bulgakov had at the same time reported at the end of June 1783 that the Turks were afraid of war. They were doing their best to conceal the loss of the Crimea, and as long as the common people did not rise and overthrow the sultan, Bulgakov thought, peace was assured.[51]

Other powers were exercising pressure in Constantinople to prevent war. In December 1782, Harris on his own initiative had assured Potemkin that Britain would view Russia's Crimean policy with a friendly eye, and the British envoy to the Porte urged peace on the Turks.[52] The new British government which came to power in April 1782 expressed itself in the same friendly terms.[53] Vergennes had at first hoped to enlist the help of Britain to bring pressure to bear on Russia, but he found Fox quite unwilling to cooperate. Subsequently, the revelation of the existence of the secret Austro-Russian treaty of May/June 1781 which committed Joseph II to come to the assistance of Russia in the event of war with the Porte, paralysed French foreign policy.[54]

Joseph II meanwhile, though greatly tempted to make gains at the expense of the Porte, did not want to run the risk of war in which Austria might have to bear the brunt of a Prussian attack, and was by no means assured of French support, or even neutrality. Nor was he willing to join France in bringing pressure to bear on Russia for fear of losing his ally to Prussia. So he was compelled to put a bold face on the fact that he came out of the crisis empty-handed.[55]

Abandoned by all the powers, and bullied by Austria and Russia, the Porte reluctantly decided in the autumn of 1783 to give in to the Russian demands. A new agreement between the two powers was finally signed on 28 December 1783/8 January 1784, which confirmed the existing treaties of 1774 and 1779 and the commercial treaty of 1783, except for those articles which dealt with the Crimea. The Porte was thus not forced to accept Russian annexation in so many words. It merely ceased to have the right to the spiritual investiture of the khan, and accepted Crimean loss of independence in silence.[56] Catherine had added over 18,000 square miles to her empire without a fight. She had also immeasurably increased her influence in Europe, and shifted the balance of power in the Black Sea decisively in her favour.

Catherine was not ungrateful. She poured out her thanks to Joseph and promised to support his schemes for aggrandisement in Germany.[57] Joseph was ready with his plans, namely the exchange of the Austrian Netherlands for Bavaria, which he had failed to achieve in 1778–9. It was essential for him to strike while Catherine might still be driven by gratitude, and before the other powers, now finally at peace since the Treaty of Versailles of September 1783, could reconstitute any system of alliances. Encouraged by the unofficial Russian response,

Joseph outlined in a letter to Catherine of 2/13 May 1784 his plan for the acquisition of Bavaria and the upper Palatinate, together with the archbishopric of Salzburg, in exchange for the Austrian Netherlands. He hoped to achieve his object by agreement with the Elector of Bavaria, and with his heir, the Duke of Zweibrücken. The exchange would in his view in no way affect the constitution of the Empire as guaranteed in the Peace of Teschen.[58]

Catherine's reply was prompt and her support was immediately offered, even to the extent of confirming that she would keep her engagements in the event of a Prussian or a French attack on Austria.[59] Joseph meanwhile brought pressure to bear on the Dutch for the opening of navigation on the Scheldt to ships of the Austrian Netherlands, hoping for support from both France and Russia. His ultimate aim was to accept the French solution for his conflict with the United Provinces in exchange for French support in arranging the exchange of Bavaria for the Austrian Netherlands.[60] The United Provinces had emerged as the principal losers in the war of American Independence. Among other casualties was their traditional alliance with England. France had helped to negotiate the definitive peace treaty between the United Provinces and Britain which put an end to the war, on 9/20 May 1784, and the Patriot Party, now in the ascendant at The Hague, had been only too happy to press for the conclusion of a more permanent defensive treaty with France. The conclusion of this treaty, in October 1784, coincided almost exactly with an 'incident' on the Scheldt, provoked by Joseph II, in which a Dutch vessel fired on an Austrian ship which had refused to stop. Both parties, the Austrians and the Dutch, appealed to France, ostensibly in the hope of preventing the outbreak of a war which no one was in fact prepared to risk. Meanwhile, Joseph II continued to explore the possibility of securing the consent of the Elector of Bavaria to the exchange project, and Catherine's envoy to a number of German courts, Count N.P. Rumyantsev, was charged with persuading the Duke of Zweibrücken, heir to Bavaria, to give his consent. France however continued to oppose the exchange, since her long-term interests were better served by the maintenance of potential client states in the Holy Roman Empire than by strengthening the Hapsburg lands.[61] The Duke of Zweibrücken, aware of French opposition to the scheme, and knowing that he could count on Prussian support, rejected the exchange proposals at the beginning of January 1785, and Joseph was induced to abandon his pet project for the time being.

Nevertheless public speculation continued rife, and Frederick II, brandishing the Treaty of Teschen, made use of the opportunity to break out of his existing isolation (Russia was after all his *only* ally) and build a system of alliances within the Empire. By July 1785 he had built up a League directed against Joseph II which was eventually joined by most of the German princes. The League was a resounding diplomatic defeat for Joseph and to a lesser extent for Catherine. In his dispute with the United Provinces too, Joseph was forced to accept a face-saving solution by which the Dutch paid a substantial indemnity but the Scheldt remained closed.

Catherine had supported her ally loyally by making representations at The Hague and trying to bully the Duke of Zweibrücken. But she had no intention of going to war over Bavaria, and once the immediate crisis was over she issued a circular to the German courts on 23 May/3 June 1785 denying any intention of overthrowing the German constitution.[62] But the formation of the League of Princes and particularly Hanover's accession led to a considerable coldness in Anglo-Russian relations which affected negotiations for the renewal of the Anglo-Russian trade treaty. It was due to expire in 1786, and in March 1785, the British envoy to St Petersburg, Alleyne Fitzherbert (the future Lord St Helens), reminded his court of the need to propose its renewal. In November 1785 the Russians appointed the usual commission to treat with him. The British hoped merely to renew the treaty of 1766 with all the advantages it gave to British trade. But Catherine had not given up the hope Fox had once encouraged of securing English acceptance of the maritime principles of the Armed Neutrality. Thus a Russian draft treaty of February 1786 came as an unpleasant shock to William Pitt, then First Lord of the Treasury – both because of the insistence on the maritime principles, and because of a new Russian condition, that Russian merchants should pay lower export dues than British merchants in Russia.[63] The accession of Hanover to the League of Princes in 1785 so irritated Catherine that she was willing to snub Britain and prepared to listen to fresh proposals for a commercial treaty with France. In June 1785, on the occasion of a journey by water through Lake Ladoga, the Volkhov, Lake Ilmen and the upper Volga, on which Catherine had invited the envoys of Britain, France and Austria to accompany her, Ségur, striking while the iron was hot (and borrowing Fitzherbert's writing desk to do so) drafted a note at Potemkin's instigation, which inaugurated negotiations for a commercial treaty between France and Russia.[64] While in autumn 1786 Pitt rejected the controversial Russian proposals out of hand,[65] the negotiations between France and Russia, prolonged over nearly eighteen months, culminated at last in the signature of a treaty on 11/22 January 1787.[66]

In the fond belief that Russia needed to export to England more than England needed to import from Russia, Pitt allowed the Anglo-Russian treaty to lapse in April 1787, just as the Russian-French treaty was ratified. Equally, Catherine and her advisers were confident that Britain could not do without Russian raw materials, and refused to yield. British merchants now had to pay duty in foreign currency, and were liable to have soldiers billeted on them. Some took out burghers' rights in order to protect themselves.[67]

In the meantime, preparation for the long-planned and often postponed visit by the empress to her domains in South Russia, and in particular to the Crimean peninsula, were reaching completion, and she set out in January 1787. By the time she returned, in autumn of that year, Russia was at war with the Porte again.

25

The Second Turkish War

Ever since the Russian annexation of the Crimea had been forced on the Ottoman Porte by the combined pressure of France and Austria,[1] the Turks had been watching for an opportunity to reverse the verdict of war. The underlying tension between the two powers was increased by Russian interference in the Caucasus and the Russian protectorate over Georgia ; by Russian meddling with the Persian trade ; by her open encouragement of subversion against the Turkish-appointed hospodars of Moldavia and Walachia ; and by the provocative behaviour of Russian consuls in the Archipelago and in Egypt.[2] In the autumn of 1786, the dispute between the two powers became even more acute. Potemkin complained that the Turks had broken an understanding of 1784 allowing Russia some say in the appointments of the hospodars in the Danubian Principalities, and when a pro-Russian hospodar fled to Russia, he was given asylum. The Turks responded by complaining that Turkish merchants paid higher duties in Russian ports than did Russians in the Ottoman Empire, and that the inhabitants of Ochakov were refused permission to procure all the salt they needed from the saltpans of Kinburn.

Russian councils in 1786 and early 1787 were very divided over policy to the Porte. A.A. Bezborodko, the *de facto* foreign minister, still favoured prudence. But in October 1786 Catherine placed Potemkin in sole charge of negotiations with the Porte, granting him wide powers to dispose of Russian armed forces as he saw fit, and even to order the recall of Ya. Bulgakov, the Russian envoy, from Constantinople – almost the equivalent of a declaration of war. Potemkin used his powers to instruct Bulgakov on 13/24 December 1786 to employ such threatening language to the Porte as to lead inevitably to misunderstandings.[3] It is unlikely that Potemkin wanted to provoke the Porte to declare war just when Catherine was setting out on her triumphal journey to the fairyland he was preparing for her.[4] But he may simply have miscalculated the impact of Russian threats. However, Russian verbal arrogance was probably merely a minor irritant compared with the actual presence of Catherine in the Crimea, inspecting her new naval base at Sebastopol, within a day's sailing of Constantinople. Potemkin had moved large numbers of troops to Kherson, the Crimea and Astrakhan'. The shipyards of Kherson and Sebastopol were ringing with the noise of the construction of Russian warships, many of which were already sailing on what had been until 1774 a Turkish lake. The presence of the Emperor Joseph implied an agreement to partition the Ottoman Empire ; the inscription over a gateway in Kherson : 'This is the road to Byzantium' confirmed it. The summoning of Bulgakov and the Austrian internuncio Herbert, from Constantinople to Kherson, underlined too emphatically the alteration in the balance of military and naval power between the two empires. The only solution might well seem a preemptive strike, before the Russian armament had time to grow further.

Joseph had embarked very reluctantly on his second trip to Russia. So far he had benefited but little from the Austro-Russian alliance, and he saw no reason to jeopardize his already delicate health in order to pander to Catherine's vanity. The active opposition of France to his project for the Bavarian exchange in 1784–5 had led him briefly to toy with a *rapprochement* with Prussia – which appeared more feasible after the death of Frederick II in August 1786. Such an alliance might help Joseph to realize his Bavarian designs, if Prussia could be compensated, probably in Poland. Kaunitz had argued Joseph out of this policy and persuaded him to tighten his links with Catherine by accepting her pressing invitation. But neither emperor nor chancellor favoured a war with Turkey which, in Kaunitz's eyes at any rate, would turn Russian attention away from the primary task of holding Prussia in check, and might also, if victorious, lead to an undesirable strengthening of the Russian Empire.[5] As a result Joseph, while in Russia, discouraged Potemkin's warlike schemes, and confided to Ségur that Austria would not tolerate further Russian expansion, particularly the occupation of Constantinople. Austria would always find 'the vicinity of the turbans less dangerous than that of the hats'.[6]

In a last effort to preserve peace, Bezborodko, Bulgakov, the internuncio Herbert, Fitzherbert, Cobenzl and Ségur met in Kherson to discuss the terms of an agreement to be submitted to the Porte, and the Austrian and Russian envoys returned to Constantinople in July. But though Bulgakov, by the lavish use of bribes, strove to postpone a breach until the following spring, or at least until the end of the present campaigning season in the autumn, it was now the turn of the Turks to raise their terms.[7] They had been steadily rearming with the help of French experts and it was now or never as far as they were concerned. Accordingly on 15/26 July a Turkish ultimatum was presented to Bulgakov : Russia was to remove her troops from Georgia and give up all claim to suzerainty ; to surrender the hospodar ; to surrender thirty saltpans near Kinburn ; to allow the appointment of Turkish consuls in the Crimea and Russia ; to allow the Porte to search Russian ships in Turkish waters and to grant other commercial rights. Without giving Bulgakov time to receive a reply from Russia, the envoy was summoned again on 5/16 August and informed that the Porte was denouncing all treaties and demanded the return of the Crimea. When Bulgakov naturally rejected these terms, he was arrested and incarcerated in the Seven Towers.[8]

In spite of the sabre-rattling which had marked most of 1787, Russia was taken by surprise when war actually broke out. From the point of view of her international position the situation was inauspicious. In the Austrian Netherlands, revolt had broken out in May, thus distracting the emperor's attention and eventually his troops. In the United Provinces, the Patriot Party had risen against the Stadholder, and insulted his wife, a sister of King Frederick William II of Prussia. The new King of Prussia was not bound by Frederick II's old antagonisms, and the disturbances in the United Provinces led to a *rapprochement* between Prussia and Britain, culminating in a treaty of alliance signed in August 1787. This new orientation opened the way for a possible Anglo-Prussian intervention in a Russo-Turkish war, and increased the fears of Joseph II of a Prussian attack on his dominions. Anglo-Russian relations had not recovered from the blow inflicted by Hanover's entry into the League of Princes, and Catherine was convinced – with some justice – that Britain had egged the Turks on to war. She accepted Pitt's assurances to the Russian ambassador in London that Britain's ambassador in Constantinople had no instructions of the kind ; but, she wrote to Potemkin, 'English foreign policy is directed not by the English government, but by the most spiteful of kings, on the instructions of Hanoverian ministers.'[9]

The Turkish declaration of war, issued on 24 August/4 September 1787, faced Austria with the decision whether or not to recognize the *casus foederis* of the Austro-Russian treaty of 1781. In the formal sense Catherine had been attacked, and Joseph was in duty bound to go to her aid. In addition, Kaunitz argued that only by joining in the war could Austria hope to ensure a 'balance of conquests' and limit Russian expansion at the expense of the Porte. On 19/30 August 1787, without waiting to be asked, Joseph wrote to Catherine declaring that her cause was his.[10] He did not yet declare war however, in the hope of mounting a surprise operation against Belgrade.

On 31 August/11 September 1787, Catherine presided at a meeting of an enlarged Council of state[11] at which she formally communicated to her advisers the Turkish declaration of war, and discussed Russian military and financial resources.[12] Though Catherine herself, because of her boundless trust in Potemkin, believed that Russia was better prepared now for war than in 1768, nevertheless, in one respect the moment could not have been worse. Owing to a patchy harvest, the price of grain had leapt prodigiously and in some areas had reached 7 rubles a chetvert'. The southern provinces through which Catherine had recently travelled were particularly fertile and do not seem to have suffered. But the spectacle of near famine in some central areas had cast a shadow over her return to Moscow.[13] Catherine's immediate response was to free the trade in grain between various gubernii, to limit distillation from corn, to order vast supplies for the capital and to postpone any increase in taxation to finance the war.[14] On 7/18 September the empress signed the Russian manifesto declaring war, which was read in Russian churches on the twelfth. 'She wept,' noted her secretary briefly in his diary on that day.[15]

In the interval between the peace of Kuchuk Kainardzhi and 1781 the annual recruit levy had been limited to one in 500. In 1782 it rose to one in 200 (one in 100 for the odnodvortsy), presumably with the annexation of the Crimea in mind. In 1783 the levy rose to two in 500 ; it was one in 500 in 1784, two in 500 in 1785 and one in 500 in 1786, giving a total number of recruits over these years of 142,911 (one in 500 produced about 18,000 recruits). On the outbreak of the war in 1787 a levy of 2 in 500 was decreed in August followed by 3 in 500 in September, which raised 92,735 men. But since kuptsy and wealthy peasants could buy themselves out for 500 rubles, exemptions often considerably reduced the total numbers called up : in 1790, for instance, of 73,651, 9,251 were exempt.[16] The army, as remodelled by Potemkin, comprised a cavalry force of 62,416 men, to which must be added the irregular Cossack forces totalling 73,651 throughout the country. The artillery had 244 field guns and 178 siege guns. The infantry totalled 218,306, including the four guards regiments, ten regiments of grenadiers, and light infantry.

The Russian navy was divided into the Baltic and the Black Sea fleets. In the Baltic naval base of Kronstadt, Russia disposed of 37 ships of the line and 13 frigates (with smaller ships). The Black Sea fleet was supposed to consist of 12 ships of the line, 20 frigates and smaller oared vessels in 1785. During the war of 1787–91, 22 more warships were under construction, as well as 12 frigates, and 17 cruisers. A flotilla of small boats was built for operations on the Danube, and a fleet of 3 frigates and a bombketch patrolled the Caspian.[17]

Potemkin, who had been president of the College of War since 1784, was appointed commander-in-chief of the Russian armies in the field, which were divided into two groups : the main Yekaterinoslav army directly under his own command, numbering some 82,000 men, which was stationed from the Caucasus along the Black Sea shore to the Bug, its right wing linking up inland with the Ukrainian army at Olviopol. The Ukrainian army, regarded as a reserve force, numbered some 40,000 men and Catherine summoned Rumyantsev to take command, though he found it very difficult to serve under Potemkin. His army was composed of three divisions extending from the Bug at Olviopol to Khotin in Turkish territory and Kamenets Podol'sk in Poland, where the junction with the Austrian forces was to be made. A corps of 12,000 under General Tekelli was to operate in the Caucasus, and two infantry, two cavalry and 27 regiments of Don Cossacks guarded the Kuban'.[18]

The first object of the Yekaterinoslav army was the capture of the great Turkish fort of Ochakov, which dominated the thirty-mile-long estuary of the Dniepr opposite the Russian fort of Kinburn, bottling up the Russian navy in the estuary and reducing the value of the main naval supply base at Kherson. Ochakov was also the key to the coast between the Bug and the Dniestr. Potemkin's strategy aimed secondly at a Russian advance over the Dniestr, and the clearing of the Turks from the Dniestr to the Pruth. While the Russians took Bender, the Austrians, advancing from Bukovina, would take Khotin, and both armies would then advance on the Danube. The Ukrainian army's role was to be secondary, covering the right flank of Potemkin's army. The Crimea was to be defended mainly by sea, but a special corps was detached under General A.S. Suvorov to defend Kinburn and Kherson. Meanwhile the main Turkish force of some 60,000 was advancing at the end of August from Adrianople to Izmail, to contain Austro-Russian forces. But the Turks relied principally on the numerical superiority of their navy of 120 ships and their inside lines. With the ships at Varna, those already in Ochakov, and the garrison of Ochakov which numbered 24,000 men, they hoped to seize Kinburn and Kherson, reconquer the Crimea, and then advance along the coast to the Bug. At the same time, forces were concentrated in Anapa, to foment rebellion against Russia in the Kuban'.[19]

Fighting began on 19/30 August 1787, when a Turkish naval detachment opened fire on two Russian frigates off Ochakov, and began the bombardment of Kinburn. Two Turkish descents on the narrow tongue of land on which Kinburn was built were beaten off in fierce fighting. Suvorov, in command, was a great believer in cold steel : 'The bullet is a fool, the bayonet a brave lad.' A Russian attack on the Turkish fleet was less successful, and operations then ceased when the estuary began to be covered in ice in October. Meanwhile the main Russian fleet sailing from Sebastopol was caught in a severe gale at sea. A ship was captured, another went down, and the rest of the fleet was dismasted or suffered heavy damage.[20]

For Catherine these were anxious days. She was without news from Potemkin for twenty-one days and finally heard that Kinburn was under attack on 22 September/3 October. To add to her worries, there was the constant uncertainty about Potemkin's health. 'Dans ce moment mon cher ami,' she wrote to him, 'vous n'êtes pas un petit particulier qui . . . fait ce qui lui plait ; vous êtes à l'état, vous êtes à moi.' 'Pray God,' she added later in the same letter, 'to give you strength and health and alleviate your hypochondria.'[21] But the uncertainty regarding the outcome of the Turkish assault on Kinburn brought Potemkin to the verge of a nervous breakdown and he asked to be relieved of his command. 'The empire will still be an empire even without Kinburn,' Catherine wrote to him, stressing the extent to which she and the empire both needed his services. The loss of his precious Black Sea fleet overset Potemkin completely. Faced with the enormous naval superiority of the Turks, he believed he would be unable to defend the Crimea, and proposed evacuating the peninsula and withdrawing to the isthmus of Perekop. He blamed himself, and again proposed throwing up his command, his rank and his privileges. Catherine's reply to her disordered friend was a masterly combination of affection, encouragement and strategic common sense. The storm was a disaster, she wrote, which harmed not only Russia but the enemy. Since neither she, nor Potemkin, had caused it, the less said about it the better. As for withdrawing from the Crimean peninsula, had Potemkin thought where to send the Black Sea fleet ? There was no need to hurry to begin the war by evacuating a province which was not even in danger. To assuage Potemkin's anxieties, she enclosed the necessary orders to enable him to hand over his command to Rumyantsev but, she concluded, in a postscript : '. . . vous êtes impatient comme un enfant de cinq ans, tandis que les affaires dont vous êtes chargé en ce moment demandent une patience imperturbable. Adieu mon ami, neither time nor distance, nor anyone in the world will change my thoughts of you and about you.'[22] By the beginning of October Potemkin had recovered sufficiently to put Catherine out of her anxieties,[23] and she set about rewarding in her usual lavish way the defenders of Kinburn.[24] At the same time she began to plan the dispatch of a fleet from the Baltic to the Mediterranean as in 1769.

Before Joseph II issued his declaration of war in February 1788, the diplomatic pattern in Europe had suffered some changes. In September 1787 Prussian troops had entered the United Provinces by agreement with Britain to restore the Stadholder's authority. The overthrow of the Dutch Patriot party was a blow to French prestige, already suffering from the gradually worsening domestic crisis. All Ségur's efforts to bring about a quadruple alliance between the two Bourbon powers and the two empires came to nothing. France could be of no help to Russia ; the hesitations in French policy revived Catherine's distrust and Russia had no wish to lose the English trade.[25]

Joseph II was far more affected however by the revelation of a far-reaching Prussian plan to profit by Austrian involvement in war with Turkey in order to secure valuable acquisitions in Poland without drawing the sword. The so-called Hertzberg plan involved the cession of the principalities of Moldavia and Walachia by the Turks to Austria ; Austria would then restore Galicia to Poland ; Prussia would receive Danzig and Thorn from Poland, while Russia would acquire Bessarabia and Ochakov. In exchange, Prussia and her allies would guarantee Turkish possessions south of the Danube. Communicated to Prussian envoys in the various capitals in December 1787, details of Hertzberg's plan leaked quickly enough to alarm Joseph at the thought of a possible war with Prussia. Catherine had no intention of fighting the Turks in order to allow Prussian aggrandisement at the expense of Poland, nor did she wish to arouse Joseph's suspicions by any double-dealing. Thus on 1/12 March 1788, Prussian proposals for a mediation and for the renewal of the long forgotten Russo-Prussian treaty, with subsidies for the existing war, were formally turned down by Russia.[26] The Russian rejection of Prussian overtures was followed by a secret formal declaration to Austria on 10/21 May 1788, by which Catherine bound herself to join with Austria to oppose, in word or deed if necessary, any Prussian attempt at aggrandisement in Poland.[27]

Both in order to guarantee Poland against Prussian aggression, and to tie the Republic more closely and more exclusively to Russia, Catherine proceeded to develop the plan for an alliance between Russia and Poland which Stanislas had so pressingly outlined in Kaniev in May 1787. In September of that year the king had forwarded a draft treaty to St Petersburg, outlining Polish hopes to join in the war against the Porte and to obtain, in addition to territorial acquisitions (Bessarabia, part of Moldavia and a port on the Black Sea), support for some strengthening of royal power, an increase in the Polish army and Russian subsidies. The alliance would have to be put through the diet in Poland by means of a confederation which would guarantee the maintenance of public order during the war.

But Potemkin was developing his own policy in Poland. He had continued to build up his estates there until he owned over 112,000 serfs. His purchases were mainly in that triangle of land in the Polish palatinate of Kiev which projected, along the banks of the Dniepr, into Russia, from Kiev to Kremenchug and down to Uman'. They were so large, including the vast estate of Smiła, that they could almost be regarded as a form of Russian annexation. Potemkin was quite open to Catherine about some of the objects of his purchases which were doubtless made with her approval. He argued that the logical consequence of the Russian alliance with the emperor was alliance with Poland. He had bought these estates because as a Polish landowner he would have the right to intervene in the Polish government, and 'in their military command'. That he might plan to set up his own principality independent of both Russia and Poland, did not escape Catherine.[28] But once secure of his territorial and financial base he toyed with several policies. On the surface he appeared to favour negotiations with Stanislas. But behind the scenes he plotted with his Polish clientèle, starting with his nephew by marriage, Count Xavier Branicki, the formation of a national 'Host' in the southeast Polish provinces, namely Volynia, Podolia and Bratslav (where Cossack traditions and Orthodoxy were still strong), which would be led by Branicki, and other Polish magnates such as Count Felix Potocki, and sundry Rzewuskis, Sapiehas and Walewskis. The Host, to be formed as secretly as possible, would then proclaim a confederation, since, as Potemkin put it, 'it was necessary that the people should force the king to their side, not the king the people'. The confederation (which the king and other magnates might be invited to join) would have as its objects the defence of Poland against Turkish incursions, the maintenance of the Roman Catholic religion, and the freedoms and prerogatives of the Polish nobility.[29] These were Potemkin's ostensible motives. But he may well have contemplated the establishment of some totally different type of 'oligarchical federation' in which he himself would have played a crucial role as a Polish magnate. His systematic recruitment of new Cossack formations provided him with a locally based armed force to assist him in carrying out his plans and in forming a Polish confederation.[30] Who can tell how much truth there was in the remark made by Potemkin's niece, Countess Alexandra Branicka, after his death, that her uncle intended 'to win over all the Cossacks, unite with the Polish army and proclaim himself king of Poland' ?[31]

Catherine, however, did not wish to sacrifice Stanislas, who remained throughout her most reliable tool in Poland.[32] Thus, when she forwarded her reply to the draft Polish treaty of alliance to Warsaw in June 1788, she agreed to the formation of a confederation under the king, and to the use of an auxiliary Polish force of 12,000, under overall Russian command, in the war.[33] But Poland was to be allowed no territorial gains and no constitutional reform, and was to harmonize her foreign policy with that of Russia. When the terms of this proposed treaty became known in Prussia, they led to an uproar. Hertzberg saw at once that it meant the end of any hope of securing Russian consent to Prussian aggrandisement at the expense of Poland. Prussian policy was immediately directed at forcing Russia to drop the proposed Polish alliance.[34]

The change in Prussian policy from the attempt to woo Russia to the formation of an anti-Russian 'front' came at a time when Catherine was particularly vulnerable. Military operations against the Turks had not gone particularly well either for Austria or for Russia in the spring and summer of 1788. An Austrian *coup de main* against Belgrade in January 1788 had failed. The Austrian strategy of extending their forces from the Adriatic to the Dniestr left them equally weak everywhere. The total force of 120,000 was divided, with the Prince of Coburg in charge of the forces in the Bukovina, destined to cooperate with the right wing of Rumyantsev's army. The emperor himself commanded the army before Belgrade.

Russian strategy was still directed primarily at the capture of Ochakov. As late as May 1788, however, Potemkin in the throes of a fresh crisis was again proposing to evacuate the Crimea, and allow the Turks to occupy it, in the hope of reconquering it later. It required all Catherine's firmness and common sense to make him see that the war was about the Crimea : its evacuation would deprive Russia of her Black Sea naval base and divide the main army from the army of the Caucasus. 'When you are sitting on a horse ; she wrote to Potemkin, 'there is no point in getting off it and holding on by the tail.'[35]

As in the previous Russo-Turkish war Catherine was planning to arouse the Christian Orthodox populations under Turkish rule to revolt against their overlord. On 17/28 February 1788 a Russian appeal was launched to the peoples of the Danubian Principalities, and Russian agents in Malta, Italy and the Greek islands were ordered to prepare the ground and purchase supplies for the despatch of a Russian fleet to the Mediterranean in order to support land operations. Admiral Greig was to direct the hoped-for risings against the Turks, particularly in Montenegro, and he was authorized to recruit men into the Russian armed forces.[36]

But the despatch of the fleet to the Mediterranean met with unexpected obstacles. Accustomed to take British friendship for granted, Catherine did not realize that her seeming *rapprochement* with France in summer and autumn 1787, coupled with lasting resentment at the Armed Neutrality of 1780, had strengthened British resolve to maintain a strict neutrality in the present war. Thus, in winter 1788, Catherine was refused permission to hire British transports, to recruit British seamen, and to use British ports, in Britain or the Mediterranean, to refit and provision her ships.[37]

It was however the threatening behaviour of Sweden which finally led Catherine to abandon the Mediterranean naval expedition. Gustavus III resented and feared Russian intrigues with Swedish noble opposition to his policy of restoring absolutism in Sweden, and with disaffected nobles in Finland.[38] Military ambition and political calculation led him to seek to strengthen his own position and authority by means of a successful war. The Russo-Turkish conflict provided the perfect opportunity to revenge himself for Sweden's previous defeats, since in a war on two fronts, St Petersburg itself might prove vulnerable, while the bulk of the Russian army was concentrated in the South.

By March 1788 Catherine had heard rumours of Sweden's armament, and of Gustavus's claim that the Russian Mediterranean expedition was in reality directed against him ;[39] the Council began to discuss the strengthening of the Russian Baltic coastline against Swedish incursions.[40] Catherine used every means to avoid a break, while Gustavus was forced to manoeuvre in such a way as to present Russia as the aggressor in order not to do too much violence to the Swedish constitution. A clumsily worded Russian note, which seemed to distinguish between the King of Sweden and his people, gave Gustavus a handle to demand the withdrawal of the Russian envoy in an ultimatum dated 12/23 June. Catherine responded in a manifesto of 30 June/11 July, in which she tactlessly pointed out that Gustavus owed his crown to Russia (the Empress Elizabeth had after all insisted in 1743 that the crown should go to Adolf Frederick of Holstein-Gottorp).[41] Gustavus in turn issued an ultimatum to Russia demanding the punishment of Razumovsky, the return of Russian Finland including Kexholm as compensation for the costs of his military preparations and the acceptance of Swedish mediation in the war with the Porte on the basis of a Russian return to the limits of 1774, or even 1768 if the Porte preferred. He too tactlessly took the credit for not having declared war on Russia in 1773–4 when Catherine was suffering from the Pugachev revolt. Even the Grand Signor, remarked Ségur, would not address a hospodar of Moldavia in such terms.[42]

In these circumstances it took only a spark to ignite the conflict. A raid by a party of so-called Cossacks from Russian Finland on Swedish territory served to justify Gustavus in treating Russia as the aggressor, even though rumours already circulated at the time that the 'Cossacks' were Swedish soldiers disguised in costumes procured from the Swedish royal opera.[43] In turn, Swedish forces bombarded the Russian fort of Nyslott on 22 June/3 July 1788.

But Gustavus had acted too soon. The Russian Mediterranean fleet had not yet left the Baltic, and Admiral Greig now had seventeen battleships and seven frigates under his command, as against the fifteen battleships and five frigates of Duke Charles of Sudermania. The two fleets met on 6/17 July off the island of Hogland. In the ensuing battle both sides suffered severely. It was a draw rather than a Russian victory,[44] but it removed for the time being any danger of a Swedish descent on St Petersburg. On 12/23 July Swedish forces under Gustavus himself laid siege to Fridrikshamm, but the battle of Hogland left him in an exposed position and he was forced to withdraw in August.

At this moment Catherine's intrigues with the Swedish and Finnish noble opposition began to bear fruit. Opposition to Gustavus's restoration of absolutism had taken different forms in Sweden and in Finland. While in the former, the nobles hankered after aristocratic constitutionalism, in Finland an autonomist movement was developing, mainly among nobles of Baltic origin. The leader of these Finnish malcontents, Goran Magnus Sprengtporten, had entered Russian service in 1786 and had put before Catherine a project for a Finnish republic under Russian protection. He succeeded in winning some support for his ideas among Finnish officers, indignant at the prospect of the invasion of their country for the third time in a hundred years. Over a hundred Swedish and Finnish officers were induced on 1/12 August to sign the pact of Anjala, which denounced Gustavus for engaging in war unconstitutionally. The conspirators sent emissaries to St Petersburg, to propose that Catherine should negotiate peace (on the basis of the Swedish frontier of 1721) with the Riksdag. This would have satisfied the Swedish noble conspirators who hoped to use a Riksdag to restrict the powers of the king, but the Finnish plotters meant to go further. Catherine now proposed that the Finns too should set up a representative body with which she could discuss peace – and autonomy.

Gustavus was rescued from his predicament, indirectly, by Catherine herself. On the outbreak of war, she had immediately called on Denmark for the assistance she was entitled to by treaty. Denmark hesitated at first, but finally declared war on Sweden at the end of August (possibly encouraged by the mutiny in the Swedish army) and thus enabled Gustavus to restore his authority over his army by appealing to Swedish patriotism, in any case outraged by the revelation of the treasonable behaviour of the Anjala conspirators.[45]

The first public manifestation of the Triple Allance between Britain, Prussia and the United Provinces was their joint offer in late August 1788 to mediate between Russia and Sweden and Russia and the Porte. The alliance emboldened two of the most enterprising English envoys abroad, Hugh Elliot in Copenhagen, and J. Ewart in Berlin, to embark in September on the rescue of Sweden from the combined Russian-Danish threat, which seemed about to destroy the balance of power in the Baltic. The Danes had invaded southern Sweden, and were rapidly advancing on Göteborg. Elliot, already profoundly anti-Russian, set out to break the Danish-Russian connection and win both Scandinavian powers to the British-Prussian alliance. On 5/16 September he threatened the Danes with the intervention of Prussia and Britain if they did not halt their advance. The next day he left for Sweden without instructions from London. His object was to browbeat Gustavus into accepting the mediation of the Triple Alliance (and thus wean him away from France). Prussia too urged mediation on Denmark with the threat of a Prussian corps and a British squadron. Elliot caught up with Gustavus at the end of September, and compelled the Danes on 28 September/9 October to agree to an armistice, which was later prolonged to the following summer. Denmark took no further part in the war.[46] Though Elliot was subsequently to some extent disavowed by his foreign sescretary, William Pitt, there is little doubt that his intervention saved Gustavus, by giving him the breathing space he needed to restore his position within Sweden and to organize a further campaign.

The offers of mediation of the Triple Alliance met with a cold reception in Russia. That Prussia should support Swedish pretensions was offensive ; and it was also dangerous. It was therefore agreed to refuse Prussian offers on the grounds that it was for Sweden to give satisfaction for her unjustified attack on Russia and that Russia would in any case have to consult her allies, Denmark and Austria. At the same time offensive action by Prussia had to be forestalled. The war with the Porte would have to become defensive, and troops would have to move into Poland to be ready for a far more dangerous enemy than the Turk.[47]

Catherine from the moment of the Swedish declaration of war, had lived through one of the most tense summers of her life. And there was still no news from the Turkish front to assuage her anxiety. Joseph II was proving once again that he was no Frederick II. On 16/27 April 1788 a small Turkish fort, Shabach, on the Save, was taken. Fever then hit the Austrian army, and by the end of August, the Grand Vizir, Yussif Pasha, with an army of 70,000 men, crossed the Temesch, and ravaged the land. Further fierce fighting in September culminated in a Turkish attack on the Austrian camp at Lugosch on the night of 9/20 September, in which Joseph only just escaped.

The Austrian forces in Bukovina were more successful. Acting in cooperation with the Russian army under Rumyantsev, their objective was the great Turkish fort of Khotin. The Austrian commander, Prince Frederick of Saxe Coburg Saalfeld, hoped to secure the surrender of the fort without a fight, hence he advanced very slowly. Meanwhile Rumyantsev crossed the Pruth but, distrusting Coburg, he too advanced slowly, mindful of the need to protect the flank of Potemkin's Yekaterinoslav army. Both the Russian and the Austrian commanders appeared willing to sacrifice the taking of Khotin to the occupation of the Danubian Principalities. After a good deal of undignified squabbling between the various commanders, and a good deal of aimless marching and counter-marching during which the main Turkish army refused battle, Khotin was finally induced to surrender on 4/15 September 1788 to the Austrian forces, who, to Rumyantsev's fury, allowed the Turks ten days to evacuate the fort with the full honours of war.[48]

Meanwhile Potemkin was conducting a leisurely siege of Ochakov. In the middle of June, he crossed the Bug with 50,000 men to surround Ochakov on land. But it was still open to the sea, and on 20/31 May a powerful Turkish fleet had arrived off the fort.[49] The Russian fleet, which had been strengthened during the winter, was divided into : the flotilla of gunboats, under Prince Charles of Nassau Siegen (with Samuel Bentham as his second-in-command) and the sailing fleet, to which the most controversial appointment was made, namely that of the American privateer hero, Paul Jones, whose services had been snapped up by Catherine. Knowing that the many British officers in the Russian Baltic fleet would refuse to serve with him, Catherine sent Paul Jones straight to the Black Sea, where even so his presence caused a certain resentment.[50]

The Turkish fleet had the advantage in battleships, and also in lighter craft ; but the Russian gunboats were better armed thanks to Samuel Bentham.[51] After some inconclusive skirmishing, battle was finally engaged between the two gunboat flotillas on 7/18 June in which the Turks were worsted. The withdrawal of the Turkish flotilla left the Russians masters of the sea. A major encounter between the main sailing fleets took place on 17/28 June and ended again with the advantage to the Russians. The Turkish admiral now decided to withdraw the remainder of the sailing fleet from the bay, but to do so he had to pass under the guns of a newly constructed Russian battery at Kinburn. Keeping too far to the north to avoid the gunfire, nine of the Turkish ships ran aground, and the Russian flotilla moved in to destroy them. The Turks were estimated to have lost a total of fifteen ships, of which ten were of some size, in the two days' fighting.[52]

What was left of the Turkish fleet now moved out into the open sea, to watch out for the Russian Sebastopol squadron and to await reinforcements. The two fleets met finally on 3/14 July off the island of Fidonisi near the Danube delta. Again the battle was inconclusive, and on 7/18 July the stronger Turkish fleet drew away while the Russian fleet returned to refit at Sebastopol.

It was now time to close the ring around Ochakov, one of the strongest forts in the Ottoman Empire with a garrison estimated at 20,000. For the next few weeks, Potemkin, who had decided against taking the fort by storm, for fear of the inevitable heavy casualties, proceeded to tighten the ring of batteries around the fort. Suvorov was placed in charge of the left flank of the Russian besieging army, and on 27 July/7 August he turned the pursuit of a defeated Turkish sally into an attack on the fortress – in which he was wounded – for which he was severely rebuked by Potemkin for disobeying orders. Whereupon Suvorov, deeply offended, begged (in vain) to be released 'to go and take the waters' for his health.

Potemkin's caution was probably justified as long as the Turkish fleet remained undefeated. In a fresh effort to relieve the fort, it appeared in the estuary of the Dniepr on 29 July/9 August but no fighting took place. During the next two months there were frequent engagements between small numbers of ships, the Russians attempting to enforce a complete blockade of Ochakov, the Turks attempting to keep communications open. The effectiveness of the Russian navy was not improved by the struggle for precedence which developed between Nassau-Siegen and Paul Jones. Both naval commanders were superseded, after two Turkish ships had succeeded in running the blockade, on 8/19 October, bringing 1,500 men into Ochakov. Rear Admiral N.S. Mordvinov now took command of the whole naval force.

There could be no further justification for postponing the assault on Ochakov since it could not be supplied by sea once the bay had frozen over. Potemkin's plan was to breach the walls of the fort on the side of the Dniepr estuary, where they were less heavily fortified, and the guns from the flotilla could be used. For more than a month the cannonade continued, until finally on 6/17 December the order for the assault was given. The fighting was extremely fierce, but after an hour and a quarter Ochakov was taken at last and the way was now open for a Russian advance towards the Dniestr and the Danube.

For Catherine the news of the capture of Ochakov which reached her on 16/27 December was one bright spot in a troubled year. 'I take you by the ears, and kiss you in my thoughts, dearest friend,' she wrote to Potemkin, aware that her hand was at last strengthened in the delicate diplomatic situation in which Russia found herself. Her first thought was for the killed and wounded, and for the brave who must be duly rewarded : half a year's pay was to be given to all those who had taken part in the siege.[53] And at last Potemkin himself would be able to leave the army and join her in the capital, to help her with the organization of the defence against Sweden, and to mourn with her the loss of her best naval commander, Samuel Greig, who had died at sea in October. Meanwhile, the Russian army was ordered to winter in Poland, where the situation was developing unpleasantly for Russia. Prussian protests at the projected Russo-Polish treaty of alliance, coming at a time when Prussia was preparing to support Sweden against Russia's ally Denmark by force, led Catherine reluctantly to abandon the alliance project in September 1788. Indeed the Prussian attitude had become extremely threatening ; Hertzberg ordered the Prussian envoy in Warsaw to prevent the confederation of the Diet ; and, if necessary, to organize a Polish counter-confederation which would invite the support of the Prussian army. It was clear that the Diet in October would see a struggle for the control of Poland between Russia and Prussia.

Polish hatred of Russia was such that only a very small party of those around Stanislas favoured the king's policy of leaning on Russia, in exchange for the very limited measure of reform Catherine would allow. The opposition to Stanislas was composed of those who hankered after the days of unfettered golden liberty, who looked to Potemkin for aid in overthrowing the king ; and those who sought for far-reaching reforms, but who realized that these could only be achieved by freeing Poland from the Russian stranglehold. This required the support of a great power – in the present context, inevitably Prussia. They had few illusions about Prussia as such, but there was hope that the Triple Alliance of Britain, the United Provinces and Prussia, could be extended into a 'federative system' comprising also Sweden, Turkey, Denmark and the Princes' League, united against the two imperial powers : a kind of 'Northern system' in reverse.

When the Polish Diet met therefore on 25 September/6 October 1788 it was almost immediately confederated, thus enabling decisions to be taken by majority vote. The Russian programme of allowing a limited increase in the army was lost sight of when on 2/13 October a Prussian declaration was read protesting against the Russian offer of alliance, and offering a Prussian one instead.[54] All the Poles' pent-up hatred of Russia now burst forth, and Stanislas's warnings of the danger of making unilateral changes in a constitution guaranteed by the empress were swept aside. During the next few months the confederated Diet proceeded to dismantle the Polish system of government as guaranteed by Russia, to the accompaniment of much verbal abuse of Russia and of Catherine. In this the Poles were secretly egged on by Prussia, who hoped to benefit from the internal turmoil in order to be invited by the Polish opposition to Stanislas to join a confederation and secure the long desired compensation in Danzig and Thorn. Alternately, during the winter of 1789, hopes were entertained in Berlin that Potemkin might persuade Catherine to reach an agreement with Prussia at the expense of Poland.

Indeed in St Petersburg, counsels were deeply divided. The increasing tension between Russia and Prussia led to acute dissension within the Russian Council between those prepared to risk a war with Prussia rather than knuckle under to her, such as A.R. Vorontsov, Bezborodko or Zavadovsky and indeed the empress herself, and those like A.A. Vyazemsky, and particularly A.P. Shuvalov, who declared that no decision on the Prussian demands should be taken without consulting Potemkin as president of the College of War. Implicit in Shuvalov's stand, though not openly stated, was the view that Potemkin might recommend peace with the Porte in order to reach an understanding with Prussia at the expense of Poland. The result of the explosion in the Council was a decision to use a more moderate tone with Prussia, and to wait for the prince to arrive, and even this 'caused many tears'[55] noted the empress's secretary in his diary.

Meanwhile events in Poland had alarmed Joseph and Kaunitz, with whom fear of Prussia was uppermost. Austria therefore began to press on the Russians the need to make peace with the Porte, on the basis of the *uti possidetis* in order to free both powers to attend to the crisis in Poland.[56] From December 1788, Count Cobenzl urged moderation on Russia, and particularly compliance with the most outrageous Polish demands such as the withdrawal of the Russian troops.[57] The Austrian pressure for peace, as well as Russia's own parlous position led the Council in December 1788 to define Russian peace terms with the Porte : in the first place Bulgakov must be released from Turkish captivity ; all treaties must be renewed guaranteeing Russia the Crimea, Taman' and the Kuban'. The cession of Ochakov and its hinterland (now that it had been conquered) up to the Dniestr was also a *conditio sine qua non*. The other matters of dispute which had led to the war could be the subject of negotiation. The possibility that Austria might have to conclude a separate peace was accepted.[58]

During the first few weeks of 1789 all were waiting for Potemkin to arrive in the capital. Catherine herself was ill ; she bewailed the prince's absence, needed his advice, but also feared that he would strive to make her change her present political system, which she had no intention of doing. The Austrian alliance, and the maintenance of Stanislas in an unpartitioned Poland, were still the main-springs of her policy, and her hatred of Prussia and contempt for its ruler mounted : 'Qu'est ce que c'est que ce petit homme, je lui apprendrai bien son métier.' Moreover Catherine was well aware that Prussia was insistently pressing her alliance on the Porte with a view to carrying out Hertzberg's famous ex-change plan in some form or another. Potemkin by all accounts was the one per-son who could have induced Catherine to reach an accommodation with Prussia at the expense of Poland (to be compensated in turn by parts of the Ottoman Em-pire). But he failed. When after a stay which lasted from 4 February to 6 May he returned to the army, the empress had won.[59] The Austrian alliance continued in-tact, and was indeed renewed by a fresh exchange of letters between Catherine and Joseph in May–June 1789. A more conciliatory tone was adopted towards Prussia, with whom some inconclusive negotiations were undertaken, and Russia agreed to withdraw her troops from Poland in order to remove any shadow of a pretext which Prussia might put forward for a breach.[60] For the time being, Catherine was compelled to pretend to take no notice of the collapse of Russian power in Poland.

Not long after Potemkin's departure for the southern front in May 1789, the precarious balance of power at court suffered a complete change when Catherine at last discovered what had been known to many for some time, that her current lover, Alexander Dmitriyev Mamonov, was betraying her. Realizing that the young man was chafing at his position, Catherine had written to him proposing an excellent marriage with an heiress, as a means of keeping him at court (though in precisely what relationship she did not specify). On hearing of Catherine's matrimonial plans Mamonov admitted that he had been in love for some time with a young princess, Darya Shcherbatova, and begged to be allowed to marry her. The news came as a complete surprise to Catherine, who was deeply hurt. There was much coming and going, long sessions between Catherine and Ma-monov, in which the empress wept bitter tears. But, she wrote to Potemkin, 'I have never tyrannized over any one', and so she summoned the two young peo-ple and betrothed them herself. To Potemkin she complained that he, who had once hinted to her that Mamonov was playing her false, had not opened her eyes to what was going on long ago. To Khrapovitsky, her secretary, she also con-fided her unhappiness, which was only too evident to him, and her shock at hav-ing been so deceived. 'Spit on him,' Potemkin had told her, when he had visited the capital that winter, but Catherine had refused to be enlightened. Now, when she poured out her grief to the one man who could understand even this particular type of disappointment, he wrote back to her : 'My dearest lady, Vous me nommés votre ami intime ; c'est vrai dans toute l'étendue du terme ; believe me, I am devoted to you without any hypocrisy . . . je ne me suis jamais trompé en lui ; c'est un mélange d'indolence et d'égoisme. Par ce dernier il était Narcisse à

outrance. Ne pensant qu'a lui, il exigeait tout, sans paier d'aucun retour. . . .'
Let Catherine marry them off, and send him as Russian envoy to Switzerland.[61]
Catherine did marry them off, but sent them to Moscow.

In her distress the empress turned for consolation to an old friend, Anna Niki-
tishna Naryshkina, and it was she who brought forward, on the very day Mamonov was dismissed, the twenty-two-year-old Platon Aleksandrovich Zubov
who was to be Catherine's last favourite. The details of Zubov's promotion,
including the gift of 10,000 rubles from Catherine to Zubov himself and the
watch worth 2,000 rubles which Zubov gave to Anna Naryshkina can be followed in Khrapovitsky's diary. On 6/17 July Catherine wrote to Potemkin,
enclosing a letter from her new favourite to the prince, which inaugurated a relationship the latter was to find anything but happy. While Catherine spoke of his
gentleness, his modesty, his desire to please Potemkin, 'le petit noireaud' as she
dubbed Zubov, began the process of procuring favours for his family and a clientèle for himself.[62]

Fortunately Potemkin was soon able to provide Catherine with the best tonic
she needed : good news from the battlefield. The removal of Russian troops from
Poland had faced him with fresh problems and had rendered the supply of arms,
recruits and food to the Ukrainian army more difficult since convoys could no
longer be sent through the territory of the Republic. Catherine decided to place
both the Ukrainian and the Yekaterinoslav armies under Potemkin, and to put
Rumyantsev in charge of the preparation of Russian defences against a possible
Prussian attack.[63] Rumyantsev took his recall extremely ill. Doubtless interpreting it as demotion, instigated by Potemkin, he replied resigning his command
and, like Suvorov, asked for leave, to 'take the waters' for his health. Catherine
granted his request, whereupon Rumyantsev settled down in Jassy for the next
eighteen months to carp and to criticize, until Catherine had finally to order him
to leave in the spring of 1790.[64] General Prince N. V. Repnin replaced Rumyantsev in command of the Ukrainian army, under Potemkin's overall direction. Four
regiments were sent to the borders of Belorussia to be on guard against Prussian
moves.

During the campaign of 1789, the Ukrainian army, acting with the Austrians
under the Prince of Coburg was to advance along the Seret. The main Russian
army under Potemkin was to seize control of the Dniestr, and both armies would
then advance on the Danube. The main Austrian army under Field Marshal G.E.
Laudon was expected to cross the Danube and attack Belgrade.[65] The campaign
began well with a lightning Russian raid on Galatz, in which vast quantities of
stores were seized. The main Yekaterinoslav army, under Potemkin, began to
advance on 11/22 May and reached Olviopol on the Bug on 27 June/8 July. On
11 July it crossed the Bug making for the lower Dniestr. A Turkish naval demonstration against the Crimea found it too well defended and failed to deflect
Potemkin from his advance.

Meanwhile Suvorov had been appointed to command the extreme left wing of the Russian forces in Byrlad, linking up with Coburg and his 18,000 Austrians. Determined to prevent a junction between the Austrians and Potemkin, the Grand Vizir advanced upon Coburg's army with 30,000 men. Coburg appealed to Suvorov for assistance and the latter arrived with 4,000 men, in time to engage the much stronger Turks on 21 July/1 August and rout them completely near Fokshany. Potemkin continued a leisurely advance, reaching the Dniestr on 12/23 August, then turning southwards towards Bender. A detachment was sent to cooperate with the fleet in taking the Turkish fort of Gadzhibey on the coast and in his rear.

Potemkin now settled down outside Bender which he hoped to take without a fight, while Repnin was involved in various skirmishes with the Turks outside Izmail, which, however, he was not strong enough to storm. The Grand Vizir again attempted to destroy Coburg's forces near Fokshany, and again Coburg appealed to Suvorov for help. In forced marches, Suvorov advanced 70 kilometres and forded two rivers in two days, joining Coburg on 10 September. The next day the combined Austrians and Russians by a combination of skilful manoeuvre and fierce fighting drove the Turks back across the river Rymnik to their rear with losses amounting to some 15,000 killed. The Grand Vizir himself resigned his command and died soon after.[66]

Potemkin did not pursue the fleeing Turks, but waited until he controlled the whole course of the Dniestr. Gadzhibey was captured on 14 September ; the Turkish fleet refused to give battle to the Russian Sebastopol fleet and sailed away to Constantinople on 23 September/2 October, leaving Akkerman at the mouth of the Dniestr defenceless. On 28 September/9 October the garrison surrendered. Bender was now completely cut off. After some parleying, the garrison of 20,000 surrendered on 3/14 November, and as Potemkin had hoped, no lives were lost. The Austrian forces too had been successful in 1789. Belgrade was captured on 19/30 September, and Coburg entered Bucarest on 4 November. Catherine was delighted with the successes of the allied armies, and awarded a ruble apiece to the Russian soldiers. Suvorov (at Potemkin's suggestion) was made a count of the Russian Empire and of the Holy Roman Empire, and allowed to add the suffix 'Rymniksky' to his name. He was also rewarded in Catherine's usual lavish way.[67]

The victorious campaign confirmed Catherine in her wish to open peace negotiations with the Porte. The Prussian attitude was still threatening, and the campaign of 1789 against Sweden had been inconclusive. Thanks to Hugh Elliot's intervention, Gustavus III had been given a breathing space during which he arrested the Anjala conspirators and effected the second political *coup d'état* of his career. At a session of the Diet, called for 6/17 February 1789, he forced through an 'Act of Union and Security' which increased the power of the Crown and reduced the privileges of the nobles. Even though Swedish finances were precarious, he determined to carry on the war. Thus in spring and summer 1789 a number of minor engagements took place in the Baltic between the Russian and the Swedish fleets. A more important battle took place on 13/24 August 1789 at Svensksund, which must be counted as a Russian victory since the Swedes withdrew, leaving the Russians free to support their armed forces in Finland by sea.[68] However, Gustavus received substantial encouragement from the Porte when a subsidy treaty was signed on 30 June/11 July 1789, by which the Turks undertook to pay Sweden one million piastres a year as long as the war lasted and ten million on the signature of peace. Sweden undertook not to make a separate peace.[69]

Strenuous efforts were being made by Catherine in St Petersburg to recruit new forces for the defence against Sweden and for the armies in the south. A recruit levy of 5 in 500 was ordered in 1789, which produced 92,822 men (of whom 6,549 purchased their exemption at 500r.).[70] But she was short of qualified generals. Musin Pushkin ('he is a canaille, forgive the word') was slow and unenterprising; even the guards regiments were complaining about him, wrote Catherine to Potemkin, asking him to send her 'some good major generals and not all Germans'.[71]

But though Catherine might desire peace, the Porte was in bellicose mood. The death of Sultan Abdul Hamid on 27 March/7 April 1789 was followed by the accession of the eighteen-year-old Sultan Selim III. He had no intention of embarking on peace negotiations. Though Austria had been successful in the 1789 campaign, Joseph II was meeting mounting difficulties in the Austrian Netherlands and his health was failing. Moreover the Porte was being systematically wooed by Prussia, hot in pursuit of Hertzberg's extravagant schemes. The Prussian minister still hoped to acquire Danzig and Thorn for Prussia, either by a war in which Prussia would form a coalition with Sweden and the Porte against Russia, or by an armed mediation between Russia and the Porte, for which Prussia would be rewarded in Poland, and Poland would be compensated by Austria. But having discovered that Hertzberg's instructions to the Prussian envoy in Constantinople involved the Ottoman loss of the Crimea to Russia, and of Moldavia and Walachia to Austria, in order ultimately to enrich the only power which was doing no fighting at all, the Turks were in no hurry to conclude negotiations with Prussia. On 13/24 October Sultan Selim issued a *hatticherif* proclaiming a Holy War, thus putting paid to the secret peace talks his more peaceloving Grand Vizir had been conducting with Potemkin for Russia and with Field-Marshal Laudon for Austria. Potemkin rejected an armistice, except as preparation for genuine peace negotiations. He defined Russian peace terms as: the renewal of all previous treaties between the Porte and Russia (including the cession of the Crimea), Turkish cession of the territory between the Dniepr and the Dniestr ; the formation of an independent principality of Dacia from Moldavia, Walachia and parts of Bessarabia, under a ruler of Orthodox faith, namely the Grand Duke Constantine ; peace with Joseph II, and the exclusion of Sweden from the negotiations. Balancing between peace with Russia or an alliance with Prussia, the Porte released the Russian envoy Bulgakov in the autumn.[72]

Meanwhile Hertzberg, exploiting Joseph's increasing difficulties in the Austrian Netherlands, gave a new twist to his scheme. Prussia would help Austria to recover the Austrian Netherlands ; Austria, in exchange, would abandon all claim to Moldavia and Walachia and return to the frontiers of the Peace of Passarowitz ; Galicia would be ceded by Austria to the Poles, and Prussia would acquire Danzig and Thorn. Turkish response to these terms was that they would make no peace without recovering the Crimea ; they asked when Prussia proposed to declare war on Austria and Russia.

In all innocence the Prussian envoy now went ahead with negotiations for an alliance between Prussia and the Porte, signed on 20/31 January 1790. He committed Prussia to declaring war, to assisting in the reconquest of the Crimea, and to guaranteeing the Crimea to the Porte in future. This was going much further than Hertzberg and his master were prepared for. The envoy was recalled and disgraced, and Frederick William delayed ratification of the treaty in order to evade 'cette terrible clause de la Crimée'.

At this critical moment, having lost control of the Austrian Netherlands and with Hungary seething with discontent, the disillusioned and heartbroken Joseph died on 9/20 February. He wrote what he knew would be his last letter to Catherine on 5/16 February, describing himself as 'le plus loyal de vos amis', 'le plus juste de vos admirateurs'.[73] To Potemkin Catherine expressed her verdict : 'I am very sorry for my ally. Strange that seeing that he was both clever and knowledgeable, there was no true friend to tell him not to irritate his subjects with things that do not matter.'[74]

Meanwhile the ring around Russia was tightened by the conclusion of a defensive treaty between Prussia and Poland on 18/29 March 1790. Stanislas had opposed it, in the belief that alliance with Prussia would spell the destruction of Poland. And in deference to Polish Patriot opinion no mention was made of the vexed question of Danzig and Thorn. But article 6 of the treaty provided for Prussian assistance, by force of arms if need be, against any attempt by a foreign power (Russia) to interfere in Poland's internal affairs in the name of a previous guarantee of the Polish constitution.[75]

It remained to be seen what the new king of Hungary and Bohemia, Leopold II, would do. France, since the outbreak of the Revolution, provided no help. The situation inherited by Leopold was so dangerous that he determined to bring the Turkish war to an end, sacrificing if need be all the Austrian conquests. One of his first steps was to invite English mediation. Peace on the basis of the *status quo* was the policy which Pitt was pressing on Prussia, and Frederick William was willing to press it on Leopold in the belief that he would not give up all the Austrian gains. But while Hertzberg hoped that '*status quo*' would not be interpreted so literally as to exclude the hoped-for Prussian acquisition of Danzig and Thorn, Frederick William still believed in war. As a result Prussia seemed to be following three policies : negotiations on the basis of the strict *status quo* ; negotiations on the basis of a modified *status quo* from which Prussia would derive advantages, and war.

Ever since she first heard of the treaty between Prussia and the Porte, in

December 1789, Catherine had been hoping that Potemkin's secret talks with the Turks would lead to peace. She too rejected an armistice. It was a choice between peace and a war on three fronts. The prince was holding his court in Jassy that winter, and did not visit the capital.[76] Waiting anxiously for news was 'like childbirth' for Catherine and to pass the time and keep up her morale she spent her evenings translating Plutarch's *Lives* with Platon Zubov. But on 13/24 March 1790 a courier arrived confirming that there would be war for a further campaigning season.[77] Meanwhile the Austrians were pressing Catherine to take steps to defend Galicia from possible Polish/Prussian attack, and to concert measures in the event of this new war.

Before the signature of the Prussian-Turkish treaty, Catherine had considered that Potemkin's Polish policy, of which she heartily approved in general, could only be implemented after peace had been concluded with the Turks. But now, evidently at his suggestion, she was prepared to support a Russian irruption into Poland to forestall a Prussian attack on Russia and to prevent Prussia from acquiring parts of Poland.[78] A rescript which had been sent to Potemkin on 10/21 January 1790, appointing him grand hetman of all the Yekaterinoslav and Black Sea Cossacks, was made public in March and Potemkin now planned, with Catherine's approval, to occupy the Palatinates of Kiev, Podolia and Bratslav, and to form a confederation of Orthodox Ukrainians 'more or less similar to that set up by Bogdan Khmel'nitsky'.[79]

Russian reluctance to commit herself to joint action against the Prussian threat contributed to Leopold's determination to get out of the war as best he could : the strict *status quo* if need be, a modified *status quo,* if possible, with a few gains from Turkey (for which Prussia might compensate herself at Polish expense).[80] Meanwhile the Triple Alliance powers, Britain, Prussia and the United Provinces, began to put pressure on Russia to accept peace on strict *status quo* terms under threat of their armed intervention.

In June 1790 war seemed about to break out between Prussia and Austria. But talks began on 16/27 June at Reichenbach in Prussian Silesia. Leopold agreed to restore all conquests to the Porte, and on 16/27 July the Convention of Reichenbach was signed, providing for an immediate armistice between Austria and the Porte, and the calling of a congress to negotiate a final peace treaty.[81] Catherine now stood alone against Sweden and Turkey, with the threat of war with Prussia and Poland, supported by Britain, looming over her.

26

The Peace of Reichenbach, the Ochakov Crisis and the End of the Turkish War

The Triple Alliance had imposed its will on Austria. It remained to be seen whether it could also impose a peace on strict *status quo* lines on Catherine II. As a first step, and in order to bring pressure on Catherine, Prussia ratified the treaty with the Porte, signed on 20/31 January 1790, precisely while the negotiations with Austria were being carried on at Reichenbach in July.[1]

But Catherine was only willing to make peace on her terms and without mediators. Meanwhile she concentrated on her nearest enemy, Gustavus III. The main thrust of Russian strategy in the campaign of 1790 was to close the Gulf of Finland to the Swedish fleet, destroy the Swedish galley flotilla, and carry the war on land into Swedish Finland. Gustavus, on his side, intended to make a determined effort in 1790 to capture St Petersburg, for which he needed command of the Baltic Sea. But Sweden was worsted in an engagement on 2/13 May between Admiral Chichagov's fleet from Reval, and the Swedish Karlskrona fleet under Duke Charles of Sudermania. An attack by the Swedish galley fleet, under Gustavus's personal command, on the Russian galley fleet outside Fridrikshamm on 4/15 May also failed.[2] A major battle between the Russian Kronstadt fleet and the main Swedish fleet took place in the Gulf of Finland on 23 May/3 June, which lasted on and off for two days. The gunfire, clearly audible in St Petersburg, even rattled Catherine's windows in Tsarskoye Selo. Neither side lost a ship, though both fleets suffered heavy casualties. Though the battle did not result in a clear victory for either power, it was Russia which benefited most from the encounter. The Reval squadron and the Kronstadt fleet were now strong enough to bottle up the Swedes in Vyborg. The initiative passed to the galley flotillas which were being used by the Swedes to land troops on the coast between Vyborg and St Petersburg. During the next fortnight a number of inconclusive engagements took place, and finally the Russian galley flotilla, now commanded by Prince Nassau Siegen, launched a major assault on the Swedish flotilla guarding the main Swedish fleet in Vyborg, to the south of Björkö Sound, on 21 June/2 July. The Swedish flotilla drew away after a while to cover the escape of the main sailing fleet which thus broke out of Vyborg and moved towards the open sea, though with the loss of twelve war ships.

The galley flotillas continued to manoeuvre among the islands and by 28 June/9 July had converged off Sveaborg, more or less where the battle of Svensksund had taken place in 1789. Inspired by the thought that 28 June was the anniversary of Catherine's accession, Nassau Siegen attempted to snatch a victory. But in deteriorating weather he was steadily driven back throughout the day with his line in disorder, while fresh Swedish forces were brought against him. On the next day the Swedes continued their pursuit, and the Russians lost approximately five frigates, and a total of 64 ships of all kinds, and 7,369 men of whom some 6,500 were taken prisoner.[3] It was the first major Russian naval defeat of the war and Nassau Siegen was in despair. He resigned his command, his honours and his rank, and asked to be court-martialled. To Catherine the defeat was a political blow and the losses in men particularly painful.[4] She put a good face on it, however, and wrote to Nassau Siegen the kind of letter which secured her such good service throughout her life. She refused to treat ill fortune as treasonable, referred to his many previous victories, encouraged her admiral to serve her again, and received him at court as usual.[5]

But the Swedish galley victory at Svensksund could not make up for the loss of the warships, which had reduced the Swedish battle fleet to less than half that of Russia. Gustavus as well as Catherine, though for different reasons, needed peace. Talks of an inconclusive kind, carried on as a result of a Spanish offer of mediation in 1790, cleared the way for direct negotiations at the small town of Verela. Efforts by Britain to keep Gustavus in the war foundered on British reluctance to give large enough subsidies in time, and the negotiations culminated in a peace hastily agreed on 3/14 August 1790. It was based on the *status quo,* with no compensations or indemnifications. But Sweden gained one advantage : the implicit acceptance by Russia of the constitutional changes introduced by Gustavus III.[6] Even so, Catherine was delighted, more particularly because Britain and Prussia knew nothing about the negotiations and had played no part in them. 'On les a joué', she exclaimed to her secretary,[7] and signed the ratification without delay. By courier she informed Potemkin at once of the news, and prayed that he would now be able to make peace with the Porte. 'We have got one paw out of the mud,' she wrote, 'when we get the other out, we will sing Hallelujah.'[8]

The uncertainty over Prussia's intention paralysed Potemkin's military activity in spring and summer 1790. Prussia had stationed 40,000 troops on the borders of Livonia, another 40,000 were concentrated in Silesia ; the reserves numbered 100,000.[9] Potemkin had to withdraw troops from Moldavia in order to guard the Polish frontier, and he remained strictly on the defensive on land while he reactivated secret peace talks with the Turks. He was now authorized by Catherine to give up the demand to create an independent principality of Dacia ; even the idea of an independent Moldavia, as an appanage for Constantine, was abandoned, out of fear that such a demand might precipitate Prussian entry into the war.[10] But if the Turks had lost an ally – Sweden – they had also lost an enemy – Austria – and they thought that they could count on Prussian help.[11]

While talks had been in progress, the Black Sea fleet, under Admiral Ushakov, had sailed on 16/27 May for the northern shore of Anatolia, raided Sinope and Samsun, then made for Anapa, where a Turkish fleet was concentrating to support a descent on the Crimea. After an inconclusive skirmish, Ushakov returned to Sebastopol, collected more ships and set sail on 2/13 July 1790. The Turkish fleet was sighted close to the Straits of Kerch, and battle was engaged on 8/19 July ; the fleets separated at dusk, with the loss of only one Turkish ship. Though on the surface inconclusive, the battle frustrated the Turkish plans for landing in the Straits of Kerch.

More important in the long run was the engagement which took place on 28 August/8 September near the island of Tendra, off Gadzhibey. At the end of the battle the Turkish fleet withdrew in disorder having lost two ships including the flagship which finally blew up.[12] The threat to the Crimea was removed and Potemkin, now that Sweden had made peace, felt free to order a general advance on land on 11/22 September 1790. His object was to capture the Turkish forts on the lower Danube and cut them off from the sea. Suvorov was ordered to attack Galatz, while the flotilla of galleys under the Neapolitan adventurer, José de Ribas, gathered in the mouths of the Danube, with the ex-Zaporozhian Cossacks and their boats, and routed the Turkish galleys in mid-October. On 18/29 October Kilia was taken followed by Tul'cha on 7/18 November and Izakchi soon after.[13] It was now the turn of Izmail.

Izmail was one of the strongest Turkish forts. Situated on the Danube, opposite the island of Sulia, its garrison numbered 35,000 with 265 guns and it was well supplied. The Russians disposed of 31,000 men and 600 guns, as well as the flotilla. The siege began on 23 November/4 December, but so little progress was made that the three generals in command called a council of war and decided to withdraw. In despair Potemkin sent for Suvorov : 'My only hope is in God and your valour ; there are too many generals equal in rank over there, and the result is always a kind of indecisive parliament.' At the same time Potemkin gave Suvorov full freedom to decide whether to carry on with the assault or to withdraw. If he thought he would fail, it would be better not to try.[14]

Suvorov, on his way to take command, met the retreating troops and ordered them straight back. He arrived before Izmail on 2/13 December 1790, looked around, set about establishing batteries and announced to Potemkin that he would storm the fort in five days' time. On 7/18 December he summoned the Turks to surrender, and began the attack at dawn on 10/21 December. By 11 a.m. three of the gates were in Russian hands, and the Turks now fought desperately for every street and every house, until they were at last induced to surrender. The Turkish losses were immense : 26,000 killed and 9,000 prisoners, and 265 guns were seized. As Suvorov had promised the soldiers – and the Turkish garrison – looting went on for three days, and amounted to some two million rubles in value in addition to prisoners and slaves, and military supplies. The capture of one of the strongest forts in Europe was a tribute to the military genius and the qualities of leadership which had already made the name of Suvorov a byword in the Russian army ; it was also one of the bloodiest battles in Russian history.[15]

Russia was still by no means out of danger. The Triple Alliance powers were committed to force her to accept peace on strict *status quo* terms. But during the autumn months all sides marked time, while preparations were made for the conclusion of the final peace treaty between Austria and the Porte at the peace congress which began its sessions only on 3 January 1791 at Sistovo, in the Turkish dominions. British policy had, for the time being, been diverted from Eastern Europe by the conflict with Spain over Nootka Sound, which threatened to lead to war between the two countries in autumn 1790, but which was finally solved at the end of October 1790 ; Spain had to climb down in view of the failure of revolutionary France to support the Family Compact. Pitt was thus free to turn his attention to Eastern European problems which had been suffering from the fluctuations of Prussian policy. Frederick William continued to urge Catherine to accept the strict *status quo* in peace negotiations with the Porte, even if he ceased insisting on Catherine's acceptance of the mediation of the Triple Alliance.[16] But he could not commit himself to war with Russia until he was certain of Austrian neutrality in such a conflict, and Leopold was a past master at evading any commitment and at delaying the deliberations of the Congress of Sistovo, hinting to Prussia that he would be neutral, assuring Catherine that he would stand by his alliance, as far as his means allowed.

Yet Prussia, behind the back of her English and Polish allies, was also making direct and secret approaches to Russia, suggesting that an understanding might be reached guaranteeing Ochakov to Russia, provided of course that Prussia received Danzig and Thorn from Poland, and proposing that Catherine should bind herself in advance by a secret convention to renew the Russo-Prussian alliance after peace had been signed with Turkey. Catherine in turn explored every loophole and even embarked on secret negotiations with revolutionary France, which came to nothing with the death of Mirabeau.[17]

It was largely British policy which kept Europe in a state of tension during the winter and spring of 1791. Pitt was not only concerned to maintain the balance of power in Europe as he saw it, in the form of the so-called federative system, uniting the Triple Alliance, Scandinavia, Poland and Turkey into a vast league directed against the two empires and the two Bourbon powers. He had also taken up the idea that Russia could be replaced in the British commercial network by Poland. If the British economy could draw from Poland the essential naval stores as well as grain and hides, then Britain would cease to be so dependent upon Russia. These ideas were strongly reinforced by J. Ewart, the British envoy in Berlin, now on home leave, who was deeply hostile to Russia. He argued that Ochakov in Russian hands would seriously menace the Ottoman Empire ; and if the Russian border advanced to the Dniestr, Poland would lose that outlet for her trade and be cut off from direct contact with the Porte. In order to achieve the new political and commercial alignment in Eastern Europe, Pitt accepted that Poland would have to cede Danzig and Thorn to Prussia. The Triple Alliance would then enforce a strict *status quo* peace on Russia, if necessary by war.[18]

Pitt's offensive against Russia was launched in January 1791. He was encouraged by Sir Charles Whitworth, the British envoy in St Petersburg, who belonged to the school anxious to see Russia 'reduced to the place she ought to hold amongst the powers of Europe'. In his reports he stressed the parlous state of Russian finances and above all of the Russian armed forces, as well as the obstinacy of the empress, who would only knuckle under to an ultimatum backed by a show of force.[19]

On 10/21 and 11/22 March, the Cabinet agreed to Pitt's policy, and the prime minister himself drafted an ultimatum to Russia, giving Catherine ten days in which to accept peace on strict *status quo* terms under threat of the despatch of British fleets to the Baltic and the Black Seas, and the advance of Prussian troops into Livonia. The British ultimatum was sent in the first place by courier on 16/27 March to Berlin.[20]

Rumours of the British-Prussian initiative reached Catherine at the beginning of the year. On 16/27 January 1791 the Council discussed defence measures against Prussian, or possibly Swedish attack.[21] Gustavus III was indeed at the moment on sale to the highest bidder. Britain was proposing that he should join the anti-Russian coalition, lend his ships or his ports, and receive subsidies in cash ; while Catherine countered by offering to pay for the upkeep of the Swedish army and fleet.[22] In the event Catherine won the auction, and at the beginning of February 1791, serious negotiations began for a new Russo-Swedish treaty of alliance, which would provide for personal subsidies for Gustavus.[23]

Potemkin meanwhile had been lingering in his luxurious court at Jassy, organizing the redeployment of the Russian army in view of the Prussian threat, and conducting a passionate love affair with his cousin by marriage, Praskovia Potemkina.[24] He had remained in the south partly at Catherine's insistence, to observe Turkish reaction to the fall of Izmail.[25] But on 28 February/11 March 1791 he arrived at last in the capital. He had already begun to feel the effects of Catherine's infatuation with Platon Zubov, which embraced also the latter's younger brother, Valerian. Already the young man was beginning to build up his own party. But there were many who, aware of the havoc caused by the young favourite, looked with greater respect on the old one, and welcomed his return. There was clearly going to be a struggle for power while Potemkin attempted to 'draw the troublesome tooth' – a pun on the Russian word *zub* (tooth).[26]

Faced with mounting pressure from the coalition against her, Catherine had also to stand up to the divided counsels and faint hearts around her. Almost alone throughout the winter of 1791 she maintained her determination never to give in to what she regarded as the outrageous and humiliating Anglo-Prussian blackmail. Potemkin's arrival gave her little comfort. With far more authority than her other advisers, since he more than any of them was aware of Russia's military weakness in the face of the Prussian army and the British fleet, he set about bullying her to agree to negotiate with Prussia. His own plans were as usual grandiose: he would organize his Cossack explosion in Polish Ukraine and prepare at the same time a more extensive partition which would buy off Prussia, reward Russia, and perhaps leave something over for himself.[27]

The process of beating down Catherine's resistance to any negotiation with Prussia was long drawn out. 'Anxiety over Prussia. It has lasted a long time. She cried,' noted her secretary in his diary. On 10/21 March the prince was heard to exclaim that Catherine 'was obstinate, listened to no advice, and that he intended to have a row with her' ; 'she is crying with vexation ; she doesn't want to climb down and make terms with the king of Prussia' ; 'unwell, stayed in bed with spasms and a bad colic' ; 'cross ; obstinacy will lead to a new war'.[28] Finally Potemkin wore Catherine down and she agreed to accept in strict secrecy the Prussian proposal to bind herself by a secret convention to the renewal of the Russo-Prussian treaty, and the cession of Danzig and Thorn, after a peace had been signed with Turkey on her conditions : the renewal of all previous treaties and the cession of Ochakov.[29]

Meanwhile Potemkin in April continued to urge the merits of a partition of Poland to the Austrian envoy, Cobenzl, stressing the importance of inducing Prussia to propose it, putting the idea forward as a means of splitting the Triple Alliance and buying off Prussia, the most dangerous member for Russia. If war with Prussia were to break out, then the prince would revert to his plan of forming a confederation with Poland which would swing the Republic over to the side of the two imperial courts.[30]

Catherine's resistance to Anglo-Prussian pressure had in part been encouraged by the refusal of her ambassador in London, S.R. Vorontsov, to believe that Britain seriously intended to send a fleet to the Baltic.[31] On 17/28 March, the day after he sent the text of the ultimatium to Russia to Berlin, Pitt put before Parliament a royal message asking for a partial mobilization of the fleet. It was approved in both Houses on 18/29 and 19/30 March, but Pitt soon found the ground crumbling under his feet. He had not prepared British public opinion for his policy, and his own colleagues were not all in favour of it. In spite of the damage to the traditional picture of Russia as a natural ally inflicted by Catherine's Armed Neutrality in 1780, commercial ties between the two countries were still so strong as to offset any growing sense of the threat of Russian power to British interests. What is more the nature of the object in dispute, Ochakov, the whereabouts of which was uncertain to most people, seemed scarcely worth such a display of sound and fury. The general feeling is well summed up in Lord Auckland's phrase : was it worth running such risks for the sake of 'taking a feather out of the cap of an old vixen, or of preserving a desert tract of ground between two rivers to the Turks . . .'.[32]

The weakness of Pitt's case, and the weakness of his defence of his case, left him open to attacks by the Whig opposition which were echoed by the newspapers, many of which took their tone from the Whig *Morning Chronicle*. Vorontsov now intervened, and most ably made use of the existence of a free press in Britain to campaign in favour of the policy of his absolute mistress. He not only supplied the Whig leaders with information on British trade with Russia, which could be used in parliamentary debates, but he also arranged for the publication of a pamphlet, *Serious Enquiries into the Motives and Consequences of the Present Armament against Russia,* which was widely read. Through various agents he helped to orchestrate a campaign of meetings throughout the country at which resolutions deploring a war which would close Russian markets to British manufactures were passed for submission to members of Parliament.[33]

Catherine had not yet received the British ultimatum though she was aware of its contents. She still held out against the arguments of Potemkin and Bezborodko.[34] She had given in on negotiating secretly with Prussia ; she would stand up to British blackmail. Orders were sent to the Russian fleet in the Baltic[35] to take up their stations in order to oppose the expected British squadron. But Pitt was already climbing down. Though he secured Parliamentary majorities on three occasions for his policy,[36] the Cabinet remained divided. 'No war with Russia' was chalked up on too many houses, and too many people objected to Britain pulling the chestnuts out of the fire for Prussia. By 20/31 March Pitt had already proposed to Frederick William II to delay the despatch of the ultimatum to Russia, and in the ensuing days he faced the fact that his policy had failed.

But Frederick William was still bent on war. He did not know that Catherine had at last consented to secret, direct negotiations with Prussia, and on 27 March/7 April, the day when the text of Pitt's proposed ultimatum was discussed in Berlin, he ordered the mobilization of 88,000 Prussians on the borders of Livonia.[37] It was Hertzberg who now opposed war; he disapproved of Prussia playing second fiddle to Britain ; acquiring Danzig by British good offices, and being pushed into war with Russia in order to give Britain control of Polish trade. Hard on the heels of the Prussian order to mobilize came the news that Pitt's policy had collapsed. On 31 March/11 April at a meeting of the Cabinet it was decided to abandon the demand for the restoration of the strict *status quo* and to propose to Russia instead a modified *status quo* which would still leave both banks of the Dniestr in Turkish hands.[38] Frederick William did not at once realize that this meant the abandonment of the whole 'exchange' plan, that there would be no British fleet in the Baltic, that the whole alliance system on which he had based his policy to Russia had crumbled. He was outraged when it at last dawned on him that he had been uselessly led into great expense before the whole of Europe.[39] Catherine's humiliating surrender to Prussia, her agreement to negotiate secretly with Frederick William, had also proved unnecessary. It was not officially communicated to the Prussian court, but unofficially, the Russian minister in Berlin, Alopeus, mentioned it to the king's confidant, Colonel Bischoffswerder, who exclaimed delightedly that had Prussia only been told ten days before, it 'would not have been dragged into supporting Pitt's schemes'. For Catherine it was a narrow escape.[40] It was also the beginning of the end for Poland. Prussia would now abandon her ally and seek her 'compensation' by agreement with Russia.

At the beginning of May Catherine herself was almost out of her anxiety. Her courage and her strong nerves had seen her through the most trying ordeal of her life. Almost alone she had maintained her confidence that Russia could stand up to the British navy and the Prussian army. Finally, on 30 April/10 May she heard that Britain had abandoned the demand for the strict *status quo,* and was sending a special envoy, William Fawkener, to negotiate a compromise.[41] Not surprisingly Catherine suffered from a physical reaction at the news. She left secretly for Tsarskoye Selo, and was ill for a while with her usual stomach disorders.[42]

When Potemkin left the southern front for St Petersburg in February 1791, he reorganized the disposition of the Russian forces to meet the impending Prussian threat. An observation corps was to be stationed along the Dvina against Prussia, and a corps in Kiev, to watch over Poland. In the event of an attack the two Russian corps were to advance into Poland and attempt a junction there. Suvorov was transferred from the south and placed in charge of the defences of Finland and the protection of the northern capital against a possible treacherous attack from Sweden. The troops on the Turkish front, under Prince N.V. Repnin, were to confine themselves to defensive operations, but they were authorized to attack the Turks across the Danube if the opportunity arose. A second army was ordered to capture Anapa in the Kuban', and the fleet was to prevent communications between the European and the Asiatic fronts. The galley flotilla was to cut communications between the Danube and Constantinople.[43]

Potemkin remained in the capital throughout the spring and summer of 1791, deeply involved in preparations for the recovery of the Russian position in Poland. The Poles themselves precipitated a crisis. The confederated Diet which had first met in October 1788 had continued in session ; under the protective umbrella of the Prusso-Polish treaty and in view of the imminence of war with Russia, it had drafted a new constitution for Poland, with the active participation of Stanislas Augustus. The adoption of the constitution by a partially renewed Diet on 22 April/3 May 1791 was hastened by the news of the impending withdrawal of the British ultimatum to Russia, and of the collapse of Pitt's policy. The new constitution, which provided for a hereditary monarchy with a Saxon candidate, was approved by the vast majority of those present ; it provided for a strengthened executive and an elected legislature, and abolished the liberum veto, the binding mandate, and confederations. Greater judicial, political and economic rights were granted to the Polish bourgeoisie, and some protection was provided for the peasantry. Stanislas at once took the oath of loyalty to the new constitution which was proclaimed throughout the country.

The Polish constitution was in no sense Jacobinical. But to Catherine there was not, in spring 1791, much to choose between revolutionary Poland and revolutionary France. Like most European rulers, she had watched the events of 1788 and 1789 with a mixture of malice, indignation, and contempt for the weakness and inadequacy of Louis XVI. 'C'est une véritable anarchie,' she exclaimed on 16/27 September 1789. 'Ils sont capables de pendre leur roi à la lanterne, c'est affreux.'[44] But as long as she was fighting on two fronts, she could do nothing to help the French monarchy ; she could not intervene in the much nearer Poland.

In the first years of the French Revolution, a considerable amount of information about events in France was disseminated in the Russian periodical press and in the pages of the St Petersburg and Moscow *Gazettes,* which increased their runs to 2,000 and 4,000 respectively. The Declaration of the Rights of Man was published in full in the St Petersburg *Gazette ;* political speeches were reported as well as horrifying news, such as the irruption of 'drunken Parisian housewives' into the very chamber of the queen at Versailles.[45] Though the accounts might be slanted, the Russian reading public was reasonably well-informed. But the Polish revolution of 3 May 1791 was a different matter. It was clearly perceived to be a 'revolution', not unconnected, in its origin, with events in France, in spite of the fact that it proclaimed a hereditary monarchy and abolished the liberum veto. In Catherine's eyes revolutionary means had been employed to introduce royal absolutism in Poland : 'Ne faut-il pas avoir le diable au corps depuis la tête jusqu'aux pieds que de manquer ainsi à son premier principe . . . Le roi de Pologne est venu leur dire comme quoi les voisins allaient de nouveau partager la Pologne et tout de suite tout le monde consenti à lui conférer le pouvoir arbitraire,' she wrote indignantly to Grimm.[46]

Under this verbiage, Catherine concealed her appreciation of the real danger in the restoration of 'absolutism' in Poland. For not only would a revived Poland escape from Russian tutelage ; a free and reformed Poland might become strong enough to act independently of her neighbours. In talks with the Austrian envoy, A.R. Vorontsov took up again the idea of partition, while Potemkin reverted to his schemes for forming a confederation in Polish Ukraine.[47] But after their initial explosion of anger, the Russians became less outspoken, and appeared to treat Polish affairs with indifference. Behind the scenes, however, the Polish revolution and the British *volte face* led to a thorough reappraisal of Russian policy towards Sweden, Poland, France, the Triple Alliance and of course the Porte.

On 14/25 May, the British special envoy, William Fawkener, arrived in St Petersburg. But before any negotiations with Britain were begun, Catherine signed a rescript on 16/27 May to Potemkin concerned primarily with military dispositions, should Britain persist in Pitt's policy of peace on strict *status quo* terms. She stressed the need to guard against Prussia, while at the same time forcing the Porte to demand peace by destroying the Turkish fleet, 'carrying terror to the Bosphorus', and capturing Anapa in the Kuban'. Yet she also indicated her belief that Britain and Prussia would confine themselves to demonstrations, and would not go to war. Hence, when peace with the Turks was achieved the Russian forces must turn upon 'new enemies' i.e. Poland. One corps would be stationed in Mogilev, one in Kiev and the main army on the Dniestr, from Bender to the Polish border. It was not advisable, continued Catherine, to break with the Poles yet, though Russia had been given plenty of grounds ; as long as the Poles did not behave in a hostile manner, and the Prussians did not introduce troops into Curland or Poland, Russia would not move. But if they did then Potemkin was authorized to cross the Polish border. Potemkin was also to endeavour to wean the Polish nation from the 'unreliable' king, by offering the Poles Moldavia (provided the Orthodox religion were maintained), a Russian alliance, and a promise not to interfere in its internal affairs. But if these methods failed, then he could resort to 'extreme measures'. These again were clearly spelled out : the change in the constitution might give ground for a 'reconfederation' organized by the pro-Russian 'aristocratic' party ; a second 'extreme measure' was the secret project for a Russian irruption into Kiev, Podolia and Volynia led by Potemkin as grand hetman of the Cossack forces of Yekaterinoslav and the Black Sea, with the object of liberating the people of 'our race and religion' and 'chasing the national enemy out of the land'. As regards partition, the emperor had declared that he had no claim as long as Prussia made no acquisitions, and Catherine laid down that Prussia should receive nothing unless a cession of territory were necessary to avoid a war. Partition would only be considered if no other means served to end the present disturbances. Potemkin was also informed of the concurrent negotiations with Sweden.[48]

It was in a rescript to her envoy in Stockholm, dated 22 May/2 June 1791 that Catherine set out the full range of her ostensible objectives regarding the French Revolution. Here she stated first that the affairs of France were the concern of all crowned heads ; secondly that all European powers should form an alliance to return his rights and privileges to Louis XVI. It was not merely a question of crushing the French Revolution, but France must be enabled to take up her place as the countervailing force to Britain and Prussia in the balance of power. Sweden was therefore offered a subsidy for the maintenance of a corps of 10,000 men until they entered France, when the cost should fall on the French king.[49] It would be naive to accept this exposition of policy at its face value. Catherine's real intention was to prevent Gustavus from concluding any alliance with Britain and Prussia, by pushing him forward into the position he coveted in any case, that of leader of the crusade against the French Revolution. Hence her offer to defend Swedish possessions in the event of a Danish attack, and her proposal that Gustavus should open talks with Spain, Sardinia and the minor German courts to organize joint action against France.[50]

Meanwhile Russia drew out the talks with Fawkener on the Russian terms for peace with the Porte.[51] But agreement was reached quickly. All efforts to get Catherine to agree that the areas to be ceded to her should remain neutral, or should not be fortified, were rejected by the empress who saw no reason why she should make sacrifices to soothe Prussian and British pride.[52] By 15/26 July the British and Prussian envoys gave their formal consent to Russian acquisition of the land between the Bug and the Dniestr, and Catherine hastened to let the Turks know their decision through the Neapolitan minister.[53] Catherine's hand in the negotiations with Fawkener was much strengthened by the arrival from London in June of a certain Robert Adair, who came as the emissary of the Whig opposition. He advised the Russians on the replies they should give Fawkener, and used his inside knowledge to assist his friends in England in their stock exchange speculations. It is not surprising that Catherine ordered a marble bust of Charles James Fox to be sent to her, from which a bronze copy was made and placed on the colonnade at Tsarskoye Selo between Cicero and Demosthenes, for 'It was his [Fox's] eloquence which persuaded England to abandon the war'.[54]

Now that the Anglo-Prussian challenge had been successfully met and overcome, there remained Poland. Catherine's official policy was for Russia to remain a peaceful spectator of events in Poland until the Poles themselves 'invited' Russian help to restore their liberties,[55] while assurances were given to Austria, which was pressing for recognition of the May Constitution, that Russia was postponing her decision but was not ill disposed.[56]

Catherine's true intentions were set out in a rescript of 18/29 July to Potemkin, prepared for him on the eve of his departure for the Turkish front. The 3 May constitution could do no good to Poland's neighbours, she wrote, Russia would have to act ; she needed a free hand in Poland and would have therefore to wait until the end of the Turkish war. When peace had been concluded and the bulk of the army was being sent back through Poland it would be possible to support the opponents of the May constitution, and implement the plans they themselves should put forward.[57] To justify intervention in Poland, Catherine argued that the Poles had broken their treaties with Russia and their own fundamental laws ; they had caused difficulties for Russia in the war with the Porte, and had even signed a treaty of alliance with the Turks. The opponents of the constitution must act before it acquired consistency, and turn to Russia as the guarantor of the previous free constitution. It was difficult to foresee the outcome of this policy, but Catherine aimed first at the restoration of the ancient constitution and the consequent permanent security of Russia. But if Prussian agreement had to be bought, then Russia would be forced to agree to a fresh partition of Poland in favour of the three allied states. Russia's frontiers would be enlarged, she would acquire more subjects of the same faith and race and Poland would be reduced to the role of a buffer state. Potemkin was authorized to discuss plans for a confederation with Felix Potocki and others whom he might win over. As for the form of government selected to replace the May constitution, Potemkin should leave it for the Poles to work out whether to adopt Potocki's plans for a federation of four hetmanates, or to revive a limited monarchy. As regards the tactics to be pursued, Catherine pointed out that it was essential for Poles to protest against the new constitution publicly, with references to Russia's guarantee ; it would be better if a confederation could be formed *before* Russian troops entered Poland. The best time to act would be *after* the signature of the peace treaty with Turkey if the confederates were ready. Finally, if Prussia wanted a new partition, and there was no other way of achieving Russian objectives, then partition would be accepted, but this must be most carefully concealed from all Poles.[58]

There has been considerable discussion among historians about the two rescripts to Potemkin on Poland. According to one theory, Catherine deliberately made Potemkin's 'alleged plenary powers a sham' by imposing many 'limiting conditions' on the policy she outlined, because the prince, by spring 1791, was suffering from general paralysis of the insane contracted as a result of an earlier syphilitic infection.[59] The significance of these rescripts has however been distorted because they have been taken out of their context, as if they were the only two instructions given to Potemkin in the course of four months. The nature of the relationship between Catherine and Potemkin must also be taken into account.

It is true that there was frequent tension between the two in spring and summer 1791. The only direct evidence of quarrels between the empress and the favourite concerns his efforts to force her to agree to secret negotiations with Prussia in March–April 1791.[60] But there are frequent references in diplomatic dispatches to Potemkin's efforts to persuade Catherine to get rid of Zubov, which led to a coldness between them. This coldness however did not affect the prince's position as Catherine's principal counsellor, president of the College of War, commander-in-chief of the theatres of war in the South, charged with the peace negotiations. There was a solidity in the link between the two which could be ruffled, but not broken by a Zubov.

It is in fact very probable that the two rescripts of 16/27 May and 15/26 July were drafted if not by Potemkin himself, at least as the result of discussion with him, and represent the minimum programme on which he and Catherine were agreed as regards Poland. Analysis of the rescripts shows that they sum up and restate previously agreed policies. In this context it may be worth pointing out that Potemkin did not in general regard a partition of Poland as the best solution for the Polish problem for reasons which were entirely his own.[61] If, as seems more than likely, he was planning for his own future in the event of Catherine's death, then judging by the available evidence he intended to leave Russia for Poland where, as a Polish magnate on the scale of the Potockis or the Czartoryskis, he could expect to play a dominant role in military and political affairs in an unreformed Poland, where his own geographical base would be in Orthodox territory. He could have no desire to see his Polish estates allocated to Russia in a partition, and placed under the sovereignty of the Emperor Paul. Nor, of course, would he be happy in the Poland of 3 May. Hence, where Potemkin was concerned – and Catherine too, as long as peace had not been signed with Turkey – the first priority was to restore the old constitution of Poland. If reformed Poland, however, were to enter the war against Russia as the ally of Prussia, then

Potemkin would lead the Orthodox Cossack rising against Poland and Polish landlords in Polish Ukraine. And finally, and only if it proved impossible to achieve Russian objects otherwise, Russia would have to form a 'Polish' confederation and invade Poland and Prussia might have to be bought off, in which case a partition would ensue. The rescript of 16/27 May outlines the policy to be pursued when it was not yet quite certain that Britain and Prussia had climbed down ; the rescript of July is more precise, but action still hinges on the signature of peace with Turkey. A few days after the signature of the second rescript, Potemkin, on 24 July/4 August, took his leave of the empress he was never to see again.

In the meantime the situation on the southern front had changed out of all knowledge. At the end of March 1791, Repnin launched a rapid raid across the Danube and briefly occupied Machin on 28 March/8 April, with heavy losses to the Turks. A skirmish near Brailov on 31 March/11 April was followed by a more serious engagement when on 3/14 June, 12,000 Russians crossed the Danube and routed 15,000 Turks at Babadag. There still remained some 30,000 Turks at Machin, and the 80,000-strong army of the Grand Vizir was said to be approaching. Repnin decided to launch a second attack across the Danube before the two Turkish armies could join forces. Russian forces crossed the river again on 23 June/4 July, and in a hard fought battle at Machin on 29 June/10 July, in which the future field-marshal Kutuzov particularly distinguished himself, the Turks were again completely routed. Meanwhile on 22 June/3 July the fort of Anapa in the Kuban' was captured by Russian forces.[62]

The series of blows inflicted on the Turks, culminating in the second battle of Machin, led the sultan, despairing now of Prussian help, to re-open peace talks with Russia. The day after the battle he sent envoys to parley with Repnin, and preliminary conditions of peace were agreed with astonishing rapidity and signed on 31 July/11 August 1791 at Galatz. On that same day the Russian Black Sea fleet won a major victory over the Turkish fleet south of Cape Kaliakra, 25 miles northeast of Varna. Neither side lost a ship, but the strategic advantage lay with the Russians in a battle in which the Russian guns could be heard in Constantinople.[63]

Travelling at great speed, Potemkin arrived at the Russian headquarters in Jassy on 1/12 August 1791, the day after Repnin had signed the preliminaries of peace. A fierce quarrel promptly broke out between the two men, of which there are several versions. According to one, Potemkin blamed Repnin for his victories and reproached him for snatching the laurels from his – Potemkin's – brow and signing a peace against Russian interests. A second version suggests that Potemkin was angered by the fact that Repnin had hastened to sign the preliminaries, well knowing that his commander-in-chief was only a day's journey away. There may be some truth in both these accounts; but Potemkin was also outraged to discover that though Repnin had secured all the obvious Russian requirements (the renewal of the Treaty of Kuchuk Kainardzhi and subsequent treaties and the cession of the territory between the Bug and the Dniestr, including Ochakov), he had agreed to the Turkish demand not to fortify the ceded territory, and he had accepted an armistice of eight months' duration. Potemkin had always opposed an armistice as a mere device to enable the Turks to draw breath ; they would now be in a position to postpone the conclusion of the final peace treaty for many months, thus depriving Russia of her long desired freedom of action in Poland.[64]

The news of the preliminary peace, which reached Catherine on 11/22 August, came as an enormous relief to her after the tensions of the last four years. But she too at once spotted the offending clauses and immediately sent orders to Potemkin to secure the reversal of these concessions, pointing out that the right to fortify the Russian border was included in the Treaty of Kuchuk Kainardzhi.[65]

A few days before the signature of the preliminaries of Galatz, the Congress of Sistovo had been brought to a close with the signature on 24 July/4 August of the final peace between Turkey and Austria, by which Austria restored almost all her conquests.[66] The Turkish plenipotentiaries then moved on to Jassy to negotiate the final peace with Russia. The Turks had succumbed to the cumulative Russian hammer blows in the summer, and to the pressure for peace in Constantinople where a serious fire had devastated large parts of the city. They feared too that when the Austrians evacuated Walachia on the conclusion of the peace of Sistovo it would be occupied by the Russians. But they were prepared to bargain as long and as hard as possible, and events played into their hands. Not only the Russian plenipotentiaries appointed by Potemkin, but the prince himself, were struck down by the fevers which had become endemic around Galatz and Jassy. Between the paroxysms of his illness, Potemkin continued to negotiate, demanding a large indemnity, the cession of Anapa, even the independence of Moldavia, aware all the time that the Grand Vizir with his large army lay just across the Danube. The progress of his illness – and his occasional recoveries – can be followed in Catherine's increasingly anguished letters and in the diary of her secretary, who recorded every adverse report with the laconic 'tears'.[67]

To the despair of his attendants Potemkin refused to take the quinine prescribed or to follow the diet ordered by his doctors. His niece, Alexandra Branicka, was sent for in the hope that she would persuade him to be treated. Oppressed by the stifling heat, Potemkin asked to be moved from Jassy to the new town of Nikolaev, founded on his orders at the mouth of the Bug. On 5/16 October, he dictated a last letter to Catherine : 'matushka, most gracious sovereign lady, I have no strength to stand any more torment ; the only hope is to leave this town . . . I don't know what will happen to me. Your eternally grateful subject.' In his own hand he scrawled 'My only hope is to leave'. He was placed in his carriage and moved off, escorted by his niece, his faithful aide-de-camp, Vasily Popov, and his doctors. But some forty versts from Jassy, the prince asked to be lifted out of the carriage and laid on the ground in the open air. Here, shortly after, he kissed his icon and died.[68]

27

The Second Partition
of Poland

Potemkin's death inaugurated a new phase in Russian foreign policy, and coincided with new problems. On 9/20 June the King and Queen of France had fled from Paris, and were ignominiously brought back from Varennes. Their capture was followed by the Circular of Padua, issued on 25 June/6 July 1791 by Leopold, appealing to all the European powers to assist in the restoration of monarchical government in France. It was a misleading appeal since Leopold had no intention of embarking on quixotic adventures. But Frederick William's willingness to assist in the task (at a price) was one of the factors which led him to advocate a rapprochement with Austria, embodied in the Convention of Vienna, of 14/25 July 1791, which was to be followed by a formal treaty. For the time being the two powers also agreed to maintain 'the' free constitution of Poland and the integrity of the republic and, in total ignorance of Catherine's views as expressed in the rescripts to Potemkin, they proposed inviting the empress to join in their accord.

The Vienna Convention was followed by the Peace of Sistovo, between Austria and the Porte and, on 31 July/11 August, the Russo-Turkish war came to an end. For a brief moment Europe was at peace. But the first shot in the campaign against revolutionary France was fired at Pillnitz in Saxony on 16/27 August, when Austria and Prussia proclaimed publicly their intention of assisting the French monarchy in terms sufficiently strong to outrage the French National Assembly, while concealing their real intention to do as little as possible.

In Russia, Catherine would not show her hand until the final peace was signed with the Turks. Meanwhile she welcomed the Declaration of Pillnitz and encouraged the German princes to turn to her as a guarantor, by the Peace of Teschen of 1779, of the imperial constitution. During the spring and summer of 1791 Osterman was kept busy pushing Britain, Prussia, Spain and Sardinia to commit themselves to fight against the French Revolution. His main success was with Gustavus III of Sweden. A treaty was signed on 7/18 October 1791; by a secret convention Russia agreed to supply Gustavus with 8,000 Russian troops and some warships, or 300,000 r.p.a. for 8 years. An invasion of France was planned for spring 1792.[1]

Both Catherine and Leopold were in favour of making a lot of noise without committing themselves to action. Louis XVI, by his formal acceptance of the new French constitution on 2/13 September 1791, made their task that much easier. Catherine expressed her contempt for this latest example of royal weakness : 'Eh bien, ne voilà-t-il pas que Sire Louis XVI vous flanque sa signature à cette extravagante constitution,' she wrote to Baron Grimm on 25 September/6 October 1791. 'Je suis dans une colère horrible ; j'ai tapé du pied en lisant ces . . . ces . . . horreurs là,' and she refused to receive the French chargé d'affaires from now on.[2]

But though Catherine declared her solidarity with all crowned heads, subsidized Gustavus, promised to join in any common action to restore the French monarchy and supplied the king's brothers with 500,000 rubles through her personal emissary, the prince of Nassau Siegen, her real views emerge much more clearly in an outburst to her secretary on 14/25 November : 'Je me casse la tête in order to push the courts of Vienna and Berlin into French affairs.' The Prussians, said Catherine, would go ahead but Austria was holding them back. 'Il y a des raisons que je ne peut pas dire ; je veux les engager dans les affaires pour avoir les coudées franches. I have much unfinished business, and it's necessary for them to be kept busy and out of my way.'[3]

It was above all with regard to Poland that the death of Potemkin affected Russian policy. There was now no one left who could hope to act the part of a great Polish magnate or aspire to make himself king. Still less was there anyone capable of filling out the charismatic role of a grand hetman of the Orthodox Cossacks. A more pedestrian, pragmatic policy would be carried out by more pedestrian, pragmatic minds.

Leopold II continued steadfastly to preach acceptance of the Polish constitution of 3 May 1791 to Catherine. No formal reply had ever been made to Kaunitz's overtures to Russia on the subject in May 1791, and the chancellor returned to the charge in November 1791. He accepted that the new constitution would have to be modified to limit the king's power and maintain the independence of the nobles. But if Poland were not given a stable government French revolutionary principles would spread to it, he pointed out.[4] Kaunitz's arguments cut no ice with Catherine, particularly as Leopold appeared so indifferent to fighting revolutionary principles at their source. On 3/14 December Marie Antoinette had written secretly to Catherine, stressing that the king had been coerced into accepting the constitution. She also urged the empress to take part in the plan for an armed congress of the powers which she had already secretly proposed to Leopold and to the kings of Sweden and Spain.[5] But Catherine had already drawn her own conclusions from Leopold's passive policy towards France : the position of the French royal family in her view was desperate ; they were as good as dead.

Early in January 1792 Catherine had the satisfaction of receiving news of the signature of the final treaty of peace with the Porte. Bezborodko had volunteered to go to Jassy on Potemkin's death. He arrived on 4/15 November and brought the negotiations to a successful conclusion on 29 December 1791/9 January 1792. The Turks silently accepted Russian annexation of the Crimea, and ceded the strip of territory between the Bug and the Dniestr, including Ochakov, to Russia.[6] Catherine was free of the Turkish threat at last. But her joy was mingled with grief at the loss of the man who had succeeded in achieving at least a small part of the 'Greek' dream. Grief however could not divert the empress from the pursuit of her aims and as part of the process of gaining elbow-room for her Polish policy, Catherine continued to drive Prussia into the anti-French coalition. She was more than irritated when the Swedes complained that the Russian assistance promised in the treaty of October 1791 was insufficient to enable the financially exhausted Sweden to launch an anti-revolutionary campaign.[7] She brought pressure to bear on the German princes of the Holy Roman Empire, at the same time as the French emigré princes were admonished to set their house in order and learn to act together. Catherine also supported the idea of calling a congress of princes to work out a common programme for the restoration of the French monarchy, either by force, or by peaceful negotiations with the National Assembly, assisted by some judiciously distributed largesse.[8] Finally, she constantly pressed Leopold II himself to have more regard to the interests of his sister, and to act consistently in defence of the monarchical principle.[9] Meanwhile, Leopold was striving to win Frederick William over to joint action against France on his own terms ; but he was forced to accept a Prussian modification of the clause in the Vienna Convention regarding the Polish constitution : it was now agreed to maintain 'a' free Polish constitution, not 'the' free Polish constitution, thus excluding any specific guarantee of the May constitution. Since the fiasco of the Triple Alliance, Frederick William saw no reason to support the new Poland. What he had been unable to obtain from the Poles, he might now obtain by agreement with the two imperial courts. On these terms the treaty of alliance between Prussia and Austria, based on the Vienna Convention, was concluded on 27 January/7 February 1792. It was modelled on the Treaty of Versailles of 1756.

Bezborodko in Jassy had continued to keep the Polish pot boiling with the leaders of the malcontents, Felix Potocki and Severin Rzewuski, who had refused to swear allegiance to the 3 May constitution, and Xavier Branicki, who had sworn, but was prepared to break his oath. The death of Potemkin left them in disarray. But Bezborodko discussed with them the plans outlined in Catherine's rescript of 18/29 July to Potemkin, and the Poles in turn developed their own views for a confederation, the future form of government of Poland (the constitution of 1773 or the 'United Provinces of Poland') and a Russian guarantee of the integrity of their country.[10]

There was however considerable divergence of views in St Petersburg on the policy to be pursued, once Potemkin's master hand had been withdrawn. Potemkin had wanted a kingdom, or the security of a great estate – partition had been for him a means, not an end. Others such as Zubov and his mentor in foreign affairs, A.I. Morkov, a member of the College of Foreign Affairs, favoured the outright annexation of the Polish Ukrainian lands. In any case an invasion of Poland was necessary to restore the ancient constitution. As for Catherine, her views were expressed in a note to the College of Foreign Affairs of December 1791, in which she bluntly stated that she would never agree to the new order which had been introduced in Poland in breach of a treaty, without consulting her, and to the accompaniment of many insults. 'We can do whatever we want in Poland,' she added, 'for the contradictory "half wills" of the Vienna and Berlin courts will only oppose us with a pile of written paper and we will finish our affairs ourselves.' When Morkov urged her to form a party in Poland beforehand and warn the other courts of her intentions, Catherine noted: 'And I say, don't say a word to the other courts; we'll always find a party when we need it. There are bound to be people who prefer the old regime. It is not just a matter of the sale of starostwas or the destruction of hetmanates. There are many pretexts as regards Volynia and Podolia, we need only choose.'[11]

Russia's Polish policy now became the object of factional struggle at court. Zubov and Morkov hoped to carry it through with a high hand, and were in charge of the military dispositions. But Catherine still leant on Bezborodko and trusted his judgment, and she wrote to him herself, urging his prompt return from Jassy at the beginning of February 1792. Bezborodko had indeed already issued a warning on 25 January/5 February 1792 that a Russian invasion of Poland might be regarded by Prussia as the *casus foederis* of the Prusso-Polish treaty, Prussia might declare war on an exhausted Russia, who would not be able to rely on Austrian help. Prussian intentions, he pointed out, must be established beforehand ; best of all would be a separate alliance with Prussia, in which both parties guaranteed each other's existing possessions (i.e. no new acquisitions). If the Prussians were convinced that the object of the Russian occupation of Poland was only the restoration of the constitution, they would be deprived of all pretext to demand Danzig and Thorn. They must realize that now that Russian hands were free, Prussia could not acquire anything except by agreement between the three powers on a partition with equal advantages to all three.[12]

Possibly as a result of Bezborodko's exhortations, Catherine now embarked on the task of persuading the two German powers to approve of her policy. On 17/28 February 1792 an answer was at long last made to Kaunitz's first formal approach on the Polish constitution as far back as May 1791. Catherine declared that she would never accept the Polish violation of the Russo-Polish treaty, and proclaimed her intention to overthrow the 3 May constitution. She hoped that Prussia and Austria would join her in issuing strong declarations in Warsaw to induce the Poles to submit. To Austrian protests, Catherine replied that Austria too was bound by treaty to the maintenance of the ancient constitution of Poland, and that Prussia would certainly join with Russia in demanding its restoration. Austrian suggestions that intervention would inevitably lead to a fresh partition were brushed aside by Catherine. Russia would on no account consent to a partition. The whole communication was couched in the unpleasantly dictatorial language tinged with irony which Catherine had become accustomed to use in international relations, particularly where Poland was concerned.[13]

Prussian complaisance was not surprising ; towards the end of January the text of a note from the empress to Platon Zubov had come to the ears of the Prussian envoy. It proclaimed Catherine's intention of sending the Russian forces returning from Moldavia through the Ukraine into Poland and continued : 'If Austria and Prussia oppose, as is probable, I shall propose to them either compensation or partition.'[14]

Just when his moderating influence was most necessary, the Emperor Leopold suddenly died on 19 February/1 March, leaving his throne to his son, an inexperienced and weak youth of twenty-four years, Francis II. A more dramatic shock was inflicted on Catherine when on 5/16 March Gustavus III was seriously wounded by an assassin at a masked ball in the Opera House in Stockholm. Gustavus survived the attack but he died on 29 March/9 April 1792. Meanwhile Felix Potocki, Sewerin Rzewuski and Xavier Branicki arrived in St Petersburg from Jassy. They were well received in the empress's intimate circle, where plans for a confederation were completed. A scheme for the government of Poland was drawn up by Catherine herself, restoring many of the features of the old constitution, but it was not formally put forward as the policy of the confederation. The actual Act of Confederation, based on an original draft of Potemkin's, was signed on 27 April/8 May in St Petersburg. It accused the 'usurpers' in Warsaw of overthrowing the constitution, but it also referred ominously to 'the contagion of democratic ideas' and the 'abolition of liberty and equality' — of the nobility, be it understood. In addition the confederates issued a demand for the aid of Catherine, the 'tutelary divinity' of Poland, and a Russian guarantee of Polish integrity. The Russian armed forces were now organized into four armies and the arrangements for the invasion of Poland, worked out mainly by Platon Zubov and Arkadiy Morkov, were well advanced when Bezborodko at last arrived back in the capital on 10/21 March from Jassy. Though his influence had been greatly undermined by Zubov, Catherine would not act without consulting him, and he persuaded her to put her Polish policy before the Council.

On 29 March/9 April 1792, for the first time in many months, the Council discussed Poland. The draft manifestos to the Poles and the orders to the military were put, in strictest secrecy, before those present. (Zubov was not a member.) The Council, evidently influenced by Bezborodko, decided that the invasion of Poland, without any preliminary conciliation of the two German courts, and particularly Prussia, was dangerous. The Prussian-Polish alliance might be invoked, and it was essential therefore to warn Berlin in advance that Russia intended only to restore the previous constitution. It would also be useful to stress Russian desire to achieve closer relations with Prussia – a hint that Prussian interests would be considered if and when the time came.[15]

In accordance with the Council's recommendations, the plan for the confederation and the invasion of Poland was communicated on 10/21 April to Berlin and Vienna. The invasion was now openly talked about in the capital. Though Bezborodko still claimed that Catherine did not wish for a partition, his own policy implied the possibility of an agreement on partition with Prussia, and Zubov and other Russians, keen to obtain lands in Poland,[16] were pressing for violent measures.[17]

On 7/18 May Russian troops crossed the Polish border, and the Russian envoy in Poland, Bulgakov, published the Russian manifesto, presenting it as the reply to the Polish communication of the May 1791 constitution which had only been made to Russia in the following December. Revolutionary France now played into Catherine's hands. On 9/20 April France declared war on Austria. The news reached Russia on 28 April/9 May, when the Russian troops were already on the move : Catherine could now be sure that neither Austria nor Prussia would interfere with the Russian invasion of Poland. The Poles accompanying the Russian forces promptly proclaimed the Act of Confederation, dating it from Targowica, just across the Polish frontier, on 3/14 May 1792 (i.e. *before* the Russian invasion) and the Russians proceeded almost without opposition to occupy the western and southern borderlands and Lithuania.[18]

While King Stanislas swore to defend the constitution, and his nephew Joseph began to organize Polish defences, Ignacy Potocki went to Berlin to invoke the *casus foederis* of the Polish-Prussian treaty. Frederick William turned him down flat, on the grounds that the constitution of 3 May had changed the situation and abrogated Prussian treaty obligations to the Polish Commonwealth. Within the limits of their small numbers (about 45,000 fit for field service to the Russians' 100,000), the Poles succeeded in putting up some military resistance, notably on 7/18 July at Dubienka where the future hero Kosciuszko opposed 19,000 Russians with 6,000 men. But the Russians succeeded in forming further confederations and in collecting signatures among magnates and gentry which gave some semblance of Polish support for their intervention.[19]

On 11/22 May the Polish Diet appointed Stanislas 'Dictator', decreed an increase in the army and then dissolved itself. It was therefore Stanislas who now directed Polish policy. Meanwhile the Russians entered Vilna, where on 14/25 June the Russian-sponsored General Confederation of Lithuania was proclaimed amid much public rejoicing. Wherever the Russian forces went, the confederates immediately rescinded all legislation enacted under the 3 May constitution, and attempted, within the limits of war, to restore some form of 'republican' government and social structure.[20] The will to win among the patriotic Poles was undermined by the total absence of allies and the desertion of the king, who was already attempting to negotiate with Catherine. At his instigation, on 11/22 June, Joseph Poniatowski, commanding the Polish armies near Ostrog, asked the Russians for an armistice of four weeks.[21] Catherine on 21 June/2 July ordered the demand to be rejected out of hand. The Poles should be told to disperse, or to submit to the lawful rule of the Confederation of Targowica.[22]

A further effort was made by Stanislas to buy off Catherine by offering the throne of Poland to her grandson Constantine in a perpetual dynastic union. Discussed at the Russian Council on 21 June/2 July, the proposal was rejected as a ploy devised to gain time and to arouse the suspicions of Vienna and Berlin. Stanislas was told to give up the advisers who had led Poland astray and to accede to the Confederation of Targowica.[23] Abandoned by Prussia Stanislas put the Russian demand to a Polish extraordinary council on 12/23 July ; faced with the overwhelming odds, seven voted in favour, five against.[24] On 13/24 July, the king acceded to the Confederation and the army was ordered to cease all resistance to Russia. Many of those who had been associated with the new constitution departed on the weary road to exile, including Joseph Poniatowski and Kosciuszko. The government was taken over by the Confederates of Targowica.

The outbreak of war with France, and the mutual jealousy between Prussia and Austria, prevented either power from taking any action when faced with Catherine's *fait accompli*. The Russians were in occupation, and both German powers were at the time negotiating alliances with Russia. The empress had refused to accede to the Austro-Prussian treaty of 27 January/7 February 1792 but was willing to conclude a bilateral arrangement with Prussia. At the same time, in order not to alienate Austria, Catherine proposed the renewal of the Austro-Russian treaty of 1781. The latter was concluded on 3/14 July 1792, and, as in 1781, guaranteed the unreformed constitution and the boundaries of Poland. The Russo-Prussian treaty was signed on 27 July/7 August, and also provided for the re-establishment of the old Polish constitution.[25]

Catherine's absorption in Polish affairs did not lead her to neglect France. Her closest ally had been Sweden. But the young Gustavus IV, under the regency of his uncle the Duke of Sudermania, had abandoned his father's policy at the very moment when France declared war. From the beginning of the campaign, Austria and Prussia had pressed for the participation of substantial Russian forces. Catherine argued that her forces were occupied putting down Jacobinism nearer home, but finally agreed in summer 1792 to give a subsidy of 500,000 rubles, a sum which the two German powers regarded as totally inadequate.[26] In the meantime tortuous negotiations took place between Austria, Prussia and Russia on the difficult problem of their 'compensation' for fighting revolutionary France. The first stage involved agreement between Prussia and Austria, and by June the new ruler of Austria, Francis II, had agreed that Prussia should seek compensation in Poland while Austria would seek to win Bavaria in exchange for the Austrian Netherlands – a complete break with the policy of Leopold II. Austria, moreover, seemed to consider that Catherine was entitled to no indemnities, but could simply be excused her promised cooperation in the war against France.[27] Catherine meanwhile hinted that Prussian compensation in Poland was negotiable provided Prussia committed herself fully to the war with France, and was gracious about the Bavarian exchange plan. But during the summer the Austro-Prussian agreement proved a broken reed when Austria started to demand immediate compensation (like Prussia) instead of being content to wait until the general reorganization of Europe after final victory over France for the implementation of the Bavarian exchange. Military events now gave the lie to politicians. Paris responded to the manifestos of the émigré princes by overthrowing the French monarchy on 10 August 1792. Shortly afterwards, Prussian forces invaded France and seized Verdun. Paris retaliated with the September massacres and the imprisonment of the royal family in the Temple. On 9/20 September the battle of Valmy took place, and the allied invasion came to an end as the Prussians withdrew to the Rhine. The French now swept rapidly forward to capture Spier, Mainz and Frankfurt ; by November they were in the Austrian Netherlands. As a result Austrian hopes for compensation at the expense of France, or by the Bavarian exchange, vanished, and her dependence on Prussian forces to continue the war with France increased. Prussia was placed in the happy position of declaring that, as a mere auxiliary in the war against France, she must receive an indemnity – in Poland – for her past efforts, before committing herself to a second campaign.

Russia was meanwhile experiencing difficulties in Poland, since the unreformed constitution could not simply be resurrected in all its glory. The confederate temporary government was riven by faction, and using its powers to pay off old scores. The dismal failure of the Austro-Prussian campaign against revolutionary France led Catherine to conclude in November 1792 that neither power was entitled to *any* compensation.[28] But pressure in favour of partition was mounting at the Russian court, where even Bezborodko and A.R. Vorontsov, who feared the aggrandisement of Prussia, were nevertheless at bottom in favour of Russian annexation of Polish lands. Catherine may also have feared that if she did not act together with Frederick William, he might act alone.[29] The confederate leaders in turn played into her hands by accusing all their opponents, however moderate, of Jacobinism, and by their manifest inability to win support in the country, let alone govern it. The victories of the French armies also encouraged the small number of real Polish Jacobins to indulge in provocative behaviour; some hotheads, with little knowledge of geography, imagined the French to be only a few miles from the Polish border.[30]

By the beginning of December 1792, Catherine decided that partition was the only solution. She did not consult Austria, in order to forestall Austrian claims to a share, and objections to the large area Russia proposed to annex. Nor did she conclude a treaty with Prussia ; she merely gave her the green light, on 5/16 December, to occupy the areas she proposed to annex. On 5/16 January, Frederick William announced to the Poles that he was about to send troops into Poland in order to protect his own lands from contamination by the Jacobinism rampant there, and on 12/23 January 1793 the second partition treaty – the St Petersburg Convention – was signed between Russia and Prussia.[31]

Though Catherine – inspired perhaps by her study of Russian history – was not averse, in her pronouncements on the subject, from speaking of the Russian 're- covery of lands inhabited by peoples of the Russian faith and race,' the actual an- nexations were justified mainly on the grounds of the political dangers to the neighbouring states from the aggressive revolutionary spirit in France. In conse- quence the treaty also committed the contracting parties, though in very unequal degree, to the continuation of the war against France. While Frederick William seemed bound by an open-ended commitment, Catherine only promised to act in accordance with existing treaties, and to police Poland. But the rewards were in inverse proportion to the degree of commitment, at any rate as regards the size of the territory annexed. Russia acquired 250,200 km.[2] with over three million in- habitants. Prussia received the coveted Danzig and Thorn, and one million in- habitants. Austria merely received assurances that Prussia would continue in the war against France, and that Prussia and Russia would support the plan for the Bavarian Exchange.

Both Russia and Prussia declared publicly that their policy was aimed at uprooting Jacobinism in Poland. Since the Polish constitution of 3 May scarcely deserves that name, these protestations have usually been regarded as pure hy- pocrisy. This underestimates the nature and the amount of information available to Catherine and her advisers at the time, and also the increasingly heated climate of ideological warfare, the bandying of slogans and words. Catherine regarded events in France with mounting horror – particularly after the flight to Varennes. The total dismantling of the social structure of the *ancien régime,* the proscrip- tion of the émigrés, the September massacres, the abolition of the monarchy were so many shattering blows to the traditional social order and form of government. It was not Catherine who became 'reactionary' in the 1790s, but France which became revolutionary. As in the days of the Pugachev revolt, when the Russian nobility proved infinitely more sensitive to the raping and disembowelling of noble women by rebellious peasants, than to the flogging and torturing of serf girls by noble lords, so Catherine was infinitely more moved by attacks on her own order. The assassination of Gustavus was evidence of a diseased political spirit ; it was followed by urgent police inquiries into reports that a Frenchman was on his way to St Petersburg to assassinate Catherine. The 'Jacobinière' of Warsaw was in correspondence with the Club in Paris, wrote Catherine to Grimm in May 1792 ; was she to abandon her friends in Poland to fight Jacobin- ism in France? No, she preferred to fight it in Poland.[32] The execution of Louis xvi made Catherine physically ill, and she took refuge in bed.[33]

There remains a final problem. Was the second partition of Poland a policy systematically pursued by Catherine from 1788 onwards ? Was it implicit in the first ? There is much evidence to suggest that at the beginning of the second

Turkish war in 1787–8, no such plan existed. Rather Russia was willing to enter into an alliance – on very unequal terms – with Poland. Once Poland adopted a pro-Prussian, anti-Russian policy in October 1788, then an invasion of Poland was undoubtedly one of many options considered by Catherine and particularly by Potemkin. With the proclamation of the May constitution in 1791, partition was openly spoken of in Russia as a means of awakening the republic to a sense of its treaty obligations. But the main thrust of Russian policy was the restoration of the unreformed constitution. Never, so long as the Triple Alliance was blackmailing her, did Catherine consider allowing Prussia to annex Polish lands. Had there been no war with France in 1792, Catherine might still have been forced, after the Russian invasion of Poland in May, to agree to share the spoils with Prussia. But once war had broken out, it was almost inevitable that 'Jacobin' Poland would be made to pay for the continuation of the war against Jacobin France.

Was the partition treaty a victory or a defeat for Russian foreign policy ? There is no simple answer to this question. How can one measure precisely the relative merits of governing undivided Poland indirectly, or acquiring vast, rich and underpopulated lands, of which the bulk of the population was easy to assimilate? In the short term the advantages were all in favour of annexation, even at the price of strengthening Prussia. Divisions in the Russian court arose rather over the *manner* of proceeding, than over the policy of partition itself. Only one critical voice was raised in Russian court circles : Simon Vorontsov, from London, throughout 1792, warned that the Russian occupation of Poland in May would inevitably lead to a partition, which he later described as 'une transaction d'une perfidie injustifiable' and an eternal shame for Russia.[34]

As her agent to put through her policy in Poland, Catherine summoned from his semi-exile in Livonia Count Ya. Sievers, who had been her right-hand man in the 1760s in the local government reforms, but who had fallen from grace over his defence of Livonian liberties. Sievers was an old friend of Stanislas Augustus. They had met in England in the 1750s. But like his predecessors, he acted in a high-handed manner in Warsaw, to all intents and purposes the final authority in the kingdom, above the confederation and the king.

In spite of the rumours which had been circulating since November 1792, the confederate leaders were thunderstruck when they heard of the Prussian invasion and they issued an appeal to arms on 11/22 February 1793, against Prussia alone. Awake at last to the impending doom, S. Rzewuski wrote to Catherine, protesting at the partition and pointing out the intolerable position in which the confederate leaders had been placed. Catherine mockingly exclaimed to her secretary that the confederates had not kept their word. She had expected confederations to spring up ahead of her troops, but they were always behind. Now she was seizing the Ukraine in compensation for her expenses and her losses in men.[35] In Poland Sievers immediately secured the withdrawal of the order for a general armament against Prussia. But the confederate leaders still asked for an assurance that Catherine would protect the integrity of Poland.

It was in vain. Sievers now pressed Stanislas to move to Grodno, the centre of the confederation. The king fought against what he suspected would be his final humiliation. But he was strangled by his debts, estimated at 34 million Polish florins, which Catherine would not pay unless he obeyed her, and he was incapable of standing up to the psychological pressure of Sievers, who alternately threatened and cajoled him.[36] Early in April Sievers arrived in Grodno, and on 27 March/7 April the Russian and Prussian manifestos proclaiming the partition were published.[37] It remained to secure Polish acceptance of their destiny.

The means chosen by Catherine were of a refined cruelty. Stanislas was to summon a Diet to Grodno, away from 'Jacobin' Warsaw. At a time when Poland was facing economic ruin, Sievers had only to postpone payment for food and fodder taken by the Russian army, or to threaten the sequestration of estates, to secure compliance with his wishes. On 3 May 1793 (the second anniversary of the May constitution) invitations to elect a new Diet were signed by the king. By a combination of force and bribery Sievers saw to it that apparently reliable deputies were elected. When they arrived in Warsaw they were entertained lavishly by the Russian ambassador and received their pay. But Sievers had no guarantee that they would do what they had been paid to do. The tasks laid upon him had been outlined by Catherine in two rescripts which are masterpieces of cynicism. He had to secure the election by the Diet of a delegation which would negotiate the treaties of cession between Russia and Poland and Prussia and Poland respectively, treaties which were to be kept entirely separate. Only when these treaties were out of the way was Sievers to deal with the future constitution of Poland, a matter from which Prussia was to be totally excluded. Finally, in a later rescript, Catherine touched on the fact that Austria, seeing the Bavarian Exchange vanish into thin air, was demanding some form of compensation elsewhere, preferably in Poland, where the city of Cracow would prove acceptable. It did not seem wise to Catherine to reduce the limits of Poland further, and she therefore proposed, instead of allowing the Austrians a share, to persuade Prussia to disgorge part of her gains in order to remove her further from the Austrian border. Sievers was therefore discreetly to encourage the Poles to oppose the cession of Czestochowa to the Prussians, while ostensibly acting as a conciliator between the two sides.[38]

The intricacies of the Polish constitution enabled the deputies to the Diet and the confederates to indulge in a number of delaying manoeuvres and intrigues; Stanislas made a bid to clear his name by publicly declaring that he would never sign a treaty giving away Polish territory. Sievers's response was to order the sequestration of the royal revenues. Russian pressure finally forced the Diet to appoint a delegation on 1/12 July. Four days later the delegates reported to the Diet the terms of the Russian-Polish partition treaty, and after stormy debates even the most patriotic Poles surrendered to *force majeure* and with twenty dissenting votes accepted the treaty, which was signed on 22 July/2 August.[39]

The outright incorporation into Russia of the rest of Poland had been considered by Catherine in May 1793. Sievers's reports, marked by his own wishful thinking, had encouraged her by suggesting that

les plus sensés d'entre les Polonois sentoient que dans la faiblesse et le néant où leur pays seroit plongé à la suite du nouveau démembrement qu'il vient de subir, il lui seroit difficile ou plutôt impossible de subsister en corps libre et indépendant. En partant de là, presque tous désireroient assés unanimement de pouvoir suivre la destinée de ceux de leurs compatriotes qui ont passé sous ma domination.[40]

Sievers himself recommended the annexation of the whole of the rump of Poland but outright incorporation would not be tolerated by Prussia as Catherine clearly realized. The same object could however be achieved by a treaty of alliance so close that while 'neither power was subject to the other', Russia and Poland should be inseparably united. No reference was made to this projected alliance in the partition treaty, and the Poles were assured in article 5 that Russia would not oppose changes in the ancient form of government to be introduced in the Diet, and would be willing to guarantee the Polish constitution.[41]

It was now Sievers's task to persuade the Poles to negotiate with Prussia, while concealing from Prussia Russian willingness to force some concessions from Prussia in favour of Poland. After even more violent outbursts of patriotic feeling Prussian negotiations with the Polish delegation began at the end of July and lasted three weeks, with Sievers acting as the honest broker. On 15/26 August the deputies put the treaty before the Diet which greeted it with even wilder scenes of outrage than it had the Russian treaty. Sievers then resorted to force. On the pretext of a plot against the king, the marshal of the Diet and the senators, he surrounded the Diet with troops, and introduced Russian officers into the chamber. The deputies were informed that no one would be allowed to leave until the treaty had been approved. The session lasted far into the night, and the deputies finally approved the treaty with five conditions, one of which, that the empress of Russia should guarantee the treaty and in particular the commercial treaty between Poland and Prussia still to be negotiated, was deliberately put forward as highly offensive to Prussia.[42]

News of this further Polish tergiversation outraged Frederick William II and his advisers, and he was persuaded to threaten immediate withdrawal from the war with France, and the breaking off of negotiations with Austria for an Austrian 'compensation', in order to use his troops to enforce his Polish claims. Whether because she really feared that Frederick William would leave the war against France, or because she wished to hasten the constitutional settlement of Poland which could only take place after the conclusion of the Prussian treaty, Catherine ordered Sievers to bring things to an end. He had already anticipated his mistress's orders, by the use of the usual methods; the arrest of four opposition leaders, the introduction of troops into the Diet, and of officers into the chamber itself for the session of 12/23 September 1793. The deputies were informed that no one would be allowed to leave until the Polish-Prussian partition treaty was approved. Once again there were scenes of violent protest. Then the deputies resorted to a different tactic : they lapsed into total silence, and sat immobile in their seats. When at 4 a.m. the Russian general threatened to bring in his troops, the marshal of the Diet found a way out: three times he asked: Does the Diet authorize the delegates to sign the treaty, and three times not one deputy replied, whereupon the marshal exclaimed 'Silence means consent,' and three days later the treaty was signed.[43]

It remained now to negotiate the treaty of alliance between Russia and the truncated rump of Poland. Using his Polish tools, Sievers soon secured a request from the Polish deputies for an alliance with Russia in precisely those terms which were set down in a Russian draft prepared by Catherine herself. It was approved unanimously with a few amendments on 5/16 October, and was followed by fresh banquets and balls at which Russians and Poles drowned the tension between them, for a while, in unbridled merriment. The treaty provided for the mutual defence of the territories of the contracting parties, the command of the army going to Russia. Russia would be entitled to introduce her forces into Poland after previous consultations with the Polish government ; she could in time of war or, in case of necessity, recruit Polish troops or increase the Polish army. Poland undertook to refrain from any alliances with other powers without Russian consent ; her envoys at foreign courts were to act with Russian envoys ; and she would be represented by Russia at courts where there was no Polish envoy. Russia guaranteed the Polish constitution which could not be altered without her consent. The Orthodox community remaining in Poland was to be subordinate to the Metropolitan of Kiev.[44]

The treaty in fact turned Poland into a Russian protectorate, but even so Catherine was not satisfied with the amendments Sievers had allowed into the text. In particular she was very angry that any Russian decision to introduce troops into Poland had been made subject to consultation with the Polish government : 'My intention', she wrote,

had been to divert the attention of other governments from the entrance of any troops into Poland, so as imperceptibly to accustom them to this in all cases. The Polish government would have been spared the inevitable explanations, if it was asked on what grounds our troops were entering ; it needed merely to reply : in accordance with the treaty, and no more. It is obvious that I would not take on the burden of defending . . . a weak state . . . unless I could count on its complete submission to my advice, plans and views. Whom should I ask to agree to the introduction of my forces ? The king ? But he has no power. The Permanent Council, or the Diet ? But then I would have to explain my reasons every time. . . .

As Catherine also pointed out, a treaty was one thing, the manner in which it was implemented was another. Sievers was instructed not to work through the king but to build up an independent party and prevent Stanislas from appearing as the spokesman of Polish national interests. He was to fill government posts with faithful and modest people, and explain to the king that in the fulfilment of the treaty he should increase Catherine's influence to the point where she had the right to appoint to important posts those people who had of late served her so well. Though many of the decrees of the confederates were now rescinded, nevertheless there was to be no persecution of Catherine's partisans for the many injustices they had committed during their brief period of power.[45]

On hearing the terms of the treaty one Polish deputy exclaimed : 'Poland has become a Russian province. We would have done better to unite entirely with Russia before, we would have maintained more of our integrity and we would have been happier.'[46] Catherine shared this opinion. She would have been glad to 'unite' with the whole of Poland, but circumstances were unfavourable. Nevertheless the total absorption of Poland remained on the agenda since as a result of developments in the war against revolutionary France relationships between the three Eastern powers had again become very tense.

28

Finis Poloniae

The French victory over Prussia at Valmy had been followed by the victory of Jemappes in November, and the Declaration of the National Assembly offering French support to all peoples willing to free themselves from absolutist governments. In December 1792, the French National Assembly proclaimed that in all territories occupied by French armies, the existing form of government would be overthrown and replaced by the sovereignty of the people. Catherine's own ideas of the policy to be pursued in relation to France are set out in a memorandum,[1] unfortunately undated, but probably written sometime in 1792, and intended for the French émigré princes. For her, the cause of the king of France was the cause of all kings, and it was necessary for the European balance of power that France should maintain her status as a great power. The disorder in France was such, wrote Catherine, that 'une révolution est indispensablement nécéssaire . . . Cette révolution ne saurait consister sans doute que dans le rétablissement du gouvernement monarchique . . . l'équilibre des pouvoirs, la noblesse, le clergé, la magistrature ne se réuniroient-ils pas sous des chefs animés d'un désir aussi légitime, aussi équitable, aussi modéré ?' There is not, in Catherine's vision of a restored monarchy à la Montesquieu, in which all ranks should also wear the corresponding external signs of distinction, any desire (as yet) for vindictive repression. A few 'scélérats' should be punished and an act of oblivion and amnesty should immediately follow for those who returned to their allegiance. Many deputies to the National Assembly, Catherine asserted, would return as soon as they felt themselves upheld ; in any case they had gone beyond their powers because the electors did not demand abolition of the monarchy, let alone of the Christian religion. One should not 'nuire à la liberté raisonnable des individus', but abolish a government incompatible with the existence of a great realm. However, it would be necessary to have 'quelque égard au cri général de la nation' against the restoration of the Parlements and in favour of liberty as against monarchy. But the demand for liberty could be satisfied by good and wise laws. Some kind of national compact was proposed by Catherine as a means of welding the émigré princes and the royal family together (the gulf separating the queen and the princes was known to all) around a programme which could be put before the nation, and great care should be taken to ensure that subsidies should be used only for restoring the monarchy and religion. The restoration could be easily achieved by the German armies and the French exiles, wrote Catherine. Though foreign troops might be more reliable at first, the exiled French nobility could form a 'Maison du Roi' which should not be disbanded even after the king's restoration.

Catherine had held back from direct intervention in the war with France while she was engaged in the invasion of Poland and preparations for the second partition. But she continued to proclaim her anti-revolutionary sentiments in order to distract the Western powers from Polish affairs. She had in any case believed all along that nothing could be achieved without Britain, and that Britain had no intention of going to war to restore the French monarchy. In autumn 1792, Catherine had approached Britain to concert measures, but even the decree opening the river Scheldt to navigation, issued by France on November 1792, did not provoke Pitt to declare war. He contented himself with the statement that British policy was concerned primarily with the security of Europe, not with the nature of the French government.[2]

The execution of Louis XVI on 10/21 January 1793, news of which reached St Petersburg on 29 January/9 February (after the signature of the Russo-Prussian partition treaty) led Catherine to take an enormous step forward in committing Russia to open hostilities against France. After consulting the Council, which drew on precedents created for the government of Tsar Aleksey Mikhaylovich by the execution of Charles I, Catherine decreed a total breach with revolutionary France. The French chargé d'affaires, Edmond Genet, had ceased to be received at court on the grounds that the king was a prisoner, ever since the flight to Varennes. He was expelled in July 1792, and diplomatic relations between the two powers were then *de facto* broken off. The empress's ukaz of 8/19 February 1793 legalized the situation. In addition she annulled the Franco-Russian commercial treaty of 1787, prohibited all trade between the two countries, recalled all Russian subjects from France, and expelled all French citizens from Russia unless they took an oath of allegiance to the French monarchy. The importation of French newspapers and books was also prohibited.[3]

The death of Louis XVI precipitated matters in England too. The French envoy was ordered to leave the country at once. The French Convention reacted by declaring war on Britain on 21 January/1 February 1793, and followed this up by declaring war on the United Provinces, Spain, Portugal and the Two Sicilies. This strengthened Catherine's hand, since Britain was in the war before any treaty had been negotiated with Russia. Six days after the French declaration of war, Russia opened talks for an Anglo-Russian treaty with the British envoy in St Petersburg, which were completed in record time by Simon Vorontsov in London. A commercial treaty was signed on 14/25 March 1793, renewing the long-lapsed treaty of 1766, as well as a second treaty binding both parties to assist each other in the war against France, not to conclude a separate peace, to close their ports to all French ships and to prohibit French trade with neutral countries. This last provision ran totally counter to the principles of the armed neutrality proclaimed by Catherine with such pomp in 1780.[4]

Nevertheless the two powers had very different ideas on how to carry the war into France. Catherine was for once prepared to supply troops, but on her terms : she would offer a Russian corps to be transported on British ships, together with a French corps of some five to six thousand. The corps would assemble in Danzig and would join the French émigré troops in the Channel Islands. The commander-in-chief would be the Comte d'Artois. The object was to effect a landing in Brittany or Normandy and secure a base in the French provinces, since the provinces, in Catherine's view, could be used to redress the balance against corrupt Paris.[5] The allied powers should put the French princes forward and assist their enterprises. For these services Catherine asked for a subsidy of 600,000 rubles and expected Britain to bear all the costs of the enterprise, which she would recover afterwards from France. To justify her demand for subsidies, Catherine pointed to the large sums she was already paying to the French émigré princes. In contrast, England could recoup herself not only by French repayments but by the annexation of French colonial territories. The role which Catherine here assumed, of political leader of the coalition against France, was rejected out of hand by Britain who refused to grant a subsidy but demanded that a Russian corps should be put at Britain's disposal. Agreement might have been reached on military cooperation, but the views of the two powers on the future of France were too far apart for political cooperation to be possible. This may well have been the result which Catherine was seeking, since it enabled her to refuse to supply any Russian troops ('as though we were Hessians'). Not only was Russia in serious financial difficulties but she needed her troops far more for Poland, to keep watch on Turkey, and as a guard against Sweden who was increasingly outraged by the high-handed manner in which the Russian navy was carrying out its task of cutting off all trade with France.

As early as January 1793, Catherine armed a squadron of twenty-five ships of the line in the Baltic to enforce the prohibition of trade with France, and the treaty with Britain obliged her to put a number of ships at Britain's disposal for her blockade of the French coasts. The instructions to Admiral Chichagov of 27 May/7 June 1793 show that the squadron was to act against Danish and Swedish ships, since both countries had refused to take part in the trade prohibition. Swedish protests were rejected on the grounds that the war against France was not governed by normal rules. The ideological element in the war, or as Osterman put it, the fact that the French were rebels, justified the detention of neutral ships and the confiscation of French goods or goods originating in France or destined to France on board neutrals, or indeed anywhere.[6]

Sweden, under the regency of the Duke of Sudermania, was clinging to her neutrality (and losing as a result the Russian subsidies promised in the treaty of

October 1791). Her policy led to increasing tension with Russia and put paid for the time being to a plan caressed by Catherine, namely to arrange a marriage between Gustavus IV and her eldest granddaughter, Alexandra Pavlovna. Alarmed by Russian naval policy, Sweden and Denmark took steps to protect themselves in the 1794 sailing season against Russian patrols and concluded a convention in April 1794 for the arming of squadrons and mutual trade protection.[7] In Western Europe, efforts to consolidate the 'first Coalition' against revolutionary France suffered from Prussian unwillingness to fight without substantial British subsidies, and the huge gap between words and deeds in Russia. A British subsidy treaty with Prussia was finally concluded in April 1794 but no formal treaty was signed with Russia, with whom disputes soon arose over the implementation of the Anglo-Russian commercial treaty.

In a time of revolutionary fervour, when French arms were so frequently victorious, Polish patriots found it intolerable meekly to accept the mutilation of their country and the servile constitutional settlement imposed upon them by Catherine. Count Sievers was recalled in November 1793, and replaced by Baron Igelstrom who was also the commander of the Russian armed forces. He now began the reduction of the Polish army to 15,000 men. Even the confederates of Targowica found the Russian yoke heavier than they had expected. In these circumstances, a resistance movement grew up inside Poland, kept alive by contact with émigré Poles, notably Kosciuszko, and directed against Russia and Prussia (but not Austria which had taken no part in the second partition). There were even some inconclusive talks with French republican leaders.

The disarming of the Polish army sparked off a rising in March 1794. Kosciuszko, who had hoped to postpone a revolt until he had received assurances of Turkish or French support, returned to Poland, took command of the Polish rebel forces and defeated a Russian detachment on 24 March/4 April 1794 at Racławice. Ten days later, Warsaw rose against the occupying power. The Russian garrison numbered 7,000 men, more than half of whom were killed or taken prisoner.[8] Igelstrom, with a few battalions, fought his way out and fled to the Prussian forces encamped in their zone nearby. By 11/22 April the revolt had spread to Russian-occupied Lithuania and even to Curland. The hetman of Lithuania, Kossakowski, who had been a fervent adherent of Russia, was publicly hanged in Vilna as a traitor. Some 4,000 Polish officers, caught in the lands annexed by Russia, made their way back to Poland and joined Kosciuszko's forces. A provisional government was quickly formed and Kosciuszko was appointed commander-in-chief of the Polish forces. Stanislas remained in Warsaw, distrusted by the Poles and patriots, in an attitude of guarded sympathy towards the revolt, but fearing, in common with many, that the 'Jacobin' element might take the upper hand, as it had in Vilna.

As in France, war against the foreign enemy went hand in hand with political revolution at home, which alienated many Poles. By 17/28 April an investigating commission had been set up to detect and punish cases of treason, empowered to arrest, interrogate, but not to try and sentence. A general armament was decreed as well as a levy of 10 per cent on income, and in an effort to win the common people to support the national cause, Kosciuszko issued on 7/18 May 1794 a manifesto in which he denounced Catherine's promises that the Polish serfs would be better treated under Russian than under Polish rule, proclaimed the personal freedom of the Polish peasants, and reduced their labour dues.[9] The manifesto was not in fact implemented, and indeed most of its provisions were extremely unpopular with the Polish gentry class, but it contributed to the Jacobin image of the Polish revolt in foreign eyes. In Lithuania, verbal imitation of the French model went much further ; the common objectives of the French and the Poles were stressed in public proclamations, and a Committee of Public Safety was set up. In Warsaw, towards the end of May, popular rioting culminated in the public hanging of Bishop Kossakowski (the hetman's brother, previously deprived of his ecclesiastical rank) and three other leaders of the pro-Russian party. A few executions took place elsewhere in Poland, but considering the heated atmosphere and the provocation, the numbers were small.[10]

The first rumblings of the Polish revolt had been disregarded in Russia, and when news of the Warsaw rising reached the capital at the end of April, Catherine as usual maintained her composure in public, but the blow to Russian prestige was severe. On 20 April/1 May the situation was laid before the Council. On the military side it was agreed to concentrate all the Russian forces in Poland in Lithuania to protect the Russian frontier, or to move them as close as possible to the Prussian frontier. Frederick William was to be invited to take charge of putting down the revolt west of the Vistula ; and the Austrians (to whom a hint was given to move troops into Poland) were to be urged to close their border in Galicia to Polish rebels. At the same time the Council recommended the sequestration of all the estates belonging to known rebels which were in Russian occupied lands.[11]

Catherine's reliance on Prussian and Austrian troops in this emergency reflects not only the extent of her disarray but also the fact that the bulk of the Russian army was at the time stationed on the Turkish border, on guard against a threat which fortunately for Russia was conjured by the diplomatic skill of her envoy to the Porte, General M.I. Kutuzov. A significant portion of these forces was now placed under Field-Marshal P.A. Rumyantsev, recalled to active service to take overall charge of the repression of the Polish revolt.[12] Prince N.V. Repnin, who was governor of the provinces formed out of ex-Polish territory, was in command of the Russian forces in Russian-annexed Lithuania. Meanwhile Frederick William, through the ubiquitous Prince of Nassau Siegen, offered Catherine military assistance and broached the subject of his reward. That the outcome of the revolt might be a further partition of Poland was clear to all, and Frederick William's despatch of Prussian troops to lay siege to Warsaw strengthened his hand. The failure of the Austrian campaign in the Netherlands against France in spring and summer 1794, coupled with the spectacle of Prussian armed intervention in Poland, led Austria to turn her eyes in that direction too. The way was clear for Catherine who, on 11/22 July 1794 openly warned Austria and Prussia that the time had come to 'extinguish the last spark of the [Jacobin] fire in Poland'.[13]

The admission of Austria to an eventual partition, a policy contemplated from the first by Catherine to keep Prussia in bounds, aroused the anger of Frederick William who hastened to send troops towards Cracow to prevent the Austrians from seizing it. On 26 May/6 June a joint Russian-Prussian force defeated a Polish army at Rawka, and the Prussians occupied Cracow on 4/15 June. Austrian forces advanced into the palatinates of Sandomir, Lublin and Volynia on 30 June/11 July and formally placed before Catherine their demand for Cracow. Both the German powers put forward large territorial claims in Poland to St Petersburg, while Catherine, secure of her own share, which her armies were occupying little by little, could play the role of arbiter.

By mid-July the war with revolutionary Poland – for a war it was – had become fiercer, and some 25,000 Prussians and 14,000 Russians were advancing on Warsaw. Defeat had exacerbated the mood of the population in the city, and extremists broke into the prison, seized a number of pro-Russian Poles and summarily hanged them. At the end of July, the siege of the city began in earnest, led by Frederick William in person, who had abandoned the fight against France for the more immediate promise of reward in Poland. But in September he was forced to withdraw his troops from Warsaw by the outbreak of a revolt in Prussian-occupied Greater Poland.

Catherine 'laughed too heartily to feel any indignation' at the spectacle of Frederick William's undignified departure from Warsaw. She soon saw that if Russia alone crushed the revolt in the capital she would be in a much stronger position to dictate a settlement.[14] The improved Russian strategic position enabled Rumyantsev to order a corps of some 13,000 men to advance through Volynia to Brest Litovsk and secure the left flank of Repnin's army in Lithuania. To command this corps Rumyantsev appointed General Suvorov, knowing, as he put it, that Suvorov's name alone would be worth several thousand men.[15] His rapidly advancing troops were successful in two minor engagements against Polish forces. Kosciuszko now concentrated on preventing a junction between the two main Russian armies, but he was fatefully defeated at Maciejowice on 28 September/9 October in a battle in which 7,000 Poles were outnumbered almost two to one, and in which he himself was wounded and taken prisoner, together with a number of other Polish military leaders.

Reinforced by troops from Lithuania, Suvorov soon felt himself strong enough to advance deeper into Poland where he planned to lay siege to Praga, the fortified suburb of Warsaw across the Vistula, and seize the bridges over the river. The Russian attack was launched before dawn on 24 October/5 November and three hours later the Russians were masters of the scene. 'The whole of Praga was strewn with dead bodies, blood was flowing in streams,' wrote Suvorov in his report.[16] Amid scenes of carnage unseen in European warfare for a long time, the remnants of the Polish forces unable to escape over the bridges into Warsaw flung themselves into the Vistula and drowned, or were hacked to death on a little tongue of land in the middle of the river. 'They're all dogs, they have fought against us, let them perish,' exclaimed one stalwart Russian soldier who used a hatchet to split open the skulls of his victims.[17] Politicians, like Bezborodko, and subsequent historians, have argued that Suvorov was unable to restrain his soldiers from taking revenge for their comrades who had perished at Polish hands during the Warsaw rising. This seems a rather far-fetched argument and does not explain the massacre of women, children, priests and nuns. Those who accepted Suvorov's offer to escape to the Russian camp sometimes saved their skins, if not their property. But some of the Bernardine nuns, together with the girls entrusted to them for education, were raped and killed. Bezborodko estimated the number of Poles killed at 20,000, the number of prisoners at 10,000. Judging by Suvorov's policy towards the Turks in the past, it was his practice to allow an initial period of licence to his soldiers, and then to clamp down completely. This view is strengthened by the fact that he warned Warsaw that it would be treated like Praga if it did not surrender.[18]

Warsaw heeded the warning. The surrender of the city and its defenders within eight days was negotiated by the city council and Suvorov undertook to protect the lives and property of the citizens. He marched in on 28 October/8 November 1794, to cries of 'Long live Catherine'. Stanislas Augustus, who had throughout remained in Warsaw, was still officially king of Poland and recognized as such by Suvorov. A Te Deum was duly sung in St Petersburg, and to the jealous fury of many senior army commanders, Suvorov was raised to the rank of field-marshal.

From the beginning Catherine had held very strong views about the nature of the Polish revolt, and the policies to be pursued in quenching it. Kosciuszko was for her the spokesman of undiluted Jacobinism, ready to murder all those who thought otherwise. His manifestos were imbued with 'French principles'; they were not issued in the name of the king, but by the leader of a 'popular' rising against established authority, who was believed to be in correspondence with Robespierre and Saint-Just. He was merely pretending to work with the king, the Church and the nobles in order to round on them and destroy them later. Kosciuszko had allegedly told the French leaders that he hoped to raise a rebellion in the Crimea and burn the Russian fleet. He was urging the French to arouse the Turks, and to send the Poles 10 million livres above the 1·3 million allegedly already sent.[19]

The behaviour, the language, and the policies of the Polish rebels served to ram home in Russia the vision of a nest of Jacobins on the very frontiers of the country. What to do with Poland became a crucial question, and opinions were very divided. England and Austria, wrote Bezborodko in April, would prefer a return to the *status quo*. Prussia wanted partition, either total, or leaving a small buffer between the partitioning powers. Bezborodko himself as early as May came down in favour of a complete partition, since there was no hope that Poland would ever be quiet and reliable. But if the 'name of Poland' were not to be destroyed forever then substantial frontier modifications should be made in Lithuania and Volynia, to recoup Russian expenses, and the Polish armed forces should be reduced to a minimum; the capital should be removed from Warsaw, and Vilna should be destroyed by fire. Russia should also become the suzerain of Curland.[20]

With the passage of time the dangers of 'Jacobinism' became ever clearer to the Russians. The 'seed' had struck such deep root that it was impossible for governments, anxious to prevent the established order from being overturned by 'absurd equality and transient freedoms', to allow a Polish government to subsist.[21] Past experience showed that it was impossible to make friends of the Poles, wrote Bezborodko, particularly since the second partition. In the event of war with the Turks they would take the Prussian side and attempt to injure Russia. The country was now too small to make an effective barrier between Russia and her neighbours, and in any case a buffer state which could be invaded at will, was but a chimaera. Ideas too could cross frontiers : 'the state of mind of the Poles, particularly the young ones, was such that the infection could easily spread ; the freedom of the peasants and such like would provoke our own village dwellers, so similar in language and habits, whereas the vicinity of Austria implied no such danger.'

Moreover Russia was stronger than any one of the German powers, and could rely on the fact that they would never unite against Russia; one at least would always be allied with Russia. These considerations led Russia to advocate the annihilation of Poland, instead of setting up a fresh confederation or creating a Russian party there.[22] The Council, in accordance with Bezborodko's usual practice of sharing responsibility, was invited to discuss his advice. It decided on 13/24 November 1794 that Warsaw could be treated as conquered territory ; private property would be respected but the city was to pay an indemnity in goods and money ; the arsenal and all military supplies should be removed ; all the regalia, banners, insignia, badges of hetmans' offices, etc. should be sent to Russia. The archives and the public library should also be removed. Suvorov was to govern by decree, and dissolve all revolutionary institutions. Those who had participated in the Warsaw rising of 6/17 April were to be arrested and sent to Russia. Warsaw was to be kept firmly in Russian hands.[23] The king was to be sent to Grodno, and since Poland was about to cease to exist, pressure was to be brought to bear on him to abdicate. Stanislas had still hoped to play some role in some kind of Poland ; he was soon disillusioned, and left unwillingly for Grodno, never to see Warsaw again.[24]

It now remained to push through the diplomatic negotiations. In autumn 1794 Catherine peremptorily invited both German powers to reduce their claims to what she considered manageable proportions. Austria gave way gracefully ;

Frederick William stuck to his full claims (cutting down the Austrian share correspondingly) and attempted to disentangle himself from the war against France in the West in order to bring his full military weight to bear in the East. Accordingly while secret negotiations began between Prussia and France, Russia and Austria reached a rapid agreement incorporated in three treaties of 23 December 1794/3 January 1795 (as with all Russian-Austrian agreements since the dispute over the alternative with Joseph II in 1781, the agreements took the form of an exchange of declarations). The agreements provided for the final partition of Poland, leaving a portion for Prussia should she later care to adhere to the treaty ; for the belated adhesion of Austria to the second partition treaty between Russia and Prussia ; and for the renewal of the treaty of 1781, namely the partition of Turkey, with an additional clause by which the signatories guaranteed each other against attack by Prussia. Russia also undertook to support Austrian claims for territorial indemnities in the West.[25] Nothing could be done to implement the treaty however, since the Prussians were in occupation of Cracow, and were still negotiating peace with France.

To make up for the impending loss of Prussia from the anti-French coalition, Britain again attempted to secure Russian forces for the fight against France. Negotiations for a treaty began in autumn 1794 but the two sides had different objects in view. Britain sought fresh forces. Catherine sought guarantees against the possibility of attack from Turkey, Sweden or even Prussia. She made it a condition that she should not supply Russian troops if she needed them for her own defence, with her involvement in Poland specifically in mind. The treaty was finally signed on 7/18 February 1795, and provided for mutual assistance in the form of an expeditionary corps (Russia) or a squadron (Britain), or an annual subsidy of 500,000 rubles. A secret article provided that though the present war against revolutionary France was, as usual, excluded from the treaty, nevertheless Russia would provide a squadron of twelve warships and six frigates to act with a British fleet in the Channel and the Atlantic but not in the Mediterranean or in non-European waters. Other secret articles provided for a British squadron in the Baltic if Catherine were attacked, and the opening of British ports to the Russian fleet in the event of a war with the Porte.[26]

These two clauses hint at further complications besetting Russian foreign policy. Relations with Sweden had continued to deteriorate since the reversal of policy introduced by the regent, Duke Charles, on the death of Gustavus III in 1792. One of the first steps taken by the regent was to dismiss Baron G.M. Armfeldt, Gustavus's favourite, who had been appointed to the regency council in the king's will, and to replace him by a favourite of his own, Baron G.A. Reuterholm, who was also a personal enemy of Armfeldt's. The latter had fled from Sweden, and had conspired to overthrow the regent and Reuterholm, conducting secret talks with Russia through one of Zubov's private secretaries. When the plot failed, Armfeldt was tried and sentenced *in absentia* for treason in July 1794. Subsequently Catherine gave him asylum in Kaluga, and all Swedish efforts to obtain his extradition were met with a blank refusal on the grounds that Armfeldt was not in Russia. Even when the regent tempted Catherine with the bait of the marriage between Gustavus IV and her granddaughter on condition of the extradition of Armfeldt, Catherine would not hear of it. The whole episode poisoned relations between the two Crowns and drove them further apart.[27]

Meanwhile, on her southern border, Russia was also faced with threatening moves by the Porte. France had been egging the Turks on to declare war on Austria, and Catherine as Austria's ally was committed to come to her aid. The 'Greek' dream began again briefly to float before her eyes. In these circumstances the protection of the British fleet in the Baltic, and the use of British ports by her own ships, provided useful guarantees. But meanwhile the first coalition against revolutionary France was crumbling away. Prussia deserted on 25 March/5 April at the Peace of Basle, and on 5/16 May the United Provinces made peace with France. Secret talks began at once between France and Spain, and in spite of all Osterman's efforts to underline that Prussian jealousy of Austria and Spanish jealousy of Britain were enabling revolutionary France to destroy the coalition, peace between France and Spain was signed on 30 June/11 July 1795. Other minor powers followed one after another, leaving Britain and Austria almost alone in the field.

The Anglo-Russian treaty now also served Catherine well in the new situation created by Prussian desertion of the war against France. Just as Prussia was free to turn on Russia in order to obtain her share of Poland, Russia had acquired a new ally. Catherine did not fail to propose to Britain that her forces might be more advantageously employed in fighting France's new ally, Prussia, than in fighting France herself.[28] During the spring and the early summer of 1795, Russian forces were massed on her borders to ward off a Prussian attack in a situation which Bezborodko regarded as more critical even than that of 1790–1.[29] Meanwhile the Austrians concentrated their troops in Bohemia, Moravia and Galicia. But in August the two imperial powers called the Prussian bluff. The partition treaty was presented almost as an ultimatum to Prussia, and Frederick William agreed to negotiate for a share of Poland. The final treaties were signed on 13/24 October 1795, based on the Austro-Russian partition treaty of 23 December 1794/3 January 1795. Austria ceded a few districts to Prussia, and finally obtained, by an arbitration award from Catherine in October 1796, the coveted city of Cracow.[30]

Russia, by the third partition, acquired Lithuania, the remaining part of Belorussia and Western Ukraine – comprising about 120,000 km.[2] and mainly Orthodox inhabitants – not a single Pole, as Catherine proudly put it. It was slightly less than the territory secured by J. V. Stalin in 1945. There remained the little problem of the Duchy of Curland which A.R. Vorontsov had pressingly urged Bezborodko not to overlook.[31] It was solved by organizing a meeting of the local Diet. The Curlanders then invited Catherine to become their overlord,[32] arranging for the abdication of Duke Peter Biron (who had inherited the Duchy from his father in 1772) and for the abdication of the existing suzerain, Stanislas Augustus, which took place on 15/26 November 1796. By a final convention signed by Paul I after Catherine's death, it was agreed that the denomination 'Kingdom of Poland' should never be used, so that all memory of a once great state should be forgotten.[33]

The main Russian supporters of the second and third partitions of Poland were lavishly rewarded by Catherine. In the period from the middle of 1795 to 28 June/9 July 1796, when Catherine signed the last land grant she ever made, ninety-six estates were distributed, totalling 130,000 male souls. Of these 121,580 were in the ex-Polish lands. Large numbers of souls went to the great military leaders, Rumyantsev, Suvorov, to the favourite P. Zubov, and his family, to the nieces of Potemkin, and smaller grants of one to four hundred serfs to deserving officers and officials. Bezborodko received 50,000 rubles and a pension of 10,000 r.p.a.

If one examines Russian foreign policy in the years 1792–6 objectively it is difficult to accept the view that Catherine's main aim was to fight the French Revolution, that Poland was of less significance, and that only the appalling financial situation and exhaustion after the second Turkish war prevented Russia from sending an expeditionary corps to France.[34] It is true that there were financial constraints on Russian freedom of action, but there is no doubt that until the fall of the French monarchy Catherine could live with the French Revolution, whereas she could not for one minute accept the Polish 3 May constitution, which challenged both the Russian power position in Poland, and the absolute monarchy she incarnated. Catherine sensed the revolutionary undercurrent in Poland – and there is no point in pretending it was not there – and she crushed the revolution where she could most easily reach it.

But the third partition of Poland did not succeed in wiping out the name of Poland forever. From 1795 onwards – like Banquo's ghost – the problem of Poland was at the centre of Russian foreign policy in Europe, and Russia could take no step without pondering the possible repercussions on the delicate balance between the three partitioning powers.

Part IX

Domestic Problems

29

Agriculture and Industry

At Catherine's accession, European Russia was an overwhelmingly agrarian country, very unevenly developed according to the nature of the soil, population density, the climate, channels of communication and the extent of a given area's integration into the national market. Russian economic historians have grouped these areas according to different criteria. The classification adopted here is that of N.L. Rubinstein.[1] The old heartland of Muscovy formed the Central Industrial Region (comprising the gubernii of Moscow, Vladimir, Yaroslavl', Kostroma and Kaluga) ; to the northwest lay the North-Western Commercial and Cottage Industrial Region (the guberniya of Tver', Smolensk, Novgorod, Pskov and St Petersburg) ; to the north was the Northern Industrial Region, including Archangel, Olonets and Vologda gubernii, and to the south, the Central Black Earth Commercial Agricultural Region, comprising Tula, Ryazan, Orel, Kursk, Tambov, Voronezh and Penza, the last four of which were still in the process of being settled and economically integrated with the rest of the country.

To the south, southwest and east lay lands which were being progressively incorporated into the Russian economic system, with the advance of settlement, the development of communications and the extension of Russian colonization. The economy of the Middle Volga area (Nizhniy Novgorod, Kazan', Simbirsk, part of Saratov) maintained its cottage industry character but was now expanding into commercial agriculture, as were the gubernii bordering on the Urals : Perm', Orenburg and Vyatka, where the main concentration of heavy industry was to be found. Little Russia and Slobodska Ukraine belonged to the fertile Black Earth zone, but their economy was still not fully integrated into the Russian Empire.[2] The Baltic provinces, the territories acquired from Poland at the first partition in 1772 and the acquisitions in 1774 at the expense of the Porte on the Black Sea, maintained their own character.

The characteristics of the regions listed above resulted in the first place from a combination of soil and climate. European Russia suffered from a climate far more severe than its western neighbours. The White Sea, the Gulf of Finland, the northern coast of the Black Sea and the Sea of Azov all froze in winter. Most of the inland lakes were also liable to freeze. Snow blanketed the whole of Russia as far south as the Black Sea for anything from three to eight months. Stretching across the country from St Petersburg to the Urals and beyond was the so-called tayga zone of coniferous trees and swamps, invaluable as a source of timber and furs, but very unsuitable for agriculture. Southwards lay a belt of mixed forest (coniferous and deciduous) stretching from Poland south to Kiev, east to Moscow and Kazan', heavily wooded still, lacking in humus and of difficult cultivation. Much of Russia was still covered by dense forests, taking up half the surface in e.g. the guberniya of Kaluga, up to three quarters in parts of Nizhniy Novgorod and Vladimir. Further south was the granary of Russia, the wooded steppe and the grassland steppe with the rich black earth extending into Siberia and to the foothills of the Caucasus and the shores of the Black Sea, leaving aside the lower reaches of the Volga which meandered through increasingly desertic saltpans to the Caspian Sea.

Population too was most unevenly distributed. The major concentration occurred in the lands of old Muscovite settlement, ranging from 2,189,768 in 1762 in the Central Industrial Region and 1,039,243 in the North-Western Commercial/Industrial Region to 413,718 in the Northern Industrial Region (only 97,329 in Olonets and 77,708 in Archangel). The population of the rich black earth belt south of Moscow, lands settled in the seventeenth century with the advance of the Russian fortified lines, numbered 2,363,051, while the middle and lower Volga reached only 615,034, Vyatka and Perm' abutting on the Urals about the same, Orenburg only 236,040, and the whole of Siberia 392,742.[3]

The amount of land at the disposal of individuals (nobles, serfs, state peasants), and the division of the peasantry between serf and non-serf varied enormously from area to area. Overall figures for the size of private estates in different parts of the country are difficult to come by. Incomplete figures show that there were for instance in Orel 10 estates of over 1,000 souls, 62 between 500 and 1,000 and 2,129 under 500, but no details of actual size are known, though clearly, judging from other figures, the majority of the estates of under 500 souls were in fact below 100 souls. In contrast, in Voronezh (an area heavily settled by odnodvortsy) there were no estates over 1,000 souls, only 2 over 500, and 424 below 500, while in Penza well over half the nobles owned fewer than 20 serfs. In the uezd of Nizhniy Lomov, one Prince Golitsyn owned more serfs than the 194 small landowners who made up 71 per cent of the local *pomeshchiki*. But there were also landowners so poor, owning fewer than 10 serfs, who received no income at all.[4] In Petersburg guberniya too, there were only seven estates of over 1,000 serfs, 14 from 500 to 1,000, and 188 below 500. In general however it can be safely concluded that the areas of old settlement around Moscow, westwards to Smolensk, northwest to Pskov and Novgorod, and immediately to the south, comprised both the highest concentration of privately owned estates and the highest concentration of large estates. For that reason the peasants were mainly serfs, reaching 82·18 per cent of the peasantry in Kaluga, 75 per cent in

Ryazan', 79·41 per cent in Smolensk, compared with 58·2 per cent in Penza, 52·55 per cent in Simbirsk, 47·26 per cent in Tambov, 18·21 per cent in Kazan', 33·91 per cent in Perm', and falling in the north and northeast to 4·89 per cent in Olonets, 2·03 per cent in Vyatka, and 0·07 per cent in Archangel.

In terms of the national economy as a whole, the landowners provided the framework within which serf agriculture developed, while the state peasants enjoyed greater theoretical freedom. Yet there does not seem to have been a great difference between the type of agriculture practised in the two economies in a given area, and in its productivity as between the two types of peasantry. In both state peasant and serf villages communal administration of the land was the norm. The landowner's land was usually divided into strips intermingled with those of the peasants, which made it very difficult for an enterprising man to break away from the traditional peasant methods of cultivation and introduce new crops or machinery.

A further limitation on agricultural progress was that the serf and the peasant used their own implements and draught animals. Throughout most of Russia ploughing was carried out with the *sokha,* which turned over the soil to a depth of only four inches. The heavy wheeled *plug* could carve a furrow seven inches deep but needed three or four pairs of oxen at least to pull it, and was therefore likely to be used only by the wealthier peasants in the Black Earth zone.

The relative paucity of livestock throughout most of Russia led to a universal shortage of manure. The harsh climate rendered the keeping of livestock particularly hazardous. In the north, where the agricultural season lasted from May until September, cattle emerged starved from the long winter, and were exhausted by the autumn. Even where the growing season was longer, as in the Black Earth belt and the Ukraine, cattle still had to be indoors for as much as six months of the year.

In view of the small part played by manure in Russian agriculture, the peasants traditionally employed the three field system rotating between winter corn, spring corn and fallow in that order. Shortage of manure might lead to soil exhaustion under this sytem, which was supplemented by others. In some areas such as the northeast the old 'slash and burn' technique was still used, bringing into cultivation the vacant land. Elsewhere, particularly in the south and southeast, there existed large reserves of unused land which were brought into cultivation at intervals, and then allowed to revert to spontaneous vegetation for ten to twenty years, the so-called long-fallow reserve.[5] There was no shortage of land in Russia in absolute terms. Leaving aside the vacant lands, which might be rented by the wealthier peasants individually, or by the peasant commune as a whole, the amount generally available per peasant was usually more than he could cultivate at any given time. But in the northwest, the north and the Central Industrial Region meadow land was in short supply, forming only 6 per cent of the total surface, rising to 8 per cent in Moscow guberniya.

The extent of the peasant's allotment varied enormously in different parts of the country, and even within the same guberniya. In the Central Industrial and western provinces it averaged 3 to 3·5 desyatinas of arable land per male soul ; it was usually more when peasants were on barshchina than when they were on obrok ; it was also more – up to 6·6 desyatinas – where there was little craft industry. In Catherine's own estates in Tula, peasants had 13 desyatinas of arable land. In the southern steppes the odnodvortsy had been allotted large grants of land for cattle raising. In Voronezh guberniya, the last to be developed (a process which continued into the nineteenth century), grants often amounted to 8 desyatinas of arable and 18 desyatinas of meadowland per male soul. Broadly speaking, in the Central Industrial Region, the northwest and the Baltic, the western parts of Nizhniy Novgorod and the north, the peasant allotment came to 3–4 desyatinas of arable per male soul, whereas in the old Black Earth zone, the east and the south it rose to 5–6 desyatinas. The allotment of meadowland was much smaller, between 0·5 and 1·5 desyatinas except in the southwest and the Volga where it rose to 3–6 desyatinas, and as high as 11 in Orenburg. But not all the allotted land was cultivated. The average was more than the tyaglo, or working unit, could physically manage. The gap between the acreage of the allotment and the amount actually cultivated might well rise to 3 desyatinas per male soul, particularly where crafts were highly developed as an alternative source of income. There were also ample reserves of forest land which could be cleared, and of virgin soil in the steppes, and even in the old heartlands of Muscovy the soil was not exhausted. The reduction of the sown area which had occurred in central Russia in mid-eighteenth century reflects the attraction of the Moscow market as an importer of the products of cottage industry and a source of employment, rather than the exhaustion of the soil.

Any attempt to make valid general statements about the state of Russian agriculture in the eighteenth century is frustrated by the patchy nature of the evidence. Governors' reports and the 'Economic Observations' attached to the Land Survey provide a good deal of descriptive data on crops and prices. But the study of the peasant economy is based almost entirely on the archives of the large serf-owners who ran their estates in a businesslike manner. There is no corresponding information either about the small serf-owners, who formed the majority, or about the villages of the state peasants. The one-sided nature of the evidence may explain the prevailing view that most of the Russian peasantry were serfs, whereas, in contrast with most European countries, nearly half the Russian peasantry in the eighteenth century had no other landlord but the state.

The principal grains grown in Russia were winter rye and spring oats, and increasingly, barley. They were grown for consumption in the poor soils of the north and in the Central Industrial Region. In the Central Agricultural Region, rye and oats formed the main crop too, supplemented with buckwheat however, and spring wheat, while in the south winter wheat was also cultivated in an economy increasingly oriented towards the market. In the southwest (for which data are still lacking), i.e. in Slobodska Ukraine and Little Russia, corn was not produced for export from the guberniya ; if anything it was imported for use by the nobility and the Cossacks in distilling.[6] In the Middle Volga, and to the east, corn was grown for export by river to St Petersburg and Moscow via Kazan'. But the whole area of Simbirsk and Saratov was still underdeveloped. Further east, the gubernii of Ufa and Orenburg grew corn for the factories in the Urals, including wheat, oats, barley, millet and buckwheat. Market gardening was frequent in the vicinity of towns. Landowners usually supplied themselves, but there was a vast market for fruit and vegetables.

In spite of the abundance of land, the combination of the brief farming season, the severe climate, the primitive agricultural implements and the shortage of manure led to the prevalence of low yields except in particularly favoured areas. In the 1760s the yields averaged not more than 1:3 or 1:4 in the Central Industrial Region and the northwest, sinking as far as 1:2 in Tver', rising to 1:6 in the intensively cultivated Baltic province of Livonia. In the Commercial Agricultural zone, yields rose to 1:6, 1:8 or even 1:9, in Kazan' as high as 1:10, and in Little Russia and Slobodska Ukraine as well. Within these averages there were considerable local fluctuations, and figures often slumped disastrously with the frequent harvest failures. These, in the eighteenth century, tended to be local. Even the frequently mentioned harvest failure of 1766 was not noticeable in many parts of Central Russia (Moscow, Novgorod, Smolensk) and only really perceptible here and there in the Central Black Earth Region and in Kazan', Nizhniy Novgorod and Orenburg.[7]

Productivity depended to a great extent on the physical and numerical strength of a *dvor,* or household. The more young men, the more land, the more cattle and hence the more manure. A strong household could achieve yields of 1:4 or 1:5 in the Central Industrial Region and 1:7 in the Black Earth zone. Production for the market could in these circumstances be envisaged. According to Rubinstein's calculations, an allotment of three desyatinas per male soul produced about 10 chetverts of rye (one chetvert = 5·77 bushels) and fifteen chetverts of oats. He assessed at 6 chetverts the tyaglo's requirements of corn for their own and their cattle's consumption, and at 5·5 chetverts the amount of seed corn required, giving a surplus of about 12 chetverts or, in a household of 3 male souls, more than 30 chetverts. In the Black Earth Region the surplus was considerably larger : the gross harvest could amount to 15 chetverts of rye and 25 chetverts of oats per male soul, and even assuming a bigger fodder consumption, the surplus would amount to 25 chetverts per male soul, or some 75 chetverts per household of three. Where more manpower was available the surplus could reach 100–150 chetverts per household. A poorly equipped household might however achieve yields of only 1:3, giving only just enough for consumption and seed corn, and leaving the peasant unprotected against a bad harvest. The widening difference in yields led to a growing economic differentiation in the villages, whether of serfs or state peasants, between rich, medium and poor peasants. The latter often rented their land to a rich peasant and either worked for him as a labourer, or sought employment in industry.

What, precisely, do these categories of rich, middling and poor peasants signify, and again how large was each category ? In the Golitsyn estate of Golun, in Orel guberniya, in 1784 there were 84 rich households (40 per cent of the total) producing 83·5 per cent of the rye, 66·6 per cent of the oats, 69 per cent of the buckwheat, and 78·6 per cent of the peas. The surplus grain per household, available for the market, was 50 chetverts – in some cases it rose to over 100, usually where the household owned a good number of draught animals (over 20 horses). The households averaged 27·6 desyatinas of their own land and 10·75 desyatinas of the landlord's land, and plenty of land for rent was available. At the other extreme, 20 per cent of the households produced less than 2 per cent of the total rye harvest, and half of these grew no corn at all. The latter had evidently made over the use of their land to their richer brethren, and worked as labourers. In the Penza estate of the Kurakin family, an area which had only just been opened up, poor peasant households numbered 64 per cent, 36 per cent were well off, but only half of them produced a surplus of corn for sale. Elsewhere in Penza, in the 1770s, on the Polyansky estate, 37 households (15 per cent) had on average 14 desyatinas of arable per household, and produced 44 per cent of the rye, owned 44 per cent of the horses, 37 per cent of the cows. As regards state peasants, an analysis of Kursk guberniya carried out by the land surveyors listed approximately 100,000 heads of household of whom approximately 20 per cent were rich (10 horses, 10 cows, 10 sheep and 50 pigs per household) and produced 600,000 chetverts of corn for sale ; 60 per cent were middling (5 horses, cows, and sheep, 25 pigs) and produced 500,000 chetverts of corn for sale while 25 per cent were poor (2 horses, 1 cow, 5 sheep, 10 pigs) and produced only 180,000 chetverts.[8] In the Volga area, between Simbirsk and Saratov, and westwards in Penza the average seemed to be 27·83 per cent of households owning one horse, 40·16 per cent owning 2 horses, and 19·16 per cent owning 3; 10·52 per cent of all households owned 4, 5 or 6 horses. In Penza in 1775, on a Saltykov estate, 44 households owned 368 horses, 208 cows, 1,112 sheep. The richest household owned per couple 30 horses, 40 cows and 80 sheep.[9]

Corn was sold either to the importing cities and gubernii of the north or to the liquor distilleries ; again prices varied enormously throughout Russia in accordance with demand, transport facilities and the quality of the harvest. Prices rose steadily during the eighteenth century : rye in the Central Industrial Region fetched 0·6–1 r. a chetvert in the early 1760s rising to 1·2 to 2 in the late 1760s, 2·6 to 5 in the mid-1780s. In Moscow guberniya prices started higher and rose faster as well as in St Petersburg where the cost of living was particularly high. Rye fetched between 2 and 3 r. a chetvert in the early sixties, 3 r. in the 1770s and 5–6 in the 1780s. In contrast in the Central Agricultural Region and on the Volga, it started at 0·6 and 0·4 respectively and rose to 1 to 2 and to 3 to 4 in the mid-1780s. Oats fetched less, falling to $0\cdot2$–$0\cdot3$ in the Mid-Volga, and rising to $1\cdot8$–$2\cdot5$ in the 1780s. Wheat always fetched a higher price – and was indeed normally cultivated for sale ; in the Central Industrial Region prices were $1\cdot5$ to 2 in the early 1760s, 3–4 in the late sixties and rose to 5 to 7 in the mid-1780s though here again, in the Central Agricultural Region and the Mid-Volga, prices were much lower, $1\cdot5$–$2\cdot5$ in the late 1760s rising to $2\cdot5$ to 5 in the 1780s.[10] There were substantial fluctuations however within each decade ; the highest prices in the 1760s were in the period 1764–5, and not in the allegedly deficitary year of 1766–7. These fluctuations were more noticeable in the consuming areas than in the producing areas, and were least noticeable in the lands which were not yet fully incorporated into the Russian market such as the southern parts of Voronezh, Khar'kov or Saratov.

Conditions in most of Central European Russia were unfavourable for cattle raising. Nevertheless, in the far north, where the land was unsuitable for cultivation, livestock farming with good European stock, imported with Catherine's encouragement, was rendered possible by the specially cultivated grasses (timothy grass, etc.). To the south and east however cattle raising went beyond the needs of the peasant household and became a commercial occupation. In southern Voronezh, odnodvortsy households had as many as 200 head of horned cattle and up to 1,500 sheep. On the estate of Turbay (Mirgorod), belonging to the Basilevskys, serf households averaged 6–7 head of horned cattle, though a few wealthy households had as many as 70 head of cattle, 30 horses, 250 sheep. (A horse was valued on average 4–7 r. in the countryside but in Moscow it could fetch 20–70 r.). Oxen were valued at 3–4 r. in Russia and rose to 10–15 r. in Kiev, probably because they were more heavily used on the land. Sheep were valued at 50–70 kopeks, rams at 30–50, pigs at 60–80k. to 1–2r. Increasing demand and better security led to intensive development of cattle raising in the Black Earth steppe of the gubernii of Kursk and Voronezh. In Kursk, it formed 20 per cent of the revenue from agricultural production, including hides and wool. Great herds of cattle would be driven to urban markets from Tambov and Slobodska Ukraine and the Volga where Saratov was a major market, and where peasants owned as many as 10–12 horses and 15–20 cows per household. In contrast, barnyard fowl were kept on a relatively small scale, averaging 5–10 hens per household, up to 15, 20 or even 50 in a rich serf's household with a few ducks or geese. In the 1780s chickens fetched 5–15 kopeks, turkeys from 20–40 kopeks in local markets.

Though agriculture was the principal activity of the Russian peasant this was supplemented, indeed overtaken at times, by the cultivation of industrial crops such as flax and hemp, used both for the production of yarn and cloth for domestic use and for sale, and for oils. These two crops were grown throughout northwest and north Russia, in the Black Earth zone of the centre and in the Mid-Volga, and spinning and weaving frequently formed part of dues exacted from the women and children of a serf village, particularly in areas like Pskov, where flax and hemp were cultivated almost to the exclusion of grain, and yarn was sold in fairs or to urban manufactories. The annual production of linen of one woman was estimated at 20–30 arshins, or 15–23 yards.[11] Landowners occasionally took part in the trade in yarn and linen, exacting high dues in kind from their serfs, and selling the produce in the capital, but in serf estates the production and trade seems to have been left very much in the hands of the wealthier serfs, who also organized the processing of hemp and linseed oils. Less widespread was the cultivation of hops beyond the Volga and in the Mid-Volga areas, and of tobacco in the Ukraine.

Other branches of peasant activity, on their own initiative, or within the framework of the landlord's economy, were rope-making, bee-keeping, and the exploitation of the huge reserves of forest in Russia. In north and northeast Russia, where landlords were few and forests vast, peasants provided charcoal, pitch, resins, and timber. Barge and boat building was also a common occupation. Timber was cut and seasoned for home consumption in construction and for export for ship building. Further south, forests were mainly in the hands of landowners who drew large revenues from their exploitation, employing hired labour where their own was not sufficient, in saw mills, ship building, etc.

Fisheries were a major source of revenue in Russia. State-owned ponds and rivers were leased to merchants or state peasants who employed hired labour ; privately owned lakes, rivers and ponds seemed to have been exploited for home consumption. Fish in some areas was often so cheap as to be unsaleable. In one respect the Russian peasantry seems to have been much better off than their Western contemporaries. There were no nationally devised and nationally imposed game laws. Landowners laid down the rules of the chase on their estates according to their fancy. It was usual to allow peasants free hunting for deer, boar, wild duck, woodcock, quail, partridge, etc. Game would be frozen and despatched to the cities ; waterfowl were so abundant that they formed part of the normal diet of the peasants, and were cheap even in the cities. Indeed food was cheaper than anywhere in Europe in the interior.[12]

The processing of agricultural products such as timber, flax and hemp, wax and tallow, and the transport and marketing of grain, cloth, etc., fall within the normal framework of an agricultural economy. But the Russian peasant, particularly in the less fertile areas, played an increasing role in industrial development at the level of the small-scale manufactory. It was peasant industry which satisfied the demand for everyday consumer goods of a simple, even coarse, quality.

Throughout Russia peasants produced ironware (nails, locks, buckles, etc.), cutlery (the village of Pavlov in Nizhniy Novgorod counted 3,000 peasants all engaged in the craft), earthenware, leather goods, wheels, bevels, carts. But in addition to these simple wares, peasant cottage industry played a big part in the production of hats, shoes, furniture, silk and cotton cloths, kerchiefs, ribbons, taffeta, etc. There were even specialists in the production of gold and silver leaf. Others tanned leather or dressed furs, manufactured printed linen or nankeen.

The growing part played by the peasantry in these fields met with the approval of the nobility, who benefited from the economic enterprise of their serfs, but created a real and acute rivalry with the merchant class since peasants working in their villages paid no town taxes. Thus the battle was engaged in the Legislative Commission of 1767 between the nobility, anxious to exploit the skill and commercial acumen of their serfs and to legalize their trade in urban centres, and the kupechestvo anxious to monopolize trade within the towns for their estate.[13] But they were also rivals in the more strictly manufacturing industrial sphere, since here the nobility enjoyed after 1762 the monopoly of the purchase of serf labour, and could often produce the raw materials on their own estates. If the rivalry was not acute, it was because the nobles and the kuptsy were active in different spheres. The former concentrated on sail cloth, linen, fine cloths, silks and luxury goods like glass, porcelain, mirrors, writing paper, etc. Moreover in general, noble manufacturing was organized on a larger scale, and nobles continued to be prominent in those branches of industry which dated back to Peter I, while kuptsy, using hired labour, predominated in the small-scale production of consumer goods and in many enterprises dating from 1762.

There was one field however in which the nobility had acquired an almost complete monopoly, namely distilling. 'Liquor', used here to describe both small beer or *vino*, produced from rye and occasionally oats, with the addition of malt, yeast and hops, and 'vodka' or spirits, which was distilled from *vino,* was an important source of national revenue. Until the mid-1750s, production had far exceeded consumption in the state-owned or -licensed *kabaki,* and much revenue was lost as a result of direct sale by producers to consumers. The monopoly of private distilling was granted to the nobles in 1754, and merchant production was phased out. The combined production of noble and state distilleries rose steadily to fill the gap left by merchant production. In 1765 nobles delivered 1,859,857 vedra (one vedro, or pail = 3·23 gallons) and the quantity rose to 2,103,325 vedra in 1775. State production served to prevent the noble distillers from arbitrarily raising the prices.[14]

The multiplicity of producers and of outlets for sale laid the whole distilling industry particularly open to bribery, tax evasion, bootlegging, etc. In accordance with her usual practice therefore, Catherine set up a commission on 23 March 1764 to study the organization of the liquor monopoly in order to increase its profitability to the state.[15] It recommended that the sale of liquor to the public should be farmed out, a policy which was put into effect in 1767.[16] Tax farmers were invited to tender for four-year contracts to sell liquor bought from government stores and collect the tax. To raise the status of the tax farmers, they were to be allowed to wear swords – if they were kuptsy – and were granted certain tax privileges as 'agents of the crown'. The status of the *kabaki,* associated with drunkenness, was also to be improved by changing their names to 'drinking houses' (*piteynyye doma*). Nobles, raznochintsy and wealthy peasants – even serfs – could act as tax farmers.

The system devised in 1765 survived in practice from 1767 when it was put into effect until 1775, when the responsibility for organizing the tax farming was laid on the local treasury boards (*kazennyye palaty*). A larger number of contracts for smaller deliveries became the norm and was enshrined in new regulations issued on 24 August 1781, which laid down that given equality of tender, preference should be given to small-scale producers and to nobles in the countryside, state peasants in state peasant districts, and townspeople in the towns. A new Code of Distilling was issued on 17 September 1791.[17]

The purchase price of liquor rose steadily throughout Catherine's reign from 85 k. a vedro in 1768 to 1 r. 10 in the 1790s (with considerable local fluctuations). Tax farmers sold to the public at 2 r. 54 a vedro in 1763 ; the price rose to 3 r. a vedro in 1768 on the outbreak of the first Turkish war, and to 4 r. in 1794. Per capita consumption per male soul is estimated to have been half a vedro or approximately 1·75 gallons per annum, at a cost of about 2 rubles.[18] If the state benefited, so did the producer. By 1795–6, nobles were producing 3,348,278 vedra of liquor (excluding Little Russia). Even where noble landowners bought grain for distilling, the profit came to roughly 1 r. 25 per vedro. Many of the great magnates added to their already substantial incomes by large-scale distilling. Prince A.B. Kurakin's share was 111,785 vedra in the 1790s, K.G. Razumovsky's was 99,200 ; on a more modest scale, the poet G.R. Derzhavin undertook in 1796 to produce 10,616 vedra ; he used the grain from his own estate of 400 souls, and bought grain for 7,000 r.[19] Tax farmers too made large fortunes and some were eventually ennobled. But illicit sale of liquor continued to be a drain on the revenue, and evasion only increased after control was decentralized in 1775 ; a large number of people could be given smaller bribes.[20]

Catherine had come to the throne with a clear sense of the need to formulate an economic policy for Russia. Her views are marked by that common-sense eclecticism typical of her general attitude to government. She believed in the primacy of agriculture as necessary to sustain life ;[21] she favoured small-scale cottage industry over large-scale manufacturing, since it kept the peasants on the land, but employed them during the long winter months. Moreover it required no state subsidies in labour or money ; wages were lower, so that goods cost less to produce ; less capital was invested so that the small-scale producer was less vulnerable to fluctuations in demand. Large factories, in Catherine's view, needed more capital and more professional staff, but suffered just as much from theft and incompetence while the work force was regimented and bullied, treated roughly and cruelly by foremen.[22]

In addition Catherine believed that 'unfree hands do not work so well as free, and the purchase of villages by manufacturers leads to the destruction of agriculture'.[23] The preference for hired labour as distinct from serf labour in industry is most clearly expressed in the instruction of the College of Manufacturers to its deputy to the Legislative Commission. The instruction pointed out that coercion had been necessary to create industry in Peter's time, but the inconvenience of coercion now outweighed its advantages. The purchase of estates by industrialists had moreover enabled them to enjoy the privileges of nobility, even to enter the military branch, thus contributing to an irremediable and undesirable confusion among the estates. The industrial enterprises had become serf-centred, and crushed the national industry ; industrial peasants had been formed into a new type of private serf, instead of increasing the number of craftsmen and prosperous townspeople. Industry, stated the instruction, should be left to itself, and everyone should be allowed to work as much as he wanted to.[24] Finally, Catherine was totally opposed to all forms of monopoly, whether in production or sale. She believed in the reduction of state interference in the production and distribution of goods, particularly consumer goods, in the encouragement of competition, and the establishment of a minimum of state supervision and regulation in the interests of the national economy on the one hand and the national revenue on the other.

Catherine was by no means alone in her views. She inherited economic advisers and economic policies from the brief reign of Peter III (such as D. V. Volkov, G.N. Teplov). On 23 March 1762 Peter had issued an ukaz condemning monopolies. It was followed by the ukaz prohibiting the purchase of serf villages by non-noble industrialists.[25] Catherine, in an ukaz of 31 July 1762, developed this policy further, and on 8 August the prohibition of the purchase of serf villages by industrialists was repeated.[26] The freedom granted to all and sundry to venture into manufacturing on any scale led to the setting up of an increasing number of enterprises. The large number of peasants who habitually left their villages to work in the service or manufacturing industries provided a pool of people with some training in a number of different industrial processes which they were able to take back to their villages when they started up on their own, employing their own family. There were also now more and better trained factory workers in the factories. The increase in the urban population and in peasant mobility made it easier for the non-noble entrepreneur to find hired labour which did not involve him in the capital expenditure of buying serf villages.[27]

An exception to the practice of freeing industrial activity was the taxation of the production of the metallurgical industries. In 1763, blast furnaces had to pay 100 rubles tax, copper foundries 5 rubles, and a charge of 4 k. per pud was levied. Taxation was doubled in 1769 in order to pay for the war.[28] But Catherine took the first possible opportunity not only to remove these special war taxes, but to proclaim freedom of industrial enterprise. The manifesto of 17 March 1775 on the occasion of the ratification of the peace with the Porte proclaimed the freedom for all, in whatever estate, to set up a workbench or industrial enterprise in any branch of production anywhere.[29] In 1779, the obligation to sell part of their production to the state was removed from the iron foundries. Five years later the last remaining state shackles on the free use of their own private property was removed from the nobility. In an ukaz of 28 June 1782, the nobles were granted the free exploitation of the subsoil and the growth on their lands, thus finally abrogating the prospecting rights which Peter I had originally imposed with a view to increasing mining, and opening the way for unshackled control by the nobles of their industrial enterprises.[30]

The impact of the liberal economic policy of the government showed itself in the increase in *otkhodnichestvo,* or leaving the village. The guberniya of Yaroslavl' provides an indication of the rhythm of growth : in 1778, 53,656 passports were issued to peasants for winter work away from the village ; in 1788 it had risen to 70,144, and in 1798 to 73,663 out of a total male population of 385,000 (in the fifth census), or some 20 per cent. The number of enterprises rose from some 600–700 in 1762 to over 2,000 in 1796.[31] As early as the 1760s 61.9 per cent of the peasantry in the vast, pre-1775 guberniya of Moscow were engaged in the weaving and spinning of linen and hemp in addition to their work on the land, and in the 1770s, 40 per cent of them were working for the market. As elsewhere, the cotton printing industry developed rapidly in the 1760s, after its foundation by the firm of Chamberlain and Cousins in 1755. As in other countries, child labour was used extensively. It was in cotton printing that the serf millionaires of P.B. Sheremet'yev's estate at Ivanovo built up their huge fortunes. The pioneer was a serf who set up shop in 1762 ; by 1774 there were already 14 manufactories engaged in weaving cloth and cotton printing, with 614 looms or presses. By the end of the century there were 49 (rising to 125 in 1825). The serf entrepreneurs employed mostly hired serf labour but in time they became serf-owners themselves, though their purchases were of course carried out in the name of their owner.[32]

Whereas Russian manufacturing industry was concentrated in the Central Industrial Region, and in or near the two capitals, the bulk of Russian heavy industry was located in or near the Urals, though there was a significant concentration of iron foundries, forges and blast furnaces around Moscow, in Tula, Pereyaslavl' Zalesskiy and Kaluga. In 1754 it was forbidden to set up new metallurgical works for a radius of 200 versts around Moscow, to ward off the depletion of the forests. This led to the decline of Tula, which did not recover when the prohibition was repealed in the early 1760s.

Transfigured by Peter I's daemonic energy, the Russian mining and metallurgical industry survived his death, and the transition from a war-time to a peace-time economy. There was no actual decline in the net output of iron and copper from private and state enterprises. A feature of the post-Petrine period was the transfer of many enterprises from state to private ownership, accompanied by an increase in government supervision and regulation. It was assumed at the time that private enterprise was more efficient ; thus, if state enterprises were not profitable, they would be better in private hands. The state would benefit by limiting itself to a supervisory role. But industries made over to private owners were bound to fulfil government contracts at fixed prices.

The transfer from state to private hands was speeded up in Elizabeth's reign, when many magnates saw the chance of making large fortunes for themselves, and some 32 enterprises were transferred to the nobility either by gift or by purchase. A number of foundries was established by ennobled business dynasties like the Stroganovs and the Demidovs.[33] These great dynasties continued to dominate the metal foundries of the Urals to the end of the century, though owing to the Russian system of inheritance, they were now divided into family groups : six Demidov families owned twenty-five foundries ; four Stroganovs owned eight.[34] But few of the nobles who merely bought themselves in to the industry (the Shuvalovs, the Chernyshevs, the Vorontsovs) were able to run them efficiently or profitably and they were eventually bought out by the state, at a loss.[35] Notable among new entrepreneurs was Savva Yakovlev, who constructed seven blast furnaces and forges on the Siberian side of the Urals between 1769 and 1779.[36] In all, between 1763 and 1796, 31 new enterprises were founded, some of which did not last. Production continued to increase rising from 60,050 tons of pig iron in 1760 to 83,705 in 1770, 110,132 in 1780 and 162,427 in 1800, outstripping production in England. Russian iron was in great demand during the two Turkish wars, but also in England during the American War of Independence.[37]

Nevertheless the metallurgical industries were experiencing an economic crisis in the 1760s and 1770s (leaving aside the damage caused by the Pugachev revolt), which can be attributed to the increasing relative cost of transport and services and the lack of technical modernization. Transport was more frequently carried out by hired labour at a higher wage, and not by 'assigned' peasants, the number of which remained static, since no more were assigned after the disturbances of 1762–4.[38] Moreover in 1769, when the obrok paid by state peasants was raised to 2 r.,[39] to pay for the Turkish war, the government raised the wages of the assigned peasants – unchanged since 1724 – to 12 k. and 6 k. per diem respectively for a peasant with and without a horse in summer, 8 k. and 5 k. in winter, plus a travel allowance of 3 k. per day.[40] The increased wage, which probably worked out at about 10–15 per cent for a peasant already faced with an increase of 100 per cent in the obrok payable to the state, brought him no relief at a time of rising food prices, while it weighed on industries already burdened by the taxes on production decreed in the early 1760s.[41] The increased pressure on the assigned peasants accounts for the speed with which they rallied to Pugachev in 1773–5.[42]

The industrial establishments of the Urals suffered widespread damage during the revolt, mainly in Bashkiria, following a line running from Zlatoust, south of Yekaterinburg, Kungur and Perm' along the Kama River. North of this line, the Russian population reacted against the Bashkirs and defended themselves and their enterprises. Some 89 enterprises suffered in varying degrees ; 25 were completely destroyed, and 35 ceased work and were looted. The total loss in human life, killed and disappeared, in the industries was estimated as 2,716. The total material losses amounted to 2,716,506 r. (which sum included over one million rubles for the destruction of peasant households). Lost production was estimated at 2,819,687 r.[43]

Already in spring 1774 the government took steps to get the industry going again and to discover the extent of the damage. Where the rebels had confined themselves to looting and firing the establishment, reconstruction could be fairly rapid. But in Bashkiria, the base of the copper industry, destruction was more thorough-going. Nevertheless, by 1776, some 30 enterprises had been rebuilt, and leaving aside a few in Bashkiria which were abandoned, 'all traces of the destruction caused by the revolt' had disappeared by 1780.[44] Unfortunately reconstruction was not accompanied by any technical innovation, either in the private or the state-owned sector.

The behaviour of the assigned peasants, their almost instantaneous flight back to their villages, or to Pugachev, led the government to take some steps to improve their condition. A manifesto of 21 May 1779[45] defined precisely the kind of work assigned state peasants could be asked to undertake in state enterprises (charcoal burning and transportation, wood cutting, transport of ore, building and repair work, etc.). Wages were also considerably increased, to 10 kopeks for a peasant on foot and 20 kopeks for a peasant with a horse per day in summer, 8 kopeks and 12 kopeks respectively in winter. A further ukaz in 1780 doubled the travel allowance per diem for a horse to 1 and 2 kopeks respectively for winter and summer. But this considerable increase in the wages and allowances was again reduced in value in 1783 when the obrok paid by state peasants was increased to 3 r., making a total charge of 3 r. 70 p.a.[46] In spite of the increased obrok, the assigned peasant was still better off than he had been in the 1760s – provided the increase was actually paid. More than half the assigned peasants (170,000 out of 230,000) did in fact work for state-owned factories, where payment could be ensured. It was more difficult to supervise the proper wages in privately owned industry, and even more difficult to ensure implementation of decrees laying down the wages of the 'possessional serfs' or skilled labour. Wages had risen since the 1760s by perhaps 20 per cent by the end of the century, but so had prices as a result of the combination of a depreciating paper currency, particularly in the 1790s, and the agricultural boom. The net result may well have been that the assigned peasants, all things considered, were relatively better off, and the possessional serfs relatively worse off at the end of the century.

Even if there were no new enterprises, and no technical innovations, Russian production of pig iron continued to expand in the last twenty years of the eighteenth century, benefiting from a rise in the price of iron consequent on rising foreign demand, and a growing market in the metalworking industries of the Central Industrial Region. In the 1780s and 1790s the industry went through a period of exceptional prosperity, in which the part played by state-owned enterprises declined steadily. In 1782, state production totalled 182,363 puds, private enterprise produced 2,876,049 puds.[47] But the failure to modernize led to the gradual overtaking of the Russian metallurgical industries by foreign competitors at the beginning of the nineteenth century.

The eighteenth century also saw some development of mining and metallurgy in Western Siberia, in the area between the Irtysh and the Yenisey, in the Kolyvan copper mines in the Altay Mountains to the south, which were the private property of the imperial family – an area larger than the whole of England. The bulk of the labour force consisted of assigned peasants from Siberia (55,306 assigned, 6,797 non-assigned).[48] But members of other social groups, exiled for settlement, could also be assigned to the mines and foundries to work off their poll-tax. Almost double the amount could be earned by peasants who hired themselves for the extremely important and relatively lucrative task of transporting the ore from the mines to the centres where smelting took place. At 6 kopeks per pud, a peasant owning 10 horses making 10 journeys could make up to 120 rubles. As a result peasants tended to invest in large numbers of horses, the wealthier owning between 50 and 100.

The whole territory and the mining complex was at first administered by the 'Cabinet', a body which dealt with the private income of the ruler, no doubt because silver and gold were mined there. The Zmeynogorskiy mines – the Potosi of Russia – produced the bulk of the gold and silver mined in Siberia, the metallic yield of this ore being particularly high in the 1770s and declining gradually in the period 1780–90, from a maximum of 1,338,753 puds of ore and 1,311 puds of silver to 1,131,466 puds of ore and 952 puds of silver in 1793. On 1 May 1779 Catherine ordered that the statute of local administration of 1775[49] should be extended to Western Siberia, and the local Mines Office was absorbed into the new treasury boards, while its judicial functions were passed to the new law courts. In 1783 Kolyvan became a guberniya divided into uezdy with a network of criminal and civil courts which could not be fully staffed. These same authorities were charged with running schools for the children of skilled workers – in 1787 there were six, with up to 800 pupils.

Further to the east were the mines of Nerchinsk. The silver mines were producing some 619 puds p.a. of silver in 1774, and gold mining started up in 1778. But the name has a sinister ring since in the eighteenth century it was to Nerchinsk – situated beyond Lake Baikal on the Mongolian border – that the worst criminals sentenced to settlement or to hard labour were sent.

Trade and Finance

Writing in 1779, Catherine painted a gloomy picture of the financial and economic situation of Russia at her accession. The bulk of the army, then in Prussia, was unpaid ; orders for the payment of 17 million rubles had been disregarded ; almost all branches of trade had been granted away as monopolies ; customs duties had been farmed out for a mere 2 million rubles, and the sixteen million rubles circulating in the country were of 12 different weights.[1] Her poor opinion was shared by her principal advisers in economic affairs, most of whom had already been influential under Peter III.[2] In an ukaz of 23 March 1762 Peter had proclaimed that 'all trade must be free', attacked monopolies, and stressed the need to develop exports, to keep Russian currency at home and to trade in Russian ships.[3] These were all policies which Catherine would pursue during her reign, and she began at once with the ukaz of 31 July 1762 which abolished almost all Crown monopolies, opened up the Chinese caravan trade to all merchants and freed trade in a number of furs. Privately owned monopolies were not to be renewed when they expired, and some were curtailed at once.[4] The ukaz bears the marks of haste, but it was the starting-point for a progressive liberalization of the Russian economy, both in production and in foreign and domestic trade. It was followed soon after by the removal of the customs from the hands of the existing tax farmer who had accumulated considerable arrears. After a devastating indictment of the system of tax farming by G.N. Teplov, it was finally decided in 1762 to keep the collection of the customs duties in government hands and Count E. Münich (son of the field-marshal) was appointed supervisor of all the customs of the empire.[5]

Catherine's own views on commercial policy were expressed in her great Instruction in 1767. She accepted regulation in the interests of trade and her model was England. 'The Liberty of Trading does not consist in a Permission to Merchants of doing whatever they please ; this would be rather the *Slavery* of Commerce : what *cramps* the Trader does not *cramp* the Trade' (article 321) ; and 'England has no tariff or fixed Book of Rates with other Nations . . . strongly jealous of the Trade which is carried on in Her Country, she rarely engages herself in Treaties with other States and depends on no Laws but her own' (article 324). It was thus the state's duty to ease the path of trade and enterprise while keeping the national revenue constantly in mind. Catherine attached so much importance to trade that she soon set up a special Commerce Commission, responsible directly to her. The terms of reference of this body, set up in December 1763, and drafted by Teplov, were : to study the present state of Russian domestic and foreign trade and to devise new legislation for its development, for the improvement of credit, the increase in the circulation of money and the better exploitation of the Crown regalia.

The Commerce Commission was purely advisory and had no executive functions and, as was so often the case in Catherine's administrative improvisations, its relationship with other policy-making or executive bodies was ill-defined. It had no monopoly of the formulation of commercial policy, which could be discussed in the Council or in the College of Commerce. Its personnel included over the years such experts as G.N. Teplov, Prince M.M. Shcherbatov, and above all A.R. Vorontsov, who was appointed in 1774 and who, as president of the College of Commerce, provided a useful overall view. Russian merchants were co-opted from time to time. The members of the commission indulged in extremely searching and exhaustive analyses of the deficiencies of Russian economic life : legal uncertainty, poor communications, the absence of banking facilities, bad and corrupt administration.[6]

One of its most important tasks throughout its existence was the formulation of Russian tariff policy and the drafting of the tariffs. The Senate had been engaged in revising the tariff of 1757 for some time, and its draft was forwarded to the commission, which proceeded to a drastic overhaul, based on a number of economic principles which it laid down. Goods were divided into categories, and the objects which duties were intended to achieve were stated in each case. The new tariff was finally promulgated on 1 September 1766, to take effect from 1 March 1767 in all the customs posts of the empire except Orenburg (for the Asiatic trade) and Siberia, Russian Finland, and the Baltic provinces which were governed by laws laid down by Queen Christina of Sweden in the seventeenth century and were therefore not included in the Russian customs area.

The new tariff was moderately protectionist in character. It facilitated the import of raw materials or semi-finished goods for processing by Russian industry ; it allowed the import of goods not produced in Russia ; goods which might be produced in Russia were charged a duty of 15 per cent, goods which actually were produced paid 30 per cent. The import of goods in which Russia was self-sufficient was forbidden or taxed at 200 per cent, as were luxuries such as cloths of gold and silver. 'Necessary' luxuries (such as silk) bore a duty of 20 per cent, but furniture and *objets d'art* and 'luxury' food and drink paid 100 per cent duty. Anticipating modern dietary theories Catherine allowed the free import of lemons and chestnuts, while sweets and preserves paid duty. Duty was to be paid in Russian currency, or in silver thalers (*yefimki,* from Joachimsthal silver) by

Russian merchants ; foreign merchants paid in silver thalers valued at 1 r. 25 k. Exports were treated in an equally flexible way. The export of corn, when the price in Russia was reasonable, was permitted free of duty ; export of salt meat, fish and caviar suffered a moderate tax, and low duties were imposed on high quality goods in order to enable Russian produce to compete in foreign markets. The tariff was to be revised every five years.[7] It is noteworthy that the tariff prohibited, or placed a heavy duty on the import of those luxury goods of particular significance to the nobility. It can therefore scarcely by said – as has been argued by some Soviet economic historians – that it was devised in the interests of the nobles. Champagne for instance paid duty at the rate of 144 per cent.[8]

On paper Russia enjoyed a balance of exports over imports which averaged 2 million r.p.a. in the period 1761–70, rising to 4·2 million r.p.a. in 1771–5 and 5·2 million in 1778–80. These figures unfortunately take no account of the vast extent of smuggling into Russia over the long unguarded land frontier with Poland,[9] which may well have been so great as to turn an export surplus into a deficit.

The tariff of 1766 was not revised until 1781, in the context of the expansion of Russian trade during the war of American independence. Then the same approach was adopted, under the inspiration of A.R. Vorontsov, as in 1766, and the new tariff was approved by Catherine on 27 September 1782.

Unlike its predecessor of 1766, the new tariff was extended to the Baltic provinces, the administration of which was integrated into the Russian Empire in the next year, though Riga was still to pay duties in silver thalers (the ruble was not legal tender in Livonia and did not become so until 1793).[10] The produce of Little Russia, Belorussia and neighbouring Poland was to be admitted into Russia proper free of duty. The specially reduced duties introduced for the Black Sea ports in 1775[11] were maintained in the tariff of 1782, and special regulations governed the Asiatic trade through Orenburg and Troitsk. Most imports paid 10–12 per cent duty, but many goods were prohibited.

The tariff of 1782 was even more liberal than that of 1766. The duty on imported raw materials was reduced to a bare 2 per cent, and the duty on semi-finished goods remained low. Luxury goods and goods consumed by the 'middling' classes (as distinct from the rich nobles) were to be taxed at 8–10 per cent, while expensive imported luxury goods which were already produced in Russia paid up to 20 per cent (furniture, high quality textiles, etc.). Commodities which, though not necessities were nevertheless in common use such as coffee, sugar and chocolate were moderately taxed. Books, pictures, musical instruments, all goods serving the arts and the sciences, and all medical instruments and medicines were duty free. The export of a number of previously forbidden items was now allowed e.g. weapons and saltpetre ; the export of salt, spirits, dyed furs, gold and silver brocade, Russian coin and objects depicting the saints was forbidden. At least half of all duties had to be paid in silver thalers, the rest in Russian rubles. Smuggling was still a problem. The reduced duties on imports did not serve to restrict its dimensions, and a new system of frontier posts at 10 versts distance was therefore set up under the overall supervision of the local treasury chambers and extended in the 1780s and 1790s to all the European frontiers of the empire. Judging by a survey made in 1795, smuggling continued unabated, with the active assistance of the frontier guards appointed to prevent it.[12]

Long tradition, enshrined in the trade treaties of 1734 and 1766, had given British merchants a dominant position in Russian foreign trade. In 1756 Britain participated in the trade of St Petersburg to the tune of 70 per cent of its exports and 20 per cent of its imports. The dominance of British trade may have been even greater, since some outwardly Russian firms were in reality British-owned. In 1773, 188 Russian firms exported through St Petersburg and 272 foreign firms, including 65 British firms.[13]

British firms had their own manufactories in Moscow, Vologda, Tula, Yaroslavl', Kazan' and even in Astrakhan', in which they processed Russian raw materials for export. They had maintained, in the commercial treaty of 1766, the right to pay customs duties in Russian currency, which put them in a strong position via-à-vis traders from other countries. Though the balance of trade between the two countries was favourable to Russia, Britain had the benefit of the freight and commission.[14]

The great weakness of Russian foreign trade was the lack of shipping. In the years 1773–7 the average number of Russian ships in *all* Russian ports was only 227, of which only some 12–15 of those over 200 tons were genuinely Russian. In contrast, in that same period, of 1,748 ships visiting Russian ports over 600 were British, as compared with 642 Dutch ships in the Russian carrying trade. In 1764 a group of Tula merchants formed an export company with a capital of 100,000 r. ; Catherine took 20 shares at 500 r., provided a frigate and reduced tariffs to encourage the venture, but it lapsed after the first attempt.[15]

The expedition of the Russian fleet to the Mediterranean in 1769 led to the appointment of consuls in a large number of Atlantic and Mediterranean ports, thus laying the groundwork for the protection of Russian shipping. By the 1780s there were 16 consuls general and 32 consuls, covering the Baltic, North Sea, the Atlantic, the Mediterranean in general and the Greek islands in particular. A major effort to break away from the dependence on British shipping was made with the proclamation of the Armed Neutrality in 1780.[16] In the ensuing years Catherine negotiated a number of trade treaties nearly all of which incorporated the principles of the Armed Neutrality. In these treaties, based on a strict equality of treatment, the contracting parties granted each other most favoured nation treatment, and agreed to lower some of the tariffs on their respective goods, if they were exported in their own ships. It was clear to all at the time that these treaties were a blow at British dominance of the Russian trade, particularly since Russia now allowed the payment of half the customs duties in Russian currency, thus reducing the value of the privilege so far enjoyed by British merchants.[17]

The demand for Russian produce during the American war and the Armed Neutrality raised Catherine's hopes of expanding her merchant marine. But Russians – apart from Livonians – were not born sailors, and the relative share of Russian shipping in the export trade remained low. In 1775 the total number of Russian ships engaged in foreign trade was 17 ; by 1780, 38 ships sailed from St Petersburg, and the fleet was expected to reach 51 in 1781. By the 1790s the number of ships flying the Russian flag had multiplied nearly tenfold. In 1794, 406 Russian ships sailed from Russian ports, but British ships still outnumbered them (1,011). The percentage of imports and exports going through Russian merchants in the port of St Petersburg increased steadily, reaching 45·6 and 22·6 respectively in 1782, and 66 and 37·4 in 1795, while the corresponding British figures were 23·4 and 55, and 29 and 60.[18]

As soon as she could Catherine endeavoured to profit from the permission granted by the Treaty of Kuchuk Kainardzhi to send merchants ships through the Straits into the Mediterranean. In 1776 she provided four frigates disguised as merchant ships for a government-backed company, but the Turks refused to allow what they regarded as warships through the Straits. In spite of this initial setback, trade in the Black Sea developed rapidly, mainly from the port of Taganrog, in the period up to 1787. In 1792, at the Peace of Jassy, Russia acquired the valley of the Dniestr, and when trade resumed again at the end of the second Turkish war, total turnover rose rapidly to over two million rubles in 1794, and a balance of trade in Russian favour of some 500,000 r. By 1796, 357 ships visited Russian Black Sea ports, 87 of which went to Odessa.[19]

Commercial relations between Russia and China were governed by the Treaty of Kiakhta of 21 October 1727, which laid down the organization of the trade caravans. Russia exported mainly furs and hides, and imported fine silks and damasks, gold and silver, tobacco, and rhubarb (a state monopoly). Participation in the caravans was thrown open to all merchants in an ukaz of 1 July 1762, but it was difficult to make use of in the tense situation which developed between China and Russia in the late 1750s, culminating in the severing of diplomatic and trade relations in 1764–8. On 4 October 1764, Catherine called a conference to discuss relations with China and preparations for a possible outbreak of war, but Russian policy remained purely defensive.[20]

The loss of customs revenue from the Chinese trade was a powerful incentive for Catherine to reopen talks with China, and negotiations actually began at Kiakhta in July 1768. On 16 October 1768 a protocol was signed incorporating amplifications and amendments to the treaty of Kiakhta. Russia agreed to remove the customs from the frontier and a procedure for the capture and exchange of fugitives and thieves was laid down. Trade was resumed soon after, but it continued to be subject to occasional vexations and interruptions on the Chinese side, notably during the two Russo-Turkish wars. By the end of Catherine's reign the trade turnover was in the region of 5 million rubles p.a.[21]

A new turn was given to Russian commercial policy in 1793 with the decision to ban trade with revolutionary France. On the one hand Catherine renewed the commercial treaty of 1766 with Britain, but made no demand for the recognition of the principles of the Armed Neutrality. On the other hand she banned all trade with France, but took the opportunity to restrict entry into Russia of large quantities of imports from other countries which thanks to the liberal tariff of 1782 undercut Russian industry. English striped woollen cloth (for petticoats) fell a victim to this new protectionism, as did glass, china, mirrors, carriages, many luxury goods such as clothes, hats, gloves, etc.[22]

In spite of the decline in the exchange rate of the ruble in the 1780s,[23] the figures for imports and exports indicate a striking increase in the total foreign trade turnover during Catherine's reign.

Total foreign trade turnover in 000r.[24]

Year	Total	Imports	Exports	Balance
1772	31,253	15,563	15,690	127
1782	40,301	19,242	21,059	1,817
1787	48,867	22,753	26,114	3,361
1792	78,218	37,521	40,697	3,176
1794	85,004	39,530	45,474	5,944
1795	90,424	36,652	53,772	11,893
1796	109,519	41,879	67,640	25,761

If foreign merchants dominated the export trade to the West, Russian kuptsy dominated the export trade to the East and South, and internal trade. Moscow was the centre, maintaining direct links with some Western lands and extending its contacts to Persia, Syria, the Greek islands and Constantinople. The removal of domestic tariffs in 1753 had given a great fillip to the internal movement of goods. At the same time the government attempted to regulate the status and procedure of traders. Merchants were not allowed to sell retail in towns in which they were not registered, peasants were allowed to trade only in villages further than 5 versts from a town, and had no access to foreign markets. Nobles were allowed to trade in the surplus from their estates, and wholesale on foreign markets.[25] Other regulations forbade the opening of shops in private houses – shops had to be concentrated in the *gostinnyye dvory* or covered markets. Trade took place to a great extent in markets and fairs of which there were several thousand a year, some of which brought merchants and goods together from all over Russia. The most famous were the Makar'yev fairs from 10 July to 17 August, but there were also important fairs at Kursk, Khar'kov, and Irbit in Siberia. Nizhniy Novgorod and Tver' became great centres for the trade in corn. Local fairs and markets maintained their importance because of the enormous transport problems of Russia. Huge distances had to be crossed, often on roads only passable by sledge in winter, hence the importance of the great and small waterways. Apart from the distribution of goods imported from the West, Russian corn, iron, hides, leather, fats, fish, caviar, wax, hemp, flax, ropes, pitch, furs, etc. made up the bulk of the trade, as well as the goods produced by peasant industry.

As the century advanced, the kuptsy's hold on internal trade came under attack from the peasant trader on the one hand and the noble on the other. Both were in a position to sell the agricultural or industrial produce of the village in the towns, without paying the taxes weighing on the registered urban taxpayers. The freedom granted to all classes to manufacture in 1775 played into the hands of the state peasants and the noble/serf complex and led to an upsurge in craft and industrial production located away from the urban centres. The rivalry between peasant and kupets was expressed in the debate in the Legislative Commission in 1767, and continued in a variety of petitions from the kuptsy to the government. Nevertheless, at no time did Catherine and her economic advisers introduce any limitation on peasant/noble trade. It is argued that this policy was enforced by her noble advisers in the interests of their own class. This was undoubtedly so, but it also benefited the vast class of state peasants and odnodvortsy as well as the serfs themselves. Though not many peasants took advantage of the right to register as members of a guild (and pay town taxes), they flocked into the towns and provided a substratum from which a new trading and industrial class could develop, more enterprising, free from the burden of servitude to the town which the Muscovite state had laid on the shoulders of the Russian bourgeoisie.

The scope of trading operations, the widening range of goods and the increasing demand certainly enabled a number of kuptsy to accumulate large fortunes – some of them were able to crown their achievement by becoming nobles either in the first or the second generation. But a process of differentiation was clearly going on within the obsolete category of kuptsy. The great merchants in the first guild were building large commercial empires, and accumulating capital ; while many registered members of the third guild were dropping back into the class of employees or even labourers, and being superseded by the new phenomenon of the unregistered peasant trader.

Among the hindrances to the rapid development of Russian trade was not only the low educational level and lack of business savoir-faire of the merchant class, but the absence of certain basic features of an advanced economy such as banks, credit, corporate institutions, joint stock companies, or even a legal definition of bankruptcy. In the 1730s the Mint had been allowed to lend money at 8 percent on the security of gold and silver objects, and did so to a very limited extent ; in the 1780s, other government institutions such as the Admiralty College and the College of Foreign Affairs also lent money, which they apparently rarely recovered. P.I. Shuvalov, the driving force in the Russian economy in the 1750s, was instrumental in 1754 in setting up the first two Russian banks, the Nobles' Bank and the Bank for the Improvement of the Trade of St Petersburg, known as the Commercial Bank. At the same time an ukaz was issued prohibiting usury.[26]

The Nobles' Bank was authorized to lend between 500 and 10,000 r. for three years at 6 per cent, on the security of landed estates assessed in terms of male serfs valued at 10 r. (as against the current market price of 30 r.). Demand soon swamped its modest resources of 750,000. Nevertheless it was by degrees allowed to give smaller loans and accept stone houses as security. One of its clients was N.I. Novikov, who borrowed 100 r. in 1768 – perhaps to start 'the Drone'. Loans became easier for the borrower as the price for serfs rose to 20 r. in 1766, and 40 r. in 1786. In principle, if landowners defaulted their estates were taken over by the Chancery of Confiscated Estates and run on behalf of the banks, allowing a tenth of the income to the owners, until the debt was paid off. But financial stability was jeopardized by the high social position of many of the heaviest borrowers, immune to the pressure for repayment. After 1775 the function of the Chancery in administering mortgaged estates was taken over by the Councils of Guardianship set up under the boards of social welfare.[27]

The banks set up in 1754 were essentially institutions intended to receive interest on loans. The reverse side of the financial operation, giving interest on deposits, was only authorized in the 1770s. The bank paid 5 per cent on these deposits but financial stability still evaded it, owing to the difficulties of recovering interest payments and loans. At intervals therefore, the state provided subsidies to ward off bankruptcy, amounting, between 1762 and 1786, to six million rubles. In 1782 the Commerical Bank was wound up and its assets of 802,000 transferred to the Nobles' Bank, which continued to function until 1786 when it was subsumed into the State Loan Bank.[28]

There were however other sources of credit. The Loan Treasury of the Foundling Homes gave short-term loans on sums up to 1,000 r. on securities in gold and silver.[29] Its scale of operations was quite substantial : loans of e.g. 808,000 r. were outstanding in 1795. The Savings Bank, also attached to the Foundling Homes, paid interest on fixed-term deposits, and only one per cent on open-ended deposits. The sum of deposits in the Moscow and St Petersburg Savings Bank was nearly equal to the capital of the Nobles' Bank, amounting in 1781 to 4·7 million r. ; in 1787, to 8·6 million r. Unfortunately the source of these savings is unknown. Some was undoubtedly merchant money – but the influx of funds into the Savings Bank and the State Loan Bank reflects the fact that these institutions were the only bodies legally entitled to pay interest.[30] It also reflects the beginning of a diversification of Russian wealth away from land and moneylenders, and into the class of *rentiers*. The Savings Bank used its funds to lend money on the security of landed estates, factories and stone houses, at 6 per cent, at first for 10 years, then five or exceptionally eight years. Its terms were on the whole less favourable than those of the Nobles' Bank, though they became easier in the 1780s, as the price of serfs rose. As with other institutions the Savings Bank proved unable to recover interest or capital on its loans and was too weak to stand up to the pressure of great magnates, including for instance Potemkin. The demand for loans was so great that having exhausted its funds, the Moscow Savings Bank proceeded to issue its own Savings Bank banknotes up to 1 million rubles to 1795. This led to the discrediting of the bank since the banknotes had no cover and were discounted at 20 or 25 per cent ; in 1795 they were bought in and the Savings Bank was prohibited from issuing any more. Counting serfs at 40 r., by the end of the century the Moscow and St Petersburg Savings Banks had lent over 14 million rubles, some of it probably to kuptsy. Similar savings bank functions were carried out in the provinces by the boards of social welfare, and the treasuries of the provincial assemblies of nobles which received money on deposit and made loans. Unfortunately almost nothing is known about the range of their operations.

It is difficult on present information to give exact figures for noble indebtedness at the end of Catherine's reign, and impossible to estimate that of the kuptsy. In 1798 the debts of serf-owners to state credit institutions (as distinct from private moneylenders) were estimated at 45·5 million rubles, or to put it differently, well over one million serfs were mortgaged, equivalent to 7 per cent of the total taxable male population.

Nor do we know to what use this extensive borrowing was put. From the evidence available, by far the largest borrowers were the great magnates and wealthy entrepreneurs. Were the large sums they borrowed spent on living in the grand western manner ? Or were they invested in new economic enterprises ? A. Kahan has suggested that it suited the government to promote the westernization of the gentry and, in common with the practice elsewhere in Europe, subsidies and loans to the gentry were provided to enable them to live according to the required standard. The method of subsidization adopted enabled the government to control the nature and extent of the subsidies and to choose the recipients.[31]

As in other countries, Russian state revenue was derived mainly from direct and indirect taxes. The principal tax was the poll-tax, introduced by Peter I, and payable by all adult males entered on the census registers, with the exclusion of certain specified categories such as nobles (who were assumed to be serving as officers or officials), soldiers and non-commissioned members of the armed forces, priests, and their immediate families, etc. There were in addition a number of indirect taxes, grouped together under the generic name 'chancery taxes' (including Peter I's famous taxes on baths, beards and old Russian costume) ; revenue from state-owned or state-regulated enterprises, customs dues, income from the liquor and salt monopolies, and obrok or dues paid by the taxable non-serf population to the state.

There was no central collection or disbursement of public monies, and many taxes were still allocated in advance to specific items of expenditure. Thus the poll-tax was allocated to the army and was collected by the College of War. Customs dues, according to Petrine legislation, went to the navy as well as part of the revenue from the liquor monopoly. The salt tax went to the upkeep of the court, and the remainder of the revenue from the liquor monopoly to the privy purse of the sovereign. Some of the smaller chancery taxes were collected and spent locally – a practice encouraged by the absence of paper money and the widespread use of very heavy copper coins, difficult to transport in any quantity.

The poll-tax was by far the largest single source of government income, amounting to some 30 per cent of the total. Fixed at 70 k.p.a. in 1725, it remained at this level to nearly the end of Catherine's reign. It was the only tax paid directly to the government by the serfs of the landowners, and by the Church peasants until they were secularized in 1764. But all the rest of the taxable population paid in addition an obrok or money due, introduced by Peter I to equalize the burdens between the serfs and the rest of the population. Originally set at 40 k. for peasants and odnodvortsy, and at 50 k. for townspeople, the obrok was raised to one ruble on 12 October 1760, doubtless because of the financial strains of the Seven Years' War. In 1764 this increase was extended to odnodvortsy and to Siberian peasants, and with the secularization of Church lands in 1764 the so-called 'economic' peasants were charged with a money due of 1 r. 50 in addition to the 70 k. poll-tax.

War caused Catherine to raise the obrok to 2 r.p.a. in 1769 ; thus from now on, court, state and Church peasants, as well as townspeople, paid 2 r. 70 p.a. and the odnodvortsy from 1765 paid the same sum or 1 r. 70 k. if they served in the militia. In Little Russia, serfs, state and church peasants and all townspeople continued to pay the lower tax of one ruble which brought in about 480,000 r.p.a., and in the ex-Polish provinces of Belorussia annexed in 1772, the tax remained at 60 k. until 1783.[32] The special double poll-tax on Old Believers brought in between 25,000 and 30,000 r.p.a., leading one to the conclusion that millions must have evaded payment.

In 1783 the poll-tax was introduced into Livonia, Little Russia and Belorussia, but not the full obrok. Cossacks and townspeople paid 1·20 r. ; peasants paid 70 k., and an obrok of 1 r. in lieu of services or payments in kind. Meanwhile in Russia proper the obrok went up again by 1 r., raising the total of obrok and poll tax to 3·70 r. The kuptsy were treated as a separate group in 1775, when the poll-tax was replaced by a tax of 1 per cent on their declared capital. In the view of Catherine's advisers the obrok paid by the non-serf population, over and above the basic poll-tax, corresponded to the money income obtained by landowners from their peasants. It could be paid in 1783 out of increasing production without burdening the peasant, in the same way as the landowner was at the time increasing the obrok he demanded from his serfs.[33]

The revenue derived from the poll-tax and the obrok rose steadily throughout Catherine's reign from 5,667,000 in 1763, to 9,275,000 in 1769 ; after the 1 r. increase decreed in that year, it rose to 12,163,000 in 1770. It remained at between 12 and 13 million to 1784, when the rise decreed in 1783 was reflected in a revenue of 21,691,000. Again it remained between 21 and 23 million rubles until 1794–5 when the last increase of Catherine's reign took place.

The second largest source of revenue was the liquor monopoly, amounting to some 25 per cent.[34] In 1763 Catherine raised the price of liquor from 2 r. 23½ per vedro to 2 r. 54 in order to help to pay for the reforms introduced in that year. The rise in price led at first to lower sales, but they soon recovered and the clear profit to the treasury rose from 4,376,000 in 1763 to some 5,081,000 in 1767–9. The price was again increased during the war, in 1771, to 3 r. per vedro, and in 1772–4 revenue averaged 6,641,000 r.p.a. By 1779 it had risen to over 9 million and it remained just under or just over that figure until 1794.

Salt, which produced about 8 per cent of the national revenue, was a state monopoly but its production and distribution were not farmed out. Some 6·7 million puds of salt were sold annually at 50 k. per pud. The cost of production came to about 1 million, and the net profit to 2·2 million rubles. On her accession, in a bid to establish her popularity, Catherine reduced the price of salt to 40 k. per pud, counting on a decline in revenue of about 600,000 r. In fact sales of the cheaper salt rose in 1763–4, and the decline proved less severe than expected. By 1771 revenue had risen again to 2 million, and in 1775 on the occasion of the end of the Turkish war, the price was again reduced to 35 k. per pud. In 1781 the production and distribution of salt, while remaining in state hands, was decentralized and placed under the treasury chambers set up by the Statute of Local Administration of 1775. But the new Salt Code of 1781 placed too great a burden on the local organs and proved unworkable. It inaugurated a slow decline in the revenue from salt. During the first 20 years of Catherine's reign the net income fluctuated between 1,510,000 and 1,900,000 r.p.a., declining in the 1780s to around 1,200,000 r.p.a. By 1790 salt was produced and marketed at a loss to the state, which realized 1,175,000 r. in 1795. Production and transport cost between 43–72 k. per pud, but the price remained unaltered at 35 k. a pud in spite of inflation. The average annual requirement was 15 pounds per person, i.e. less than 15 kopeks. It was the cheapest salt in Europe. The price was eventually raised to 1 r. per pud in 1810.

The government could also count on revenue from state gold, silver and copper mines, from the minting of gold and silver coins and from the tax on metals produced in privately owned enterprises. Average annual revenue in the 1770s was 1,350,000 r. Finally there were the miscellaneous 'chancery taxes'. These included taxes on inns, stamped paper, failure to attend confession once a year, the cost of peasant passports, and a host of others, some purely local, some dating back to the sixteenth century and never repealed. In addition there were taxes on business transactions, on buying and selling houses, on contracts for sale or purchase (12 per cent of the value of the object sold), on wills (5 k. per desyatina bequeathed) on inheritance (3 k. per chetvert' of land), on the use of state land without a proper title, on promotion in the Table of Ranks (these taxes, based on salaries, were allocated to the medical care of the people concerned), on the granting of patents for titles of nobility, and on the granting of estates. These taxes gave rise to endless complaints since they were collected quite arbitrarily. It was discovered in 1782, for instance, that Little Russia never used any stamped paper, because the then hetman, Kyrill Razumovsky, had decreed in the 1750s that as Little Russia never had used stamped paper, it was not going to start under his administration.[35]

Still under the same general heading of chancery taxes came the revenue from leases of government-owned or -controlled enterprises, such as fisheries, flour-mills, public baths, etc. The total income from these sources was estimated in 1762 at 675,000 r., rising to one million in 1766; 1,468,000 in 1768; 4 million in 1789; and 5,700,000 in 1795. The total made up roughly 4–6 per cent of national income.[36] To these sources of income must be added the customs duties from all foreign trade, which rose steadily from 3,072,000 r. in 1763 to 4,963,000 in 1783, reaching 7,228,000 in 1792, and dropping to 6,470,000 in 1796.

To sum up, the poll-tax provided broadly 30 per cent of the revenue, the liquor monopoly 25 per cent, the salt monopoly in the earlier years 7–10 per cent and customs dues another 9–10 per cent. The total income in 1763 has been estimated at 18·5 million gross, though much of it was still in arrears. The gross total went up to 30·7 million in 1773, 51·1 million in 1784 (after the rise in the obrok in 1783), 57·9 million in 1793, 71·9 million in 1795 (again after a rise in the obrok in 1794). But these figures totally ignore the costs of collection. The actual revenue for the above years as given by economic historians is 1763 : 14·5 million ; 1773 : 25·6 million ; 1784 ; 40·5 million ; 1793 ; 41·3 and 1795 ; 55·1 million. The costs of collection rose steadily as a percentage of revenue obtained, from 25 per cent approximately in 1763 to over 37 per cent in 1796.

Catherine's first reform of the bureaucracy in 1763 was very costly, since it ordered the payment of salaries to previously unpaid public officials and introduced a number of new or increased taxes to pay for them as from 1 January 1764.[37] These included 30 k. per vedro on liquor, 3 k. per chetvert' of land on wills, mortgages or pledges, plus a percentage on the value of the transaction (10 k. to 10 r., 50 k. to 100, 1 r. to 1000 r.), extended also to transactions by the Nobles Bank and the Commercial Bank ; a tax of 8 per cent was to be levied on the negotiation of bills of exchange, petitions were to be taxed at 25 k., and at 3 r. and 6 r. on appeal and the cost of stamped paper was to be doubled. Industry was to be charged with either one per cent of the capital employed or 1 r. per workbench; forges were to pay 100 r. per furnace, passports were raised to 10 k. per year, 50 k. for 2 years. The taxes on appointment in the Table of Ranks were laid down, ranging from 25 k. for a subaltern and 1 r. for a captain to 30 r. for a major general, 50 r. for a full general (known in Russia by the picturesque title of *generalanshef*) and 100 r. for a field-marshal. Taxes on the grant of an estate were fixed at 25 k. per soul (5 r. per haken in Livonia), and on titles at 100 r. for a count, 50 r. for ennoblement. The revenue from all these taxes, expected to reach 615,000 r. in 1764, was to be devoted to the new salaries. These were estimated to require 1,144,000 r.p.a., but in 1765 already cost nearly 2 million rubles. The new taxes however raised revenue by over 3 million rubles to 21.9 million in 1764 and it was further increased when the secularization of Church lands took place in 1764 by 1,366 – 1,530,000 r.p.a., of which 500,000 r.p.a. was allocated to church and monastic expenses, and 120,000 to charity.

In the first four years of her reign, by careful housekeeping, Catherine was able to keep expenditure below revenue, and even to put by a little. Her relative parsimony at this stage of her career aroused criticism among those accustomed to the lavishness of Elizabeth's years.[38] From 1763, expenditure under the main heads of government rose as follows (in hundred thousands):[39]

Year	Court	Army	Navy	Central and local admin.	Costs of revenue collecting	Total
1763	1,648	7,920	1,200	4,020	2,443	17,235
1768	2,790	10,013	1,313	4,525	4,992	23,633

The outbreak of war in 1768 led to an immediate consideration of the means to finance it. Catherine started out with a reserve of 8·5 million rubles.[40] Rejecting any increase in the poll-tax which would hit the landowners as well as the rest of the population, she preferred to raise the obrok paid by all the non-serf taxable population and the liquor tax.[41] A special levy of 115,000 thalers was imposed on the Baltic provinces,[42] and a number of special war taxes were imposed on factories and the merchant class, whose obrok was raised by 18 k.[43] The special war taxes raised approximately 500,000 r.p.a. But the cost of supplying armies in the field (though reduced by the Russian habit of living off occupied land, e.g. in Moldavia), and above all the cost of the many naval expeditions to the Mediterranean seriously stretched Russian resources. The deficits were partly met by Prussian subsidies, totalling 1,200,000, paid with great anguish by Frederick II over the duration of the war. In addition Catherine borrowed money in the United Provinces and in Genoa.[44] But the main new device she employed was the issuing of paper money, or assignats.

The use of paper money had been considered before in Russia to replace the heavy copper coinage. Bills of exchange had been introduced in Elizabeth's reign, but only for use by merchants in transactions between the capital and certain provincial cities, at a discount of 6 per cent. In May 1762 Peter III had replaced the bills of exchange by banknotes payable to bearer in full on demand in copper, but Catherine had not confirmed this ukaz. It was Vyazemsky who revived the proposal to issue paper money in the Council of State on 17 November 1768, and the manifestos setting up the assignat banks in Moscow and St Petersburg were issued on 29 December 1768.[45]

The operation was initially very successful. Banks were set up in the two capitals where copper money could be exchanged for assignats in denominations of 5 r. and over. The government accepted payment of dues and taxes in assignats. The number of assignats was kept low, at about 5 per cent of the annual revenue ;

by the end of the war in 1774, some 20 million r. of assignats had been issued, and their value oscillated between 101–3 k. to the silver ruble. The stability of the currency was tempting, and a further 3.5 million r. of assignats were issued in 1775 and 1776 without monetary cover ; after that no more were issued until 1781.

The first Turkish war was thus financed without permanently overburdening the population. War taxes were heavy and the suppression of the Pugachev revolt added to the government's expenditure, while the low interest loan of 1,500,000 r. to the victims of the revolt was repaid very slowly. But in the manifesto of 17 March 1775 celebrating the end of the war all the special taxes were repealed, and some old taxes such as the tax on baths were abolished.[46]

During the next five years Catherine reverted to good housekeeping. In 1774–8, three million r. of loans were paid off (the Turkish war indemnity was used for the purpose) and the balance of 4.4 million was converted in 1779 for a further ten years from 5 to 4 per cent – a conversion which was easily carried out and reflected the high financial standing of Catherine's government. Moreover, with the restoration of internal and external peace in 1775 to 1786, the armed forces were reduced in size to below what they had been before 1768. Whereas the recruit levy had averaged 5 men in 300 in the period 1765–8, and in 1770–74, 10 in 300, it dropped in 1775–86 to one in 100, and the costs of the army were correspondingly reduced in relative terms, while fewer productive workers were taken off the land or industry.[47]

Nevertheless, by the early 1780s, government expenditure was creeping up. The gradual implementation of the Statute of Local Administration entailed a steady increase in the proportion of the annual revenue devoted to provincial government from 37·5 per cent in 1763 to 54·2 per cent in 1781.[48] The influx of personnel into the provinces led to a good deal of local inflation which unbalanced the relation between silver rubles and assignats. Large sums were also devoted to naval expenditure in 1779–82 because of the squadrons commissioned to carry out the policy of the Armed Neutrality.[49] Two new issues of assignats were therefore made of 5·5 and 7 million rubles in 1781 and 1782, and two new foreign loans, of 4·5 million rubles.

In spring 1783 a secret commission was set up to examine ways of increasing revenue, composed of A.A. Vyazemsky, A.P. Shuvalov (the director of the assignat bank), A.R. Vorontsov and A.A. Bezborodko. It recommended a number of measures such as raising the obrok paid by the taxable non-serf population to 3 r., and the extension of the poll-tax to Livonia and Little Russia.[50] Kuptsy would be allowed to buy themselves out of the recruit levy for 500 r., and on[51] 1 May 1783 a number of other taxes were approved which were expected to raise a further seven million r.p.a. But the extra revenue was soon swallowed up by the expenses of the annexation of the Crimea and the settlement of New Russia and the territories under Potemkin's jurisdiction. Income was steadily being outdistanced by expenditure. Vyazemsky continued to propose increased taxation, including raising the poll-tax to one ruble and passing the costs of local administration to the gubernii (according to the number of souls). Others, including Bezborodko, argued that heavy taxation led ultimately to a reduction in the tax-paying capacity. It was more important to stimulate the production of wealth and to reduce the costs of collection of taxes, and of accounting. Nevertheless, at a time when vast sums of money, over and above what had been budgeted for, were being put at the disposal of Potemkin for the building of the Black Sea fleet and the organization of Catherine's journey to the Crimea, clearly expenditure was going to prove difficult to control.

Catherine finally fell in with Bezborodko's proposal to 'increase' wealth. But the means chosen was the reorganization of the assignat banks and the printing of more money. A commission was formed in April 1786, consisting of the same people as in 1783 with the addition of P. V. Zavadovsky, and the empress's current favourite, A.P. Yermolov. The cautious Vyazemsky was again overborne in favour of issuing a large sum in assignats which the government would then borrow. A manifesto was accordingly issued on 28 June 1786, setting up a new State Loan Bank and solemnly promising that the number of assignats in circulation would never increase above 100 million rubles.[52] Of these 33 million were to be devoted to loans, repayable over 20 years, at 8 per cent, of which 22 million were destined to the nobility and 11 million to the towns. The 22 million allocated to the nobles would subsume the 4·5 million already advanced to them by the assignats banks.[53] The State Loan Bank could also take deposits at 4·5 per cent. On this calculation 17 million rubles were held in reserve. The interest received on the loans to the nobles and the towns was intended to be used to pay off the debts of the cabinet or privy purse, and the state loans.

The weaknesses of the scheme were many. It identified paper money with wealth ; it assumed that all debts and interest would be punctually paid ; and it assumed that the nobles and the towns would immediately take up the full amount of the loans and pay interest to the state.

The outbreak of war in 1787 brought down the whole edifice. Hostilities with Turkey and Sweden, the war with Poland and the final partition, as well as subsidies to the French royalist forces, raised Russian expenditure on the armed forces to an average of 40–42 million r.p.a. in the years 1788–95. The deficit which had amounted to one million rubles in 1781 reached 6 million in 1784 and 11 million in 1787. By 1791 it reached 25·4 million, but fell again to 13·1 in 1794.

Russia had begun to live a hand to mouth existence in the financial sense. The reserves set aside by the State Loan Bank were exhausted in the first year of the war. The sums theoretically available for interest-producing loans to the nobles and the towns were raided and used up on current expenses. By 1788 already copper money began to be scarce and assignats fell to 108 k., and 109 k. in 1789. In endless discussions in the Council, Vyazemsky represented the voice of caution and high taxation. At various intervals he proposed raising to 500 r. the price of immunity from the recruit levy. This was rejected on the grounds that the armed forces needed the manpower, and that the cost to the peasants, which would work out at about 5 r. per soul (with a call-up of one per hundred) would be too heavy for them to bear. Alternatively Vyazemsky proposed a once for all tax of one ruble on all peasants and meshchane, and 5 r. on kuptsy. In Livonia, Belorussia and Little Russia a special one ruble tax should be paid in view of the fact that they did not suffer from the recruit levy. Vyazemsky's proposals were again rejected on a number of grounds. His opponents estimated that the peasants, including serfs, paid out approximately 8–10 r.p.a. in taxes and obroki to the state and landowners. To increase this by one ruble as proposed by Vyazemsky would be too heavy a burden, and when imposed on the serfs would in fact be borne by the landowners. There would be constant arrears, and the income would exist only on paper. Special taxes on the non-Russian provinces were not advisable, particularly in areas bordering on Poland, where the Russian government was anxious to cultivate the image of a better Russian than Polish administration. The other members of the Council proposed reviving the taxes on industry of the first Turkish war, raising the poll-tax by 30 k. and the tax on the kuptsy to 2 per cent of capital, raising the liquor tax and finally a form of income tax on the nobility, excepting serving officers, amounting to 20 per cent of salaries and pensions above 500 r.p.a., 10 per cent of salaries between 100 and 500 r.p.a. and nothing on salaries under 100 r. A fifth of the expenses for the table allowed to officers and officials should also be levied. Finally it was proposed to levy a rate on inhabited dwellings in towns.[54]

These interesting proposals, which weighed on all classes of society (except the Church), were not pursued. Instead Catherine attempted to close the gap by foreign loans and by issuing assignats up to 156·7 million in circulation, i.e. 50 million more than was authorized by the manifesto setting up the State Loan Bank. In the years 1787–92 loans totalling more than 39 million rubles were negotiated abroad. By 22 April 1790 the Council agreed that certain government offices, notably the Admiralty, should be allowed to pay its debts by deferred warrants at 0.5 per cent per month. Russia was well on the way to creating both an internal and an external debt.

By 1794, increased taxes could no longer be postponed. A number of proposals were discussed at a meeting of the Council on 4 May 1794, including a tax on windows, and a tax of 10 r. on owning more than one pair of horses in the two capitals. Catherine finally agreed to the increase of the poll-tax by 30 k., in view of the general rise in prices and profits since it was first introduced by Peter I. The poll-tax paid by townspeople rose to 1 r. 80 k., stamped paper was doubled, as were the taxes on patents and diplomas of nobility. The cost of passports went up to 1 r. for the first year, 2 r. for the two years and 4 r. for the third year. Kuptsy were to pay death duties of one per cent of their capital and the taxes on factory-owners who had been granted assigned peasants or state forests were to be increased. The proposal to tax horses and windows aroused no enthusiasm, and the procurator general was instructed to investigate instead means of freeing the state treasury from payment of salaries to assessors elected by nobles, townspeople and common people (except for the salary of the land captain) to the courts in the provinces. Finally the Council proposed the sale of vacant state lands, which would provide a capital sum, the interest on which could serve as a reserve for emergencies. To start with, such sales would take place only in Orel and St Petersburg gubernii. A new census was also ordered in view of the evidence of a rising population provided by the parish registers.[55]

The financial disarray evidenced by this series of expedients was compounded by the decline in the rate of exchange of the ruble, partly originated by the evident decline of Russia's favourable balance of trade. The decline of the rate on the Amsterdam market to 39 stivers to the ruble in 1774 was thought to be due to a temporary deficit in the balance of trade. The rate however continued to decline (possibly reflecting the issue of assignats) to 36·5 in 1784, and even to 30·25 in 1788. The expenses of the war, and the large Russian foreign loans led to a new low in 1792, at 22·5. There is no doubt that this fall in the ruble was one of the elements which contributed to the promulgation of the new restrictive trade tariff of 1793. Ostensibly designed to ban trade with France, it limited imports to the extent that the rate of exchange rose to 24·5 stivers in 1793 and to 27 in 1794. But the loss of foreign confidence in the ruble rendered borrowing abroad all the more difficult, and repayment more onerous.

The financial policy of Catherine's last years has been severely criticized by the only historian to make a scholarly study of it, namely N.D. Chechulin. In his view, though one could not expect Catherine and the government to be expert political economists, yet once the disastrous effects of printing money had been observed, they should have known better than merely to print more. Reducing government expenditure particularly on unnecessary items such as wars and the court, and increasing taxation, would have been preferable. As it was, the people were ground down by taxes, the economy remained stagnant, and there was no increase in the national wealth.[56]

The picture of grinding taxation and economic stagnation has not, however, been endorsed by later historians. There was undoubted economic expansion in the last third of Catherine's reign.[57] According to the calculations of a modern Western economic historian, using data provided by Soviet historians, the rise in the poll-tax paid to the state and the obrok paid to the landowners needs to be adjusted in terms of the decline in the value of the ruble. Hence the poll-tax of 70 k. in the 1730s was only 16.8 k. in the 1790s. The real burden of taxation weighing on the private serf, thus adjusted, is given as (1730 = 100) 81·3 in the 1760s, 79·6 in the 1780s and 77·7 in the 1790s.[58]

Finally, in what way was the Russian revenue spent? Leaving aside special expenditure on war and on the interest on foreign loans, the following table gives the percentages over the years 1762–73 and 1781–96.

TRADE AND FINANCE
1762–73

Court	10·7% of all expenditure
Army	39·5%
Navy	6·5%
Internal administration	43·3%

1781–96

Court	11·2% of all expenditure
Army	31·9%
Navy	8·8%
Internal administration	48·1%

Taking the first and last year however of these two periods the following changes can be observed:

	Court	Army	Navy	Internal administration
1763	9·5%	45·9%	7·1%	37·5%
1773	9·5%	34·5%	4%	52%
1781	11·5%	26·3%	8%	54·2%
1796	11·8%	28·4%	9%	50·8%

Total revenue more than quadrupled in the period 1762–96, from 17,235,000 to 73,970,000 r. Expenses on the court are clearly high, but no higher than that of the court of France in the eighteenth century. Moreover 'the court' covered a large variety of activities ranging from the imperial palaces to the theatres, picture galleries, public and semi-public functions, pensions, patronage of arts and letters, etc. The increase towards the latter half of the reign may also reflect in the 1780s the influence of the extravagant Potemkin ; in the 1790s, the separate households of Alexander and Constantine.

What is noteworthy is that the percentage devoted to the army declined throughout the reign. In spite of Catherine's bold foreign policy, and the need to keep the army in fighting trim, it proved possible to increase considerably the sums spent on civilian as distinct from military objects. In absolute terms, expenditure on the army rose from 7,920,000 in 1763 to 21,000,000 in 1796. But internal administration rose far more dramatically, from 4,020,000 in 1763 to 30,231,000 r.p.a. To this must be added the grants to churches and monasteries, which rose from 470,000 in 1781 out of a total of 40,960,000 to 820,000 in 1796 out of a total expenditure of 78,160,000 r.; expenditure on public education, foundling homes and the ransom of prisoners (outside the measures laid down in the Statute of 1775), which rose from 540,000 r.p.a. in 1781 to 1,340,000 in 1796 ; and expenditure on ports, canals, roads and buildings which rose from 1,950,000 in 1781 to 4,700,000 in 1796.[59] It is remarkable that, when so much time, money and attention had to be devoted to war, nevertheless Catherine devoted not only a great deal of attention but an increasing proportion of the national revenue to the improvement of internal administration.

The Foundation of the
Russian Educational
System

Throughout her reign Catherine was passionately interested in education, which she firmly believed could remodel human nature. With the passage of time, she came to regard herself as a great expert in the field. At her accession, primary schools, where they existed, were mostly run by parish priests. Minor clerics took pupils in towns or ran day or boarding schools on an *ad hoc* basis. So occasionally did the wives of kuptsy or non-commissioned officers. Landowners occasionally set up schools on their estates, and on some court estates there were primary schools to train peasants in literacy and the basic skills necessary for the exploitation of the estate.

Secondary education was based on the diocesan grammar schools established in the reign of Peter I, modelled on the classical grammar schools common all over Europe.[1] By 1764 there were 26 such schools with some 6,000 pupils, mainly drawn from the clerical estate. Children from other walks of life occasionally received a classical education in these schools, and went on to careers in the armed forces or formed the nucleus of the professional classes in the third estate. Peter I had ordered monasteries and dioceses to set up so-called 'cypher schools' to train boys from the age of 10 to 14, in skills necessary for naval service. They were not popular, and were eventually merged with the more successful and longer-lasting army garrison schools, which provided an elementary education for the children of poor nobles and officers, Church nobles, private soldiers and non-commissioned officers, vagrants and orphaned children, who were subsequently incorporated in the army.[2]

A gymnasium was attached to the Academy of Sciences in St Petersburg, but it proved difficult to recruit pupils. In 1747, new statutes laid down that the Academy should provide 20 scholarships for the gymnasium, open to all classes of society except those who paid the poll-tax (i.e. excluding almost everyone except nobles, raznochintsy such as soldiers' children and children of non-commissioned officers, priests and some Church servants). Nobles and raznochintsy could also attend on a fee-paying basis. But the gymnasium continued to be filled mainly by people of humble extraction including the children of the household serfs of the president of the Academy, Kyrill Razumovsky.[3]

The gymnasium was supposed to prepare children for the 'university' attached to the Academy. It failed dismally in this task ; in spite of the scholarships provided by the Academy, which were worth 100 rubles per annum in 1760, there were practically no students.[4] The same need to set up secondary and university teaching simultaneously was felt when Moscow University was founded in 1755. Two gymnasia were established, one for nobles, one for non-nobles, and graduates from both were taught together at the university. The conditions of entry to the non-noble gymnasium were much more flexible than in St Petersburg, reflecting no doubt the influence of the prime mover in the whole scheme, the polymath Lomonosov. The non-noble gymnasium was open to pupils of all classes, including children of serfs freed by their owners in order to enable them to be educated. Such pupils had to bring with them their letters of emancipation, which were returned to them on completion of their studies, 'so that no one could reduce them to bondage again'.[5]

As in St Petersburg, the first year's intake of students into Moscow University had to be drawn from the classical grammar schools ; but subsequently the gymnasia provided recruits for the university, though the numbers continued small, averaging twenty a year in the period 1756–74.[6] Until 1767, the teaching was mainly in French or Latin. Most of the students came from poor families, but many made distinguished careers, notably the publicist N.I. Novikov, the dramatist D.I. Fonvizin, and greatest of all, G.A. Potemkin. Fonvizin has left a brief and very unflattering description of the way his teacher helped students to cheat their way through examinations ; but he remembered with gratitude the fact that he had been taught Latin in the gymnasium, and had thus laid the foundations for his future self-education.[7]

In 1758, the Academy of Arts was founded in St Petersburg, and provided a further avenue for advancement to the non-nobles, the raznochintsy, and even serfs given their letters of emancipation. The first intake of students was drawn from the same varied background as in the St Petersburg Academy of Sciences, and the students were taught painting, architecture, sculpture, engineering, music, etc.

There were in addition in Russia at mid-century a number of professional training schools, mainly preparing officers for the armed forces, such as the Army and the Navy Cadet Corps, and the Engineering and Artillery Schools. These schools had moved away from the narrowly utilitarian curriculum originally devised for them. The Noble Army Cadet Corps, in particular, founded in 1731 for 200 pupils, acted as a forcing house for the first generation of Russian intellectuals.[8] The Cadet Corps attracted many pupils, since they graduated as officers, and by 1762 it had 600 pupils.

State schools and private establishments were not the only means by which the benefits of education were spread in Russian society. The practice of engaging tutors was widespread among the nobility, though unfortunately the foreign tutors more often than not proved both morally unsuitable and intellectually unqualified. A brief glance at the memoir literature of the time suggests that between a school and a private tutor there was little to choose in terms of brutality to children, and not much in terms of pedagogical skills. Alarmed by the influx of French adventurers, the government issued a decree in 1758 insisting that potential tutors should first be examined by the Academy of Sciences in St Petersburg and the University of Moscow to pronounce on their fitness to teach.[9]

From the moment she seized power, Catherine had manifested an interest in education. 'La manie de cette année [1762] est d'écrire sur l'éducation,' she wrote ; and the object was 'la fabrication de l'homme idéal et du citoyen parfait'.[10] The dominant intellectual influences in these early years of her reign were Locke (whose *On Education,* had been translated in 1759) ; Fénelon, whose *Télémaque* and *Traité de l'education des filles* had been translated several times by mid-century, and the *Encyclopédie.* Rousseau's influence was ambiguous. Though the banning of *Emile* in 1763 had in all likelihood little to do with his educational theories, Catherine did not care for them : 'Je n'aime point surtout cette éducation d'Emile',[11] moreover, in so far as Rousseau denied the power of formal education to 'educate', his ideas were rejected. It was regarded as axiomatic that education would be a powerful force for the creation of the 'ideal man and perfect citizen', since there were no 'innate ideas'.

In 1763, Catherine appointed I.I. Betskoy to be her principal adviser in the field of education, as well as director of the Cadet Corps, president of the Academy of Arts and charged with the supervision of palaces and public buildings. Though a man of considerable culture, humanity and good intentions, he seems also to have been fussy, vain and impractical. Nevertheless, he was to remain for years one of Catherine's closest collaborators.[12] Through him she collected information from Russia and from other countries on educational principles and establishments.

It was typical of Catherine that her first step in the field of education was to set up a commission, composed of G.N. Teplov, T. von Klingstedt, F.G. Dilthey (professor at Moscow University) and the historian G. Müller. The Rev. Daniel Dumaresq, who had been chaplain of the English factory until 1762, was recalled to Russia by Catherine in 1764 and appointed to the commission. The commission studied the reform projects which had been put forward by I.I. Shuvalov under Elizabeth, and under Peter III, and submitted its own recommendations for the establishment of a general system of education for all Russian Orthodox subjects except serfs from age of 5–6 to 18.[13] Nothing was done however to implement the many plans put forward by the commission, in all probability because its deliberations were overtaken by the calling of the Legislative Commission.

Education was touched on in Catherine's Instruction only briefly, merely to proclaim that it was necessary, and to put forward a few general principles of what it should contain, not how it should be organized. Catherine admitted that it was impossible for the state to provide universal education for a 'numerous People . . . in Houses regulated for that Purpose'.[14] But one of the sub-commissions set up by the Legislative Commission was charged with the preparation of plans for a system of national education. It received a special instruction from Catherine, in which she pointed out that education in the home had been referred to another sub-commission and that its task was to concern itself not with the subtleties of sciences but with primary, secondary and higher education designed to teach children the duties of those who have to live in society. This implied the setting up of schools in towns and villages in which the catechism and the laws would be used as textbooks.[15]

The sub-commission on education was charged first of all with collating all references to education in the instructions submitted by deputies from the various estates and institutions. There were not many, but where education was mentioned, the instructions painted a gloomy picture of the existing facilities in the provinces and complained that the nobility could not serve the state unless the state saw to their education. In Vereya, the nobles complained that the illiterate children of poor nobles, unable to afford school in the capitals, had to enlist in the army as private soldiers. The townspeople too complained of the shortage of schools, but seemed less convinced of the need for the state to provide them. Least of all was said about the education of the peasantry though a few local government offices, a few nobles (including the favourite, G.G. Orlov), a bishop and some of the peasant deputies urged the necessity to set up parish schools for peasant children from the age of 5 to 12 to attend in winter.[16]

The sub-commission started its labours in May 1768 and extended its search for models to English universities, the Prussian system of national education and 'Irish schools'. It also studied the various projects of Catherine's first commission on education, but by the time the sub-commission's activities ground to a halt in 1771, nothing had been put into a form which could be presented to the empress as a finalized plan. But if the search for a model system of education had produced no results in ten years, Catherine had achieved some progress on the definition of educational principles and the establishment of individual institutions or the reform of others, in which they could be applied.

On 12 March 1764, Betskoy's *General Plan for the Education of Young People of both Sexes,* approved by Catherine and possibly dictated in part by her, was published.[17] It set out the principles which, in theory, were to be applied in all Russian educational institutions. The emphasis was on the creation of a 'new kind of person', a new generation, which could only be achieved by isolating the child completely from the age of 5 to 21 from the harmful influences of parents and an illiterate, brutal and corrupt society. Schools were to stress not professional or vocational training but the creation of good citizens and accomplished human beings. Education was to be by precept and moral persuasion. Two years later Betskoy produced a continuation of the general plan dealing with the physical aspect of the education of children from birth to youth. The instructions, 'selected from the best authors', emphasize hygiene, simplicity, fresh air, loose clothing, well-fitting and low-heeled shoes, etc. Locke's acceptance of corporal punishment is rejected :

Children must almost never be beaten, and the example of cruel punishments by mindless and savage schoolmasters must not be followed, since by such punishments children are humiliated and lowered : a slavish cast of mind and baseness is bred in them, they learn to lie and sometimes acquire serious vices. All forms of beating, apart from the pain, are, in accordance with all knowledge of all physical principles, harmful to health.[18]

The purpose of these regulations was didactic. They were to be printed and distributed to all the relevant government offices throughout the country, and to the Holy Synod.

Practice followed hard on the heels of theory. The decree setting up a Foundling Hospital in Moscow, to which a women's lying-in hospital was attached, had been signed in June 1763 and it opened its doors in April 1764. The Foundling Hospital was to be a private foundation, not a state body, i.e. it was placed directly under the empress and was not accountable to any government institution. It received no public money and was to rely on subscriptions from society, the operations of an insurance fund to provide pensions for widows with which it was also charged. In its first years the hospital was very well supported. Catherine and Paul gave lavishly ; so did the Metropolitan Dmitry (40,000 rubles) and Prince D.M. Golitsyn (22,000 r.) ; a Moscow merchant gave the interest on 180,000 r. for eight years. When gifts began to decline, the hospital lived off the various 'privileges' it had been granted such as the proceeds of taxes on playing cards.[19]

The Foundling Hospital not only represented an opportunity for new educational theories to be tried out. It also fitted into Catherine's general concern with population policy, and in particular with the fashionable effort to create a third estate in Russia. All abandoned children, whether illegitimate or legitimate, would be received in the hospital, and precautions were taken to ensure that on leaving they were free and remained free. They were to be trained in a craft or a skill, while the brighter children would go on to Moscow University or the Academy of Arts. Girls were given a dowry of 25 r. on marriage ; and all were provided with one ruble on leaving to tide them over.

The hospital had difficulty in providing the kind of education in the kind of conditions which Betskoy's *General Statute* had laid down. Moreover, it suffered from the same initial tragedies which plagued foundling hospitals in other countries, namely the very high mortality rate.[20] Archdeacon Coxe visited it in 1778, and was favourably impressed. The dormitories were large and airy ; each child had its own bed, clean linen was frequently provided, and there were no unwholesome smells. Cradles were not allowed and rocking was particularly forbidden. Infants were not tightly swaddled according to the custom of the country but loosely dressed. Coxe was struck by the spontaneity with which the children crowded around the director, taking hold of his arm, pulling at his coat, kissing his hand. He could not, he said, judge if they were well instructed ; but he could see that they were healthy and happy. He was less satisfied with a performance of Rousseau's *Le devin du village* which they put on for him, since all this singing and dancing 'must unavoidably take off their attention from the manufactures'.[21]

The general principles governing the setting up of foundling hospitals in Russia were duly published by Betskoy in 1767,[22] and were followed by the setting up of such hospitals in St Petersburg and in a number of other towns. Some were founded by nobles, others by priests or peasants, one by a serf, all at their own expense.[23] After the local government reform of 1775, they came under the general supervision of the boards of social welfare and the local governors as and when these boards were established.[24]

May 1764 saw the foundation of the first Russian school for girls. The Smol'nyy Institute for Noble Girls was broadly modelled on Madame de Maintenon's Saint Cyr. The curriculum included scripture and the catechism, but also good manners and morals, foreign languages, music and dancing. It was followed by the Novodevich'ye Institute for Girls of the Third Estate. They were given the same kind of education, though in their case genealogy, for instance, was omitted.[25]

Catherine turned her attention next to the Army Cadet Corps for which new regulations were issued in 1766.[26] It was now to take children from a very young age, and educate them until the age of twenty-one. The curriculum was broadened to include natural sciences, philosophy, ethics, history, international law, etc. Though the Cadet Corps remained primarily a professional military school, it became to some extent also a 'political and civil school',[27] modelled on the Ritterakademie such as the Berlin Académie des Nobles, or even more the École Militaire Royale in Paris.

Though no progress was made toward a national school system during the war of 1768–74, Catherine continued to follow educational theory and practice in other countries, notably the work of Johann Basedow in Germany. Basedow had set up his 'Philanthropin' in Dessau in 1774, which attracted immediate attention. Simplicity, the open air life, teaching about *Realien* or real things, learning by play, co-education and non-denominational religious instruction give an astonishingly modern sound to Basedow's ideas. Catherine encouraged one of his disciples, Wolcke, to open a 'Philanthropin' in St Petersburg, ordered large numbers of copies of his works which were distributed in Russia and sent him a substantial monetary gift, as did the Grand Duke Paul.[28] It was however Diderot who pointed most clearly to the fact that what Russia needed was not theorizing about education but theorizing about educational systems which, in his view, was done better in Germany than in France and by Protestants than by Catholics. At any rate in his *Essai sur les Etudes en Russie,* sent to Catherine in 1773, Protestant Germany is put forward as a model.[29]

In 1775 Catherine took up the question of education again in the context of the

Statute on Local Administration. The obligation to establish schools at guberniya and uezd level was laid on the boards of social welfare which were to be set up with the participation of elected representatives of the three free estates (article 388 of the Statute). The boards were given an initial sum of 15,000 rubles, partly for capital expenditure and partly for recurrent expenditure out of interest. In addition many of the fines inflicted by the law courts were to be paid over to the boards for the use of the schools.

As the new institutions were progressively introduced in the gubernii, existing schools were taken over, or new ones established by the boards. How successful the various boards were depended a great deal on the local governors, and the cooperation, personal and financial, of the local nobility. A tour of inspection, carried out by Catherine herself in northwest Russia in 1780 gives some idea of what had been achieved in five years, and of what still had to be done. In Pskov for instance, her officials told her that the nobles had produced a very decent sum for a school but that there was as yet no school for the townspeople. Catherine at once gave 1000 r. for the town school, 500 r. for a seminary, 300 r. for the orphanage, 400 r. for the almshouse.

The town of Polotsk, until it became Russian at the first partition, was a town in name only, with almost no townspeople apart from Jews. But in 1780 there were 6 schools in the guberniya with 300 noble pupils and 130 townspeople's children. Mogilev already had 34 schools with 858 pupils in the guberniya, Smolensk had 12 urban schools (apart from the classical grammar school) for 359 townspeople's children. In Novgorod guberniya which had 350,816 inhabitants, there were 10 urban schools with a total of 1,173 pupils. The capital of the board of social welfare had risen to 27,000 rubles.[30] The nobles of Kursk and Orel had contributed 10,000 rubles for educational purposes by 1783.[31]

In St Petersburg, both state and private initiative was reflected in educational development. In 1777, a 'commercial' school for the kuptsy was set up on state initiative. In the same year, the publicist N. Novikov announced that the profits from his new venture, the publication of a monthly periodical entitled *Utrenniy Svet* ('Morning Light'), of a strongly Masonic cast, would be devoted to the setting up and maintenance of two schools in the capital. In November 1777, the first of these, St Catherine's (the name is suggestive), a school for day pupils and boarders of both sexes and all free classes, both fee-paying and with free places, was founded, attached to the church of the Madonna of Vladimir ; a second school, St Alexander's, was founded in August 1778, on the same lines. Both schools were solemnly inaugurated by Archbishop Gabriel in full canonicals, supported by the ecclesiastical hierarchy; and they were maintained by donations from charitably inclined lay and clerical patrons, including one of Catherine's secretaries, and even the head of the Secret Investigation Section of the Senate, S.I. Sheshkovsky. In 1781 the two schools had 95 pupils.[32] So successful were the schools in collecting donations, that in the end it was they which subsidized the periodical 'Morning Light,' and not the other way round as originally intended.[33]

In St Petersburg Catherine founded at her own expense in 1781 a school attached to the St Isaac's Cathedral.[34] Six more schools were founded in the same year, attached to churches, financed by, and under the supervision of, the board of social welfare. Pupils were mainly drawn from the merchants, children of officers, clerks, soldiers, court officials and servants of nobles. By 1781 there were 486 pupils (of which one twelfth were girls) and the board of social welfare in St Petersburg had raised the capital sum at its disposal to 31,663 r. from private benefactors and official sources.[35]

By the late 1770s, Catherine had moved away from the consideration of general principles of education as expressed in Betskoy's Statutes. She had realized that since the Statute of 1775 required all guberniya and uezd towns to establish schools it was necessary for the state to provide guidance on a general system of education, rather than allow schools to be set up in a haphazard manner. Moreover her interest in pedagogical methods had now been aroused – an aspect of education which had barely been touched on in the earlier Statutes.[36] It was not merely Diderot who directed her attention to German models, by which the state created useful and loyal citizens. The Prussian educational system was founded in 1769, the Commission of National Education was set up in Poland in 1773, when the Jesuit schools were closed. And more important still, Catherine heard at first hand from Joseph II, on his visit to Russia in 1780, of the successful reorganization of Austrian education in 1774 which had also been rendered necessary by the dissolution of the Jesuit order. Austria had adopted the methods devised in Prussian Silesia by the Augustinian abbot, Johann Ignaz von Felbiger, and borrowed the man himself. His new teaching methods involved the provision of uniform textbooks and the organization of the teaching of the same subject to a number of children at the same time. Children were taught by reading aloud together, by memorizing, based on the use of tables, using the initial letters of words as mnemonics, and by question and answer. The advantages of this method were that all children were involved simultaneously in the process of learning.[37]

An advisory commission was set up by Catherine in 1782, to study the various models of educational systems. The leading spirit was the distinguished mathematician, F. Aepinus, at one time a tutor of the Grand Duke Paul, and later head of the code-breaking section in the College of Foreign Affairs.[38] Aepinus came out strongly in favour of the adoption by Russia of the Austrian three-tier model of *trivial, real* and *normal* schools at village, town and provincial level, and he suggested to Catherine that she should ask Joseph II to send her an adviser, Orthodox in religion and with a knowledge of a Slavonic language. Catherine followed his advice. The Felbiger method, with its emphasis on uniformity, was well suited to the cultural integration of a multi-language and multi-cultural empire. Accordingly Joseph II, on the recommendation of Felbiger himself, sent F.I. Jankovich de Mirjevo, who had taken a leading part in introducing the Austrian reformed system into the Serbian speaking and Orthodox parts of the Hapsburg lands. He arrived on 4 September 1782, was received by Catherine on 6 September, and on 7 September an ukaz was issued setting up the Commission on National Schools under the ex-favourite, P.V. Zavadovsky.[39]

The commission was charged with the setting up of a network of schools, training the teachers and providing the textbooks. A high school was opened in St Petersburg in 1783 with a teachers' training school attached to it. Meanwhile Jankovich saw to the translation and adaptation of a whole range of textbooks by, or approved by, Felbiger from the German or the Serbian, on such subjects as history, geography, the three Rs, Latin, Greek, grammar, etc.[40] Jankovich also produced a catechism which was highly approved of by Aepinus and presumably by Catherine. He had 'tellement écarté tous les points de controverse en s'attachant à la morale la plus pure qu'il n'y avoit aucune des religions chrétiennes qui ne puissent faire usage de ce catechisme'.[41]

Meanwhile the commission extended its control over all existing private schools in Russia to ensure that they should conform to the national pattern. In the course of 1782 the new teaching methods were introduced into the schools of the capital. In 1784 the commission was ordered to inspect all private schools and boarding schools (of which there were then twenty-six in St Petersburg alone, though mainly for foreigners) and examine their teachers. As a result of this inspection one foreign school was closed and the rest were placed under the commission. All the Russian private schools were closed and their pupils advised or compelled to transfer to the new national schools, which were opened in the two capitals from 1783 onwards. The two schools opened by Novikov and his circle were now absorbed into the state system.

It is a commonplace of Russian and Soviet historiography that Catherine deliberately sought to stifle Novikov's work of 'enlightenment'. A note of hers has survived in which she asked for an inquiry to be made into the schools maintained by 'Morning Light', 'their needs and deficiencies'.[42] This has been interpreted as singling out Novikov's schools for particular condemnation. But since all private schools were at the time being integrated into the state system, it would be more surprising if the 'Morning Light' schools were excluded from the process.[43] In October 1785 the commission was ordered to inspect all the Moscow schools and ensure that only authorized books were used in teaching.[44]

On 5 August 1786 the Russian Statute of National Education was promulgated. It provided for the setting up of a two-tier network of high schools and primary schools in guberniya capitals and primary schools in uezd towns, free, open to all the free classes in the country and co-educational. No provision was made for rural schools, though these had figured in Catherine's early drafts. The Commission on National Schools supplied the funds for the initial capital expenditure, but thereafter the local boards of social welfare were supposed to provide funds for the maintenance of the schools from the interest on their capital and from donations from the public.

The Statute regulated in great detail the subjects to be taught at every age and the method of teaching. The primary schools, comprising two classes, each of one year, concentrated on reading, writing and arithmetic, with religion and moral education. The high schools comprised four classes, (the last of two years) and taught in addition geometry, architecture, mechanics, physics, history, geography, drawing, and languages useful for Russians such as Latin, Greek in the southern gubernii of Russia, Tartar and Arabic in the southeast, and Chinese in Irkutsk and Kolyvan. French was relegated to private tuition probably because the nobility would learn it at home and others did not need to.[45]

In addition to the textbooks diligently translated by the commission, teachers were provided with guidance on the moral duties of a teacher. The 'Guide to Teachers' issued in Russian in 1783 was based on a Serbian translation of a work by Abbot Felbiger. It set out in all the detail beloved of Catherine the qualities of the ideal teacher : he was to be Christian, honourable, loving (in a dignified way), bold, patient, zealous, unprejudiced and condescending ; he was to remember that his role was not merely to impart knowledge, but to 'educate' or bring up. His every step, and his every gesture must therefore be carefully calculated to fulfil that aim.[46]

Pupils too were provided with guidance over and above the catechism, namely the little book based on another work by Felbiger, entitled 'The Duties of a Man and Citizen' published in 1783, designed to inculcate respect for the law and the government. It was divided into four parts : chapter 1 dealt with duties to God and man ; chapter 2 with health and hygiene ; chapter 3 with duties to society, and chapter 4 with domestic economy. The child is enjoined to love God (but not specifically the Christian God), and to be dutiful. Most interesting is chapter 3, which explains the formation of society (people come together because they need each other's help). Some groups place themselves under one leader. In other groups 'several people concern themselves with the general welfare, and have that power which in a realm belongs to a ruler. These societies are called republics.' But whether one or many rule, all must obey. The authority of Holy Writ is quoted for the statement that rulers would not be where they are if God had not willed it. Their power is established by God for the welfare of those they rule over, and they must rule justly, with the well-being of their subjects in mind. The book preaches acceptance of the division of society into estates and contentment with one's lot in life. Society is made up of masters and servants, even masters and slaves, each with his role to play. Various propositions of this kind are buttressed by quotations from the New Testament.[47]

In spite of its reliance on the authority of the Bible, the tone of 'The Duties of a Man and Citizen' was entirely secular. It might be designed to create obedient citizens, 'but the language is the language of the enlightenment'. The people must be taught to believe that 'those who give orders know what is useful to the state, their subjects and all civil society in general, that they do not wish for anything but that which is generally recognized as useful by society'.[48] It was above all this secular tone of the Statute of 1786, and of all the material it published, which shocked the nineteenth-century Minister of Education, Dmitry Tolstoy. 'In the 113 articles of the Statute the Church is not mentioned,' he wrote in 1886, 'as though the Christian and moral enlightenment of the people were none of its concern.'[49] Religion was taught in the new schools, but not by priests, in textbooks provided by the commission, not by the Church.

In the 1760s, Catherine had had the opportunity to use the Church as the instrument with which to develop Russian education. Proposals had been put before her by the Commission on Church Estates in the 1760s for the reform of the grammar schools and the establishment of a clerical academy in Moscow. They were forwarded eventually to the sub-commission on education of the Legislative Commission, and ended there. Again in 1771 a project for national education run at all levels by the Church had been put before the empress.[50] Under the enlightened guidance of Archbishop Platon, the standards of the church grammar schools improved somewhat, and numbers rose from 6,000 at Catherine's accession to 11,329 in 1783.[51] But the educational level of the priesthood continued so low that there was no incentive for Catherine to overcome her latent distrust of the priesthood and employ priests as primary school teachers. The tone of her own pedagogical works, such as 'An Elementary Civil Primer,' written for her grandchildren, is totally secular. In a series of 210 moral maxims, graded in Catherine's view to a child's understanding, God is mentioned only twice : in No. 35 : 'God alone is perfect', and in No. 111, 'Honour God first, then your parents', where the maxim is attributed to Xenocrates. Jesus Christ is not mentioned at all, while Socrates, Plato, Alexander the Great, Julius Caesar are all drawn upon. The question 'What is a hero ?' is asked, never 'what is a saint ?'[52]

In one other respect Catherine's pedagogical principles as expressed in the Statute of 1786 were in advance of the principles and practice of her times. Corporal punishment of any kind, even pulling the children's hair, was completely forbidden in her schools.[53]

The Statute of 1786 required the governors in 25 gubernii to proceed at once with setting up the new schools, and in 1788 the opening of schools was ordered in a further 16 gubernii,[54] including the Baltic provinces, the three Little Russian gubernii, Tobol'sk and Irkutsk. In 1786 there were already 165 schools with 394 teachers, 10,230 boys and 858 girls ; by 1792 numbers had almost doubled to 302 schools, 718 teachers, 16,322 boys and 1,178 girls. The numbers dropped after Catherine's death but rose again in 1800, and by the end of the century there were 315 schools, 790 teachers, 18,128 boys and 1,787 girls. All ten uezdy in Moscow guberniya had schools by 1800, in Ryazan all twelve.[55]

The Commission on National Schools continued to operate as a kind of Ministry of National Education though its functions seem to have been mainly supervisory and judicial ; it was charged with the coordination of curricula, qualifications of teachers, promotion, salaries, textbooks, etc. It provided the initial capital expenditure for the schools, but afterwards the boards of public welfare were supposed to use their own resources. The governors in the gubernii retained overall supervision of the schools, which were to be supervised locally by a director who was a member of the board of social welfare and in the uezdy by an appointed inspector ; it was the duty of the police office (*uprava blagochiniya*) to see that no schools were opened without the permission of the board – and the board was to ensure that only the textbooks and teaching methods prescribed by the commission were used.[56] The teachers in the top two classes of guberniya high schools were paid 400 r.p.a., with lodging, heating and light, and proportionately less for the lower classes and the primary schools. The high school teacher started in the twelfth rank in the Table of Ranks ; other teachers started in the fourteenth or lowest rank. With the automatic system of promotion in force in Russia, a high school teacher could acquire hereditary noble rank (*kollezhskiy assessor,* eighth rank) after 22 years' teaching, a junior school teacher after 36 years.[57] The teaching profession was thus the first civil, professional, functional corps to be set up in Russia. As usual with government employees, teachers were bound to their service and came under the jurisdiction of the Commission on National Education. To prevent the flight of school teachers from the service after they had reached noble rank, those educated at the cost of the state were forbidden to leave. Teachers committing misdemeanours were punished – sometimes very severely – by order of the commission.[58] A teacher who got drunk (a very common failing) could be sentenced to detention on bread and water. For more severe offences teachers could be sentenced to serve as common soldiers.[59]

At the same time as the national network was being set up, Catherine turned a coldly critical eye on the institutions established in the 1760s under Betskoy's inspiration, and which had signally failed to produce a new race of men (or women). The Commission on National Schools was ordered in April 1783 to inspect the Smol'nyy Institute for girls. It reported that the teaching was mainly in French, there was no proper timetable, and the teachers were poorly qualified. The commission set about reforming this situation by introducing teaching in Russian, a fixed timetable, and its own teaching methods as laid down by Jankovich de Mirjevo, who also supplied a special 'Instruction' to teachers.[60] The Military and Naval Cadet Corps were reformed at the same time, and some of the less military subjects, such as sculpture, were cut out of the curriculum ; the number of lessons per week, which had risen to forty-five, was also reduced.[61]

The most important questions now arise: how successful was this educational programme? How effective were the pedagogical principles, and how widely were they applied? The judgment of the nineteenth century was highly critical. Catherine was always accused of failing to make enough money available to support her educational programme. It would require a more detailed study than has as yet been made of the financing of education in Russia to elucidate this question. Much larger sums were made available for the special and professional schools in the capital than for the national schools, ranging from the interest on 2.5 million r.p.a. for the schools for noble and non-noble girls (which at the usual rate of 6 per cent would give them an income of 150,000 r.p.a. together) to the 46,000 r.p.a. allotted to the Naval Cadet Corps in 1783, which rose to 187,000 r.p.a. in 1792.[62] It is probable that the government had little experience of the actual financial needs of schools.[63]

As regards the contribution of society, the response was doubtless uneven, and much depended on the local governor. A.P. Mel'gunov, the governor of Yaroslavl', inspired the inhabitants of his guberniya to put up 30,000 r., and a stone house worth 20,000 r. ; in addition he founded a school for all poor children of both sexes (excluding serfs), joined to an almshouse for orphans, widows with small children, and the old and crippled, for which local nobles and merchants raised a further 30,000 r. which provided the keep for 40 children.[64] By the end of the century the nobility of Tver' had advanced 77,000 r. for education, Penza levied a tax on the nobles of 5 kopeks per male soul, which produced 9,000 r.[65] In Ryazan', a stone house was built by the governor, of which the upper floor was reserved for assemblies of the nobility, balls and masquerades, and the ground floor provided rooms for a *pansion* for well-born children.[66] This was better for the children no doubt than the school lodged under the same roof as an eating house, a cookshop and an alehouse ![67] If serfs belonging to private owners were – in theory – excluded, girls were specifically included. John Parkinson, present at one of the twice-yearly public examinations of the pupils in Astrakhan' in 1791 was 'surprised to see four girls in the first class'.[68] But numbers were not everything. Many nobles were reluctant to send their children to the national (and classless) schools ; private education too, therefore, received a fillip, and an increasing number of private boarding schools was founded. The poet Derzhavin, when governor of Tambov, pandered to this class exclusiveness by arranging that teachers from the national school should, for a moderate sum, teach grammar, arithmetic and geometry in his own home to girls and boys whose parents found it improper for them to attend public schools.[69]

Two years after the inauguration of the educational programme a member of the commission was sent on a tour of inspection and brought back a somewhat depressing picture. Society's response to the state programme had been patchy. While the nobility, and the more enlightened urban dwellers, had put up quite generous sums of money for the schools, most of the merchants and townspeople regarded the education in the humanities provided by the third and fourth classes of the high schools as utterly useless. 'It was well known that to secure a job in the civil service, good penmanship was all that was required,' was the common view. The townspeople also turned against the junior schools with their new-fangled pedagogical methods, and their conglomeration of poor nobles, peasants, soldiers' children, etc. It also proved difficult to recruit qualified people to the boards of social welfare designed to supervise the schools.

To what extent did this lukewarm social response arise from lack of consultation and the repression of social initiative, as some historians have argued ? There is no doubt that Catherine's policy, as carried out by the commission, aimed at complete control of education and the establishment of uniformity throughout the country. Underlying this monopolistic attitude was the firm conviction that the government was more enlightened than society, a view which many of Catherine's foreign advisers, from Diderot to 'Estimate Brown', ceaselessly dinned into her ears, and in which she was only too prone to believe.[70] Precisely because the government knew best, it was essential to ensure that its model was followed universally and that individuals should not be allowed to teach according to their fancy, but only if they avoided all 'widely nonsensical ideas thought up by deceit and ignorance' or 'strange subtle philosophizing'.[71] The first of these warnings was directed against ecclesiastical obscurantism, the second against Masonic obscurantism. Both reflect Catherine's determination to put Russia's children on a strictly rationalist diet, incorporating a useful dose of utilitarian religion. Nevertheless, it would be hard to defend the view that more would have been achieved had 'society' been left free to act according to its own lights. It had not achieved very much before 1786 and the initial response was in fact surprisingly good.

Does Catherine's choice of the Austrian model signify that she had abandoned her earlier interest in education as a means of developing the 'all round man' in favour of a system which taught that the purpose of education was the creation of quiet and useful citizens ? 'In the search for an alternative to the old rote memorization of classical texts in grammar schools Catherine selected not the Lockian or Rousseauian "natural" education, but a very Germanic regimen of discipline, repetition and order,' writes a modern expert.[72] Where, one might ask, was there a school, let alone an educational system, run on Rousseauian lines ? Catherine saw no incompatibility between the education of the 'all round man' and the education of good and useful citizens, content, each in his own station, to develop his maximum potential. The principles she chose to inculcate by means of 'The Duties of a Man and Citizen' were certainly designed to promote willing obedience to rulers and acceptance of a static, hierarchical society. Even so it was rumoured, in the winter of 1794, that the book had been withdrawn as subversive. This was not the case, and it was reprinted eleven times until 1819, when it was finally banned by Metropolitan Filaret, who held that consciousness of one's duties should be based on religion and not on secular morality.[73]

The imposition of a uniform system of education was a logical development from the attitude of mind already shown by Catherine in the implementation of the Statute of Local Administration. Just as it was extended to areas like Livonia and Little Russia with little regard to long established tradition, so the new curricula and the new pedagogical principles were applied throughout Russia, in private or state schools, whether the language of instruction was Russian, German or Tartar.[74]

To what extent were the pedagogical principles of the Statute actually applied ? Was the banning of corporal punishment effective ? There is not much evidence to go upon, but Baron Shteyngel, the future Decembrist, described with feeling the ill-treatment he was subjected to in the Naval Cadet Corps in the 1780s.[75] Given the principal defect of Russian schoolteachers – drunkenness – it is likely that brutality to children continued unabated. It was taken for granted throughout Europe at the time.

The children being educated in the newly founded national schools by no means exhausted the number of those receiving primary or secondary education outside the home in Russia. Some 1980 pupils were attending the professional schools of the armed forces, and some 12,000 were being educated in the garrison schools ; all told, including technical schools, seminaries, and grammar schools, some 62,000 children were being educated in some 549 state institutions at the end of Catherine's reign.[76] There are no figures at all for the educational facilities in the countryside, but some undoubtedly existed, if on an intermittent basis. The numbers were a drop in the bucket in relation to the size of the population ; but a beginning had been made. Education is a very long-term process, and the crop of Catherine's sowing was to be gathered by Alexander I.

No effort was made at this time to set up universities. Catherine had invited the commission to prepare plans for universities in Pskov, Chernigov and Penza which should include a faculty of medicine and exclude theology in accordance with Russian practice.[77] Pskov would serve both the Baltic provinces and northern Russia ; Chernigov would rival Kiev for Little Russia ; Penza would provide an alternative to Kazan'. Nothing came of these plans and indeed on the whole, seeing how difficult it was to recruit enough students for Moscow University, it was wiser to concentrate resources lower down the educational ladder.[78] But throughout Catherine's reign a constant stream of Russian dvoryane, raznochintsy and sons of priests were sent, at their parents' or at government expense, to study at foreign universities. In 1764, Catherine followed her usual practice and set up a commission to select suitable students for foreign study. A first group departed in November 1765 for London, which included the younger brother of the future Metropolitan Platon. A number were entered in Oxford colleges, for the study of Greek, Hebrew, French, moral philosophy, and mathematics. Not all were able to finish the course, some fell ill, others got into debt. But two Russian students were awarded their MAs in 1775.[79] More well known are the adventures of the Russians who studied at Glasgow under Adam Smith (Desnitsky and Tret'iakov)[80] and of the group which was sent to Leipzig in 1766, and which included the young Radishchev. Others were sent to Paris, Strasbourg and Jena. In 1785–7, 44 Russian students were studying in Strasbourg ; in 1796, the year in which the Emperor Paul I recalled all Russian students from abroad, 65 were studying at Jena, 36 at Leipzig. It was left to Alexander to develop Russia's universities.

32

Catherine's Religious Policy

The ease with which Catherine passed from Lutheranism to Orthodoxy before her marriage to Peter Fyodorovich suggests that religion sat lightly upon her. Throughout her life she was probably an agnostic. Divine Providence figures prominently in her official pronouncements and her private correspondence and she was most punctilious in the discharge of her frequently onerous Orthodox religious duties, but she was untouched by the deeper springs of spiritual experience ; mysticism was merely obscurantist mumbo-jumbo to her. And, since she was totally unmusical, religious services made little appeal to her imagination or her senses. As a rational being, she believed neither in forcible conversion nor in the persecution of religious minorities, provided that her subjects all had a religion, and fulfilled the religious duties it imposed upon them. Religion was to her a valuable element in the preservation of public order and the maintenance of public and private morality, but it should never be allowed to rival the influence of the government.

The empress's views were put before the public in articles 494–6 of her great Nakaz. Here Catherine expressed strictly utilitarian as distinct from theological maxims. She stressed the need for a 'prudent' religious toleration in the interests of public security in a multinational empire, and in article 494 she added : 'The human Mind is irritated by Persecution, but the permission to *believe* according to *one's Opinion* softens even the most *obdurate* Hearts. . . .'[1]

Though *ad hoc* decisions regarding individual religious communities were taken in the intervening years, it was not until 13 June 1773 that a statement of general religious policy was issued by Catherine. It was no formal 'patent' of religious toleration in the manner of Joseph II. Rather, in typically Russian manner, religious toleration was proclaimed indirectly in the context of the granting of building permits for mosques. The ukaz proclaimed that 'As Almighty God tolerated on earth all faiths tongues and creeds, so Her Majesty, starting from the same principles, and in accordance with His Holy Will, proposed to follow in the same path'. The Holy Synod was thereupon ordered to issue directions to the ecclesiastical authorities throughout the land to leave matters concerning other faiths, including the building of their places of worship, entirely to the civil authorities.[2]

The first issue of religious policy to face Catherine on her accession arose over the Jews. There were very few Jews in Russia, where settlement had not been allowed in Muscovite days. But Jews had settled in Polish Ukraine, and a few communities in Little Russia had survived the ferocious pogroms carried out by Bogdan Khmel'nitsky's Cossacks in the seventeenth century. A few Polish Jewish prisoners of war had settled in Russia proper and their presence was winked at, but Jews were not allowed into Moscow. Catherine I issued an ukaz in 1727 ordering the expulsion of all Jews from Russia and Little Russia – a law which was not implemented since Jews were far too necessary to the Little Russian economy.[3] Eighteenth-century religious intolerance reached its zenith when a Jew was convicted in 1738 of having converted a naval officer to Judaism. Both were burnt alive in public on 15 July 1738 in St Petersburg.[4] A more effective edict of expulsion was dictated by Elizabeth in 1742, and by her order the distinguished Sephardi court physician, Antonio Nuñes Ribeiro Sanchez, was forbidden to return to his post in Russia and deprived of his honorary membership of the Academy of Sciences.[5]

Four or five days after her accession Catherine attended a routine session of the Senate, to find on the agenda a proposal dating from Peter III's days to admit Jews to settle in Russia. The empress doubted the wisdom of beginning her reign with a measure marking such a deviation from her proclaimed intention of defending the Orthodox faith. She was rescued from her predicament by a senator who proposed examining Elizabeth's decision on a previous project of the same kind. On reading the late empress's words : 'I wish to derive no benefit from the enemies of Jesus Christ', Catherine was emboldened to postpone the question.[6] The manifesto inviting foreigners to settle in Russia, issued on 4 December 1762, explicitly excluded Jews.[7]

But Catherine saw in Jewish settlement a means of increasing the deplorably small numbers of the Russian third estate, and a useful contribution to the colonization of the empty lands of New Russia. For simultaneously with the exclusion of Jews in the manifesto of December 1762 came an instruction to the authorities in South Russia to admit settlers without enquiring into their 'race or creed', the formula usually used in the particular case of Jews.[8] In 1764 Catherine ordered Prince Dashkov, with the Russian army in Poland, to take under his protection Jews wishing to emigrate to Russia.[9] The first specific permission to Jews to settle in New Russia was granted in 1769.[10]

Nothing more clearly indicates the limitations on absolute power than the clandestine means adopted by Catherine to promote Jewish settlement in Russia. In April/May 1764, in a private letter drafted by G.G. Orlov, Catherine's main collaborator in the field of foreign settlement, the empress ordered Governor Browne of Livonia to allow a small number of traders (evidently Jews) from New Russia to reside in Riga, and also to give passports to two or three people, proceeding from Mittau to St Petersburg, 'without stating their race or creed'. In a postscript in German in her own hand Catherine added : 'If you don't understand me it won't be my fault . . . keep all this secret.'[11] In this way seven Jews, including a rabbi, were smuggled into the capital and lodged for a time with Catherine's confessor, while the court pretended not to notice their religious beliefs.[12]

The presence of Jews in Riga charged with the recruitment and transport of Jewish settlers in South Russia led to the reopening of the question of the status of Jewish settlers in the Baltic provinces. The uncontrolled influx of Jews to Riga 'on their way to New Russia' alarmed the town council, which reverted to the old practice of setting up a special Jewish 'inn' outside the city, where all Jews were to reside except those who bought exemption from the restriction for the sum of 100 thalers. By 1765 there were 36 resident Jews in the city. On 8 February 1766, Browne issued a patent which limited Jewish activity to Riga alone. Here they could trade in a number of commodities (excluding second-hand junk) through Riga merchants. Unless they were exempted, they were to lodge outside the walls. In the rest of Livonia Jews were not allowed to reside or to be employed in any service.[13]

The rights of the Jews in the Baltic provinces to a permanent residence received a clearer formulation when in 1783, by a convention between Curland and Russia, a small slice of land around Schluck was ceded by the former principality to Livonia. In 1785, Catherine allowed it to be settled by people 'without distinction of race or creed'. The Riga Jews now registered mainly in Schluck, apart from the privileged *Schützjuden* or exempted Jews who were allowed to live in the city.[14] Thus in Livonia, where there was a well organized urban estate, and where there was no need to increase the numbers of the third estate artificially, Catherine contented herself with a moderate dose of toleration, sufficient to benefit trade, and to give some legal security to those engaged in it, but not sufficient to give the Jews permanent residential status or equality of treatment throughout the provinces.

The annexation of parts of Poland-Lithuania in 1772 created a quite different set of problems. In spite of their sufferings at the hands of Ukrainian Cossacks, Polish Catholics, Lutheran Swedes or Orthodox Russians, there were sizable Jewish communities, in some towns even outnumbering the Christian population.[15]

The traditional Jewish organization developed over the centuries was the kahal, an elected body usually presided over by a rabbi, which administered all the affairs of the Jewish community in a given locality and was responsible to the Crown for the payment of taxes and the performance of services. In small villages there were sub-kahals. Representatives of the kahals acted as pressure groups on the Polish Diet in the interests of Polish Jewry as a whole.[16]

The manifesto announcing the annexation of the Polish Belorussian provinces specifically included the Jews as recipients of the empress's grace and favour.

They were assured of their existing, i.e. Polish, rights to the free exercise of their religion and to their property.[17] Though the criteria for defining a Jew were never specifically spelled out, they were purely religious. A Jew converted to Orthodoxy ceased to be a Jew in the legal sense.[18] But Russian policy towards its new Jewish subjects was torn between two opposing trends : the need to preserve the kahal, with authority over the community to carry out the functions which the state administration was not yet able to undertake ; and the wish to break down Jewish separatism, perpetuated by the autonomous institution of the kahal, and to incorporate the Jews in the general urban estate.

The Russian government at first maintained the kahal organization, and bound the Jew to his kahal as the kupets or the meshchanin was bound to his magistrat or his ratusha. He was subject to its authority not only in spiritual matters but in judicial, financial and administrative matters. He paid a poll-tax of one ruble per male soul, and a tax in lieu of the recruit levy. Jews residing on privately owned estates came under the jurisdiction of the landowner, as in Polish times.

The introduction of the Statute of Local Administration into the new guberniya of Mogilev and Polotsk from 1778 onwards led to a greater integration of the Jews into the Russian state. Lawsuits between Jews and Christians or concerned with bills of exchange were now to be tried by the magistraty, for town-dwellers, and the lower peasant courts for country-dwellers. In January 1780 the Jews of Mogilev and Polotsk were allowed to register as kuptsy or meshchane, according to their capital and, in the case of the former, to pay the tax of one per cent on declared capital like the Russian kuptsy instead of the poll tax.[19] In 1783 Jews were ordered to pay the same taxes as Russians directly to the Russian magistraty, which took over the issuing of passports from the kahals. Jews took part in local elections in 1783 and in some cases were elected to local offices. In response to protests from local opinion, possibly even from local officials, Catherine ordered the governor of Mogilev and Polotsk, then General P.B. Passek, to see to it that elected Jews should be allowed to carry out their duties.[20] But local anti-semitism was very strong, and in areas of Jewish predominance elections were carried out in separate curia weighted in such a way as to ensure that Jews were not elected to the major posts. Thus, though 25 Jewish officials were elected in Mogilev guberniya, including 7 'burgomistry' or members of the ratushi, not one Jew was elected to the magistrat of the city, though there were 375 Jewish kuptsy and only 196 Christian kuptsy, and 2,709 Jewish meshchane as against 2,703 Christians.

Barely two years later, in 1785, the civil rights of the Jews in Mogilev and Polotsk were disputed when the Charter to the Towns extended the range of institutions to which Jews, as members of the urban estate, could elect deputies. The magistraty and the administration frequently proved unwilling to extend these rights to their Jewish fellow-citizens. It needed a personal rescript from Catherine in 1786 to the governor-general of Mogilev to call the magistrat to order.

Whether it was effective remains open to doubt. At the same time Catherine utterly refused the Jewish request to remain under their own judicial authorities.[21] Assimilation was the order of the day.

But the seemingly liberal provisions which gave the Jews the same status in law as the Christian urban population, subjected the Jews to disabilities they had not known in Poland, but which weighed on the Russian urban estate, namely the restrictions on movement imposed by registration in a town. An ukaz ordering all registered townspeople to leave the countryside and move to the towns hit the Jews particularly hard, and indeed seemed almost aimed at them.[22] Many of them lived in the countryside, where they made a living by acting as the agents of landowners, and leasing from them the distilling and sale of liquor. The towns were mostly small and wretched agglomerations of wooden houses where Jews would find it difficult to make a living. They were also hit by the enforcement in 1783 in Belorussia of the Liquor Code of 1781, which repeated the prohibition of the distilling of liquor by all non-nobles, whether 'kuptsy, meshchane or yids'.[23]

Deputies of the kahals appealed to Catherine against these disabilities, and an ukaz was eventually issued on 7 May 1786 which was the first official statement of the civil equality of the Jews in Europe.[24] It recognized that Jews were subjects of the Crown with the right to enjoy the privileges appropriate to their status and occupation. Jews were to be allowed to lease distilleries and taverns on the same terms as anyone else. As a result their presence in the countryside would be unofficially tolerated. They were to elect representatives to all relevant urban institutions 'in equal proportion to other groups' and were placed under the jurisdiction of the guberniya courts. The kahals would still perform the function of the *mirskiy skhod* in Christian communities in allocating the payment of the poll-tax within the Jewish communities. Decisions on matters of religion and ritual were also reserved to them, as well as some of the functions of a board of social welfare.

The legislation of the 1780s gave some security and status to the Jewish community, at any rate within the ex-Polish provinces. No wonder that when Catherine visited Mogilev in 1780, in company with the Emperor Joseph II, the Jewish street decorations and fireworks arranged to celebrate the occasion were the most lavish and striking.[25] Nevertheless, though the government may have intended to create stable conditions for the development of a Jewish urban estate, there was frequently such ambiguity and lack of precision in the decrees it issued, that it was easy for anti-semitic governors or local authorities to get around them.[26]

In the 1790s Russian policy underwent a change which has never been adequately explained. The Jews of Belorussia petitioned in December 1789 to be allowed to register as merchants outside Minsk and Polotsk, and a small group of very rich merchants had in fact settled in Moscow. The Muscovite kuptsy, jealous of any commercial rival, whether an Orthodox peasant or a Belorussian Jew, complained to the Senate in 1790, not, as they were careful to point out, on grounds of religious prejudice, but on grounds of the harm done to trade by 'deceitful' and 'fraudulent' rivals.

The complaint of the Moscow merchants was considered by the Council on 7 October 1790, when it was argued that no existing law permitted the settlement of Jews in towns in the interior of Russia, where moreover their presence was of no particular benefit. Hence it was decreed that Jews should be allowed to settle freely in Belorussia, and settlement was also opened to them in Yekaterinoslav and Tauris (Crimea).[27] There was at this time however, no specific intention of limiting Jewish settlement any more than Orthodox Christian settlement was already limited. The difficulties facing members of any estate other than the nobility in moving about in Russia should be remembered. Jews were being directed to a wide, underpopulated area, within which they would have more freedom of movement than Russian kuptsy enjoyed in Russia proper. (Potemkin had always welcomed anyone to his lands, and was said at one time to have proposed forming a special regiment to be known as the 'Israelovsky.')[28]

With the second and third partitions of Poland, new areas with substantial Jewish populations were annexed by Russia (the gubernii of Volynia and Podolia in 1793, the gubernii of Vilna and Grodno in 1795). In general the same civil and religious rights were extended to these Jews as in Belorussia. But in 1794 Catherine inaugurated a major departure from previous Russian policy. An ukaz of 23 June 1794 decreed that the Jewish population should pay double the tax paid by the Christian members of the corresponding estate.[29] At the same time the area of authorized Jewish settlement was widened to include the three guberniya of Little Russia (Kiev, Chernigov and Novgorod Seversk).

Various explanations of the decree of 1794 have been put forward. Did it represent a beginning of government anti-semitism ? Was it a purely revenue raising measure during a financial crisis designed to offset Jewish exemption from the recruit levy ? Did it represent fear of the Jews as carriers of the seditious ideas of the French Revolution ?[30] Or did it respond to the desire of the government to move people from the more densely populated western borders to the lightly settled southern lands acquired from the Porte at the peace of Jassy ? For those who emigrated escaped all taxation for a while, and in the long run contributed to the development of one of the great cities of Russian Jewry, Odessa.[31]

Russian relationships with Moslems were of much longer duration and much closer than with the Jews. They began when the Golden Horde was converted to Islam in the fourteenth century, and were intensified after the conquest of the Tartar khanates of Kazan' and Astrakhan' in the sixteenth century by which Russia acquired a large number of Moslem subjects. During the seventeenth century severe measures to promote conversion to Orthodoxy and punish relapse into Islam were enacted by the state, such as the stake for Moslems who seduced

Christians from their faith. By the end of the century the Moslems had almost ceased to be urban and had become mainly rural communities, deliberately turned in upon themselves.

Peter I used such inducements as grants of money and clothing, tax exemptions or exemptions from the recruit levy, as well as coercion, to promote conversions to Christianity. The Commission for the Conversion of Those of Other Faiths in Kazan', Nizhniy Novgorod, and elsewhere, was set up in 1731, renamed in 1740 the Office of the Converted. It was charged with overall responsibility for the civil and religious administration of Islamic communities. It performed its duties with great brutality in areas of Moslem settlement : children were kidnapped, adults were forcibly christened, mosques were destroyed.[32]

Catherine's first step in relation to Islam was to abolish the Office of the Converted in 1764.[33] Converted Tartars were placed on an equal footing with other state peasants, though they were freed from the poll-tax and the recruit levy for a further three years. The removal of the pressure upon the converted led to a massive falling off among them and a revival of Islam. The new attitude of the government was further manifested when the Moslem Tartar population of the Volga and the Urals was invited to send deputies to the Legislative Commission, in December 1766.[34] The deputies came duly supplied with instructions from their electors, in which they set out their needs and grievances. These were mainly of an economic kind, including complaints about land seizures, or limitations on Tartar economic activity as well as complaints about religious persecution. The deputies asked for removal of these economic restrictions, the restoration of the rights of Tartar nobles, and legalization of Islam.[35] In the debates, two Moslem deputies reacted strongly against the suggestion that their evidence on oath should be treated as on a level with that of Russian schismatics and stressed the trustworthiness of an oath on the Koran.[36]

Catherine herself was favourably impressed by Kazan' which she visited in 1767. It was a town, she wrote to Nikita Panin on 27 May 1767, 'which could well be the capital of a kingdom'. She lodged in the stone house of a merchant, with 'nine rooms one after another, all hung with silk ; the armchairs and the sofas are gilt, and there are looking glasses on marble tables dotted around'.[37] While in Kazan', Catherine received representatives from the various estates, and authorized the building of a mosque.[38]

The edict of religious toleration, if one may so describe it, originated in 1773 precisely over the question of the construction of mosques, and it inaugurated a new period in the life of the Moslem community in Russia.[39] Religious persecution formally was abandoned in favour of passive toleration. It was followed by an ukaz in 1776 which repealed the limitations on Tartar economic activity.[40] With the annexation of the Crimea, and probably largely because Catherine and Potemkin saw eye to eye, a more systematic policy began to be adopted. Both saw the need to win over the Tartar religious and secular élite in the peninsula, where there were some 1,500 mosques and about 25 per cent of the land belonged to mosques or religious foundations.[41] Hence the existing Moslem organization was left untouched, and the Orthodox Church was not allowed to interfere in spiritual matters.

The initiative in organizing the central administration of the Moslem population in Russia belongs to an enterprising governor of Orenburg, Igelstrom, who came to the conclusion that Russian support of Islam might cure the Tartar tribes of their nomadic ways. In the autumn of 1785 Catherine accepted his recommendations, which led to the construction of large numbers of mosques, as well as caravanserais and schools.[42] In 1786, Moslem schools were placed under the Commission on National Schools which was charged with printing books at Russian expense in Russian and Tartar, now granted the status of the official language of the Moslems.[43] Finally, in 1788–9, a central administration for the Moslem community throughout the empire was established in Orenburg (later in Ufa), which was given responsibility for the whole Moslem community within the empire, paralleling the Holy Synod for the Russian Orthodox, though not with the same status. This took the form of the 'Moslem Spiritual Assembly', whose functions were to supervise religious life, to examine the qualifications of mullahs and to make appointments, and to superintend schools, which must be attached to a mosque. The Spiritual Assembly dealt with matters of dogma, marriage and divorce. Civil cases involving Moslems were to go before the Russian secular courts. The Moslem mufti, or chief of the Assembly, together with other high Moslem officials, was given noble status and allowed to own estates with Moslem peasants. No mullahs or ulemas were to be allowed to enter Russia from the Ottoman Empire or Bokhara.[44]

The Charter to the Moslem Spiritual Assembly served to legalize and give shape to Moslem religious and cultural life in Russia up to the Bolshevik Revolution.[45] It provided a system of assimilation of the Moslem Tartars into the Russian state through their own leadership. At this stage, 'Russification' in the cultural sense was only pursued to the degree necessary to maintain administrative control. Russian was to be the official language of the Spiritual Assembly (with Tartar translations), but the Moslem community continued to use its native speech in all other contexts.

The elimination of religious dissent, and the incorporation of the Moslem religious élite into the Russian state, did much to promote growth and stability in areas of Tartar settlement. Gradually the noble class faded out of the picture, and as trade with Central Asia became the predominant activity, a large class of kuptsy developed, which benefited from the new regime.[46]

In dealing with Jews and Moslems, Catherine had enjoyed a completely free hand, since these were religious communities with no supreme head (Judaism) or with a supreme head who could be disregarded (the Ottoman sultan). The Catholic community in Russia raised more complex problems since it had a supreme head outside the borders of the Russian Empire whose authority could not be totally disregarded.

It was the influx of foreigners in seventeenth-century Russia, often Scottish Catholics like Patrick Gordon, which led to the demand for the provision of churches and schools. A couple of Jesuit fathers managed to found a church and a school unofficially in 1685, but Patriarch Joachim persuaded Peter I to expel the Jesuits in 1689. The vast recruitment programme of foreign specialists led Peter in 1702 to enact general religious toleration (implicitly limited to the Christian faith), though all forms of proselytizing were forbidden. Members of various religious orders began to appear in small numbers in Russia, and priests were allowed to stay as chaplains or preceptors in private houses.[47] Mixed marriages were authorized in 1721, provided there was no conversion of the Orthodox parties and the children were brought up in the Orthodox faith.[48]

The Catholic communities in Russia seem to have been particularly unfortunate in their choice of priests, since there was constant dissension between the priests and the faithful, and between the priests of the different orders, more often than not over Church funds and property, on which the Russian authorities were called to pronounce. The most serious of these undignified squabbles occurred not long after Catherine's accession, in 1766.[49] The empress was delighted to intervene, and, without consulting any Catholic authorities, she issued her Regulations for the Catholic Community in Russia on 12 February 1769. She asserted her intention not to interfere in matters of Catholic dogma, and then laid down that there should be six Franciscan priests ; the community should elect a superior, and eight syndics, or elders to assist the superior in managing the community's financial affairs ; there should be a school for Catholic children (no others could attend) ; buildings and property would be exempt from town taxes ; priests should undertake not to proselytize ; and finally disputes would be referred to the Justice College for Livonian, Estonian and Finnish Affairs (which already dealt with matters concerning the Lutheran religion).[50]

Catherine II had thus rejected the right of Rome to appoint priests or control Catholic property in Russia. To a Russian Orthodox historian like D.A. Tolstoy, her policy represented the wise assertion of the control of the state over the Roman Catholic community in Russia, which was now protected from the arbitrary behaviour of its priests.[51] To a Catholic historian like P. Pierling, this same measure was an example of Russian despotism, which deprived Rome of the right of appointment, and the validity of which was never recognized by the Holy See, among other reasons because it undermined Roman superiority by encouraging the participation of elected representatives of the community in the management of their affairs. Nevertheless, in spite of efforts by Rome in subsequent years to get Catherine to modify them, the Regulations of 1769 were adopted in practice and even survived the concordat concluded between Russia and Rome in 1847.[52]

It was again the first partition of Poland which opened up a completely new scene. Russia now found herself ruling over some 100,000 Roman Catholic subjects as well as some 800,000 Uniats or Catholics of the Eastern Rite. This presented the Russian government with a threefold problem. In the first place the independence of the Catholic communities of Belorussia from the Polish hierarchy had to be secured ; secondly a new Catholic Eastern Rite hierarchy and establishment had to be devised and the relations between this new ecclesiastical organization, the Russian state and the Holy See, had to be defined. And thirdly, Russia was faced almost at once with the question whether to obey the Papal decree dissolving the Jesuit order, a decree extorted from the Pope under French and Spanish pressure in the Papal Bull of 21 July 1773 (NS), *Dominus ac Redemptor*.

In the manifesto proclaiming the annexation of Belorussia, Catherine had undertaken to respect the religion of its inhabitants, and in the treaty with Poland of September 1773, she bound herself to maintain the *status quo* with regard to the Catholic religion. But the Russian tradition, by now well established, of state domination over the Church signified that Catherine would interpret the words *status quo* in her own way, namely the exclusion of any independent external (or internal) control of ecclesiastical institutions. This meant that Russian Catholic subjects would enjoy freedom of worship and that the state would not interfere in matters of dogma. But the same principles which governed the state's relations with the Orthodox Church would govern its relations with Rome. Indeed, in one sense Russian policy towards Catholics was to be even more arbitrary, since there was not even a Holy Synod to act as a channel and a brake.

With total disregard for Rome therefore, and without any consultation with any Catholic ecclesiastics, on 14 December 1772 Catherine issued an ukaz which regulated the status of Roman Catholics in Belorussia and throughout Russia, and removed them completely from the authority of bishops or abbots located in Poland. A new bishopric of Mogilev was established to which Stanislas Siestrencewicz-Bohusz was appointed. The diocese of Mogilev was to comprise all the Roman Catholics in the Russian Empire, wherever they might be, and all Roman Catholic monasteries were placed under the bishop's authority (contrary to the usual Roman Catholic practice). The bishop was to be assisted by an elected consistory (in the Protestant manner) which was to administer Church property in accordance with the Regulations of 1769. The bishop was granted the princely salary of 10,000 r.p.a. by the state. In disputes regarding non-dogmatic issues, the courts of first and second instance were to be the Justice College for Livonian, Estonian and Finnish Affairs and the Senate respectively. The property of monks who had not sworn allegiance to Catherine, and of monasteries over the Polish border was confiscated. In 1786, the Church was forbidden to acquire estates, but individual priests and bishops were still allowed to own land in their personal capacities.[53] Catherine also adopted the practice, later confirmed by an ukaz, of refusing to promulgate papal bulls or briefs until they had been examined by the Senate.[54]

Catherine's high-handed and unilateral arrangements for the Latin Church outraged the Papacy, particularly the institution of a bishop, the determination of the size of the see, and the subordination of the Church in the judicial field to a secular College. The bishop, Siestrencewicz, who needed to receive confirmation from the Pope, manoeuvred unhappily between St Petersburg and Rome, doctoring his reports as required. But there was little the Pope could do, since he was in the awkward position of needing Catherine's assistance in the suppression of the Jesuit order.

There were four Jesuit colleges, two residences, and fourteen missions in the Polish lands annexed by Russia, including the great Jesuit College of Polotsk, founded by Stephen Bathory, with its library of 35,000 books ; and there were some 200 Jesuits of whom 98 were priests.[55] Catherine had at first ordered Z.G. Chernyshev, the governor-general of Mogilev and Polotsk, to keep an eye on the Jesuits as 'the most sly of all the Latin Orders'.[56] The Jesuits however seemed willing to obey the orders of Rome, and to dissolve themselves. Three of them were summoned to St Petersburg after they had taken the oath of allegiance to Russia, and Catherine was favourably impressed by their intellectual ability and worldly savoir-faire.[57]

What to do about the Jesuit order now became a matter of discussion at court. Zakhar Chernyshev wished to keep them in being since he valued their capacities as educators. So apparently did G.N. Teplov. But Nikita Panin had a poor opinion of 'un conventicule de prêtres, qui pour surplus de disgrâce, s'acquittent mal de l'instruction de la jeunesse'.[58] What finally decided Catherine at this moment can only be surmised. It would certainly be difficult to replace the Jesuit colleges without 'importing' priests from Poland or elsewhere, and Catherine may have preferred therefore to win to herself the loyalty of those whom Rome had discarded. On the other hand the temptation to assert the power of Russia *vis-à-vis* the Papacy must not be underestimated. Catherine's attitude towards Rome was in many ways similar to that of Maria Theresa, but as an Orthodox monarch she could allow herself to indulge in irony at the expense of the Holy See.

In November 1773 Catherine decided not to promulgate the Papal Bull dissolving the Jesuit order in her territories, and by doing so she provided eventually for the continuous existence of the Jesuits. As Zakhar Chernyshev remarked to the Jesuits who had been prepared to obey Rome, 'Croyez moi, les souverains Pontifes nous saurons gré un jour de vous avoir conservés.'[59] Thus, while Pope Pius VI was seeking to persuade Catherine to modify her reorganization of the Catholic hierarchy and, under Bourbon pressure, to secure her agreement to dissolve the Jesuit order in her lands, the empress set about giving the order a privileged status in the empire. Alone among religious orders, they were excluded from the jurisdiction of Bishop Siestrencewicz ; they elected their own provincial and were given control of their property. An even more controversial move occurred in 1777, when Catherine authorized the setting up of a Jesuit noviciate in Polotsk, which acted as a recruiting ground for the order.[60] In 1780 on the occasion of her meeting with Joseph II, Catherine visited the Jesuit college in Polotsk and was deeply impressed by their activities. For the rest of her reign, the Jesuits enjoyed her protection. The efforts of the Papacy to contest her decisions and to bargain with her were curtly rejected. As far as she was concerned, she protected the Jesuits 'because they benefited that region, and were far more useful than other Roman orders, which did nothing but cut themselves off from any useful social activity.'[61] Her protection extended to the point of ordering the withdrawal from circulation of a highly critical *History of the Jesuit Order* which had been published by N.I. Novikov in the early 1780s.[62]

Though by the mid 1770s the Pope had been manoeuvred into recognizing Siestrencewicz as bishop of Mogilev, Catherine sought further promotion for him. She could always bring pressure to bear on Rome by threatening the Catholics of the Eastern Rite. In common with most contemporary Orthodox officials and with subsequent Orthodox historians, Catherine regarded the Uniat religion as an unhappy marriage of the dogmas of one faith with the ritual of another, an artificial creation, specially invented to seduce the Orthodox population of Belorussia from their allegiance to Moscow: the faithful could only too easily be misled by the wolf in sheep's clothing.

The Uniat bishop, J. Smogorzewski, had remained in Poland at the first partition, and Catherine naturally rejected the authority of a bishop beyond her borders. Treating the Uniats precisely as she had treated the Roman Catholics, she set up a new Uniat bishopric of Polotsk with jurisdiction over all Uniats within Russia and over the Uniat Basilian order. Uniat property was to be managed in accordance with the Regulations of 1769. But Catherine left the see vacant, while a consistory ran the bishopric.[63] When the Pope pressed for the appointment of a Uniat bishop, Catherine asked him to raise Bishop Siestrencewicz to the rank of archbishop. When the Pope delayed, she went ahead and made the Roman see of Mogilev into an archbishopric on her own authority, and Siestrencewicz-Bohusz was installed on 20 February 1782. It was Catherine's turn now to ask the Pope for the pallium for her new archbishop, a man deeply distrusted in Rome as potentially 'un nuovo papa dell' impero russo'. This was precisely the threat which Catherine now brandished. In a strongly worded rescript to her ambassador in Warsaw, Count Stackelberg, through whom negotiations with the nuncio in Poland were being conducted, she declared that unless her wishes were complied with the Pope would be deprived of all authority, the Roman Church would be proscribed as incompatible with the laws of the Russian state, and Belorussia would be lost to Rome, since its people 'n'attend qu'un signe pour se déclarer orthodoxe'.[64]

The threat worked, and in January 1783, Rome gave in. A papal legate was sent to Russia, and on 15/26 December 1783 final agreement was reached on the archbishopric of Mogilev, and the new archbishop was consecrated on 10 January 1784. Even so, however, Catherine had succeeded in forcing a modification of the form of oath sworn by the archbishop. The formula 'Je persécuterai et j'attaquerai de mon possible les hérétiques, les schismatiques, et les rebelles contre Notre Seigneur et contre ses dits successeurs' (the Popes) was contrary, declared Catherine, to the sovereign rights of the Russian Empire, 'et blesse les égards indispensables qu'une religion tolérée est dans le cas d'observer vis à vis de la religion dominante du pays où elle se trouve établie'.[65] The oath was duly modified. Not unrelated to the yielding disposition of the Papacy was the appointment by Catherine in 1784 of a Uniat bishop, Irakli Lisovsky, in charge of all secular and regular Uniat clergy. Catherine, satisfied, pressed for the award of a cardinal's hat to Siestrencewicz-Bohusz. The Pope rejected the request on the grounds that no cardinals were appointed where the head of state was not a Catholic.[66]

The second and third partitions led to no change in Catherine's policy, but enormously widened the area of its application. Six Latin dioceses and four Uniat dioceses were absorbed into Russia. Catherine, again on her own initiative, set up three new Latin dioceses on the ruins of the old, namely Inflyandiya (with its seat in Vilna), Pinsk, and Letychev; the new bishops were paid salaries of 3000–4000 r.p.a. by the state and were placed on a footing of equality with the archbishop of Mogilev.[67] The position of the Uniats became extremely vulnerable. If ever they had persecuted the Orthodox, it was now their turn to be harassed. Before long, in all Podolia there was not one Uniat parish church. Many Uniat bishoprics became superfluous and were abolished as the Uniats 'returned in droves' to the Orthodox confession. It was only the continued presence of the Jesuits, argues the Russian historian Tolstoy, which prevented the whole of Belorussia from reverting to Orthodoxy.[68] The four Uniat bishoprics in ex-Polish lands were simply abolished now, and the whole Uniat communion was placed under the Uniat bishop of Polotsk, Lisovsky. Papal approval of Catherine's unilateral dispositions was negotiated only in the reign of Paul I, by the papal legate, Archbishop Litta.[69]

To sum up, Catherine, whether influenced by the secular spirit of the Enlightenment or, as seems more probable, by the Russian tradition of the supremacy of the state over the Church, organized the Catholic communities in her empire in the manner which suited her best. She reserved to the state the right to determine which issues pertained to dogma and ritual, in which the state would not interfere, and which issues pertained to the organization and finances of the community, over which she exercised control. She also asserted the right of the state to decide on the size and authority of dioceses, and the appointments to be made to bishoprics ; she placed non-Orthodox communities under Russian secular courts, and she interposed the authority of the state between the Pope and the Catholic hierarchy within Russian borders, even in traditionally Catholic areas such as the annexed Polish lands.[70]

Protestant communities presented no such problems. Not that the Orthodox Church approved of the Reformation. On re-baptism into Orthodoxy, a Protestant had to damn Luther in so many words. Disputes between the Orthodox and the Protestants led to violence and the destruction of the Protestant churches on several occasions, but they were rebuilt, in the suburbs outside the walls of Moscow, where the whole foreign settlement was transferred in 1652. The revocation of the Edict of Nantes in 1685 led to the promulgation of an edict of tolerance of Protestants and an invitation to Huguenots to settle in Russia in 1689. The status of Protestants was further secured by Peter I's manifesto to foreigners in 1702, promising freedom of conscience. The number of Protestants within the borders of the Russian Empire increased rapidly under Peter, not only by immigration but as a result of the conquest of the Baltic provinces, and the large number of Swedish prisoners of war who decided to settle in Russia. Many high officials in Peter's intimate circle were also Protestants. To the dismay of the Orthodox hierarchy, Peter even guaranteed the maintenance of Lutheranism as the official religion in Livonia, Estonia and Russian Finland.

These Baltic communities were organized into consistories, and placed under the College of Justice for Livonian, Estonian and Finnish Affairs. Otherwise there was no overall organization of Lutheran and Reformed communities which remained independent of each other, and recruited their own clergy from Germany. Protestant communities became far more numerous in the second half of the eighteenth century as a result of the programme of colonization and the increasing number of German settlers in towns throughout Russia. By the 1790s, St Petersburg contained a total of some 20,000 Protestants of various kinds and the school attached to the Lutheran Church of St Peter had acquired a reputation for scholarship.[71]

There remained one religious community of which the head was a foreign sovereign, namely the Anglican community. But no eighteenth-century Russian ruler made any effort to assert state control over what was in a real sense an English club. An independent Anglican congregation was first formed in 1706 in Moscow, but moved in 1723 to St Petersburg when the English factory was transferred from Archangel to the new capital. From then on, it was the English factory, or the Russia Company, which appointed and maintained the chaplains to the British community and both the Russia Company and the factory subscribed the sums required to build a chapel and a residence in St Petersburg, which was opened in 1754. One of the chaplains, the Reverend Daniel Dumaresq, appointed in 1747, and who remained, with interruptions, in Russia until 1762, was well known to Catherine II. She consulted him on the education of the grand duke, and sent for him in 1764 to form part of a commission for the study of educational reform.[72]

Most of the Anglican chaplains were men of merit and two of them were particularly distinguished for the work they did to familiarize the British public with Russia and the Russian Orthodox Church. John Glen King published *Rites and Ceremonies of the Greek Church in Russia* in 1772, and William Tooke, chaplain from 1771 to 1792, translated many works on Russia and was himself a member of the Free Economic Society of St Petersburg.

Political issues did not obtrude into the status of the Anglican community in Russia, since in an ill-defined way, though it was in no sense an official body, the church served to some extent as the Embassy chapel, with a special pew for the British ambassador.[73]

It was not only the foreign religious confessions which benefited from the more tolerant climate of the 1770s. Steps were taken to win over the Old Believers, who whether 'priested' or priestless, played a significant part in the economic development of Russia. Indeed their role has been compared to that of the Puritans in England or the Calvinists in Europe in the development of Western economies.

The main centres developed in Moscow from the 1770s onwards. One of the most puritanical sects, which eschewed private property, inheritance and Western indulgencies such as tobacco and potatoes, alcohol and tea, and Western-style clothing, set up a community in 1771 around its cemetery in the suburbs of Moscow, at Preobrazhenskoye. A priested community set up a parallel community at Rogozhsk. These settlements were actively encouraged by Grigory Orlov, and tacitly accepted by Catherine. The Old Believer cemeteries which were social, religious and welfare centres for the communities soon turned into financial and entrepreneurial power houses. Old Believers flocked in increasing numbers back to Moscow. Their ascetic way of life, religious and moral discipline, and strict observances soon enabled them to accumulate capital. The Old Believer communities throughout Russia provided them with a network of reliable agents almost everywhere. Old Believers even had a secret language of their own. This explains the growing importance of Old Believers, whether serfs or state peasants, in for instance the great textile centre of Ivanovo, in manufacturing, and in trade throughout south Russia and the Urals.[74]

The policy pursued by Catherine, which seems to have originated with Rumyantsev in Little Russia, supported by Potemkin in the capital, was a compromise by which Old Believers would preserve their own ritual, while acknowledging the authority of the Orthodox Church. It is known in Russia as *yedinoveriye*. Discussions first began in 1781, with an Old Believer, Abbot Nikodim, in Little Russia, and were carried on in St Petersburg by Potemkin. The Old Believer request for all of them to be placed under one bishop dependent directly on the Synod, regardless of where they lived, was rejected by Potemkin as contrary to Church law. But he found a way to meet their wishes when the new see of the Crimea was set up, in his own guberniya, and all Old Believers were placed under the bishop. They thus escaped the jurisdiction of the bishops in their place of residence. Potemkin's partiality for the Old Belief, and his desire to populate his vast empty lands, led him to set up in 1785 a *yedinoveriye* monastery and a number of Old Belief parish churches in the diocese of the Crimea in order to win them over. In other respects their position improved : they were no longer compelled to wear distinctive clothing ; they were, as from 1782, not to be called schismatics, and in 1785 public office was opened to them. They were of course allowed to wear beards and traditional Russian clothes, since Peter I's prohibitions were no longer being enforced.

By no means all the Old Belief communities were won over by these reforms. They were most successful with well established 'priested' communities, and with the economically prosperous. Among the poorer communities they were at times rejected with violence, and on the whole they failed with the priestless. The whole *yedinoveriye* movement in any case lost momentum with the death of Potemkin.[75]

The numbers of Old Believers have never been accurately stated in eighteenth- or nineteenth-century population statistics. They may well have reached 20 per cent of the peasantry. By the eighteenth century there were but few among the nobility but a sizable number in the merchant class. They played an increasingly important role in Russian social and economic history and survive in the Soviet Union to this day.

Part X

The Declining Years

33

The Role of Freemasonry

Probably nowhere in Europe did Freemasonry play so big a part in the development of the cultural life of three or four generations as it did in Russia. This may reflect the relative poverty and lack of originality of the essentially derivative culture of eighteenth-century Russia ; it may also reflect the absence of Orthodox works of theology or piety, accessible in language and style to the layman, of sufficient intellectual rigour or emotional depth to satisfy a more discriminating public. The introduction of the Masonic movement into Russia is sometimes dated to the late seventeenth century ; sometimes it is attributed to Peter I. At one time the grandmaster was General James Keith, who entered Russian service in 1728 and left for Prussian service in 1744. At first the movement spread mainly in the foreign communities, but by the 1760s, Elizabeth's Secret Chancery already recorded that a number of high government servants were Masons, notably the brothers Zakhar and Ivan Chernyshev, R.L. Vorontsov, the brothers P.I. and I.I. Melissino, Prince M.M. Shcherbatov, the two Panins. Various prominent Golitsyns and Trubetskoys in the Guards and the Cadet Corps were also members, as well as some non-nobles. In the reign of Elizabeth many in Church and government believed that the object of the Masons was to build Babylon, the Throne of Antichrist, and that Masonic rites were not only blasphemous but bloodthirsty.[1] Peter III was reputed to have held Masonic meetings in his palace at Oranienbaum.[2]

Very little is known about the membership and organization of Masonry in Catherine's early years, though it appears that young officers who were also interested in the arts and writers, actors, artists and musicians found a meeting-place in the lodges. By the mid-1770s the grandmaster was I.P. Yelagin, director of court theatres and spectacles and of the administration of court properties. He controlled some fourteen lodges, some German, some English, some bilingual with Russian. The lodges belonged to the system of 'lax observance' limited to three degrees, apprentice, journeyman and master. But as elsewhere, the desire to increase the mystery and multiply the number of degrees developed in Russia. Baron Reichel, who entered Russian service in 1770, brought with him from

Brunswick the Zinnendorf system, and won over many of Yelagin's lodges. In 1776 the two groups were united, and came under the overall direction of Duke Ferdinand of Brunswick.

Even so, the Reichel system proved too pragmatic and lacking in ritual and esoteric lore to satisfy adepts who sought in Freemasonry what the Church could no longer give them. The disappointed found an answer in the Order of the Temple, or in Rosicrucianism. The Templars purported to be a revival, or a continuation, of the order destroyed in 1307. The order was strictly hierarchical and composed of many degrees. It had great success in Sweden, and was imported from there by Grand Duke Paul's friend, A.B. Kurakin, in 1776–7. It took root in Russia when Gustavus III paid a visit in summer 1777 bringing with him the most important Masonic constitutional documents. Efforts to unite all Russian lodges under one system and one grandmaster, the Duke of Sudermania, brother of the King of Sweden, failed however, when Yelagin sensed the unwisdom of allowing the direction of a movement, of which the deputy grandmaster was the man in charge of Russian foreign affairs, Nikita Panin, to pass into foreign hands.[3] The two Masonic systems remained separate therefore, and Prince G.P. Gagarin, ober-prokuror in the Senate and a friend of Paul's, became head of the Swedish system in Russia. Two nephews of Nikita Panin, Prince A.B. Kurakin and Prince N.V. Repnin, were at one time members of the Swedish order, to which some seventeen lodges adhered for shorter or longer periods in the 1780s.

If the Swedish-directed lodges of strict observance aroused some fears that they were Jesuit-inspired, Catholic and absolutist in tendency, it was their possible *political* implications, rather than their esoteric aspects which alienated Russians, and many moved in time to other systems. Ultimately the most influential of the Russian Masonic groups flourished in Moscow ; it broke from the Swedish system in 1781 and set up a new 'scientific' lodge, 'Harmony', of which N.I. Novikov became a member, and I.G. Schwarz the moving spirit.[4]

Schwarz, a Transylvanian by birth, arrived in Moscow in 1779, to take up a post as professor of German in the gymnasia of Moscow University, a post probably secured through his Masonic connections. Schwarz's real allegiance was to Rosicrucianism of which the leaders at the time were J.C. von Wöllner and J.C.A. Theden, a surgeon, both of whom were attached to the court of the Crown Prince of Prussia. Schwarz visited Germany from summer 1781 to February 1782, and on his return, the Harmony Lodge was reorganized as a Rosicrucian centre, subordinated to Theden and Wöllner. Schwarz himself was empowered to recruit Masons and direct their activities, and he was to send to the superior in Prussia an annual report on newly admitted brothers, and ten rubles for each new recruit. Then, at the Wilhelmstadt convention of Masons in 1782, Schwarz secured the recognition of Russia as the eighth province under the grandmaster of European strict observance Masonry, Duke Ferdinand of Brunswick. Thus, though apparently affiliated to strict observance European Masonry under Duke Ferdinand, Schwarz's circle was in fact, and possibly without the knowledge of most of its members, subordinated to the Berlin Rosicrucians. In the official chapter of the eighth province of European Masonry, the post of provincial grandmaster was not filled. It was hoped that the Grand Duke Paul might occupy it. But Schwarz became chancellor of the Rosicrucians, and *de facto* head of an expanding network of provincial lodges ; he alone knew the full list of Rosicrucians, and only the masters of the sixty lodges eventually founded knew that Rosicrucianism was the central purpose of their system.[5]

It was through his Masonic connections that Novikov was offered the lease of the Moscow University Press in 1779, and hence transferred his operations to the old capital. Catherine's edict of 1783 which allowed individuals to set up printing presses provided they registered them with the police led to a proliferation of presses in the capitals and the provinces of which the Rosicrucians took full advantage. Novikov and I. V. Lopukhin set up private printing presses of their own. In 1784 the Rosicrucians set up a joint stock publishing company, the Moscow Typographical Company (which supplied detailed reports on its activities to its Prussian Masonic superiors) which was registered with the police. Novikov also maintained a secret, unregistered press on which occult and Rosicrucian literature was published in Russian translation, at the behest of the Prussian Rosicrucians. I. Lopukhin also set up his own secret press, on which he printed mystical and alchemical works. These books bore no indication of their place of publication, and were not submitted to the police chief before printing.

The existence of the presses served as a focus around which to concentrate the educational activities of Novikov and Schwarz. In November 1779 a 'Pedagogical Seminar' was set up attached to Moscow University, with the object of training teachers. It was maintained by private benefactions from prominent Masons, under the direction of Schwarz. The original number of six students had expanded to 30 by 1782, at a cost per student of 100 rubles p.a. The setting up of the seminar was followed by the establishment of the Society of University Graduates in March 1781 designed to fulfil two functions : the selection and preparation of materials for publication in periodicals and by the presses, and the cultivation of a high moral tone among the members, which would lead them eventually to join the Rosicrucian movement. A special translators' seminar was set up and a house was bought for students in both seminars, in which Schwarz and a secret German press were also lodged. The edifice of Masonic university activity was crowned by the opening of the Friendly Learned Society of Moscow in 1782 under the patronage of the governor-general, General Zakhar Chernyshev (a Mason) and Archbishop Platon. The Society was to act as a forum for the cultural life of Moscow, but it also subsidized students attending courses at the university and published and distributed textbooks. Masonic ideals were propagated in many literary works of the time, as well as in the Masonic songs which accompanied Masonic rituals. Not surprisingly the first of Mozart's operas to achieve popularity in Russia was *The Magic Flute*.[6]

Since he had moved to Moscow in 1779, Novikov had enormously expanded his publishing output. The University Press made a considerable profit from the publication of a programme of translations ranging from Blackstone's *Commentaries on the Laws of England* (commissioned by Catherine) to Bunyan's *Pilgrim's Progress, Emile,* by Rousseau, the *Discourse against Atheism* of Grotius, translated by Archbishop Ambrosius of Moscow. Novikov continued to edit and contribute to a number of periodicals, some with a pronounced Masonic cast, some catering to the developing interest in economic or cultural affairs, such as *Gorodskaya i derevenskaya biblioteka* ('Town and Country Library'), or *Pokoyushchisya trudolyubets* ('The Busy Man at Rest') and perhaps most noted of all ; his series for children, *Detskoye Chteniye*. His interest lay not only in publication, but in distribution, and he took a prominent part in the development of the book trade throughout provincial Russia.

At a time when the productions of most of the provincial presses were unable to find a commercial outlet, censorship records show that Novikov's publications were on sale in a number of important provincial towns, from Archangel to Tambov, from Nizhniy Novgorod to Irkutsk. These provincial centres of the book trade were nearly all towns in which there were Masonic lodges, often under the direction of the Moscow Masons, and many of those who supervised and supplied the book stores were active Masons.[7]

But there was another side to Novikov's publishing activity. The secret presses which he and his colleague Lopukhin maintained produced a constant stream of mystical, Masonic, and occult works such as Saint Martin's *Des erreurs et de la vérité,* the *New Chiropaedia* of A.M. Ramsay, the works of Miguel de Molina and Madame Guyon, William Hutchinson's *Spirit of Masonry,* Arndt's *True Christianity,* and *The Imitation of Christ* of Thomas à Kempis. Both the secret presses and the Typographical Company operated under the control of the Rosicrucian order. Schwarz died in 1784, but he was replaced by Baron Schröder, who reported to his superiors in Prussia, Wöllner and Theden, to whom the sums collected from the Russian brethren on various pretexts were forwarded.[8]

Catherine's attitude to Freemasonry, to which so many of her courtiers belonged, was marked at first by an amused tolerance. But her distaste became acute as a result of the visit to St Petersburg in 1779 of Count Cagliostro, the Sicilian charlatan Giuseppe Balsamo, a pseudo-alchemist rather than a Freemason. In 1780 she published an anonymous attack on the 'absurd society' and later satirized Cagliostro under the name of Kalifankerstan in her play 'The Deceiver', in which he is shown embezzling gold from his victims. The play was performed in 1786, and translated into French and German. Catherine reverted to the theme in two plays of 1785–6, which were also performed in the two capitals.[9] Like many outside the Masonic movement, Catherine could not distinguish between the dangerous and revolutionary 'illuminati' who had been broken up in Bavaria as recently as 1784, the Martinists or followers of the mystic Saint Martin,[10] and the Prussian-controlled Rosicrucians, oriented towards the inner life.

It is a long-established tradition of Russian and Soviet historiography that

Novikov, from the beginning of his career as a publisher and editor in 1769, was persecuted by an increasingly reactionary empress who would allow no independent social initiatives to thrive.[11] But it was not Novikov's Masonic or reforming activity which led to his first brush with the government, but a straightforward breach of copyright. The Commission on National Schools complained in August 1784 that Novikov had printed two school textbooks in breach of the exclusive licence given by the commission to another printer. Novikov, though he alleged that he had been authorized by the governor-general to print the books, was ordered to withdraw them, and suffered financial loss. But this was no specific and unprecedented attack on his press, since other publishers had in similar circumstances been treated in exactly the same way, as part of the process of establishing copyright in Russia.[12] Shortly afterwards Catherine's attention was drawn, possibly by Jesuit sympathizers, to the publication, in one of Novikov's periodicals, of an 'abusive' history of the Order of Jesus. It portrayed the Jesuits as faithless, devious, power-seeking, aiming to set up a state within a state, in fact it gave what many 'enlightened' minds considered to be an 'objective' account of the Jesuits. Catherine ordered the history to be withdrawn, since 'having given her protection to the Jesuits' she could not 'suffer them to be reviled'.[13] Catherine was here extending to the Jesuits the same protection as the existing Russian censorship regulations afforded to all religious institutions.

But it was in 1785, precisely when Catherine was churning out her theatrical satires on Freemasonry, that her attention was drawn to the nature of some of the books Novikov published on the University Press. In December 1785, Governor-General Bruce and Archbishop Platon of Moscow were ordered to inspect the books published by Novikov, to ensure that they contained no 'ravings', 'stupid lucubrations' or 'schism', and the archbishop was ordered to test Novikov's beliefs as a Christian.

Novikov passed the test of his faith with flying colours. Would that there were more Christians like him, concluded the archbishop. As for his publications, after expressing his disapproval of the 'heinous and fanatical products of the so-called enlightenment . . . which should be uprooted like the tares among the good seed', Platon listed twenty-three books which he thought likely to induce error – for instance one entitled *On the Ancient Mysteries and Secrets of All Peoples* which 'praised pagan rites found sinful by the Church, and declared that the Church derived its ritual and its sacraments from paganism'.[14]

Of the twenty-three books listed by Platon, Catherine banned only six, all of them Masonic, including the *New Chrysomander,* the specifically Rosicrucian text brought by Schwartz from Germany in 1782, and the *Chemical Psalter,* one of the many pseudo-Paracelsuses in circulation. The remaining books were to be allowed to circulate freely, whether 'enlightened' (Voltaire), Masonic, or merely bawdy.[15] But evidently Catherine was not happy about the kind of Masonic influences emanating from Moscow. In January 1786, she ordered the police chief of Moscow to 'inspect a hospital and schools (if there are any) set up by these new sectarians, to ensure that no schism, vanity or deceit should creep in'.[16] At the same time he was ordered to summon Novikov and warn him that he enjoyed the lease of the University Press in order to publish books useful and necessary for society, and not in order to issue books 'full of a new schism in order to deceive and entrap the unwary'.[17] There were, however, no schools, and there was no hospital, only a small sick bay for the workers in the press.[18] But Novikov was incautious enough to keep a secret stock of the banned books which he subsequently allowed to be sold in Moscow and at country fairs.

It proved only too easy to feed Catherine's distrust of the Moscow Rosicrucians, though the next step was not aimed at them. Her confessor, I. Pamfilov, was in frequent correspondence with the Archpriest Peter Alekseyev of the Moscow Archangel Cathedral, an unquiet and unpleasant schemer, at daggers drawn with Archbishop Platon. It was probably through Pamfilov that Catherine was informed about the large number of works of a religious character which were being printed on secular presses, in defiance of the official – and lucrative – monopoly of the Holy Synod press.[19] At any rate, on 27 July 1787, soon after Catherine's last visit to Moscow, she ordered a list of all such books to be made and prohibited the publication of all prayer books, church books or religious works except by authorized presses such as the Holy Synod and the Commission on National Schools. It was found that, in Moscow alone, 313 titles of religious works had been published by secular presses (166 of them by Novikov), and others were listed in St Petersburg and a number of provincial centres. In September 1788, Catherine, having studied the reports of the ecclesiastical censors, ordered the return of 299 of the 313 Moscow titles to their owners, banned 14 titles, and decreed that in future all religious works should be submitted to the Synod (and not merely to the police boards) before publication. The 299 titles included works by many leading Russian metropolitans and archbishops, including Platon himself. The 14 banned titles were condemned on religious, not political grounds. They included A.M. Ramsay's *New Chiropaedia* (banned for the second time), and a translation by A.M. Kutuzov (a devout Rosicrucian and a friend of Radishchev's) of Klopstock's *Messias* which was found to contain 'expressions contrary to Holy Scripture, and derogatory to the divinity'. Of the fourteen banned books, eleven titles had been published by Novikov, and were mainly Masonic.[20] This further evidence of what Catherine considered to be Novikov's religious sectarianism ('il est un fanatique') determined her not to renew his lease of the Moscow University Press when it should expire in 1789.[21]

Meanwhile Novikov, as a result of the impounding of his stock of books in 1787, began to experience serious financial difficulties, both in the Typographical Company and with the University Press, the affairs of which were not kept separate. Since the Rosicrucians had invested large sums in the Typographical Company, their relations with Novikov, and Novikov's own relation with his German superiors, grew more tense. Baron Schröder demanded the return of the monies he had invested, and finally the Berlin superiors proclaimed a *silanum* or suspension of all Masonic activities in Russia. The death of Frederick II, and the accession of Frederick William II in 1786, led to further changes in the relationship between Moscow and Berlin. J.C. von Wöllner, the leader of the Rosicrucians, who became one of Frederick William's ministers, now maintained the Rosicrucian contacts through Prince N. Trubetskoy rather than through Novikov.[22] In 1787 A.M. Kutuzov went to study Rosicrucian lore in Berlin ; in 1788, M.I. Nevzorov and V. Ya. Kolokol'nikov went there at the expense of the Moscow Masons to study chemistry as the basis of alchemy.

In spite of his financial difficulties, in the summer and autumn of 1787 Novikov carried out local relief work during the famine which beset Moscow guberniya. He set about it with his usual mixture of idealism, enterprise and financial inefficiency, with the idea of creating a long-term viable system of public relief. With the aid of substantial sums amounting to more than 50,000 rubles, borrowed from a Masonic friend, he provided grain and seed corn to some hundred private and state-owned villages and set up magazines on his estate from which seed corn was distributed in subsequent years. The supplies of corn were to be repaid in cash or in labour on Novikov's own estate of Avdot'ino, in his spinning and weaving workshops, brick kilns or building enterprises, which benefited his serfs as well as himself. Novikov spent much of the autumn of 1787 and the spring of 1788 in these activities, and after he lost the lease of Moscow University Press in 1789, he spent an increasing amount of time on his estate.[23] The Typographical Company was also wound up in 1791, by which time it was very seriously in debt.

Meanwhile Catherine was becoming increasingly suspicious of the activities of the Masons in general and of the Moscow group in particular, suspecting them of secret links with revolutionary activity abroad. In March 1790 she ordered the newly appointed governor-general of Moscow, Prince A.A. Prozorovsky, to institute a secret surveillance of the Moscow Masons ; and later in the year she ordered General P.I. Melissino, who had founded his own, completely national, Masonic order in St Petersburg, to close it down.[24]

Here again, Archpriest Alekseyev may have played a fateful part. In pursuit of his vendetta against Metropolitan (as he now was) Platon, he collected evidence that Platon had permitted the recruitment of seminarists who had been trained in 'Martinism' by Schwartz and his followers, and in doctrines on the natural state of man 'incompatible with a monarchical government'. These seminarists, he reported, were now parish priests spreading Martinist doctrines. Alekseyev also alleged that books were still secretly being printed in Novikov's house.[25]

Possibly as a result of complaints arising from the winding up of the Typographical Company, in November 1791 Catherine ordered Prozorovsky to inspect Novikov's activities on his estate : what kind of buildings was he putting up, what were his enterprises, what life was he leading ?[26] Then, in March 1792, Gustavus III of Sweden was assassinated. In that same month Nevzorov and Kolokol'nikov, the two Russians who had been studying chemistry abroad, returned to Russia. They were promptly arrested on the suspicion that they had been in Paris and had joined in revolutionary demonstrations.[27]

Their arrest was followed, chronologically, by an order to Prozorovsky on 13 April 1792 to investigate whether a book on the Old Believer martyrs of the Solovetsky Monastery, 'full of lying miracles and insults to our church and government' had been published by Novikov (can one detect here again the hand of Archpriest Alekseyev ?), who was suspected of running a secret press on his country estate.[28] Prozorovsky, whom Potemkin had described as Catherine's 'oldest gun' (he was only fifty-eight), who would undoubtedly hit the target, but perhaps 'spatter her reputation with blood',[29] found no trace of the book on Old Believers in Moscow. But he did find on sale a copy of one of the six books banned in 1786. This was enough. He seized all Novikov's stock of books in Moscow, and sent his minions to examine the books and papers in the country, and to bring Novikov himself to the capital where he was placed under house arrest.

Prozorovsky's first reports to Catherine confirmed that Novikov had continued to publish and sell forbidden occult and Masonic works,[30] whereupon Catherine ordered him to be brought before the proper court (staffed by 'reliable' people), which should also investigate the suspiciously large sums of money he had disposed of in his relief work.[31] But as Prozorovsky delved deeper he discovered evidence that the Rosicrucians had been directed from abroad by Wöllner, and that the Grand Duke Paul had been approached to to join the order, even to lead it in Russia. Among the papers found by Prozorovsky was a memorandum by the architect V. Bazhenov, also a fervent Mason, who had visited Paul three times, in 1784, 1787 and 1791, and presented him with devotional books published by Novikov, as a means of initiating contact.[32]

Prozorovsky disliked and despised Novikov ; he thought him a sly, cunning and insolent rascal, too devious for a simple soldier like himself to deal with. He was lost in the intricacies of the Masonic world ; he believed that Novikov and his ilk were egalitarians in the guise of lovers of humanity, guilty of bribing the censors and the Secret Chancery.[33]

Prozorovsky's further reports led Catherine to agree that it was inadvisable to bring Novikov to trial before the ordinary courts. She ordered him to be sent under strong escort, by a roundabout and secret route, to Schlüsselburg, where Sheshkovsky, head of the security section in the Senate, would take on the investigation. The charges levied against Novikov were now far more serious ; they included the holding of secret meetings, with oaths on the gospels, etc., at which the misguided were induced to promise eternal submission to the order of the Rosicrucians ; placing themselves under the authority of the Duke of Brunswick ; carrying on a secret correspondence with the Prince of Hesse Cassel and the Prussian minister Wöllner in cypher, 'at a time when the Prussian court was acting in a completely hostile manner to Russia' ; using various means to entrap 'a certain person' (Paul) into their sect ; publishing forbidden and corrupt books, and setting up 'archbishoprics', 'dioceses' and 'rituals' outside of Holy

Church.[34] Without any formal trial, Novikov was sentenced in August 1792 to fifteen years' imprisonment in Schlüsselburg. He was allowed to keep with him his private physician, the Rosicrucian M.I. Bagryansky, and his serf servant. On Sheshkovsky's orders, they were each allowed one ruble per day for their keep (365 r. = £90 approximately) which was doubled at the request of the commandant, a bare three weeks before Novikov was released from confinement on the death of Catherine in November 1796.[35]

The traditional view of the imprisonment of Novikov[36] does not take into account Catherine's extreme sensitivity about anything to do with Paul. It is clear from Novikov's evidence that as early as 1781–2 the correspondence between Schwartz and his German superiors expressed the hope that Paul would join the order – possibly during his foreign travels in 1781. After his first visit to Paul in 1784, Bazhenov's memorandum, summarizing these same hopes, had been paraphrased by Novikov and forwarded through Schröder to Wöllner in Berlin, thus in a sense placing the operation of winning over the grand duke under Prussian direction. It was also clear from Novikov's evidence to Sheshkovsky that he had reported regularly to Schröder on his publishing programme, which he had placed under the latter's control, as well as on his Masonic spiritual exercises.[37]

Though one can scarcely speak of a Pauline party, Catherine certainly sensed the existence of a trend in Russian society opposed to her own policy and style of government, and pinning its hopes to a future tsar. Paul himself, though not averse to criticizing his mother's policies and her public and private servants, seems to have stopped short of encouraging real sedition, except perhaps in his secret contacts with the Prussian court.[38] But he cultivated his popularity by underlining his links with the traditional Russian way of life which lingered among the merchant and burgher class, reproducing that same polarization which had arisen between Peter I and Aleksey Petrovich, down to his expressed preference for Moscow over St Petersburg.[39]

There is little direct evidence of the political opinions of the Moscow Rosicrucians, though by their behaviour one can deduce that they were not interested in political change so much as in social reform by means of philanthropy. In a purely Russian context they represent a throwback to the moral standpoint of the Jansenists, an influence already perceptible in Novikov's journal *Utrenniy Svet* which published selections from classical moral philosophy, from Bacon, Grotius, Christian Wolf and above all, from Pascal.[40] The austere and high-minded Masons rejected Catherine's blatant disregard for the rules of Christian marriage, which contrasted so strikingly with the seeming domestic bliss of the Grand Duke Paul.[41] Novikov, for instance, displayed portraits of the grand ducal couple on the walls of his country house, but no mention is made in the inventory of his belongings of a portrait of the empress.[42] The Rosicrucians also sang hymns of greeting to Paul :

> In you Paul we see
> A pledge of heavenly lore.
> In your wonderful union

We read the sign of the angel.
When you are adorned with the crown
You will be our father.[43]

In so far as members of a Pauline Masonic movement can be pinpointed, one can name Paul's childhood friends, the Kurakin brothers, Nikita Panin and Peter Panin, and Admiral S. Pleshcheyev, Paul's naval adjutant. Pleshcheyev travelled in France in 1788–9, called on Saint Martin in Strasbourg, and joined the secret mystical society founded by Count Grabyansky in Avignon, which he introduced into Russia. The society went by the name 'People of God' or 'New Israel' ; it had few members in Russia, but one was Panin's nephew by marriage General Prince N. V. Repnin.[44] Was Paul a Mason ? He denied it. But he was certainly attracted to some aspects of mystical religion, possibly even to the occult. That he sensed the part his own involvement had played in Novikov's downfall is suggested by the fact that one of his first actions on his accession was to order the immediate liberation of Novikov. He also ordered all the papers in the Novikov case to be sent to him, and they were found locked in a casket in his room at his own death. On his return to the capital Novikov resumed his Masonic activities, but though he was only fifty-three, his publishing days were over.[45]

The moral opposition to Catherine and what she stood for may have enjoyed considerable support in the Church and among Old Believers. The subject has been neglected in modern scholarship. But this may explain why someone like Metropolitan Platon, in spite of his disapproval of Masonic occult literature, felt closer to Novikov and his friends than to the secular 'enlightenment' of Catherine, particularly in the educational sphere. The empress herself had been bitterly hurt when that other paladin of freemasonry, Gustavus III, had attacked her 'atheistic and idolatrous' school programme.[46] At the same time, against the background of the French Revolution, the assassination of Gustavus and the threats against her own life, the existence of a group, orchestrated by her enemies the Prussians, apparently disposing of large funds, (Novikov had debts of over 700,000 r.), inspired by Masonic tenets which could range from extreme egalitarianism to alchemical and occult 'lucubrations', apparently ready to dethrone her in the interests of Paul, may have seemed a more real threat to the ageing Catherine than can be appreciated today.[47]

There are still inexplicable features about Catherine's treatment of Novikov, notably the severity of his punishment compared to the leniency with which others among the Moscow Rosicrucians were treated, such as N. Trubetskoy, I. Lopukhin, and I. Turgenev, who were merely rusticated on their country estates. It is true that these three had not been directly involved in the effort to enlist Paul in the Masonic movement. But the architect Bazhenov, who had visited Paul on Novikov's behalf, seems also to have escaped scot-free. Perhaps the first three were let off because they belonged to the highest aristocracy, and the last because he was too lowly.[48] The eddies of the Novikov affair spread fairly widely. A number of booksellers were arrested and interrogated but they were all released with a warning. Some 20,000 copies of the mainly Masonic works confiscated when Novikov was arrested were burnt in 1793 ; the inoffensive theological works were handed over to the Zaikonospassky monastery or to the university.[49]

It has been frequently suggested that Novikov was hounded until some valid reason could be found to arrest him, in order to cut short his independent social and publishing activity. The evidence does not sustain such an interpretation. The only works he published which were ever banned were those of a Masonic character, judged harmful even by Archbishop Platon. In common with other publishers, he was forbidden to break the monopoly of the Holy Synod for the publication of religious works, and it was only the discovery of his secret correspondence with the Prussian masters of the Rosicrucians which precipitated his final downfall. But it was a sad end for one of the great figures of the Russian world of letters who left a lasting impression on those who knew him, and on those who benefited from the work of disseminating knowledge which he had so successfully undertaken.

34

The Birth of the Intelligentsia

The years from 1775 to 1787, during which Russia was at peace, mark the apogee of Catherine's reign. She herself, aged forty-six in 1775, was at the height of her powers, intellectually alive, physically vigorous and sensual, completely confident in her capacity to govern her vast empire and establish its administration on a solid bureaucratic basis. But her absorption in domestic reform and foreign policy did not lead Catherine to neglect the equally important task of leading and guiding Russian culture. She fully understood the importance of using all the arts in the furtherance of her political ascendancy, and she was in addition genuinely interested in architecture, painting and sculpture. Like her predecessors, she was a passionate builder: 'La fureur de bâtir est chose diabolique,' she wrote to Grimm in 1779 ; 'cela dévore de l'argent et plus on bâtit, plus on veut bâtir, c'est une maladie comme l'ivrognerie.'[1]

But architecture was not merely self-indulgence. It was envisaged not only in relation to the authority of the crown, as symbolized in imperial palaces and summer follies. It served also to give physical embodiment to the increasing range of functions the government was creating for, and delegating to, the towns throughout the whole country. As far back as 1762, Catherine set up a commission on the building of St Petersburg and Moscow, under Zakhar Chernyshev, I.I. Betskoy, and Prince Dashkov, which continued in being throughout her reign. Under its auspices the embankments of the Neva and the canals were faced with granite, stone bridges were built, many streets were paved. The commission also promoted and supervised the construction of handsome private and public buildings.

When, in May 1763, the town of Tver' was destroyed by fire, the commission was charged with planning its reconstruction. This was its first venture into town planning.[2] But this aspect of its work vastly increased with the Statute of 1775 which required the provision, in the newly created or 'promoted' towns, of a whole range of public buildings, a governor's palace, law courts, schools, hospitals, orphanages, a house of assembly for the nobles, etc. Town planning was conceived of rationally : areas were zoned as residential or business. The monuments of old Russia were usually preserved, but the new pattern involved large squares, broad spacious avenues, with plenty of space between the houses to reduce the risks of fire. Public buildings and churches were situated in the centre surrounded by the solid stone houses of nobles and merchants, and further out of the modest wooden homes of the poorer classes. Contemporary travellers were often impressed with the results. Miranda spoke highly of Sevsk, and particularly of the rebuilt Tver'. In Krestsy, which he regarded as well built, there was a handsome main street, with the church well placed at one end, and well lit at night, but Novgorod he found a sad and decayed city. The regulations regarding paving, lighting and sanitation issued by the commission were however well ahead of the normal standards of the Russian people, and represent an ideal Catherine hoped to achieve rather than the reality of the Russian streets.[3]

Almost from her accession Catherine had reacted against the lush baroque which Bartolomeo Rastrelli so amply provided for Elizabeth Petrovna. The architects who worked for her in St. Petersburg introduced the new classical style : A. Velten, A. Rinaldi, J.-B.M. Vallin de la Mothe and the Russians, M.F. Kazakov, I.Ye Starov and V.I. Bazhenov. Bazhenov studied in France and Italy, and distinguished himself in Russia with several magnificent designs which were never carried out. A devout Freemason, he was in his later life influenced by the desire to conciliate neo-gothic with traditional Russian styles. He worked mainly in Moscow and influenced the Russian architects engaged in building country houses for the nobility. Starov had also studied in Italy and he was responsible for the great Tauride Palace built for Prince Potemkin in 1783–8, with its magnificent central hall of columns opening on to an enormous winter garden. The closest exponents of Catherine's personal tastes were the Scot, Charles Cameron, who remodelled her private apartments in Tsarskoye Selo in the 1780s in the Adam tradition, and built the elegant palace of Pavlovsk for the Grand Duke Paul ; and Giacomo Quarenghi, the Italian, who built the Palladian Hermitage theatre for Catherine, in the style of the theatre of Vicenza, where her own plays and operas were performed.

So much building provided a tremendous fillip not only to painting and sculpture, but to the decorative arts, to cabinet making, porcelain, china, glass, mirrors, tapestries and fine clothes. The massive purchases of Catherine which laid the foundations for the magnificent Russian collections of paintings, opened up a whole new range of visual perceptions to Russian artists who had not studied abroad. Catherine bought Pierre de Croizat's collection in 1772, and doubtless with a touch of malice, that of the Duc de Choiseul in the same year. She swooped on the Houghton collection, built up by Sir Robert Walpole, when it was sold by his spendthrift heir in 1779. Many foreign painters worked in Russia in her reign including Rotari, Torelli, Lampi, Roslin, and in 1795 for a short time Mme Vigée Lebrun. The empress patronized Russian painters as well : F.S. Rokotov, D.G. Levitsky both painted her. M. Shibanov, who had been a serf of Potemkin's, painted the well-known portrait of the empress in the travelling dress she wore on the journey to the Crimea, as well as scenes of peasant life.

F.I. Shubin, the most outstanding sculptor, studied with Pigalle in Paris and with Nollekens in England, and has left portrait busts of most of the great magnates of Catherine's court. But the most remarkable single work produced in Catherine's reign was Falconet's great statue of Peter I, commissioned by Catherine, with which she boldly asserted her claim to equality with him in the lapidary phrase *Petro Primo Catharina Secunda*.

Whereas in Elizabeth's time, not even the empress had enough furniture to equip her palaces, and provincial nobles lived in austere wooden simplicity, standards of domestic elegance and comfort rose steadily among the urban nobles, officials and merchants, and began to rival those of Western Europe among the élite of the two capitals. Around St Petersburg and Moscow, magnates built summer palaces or country houses, as for instance the elegant mansion of Princess Dashkova at Kirianovo near St Petersburg, or the even more palatial dwelling near Moscow where Alexander Vorontsov enjoyed the performances of Fonvizin's plays put on by his serf actors and actresses. Bureaux, consoles, settees and sofas were imported or made in the contemporary European style by Russian craftsmen, while at the same time traditional Russian carpentry and woodwork found an expanding market. Porcelain and faience displaced wood on the tables of all but the peasantry and were made in the state factory near St Petersburg, or in that of the Englishman Francis Gardner, near Moscow.

More ephemeral arts were used by Catherine (as by her predecessors) as part of the process of winning popular acceptance of her rule. Victories and anniversaries were celebrated with pageants, triumphal arches, processions, illuminations, fireworks, food and, above all, drink. Events were dramatized, the moral pointed in symbolic representations. Like Elizabeth of England – if with less reason – Catherine was portrayed sometimes as Astraea, the just virgin of the Golden Age ; more often she was *Minerva triumphans,* both warrior and lawgiver, standing with the 'Great Instruction' in her hand. There was indeed throughout eighteenth-century Russia a belated echo of the political use of court spectacle as it had developed in the Renaissance and which reached its apogee at the court of Louis XIV.[4] Catherine consciously used spectacle in much the same way and with much the same objects as Louis XIV, and, it must be added, with much the same success.

Music continued to thrive, both as an element in court spectacles and in private society. Catherine needed composers to put her libretti to music, but the real patron was Potemkin, a man of far richer and more complex gifts than his public life attested. He tried to persuade W.A. Mozart to enter Russian service, and he succeeded in persuading Mozart's contemporary, Vicente Martin y Soler, to come to Russia. Sarti and Paisiello both worked for him. It was Sarti who set the traditional Russian Te Deum to music for Potemkin, to the accompaniment of salvoes of gunfire – a setting which Catherine much appreciated though she regretted that such an accompaniment rendered this version unsuitable for performance in church.[5]

After her initial venture into journalism in 1768–9, Catherine herself never again edited a journal, directly or indirectly, though she continued to contribute to journals published by others. The Academy of Sciences was enlivened in December 1782 when Catherine appointed a new director, none other than Princess Catherine Dashkova, the sister of Simon and Alexander Vorontsov.[6] The widowed princess, kept at a distance by Catherine for some time after the *coup d'état* of 1762, had spent many years in foreign travel, partly for her own pleasure, partly for the education of her son. A quarrelsome, mean, vain and cantankerous woman, Dashkova was nevertheless a genuinely cultivated person, with wide-ranging literary and scientific interests, many friends in the cosmopolitan intellectual world and a great deal of energy. It was a tribute to Catherine's perception and to her disregard for current prejudices, that she appointed a woman to take charge of an institution regarded as a male preserve. It was also her way of keeping a busybody busy.[7] Under Dashkova's energetic leadership the academy was galvanized into new life, however many enemies the princess made in the process.

The same confidence in Dashkova's powers was shown by Catherine when she appointed her president of the Russian Academy of Letters, founded in 1783. The Russian language still suffered from the lack of grammatical rules and precise definitions of the meaning of words. The first tasks therefore of the new academy were to produce a dictionary and a grammar. Dashkova distributed the work of preparing the dictionary among the most distinguished literary figures of the time, and the six volumes of the first academy dictionary appeared between 1789 and 1794. It was much criticized since Dashkova had adopted the etymological instead of the alphabetical order for the arrangement of words, but nevertheless it occupies an honoured place as the first attempt at classifying concepts in the Russian language.

As an offshoot of the Academy of Letters, Dashkova edited, in 1783–4, together with O.P. Kozodavlev (subsequently a leading figure in the Commission on National Schools) a magazine entitled *Sobesednik Lyubitely Russkogo Slova* ('The Companion of Lovers of Russian Literature'). Catherine contributed a regular feature, 'Facts and Fancies', to this journal. But she used it also to publish her extensive writings on what had become her major interest, Russian history.

This was a subject which had always attracted her. Providing Russia with a proper history, properly written, was part of the process of attaining equal consideration in the West. In 1766, Catherine appointed G. Müller (Miller) director of the archives of the College of Foreign Affairs, and she later appointed Prince M.M. Shcherbatov (a man for whom she had no personal sympathy) as official Russian historiographer, allowing him free access to official archives, and she purchased Shcherbatov's extensive collection of manuscripts from his heirs after his death in 1790.[8] She assisted Novikov by opening the state libraries and archives from which he drew the documents published in his *Drevnaya russkaya vivliofika*.

Catherine's own 'Notes on Russian History,' the first part of which were published in *Sobesednik,* are didactic in tone, designed to counter the biased accounts of foreign historians, and to emphasize the constructive role of Russian princes. [9] Her approach was that of an amateur, but she genuinely attempted to collect and use source materials, to distinguish myths from facts, to assess the value of evidence, to discuss different theories of early Russian development, and to provide information. She also firmly located Russia in Europe, to the extent of providing, for each period she treated, a table of contemporary Western rulers and popes, as well as patriarchs.

Catherine's interest in history was reflected in her later plays, in which incidentally, she broke new ground by abandoning the dramatic unities and openly modelling herself on Shakespeare. Her play 'From the life of Ryurik, an imitation of Shakespeare, without the dramatic unities', was published in 1788, though never performed. She drew on a mythical element in the genealogy of Ryurik (too mythical for her to include it in the 'Notes on Russian History'). [10] In this tale, Ryurik has a young first cousin, Vadim, a Slavonic prince, who raises Novgorod against the incoming Vikings under Ryurik who have been invited to bring order to the land. Ryurik (Catherine) sends an army to put down the revolt, Vadim is forgiven, and won over by Ryurik's magnanimity to become the first of his loyal subjects. [11] 'Ryurik' was followed in 1787 by two more libretti on historical subjects, set to music by court composers, and appositely enough, by an unfinished drama on the Russian Grand Prince Oleg, who led a successful assault on the Byzantine Empire in 900. In 1789, in the throes of the war with Sweden, Catherine threw herself into a veritable whirlwind of literary and historical activity, partly to dull the edge of anxiety, partly because 'since I can't occupy myself with legislation, I think I may take up history'. [12] She found relief in the composition of a comic opera, *Gorebogatyr,* to music by Martin y Soler ('Knight of Mischance' would be a fair translation), in which Gustavus III was satirized in a tedious and tasteless manner. [13] Catherine however was delighted with the success of her production in the private theatre of the Hermitage in December 1788, and was with difficulty persuaded not to allow public performances in St Petersburg until Potemkin should have expressed an opinion. When the prince did see the opera, on his return to the capital, he pronounced himself against public performance and *Gorebogatyr* was eventually shown only in Moscow where it was less likely to offend Swedish susceptibilities. [14] In 1791, Catherine dug out her play on Oleg, and it was set to music by Sarti and performed as an operatic ballet with lavish costumes. The ballet programme pointed the moral : Catherine was portrayed as the heir to Oleg in the campaign for Constantinople. [15]

Much as Catherine enjoyed writing, her role as a creative force in Russian literature is but marginal. But her constant patronage and lively interest undoubtedly encouraged the Russian drama, both comedies and tragedies, in the 1780s and 1790s. The first play, in time and in quality, was *Nedorosl'* ('The Minor') by Denis Fonvizin. It was performed, thanks to Catherine's support, in September

1782 in St Petersburg[16] and in 1783 in Moscow, and was a tremendous success in both capitals. The play dealt with two main themes : parental failure to educate children properly (the uncouth and spoilt 'minor', Mitrofan) and the gross inhumanity of primitive serf-owners towards those in their power, illustrated by the character of Prostakova, who delivers herself of the classic phrase : 'Of what use is the freedom of the nobility if we are not free to whip our serfs ?' Fonvizin himself, though hostile to Catherine and particularly to Potemkin, had still sufficient faith in the reforming power of absolute monarchs to end his play with the official sequestration of Prostakova's estates, on the grounds of her ill-treatment of her peasants, in accordance with a law enacted by Peter I, and re-enacted by Catherine in 1775 in her Statute of Local Administration.[17]

After the Police Ordinance of 1782 the censorship of printed works lay with the chiefs of police. But the local governors could and did exercise their own arbitrary judgment in the case of plays. Thus it was General Ya. Bruce, governor-general of Moscow, who halted the performance of the play *Sorena i Zamir* by the blind playwright N.M. Nikolev in 1785. In this play a pair of lovers are at the mercy of a tyrannical Russian prince. In the lovers' repeated declamations against tyranny Soviet critics have read a complete political programme (in spite of the fact that similar tirades can be found in Corneille, and Racine), contrasting Russian despotism with the free political organizations of the nomadic Polovtsians. Catherine did not see it that way. When Bruce drew her attention to the more daring remarks, she did not regard them as alluding to herself. The author, she replied, was protesting against the arbitrary behaviour of tyrants, while 'she was regarded as a mother'.[18] It was indeed during this period that translations of most of Voltaire's tragedies were published in Russia, many of them, such as *La Mort de César* and *Brutus,* by Novikov. Voltaire's 'Roman' tragedies included lengthy tirades against tyranny and in favour of freedom, but they easily passed the censorship.[19] In fact the theatre, whether as classical tragedy, bourgeois comedy, satire or comic opera, enjoyed considerable freedom, provided performances complied with the Police Ordinance and the regulations for theatres.[20]

An ukaz of profound significance in the Russian cultural scene was issued on 15 January 1783, authorizing anyone to establish a printing press, provided the police were notified of its existence, and manuscripts were submitted to the local police boards for approval. The ukaz represents the coming of age of Russian intellectual life. Thus far the government had led Russian intellectuals by the hand, educating them, providing translations for them, employing them, printing their works on government presses. Now, at last, the government recognized that intellectual and literary life had acquired its own momentum, it could stand on its own feet and look after itself ; it had become an independent and creative critical force. Printing presses sprang up all over Russia, some run by nobles on their estates, some run by kuptsy or by foreigners in the cities.[21]

The periodical press received a new lease of life as a result of this ukaz. In distant Tobol'sk, a new journal, *Irtysh prevrashchayushiisya v Ipokrenu* started up in 1789 ('The Irtysh transformed into the Hippocrene'). Among those whose efforts were unsuccessful was Fonvizin. He had resigned from government service when Nikita Panin was removed from office in summer 1781, and he travelled abroad in 1784–5. He had hoped to edit a new journal, 'Starodum or the Friend of Honest People', but at some time before 1788, the chief of police of St Petersburg forbade publication. It is clear from the materials Fonvizin had already prepared that he would be indulging in *satira na litso* or personal satire which Catherine had condemned in the 1760s. It is possible that this led her to refuse to authorize Fonvizin's new journal.[22]

But the 1780s and 1790s saw the publication of journals of all kinds, some designed purely for entertainment, others with a serious purpose. Many were short-lived, but the *genre* as such was now quite independent of government patronage and government printing presses. Among the most outstanding was the monthly *Pochta Dukhov* ('The Courier of the Spirits') edited by the young I.A. Krylov (he was barely twenty) in 1789. Of modest origins, Krylov was nevertheless not unknown. At the age of nineteen he had written a comic opera in which he cruelly mocked Knyazhnin, and his wife, herself a poet. He made many enemies, and found his path in the theatre blocked. The affiliation of *Pochta Dukhov* with the journals of the 1760–70s (nobably Emin's *Adskaya Pochta*) is clear, and it indulged in the same kind of sharp polemics with contemporary literary figures (in this case Knyazhnin), as well as in biting satire, placed in the mouths of nymphs or devils, directed both at personalities and at vices, and attacking the classic targets of Russian satire, above all the abuses of serfdom. Twenty years later Krylov was indeed producing the same type of 'anti-establishment satire' which Novikov had first launched in *Truten'* at much the same age. Even more radical and more outspoken, Krylov's journal did not last for the promised twelve issues, and ceased publication in August 1789. It is usually assumed, without adducing any evidence, that it was closed by order of Catherine. Two years later, in February 1792, Krylov published on his own press in St Petersburg a journal, *Zritel'*, ('The Spectator') which contained contributions by himself and by others, mixing original work, literary criticism and satire. The scandal surrounding the arrest of Novikov in 1792 led to an official search of Krylov's press, but he continued to publish his most biting pieces in *Zritel'* until the journal closed at the end of the year.[23] It was succeeded by the 'St Petersburg Mercury' which can scarcely be called satirical and published fewer and fewer items by Krylov. It lasted only a year, and thereafter Krylov disappears for a while from the annals of Russian literature, to reappear in the nineteenth century as the great fabulist.

One more name must be mentioned in this brief survey of the role of periodicals in the 1780s and 1790s : that of N.M. Karamzin. Born in 1766, Karamzin was educated in Moscow where he gravitated towards the Masonic circle, and edited the journal *Detskoye chteniye* ('Readings for the education of a child's heart and reason') published by Novikov, the first serial publication specially written for children, in a spirit of complete acceptance of the social and political order of the day. Diverging in 1789 from his Masonic friends, Karamzin left in May for a tour through Germany, Switzerland, France and England. Judging by what he wrote – some years later admittedly – he was not an enthusiast for revolutionary France ; nor was he very taken with England. On his return to Russia he founded the *Moskovskiy Zhurnal* ('Moscow Journal'), in 1791 in which he published his own prose and poetry, the works of others, book reviews, literary criticism, translations of foreign works. *Moskovskiy Zhurnal* achieved a *succès d'estime,* but it secured only 300 subscribers and Karamzin had to close it down after a year. Nevertheless, the journal served as a model for the great literary journals of the nineteenth century. In its pages Karamzin published his 'Letters of a Russian Traveller,' describing his foreign travels, and his famous short story 'Poor Liza', the best known example of the literature of sensibility written in a pleasing and elegant style.

One of the first and best contributors to Dashkova's *Sobesednik* (as later to Karamzin's *Moskovskiy Zhurnal*) was the greatest lyric poet of late eighteenth-century Russia, G.R. Derzhavin. The son of a poor noble, an army officer with only a few serfs, Derzhavin came up the hard way. He served for ten years as a private in the Preobrazhensky Guards Regiment, and, as a sergeant in the guards (equivalent to commissioned rank in the army), he took an active if inefficient and quarrelsome part in the suppression of the Pugachev revolt.[24] After much cultivation of favourites in antechambers, Derzhavin at last received a grant of an estate (in miserable Belorussia !) as a reward for his services in 1774–5. But having succeeded in the difficult task of alienating both General P.I. Panin and General P.S. Potemkin, he was urged to transfer to the civil administration and was appointed governor of Olonets in 1783. He got into trouble, among other reasons for failing to denounce as *lèse-majesté* the frivolous behaviour of a junior who had allowed a bear to sit on the throne reserved for the empress, or her representative the governor, and was moved to Tambov, where he got into trouble again. For a short time, in 1792, he was appointed secretary to Catherine to receive petitions, but the empress soon decided that he would do better to stick to poetry.[25]

It was Derzhavin's gay and witty ode, 'Felitsa', which he published in *Sobesednik* in 1783, which attracted Catherine's attention. 'Felitsa' was presented as a poem translated from the Arabic, addressed to the wise princess of the Kirghiz Kaysak horde, who had herself guided the steps of the tsarevich Khlor to wisdom – an allusion to Catherine's tale of the 'Search for the Rose without Thorns' written for her grandson Alexander. Derzhavin steered a perfect course between flattery and satire, so that not even the verses aimed at Potemkin and other favourites caused offence. The ode was an instant success ; Catherine was delighted, Potemkin was amused, and Derzhavin's place in Russian literature was assured.

Closer acquaintance with the court, and with Catherine herself, induced in

Derzhavin a more sceptical attitude to rulers and magnates, but he continued to write odes on important events such as the capture of Izmail. His greatest ode, 'The Waterfall', written on the death of Prince Potemkin, is an allegory of human fate, the river which throws itself into the valley, then loses itself in the depth.

Derzhavin was a genuine poet, not a politician, a courtier or a bureaucrat. Within the general framework of the classical tradition – and often outside it – he could be magniloquent or gently lyrical, satirical and witty, bucolic, amorous or patriotic. He was always conscious of the basic dignity of man and of human joys, and though he did not oppose the Russian political and social system as such, he reacted passionately against the corruption and the servility of court life. In a versification of Psalm 81, 'To rulers and judges', he attacked the unjust, and called upon God to rise and condemn the wicked rulers. The poem, originally written in 1780, was published in 1787. But by 1795 it brought down on Derzhavin the accusation of Jacobin sympathy, largely because the psalm had by then been given wide currency by the Jacobins themselves in Paris.[26] Other poets were more cautious, like V. V. Kapnist, who wrote but did not publish his 'Ode on Slavery'.[27] In 1793–4 he completed his best known play, 'Chicane', a satire on the bureaucracy which again was not published or performed until 1799.

If, under the active patronage of Catherine, Russian intellectual life became richer and more varied, it also, particularly after the ukaz permitting the setting up of private presses, became much more independent of the government, even critical of it, as a new and younger generation of writers, addressing a vastly enlarged reading public, came to the fore. This increasing independence was in part the consequence of a growing maturity and versatility in a more differentiated and pluralist society, where the leisure essential for the development of cultural pursuits was at last available, at least to the élite class. In part the new trend was also a response of educated Russians to foreign intellectual currents and to foreign political events, to the really massive programme of translations, and to the American and French Revolutions.

The French Revolution eventually awoke Catherine to the dangers for absolute monarchy implicit in much of the thought of the *philosophes* she had so greatly admired. According to Ségur, the fall of the Bastille was greeted with dismay by the court, with enthusiasm by the common people in St Petersburg. 'French, Russians, Danes, Germans, Englishmen, Dutch, all congratulated each other in the street, embraced each other, as though they had been freed from a chain too heavy to bear.'[28] It is unlikely that the full implications of the fall of the Bastille were clear to the Russian man in the street, but the emptying of a prison, any prison at any time, was likely to arouse popular enthusiasm.

In the first two years of the French Revolution a considerable amount of information about events in France was freely disseminated in the Russian periodical press and in the pages of the St Petersburg and Moscow *Gazettes,* which increased their circulation to 2,000 and 4,000 respectively. The Declaration of the

Rights of Man was published in full in the St Petersburg *Gazette* ; the speeches in and the decrees of the National Assembly were reported and a mass of revolutionary literature of all kinds and qualities circulated fairly freely.[29] The demand for the classics of the Englightenment increased enormously, and the greatly enlarged network of publishers and bookshops facilitated their distribution. The commandant of the Cadet Corps arranged a special display in its library of all the relevant revolutionary literature which was hotly debated by the young cadets. The slogans of the French Revolution found an echo in the Russian urban and commercial world and occasionally even among literate or illiterate peasants.[30] Two young Golitsyns took part in the storming of the Bastille ; a young Stroganov attended meetings of the Jacobin club in Paris with his tutor, Gilbert Romme.[31] Revolutionary songs like 'Ça ira' were sung in the presence of the empress.

Until his capture at Varennes in June 1791 Catherine could still regard Louis XVI as a free agent. But after his return to Paris, and particularly after the September massacres of 1792, the coming to power of the Jacobins, and the proclamation of the Republic, it was impossible to harbour any illusions about the revolutionary nature of the French regime and the ease with which its principles could cross frontiers. The surviving supporters of the 'aristocratic constitutionalism' of the 1760s, such as the Vorontsovs and the remnants of Panin's clientèle, could see themselves as legislators in a constitutional monarchy ; but they turned against the excesses of the Jacobins and were driven to increasingly conservative positions, Fonvizin to defend serfdom, P.S. Potemkin to turn against Rousseau, most of whose works he had translated into Russian. The younger intellectuals among the guards officers, educated nobles and the increasingly numerous class of raznochintsy active now in the professions, business, state and private bureaucracies, were a more fertile ground for revolutionary principles. Catherine's government offered them little in the way of political excitement, and the stirring events enacted in France inflamed many a heart, starting with that of Grand Duke Alexander himself.

Less resilient than in her younger days, faced with a new type of danger which none of the governments of the *ancien régime* knew how to avert, and surrounded by lesser minds than those which had shared her years of triumph, Catherine now saw dangers in the written word which she had not perceived before, and proceeded to limit the freedom of expression she had encouraged for most of her reign. Among the first to suffer was A.N. Radishchev.

The eldest of the eleven children of a wealthy landowner (with over three thousand serfs), Alexander Radishchev, born in 1749, was chosen at the age of seventeen, with five other young men, to study at Leipzig University at state expense. In spite of their ill-treatment at the hands of the totally unsuitable, brutal and corrupt Major-General Bokum, who was placed in charge of the party, the young men were provided with an excellent education, and the opportunity to study with some of the most renowned German thinkers of the day. At the same time, since they all read French, they devoured the latest Parisian productions.

In 1771 Radishchev returned to Russia, where he served first in the Senate, then on the military legal staff of General Ya. Bruce, commanding the military district of Russian Finland. During this period he was commissioned by Novikov to translate Mably's *Observations sur l'histoire de la Grèce* with its idealization of republican Sparta. In the relatively relaxed climate of the 1770s, Radishchev's personal annotations to his somewhat free translation of Mably caused not a ripple, even when he claimed that 'the injustice of the ruler gives to the people, as his judges, the same, even more rights, than the law gives to the ruler over criminals'.[32]

In 1775, Radishchev married and resigned from service. But two years later, unable to make ends meet on an income from 300 serfs, he returned to the capital to a post in the College of Commerce, where he won the friendship of Alexander Vorontsov, who was to remain his patron in the dark days to come. By 1790, he had become director of the St Petersburg Customs, in the sixth rank of the Table of Ranks.

In 1789 Radishchev, who had previously made sporadic contributions to the periodical journals, published anonymously a biography of a fellow-student in Leipzig, F. Ushakov, who had died there of syphilis. It is both a personal tribute and an intellectual biography of a young man who died as a result of self-indulgence, before he could enrich Russia with his talents. It caused no particular stir, in spite of its many tirades against despotism, war, the corruption of courts, etc. Encouraged in all likelihood by the reception of the 'Life of Ushakov', Radishchev set about printing (on a press which he bought for himself), and distributing through book sellers, his main work, 'A Journey from St Petersburg to Moscow.' It appeared in May 1790, at a critical juncture in the war with Sweden, and when Austria was about to abandon the fight against the Turks.

Modelled in outward form on Sterne's *Sentimental Journey*, Radishchev's book expresses in the language of sensibility a passionate critique of the evils man inflicts on man, including serfdom, and an equally passionate belief in the ability of man to find within himself the means – truth, justice – to achieve reform. In episodes arising at each staging post he describes the inhumanity of the recruit levy, the abuse of serf labour, the defenceless state of serf women belonging to lecherous landlords, the verdicts of corrupt judges and the sufferings of honest ones. He uses the technique of the 'bundle of papers found by accident' to produce a plan for the emancipation of the serfs, preceded by a devastating indictment of slavery in general and Russian serfdom in particular. He issued the warning : 'Do you not know . . . what destruction threatens us and in what peril we stand ?' And he went on to stress that the serfs, driven desperate by oppression, and with no glimmer of hope for the future, were merely waiting their chance to revolt. Then 'the destructive force of bestiality' would break loose, 'round about us we shall see sword and prison. Death and fiery desolation will be the meed for our harshness and inhumanity.' Radishchev openly referred to the horrors of the Pugachev revolt, in which the serfs 'had spared neither sex nor age' and 'had sought more the joy of vengeance than the benefit of broken shackles'. The danger was mounting, he warned, and the serfs would respond to the appeal of the first demagogue. . . . Realizing that 'the supreme power was not strong enough to cope with a sudden change of opinions', Radishchev proposed a gradual emancipation of the serfs. All domestic serfdom should be abolished at once, but peasants should first be granted full ownership of their private plots and then be allowed to buy their freedom for a fixed sum. Other targets of Radishchev's criticism were ranks awarded merely for court service, and censorship, even of pornography : let venal girls be censored, but not the productions of the mind, however dissolute, since no book has ever infected anyone with venereal disease.[33]

Radishchev submitted his book anonymously to the chief of police of St Petersburg in charge of censorship, who took it, after a cursory glance, to be no more than a travelogue à la Sterne, approved it, and returned it to the customs office, whence it had been submitted. Radishchev took the opportunity to add a few more passages, including a reference to the French Revolution, before printing and distributing it.

Catherine read the 'Journey' in June 1790, when she was already beginning to exercise a secret quarantine against possible French contagion. In April 1790, orders had been issued to guard against the machinations of a club set up in Paris to organize foreign propaganda. The police were told to keep a discreet watch on its possible activities in Russia and to forbid all secret meetings and conventicles of Masonic lodges and other such 'concealed and absurd gatherings'.[34] Catherine's views on Radishchev's 'Journey' can be followed in her secretary's diary and above all in her own marginal notes on her copy of the book.[35]

The empress commented adversely on Radishchev's criticism of landowners and on his emotional portrayal of the conditions of the serfs, which she utterly rejected since, in common with many Russians, including e.g. Fonvizin, she sincerely believed that 'the Russian peasants under good masters were better off than anywhere in the world'.[36] She merely noted Radishchev's proposals for emancipation, but was outraged by his warnings of the impending revenge of the serfs. She saw in him a man worse than Pugachev (whom Radishchev *had* condemned), inciting the peasants to bloody rebellion. Not only peasants, but the people in general were being roused to disregard the authority of rulers, tsars, emperors, magnates and officials, noted Catherine, and Radishchev was comparing himself to Franklin as 'the inciter to rebellion'. Here Catherine detected the 'French poison' with which Radishchev was infected and which manifested itself even more clearly in several stanzas of an Ode to Liberty which he had included in the 'Journey.' The poem was originally written in 1781–3, with reference to the American Revolution, and contained lengthy tirades against the despotism of priests and kings. Radishchev calls on the spirits of Brutus and Wilhelm Tell, and praises Cromwell by whom the 'king was brought to the block'. But Cromwell also incurs the writer's condemnation for having seized power from Charles I, and destroyed the freedom of England. On the well-known allegorical scene of the dream, in which a blind ruler is portrayed sitting in glory, surrounded by sycophantic courtiers, and is suddenly enabled to see by the pilgrim Truth the dreadful reality, the poverty and corruption, the horrors of war, where the commander-in-chief, instead of fighting, 'wallows in luxury and pleasure', Catherine merely remarked : 'The author is maliciously inclined.' It was not therefore this particularly savage denunciation of her own government and of Potemkin which aroused her anger, it was the effort to introduce French revolutionary principles into Russia : the violent overthrow of established authority and of the social order.[37]

It did not take long for Catherine to identify the author, and Radishchev was soon arrested and taken to the Peter and Paul fortress. Here he was interrogated at length by Sheshkovsky (head of the Secret Expedition of the Senate) who based many of his questions on Catherine's marginal notes. Radishchev was not, according to all the available evidence, subjected to any physical duress let alone any form of torture, though incarceration in the grim fort was in itself a terrifying enough experience.

Radishchev's answers and admissions suggest that his arrest aroused him out of a dream world into the world of reality ; he woke up to the unwisdom of the manner in which he had expressed himself, particularly in the heated atmosphere of the 1790s.[38] He declared that his main object had been the winning of literary acclaim. He denied any intention of attacking the present Russian form of government, and the Statute of 1775 in particular ; he intended only to point to certain practical shortcomings, as reported by public opinion. He had not intended to arouse peasants against landowners ; he had only wished to force bad landowners to be ashamed of their cruelty. He admitted that he hoped for the freedom of the serfs, but by means of legislative action such as that already undertaken by the empress, when she had banned the sale of serfs or the assignation of state peasants to industrial entrprises, or when she had regulated the treatment of industrial serfs, or forbidden the corporal punishment of soldiers without a court martial.

Without thus going back on the substance of what he had written, Radishchev, aware of the possible consequences to his family, did his best to minimize its consequences by admitting that his language had been exaggerated and insulting, and his accusations against government officials wild. He threw himself on Catherine's mercy. But in spite of his appeals, he was tried by the St Petersburg criminal court on charges of sedition and *lèse majesté,* and sentenced to death on 24 July 1790, a sentence which had to be passed to the Senate and the empress for confirmation. The Senate, as might be expected, confirmed the verdict on 8 August. Not until 4 September was Radishchev put out of his misery, on hearing that Catherine had commuted the death penalty, on the occasion of the peace with Sweden, to the loss of his status as a noble, and ten years' exile in Ilimsk, a remote fort in Siberia.[39] Roughly dragged away in chains almost at once, Radishchev's lot was much alleviated thanks to A.R. Vorontsov. When he informed Catherine that the condemned man was in irons, she ordered them to be removed at once ; and Vorontsov gave Radishchev a total of 500 rubles to equip him with adequate clothing and supplies.[40] He was allowed to break his journey several times – he took sixteen months to reach Ilimsk – and Vorontsov gave him an annual allowance of 500, then 800, then 1000 rubles during his exile.

Radishchev was eventually joined by his younger children, and his sister-in-law, who bore him three children in Siberia, but whom as his deceased wife's sister he could not marry. He built himself a new, commodious wooden house, into which he moved with his servants and the books with which Vorontsov supplied him. The climate was appalling, the company non-existent in a settlement of some 300 people, but Radishchev devoted himself to natural science and the study of the surrounding native peoples. By twentieth-century standards his fate was not cruel ; his exile in Ilimsk lasted only five years, and on the accession of Paul in 1796 he was allowed to return to his estates. He published no more during Catherine's lifetime, but his 'Journey,' and the harsh sentence he suffered, resounded through Russian intellectual life at the time and ever since. Though all unsold copies of his book were destroyed (only eighteen are extant), news of it spread like wildfire. It rapidly acquired black market value. Manuscript copies circulated throughout the country and it was widely, if secretly, read in educated circles in the capital and in the provinces : an eighteenth-century example of *samizdat*.

Catherine's increasing sensitivity to the portrayal of political conflict, in literature or drama, was illustrated again in 1791, when a play 'Vadim of Novgorod', by Ya. B. Knyazhnin, the author of the highly successful comic opera 'The Misfortunes from a Carriage' was produced. The play had been written in 1789, and reworked the theme Catherine herself had treated in her *Ryurik*. But while in both plays Ryurik appears as the 'foreign' enlightened, absolute monarch, the chosen of the people, Vadim was portrayed by Knyazhnin as the champion of free republican institutions, while to Catherine he was a self-centred, ambitious and even frivolous challenger of legitimate authority. The tirades of Knyazhnin's hero would have passed unnoticed in 1785, but in the heated intellectual climate of post-revolutionary Europe, Vadim's defiance of the monarchical principle incarnated in Ryurik could not be allowed to pass. Knyazhnin withdrew the play from production before he himself died in 1791. But it was published in 1793 (after it had been passed for censorship by none other than O.P. Kozodavlev, a member of the Commission for National Schools) by Princess Dashkova, both separately and in one of the issues of *Rossiyskiy teatr* ('Russian Theatre'), an anthology of Russian plays.

Catherine bitterly upbraided Dashkova for publishing 'des injures et des atrocités contre moi', and ordered the Senate to seize and destroy all copies, whether in private hands or in shops, of a work full of 'expressions directed against the sovereign authority'.[41] It proved impossible to recover all the copies of *Vadim,* which continued to be widely read. A discreet inquiry was made into Knyazhnin's unpublished works, which showed that though he was far from a revolutionary he believed, like Radishchev, that reforms should be undertaken in Russia in order to forestall too sharp a break with the past.[42]

As the excesses of the French Revolution grew more horrifying for absolute monarchs, with the trial and execution of the king and queen, and the indiscriminate massacres by the guillotine, so the climate in Russia grew more repressive. In 1793 Catherine ordered provincial governors to forbid the publication of books 'which appeared doubtful, likely to corrupt morals, concerned with the government and above all dealing with the French revolution and the execution of the French king'.[43]

The 1790s saw a number of arrests and convictions for political offences of less resonance than that of Radishchev, but just as symptomatic of the gulf which was opening up between the empress and the younger generation of intellectuals. The twenty-two-year-old Major B.R. Passek, arrested in 1794, was found in possession of a manuscript copy of Radishchev's 'Journey.' He alleged that he had read the printed version at Prince Potemkin's and therefore did not realize it was a forbidden work ! He had, he said, bought the manuscript copy for a few rubles in the market at Jassy after the prince's death. Charged with writing anti-monarchical poems, he was sentenced to serve in a Baltic provincial regiment and forbidden to visit the two capitals.[44] Some half dozen cases all told are known of the arrest of outspoken writers of memoranda or literary works, some of them young officers, who were sentenced to varying terms of imprisonment. F.V. Krechetov, an officer probably of non-noble origin, remarkable for his passionate interest in education, his appeal to women, and his opposition to war, was denounced in April 1793 by a serf for his revolutionary incitement to peasants and soldiers to overthrow the government, and for using insulting language about the empress, who 'lived a dissolute life, did not know how to govern, and used hirelings to do so, . . . and who should be deprived of the throne as a murderess and shut up in a monastery'. Her Nakaz was mere words which she had been unwilling or unable to implement ; her reforms were inspired by the need to reinforce the might of the Crown, shaken by 'Emelka' Pugachev. Krechetov's papers, and the lengthy investigation in which he openly stated his views, showed him to be an anti-clerical, Christian egalitarian republican. He admitted attempting to seduce soldiers from their oath of allegiance, and encouraging them to free the serfs. He hoped to see a revolutionary movement like the French one in Russia, leading to an assembly of representatives of the people, a new constitution, and the overthrow of the monarchy. As for the empress, 'let her sit in a cage' and watch what the revolutionaries were doing through the bars. Without a formal trial Krechetov was sentenced to imprisonment, and forbidden visitors or writing materials. He was transferred from the Peter and Paul fortress to Schlüsselburg in December 1794 ; released by Alexander I in 1801 he disappears from recorded history.[45]

Not only did Catherine take steps to repress the writers. The free flow of French revolutionary literature, indeed of all foreign literature, was dammed, and the empress now condemned the works of the Enlightenment she had done so much to propagate. Voltaire himself was consigned to the flames with the enthusiastic cooperation of General Prozorovsky, who made a bonfire of 825 copies of 67 titles in 1793–4.[46] The 'absurd' new French revolutionary calendars were banned, but clandestine sales continued unabated, and included also pictures of the execution of the French royal family, imported into or produced within Russia. Prozorovsky, and Prince N.V. Repnin, now governor-general of the Baltic provinces on the death of Browne, directed Catherine's attention also to the flood of imports of caricatures satirizing European rulers, and of symbols of the Revolution such as playing cards with portraits of revolutionary leaders. A model of a guillotine was discovered in May 1794 on board a Danish ship, and was promptly burnt. Less easy to detect was imported writing paper, already in circulation, using as a watermark the tree of liberty and the word 'Liberté'. The only way to put a stop to French revolutionary propaganda was to seal Russia's borders – and this was effectively decreed in September 1796. All imported literature now had to be checked at three points of entry : Riga, Odessa and the Polish border, where censors were established to examine all imports, and weed out and burn all politically undesirable material.[47] Even so, Radishchev could read *Père Duchesne* in distant Ilimsk, and the appeals of Jean Carr to overthrow royal despotism in favour of popular sovereignty found a ready audience in Russia.[48] The teaching of French too came under attack. Conservative opinion also found expression in a large number of works of which the generic title might be 'Voltaire unmasked'.[49]

There is no doubt that the 1790s represent the parting of the ways between the government and the intellectuals of Russia – those whom it is now permissible to term the intelligentsia. There were several reasons for the growing estrangement between Catherine and the younger writers of the 1790s. In the first place the empress herself had, with age, become less receptive to new ideas ; moreover she was surrounded now by inferior minds – a Platon Zubov for a Potemkin – who pandered to her nervous fears, and to the intellectual arrogance which had grown more marked with age and success.

Secondly, the ideas which had most strongly attracted Catherine in her prime offered patterns of modernization which could be adapted to the social and political organization of a backward and unwieldy polity like that of Russia. Montesquieu, the principal French influence on Catherine, and the German cameralists such as Bielfeld, provided Catherine with models, which she adapted in her own way in the Police Ordinance of 1782 and the Charters of 1785. Yet French thought, basically iconoclastic, served also to inspire other, more radical, political movements. Even Montesquieu, the exponent of a society grouped into estates, of absolute monarchy according to fundamental laws, or of aristocratic constitutionalism, could be used as the banner for rebellious *parlementaires,* or for constitutional monarchists. The 'constructive' thinkers of Catherine's prime were revealing by 1789 their more dangerous implications, with which the ageing empress could have no sympathy : the abolition of the legal structuring of society, social egalitarianism, the limitation of absolute power, the representation of individual opinion, as opposed to corporations, interests, or orders. Moreover, this new ideology was showing to the privileged classes of Europe, including its rulers, a particularly ugly face : the indiscriminate appetite of the Terror for young and old, men and women affected the upper classes much as Dachau or Auschwitz affected twentieth-century public opinion.

Thirdly, the nature of Russian educated society had changed considerably in the thirty years since Catherine had begun to rule Russia. Partly as a result of the policies of her predecessors, partly in consequence of her own, the court was relatively less important as the centre and focus of cultural life which was now far more diffused throughout society in both the capitals and the provinces. Though figures are not available, it is clear that by the 1790s Russian society had become far more differentiated. There were more middle-rank educated nobles and more raznochintsy ; there was a far greater variety of 'middle-class' occupations requiring literacy, indeed higher education, such as professors, teachers, doctors, architects and artists, businessmen, surveyors, technicians of various kinds, who did not fit easily into the simple Russian social pattern of warrior – merchant – cultivator of the soil. To such people, who suffered only too often from the arrogance and injustice of those who were socially superior if culturally inferior to them, the tenets of the French Revolution offered a heady and intoxicating brew. But even those, like for instance Karamzin, in whom these tenets aroused only a passing enthusiasm, began to harbour a weary distaste for the vituperative sabre-rattling which emanated from the court and government circles, and the petty persecutions indulged in by the police.

But it would be misleading to leave the Catherinian literary scene on such a negative note. It was in every respect an invigorating and creative period. The fact that the empress herself wrote, however badly, made literature and drama respectable. Her patronage was a driving force and an encouragement. The Russian theatre saw in her reign the development of indigenous comedy with Fonvizin, Kapnist and Knyazhnin ; original lyrical and elegiac poetry with Derzhavin ; a new and purer literary language with Karamzin. And apart from the major writers, a whole school of novelists, ranging from the sentimental to the social, of satirists, poets and Ossianic bards, and of journalists flourished with varying and intermittent public acclaim. Many of the writers of the 1780s and 1790s survived into the freer climate of Alexander I's earlier years and paved the way for the literary explosion of nineteenth-century Russia.

35

Social and Economic Changes 1775–96

The second Turkish war, Poland and the French Revolution absorbed Catherine's declining energies in the last nine years of her reign to the almost total exclusion of major domestic reform. The postponement of many plans existing in draft may have reflected Catherine's awareness of the need for Russian society to assimilate the very substantial amount of legislation enacted in previous years and which was still being implemented. It took twenty years for the Statute of 1775 to be applied throughout Russia ; the General Land Survey rumbled on into the nineteenth century. The inadequacies in the drafting of many laws, notably the two Charters of 1785, meant that Catherine was frequently concerned with their interpretation. She was also kept constantly busy with petitions, proving herself more willing than her predecessors to deal with those addressed directly to her. After Vyazemsky's retirement in 1792, procedure in the Senate slackened. But Catherine examined all criminal cases referred to it, and repeatedly ordered the Senate to re-examine or speed up its decisions. In all, it is estimated that the Senate dealt with some 120–150,000 cases during Catherine's thirty-four year reign, of which 11,456 were still undecided at her death, i.e. slightly more than one year's intake. But the growing backlog is not merely an indication of a declining attention to duty. It reflects the increase in cases coming up from the much larger number of government instances set up during her reign. The empress did what she could to speed matters up ; in summer 1792 she threatened to deprive senators of their month's holiday in the summer if a given case was not decided by then, and in 1794, she actually deprived the second Department of the Senate of its summer leave.[1] But judging by the accounts of contemporaries, even of those well disposed to Catherine, the slackening of central control was reflected not only in civil life but in the army too. Bribery was rife, and fortunes were made out of the sums allotted for regimental keep.[2]

During Catherine's long reign Russian society changed a great deal. Peter I's reforms were still working their way through its various levels in ever widening circles, when they were overtaken by the second great wave of reforms initiated by Catherine herself. Apart from changes resulting from the conscious effort to remodel the social structure from above, economic developments and closer commercial integration and political cooperation with the rest of Europe were contributing to the emergence of an infinitely more complex society. The legal differentiation between estates was being slowly whittled away, but economic, social and cultural differentiation between estates and within estates increased enormously, accompanied by a substantial growth in population and the formation of new functional subgroups.

The years 1786–96 saw a striking expansion of the Russian economy in spite of the war. This was partly the result of the colonization of the lands in the south and the annexation of the Crimea ; it was also the result of the General Land Survey which led to the purchase or renting of so much new land in central Russia, and a striking increase in the sown area. In the guberniya of Moscow it rose by 60 per cent thanks to the proximity of the Moscow market. In the Central Industrial Region, the North West Commercial/Industrial Region and Tula guberniya, it rose by 30–40 per cent in the 1780s and by 5–20 per cent in the 1790s. It doubled in Pskov guberniya (which supplied St Petersburg) and increased by 90 per cent in St Petersburg guberniya. In the Central Agricultural Region, the average rise was between 60 and 100 per cent ; in Ufa up to 120 per cent, in Saratov, 100 per cent.[3] Indeed the shortage and high prices which prevailed in Moscow in 1787 were due in great part to the expansion of the agricultural market, and not to harvest failures which were rare in the eighteenth century, and occurred more often in the recently acquired lands than in the old heartlands of Russia.

The leaders in this agricultural expansion were the landowners, or at any rate those with enough labour and access to capital. The proportion of their estates reserved for demesne production for the market, by obrok or barshchina, grew, and whereas in the 1750s landowners had been primarily concerned with the better exploitation of their serfs, they now showed an increasing interest in improved methods of cultivation, new machinery and better seed.[4]

The search for increased income and the direct exploitation of the estate by the owner led to a gradual swing away from obrok to barshchina, particularly intensive in the period 1780–90. It could take the form, in distilleries, brick kilns, sawmills, etc. of *mesyashchina,* removing the peasant from the land and putting him on whole-time work in the enterprise for his keep. This form of labour was regarded as particularly oppressive, since barshchina was still (except at harvest time) normally held to three days a week. Barshchina had now on the surface become more profitable than obrok, though it required more – and more expensive – organization.[5]

Where obrok was in use, landowners raised it considerably in the last twenty years of the century. In the 1780s the average was 3–5r. rising at times to 10r. ; in the 1790s the average was 5r. rising to 20r. per tyaglo. The rise reflected in part the decline in the value of money ; but the increase in agricultural prices stimulated production and hence the sale of grain. Yet in spite of the interest shown by landowners in maximizing their agricultural income, and in spite of the really large amount of vacant land brought under the plough, at the end of the century, landowners held 18 per cent of the land in the Black Earth areas and the peasants 72 per cent. It was not until the nineteenth century that the landowners pushed back peasant ownership to 51 per cent.[6]

One consequence of increased agricultural exploitation was increasing peasant unrest. Though it never reached the proportions of the revolts of the 1760s and the Pugachevshchina, peasants rioted from time to time, usually against specific local grievances such as the change from obrok to barshchina or the introduction of manufactories on the estates. The most violent and persistent outbreaks occurred in 1797, after Catherine's death, spreading over some thirty-four gubernii of European Russia. They were a manifestation of resentment at economic exploitation, but they also fit into the peasant pattern of expectation of better things from a new ruler.[7]

A second consequence of agricultural expansion was the growing economic differentiation within the peasantry, both among serfs and state peasants. The nature of agriculture was such that a strong family unit would grow steadily richer, while the incompetent or unlucky sank into the position of landless labourers. What remains extremely difficult to assess is the standard of living of the Russian peasantry, in absolute and comparative terms, and bearing in mind differences of climate and soil fertility.

The discomforts of the wooden *izba* or peasant hut (available in prefabricated form on the outskirts of many villages at 24 r.)[8] was a cultural rather than an economic fact. Peasants lived in close proximity with their animals during the long, dark winter ; dirt, stench, fleas and smoke were a perpetual accompaniment to this huddled existence, in which a large part of the interior might be taken up by a stove, and of the rest by a loom. The judgments of foreign travellers, forced to sleep overnight in peasant huts, vary considerably according to their countries of origin and the areas of Russia they visited. Chappe d'Auteroche's grim picture of Siberian peasants (illustrated by the titillating, highly artificial drawings of Le Prince) is contested by Gilbert Romme, the future Jacobin, who travelled in Siberia in the 1780s. In his eyes, the Siberian peasant, though unfree, lived better and had more land than the French peasant near Versailles.[9] The South American Miranda, who travelled from Kherson to Moscow and hence to St Petersburg, was sometimes shocked at the dirt, sometimes surprised at the spaciousness and cleanliness of peasant huts, particularly in Northern Russia. His standard of comparison was his native Venezuela, Spain or Italy.[10] John Parkinson, travelling from Perm' to Tobol'sk in the 1790s, was frequently critical, but one cottage 'would have been no disgrace to Norway'. Moving down the Volga towards Astrakhan', Parkinson was struck by 'the goodness and neatness' of the people's best clothes, and contrasted them favourably with the 'rags and tatters of the populace in Italy'.[11] Sundays and the many religious holidays provided occasions for the people to wear their festive costumes, elaborately embroidered and hung with gold coins.

The Russian peasant diet of *kasha,* rye bread, sausage, cabbage and cucumber, enlivened by berries and mushrooms, wildfowl and sometimes other game, and coarse pressed caviar during the long religious fasts, was undoubtedly monotonous, but it was healthy. In some parts of the country, notably the Ukraine, 'pears, apples and plumbs' could be bought for one kopek for fifty, and melons and water melons were one kopek each, wrote Maria Guthrie in 1795–6.[12] It seems that in many parts of Russia all but the very poorest peasants fed well enough in normal times, even if they lived in squalor.

Food is not all. Infantile mortality was very high and led to a custom much frowned on by the Church, namely the marriage of small boys to nubile girls who gave birth to several children by their fathers-in-law before their own marriage was consummated.

Life for the Russian peasant was undoubtedly hard, in many cases miserable. Field work during the short agricultural season was long and back-breaking. But the picture of Russian serf life as one of grinding oppression punctuated by the rise and fall of the knut is distorted. There were occasional local food shortages and much distress, but never the nation-wide famines familiar in the nineteenth and twentieth centuries. There were cruel landlords, but most of them, most of the time, behaved with a rational appreciation of their own self-interest.

The records of the Sheremet'yev estate at Ivanovo show that in twenty years, from 1790 to 1809, 109 people out of a population of 9,204 were punished for a total of 851 offences, the most frequent by far being drunkenness. Corporal punishment was inflicted 407 times, oral reprimands 277 times. Other cases were dealt with by fines, 3 days on bread and water, etc.[13] Moreover the brutal punishments inflicted on serfs (or peasants, soldiers, even priests) have to be seen in the context of the times.

Catherine herself was one of the earliest critics of the array of instruments of punishment to be found in the great houses in Moscow.[14] And it is essential in order to give a balanced interpretation of her attitude to serfdom, to rescue from oblivion those legal barriers to the process of enserfment in Russia which she introduced. Until her reign the various methods of enserfment included the poll-tax census, which could more or less accidentally register a man as a serf to a particular person; taking in orphans or illegitimate children who could be enserfed to those who fostered them; the enserfment of prisoners of war; marriage to a serf; assignment of supernumerary priests or Church servants as serfs. All these means of enserfment were gradually stopped, as occasion arose, by legislation. As early as 1763, the rules for the foundling homes ensured that their inmates should be and should remain free. By 1767 it was forbidden for foster parents to enserf illegitimate children. In 1781 the enserfment of prisoners of war, whatever their religion, was prohibited. It also became the practice that the marriage of a free man to a serf woman freed the serf woman (sometimes for a payment) and in some cases, if a free woman married a serf, she freed her husband.[15]

The most specific enactment prohibiting enserfment was a clause in the manifesto celebrating the end of the first Turkish war on 17 March 1775.[16] The manifesto is of considerable importance in the history of human rights in Russia, since before it was issued there was no general legal protection of the individual against the vagaries of the poll-tax census. Russian nineteenth-century historians have frequently condemned this law as purely negative in scope ; it prevented enserfment but did nothing to promote freedom. However since as many as 830,151 free men were arbitrarily enserfed by census-takers between the first and second censuses in 1721 and 1741, by being registered to owners, the manifesto may well have helped to stop a sizable hole.[17] Even Catherine's critics admit that in practice she decided 'doubtful cases in favour of freedom',[18] and by enforcing the limitation of ownership on serfs to hereditary nobles, she reduced the numbers entitled to own them.

The manifesto of 17 March 1775 is important in another respect. Until then, the status of an emancipated serf was not clear in law. Freed domestic serf servants could merge into the townspeople (meshchane, or raznochintsy). But a free peasant on private land was an anomaly, and the manifesto laid down that he must at once choose a new 'status', as a state peasant or a townsman, since he must be registered somewhere to ensure payment of the poll-tax.

A freed serf, however, could not own agricultural land as an individual, isolated from his commune, since this was a privilege reserved to the nobility. Thus it continued to be impossible to emancipate an individual peasant with land. Nor in the existing state of the law was it possible to emancipate a whole village with land. Catherine has never been given the credit for the original proposal put forward in the Project for the Rights of the Nobles in the Legislative Commission in 1767, allowing them to set up 'free villages', i.e. communities of free peasants with the right of ownership or use of land. The details of the plan remain obscure. What was to be the relationship between the landowners and the free village ? Was it to parallel that between the state and the state peasant? Or was it to be a purely commercial relation, the peasants paying rent to the landowner and the poll-tax to the state ? As a *ballon d'essai* it failed and was buried under the first Turkish war and the Pugachev revolt. But it may be the source of the Law of Free Cultivators enacted in 1803 which enabled landowners to free whole villages with land by agreement with the peasants.[19]

Catherine's personal commitment to the ideas of the Enlightenment has often been brushed aside as hypocrisy because she did little to alleviate the lot of the peasants, let alone emancipate them, and because she 'introduced' serfdom into Little Russia in 1783. Indeed throughout her reign, the ukaz of 22 August 1767,[20] originally introduced as a temporary measure and which prohibited all complaints against landowners, remained unrepealed.[21] Yet in Catherine's memoirs there is a genuine expression of deep concern at the ill-treatment of domestic serfs, accompanied by a most revealing comment on the lack of support her initiatives in favour of the serfs received at the Legislative Commission in 1767–8.

'A peine ose-t-on dire qu'ils [the serfs] sont hommes comme nous, et quand je le dis moi-même, c'est au risque de me voir jeter des pierres [stones were indeed thrown at the Palace in Moscow in 1767 and much alarmed Catherine] ; que n'aye-je pas eüe à souffrir de la voix d'un public insensé et cruel, lorsque dans la Commission des Loix on commença à agiter quelque question relative à cet objet, et que le vulgaire noble, dont le nombre étoit infiniment plus grand que ne l'aurois jamais osé supposer, parce que j'estimois trop les gens qui m'entouroient journellement commença à se douter que ces questions pourroient amener quelque amélioration dans l'état présent des cultivateurs! . . .

Even the kindest of men, Count A.S. Stroganov, continued Catherine, 'defended the cause of servitude with passion and fury. There were not twenty people at that time, who thought on that subject like human beings.'[22]

Catherine's words illustrate the extent of her disillusionment when she first met the mass of Russian nobles instead of the élite which normally surrounded her at court. She was far too realistic a ruler to ignore the opinion of the dominant social estate. But one may speculate on what steps she might have taken had the Pugachev revolt not pushed the problem of public order into the forefront, in a system in which the only agents the government could employ were nobles. For she used the Statute of Local Administration of 1775 to introduce some protection for serfs against ill-treatment by landowners. Governors-general were empowered, for the first time, to prosecute landowners charged with cruelty or oppression, and their estates could be removed from them and run by the local boards of guardians.[23] Some such prosecutions are known, but the treatment of complaints by serfs against landowners after the promulgation of the Statute of 1775 has not been studied.[24] Behind the scenes, Catherine continued to try to influence noble behaviour, and she is known to have arranged to buy out landowners reputed to ill-treat their serfs.[25]

Contrary to what is frequently asserted, Catherine did not convert large numbers of state peasants into privately-owned serfs by making grants of settled land to her favourites and high officials. The 400,000-odd male serfs she is known to have granted throughout her reign came mainly from lands annexed from Poland. Some 192,000 were given away in Belorussia, between 1772 and 1795.[26] Between 1795 and Catherine's death in November 1796 grants totalling 121,580 male souls were made in the lands acquired in the second and third partitions of Poland. Thus of the total of 400,000 male souls distributed, some 314,220 came from ex-Polish territories ; 34,401 came from the Baltic provinces, and Little Russia, and 60,000 from other sources.[27]

Catherine had given up the attempt to introduce a 'Charter to the Free Rural Dwellers' (i.e. the state peasants), parallel to the Charters to the Nobility and the Towns, but she intervened in a decisive way in the economic organization of the peasantry in north and northeastern Russia. Starting from local complaints of shortage of land in the guberniya of Olonets, emanating from the poorer peasants, the governor recommended a redistribution of all land in the communes, regardless of ownership, purchase or lease, to ensure that all peasants had enough to pay their taxes. The wealthier peasants protested loudly at what seemed an unjust confiscation of the product of their labour, but the government supported the governor's view that the equalization of land-holdings was essential to equalize the burden of taxes. The measure was introduced in the guberniya of Olonets and Archangel in the 1780s and 1790s, though it affected only land subject to the control of the commune, not land acquired by the peasant on his own account. Government policy provided yet one more example of the coincidence of the peasant sense of justice with the state's need for revenue at the expense of the economic enterprise of the individual.[28]

The second half of Catherine's reign also saw significant changes in the estate of the townspeople. The easier climate following on the Statute of 1775 led to a large influx of state peasants into the towns. A barrier to this uncontrolled influx was established in 1782 when it was decreed that incoming peasants would have to pay the poll-tax in their village of origin as well as in the towns until the next census.[29] But immigration from the country continued, and the towns also grew as more nobles built houses and settled in country towns.[30] By the end of the century the town population is variously estimated to have risen to 4·1 per cent of the taxable population or 7·5 per cent (according to one authority even 8·3 per cent) of the total population of the country.[31] Within the towns, the registered kuptsy and meshchane came to about 35 per cent of the actual inhabitants of a town ; nobles, priests and officials made up 7·5 per cent, peasants some 32 per cent and raznochintsy, retired soldiers, etc., 25 per cent.[32]

Within the ranks of the strictly trading class, the kuptsy, wealth was being increasingly concentrated in a small group at the top. In St Petersburg in the 1780s 3·7 percent of the kuptsy owned over a quarter of the total number of shops ; the ennobled Savva Yakovlev owned 9 per cent,[33] while at least 2,000 peasants, trading on their own, owned shops in the name of kuptsy. This proliferation originated with an ukaz of 8 June 1782 which authorised kuptsy to open shops in their own houses, instead of concentrating all trade as previously in the *gostinnyye dvory* or large-scale covered bazaars.[34] The differentiation in wealth was facilitated by the gradual raising from 500 r. in 1775 to 2,000 r. in 1794 of the capital necessary to become a member of the third and lowest guild, which forced small-scale businesses down into the ranks of the meshchanstvo.

With the Statute of Local Administration of 1775, the Police Ordinance of 1782 and the Charter to the Towns, some of the burdens previously borne by town-dwellers as unpaid agents of the government were shifted either to paid elected functionaries or to the treasury chambers and police boards. But economic rewards for achievement were not enough to satisfy merchant aspirations, since they could not take forms which raised human dignity. Merchants who had made fortunes sought social recognition too: the right to wear swords, to ride in carriages, to be freed from humiliating personal services, above all from the recruit levy (with service as a common soldier) and corporal punishment. These aspirations were recognized by Catherine. She favoured ennobling rich merchants, for 'un marchand trop riche est dans le commerce comme une sangsue'.[35] By creating the social group of the 'eminent citizens', abolishing corporal punishment for the urban élite, and allowing its members to purchase immunity from the recruit levy, and ennobling a number of them, she reduced the cultural gap which separated the rich merchant class from the court nobility.

It was the noble estate which underwent the greatest change in the thirty-four years of Catherine's rule, in terms of numbers, and social role. The Russian nobility in Russia proper numbered 84,066 in 1782 and 111,600 in 1795. The increase in the number of Russian nobles was partly due to natural growth, partly to the extension of noble rights to Cossack and Tartar officers, partly to the freedom with which noble rank was granted by Potemkin to promoters of settlement in New Russia. To these figures must be added nobles in the lands acquired from Poland at the partitions, totalling some 250,974 by 1795, or 66·22 per cent of the total number of nobles in the Russian Empire.[36]

There is little information about the distribution of wealth in this new nobility. But judging by the situation in the early nineteenth century nearly half of the total noble estate was composed of personal nobles, i.e. officers and officials who had been promoted, but who were not allowed to own land with serfs, and whose children were not nobles. As a result of this vast influx of personal nobles, the estate as a whole became much less homogeneous. At the bottom end there developed a new social group, legally noble, yet making a living by employment in the armed forces, the bureaucracy, business, education, medicine, journalism, translation, the Academies, etc., and merging imperceptibly with the class of raznochintsy, or men without a *chin*, to which, if they were only personal nobles, their children would belong. This essentially urban group of landless personal nobles, and poor hereditary nobles, played no part, except as salaried employees, either in the elective local institutions established in 1785, or in the Noble Assemblies. These bodies became more clearly than before the preserve of people who were both nobles *and* landowners with an official *chin* and an income ranging from 100 r. to tens of thousands.

At the other extreme, the great magnates grew steadily richer, since they were the principal beneficiaries of imperial generosity, and were in a position to exploit their agricultural and industrial wealth effectively. They had also, as in France or England, learnt the art of living with huge debts. They were responsible for the enrichment of the countryside and the two capitals with handsome and well furnished buildings, and showed more of a social conscience than they are usually credited with in their patronage of private charity (schools, hospitals, etc.). Many of them hankered after a political power which would reflect their social and economic status, and envied the British peerage above all (the fate of the French aristocracy was too dreadful to contemplate). The man most deeply

→ aristocratic constitutionalism .

imbued with these notions, S.R. Vorontsov, spent most of his time as ambassador to England, and could only watch helplessly from a distance while Potemkin swamped his cherished noble estate with promoted officers and officials.[37]

How deep was the cultural gulf which now began to separate the Russian nobles from their peasantry and from the meshchantstvo? It is generally assumed that the nobility was totally alien in speech (French), clothing (uniform), and culture (cosmopolitan) from the common people. The great magnates doubtless receded into a distant horizon of stone palaces, gardens in the English manner, pavilions, follies and serf theatres,[38] though it is difficult to conceive of a Potemkin, an Aleksey Orlov or a Suvorov as unable to communicate with the common man. But the assumption of a total cultural incomprehension exaggerates the extent of the assimilation of Western culture by the nobility. The court spoke French of course in the presence of foreigners. But most of Catherine's private and official correspondence with Russians is in Russian, and it is fair to assume that Russian was still spoken more frequently than French. Most of the nobles were too poor to spend money on any but the most basic requirements and the rural nobles at any rate were closely linked to peasant language and values in their childhood. S.T. Aksakov's description of his grandfather does not suggest that he was more than a peasant writ large.[39]

All classes of society, but above all the noble and urban élite, benefited somewhat from the gradual softening of manners and the elimination of the worst excesses from the treatment of those convicted or merely accused of crime. Such a trend had already emerged under Peter III, with the abolition of the Secret Chancery, and modifications in the corporal punishment of soldiers and sailors.[40]

Catherine's reign saw developments in three directions : the attempt to define crime ; the almost total elimination of torture ; and the definition and regulation of punishment including the reduction of corporal punishment, particularly for women. It is under Catherine that the concept of crime, not merely as failure to obey the will of the ruler (governor, director of a factory), but as failure to comply with the law, was first introduced though it took a long time for it to spread through the law courts and society.

As early as December 1762 Catherine issued secret orders that torture was to be used very sparingly in order not to let the innocent suffer.[41] As she became more confident she came further into the open, and in Chapter x of her Great Instruction, published in summer 1767, torture was roundly condemned. In an ukaz of 13 November 1767 Catherine ordered that the principles of her Instruction should be followed, and forbade the application of torture, even where it was allowed by law, without reference to the local governors. It was used in the repression of the Pugachev revolt, with Catherine's reluctant consent,[42] but several ukazy prohibited torture in the armed forces, culminating in an ukaz of 1 January 1782, which again ordered the principles of the Great Instruction to be followed, and forbade torture in military and naval courts without reference to the Colleges of War and Admiralty respectively.[43] The frequent amnesties, notably in 1775, 1787 and 1794, also freed convicts from that part of their sentence. On the other hand nostril clipping and branding continued as part of normal penal policy, and in the army, the fearsome punishment of running the gauntlet.[44]

The most defenceless category of all, the serfs, remained at the mercy of their landowners ; their only protection, and it was not very reliable, was the gradual refinement of manners, heart and feeling among the more educated nobles. But the actual power of landowners to inflict punishment or to give vent to sadistic impulses remained unchecked by law. Only if cruelty to serfs created a public scandal or resulted in death were cases punished.

It was of course one thing to ban torture, brutality in the armed forces, or corporal punishment in schools, by law, it was quite another to enforce this ban, given the general level of civilization of Russian officialdom. Many even among the highest officials in the land failed to grasp the meaning of legality. A case in point is narrated by the Freemason I. V. Lopukhin, who was a judge in the Moscow criminal court. It was well known that fifty strokes of the knut amounted to a death sentence[45] – hence Lopukhin, knowing that there was no death penalty in Russia, invariably gave a lesser sentence. He was harshly rebuked by General Ya. Bruce, the governor-general of Moscow, who argued that in heinous crimes, even though there was no legal death penalty, Lopukhin should pass such a sentence as to ensure that death would follow. After long arguments, Lopukhin finally persuaded Bruce that he was bound to apply the law as it stood, and Bruce ceased to interfere with his sentences.[46] A.P. Mel'gunov, when governor of Yaroslavl', also attempted to enforce obedience to the provisions of the law : he fined the local judges of the criminal court because they had sentenced a criminal to corporal punishment in 1787, contrary to the provisions of the manifesto of 28 June 1787 of that year, issued on the twenty-fifth anniversary of Catherine's accession, and which granted an amnesty for many crimes, and commuted all pending sentences of corporal punishment.[47] The extent to which the concept of the primacy of law was alien to Russian political culture is well illustrated by the episode in A. Radishchev's 'A Journey from St Petersburg to Moscow,' in which the judge 'puts away his law books' and acquits a serf of murdering a landowner because he was morally justified.[48] If the highest officials in the realm could show such a singular failure to appreciate the *meaning* of law, it is not surprising that lower down the scale disregard of its niceties was widespread. In general, the lower the court, the harsher the penalties to which people were sentenced.[49]

The movement towards a more humane approach in penal practice, prisons, schools, hospitals, workhouses, etc. has been studied by two impartial observers, Archdeacon W. Coxe, who travelled in Russia in 1778, and John Howard, who died in Kherson in 1792. They do not suggest that Russia was either better or worse than the many other countries they visited. Some prisons were overcrowded, stuffy, dirty and offensive, others less so. In Kronstadt when Howard visited it, there were 155 prisoners, comprising 'slaves indebted to the government', malefactors, and 117 peasants sent by their lords (i.e. under the ukaz of 1 January 1765 authorizing serfs to be sent to hard labour in admiralty establishments). According to Admiral Samuel Greig, convicts were allotted 3 r.p.a. for clothing, which seemed adequate, and 2 k. per day for food (2 k. could buy 3 lb 10 oz of coarse bread). Elsewhere Coxe saw prisoners guilty of 'great crimes' chained to logs, or with irons round their necks. In the main Moscow prison, which had room for 800, there were only 97 when Coxe visited it, a convoy of 248 having just been sent to Siberia. The prisoners seemed to Coxe reasonably well fed ; peasants were allowed to enter the outer courtyard and sell bread and kvass to the inmates. Gaol-fever was unknown, partly because the prisons had open yards and baths, partly because of the diet. In 1788 in the main St Petersburg prison there were 133 prisoners, including 14 nobles and officials, 17 raznochintsy, 14 kuptsy and meshchane, 27 peasants and servants, 33 debtors and 7 women. For a large city the numbers are not overwhelming. Miranda, also an indefatigable visitor of prisons, found 41 men and 55 women in the St Petersburg House of Correction in 1787, while in the workhouse there were 139 men and 39 women, working off their sentences at the rate of 5 kopeks a day.[50]

Prison reform of course attracted Catherine. John Howard's ideas were known in Russia in the 1780s, and they were popularized in 1791, in the first law journal ever published there entitled 'Theatre of study of the law or readings for judges and all lovers of jurisprudence. . . .' In its fourth issue the journal published long quotations from Howard's description of English prisons and his proposals for their reform. The empress herself, some time after 1775, drafted a plan for prison reform, in her usual meticulous detail, dividing the convicted from those awaiting trial, men from women, criminals from debtors. Article 41 of the draft laid on the prison administration the duty of informing prisoners within three days of the offences with which they were charged.[51] Some of the provisions of this draft were eventually carried out in the new prison erected in Moscow after 1775, which Howard visited, notably the separation of the convicted from those awaiting trial and of men and women. Howard also visited the elegant House of Correction constructed in St Petersburg in 1781. Elsewhere however Russian prisons continued to fall well below the level of the capital, notably in forced labour prisons such as Rogervik which could hold up to a thousand convicts.

The security organ was the so-called 'Secret Expedition' in the Senate which had taken over from the Secret Chancery when it was abolished in 1762, and which had also taken over S.I. Sheshkovsky, who eventually became its head. Descended from an ennobled official, Sheshkovsky had served in the security organs since the age of sixteen, and was reputed to be a skilled interrogator. The Secret Expedition held its sessions in the Peter and Paul fortress in St Petersburg and in the Lubyanka prison in Moscow.

There is very little evidence of how this institution operated and how many people passed through its hands.[52] Sheshkovsky played a part in the Mirovich affair, in that of Metropolitan Arseniy of Rostov, and subsequently in the interrogation of Pugachev, of Radishchev and of Novikov. Was torture used? One of the nineteenth-century historians of the Secret Expedition states that under Catherine none of the tortures in use under Elizabeth and Anna were used, but there was 'coercion' (*pristrastiye*), i.e. whipping and caning.[53] This is confirmed by a report by A.A. Vyazemsky of the interrogation of a drunken soldier in 1778, who had declared that Peter III was alive in the Crimean steppes. 'Coercion has been used', he wrote, but 'not as before, not torture, only a beating'. In none of the cases of nobles and officials interrogated by Sheshkovsky is physical, as distinct from moral violence, known to have been used. If it had been, there is no doubt that direct evidence would have survived, particularly in the case of highly placed victims such as Radishchev. Most of the tales about Sheshkovsky start with the words 'they say' or 'there is a tradition'. Even the case of young Baroness Elmpt, allegedly delivered over to him for a whipping because of some scurrilous cartoons about the empress, her officials and her favourites, is unsubstantiated.[54]

Obviously it was the court élite, the high officials, the wealthy, who benefited from the more gentle climate and the gradual emergence of a new concept of legality in the relations between the state and the people and the different kinds of people. Wider circles would profit from Catherine's efforts to improve hygiene and sanitation, reduce the risk of fire and industrial pollution and improve drainage. Hospitals and apothecaries were set up, and centres in which inoculation against smallpox was dispensed. At first parents were paid to bring in their children. Subsequently the practice was introduced into the national schools. A 'smallpox' house was set up in Kazan' in 1771, in Irkutsk in 1772 and dealt with 15,500 in five years. The wealthy were usually inoculated at home.[55]

Some of the hospitals were visited by Coxe and Howard who provide interesting and sometimes surprising comments. Howard inspected the Paul and Catherine hospitals in Moscow and 'wished the same attention to cleanliness' were given in English hospitals. Coxe was even more enthusiastic. He describes a ward, 'neatly papered', with nine beds with linen curtains. Each patient was allowed a linen bedgown, a glass tumbler, and there was a small table between each bed with a little bell on it. This description corresponds in almost every particular with the plan laid down by Catherine in the Statute of Local Administration of 1775. There were 150–200 patients in the Catherine Hospital, 52 in the Paul Hospital. Both were 'fine institutions', more like private houses than hospitals, wrote Coxe.[56] The two hospitals were clearly unique, models for others to follow. Other hospitals did not live up to these standards, except for the lying-in hospital, attached to the Foundling Home.

The total transformation of the social habits and the physical environment of a society is a slow process. In the thirty-five years of Catherine's reign the Russian educated population had moved closer to the general patterns of European ways of life by a combination of economic development, functional differentiation, and Western cultural penetration ; above all however, there was the constant direction given from above, encouraging the new ideas and new manners to spread in ever widening circles downwards through society, and providing, where possible, many of the necessary facilities and external manifestations of a new, more humane approach to individual human beings.

Epilogue

The disappearance of Potemkin in October 1791 was like the fall of a mighty oak, leaving a vast gap both in Catherine's public life and in her private life. For seventeen years he had dominated the Russian scene, and had inevitably become the target of the envy, even the hatred, of those he had displaced, of those who had not benefited from his patronage and of those who resented his arrogant assumption of omnipotence. Increasingly, as they both grew older, Catherine treated Potemkin as a prince consort. When he arrived in the capital, in winter 1789, she called on him publicly in order to emphasize his status. The following note is typical of their private relationship. 'I would come to you but I hear you are being shaved and the archbishop's with you.' The roads were specially lit up for him, royal escorts were provided wherever he went. His requests for money were almost always met, and Catherine had just given him in 1790 the new Tauride palace built by the Russian architect Starov. Contemporaries rarely if ever put into words the supposition that the two were married. But the jaundiced Saxon envoy, Helbig, remarked that their relationship was shrouded in mystery. 'One cannot discern how far the empress and Prince Potemkin act together, or differ in their views.'[1]

Platon Zubov, in his old age, once burst out against the Prince: 'Though I won a semi-victory over him, I could not remove him from my path ; and it was essential to remove him, because the empress always met his wishes half-way, and simply feared him as though he were an exacting husband. She loved only me but she often pointed to Potemkin as an example for me to follow. It is his fault too that I am not twice as rich as I am.'[2]

Potemkin's ambitions, for instance to become king of Poland, were matters of common gossip. Nikita Panin had long ago taken the credit of preventing him from securing the Polish crown in 1775.[3] But Potemkin's own words are rarely quoted. All the more interesting therefore is the brief snatch of dialogue reported by the Prince de Ligne in 1788 : 'I will make you hospodar of Moldavia and Walachia,' said de Ligne to the prince. 'Je me moque bien de cela,' replied Potemkin. 'Je parie que je serai roi de Pologne si je le voulais ; j'ai refusé d'être duc de Courlande ; *je suis bien plus que tout cela.'* (Author's italics.)[4] Did he mean that he was emperor consort ? He behaved like one, and the people 'saw in him their ruler'.[5]

It was doubtless Catherine's dependence on Potemkin as consort *de facto* if not *de jure* which explains the self-confidence, and indeed arrogance, with which he acted, and the hatred and distrust he inspired. But he provided Catherine with the unconditional devotion she needed, and he made her laugh. He was larger than life, and it is a tribute to his overpowering personality that so many legends grew up around him. Many, like the British envoy, James Harris, the Comte de Ségur or the Prince de Ligne, fell victim to his charm. A man of wide knowledge, he was more than anyone at Catherine's court familiar with the native roots of Russian culture in Church Slavonic and Greek, and he was less touched by the intellectual aridities of the Enlightenment. But he was hated by those he had superseded or dislodged from power, the Panins, the Chernyshevs, the Orlovs.

The emotions he aroused in his lifetime have clouded subsequent historiography and prevented an objective judgment of his services to Russia. Only recently has his work as governor-general of New Russia been studied in his own papers, and a more positive estimate of his role in developing previously unsettled lands been given.[6] Similarly, Potemkin, unlike Suvorov, or Rumyantsev, still awaits his military biographer. He has been charged with laziness, dilatoriness, the invention of enemies where none existed – though never with personal cowardice.[7] Failure to take him seriously as a soldier has led historians to overlook the fact that he was the first modern Russian general to command not just one army but several theatres of war, ranging from the Danubian Principalities and Bessarabia, to the Crimea and the Caucasus, and with the additional task of integrating the operations of the Black Sea fleet (which he had created) into overall Russian strategy and acting jointly with an ally, Austria. His task was much more complex than that of Rumyantsev in the first Turkish war, who commanded one army only, in Moldavia.

In addition Potemkin had to defend territories which were now Russian (Crimea) from Turkish seaborne attacks, and to govern the large areas of New Russia of which he was viceroy. Furthermore, in the first Turkish war, Russia had for most of the time no fear of an attack in the rear. Only in 1771–2 did Austria seem briefly to threaten, and she was held in check by the Russo-Prussian alliance and bought off by the partition of Poland. But in the second war, from 1788 onwards, Russian military operations had always to be conducted with an eye to the threatening situation in the rear. These diplomatic pressures on the commander-in-chief escaped the notice of the censorious Russian and foreign experts. As a commander in the field, Potemkin certainly preferred to force the surrender of Turkish forts by overwhelming numbers in order to avoid bloodshed. Not for him the butchery of Izmail. As a military administrator his correspondence reflects a constant care for the welfare of the soldiers, and contemporary accounts suggest that his armies were well supplied. He was in general loved by the soldiers, who praised him 'because they don't beat us on exercises as they used to, and they don't worry about superfluous cleanliness'. The officers were less enthusiastic about the uniforms of coarse cloth which meant that they could not be distinguished from the lower ranks. On the other hand the occupied territories, Bessarabia and Moldavia, were ruthlessly exploited, and anxious only to see the back of the Russian armed forces.[8]

One of the ways in which Potemkin can be justifiably charged with exercising a nefarious influence on Catherine and her court was in encouraging, by his example, the outrageous luxury which marked the last years of her reign. The expenses of the war, the partition of Poland, and the deepening financial crisis had no effect on the balls, court spectacles and masquerades, the regular entertainments provided by the empress herself and by her leading and wealthier courtiers at which Potemkin might appear 'resplendissant comme une gloire'.[9] The feast which Potemkin himself gave in his new palace on 28 April 1791, to celebrate the birthday of the empress, has been described so often that few details need be given here. Three thousand guests were invited, minuets were danced by the Grand Dukes Alexander and Constantine, plays were performed in the vast palace, with its covered winter garden, fountains and statues. Catherine stayed until two in the morning, contrary to her usual practice, and when she finally bade her host farewell, Potemkin fell on his knees before her and both were moved to tears.

The striking nature of this scene and the death of Potemkin six months later have led many subsequent writers to read a fond and emotional farewell into it. They have seen an empress, weary of her great favourite, yet still touched by his attentions to her ; a favourite, aware that he had failed to win his mistress away from her young lover. Such an interpretation is pure hindsight. Catherine and Potemkin were both easily moved to tears. His beautiful feast was a heartfelt answer to her endless generosity towards him, an expression of his love and gratitude. But politics came first for both of them, and Potemkin stayed in the capital until he knew that Russia was safe from the Triple Alliance and until policy towards Poland had been agreed. When he left for the south, neither the empress nor the prince expected that they would never meet again, and his position as president of the College of War and principal counsellor of Catherine remained unshaken.

This explains the shock of his death. When Catherine received the news, coming after reports that he was better, she was overwhelmed, and had to be bled. 'How can I replace Potemkin,' she wailed to her secretary. 'It won't be the same. Who would have thought that Chernyshev and other old men would outlive him ? Yes, I am old. He was a real nobleman, an intelligent man, he did not betray me, he could not be bought.'[10] Though government had to continue, social life was suspended. Court receptions at the Hermitage, and even Catherine's small private parties, attended by fifteen to twenty people, were abandoned. The empress wept when the peace treaty with Turkey was put into her hands on 6/17

January 1792 ; there were no public rejoicings beyond a salute of 101 guns, and prayers were said privately in the palace. Catherine angrily waved aside all toasts at dinner. At the beginning of February, A.N. Samoylov, Potemkin's nephew, arrived with the Turkish ratification ; all present were dismissed, and Catherine remained alone to cry with him.[11]

The death of Potemkin totally altered the power structure in St Petersburg, and led to a regrouping of the various factions. He had been the mainspring for so long, the ultimate authority, under the empress, that the government was left in some disarray. In the next two or three years, new figures emerged to share out his inheritance, but independently of his death there was a considerable renewal of personnel owing to the death or retirement of many of Catherine's long-serving high officials. Ivan Orlov died in 1791 ; so did General Ya. Bruce and Potemkin's cousin M.S. Potemkin ; A.A. Vyazemsky died in January 1793 and in September A.N. Samoylov was appointed to replace him, though without his financial responsibilities. Of all those who had been close to Catherine on the great day in June 1762, only Kyrill Razumovsky, Fyodor Baryatynsky and Aleksey Orlov survived. Catherine was surrounded by newer and younger faces.

The great men of her prime had not always agreed with each other and with Potemkin. But a division of labour between the principal figures and their membership of the Council had given a great deal of stability to the process of government. From 1781 onwards, though I.A. Osterman, as vice-chancellor, continued in nominal charge of the College of Foreign Affairs, A.A. Bezborodko, as the senior member, was the dominant figure in foreign policy. Vyazemsky had dealt with home affairs, A.R. Vorontsov with trade and Potemkin with the armed forces and the new lands. Vorontsov opposed Potemkin on principle, but was bound by close ties of friendship with A.A. Bezborodko and P.V. Zavadovsky (education and banking), while Vyazemsky was suspected of supporting Potemkin.

The young Platon Zubov (he was twenty-four in 1791) had been used by Catherine, as she used his predecessors, as a channel for requests and petitions, but he had almost at once begun to intrigue not only against Potemkin but also against Bezborodko – so much so that Bezborodko positively welcomed Potemkin's return to court in March 1791. But when he left for Jassy to conclude the peace treaty, Bezborodko left the way open for Zubov. At first Catherine seems mainly to have wanted to confide in the young man, to have someone always to hand with whom to discuss government problems. But she soon endeavoured to make a silk purse out of a sow's ear, and began to train the *dura-leyushka* (little fool), as Khrapovitsky called him, in statecraft.[12]

The difficulties which the young, incompetent and inexperienced Zubov met were alleviated by his alliance with Arkadiy Ivanovich Morkov, Bezborodko's junior in the College of Foreign Affairs. These two were joined for a while by V.S. Popov, who had been head of Potemkin's chancery, and now put himself forward as the custodian of the prince's political last will and testament. If anyone dared to query any aspect of past administration, he would report to the empress that Potemkin was being maligned, and an embargo would promptly be placed on any further discussion.[13]

Bezborodko had, until then, been almost indispensable. Efficient, prompt in the despatch of business (though in nothing else), he was notorious for an outstanding memory and he shared with Potemkin a unique mastery of the Russian language. He could reduce a chaotic mass of papers to a clear summary, and draft ukazy correctly. Never a favourite in the technical sense (he was a gross man with a reputation for somewhat sordid alliances and a penchant for low company), he was not a man of original political convictions like N.I. Panin, or Potemkin, but an excellent executor of Catherine's intentions. Catherine trusted him, and liked him better than the stand-offish Vorontsovs. (Simon Vorontsov could still in 1796 speak of the day when Catherine seized power and he was briefly arrested as 'le jour horrible', 'l'abominable jour de la révolution même'.)[14] He now found that he was expected to pay his court to young Zubov. Matters of foreign policy ceased to come before the Council but were decided by the cabal of Zubov and Morkov. The hopes which he, Alexander Vorontsov, and N.I. Saltykov had harboured, of taking over Potemkin's gubernii, had been frustrated when Catherine entrusted them at first to Popov under her own direction. Bezborodko began to speak of retiring, while Alexander Vorontsov went on prolonged leave in July 1792.[15]

The rapid rise of Zubov is the measure of Catherine's own decline. Pushed from behind at first by N.I. Saltykov (who got the College of War on Potemkin's death), with whom the young Zubov's father was closely connected, the favourite brought with him the usual cohort of greedy relations. One brother married Suvorov's niece, another a daughter of A.A. Vyazemsky. The youngest, Valerian, was much loved by Catherine, to the extent that gossip averred that he shared her favours. This is not however consonant with Catherine's sexual psychology, whereas a warm and admiring affection for a handsome and bold youth was typical of her. A sister of Zubov's, married to A.A. Zherebtsov, became the mistress of the English envoy, Charles Whitworth.

Platon unfortunately lacked the intelligence and good breeding to carry off the unusual situation with a high hand. He was a young man of limited education and attainments whose ambitions swelled as he climbed higher. Guided by N.I. Saltykov and A.I. Morkov, he succeeded in mastering some of the administrative techniques of Catherine's government, and became in rapid succession grand master of the Ordnance, governor-general of New Russia and Crimea, a senator, knight of many Russian orders and finally prince of the Holy Roman Empire. He was also notorious for his passion for money. He boasted that he was responsible for giving Russia fertile inhabited lands (in Poland, of which he had his fair share), while Potemkin had endowed her only with fever-ridden deserts. The great magnates of the land found it necessary to attend Zubov's levées and wait upon his caprices ; the future Marshal Kutuzov would pour out his coffee and carry it to him as he lay in bed.[16] What had been tolerable in a Potemkin became insupportable in a young man who was only twenty-nine when Catherine died, and who surrounded himself with second-rate minds.

Some of the acerbity in the memoirs written about this period must be discounted, because their authors belonged to a much younger generation (e.g. Rostopchin, Grand Duke Alexander himself) who had never known Catherine in her heyday, and who in any circumstances would have felt the desire for something new which affects the young and ambitious at the end of a long reign. Potemkin too was not spared by them. But Zubov inflicted far greater damage on Catherine's prestige than Potemkin ever had. The prince had reached the rank of lieutenant-general in army service and on the battlefields before he became favourite. The ten years which separated him from Catherine acquired less significance as they both grew older. By the time of his death, Potemkin, middle-aged, stout and hypochondriacal, was a great man in his own right. Hated he may have been by the court. But it is possible that his presence by Catherine's side was a stabilizing fact in the nation at large. He satisfied in part the Russian desire to be ruled by a man, and he knew how to talk to the common people with that mixture of authority, joviality and kindness which could win their allegiance. Zubov, young, lightweight and arrogant, and thirty years younger than Catherine, could only tarnish her reputation.

Marriage and maternity had provided Catherine with but few joys, but grandmotherhood made up for it in full measure and she proved a delightful companion to all small children. S.N. Glinka described how, when Catherine visited Belorussia in 1780, his father, the local land captain, presented his children. Catherine took one of them on her knee and he began to play with the sash of her order, and exclaimed : 'Granny, give me the star !' Catherine replied : 'One day you will have your own sash and star,' and promptly entered him in the Cadet Corps. She had frequently visited the Cadet Corps with Grigory Orlov, when her son Aleksey Bobrinsky was a pupil. In later years some twenty of the smaller children were invited each Sunday to play with her own grandchildren. Catherine would join in the games, and again, when one boy's suspenders broke, she sat him on her knee, retied them, kissed him and gave him a bag of sweets.[17]

The empress had removed her two eldest grandchildren from their parents at birth, and took a passionate interest in their upbringing. She explained her methods, in which she took great pride, to Baron Grimm. The children were to have a simple, spartan life : plenty of fresh air, loose clothing (Catherine invented a special one-piece garment of which she sent the design to Gustavus III when she heard he was setting up his nursery),[18] good plain food, plenty of play. They slept on flat beds with leather mattresses, not in cradles. The temperature of the room was kept at 14–15 degrees, and no more than two candles could be lit at a time to keep the air fresh. A balustrade prevented people from approaching too near the infant grand princes. The babies were bathed every day, in cold water as soon as they were old enough. In every way in fact their upbringing differed from that inflicted on Paul by the Empress Elizabeth. If Alexander's wet nurse was a Russian, he was provided with an English nanny (perhaps the first in Russia) who had Catherine's full confidence. Constantine was given a Greek nurse, to prepare him for his future destiny as ruler in Constantinople.[19]

In spite of her many occupations Catherine always found time to play with her favourite grandson and to teach him his letters. Her delight in him can be followed in her letters to Baron Grimm. She wrote fairy stories, moral tales and tales from Russian history for the children – indeed she was probably the first person to write secular educational works specifically for children in Russia, works which were of course published and available to a generation of Russian children. The influence of *Emile* can be perceived in the encouragement given to the children to play mechanical games (she asked Grimm to send her a 'printing machine with plenty of letters' for Alexander) and to till their own little gardens and grow their vegetables.

In 1783, Catherine appointed General N.I. Saltykov as tutor to the grand princes. His role was that of N.I. Panin in Paul's youth, and the appointment was above all made because he was a skilful courtier, acceptable to Paul, and a master at manoeuvring between the court factions. Catherine provided Saltykov with a long instruction setting out the educational principles he was to follow, most of which would be endorsed by contemporary paediatricians. The document is typical of Catherine's pedantic attention to detail, and reflects her particular interest in education in the early 1780s. Education was not merely instruction. The children were to be encouraged by firmness and kindness to be truthful, stoical and courageous.[20]

It was Baron Grimm who brought to Catherine's attention the Swiss pedagogue, César de la Harpe, whom she put in charge of the actual instruction of the grand dukes. From the purely personal point of view, a better choice could not have been made. La Harpe's Swiss republican virtue rendered him immune to corruption by a court, and his genuine gifts as a teacher won him Alexander's respect and affection and the trust of Catherine II. Also typical was Catherine's choice of religious instructor for her grandsons, namely A.A. Samborsky, who had been sent to study agronomy in England, married a Miss Fielding, and became chaplain to the Russian Embassy in London. He was allowed by Catherine to shave and wear secular dress, as a result of which the purity of his Orthodoxy was suspect to the conservative hierarchy. The Metropolitan of Novgorod refused to conduct services with him ; he had heard that the people believed that the harvest had failed because Samborsky did not wear a beard, and accused him of starting a new heresy.[21]

The four daughters who followed Alexander and Constantine into the world were left to the care of their parents, but the fate of the two eldest boys was a matter of constant strife between the empress and the grand ducal couple. Catherine had planned to take the two boys with her to the Crimea in 1787, because she did not wish to leave them in Paul's guardianship. This proposal was the subject of acrimonious dispute with Paul and Maria, who were remaining behind. Catherine consoled them in her usual ironical tone with the thought that the presence of their younger children would assuage their grief at the absence of the two elder ones. Her own plans were frustrated however when the two boys went down with measles.[22]

It was not surprising that Catherine should refuse to allow her son to join her on the Crimean voyage. 'Die schwere Bagage'[23] ('the heavy luggage') as she unkindly described the couple to Grimm would have cast a blanket of gloomy disapproval over what was essentially Potemkin's show, and Paul could be trusted to take offence at every fancied slight. On the outbreak of war, in September 1787, Paul asked to join the army as a volunteer, 'Voilà un embarras de plus pour vous que je serai enchantée de vous épargner,' wrote Catherine to Potemkin and at first she refused. When Paul returned to the charge, she gave in, but was then delighted to seize on the pretext of the grand duchess's pregnancy to rescind her permission on the grounds that Paul might jeopardize a precious Romanov life if he deserted his wife at this moment.[24] About to depart again, in June 1788, after the birth of his fourth daughter, Paul was detained by the outbreak of war with Sweden.

Catherine was more willing to allow Paul to visit the Swedish front and Paul left on 1 July 1788. His stay was short. He quarrelled with the commander-in-chief, Count V.P. Musin Pushkin ; he was horrified to find that the hastily assembled forces in Finland did not live up to the parade-ground standards of Gatchina, and he was not allowed to discuss military operations. By mid-September, when the troops went into winter quarters, Paul was back in the capital. He never went to the war again.[25]

On her return from the Crimea Catherine began to think seriously of disinheriting Paul and passing the succession straight to Alexander, then only eleven years old. In law she was perfectly entitled to name her own successor, and one day she read out to her secretary a passage from the 'Law of the Monarch's will', the document which justified Peter I when he disinherited his son Aleksey Petrovich. She drew attention to the 'false opinion' which Peter I too had disclaimed, that the throne must go to the eldest son, and sent for the ukazy in which her predecessors had settled the succession. On another occasion, she justified Peter I's treatment of Aleksey, since he was ungrateful, disobedient, and incapable, he listened to flattery and 'nothing pleased him more than criticisms of his glorious father'.[26] It is perfectly probable that Catherine knew something – by means of intercepts – of Paul's almost treasonable relations with Frederick William II through the Prussian envoy Baron Keller. Paul made it perfectly clear that he resented the *coup d'état* of 1762. 'Ce n'est pas à moi de juger si ce qu'on a fait il y a vingt-quatre ans était juste. . . . Que ceux qui ont agi alors interrogent leur conscience ; je ne veux pas me brouiller avec la mienne.' He expressed his disapproval of Catherine's policies, and remarked on the extent of his popularity in Moscow, and the uneasiness it aroused in the empress.[27] However, in spite of the opinion current among some diplomats that Paul might, if his own safety required it, or if he was urged by the general desire of the people, lead a movement against the empress,[28] in fact he never contemplated translating words into deeds.

But he was afraid of being disinherited. In 1788, when he believed he was leaving for the army, he dictated a will instructing his wife to secure the empress's papers at once in the event of her death in order to ensure that no testament of Catherine's should affect his claim to the throne. In the meantime Paul wrote many drafts of a law of succession for Russia, abrogating Peter I's disastrous introduction of the free choice of heir in favour of hereditary succession in the eldest son and the almost total exclusion of women from the throne of Russia.[29]

The deficiencies of Catherine's system of education of her grandchildren was revealed to all but the doting grandmother when they were in their teens. Adolescents normally go through a phase of revolt against their parents. Catherine had usurped the role of the parents and the revolt was directed against her. The warm, almost stifling, affection she surrounded them with, the high expectations and great demands she made of them led them secretly to seek refuge from her overwhelming femininity in the masculine world of their father. At Gatchina, strict etiquette and punctuality reigned instead of informality and ease. But both boys enjoyed the military drill, the 'paradomania', the opportunity to learn the arts of warfare.

But it also became evident as Alexander grew older that he began to repudiate his grandmother's private and public conduct. Implicit in much of La Harpe's teaching, with its strong emphasis on private and public morality, was a condemnation of political absolutism, favouritism and all it implied, and of Catherine's totally amoral foreign policy.[30] Republican austerity was a standing reproach to the luxury and license of Catherine's court. The empress herself presented a glaring example of the divergence between theory and practice as she carefully expounded the merits of the French constitution of 1791 to her grandson.

Torn between his father and his grandmother, Alexander soon learned to adapt himself to the company he was in, to conceal his thoughts and feelings under a protective covering. He listened to, and agreed with, his father's diatribes against Catherine's past and present domestic and foreign policies, then, back at court, he concurred with all Catherine's views. Above all however Alexander grew to hate and despise the system of favouritism, and more particularly Platon Zubov himself. He detested the accumulation of power in unworthy hands, and the corrupt use which the Zubovs made of it. He despised the courtiers who flocked to Platon Zubov's antechamber and waited on the young man for favours, and he grew to despise the grandmother who allowed all this to happen.[31] Catherine never realized the extent to which her idolized grandson wanted to escape from her influence. With Constantine, Catherine's methods were even more of a failure. There was in him that same underlying streak of violence, and in Constantine's case even brutality, as in Paul (a confirmation perhaps of true Romanov descent from Peter I through Peter III) which none of his tutors was able to tame. He could express himself with shocking coarseness about his grandmother and her lovers.

Anxiety about the future of the dynasty led Catherine to a decision which placed a further strain on her beloved grandson. Reverting to her own experience as a fourteen-year-old bride, she saw nothing unnatural in providing Alexander with a wife when he was barely fifteen, in the hope of strengthening his position as heir apparent. After the usual inspection of the minor German courts, Catherine's choice fell upon the princesses of Baden, Luise and Frederika, who were despatched to Russia in October 1792 on a visit, the purpose of which was well understood by all. Princess Luise proved to be a charming, well-mannered child, and Alexander was eventually induced to admit that he felt some admiration for her. In January 1793 Luise accepted Orthodoxy and became the Grand Duchess Elizabeth Alekseyevna on her betrothal, and the wedding took place in September 1793. The groom was fifteen, the bride fourteen. They were both far too young in every way for the responsibilities of marriage. Elizabeth was a shy, romantic girl who fell deeply in love with the handsome young prince, while Alexander was incapable as yet of living at the emotional altitudes inhabited by Elizabeth, and responding to her need for tenderness. He was still more at home in the masculine company of Gatchina and had little time for sentimental delicacy. The young couple enjoyed the balls and gay pastimes of Catherine's court ; they offended the staid and elderly by their unconventionality, and Alexander hid even from Catherine an incipient trend towards dandyism which manifested itself in cravats tied so high that he could not trim his beard. Their situation became very difficult when Platon Zubov developed a passion for the grand duchess which required her to manoeuvre with great care amid the pitfalls of the court. And unfortunately for the grand duchess, she produced no heir.

Meanwhile Paul's behaviour had become increasingly eccentric. His previously unclouded marriage was now overshadowed by his infatuation with one of his wife's maids of honour, a plain, but evidently witty and attractive woman, Catherine Nelidova. Paul's insistence that all the members of his court should show her greater deference than to the grand duchess split the already small circle of his friends, and aroused Maria Fyodorovna to furious jealousy. Nelidova refused to become Paul's mistress, and the prospect of a new Madame de Maintenon could only be strengthened when the favourite asked for permission to retire to the Smol'nyy Convent for Noble Girls where she had herself been educated, and whence she continued to dominate the grand duke. When Paul, during one of his periodic fits of sulking, refused to attend Alexander's wedding, Maria Fyodorovna put her pride in her pocket and appealed to Nelidova to persuade him to behave.[32]

Paul's attitude to the French Revolution was more extreme than Catherine's. He had been worked upon by French émigrés, notably Count Esterhazy, the agent of the royal family, who convinced him of the need to rule with a rod of iron. He saw Jacobins everywhere. The slightest failure to comply with an order, however absurd, was interpreted as Jacobin insubordination. Pantaloons and round hats (as distinct from the tricorne) were banned from Gatchina – allegedly as the costume of the sansculottes. To Catherine Paul preached the need to dispel revolutionary talk with a few broadsides – to which the empress replied that if he tried to fight ideas with guns his reign would be short.[33]

The obsessive fear of being disinherited contributed powerfully to the perpetual state of tension of Paul's already unbalanced temperament, while Catherine in turn feared that if Paul inherited the throne her whole political system would be changed and Russia would become 'a Prussian province'.[34] The wedding of Alexander, which seemed to imply, if not a legal majority, at least a greater degree of maturity, gave Catherine the opportunity to sound out opinion at court, and above all to sound out Alexander himself. The instrument Catherine chose, with this latter purpose in mind, was none other than La Harpe. He was summoned in October 1793 to an audience with the empress, during which, for two hours, Catherine tried to make La Harpe agree to talk to Alexander, without actually saying it in so many words. All her wiles failed to breach his solid republican virtue. He refused to admit that he understood what she asked of him ; but he had understood only too well, and he also realized that should any plot to disinherit Paul fail he, as the foreigner suspected of Jacobinism, would be cast for the role of scapegoat. A year later, La Harpe was released from his post in circumstances which implied his dismissal, but he did not in fact leave Russia until he had visited Paul and given him some sound advice on how to treat his sons and trust in their loyalty to him. It is ironic that Paul subsequently deprived La Harpe of his pension.[35]

La Harpe's account of this incident suggests that a number of people were in the empress's confidence, but the evidence is very tenuous and indirect. According to one account, Catherine raised the question of the succession in the Council in 1794. All the members agreed to exclude Paul from the throne except Count V.P. Musin Pushkin (regarded by Paul as a bitter enemy !) or, in another version A.A. Bezborodko who argued that it would be dangerous to interfere with the succession after Paul had for so long been treated as heir apparent.[36]

Catherine seems to have tried again in summer 1796. According to a much later, and somewhat garbled account, she attempted to secure Maria Fyodorovna's signature to a document pressing Paul to give up his rights. The grand duchess indignantly refused, but Paul found the document among Catherine's papers after her death, and was furious that his wife had been consulted and had concealed it from him.[37]

Catherine, in her prime, was able to get through an astonishing amount of work. An early riser, her day began at 5 a.m. (as she grew older she got up at 6), when she rose and lit the fire in her stove herself in order not to disturb her servants. She then settled down to reading and writing, downing several cups of strong black coffee. At 9 o'clock she put aside her pen, and received government officials, read or listened to their reports, signed ukazy, granted audiences, until 1 p.m., when she retired to dress for dinner (served at 2 p.m. since the outbreak of the Swedish war in 1788). She did not indulge in long and complicated levées, but dressed in the privacy of her room, and only appeared in the 'public' dressing room for the final touches to be given to her toilette : the placing of a lace or lawn cap, adorned with diamonds, on her lightly powdered hair. Since she had put on weight, at informal meetings she usually wore a loose silk gown ; but she had prescribed as formal court dress the old style Russian boyar lady's gown (to the fury of those who followed French fashions), which also hung loose from the shoulders.

Except on fast days, when she dined in private, there were usually anything between ten and twenty guests, belonging to the highest ranks or to the small circle of Catherine's closest personal friends which included some foreigners, notably Miranda, during his stay. The empress was not particular about food, the guests were accustomed to the spartan and poorly prepared meals served at the imperial table, and frequently adjourned to the apartments of the favourite or of other courtiers resident in the palaces, who maintained an open table. Catherine was also abstemious, and only at the end of her life did she take an occasional glass of Madeira on medical advice.

After dinner Catherine read, or was read to while she sewed or embroidered ; or she entertained special distinguished visitors, such as Diderot or Grimm. Then back to work with her secretaries, listening to dispatches or reports. An hour or two would perhaps be spent playing with her grandchildren. Then, at 6 p.m., if there was a court reception, she would 'circle' among her guests in her various drawing rooms in the Winter Palace, then sit down to cards with her courtiers or some chosen foreign diplomats. Supper would be served, but Catherine never partook of it, and at 10 p.m. she withdrew to her own rooms. When there was no official court reception, Catherine entertained those who had the entrée in the Hermitage, her own favourite winter residence, adjacent to the Winter Palace. Here all formality was banned and it was forbidden to rise when 'Matushka' stood up. There were pictures and engravings to examine ; the company might indulge in games, cards, charades, or there might be a concert or a performance of a French or Russian play.

In her younger days, Catherine had frequently accepted invitations to the town or country houses of her friends. She even attended public masquerades, and was not above dressing and behaving like a man. On one occasion, she pursued a young woman with her attentions to the extent that her victim rounded on her and, to her annoyance, snatched off her mask. Sir James Harris's sister Gertrude saw her at a masquerade at court in 1778 : she was 'very fine in a Venetian domino and Hat ornamented with diamonds, the loupe composed of a single row of large ones and an prodigious fine one for the button. She looked well but so like a man, I did not at first distinguish her from the foreign ministers, Prince Potemkin and other men she was at Macao with.'[38]

As she grew older, Catherine kept more to her own palaces. She spent the winter in the Winter Palace in St Petersburg. After Potemkin's death she spent a few weeks in spring and autumn in the Tauride Palace which she had repurchased from his estate, and the summer in her favourite dwelling at Tsarskoye Selo, in the suite of rooms decorated for her in cool classical style by Charles Cameron, who had also designed a special ramp to ease her descent to the park. Life in Tsarskoye Selo was particularly informal and gay. The young grand dukes, and after their respective marriages, their wives, provided entertainment in the form of concerts (Alexander played the violin) and theatricals. Paul and Maria Fyodorovna spent the summer at Pavlovsk and cast no shadow on the informality of Catherine's court. Inevitably political and amorous intrigue provided a counterpoint to the smiling surface, as courtiers manoeuvred to gain favour with the empress or the favourite.[39]

A feature of Russian eighteenth-century absolutism was the lack of barriers between the public and the imperial family. Imperial palaces and parks, in the capital and in the countryside, were open to the 'decently' dressed public. In court masquerades, as Gertrude Harris described in 1778 :

In the salon d'Appolon and the two rooms before, the bourgeoisie and other people of a lower class dance. The Empress, and other of her servants were dancing in masquerade habits in these apartments, we went into the gallery to view the Coup d'Oeil from thence, here all sorts of people seem'd to be admitted but they were very quiet and civil.[40]

Miranda too describes an entertainment in Pavlovsk at which at least six thousand people who had come out from the capital were dancing or promenading, including many respectable kuptsy wearing traditional Russian costume.[41] The park at Tsarskoye Selo was open to the public. One day, Catherine was seated on a bench with her faithful personal maid after their early morning walk. A man passed by, glanced contemptuously at the two elderly ladies, and failing to recognize the empress, walked on whistling as he went. To her indignant maid Catherine merely remarked : 'What do you expect, Maria Savichna, twenty years ago this would not have happened. We have grown old. It is our fault.'[42]

The strains of the years 1787–91, when Catherine had suffered the personal shock of her betrayal by Dmitriyev Mamonov, had heard the Swedish guns rattle the windows in St Petersburg, had held out alone against the blackmail of the Triple Alliance, and had finally lost her greatest support in life, Potemkin, had told on her health. She had always had a tendency to headaches and nervous indigestion and she now suffered from frequent colics, colds and rheumatism. She had grown so stout as to find climbing stairs exhausting, and by summer 1796 she was suffering from open sores on her legs. Though small, she was very impressive on public occasions in spite of her bulk, holding her head high, both gracious and dignified. In private she still charmed all those who met her by the simplicity of her manner and the vivacity of her mind.

The hopes which Catherine had once entertained of a marriage between her eldest granddaughter Alexandra Pavlovna, and the young king, Gustav Adolf IV, seemed to vanish when the regent started negotiating a marriage alliance with a princess of Mecklenburg Schwerin which culminated in a public announcement in November 1795. At the same time, in June 1795 Sweden had recognized the French Republic ; she followed this up with a treaty of alliance, by which Republican France resumed the traditional French policy of paying subsidies to Sweden.[43] Catherine was by now so bitterly offended with Sweden that she utterly refused to receive the Swedish envoy sent to announce the engagement of the young king.

Nevertheless the empress was still determined to force through the Swedish marriage of her granddaughter which, by linking the two reigning houses, might wean Sweden from hopes of revenge, and at the same time reduce the threat to St Petersburg from Swedish forces in Finland. A series of threatening troop movements in Livonia and Russian Finland, carried out in March 1796, served her purpose. By the beginning of April the regent had agreed to postpone the marriage of the King of Sweden until his majority – the first step in breaking the Mecklenburg entanglement. On 15/24 August, the second stage was embarked on : the young king and his uncle arrived on a visit to St Petersburg, incognito, under the names of Count Haga and Count Vasa.

Impressed by the charms of the young Grand Duchess Alexandra, Gustav Adolf, who was chafing at his uncle's policy, soon declared himself to Catherine. While ball followed ball, and Gustavus was seen to whisper sweet nothings in Alexandra's ear, negotiations for the marriage and the Russo-Swedish alliance which it would entail began. The question of the right of the grand duchess to practise her religion as Queen of Sweden was considered by the Russin negotiators as solved in accordance with the agreements reached earlier in abortive negotiations in 1794, which stated that no obstacle would be placed in her way.

Catherine has left her own account of subsequent events ; the king had at first made difficulties over the religion of his future queen, but on 2/13 September, he had assured Catherine that he had been convinced by the arguments put before him that there was no objection to Alexandra continuing in the Orthodox faith. Catherine thereupon proposed to hold the Orthodox betrothal ceremony on 8/19 September 1796 before a ball to be given in the Tauride Palace. Only the two families and the plenipotentiaries were to be present, and they met at 12 noon to sign the treaty first. It was then discovered that the clause on religion was missing from the text. Gustav Adolf IV had apparently removed it, in order to discuss the matter further with the empress. During the long hours that followed, Catherine made several attempts to persuade Gustav to agree to a clause promising the grand duchess the right to practise her religion. He refused utterly to go beyond the formula 'que Madame la Grande Duchesse ne serait jamais geneé dans sa conscience en ce qui regarde la religion, . . .' By 10 p.m. Catherine and the grand duke agreed to announce that the empress was not feeling well and that the betrothal was to be postponed.[44]

On the following morning Catherine briefly saw the regent, who was in despair, and the king, who was as 'stiff as a ramrod', and kept on repeating : 'Ce que j'ai écrit, je l'ai écrit – je ne change jamais ce que j'ai écrit.' He was, said Catherine, rude, obstinate and opinionated. After an hour they withdrew, the regent in tears.[45] That night there was a formal court ball given by the Grand Duke Alexander. Since the court was in mourning for the Queen of Portugal, Catherine appeared in deep black which was most unusual for she usually wore grey mourning. She was pale and looked as though she had not slept. To the grand duchess's lady-in-waiting she remarked that the ball seemed more like a German wake, everyone in black clothes and white gloves.[46]

A few days later the treaty, including the clause on religion, was signed, in order to save face all round, but its implementation was made subject to ratification by Gustav Adolf when he came of age two months later. It was clear to all that he would not ratify it. The episode proved to both Russians and Swedes that the policy pursued by the regent of delivering Gustav Adolf to a rigorist pastor had left a deep imprint on the young man who was already showing signs of mental derangement. It was only discovered later that during the long sessions in which he had appeared to be wooing the grand duchess, he was in fact endeavouring to convert her to Lutheranism.[47]

The account which Catherine gave of the whole painful story was deliberately deprived of all drama. But she never recovered from the shock of the public humiliation inflicted on her by a lad of seventeen. To many onlookers she seemed at the time, on 11/22 September, to have suffered a slight stroke. That night she suffered a spell of dizziness. For the next few weeks she went out little, received few people, and spent most evenings in her bedroom. One gleam of light came from her latest military venture. In mid-1795 the Shah of Persia, Aga Mohammed Kadzher, had invaded the Caucasian principalities with a view to reasserting Persian suzerainty over these mountain kingdoms. To counter his claims a Russian expeditionary corps of some 30,000 troops under Valerian Zubov, the favourite's brother, had been sent in spring 1796, and swiftly occupied Derbent, moved on to Baku, and prepared to invade Persia. It seemed as though here again fortune smiled on Catherine's arms.

There is some evidence that Catherine, alarmed at her own failing health, again attempted in September to win Alexander's consent to a plan to pass over Paul and leave the throne to him. A few days after the breaking off of Alexandra Pavlovna's betrothal, Alexander was shown a number of important papers by his grandmother. He wrote to Catherine – possibly after having consulted the Grand Duchess Maria Fyodorovna – expressing his entire agreement with the contents of the papers shown to him, and his gratitude to Catherine for all she had done and intended to do for him.[48] His letter might represent a reply to the empress's proposals in terms so ambiguous as to leave her under the illusion that he had accepted them. Rumours were by then circulating freely around the court that Catherine intended to proclaim her grandson heir either on her name day, on 24 November/5 December, or on New Year's Day 1797.

Alexander had no intention of falling in with Catherine's wishes. He had no desire to injure his father ; at that time he did not even wish ever to reign. In a burst of adolescent romanticism he hoped merely to endow Russia with a 'free' constitution and withdraw with his wife to the banks of the Rhine, or to America, to be free and happy.[49]

On 2/13 November Catherine appeared in public for the last time. The next two days she spent in seclusion, but worked as usual. On 5/16 November she rose at her normal time, but in the course of the morning withdrew into her privy closet. When she did not emerge, her valet and her maid forced open the door, and found that she had fallen down behind it, the victim of a massive stroke. She was transported to her bedchamber, but her servants found the inert body too heavy to lift, and she was placed on a mattress on the floor, and bled by Dr Roggerson.

The empress was not yet dead. But who was to succeed her? Alexander was out walking on the quays ; a message brought him hastily back. The highest officials at court, Platon Zubov, Bezborodko, General N.I. Saltykov (president of the College of War), the procurator general, A. Samoylov, Aleksey Orlov, at the time in St Petersburg, and the metropolitan concurred in the need to send for the Grand Duke Paul at once.

Intrigues sprang up on all sides. General Saltykov would not admit Alexander to his grandmother's bedside, fearing that the grand duke might proclaim himself. Meanwhile Platon Zubov's brother, Nicolas, galloped to Gatchina to notify the grand duke. Alexander in turn sent his own messenger, Count F.V. Rostopchin, to his father to ensure that the distrustful Paul should not suspect his son of attempting to seize the throne.

Paul was alarmed at first by the arrival of Nicolas Zubov because he feared that a posse had been sent to arrest him. But Zubov's news promptly made him swing to the opposite extreme of exaltation at the prospect that power was at last going to be his. The grand ducal couple arrived in the Winter Palace at about 9 p.m. They were greeted by Alexander and Constantine who had already changed into the 'Gatchina' uniform, in the Prussian style, with tightly buttoned tunics, thigh boots and gauntlets – uniforms which had not previously been allowed outside the precincts of Gatchina and Pavlovsk.

Catherine still lay, breathing heavily, on a mattress on the floor of her bedroom. Her dying hours were a period of intense anguish and anxiety. Would she regain consciousness for long enough to disinherit her son in favour of Alexander ? Would she recover ? Would she linger on, semi-paralysed, for weeks, imposing a regency ? Courtiers anxiously weighed the advisability of declaring their allegiance to Paul too soon – or too late. Meanwhile the Grand Duke Paul established himself in Catherine's dressing room, beyond her bedchamber. All those who came to seek his orders had to pass by the couch of the dying empress, over which her personal maid and her ladies-in-waiting sobbed out loud. The men of Gatchina arrived one after the other, to pay their respects to the rising sun to whose chariot they had long ago attached their fortunes, while Catherine's courtiers wondered where these savage 'goths' had emerged from.

On 6/17 November the archbishop administered the last sacraments. At some time in the afternoon the Grand Duke Paul sent for A.A. Bezborodko and instructed him to prepare the manifesto announcing his accession. According to tradition, at this meeting, Catherine's testament, passing over Paul in favour of Alexander, was destroyed in a moment of silent complicity between the two men.[50] Catherine still lay agonizing on the floor, without recovering consciousness, and finally died at 9.45 p.m., thirty-six hours after she was struck down.

The new regime made itself immediately felt. Prince Fyodor Baryatynsky, the Master of the Household, who had been one of Peter III's assassins at Ropsha in June 1762, was dismissed from his post. The oath of loyalty was administered to the high officials in the church of the Winter Palace, a ceremony which continued until 1 a.m. Observing that Aleksey Orlov was not among those who swore allegiance, Paul sent F. Rostopchin and the chief of police to Orlov's lodgings to make him swear at once. Orlov, who had left the Winter Palace before the empress's death, had no hesitation, but his prompt compliance did not save him from Paul's last strange revenge.

On 8/19 November the tomb of Peter III in the Alexander Nevsky monastery on the outskirts of the capital was opened in the presence of the new emperor, his family, and his court. Since it contained only bones (the body had not been embalmed) the coffin was closed again. On 2/13 December a solemn procession left the monastery, through avenues lined by the guards regiments : the coffin of Peter III was carried to the Winter Palace followed by Paul and his family on foot and in deep mourning. Two ghosts of the past were made to walk in the procession : Fyodor Baryatynsky, and Aleksey Orlov, head erect, looking neither to right nor left, and bearing the dead emperor's crown on a cushion before him. The coffin of Peter III was placed beside that of Catherine on two great biers in the Winter Palace, while the public were invited to pay their respects. They were transported to the Peter and Paul fortress on 5/16 December when, at a joint funeral, Catherine was interred beside the husband she had dethroned. Court mourning was ordered for Peter III and Catherine II.

A court poet immortalized the scene : 'Two graves and hearts, separated by fate/Are joined together by their son, model of tsars. . . .'[51]

Among those who knew her well, and among the courtiers who were the recipients of her bounty, Catherine left a glowing memory. Lower down the social scale evidence is more scanty. In Ukrainian folksong, she is reviled as the woman who tamed the Cossack Hosts and fastened the Little Russian peasant to the soil : 'Katerina, devil's mother, what have you done ! To the wide steppe and the gay land you have brought destruction,' runs a popular Ukrainian song. Catherine was doubly the target of popular verse and satire. As long ago as the 1730s, a peasant had refused to drink to the health of the Empress Anna : 'we haven't got a tsar now, what does a baba know, she has more hair than wit.' He thus expressed a man's deep distrust of a woman on the throne.[52] But a shameless woman, who went from lover to lover, aroused even deeper feelings in male-dominated peasant society. The vices of the woman are condemned in folk tradition, the virility of the men envied and admired. To Pugachev's followers Catherine was the 'trollop tsaritsa'. A poem celebrating her short stop in Glukhov in the Ukraine in 1787 ends with the local official asking her how many servants she will require. 'As it is the great fast,' the empress replies, 'and as I am tired with the journey, three will be enough.'[53] On the Russo-Finnish border, a number of lewd folk tales celebrating the prowess of Catherine's lovers and the lasciviousness of the empress survive to this day.[54] Legends about her were legion, none perhaps more outlandish than one current among Old Believers in the early nineteenth century, that she was the mother of Napoleon.[55]

In the long run, morality will not be trifled with. Retribution overtook Catherine, and she was condemned by one of those she had loved most, her grandson Alexander. The education she gave him, coupled with his own temperament, combined to make him reject her amoral foreign policy, her immoral private life and her secular, rationalistic cast of mind. In later years Alexander was curt and stand-offish with those who approached him, as he travelled about Russia, in order to recall the glorious days of his grandmother. Even when he did justice to her qualities as a ruler, he could exclaim, as in 1815, 'quant au développement moral, elle était au même point que son siècle. Nous étions philosophes et la divine essence du christianisme se dérobait à nos égards. Je sentais le vide dans mon âme et un vague pressentiment me suivait partout.'[56]

All those who worked with the empress, in whatever capacity, found her reasonable and understanding. Her servants loved her. She would overlook any little social clumsiness, and was too certain of her own greatness to take offence at small slights. She would discuss policy on equal terms, listen to argument, change her mind. Seldom was she arrogant or overbearing, though as she grew older, she was occasionally impatient, and at times even lost her temper. Behind this agreeable exterior there was however an iron will, the will which had carried her to power, the self-control which kept her there.

Yet she rarely misused power. Time and again, when the Senate referred some matter for her decision, she would send it back on the grounds that it was for the Senate to apply the existing law. She could be misled into injustice, but she sought justice and believed herself to be acting justly. Her attitude to absolute rule was explained some years after her death by Potemkin's factotum, V.S. Popov, to the young Emperor Alexander :

Nothing left a greater impression on my mind than the following conversation [with Catherine] :

The subject was the unlimited power with which the great Catherine not only ruled her own Empire but ordered things in other countries. I spoke of the surprise I felt at the blind obedience with which her will was fulfilled everywhere, of the eagerness and zeal with which all tried to please her.

'It is not as easy as you think,' she condescended to reply. 'In the first place my orders would not be carried out unless they were the kind of orders which could be carried out ; you know with what prudence and circumspection I act in the promulgation of my laws. I examine the circumstances, I take advice, I consult the enlightened part of the people, and in this way I find out what sort of effect my law will have. And when I am already convinced in advance of general approval, then I issue my orders, and have the pleasure of observing what you call blind obedience. *And that is the foundation of unlimited power.* But believe me, they will not obey blindly when orders are not adapted to the customs, to the opinion of the people, and if I were to follow only my own wishes not thinking of the consequences.'[57]

Conclusions

Catherine's long reign was marked by so many major enactments that it is almost equal in significance in Russian history to that of Peter the Great. She set herself the task of continuing his policies but by diametrically opposite means. Thus where Peter indiscriminately imported the form and the substance of European thought and customs, Catherine neglected the form and went for the substance. Where Peter denigrated Russia in the interests of westernization, Catherine, the foreigner, extolled the native virtues of Russia and Russians, and imbued them with a high sense of their equality with, if not their superiority over, Western Europe. Where Peter used terror, Catherine used persuasion.

Though the empress was by no means immune from criticism during her lifetime – indeed she tolerated criticism more than any of her predecessors – yet it was coupled with a degree of admiration for the qualities none could dispute in her : application, seriousness, sagacity, good judgment of men, generosity of spirit, and the ability to bring out the best in those who served her. The brief reign of Paul I served to underline even more strongly the merits of his mother's rule, in spite of the general dissoluteness of the court which the empress's own conduct seemed to authorize. The historian Karamzin gave vent to this appreciation both in his eulogy of Catherine, published in 1802, and in the 'Memoir on Ancient and Modern Russia' he wrote for Alexander I in 1810. An aristocratic conservative, he could condemn Catherine's foibles and stress the disparity between her aims and her achievements, but he welcomed the fact that the upper classes at least no longer felt themselves to be slaves, and concluded that 'should we compare all the known epochs of Russian history, virtually all would agree that Catherine's epoch was the happiest for Russian citizens . . .'[1]

Later writers have judged Catherine more harshly. Pushkin, who had every reason to loathe and despise a dissolute court, set the tone when he accused her of being merely a 'Tartuffe' in petticoats. Nineteenth- and twentieth-century historians have ever since then dismissed her dialogue with the *philosophes* as sheer hypocrisy, her *Nakaz* as a farce, written to win acclaim in the West while leaving her subjects sunk in lawlessness and injustice. Above all, Catherine's claims to greatness as a ruler are dismissed because in spite of the major reforms she introduced into nearly all spheres of Russian government, she did not emancipate the serfs or even regulate their relationships with the landowners.

If one is to analyse the significant aspects of her reign, three areas of her activity spring to mind : her relations with the philosophes and the Enlightenment in general ; her social policies ; and her foreign policy.

It is a fallacy of course to judge Catherine as a ruler by the discrepancy between the principles expounded in her Nakaz and the reality of Russia. The Nakaz was not a programme for legislation, but a statement of the ideals which a society should strive to implement. It was primarily intended to mould public opinion, to put before the ruling groups in Russia new ideas and new attitudes. Its principles were sometimes referred to in subsequent decrees, both during Catherine's reign and later, mainly in the field of penal law, and always in the direction of softening its harshness and reducing its cruelty. No study has yet been made of the extent to which the spirit of the Nakaz imbued Catherine's subsequent legislation, but it can be argued that her policy towards the free estates of the realm and towards the judiciary was throughout imbued with the ideas she first put forward in 1767–8.

There is no point in posing the classical question : was Catherine II an enlightened despot ? Such questions serve only to prolong an obsolete debate. Catherine was a child of her time, and she genuinely enjoyed intellectual activity, contact with sharp and witty minds, with political thinkers, with literature and drama. Her correspondence with Grimm reflects the wide range of her artistic interests, and there is no doubting the genuineness of her intellectual commitment, whatever the quality of her own writings. Inevitably her analysis of society as well as her political programme was influenced by the literature she read. Thus the theoretical background of her legislation can be found in the *Encyclopédie,* in Montesquieu and Blackstone, and in German cameralist thought. She came to believe that it was the duty of the ruler to regulate the lives of the people in order to facilitate the proper performance by each of his allotted function in the interests of the military and economic power of the state. The increasing effectiveness of that power was accompanied by the increasing standardization of the rights and duties of the population. On the other hand Catherine also believed in the hierarchical division of society into orders and estates, each with its own rights and privileges and its corresponding obligations. It was for the ruler, however, to set in motion the machinery of social change – the estates were only subordinate and willing partners. It is this varying combination of cameralism with a society of 'estates' which gives a unique flavour to Catherine's government, which leant sometimes one way, sometimes another.

More typical of the cameralist approach in Catherine's style of government was her systematic search for uniformity, in total disregard for the human feelings involved. The abolition of special jurisdictions, such as those of the Manufacturing College, the College of Mines or the Votchina College, may have served the positive purpose of bringing individuals together under the same law (though the clerical estate, the university community and school teachers continued to come under the jurisdiction of the Holy Synod, the university and the Commission on National Schools, respectively). But the extension of Russian local administration and social organization to the whole of European Russia, with a total disregard for ethnic boundaries and local traditions, points to a lack of imaginative understanding implicit in a purely rational concept of good government. Catherine's attitude to the liberties of the Baltic provinces and Little Russia was as insensitive as that of Joseph II to the Austrian Netherlands and Hungary. If she was successful where he failed it was because the Baltic provinces and Little Russia were both isolated and weak. In the same way, the introduction of the poll-tax into Little Russia at the same time as it was introduced into the Baltic provinces shows a failure to distinguish between the structure of the peasantry in the two areas. The status of the Baltic peasant, already a serf fully in the power of his landowner, would be unaffected ; but the status of the Little Russian peasant would be infinitely lowered by the loss of his cherished right to move.

Still in the field of social policy, there has been much discussion on the nature of the corporate bodies set up by Catherine in 1775 and 1785 for the nobility and the towns. To what extent was she intending to introduce into Russia social institutions sufficiently autonomous to act in partnership with the central government ? Or did Catherine merely call upon the social estates to supplement the work of the bureaucracy simply because the bureaucracy was still too small and inefficient to carry out the goals of the state ? These questions cannot be easily answered, since Catherine's political ideas and political practice fluctuated according to circumstances during her long reign. She undoubtedly hoped to mobilize local initiative and promote voluntary social activity and enterprise – always provided that it fitted into the rational and secular framework she had provided. But, as other authoritarian rulers before and since, she found it difficult to keep the fine balance between freedom and repression, to teach people to act freely in an unfree society. Historians have sometimes assumed that she intended to create genuine corporate institutions with some degree of autonomy, a rudimentary *Ständestaat,* just when enlightened monarchs like Joseph II were emptying such corporate institutions as survived in their dominions of all political content. More convincing is the view that she thought not of a *Ständestaat,* but of a *Ständegesellschaft,* not a state based on 'estates' but a society based on 'estates'. Estates were a necessary part of the social order, and should be fostered, even created where they did not exist, in order to enable the government to communicate with organized social groups throughout the country. Thus the reform of 1775 strengthened a weak social organization in Russia, whereas its introduction in 1783 in Livonia served to weaken well-established and over-powerful noble and urban political and corporate bodies.

Did Catherine however favour this kind of *Ständegesellschaft* merely because the Russian bureaucracy was still too weak to fulfil its tasks ? Certainly the type of well-regulated state envisaged by the cameralists required for its smooth functioning the services of an increasing number of officials trained in the systematic performance of duties and bound by ties of dependence to the state as employer. State control of government employees was easy to achieve in Russia by means of the Table of Ranks and because of the total absence of the system of the sale of offices. While one cannot speak of a bureaucracy in the modern sense in eighteenth-century Russia, nevertheless the proportion of government officials entering the service directly as civilians steadily increased, particularly in the latter half of Catherine's reign.[2] They were by now mostly better educated, and usually better paid, even if they remained totally untrained in administrative practices and lacking in the service ethic and in *esprit de corps*. Were they equipped to act as the government's sole partner ?

In a very perceptive essay on Catherine's reign, the German historian Dietrich Geyer wrote that it was impossible in Russia to replace a corps of noble landowners by a body of state servants owing allegiance only to the state (as in Austria or Prussia) because such a body did not yet exist. As a result Catherine was forced to weld her administration not to a bureaucracy but to the existing noble 'estate' organization. Only if it could be freed from the noble estate could an efficient dynamic bureaucracy emerge, argues Geyer, and bring about an improvement in Russian administration. Since the social structure did not change, however, the bureaucracy remained welded to the nobility and Russia remained in a state of paralysis.[3]

The flaw in this analysis lies in the assumption that a bureaucracy is a necessary instrument of administrative change, indeed that no improvement can be achieved without a bureaucracy. Yet there were other models in the eighteenth century than Prussia and Austria, and other political writers than the cameralists. This is where one must return again to Montesquieu, and to his disciple Blackstone. Montesquieu guided Catherine to England. From England she borrowed the equity court and the attempt to introduce a sort of habeas corpus. She may well have thought the English model, with its strong reliance on the country gentry, more appropriate to the large underpopulated Russian countryside than the Prussian/Austrian bureaucratic model. The *modus operandi* of the *zemskiy ispravnik* and the lower land court, as outlined in the Statute of 1775, has certain similarities with that of the justices of the peace and the magistrates' courts.[4]

In this context a word can be said about a judgment which is frequently passed on Catherine's policy, namely that she was forced, because of her political dependence on the nobility, to increase their powers over their serfs, or that after the revolt of Pugachev, she formed an alliance with the nobility for the government of Russia, based on a common fear of peasant revolt. Both these statements simplify out of all recognition a very complex situation. Precisely when her hold on the throne was most tenuous, in the first few years of her reign, Catherine made the fewest concessions to the nobility, both in terms of grants of land, and political weight. In addition, much of the content of the Statute of 1775 had been adumbrated during the sessions of the sub-commissions of the Legislative Commission, before the Pugachev revolt.

There was always an alliance between the Crown and the nobility in eighteenth-century Russia, for particular purposes. But it was not an alliance between equals, and it implied no dependence of the Crown on the nobility, no sharing of political power. What happened was a delegation by the Crown to the nobility of certain functions it could not hope to fulfil by means of a non-existent bureaucracy it could not afford to pay. The policy goes back at least to Ivan the Terrible and the establishment of local organs to control brigandage. Peter I tried and failed to get the provincial nobility to take a share as an 'estate' in local administration, and fell back on a bureaucratic order which collapsed under its own weight in 1727. It was only in 1775 that Catherine devised a system of delegation to the provincial nobility on an elective, temporary and salaried basis which proved lasting. But the state kept its grip on the noble estate, since it was the state which granted *chin*, and thus controlled the social status of all but the great magnates. Since social status cut across title and wealth, it was impossible for hereditary peer groups to form and to develop social cohesiveness or political solidarity. There is no doubt that like *mestnichestvo*, to which it was a worthy successor, the Table of Ranks promoted intense rivalry and petty squabbling within the civil and the armed services. It placed the ultimate control of society firmly in the hands of the ruler, since he controlled both entry into the nobility and promotion within it. The Table of Ranks remained the main instrument for the preservation of a service-bound society and inevitably prevented the emergence of a truly free society.

Thus it was not fear of the nobility which prevented Catherine from intervening decisively in the vexed field of serfdom. It was rather the conviction, particularly deeply rammed home by the Pugachev revolt, that the time was not yet ripe to tackle a problem so closely linked with public order, finance and military strength. Russia was not yet rich enough, nor well-governed enough, there was indeed not *enough* government throughout the country, to enable it to cope with the massive social upheaval implicit in a change in the status of the serfs. Even the regulation of relationships on the Livonian pattern might have set off large-scale social disturbances. Yet where Catherine could narrow down the range of those entitled to own serfs, reduce the ways by which people were enserfed, and increase the security of those who had been freed, she did so. The empress's remark to the Baltic official, Dahl, comes to mind : 'Wherever you touch it [the peasant question], it does not yield.'[5]

In one other most important field Catherine's influence was in the long run positive. She left a lasting mark on the organization of the law courts in Russia, setting up a system which lasted almost unchanged until the great reforms of 1864. The new network of courts brought justice much nearer the population even if the division into estates courts was contrary to past Russian practice. It is clear from studies of actual court cases that this division broke down in practice, just as the equity courts came to be used as merely a speedier and more effective civil criminal court.[6] But in spite of the greater emphasis on legality fostered by Catherine the attitude of Russian society and of the bureaucracy to law and justice remained largely unchanged in her lifetime. The very idea of legality, of a system of formal rules valid yesterday, today, and tomorrow for everyone, was quite alien to Russian society at all levels. Law in eighteenth-century Russia was, as one historian has put it, more like a moral ideal. 'That is why so many of the statutes of Russian law throughout the period 1711–1905 were not enforceable legal rules but exhortations to behave or work according to this or that ideal.'[7] The study of native Russian law did not even begin until the late 1780s and the lack of trained lawyers made itself felt not only in the administration of justice but in the actual drafting of the laws.

In one important respect the reign of Catherine II stands out like a shining beacon between the world of Peter I and the military despotism of the nineteenth century. It was an increasingly civilian society and government. The increase in direct civilian entry into the bureaucracy, coupled with the growth in its relative weight in the administration contributed to a process which can best be described as the demilitarization of the Russian government. In Peter I's day the military, and more particularly guardsmen, were used extensively as direct and effective agents of the tsar's will. In mid-century, the upper levels of government service were overwhelmingly staffed by men with some military experience, trained in unquestioning obedience and in the rough enforcement of orders on the civil population. Under Catherine administration acquired more civilian overtones, because more civilians were engaged in it. (It is noteworthy that as early as 1764 the collection of the poll-tax was removed from the soldiers and placed in the hands of the civil administration.)[8] The larger number of officials employed in the separate judicial branch of administration contributed to this process of demilitarization which constitutes an extremely important, though frequently overlooked, element in the development of civilized society.

But it was not merely a question of separate military and civilian chains of command. A new spirit was abroad. The demilitarization of administration and society was the corollary of the presence of a woman on the throne. Catherine could not command armies in the field, nor interest herself in the minutiae of uniforms, parades, the language of military orders (in Gatchina the German *Marsch* was used instead of the Russian *stupay*). These tasks were delegated by her to the heads of the College of War, in fact during most of her reign to Potemkin. A civilian bureaucracy was bound in the event to develop with the increase in the number of posts. But the 'civil' cast of mind developed in the administration and even more in society because the supreme autocrat was a civilian, with overwhelmingly civilian interests, who actively encouraged the process.

On the surface, judging by the size of her conquests, Catherine's foreign policy was extremely successful. Yet it is here, in the field in which she prided herself most on her skill, that she did the greatest disservice to Russia. Whereas in domestic policy her instinct was sure, and she knew how to conciliate opinion, in foreign affairs she was both brash and brutal. As a result twice she brought war on herself when she was not yet ready for it, and she was inveigled into allowing Prussia to intervene in Poland and ultimately to share in its destruction. The authoritarian and disagreeable tone adopted towards the Poles foreshadows the Stalinist style of diplomacy in the twentieth century. Catherine was fortunate in that the victories of her armies covered up the flaws in her diplomacy.

Total consistency of opinion or action cannot be expected in a long reign. Catherine was diverted by war in 1768 from a process of domestic reform on which she had embarked when she summoned the Legislative Commission. The Commission did not live up to her expectations as an instrument of social change, so she altered her approach in the ensuing years. Again in 1787 she was diverted by war from completing her plans for central government reform, possibly for a charter to the state peasants. Her opinions and her priorities changed as she grew older and fatigue began to tell upon her. She could not be everywhere, supervise everything, and she tended to content herself with issuing statutes and laws in the fond hope that they would be carried out in her spirit. But many of her projects ranged far ahead of the capacity of Russian society to execute them. More than most European rulers she suffered from the limited cadres she could call upon. The long periods in office of her more important officials not only reflect her confidence in them, her lack of caprice, but also the shortage of really competent people with whom to replace them.

With all her inconsistencies, her overweening confidence in her powers, her certainty that she was – nearly always – right, Catherine nevertheless rendered signal service to Russia. Her greatness lies not so much in her territorial acquisitions but in the new relationship between rulers and ruled which she fostered. Starting with the Legislative Commission the idea of national debate became conceivable. Imperfect as many of Catherine's great enactments were, they were carefully elaborated and she was rarely arbitrary in their implementation. Instruments of public control were multiplied and penetrated deeper into society, new concepts of justice and legality were put before an untutored public. Russian society relaxed in a new-found sense of security. Justice was brought nearer the people and mistakes were not treated as crimes. (One need only contrast the freedom and authority with which Catherine's councillors and governors spoke and wrote to her with the nervous hysteria typical of Paul's court, to measure the gulf between the mother and the son.) The élite of Russian society basked in a new-found sense of freedom and self-respect, and the area of private as distinct from state activity expanded immeasurably. Learning thrived, and the court itself acted as the source of literary, artistic and musical patronage. A hundred years later, and with a lighter touch, as befits a woman, Catherine did for Russia what Louis xiv had done for France before he became the prisoner of Versailles.

CONCLUSIONS

There were shadows on this picture. Reality fell far short of the hopes expressed in legislation. Corruption was widespread, particularly in the last years of Catherine's reign. Justice was often venal, brutality all too common. The mainsprings of government activity and supervision over its effectiveness slackened with the death of the older generation of Catherine's servants. By modern standards too much of the national revenue was spent on 'glory', often merely military glory, too little on justice and administration. But for a brief period, at the end of the eighteenth century, Russia and Western Europe converged : the spatial abyss and the lag in time were reduced. After Catherine's death their ways diverged again. Many of her enactments were repealed or their spirit was changed out of all recognition under Paul. And though the separation between the civil government and the military remained, both Paul and Alexander, when their turn came to rule, revived the supremacy of the military over the civil which gave its tone to Russian society, the 'paradomania' which reached its apogee under Nicolas I. With the advance of the nineteenth century, Russia and the West moved further and further apart ; the tempo of Russian development slowed down, while that of European growth accelerated until the yawning gap was revealed by the Crimean war. Those who remembered Catherine's rule looked back on it then as a time when autocracy had been 'cleansed from the stains of tyranny',[9] when a despotism had been turned into a monarchy, when men obeyed through honour, not through fear.

Maps

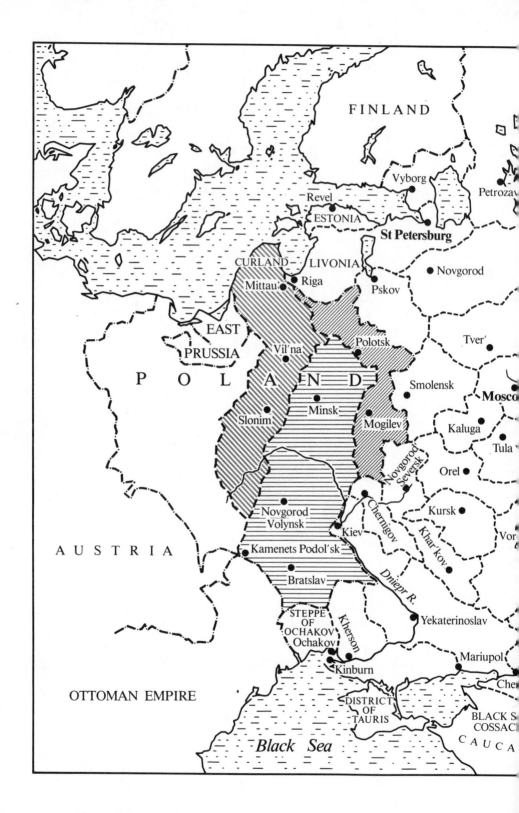

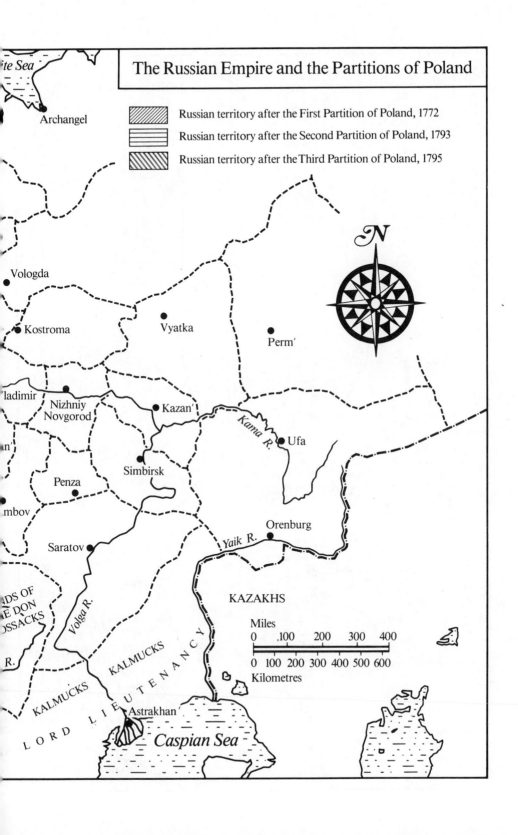

The Russian Empire and the Partitions of Poland

Russian territory after the First Partition of Poland, 1772

Russian territory after the Second Partition of Poland, 1793

Russian territory after the Third Partition of Poland, 1795

ite Sea

Archangel

Vologda

Kostroma

Vyatka

Perm'

'ladimir

Nizhniy
Novgorod

Kazan'

Kama R.

Ufa

an'

Simbirsk

Penza

mbov

Saratov

Orenburg

Yaik R.

KAZAKHS

IDS OF
IE DON
OSSACKS

Volga R.

KALMUCKS

KALMUCKS

L O R D   L I E U T E N A N C Y

KALMUCKS

Astrakhan

Caspian Sea

R.

Miles
0   ,100   200   300   400

0   100 200 300 400 500 600
Kilometres

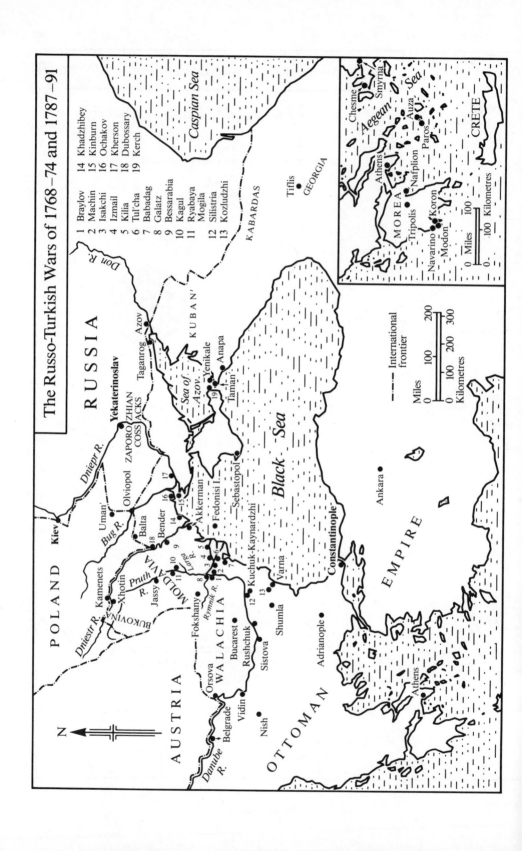

The Russo-Turkish Wars of 1768–74 and 1787–91

1 Braylov
2 Machin
3 Isakchi
4 Izmail
5 Kilia
6 Tul'cha
7 Babadag
8 Galatz
9 Bessarabia
10 Kagul
11 Ryabaya Mogila
12 Silistria
13 Kozludzhi
14 Khadzhibey
15 Kinburn
16 Ochakov
17 Kherson
18 Dubossary
19 Kerch

POLAND

RUSSIA

Dniepr R.

Kiev

Yekaterinoslav

Uman'

Olviopol

Bug R.

Balta

ZAPOROZHIAN COSSACKS

Taganrog   Azov

Don R.

Sea of Azov.

KUBAN'

Kamenets

Dniestr R.

BUKOVINA

Xhotin

Jassy

Pruth R.

MOLDAVIA

Fokshany

Rymnik R.

Lurga R.

Bender

Dubossary 18

14

10

11

9

8   12   3 4 5
         6
         7

13   13

Akkerman

Fedonisi I.

Sebastopol

15
16
17

Kuchuk-Kaynardzhi

Varna

Shumla

Bucarest

Rushchuk

WALACHIA

Orsova

Sistova

Vidin

Belgrade

Nish

AUSTRIA

Danube R.

OTTOMAN

Adrianople

Constantinople

Black Sea

Yenikale

Anapa

19

Taman

KABARDAS

Tiflis

GEORGIA

Caspian Sea

EMPIRE

Ankara

Athens

N

International frontier

Miles   0   100   200

Kilometres   0   100   200   300

Chesme

Smyrna

Aegean Sea

Athens

MOREA

Tripolis

Navarino

Modon

Koron

Nafplion

Auza

Paros

CRETE

Miles   0   100

Kilometres   0   100

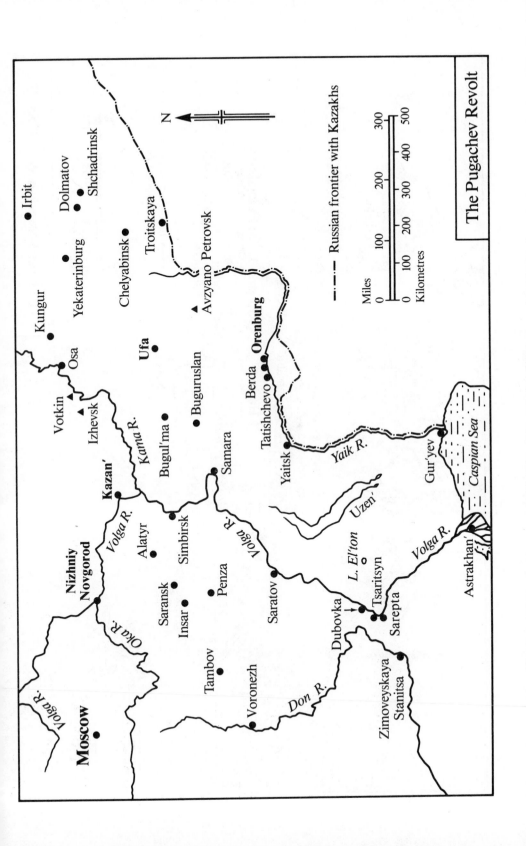

The Pugachev Revolt

Moscow
Nizhniy Novgorod
Kazan'
Volga R.
Oka R.
Don R.
Volga R.
Voronezh
Tambov
Insar
Saransk
Penza
Alatyr
Simbirsk
Saratov
Volga R.
Zimoveyskaya Stanitsa
Sarepta
Tsaritsyn
Dubovka
L. El'ton
Uzen'
Astrakhan'
Caspian Sea
Gur'yev
Volga R.
Yaik R.
Yaitsk
Tatishchevo
Berda Orenburg
Samara
Buguruslan
Bugul'ma
Kama R.
Izhevsk
Votkin
Osa
Kungur
Ufa
Yekaterinburg
Chelyabinsk
Avzyano Petrovsk
Troitskaya
Irbit
Dolmatov
Shchadrinsk
N

—·—·—· Russian frontier with Kazakhs

Miles
0   100   200   300
0   100   200   300   400   500
Kilometres

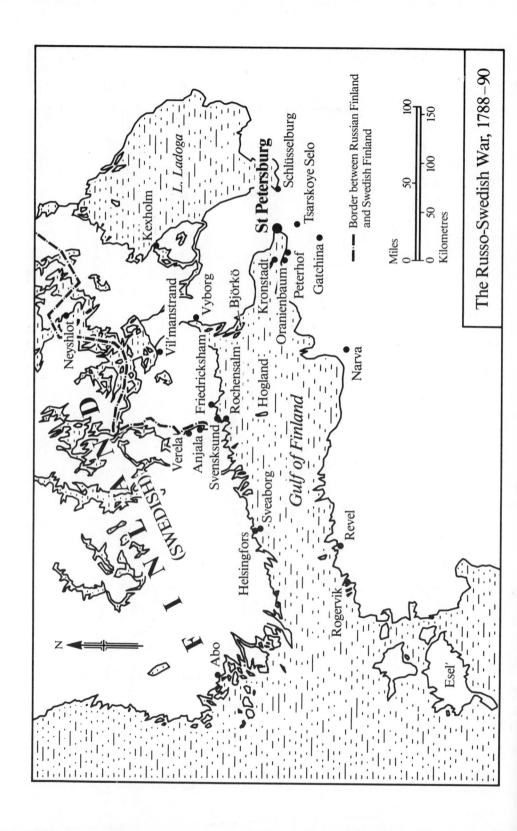

The Russo-Swedish War, 1788–90

F I N L A N D (SWEDISH)

Abo

Helsingfors

Sveaborg

Svensksund
Anjala
Verela
Rochensalm
Friedricksham
Vil'manstrand
Vyborg
Björkö
Kronstadt
Oranienbaum

Neyshlot

Kexholm

L. Ladoga

St Petersburg

Schlüsselburg
Tsarskoye Selo
Peterhof
Gatchina

Hogland

Gulf of Finland

Narva

Revel

Rogervik

Esel'

N

Miles

Kilometres

Border between Russian Finland
and Swedish Finland

0   50   100
0   50   100   150

Glossary

ataman, elected or appointed Cossack leader

barshchina, labour dues

boyarskiye deti, (literally, boyar's children) seventeenth-century term used for lowest rank of military servitors, usually landless

chelobit'ye, (literally, beating one's forehead) a petition

chin, a rank in the Table of Ranks

chinovnik, a person with a rank in the Table of Ranks, usually applied to an official or bureaucrat

duma, town council

dvoryanin ; dvoryane ; dvoryanstvo, noble ; nobles ; nobility

esaul, Cossack rank corresponding to captain

guberniya, province governed by a gubernator (governor)

haydamachestvo ; haydamaki, brigandage ; brigands, in the Ukraine

hetman, elected or appointed leader of the Ukrainian and Zaporozhian Cossacks

izba, peasant hut ; also used of administrative offices

khata, peasant hut (Ukraine)

khorunzhiy, lowest commissioned rank in Cossack regiments, i.e. ensign or cornet

khutor, Ukrainian farmstead

kupets ; kuptsy ; kupechestvo, merchant ; merchants ; collective merchant estate

magistrat, urban council elected by merchants with administrative and judicial functions

meshchanin, meshchane, meshchanstvo, common people registered as town-dwellers

mestnichestvo, seventeenth-century system of social and service hierarchy in order of the rank in service of one's father and family, abolished in 1682

mirza, landowner or noble in moslem Tartar areas

namestnichestvo, lord lieutenancy, area governed by a namestnik (lord lieutenant), usually two gubernii

oblast', region, area of administration smaller than a guberniya, larger than a uezd (q.v.)

obrok, money dues

odnodvorets, odnodvortsy, owners of single homesteads serving for their land in the militia

polk, regiment ; in the Ukraine, a military/administrative unit commanded by a colonel

pomeshchiki, owners of a pomest'ye, i.e. landowners

pomest'ye, pomestiya, originally an estate held on a service tenure, applied in the eighteenth century to any estate

posad, urban settlement

posadskiye lyudi, registered people of the posad, i.e. town-dwellers

prikaznyye lyudi, people serving in a prikaz or government office ; clerks, copyists, etc. in junior posts in the bureaucracy, below the Table of Ranks, belonging to the estate of chancery servants

Prikaz Obshchestvennogo Prizreniya, Board of Social Welfare

ratusha, from Ger. *Rathaus,* town council in small settlements

raznochinets, raznochintsy, people who have no chin in the Table of Ranks, are not peasants and are not registered in any specific estate

samoderzhaviye, literally, Gk. autocracy, used in eighteenth century for sovereignty

shlyakhetstvo, collective noun for nobility, of Polish origin, used at the beginning of the eighteenth century

shtat (shtaty), establishment ; **zashtatnyy,** not on the establishment

skhod (mirskiy, posadskiy), village or town assembly

sloboda, suburb

sosloviye, soslovnyy, an 'estate' or belonging to an 'estate', i.e. noble, burgher, priesthood

sostoyaniye, as previous entry

starosta, elder

starshina, collective noun for higher Cossack officialdom

treby, dues paid to the clergy

tsekh, craft union

tyaglo, taxable unit, usually a couple ; taxable population

uezd, district

votchina, allodial patrimonial estate

voyevoda, governor of a district

vygonnyye zemli, lands belonging to a town

zemskiy ispravnik, lowest-level rural appointed official : land captain

Weights and Measures

1 arshin	28 inches
1 desyatina	2.7 acres
1 chetvert' (area)	0.5 desyatinas
1 chetvert' (vol.)	5.75 bushels
1 pud	40 Russian pounds = 36 pounds avdp.
1 verst	0.663 miles
1 haken (Livonia)	measure of area of land producing an income of 60 rubles
1 vedro	2.7 gallons

Notes

Note : details of place and date of publication will be found in the Bibliography.

Abbreviations used

AAE	*Archives des Affaires Etrangères,* Quai d'Orsay, Paris
AGS	*Arkhiv gosudarstvennogo soveta*
AHR	*American Historical Review*
AKV	*Arkhiv knyazya Vorontsova*
ChIOIDR	*Chteniya v imperatorskom obshchestve istorii i drevnostey rossiykikh*
CMRS	*Cahiers du Monde russe et soviétique*
EHR	*English Historical Review*
FOG	*Forschungen sur Osteuropäischen Geschichte*
HZ	*Historische Zeitschrift*
IPS	*Istoriya pravitel'stvuyushchego senata*
IZ	*Istoricheskiye zapiski*
JGOE	*Jahrbücher zur Geschichte Osteuropas*
OZ	*Otechestvennyye zapiski*
PCFG	*Politische Correspondenz Friedrichs des Grossen*
PSZ	*Polnoye sobraniye zakonov imperii rossiyskoy*
RA	*Russkiy Arkhiv*
RS	*Russkaya Starina*
SEER	*Slavonic and East European Review*
SIRIO	*Sbornik imperatorskogo russkogo istoricheskogo obshchestva*
VI	*Voprosy istorii*
ZhMNP	*Zhurnal Ministerstvo Narodnogo Prosveshcheniya*
ZOOID	*Zapiski odesskogo obshchestva istorii i drevnostey*

Preface

1. Volume III, part 10 of the *Allgemeine Geschichte,* edited by Wilhelm Oncken.

2. A twelfth volume also appeared in 1900 containing a survey of opinion on Catherine in world literature.

3. See Bibliography.

4. Ibid.

5. Ibid.

Prologue

1. Hetman was the traditional title of the elected leader of the Cossacks in the Ukraine, an area which stretched from Poland to the Don. The name Little Russia applies to part of the Ukraine which came under Russian suzerainty in 1654. The title of hetman had been revived under the Empress Elizabeth. See below, Chapter 4.

2. For Catherine's *Mémoires* I–IV, see *Sochineniya,* Vol. XII, ed. by A.N. Pypin, with extensive discussions of the various versions and bibliographical notes. There is an English translation by M. Budberg, ed. by D. Maroger, London, Hamish Hamilton, 1955, which is rather unsatisfactory since no indication is

given of the way in which the various original versions have been merged into one text.

3. V.A. Bil'basov, *Istoriya Yekateriny II,* I, p. 7.

4. Catherine, *Mémoires,* I, op. cit., pp. 20ff.

5. Ibid., p. 33.

6. Bil'basov, I, p. 32.

7. Ibid., p. 34. He did not propose on any account to allow one of his own sisters to marry into Russia. See *PCFG,* II, p. 458.

8. Bil'basov, I, pp. 43–4.

9. See Frederick to Mardefeld (Prussian envoy), 14 January 1744 : 'La princesse Johanne Elisabeth sera une corde de plus à notre arc pour culbuter Bestuschew.' Ibid., p. 63, n. 1.

10. Ibid., pp. 36–8.

11. Bil'basov, I, pp. 88ff, and p. 93.

12. The historian Bil'basov adds that Peter was 'cruel with people and found pleasure in torturing animals' (I, p. 94). This is not borne out by Catherine's memoirs, passim, which suggest rather that he was insensitive to pain in others, and that he could be cruel when frightened.

13. Bil'basov, I, p. 124.

14. *Mémoires,* I, pp. 60–2 ; IV, pp. 215–16 ; Bil'basov, I, pp. 156–7, n. 1.

15. *Mémoires*, I, p. 62 ; IV, p. 216.

16. *PSZ*, No. 9123, 16 March 1745 authorized the advance payment of salaries to those in the first four ranks to enable them to spend in the manner proposed in ibid., No. 9124.

17. *Mémoires*, I, p. 69 ; II, p. 75 ; III, pp. 172–3 ; *Memoirs*, ed. by Maroger, p. 99.

18. *Mémoires*, IV, pp. 293–4.

19. But see Bil'basov, I, p. 276.

20. Bil'basov, I, pp. 317ff; *Mémoires*, IV, p. 348.

21. *Mémoires*, IV, pp. 272, 309, and see Bil' basov, I, pp. 286 and 287, n. 1.

22. Ibid., p. 28.

23. *Mémoires*, IV, p. 315.

24. *Memoirs*, ed. D. Maroger, p. 301.

25. *Mémoires*, IV, p. 295. Hanbury Williams described Peter as 'unfit either to govern an Empire or to furnish a succession'. Whereas of Catherine he said 'the first she will do hereafter, the last she has already done without the assistance of her husband'. See Williams to Holdernesse, 4, July 1755, quoted in H. Kaplan, *Russia and the Outbreak of the Seven Years' War*, pp. 103 and 106, n. 13.

26. Stanislas Poniatowski, *Mémoires*, I, pp. 136–7.

27. Ibid.

28. See Earl of Ilchester, *Correspondence of Catherine the Great with Sir Charles Hanbury Williams*, pp. 77ff, 23 August 1756.

29. Bil'basov, I, p. 348, n. 1 speaks of one loan of a thousand ducats on 21 July 1756, and one on 11 November of 44,000 rubles. Hanbury Williams secured IOUs signed by Catherine guaranteeing repayment. In 1764 when Catherine did indeed attempt to repay these loans the British government refused to accept the money. (*SIRIO*, 12, pp. 162–4.)

30. See L. Jay Oliva, *Misalliance, A Study of French Policy in Russia during the Seven Years' War*, pp. 46ff.

31. Chapter XIX of the *Cambridge Modern History*, VII, pp. 458–9.

32. See Earl of Ilchester, op. cit., p. 77.

33. *Mémoires*, IV, pp. 408–9.

34. The grand ducal couple may also have feared a plot to eliminate both of them in favour of Ivan Antonovich, directed by the Francophile party at court, who would seek thus to perpetuate their ascendancy. Ilchester, op. cit., p. 105, does not to my mind refer to Catherine's ambition to seize the throne for herself, but rather to make sure that Peter would inherit.

35. *Mémoires*, IX, p. 387.

36. See Bil'basov, I, p. 368, n. 1.

37. According to Hanbury Williams, quoted by H. Kaplan, *The Outbreak of the Seven Years' War*, p. 109, n. 21. See also V. Cronin, *Catherine, Empress of all the Russias*, pp. 119–20. Elizabeth herself had been born before Peter married her mother.

38. See e.g. *Zhizn' i priklyucheniya Andreya Bolotova*, pp. 132.

Chapter 1. Catherine's *coup d'état*

1. Bil'basov, II, pp. 693–4.

2. *Zhizn' i priklyucheniya Andreya Bolotova*, pp. 125–7.

3. *PSZ*, XV, No. 11, 445, 21 February 1762 ; V. Samoylov, 'Vozniknoveniye taynoy ekspeditsii pri Senate'.

4. N.B. Golikova, 'Organy politicheskogo ssyska i ikh razvitiye v XVII–XVIII vv'.

5. *PSZ*, XV, No. 11, 444, 18 February 1762.

6. See Chapter 5 for a fuller analysis.

7. Solov'yev, XIII, p. 12 ; for a more detailed account, see M. Raeff, 'The Domestic Policies of Peter III and his Overthrow'.

8. M.M. Shcherbatov, *On the Corruption of Morals in Russia*, pp. 232–3.

9. See the discussion of this question in N.L. Rubinstein, 'Ulozhennaya Kommissiya 1754–1766 gg. i eyo proekt novogo ulozheniya'. Rubinstein rejects Glebov's authorship, but the elimination of all of the economic privileges demanded by the nobility from the manifesto inclines me to the belief that it emerged from someone who had been close to Elizabeth's minister Peter Shuvalov, like Glebov.

10. Raeff, op. cit.

11. Solov'yev, XIII, pp. 66–7 ; Bolotov, pp. 171–2 ; I. Smolitsch, *Geschichte der russischen Kirche*, p. 145.

12. *PSZ*, XV, No. 11, 460, 5 March 1762.

13. Solov'yev, XIII, pp. 66–7 ; Bolotov, II, pp. 171–2 ; I. Smolitsch, op. cit., p. 145.

14. *PSZ*, XV, No. 11, 481, 21 March 1762.

15. *PSZ*, XV, No. 11, 503, 15 April 1762.

16. Solov'yev, XIII, 61ff.

17. Ibid., pp. 33ff.

18. For the text of the treaty of peace and the concurrent treaty of alliance, see Martens, *Recueil*, V, pp. 367ff and 389ff.

19. Solov'yev, XIII, p. 73.

20. *PSZ*, XV, No. 11,538, 18 May 1762. The other members were: Prince N. Yu. Trubetskoy, the chancellor, now Count M.R. Vorontsov, General A. de Villebois, General M.N. Volkonsky, General A.P. Mel'gunov, and D.V. Volkov.

21. Raeff, op. cit.

22. See e.g. the reports of the Danish envoy, G.C. Haxthausen, in *RS*, February 1915.

23. Ch. de Rulhière, *Histoire et Anecdotes sur la Révolution de Russie en l'année 1762*, pp. 50ff.

24. A.T. Bolotov, quoted in Solov'yev, XIII, p. 71.

25. A.G. Bobrinsky was entrusted to Catherine's valet Shkurin to bring up, and subsequently entered the Cadet Corps, and the Guards. He travelled abroad in the 1780s, sowing a substantial crop of wild oats, and was recalled to Russia in 1787. Catherine ordered him to reside in Reval, and he only visited the court briefly when he married in 1796. He was called to the capital by Paul who treated him as a brother, but finally aban-

doned St Petersburg and withdrew to Reval for good in 1798.

26. H. Fleischhacker, 'Porträt Peters III'.

27. For Panin's activities in Sweden, see J.R. Danielsson, *Die Nordische Frage in den Jahren 1746–51* ; W. Krummel, 'Nikita Ivanovič Panins aussenpolitische Tätigkeit 1747–51'.

28. D.L. Ransel, *The Politics of Catherinian Russia. The Panin Party,* p. 33ff. Panin was given a salary of 4,000 r.p.a. and a grant of 14,000 r. to pay his debts. *AKV,* XXI, M. Deyev to A.R. Vorontsov, 18 July 1760.

29. See below, Chapter 2.

30. Ransel, op. cit., pp. 62–3 ; A.F. von der Asseburg, *Denkwürdigkeiten,* Berlin, 1842, p. 317.

31. Many of the plotters were linked by family ties : Dashkova's husband was the son of a first cousin of Nikita Panin's ; by some she was reputed to be his mistress, by others his daughter, allegations which she repudiated violently. Prince Dashkov was also a nephew of Prince N.M. Volkonsky, who was in turn a nephew of Bestuzhev Ryumin's. On the plan for a regency see Dashkova's *Memoirs,* ed. by K. Fitzlyon, pp. 61–4.

32. A.T. Bolotov, *Zhizn',* II, p. 133.

33. Dashkova, *Memoirs,* pp. 78–9.

34. A.T. Bolotov, *Zhizn',* II, pp. 129–30, 169. The difficulty of sorting out family groupings in the tight court circle is illustrated in the case of Korf, who had married Catherine Skavronskaya, a first-cousin of the Empress Elizabeth, and of Peter III's mother, and sister of the wife of the chancellor, M.R. Vorontsov. Vorontsov's daughter married A.S. Stroganov, a partisan of Catherine's, but was for some years the mistress of Nikita Panin.

35. Bil'basov, I, pp. 471–2.

36. There is some divergence between the many accounts of the plot which have survived. See Bil'basov, II, pp. 467ff, for a thorough discussion of the value of these accounts and of those by eye-witnesses. Catherine's own account is in a letter of 2 August 1762 to Stanislas Poniatowski (*Sochineniya,* ed. Pypin, XII, pp. 547ff). It is a partial account, stressing the services of the Orlovs, but it is one of the earliest and hence one of the freshest.

37. Including Simon Vorontsov, the brother of Peter's mistress and of Catherine's devoted adherent, Princess Dashkova, who was never reconciled to Catherine's usurpation.

38. Catherine to Poniatowski, 11 October 1762, *SIRIO,* 46, p. 285.

39. Bil'basov, II, p. 36 ; *SIRIO,* 7, pp. 101ff.

40. A.S. Pushkin, *Polnoye Sobraniye Sochineniy,* XII, p. 177.

41. A.F. von der Asseburg, op. cit., pp. 315ff.

42. The unfortunate Ivan Antonovich was briefly moved out to Kexholm. Two deposed emperors in one fortress was too much.

43. *AKV,* XXI, p. 89; Dashkova, *Memoirs,* p. 90 and n. 1.

44. Solov'yev, XIII, pp. 114–15. In an undated letter from Ropsha Aleksey Orlov warned Catherine that Peter was 'mortally ill'. See *Sochineniya,* XII, p. 767.

45. Dashkova, *Memoirs,* p. 89.

46. For details of the awards estimated at over one million rubles, see Bil'basov, II, pp. 93–4; ibid., pp. 508ff for promotions. See also *SIRIO,* 7, pp. 108–9.

47. Catherine to Poniatowski, 2 August 1762, *Sochineniya,* XII, pp. 547ff.

48. Subsequently the tavern-keepers were compensated at state expense. Bil'basov, II, pp. 80–2.

49. Ibid., p. 78, n. 1.

50. Catherine's manifesto of 7 July 1762 exonerated Peter III's ministers for his mistakes, Bil'basov, II, pp. 84ff. On the consequences of Bestuzhev's return, see Solov'yev, XII, p. 455 ; XIII, p. 125 ; *SIRIO,* 7, pp. 141–3.

51. Volkov was honourably exiled to the post of governor of Orenburg, but returned in December 1763.

52. Ransel, op. cit., p. 106, suggests that there was a 'party' around the Orlovs, but provides no evidence and mentions no names.

53. Bil'basov, II, pp. 188ff. The exiles were allowed to receive 10 kopeks a day from their families for the maintenance of two servants. Khrushchev eventually escaped to France with the adventurer Beniowsky (op. cit., p. 199, n. 2).

54. Khitrovo had been granted 800 serfs for his part in Catherine's *coup d'état* (*SIRIO,* 7, p. 109) ; two other participants in the so-called plot had received 600 serfs and 6,000 rubles (N. Roslavlev) and 800 serfs (M. Lazunsky). They had apparently asked Catherine for more and she had refused. (See her note to her secretary I.P. Yelagin, 25 February 1763, *SIRIO,* 7, p. 234.)

55. See note by G.G. Orlov, 26 May 1763, *SIRIO,* 7, pp. 290–1 ; Solov'yev, XIII, pp. 208ff ; Bil'basov, II, pp. 273ff.

56. Bil'basov, II, pp. 330–1 ; cf. Solov'yev, XIV, pp. 25, 77.

57. Undated note from Catherine to Nikita Panin, *SIRIO,* 7, p. 364.

58. Bil'basov, II, pp. 343–4 ; see also D. Ransel, 'Catherine's Instruction to the Commission on Laws'.

59. Bil'basov, II, pp. 381–2. By 'Roman' general Mirovich presumably referred to the fact that Catherine's brother had served in the Austrian army for a brief period, when Zerbst was occupied by Prussian troops.

60. Catherine to Panin, 10 July 1764, *SIRIO,* 7, p. 365. On the rumours of plots while Catherine was in Livonia, see Ransel, *The Politics,* pp. 170–3, and 173, n. 4. Bil'basov, II, p. 347 quotes an example which states : 'the time for revolt is growing near.' Zakhar Chernyshev, Aleksey Razumovsky and Grigory Orlov were to be quartered, the empress sent back to her own country, and the 'throne of the tsars should be confirmed to the pure and innocent Ivan Antonovich'.

61. Bil'basov, op. cit., p. 386, n. 4.

62. For his appointment, see below, Chapter 3.

63. The death penalty had never been formally abolished in Russia, but the Empress Elizabeth had made it a practice not to confirm death sentences, so that in effect they were no longer inflicted (though death might actually occur as the result of some of the punishments in use, such as the knut).

64. The view that Catherine engineered the plot and then threw Mirovich to the wolves seems to rest on the fact that she refused to allow him to be tortured to reveal his accomplices.

Chapter 2. The Reform of the Central Government Institutions

1. *PSZ*, xv, No. 11,647, 20 August 1762.

2. *PSZ*, xv, No. 11,643, and see below, Chapter 7.

3. *PSZ*, xvi, No. 11,707, 11 November ; *SIRIO*, 7, pp. 159ff. See Bil'basov, II, p. 241, n.5 ; *PSZ*, xvi, No. 11,985, 8 December 1763 and *SIRIO*, 7, pp. 327–8. A commission for the building of St Petersburg and Moscow was set up on 11 December 1762, *PSZ*, xvi, No. 11,723.

4. Catherine seems to have been aware of the parallel between her situation and that of the Empress Anna Ivanovna in 1730. Soon after her accession she examined the papers concerning Anna's accession and sealed them up with a note saying : 'Not to be shown to anyone without a special ukaz.' See Korsakov, *Iz zhizni* . . . , p. 374.

5. Bil'basov, II, pp. 83ff. The manifesto was excluded from the collection in *PSZ*.

6. *SIRIO*, 7, pp. 202ff for the full text. See M. Raeff, *Plans for Political Reform in Imperial Russia, 1730–1905*, pp. 56ff for an abridged English version.

7. For an examination of the procuracy see Chapter III.

8. The latest and most complete study is in D. Ransel, 'Nikita Panin's Imperial Council Project and the Struggle of Hierarchy Groups at the Court of Catherine II', which should be read in conjunction with his 'Memoirs of Count Münnich', and *The Politics of Catherinian Russia, The Panin Party*.

9. See e.g. Bérenger to Choiseul, 16/27 July 1762, who speaks of a council 'que l'impératrice propose d'établir', *SIRIO*, 140, pp. 29ff.

10. *SIRIO*, 7, p. 143.

11. Solov'yev, XIII, p. 126. Teplov, who was very close to Panin, may have hoped to become secretary of the council.

12. V.A. Petrova, 'Politicheskaya bor'ba vokrug Senatskoy reformy 1763 goda'.

13. Breteuil to Choiseul Praslin, 3 February 1763, *SIRIO*, 140, p. 151.

14. Breteuil to Choiseul Praslin, 3 February 1763, *SIRIO*, 140, p. 151.

15. Ibid.

16. Breteuil to Choiseul Praslin, 23 February 1763, *SIRIO*, 140, pp. 160ff.

17. Instruction to A.A. Vyazemsky, April 1764, *SIRIO*, 7, p. 345.

18. Published in L.K. Blum, *Ein russischer Staatsmann*, I, p. 144.

19. Instruction to Vyazemsky, op. cit., in n. 17 ; but see also Catherine's Instruction to the Commission on the Code of Laws, Reddaway, *Documents*.

20. 'Panin ne veut pas d'un pareil conseil,' wrote Breteuil to Choiseul Praslin, 23 February 1763, op. cit., n. 16.

21. The members were : Count K.G. Razumovsky, Count A.P. Bestuzhev Ryumin, Prince N.M. Volkonsky, Nikita I. Panin, Prince Ya.P. Shakhovskoy, Count Z.G. Chernyshev, Count M.L. Vorontsov. The Secretary was G.N. Teplov. See Bil'basov, II, pp. 243ff ; *PSZ*, xvi, No. 11,751 ; *SIRIO*, 7, pp. 232ff.

22. *SIRIO*, 7, p. 279.

23. Bil'basov, II, p. 206.

24. V.A. Petrova, 'Politicheskaya bor'ba . . .', p. 60.

25. *PSZ*, vi, No. 3978, 27 April 1722. Representations should not be confused with the 'droit de remontrance' enjoyed by the French *parlements*.

26. Bil'basov, II, p. 246. On 18 August 1763, Catherine ordered the Senate to meet three times a week until a backlog of 148 imperial ukazy which had not yet been put into effect should have been cleared. *IPS*, 2, pp. 335–6.

27. *SIRIO*, 7, pp. 345ff.

28. Ibid., and *PSZ*, xv, No. 11,989 ; *SIRIO*, 27, p. 165.

29. See below, Chapter 6.

30. *IPS*, 2, p. 388.

31. A.D. Gradovsky, 'Verkhovnoye upravleniye Rossii i general prokurory', p. 234, n.2.

32. See discussion in D. Ransel, *The Politics* . . . , pp. 161–2.

33. *IPS*, 2, p. 390.

34. See the comment by the French chargé d'affaires : 'Ce corps [the Senate] n'a plus de consistence ; c'étoit le seul tribunal qui put opposer une barrière aux entreprises du trône. Aujourd'hui ses membres . . . ont perdu toute l'unité qui faisoit leur force . . . Les senateurs sont devenus des commis isolés qui ne pourront désormais s'assembler pour déliberer en concert sur un même objet que sous le bon plaisir de la Despote . . .', *SIRIO*, 140, p. 350, Bérenger to Choiseul Praslin, 5 March 1763.

35. See above, Chapter 1, pp. 33–4.

36. For the treatment of foreign policy see Chapter 12 below.

37. In the protocols this meeting was described as 'a conference'. This gave rise at the time to considerable confusion as many foreign envoys assumed that Panin's Council had been set up at last (see e.g. the Prussian envoy Count Solms to Frederick II, *SIRIO*, 22, p. 137, 10/21 October 1763) as a permanent feature of

Russian government, recalling the Conference of Elizabeth.

38. See Bérenger to Choiseul, 16/27 July 1762, *SIRIO*, 140, pp. 29–30, and Breteuil to the same, 9/20 December 1762, pp. 135–7.

39. *SIRIO*, 7, p. 201.

40. See below, Chapter 3.

Chapter 3. Local Administration and the Procuracy

1. Seven offences were punishable with death by shooting ; 11 by beheading, 25 by hanging, 6 on the wheel, 8 by quartering, 4 by burning. In addition 9 offences were punishable by mutilation, 41 by corporal punishment, 8 by prison, 9 by hard labour, 29 by confiscation of property, 5 by deductions from salary, and 21 by fines. See M. Gernet, *Istoriya tsarskoy tyur'my*, I, p. 155.

2. There were usually not many prisoners at any one time in these monasteries, which also harboured criminal lunatics, plain lunatics, convicted priests, sectaries, sexual offenders, drunks and retired soldiers.

3. Cf. Bolotov, quoted in Gernet, I, p. 55.

4. For a description of the Table of Ranks see Chapter 4.

5. The general disinclination to serve in local administration can be explained by the fact that such service usually came after long years of military service. Data referring to some 30 per cent of the incumbents of second rank posts in the years 1727–40 show that over 70 per cent were between 50 and 70 years old. Of 185 voyevodas in 1745, 90 were between 50 and 70. Cf. Got'ye, I, pp. 217–18. By the 1760s the average age was somewhat younger.

6. Got'ye, I, p. 231.

7. Got'ye, I, pp. 268ff. *IPS*, II, pp. 265ff. The ukaz limiting promotion to the post of secretary to nobles except *in cases of* unusual merit dated from Peter I (1724).

8. N.F. Demidova in 'Byurokratizatsiya gosudarstvennogo apparata absolyutisma v XVII–XVIII vv' disputes this point with Got'ye (I, p. 260), to my mind unconvincingly.

9. This exclusion applied to townspeople, court peasants, Church peasants, monastery peasants and private serfs. In 1766 soldiers' children were excluded. (Got'ye, I, p. 262.)

10. *PSZ*, XIV, No 10, 473, 11 October 1755.

11. Demidova, op. cit., p. 236.

12. 'Dovol'stvovat'sya ot del' is the expressive but untranslatable Russian phrase, supplemented by 'let petitioners give what they can'.

13. Demidova, op. cit., p. 232. In Moscow a secretary received 150 r.p.a., chancery clerks 80 r.p.a., under clerks and copy clerks 30 r.p.a. In the provinces salaries could be much lower, e.g. clerks, 31 r.p.a., or even 18 r.p.a. The lowest levels, such as guards and soldiers, were paid about 6–7 r.p.a., less than 2 kopeks a day. Cf. Got'ye, I, pp. 295ff.

14. Governors of the major cities received over 2,500 r.p.a. (St Petersburg, Riga and Reval) ; in other gubernii the salary was 809r. 50 k. p.a. A town voyevoda received 150 r.p.a. and a voyevoda in a townlet 60 r.p.a. (corresponding to the ranks of major and lieutenant). Got'ye, I, p. 33.

15. Got'ye, I, p. 277, n. 1.

16. See Got'ye, II, pp. 161ff.

17. Got'ye, II, pp. 187ff. *PSZ*, XLIV, II, No. 11,991.

18. *PSZ*, XVI, No. 12,175, 7 June 1764.

19. 'I have the honour to inform you. . . . that you have been appointed to. . . . I congratulate you on your appointment, and believe that in this new post you will carry out your duties according to the laws as your duty and your oath of loyalty bind you.' Got'ye, II, p. 11, n.1.

20. Quoted in Got'ye, II, p. 183, ironically enough from a letter of A.I. Glebov to Catherine. Glebov was shortly to be disgraced for fraud and embezzlement.

21. See Demidova, *Byurokratizatsiya*, pp. 230 and 239 ; Kulomzin, *SIRIO*, 5, pp. 228–9 and Got'ye, I, pp. 187 and 297. Salaries of governors of gubernii rose from 809.50 r.p.a. in the period 1727–63 to 1,875 r.p.a. ; salaries of their deputies from 300 to 600 r.p.a. ; of provincial voyevodas from 300 to 600 r.p.a. At the lower level, secretaries of guberniya chancelleries now received 300 r.p.a., protocolists 200, other senior clerical staff 100 to 150 r.p.a. ; copy clerks 60, and executioners 12 r.p.a.

22. The Russian nineteenth-century bureaucracy has a very poor reputation. The fact that the salaries laid down by Catherine II in 1763 (and 1775) were not effectively raised until the mid-1830s, may go some way to explain this. Cf. Hans Joachim Torke, 'Das Russische Beamtentum in der ersten Hälfte des 19. Jahrhunderts', p. 188.

23. Got'ye, I, p. 187.

24. Cf. Got'ye, I, pp. 66–8 ; II, pp. 185ff. Gradovksy, op. cit., p. 234. For the 'Instruction', see *PSZ*, XVI, No. 12,137 ; *SIRIO*, p. 352.

25. Got'ye, II, p. 186.

26. See Chapter 2.

27. *SIRIO*, 7, pp. 354ff.

28. *PSZ*, XVI, no. 11,759, 17 February 1763.

29. Got'ye, II, p. 37.

30. The salary was now raised to 450 r.p.a. (plus a special responsibility allowance of 9.50 r.p.a.) for guberniya procurators. Provincial procurators ranked as majors with a salary of 375 r.p.a.

31. See Yu. R. Klokman, 'Gorod v zakonodatel'stve russkogo absolyutizma', p. 335.

Chapter 4. The Baltic Provinces and Little Russia

1. 'Finland' was of course Russian Finland.

2. Smolensk had been ceded permanently to Russia in 1686 by Poland-Lithuania, and still enjoyed a special status. The nobles, as late as 1750, served from May to September in a militia, without pay. The merchants were still allowed to own serfs long after this right had been abolished in Russia. See A. Romanovich Slavatynsky, *Dvoryanstvo v Rossii*, p. 123 ; Semevsky, *Krest'yane*, I, p. v.

3. *SIRIO*, 7, pp. 345ff.

4. For Catherine's letter, undated, but by inference 18 December 1762, see K. Blum, *Ein russischer Staatsmann*, I, p. 436. For the charter to Livonia see *PSZ*, XVI, No. 11,727 ; a similar charter was issued to the nobles of Estonia on 21 September 1763, ibid., No. 11,993.

5. See below, Chapter 5.

6. *SIRIO*, 7, pp. 120, 349.

7. To Nikita Panin, July 1764, *SIRIO*, 7, p. 368.

8. For the most recent scholarly investigation into Catherine's relations with Livonia, see H. Neuschaeffer, *Katharina II, und die baltischen Provinzen*, 1975 ; for Catherine's journey, see pp. 379ff.

9. See below, Chapters 11 and 12.

10. The most up-to-date summary on Eisen is in Neuschaeffer, op. cit., pp. 247ff and 389ff.

11. Vol. IX, pp. 491–527. Eisen later strongly objected to this addition to his article. Neuschaeffer, op. cit., pp. 391–2.

12. O. Zutis, *Ostseyskiy vopros v XVIIIm veke*, pp. 345ff.

13. For Eisen's work in Russia, see below, Chapter 8.

14. It is very difficult to find an objective portrayal of the condition of the serfs in Livonia. Nationalist prejudice has distorted the accounts of the eighteenth-century officials and publicists, nineteenth-century Russian and German historians, and Soviet historians. Russians stress the misery of the peasantry under their German masters ; Germans point to what they regarded as the far lower standard of living of the Russian serfs.

15. George Browne, a Roman Catholic Irishman born in Co. Limerick in 1698.

16. Neuschaeffer, op. cit., pp. 413ff ; see also L.A. Loone, 'Krest'yanskiy vopros v obshchestvennoy mysli Pribaltiki'.

17. Zutis, op. cit., p. 353 ; Neuschaeffer, op. cit., pp. 420ff.

18. See N.D. Chechulin, *Nakaz Imperatritsy Yekateriny II*, p. xxxiii.

19. See below, Chapter 27.

20. V.M. Kabuzan, *Izmeneniya v razmeshchenii naseleniya Rossii v, XVIII – pervoy polovine XIX v*, pp. 87–91.

21. On the Razumovskys, see A.A. Vasil'chikov, *Semeystvo Razumovskikh*.

22. Hetman Mazeppa is said to have owned 19,654 homesteads in different polki, totalling some 100,000 dependent peasants. He also owned 20,000 serfs in Russia proper. *Ocherki*, p. 521.

23. Of 6952 homesteads and 5,469 khaty in 1751, only 2,661 homesteads and 1,273 khaty were left in 1764. *Ibid.*, p. 581.

24. For the best and most recent account of Little Russia, see Z. Kohut, *The Abolition of Ukrainian Autonomy, 1763– 86. A Case Study in the Integration of a non-Russian Area into the Empire*.

25. See B. Nolde, *La Formation de l'Empire russe*, II, pp. 46ff.

26. A number of Don Cossacks had been resettled in 1731 on the Volga, between Tsaritsyn and Kamyshin, with their centre in Dubovka. The number of serving Cossacks oscillated between 33,354 (1768) and 21,990 (1781). Numbers rose in war-time.

27. I.G. Rozner, *Yaik pered bur'ey*, passim. There were also small Cossack units in various towns in Siberia, but their status was quite different since they had no Cossack 'lands'. There was also a detachment on the Terek river.

28. For Teplov's memorandum, see Solov'yev, XIII, pp. 340ff ; Kohut, pp. 93ff, and notes 53, 54, 56. I accept Kohut's dating.

29. N.D. Polonska-Vasylenko, 'Iz istorii yuzhno-Ukrainy v XVIII v : zaseleniye novorossiyskoy gubernii (1764–75)', *IZ*, No. 13, 1941, pp. 130ff.

30. *Dnevnyye zapiski malorossiyskogo podskarbiya general'nogo Yakova Markovicha*, 2 vols, Moscow, 1859, II, p. 387 ; Vasyl'chikov, *XVIIIvek*, p. 590 ; Kohut, op. cit., pp. 85ff.

31. Bil'basov, op. cit., II, p. 454 ; Markovich, op. cit., II, p. 653.

32. *PSZ*, XVI, No. 11,911, 4 September 1763 ; No. 12,143, 28 April 1764.

33. *PSZ*, XVI, No. 11,987.

34. The Saxon envoy, Count Sacken to Count Flemming, 21 September 1763, quoted in Bil'basov, II, p. 430, n. 1.

35. For Catherine's consultations see her note to her secretary, A.V. Olsuf'yev, of 17 February 1764 in *RA*, 1863, pp. 42ff, 184.

36. Solov'yev, XIII, pp. 343–4, undated.

37. Ibid. According to Vasil'chikov, *Semeystvo Razymovskikh*, p. 596, the papers on the abolition of the hetmanate bore the inscription in Catherine's hand : 'keep secret'. It would be interesting to know if they are available now.

38. Kohut, op. cit., p. 113 ; Ségur, *Mémoires*, II, p. 252.

39. *PCFG*, 22, p. 310 and p. 375, n. 1. Rumyantsev's refusal to return to Russia was not unconnected with a liaison with a lady who lived in Danzig.

40. *SIRIO*, 7, pp. 102–3, footnote, undated.

41. Kohut, op. cit., pp. 113–14.

42. *SIRIO*, 7, pp. 376ff.

43. The instruction to Rumyantsev was drawn up by Catherine's secretary, A.V. Olsuf'yev, on lines laid down by her. See *RA*, 1863, p. 189.

44. See below, Chapter 7.

Chapter 5. The Nobility

1. Russian dvoryane adopted the 'von' in German and the 'de' in French in order to stress the similarity with the German and French nobility, though the *particule* plays no role in Russian nomenclature. Territorial or family links were expressed by the genitive *ov*, or the adjectival ending *skiy*.

2. Russian 'princes' were descendants of Ryurik, Gedimin of Lithuania or tartar khans. The title could not be granted by tsars, and in the eighteenth century it was procured from the Holy Roman Emperor. Bearers of these titles were not princes of the Russian but of the

Holy Roman Empire. The princely title was in fact only awarded once (by Peter I to Alexander Menshikov) until the reign of Paul I in 1796. All other princely titles awarded in the eighteenth century were imperial. But the title of count was frequently awarded, and the title of baron – less esteemed – crept in from Livonia. Titles were accompanied by the introduction of honorific forms of address copied from the German. There was no title corresponding to knight since orders of chivalry had been unknown, and therefore there was no honorific description of a man on horseback. The title *kaval'er* was imported from the West. The use of coats of arms, which had begun to creep into Russia in the seventeenth century from Poland and the Ukraine, was also regulated by Peter I.

3. V.M. Kabuzan, *Narodonaseleniye Rossii v XVIII v. pervoy polovine XIXV*, p. 154. Using a different set of figures V.I. Semevsky in *Krest'yane* I, p. 31 shows that in 1777, 32 per cent of the nobles owned fewer than 10 serfs.

4. Quoted in S.A. Gukovsky, *Ocherki po istorii russkoy literatury i obshchestvennoy mysli XVIII veka*, p. 26.

5. A.V. Romanovich Slavatynsky, *Dvoryanstvo v Rossii ot nachala XVIII veka*, p. 64.

6. See G.P. Karnovich, *Zamechatel'nyye bogatstva chastnich lits v Rossii*.

7. See Christopher Marsden, *Palmyra of the North*, for a highly readable account of eighteenth-century court life and N.D. Chechulin, *Russkoye provintsial'noye obshchestvo vo vtoroy polovine XVIII veka*, for provincial society. See also the *Memoirs* of A.T. Bolotov, passim. As late as 1748, the wearing of Muscovite clothing could bring in 50,000 r.p.a. in fines in Belgorod. Romanovich Slavatynsky, p. 543, n. 38.

8. An attempt to regulate the employment of foreign tutors and to register their qualifications was made in 1757. Cf. *PSZ*, xv, No. 10,724, 5 May 1757.

9. V. Bochkarev, in 'Kul'turnyye zaprosy russkogo obshchestva nachala tsarstvovaniya Yekateriny II po materialiam zakonodatel'noy kommissii 1767 goda' (*RS*, January 1915, pp. 64–72), analysed the percentage of illiteracy among nobles signing their *nakazy* to the Legislative Commission of 1767. According to this source the highest percentage of illiteracy was in Orenburg (60 per cent), followed by Archangel (28·09 per cent) ; Moscow, 17·88 per cent ; Smolensk, 9·22 per cent ; Malorossiya, 5·99 per cent ; St Petersburg, 4·88 per cent ; Kiev and the Baltic Provinces, 0 per cent.

10. See S.A. Gukovsky, *Ocherki po istorii russkoy literatury XVIII veka. Dvoryanskaya fronda 1750kh-1760kh godov*, p. 17.

11. S.M. Troitsky, *Russkiy Absolyutizm i dvoryanstvo*, pp. 215–22 ; A. Czartoryski, *Mémoires*, I, p. 301.

12. See above, Chapter 2, pp. 43 ; R.E. Jones, *The Emancipation of the Russian Nobility 1762–1785*, pp. 94–5, 108ff.

13. Breteuil to Choiseul Praslin, 28 October 1762 NS. Quoted in Bil'basov, II, p. 242, no. 2 and p. 621.

14. *PSZ*, xvi, No. 11,751. See *SIRIO*, 7, p. 233, undated note to N.I. Panin, and Bil'basov, II, p. 243.

15. See Chapter 2.

16. *SIRIO*, 7, pp. 232–3.

17. See A.N. Kulomzin, 'Pervyy pristup', pp. 26–34.

18. Ibid., pp. 36–73.

19. See Raeff, 'The Domestic Policies,' pp. 1293–4, for mention of plans by the Senate to professionalize the civil service in April 1762, and to upgrade the status of the civil branch. This sort of thinking may also have been in Panin's mind.

20. *AKV*, xxiv, pp. 518–19, n.d. Vorontsov russifies the French phrase 'eriger une terre' into 'znatnyia votchiny dvoryan erizhirovat'ili v dostoinstva vozvesti . . .'.

21. *SIRIO*, 7, p. 238.

22. See original text with Catherine's marginal comments in Kulomzin, 'Pervyy pristup', pp. 38ff ; corrected version in *SIRIO*, 7, pp. 238ff.

23. There is a striking similarity between the approach of the commission to freedom from service and the nobility's approach to the emancipation of the serfs. Servitude for the nobility was justified by the fact that they had previously been uneducated and unwilling. Freedom was justified by their present enlightenment. The serfdom of the serfs was justified by their present lack of enlightenment. When they too were 'enlightened' then they might deserve freedom.

24. Kulomzin, op. cit., p. 48.

25. Article 19, with a long explanation going back to Augustus Caesar.

26. *SIRIO*, 7, pp. 264–5 ; Romanovich Slavatynsky, op. cit., p. 202. As late as 1764 however Breteuil reported on the discontent of the Russian nobles : 'Quant à la noblesse, elle voit avec douleur et colère les difficultés et les retards que sa souveraine apporte à la confirmation de la liberté accordée par Pierre III et des privilèges dont cette liberté veut être appuyée pour devenir fondamentale et anéantir pour jamais le despotisme. . . .' *AAE*, Mémoires et Documents, Breteuil to Choiseul Praslin.

27. There is some divergence of opinion regarding the number of nobles who flocked to the provinces as a result of the manifesto. Chechulin (*Provintsial'noye obshchestvo . . .*), and particularly Korf (*Dvoryanstvo . . .*) have argued that a great change occurred in provincial life. Got'ye, II, pp. 120ff, argues that before 1762, many nobles were active in provincial life. Others argue that the manifesto itself was an intelligent move designed to demobilize the surplus officers in service during the Seven Years' War. See Raeff, op. cit., pp. 1293–4.

28. *Sochineniya*, VIII, pp. 276–8. Cf. : 'Thus a significant proportion of the nobility [in the eighteenth century] failed to understand the position of their estate which had developed historically. . . .'

29. The Russian word *razkreposhcheniye*, or 'deserfing' as opposed to 'enserfing' is often used to describe this process.

NOTES

Chapter 6. The Towns, the Peasants, and the Land

1. *Ocherki*, pp. 151–2. Twelve towns had between twelve and thirty thousand inhabitants ; 21 towns about 10,000 and 33 towns between 3,000 and 8,000.

2. See A.A. Kizewetter, *Posadskaya obshchina v XVIII veke*, pp. 101–2 ; V.M. Kabuzan, *Izmeneniya v razmeshchenii naseleniya Rossii v XVIII veke*, p. 90. On the towns see also G. Rozman, *Urban Networks in Russia, 1750–1800*, p. 105 ; Rozman estimates the total urban population (as distinct from the urban 'estate') at 8·9 per cent of the population of Russia.

3. Yu. R. Klokman, *Ocherki sotsial'no-ekonomicheskoy istorii gorodov severozapada Rossii v seredine XVIII veka*, p. 120 ; Kizewetter, op. cit., pp. 83–5 gives 269 official towns in 1738.

4. Private towns survived only on the western borders of Russia and in Little Russia and had their origin in a non-Russian feudal system. See K.N. Serbina, *Ocherki iz sotzial'no-ekonomicheskoy istorii russkogo goroda*, and I.I. Dityatin, *Ustroystvo i upravleniye gorodov v Rossii*, I, pp. 342–3.

5. Kizewetter, op. cit., pp. 145–6, 162ff. In the 1760s there were 396 members of tsekhi in Moscow, 154 in Novgorod, 29 in Tambov.

6. Kizewetter, ibid., pp. 628ff.

7. Ibid., pp. 176ff.

8. Yu. Got'ye, *Istoriya*, I, p. 344. A rich merchant might pay a poll-tax of anything between 9 and 120 rubles. A merchant in the third guild might be assessed at 30 kopeks instead of 1r. 24. Kizewetter, op. cit., p. 610.

9. In Olonets, in the 1760s, up to 3,000 registered kuptsy lived as much as 1,500 versts away from the town, cultivating the soil and trading in agricultural produce. Klokman, *Ocherki*, p. 64.

10. E.I. Indova, 'Rol'dvortsovoy derevni pervoy poloviny XVIII veka v formirovaniye russkogo kupechestva', p. 207.

11. Klokman, *Ocherki*, pp. 142–3.

12. See Chapter 5 and N.L. Rubinstein, 'Ulozhennaya Kommissiya', *IZ*, pp. 218ff : 'uravnitel'noye i bezobidnoye raspolozheniye' is the phrase used.

13. Nobles were not allowed to register in towns as merchants ; Romanovich Slavatynsky, op. cit., pp. 264ff.

14. See Yu. Got'ye's review of A. V. Florovsky's *Iz Istorii* in *ZHMNP*, November 1916, pp. 83ff.

15. Semevsky, *Krest'yane*, I, p. 214. In 1762 a noble, Nesterov, whose serf had died under punishment, was sentenced to perpetual hard labour in the mines of Nerchinsk, and to the loss of his civil personality. His estate was to go to his heirs. See *PSZ*, xv, No. 11,450, 25 February 1762.

16. See M.N. Gernet, *Istoriya tsarskoy tyur'my*, I, pp. 66ff. Some fifty of these codes have been found. See Rubinstein, *Sel'skoye Khozyaystvo*, pp. 132ff, and V.A. Aleksandrov, *Sel'skaya obshchina v Rossii xvii–nachalo xix v*, pp. 319–22.

17. Owners sometimes freed the old and useless because then they ceased to be responsible for their welfare. This was freedom for the owner, not the serf.

18. *PSZ*, xv, No. 11,429, 31 January 1762.

19. An enormous amount of material is available on Russian economic life as a result of various Senate inquiries, the *ankety* of the procurator general, reports of governors, and the economic observations attached to the General Land Survey (see below, pp. 108–10).

20. See Catherine's remarks in her Instruction, articles 269–71, in Reddaway, *Documents*, p. 258.

21. See Rubinstein's table for the guberniya of Moscow, op. cit., p. 102.

22. See Rubinstein's criticism of V.I. Semevsky's figures, op. cit., pp. 92ff, and the summary of the problem in M. Confino, *Domaines et Seigneurs en Russie au XVIIIe siècle*, pp. 186ff.

23. Rubinstein, op. cit., pp. 96–8.

24. This section is largely based on Semevsky, *Krest'yane*, II, pp. 1–184.

25. E.I. Indova, *Dvortsovoye khozyaystvo v Rossii – pervaya polovina XVIII veka*, provides an excellent introduction.

26. See S.I. Volkov, *Krest'yane dvortsovykh vladeniy Podmoskov'ya v seredine XVIII veka*, pp. 161ff.

27. Indova mentions codes of 1743, 1756 and 1764 but does not publish them (op. cit., pp. 304–5).

28. Semevsky, op. cit., II, p. 25.

29. Indova, op. cit., pp. 280ff.

30. These included the *pakhotnyye soldaty* (soldier farmers), *staryye sluzhilyye lyudi* (old time service men) and *pantser boyare*, the name given to odnodvortsy in the western provinces.

31. Semevsky, op. cit., II, p. 726, n. 2.

32. Ibid., pp. 733ff.

33. For details see Semevsky, op. cit., I, p. 110.

34. See for instance the demands put forward by state peasants and odnodvortsy for land equalization in the Legislative Commission of 1767 (see below, Chapter 11).

35. Semevsky, op. cit., I, p. 122 ; Aleksandrov, *Sel'skaya obshchina* provides an excellent modern treatment of the commune. Unfortunately there are very few sources for the state peasants or for small estates.

36. Ibid., pp. 458–9, and n. 2 ; *PSZ*, xiii, No. 9,954, 12 March 1752.

37. *Ocherki*, p. 118. R. Portal, *L'Oural au XVIIIe Siècle*, Paris, 1950, pp. 217–18.

38. Portal (op. cit., p. 249) estimates the purchasing power *per diem* of salaries in the Urals as follows:

	r.p.a.	p.diem	rye	wheat flour	meat
Apprentices:	12	3k⅓	10–12 kg	5 kg	2–3 kg
Skilled Workers:	18	5k	16–20 kg	8 kg	3–4 kg
Masters:	30	8k⅓	27–32 kg	13 kg	4–6 kg

He warns however that these figures may be inflated since they probably represent wholesale prices and refer to a fertile area.

39. Semevsky, *Krest'yane*, I, p. 479, n. 4, ukaz of 15 September 1763, not in *PSZ*.

40. See E.I. Zaozerskaya, 'Le salariat dans les manufactures textiles russes au XVIIIe siècle'.

41. Semevsky, *Krest'yane*, II, p. 314.

42. Portal, op. cit., p. 280.

43. The total number of serfs bought by all types of industrial enterprises is variously estimated at 85,000 (1720–50) by the Soviet historian Zaozerskaya, and 60,000 (1700–60) by Semevsky. See A. Kahan, 'Continuity in Economic Activity and Policy during the Post Petrine Period in Russia'.

44. See V.B. Elyashevich, *Istoriya prava pozemel'noy sobstvennosti v Rossii*, II, p. 1.

45. See N.F. Demidova, 'Byurokratizatsiya gosudarstvennogo apparata absolyutizma v XVII–XVIII vv', at p. 219.

46. See I.G. German, *Istoriya russkogo mezhevaniya*, p. 190 and S.M. Troitsky, 'K probleme konsolidatsii dvoryanstva v Rossii v XVIII veke' at p. 132.

47. *PSZ*, XII, No. 9,267, 14 March 1746.

48. *IPS*, II, p. 404. German, op. cit., pp. 174–83. 'Dacha' was the term used to describe a bloc of land comprising several villages within which there might be several pomestiya or estates. Since the pomest'ye consisted of a number of households and a variable amount of land, sufficient to produce a given quantity of corn, the acreage was not delimited precisely, and there could be much vacant land within a dacha.

49. See Chapter 7.

50. The standard work on the General Land Survey is that by German quoted in n. 46. See Rubinstein, op. cit., pp. 64ff. for examples of acquisitions by individuals.

51. Descendants of clerks and ecclesiastics who had received formal land grants were allowed to keep their small patrimonies, *PSZ*, XV, No. 10,796, 6 February 1758. In Little Russia, which was not affected by the Survey in Catherine's lifetime, in the guberniya of Kiev in 1795, 13 serfs, 212 townspeople, 3744 Cossacks, 833 raznochintsy and 122 chancery clerks were still registered as pomeshchiki or landowners – a total of 4,947 in an alleged noble population of 22,562 nobles in Left Bank Ukraine. (Kabuzan and Troitsky, 'Izmeneniya v chislennosti, udel'nom vese i razmeshcheniya dvoryanstva v Rossii 1782–1858gg', pp. 153–8, Tables.)

52. Rubinstein, op. cit., pp. 28ff.

53. For details of payment and large purchases, see ibid., pp. 38ff.

Chapter 7. The Orthodox Church

1. On 15 July 1762 Catherine repealed Peter III's decree forbidding the building of private chapels. *PSZ*, XV, No. 11,612. See Chapter 1.

2. Smolitsch, op. cit.

3. Ibid., p. 115.

4. Smolitsch, p. 409 ; *PSZ*, XIX, No. 13,986, 25 May 1773.

5. See the very thorough study by G.L. Freeze, *The Russian Levites – Parish Clergy in the Eighteenth Century*, for much new information on this subject.

6. Smolitsch, pp. 709–10.

7. A. Kartashov, *Ocherki po istorii russkoy tserkvi*, II, p. 449 ; see also Smolitsch, op. cit., p. 346.

8. Reddaway, *Documents*, pp. 7–8, 17/28 November 1765.

9. *PSZ*, XV, No. 11,643.

10. Kartashov, II, p. 450 ; Ransel, *The Politics . . .*, pp. 140–2.

11. *PSZ*, XV, No. 11,716, 29 November 1762.

12. Kartashov, II, p. 460ff ; Bil'basov, II, p. 261 ; G.M. Soldatov, *Arseniy Matseyevich, mitropolit Rostovsky, 1706–1772*, pp. 112–20 ; see also V.S. Ikonnikov, 'Avtobiograficheskoye pokazaniye Arseniya Matsiyevicha'.

13. Soldatov, op. cit., pp. 120–3.

14. Kartashov, II, p. 464. See also Solov'yev, VIII, pp. 200ff.,., particularly p. 206.

15. Kartashov, II, pp. 472ff. ; Soldatov, pp. 90ff.

16. *PSZ*, XVI, No. 11,814, 12 May 1763.

17. *PSZ*, XVI, No. 12,060, 26 February 1764 and *Kniga shtatov*, XLIII, pt. III.

18. Smolitsch, op. cit., p. 350, n. 570.

19. See *PSZ*, XVI, No. 12,060 ; XLIII, pt. III, and XVI, No. 12,121 of 31 March 1764.

20. N.D. Chechulin, *Ocherki po istorii russkikh finansov v tsarstvovaniye Yekateriny II*, pp. 138–9, 315–16. After 1784 there are no separate figures for income from Church peasants. For the organization of the College of Economy and the administration of the Church peasants, see Chapter 8.

21. See below, Chapter 20.

22. See *SIRIO*, 7, pp. 316, 317 for Catherine's instructions of 19 August and 4 September 1763. Potemkin held this office until 25 September 1769, by which time he had volunteered for the army.

23. *PSZ*, XVI, No. 11, 746, Catherine's instruction to the Holy Synod, 3 February 1763.

24. *PSZ*, XVII, No. 12,570, 12,659, 12,711, 12,929 ; XVIII, 12,925. The allotment was laid down in the General Land Survey (see Chapter 6).

25. V.I. Semevsky, 'Sel'skiy svyashchennik vo vtoroy polovine XVIII v' ; Freeze, op. cit., pp. 164ff.

26. Ibid. The income from dues was extremely small, averaging from 1–4r.p.a. for the entire staff of a parish church. Freeze, op. cit., pp. 166–7.

27. Freeze, op. cit., p. 40.

28. *PSZ*, XVIII, No. 12,909.

29. *PSZ*, XXIII, No. 17,004, 11 December 1791.

30. For example, Metropolitan Paul of Tobol'sk who was removed from his see in 1768.

31. Freeze, op. cit., pp. 210ff.

32. See J. Billington, *The Icon and the Axe* pp. 201–2, and Chapter 15, n. 88.

33. On Tikhon, see N. Gorodetsky, *St Tikhon Zadonsky, Inspirer of Dostoyevsky*.

34. See in general on this subject J. Billington, op. cit., pp. 200ff and 238–40, and the literature cited in the notes.

35. Andreyev, op. cit., pp. 126ff. Potemkin's presence in the Synod explains this leniency, according to Andreyev.

36. See Andreyev, op. cit., pp. 241ff, and 263ff. See also F.C. Coreybeare, *Russian Dissenters*, Part II, pp. 261ff, and Part III, 339ff. Selivanov's ultimate fate illustrates Paul I's strange psychology. He sent for Selivanov from Siberia, but, after an interview, had him locked up in a lunatic asylum, from which he was released by Alexander. Coins with the head of Peter III (rare in Russia) were collected by skoptsy.

Chapter 8. Industrial and Agrarian Unrest : Repression and Reform in the 1760s

1. *SIRIO*, 10, p. 380, 20 September 1769.

2. Semevsky, *Krest'yane*, II, p. 403.

3. Including N.I. Panin, G.N. Teplov, D.V. Volkov, etc. See e.g., ibid., p. 351.

4. Ibid., pp. 403–4. The senators showed remarkable abnegation, seeing that some of them were owners of industrial enterprises with assigned peasants.

5. *SIRIO*, 7, pp. 188ff. Instruction to Prince A.A. Vyazemsky, 6 December 1762.

6. Portal, op. cit., p. 299 ; *PSZ*, XVI, No. 11,790, 9 April 1763 ; Semevsky, *Krest'yane*, II, pp. 405ff.

7. The last assignment had been made in 1760 ; ibid., p. 413.

8. Peter Shuvalov, who had taken over the Kamsk and Goroblagodatsk foundries, died owing 600,000 rubles to the state. Enterprises taken over by the Vorontsovs and the Chernyshevs were also eventually retaken by the state at a considerable loss. Semevsky, op. cit., II, p. 413 and n. 1 ; See also N.I. Pavlenko, *Istoriya metallurgi v Rossii XVIII veka*, p. 473.

9. Semevsky, *Krest'yane*, II, pp. 414, 432 ; *SIRIO*, 2, p. 280 ; ibid., p. 32.

10. See below, Chapter 16.

11. Kartashov, II, p. 250.

12. See above, Chapter 7 and *PSZ*, XVI, No. 11,814, 12 May 1763, and No. 11,844, 6 June 1763.

13. In January 1763, 77 peasants of the Novodevichiy monastery were whipped for petitioning the Empress personally. Semevsky, op. cit., II, p. 244, n. 2.

14. See above, Chapter 7.

15. *PSZ*, XVII, No. 12,060.

16. According to the ukaz, 910,866 peasants ; according to Semevsky, 999,761 (op. cit., II, p. 254).

17. *PSZ*, XVI, No. 12,226 ; see also No. 12,745.

18. V.V. Mavrodin, *Krest'yanskaya voyna . . .*, I, p. 419, quoted seven cases of seizures in 1771–2.

19. See my article, 'Catherine II and the Serfs : A Reconsideration of some Problems'.

20. Semevsky, op. cit., I. p. 441 ; N.L. Rubinstein, 'Krest'yanskoye dvizheniye v Rossii vo vtoroy polovine XVIII veka'. Mavrodin, op. cit., p. 376, gives only seven risings in 1768, and four in 1769.

21. For comparison, in the period 1835–54, there were 144 murders of landowners, and 29 of government officials. See I.I. Ignatovich, *Pomeshchishchiye krest'yane nakanune osvobozhdeniya*, p. 327.

22. Semevsky, op. cit., I, pp. 414ff ; Mavrodin, I, p. 350 quotes three murders in Kazan' in 1764–5.

23. *Osmnadtsatyy vek*, III, p. 390, undated but probably 1767.

24. M.T. Belyavsky, *Krest'yanskiy vopros nakanune vosstaniya Pugacheva*, p. 50 ; Semevsky, op. cit., I, pp. 419ff.

25. *PSZ*, XVI, No. 11,875 ; Belyavsky, op. cit., pp. 51–2.

26. Semevsky, I, p. 427–8.

27. Mavrodin, I, p. 347, quoting unpublished dissertation by T.P.Rzhanikova.

28. Peasant flight in the period 1730–50 is studied by P.K. Alefirenko in *Krest' yanskoye dvizheniye i krest'yanskiy vopros v Rossii v 30-50-kh godakh XVIII veka* ; Mavrodin, I, p. 342 gives 320,000 male souls in flight in 1727–41.

29. Solov'yev XIII, pp. 228–30.

30. Solov'yev, XIII, pp. 230–1.

31. *PSZ*, XVI, No. 11,815 ; Semevsky, op. cit., I, p. 400 ; Belyavsky, op. cit., p. 42 gives 12,000 peasants who had returned from Poland among assigned peasants in Siberia.

32. *PSZ*, XVII, No. 12,748 ; XVIII, Nos. 13,074 and 13,287 ; Semevsky, I, p. 166, n. 2.

33. *PSZ*, XVIII, No. 13,103, 18 April 1768.

34. Mavrodin, op. cit., I, p. 352 ; Mavrodin admits that the majority of brigands were criminals, but he does not study the materials in the archives referring to these bands and limits his interest only to those cases in which a discriminating scholar can detect real class war motives.

35. Mavrodin, I, pp. 347ff.

36. V.A. Golobutsky, *Zaporozhskoye Kazachesvtvo*, and K.G. Guslitsky, *Koliivshchina*.

37. *PSZ*, XV, No. 11,577, 19 June 1762 ; No. 11,593, 3 July 1762.

38. *PSZ*, XVII, No. 12,311 ; M.T. Florinsky in *Russia ; a History and Interpretation*, I, p. 572 states that this decree 'gave owners power to sentence serfs to penal servitude in Siberia and then to claim them back'. L. Kochan in *The Making of Modern Russia* makes the same error, as does Belyavsky, op. cit., p. 268.

39. *PSZ*, XVI, No. 12,316, 19 January 1765.

40. See 'Sobornoye ulozheniye tsarya Alekseya Mikhaylovicha 1649 goda' in *Pamyatniki russkogo prava*, ed. K.A. Sofronenko, VI, pp. 29 and 34.

41. Semevsky, I, p. 374 ; and see Chapter 11.

42. Ibid., p. 414.

43. See my article referred to in n. 19 above.

44. *PSZ*, XV, No. 11,116, 13 December 1760. The ukaz laid down that serfs were to be under 45, accompanied by their wives and small children for whom the state would pay 50 rubles for boys from 5 to 15 and half this sum for girls. Owners were to supply 20–30r. for expenses and footwear.

45. See my article referred to in n. 19.

46. G. Macartney, *The Present State of Russia*, p. 23 ; Semevsky, 'Razdacha naselennykh imeniy pri Yekaterine', pp. 204–77.

47. Portal, op. cit., p. 293.

48. See note 37.

49. *SIRIO*, 7, p. 322 ; M.M. Shtrange, 'Istoriya odnogo podlozhnogo ukaza 1763 g,' pp. 310–4.

50. Quoted from *Khrestomatiya po russkoy literatury XVIII veka*, pp. 262ff. There is no evidence that this anonymous work was written by a serf. Among rumours which circulated at the time was one that an 'Instruction' (Catherine's great Nakaz ?) included the order that barshchina should be limited to two days a week. See Semevsky, op. cit., I, p. 66 ; A.V. Florovsky, *Iz istorii*, p. 24.

51. Quoted in Semevsky, *Krest'yanskiy vopros*, p. 8.

52. *SIRIO*, 7, p. 84, undated, probably 1761.

53. Zutis, op. cit., pp. 334ff. Neuschaeffer, op. cit., pp. 400–413 ; Semevsky, *Krest'yanskiy vopros*, I, pp. 13ff.

54. On Golitsyn see I.S. Bak, 'Dmitry Aleksandrovich Golitsyn', p. 258 ; and see Semevsky, *Krest'yanskiy vopros*, I, pp. 23ff, and by the same author, 'Krest'yane dvortsovogo vedomstva'.

55. See the excellent study by M. Confine, *Domaines et seigneurs en Russie vers la fin du XVIIIe siècle*.

56. Semevsky, *Krest'yanskiy vopros*, I, p. 48.

57. Polenov had studied jurisprudence in Strasbourg and Gottingen ; for examples of the extensive cuts to his essay see Belyavsky, *Krest'yanskiy vopros*, pp. 293ff.

Chapter 9. The Legislative Commission of 1767

1. *PSZ*, XVII, No. 12,801, 14 December 1766.

2. The Code of 1649 had been drafted and approved by a 'Zemskiy Sobor' or Assembly of the Land, composed of representatives of the government, the Church and the free estates of the realm.

3. See the survey in V.N. Latkin, *Zakonodatel' nyye kommissii v Rossii v XVIII st.*

4. *PSZ*, XVII, No. 12,801.

5. Latkin, op. cit., p. 127.

6. In the event the courts tended to interpret this immunity as applying only to deputies who had taken an active part in proceedings. See M.A. Lipinsky, 'Novvye dannyye dlya istorii Yekaterininskoy kommissii', at p. 236 ; *SIRIO*, 10, p. 139, para 6, for Catherine's views.

7. *PSZ*, XVII, No. 12,801 ; the salaries of the deputies on 37r.p.a. were raised to 50r.p.a. in September 1767 (*PSZ*, XVIII, No. 13,007, 9 September 1767).

8. Everett M. Jacobs, 'Soviet Local Elections – What they are and what they are not', p. 61.

9. *PSZ*, XIX, No. 13,953, 28 February 1773.

10. See *PSZ*, XVII, No. 12,801, 14 December 1766 ; A.V. Florovsky, *Sostav*, p. 588.

11. See the interesting example of the nakaz or instruction from the chief of police which deviated in many important ways from Catherine's own views as expressed in her Great Instruction (see Chapter X). Cf. K. Papmehl, 'The Problem of Civil Liberties in the Records of the Great Commission'.

12. Two hundred and four women landowners registered their votes in the election. See Florovsky, *Sostav*, pp. 263ff.

13. Ibid.

14. Ibid., pp. 152–3.

15. Latkin, op. cit., p. 209. Florovsky, p. 207, estimates that only one quarter of the noble landowners in each district took part in the elections.

16. V. Sergeyevich in 'Otkuda neudachi yekaterininskoy zakonodatel'noy kommissii', pp. 217–18, makes the point that since there was no 'opposition' to the government there was no need for the government to intervene in the elections.

17. Ibid., p. 211.

18. V. Bochkarev, 'Kul'turnyye zaprosy russkogo obshchestva', pp. 325ff.

19. This view was disputed by V. Latkin, op. cit., at first, and upheld by I.I. Dityatin (*Ustroystvo i upravleniye gorodov v Rossii*, I, pp. 388ff) and M.A. Lipinsky, op. cit. See also A.A. Kizewetter, 'Proiskhozhdeniye gorodskikh deputatskikh nakazov v yekaterininskuyu kommissiyu' in *Istoricheskiye Ocherki*. The most recent study is F.-X Coquin, *La Grande Commission Legislative (1767–1768). Les cahiers de doléances urbains*, pp. 29ff and p. 39, n. 63.

20. See the table in Coquin, op. cit., p. 51. Merchant exclusiveness predominated in the gubernii of Moscow and Novgorod. Peasants took part in the election of 33 urban deputies. But it must be stressed that all conclusions on the participation of electors must be tentative in view of the patchy nature of the evidence.

21. Florovsky, *Sostav*, p. 386.

22. Lipinsky, op. cit., p. 264.

23. Kizewetter, 'Proiskhozhdeniye, . . ', pp. 209–41.

24. Sergeyevich, op. cit., p. 202 ; P. Kudryashev, 'Otnosheniye naseleniya k vyboram v Yekaterininskuyu kommissiyu', at p. 110.

25. Some sixteen towns all told were at some time represented by a noble. The number fluctuated owing to the practice of transferring the mandate to another person. See Belyavsky, *Krest'yanskiy vopros*, p. 74.

26. The deputy for the state peasants of Archangel, I. Chuprov, brought some 500 petitions with him. The bulk of the published petitions will be found in *SIRIO*, 105 and 123. See also Belyavsky, op. cit., p. 119.

27. Ya. Zutis, *Ostseyskiy vopros v XVIII veke*, pp. 361ff.

28. Solov'yev, XIV, p. 36.

29. Catherine to Governor-General Browne, in A.V. Florovsky, *Sostav*, pp. 242–3.

30. Catherine to A.A. Vyazemsky, 16 June 1767, *SIRIO*, 10, p. 213.

31. Ibid., pp. 285ff.

32. Solov'yev, XIV, pp. 38–9.

33. Ibid., pp. 39–40.

34. Ibid., pp. 45–6. The civil court condemned the accused to exile ; the military court condemned 33 out of 36 to death. The Senate reduced the sentence, and Catherine pardoned the culprits in 1770. See Kudryashev, op. cit., at p. 533.

35. Solov'yev, XIV, p. 41.

36. Kohut, *The Abolition of Ukrainian Autonomy*, pp. 138ff.

37. Kudryashev, op. cit., pp. 112ff.

38. Ibid., p. 120.

39. Ibid., p. 111.

40. Solov'yev, XIV, pp. 48–9 ; Florovsky, *Sostav*, p. 400, n. 1.

41. These figures are taken from the list in Belyavsky, op. cit., pp. 355ff. They do not coincide exactly with the figures given by the same author in the tables on pp. 81ff.

42. For Catherine's letters describing her journey, see *SIRIO*, 10, pp. 183ff. See also Reddaway, *Documents*, pp. 17–18.

Chapter 10. The Great Instruction

1. *PSZ*, XVII, No. 12,801.

2. Altogether at least 25 editions in nine languages were published between 1767 and 1797. See W.E. Butler, 'The Nakaz of Catherine the Great' in *The American Book Collector*, XVI, No. 5, 1966, pp. 18–21. The Nakaz was banned in France.

3. *SIRIO*, 1, p. 268, Catherine to Madame Geoffrin, 28 March 1765.

4. *Sochineniya*, ed. by Pypin, XII, pp. 524–5.

5. Quoted in Solov'yev, XIV, pp. 265–6 ; cf. *SIRIO*, 20, p. 236, 17 October 1767.

6. F. Taranovsky, 'Politicheskaya doktrine v nakaze Imperatritsy Yekateriny II' ; M.M. Shcherbatov, 'Zamechaniya na Bol'shoy Nakaz Yekateriny.'

7. See N.D. Chechulin, 'Ob istochnikakh Nakaza'.

8. Catherine has been charged by no less an authority than Franco Venturi with having distorted the thought of Beccaria. She may well have been influenced – if she needed influencing – by Melchior von Grimm's review of Morellet's translation into French. Grimm attacked the whole theory of the social contract 'dont je n'ai jamais trouvé trace dans l'histoire de l'homme . . . et sur lequel M. J.-J. Rousseau bavarde si éloquemment depuis quelques années'.
(*Correspondance Littéraire*, 1 December 1765, quoted in *Cesare Beccaria*, op. cit., ed. F. Venturi, p. 338.)

9. The second volume of Bielfeld's *Institutions* appeared in Russian in 1775. See N.D. Chechulin, *Nakaz Imperatritsy Yekateriny II dannyy kommissi po sochineniyu proekta novogo ulozheniya*, p. cxxiv.

10. A.H. Brown, 'S.E.M Desnitsky, Adam Smith and the Nakaz of Catherine II'.

11. All quotations from Montesquieu's *L'Esprit des Lois* are from the Garnier edition, Paris, 1961. All quotations from Catherine's Instruction are from the English translation by M. Tatishchev, reprinted by W.R. Reddaway in *Documents*. For article 5 of the Instruction see Montesquieu, Livre I, Ch. III, Garnier edn., p. 10.

12. Article 9 : 'The sovereign is absolute.' But see French version : 'le monarque de Russie est souverain', in 1769 St Petersburg edition ; Russian version ; 'gosudar' st' samoderzhannyy'.

13. Livre VIII, Ch. XXI, p. 134.

14. *RS*, XII, 1875, pp. 384ff, probably dating from the 1760s since there is a reference to the Nakaz.

15. Livre II, Ch. IV, pp. 19–22.

16. *Nakaz*, Chapter III, articles 18, 19 and 20. The semantic problem is here particularly acute. The Russian text has : 'pravitel'stva' ; the English text has 'courts of judicature' ; the French has 'Tribunaux'.

17. *Nakaz*, Chapter IV ; Livre VI, Ch. IV, at p. 21. D. Ransel, in *The Politics*, p. 179, n. 30, seems to accept that Catherine perverted Montesquieu's idea and 'located the depository of laws in the bureaucracy'. But the *parlements* were royal tribunals to which, in the Russian context, the Senate was the nearest parallel.

18. 'Protiv ulozheniya', Chapter III, article 21.

19. 'Ne mogut peremenit'sya' : 'Cannot be altered'. See Chapter XIX, articles 440–46.

20. Livre XI, Ch. VII, pp. 174–5.

21. Article 149 ; the whole of Chapter X of the Nakaz from which this article is quoted is strongly influenced by Beccaria's *Dei delitti e delle pene*.

22. Beccaria, *op. cit.*, p. 16. 'C'est rompre la digue qui s'oppose au torrent des opinions.'

23. Montesquieu, Livre III, Ch. IV, Garnier edn, p. 200.

24. Beccaria, XXI, 'Pene dei Nobili'.

25. Livre XI, ch. VI, 'de la constitution d'Angleterre', p. 166.

26. Article 260 ; cf. Montesquieu, Livre XV, Ch. XVIII, pp. 269–70.

27. Articles 36–39 ; cf. Livre XI, Ch. III (Garnier edn, p. 162), and also in article 39, Livre XI (Garnier edn, p. 164).

28. Montesquieu, Livre XII, Ch. V, p. 201. See also Chapter XXI.

29. Catherine, *Sochineniya*, XII, p. 524.

30. Ibid.

31. Chechulin, op. cit., p. xciii ; A.V. Florovsky, *Iz istorii yekaterininskoy kommissii 1767 goda*, pp. 10–11.

32. Catherine, *Sochineniya*, XII, p. 524.

33. Livre XV, Ch. XVIII, Garnier edn, p. 270. All the general observations on slavery in the classical world in the original Chapter XI of the Instruction are taken from Livre XV. For the original text of Chapter XI see *SIRIO*, pp. 152ff.

34. Such a law was in fact enacted in 1775 (*PSZ*, XX, No. 14,275, 17 March 1775).

35. See above, Chapter 4 and see Chechulin, op. cit., p. xxxiii.

36. *SIRIO*, 10, pp. 82ff.

37. G. Sacke, *Die Gesetzgebende Kommission Katharinas II*, pp. 76ff.

38. See the reports of Beausset in *SIRIO*, 141, passim. And see G. Macartney, *The Present State of Russia*, p. 28.

39. Ya. Zutis, *Ostseyskiy vopros v XVIIIm veke*, pp. 311ff ; see also M.T. Belyavsky, *Krest'yanskiy vopros . . . .* , p. 37.

40. See Chapter 8.

41. *AAE*, Mémoires et documents, *Description politique de la Russie*, 1767 ; folio 110ff.

42. In May 1868 the Imperial Russian Historical Society asked for permission to publish the materials of the Legislative Commission of 1767. Alexander II asked Prince P.A. Vyazemsky to check whether there would not be inconveniences in publishing the history of the Commission owing to the 'delicacy and political significance of some of the questions which were raised in the Commission'. A.V. Florovsky, *Iz istorii*, p. 228 ; cf. Belyavsky, p. 101.

43. Cf. Shirley, quoted in Sacke, p. 98. 'Cedant arma togae' was invented here, wrote Cathcart to Weymouth on 19/30 August 1768. 'There was not a black gown or anything that looked like a lawyer in the house.' (*SIRIO*, 12, p. 355.)

44. In his annual report for 1764, Breteuil reported Panin as one of the disgruntled : 'M. Panin m'en a dit plus qu'il ne faut pour m'assurer de ses regrets et de ses dispositions, et pour que je ne doive pas douter qu'il seroit aisé d'aider à la chute de cette princesse.' *AAE* Mémoires et documents, xI, 1764.)

45. Chechulin, op. cit., p. cxlvii ; *PSZ*, xVIII, No. 12,977, 24 September 1767.

46. P.I. Shchegolev, *Dekabristy*, Moscow, Leningrad, 1926, p. 166.

Chapter 11. The Great Debate

1. *PSZ*, xVIII, No. 12,948, 30 July 1767 ; ibid., No. 12,950, same date.

2. G. Sacke, *Die Gesetzgebende Kommission*, p. 104.

3. *SIRIO*, 4, p. 52.

4. *SIRIO*, 4, pp. 48–9. Vyazemsky had been ordered to appoint four legal experts to his staff. One of them was Charles de Villiers, on whom see A. Florovsky, 'Un légiste français au service de la tsarine Catherine II'.

5. *SIRIO*, 10, p. 231. Sacke, op. cit., pp. 22ff has argued that these protocols are not a reliable account of what occurred in the debates since 'zweifellos' they were censored by Catherine or Shuvalov, and 'oppositional speeches' were eliminated. Since there were no shorthand writers, evidently the journals provide incomplete summaries and collated reports rather than transcripts. But there is no evidence for political censorship. However Sacke has performed a useful service

in pointing to omissions in the journals, and to the poor quality of the editing of some of the earlier volumes on the Commission published by the Imperial Russian Historical Society.

6. It has been argued that the predominance of high government servants in the sub-commissions, or nobles with high service ranks, reflects a conscious effort to give a class bias to legislation. For a sensible discussion of this point see Kerry R. Morrison, 'Catherine II's Legislative Commission : An Administrative Interpretation'.

7. *SIRIO*, 10, p. 230, article 23. The assembly voted against Glazov's exclusion, and in favour of an apology and fine by 323 to 105. See ibid., 4, pp. 108 and 131, and fuller version in Solov'yev, xIV, pp. 117ff.

8. For instance the deputy from the peasants of the Goroblagodatsk foundry took the opportunity to return to his 'constituency' in the interval created by the transfer of the assembly from Moscow to St Petersburg. He invited the local peasants to meet in their village assemblies, and let him know of any further grievances they might have ; in order to enable them to meet, he issued 'an instruction' that uezd electors should be freed from factory work and from transport and communal dues, and collected 20 rubles from the peasants to pay for his journey from and to the capital. The manager of the enterprise, General Irman, reported this as interference with the management of the foundry, and the Senate condemned the deputy to loss of his status, his badge, and to repayment of the money. Catherine confirmed the verdict on 22 August 1768, but added that the money should only be returned if the peasants asked for it, since they should not have obeyed the deputy's orders any more than he should have given them. (See fullest, though incomplete, account in Belyavsky, *Krest'yanskiy vopros*, pp. 179ff).

9. *SIRIO*, 4, pp. 57 and 62, note ; for fuller text and discussion see Sacke, pp. 132ff.

10. It has been frequently suggested that the fact that 'only 12' peasant nakazy were read out in the Commission reflects the class bias of the Commission. But no noble or urban nakazy were read out at all.

11. See *SIRIO*, 4, pp. 137–47, and ibid., 8, pp. 20–34 for these lists of laws.

12. *SIRIO*, 4, p. 221, for resolution of 8 October 1767, and ibid., 8, pp. 321–4.

13. *PSZ*, xVIII, No. 12,956, 11 August 1767.

14. Sacke, op. cit., p. 146.

15. *SIRIO*, 8, p. 324.

16. Sacke, op. cit., pp. 146–7 ; Florovsky, *Sostav*, p. 530.

17. *SIRIO*, 4 pp. 49ff. The theoretical exposition in this document reflects Catherine's reading of Montesquieu and Bielfeld. The total number of sub-commissions eventually set up was 19, each composed of five members.

18. *SIRIO*, 10, p. 270.

19. *SIRIO*, 10, pp. 297–9, 16 July 1768. A further instruction to Bibikov, amplifying that of 16 July,

was issued by Catherine on 13 August 1768. Here again she outlined the stages to be gone through before a vote was taken on a draft law. But it must be emphasized that a vote was not the expression of a decision but of an opinion. Ibid., pp. 299ff.

20. *SIRIO*, 36, p. 146.

21. Belyavsky, *Krest'yanskiy vopros*, p. 277 ; *SIRIO*, 36, p. viii.

22. *PSZ*, XIX, Nos. 13,746, 13,793, 13,845, 1 February, 1 May and 1 September 1772, and No. 13,893, 1 February 1773. See also No. 13,938 on the election of deputies from territories annexed at the first partition of Poland.

23. Belyavsky, op. cit., p. 253.

24. Sacke, op. cit., pp. 147ff ; Florovsky, *Sostav*, p. 535 ; Lipinsky, *Novyye dannyye*, p. 233. Twenty-nine deputies were specifically recalled to their duties on 22 December 1768 (*SIRIO*, 36, pp. 149–51).

25. Sacke, pp. 149. Belyavsky estimates that in the course of 1768 fifty-eight 'anti-noble' speeches were made by a total of 26 deputies. This scarcely confirms the existence of a formidable anti-noble bloc (p. 253).

26. Sacke, op cit., p. 155.

27. Belyavsky, op. cit., p. 253.

28. V. Sergeyevich, *Otkuda neudachi*, p. 237.

29. Cf. the same conclusion in Kerry Morrison, op. cit., p. 480 ; see also Sergeyevichch, op. cit., pp. 260–1.

30. Sergeyevich goes so far as to call it government-sponsored, op cit., p. 237. See *SIRIO*, pp. 575ff, for the text and amendments proposed by the directing sub-commission.

31. Sergeyevich, op. cit., p. 244.

32. *SIRIO*, 4, p. 200.

33. Ibid., pp. 187ff.

34. *SIRIO*, 8, pp. 335, 339.

35. Ibid., p. 350.

36. For Zolotnitsky's speech see *SIRIO*, 36, p. 332; for Poletika's speech, ibid., pp. 341ff. For the report by Ungern Sternberg and Löwenwolde to their electors, see Sacke, op. cit., pp. 159ff, and *SIRIO*, 36, pp. 359ff, and 371ff.

37. *SIRIO*, 32, pp. 345–6. Matters *kasayushcheyesya do pravleniya.*

38. The nobility of Smolensk attempted to state their case for the preservation of rights granted by the kings of Poland. See Dukes, p. 157, n. 3, and in addition to references given there see *SIRIO*, 32, p. 319.

39. *SIRIO*, 36, pp. 300–1. Two Yaik Cossacks, Ivan Tambovtsev, and I. Akutin 'adhered' to Antsyferov's opinion. So did T. Padurov, deputy of the Orenburg Cossacks, who was to become one of the leaders of the Pugachev revolt. *SIRIO*, 32, p. 208.

40. *SIRIO*, 36, p. 13. Korob'in, an artillery officer, had not been elected, but the mandate of the elected deputy had been transferred to him, probably around December 1767.

41. Vasily Tambovtsev of the Yaik Cossacks objected to a clause in the draft which entitled all the no-

bles to be received at court. He argued that since the ruler was sovereign only he could decide whom to 'admit to his house'. No one had the right to draft a law on this subject and thus place an obligation on the sovereign. Eighteen non-nobles supported his opinion. *SIRIO*, 32, p. 296.

42. *SIRIO*, 4, pp. 165ff, 179ff, 212ff.

43. *SIRIO*, 32, p. 54.

44. *SIRIO*, 32, p. 406, 5 May 1768.

45. For the nakaz of the nobles of Kozlov see *SIRIO*, 32, p. 420.

46. Ibid., pp. 475ff.

47. Ibid., pp. 486ff.

48. There is a good deal of confusion about Ya. P. Kozel'sky. Was he the same person as the Ya. P. Kozel'sky who published his *Philosophical Considerations* in 1768, and who subsequently enjoyed a distinguished career as a translator, writer and bureaucrat ? According to the latest Soviet scholarship, there were three sons of Paul Kozel'sky, who were all three called Yakov, according to 'an unusual but genuine Ukrainian custom'. The middle Kozel'sky is the writer, and his younger brother is the army officer, who made a brief appearance on the historical stage in the Legislative Commission. The arguments in favour of two, let alone three, brothers of the same name are rather far-fetched and seem to stem from a refusal to recognize that the champion of the serfs in 1768 could possibly have had a perfectly respectable government career afterwards, . when he should by rights have been disgraced. See the various arguments in the introduction by S. V. Paparigopulo in S.A. Pokrovsky (ed.), *Yuridicheskiye proizvedeniya progressivnykh russkikh mysliteley*, pp. 594ff, n. 1 ; see also by the same author, 'O dvukh Ya. P. Kozel'skikh'.

49. *SIRIO*, 32, p. 580. Article 15 stated that the purchase or sale of free estates was allowed duty-free.

50. *SIRIO*, 32, pp. 233ff ; 36, pp. 309ff.

51. *SIRIO*, 36, pp. 27–8.

52. *SIRIO*, 36, p. 29.

53. See A. Brückner, *Katharina die Zweite*, pp. 480–1 ; P. Milyukov, *Ocherki po istorii russkoy kul'tury*, p. 362.

54. A. Florovsky, *Iz istorii*, pp. 225ff.

55. Belyavsky, op. cit., p. 246. Belyavsky produces no evidence to support his allegation. V.I. Nedosekin, in 'O diskussii po krest'yanskomu voprosu v Rossii nakanune vosstaniya Pugacheva', denies that Korob'in was a liberal at all but portrays him as concerned to improve the status of the serfs merely in order to strengthen serfdom, in which he supported Catherine. Nedosekin proves that he was not forced to give up the mandate (p. 343). The popularity of Korob'in's views in the assembly as a whole is reflected in the votes cast for him in two elections to sub-commissions : 174 out of 287 on 5 May 1768, the day he first spoke, and 260 out of 306 on 14 May 1768. These figures are adduced by Nedosekin to prove that Korob'in must have pleased the nobles ; by Belyavsky to prove that he pleased the non-noble deputies. See also Sacke,

op. cit., n. 44, and for an almost contemporary recollection, where Korob'in appears as an opponent of serfdom, Vinsky, *Moe vremya*, Introduction by I. de Madariaga, pp. 5–6.

56. See Dukes, op. cit., p. 220, who makes the same point. In the *Zapiski o zhizni i sluzhbe Bibikova*, written by the son of the marshal of the Commission, the author states (p. 41) that his father, who had been the deputy of the nobility of Kostroma, had wished to include in their nakaz 'the setting up of free peasants' almost in the same way as 'free agriculturalists' were set up by Alexander I, but had not been allowed to do so. The connexion between Alexander's law of 1803 and the project for setting up villages deserves study.

57. *SIRIO*, 32, p. 283. This clause in the draft had evidently provoked dissension in the directing subcommission, judging by a note in the margin : 'this article is excluded entirely from this draft since it belongs to the sub-commission on justice'. (Ibid., p. 584.)

58. For published peasant nakazy see *SIRIO*, 115 and 123.

59. The summary was prepared by R.L. Vorontsov, A.S. Stroganov, and P. Orlov. Belyavsky, *Krestyanskiy vopros*, pp. 114, 129–30, states that the summary softened peasant criticism and anti-noble feeling (n. 23) ; it has not been published.

60. Belyavsky, op. cit., p. 362.

61. Ibid., p. 178, table analysing the composition of the sub-commission by estates.

62. The extension of Vyazemsky's reforms to other state foundries was not completed until 1767. See above, Chapter 8.

63. The length of peasant memory is reflected in the nakaz of the Yeniseysk state peasants, in which the misdeeds of a voyevoda as far back as 1728 were duly recounted.

64. *SIRIO*, 43, pp. 199ff., art. 6. Article 10 requested the establishment of a Mining and Smelting Cadet Corps for the children of mine-owners and owners of foundries.

65. Andrushchenko, *Krest'yanskaya voyna*, pp. 104–5 ; *SIRIO*, 115, pp. 264ff.

66. *SIRIO*, 43, pp. 204ff at p. 207. This nakaz is a general survey of the importance of manufacturing to the national economy. It was in all likelihood drafted by D. Volkov, whose views it reflects.

67. *SIRIO*, 4, pp. 88–91 ; ibid., 8, pp. 332–5 ; cf. Semevsky, *Krest'yane*, II, p. 436.

68. *SIRIO*, 8, pp. 89ff.

69. Odnodvortsy deputies spoke 84 times in the full assembly.

70. Belyavsky, op. cit., p. 101.

71. On the Land Survey see Chapter 6.

72. *SIRIO*, 32, pp. 513ff.

73. Nachertaniye, *PSZ*, XVIII, No. 13,095, 8 April 1768 ; cf. Florovsky, *Iz istorii*, p. 156.

Chapter 12. Foreign Policy: from Peace to War

1. *SIRIO*, 48, pp. 9ff. The questionnaire was drafted by M.L. Vorontsov.

2. *SIRIO*, 27, p. 170, Note by Catherine, after May 1771.

3. *SIRIO*, 48, pp. 9ff.

4. *SIRIO*, 7, p. 91. Cf. Bil'basov, II, p. 298.

5. Bil'basov, II, pp. 305–6. See also his 'Prisoyedineniye Kurlyandii' in *Istoricheskiye Monografii*, II, pp. 205–66.

6. See for instance Catherine to Count Keyserling in Warsaw, 1763 : . . . 'mon but est d'être liée d'amitié avec toutes les puissances et même jusqu'à la défensive afin de pouvoir toujours me ranger du côté du plus opressé et être par là l'arbitre de l'Europe.' Solov'yev, XIII, pp 291–2.

7. It had been included in Peter III's treaty of alliance with Prussia in March 1762.

8. *Sochineniya*, ed. by Pypin, XII, p. 547.

9. For the most recent treatment of Anglo-Russian negotiations see H.M. Scott, 'Britain, Poland and the Russian Alliance'.

10. *SIRIO*, 48, pp. 298ff for the protocols of the conference of 4/15 February 1763.

11. *SIRIO*, 51, pp. 6ff. Present on this occasion were Bestuzhev Ryumin, the vice-chancellor, A.M. Golitsyn, N.I. Panin, Ya.P. Shakhovskoy, I.I. Neplyuyev, G.G. Orlov, and A. Olsuf'yev ; Z. Chernyshev was called in to discuss military matters. Ransel, *The Politics*, p. 131, is misled by the reports of foreign envoys, who themselves were misled into thinking that a new institution, a 'Conference' on the lines of the Elizabethan 'Conference', had been set up by Catherine. But it was Catherine's normal practice to call together a number of her advisers to discuss major issues on an *ad hoc* basis. The word 'conference' simply describes a meeting, and has no institutional significance whatever in this context. There is therefore no question of Catherine 'finally deciding to abolish the conference' and working through Panin alone.

12. The title (for it was not a post) of chancellor had been attached in 1709 to the chief minister and head of the Posol'skiy Prikaz, or Office of Ambassadors. When the College of Foreign Affairs was established by Peter I, the chancellor became its president and the vice-chancellor its vice-president. Catherine never appointed a chancellor, though Panin was eventually raised to the first rank in the Table of Ranks, equivalent to a field marshal.

13. For Austrian policy see A. Beer, *Die erste Theilung Polens*.

14. See H.M. Scott, op. cit., n. 9 above, and M. Roberts, *Splendid Isolation, 1763–1780*.

15. See *PCFG*, 23, p. 216 Finckenstein to Frederick II, 14 December 1763, p. 218, Frederick to Solms (in St Petersburg), 17 December 1763. F. de Martens, *Recueil*, VI, L'Allemagne.

16. Martens, op. cit., pp. 11ff and 25ff. See also H.M. Scott, 'Frederick II, the Ottoman Empire and the Origins of the Russo-Prussian Alliance of April 1764'.

17. Solov'yev, XIII, p. 361 ; see also H. Kaplan, *The First Partition of Poland*, p. 33.

NOTES

18. *Correspondance inédite du Roi Stanislas Auguste Poniatowski et de Madame Geoffrin, 1764–1777*, p. 101, 9 September 1764.

19. See S. Askenazy, *Die letzte polnische Königswahl*, pp. 101–2 ; A. Beer, op. cit., I, p. 161 ; Solov'yev, XIII, pp. 353ff.

20. The standard works on this subject are N.D. Chechulin, *Vneshnyaya politika Rossii v nachale tsarstvovaniya Yekateriny II, 1762–1774*, and P.A. Aleksandrov, *Severnaya Sistema*. For a review of more recent literature see D.M. Griffiths, 'The Rise and Fall of the Northern System : Court Politics and Foreign Policy in the First Half of Catherine II's Reign'.

21. Solov'yev, XIV, pp. 176–8.

22. For the negotiations with Denmark see O. Brandt, *Caspar von Saldern und die Nordeuropäische Politik im Zeitalter Katharinas II*. Saldern, a Holsteiner himself, was supposed to be negotiating on behalf of Russia, but since he wanted Holstein to be transferred to Denmark, he worked closely with the Danish minister, Count Bernstorff, and was amply rewarded for his services. See *Danske Tractater*, pp. 183–201 ; 229–62.

23. *SIRIO*, 12, p. 232, to Grafton.

24. For the latest study of Macartney's mission in Russia, see M. Roberts, 'Macartney in Russia'. See also Martens, *Recueil*, IX, L'Angleterre, pp. 228ff.

25. *SIRIO*, 12, p. 221, Grafton to Macartney, 29 September 1765.

26. Ibid., pp. 264ff., and see K. Rahbek Schmidt, 'The Treaty of Commerce between Great Britain and Russia 1766 ; A Study in the Development of Count Panin's Northern System', *Scandoslavica*, I, 1954, pp. 115ff and Roberts, op. cit., n. 24.

27. *SIRIO*, 67, p. 373, Panin to Macartney, 30 April 1767.

28. Macartney bribed Saldern (already the recipient of Danish money) who had access to Panin, but this had no effect on his negotiations. See W. Reddaway, 'Macartney in Russia, 1765–67', at p. 281 and note ; Buckinghamshire, II, p. 106, pp. 228–9 ; *PCFG*, 22, p. 373, Frederick to Goltz, 7 December 1762 ; ibid., 23, p. 42, the same to the same, June 1763.

29. E. Amburger, *Russland und Schweden, 1762–1772. Katharina II., die Schwedische Verfassung und die Ruhe des Nordens*, pp. 51–2 ; *SIRIO*, 48, pp. 9ff.

30. Amburger, op. cit., pp. 69–70 ; *SIRIO*, 48, p. 70, Rescript to Osterman in Stockholm, 13/24 August 1762.

31. For the most recent study see M.F. Metcalf, *Russia, England and Swedish Party Politics, 1762–1766*. Metcalf estimates that Osterman received 350,000 rubles, and Goodricke £17,300, much of which was used to feed and provide transport for nobles (pp. 253ff).

32. L. Jacobsohn, *Russland und Frankreich in den ersten Regierungsjahren der Kaiserin Katharina II., 1762–1772*, pp. 24ff.

33. Metcalf, op. cit., passim. Amburger, op. cit., pp. 157–8.

34. Jacobsohn, op. cit., pp. 24ff.

35. When Durand was appointed to Russia in 1772 his credentials were drafted in Latin, a less pure language than French, which permitted the adjective 'imperialis' to qualify 'maiestas'. See *SIRIO*, 67, pp. 1–5, Panin to D.A. Golitsyn, Paris, 12/23 April 1766 ; *PCFG*, 32, p. 500, Frederick II to Edelsheim, 20 September 1772.

36. Solov'yev, XIII, pp. 129ff ; XIV, p. 358.

37. Stanislas to Rzewusky, 15/26 September 1766, *SIRIO*, 67, p. 138.

38. The 'liberum veto' was the right of any deputy to the Diet to object to the enactment of any measure. Since decisions had to be taken by unanimity at ordinary Diets, this meant the throwing out of any measure under discussion, and had come also to signify the abrogation of all measures already agreed upon at a Diet.

39. 'Forming a confederation' was a constitutional means of revolting against the king or the existing government in Poland.

40. *SIRIO*, 67, pp. 76ff, 15/26 August 1766, Rescript to Repnin ; for the French text of the Declaration ibid., pp. 84ff. English translation in H. Kaplan, *The First Partition of Poland*, pp. 219ff ; a copy of the Declaration was forwarded to the Russian envoy in London, asking him to procure English *written* support for it in Poland ; verbal support had already been promised. See *SIRIO*, 67, pp. 63ff ; Kaplan, op. cit., p. 54.

41. *SIRIO*, 67, p. 108, Panin to Repnin, 2/13 September 1766.

42. Solov'yev, XIV, pp. 150ff.

43. *SIRIO*, 67, p. 178ff, Rescript of 6/17 October 1766.

44. *PCFG*, 25, passim, and specifically pp. 281–2, Frederick to Solms, 15/26 October 1766.

45. Kaplan, op. cit., p. 60, n. 10 ; Beer, *Die erste Theilung*, p. 188.

46. Stanislas burst into tears when Repnin congratulated him on the abolition of majority voting, Solov'yev, XIV, pp. 158ff, Repnin to Panin, 11/22 November 1766.

47. Ibid., and Beer, op. cit., pp. 201–2.

48. *SIRIO*, 67, p. 149, Catherine to Stanislas, 6/17 October 1766 ; ibid., p. 204, comment on Repnin to Panin, 9/20 November 1766.

49. *SIRIO*, 67, pp. 409ff, Panin to Repnin, 14 August 1767.

50. *SIRIO*, 67, pp. 205ff, Rescript to Repnin and Panin to Repnin, 24 December 1766/4 January 1767.

51. Solov'yev, XIV, pp. 184–5 ; *SIRIO*, 67, pp. 301ff, N. Panin to Repnin.

52. Nothing would please him more, wrote Panin, than to see the Orthodox bishop of Belorussia, however unworthy as an individual, take his seat in the Polish Senate. But he gave up the demand when Stanislas offered to grant similar rights to Uniat bishops. 'We don't want these renegades to obtain by imperial protection the advantages they have not so far been able to obtain from the Republic by going over to Rome.' (*SIRIO*, 67, p. 464, Panin to Repnin, 21 September 1767 ; pp. 388ff, 26 June 1767.)

53. The intervention of the Papal nuncio led Panin

to instruct Repnin to attempt to persuade the king and
the Polish primate to point out to the Pope that 'popes
no longer governed affairs according to their own caprice ; that by his ardour, which was out of place, he
might do more harm than good to the Catholic faith,
and lead to the withdrawal of Poland from its obedience
to Rome ; that we [Russia] had sufficient means and
strength in Poland to order everything there, and we
might decide to destroy Papal power there and establish
an independent hierarchy if he continues his unworthy
actions.' Repnin was to point out to the king that Poland would become enslaved to the papacy 'at a time
when all other Catholics are freeing themselves from
this infection' (Solov'yev, XIV, 228–9). Repnin however realized that this was going too far.

54. Solov'yev, XIV, pp. 212ff, undated.

55. See K. Lutosłanski, *Recueil des actes diplomatiques, traités et documents concernant la Pologne*, I, pp. 25ff, Nos 22 and 23.

56. Martens, *Recueil*, VI, L'Allemagne, pp. 43ff.

57. See Chapter 8, pp. 129–30.

58. *SIRIO*, 141, p. 475, Rossignol to Choiseul,
11/22 November 1768.

59. Solov'yev, XIV, pp. 251ff.

60. *PCFG*, 26, pp. 498–9. Frederick to Solms, 26
November/7 December 1768.

Chapter 13. The First Turkish War

1. *SIRIO*, 10, p. 302 ; Solov'yev, XIV, p. 301.

2. See Chapter 2, pp. 40–1.

3. *AGS*, I, p. 11.

4. Account constructed from reports of foreign
envoys in *SIRIO*, 109, pp. 333ff ; ibid., 141, pp.
493ff ; ibid., 37, pp. 188ff. It may be added that Frederick II thought Rumyantsev to be the best general, and
Chernyshev a better man than Panin to be placed in
charge of military operations (PCFG, 28, 19ff, Frederick to Solms, 8 January 1969, pp. 54ff, 22 January
1969). Field-Marshal Golitsyn was incidentally the
brother-in-law of Rumyantsev, who detested him.

5. *AGS*, I, pp. 1ff ; *SIRIO*, 10, p. 310.

6. The treaty of Belgrade was concluded at the end
of the war with Turkey, 1736–9.

7. Yu. R. Klokman, *Fel'dmarshal Rumyantsev v
period russko-turetskoy voyny 1768–1774 gg*, pp.
35–6 ; L.G. Beskrovnyy, *Khrestomatiya po russkoy
voyennoy istorii*, pp. 202–3.

8. Solov'yev, XIV, p. 286 ; L.G. Beskrovnyy,
Russkaya armiya i flot, p. 294.

9. Klokman, op. cit., p. 66. The standard account
by A. Petrov, *Voyna Rossii s Turtsiey i pol'skimi konfederatami*, has not been superseded.

10. *SIRIO*, 10, p. 389, 14/25 December 1769.

11. Klokman, op. cit., p. 96 for the losses of
both sides.

12. *Fel'dmarshal Rumyantsev, Sbornik Dokumentov i materialov*, ed. by N.M. Korobkov, rescript from
Catherine to Rumyantsev, 2/13 August 1770, pp.
191ff.

13. *AGS*, I, pp. 1–5, 4/15 November ; pp. 8–11,

12/23 November 1768 ; for rescripts to A.G. Orlov
throughout the war, see *SIRIO*, 1, pp. 2ff.

14. See A.G. Cross, 'Samuel Greig, Catherine the
Great's Scottish Admiral'.

15. 'Pis'ma Imperatritsy Yekateriny II k Grafu
Ivanu Grigor'yevichu Chernyshevu 1764–1773', at p.
1321.

16. *SIRIO*, 141, p. 561, 23 May 1769.

17. *SIRIO*, 87, p. 473, Panin to Chernyshev,
18/29 July 1769. Russian instructions to privateers,
mainly Greeks, operating in the Aegean, were modelled on the English. See *SIRIO*, 1, p. 22, Catherine to
A. Orlov, 11/22 August 1769.

18. Solov'yev, XIV, pp. 301ff ; the standard modern work is Ye. V. Tarle, *Chesmenskiy boy : pervaya
russkaya ekspeditsiya v Arkhipelag 1769–74*, pp. 28ff.

19. M.B. Petrovich, 'Catherine II and a Fake Peter
III in Montenegro'.

20. Solov'yev, XIV, pp. 377ff. Aleksey Orlov to
Catherine, undated.

21. Ye. Tarle, op. cit., pp. 45ff. The standard account with map is in R.C. Anderson, *Naval Wars in the
Levant*, pp. 287ff.

22. Solov'yev, XIV, p. 383.

23. *SIRIO*, 1, pp. 61–2, Catherine to A. Orlov.

24. *AGS*, I, pp. 368ff, 8/19, 10/21, 14/25, 17/28
March, 21 March/1 April and 23 March/3 April 1771 ;
SIRIO, 1, pp. 65ff rescripts to A.G. Orlov, 22 March/2
April 1771.

25. Beskrovnyy, *Russkaya armiya i flot*, pp. 295ff.

26. *AGS*, I., p. 67, 11/22 November 1770 ; pp.
368ff (see n. 24) ; *SIRIO*, 1, p. 69, Catherine to Orlov,
22 March /2 April 1771.

27. Solov'yev, XIV, pp. 450–1.

28. A.W. Fisher, *The Russian Annexation of the
Crimea, 1772–1783*, pp. 40ff.

29. See below, Chapter 14.

30. *PSZ*, XVIII, No. 13,194, 13 November 1768,
No. 13,303, 27 May 1769 ; S.M. Troitsky, *Finansovaya politika russkogo absolyutizma XVIII veka*, pp.
142ff. Payments to assigned peasants were raised to 6
k.p.d. and 12 k.p.d. (with horse) in summer and 5 and
8 k.p.d. in winter, with an allowance of 3 k.p.d. for
travel estimated at 25 versts a day.

31. Beskrovnyy, op. cit., pp. 295ff.

32. See Chapter 7, p. 117.

33. P. Alefirenko, 'Chumnyy bunt v Moskve v
1771 g.' 161 of those arrested were eventually tried and
sentenced to the usual forms of corporal punishment
and hard labour. For those interested in the composition
of rioting crowds, Alefirenko provides details. Mavrodin, op. cit., I, p. 458 analyses the extent to which the
riot can be regarded as an early example of political activity by an industrial proletariat (there were 12 factory
workers among those arrested).

Chapter 14. The Impact of the War on Russian
Foreign Policy

1. Amburger, op. cit., p. 184.

2. See Chapter 13, pp. 205–6.

3. See Chapter 12 for the exchange treaty ; see also Amburger, op. cit., pp. 189–90 ; *SIRIO*, 87, pp. 246ff, Panin to Filosofov, 21 December/2 January 1769.

4. *SIRIO*, 87, p. 335, Catherine to Panin, n.d. on Filosofov to Panin, 13/24 February 1769.

5. Amburger, pp. 194ff.

6. Solov'yev, xiv, pp. 351, Osterman to Panin, 21 February/3 March 1768.

7. Amburger estimates that more than five million silver thalers had entered the country, pp. 223ff.

8. Ibid., p. 192.

9. *SIRIO*, 87, pp. 299ff., Panin to I.G. Chernyshev, 2/13 January 1769 ; Solov'yev, xiv, pp. 260ff, 355.

10. *PCFG*, 28, pp. 406ff, Frederick to Solms, 28 June 1769.

11. Ibid., 29, pp. 11ff.

12. Frederick to Rohde, 20 September 1769, *PCFG*, 29, p. 89.

13. Solov'yev, xiv, pp. 340ff ; F. de Martens, *Recueil*, 6, pp. 48ff. For the secret article see A. Geffroy, *Gustave III et la cour de France*, i, p. 39, n. 1.

14. F. de Martens, *Recueil*, 6, p. 11, and *Danske Tractater*, p. 229.

15. *SIRIO*, 87, pp. 372ff. Solov'yev, xiv, 328ff.

16. See Chapter 12 for the effect of the plague in Russia.

17. Kaplan, op. cit., pp. 126–7 ; Solov'yev, xiv, pp. 401–2.

18. *PCFG*, 29, p. 520.

19. *AGS*, 1, pp. 52–4, 12/23 August 1770 ; p. 56, 26 August/6 September, and p. 59, 13/24 September 1770.

20. *PCFG*, 30, pp. 101ff, conversations between Kaunitz and Frederick ii, 3 and 4 September 1770.

21. Solov'yev, xiv, p. 401.

22. *SIRIO*, 97, pp. 138–9, Catherine to Rumyantsev, 17/28 September 1770.

23. *AGS*, i, pp. 59–61.

24. *PCFG*, 30, pp. 357, 361, 3 January 1771.

25. Solov'yev, xiv, p. 444, undated.

26. *PCFG*, 30, pp. 460ff.

27. Lynar was a Dane who had played a part as an intermediary in the negotiation of the convention of Klosterseven between the Duke of Cumberland and the French commander in 1757.

28. See Chapter 12, p. 189.

29. *PCFG*, 29, pp. 462ff, Nugent to Kaunitz, 25 May 1770.

30. *PCFG*, 30, pp. 406ff, Prince Henry to Frederick ii, 8 January 1771.

31. *SIRIO*, 37, pp. 339–40, Solms to Frederick, 28 December 1770/8 January 1771.

32. *SIRIO*, 37, pp. 391–2, 20 February 1771.

33. *SIRIO*, 37, pp. 366ff, Solms to Frederick, 1/12 February 1771.

34. *PCFG*, 30, pp. 482ff, to Solms, 27 February 1771.

35. See 'Exposé des droits de Sa Majesté le Roi de Prusse sur le duché de Pomerellie . . .' in Hertzberg, *Recueil de Déductions*, i, pp. 324ff.

36. *SIRIO*, 37, pp. 459ff, Solms to Frederick, 19/30 April 1771 ; van Swieten quoted in Finckenstein to Frederick, 13 May 1771, *PCFG*, 31, pp. 148–9.

37. *AGS*, i, 17/28 March 1771, pp. 371ff ; *SIRIO*, 97, pp. 246ff, 256, rescript to A.G. Orlov, 22 March/2 April 1771.

38. *AGS*, i, pp. 80ff, 9/20 May 1771, quoting Kaunitz to Lobkowitz of 2 May 1771, NS ; see also Joseph ii to Leopold, 2 May 1771 in Arneth, *Maria Theresia und Joseph* ii, ii, pp. 338ff.

39. *SIRIO*, 97, pp. 258ff, Panin to Saldern, 29 April/10 May 1771 ; cf. Lobkowitz to Kaunitz 26 April 1771, *SIRIO*, 109, pp. 524ff.

40. *AGS*, i, pp. 82–3, 16/27 May 1771.

41. *PCFG*, 31, pp. 196–7, Frederick to Rohde, 16 June 1771 ; pp. 202–4, to Solms, 19 June 1771 ; pp. 223ff, 3 July 1771.

42. *PCFG*, 31, p. 235, n. 2, quoting Kaunitz to Lobkowitz, 1 July 1771.

43. G.F. de Martens, *Recueil de Traités*, ii, 1771–9, pp. 19ff.

44. *PCFG*, 31, pp. 305ff, Frederick to Solms, 14 August 1771.

45. *AGS*, i, pp. 117–18, 31 October/11 November 1771.

46. *SIRIO*, 37, p. 527.

47. *AGS*, i, pp. 104–6, 22 August/2 September 1771.

48. *PCFG*, 31, pp. 399–401, Frederick to Solms, 25 September 1771.

49. *PCFG*, 31, pp. 363ff, account by Rohde of a conversation with Maria Theresa on 5 September 1771.

50. *AGS*, i, pp. 115–16 ; cf. *PCFG*, 31, p. 443, n. 1, Solms to Frederick, 12/23 September 1771.

51. *AGS*, i, pp. 122ff.

52. Ibid., pp. 119ff, 10/21 November 1771.

53. See Beer, op. cit., pp. 100, for Kaunitz's analysis of Austrian policy in September 1771 ; see also Solov'yev, xiv, p. 498.

54. *SIRIO*, 97, pp. 501ff : draft letter from Panin to D.M. Golitsyn (Vienna), 5/16 December 1771 ; pp. 508ff, réponse personnelle of the empress to a personal letter from Maria Theresa and Joseph, 6/17 December 1771.

55. *AGS*, i, pp. 145–6 ; see also Beer, op. cit., pp. 168ff. Frederick of course would have nothing to do with exchanging the Austrian share of Poland for Silesia and Glatz. See *PCFG*, 31, pp. 722ff, van Swieten to Kaunitz, 4 February 1772.

56. For the texts see Lutosłanski, pp. 36ff, Nos 30 and 34. Russia acquired 93,000 km.^{2} from Poland.

Chapter 15. From the Partition of Poland to the Peace of Kuchuk-Kainardzhi

1. A. Beer, *Die erste Theilung Polens*, ii, pp. 248–52.

2. *SIRIO*, 1, pp. 77–8. Rescript of 31 December 1771/11 January 1772 to A.G. Orlov ; E.I. Druzhinina,

Kuchuk-Kainardzhiskiy mir 1774 goda, pp. 151–2, re-script of 3/14 January 1772 to P.A. Rumyantsev. For text see A. Petrov, *Voyna Rossii,* IV, Appendix, pp. 187–92.

3. Druzhinina, op. cit., pp. 156–9.

4. Ibid., p. 160.

5. *AGS,* I, p. 195, 27 August/7 September 1772.

6. Druzhinina, op. cit., p. 180.

7. See Chapter 17 for the court crisis of 1772–74.

8. *AGS,* I, pp. 197–8, 1/12 September 1772.

9. Ibid., pp. 201–2, 10/21 September 1772 and see V.L. Ulyanitsky, *Dardanelly, Bosfor i Chernoye More,* p. 408.

10. See Chapter 13, p. 213.

11. Druzhinina, op. cit., p. 215 (who is critical of Catherine's bellicosity and sides throughout with the so-called 'Panin group' – why it is difficult to see, since it was Catherine's persistence which won Russia so much territory) ; see also the paraphrase in *AGS,* I, p. 224, 2/13 January and 3/14 January 1778.

12. Ibid.

13. M. Roberts, 'Great Britain and the Swedish Revolution' at p. 14. See also Gunning to Suffolk, 14/25 September 1772 in *SIRIO,* 10, pp. 320ff.

14. *SIRIO,* 19, pp. 305ff. Déclaration faite au roi de Pologne. Copy delivered to Suffolk by Musin Push-kin on 30 September 1775. For the joint declaration by the three courts see Lutosłanski, *op. cit.,* p. 45, No. 38, 18/29 September 1772.

15. Solov'yev, XIV, pp. 578, Lutosłanski, op. cit., p. 47. No. 39, Protestation du Ministère de Po-logne, 17 October 1772, NS. *SIRIO,* 118, Contreprojet d'une déclaration à remettre au Roi et à la république de Pologne, 14/25 December 1772. See also Panin to Stackelberg 23 December 1772/3 January 1773, *ibid.,* pp. 304 and 31 March/11 April 1773, pp. 378ff.

16. *SIRIO,* 118, pp. 338ff. for the draft with Cath-erine's comments, enclosed in Panin to Stackelberg, 24 February/7 March 1773 ; *ibid.,* 52, pp. 317–34 for the final version. For the decision on the armed forces see *ibid.,* 118, pp. 372ff. Panin to Stackelberg, 21 March/2 April 1773.

17. For the above see J. Lelewel, *Histoire de Po-logne,* II, Paris/Lille, 1844, pp. 78–83 ; Kaplan, *op. cit.,* pp. 174ff. For the texts of the treaties, all dated 7/18 September 1773, see Lutosłanski, op. cit., pp. 66, No. 53, Russia ; p. 71, No. 54, Prussia and p. 75, No. 55, Austria.

18. Lutosłanski, op. cit., pp. 81–2, and pp. 82–3, No. 59.

19. See W.P. Reddaway, 'Great Britain and Po-land, 1762–72' ; W. Konopczynski, 'England and the First Partition of Poland' ; D.B. Horn, *British Public Opinion and the First Partition of Poland ;* E. Burke, *Correspondence,* I, p. 403.

20. M. Tourneux, *Diderot et Catherine,* p. 252.

21. On the alleged secret treaty between Sweden and the Porte see *AGS,* I, pp. 237–8, 18/29 March 1773, and 238–9, 21 March/1 April 1773. On 26 March/6 April 1773 the Council discussed the break-down of the peace talks (Ibid., p. 239–40) ; for instruc-tions to Osterman of 28 March/8 April 1773 see *SIRIO,* 118, pp. 374.

22. M. Roberts in 'Great Britain and the Swedish Revolution' (p. 19, and n. 87) states that English policy was to make Russia believe that a French fleet might be allowed to appear unchallenged in the Baltic. If this was so, British ministers were singularly unsuccessful in convincing the Russian envoys to report this to their courts. See *AGS,* I, pp. 225–6, session of 14/25 Jan-uary 1773 and particularly pp. 228, session of 28 Jan-uary/8 February.

23. *SIRIO,* 19, pp. 265ff. Instructions to Gun-ning. See also pp. 289–90. Cathcart to Gunning in Gunning to Suffolk, 13/24 July 1772 ; pp. 333ff ; Suf-folk to Gunning, 10 November 1772 ; pp. 348ff., Gunning to Suffolk, 29 March/9 April 1773.

24. *SIRIO,* 19, pp. 358ff, Gunning to Suffolk, 24 May/4 June 1773 ; pp. 371ff, 16/27 July 1773 ; pp. 374–5, Suffolk to Gunning, 27 August 1773, NS.

25. M.S. Anderson, 'Great Britain and the Rus-sian Fleet'.

26. *AGS,* I, pp. 232–3.

27. Petrov, *Voyna Rossii,* IV, p. 5.

28. Klokman, op. cit., quoting correspondence of Rumyantsev and Nikita Panin in *RA,* 1882 and *Pere-piska imperatritsy Yekateriny s grafom Rumyantsevym Zadunayskim,* pp. 1 ff ; see also *Perepiska Yekateriny II s raznymi osobami,* and *Fel'dmarshal Rumyantsev, Sbornik Dokumentov i materialov,* pp. 235–6.

29. *SIRIO,* 13, pp. 349ff. Klokman uses this letter (op. cit., pp. 145–6) in a most disingenuous way and goes so far as to say that Catherine 'refused categorically' to raise the numbers of Rumyantsev's army.

30. L. Beskrovnyy, op. cit., pp. 295ff.

31. *AGS,* I, pp. 256–7, 27 August/7 September 1773.

32. *AGS,* I, pp. 264ff. See the discussions at the sessions of 11/22, 14/25, and 18/29 November 1773 ; 23 December 1773/3 January 1774 ; pp. 271ff, 9/18, 13/24, and 16/27 January 1774.

33. Petrov, op. cit., V, pp. 119ff.

34. *PCFG,* 34, pp. 294–5, Solms to Frederick, 9 November 1773 ; 35, p. 158, Zegelin to Frederick, 3 February 1774 ; *AGS,* I, pp. 264–8, 11/22, 14/25 and 18/29 November 1773.

35. *AGS,* I, pp. 273–4, 10/21 March 1774 ; Pe-trov, op. cit., V, pp. 7ff ; Zegelin to Rumyantsev, 8/19 March 1774, Appendix 3, pp. 120–1.

36. Panin had proposed this in the autumn when he was trying to scale down Grigory Orlov's ambitious demands for all the land between the Dniestr and the Dniepr. See Druzhinina, op. cit., p. 256 ; Petrov, op. cit., V, Appendix 7, pp. 130 ff ; Rescript of 7/18 April 1774, pp. 138ff.

37. *Fel'dmarshal Rumyantsev,* pp. 247, No. 112. Rumyantsev to Grand Vizir 28 June/9 July 1774.

38. Ibid., pp. 248ff. Rumyantsev to Catherine 17/28 July 1774.

39. Ibid.

40. The text of the treaty can be found in E. Druzhinina, op. cit., pp. 349ff. Russia received Azov and its surroundings, Kerch, Yenikale, Kinburn and the coast between the Bug and the Dniepr. Crimea was to be sovereign and independent under an elected Chinghisid khan except in religious matters and all Turkish garrisons were to be withdrawn. Other important clauses in the treaty provided for free passage through the Straits for Russian merchant shipping ; it allowed Russia to trade by land and sea on most favoured nation terms within Ottoman territory ; merchants could reside in each other's lands, and Russia could appoint consuls and vice-consuls where necessary in her view (art. 11). Article 14 allowed Russia to erect a Greek Orthodox Church for the general public over and above the private chapel of the envoy. Article 7 was in the long run to prove also of great significance. It ran as follows : 'The Sublime Porte promises to defend the Christian faith and its churches ; in the same way it grants to the Ministers of the Russian Court to make representations in all circumstances in favour both of the church mentioned in article 14 and of those who serve it, and it promises to listen to such representations as those made by a sincerely friendly neighbour.' It will be observed that according to this text, the Russians had only the right to make representations on behalf of *one* specific Greek Orthodox church, and not in favour of the Greek community as a whole or the Christians as a whole. Article 13 returned a number of Caucasian strongholds taken by Russia to the Porte.

41. On 7/18 February 1771, Orlov defended the view in the Council that the Russian frontier with Poland should run along a river. Tantalizingly the record continues : 'On this subject there were many political arguments in the Council, and the master of the ordnance [Orlov] was asked to submit his opinion in writing.' The 'opinion' has not been published. *AGS,* I, p. 74.

42. See e.g. *PCFG,* 30, p. 417, Prince Henry to Frederick II, January 1771.

43. See Solov'yev's speculations on this point, XIV, pp. 468ff.

44. Joseph II had decided to occupy a part of Moldavia and not Little Walachia, which was originally to be ceded to Austria by the Porte in the treaty of 6 July 1771, NS. The Austrian occupation of the area in Moldavia between Siebenburgen and the Polish border, including Cernauti and Suceara, took place by direct agreement with Rumyantsev (unbeknown to his court) in August 1774. The Porte was in no position to object, and on 7 May 1775 a treaty of cession was concluded, followed a year later by a border convention.

Chapter 16. The Revolt of the Cossacks and the Peasant War

1. The instructions of the Don, Yaik and Zaporozhian Cossacks have not been published in full though they have been used in secondary works, by e.g. Roz-ner, Golobutsky, Pronshteyn and Andrushchenko. For debates, see *SIRIO,* 32, p. 169, 10 July 1768, and 36, p. 296 for the views of the Zaporozhian Host ; see also Kohut, op. cit., pp. 208ff.

2. A.P. Pronshteyn, *Zemlya Donskaya v XVIII veke,* p. 236 and n. 1.

3. Ibid., pp. 297ff ; A.A. Karasev, 'Atamanyefremov'.

4. For events on the Yaik river, see I.G. Rozner, *Yaik pered buryey ;* and his 'Yaitskoye kazachestvo nakanune krest'yanskoy voyny 1773–5'. See also A.I. Andrushchenko, 'Klassovaya bor'ba yaitskikh kazakov nakanune krest'yanskoy voyny 1773–5'.

5. A most perceptive analysis of 'pretenderism' is by K.V. Chistov, *Russkiye narodnyye sotsial'no-utopicheskiye legendy.*

6. Rozner, *Yaik pered buryey,* p. 168. It was rumoured that I. Ulyanov, one of the leaders of the 'disobedient' faction of the Yaik rebels, had given shelter to a 'Peter III' as far back as 1762.

7. The literature on the Pugachev revolt is vast. For the account given here see N. Dubrovin, *Pugachev i ego soobshchniki,* still essential reading ; Mavrodin, *Krest'yanskaya voyna v Rossii,* 3 vols, but particularly Vol. I, pp. 503ff ; A. Andrushchenko, *Krest'yanskaya voyna ;* for documents, including interrogations of rebel prisoners, see the invaluable three-volume collection, *Pugachevshchina ;* A.S. Pushkin, in *Istoriya Pugacheva,* makes use of documents which have since disappeared. The most complete recent treatment is J.T. Alexander, *Autocratic Politics in a National Crisis : the Imperial Russian Government and Pugachev's Revolt* and see by the same author 'Recent Soviet Historiography on the Pugachev Revolt : A Review Article'.

8. Rozner, *Yaik pered buryey,* p. 168. His ambitions were realized nearly a century and a half later by another Ul'yanov.

9. See Mavrodin, II, p. 94 ; *Pugachevshchina,* II, p. 127. Some Cossacks admitted that they accepted Pugachev through fear : Andrushchenko, op. cit., p. 31.

10. A disadvantage in a tsar which Pugachev countered by scribbling gibberish on bits of paper and producing them as 'foreign languages'. One of his followers was convinced that he was a German since he had heard him speak the language (as of course Peter III did). Mavrodin, II, p. 101, n. 49.

11. Kar was court-martialed and eventually cashiered. Some historians attribute the severity of his punishment to the fact that the failure to defeat Pugachev demonstrated to the public that the rising was really serious.

12. Andrushchenko, op. cit., p. 59, n. 3, suggests that a 'Senate' may also have been set up by the rebels, but there is no evidence of its activities.

13. *Pugachevshchina,* I, pp. 147–8.

14. Ibid., p. 172. Fines were also imposed. Soviet historians regard this as 'mobilization' as distinct from the tsarist recruit levy. See Mavrodin, II, p. 474, n. 77.

15. Women were raped and beaten to death, men were hanged head down. The commandant of one of the forts taken by the rebels was flayed alive, his wife slashed to death, and his daughter taken by Pugachev for himself. She was subsequently shot by Cossacks jealous of her influence with Pugachev. See A.S. Pushkin, 'Istoriya Pugacheva', p. 667.

16. Pushkin, op. cit., p. 670. Mavrodin and Andrushchenko are almost entirely silent on the organization of Pugachev's court as distinct from his 'College of War'.

17. Pushkin, op. cit., p. 670. Pushkin adds that Pugachev, as an Old Believer, did not attend church. But there is no evidence that he was a sectarian.

18. See A. Donnelly, *The Russian Conquest of Bashkiria, 1552–1740*.

19. See Andrushchenko, op. cit., pp. 254–6 for an example.

20. The government forces were commanded by Ya. de Castro de la Cerda, a rare example of a Spaniard in Russian service.

21. *SIRIO*, 13, pp. 367ff.

22. J.T. Alexander, *Autocratic Politics*, pp. 70, 89 and 280, n. 3.

23. Ibid., p. 96.

24. Andrushchenko, op. cit., pp. 326–7, Table 1, and pp. 135–6.

25. Mavrodin, III, pp. 35ff.

26. 'Ibo raseyskiy narod ne voyn ; raseyskiy narod prosto baran', quoted in Mavrodin, III, p. 28, n. 96.

27. Ya. K. Grot, *Materialy* I, p. 16, Bibikov to Catherine, 7 April 1774, Catherine to Bibikov, 20 April.

28. Mavrodin, III, p. 383 ; Alexander, op. cit., p. 90.

29. *RA*, 1886, pp. 388ff, at pp. 390 and 397. Dubrovin, op. cit., II, p. 257, suggests that Bibikov deliberately omitted details of punishments inflicted on captured rebels from his reports to Catherine.

30. Dubrovin, II, pp. 257, 259, 291.

31. Mavrodin, III, pp. 46–7, suggests that it was the wealthy Bashkirs who now fell away, but does not adduce enough evidence to make this view convincing.

32. Dubrovin, III, p. 94.

33. *Pugachevshchina*, II, pp. 188.

34. Ibid., pp. 226, 390.

35. S.I. Tkhorzhevsky, *Pugachevshchina v pomeshchishchey Rossii*, pp. 30ff.

36. In Voronezh guberniya, of 393 estates ravaged by the rebels, 384 were on barshchina, only 9 on obrok (ibid., p. 36).

37. *Pugachevshchina*, I, pp. 40–41, dated 31 July 1774 ; Mavrodin, III, p. 132, publishes a slightly different text dated 28 July.

38. Owners of large estates were of course more likely to be absentees. For analyses of numbers of estates, destroyed and owners killed in relation to size of estate, see Tkhorzhevsky, op. cit., pp. 115ff.

39. Dubrovin, III, passim.

40. Ibid., p. 125.

41. See Chapter 15.

42. See *Pugachevshchina*, II, p. 233, P. Golitsyn to P. Panin, 16 August 1774 : . . . .' some [Don Cossacks] will join the miscreant unless they are held back from doing so by the news of the peace.' A.P. Pronshteyn, the historian of the Don Cossacks, endeavours to prove that the Don Cossacks actively sided with Pugachev in the last stages of the revolt ; like Mavrodin, he identifies those who sided with the government as the 'wealthy' Cossacks. His thesis is unproved ; he does not mention that Pugachev's forces ravaged a number of Don Cossack settlements in the Upper Don, for which see Dubrovin, III, p. 223.

43. Dubrovin, III, p. 225.

44. *Pugachevshchina*, II, pp. 224ff, testimony of Pustobayev.

45. Ibid., pp. 141ff, interrogation of Ivan Tvorogov.

Chapter 17. The Court Crisis of 1773–4 and the Restoration of Order

1. In the event of Paul's death the legitimate heir would be a younger brother or sister of Ivan Antonovich.

2. Khrapovitsky, *Dnevnik*, pp. 434–5, 20 July 1793.

3. On Aepinus see R.W. Home, 'Science as a Career in 18th Century Russia : the Case of F.U.T. Aepinus'.

4. D. Kobeko, *Tsarevich Pavel Petrovich*, pp. 67ff.

5. See Chapters 4 and 9.

6. I have found no contemporary mention of an illness which could have covered up a pregnancy in the years 1762–72. The Alekseyev girls are mentioned in Gunning to Suffolk, 28 July/8 August 1772, *SIRIO*, 19, pp. 296ff ; see also Corberon, *Journal Intime*, I, p. 135, n. 1. One of the Alekseyev girls subsequently married the German dramatist M. von Klinger, who rose in the service of the grand duke. The second married General Buxhoevden. See Kobeko, op. cit., p. 277.

7. *Sochineniya*, XII, p. 170.

8. Solov'yev, XV, pp. 156ff. K.V. Sivkov in 'Taynaya ekspeditsiya . . .', and V.S. Dzhincharadze, 'Iz istorii' add astonishingly little to what is known from Solov'yev. See also Solms to Frederick, 7 July, *PCFG*, 32, pp. 347–8.

9. Ransel, *The Politics . . .* , p. 232, and note 13. The Swedish envoy reported the presence of Potemkin in a dispatch of July 1772. This is one of the few clues to a much earlier relationship between Catherine and Potemkin than is usually suggested.

10. As late as 25 June/6 July 1772, Catherine was writing of Orlov in glowing terms to her friend Mme von Bielke (*SIRIO*, 13, pp. 258–61).

11. *SIRIO*, 13, pp. 270–2. On Zakhar Chernyshev's support for Orlov see Gunning to Suffolk, 5/16 January 1773, *SIRIO*, 19, pp. 339–40 ; 28 May/8

June 1773 ; ibid., pp. 364ff ; 20 September/1 October 1773, pp. 377ff.

12. *SIRIO*, 13, pp. 274 and 275–6. The Director of Posts failed to carry out Catherine's order to burn her note to him.

13. Brandt, op. cit.

14. *SIRIO*, 72, pp. 373ff, Solms to Frederick, 14/25 July 1773 ; pp. 384ff, 30 July/11 August 1773. For a brief survey of the sources on Saldern's intrigues, see J.T. Alexander, op. cit., p. 268, n. 69.

15. *PCFG*, 34, pp. 190ff, Frederick to the Landgräfin of Hesse Darmstadt, 5 October 1773, NS.

16. *Danske Tractater*, p. 322.

17. Ransel, *The Politics . . .* , pp. 237–8.

18. Ibid., and see *SIRIO*, 72, pp. 384ff, Solms to Frederick 30 July/10 August 1773 ; *SIRIO*, 13, p. 361, Catherine to Mme von Bielke, 6/17 October 1773.

19. Ukaz of 31 May/10 June 1773 ; see also *SIRIO*, 72, pp. 356–7, Solms to Frederick, 21 May/1 June 1773.

20. Kobeko, op. cit., p. 70.

21. Panin to Solms, in Solms to Frederick, 14/25 July 1773, *SIRIO*, 72, pp. 372ff. See also D.I. Fonvizin to his sister in *Sobraniye Sochineniy*, II, pp. 353ff, n.d.

22. Panin was also given a house, a year's food and supplies from the court, and the use of court carriages and livery. See Fonvizin, op. cit., pp. 406ff, 28 September 1773. Panin distributed the 9,000 peasants among his underlings at the College of Foreign Affairs, Fonvizin, Bakunin and Oubri.

23. Kobeko, op. cit., pp. 95ff.

24. For the instructions to N.I. Saltykov, see *RA*, 1864, p. 482. The wife of Field-Marshal Rumyantsev was appointed Mistress of the Household.

25. There is no modern scholarly biography of Potemkin. The most useful are still A. Brückner, *Potemkin*, St Petersburg 1891 ; T. Adamczyk, *Fürst G.A. Potemkin*, Emsdetten, 1936 ; A.N. Fateyev, *Potemkin Tavricheskiy*, Prague, 1945.

26. 'Kammerjunker' was a gentleman of the bedchamber ; 'Kammergerr', a more senior rank, was equal to chamberlain.

27. Potemkin to Catherine, 24 May 1769, *RS*, 23, pp. 716–17.

28. J.T. Alexander, *Autocratic Politics . . .* , p. 279, n. 54.

29. See n. 9 above.

30. According to J.T. Alexander, other letters from Potemkin to Catherine dating from this period are preserved in the Central State Archives of Ancient Documents in Moscow, but the Soviet authorities do not allow them to be studied (op. cit., p. 279, n. 54).

31. He was granted 20,000 r.p.a. and 100,000 r. for a house. He retired to Moscow and died there in 1803.

32. *SIRIO*, 19, p. 413, Gunning to Suffolk, 6/17 May 1774.

33. Ibid., p. 405 ; see also p. 457, 7/18 March 1774.

34. *PCFG*, 35, pp. 215ff, 30 March 1774.

35. *SIRIO*, 19, pp. 415ff ; Gunning to Suffolk, 13/24 June 1774 ; pp. 420ff, 15/26 July 1774. See also Catherine to Potemkin, n.d. in G. Ouvrard, *Lettres d'amour de Catherine II à Potemkine*, p. 162.

36. Aleksey Orlov performed one last service for Catherine before retiring permanently from government service. He organized the kidnapping of the so-called Princess Tarakanova (a name she never used) who had been proclaimed by a group of confederate Poles led by Prince Karl Radziwill to be a daughter of the Empress Elizabeth. The peace of Kuchuk Kainardzhi put paid to any hope of procuring Turkish support for her claims. The 'princess' was lured on board Orlov's flagship at Leghorn in the belief that he would support her cause. She was arrested, and escorted to Russia by Admiral S. Greig. She arrived in June 1775 in the capital and died of consumption in the Peter and Paul fortress in December 1775. Her statements under interrogation and her letters to Catherine are printed in *SIRIO*, 1, pp. 169–96. Her appeals against the harsh conditions in which she was kept make heart-rending reading ; but she refused to say who she really was, and her secret died with her.

37. *AGS*, I, p. 454.

38. Ibid., and cf. *SIRIO*, 6, pp. 74ff, Nikita Panin to Peter Panin, 22 July 1774.

39. Urged on by Nikita, Peter Panin had at once written from Moscow to offer his services ; *SIRIO*, 6, pp. 78ff, 26 July 1774.

40. Ibid., pp. 76ff, Peter Panin to Nikita Panin, 26 July 1774.

41. *SIRIO*, 13 pp. 420, undated, July 1774.

42. *SIRIO*, 13, pp. 427, 428 ; ibid., 6, p. 81, rescript of 29 July 1774 ; p. 83, open ukaz of 29 July 1774 ; p. 86. Nikita Panin to Peter Panin, 2 August 1774.

43. *SIRIO*, 13, p. 421, 29 July 1774.

44. E.S. Shumigorsky, *Imperator Pavel I. Zhizn' i tsarstvovaniye*, p. 23.

45. Derzhavin, op. cit., v, p. 498.

46. It was typical of Suvorov's strange sense of humour that when travelling from the Danubian army to join Peter Panin he occasionally gave himself out as Pugachev. Cf. Dubrovin, op. cit., III, p. 254.

47. *Pugachevshchina*, III, p. 467.

48. Ibid., p. 440, No. 165 for an example. More serious was the death under torture of Pugachev's secretary of the War College, A.I. Dubrovsky, whom Paul Potemkin was thus unable to interrogate.

49. Mavrodin, III, p. 403 ; see also Catherine to G.A. Potemkin ; undated but September 1774 : 'My love, Paul [Potemkin] is right. Suvorov had no more part in this [the capture of Pugachev] than Thomas [her dog] ; he arrived at the end of the fight and after the capture of the miscreant. I hope that all Paul's quarrels and dissatisfactions will come to an end when he receives my orders to go to Moscow.' *SIRIO*, 13, pp. 446–7.

50. Mavrodin, III, p. 403.

51. Alexander, op. cit., pp. 212–3.

52. Dubrovin, III, pp. 292ff ; Derzhavin, op. cit., v, p. 288.

53. *SIRIO*, 6, pp. 116–17, 25 August 1775.

54. Ibid., pp. 145ff, 17 September 1774.

55. *Pugachevshchina*, III, pp. 390ff gives an account of such a pacification ; see also ibid., pp. 463–4.

56. Mavrodin, III, pp. 434–5.

57. Dubrovin, III, p. 356 ; *Osmnadstatyy vek*, I, p. 139.

58. Catherine to Volkonsky, 1 January 1775, ibid. ; undated to Vyazemsky in Mavrodin, III, p. 42.

59. Alexander, op. cit., p. 301, n. 6 ; p. 186.

60. The accused were grouped into categories (*sorty*) according to their guilt. Pugachev himself was regarded as *vne sortov (hors série)*.

61. Mavrodin, III, pp. 419, 425. But in the case of Deputy Davydov, which had arisen earlier, Catherine allowed Panin to go through the ritual of the death sentence but to reprieve him at the last moment and send him to hard labour in Riga. ('Posobniki i storonniki Pugacheva. Ocherki i razskazy', *RS*, No. 17, 1876, pp. 53ff at p. 65.)

62. A.T. Bolotov, *Zapiski*, III, pp. 189–92.

63. See *Annual Register*, 1774, p. 155, quoted in Alexander, op. cit., p. 305, n. 46.

64. *SIRIO*, 27, Catherine to Mme Bielke, 6 March 1775, pp. 31–2. The means Catherine used to achieve her end have been finally illuminated with the publication of the relevant documents by R. V. Ovchinnikov in 1966, 'Sledstviye i sud nad E.I. Pugacheva'.

65. *Pugachevshchina*, III, p. 468.

66. M. Gernet, *Istoriya tsarskoy tyur'my*, I, p. 207.

67. Andrushchenko, pp. 299ff, 308ff. The Bashkir leaders were not included in the general amnesty of March 1775, for which see below.

68. See *AGS*, I, p. 456, session of 9 February 1775.

69. *PSZ*, xx, No. 14,275, 17 March 1775. The amnesty had originally extended to fugitive serfs who returned within the year, but as a result of debate in the Council, privately-owned serfs were excluded from this clause. *AGS*, II, p. 749, 12 March 1775.

70. See Chapter 10 for discussion of this unpublished article.

71. *PSZ*, xx, No. 14,275.

72. *PSZ*, xx, No. 14,294, 6 April 1775.

73. *Pugachevshchina*, III, p. 389. It is probable that a far less detailed record was kept of the women who perished in one way or the other on both sides.

74. See the summary in Alexander, op. cit., pp. 211–12.

75. *SIRIO*, 6, pp. 217–18, P.S. Zavadovsky to P.I. Panin, 19 November 1775 ; Alexander, op. cit., p. 220, gives 1,230 families.

76. S. Ya.Borovoy, *Kredit i banki v Rossii*, p. 59.

77. *Pugachevshchina*, III, pp. 385ff.

78. See the table in N.I. Pavlenko, *Istoriya metallurgii v XVIII veke*, pp. 475ff. Alexander in *Emperor of*

the Cossacks, p. 196 gives total damage to private property excluding industry as 5,685,000r. and to state property 613,000r.

79. *SIRIO*, 6, pp. 135–6, Catherine to Panin, 16 September 1775 ; ibid., pp. 121ff, ukaz to P.I. Panin of 2 September 1775 ; ibid., p. 213. Peter Panin's power to inflict death penalties had already been withdrawn before the amnesty of March 1775 (ibid., 207, ukaz of 16 February 1775).

80. The various reports submitted to Catherine are carefully analysed in Alexander, *Autocratic Politics*, pp. 192ff. See also Mavrin to Paul Potemkin, 15 September 1774 in Ovchinnikov, op. cit., No. 3, March 1766, pp. 131–2.

81. *Pugachevshchina*, I, pp. 31–2. Soldiers were offered rewards in cash and kind, and 'rank', and their descendants were promised 'the first place in the state'

82. Andrushchenko, p. 127.

83. Padurov's statement in *Pugachevshchina*, II, pp. 187–9 ; it is doubtful whether Pugachev was himself an Old Believer. He was incidentally somewhat puzzled to explain to his Cossack wife, Yustinya, why, unlike previous Russian tsars, he was not clean shaven.

84. Mavrodin, III, p. 94.

85. *Pugachevshchina*, I, pp. 74–5.

86. Ibid., III, p. 7.

87. It must be noted however that only a selection of the documents has been published and that in any case those interrogated endeavoured to minimize their guilt and to shift the blame elsewhere.

88. Andrushchenko, op. cit., p. 119.

89. *Pugachevshchina*, III, p. 8, describing events on the estate of the parents of N.M. Karamzin, the future historian.

90. Ibid., III, pp. 102–3, 109, for examples.

91. Dubrovin, I, p. 189.

92. *Pugachevshchina*, II, pp. 187ff, at p. 189.

93. According to E.I. Indova, A.A. Preobrazhensky, and Yu. A. Tikhonov in 'Narodnyye dvizheniya v Rossii XVII–XVIII vv', p. 77, three million peasants were involved of whom 40 per cent were serfs. According to J.T. Alexander, over 200,000. An analysis of a sample of 4,638 prisoners shows 27 per cent Cossacks, 22 per cent native peoples, and 29 per cent peasants (of all kinds). See Alexander, *Emperor of the Cossacks*, p. 187. In the province of Ufa there were 86,579 male souls almost all of whom took part in the revolt. Of these 10,772 were Russians, and of these only 1,284 male souls were privately-owned serfs. Andrushchenko, p. 137.

94. One need only point to the damage caused by football fans descending on one small town.

95. See below, Chapter 23.

Chapter 18. The Reform of Local Administration in 1775

1. See Chapter 11.

2. D.I. Ilovaysky, *Sochineniya*, Moscow, 1884, pp. 537–8. Writing to Voltaire, on 22 July/2 August

1771, Catherine remarked that she had reread her Instruction, in hopes of starting work soon again on a Code. See Reddaway, *Documents*, pp. 124ff.

3. *PSZ*, XVI, No. 12,259, 11 October 1764.

4. See mainly Got'ye, op. cit., II, pp. 215ff, and p. 223, n. 3 ; I, pp. 113–15.

5. The sub-commission was composed of Count A. Shuvalov, deputy of the free farming soldiers of Orel province ; Count I. Golovkin, deputy of the Finnish nobility ; A. Naryshkin, deputy of the nobility of Staritsky ; F. Verigin, deputy of the Derevsk pyatina of Novgorod and Baron Löwenwolde, deputy of the Estonian nobility. *SIRIO*, 32, pp. 22ff.

6. See M.P. Pavlova Sil'vanskaya in 'Sotsial'naya sushchnost' oblastnoy reformy Yekateriny II' in *Absolyutizm v Rossii*, pp. 460–91, at p. 462.

7. The text of the three lessons is printed in Got'ye, II, pp. 295ff. In his otherwise very useful article, 'Catherine II and the Provincial Reform of 1775 : A Question of Motivation', R.E. Jones makes no mention of these lessons. But they rather undermine his statement that 'until 1774 there was no indication that Catherine was actually planning to undertake a comprehensive reform of local administration' (p. 506).

8. Got'ye, II, p. 241. In 1763 and 1764 Catherine had already ordered the drawing up of maps, but evidently they had not arrived yet. In later years she saw to it that maps of the new 'namestnichestva' should be made, which were of high quality. See e.g. E. Druzhinina, *Severnoye Prichernomo'ye*, pp. 7ff.

9. I have drawn very largely on the work of Got'ye in these pages, notably II, pp. 234ff. Got'ye points out (p. 248, n. 6) that unfortunately the actual texts of the 'answers' of the sub-commission and of the projects they discussed cannot be found in the archives. Their work has to be reconstructed from the daily journals of their meetings.

10. *PSZ*, XVIII, No. 13,119, 21 May 1768 ; No. 13,600, 29 April 1771 ; No. 13,661, 25 September 1771.

11. See V. Grigor'yev, *Reforma mestnogo upravleniya pri Yekaterine II. Uchrezhdeniye o guberniyakh 7 noyabrya 1775g*, pp. 102ff : see also U.L. Lehtonen, *Die Polnische Provinzen Russlands unter Katharina in den Jahren 1772–1782* E.P. Zakalinskaya, *Votchinnoye khozyaystvo Mogilevskoy gubernii vo vtoroy polovine XVIII veka ; Belorussiya v epokhu feodalizma*, Vol. 3 ; Got'ye, II, pp. 254ff, who points to Polish influence.

12. *SIRIO*, 27, pp. 9–10 ; see also *AGS*, I, pp. 455–6, session of 18/29 December 1774 and *PSZ*, XVIII, No. 14,230.

13. *SIRIO*, 6, p. 135.

14. Pavlova Sil'vanskaya, op. cit., pp. 464ff.

15. See *SIRIO*, 6, p. 179 for Peter Panin's report on Meshchersky's plan ; ibid., for Catherine's authorization, 20 November 1774. See also R.E. Jones, op. cit., p. 206.

16. See *SIRIO*, 5, pp. 122–7 ; Jones, op. cit., pp. 206–7.

17. Ya.Ya.Zutis, *Ostseyskiy vopros*, pp. 389ff ;

Pavlova Sil'vanskaya, op. cit., p. 473, and by the same author, 'Sozdaniye v 1775 godu soslovnykh sudov dlya krest'yan'.

18. J. Alexander, op. cit., p. 240.

19. See Chapter 4.

20. K. Blum, *Ein russischer Staatsmann*, 2 vols, 1857, I, pp. 25ff.

21. *SIRIO*, 23, p. 52, 4 August 1776.

22. Jones, op. cit., pp. 213–14 accepts Grigor'yev's view of Desnitsky's participation, but no evidence has ever been adduced.

23. *PSZ*, XIX, No. 14,231.

24. Grigor'yev, *Reforma . . .* , pp. 116–17 is the only author to mention this ukaz. Pavlova Sil'vanskaya notes however that before the Pugachev revolt Catherine was already collecting material with a view to improving the lot of the state peasants, and had noted down a few possible measures. A.A. Vyazemsky had also written a memorandum for her on the administration of state peasants and serfs, and on his administration of his own peasants. This material remains unpublished ('Sotsial'naya Sushchnost', p. 484).

25. *PSZ*, XX, Manifesto of 17 March 1775, No. 14,275, amplified in the ukazy of April and No. 14,327, 25 May 1775.

26. The 184 kuptsy of Smolensk produced 1,920 r.p.a. of revenue under the new system, in 1775 – considerably more than when they merely paid the poll-tax. Cf. Yu. R. Klokman, *Sotsial'no ekonomicheskaya istoriya russkogo goroda, vtoraya polovina XVIII veka*, p. 135.

27. Klokman, op. cit., p. 91. Figures are from two different reports of the third census of 1761–7.

28. *PSZ*, XX, No. 14,392, Chapter 4, paras 81, 82.

29. See *PSZ*, XIV, No. 10,486, 1 December 1755 and XVII, No. 12,721, 10 August 1766 ; and Grigor'yev, op. cit., p. 115.

30. See M.P. Pavlova Sil'vanskaya, 'Sozdaniye v 1775 godu soslovnykh sudov dlya krest'yan'.

31. Grigor'yev, op. cit., pp. 25 1ff. Other writers have pointed to similarities with the Ukrainian Code of Glukhov of 1743 (see Chapter 4). See also Pavlova Sil'vanskaya, 'Sotsial'naya Sushchnost', pp. 485ff.

32. There is evidence that Catherine contemplated setting up a central equity court, to which appeals from the lower equity courts could be referred, and which would form part of a central chancery court. This project never materialized ; one reason, given by Catherine, for multiplying her equity courts was that 'Since England is small there is no inconvenience if all these matters are dealt with in London, but it is not practical to drag people to the capital from the ends of the earth ; to deal locally with arranging and judging current affairs is more practical.' (Ibid., p. 488.) Pavlova Sil'-vanskaya assumes however that the English Chancery Court 'had the right to confirm or reject the ukazy of the king of England', and interprets the fact that Catherine refrained in the end from setting up such a central equity court as further evidence of her desire not to weaken the autocracy, but merely to create 'powerless auxiliaries of

the "estate" courts', cf. op. cit., p. 488. But if these courts were supposed to grant bail, they had to be local.

33. The land commissar's functions seem to be based on a combination of the Kreis Kommissar in Livonia, and the instruction which was issued in May 1774 to special commissars set up in the guberniya of St Petersburg in 1771 during the crisis caused by the plague in central Russia. Pavlova Sil'vanskaya, op. cit., pp. 472–3.

34. Pavlova Sil'vanskaya, p. 472, without giving date ; Jones, op. cit., p. 214, n. 8, also undated.

35. Seeing that there was also a 'town chief' (*gorodskaya glava*) I have translated *gorodnichi* as provost.

36. The word *stryapchiye* has no satisfactory translation. Attorney or advocate implies legal training, which they did not have. 'Prosecutors' narrows down their function too much. The word 'pleader' comes closest to the original.

37. The Statute also spelled out a model constitution for the running of hospitals, going into such detail as the following : 'beside the bed of each sick person there should be a small table covered with oil cloth and on it a pewter jug and mug and a little bell to summon the attendant'. Smoking was to be permitted in the wards only twice a day.

38. This is one of the first cases in Russian legislation when the number of strokes to be inflicted in punishment is specified.

39. Chapter IV, art. 27 : 'All other courts of Judicature may, and ought to remonstrate with the same propriety to the Senate, and even to the Sovereign himself, as was already mentioned above.'

40. I have not come across any studies of the activity of a land commissar in an area where there were no noble estates. This is a subject deserving of further research.

41. See the discussion of this question in Jones, op. cit., p. 192, who points to the influence of Livonian example as mediated by Sievers. See also Blum, op. cit., II, pp. 85ff.

42. See the careful analysis by Pavlova Sil'vanskaya, op. cit., pp. 475ff. The request that members of the magistraty should be allowed to wear swords was not as yet granted.

43. *AGS*, II, pp. 208–9, and Blum, II, p. 66.

44. Grigor'yev, op. cit., pp. 31ff ; R.E. Jones, op. cit., p. 222.

45. This did not happen everywhere ; see Klokman, *Sotsial'no ekonomicheskaya istoriya russkogo goroda*, p. 103.

46. Ibid., pp. 103–4.

47. Cf. R.L. Vorontsov (Vladimir) to Catherine, June, 1779, quoted in Klokman, op. cit., p. 126.

48. Existing sources and secondary works do not however explain exactly what happened to a town which ceased to be on the establishment. Did its inhabitants revert to the status of state peasants ? Did they lose their ratushi ? Or did they survive as towns even if they were not centres of an uezd ?

49. Cf. Yu. R. Klokman, op. cit., on whom I have largely drawn in the preceding pages. Klokman is more inclined to stress the positive contribution the reform made to the development of the bourgeoisie than is Pavlova Sil'vanskaya ('Sotsial'naya Sushchnost', pp. 490), who stresses the view that the 'soslovnoye' or 'estate' organization of urban government tended rather to prevent the development of the bourgeoisie. On the whole I find Klokman more convincing, particularly in view of the evidence he adduces of the economic development of towns after the reform ; op. cit., pp. 207ff.

50. See e.g. Bolotov, *Zapiski*, Vol. III, pp. 720–25 for a description of events in Tula. Sievers reported that 625 nobles turned up in Novgorod for the opening ceremonies (cf. Got'ye, II, pp. 272ff, and n. 2, p. 273).

51. D.A. Korsakov, *Sbornik materialov po istorii Kazanskogo Kraya v XVIIIv*, pp. 123ff.

52. Cf. *Sochinenyiya Derzhavina*, VI, pp. 540ff.

53. R.E. Jones in 'Catherine II and the Provincial Reform' points to the comparison with Prussia which employed 14,000 officials.

54. Figures from R.E. Jones, op. cit., p. 511.

55. Some of the increase is accounted for by the greater extent of Russian territory in 1796, some of it by the decline in the value of the ruble.

56. For the full account see *SIRIO*, 1, p. 384, 'Dnevnaya zapiska puteshestviya Imperatritsy Yekateriny II v Mogilev'. Grants in Staraya Russa for example amounted to 2,000 rubles for the building of 100 stone houses ; to the skilled workers (*masterovyye*) of the saltpans, 1,000 rubles ; to the town school (122 pupils), 200 rubles ; to the four almshouses, 100 rubles each ; 300 rubles to the monastery.

57. I have drawn on a seminar paper, delivered at the seminar on international history of the Institute of Historical Research, University of London, by Dr J. Hartley, who has carried out research for a Ph.D. on the implementation of the Statute of 1775 and the Charters of 1785, and whose conclusions have proved novel in many respects. Jones, op. cit., p. 229 states that the equity courts ceased to function after a few years. In fact, with a brief interval during the reign of Paul, they continued to function until 1864.

58. G.S. Vinsky, *Moye vremya*, p. 42.

59. Cf. Got'ye, op. cit., II, pp. 277ff. Vinsky (b. 1752), who wrote his memoirs in 1813, was very critical of the reform of 1775. He notes, as a positive factor, that it provided a means of earning a living to many poor families since the salaries were good enough by contemporary standards, even if the peasants soon felt the difference in that they had to produce fifteen and not three sheep a year to grease local palms (*Moye vremya*, p. 40). Elsewhere he notes that bribery was not important either in its amount or in its consequences, since it occurred mainly in lawsuits (!), or in order to obtain government contracts. Sale of office was unknown in Russia, he adds, and patronage rather than bribery was the only way to achieve promotion in those days (p. 46).

NOTES

Chapter 19. The Reforms of the 1780s

1. See Chapter 1, p. 25.

2. See Chapter 4, p. 56.

3. See Chapter 12, pp. 151–2, 157–8. It is possible that Catherine wrote this supplement in answer to the Instruction submitted to the Legislative Commission by the Chief Police Administration, for which see *SIRIO*, 43, pp. 296ff. For a study of this instruction see K. Papmehl, 'The Problem of Civil Liberties in the Records of the "Great Commission" '

4. Reddaway, *Documents*, p. 295, article 530.

5. Research on the origins of the Police Ordinance of 1782 has been relatively neglected, but see the fundamental study by M. Raeff, 'The Well Ordered Police State and the Development of Modernity in Seventeenth and Eighteenth-Century Europe : An Attempt at a Comparative Approach', at p. 1,235 for discussion of seventeenth- and eighteenth-century precedents. Diderot's 'Essai sur la Police de la France depuis son Origine jusqu'à son extinction actuelle' (*Mémoires pour Catherine*, ed. P. Vernière, pp. 1ff) has nothing to do with the police.

6. The otherwise useful article by J.P. LeDonne, 'The Provincial and Local Police under Catherine the Great, 1775–1796', fails to bring out this positive aspect of the police in the eighteenth century and regards it merely as an instrument of coercion.

7. J.B.C. Le Maire, 'La Police de Paris, Mémoire inédit composé par ordre de G. de Sartine sur la demande de Marie Thérèse'.

8. *PSZ* xxi, No. 15,379, 8 April 1782.

9. J.P. LeDonne, op. cit., p. 519.

10. Ibid., Ch. D, article 41, paras 1 to 14. The police board was also instructed to watch over widows and orphans, the poor, maimed, foreigners, and in general to listen impartially to all complaints by rich and poor, high and low. Compare Nicholas I's view of the function of his gendarmerie.

11. *PSZ*, xxi, No. 15,379, article 83. This article reflects the simultaneous work being carried out on the Statute of National Education, see below, Chapter 31.

12. Ibid., article 262.

13. *PSZ*, xxi, No. 15,146, 2 April 1781.

14. These are also functions of the police in Nicolas de La Mare's *Traité*.

15. *PSZ*, xxi, No. 15,634, 15 January 1783.

16. See e.g. N.B. Golikova, 'Organy politicheskogo syska i ikh razvitiye v xvii–xviii vv' in *Absolyutizm v Rossii*, pp. 243ff, at p. 278 : 'Though neither the Statute of Local Administration nor the Police Ordinance openly and directly mention political crime, there is no doubt that the main type of activity against which the apparatus of the guberniya was directed was precisely political crime.' Golikova adduces no evidence for this statement which is itself purely political.

17. *PSZ*, xx, No. 14,816, 25 November 1778 ; Jones, *The Emancipation*, p. 266 rightly attaches much importance to this decree.

18. *PSZ*, xxi No. 15,100, 24 March 1781 ; No. 15,280, 18 November 1781 (an answer to questions submitted by G.A. Potemkin) ; No. 15,477, 25 June 1782, and No. 15,763, 19 June 1783.

19. The economic rights listed here had already been granted to the nobles and other land-users in a manifesto of 28 June 1782, *PSZ*, xxi, No. 15,447.

20. This latter argument is put forward by R. Pipes, *The Ancien Regime in Russia*, pp. 135ff. His view is not shared by S.M. Troitsky, *Russkiy absolyutizm i dvoryanstvo*, pp. 152–3, who states that it remained for the government to decide whether to promote or not. I find Troitsky's argument more convincing.

21. The principle of dividing the nobility into separate groups had already been accepted in 1768. See E.I. Indova, 'K voprosu o dvoryanskoy sobstvennosti v Rossii v pozdnii feodal'nyy period' at p. 276, n. 17.

22. After three generations had risen successively to personal nobility the next generation could petition to be raised to hereditary nobility, or if father and son had both served for twenty years the grandson could petition for 'real' nobility (article 20).

23. See Chapter 20.

24. The wording of the Charter is particularly obscure with reference to age and property qualifications. It is not clear from article 62 if a noble with an income of less than 100 rubles from land but over the age of 25 can be elected, though it is quite clear that a noble who had not reached basic commissioned rank (14th) could not be elected regardless of the extent of his estates. Seeing that estates were usually family properties there must have been a large number of young men who owned none in their own right.

25. R.E. Jones, op. cit., p. 291 ; G.L. Yaney, *The Systematization of Russian Government*, p. 143, states that the Charter 'formally recognized the serfs as their [the gentry's] private property'.

26. Romanovich Slavatynsky, p. 378. Count Bludov is said to have seen this document.

27. See Chapter 13.

28. A.N. Filippov, 'K voprosu o pervoistochnikakh Zhalovannoy gramoty dvoryanstvu 21 aprelya 1785 goda'.

29. *SIRIO*, 36, pp. 275ff. An earlier draft by Baron Ungern Sternberg had proposed setting up courts of first instance composed of serf elders, with appeal to the landowner, and finally to a special governmental court in each province, but these courts disappeared from the draft finally put forward. For Ungern Sternberg's draft see ibid., pp. 259ff, and discussion in Florovsky, *Iz istorii*, pp. 166ff, and Semevsky, *Krest'yanskiy vopros*, pp. 126ff.

30. See *SIRIO*, 20, pp. 447ff. The editor of this volume points out that until Catherine set about it, no one had ever thought in Russia of codifying the laws dealing with the state peasantry and clarifying their rights and privileges.

31. See the fundamental work by A.A. Kizewetter, *Gorodovoye Polozheniye Yekateriny II 1785 g*,

Moscow, 1909, p. 134, n. 2. Kizewetter's work is very out of date, but it has not yet been superseded. J. Hittle's *The Service City,* appeared too late for me to be able to make much use of it.

32. Klokman, *Sotsial'no-ekonomicheskaya istoriya russkogo goroda,* pp. 109ff, unfortunately undated.

33. Kizewetter, op. cit., pp. 186ff.

34. Ibid., p. 269, quoting from one of the early drafts of Catherine's Nakaz.

35. *PSZ,* xxii, No. 16,188, 21 April 1785.

36. See for the nobility, Romanovich Slavatynsky, op. cit. ; S.A. Korf, *Dvoryanstvo i ego soslovnoye upravleniye za stoletiye 1762–1861.* For the towns, I.I. Dityatin, *Ustroistvo i upravleniye gorodov v Rossii ;* M.G. Ryndzyunsky, *Gorodskoye grazhdanstvo doreformennoy Rossii.*

37. R.E. Jones, *The Emancipation . . . ,* p. 233, quoting a note prepared for Catherine. Jones, in accordance with the irritating Soviet practice, gives no details of the document he is quoting – neither date, nor description. In the same period 2,704 peasants and 3,851 townspeople were elected, out of a total of 15,000 added to provincial government. Over 10,000 out of 15,000 were thus elected officials.

38. Klokman, op. cit., p. 118 wrongly states that only those with a capital not less than 5,000 rubles were allowed to be elected.

39. Kizewetter, op. cit., pp. 447ff.

40. Pavlova Sil'vanskaya, op. cit., p. 483, with whom I concur.

41. See E. Amburger *Geschichte der Behördenorganisation Russlands von Peter dem Grossen bis 1917,* pp. 118–19 ; N.P. Yeroshkin, *Istoriya gosudarstvennykh uchrezhdeniy dorevolyutsionnoy Rossii.*

42. See discussion in M.V. Klochkov, *Ocherki pravitel'stvennoy deyatel'nosti vremeni Pavla I,* pp. 143ff.

43. These budgets have been published by A.N. Kulomzin in *SIRIO,* 5 and 6.

44. The Statskontora was abolished in 1780 ; the Kammer kollegiya in 1784 and the Revizion kollegiya in 1788 ; Amburger, op. cit., p. 119.

45. See James A. Duran, 'The Reform of Financial Administration in Russia during the Reign of Catherine II'. The standard work is N.D. Chechulin, *Ocherki po istorii russkikh finansov v tsarsvovaniye Yekateriny II.* The more modern study by S.M. Troitsky, *Finansovaya politika russkogo absolyutizma v XVIII veke,* does not go beyond the middle of the century.

46. See the new material published by M. Raeff in 'The Empress and the Vinerian Professor'. Raeff uses the translation 'Chief Executive Chamber' but to my mind this does not convey the notion of a judicial institution implicit in that untranslatable word *'rasprava'.*

47. Raeff notes the similarity between Catherine's approach and that of Valuyev or Loris Melikov in the reign of Alexander ii, or Bulygin in the reign of Nicholas ii (p. 35). The Chamber was also allotted certain

functions in the event of a regency or the extinction of the dynasty.

48. Khrapovitsky, *Dnevnik,* p. 32, 16 April 1787.

49. N.M. Korkunov, *Dva proekta preobrazovaniya Senata vtoroy poloviny tsarstvovaniya imperatritsy Yekateriny II (1788 i 1794 godov).*

50. Khrapovitsky, *Dnevnik,* p. 71, 27 March 1788.

51. Korkunov, op. cit. ; Korkunov dates the project for a supreme court 1794. But Catherine was already using the term *general'nyy sud* in the 1780s. See Khrapovitsky's diary for 16 April 1787 (p. 32) : Catherine spoke to him of the 'Raspravnaya Palata' and the 'General'nyy Sud'. Unfortunately Korkunov does not give his reasons for his dating of the drafts, nor does he say where he found them. It may be added that among other reforms begun but not promulgated in Catherine's reign was a Digest of Laws issued by her, and a description of the form of government of Russia. See A. Lappo-Danilevsky, 'Sobraniye i svod Zakonov imperii rossiyskoy, sostavlennyye v tsarstvovaniye Yekateriny II'.

Chapter 20. The Integration of Little Russia and Livonia into the Russian Empire

1. See G.A. Maksimovich, *Deyatel'nost' Rumyantseva Zadunayskogo po upravleniyu Malorossii,* pp. 88ff and 110ff ; V.G. Ruban, *Kratkaya letopis' Malyya Rossiyi s 1506 po 1776 god,* pp. 232–3.

2. V.A. Myakotin, *Ocherki sotsial'noy istorii Ukrainy v XVII–XVIII vv,* pp. 259ff : the arrears amounted to 79,703r. in 1768 and reached 177,142r. in 1770. See also by the same author *Prikrepleniye krest'yantsva levoberezhnoy Ukrainy v XVII–XVIII vv,* pp. 125–6.

3. Kohut, op. cit., p. 129.

4. Maksimovich, op. cit., pp. 346ff. See also *Ocherki,* p. 584.

5. D. Miller, *Ocherki iz istorii i yuridicheskogo byta staroy Malorossii. Prevrashcheniye kozatskoy starshiny v dvoryanstvo,* p. 26. For a vivid picture of Glukhov in the 1760s and of the experiences of a poor Ukrainian noble youth in a guards regiment, see G.S. Vinsky, *Moe vremya, passim.*

6. See Chapter 9 for the elections in Little Russia and Chapter 11 for the debates. The Little Russian nakazy are analysed in Maksimovich, op. cit. ; Kohut, op. cit., pp. 386ff ; and D. Miller, op. cit.

7. Miller, op. cit., pp. 36ff.

8. Miller, op. cit., p. 30, quoting Rumyantsev to A.A. Vyazemsky, of 3 May 1774. An ukaz of 21 February 1769 had decreed that Little Russian officers could keep the 'rangovyye' lands in addition to their salaries, as pomestiya, but they were not to be regarded as hereditary, only as attached to the *chin (PSZ,* xviii, No. 13,260).

9. Kohut, op. cit., pp. 228–31.

10. *PSZ,* xxi, No. 15,478, 27 July 1782.

11. *PSZ,* xxi, No. 15,265, 26 October 1781.

12. Kohut, op. cit, p. 270 and n. 153. Miller, op. cit.

13. O. Ohloblyn, 'Ukrainian autonomists of the 1780s and 1790s and Count P.A. Rumyantsev Zadunaysky'.

14. *PSZ*, XXII, No. 16,776, 11 June 1789. The concrete case on which the Senate acted was one of a Tartar murza whose status was doubtful.

15. Miller, op. cit., pp. 64ff. Of 5,948 claims approved in Novgorod Seversk, 9 were priests, 1,095 were raznochintsy, 4,414 were Cossacks, 87 were state peasants, 83 had been 'enserfed' by their own families.

16. Nicholas I decreed that all except the lowest Little Russian ranks entitled holders or their descendants to be recorded in the Genealogical Books of the provincial assemblies. Miller, op. cit., pp. 84ff., and Chapter IV, and see Kohut, pp. 319ff.

17. Kohut, op. cit., pp. 246ff.

18. The same policy was applied in Great Russia but was implemented with less haste. Ibid., p. 254 ; cf. *PSZ*, XXII, No. 16,174, 27 March 1785.

19. *PSZ*, XXII, No. 16,375, 10 April 1786, to the Synod. A further ukaz of 25 April 1788 (No. 16,649) extended the secularization of Church lands to the guberniya of Khar'kov, Kursk and Voronezh, and to Yekaterinoslav.

20. *PSZ*, XXII, No. 16,374, 10 April 1786, to the Senate. See Kohut, op. cit., pp. 260ff. for the problems caused by the need to provide for supernumerary monks and nuns.

21. Miller, op. cit., pp. 48–9.

22. Miller, op. cit., p. 70. In Chernigov guberniya 8,942 serfs of both sexes were owned by clerics. I have not followed up the subsequent fate of clerical landowning, but it is likely that the pressure on churchmen to dispose of their estates increased.

23. See p. 308 above.

24. *PSZ*, XXI, No. 15,724, 3 May 1783.

25. Druzhinina, in *Severnoye Prichernomor'ye*, pp. 195–6 and n. 30 states that the similar ukaz of December 1796 in New Russia cannot be regarded in itself and alone as amounting to the introduction of full-scale serfdom.

26. Kohut, op. cit., p. 377. Cases of peasant unrest nearly always turn out to be Cossack-led or inspired or both. Ibid., p. 379, n. 216, a significant and usually neglected fact.

27. *PSZ*, XXI, No. 15,724, 3 May 1783, article 12 ordered the elimination by state purchase of noble and chinovnik land from towns and cities ; ibid., No. 15,907, 17 January 1784 ordered the recovery of settled land from non-nobles.

28. *Zapiski Sergeya Alekseyevicha Tuchkova, 1766–1808*, pp. 5ff, 17ff.

29. See Kohut, *op. cit.*, pp. 309ff., who discusses the literature on whether it was Pyotr, Mikhail or Vasily Kapnist who visited Hertzberg in Berlin, and comes down in favour of Vasily. Since Vasily Kapnist was a mason of the Rosicrucian persuasion, he would have access to high court officials.

30. See *Besedy imperatritsy Yekateriny II s Dalem, 1772–1777, RS*, 1876, 17, September, p. 17, entry for 4 February 1777.

31. See Chapter 4.

32. See Ya. Zutis, *Ostseyskiy vopros*, pp. 514–16.

33. *Besedy imperatritsy s Dalem*, p. 17.

34. Zutis, op. cit., pp. 484–9.

35. Zutis, op. cit., pp. 196ff. Zutis gives figures, which he regards as underestimates, of the number of estate-owners concerned : in Livonia there were 329 allodial estates, 139 (or 141) feudal, and 5 doubtful ; more than half the feudal estates had passed in an 'illegal way' to their then holders. In Estonia there were only 43 feudal estates ; in Esel, six. But see the somewhat different figures in F. Bienemann, *Die Statthalterschaftszeit in Liv und Estland, 1783–1796*, p. 52.

36. Bienemann, op. cit., pp. 50–51. It must be said that proof of ownership was difficult in Livonian law since there were about 24 different laws on which possession could be grounded.

37. The Memorandum is printed in full in Bienemann, op. cit., pp. 58–62, under the title 'Anmerkungen betreffend der neuen Etat liefländischen gouvernements'.

38. Bienemann, op. cit., p. 62, 'Sentiment der Herren Landräthe v. Berg und Baron Schoultz zu den ''Anmerkungen'' '.

39. Zutis, op. cit., pp. 505ff ; Bienemann, op. cit., pp. 65ff ; Bezborodko to A.R. Vorontsov, *AKV*, XIII, p. 15, No. 9, 12 May 1780.

40. Bienemann, op. cit., pp. 68ff.

41. *PSZ*, XX, No. 15,278, 16 November 1781 ; No. 15,296, 10 December 1787.

42. Bienemann, pp. 82ff.

43. Bienemann, *op. cit.*, pp. 74ff. Von Rosenkampf was sentenced by the Riga High Court on 8 June 1783 to lifelong imprisonment for forgery. He died in gaol.

44. Ibid., pp. 85–6.

45. Ibid., pp. 88–9 ; Zutis, pp. 514ff.

46. Ibid., p. 91.

47. *PSZ*, XX, No. 15,606, 3 December 1782.

48. Bienemann, p. 114.

49. Legal restrictions remained in testamentary dispositions of landed estates, but these too no longer differentiated between pomest'ye and votchina land. *PSZ*, XX, No. 15,719.

50. *PSZ*, XX, No. 15,724, 3 May 1783, that same ukaz which introduced the poll-tax into the guberniya formed out of Little Russia, and into Mogilev and Polotsk, the ex-Polish lands. Peasants were to pay 70 kopeks, townspeople 1 r. 20, merchants one per cent of capital, on all of which there was a surcharge of 2 kopeks per ruble.

51. Blum, *Ein russischer Staatsmann*, II, pp. 449ff ; Ya. Sievers, who on the whole accepted the Statute he had done so much to introduce into Russia, wrote to Catherine on 4 May 1783, protesting against the poll-tax and the complete upheaval in property values consequent on the new system of taxation.

52. *PSZ*, xx, No. 15,776, 3/14 July 1783 ; German translation 20 July 1783. For the manifesto of 14 December 1766, see chapter 9.

53. Bienemann, pp. 163ff, and particularly the Senate ukaz to Browne of 19 March 1784, reproving him sharply for departing from the clauses of the Statute. Russian insistence on the appointment of Russians to the board of administration (*gubernskoye pravleniye*) or to the high court also caused alarm. (Cf. Bienemann p. 157.) A. Bekleshev was appointed governor under Browne in 1784.

54. Ibid., p. 152.

55. Zutis, pp. 548–9, quoting other historians, states that on the whole the increase in registration of labour dues did not benefit the serfs ; but he adduces no evidence.

56. Zutis, pp. 551–4, points out that there was no law establishing *serf* peasant assessors, but notes that even in the days of the Livonian Order there were peasant *'rechtsfinder'*, who were originally judges. Their functions had been reduced with time but they could still be called as witnesses and appear to have been effective as representatives of peasant needs.

57. Zutis, pp. 569ff. for a detailed analysis of the Livonian criticisms of the Charter. See also Beinemann, p. 264.

58. See Chapters 4 and 9.

59. The Livonian nobles were particularly disturbed by the traffic in Russian noble patents which had already begun. (See Bienemann, p. 274.) Zutis, pp. 569ff. prints a detailed analysis of Livonian criticisms of the Charter in the Memorandum of 29 November 1786 which Bienemann had not been able to find (p. 264).

60. Ibid., p. 268.

61. Ibid., pp. 282–3.

62. Ibid., pp. 283–4.

63. Bienemann, p. 284. Ya Sievers had the courage to write to Catherine on 29 September 1786, more in sorrow than in anger, bewailing that she had been so misled by her advisers on the Livonian constitution. He did not propose restoring the Landtag, but he asked for relief from the deliveries of food and forage in kind from the peasants.

64. Bienemann, p. 266.

65. Zutis, p. 585.

66. Zutis, pp. 582–3.

67. Events followed a similar course in Estonia. A petition opposing Catherine's Charter to the Nobility was presented to Browne on 16 December 1786. A second petition submitted to Browne on 3 March was forwarded to Catherine on 31 March 1786, and met with the same fate as the Livonian petitions. In Curland, annexed by Russia in 1793, the reform was introduced on 27 November 1795 (ibid., p. 448, n. 1).

Chapter 21. Court and Culture

1. Bil'basov, I., pp. 226–8. Catherine almost precipitated a strike by her refusal to grant automatic promotion in the Table of Ranks to the rank of captain or colonel to waiters, valets, and other court servants, who had been accustomed to climb up in this way to posts as voyevodas.

2. Zapiski Derzhavina, *Sochineniya*, VI, p. 434.

3. M. Burgess, 'Russian Public Theatre Audiences of the 18th and Early 19th Centuries'.

4. R.A. Mooser, *L'opéra comique français en Russie au XVIIIᵉ siècle*, p. 28.

5. D.J. Welsh, *Russian Comedy 1765–1823*, pp. 20–1.

6. According to Welsh, op. cit., p. 29, *Brigadir* was not performed until 1772 at court and in public until 1780 because Catherine found it too daring. No evidence has been adduced by the Russian historians of literature whom he quotes for these statements. According to other authorities, it was only 'thanks to Catherine that these plays could be performed at all'. (Quoted in K.A. Papmehl, *Freedom of Expression in Eighteenth-Century Russia*, p. 105.)

7. See G. Seaman, 'Folk-Song in Russian Opera of the Eighteenth Century'.

8. *Zapiski Stehlina o Petre III*, quoted in T. Livanova, *Russkaya muzykal'naya kul'tura XVIII veka*, ii, p. 401.

9. R. A. Mooser, op. cit., pp. 32ff.

10. Galuppi was followed as Kapellmeister by Tomaso Traetta (1768–76) ; Giovanni Paisiello (1776–84) ; Giuseppe Sarti (1784–88) ; Domenico Cimarosa and Vicente Martin y Soler (1788–91 and 1788–94).

11. Quoted in Livanova, op. cit., II, p. 406.

12. Ibid., pp. 124–5.

13. Miranda, *Archivo*, II, p. 247.

14. General P.S. Potemkin translated the *Discours sur l'inégalité* and *La Nouvelle Héloïse* ; the *Confessions d'un vicaire savoyard* appeared anonymously in 1777.

15. T.A. Afanas'yeva, 'Reyestry knig XVIII v. Moskovskoy Sinodal' noy Tipografii'.

16. I.F. Martynov, 'Kniga v russkoy provintsii 1760–1790kh gg. Zarozhdeniye provintsial'noy knizhnoy torgovli'.

17. I.F. Martynov, 'Notes on V.P. Petrov and his Stay in England (New Materials)'.

18. See S.L. Baehr, 'The Masonic Component in Eighteenth-Century Russian Literature' in *Russian Literature in the Age of Catherine the Great*, ed. A.G. Cross.

19. See Yu. D. Levin, 'Angliyskaya prosvetitel'skaya zhurnalistika v russkoy literatury XVIII veka'.

20. *I to i syo ; Ni to ni syo ; Smes' ; Truten' ; Adskaya pochta.*

21. Novikov, like Potemkin, got very high marks at first and ended up by being expelled for non-attendance or laziness. But Novikov may have been affected by family difficulties requiring his presence.

22. The fact that he retired is merely stated by G. Makogonenko in *Nikolay Novikov i russkoye pros-*

veshcheniye XVIII veka, and no explanation is attempted.

23. G. Jones, 'Novikov's Naturalized Spectator'.

24. G.J. Jones, 'The Polemics of the 1769 Journals : A Reappraisal', forthcoming. Dr Jones has kindly allowed me to make use of a MS copy of this article, on which I have drawn extensively.

25. G. Jones, 'The Closure of Novikov's *Truten*' '.

26. Reprinted from the issue of 27 April 1770, in *Khrestomatiya po russkoy literatury XVIII veka.*

27. The editor of 'The Painter' declared his intention of being guided by the author of *O vremya,* a play by the empress satirizing the provincial gentry.

28. 'The Painter' in book form was reprinted again five times in Catherine's reign, the last edition being in 1793, after Novikov's arrest and imprisonment (see below, Chapter 33).

29. In his play *Dido,* Knyazhnin makes a group of Carthaginians plot to dethrone Dido out of hatred for her 'Trojan' favourite. In his *Russkiy teatr v vtoroy poloviny XVIII veka,* p. 86, Vsevolodsky Gerngross states that Catherine did not understand that this referred to her, and regarded the tragedy as a panegyric. Ransel, *The Politics . . . ,* pp. 216ff, also suggests that there was a 'literary opposition' to Catherine, because she appeared to have moved away from a policy of domestic reform to one of military aggression. However, Dr Jones's article cited in n. 24 shows that there is no evidence for such an 'opposition'.

30. See K. Papmehl, op. cit., pp. 37ff.

31. Dispatches of this period confirm the great freedom with which Russians spoke of public affairs in front of foreigners. But see also W. Richardson, *Anecdotes of the Russian Empire,* pp. 103–4 and 244ff.

32. *PSZ,* xix, No. 13,572, 1 March 1771.

33. I have not found any reference to an ukaz forbidding Russians to set up printing presses. The fact that they did not set them up reflects a state of mind rather than the existing law. In 1776 a second press was authorized to print foreign and Russian works ; religious works were to be submitted to the Holy Synod for approval.

34. Papmehl, op. cit., pp. 75–6.

35. See *SIRIO,* 7, passim for the correspondence between Catherine and d'Alembert, and C. de Larivière, *La France et la Russie au XVIIII*ᵉ *siècle,* Paris, 1909, pp. 1–69.

36. On Pictet, see N. Hans, 'François Pierre Pictet, Secretary to Catherine II'.

37. '. . . il ne me restait plus que cette tête couronée, il m'en faut une absolument' (Voltaire to Madame d'Argental, 13 August 1763, quoted in A. Lortholary, *Le mirage russe en France au XVIII*ᵉ *siècle,* p. 93).

38. *SIRIO,* 23, p. 84.

39. Lortholary, op. cit., pp. 110ff.

40. Voltaire to Catherine, 3 January 1773, quoted in Reddaway, *Documents,* pp. 177–8.

41. A.M. Wilson, *Diderot,* pp. 466–7 ; Lortholary, op. cit., pp. 97ff.

42. 'Tout est à faire dans ce pays . . . Pour parler mieux encore . . . tout est à défaire et à refaire. . . . Vous sentez bien qu'il est impossible que le despotisme arbitraire, l'esclavage absolu et l'ignorance n'aient pas planté des abus de toute espèce . . .' 19/30 October, quoted in Larivière, op. cit., pp. 98–9.

43. Larivière perpetuates a misunderstanding about this episode by asking rhetorically : 'Eut-elle [Catherine] jamais la pensée de l'appeler à présider les séances de cette grande assemblée des notables ou de lui donner la présidence de ses travaux? Rien n'est moins sur . . .' (op. cit., p. 92). By posing the question however, Larivière is able to argue that Mercier was dismissed from Russia because his 'Argus' eyes were feared by the Russian empress, and because she suspected that he would deprive her of the credit of drafting her Code of Laws.

44. *Voyage en Sibérie,* I, pp. 118, 122, 220.

45. 'Livre de mauvais goût, de mauvais ton et de mauvaises moeurs . . . d'un ignorant qui veut se donner les airs d'un philosophe,' wrote Grimm in the *Correspondance Litteraire,* when he was not yet on the Russian payroll, quoted in Lortholary, op. cit., p. 196.

46. 'L'Antidote est . . . le plus mauvais livre qui soit possible pour le ton, le plus mesquin pour le fond, le plus absurde pour les prétensions. . . . Celui qui a refuté Chappe est plus méprisable par sa flagornerie que Chappe ne l'est par ses erreurs et ses mensonges,' wrote Diderot to Grimm on 4 March 1771. It was apparently also Diderot who reviewed the *Antidote* in the *Correspondance Littéraire* (January 1772, ix, p. 414). Lortholary, op. cit., pp. 197, and 365, n. 131.

47. 'L'Antidote', *Sochineniya,* ed. Pypin, vii, p. 9.

48. *SIRIO,* 13, pp. 68–9, n. 4. to a letter from Catherine to Voltaire, dated 3/14 March 1771, in which Catherine refers to 'un nouveau St. Bernard qui prêchait une croisade en esprit contre moi. . . '.

49. Ibid., pp. 36ff, to Madame Bielke, 13 September 1770.

50. AAE, *Correspondance Politique, Russie,* Durand to d'Aiguillon, 6 November 1773 : 'J'ai dit a Monsieur Diderot ce que j'attendai d'un françois. Il m'a promis d'effacer, s'il étoit possible, les prejugés de cette princesse contre nous, et de lui faire sentir ce que sa gloire pourroit acquérir d'éclat par une union intime avec une nation. . .'

51. Catherine to the French ambassador, comte de Ségur, in 1785, quoted in L.P. de Ségur, *Mémoires, Souvenirs ou Anecdotes,* iii, p. 37.

52. The story is alleged to have been told by Catherine to Madame Geoffrin, but the original letter has never been found.

53. See M. Tourneux, *Diderot et Catherine II,* for Tourneux's introduction ; a more up-to-date and correct edition of the text of Diderot's *Mémoires pour Catherine II* is the edition by P. Vernière, Garnier, Paris, 1966. See also G. Haumant, *La Culture française en Russie ;* 'Celui-ci [Diderot] voulait y comprendre l'anatomie, jusques et y compris les détails intimes que

la sagesse de toutes les nations écarte de l'enseignement' (pp. 92–3).

54. A. Wilson, op. cit., pp. 646ff.

55. See below, Chapter 31.

56. See the edition by P. Vernière in D. Diderot, *Oeuvres Politiques*, Garnier edition, pp. 331–458.

57. *SIRIO*, 23, Catherine to Grimm, 28 October 1785–23 November 1785, at p. 372.

58. On Ya. P. Kozel'sky, see Chapter 11.

59. *Principes de la Philosophie Morale*, a translation of *An Inquiry Concerning Virtue* by Anthony Ashley Cooper, 3rd Earl of Shaftesbury, 1745, n.p.

60. Ya. P. Kozel'sky, *Filosofskiye predlozheniya*, No. 438, in S.A. Pokrovosky, op. cit., pp. 338ff.

61. See for details of Desnitsky's career in Scotland and his relations with the Scottish Enlightenment, A.H. Brown, 'Adam Smith's first Russian Followers' and 'S.E. Desnitsky, Adam Smith and the Nakaz of Catherine II', and the literature cited there.

62. *Dokumenty i materialy po istorii Moskovskogo universiteta vtoroy poloviny XVIII veka*, III, 1767–1786, Moscow, 1963, p. 75, No. 42, 17 August 1767, and p. 141, No. 90, 17 May 1768 (wrongly dated 1767).

Chapter 22. Favouritism

1. Catherine to Potemkin, 1774 in *Sochineniya*, ed. by Pypin, XII, pp. 687ff.

2. Ibid., pp. 795–6.

3. G.Ouvrard (ed.), *Lettres d'amour de Catherine II à Potemkine, correspondance inédite*. Unfortunately this is an extremely bad edition. The letters seem to be undoubtedly genuine. Ouvrard says that he brought them out of Russia and that he published them in the order in which they were written. In fact they are not printed in chronological order, and the editor has improved Catherine's French spelling.

4. See account in G. Soloveytchilk, *Potemkin*, pp. 100–2 ; Ouvrard, p. 194.

5. Ouvrard, pp. 189 ; 191–2 ; 67–8.

6. Kobeko, op. cit., pp. 103ff ; see also *RS*, 1874, IX, pp. 678ff ; E. Shumigorsky, *Imperator Pavel' I.*, pp. 34ff.

7. Otherwise insignificant, Aleksey Razumovsky, who became Russian ambassador to Vienna, has been immortalized by Beethoven.

8. Kobeko, op. cit., pp. 120ff ; for court gossip as it changed day by day there is no better source than the *Journal Intime du Chevalier de Corberon, 1775–1780*, vol. I, pp. 221ff. Corberon is often wrong on facts, but he records what he and others believed to be true.

9. Corberon, I, pp. 230–1 ; but see Catherine to Mme Bielke, 28 April/9 May 1776, *SIRIO*, 27, pp. 79ff, and ibid., pp. 95ff, for her confirmation that the grand duchess suffered from a physical malformation.

10. *SIRIO*, 27, pp. 78–9.

11. Ouvrard, *passim*.

12. *Ibid.*, p. 189.

13. See A.I. Samoylov, 'Zhizn' i deyaniya gen-erala fel'dmarshala Knyazya Grigoriya Aleksandrovicha Potemkina Tavricheskogo', in *RA*, 1867, at pp. 587ff.

14. Ségur, op. cit., 2, pp. 254ff. See also Harris to Lady Harris, 20/31 August 1781 in Madariaga, *Armed Neutrality*, p. 341, n. 15, and *Zapiski L.N. Engel'gardta*, p. 389.

15. Ségur, op. cit., pp. 254ff.

16. See e.g. Sir James Harris, *Malmesbury Diaries*, I, p. 327, Harris to Stormont, 21 July/1 August 1780.

17. Some of Potemkin's letters to his niece Varvara have survived as examples of the love letters of the eighteenth century. See A. Brückner, *Potemkin*, pp. 259ff.

18. *Zapiski L'va Engel'gardta, 1766—1836*, pp. 116ff.

19. The fullest, if very hostile, contemporary account of Potemkin's life is to be found in the periodical *Minerva*, ed. by J.W. Archenholz, Hamburg/Berlin, 1797–1800.

20. See the penetrating pen portrait by J.E. von Goertz, Prussian envoy from 1779 to 1785 in his *Mémoire sur la Russie*, pp. 41–2.

21. Potemkin's fortune at his death was estimated at over 7 million rubles, excluding the Tauride Palace. See E.P. Karnovich, *Zamechatel'nnyye bogatstva*, p. 314, and Brückner, *Potemkin*, p. 274.

22. See I.R. Christie, 'Samuel Bentham and the Western Colony at Krichev, 1784–87', and the work of E.P. Zakalinskaya, *Votchinnyye khozyaystva Mogilevskoy gubernii vo vtoroy polovine XVIII veka*.

23. See V. Bil'basov, 'Prisoyedineniye Kurlyandii' in *Istoricheskiye Monografii*, II, pp. 205–66, at pp. 236ff.

24. Rumours quoted as quite unsubstantiated in Brückner, *Potemkin*, p. 64.

25. *Malmesbury Diaries*, I, pp. 428ff, Harris to Stormont, 25 June/6 July 1781.

26. Cobenzl to Joseph, 12 September 1781, Beer-Fiedler, I, p. 226.

27. Corberon, *Journal Intime*, II, p. 370, 23 September 1780. Unfortunately the editor of AGS has omitted all sessions dealing with foreign policy for the period 1774–87.

28. See e.g. Beer-Fiedler, p. 302, Joseph to Cobenzl, 19 February 1782 ; on the preparation for the journey see N. Shil'der, *Imperator Pavel Pervyy*, St Petersburg, 1901, pp. 146ff and pp. 542ff.

29. See D.M. Griffiths, 'The Rise and Fall of the Northern System', pp. 547–69 and pp. 562ff ; see also J.E. von Goertz, *Mémoire sur la Russie, 1788*, p. 59, and below, pp. 386–7.

30. The grand duchess feared for the life of her children who were to be innoculated against smallpox. For a description see Griffiths, op. cit., p. 364 and *FO* 65/4 Harris to Stormont No. 137, 17/28 September, and No. 156 21 October/1 November 1781.

31. Beer-Fiedler, Cobenzl to Joseph, 4 December 1781, I, p. 262.

NOTES

32. Beer-Fiedler, p. 115, Leopold of Tuscany to Joseph, 5 June 1782 ; see below, pp. 385ff.

33. Shil'der, op. cit., p. 555.

34. I.M. Dolgoruky 'Kapishche moego serdtsa' *RA*, 1890, I, 164 ; Catherine to Paul, 25 April 1782, *SIRIO*, 9, pp. 145ff, 7 June 1782, ibid., pp. 157ff ; Goertz, *Mémoire sur la Russie,* p. 58.

35. *Malmesbury Diaries,* II, pp. 8ff, to Grantham, 1/12 November 1782.

36. 'Zapiski F.N. Golitsyna,' at p. 1284 ; Shumigorsky, *Imperator Pavel,* appendix, pp. 2–3, 20.

37. See D.I. Fonvizin, 'Zhizn' grafa Nikity Ivanovicha Panina', in *Sobraniye Sochineniya,* pp. 279–90.

38. Ibid., p. 254–67 ; see for English version, M. Raeff (ed.), *Russian Intellectual History, An Anthology,* Harcourt Brace and World Inc., 1966, pp. 96–105.

39. E.S. Shumigorsky, *Imperator Pavel,* I, Appendix ; A copy of Fonvizin's *Discourse* was found among Nikita Panin's papers ; earlier Ms copies circulated among the Decembrists and gave rise to many legends. For a recent analysis, see D. Ransel, 'An Ambivalent Legacy : The Education of Grand Duke Paul'.

40. On the light cavalry see Count S.R. Vorontsov in *AKV,* 10, p. 479 ; and Prince Yu. V. Dolgoruky in *RS,* 1889, vol. 63, p. 509. On his 'passion for Cossacks' see Bezborodko to A.R. Vorontsov, *AKV,* XIII, pp. 227. There was undoubtedly some affinity between Potemkin and the Cossack way of life, which also found expression in his very tolerant policy with regard to Old Believers. See Dubrovin, *Bumagi Potemkina,* Vyp. 1, p. 119, Potemkin's report to Catherine, 10 August 1785.

41. '. . . pour se faire aimer du soldat [il] a diminué l'autorité de l'officier. . . ', wrote the Duc de Richelieu, *Journal de mon voyage en Allemagne,* 2 September 1790. *SIRIO,* 54, at p. 149.

42. *RS,* VII, pp. 722–7 ; see also *RA,* 1888, II, pp. 364–7. Already in 1775, Potemkin had issued orders banning powder, ribbons, and curls in all calvalry and pike regiments under his command. *Bumagi Potemkina,* I, p. 38.

43. And see also Arneth, *Briefwechesel,* Joseph II to Field-Marshal Lacy, pp. 354ff.

44. See *PSZ,* xx, No. 14,890. June 1779.

45. See A.I. Samoylov, 'Zhizn' i deyaniya generala fel'dmarshala Grigoriya Aleksandrovicha Potemkina Tavricheskogo,' *RA,* 1867, pp. 581–2 ; pp. 1229ff.

46. *Zapiski L'va N. Engel'gardta,* 1766–1836, p. 130.

47. Shil'der, *Pavel I,* pp. 192–3. See also the Memoirs of M. Garnovsky, *RS* XVI, p. 7.

48. *RBS,* entry P.V. Zavadovsky.

49. *RBS,* entry S. Zorich ; see also *Malmesbury Diaries,* I, pp. 172–3, Harris to W. Eden, 2/13 February 1778 ; p. 174, Harris to Suffolk, same date and p. 200, 12 May/2 June 1778.

50. *Malmesbury Diaries,* I, pp. 227–8, Harris to Suffolk, 29 January/9 February 1779.

51. Rimsky Korsakov died a very old man in 1831. The relationship between Stroganov, his wife and the ex-favourite was most picturesque but there is no room to go into it here.

52. *SIRIO,* 23, pp. 316ff ; 7/18 June 1784, continued 2/13 July.

53. Ibid., pp. 317–18, 9/18 September 1784 ; Beer-Fiedler, I, p. 17, Cobenzl to Joseph, 5 May 1780.

54. Ibid., pp. 321–2, 19/30 September 1784 ; pp. 334ff, 22 April/3 May 1785 ; pp. 344ff, 28 June/9 July 1785.

55. Yermolov subsequently settled in Vienna. He acquired the estate of Frohsdorf in Styria, later the residence of the Comte de Chambord. Two of his sons were educated in Austria as Catholics, and Yermolov died there in 1834.

56. Khrapovitsky, *Dnevnik,* pp. 290ff ; see below, pp. 407–8.

57. C.F.P. Masson, in his *Mémoires Secrets sur la Russie,* anon, Paris 1800 edition, Vol. I, p. 163, refers to Catherine's 'petite société' in which the 'Cybele of the North' celebrated her 'secret mysteries'. In my copy of this book, which once belonged to James Harris, first Lord Malmesbury, the owner has written in the margin at this point : 'mensonges'. See also the extraordinary *La Messaline du Nord,* by 'VR' (a Lady), 1834.

58. Ségur, *Mémoires,* III, p. 18.

59. *SIRIO,* 23, p. 334, Catherine to Grimm, 22 April 1785. The story of Catherine indulging in repartee too vulgar to be printed, as told in Corberon, *Journal Intime,* II, pp. 137–8, seems in the circumstances unlikely.

60. Ségur, *Mémoires,* III, pp. 183–4. But then Joseph did not care for 'La Princesse de Zerbst Catherinisée' either.

61. *SIRIO,* 23, pp. 316–17, 7/18 June 1784, to Grimm.

62. *Malmesbury Diaries,* II, p. 10, Harris to Grantham, 4/15 November 1782.

63. *SIRIO,* 23, pp. 274–5.

64. J.P. LeDonne, 'Appointments to the Russian Senate, 1762–1796' ; in this article the author has attempted to analyse family grouping within the Senate, dividing the membership broadly into a Panin and a Vyazemsky group. This is a useful approach, but where families are so closely connected it is often difficult to establish allegiance to one or another group. LeDonne does not mention a Potemkin group at all.

65. It is unfortunate that in his otherwise very useful edition of M.M. Shcherbatov's *On the Corruption of Morals,* A. Lentin has confused ennoblement with the granting of a title. This renders his analysis of 'Old and New Nobles' (Appendix II, pp. 302ff) highly misleading. Descendants of previous princely families are described as having been ennobled before the reign of Peter I, whereas they were of course never *ennobled* at all ; others are considered to have been ennobled on the day they received a title ; and a third group, comprising

such old non-titled noble families as the Zinov'yevs, Bibikovs, Zagryazhskys, Mel'gunovs, Ushakovs, Adadurovs, etc., are described as non-noble, whereas they were born dvoryane.

Chapter 23. The Viceroy of the South

1. *PSZ*, xx, No. 14,252, 14 February 1775.

2. *SIRIO*, 27, p. 37, for Catherine's approval of Potemkin's recommendation ; *PSZ*, xx, No. 14,235, 15 January 1775 ; No. 14,464, 5 May 1776.

3. *PSZ*, xx, Nos. 14,251 and 14,252, 15 February 1775 ; A.P. Pronshteyn, *Zemlya Donskaya v XVIII veke*, pp. 240ff. The cadastral survey of the Host's lands, begun in 1766, was completed in 1786, and a charter guaranteed these lands to the Host in 1793. Cossack lands could not thereafter be sold, though more land could be bought. Ibid., pp. 33–4.

4. Pronshteyn, op. cit., pp. 179–80. This gave noble status to 89 officers in 1776, 95 in 1777, 138 in 1788 and 206 in 1796.

5. See *AGS*, II, pp. 219–20, sessions of 8, 12, 19 May 1774 ; 16 June 1774 ; p. 222, 7 May 1775. Cf. Nolde, *La formation de l'Empire russe*, II, p. 108. *SIRIO*, 135, p. 353.

6. *AGS*, II, p. 221, 19 February 1775.

7. V.A. Golobutsky, *Chernomorskoye kazachestvo*, pp. 109ff and the almost identical account in his *Zaporozhskoye kazachestvo*, pp. 421ff. Kal'nyshevsky owned horses, horned cattle and corn to the value of 38,718 rubles when his wealth was confiscated (*Ocherki*, p. 586, n.1). See also P.S. Efimenko, 'Kal'nyshevsky, poslednyy koshevoy ataman zaporozhskoy sechi',' and M.N. Gernet *Istorya tsarskoy tyur'my*, I, pp. 174–9.

8. *PSZ*, xx, No. 14,354.

9. Nolde, op. cit., II, pp. 113–4 ; D. Bagaley, 'Nasledniki Zaporozhskikh zemel''.

10. Catherine II, *Sochineniya*, ed. by Pypin, XII, p. 615 ; *PSZ*, XVI, No. 11,720, 4 December 1762.

11. *PSZ*, XVI, Nos. 11,879, 11,811 and 11,890.

12. See R. Bartlett, *Human Capital*, for the most up to date and complete study of Catherine's immigration and settlement policy.

13. There are many accounts by visitors to Sarepta. J. Parkinson noted in 1792 : 'We stopped at an inn where the accommodations would do credit to a good inn in England. . . . We took our departure from Sarepta to which I never saw a place equal for the goodness of the people and for all the comforts of life.' (*A Tour of Russia, Siberia and the Crimea, 1792–4*, pp. 142ff.)

14. Bartlett, op. cit., pp. 81ff.

15. *PSZ*, XVI, 12,099, 22 March 1764 ; see also No. 12,180 for the extension of the plan to Slavyano-Serbia. Cf. N. Polonska Vasylenko, 'The Settlement of the Southern Ukraine 1750–1775', and the earlier version published in *Istoricheskiye Zapiski*.

16. Bartlett, op. cit., pp. 126ff ; *Bumagi Potemkina*, I, p. 54, Potemkin to General Muromtsev, 31 August 1775. See also H. Auerbach, *Die Besiedlung*

der Süd Ukraine in den Jahren 1774–78, Veröffentlichungen des Osteuropa Instituts ; E.I. Druzhinina, *Severnoye Prichernomor'ye, 1775–1800*, pp. 64–5.

17. Druzhinina, op. cit., p. 67.

18. Druzhinina gives the following figures for the population in the fourth census of 1782 in the two gubernii of Azov and New Russia : 365,457 male souls, or 529,538 of both sexes. (It must be remembered that when the two gubernii were formed parts of the more densely populated South Ukraine had been incorporated (see op. cit., p. 69).) Of the 365,457, 195,815 were state peasants, and 132,202 free peasants settled on private land. There were about 10,000 colonists and only 4,514 serfs. See also pp. 161–2.

19. The founder of Kherson was Ivan Abramovich Gannibal, the son of Peter I's 'moor' and grandfather of the poet Pushkin. See on Kherson H. Halm, *Gründung und erstes Jahrzehnt von Festung und Stadt Cherson 1778–1788*. The building cost many lives owing to the unhealthy conditions in which conscripted soldiers worked. They were paid 5 k. per day, or 10 k. if they worked in stone. Op. cit., pp. 49–50.

20. Specially devised mechanisms to give buoyancy to ships. *OED*.

21. Halm, op. cit., p. 48.

22. Druzhinina, op. cit., p. 83.

23. According to O. Markova, 'O neytral'noy sisteme i franko-russkikh otnosheniyakh. Vtoraya polovina XVIII v.' Potemkin hoped to establish friendly relations with Ethiopia in order to open up Russian trade in the Red Sea (p. 47).

24. See Chapter 24, and A. Fisher, *The Russian Annexation of the Crimea, 1772–1783*, Cambridge, 1970 ; the number of emigrants is variously given as 300,000 or 150,000–200,000, pp. 142–6. V. Zuyev, who was there in 1782, estimated the population then at about 50,000 (*Puteshestvennye zapiski Vasilya Zuyeva ot St Peterburga do Khersona v 1781 i 1782 goda*).

25. *PSZ*, XXI, No. 15,707, 8 April 1783. See also *SIRIO*, 27, p. 244, draft manifesto 8 April 1783, in rescript to G.A. Potemkin.

26. *PSZ*, XXII, No. 15,920, 2 February 1784.

27. *PSZ*, XXII, No. 15,925, 8 February 1784. Fisher (op. cit., p. 142) points out that Catherine had discovered in the Legislative Commission of 1767–8 that 'the use of Russian administrators was not satisfactory in native regions, particularly in settling minor judicial matters'. Local native elders had now been placed in charge of civil disputes between natives in the Volga area. Suits between natives and Russians went before Russian military courts.

28. Fisher, op. cit., p. 143. Cf. *Rasporyazheniya Potemkina*, p. 304.

29. *PSZ*, XXII, No. 15,936 ; *Rasporyazheniya Potemkina*, p. 303, Catherine to Potemkin, 30 May 1784.

30. *SIRIO*, 27, p. 300, Catherine to Potemkin, 1 March 1784, and appendix providing for five 'divisions,' of 207 officers and men each, at a total cost of 41,450 in salaries, varying from 300 r. for one major to 35 r.p.a. for private soldiers.

31. C. Lemercier-Quelquejay, 'Les Missions Orthodoxes en Pays Musulmans de Moyenne et Basse-Volga, 1552–1865'.

32. There were over 1,500 mosques in the Crimea in 1783, and the lands belonging to the clergy amounted to about 25 per cent of the land in the khanate. Fisher, op. cit., p. 9, and n. 2, and p. 149.

33. Druzhinina, *Severnoye Prichernomor'ye*, pp. 119–20 for details of grants ranging from 53,000 desyatinas to Vasily Popov, head of Potemkin's Chancery, 73,000 to Potemkin himself, on which he proposed to establish a model farm, grants to army and naval officers, diplomats, etc. See also Fisher, op. cit., p. 147.

34. A.A. Skal'kovsky, *Khronologicheskoye obozreniye istorii Novorossiyskogo kraya 1730–1823*, Pt. I, p. 221, quoted in Druzhinina, op. cit., p. 122.

35. Druzhinina, op. cit., p. 128. See *Zapiski Mertvago*, p. 180. *Rasporyazheniya Potemkina*, XII, p. 315.

36. Fisher, op. cit., p. 147, quoting P.D. Sumarokov, *Dosugi krymskogo sud'i ili vtoroye puteshestviye v Tavridu*, St Petersburg, 1803–5, p. 185, gives 8,746 serfs. This is an astonishing figure which clashes with the 226 given by Skal'kovsky for 1793.

37. Druzhinina, op. cit., pp. 78ff, 89ff. For the development of foreign trade see Chapter XXX.

38. Nolde, op. cit., pp. 193–4. See also *Arkhiv Mordvinovykh*, III, p. 195.

39. Nolde, op. cit., pp. 189–90.

40. By 1784 the original Yekaterinoslav had 2,194 inhabitants and two schools. Druzhinina, op. cit.

41. For the following remarks, see R.E. Jones, 'Urban Planning and the Development of Provincial Towns in Russia, 1762–1796'.

42. Druzhinina, op. cit., p. 176, no. 72, and p. 232 for a plan of the projected city, which included three separate hospitals. Potemkin started recruiting teachers for his university long before the city existed except on paper.

43. *SIRIO*, 27, pp. 230–31. According to M. Raeff, in 'The Style of Russia's Imperial Policy and Prince G.A. Potemkin', p. 51, n. 60, 'The Medico-Surgical School in Simferopol established in the 1790s owes its origin to Potemkin's educational designs.'

44. Druzhinina, op. cit., pp. 150, 154–5, Table 3, and 200, Table 5. See also p. 152, for Table 2, which lists 2,209 inhabited 'points' in the namestnichestvo, of which 1,863 were privately owned villages and hamlets.

45. Bartlett, op. cit., p. 171. A manifesto of July 1785 again invited foreign colonists to settle in Russia. Some 700 came from Danzig, and a number of Mennonites subsequently settled there. Druzhinina, pp. 165–6.

46. *PSZ*, XXII, No. 16,603. Its provisions were applied to the state peasants in other guberniya in 1790.

47. Druzhinina, op. cit., pp. 167ff.

48. M. Raeff, 'In the Imperial Manner', p. 30. I cannot see why Raeff assumes that Potemkin's main purpose was *'only* to enhance the glory of his sovereign, to demonstrate his own talents and power and to indulge his passion for luxury and magnificent display' (my italics). It is impossible, in someone so imaginative as Potemkin, to pigeonhole his motives so neatly.

49. A vast amount of published material (and presumably of unpublished material) exists on Potemkin's administration, the history of which remains to be written. I have drawn upon M. Raeff's perceptive article (see n. 43) though I do not always agree with him.

50. Arneth, *Briefwechsel*, pp. 353ff, Joseph II to Field-Marshal Lacy, 19/30 May 1787.

51. Miranda, *Archivo*, II, pp. 204ff, 22 November 1786.

52. *SIRIO*, 27, p. 265.

53. *SIRIO*, 97, pp. 288–317; Nolde, op. cit., II, pp. 86–7.

54. See Chapter 11.

55. Nolde, op. cit., pp. 341ff.

56. Khrapovitsky, *Dnevnik*, p. 1, April 1782.

57. In addition to Nolde, op. cit., see D.M. Lang, *A Modern History of Georgia*, and W.E.D. Allen, *A History of the Georgian People*.

58. X. Liske, 'Beiträge zur Geschichte der Kaniower Zusammenkunft (1787) und ihr Vorläufer'.

59. For descriptions of Kiev at this time see Ségur, *Mémoires*, III, pp. 41–2 (on Rumyantsev) and Miranda, *Archivo*, II, pp. 254ff. See also Prince Charles de Ligne (Joseph II's special envoy), *Mémoires et Mélanges Historiques et Littéraires*, II *passim*; Khrapovitsky, *Dnevnik*, passim.

60. See *Zhurnal Vysochayshego puteshestviya eya Velichestva Gosudaryni Yekateriny II samoderzhitsy vserossiyskoy v poludennyye strany Rossii v 1787 godu*, Moscow, at the University Press of N.I. Novikov, passim, and Ségur, *Mémoires*, III, pp. 8ff and particularly p. 96.

61. Ségur, *Mémoires*, III, p. 112.

62. *Lettres et Pensées du maréchal Prince de Ligne*, ed. by Baronne de Stael Holstein, I, pp. 137ff.

63. Ségur, *Mémoires*, III, pp. 66–7, 112–13, 120–3.

64. Quoted in Vasil'chikov, *Semeystvo Razumovskikh*, I, pp. 370–1, dated 22 June 1782.

65. See V. Chertkov's Instructions, dated 31 May 1787 for the passage of the empress through the governor-generalship of Khar'kov, ordering the streets to be cleared of beggars and the people to appear in their best clothes, in P. Bartenev, ed., *Osmnadtsaty y Vek*, I, pp. 306ff. See for a modern example Frances Donaldson, *Edward* VIII, p. 65 : when the Royal Family visited Kennington, 'a number of empty houses in Kennington Road were made to appear as if they were tenanted . . . by having curtains put up'.

66. Miranda, *Archivo*, II, p. 324, 9 May 1787, NS.

67. See Liske, op. cit., pp. 494ff, and Khrapovitsky, *Dnevnik*, pp. 33, 25 and 2 April 1787.

68. Druzhinina, *Severnoye Prichernomor'ye*, pp. 173–4. Miranda was told that the population numbered some 40,000 all told. *Archivo*, II, p. 216.

69. According to Brückner, however, Potemkin's officials took care that no complaints against him should reach the empress's ears. See A. Brückner, 'Puteshestviye Yekateriny II v poludennyy kray Rossii v 1787 godu', at p. 10.

Chapter 24. Between the Wars: Foreign Policy in the 1780s

1. J.W. Zinkeisen, *Geschichte des Osmanischen Reiches in Europa*, vol. 6, pp. 86. See also *SIRIO*, 145, p. 45ff. Catherine to Rumyantsev, 8 March 1776; *AGS*, I, p. 291, 6 October 1774.

2. Declaration for the Crimeans issued by P.A. Rumyantsev, approved by Catherine II, 6 October 1776, *SIRIO*, 145, pp. 240–1.

3. Fisher, *Annexation of the Crimea*, pp. 94–5. Cf. also Solov'yev, xv, pp. 195ff.

4. *SIRIO*, 19, pp. 463–506, Sir Robert Gunning's correspondence.

5. W. Stribny, *Die Russland Politik Friedrichs des Grossen, 1764–1786*, pp. 90–1.

6. See Chapter xv.

7. Text in F. de Martens, *Recueil*, Vols 5–6, *L'Allemagne*, pp. 101ff. The treaty was identical with that of 1769, except that it guaranteed the Grand Duke Paul's German possessions to the younger branch of the family, and it guaranteed the treaty of February 1772 (the partition of Poland). A separate Act was signed dealing with the Prussian ratification of the treaty of 11/22 August 1776 on the borders between Poland and Prussia in Berlin on 13 April 1777.

8. A. Rambaud (ed.), *Recueil des Instructions, Russia*, pp. 337ff. Vergennes to Corberon, 28 December 1777.

9. Stribny, op. cit., p. 107.

10. Fisher, op. cit., pp. 106–9. Zinkeisen, op. cit., 6, pp. 208ff.

11. For the text of the treaty of Ainalikawak see G.F. de Martens, *Recueil*, Supplément, 3, p. 653.

12. See Fisher op. cit., pp. 100ff; Nolde, op. cit., pp. 140–52; Bartlett, op. cit., pp. 130–1 gives a different figure : $1,386.

13. The colonists were exempt from all taxes for 10 years and after that, merchants would pay the tax usual in Russia (1 per cent of their capital) townspeople would pay 2 rubles per household and peasants 5 kopeks per desyatina, the first case to my knowledge of a straightforward land tax introduced in Russia. The colonists were exempted for ever from billetting and the recruit levy. The initial resettlement was as usual full of difficulties since promises were not fulfilled. But the colonies flourished after these initial setbacks.

14. Stribny, op. cit., pp. 113ff. And see the instructions for N.P. Rumyantsev, in 23 December 1785, on his appointment as envoy to Berlin in A. Tratschewsky, *Der Fürstenbund*, p. 495.

15. For the detailed account of the conflict and the peace, apart from the political correspondence of Frederick II, PCFG, vols. 41–43 ; see A. Unzer, *Der*

Friede von Teschen ; E. Reimann, *Geschichte des Bairischen Erbfolgkrieges* ; P. Oursel, *La diplomatie française sous Louis XVI : Succession de Bavière et paix de Teschen*. For the Russian documents, see *SIRIO*, 65, correspondence of Prince N.V. Repnin.

16. I. de Madariaga, *Britain, Russia and the Armed Neutrality of 1780*, pp. 44–6.

17. Op. cit., p. 52.

18. For a general discussion of the issues involved see ibid., pp. 57ff.

19. For the text of the Anglo-Russian treaty see F. de Martens, *Recueil*, 9, p. 242. When the treaty of 1734 was renewed in 1766, both the British envoy and the secretary of state, Lord Sandwich, were under the impression that 'we are now the judges of what shall be deemed ammunitions'. But article xi makes it quite clear that apart from specific contraband items 'neither the ships nor passengers, nor the other merchandise found at the same time, shall be detained or hindered from prosecuting their voyage'.

20. See Madariaga, op. cit., Chapter 3.

21. Of the five principles put forward two were highly controversial, namely the universal application of the principle 'free ships free goods', and the equally universal extension of the definition of contraband, as laid down in articles x and xi of the Anglo-Russian treaty of 1776. For the text see Madariaga, op. cit., p. 172.

22. The full text of all these treaties will be found most conveniently in James Brown Scott (ed.), *The Armed Neutralities of 1780 and 1800*, pp. 295ff, 307, 311, 321–2.

23. See A. von Arneth, *Maria Theresias letzte Regierungszeit*, 4, pp. 667–70 for an account of the emperor's decision.

24. For the most recent survey see Edgar Hösch, 'Das sogenannte griechische Projekt Katharinas II, Ideologie und Wirklichkeit der russischen Orientpolitik in der zweiten Hälfte des 18. Jahrhunderts' ; O.P. Markova, 'O proiskhozhdenii tak nazyvayemogo grecheskogo proekta (80e gody XVIII v)'.

25. *SIRIO*, 27, p. 180; M. Raeff. 'In the Imperial Manner', p. 5, n. 6.

26. A. von Arneth, *Joseph II und Katharina von Russland, ihr Briefwechsel*, p. 11, Catherine to Joseph, October 1780.

27. Madariaga, op. cit., pp. 302ff.

28. For a more detailed study see Madariaga, 'The Secret Austro-Russian Treaty of 1781'.

29. For the text of the letters see A. von Arneth, *Joseph II und Katharina von Russland, ihr Briefwechsel*, pp. 67ff, where Joseph's letters are dated 20 and 21 May, though they should correctly be dated 18 May : Catherine's letters were dated 24 May/4 June 1781.

30. The Russian convention with Portugal was signed on 24 July 1782; that with the Kingdom of the Two Sicilies in February 1783. For texts see Scott, *Armed Neutralities*, pp. 420, 433.

31. Madariaga, op. cit., pp. 320–1, 340–1. For texts of treaties see Scott, *Armed Neutralities*, pp. 397, 403, 405, 409. Austrian accession in view of the unre-

solved dispute over the alternative also took the form of an exchange of acts of accession and acceptance.

32. See V.A. Ulyanitsky, *Russkiye Konsul'stva za granitsey v xviii veke*, vol. 2, appendix 128, pp. DLXXVff. For the statement of general principles Russia intended to apply in all commercial treaties, see F. de Martens, *Recueil*, 2, p. 143, Note for Count Cobenzl, 9 September 1782. The first commercial treaty was concluded with Denmark on 8/19 October 1782, and in Articles 16 and 17 confirmed the adherence of the two parties to the principles of the Armed Neutrality (of the wisdom of which the contracting parties were firmly convinced). The treaty of Armed Neutrality with Portugal was followed by a commercial treaty with the Porte (10/21 July 1783), with Austria (1/12 November 1785), with France (31 December 1786/11 January 1787), with the Two Sicilies (6 January 1787) and with Portugal (9/20 December 1787). The principles of the Armed Neutrality were repeated in all these commercial treaties.

33. I. de Madariaga, 'The Secret Austro-Russian Treaty of 1781'.

34. Madariaga, *Armed Neutrality*, pp. 497–8.

35. Arneth, *Briefwechsel*, pp. 143ff, 10/21 September 1782. See also p. 134, the same to the same, 15/26 June 1782.

36. Ibid., pp. 169ff, Joseph to Catherine 13 November 1782. See also Beer-Fiedler, I, p. 345, Joseph to Cobenzl, 22 November 1782 ; pp. 367ff, 24 February 1783.

37. Zinkeisen, *Geschichte*, VI, 349, 383, for the simultaneous Austrian and Russian memorials of August 1782.

38. Nolde, op. cit., pp. 163–4 ; *SIRIO*, 27, pp. 221–5.

39. Harris to Grantham, 18/29 January 1782 in *Malmesbury Diaries*, II, pp. 27ff ; Arneth, *Briefwechsel*, pp. 188ff, Joseph to Catherine, 25 February 1783; Beer-Fiedler, I, pp. 407ff, Cobenzl to Joseph II, 10 May 1783.

40. Catherine may have been influenced to abandon her protégé Shagin Girey by the ruthless cruelty with which he treated his opponents. She instructed Potemkin to make sure that the Russian forces in the Crimea were dissociated from Shagin Girey's repressive policies, and ordered her envoy to protest personally to the khan. See Fisher, op. cit., p. 132–3 ; *SIRIO*, 27, pp. 231–2, Catherine to Potemkin, 7/18 February 1783.

41. The manifesto can be found in *PSZ*, XXI, No. 15,707, 8 April 1783. It was accompanied by the draft of a 'plakat' to be issued by Potemkin, summoning the Crimeans to take the oath of allegiance to Catherine within a month.

42. *SIRIO*, 27, pp. 240ff.

43. Catherine to Joseph II, 7/18 April 1783, Arneth, *Briefwechsel*, pp. 195ff.

44. Catherine to Potemkin, 14/25 April (Good Friday) 1783, *SIRIO*, 27, pp. 250–3.

45. Catherine to Potemkin, 24 April/5 May 1783.

SIRIO, 27, pp. 253–4 ; 26 May/6 June 1783, ibid., pp. 259–60 ; S. Oakley, 'Gustavus III's Plans for War with Denmark in 1783–1784', pp. 271ff.

46. Catherine to Potemkin, 5/16 June 1783, *SIRIO*, 27, pp. 261–2.

47. Oakley, op. cit., p. 277.

48. Catherine to Potemkin, 15/26 July 1783, *SIRIO*, 27, p. 269.

49. The same to the same, 20/31 July 1783, *SIRIO*, 27, p. 270, acknowledging Potemkin's report of 10/21 July 1783.

50. The same to the same, *SIRIO*, 27, p. 264, n.d. and 10/21 July 1783, ibid., p. 268, and n. 1. For the text of the commercial treaty see *PSZ*, XXI, No. 15,757, and see Zinkeisen, op. cit., VI, pp. 404ff.

51. Ibid., p. 268, n. 1, Bulgakov's report of 15/26 June 1783. See also Nolde, op. cit., pp. 170ff ; 'Iz bumag Ya. I. Bulgakova' in *Russkiy Arkhiv*, 1905, 7, pp. 337–408 ; and Bulgakov's reports to Catherine in *SIRIO*, 47, 1779–1798.

52. *SIRIO*, 47, pp. 44–7, Bulgakov to Catherine 1/12 December 1782.

53. Madariaga, op. cit., pp. 430ff.

54. R. Salomon, *La politique Orientale de Vergennes*, pp. 134ff ; Madariaga, 'The Secret Austro-Russian Treaty of 1781'.

55. See M.S. Anderson, 'The Great Powers and the Russian Annexation of the Crimea, 1783–4'.

56. For the text of the treaty see *SIRIO*, 47, pp. 100–101, enclosed in Bulgakov to Catherine, 28 December 1783/8 January 1784, ibid., pp. 98–100.

57. Arneth, *Briefwechsel*, June 1783, p. 205.

58. Arneth, *Briefwechsel*, pp. 224ff. See also Arneth et Flammermont, Kaunitz to Mercy, 2 August 1784, summary, p. 275, n. 3.

59. Beer-Fiedler, I, p. 467, n. 1, Catherine to Prince D.M. Golitsyn in Vienna 15/26 May 1784. And see Arneth, *Briefwechsel*, Catherine to Joseph, 23 May/3 June 1784, pp. 229ff, and Rescript to Golitsyn of 22 May/2 June, quoted in A. Trachevsky, *Soyuz knyazyey*, p. 120.

60. L. von Ranke, *Die deutsche Mächte und der Fürstenbund*, p. 144.

61. See S.T. Bindoff, *The Scheld Question*, pp. 140ff and Arneth and Flammermont, pp. 308ff, and p. 365, n. 2, Mercy to Kaunitz, 31 December 1784.

62. Trachevsky, p. 173–74. Stribny, op. cit., p. 225.

63. For these negotiations see John Ehrman, *The British Government and Commercial Negotiations with Europe, 1783–1793*, pp. 92ff.

64. L.-P. de Ségur, *Mémoires ou Souvenirs et Anecdotes*, vol. 2, pp. 314ff, 330ff.

65. Ehrman, op. cit., pp. 107–8.

66. F. de Martens, *Recueil*, 13, pp. 194ff. The treaty has to be seen in the context of the other commercial treaties negotiated at this time by Catherine (see n. 32). It provided for most favoured nation treatment in both countries, and reduced the duties on a number of goods, notably French wines. French traders were al-

lowed to pay dues in Russian currency instead of in rix-dalers as previously. Merchants in both countries would be under the jurisdiction of the local courts for disputes with natives of the country. Throughout the treaty strict reciprocity was observed, regardless of whether it had any practical application. Catherine's principles of the armed neutrality were also included as article 27.

67. Ehrman, op. cit.

Chapter 25. The Second Turkish War

1. See Chapter 24.

2. J.W. Zinkeisen, *Geschichte des Osmanischen Reiches in Europa*, 6, pp. 515ff and H. Uebersberger, *Russlands Orientpolitik in den letzten zwei Jahrhunderten*, 1, pp. 370ff.

3. 'Sobstvennoruchnyye bumagi Knyazya Potemkina', *RA*, 1865, pp. 740ff, extract of Catherine's instructions to Potemkin of 16/27 October 1786 ; pp. 721ff, Potemkin to Bulgakov, 13/24 December 1788. Potemkin admitted to Ségur that he had allowed himself to become too heated. (See Ségur, *Mémoires*, III, pp. 74ff.)

4. As late as 7/18 January 1787 Potemkin ordered Bulgakov to procure an exact copy of the sultan's state yacht, down to the last detail of the furnishings, and send it to Sebastopol. ('Sobstvennoruchnyye bumagi', *RA*, 1865, p. 742.)

5. K.A. Roider, 'Kaunitz, Joseph II and the Turkish War'.

6. L.P. de Ségur, *Mémoires, ou Souvenirs et Anecdotes*, III, pp. 176ff.

7. Zinkeisen, op. cit., p. 624.

8. A.N. Petrov, *Vtoraya turetskaya voyna v tsarstvoyaniye Yekateriny II 1787–1791 gg*, 1, p. 53 ; A. Brückner, 'Razryv mezhdu Rossiey i Turtsiey v 1787 godu', p. 134, n. 2. Brückner, op. cit., pp. 149ff suggests that Bulgakov, urged by Potemkin, in addition to the moderate programme agreed upon at Kherson, put forward in secret utterly unacceptable demands, such as the cession of Bessarabia and the port of Bujukdere. His only evidence is that Prince M.M. Shcherbatov alleged that these demands were put forward by Russia, and naturally refused by the Porte. But Shcherbatov was not in a position to know, and it is evident from all that went before and came after that Potemkin did not want war just then.

9. *SIRIO*, 27, pp. 425ff, 24 September/4 October 1787, at p. 427.

10. Arneth, *Joseph II und Katharina von Russland*, p. 300.

11. *AGS*, 1, p. 429, Ya. Bruce, N.I. Saltykov, V.P. Musin Pushkin, A.P. Shuvalov, A.R. Vorontsov, S.F. Strekalov and P.V. Zavadovsky were appointed to the Council.

12. *AGS*, 1, pp. 459–65.

13. Ségur, op. cit., III, p. 203. Herrmann, *Geschichte des Russischen Staates*, VII, p. 153 ; Brückner, *Razryv*, p. 163, who notes that prices had risen from 86

k. a chetvert' in 1760 to 2 r. 19 in 1773 and 7 r. in 1787.

14. See Khrapovitsky, *Dnevnik*, p. 80, 20 September 1787 ; Rubinstein, op. cit., p. 371 ; *SIRIO*, 27, p. 489 Catherine to Potemkin, 26 January 1788, p. 478, 26 February 1788 : 'now is not the time for taxes ; the harvest has failed and there are many arrears anyhow.'

15. Ibid., p. 49, 12 September 1787 ; *PSZ*, xxv, No. 16,567, September 1787.

16. L.G. Beskrovnyy, *Russkaya armiya i flot v XVIII veke*, pp. 296–7. In the 1790s about 3·1 per cent of the population was subjected to military training (ibid., p. 302).

17. Ibid., pp. 334–6.

18. See Petrov, op. cit., pp. 77–83 ; Beskrovnyy, op. cit., pp. 520 ff. In *Fel'dmarshal Rumyantsev, Sbornik dokumentov i materialov*, p. 251, n. 1, different figures are given for the size of the armies. I have preferred those given by Petrov and Beskrovnyy.

19. Petrov, p. 76.

20. Petrov, op. cit., pp. 94–102 ; Beskrovnyy, op. cit., pp. 526–9 ; see also I.R. Christie, 'Samuel Bentham and the Russian Dnieper Flotilla'.

21. *SIRIO*, 27, pp. 425ff, Catherine to Potemkin, 24 September 1787.

22. S.M. Solov'yev, *Istoriya Padeniya Pol'shi*, p. 176, Potemkin to Catherine, 24 September 1787 ; *SIRIO*, 27, p. 428, Catherine to Potemkin, 25 September 1787 ; p. 433, 2 October 1787.

23. *SIRIO*, 27, p. 436, Catherine to Potemkin, 9 October 1787. As for his 'spasms', Catherine wrote, he would do better to improve his diet since they were probably due to wind.

24. *SIRIO*, 27, p. 428, Catherine to Potemkin. The men were given 1 r. each, the n.c.o.'s 2 rubles each. Various decorations were distributed, and Suvorov was to be given 10,000 r. in cash or in some suitable object.

25. D. Gerhardt, *England und der Aufstieg Russlands*, pp. 200–203. See *SIRIO*, 27, p. 444, Catherine to Potemkin 4/15 November 1787 – 'it is better to cope with France and England without an alliance'.

26. R.H. Lord, *The Second Partition of Poland*, p. 77. The fact that Potemkin, around November 1787–January 1788 seemed to favour a Prussian alliance is evidently not unconnected with his own plans for Poland. Ibid., pp. 86–7.

27. Ibid., p. 60, and p. 509 for the full text of the declaration, printed for the first time by Lord.

28. Solov'yev, *Istoriya Padeniya Pol'shi*, p. 198, Potemkin to Catherine, n.d. Lord, p. 514. See also Khrapovitsky, *Dnevnik*, p. 16, 16/27 March 1787, and Potemkin to Catherine 27 March/7 April 1788 in *Bumagi Potemkina*, VI, pp. 252ff.

29. See *RA*, 1874, II, pp. 270ff for Potemkin's memoranda to Catherine, n.d. but presumed to be around January 1788. Branicki had already proposed something similar directly to Catherine in September 1787, possibly at Potemkin's instigation, and had been turned down by the empress. Lord, p. 84, n. 2.

30. Lord, op. cit., Appendix III, pp. 515–16, refers to these plans. See also Kohut, op. cit., pp. 299–300.

31. Quoted in Lord, op. cit., p. 513, n. 2.

32. See her comments on Potemkin's outline of the aims of his confederation. *RA*, 1874, Potemkin's memorandum, and Catherine's comments numbered alphabetically.

33. Catherine to Potemkin, 16/27 May 1788, *SIRIO*, 27, p. 489, urging him to persuade Branicki to fall in with her own plans.

34. Lord, op. cit., pp. 88–90.

35. *SIRIO*, 27, pp. 480ff, Catherine to Potemkin, 27 May 1788.

36. The detailed instructions given to Greig are printed by Petrov, Appendix 9 of 5 June 1788. For Greig's own plan of 1783 see p. 116. See also Gerhardt, op. cit., p. 205, and *AGS*, I, p. 539, 21 February/3 March 1788, Instructions to General Zaborovsky, commander of the land forces in the Mediterranean. Aleksey Orlov had been invited by Catherine to take command but he had refused to serve again.

37. Gerhardt, op. cit., p. 208. In some cases British seamen were bodily removed from Russian merchant ships by British warships ; ibid., p. 208, n. 63.

38. A. Brückner, in 'Schwede und Russland, 1788', points out that during the Swedish diet of 1786 the opposition met in the house of the Russian envoy (p. 342).

39. *SIRIO*, 27, p. 487, Catherine to Potemkin, 24 March 1788 ; p. 490, 27 May 1788.

40. *AGS*, I, p. 549, 20/31 March 1788 ; p. 552, 23 March/3 April and 27 March/7 April.

41. *PSZ*, XXII, No. 16,679.

42. Ségur, op. cit., III, pp. 315–16 ; Brückner, op. cit., p. 365. The propaganda war was carried on by Gustavus in a 'Declaration' of 10/21 July 1788, printed in Helsinki, listing Swedish grievances, to which Catherine drafted an answer in German which was anonymously circulated in September 1788.

43. Brückner, op. cit., p. 393 ; Ségur, op. cit., III, p. 325.

44. R.C. Anderson, *Naval Wars in the Baltic*, pp. 243ff. In his report to the empress, Greig described the encounter as a Russian victory (*AGS*, I, p. 582, 10/21 July 1788) ; so does Beskrovnyy, op. cit., p. 577. Anderson regards it as a draw.

45. See C. Nordmann, *Grandeur et Liberté de la Suède*, pp. 380ff ; Hugues Colin du Terrail, *La Finlande et les Russes depuis les Croisades Suédoises*, pp. 97ff. Beskrovnyy, op. cit., pp. 576ff ; *AGS*, I, p. 589, 3/14 August 1788.

46. Gerhardt, op. cit., p. 228. On the offer of mediation of the Triple Alliance see *AGS*, I, p. 603, 4/15 September 1788 and p. 606, 18/29 September 1788.

47. *AGS*, I, p. 606, 18/29 September 1788.

48. Zinkeisen, *Geschichte*, v, pp. 650ff ; Petrov, op. cit., p. 150ff ; Beskrovnyy, op. cit., pp. 535ff.

49. R.C. Anderson, *Naval Wars in the Levant*, p.

323 gives different estimates of the strengths of the fleets from those in contemporary accounts (Suvorov, Paul Jones, Nassau Siegen).

50. Christie, 'Samuel Bentham and the Dniepr Flotilla', p. 185 ; Potemkin to Catherine, 15/26 June 1788 in 'Imperatritsa Yekaterina II i Knyaz' Potemkin Tavrichesky, podlinnaya ikh perepiska', p. 470 ; *SIRIO*, 27, p. 474, Catherine to Potemkin 13/24 February 1788 ; p. 475, the same to the same, 22 February/4 March 1788.

51. Christie, op. cit.

52. Account taken from Anderson, Christie and Petrov.

53. Potemkin to Catherine, 7/16 December 1788, 'Perepiska', *RS*, XVI, p. 23 ; Catherine to Potemkin, 16/27 December, *SIRIO*, 27, p. 536.

54. *AGS*, I, pp. 619–27, 16/27 October 1788.

55. Khrapovitsky, *Dnevnik*, p. 185, 3/14 November 1788 ; *AGS*, I, p. 630, 2/13 November 1788, and the separate minute of A.P. Shuvalov's views. See also 'Zapiski M. Garnovskogo,' 1787–90 in *RS*, XVI, 1876, pp. 225ff, 7 November 1788. Garnovsky was Potemkin's agent in the capital and his reports were destined to keep his master in touch with court intrigues. As a result they may well have tended to emphasize evidence of hostility to Potemkin.

56. Lord, op. cit., p. 106. Efforts to bring Spain and France into an alliance with the two empires were again made at this time but led nowhere. See ibid., n. 2 for the relevant sources, and the discussion in the Council of State on 14–16/25–27 December 1788 in *AGS*, I, pp. 638ff.

57. Lord, op. cit., p. 108.

58. *AGS*, I, pp. 638ff, 14–16/25–27 December 1788, and pp. 649ff, draft treaty of peace with the Porte.

59. Garnovsky, *RS*, XVI, p. 235, 21 January/1 February 1789. Solov'yev, *Istoriya Padeniya Pol'shi*, p. 198, Potemkin to Catherine, n.d.

60. Lord, op. cit., pp. 109–11, who quotes from memoranda prepared by Bezborodko for Catherine setting out the possibilities of using Prussia to make peace with Sweden and Turkey, and allowing her some compensation in Poland (*RA*, 1875, ii, pp. 36ff). See also Bezborodko to S.R. Vorontsov (London), October 1789 in *SIRIO*, 26, pp. 415ff and Zinkeisen, VI, pp. 728ff. The exchange of letters between Joseph and Catherine is in Arneth, p. 333, Joseph to Catherine, 20 May 1789 and p. 335, Catherine to Joseph, 30 May/11 June 1789.

61. See Garnovsky, 'Zapiski', *RS*, XVI, p. 399, 21 June 1789 ; Khrapovitsky, *Dnevnik*, pp. 290–4, entries for 18 to 23 June 1789 ; *SIRIO*, 42, pp. 21–3, Catherine to Potemkin, 14 July 1789 ; *RA*, 1765, pp. 768ff, Potemkin to Catherine, 1789, n.d. He uses the quite untranslatable address: 'Matushka rodnaya'.

62. *SIRIO*, 42, p. 21, Catherine to Potemkin, 14 July 1789 ; p. 23, 5 August 1789 ; p. 24, 12 August 1789, where she describes Zubov as 'un enfant fort aimable et qui a un désir sincère de bien faire et de se

bien conduire . . . j'espère qu'il ne se gâtera pas. . . .'
According to Garnovsky, he was supported by A.A.
Vyazemsky and N.I. Saltykov (the master of the household of Alexander and Constantine).

63. See *SIRIO*, 42, 2, early 1789, n.d. Khrapovitsky, *Dnevnik*, p. 246, 29 January 1789, where Catherine expressed her dissatisfaction with Rumyantsev, and *Fel'dmarshal Rumyantsev, Sbornik dokumentov*, pp. 304, Catherine to Rumyantsev, 8/19 March 1789.

64. See Rumyantsev's further letters to Catherine of 7/18 May 1790 and 15/26 July 1790 in *Fel'dmarshal Rumyantsev, Sbornik dokumentov*, pp. 314–15, and *SIRIO*, 42, pp. 75–6, Catherine to Potemkin, 19 April 1790 and 6 September 1789 in 'Perepiska', *RS*, XVII, p. 35. Petrov, pp. 23–4, suggests that Rumyantsev's 'advanced years' (he was 64) and 'poor health' had deprived him of his previous energy and of the capacity for bold deeds.

65. Petrov, II, pp. 6–9.

66. Petrov, II, pp. 27ff, and Beskrovnyy, pp. 539ff.

67. Petrov, II, pp. 76ff, pp. 90–2. Suvorov was given an inscribed sword for the battle of Fokshany (as was Coburg) and the further expensive presents ('a cart load of diamonds') are described in Catherine's letters to Potemkin of 26 September, 5 October and 18 October 1789, *SIRIO*, 42, pp. 37, 39 and 43–4. For Potemkin's proposal to grant Suvorov the title of count and the suffix Rymniksky, see *RS*, XIV, p. 222, to Catherine, 22 September 1789.

68. R.C. Anderson, *Naval Wars in the Baltic*, pp. 254ff.

69. For the text see *Consolidated Treaty Series*, Vol. 50, pp. 435ff.

70. Beskrovnyy, pp. 297, 299.

71. Khrapovitsky, *Dnevnik*, p. 306, 3 September 1789 ; *SIRIO*, 42, p. 48, 25 November 1789.

72. The Prussian negotiations at the Porte can be followed in Zinkeisen, op. cit., pp. 690ff. see also *SIRIO*, 42, p. 48, Catherine to Potemkin, 25 November 1789 ; p. 52, 7 December 1789 and n.d. December 1789 ; *SIRIO*, 29, p. 418, Bezborodko to S.R. Vorontsov, 20/31 December 1789.

73. Arneth *Briefwechsel*, p. 349.

74. *SIRIO*, 42, pp. 58–9, 6/17 February 1790.

75. *AGS*, I, p. 757, 20/31 December 1789 ; *SIRIO*, 29, p. 418, Bezborodko to S.R. Vorontsov, 20/31 December 1789. For the text of the treaty see Martens, *Recueil*, IV, pp. 471ff. Polish hopes of English participation in the alliance were dashed by Pitt's indifference to continental entanglements.

76. Khrapovitsky, *Dnevnik*, p. 318, 23 November 1789.

77. Ibid., p. 320, 19, 23, 24 December 1789 ; p. 321, 31 December 1789 ; p. 322, 12 January 1790 ; p. 327, 7 March 1790.

78. *SIRIO*, 42, p. 50, Catherine to Potemkin, 2/13 December 1789.

79. *SIRIO*, 42, p. 57, Catherine to Potemkin. For the secrecy surrounding this rescript see 'Zapiski Gar-

novskogo', *RS*, XVI, p. 426, 21 March 1790. Bezborodko to S.R. Vorontsov, 20 April/1 May 1790, and Potemkin to Catherine, 18/29 March 1790, *RA*, 1865, pp. 730ff. See also *SIRIO*, 29, pp. 71–3 ; Lord, p. 139, suggests that Catherine disapproved of Potemkin's plans in 1790. There is no doubt that she did so earlier, but by 1790 she seems on the contrary to have approved of them.

80. Lord, p. 142.

81. Lord, pp. 144–9 ; see *Consolidated Treaty Series*, 51, pp. 23ff for the text of the Convention. Khotin and parts of Moldavia and Wallachia were to remain in Austrian hands until the end of the war between Turkey and Russia.

Chapter 26. The Peace of Reichenbach. The Ochakov Crisis and the End of the Turkish War

1. Zinkeisen, *Geschichte*, VI, p. 781.

2. Details of naval battles are taken from Beskrovnyy, op. cit., and R.C. Anderson, *Naval Wars in the Baltic*.

3. Beskrovnyy, pp. 590–1 ; Anderson, pp. 283–93.

4. *SIRIO*, 42, p. 91, Catherine to Potemkin, 17/28 July 1790.

5. On Nassau Siegen see Marquis d'Aragon, *Un paladin du XVIIIe siècle. Le Prince Charles de Nassau-Siegen d'après sa correspondance originale inédite de 1784 à 1789*, Paris, 1893. For his letter to Catherine and her reply see *SIRIO*, 1, pp. 210ff, and see also *SIRIO*, 42, p. 91, Catherine to Potemkin, 17 July 1790 and pp. 102ff, 29 August 1790.

6. For the text see *Consolidated Treaty Series*, 51, pp. 47ff. For the role of Spain, see Ana Maria Schop Soler, *Die Spanisch-Russischen Beziehungen im 18. Jahrhundert*, pp. 153ff and *SIRIO*, 29, p. 71, Bezborodko to Igelstrom, 13/24 April 1790.

7. Khrapovitsky, *Dnevnik*, p. 343, 5/16 August 1790.

8. *SIRIO*, 42, p. 99, Catherine to Potemkin, 5 August 1790.

9. Petrov, II, pp. 101–2.

10. Beskrovnyy, p. 552, rescript to Potemkin, March 1790 (no precise date given).

11. *Bumagi Potemkina*, 8, pp. 127ff, Potemkin to the grand vizir, 1 August 1790, and letters to Lashkarev of 2, 8, 29 August 1790 and 7 September 1790.

12. Beskrovnyy, p. 553–7 ; Anderson, *Naval Wars in the Levant*, pp. 334–41.

13. Petrov, II, pp. 147ff.

14. *Bumagi Potemkina*, 8, p. 191. Order to Suvorov, 25 November/6 December 1790 ; Petrov, II, p. 173.

15. Beskrovnyy, pp. 562–3. Elsewhere in 1791, a Russian corps had advanced in winter weather from the Kuban' on Anapa, but supplies had run out, and the men had been forced to march back, with some 2,000 casualties. Catherine was furious at the useless loss of lives and the commander was court-martialled and

cashiered. The troops in the Caucasus were more successful in September 1790, defeating a Turkish force, crossing the Kuban' and ravaging the countryside. Petrov, II, p. 43 and pp. 162–3, and see *SIRIO*, 42, p. 79, Catherine to Potemkin, 14/25 May 1790.

16. *AGS*, I, pp. 819ff, 9/20 December 1790.

17. See S.R. Vorontsov in *AKV*, VIII, p. 22, and see K.E. Dzhedzhula, *Rossiya i velikaya frantsuzskaya revolyutsiya*, pp. 281–3.

18. See J. Łojek, 'The International Crisis of 1791 : Poland between the Triple Alliance and Russia'.

19. Łojek, op. cit., pp. 26, 36.

20. For the text see Łojek, op. cit., p. 39, n. 92.

21. *AGS*, I, pp. 826ff.

22. Lord, pp. 166ff ; Khrapovitsky, *Dnevnik*, p. 356, 2 February 1791.

23. Khrapovitsky, *Dnevnik*, p. 357, 11 February 1791.

24. See his letters to her in Brückner, *Potemkin*, pp. 259ff.

25. *SIRIO*, 42, pp. 135–6, 22 January/2 February 1791.

26. See the biography 'Knyaz' Platon Aleksandrovich Zubov 1767–1822'. Platon Zubov had 3 brothers and 3 sisters. His father was a wealthy man, who had also been the manager of the estates of N.I. Saltykov, the tutor to the young grand dukes.

27. Lord, pp. 180ff.

28. Khrapovitsky, *Dnevnik*, p. 359, 15, 17, 22, 23 March 1791 ; Solov'yev, *Istoriya Padeniya Pol'shi*, p. 219.

29. Lord, p. 181, and Appendix 5, Osterman to Alopeus (Russian envoy in Berlin) 14/25 March 1791. See also Bezborodko to S.R. Vorontsov, 7/18 March 1791 in which he points to the exercise of Potemkin's influence because of his 'well known predilection for England' ; *SIRIO*, 29, p. 110 (cf. *AKV*, XIII, pp. 177–81).

30. Lord, p. 181 and note 3, quoting Cobenzl's dispatches.

31. *AGS*, I, p. 839, 6/17 March 1791.

32. Quoted in Lord, p. 164.

33. See e.g. The *Norwich Chronicle* of 21 April 1971. See also *AKV*, IX, pp. 191–3, S.R. Vorontsov to A.R. Vorontsov, 11/22 April and 15/26 April 1791.

34. Khrapovitsky, *Dnevnik*, p. 361, 9/20 April 1791. News of the king's message to Parliament had reached Russia by 7/18 April : see *AGS*, I, p. 842, 10/21 April 1791.

35. *AGS*, I, p. 847, 19/30 April 1791, a meeting attended by Admirals Chichagov, Kruze and Nassau Siegen ; p. 848, 24 April/5 May 1791.

36. See Gerhardt, op. cit., p. 364, n. 269.

37. Lord, op. cit., p. 187.

38. See Gerhardt, op. cit., pp. 368ff.

39. See Lord, pp. 188ff and Gerhardt, pp. 370–1. The decision to abandon the armament of the fleet was taken by 25 April/6 May, but was not fully appreciated by Frederick William until June.

40. See B. Dembinski, *Documents relatifs à*

l'histoire du deuxième et troisième partages de la Pologne, I, 1788–91, p. 126, Alopeus to Osterman, 28 March/8 April 1791 ; p. 144, the same to the same, 20 April/1 May 1791.

41. Khrapovitsky, *Dnevnik*, p. 362, 30 April/11 May 1791 ; *AGS*, I, p. 850, 1/12 May 1791. Vorontsov's efforts were rewarded in Catherine's usual lavish manner : an increase of 6,000 r.p.a. in his salary and the Order of St Vladimir first class (*SIRIO*, 26, p. 426, Bezborodko to S.R. Vorontsov, 11/22 October 1791).

42. Khrapovitsky, *Dnevnik*, p. 362, 1/12 May 1791, 2/13, 3/14 May 1791.

43. Petrov, op. cit., pp. 196–7.

44. Khrapovitsky, *Dnevnik*, p. 366, 16 September 1789.

45. M.M. Shtrange, *Russkoye obshchestvo i frantsuzskaya revolyutsiya*, pp. 47ff ; p. 60.

46. *SIRIO*, 23, p. 567.

47. Lord, p. 207, n. 2, Cobenzl's dispatch of 13 May 1791.

48. *RA*, 1874, II, pp. 246–58 ; See also X. Liske, 'Zur Polnischen Politik Katharinas II, 1791'.

49. Dzhedzhula, op. cit., p. 296. The ukaz may be of 15/26 May ; the author does not state which calendar he is using.

50. See the discussion in *AGS*, I, pp. 854–8, 19/30 May 1971.

51. *AGS*, I, p. 858, 19/30 May 1791.

52. *AGS*, I, p. 863, 23 June/4 July 1791.

53. Khrapovitsky, *Dnevnik*, p. 366, 11/22 July 1791. G.F. de Martens, *Recueil*, V, pp. 59ff. Russian Note of 10/21 July ; rescript to Potemkin of 18/29 July 1791 in *SIRIO*, 29, pp. 119–20.

54. Gerhardt, op. cit., 379–80, quoting Adair to Fox of 17/28 July 1791. Khrapovitsky, *Dnevnik*, pp. 363, 16/27 June 1791.

55. Solov'yev, *Istoriya Padeniya Pol'shi*, p. 247.

56. Lord, p. 208.

57. See e.g. Felix Potocki to Potemkin, 3/14 May 1791, in Lord, Appendix IX, p. 527.

58. *RA*, 1874, II, pp. 281–9, and Liske, op. cit., pp. 295ff.

59. See J. Łojek, 'Catherine II's Armed Intervention in Poland : Origins of the Political Decisions at the Russian Court in 1791 and 1792', pp. 580–2. Lord, pp. 246–7 and 247, n. 1, argues that only the rescript of 16/27 May was 'a sham' ; the theory that both rescripts were 'unreal' was put forward by the Polish historian S. Askenazy.

60. Łojek in particular relies on the dispatches of the Polish envoy Deboli, who according to Bezborodko was behaving in an outrageous way, and maligning Russia in general and the prince in particular in every possible way (*SIRIO*, 26, p. 308, Bezborodko to Potemkin, 16/27 September 1791). On the other hand Zubov was certainly trying to undermine the influence of Catherine's advisers, one of the main sufferers being Bezborodko himself (ibid., p. 423, to S.R. Vorontsov, 7/18 March 1791).

61. See G. Helbig in *Minerva*, 1797, III, p. 266,

note : Potemkin wanted neither 'Theilung' nor 'Vernichtung'.

62. Petrov, pp. 196–223.

63. Anderson, *Naval Wars in the Levant,* pp. 343–4. *SIRIO,* 29, pp. 121–2, Bezborodko to A.R. Vorontsov, early August 1791.

64. Petrov, p. 245 quoting the *Memoirs* of F.P. Lubyanovsky and A. Brückner, *Potemkin,* pp. 209–10 ; see also Bezborodko's criticisms of Repnin's peace terms in Bezborodko to Zavadovsky, 12/23 November 1791, *SIRIO,* 29, pp. 143ff.

65. *AGS,* 1, pp. 879–90, 11/22 August 1791 ; *SIRIO,* 42, pp. 194–5, Catherine to Potemkin, 12/23 August 1791, and *SIRIO,* 29, pp. 122–3, rescript to Potemkin of the same date.

66. For the text see *Consolidated Treaty Series,* Vol. 51, pp. 211ff.

67. See *SIRIO,* 42, pp. 195–203, letters written between 28 August/8 September 1791 and 3/14 October 1791 when the prince was already dead. See also Khrapovitsky, *Dnevnik,* p. 375, 16/27 September, p. 375, 3/14 October, 11/22 October 1791.

68. See the detailed account of Bezborodko to Zavadovsky, 12/23 November 1791, *SIRIO,* 29, pp. 143ff and Brückner, *Potemkin,* pp. 214–22. The prince's illness was in all probability malaria. Potemkin's tomb in Jassy was later moved to a vault in the church of St Catherine at Kherson. In 1798, the Emperor Paul ordered it to be covered up with earth and all trace of its presence removed. The memorial set up by Catherine was also destroyed. Ibid., pp. 228–9.

Chapter 27. The Second Partition of Poland

1. *Consolidated Treaty Series,* 51, pp. 251ff. See also Comtesse Brevern de la Gardie, *Un ambassadeur de Suède à la cour de Catherine II,* 1, *1790–1793,* pp. 141ff, 14/25 May 1791. P.K. Alefirenko, 'Pravitel'stvo Yekateriny II i frantsuzskaya revolyutsiya', pp. 206–51.

2. *SIRIO,* 23, p. 560 ; 29, p. 547.

3. Khrapovitsky, *Dnevnik,* 21 October/1 November 1791, pp. 379–80, 386.

4. See Lord, pp. 223–4 ; Solov'yev *Istoriya Padeniya Pol'shi* where a fuller summary of Kaunitz's instruction to Cobenzl of 12/23 November 1791 is given.

5. Dzhedzhula, op. cit., pp. 322–3.

6. For the exchange of correspondence between Catherine and Bezborodko, see *SIRIO,* 29, pp. 131–208, and ibid., pp. 548ff. For the treaty see *Consolidated Treaty Series,* Vol. 51, pp. 279ff.

7. Dzhedzhula, op. cit., p. 298 ; cf. Brevern de la Gardie, *Un ambassadeur de Suède, passim ;* Beer, *Leopold II, Franz II and Catharina,* pp. 157–8, Catherine to Frederick William, 28 September/9 October 1791.

8. Catherine to N.P. Rumyantsev, in Frankfurt am Main, 30 October/10 November 1791, *RS,* 1892, 10, pp. 16ff. Rumyantsev was envoy to the emigré princes.

9. See *SIRIO,* 29, pp. 176ff, Catherine to Bezborodko, n.d., but late November 1791, in which Catherine writes scathingly about the 'weathercock' Leopold. Dzhedzhula, op. cit., p. 306, seems to think this letter was addressed *to* Leopold, in which he is quite mistaken. His subsequent statement, based allegedly on archival sources, that to every demand by Catherine to fight the French revolution, Leopold replied by asking for parts of Poland is utterly ludicrous. Dzhedzhula is evidently unacquainted with Lord's classic work (ibid., pp. 306–7). When he insisted that he could not act until Polish affairs were settled, what Leopold sought was not a partition of Poland, but a formal Russian acceptance of the May constitution.

10. *SIRIO,* 29, p. 136, Bezborodko to Catherine, 5/16 November 1791 ; cf. Catherine to Bezborodko, 19/30 November, ibid., pp. 149–50 ; 168–9, Bezborodko to Catherine, 21 November/2 December 1791. Bezborodko's report confirms that this rescript was in fact meant to be acted upon, and was not 'fictitious' (Łojek, op. cit., at p. 580) ; Lord, pp. 250–1.

11. Catherine to Bezborodko quoted in Solov'yev, *Istoriya,* pp. 258–9, and in *SIRIO,* 29, pp. 175ff. n.d., but late November 1791.

12. Bezborodko to Catherine, 25 January/5 February 1792, Lord, Appendix 10, pp. 528–30.

13. Lord, pp. 253–4.

14. Lord, p. 237. Historians differ as to whether the Prussian envoy was deliberately allowed to see this note as part of a plot by Zubov (Łojek's version, op. cit., p. 583) or whether it merely came to Goltz's ears in the course of the usual leakages (Lord, Appendix VIII, pp. 525–7, which I find more convincing).

15. *AGS,* 1, pp. 906–8, 29 March/9 April 1792. See also *AKV,* XIII, pp. 225ff. Bezborodko to S.R. Vorontsov, 15/26 May 1792. Łojek (op. cit., pp. 585–6, and n. 31) states that the first set of minutes of this meeting were withdrawn at Catherine's insistence because they expressed opposition to her policy, but he does not give his evidence for this statement. The actual minutes clearly show a disinclination to invade Poland before reaching an agreement with Prussia, not a refusal to contemplate *any* invasion or partition of Poland. See also Khrapovitsky, *Dnevnik,* p. 394, 3/14 April 1792, noting Catherine's annoyance at the recommendations of the Council.

16. On the acute shortage of lands for distribution as rewards in the 1790s, see my article 'Catherine II and the Serfs'.

17. Brevern de la Gardie, p. 265, Stedingk to Gustavus IV, 18–19/29–30 April 1792, p. 268.

18. For the text of the instructions to Generals Kakhovsky and Krechetnikov, the Russian manifesto, and the Act of the Confederation of Targowica, see *SIRIO,* 47, *Dela Pol'shi* pp. 241ff, 293ff, and 310ff.

19. Catherine had commissioned a certain Baron de Bühler to take charge of the 'political' work which the army commanders could not themselves carry out. For his instructions see *SIRIO* 47, pp. 293ff, 19/30 April 1792. Bühler was to keep an eye on the activity of the confederates.

20. *SIRIO,* 47, p. 396, Account of the proclamation of the General Confederation of Lithuania.

21. *Ibid.,* pp. 391–2.

22. Ibid., p. 400, Catherine to General M. V. Kakhovsky, 21 June/2 July 1792.

23. *AGS,* I, pp. 922–7 ; Lord, pp. 292–4.

24. J. Łojek, *Upadek Konstytucji 3 Maja,* Wrocław, 1976, p. 240.

25. For texts, see *Consolidated Treaty Series,* Vol. 51, pp. 359ff ; pp. 399ff.

26. P.K. Alefirenko, 'Frautzuzskaya revolyutsiya 1789 goda', p. 220. Catherine was committed by the treaty with Austria to supply 12,000 troops or 400,000 r., but she raised the sum by 100,000 r. See *AGS,* I, pp. 931–5, 12/23 July 1792.

27. Lord, pp. 319–20.

28. Lord, p. 551, 29 October/8 November 1792.

29. *AKV,* 13, p. 268, Bezborodko to Rumyantsev, 27 January 1793 ; and see Kostomarov, op. cit., pp. 430–1, Catherine to Sievers, 22 December 1792/2 January 1793.

30. Solov'yev, *Istoriya,* p. 297, Bulgakov to Osterman, 30 October/10 November 1792.

31. See Kostomarov, pp. 447–8 for the Russian manifesto of 27 March/7 April 1793. Here Catherine justifies annexation by the need to protect peoples which had once formed part of Russia and were of one faith against godless Polish Jacobinism. For the treaty see *Consolidated Treaty Series,* Vol. 51, pp. 449ff.

32. See *SIRIO,* 23, p. 565, Catherine to Grimm, 3/14 April 1792. Khrapovitsky, *Dnevnik,* p. 395, 8/19 April 1792.

33. Ibid., p. 420, 2/13 February 1793.

34. *AKV,* 9, S.R. Vorontsov to A.R. Vorontsov, p. 239, 26 May/6 June 1792 ; p. 302, 26 April/7 May 1793.

35. Khrapovitsky, *Dnevnik,* p. 422, 24 February 1793.

36. See Blum, *Ein Russischer Staatsmann,* p. 486 ; Kostomarov, op. cit., pp. 438–43.

37. Kostomarov, op. cit., pp. 447–52.

38. The two rescripts of 26 May/6 June and 23 June/4 July 1793 are printed in Lord, Appendix XVIII, pp. 552ff.

39. See Kostomarov, op. cit., pp. 476, 486.

40. Lord, Appendix 18, pp. 552ff, Catherine's rescript of 26 May/6 June.

41. For text of treaty see *Consolidated Treaty Series,* Vol. 52, pp. 83ff.

42. Kostomarov, op. cit., p. 515.

43. Kostomarov, op. cit., pp. 526–30, where the treaty is also printed ; see also *Consolidated Treaty Series,* Vol. 52, pp. 137ff, 14/25 September 1793.

44. For text see *Consolidated Treaty Series,* Vol. 52, pp. 165ff, 5/16 October 1793.

45. For the rescript to Sievers, unfortunately undated, see Kostomarov, op. cit., pp. 536–8.

46. Ibid., p. 534.

Chapter 28. Finis Poloniae

1. *RA,* 1866, 3, pp. 399ff. Catherine in this memorandum speaks of the ease with which 10,000 men could slice through France ; the royal family are regarded as prisoners but France is still a monarchy. See also Esterhazy, *Mémoires,* p. 321, where Catherine stresses the importance of the restoration of the *Parlements* and the three orders, 'sans quoi point de monarchie'. She also urged an amnesty, since the position of a ruler who recovered his throne with the help of foreign troops was bound to be delicate.

2. *SIRIO,* 42, p. 337, Catherine to Zubov, undated. Grenville to Whitworth, 29 December 1792, quoted in the *Cambridge History of British Foreign Policy,* Ward and G.P. Gooch, pp. 229–30.

3. *AGS,* I, pp. 95 1ff, 31 January/11 February 1793 ; *PSZ,* XXIII, 8 February 1793.

4. Text in *Consolidated Treaty Series,* Vol. 51 pp. 491ff.

5. See her memorandum in *RA* quoted in note 1 above. The Comte d'Artois visited St Petersburg in March 1793. Catherine regarded his journey as useless and thought the money could have been better spent. But she welcomed him as a king's brother, with the same ceremonial as had been used for Prince Henry of Prussia. See Esterhazy, *Mémoires,* pp. 346ff.

6. Alefirenko, 'Frautzuzskaya revolyutsiya', pp. 227–8, 232ff.

7. Brevern de la Gardie, *Un ambassadeur,* 2, pp. 25ff, despatches of 11, 16, 20, 21 April 1794 ; *AKV,* 13, p. 284, A.A. Bezborodko to A.R. Vorontsov, April 1794.

8. According to Kostomarov, op. cit., p. 578, 2,265 were killed, 121 wounded and 1,764 taken prisoner.

9. Ibid., pp. 591ff, for full text.

10. I am making no attempt to tell the story of the Polish rising, but concentrating instead on what it must have seemed like in the eyes of Catherine and her court.

11. *AGS,* I, pp. 978–80 ; *AKV,* 13, p. 284, A.A. Bezborodko to A.R. Vorontsov, April 1794, OS.

12. *Fel'dmarshal Rumyantsev, Sbornik dokumentov,* p. 316, Catherine to Rumyantsev, 25 April/6 May 1794. Dzhedzhula, op. cit., pp. 408–9 for unsuccessful French efforts to stir up the Turks against Russia.

13. R.H. Lord, 'The Third Partition of Poland'.

14. *SIRIO,* 23, p. 610, Catherine to Grimm, 3/14 September 1794 ; see also Brevern de la Gardie, *Un ambassadeur,* 2, pp. 88–90, 8/19 September 1794 ; *AKV,* 13, p. 310, A.A. Bezborodko to A.R. Vorontsov, 25 September/6 October 1794.

15. *Fel'dmarshal Rumyantsev, Sbornik dokumentov,* p. 319, Rumyantsev to Suvorov, 7/18 August 1794.

16. Quoted in Kostomarov, op. cit., p. 653.

17. Ibid.

18. See e.g. *AKV,* 13, p. 315, Bezborodko to A.R. Vorontsov, 9/20 November 1794, and P. Longworth, *Suvorov,* pp. 204–7.

19. See *SIRIO*, 23, pp. 600, 611, Catherine to Grimm, 31 March, 3 April 1794 ; *AKV*, 13, p. 284, Bezborodko to A.R. Vorontsov, April 1794 ; pp. 288ff, n.d., probably early May OS.

20. *AKV*, 13, pp. 294ff, May 1794, A.A. Bezborodko to A.R. Vorontsov.

21. Ibid., pp. 301ff, A.A. Bezborodko to A.R. Vorontsov, 15/26 July 1794.

22. *SIRIO*, 16, pp. 57ff, pp. 61ff. A.A. Bezborodko to N.V. Repnin, 26 November/7 December 1794.

23. *AGS*, I, p. 991, 13/24 November 1794 ; *AKV*, 13, pp. 318ff, A.A. Bezborodko to A.R. Vorontsov, 16/27 November 1794.

24. *AKV*, 13, pp. 321–6, A.A. Bezborodko to A.R. Vorontsov, 29 November/10 December 1794.

25. For the treaties see *Consolidated Treaty Series*, 52, pp. 285ff.

26. Alefirenko, op. cit., pp. 238–9. For the text of the treaties see *Consolidated Treaty Series*, Vol. 52, pp. 315ff.

27. Brevern de la Gardie, *Un ambassadeur, passim*.

28. Lord, op. cit., p. 496.

29. *AKV*, 13, pp. 347–8, A.A. Bezborodko to A.R. Vorontsov, 11/22 July 1795.

30. For texts see *Consolidated Treaty Series*, Vol. 53, pp. 1ff. For the award of Cracow, 10/21 October 1796, see ibid., pp. 301ff.

31. *AKV*, 13, pp. 460ff., A.R. Vorontsov to A.A. Bezborodko, n.d. 1794.

32. Lord, op. cit., p. 498.

33. For the conventions see regarding Poland *Consolidated Treaty Series*, Vol. 53, pp. 345ff ; for Catherine's acceptance, pp. 365ff. For the disappearance of the name of king of Poland, ibid., pp. 411ff, 15/26 January, 1797.

34. This is the general tenor of Dzhedzhula's *Rossiya i velikaya frantsuzskaya burzhuaznaya revolyutsiya*. His argument is very far-fetched and is intended to exonerate Russia from the odium of initiating the second and third partitions of Poland.

Chapter 29. Agriculture and Industry.

1. N.L. Rubinstein, *Sels'koye Khozyaystvo Rossii vo vtoroy polovine XVIII v*, Moscow 1957, pp. 21ff, a work on which I have drawn extensively in this chapter.

2. Economic character does not of course coincide neatly with the borders of a guberniya, and the classification given above is somewhat rough.

3. Figures taken from Kabuzan, *Izmeneniya*, pp. 83ff, adapted to the classification of economic regions made by Rubinstein.

4. See V.I. Semevsky, *Krest'yane*, I, p. 31 and S.I. Tkhorzhevsky, *Pugachevshchina v pomeshchichey Rossii*, pp. 32ff.

5. See A. Kahan, 'The Costs of Westernization : The Gentry and the Russian Economy in the Eighteenth Century' and M. Confino, *Domaines et Seigneurs en Russie vers la fin du XVIIIe siècle*, pp. 126–7. The problem is expounded in greater detail in the same author's *L'assolement triennal*.

6. Rubinstein, op. cit., p. 261.

7. Rubinstein, op. cit., pp. 363ff ; Rubinstein uses the replies to a questionnaire sent to governors in the provinces in 1767 to inquire into the reasons for the rise in the cost of corn, and rejects the conclusions of other Soviet economic historians such as e.g. P. Lyashchenko, who assumed a decline in Russian agriculture in the eighteenth century. The Senate concluded that the rising price of corn in Moscow was caused by rising demand in the industrial centre of the country, which led to rising prices in the producing areas. Ibid., p. 79.

8. Rubinstein, op. cit., pp. 254ff and table at p. 258.

9. Tkhorzhevsky, pp. 43–4. Tkhorzhevsky notes that peasants on the Kurakin estate in Penza (303 households with 937 male souls) owned considerably more livestock in 1774, on the eve of the Pugachev rising than they owned in 1916 (2·18 horses per household in 1774, 0·94 in 1916 ; 1·79 foals and 0·35 ; 1·42 cows and 0·77 ; 11·33 sheep and 4·73 ; 1·90 pigs and 0·23). See also Rubinstein, op. cit., p. 293.

10. Prices taken from Rubinstein, p. 413, and App. III.

11. Rubinstein, op. cit., pp. 267ff. One pud of flax was valued at 1·50 r. Production could rise to 100 arshins a year ; cf. p. 305.

12. H. von Storch, *Tableau historique et statistique de l'Empire de Russie*, Vol. 1, p. 55 and Vol. 2, Ch. I, 'De la Chasse.' See p. 8 : 'Jusqu'à présent la chasse est libre en grande partie dans toute l'étendue de l'Empire. Peu de seigneurs interdisent à leurs paysans le port d'armes.' See also *PSZ*, XVII, No. 12,348, 5 March 1765.

13. See V.N. Yakovtsevsky, *Kupecheskiy kapital v feodal' no krepostnicheskoy Rossii*.

14. N. Pavlenko, *Istoriya metallurgii*, pp. 440ff.

15. See *PSZ*, XVI, No. 12,105.

16. See S.M. Troitsky, *Finansovaya politika russkogo absolyutizma*, p. 158 ; *PSZ*, XVII, No. 12,444, 1 August 1765, and No. 12,446 of the same date. The Ustav or Regulations for distilling were issued on 9 August (No. 12,448).

17. See J.P. LeDonne, 'Indirect Taxes in Catherine II's Russia. The Liquor Monopoly'.

18. LeDonne, op. cit., p. 195, No. 58.

19. N.I. Pavlenko, *Istoriya metallurgii*, p. 449.

20. See N.D. Chechulin, *Ocherki po istorii russkikh finansov v tsarstvovaniye Yekateriny II*. The Baltic provinces, Little Russia and Belorussia (from 1772) enjoyed the free sale of liquor or very light taxes (p. 164).

21. See the Great Nakaz in Reddaway, *Documents*, articles 294, 313 and 606.

22. See Catherine's comments on a report of the College of Manufactures, quoted by K. Lodyzhensky, *Istoriya russkogo tamozhennogo tarifa*, St Petersburg, 1886, pp. 107–8, quoting *RA*, 1868, p. 503.

23. Marginal note on a report of the College of

Manufactures quoted in A. V. Florovsky, *Iz istorii*, p. 219, n. 2.

24. *SIRIO*, 43, pp. 204ff.

25. *PSZ*, xv, No. 11,489 ; No. 11,490, 29 March 1762 ; see Chapter 1.

26. *PSZ*, xv, No. 11,630, 31 July 1762 ; No. 11,635 of 8 August 1762.

27. Catherine continued to favour the use of hired labour. 'As regards the purchase of villages for factories etc. . . . abide firmly by my decision of 1762,' she noted on a Senate report of 1769 (*SIRIO*, 10, p. 380). See also E.I. Zaozerskaya, 'Le salariat dans les manufactures textiles russes au XVIIIe siècle'.

28. See Portal, op. cit., p. 322.

29. *PSZ*, xx, No. 14,275.

30. Portal, p. 390 ; *PSZ*, xxi, No. 15,447.

31. Tugan Baranovsky, *Russkaya fabrika*, Introduction, gives 984 and 3,161 respectively, but his figures have now been revised downwards, though there is still much debate. See Blum, op. cit., pp. 293–4.

32. *Ocherki*, pp. 94ff.

33. N.I. Pavlenko, *Istoriya metallurgiyi*, pp. 464ff.

34. R. Portal, *L'Oural*, Tables, pp. 351–4.

35. N.I. Pavlenko, op. cit., pp. 327ff.

36. Portal, op. cit., pp. 302ff.

37. *Ocherki*, p. 101, Table, and Portal, op. cit., p. 156 and Table for exports.

38. Portal, op. cit., p. 320.

39. See Chapter 13.

40. *PSZ*, xviii, No. 13,303, 27 May 1769.

41. Portal, p. 322.

42. See below, Chapter 16.

43. N.I. Pavlenko, *Istoriya metallurgii*, table at pp. 475ff Pavlenko argues that damage was much less than these figures suggest.

44. Portal, op. cit., pp. 341–3.

45. *PSZ*, xx, No. 14,878.

46. *PSZ*, xxi, No. 15,724, 3 May 1783.

47. Portal, p. 359.

48. Z.G. Karpenko, *Gornaya i metallurgicheskaya promyshlennost' zapadnoy Sibiri v 1700–1860 godakh*.

49. See Chapter 25 ; *PSZ*, xx, No. 14,868.

Chapter 30. Trade and Finance

1. *SIRIO*, 27, p. 170, after 21 May 1779.

2. N.N. Firsov, *Pravitel'stvo i obshchestvo v ikh otnosheniyakh k vneshney torgovle Rossii v tsarstvovaniye Imperatritsy Yekateriny II*.

3. *PSZ*, xv, No. 11,489. The discrimination against Archangel introduced by Peter I in the interests of St Petersburg was also removed.

4. *PSZ*, xv, No. 11,630.

5. *PSZ*, xvi, No. 11,975, 20 November 1763 ; Firsov, op. cit., pp. 178ff.

6. See the standard work by A. Lappo Danilevsky, 'Die russische Handelskommission von 1763–1796' pp. 176–213 ; and cf. W. Daniel in 'The Merchantry and the Problem of Social Order in the Russian State : Catherine II's Commission on Commerce'.

7. *PSZ*, xvii, No. 12,735, 1 September 1766.

8. S.A. Pokrovsky in *Vneshnyaya torgovlya i vneshnyaya torgovaya politika Rossii* makes this point as against the views of the author of the standard economic history of Russia, P. Lyashchenko.

9. Smuggling was not a uniquely Russian phenomenon. In the early 1780s the value of goods smuggled into England is estimated at £2–3 million p.a. at a time when official imports totalled at most £12–13 million p.a. See J. Ehrman, *The Younger Pitt, The Years of Acclaim*, Constable, 1969, p. 241.

10. *PSZ*, xxiii, No. 17,117, 15 April 1793, ukaz authorizing Riga traders to pay duties in Russian currency, at 2 r. 50 k. per thaler.

11. *PSZ*, xx, No. 14,335, 4 August 1775.

12. Firsov, op. cit., pp. 185ff.

13. *Ocherki*, p. 128. See also N.L. Rubinstein, 'Vneshyaya torgovlya Rossii, i russkoye kupechestvo vo vtoroy polovine xviii veka'.

14. In 1770–2 Russia exported £1,110,093 worth of goods to England, and imported £145,125 from England. In 1779 the figures were £1,201,377 and £306,072 respectively (H. von Storch, *Historisches Gemälde*, vi, p. 21).

15. Storch, vi, p. 6.

16. See Chapter 24.

17. See Chapter 25 and note 36. The exception was the commercial treaty with the Porte. The principles of the Neutral League were incorporated in the Russian Instruction to Privateers issued on the outbreak of war on 31 December 1787.

18. See Storch, op. cit., *Supplement Band*, Table vii D, and Rubinstein, op. cit., p. 348.

19. Ibid., vii, pp. 113ff.

20. *SIRIO*, 57, pp. 37–47.

21. See C.M. Foust, *Muscovite and Mandarin, Russia's Trade with China and Its Setting 1727–1805*, on which I have based this section.

22. Firsov, op. cit., pp. 339ff. Cf. Brevern de la Gardie, *Un ambassadeur* ii, pp. 19ff, 23 March 1794.

23. See below, p. 486.

24. Figures from Storch, op. cit., Tables xa, and XI.

25. *PSZ*, xiv, No. 10,486.

26. S. Ya. Borovoy, *Kredit i banki Rossii (seredina xvii v–1861 g.)*, Moscow 1958, pp. 44–5.

27. A 'Copper Bank' existed briefly in 1758–62. Its function seems to have been mainly to lend money to P.I. Shuvalov and other magnates at 4 per cent.

28. See below, pp. 484–5. The six million rubles include 1·5 million advanced to compensate for damage caused by the Pugachev revolt.

29. *PSZ*, xix, No. 13,909, 20 November 1772.

30. Borovoy, *Kredit i banki*, pp. 67–72, on whom this is largely based.

31. A. Kahan, op. cit., p. 65. Kahan estimates the number of serfs mortgaged at 708,000, taking the

price of the serf at 60 r. at the end of the century. But many had been mortgaged earlier at lower rates.

32. *PSZ*, xv, No. 11,120 ; See S.M. Troitsky, *Finansovaya politika russkogo absolyutizma XVIII veka*, pp. 121, 142ff, and also *PSZ*, xviii, No. 13,194, 13 November 1768. There were a few minor variations, e.g. in Slobodska Ukraine.

33. *AGS*, ii, p. 416, 1 May 1783.

34. For the organization of production and distribution, see Chapter 29.

35. N.D. Chechulin, op. cit., p. 245, on whom these pages are largely based. Chechulin's is still the standard work drawn upon by Soviet historians.

36. Ibid. A few figures may prove of interest : the tax on baths produced in one (unspecified) year 21,925 r., with arrears of 13,061. The tax on promotion in the Table of Ranks produced 9,200 r. in 1775.

37. *PSZ*, xvi, No. 11,988, 15 December 1763.

38. See e.g. G. Macartney, *An Account of Russia*, 1768, p. 124 and the reports of Baron de Breteuil in *SIRIO*, 140, passim.

39. Table in Chechulin, p. 283.

40. See A.A. Vyazemsky's report in Chechulin, op. cit., p. 272.

41. See above, pp. 479–80.

42. *AGS*, ii, pp. 405–6, 17 November, 8 and 29 December 1768 ; cf. *PSZ*, xviii, No. 13,222, 30 December 1768.

43. *AGS*, ii, p. 410, 11 July 1769.

44. Seven million gulden (3·7 million rubles) were borrowed at 5 per cent on 2 April 1769 through the Dutch firm of de Swets for 10 years, secured on the Baltic customs dues. The loan was not taken up at once ; 4 million g. were called on in 1769, 1·5 million in 1770–1 and 2 million in 1772. A further 1,170,000 rubles were raised in Genoa in 1771–2. The Genoese loan of 1,170,000 r. was drawn on even more slowly, and was totally repaid by 1776. Chechulin, op. cit., p. 326.

45. *AGS*, ii, p. 517 ; *PSZ*, xviii, Nos. 13,219 and 13,220.

46. *PSZ*, xx, No. 14,275.

47. Chechulin, pp. 281 and 331.

48. Ibid., p. 313.

49. See Chapter 24.

50. Chechulin, p. 332 ; see above, p. 479 and see also Chapter 20, for the impact of these measures.

51. *AGS*, ii, p. 415, 1 May 1783 ; *PSZ*, xxi, No. 15,720 and 15,724, 3 May 1783 and *SIRIO*, i, pp. 297–312.

52. *PSZ*, xxii, No. 16,408.

53. This figure of 4,500,000 includes 1·5 million r. advanced to *all* those who suffered from the Pugachev revolt. *AGS*, i, 2, p. 442.

54. *AGS*, i, 2, passim for many debates on financial problems, and p. 466, 25 September 1789 for the above discussion.

55. *AGS*, i, 2, pp. 505–9, 4 and 8 May 1794. It is not clear whether these proposals to sell state lands were acted upon.

56. Chechulin, op. cit., p. 374.

57. See Chapter 35 for a fuller discussion.

58. A. Kahan, 'The Costs of Westernization', op. cit.

59. Figures for the period 1763–73 are not always available. All figures are taken from Chechulin, op. cit., pp. 282ff, but he himself points out that there are yawning gaps which he has had to bridge by means of intelligent assumptions. It is perhaps time for his work, thorough as it is, to be revised according to modern economic techniques.

Chapter 31. The Foundation of the Russian Educational System

1. See M. Okenfuss, 'The Jesuit Origin of Petrine Education'.

2. Children had frequently to be sent from a long distance to attend these schools, and in order to prevent them from running away, they were lodged in prisons or kept under guard. See in general the survey by D.A. Tolstoy (the Minister of Education under Alexander ii), *Vzglyad na uchebnuyu chast' v Rossii v XVIII stoletiya do 1872* in *Sbornik otdeleniya russkogo yazyka i slovesnosti imperatorskoy akademii nauk*, p. 3.

3. D.A. Tolstoy, 'Akademicheskaya gimnaziya v xviii stoletiye'. In the fifteen years 1751–65, of 590 pupils who passed through the gymnasium, 80 were poor, mainly landless nobles ; 22 were kuptsy, 13 came from the clerical estate, 80 were children of clerks. The largest group, 132, was composed of soldiers' sons ; 50 were sons of craftsmen in the Academy or the Admiralty ; 16 were children of household serfs, 2 were children of peasants, 93 were foreigners and 23 miscellaneous. M. Shtrange, *Demokraticheskaya intelligentsiya v Rossi v XVIII veke*, p. 120.

4. D.A. Tolstoy, 'Akademicheskiy universitet v xviii stoletiye'.

5. M.T. Belyavsky, *M.V. Lomonosov i osnovaniye Moskovskogo universiteta*, p. 293.

6. In 1759, 18 pupils entered the university ; in 1760, 20 ; 1763, 25 ; 1764, 23 ; 1769, 18 ; a total of 318 in the period 1756–1775.

7. D.I. Fonvizin, *Sobraniye Sochineniy*, ii, pp. 87–8.

8. Among its graduates in mid-eighteenth century were the poets Sumarokov and Kheraskov, I.P. Yelagin and A. Olsuf'yev (both to become secretaries of Catherine ii).

9. See *Dokumenty i materialy po istorii Moskovskogo Universiteta v vtoroy poloviny XVIII veka*, iii, p. 49.

10. S.V. Rozhdestvensky, *Ocherki po istorii sistem narodnogo prosveshcheniya v Rossii v XVIII–XIX vekakh*, Vol. 1, p. 314.

11. Catherine to Madame Bielke, 13 September 1770, *SIRIO*, 13, pp. 36–7.

12. He was reputed to have been the lover of Catherine's mother, the Princess of Anhalt Zerbst, both on her visit to Russia in 1744 and after the death of her

husband ; it was also rumoured that he was Catherine's father which was most improbable.

13. Ibid., pp. 272ff. Dilthey produced a separate plan for schools of four different levels, the lowest of which was for serf *d'yad'*ki, i.e. serf servants of noble children. See also N. Hans, 'Dumaresq, Brown and some Early Educational Projects of Catherine II'.

14. W. Reddaway, *Documents*, pp. 271–2, Chapter XIV, articles 347–56.

15. See W. Reddaway, *Documents*, Chapter X, article 158.

16. According to M.D. Kurmacheva in 'Problemy obrazovaniya v ulozhennoy kommissii 1767 g., *Dvoryanstvo i krepostnoy stroy Rossii XVI–XVIII vv.*, pp. 240–64, problems of education were mentioned only in 83 nakazy or less than 10 per cent of the total. For an analysis of the demands in the noble nakazy see P. Dukes, *Catherine the Great and the Russian Nobility* . . . , pp. 189ff.

17. *PSZ*, XVII, No. 12,103, 12 March 1764 : 'General'noye Uchrezhdeniye o vospitanii oboego pola yunoshestva.'

18. *PSZ*, XVII, No. 12,785, 16 November 1766, article 88. However not all recommendations would be so acceptable today : all musical wind instruments were regarded as harmful to health but a moderate medicinal use of tobacco was advised for those of phlegmatic temperament, or those given to head colds (article 118).

19. *PSZ*, XVI, No. 11,908, 10 June 1763 ; ibid, XIX, No. 13,909, 20 November 1772.

20. 14·03 per cent in 1777 ; 7·45 per cent in 1778 ; 8·65 per cent in 1786. Mortality was even higher in the nineteenth century. See P.M. Maykov, *Ivan Ivanovich Betskoy, Opyt ego biografii*, pp. 162–3.

21. W. Coxe, *Travels*, I, p. 350; Coxe, *Account of the Prisons and Hospitals in Russia, Sweden and Denmark*, p. 18.

22. These were Parts II and III of the General Plan for the Education of Young People ; *PSZ*, XVIII, No. 12,957, 13 August 1767.

23. Maykov, op. cit., p. 148. n. 1.

24. For Maykov, it is axiomatic that such a supervision implied less social participation and hence the eventual decline of the hospitals. His conclusion cannot be accepted without further research.

25. *PSZ*, XVI, No. 12,154, 5 May 1764, sets out here too the principles to be followed. Children were to enter at 6 years of age, and their parents were to agree on no account to remove them until they reached 18.

26. *PSZ*, XVII, No. 12,741, 11 September 1766 ; new regulations for the school attached to the Academy of Arts were also drafted.

27. *PSZ*, XVII, No. 12,338, 7 March 1765, quoted in Shtrange, op. cit., p. 78.

28. Basedow's main works were *Vorstellung an Menschenfreude* (1768) ; *Methodenbuch für Väter und Mütter der Familien und Völker* (1770) and *Das Elementarbuch für die Jugend und für Ihre Lehrer* (1774). See Rozhdestvensky op. cit., p. 317. The *Methodenbuch* was translated into Russian in 1771.

Wolcke ran one of the most reputable boarding schools in the capital from 1784 to 1801. See M. Woltner, *Das Wolgadeusche Bildungswesen und die russische Schulpolitik*.

29. 'Essai sur les Études en Russie' in D. Diderot, *Oeuvres Complètes*, III, pp. 415–28. Diderot's 'Essai' seems to have impressed Catherine more than his *Plan d' une université en Russie*, which she forwarded to her in 1776.

30. *SIRIO*, 1, pp. 384ff. 'Dnevnaya zapiska puteshestviya E.I.V. chrez Pskov i Polotsk v Mogilev . . .' At every stop Catherine gave generous sums to support schools and almshouses, and to assist in putting up stone buildings.

31. Rozhdestvensky, op. cit., p. 450.

32. W. Gareth Jones, 'The *Morning Light* Charity Schools, 1777–80'. In 1780, St Catherine's cost 499 r. 90k. and St Alexander's 1,398r.

33. Gareth Jones, op. cit.

34. *PSZ*, XXI, No. 15, 121, 16 February 1781. See also A. Voronov, *Istoriko-statisticheskoye obozreniye uchebnykh zavedenii St Peterburgskogo uchebnogo okruga s 1715 do 1828 god vklyuchitel'no*, p. 10.

35. Catherine gave 1000r. to 'her' school and 600r. to each of the other six schools. Paul gave 2,000r., Voronov, op. cit., p. 12.

36. A point made by Max J. Okenfuss in 'Education and Empire : School Reform in Enlightened Russia', p. 48.

37. In his 'plan d'une université pour le gouvernement de Russie' Diderot recognized that private education was best, but the bulk of a nation could not afford it ; the state should therefore provide universal elementary education by teachers paid by the state (*Oeuvres Complètes*, III, pp. 429ff). Similarly J.G. Justi in *Die Grundsätze zu der Macht und Glückseligkeit der Staaten* stressed the fact that if the state wanted good and loyal citizens it must create and direct a system of education (see Rozhdestvensky, op. cit., p. 387ff). There was not much difference between the ideas of the French and the German *philosophes* in this field. Okenfuss, op. cit., is very scathing about the methods of Felbiger. But his judgments seem to me to be based on contemporary American ideas of education, and pedagogy is a field in which fashions change remarkably quickly.

38. Other members were Field-Marshal A.M. Golitsyn, I.I. Melissino, then director of the Noble Cadet Corps, and the geographer and explorer S. Pallas. On Aepinus, see R.W. Home, 'Science as a Career in Eighteenth-Century Russia : The Case of F.U.T. Aepinus'.

39. The other members of the Commission were Aepinus, P.I. Pastukhov (a secretary of Catherine's) and Jankovich who was co-opted as the expert adviser. See *PSZ*, XXI, No. 16,507, 7 September 1782.

40. Jankovich left the Commission in 1785 to concentrate on directing the teacher training school and was replaced by O.P. Kozodavlev ; he returned later to the Commission. See also Voronov, op. cit., pp. 10–1.

Twenty-seven textbooks were ready by 1786 : ibid., p. 38 and n. 2.

41. Beer-Fiedler, p. 399, Cobenzl to Joseph II, 15 March 1783.

42. G. Vernadsky, *Russkoye Masonstvo v tsarstovovaniye Yekateriny II*, p. 206, n. 3.

43. The German school attached to St Peter's Lutheran church was also ordered to conform to the national pattern in an ukaz of 7 September 1783. See W. Gareth Jones, op. cit., and Rozhdestvensky, op. cit., pp. 14–16.

44. *PSZ*, XXII, No. 16,058, 5 September 1784; No. 16,275, 7 October 1785.

45. *PSZ*, XXII, No. 16,421. The Statute included an instruction on the teaching of foreign languages, with a detailed timetable. I. Matl' in 'F. Ya. Yankovich i avstro-serbsko-russkiye svyazi v istorii narodnogo obrazovaniya v Rossii' suggests that French was excluded as the language of subversive thought (p. 80).

46. I have used the third edition : *Rukovodstvo uchitelyam pervago i vtorago rozryada narodnykh uchilishch Rossiskiya imperii, izdannoye po vysochayshemu poveleniyu tsarstvuyuschiya imperatritsy*, St Petersburg, 1794, 145pp. Tables. unbound, 2 kopeks.

47. I have been unable to see a copy of this work, which was based on *Rukovodstvo k chestnosti i pravosti* in Serbian, based in turn on a work by Felbiger, *Anleitung zur Rechtschaffenheit*, which I have not been able to track down either. Extracts of the Russian version can be found in German in *Russische Bibliothek*, ed. H.L.C. Bacmeister, Vol. 9, pp. 19ff ; in Russian in M.I. Demkov, 'Istoriya russkoy pedagogiki', II, *Novaya russkaya pedagogika, XVIII vek*, and in N.I. Zhelvakov, *Khrestomatiya po istorii pedagogiki*, IV, pt. 1, pp. 172ff. See Okenfuss, op. cit., for a full discussion. The complete text, unfortunately without the footnote references to the relevant biblical passages, has now been published in English translation by J.L. Black, *Citizens for the Fatherland*, a work which appeared too late for me to make use of it.

48. Rozhdestvensky, op. cit., pp. 565ff.

49. D.A. Tolstoy, 'Gorodskiye uchilishcha v tsarstovovaniye Yekateriny II'.

50. Rozhdestvensky, op. cit., pp. 309ff.

51. Demkov, op. cit., pp. 395ff.

52. *Grazhdanskoye nachal' noye ucheniye*, 2 parts, 1781 and 1783.

53. *Rukovodstvo*, p. 106. So also were dunce's caps, ass's ears, etc.

54. *PSZ*, XXII, No. 16,726, 3 November 1788 (cf. No. 16,147).

55. Rozhdestvensky, op. cit., p. 606.

56. The firm of Breitkopf was licensed to publish these textbooks in St Petersburg : *PSZ*, XXII, No. 16,086, 1 November 1784. The Lutheran St Peter's Church in St Petersburg was given overall supervision of all German language schools in Russia, and published German translations of the textbooks. Woltner, op. cit., pp. 36–7.

57. Statute of 1786, and *PSZ*, Kniga shtatov, Vol.

44, p. 200. See also *PSZ*, XXII, No. 16,930, 16 December 1790, Rozhdestvensky, pp. 581ff.

58. Ibid., pp. 584ff. Tolstoy, *Gorodskiye uchilishcha*, pp. 112–3.

59. Tolstoy, ibid.

60. Tolstoy, *Vzglyad*, pp. 54–5.

61. Ibid., pp. 22ff. The other state educational establishments, such as the Naval Cadet Corps, the Artillery and Engineering Schools, the Corps of Pages, the School of Mines and the Medical Schools (which were attached at first to hospitals) were all reformed in the course of the 1780s and brought into line with the relevant elements in the new plan.

62. Tolstoy, *Vzglyad*, passim ; Okenfuss, op. cit., p. 63, n. 89, states that a 2 per cent tax on imports and a 1 per cent tax on exports was levied in the port of St Petersburg to a total of 10,000 r.p.a. for schools. Other port cities imposed similar duties.

63. In the 1760s, Professor Dilthey thought that 3 universities, 9 gymnasia, 21 minor schools, 2 peasant schools and a central government educational administration could be run on 104,721 r.p.a. with 150,000 r. for the initial buildings. The budget for a high school was given as 2,500 r.p.a. (Rozhdestvensky, op. cit., p. 597). A schoolmaster received 400 r.p.a. for the two senior classes in high schools, 200 r.p.a. for the second year and 150 r.p.a. for the first year. In the junior schools, teachers were paid 100 r. for the first year and 150 r.p.a. for the second. Teachers of languages received 300 r.p.a. and teachers of dancing 60 r.p.a. Tolstoy, *Gorodskiye uchilishcha*, p. 113, n. 1. For comparison it may be noted that primary school teachers received on average 200–250 r.p.a. in 1898 ; at an urban school, a highly qualified teacher received 600 r.p.a., others 480 r.p.a. in 1892. (*See Board of Education Report*, pp. 261ff.)

64. *PSZ*, XXII, No. 16,344, 10 March 1786, and G. Vernadsky, *Russkoye Masonstvo v tsarstvovaniye Yekateriny II*, pp. 203–4.

65. Rozhdestvensky, op. cit., pp. 602ff.

66. *Istoricheskaya Zapiska Ryazanskogo muzhskogo gimnaziyon*, Ryazan, 1904, p. 6.

67. *PSZ*, XXII, No. 16,443, 22 October 1786, ukaz ordering this to stop at once ; Rozhdestvensky, op. cit., p. 602.

68. Parkinson, op. cit., p. 177. However, according to I. Dubasov, *Ocherki iz istorii Tambovskogo kraya*, from 1788 to 1804, in Orel, of 3,008 pupils, 1,041 or 34 per cent were serfs. See also Semevsky, *Krest'yane'*, I, p. 286 on the presence of serf children in schools.

69. Derzhavin, *Sochineniya*, V, p. 557.

70. See for instance Diderot, 'Plan d'une université pour le gouvernement de Russie' : 'elle [Sa Majesté] a devant elle un champ vaste, un espace libre de tout obstacle sur lequel elle peut édifier a son gré . . .' (*Oeuvres*, III, p. 441); and N. Hans, 'Dumaresq, Brown and Some Early Educational Projects of Catherine II', for the expression of very similar ideas.

71. *PSZ*, XXII, No. 16,344, 10 March 1786, warn-

ing A.P. Mel'gunov ; No. 16,362, 27 March 1786, to governor Bruce of Moscow, warning N.I. Novikov.

72. Okenfuss, op. cit., p. 51.

73. Parkinson, op. cit., pp. 223. The book was pulped and sold at 50 kopeks a pud. See Zhelvakov, op. cit., pp. 172ff and 197, n. 10.

74. Most non-Russian languages had as yet no written alphabet, or were still in the process of evolving one. There could therefore be no question of translating and printing the textbooks into native languages, other than e.g. Tartar. But Russian was now taught in schools in the Baltic provinces.

75. 'Zapiski Barona Shteyngelya', pp. 283ff. Fagging was also practised in the Kronstadt Naval Cadet Corps, reflecting perhaps the strong British influence in the Russian navy.

76. According to another calculation, between 1782 and 1800, 176,730 scholars passed through the national schools of which 7 per cent (12,595) were girls. *Board of Education Report*, p. 28.

77. *PSZ*, XXII, No. 16,315, 29 January 1786.

78. The outbreak of war in 1787 may have led to the postponement of any action.

79. See A.G. Cross, 'Russian Students in Eighteenth-Century Oxford (1766–1775)', *Journal of European Studies*, V, 1975, pp. 91–110.

80. See A.H. Brown, 'S.E. Desnitsky i I.A. Tret'iakov v Glazgovskom universitete, 1761–1767'.

Chapter 32. Catherine's Religious Policy

1. Reddaway, *Documents*, p. 209.

2. *PSZ*, XIX, No. 13,996, 23 June 1773. A dispute had arisen between the governor of Kazan' and the ecclesiastical authorities. The former, relying on the relevant articles of Catherine's Nakaz, had given permission for the building of two mosques.

3. Yu. Gessen, *Istoriya Yevreyskogo naroda v Rossii*, I, pp. 9ff. In 1740, 292 men and 281 women living in 130 homes were ordered to leave Little Russia.

4. *PSZ*, X, No. 7,612, 3 July 1738.

5. *PSZ*, XI, No. 8,673, 2 December, 1742.

6. *Sochineniya Yekateriny*, ed. by Pypin, XII, p. 570.

7. *PSZ*, SV, No. 11,720.

8. Bartlett, op. cit., p. 90.

9. *SIRIO*, 51, p. 440.

10. Bartlett, *ibid.*, (*PSZ*, XVIII, No. 13,383, 16 November 1769). Jewish prisoners of war were allowed to settle (see Yu. Gessen, *Zakon i zhizn', kak sozidalis' ogranichitel'nyye zakony o zhitel'stve v Rossii*, p. 18).

11. Gessen, *Zakon i zhizn'*, pp. 16–17.

12. Ibid., quoting Catherine to Diderot.

13. A. Buchholtz, *Geschichte der Juden in Riga*, pp. 64, 67–9, 123–8.

14. Ukaz to Governor-General Browne of 4 February 1785, *PSZ*, XXII, No. 16,146 ; see Buchholtz, op. cit., pp. 69ff. The numbers involved were very small : in 1805 there were 89 Jewish kuptsy in Schluck and 44 meshchane.

15. Gessen, *Istoriya*, p. 58 and No. 33. In 1784 the total registered Jewish population in Mogilev guberniya was 1,161 Jewish kuptsy (321 Christians) and 14,258 Jewish meshchane (7,126 Christians). In Polotsk it was 467 Jewish kuptsy and 646 Christians ; 6,955 Jewish meshchane and 7,824 Christians. In Polotsk guberniya Jews formed 2·76 per cent of the total population and 37 per cent of the urban population. However, I. Levitats, *The Jewish Community in Russia 1772–1844*, p. 18 stresses the unreliability of figures.

16. Gessen, *Istoriya*, pp. 30ff.

17. *PSZ*, XIX, No. 13,850, 16 August 1772. From now on the offensive *zhid* disappeared in theory, from Russian ukazy and was replaced by the neutral *yevrey*.

18. This point is clearly brought out in the ukaz of 17 October 1776. See J.D. Klier, 'The Ambiguous Legal Status of Russian Jewry in the Reign of Catherine II'.

19. *PSZ*, XX, No. 14,962, 7 January 1780 ; XXI, No. 15,130, 10 March 1781.

20. Gessen, *Istoriya*, p. 58 and n. 33.

21. *PSZ*, XXII, No. 16,391, 7 May 1786. In no other European country except Tuscany were Jews granted these municipal rights. See S.W. Baron, *The Russian Jew under Tsars and Soviets*, p. 18.

22. Gessen, *Istoriya*, I, pp. 74–7.

23. See J.P. LeDonne, 'The Liquor Monopoly in Catherine's Russia' ; Gessen, *Zakon i Zhizn'*, p. 33.

24. R. Pipes, 'Catherine II and the Jews' ; *PSZ*, XXII, No. 16,391, 7 May 1786.

25. *SIRIO*, 1, pp. 384ff. 'Dnevnaya Zapiska puteshestviya Imperatritsy Yekateriny II.

26. The extent to which the provisions of the ukaz of May 1786 were actually carried out needs further research.

27. *PSZ*, XXII, No. 17,006, 23 December 1791. See also *AGS*, I, pp. 365–68.

28. For Potemkin's views, see Prince de Ligne, *Mémoires*, II, p. 103ff, to Joseph II.

29. *PSZ*, XXIV, No. 17,224, 1 July 1794. Gessen, *Istoriya*, I, p. 86, and n. 11.

30. Pipes, op. cit., stresses this last aspect of Catherine's policy. I find his argument unconvincing since the presence of Jews in Moscow would surely be *less* dangerous than on the border areas of the Empire. The fact that all *foreign* Jews were ordered to leave Russia in 1792 reflects suspicion of foreigners rather than of Jews.

31. It should be noted that Jews continued to be exempt from the recruit levy (on payment of a special tax) (*PSZ*, XXIII, 21 January 1796).

32. C. Lemercier Quelquejay, 'Les Missions Orthodoxes en Pays Musulmans de Moyenne et Basse Volga 1552–1865' ; S.A. Zenkovsky, *Pan-Turkism and Islam in Russia*.

33. *PSZ*, XVII, No. 12,721, 2 April 1764.

34. Among the 52 deputies of the non-Russian peoples, there were 20 Tartars and 2 Bashkirs. Of the Tartars 3 were Christians and 17 Moslems. See Florovsky, *Sostav*, p. 469.

35. Some of these nakazy have been published in *SIRIO*, 115, pp. 304ff. They show some evidence of coordination between the various groups in Kazan' province.

36. *SIRIO*, 14, pp. 135, 156–9.

37. *SIRIO*, 10, p. 202.

38. Zenkovsky, op. cit., p. 17.

39. *PSZ*, xix, No. 13,996. See above, p. 503. The Tartar language was taught to *Christian* pupils at the Kazan' gymnasium from 1769. Lemercier Quelquejay, op. cit., p. 395.

40. *PSZ*, xx, No. 14,540, 22 November 1776.

41. See A.W. Fisher, 'Enlightened Despotism and Islam under Catherine ii'.

42. *PSZ*, xxii, No. 16,255, 4 September 1785.

43. Decrees of 25 February 1782 and 2 May 1784 authorized the building of mosques in the lands of the Kirghiz. Lemercier Quelquejay, op. cit., p. 393.

44. See *PSZ*, xxii, No. 16,710, 22 September 1788 ; No. 16,711, and xxiii, No. 16,759, 20 April 1789.

45. Zenkovsky, op. cit., p. 18.

46. Trade turnover increased from 83,000 r. in 1773–7 to 624,000 in 1793–7 and 11,336,000 r. in 1830. Zenkovsky, op. cit., p. 20. Nineteenth-century Russian historians such as D.A. Tolstoy were extremely critical of this tolerant policy, and of the use of Tartar mullahs to 'Russianize' the Tartars ; cf. Fisher, op. cit., p. 551, quoting D.A. Tolstoy, who edited the papers of Count Igelstrom (*RA*, 1886, xi, p. 346).

47. The story of the Roman Catholics in Russia has been studied by P. Pierling, *La Russie et le Saint Siège*, and D.A. Tolstoy, *Rimskiy Katolitsizm v Rossii, Istoricheskoye izsledovaniye*, (first published in French in 1863–4). Pierling writes as a fervent papalist, Tolstoy as a nationalist Orthodox. It is often difficult to reconcile their respective versions. An effort has been made to do so here. M. Moroshkin, *Jezuity v Rossii s tsartsvovaniya Yekateriny II i do nashego vremein*, is deeply biased against the Jesuits, as is Tolstoy. Cf. also J.J. Zatko, 'The Organization of the Catholic Church in Russia, 1772–84'.

48. *PSZ*, vi, No. 3,814, 18 August 1721, authorizing Swedish prisoners of war to marry Russian women. The decree was passed to enable Peter i's daughter Anna to marry the Duke of Holstein.

49. *PSZ*, xvii, No. 12,776, 6 November 1766.

50. *PSZ*, xviii, Nos. 13,251, 13,252.

51. Tolstoy, ibid., pp. 178–9.

52. Pierling, op. cit., v, p. 16.

53. *PSZ*, xviii, No. 13,580 ; xix, No. 14,073, 22 November 1773 ; xxii, No. 16,616, 26 January 1788 ; Tolstoy, op. cit., p. 43. It is known that Catherine's ecclesiastical policy in Poland was influenced by Z.G. Chernyshev (the governor-general of the two new gubernii), Saldern, at that time negotiating in Poland and G.N. Teplov, who in this field too showed himself a furious disciple of the Enlightenment.

54. Tolstoy, p. 22 ; *PSZ*, xxi, No. 15,326.

55. M. Moroshkin, *Jezuity v Rossii*, pp. 53–4 and 54, n. 3.

56. *PSZ*, xviii, No. 13,808.

57. Tolstoy, p. 45.

58. *SIRIO*, 1, p. 478. Panin to Stackelberg 23 October 1779.

59. Pierling, v, p. 52.

60. See the discussion in Pierling, pp. 95ff and Tolstoy, p. 19. *PSZ*, xix, No. 14,582, 16/27 February 1777.

61. Catherine to Stackelberg (Warsaw) 14 February 1780, *SIRIO*, 1, p. 488.

62. Tolstoy, op. cit., pp. 83ff. *SIRIO*, 27, p. 238, Catherine to (?) n.d. but before September 1786.

63. Pierling, op. cit., pp. 116ff. *PSZ*, xxi, No. 15,326, 17/28 January 1782 ; No. 15, 346, 14 February 1782. The archbishop was given unlimited power over the secular and regular clergy within the Russian Empire directly under the Senate and then the empress. This ukaz was quoted in France by the constitutional clergy in 1792 as evidence that the Papacy had once given its approval to a 'civil constitution' of the clergy. Ibid., p. 144.

64. Pierling, p. 123. *SIRIO*, 1, pp. 525, 4 November 1782.

65. Tolstoy, op. cit., Appendix pp. 6, 36 and n. 2 ; Catherine also ordered the omission of a sentence to the effect that the archbishop would not alienate Church property without the permission of the Pope. Papal approval of Catherine's dispositions was given in two briefs of 17 January 1784, *Pastoralis Sollicitudo* (antedated 26 April 1783) and *Onerosa pastoralis officii* (antedated 19 December 1783). See the Rt. Rev. C. Sipovic, 'The Diocese of Minsk, its Origin, Extent and Hierarchy'.

66. Tolstoy, op. cit., p. 38.

67. Ibid., pp. 44. *PSZ*, xxiii, Nos 17,370, 17,380, 6 September 1795.

68. Tolstoy stresses that the Russian administration was ordered to use no violence. It is however hard to accept that in annexed Poland the conversion of approximately 3.5 million from the Uniat to the Orthodox religion was achieved without any kind of pressure.

69. Sipovic, op. cit., pp. 181–2.

70. Catherine had every intention of proceeding in Poland as in Belorussia, namely eliminating all monasteries devoted to the contemplative life as 'idle and useless' and keeping only those devoted to useful social purposes. Death prevented the carrying out of this policy. The attitude of Russian officials to Church property is reflected in the words of Prince N.V. Repnin, governor of Pskov : 'the property of monasteries is state property, allotted to them for sacred purposes.' That much monastic property was the gift of private individuals did not cross his mind (Tolstoy, op. cit., pp. 45–6 and 48, no. 2.

71. See Erik Amburger, *Geschichte des Protestantismus in Russland*, Evangelisches Verlagswerk, Stuttgart, 1961.

72. See Chapter 31.

73. See A.G. Cross, 'Chaplains to the British Factory in St. Petersburg 1723–1813' and the references

quoted by him to his own articles and to other published works.

74. See R. Portal, 'Aux origines d'une bourgeoisie industrielle' and W. Blackwell 'The Old Believers and the Rise of Private Industrial Enterprise in Early 19th-Century Moscow'.

75. See V.V. Andreyev, *Raskol i ego znacheniye v narodnoy russkoy istorii, istoricheskiy ocherk*, pp. 294ff.

Chapter 33 The Role of Freemasonry

1. See the reactions of Derzhavin's aunt in his *Sochineniya*, v, pp. 437–8, and see A.N. Pypin, *Russkoye masonstvo XVIII i pervaya chetvert' XIX v.*, pp. 96ff.

2. See G.V. Vernadsky, *Russkoye masonstvo*, pp. 8–9.

3. See for instance the instructions to the Directorate issued by the Duke of Sudermania, para 5 : '. . . all chapters throughout this Russian Empire are bound in everything and without delay to obey the Directorate, to present detailed reports of their state, of the nature of their work, of their economic affairs, of their enterprises and how they fulfil the instructions of the Directorate.' Vernadsky, op. cit., pp. 45ff. and see M.N. Longinov, *Novikov i Moskovskiye martinisty*, pp. 110ff, for Catherine's orders to the police chief in St Petersburg to examine the correspondence between the Duke of Sudermania and the Russian lodges.

4. Among the members were the curator of Moscow University, M. M. Kheraskov, his half-brother, Prince N.N. Trubetskoy, Prince A.A. Cherkassky, I. P Turgenev, and the judge of the criminal court, I.V. Lopukhin, some of whose masonic devotional works have been translated into English.

5. See In-ho L. Ryu, 'Moscow Freemasons and the Rosicrucian Order', which provides a valuable corrective to the idealization of Schwarz common in nineteenth-century historiography, and on which I have drawn extensively.

6. Vernadsky, op. cit., pp. 207ff. See also S. Baehr, 'The Masonic Component in Eighteenth-Century Russian Literature' and M. Green, 'Masonry, Kheraskov and Mozart : A Footnote'.

7. See I.F. Martynov, 'Kniga v russkoy provintsii 1760–1790kh gg. Zarozhdeniye provintsial'noy knizhnoy torgovli', pp. 118–19.

8. In-ho L. Ryu, op. cit., p. 219 and n. 50.

9. *Tayna protivu nelepogo obshchestva*, which was also published in French and German ; *Obmanshchik* ('The Deceiver') was performed on 2 February 1786 ; *Obol'shchennyye* ('The Deceived') and *Shaman Sibirskiy* ('The Siberian Shaman') were performed in the same year. See G.H. MacArthur, 'Catherine II and the Masonic Circle of N.I. Novikov', for further details on Catherine's attitude to freemasonry.

10. Louis Claude de Saint Martin, author of the treatise *Des erreurs et de la verité*, published in 1775.

11. See above, Chapter 31.

12. V.A. Zapadov, 'K istorii pravitel'svennykh presledovaniy N.I. Novikova'.

13. M. Longinov, *Novikov i Moskovskiye Martinisty*, Appendix 016, ukaz to N.P. Arkharov, 23 September 1784 and *SIRIO*, 27, p. 338, Catherine to unnamed person, n.d. From this last note it would appear that Catherine did not know the publisher of the History. See Chapter 32.

14. Zapadov, op. cit., pp. 39ff.

15. *PSZ*, XXII, No. 16362, 27 March 1786.

16. *SIRIO*, 27, p. 362, Catherine to P. V. Lopukhin, 23 January 1786.

17. Ibid., p. 363.

18. See the report from P. V. Lopukhin to Catherine, 30 January 1786 in G. Makogonenko, *Izbrannyye Sochineniya N.I. Novikova*, pp. 581ff.

19. See A.I. Korsanov, 'Petr Alekseyev, Protoerey Moskovskogo Arkhangel'skogo sobora, 1727–1801' ; see also 'Iz Bumag protoereya Petra Alekseyeva'. Alekseyev denounced Platon as too favourable to the French Enlightenment. He had been involved in unseemly quarrels over religious precedence with Platon's brother, also an archpriest.

20. Zapadov, op. cit., pp. 41ff. Among presses which had published religious works, and were forbidden to do so in future were the Academy Press, the Cadet Corps Press, the Senate Press, etc. Zapadov points out that contrary to previous assumptions the 313 titles were not burnt ; the books, other than the 14 banned titles, were eventually returned to their owners.

21. Khrapovitsky, *Dnevnik*, p. 173, 15 October 1788.

22. In-ho L. Ryu, op. cit., pp. 228–9.

23. M.T. Belyavsky, 'Novikovskoye Avdot'ino v 1792'.

24. See A. Pypin, *Russkoye Masonstvo*, pp. 500 and 521.

25. 'Iz bumag protoereya Petra Alekseyeva', pp. 76ff, and note of 17 August 1790 to procurator Kolychev in Moscow, p. 78.

26. *SIRIO*, 29, p. 96, Bezborodko to Prozorovsky, 15 November 1791. I.V. Lopukhin believed that Bezborodko and Arkharov (the St Petersburg chief of police) had been sent to Moscow in spring 1791 to investigate the Moscow Masons. See *Zapiski I.V. Lopukhina*, pp. 36–7.

27. Pypin, op. cit., p. 522.

28. Ukaz to Prozorovsky, in M.N. Longinov, op. cit., p. 061.

29. Longinov, op. cit., p. 301.

30. Reports of 25 and 26 April 1792, Longinov, op. cit., pp. 065–6, 067–8.

31. *Izbrannyye Sochineniya*, N.I. Novikova, ed. G. Makogonenko, p. 599.

32. For the most recent discussion and dating see V.A. Zapadov, *op. cit.*, p. 47. Khrapovitsky, *Dnevnik*, pp. 399–400, 26 May 1792. The memorandum stated that Paul was not yet a Mason.

33. Prozorovsky to S. Sheshkovsky, 17 May 1792, *SIRIO*, 2, pp. 104–5. See also J. Parkinson, *Tour of Russia*, p. 215 : 'Prince Gagarin, having been

Grand Master of the Free Masons at Moscow pretends to know for certain that the Jacobin principles had their origin in meetings of that society.'

34. Ukaz of 1 August 1792 to Prozorovsky, in *Izbrannyye Sochineniya*, ed. Makogonenko, pp. 671–2. For Catherine's close interest in the interrogation of Novikov, see her own lists of questions to be put to him in *SIRIO*, 42, pp. 224–6.

35. See M. N. Gernet, *Istoriya tsarskoy tyur'my*, I, pp. 236 and 244. The commandant supplied interesting figures on the cost of living : meat cost 6 kopeks a pound ; white bread, 3 kopeks a pound, butter 15 kopeks a pound, ¼ lb tea cost 75 kopeks, sugar 55 kopeks a pound and eggs 15 kopeks each.

36. For the latest expression of this view in English see G. H. McArthur, 'Catherine II and the Masonic Circle of N.I. Novikov', p. 546.

37. *SIRIO*, 2, p. 156 and n. 59 ; Pypin, op. cit., p. 520.

38. See J.E. von Goertz, *Mémoire sur la cour de Russie*, p. 58. The Russian envoy to Berlin in 1789, M.M. Alopeus, was in correspondence with Paul and was a close friend of Bischoffswerder ; see also G. Vernadsky, *Russkoye masonstvo*, p. 231.

39. Miranda, *Archivo*, II, pp. 385, 394.

40. See V. Bogolyubov, *N.I. Novikov i ego vremya*, p. 273. The Rosicrucians are perhaps also precursors – in the Russian context again – of the High Evangelical movement in late eighteenth- and early nineteenth-century England which reacted against the intellectual and sexual libertinism of the Enlightenment.

41. See Epilogue for Paul's peculiar domestic life.

42. See Belyavsky, op. cit., pp. 58–9.

43. From *Magazin Svobodokamenshchikov*, Vol. 1, pt. 1, p. 132.

44. Vernadsky, op. cit., pp. 82–3. Pypin, op. cit., p. 520. See also Catherine's specific orders to inquire into the activities of Repnin, Pleshcheyev and Kurakin in *SIRIO*, 42, pp. 225–7.

45. When he was released from Schlüsselburg, Novikov gave a dinner to his country neighbours, at which the 16-year-old serf who had accompanied him in prison was given a place of honour. But Novikov was sufficiently a child of his age to sell this same serf later for 2,000 rubles because his affairs were in disorder. See P.A. Vyazemsky, *Zapisnyye Knizhki* (1813–1848), pp. 110–11.

46. Khrapovitsky, *Dnevnik*, p. 218, 24 December 1788.

47. Belyavsky, op. cit., p. 39. See also Dzhedzhula, op. cit., pp. 246ff. for the threats to Catherine's life.

48. Strangely enough Bazhenov was designing a house for Prozorovsky – could this have influenced his fate ?

49. Prozorovsky reported to Catherine that 1,965 books were given to the seminary, 5,194 to Moscow University and 18,656 were destroyed as 'harmful'. See G.N. Moiseeva, 'Dopol'nitel'nyye dannyye k ob-

stoyatel'stvam presledovaniya N.I. Novikova', at p. 150.

Chapter 34. The Birth of the Intelligentsia

1. *SIRIO*, 23, p. 157.

2. For a brief and sympathetic account see R.E. Jones, 'Urban planning and the Development of Provincial Towns in Russia, 1762–1796'.

3. Ibid., and Miranda, *Archivo*, II, passim.

4. For a most perceptive treatment, see Stephen L. Baehr, ' "Fortuna Redux" : The Courtly Spectacle in Eighteenth-Century Russia', paper read at the international conference, 'Great Britain and Russia in the Eighteenth Century : Contacts and Comparisons', held at the University of East Anglia, 11–15 July 1977 published in the book under the same title edited by A.G. Cross. Baehr gives a delightful example of the allegorical and didactical ballet in 1768, entitled 'Prejudice Overcome'. Here, Minerva, sitting in the Temple of Aesculapius, agrees to be inoculated ; she then convinces Ruthenia, sitting in the Temple of Ignorance, of the need to be inoculated, and the two dance. (Shades of the Crummles.)

5. *SIRIO*, 42, p. 101, Catherine to Potemkin, 9 August 1790.

6. See the account given by Princess Dashkova in her *Memoirs*, ed. K. Fitzlyon, pp. 203ff.

7. 'Elle n'a pa le temps de tripoter, ayant un gros morceau dans la bouche qui tient les mâchoires en respect.' Catherine to Grimm, 29 April 1783 in *SIRIO*, 23, p. 277. The ukaz appointing Dashkova is dated 24 January 1783.

8. On Shcherbatov, see V.A. Myakotin, *Iz istorii russkogo obshchestva*, Etyudy i ocherki. I have not been able to make use of the unpublished dissertation by J. Afferica (Columbia University), but see her 'The Formation of the Hermitage Collection'.

9. *Sochineniya Yekateriny II*, ed. Pypin, Vols. VIII–XI at VIII, p. 5. Much of Catherine's historical work remained unpublished during her lifetime and first saw the light in Pypin's edition of her works.

10. So she said in a letter to Grimm, *SIRIO*, 23, pp. 638–9, 25 May 1795.

11. *Sochineniya Yekateriny II*, ed. Pypin, II, pp. 219–51.

12. Khrapovitsky, *Dnevnik*, p. 318, 1 December 1789.

13. Ségur, *Mémoires*, III, p. 324. Ségur found the spectacle deplorable, but the Grand Duke Paul was delighted with it. (Khrapovitsky, *Dnevnik*, p. 248, 1 January 1789.)

14. Khrapovitsky, *Dnevnik*, p. 243, 25 January 1789 ; p. 249, 5 and 6 February 1789.

15. Stephen A. Baehr, ' "Fortuna Redux" '. Catherine also wrote in these years a successful comic opera, *Fevey*, based on a fairy tale she wrote for her grandchildren. Her last work was 'Fedul and his Children', a comedy of peasant life, largely put together from peasant songs, by her secretary, in a plot devised by herself.

NOTES

16. R.I. Semyontkovsky, 'Nash pervyy skeptik (O Fonvizine)' ; K.V. Pigarev, *Tvorchestvo Fonvizina,* p. 209.

17. The play was performed twenty times in St Petersburg, at the court theatre and at Gatchina, for Paul, and twenty-six times in Moscow in the period 1782–1799. See V.N. Vsevolodsky Gerngross, *Russkiy teatr vtoroy poloviny XVIII veka,* p. 224. It was also staged by A.R. Vorontsov in his serf theatre.

18. Quoted in K.A. Papmehl, *Freedom of Expression in Eighteenth-Century Russia,* p. 106, and no. 64.

19. See P.R. Zaborov, *Russkaya literatum i Vol'œ ter,* p. 44.

20. *PSZ,* xxi, No. 15,783, 12 July 1783.

21. *PSZ,* xxi, No. 15,634. Between January 1783 and September 1796, 13 presses were set up in St Petersburg, a similar number in Moscow, and eleven in the provinces, including one in Tobol'sk. (*Svodnyy Katalog russkoy knigi grazhdanskoy pechati XVIII veka,* pp. 288ff).

22. The evidence for this episode remains obscure. Fonvizin could have started up his journal without formal permission, and no information has been published on the reasons why it was forbidden (if it was). The only source available is a letter from Fonvizin to P.I. Panin, dated 4 April 1788, which does not make it clear when, between 1783 and 1788, permission was refused, nor whether Catherine was consulted. For Fonvizin's letter, see *Sobraniye Sochineniy,* ii, p. 356.

23. See Chapter 33 for the arrest of Novikov.

24. See J.T. Alexander, *Autocratic Politics,* p. 179.

25. Khrapovitsky, *Dnevnik,* p. 301, 1 August 1789.

26. See *Sochineniya Derzhavina,* Vol. 1, pp. 57–8, and p. 58, no. 1.

27. Kapnist, Ode is said, in Soviet historiography, to refer to the 'extension of serfdom' to the Ukraine in 1783. It is more probable that it refers to the introduction of the Statute of 1775 and the destruction of Ukrainian 'political liberties'.

28. Ségur, *Mémoires,* iii, p. 434.

29. According to K.E. Dzhedzhula, *Rossiya i velikaya frantzuszkaya burzhuaznaya revolyutsiya kontsa XVIII veka,* p. 396, it was possible to buy many pamphlets and brochures, the decrees of the French National Assembly, caricatures and cartoons, and such periodicals as *Père Duchêne, L'Ami du Peuple, Le vieux Cordelier, La révolution de Paris,* etc.

30. But I cannot follow Dzhedzhula's assertion that Russia was 'as affected' by the French Revolution as the countries bordering on France. It is impossible to prove any direct connection between any of the rural disturbances in Russia during the 1790s and events in France. Fears of the landowners are not evidence of the motives of peasants. See op. cit., pp. 146ff, and 155ff.

31. On Romme see A. Galante Garrone, *Storia di un rivoluzionario ;* on the Cadet Corps see Dzhedzhula, op. cit., p. 255.

32. Radishchev, *Sochineniya,* i, pp. 229ff.

33. The most accessible text of the 'Journey' is that translated by L. Wiener, and edited by R.P. Thaler, which gives both Russian and English texts and Catherine's marginal comments. See *A Journey from St. Petersburg to Moscow,* p. 171.

34. Quoted in M.M. Shtrange, *Russkoye obshchestvo i frantzuszkaya revolyutsiya,* p. 78, without any indication of the nature or precise date of the document quoted.

35. Khrapovitsky, *Dnevnik,* pp. 338, 24 June 1790; 339, 1 July 1790; 340, 7 July 1790.

36. Fonvizin, *Sobraniye Sochineniy,* ii, p. 466, to P.I. Panin, Paris 20/31 March 1778 and Radishchev's *Journey,* tr. Wiener. Catherine's marginal comments, pp. 239ff, conveniently correlated with the pages of the English text.

37. See her remarks on a short pamphlet by Radishchev entitled 'A Letter to a Friend living in Tobol'sk', written in 1782, and published early in 1790, but which Catherine read after the 'Journey': 'it is evident from the places I have underlined that his thoughts have long been inclined in this direction, and that the French revolution decided him to come forward as the first instigator . . . we must find the others, a couple are being sent from France.' (D.S. Babkin, *Protsess Radishcheva,* p. 164.)

38. Catherine detected the influence of Raynal's ideas on Radishchev, and he admitted to it. Subsequent historians of Radishchev have tended to reject any overwhelming influence. See D. Lang, *The First Russian Radical,* pp. 247, 132, 297, 115; A. McConnell, *A Russian Philosophe,* pp. 69–70, and p. 69, notes 1 and 2.

39. Babkin, *Protsess Radishcheva,* p. 282.

40. Ibid., pp. 282; 320, A.R. Vorontsov to the governor of Tver', 12 September 1790.

41. See Dashkova, *Memoirs,* p. 243; Dzhedzhula, op. cit., pp. 221ff, and *AKV,* 12, p. 381, Bezborodko to Troshchinsky, 14 November 1793. Dzhedzhula, p. 222 repeats the allegation that Knyazhnin was interrogated by Sheshkovsky in the Secret Expedition, in 1790, and died as a result of torture. He adduces no evidence to support this tale, based on a slightly different story repeated by Pushkin. If Knyazhnin had really died as a result of such interrogation, his play would not have been published in 1793.

42. Dzhedzhula, op. cit., pp. 225–6. E. Yefremov, 'Ya. B. Knyazhnin, Vadim Novgorodskiy'.

43. P.K. Alefirenko, 'Obshchestvennoye dvizheniye v Moskve vo vtoroy polovine xviii st.'.

44. On Passek see L. Svetlov, 'A.N. Radishchev i politicheskiye protsessy kontsa xviii veka'. Passek's own memoirs are printed in *RA,* 1863, Nos 5–6. See also Dzhedzhula, op. cit., pp. 177ff. Passek defended his views by referring to Catherine's Nakaz.

45. See Svetlov, op. cit., pp. 52ff. and Dzhedzhula, op. cit., pp. 214ff.

46. Dzhedzhula, op. cit., p. 256; Alefirenko, op. cit., p. 533.

649

47. Dzhedzhula, op. cit., pp. 256ff; *PSZ*, XXVIII, No. 17,508.

48. This revolutionary speech, entitled *L'Orateur des Etats Généraux Français*, was frequently translated into Russian (see for instance Vinsky, *Moe Vremya*, p. xii).

49. Dzhedzhula, p. 264. Dzhedzhula's work should be used with caution. His references are inadequate and he often relies on secondary sources which do not amount to more than the accumulation of gossip. See also Zaburov, op. cit., pp. 71ff.

Chapter 35. Social and Economic Changes 1775–96

1. *IPS*, II, pp. 343–4, 418.

2. Miranda, *Archivo*, II, p. 313.

3. N. Rubinstein, op. cit., pp. 329ff. and Table, pp. 330–1. A special Commission on Corn had been set up in 1786–8 under A.R. Vorontsov, and its figures show that high prices prevailed mainly in Moscow and St Petersburg owing to difficulties of transport. There were poor harvests in 1787 in Voronezh, Tambov, Simbirsk and Ufa, but in other gubernii they were normal. Ibid., pp. 370–1.

4. Ibid., pp. 145–6.

5. Ibid., pp. 129–30 ; in 1806, on an estate belonging to V.G. Orlov, income from barshchina amounted to 216,239r., with expenses of 106,280r. ; on an obrok of 10r.per male soul income came to 110,930r., with expenses of 2,800r.

6. N.A. Tsagolov, *Ocheriki russkoy ekonomicheskoy mysli perioda padeniya krepostnogo prava*, pp. 38–51, 53–56. Quoted in T. Simmons, *The Emancipation of the Serfs*, pp. 42ff.

7. See N.L. Rubinstein, 'Krest' 'yanskoye dvizheniye v Rossii vo vtoroy polovine XVIII veka'. There were outbreaks in Novgorod and Tver' in the 1780s, and a major disturbance in Turbay in the Ukraine.

8. Miranda, *Archivo*, II, pp. 371, 376.

9. See I. Lubimenko, 'Un académicien russe à Paris, d'après ses lettres inédites', p. 139.

10. Miranda, op. cit., p. 370 (Tver'), pp. 373–5 (Spasskaya Polest').

11. J. Parkinson, *A Tour of Russia, Siberia, and the Crimea, 1792–1794*, pp. 122, 142, 152.

12. See Maria Guthrie, *A Tour of the Crimea*, p. 4. On the Russian diet, see the table printed by J. Blum, *Lord and Peasant in Russia*, p. 317, based on the work of F. Le Play, and showing that in 1856, the diet of an ironsmith and a carpenter in the Urals was healthier and more abundant than that of contemporary and comparable English and French workers who, however, earned more.

13. Quoted in J. Blum, *Lord and Peasant*, p. 432.

14. *Memoirs*, IV, p. 169.

15. See M. Vladimirsky Budanov, *Obzor istorii russkogo prava*, pp. 235ff., and the convenient summary by A. Lappo Danilevsky, 'The Serf Question in an Age of Enlightenment'.

16. *PSZ*, XX, No. 14,275, 17 March 1775 as amplified in ibid., No. 14,294, 6 April 1775 and 15,070, 5 October 1780.

17. Kabuzan, *Izmeneniya*, p. 7.

18. Lappo Danilevsky, op. cit., p. 277.

19. *PSZ*, XXVII, no. 20,620, 20 February 1803.

20. See Chapter 8.

21. References to this ukaz are rare, but Metropolitan Platon criticized it severely in 1787 to Miranda. See *Archivo*, II, p. 359.

22. *Sochineniya*, XII, p. 170.

23. V.I. Semevsky, 'Krepostnyye krest'yane pri Yekaterine', p. 671.

24. See Semevsky, *Krest'yane*, I, pp. 208ff. In 1778 Archdeacon Coxe saw a noble in the Kaluga prison in Moscow, serving a sentence of perpetual imprisonment 'for having serfs whipped until they died'. See *An Account of the Prisons and Hospitals in Russia, Sweden and Denmark*, p. 11.

25. P. Bartenev, *Osmnadtsatyy vek*, 3, p. 346, Catherine to the chief of police, N. Arkharov, 11 March 1794.

26. On Catherine's policy of introducing Russian landowners into Belorussia see Dashkova, *Memoirs*, ed. Fitzlyon, p. 196.

27. See my article, 'Catherine II and the Serfs : A Reconsideration of Some Problems'.

28. Semevsky, *Krest'yane*, II, pp. 604–95.

29. *PSZ*, XXI, No. 15,000, 2 July 1782.

30. Klokman, *Sotsial'no ekonomicheskaya istoriya russkogo goroda*, p. 269 gives the figures for Nizhniy Novgorod in 1789 : there were 1,957 houses, of which 217 belonged to nobles, 184 to the priesthood, 103 to officials, 141 to kuptsy, 60 to craftsmen, 641 to townspeople, 414 were used by soldiers, 91 by the post service, 13 by labourers and 93 by peasants.

31. Ibid., p. 316, and n. 6.

32. I have used here the figures given by G. Rozman, *Urban Networks in Russia 1750–1800 and Pre-Modern Periodization*, 1976, p. 105.

33. V.N. Yakovtsevsky, *Kupecheskiy kapital v feodal' no krepostnoy Rossii*, pp. 45ff, 144ff.

34. Ibid., p. 169 (*PSZ*, XXI, No. 15,462). These bazaars still survive as GUM in Moscow and the Gostinnyy Dvor in Leningrad.

35. *SIRIO*, 42, p. 292, to A.A. Bezborodko, about 1791.

36. V.M. Kabuzan and S.M. Troitsky, 'Izmeneniya . . .', Table 1.

37. *AKV*, 9, pp. 269–70, 7/18 November 1792, S.R. Vorontsov to A.R. Vorontsov.

38. At the end of the eighteenth century, up to 1840, about 170 serf treaties were active with 2000 actors and musicians. M.D. Kurmacheva, 'Krepostnaya intelligentsiya v Rossii XVIII Veka'.

39. S.T. Aksakov, *Detstvo Bagrova Vnuka*, passim.

40. *PSZ*, XV, No. 11,467, 9 March 1762. It is difficult to appreciate the exact significance of the replacement of one instrument of punishment by another since

the large variety are all translated in English by sticks, rods and canes.

41. *PSZ*, xv, No. 11,717, 2 December 1762.

42. See above, Chapter 17.

43. *PSZ*, xxi, No. 15,313.

44. On this subject see in general N. Yevreinov, *Istoriya telesnykh nakazaniy*, pp. 72ff.

45. Though Archdeacon Coxe heard of one man who survived after 333 strokes. In 1778, he adds, three people died as a result of the knut. *Account of the Prisons*, p. 2, note.

46. I.V. Lopukhin, *Zapiski*, pp. 12–14.

47. See L. Trefoleyev, 'Aleksey Petrovich Mel'gunov', and *PSZ*, xxii, No. 16551, 28 June 1787.

48. A.N. Radishchev, 'A Journey', pp. 91ff.

49. Brutal punishments were common throughout Europe. For purposes of comparison, see C. Woodham Smith's account of the Duke of Kent's 'reign of terror' in Gibraltar in 1803, when a sentence of 999 lashes was imposed and carried out (*Queen Victoria, her Life and Times, 1819–1861, pp. 20*–21). In March 1817 a woman was flogged through the streets of Inverness for the third time in two weeks for intoxication and bad behaviour. *The Observer* of 30 March 1817 protested.

50. W. Coxe, *Account of the Prisons and Hospitals in Russia Sweden and Denmark*, London 1781 pp. 9ff, and M. Gernet, *Istoriya tsarskoy tyur'my*, I, p. 118. Miranda, op. cit., p. 465.

51. Gernet, op. cit., pp. 109ff.

52. There is no study comparable to N. Golikova's *Politicheskiye protsessy pri Petre*. K.V. Sivkov wrote a doctoral thesis on the subject which has not been published. But a number of articles by him deal with various aspects. See in particular his ''Taynaya ekspeditsiya, ee deyatel'nost' i dokumenty'' ; see also the more recent work by V.Z. Dzhindzharadze, 'Iz istorii taynoy ekspeditsii'.

53. A.N. Korsakov, 'Stepan Ivanovich Sheshkovsky, 1727–1794, Biograficheskiy Ocherki'.

54. *Zapiski L.N. Engel'gardta*, p. 58 states that she was birched by the Mistress of the Household.

55. H. von Storch, *Tableau historique et statistique*, I, p. 327.

56. Coxe, *Account of the Prisons . . . .*, pp. 20ff ; Howard, *The State of Prisons*, pp. 75ff. Miranda, op. cit., pp. 422, 465, found the Catherine Hospital one of the best in Europe.

Epilogue

1. SIRIO, 42, p. 392. E. Herrmann, *Diplomatische Correspondenz aus der Revolutionszeit, 1791–1797*, p. 102, Helbig's despatch of 7/18 March 1791. See also Brevern de la Gardie, *Un ambassadeur*, I, pp. 96ff, desptaches of 17 March, 24, 25 March, 1 April 1791, etc.

2. 'Knyaz' Platon Aleksandrovich Zubov', 1767–1822', *RS*, 17, at p. 43.

3. E. Herrmann, op. cit., p. 106, von Volkersahn (Saxon envoy) 16/27 October 1791, quoting the Polish chargé d'affairs, Deboli.

4. Prince de Ligne, *Mémoires*, p. 143, November 1788.

5. E. Herrmann, op. cit., p. 102, Helbig, 7/18 March 1791. 'Er zeigt sich in den Glanze – und mit der Begleitung eines Souverains und das Volk scheint in ihm seinen Herrn zu sehen.'

6. See in particular, E.M. Druzhinina, *Severnoye Prichernomor'ye, 1775–1800*, which in accordance with Soviet practice lays no particular stress on individual achievement, but indirectly casts much light on Potemkin's activity. See also M. Raeff, 'The Style of Russia's Imperial Policy and Prince G.A. Potemkin.'

7. See Petrov, *Vtoraya turetskaya voyna*, passim. A. Petrushevsky, *Generalisimus Knyaz' Suvorov*, passim. See also Prince de Ligne, *Mémoires*, II, p. 104. When Potemkin told de Ligne that the Turks had 12,000 men in Bender, 6,000 in Khotin, and that the Dniestr was well guarded, all of which was true, de Ligne dismissed it as fancy.

8. On Potemkin as commander-in-chief see the introduction by D.F. Maslovsky to *Pis' ma i bumagi A.V. Suvorova, G.A. Potemkina i P.A. Rumyantseva, 1787–1789 gg. Sbornik voyenno istoricheskikh materialov*, Vol. 4. See also *AKV*, 13, pp. 223ff, Bezborodko to A.R. Vorontsov, 17/28 November 1791.

9. Stedingk, and his secretary Jennings, provide full descriptions of the endless parties and receptions given for Potemkin at this time, and of the prince's own magnificent appearance. Brevern de la Gardie, op. cit., pp. 98ff, 101ff, 103ff, 105 ff. See also V. Esterhazy, *Lettres à sa femme, 1784–1792*, passim.

10. Khrapovitsky, *Dnevnik*, pp. 377–8, 16/27, 17/28 18/29 October 1791. Catherine refers here to Ivan Grigor'evich Chernyshev, head of the Admiralty College.

11. Khrapovitsky, *Dnevnik*, pp. 388, 6/17 January 1792 ; 380–9, 30 January/10 February 1791.

12. Khrapovitsky, *Dnevnik*, p. 378, 17/28 and 18/29 October 1791. Catherine's impatience with Zubov's amateurishness is evident at times.

13. *SIRIO*, 29, pp. 225ff., Bezborodko to S.R. Vorontsov, 15/26 May 1792.

14. *AKV*, 8, pp. 1ff, Autobiographical note by S.R. Vorontsov.

15. *AKV*, 13, p. 243, Bezborodko to S.R. Vorontsov, January 1792 ; p. 254, 15/26 May 1792 and *AKV*, 9, A.R. Vorontsov to S.R. Vorontsov, p. 247, 25 June/6 July 1792 ; p. 257, 14/25 August 1792.

16. *AKV*, 8, p. 110, F.R. Rostopchin to S.R. Vorontsov, 14/25 September 1795.

17. S.N. Glinka, *Zapiski*, St. Petersburg 1895, pp. 25–6, 31. Bobrinsky, it should be remembered, turned into a spendthrift and dissolute young man. Catherine's two sons brought her no happiness.

18. See *SIRIO*, 23, Catherine to Grimm, p. 205.

19. N.K. Shil'der, *Imperator Aleksandr Pervyy*, Vol. I, pp. 6ff ; Khrapovitsky, *Dnevnik*, p. 434, 20 July 1793; p. 312, 9 October 1789.

20. *SIRIO*, 27, pp. 301–30, 13 March 1784.

21. Garnovich, M. *Zapiski, RS*, 16, p. 13.

22. Shil'der, *Imperator Pavel Pervyy*, p. 199 and n. 1 ; pp. 201ff, 556–7.

23. *SIRIO*, 23, p. 621, 6 April 1795.

24. Shil'der, *Imperator Pavel*, pp. 209ff. and footnotes ; *SIRIO*, 27, pp. 428, 466, 469.

25. Shil'der, p. 225. Paul's return may have been hastened by the efforts of the Duke of Sudermania to open direct talks with him, efforts which Paul correctly reported at once to his mother.

26. Ibid., pp. 216ff.

27. Ibid., p. 559, despatch of Baron Keller, 3/14 February 1787.

28. See Keller's despatch quoted in the previous note.

29. Ibid., pp. 217ff.

30. J.C. Biaudet and F. Nicod, *Correspondance de Frédéric César de la Harpe et d'Alexandre I*, p. 14.

31. See e.g. Shil'der, *Imperator Aleksandr*, I, p. 276, Alexander to V.P. Kochubey, 10 May 1796. See also *Memoirs of Prince Adam Czartovyski*, 2 vols, London 1888, I, p. 115.

32. Shil'der, *Imperator Pavel*, p. 252.

33. Ibid., pp. 246ff. *AKV*, 8, p. 7. Rostopchin to S.R. Vor'ontsov, 6/17 July 1793.

34. Quoted in Shil'der, *Imperator Pavel*, p. 253, n. 1.

35. See Shil'der, op. cit., pp. 255ff., and La Harpe's letter to N.I. Saltykov of 24 July 1794 at p. 259, n. 2. See also *Mémoires de F.C. de la Harpe, écrits par lui même*, and Biaudet and Nicrd, *Correspondance de la Harpe*, I, pp. 406–9.

36. Shil'der, op. cit., p. 255 ; the alleged source of the story is the man who was then secretary of the Council.

37. Shil'der, *Imperator Aleksandr*, p. 278, quoting an undated account by Anna Pavlovna, Queen of the Netherlands.

38. Gertrude Harris, *Diary*, 18/29 January 1778, *PRO*, 30/43.

39. Contemporary memoirs, e.g. of Mme Vigée Lebrun, Count Esterhazy, Countess Golovina, Adam Czartoryski, bear witness to the ease of life in Tsarskoye Selo.

40. Gertrude Harris, *Diary*, ibid.

41. Miranda, *Archivo*, II, p. 394 ; see also Engel'gardt, *Zapiski*, pp. 46–9.

42. Quoted in K. Waliszewski, *Le Roman d'une Impératrice*, 1892, p. 514.

43. *Consolidated Treaty Series*, 52, pp. 477ff., 3/14 September 1795.

44. *SIRIO*, 9, pp. 300ff, Catherine to General Budberg, 17/28 September 1796.

45. Ibid.

46. *Zapiski grafini Golovinoy*, ed. E.S. Shumigorsky, St Petersburg, 1900, p. 87.

47. *SIRIO*, 9, p. 316, Catherine to Budberg, 19/30 September 1796.

48. Shil'der, *Imperator Aleksandr*, p. 279.

49. See e.g. Shil'der, *Imperator Pavel Pervyy*, p. 273, n. 1 ; cf. also A. Czartoryski, *Memoirs*, I, p. 268. Interesting confirmation of the rumours is given by A.T. Bolotov, *Pamyatnik istekshikh vremyon*, quoted in Shil'der, op. cit., p. 275, n. 1.

50. According to other accounts it was F. Rostopchin and A.B. Kurakin who examined Catherine's papers in the presence of Alexander.

51. Quoted in Shil'der, *Imperator Pavel Pervyy*, p. 310.

52. P.K. Alefirenko, 'Krestyanskiye dvizheniya' . . . , p. 305. The Russian 'long in hair and short in wits' is almost identical with the Shakespearean version I have used.

53. G.A. Gukovksy, 'Podpol'naya poeziya XVIII veka'. Soviet moral censorship is such that this poem consists very largely of dots. I must thank my ex-colleagues Dr M. Kirkwood and Dr J. West for providing me with a complete version.

54. Information from Dr M. Branch.

55. A. Andreyev, *Raskol*, p. 277.

56. Shil'der, *Imperator Aleksandr Pervyy*, pp. 239–40, n. 218.

57. Quoted in Shil'der, *Imperator Aleksandr Pervyy*, pp. 279–80.

Conclusions

1. N.M. Karamzin, *Memoir on Ancient and Modern Russia*, p. 134.

2. W.M. Pintner, 'The Social Characteristics of the Early 19th Century Russian Bureaucracy', pp. 429–43. In the central government agencies civilian entry rose from 62·5 per cent in 1770–79 to 71·9 per cent in 1790–99, and in the provincial agencies from 9·4 per cent in 1770–79 to 15·2 per cent in 1790–99.

3. D. Geyer, ' "Gesellschaft" als staatliche Veranstaltung'.

4. Catherine's remarks on the zemskiy ispravnik and the English sheriff are in *RA*, 1908, p. 169.

5. 'Besedy imperatritsy Yekateriny II s Dalem', 31 December 1774 (p. 14), when Catherine incidentally remarks that the Empress Maria Theresa 'in spite of all her efforts has not made any progress' in the matter of the peasantry.

6. J.H. Hartley, seminar paper at the Institute of Historical Research, London, June 1979.

7. G.L. Yaney, *The Systematization of Russian Government*, pp. 20–1.

8. *PSZ*, XVI, No. 12,138, 22 April 1764.

9. Karamzin, op. cit., p. 131.

Bibliography

The Bibliography for a work of this kind is so vast that it would fill a companion volume. I have therefore endeavoured to cut it down by mentioning only those works cited in the text or the footnotes ; those works which I have found particularly illuminating, and relatively unfamiliar works which have helped to fill in the background.

Some aspects of the reign of Catherine have been extensively studied in the West by authors who have published very full bibliographies of their subjects. It seemed pointless to duplicate these, and I would accordingly refer readers to the works by J.T. Alexander and D. Peters for bibliographies of the *Pugachevshchina* ; to works by P. Dukes, R.E. Jones and M. Raeff on the nobility ; to the recent study by J.L. Black on education ; to the entries under J.M. Hittle and B. Knabe on towns ; to the unpublished dissertation by Z. Kohut for works on the Ukraine ; to N.N. Bolkhovitinov's work and to my own on foreign policy, and to the work of K.E. Dzhedzhula on Russia and the French revolution.

A selection of documents dealing with the Legislative Commission of 1767 has been published in several volumes of *SIRIO,* as well as some of Catherine's private and official – mainly diplomatic – correspondence, and letters and papers concerning the second and third partitions of Poland. In addition a vast amount of official and private correspondence has appeared in dribs and drabs, scattered over the pages of a number of historical journals, such as *Russkiy Arkhiv, Russkaya Starina,* etc. Unfortunately the bulk of Catherine's official correspondence dealing with domestic policy remains unpublished, though some of her drafts of laws have been the object of illuminating studies by e.g. M. Raeff, R.E. Jones or N.P. Pavlova Sil'vanskaya. But there are very serious gaps in the understanding of the empress's motives, or the sources of her inspiration, in some of the most important legislation of her reign.

In the interests of brevity I have not listed separately the documentary sources contained in the major collections such as the 148 volumes of *SIRIO,* or the even larger collection of *ChIOIDR,* and have listed only such sources as I have found useful from *Russkiy Arkhiv* and other historical journals.

Published documents and contemporary sources

Aleksandrova, E., 'Frantsuzskaya revolyutsiya 1789 g. v doneseniyakh russkogo posla v Parizhe, I.M. Simolina, *'Literaturnoye Nasledstvo,* 29–30, Moscow, 1937, pp. 343ff, 524ff.

[Alekseyev, P.] 'Iz bumag protoyereya Petra Alekseyeva', *RA,* 1882, II, pp. 76ff.

[Alexander I] *Correspondance de Frédéric César de la Harpe et Alexandre I,* ed. J.C. Biaudet and F. Nicod, 2 vols, La Baconnière, Neuchatel, 1978.

[Arkharov, N.P.] 'Iz bumag Nikolaya Petrovicha Arkharova', *RA,* No. 9, 1864, pp. 874ff.

Arkhiv gosudarstvennogo soveta, I, 2 vols, Sovet v tsarstvovaniye Yekateriny II, 1768–1796, ed. I.A. Chistovich, St Petersburg, 1869.

Arkhiv grafov Mordvynovykh, ed. V.A. Bil'basov, 10 vols, St Petersburg, 1901–3.

Arkhiv knyazya Vorontsova, ed. P. Bartenev, 40 vols, Moscow, 1870–95.

Arkhiv voyenno pokhodnoy kantselarii grafa P.A. Rumyantseva Zadunayskogo, ChIOIDR, 1865, No. 1, pp. 1–270 ; No. 2, pp. 1–310.

Asseburg, Freiherr Achatz Ferdinand von der, *Denkwürdigkeiten,* intr. by K.A. Varnhagen von Ense, Berlin, 1842.

Bibikov, A.A. *Zapiski o zhizni i sluzhbe Aleksandra Ilicha Bibikova,* Moscow, 1817.

Board of Education, *Special Reports on Educational Subjects,* vol. 23, Education in Russia, Cund. 4812, 1909.

BIBLIOGRAPHY

[Bolotov, A.T.] Zhizn' i priklyucheniya Andreya Bolotova, 1738–1793, 3 vols, Leningrad, 1931 ; ORP reprint, 1973.

Bruce, P.H., *Memoirs*, London, 1782.

[Buckinghamshire, John, Second Earl of] *The Dispatches of John, Second Earl of Buckinghamshire, 1762–65*, ed. A. Collyer, London, 1900.

[Bulgakov, Ya. I.] 'Iz bumag Ya. I. Bulgakova,' *RA*, 1905, No. 7, pp. 337–408.

[Catherine II] 'Besedy imperatritsy s Dalem, 1772–1777, *RS*, No. 17, pp. 1–20.

———— *Bibliothek der Grossfürsten Alexander und Konstantin, I.K. M. d.K. a. R.*, 4 vols, Berlin, 1784.

'Caterina e Aleksandr A. Vjasemkij', *Annali*, sezione slava, II, Naples, 1951, pp. 203–11.

Correspondence of Catherine the Great with Sir Charles Hanbury Williams, ed. the Earl of Ilchester, Thornton Butterworth Ltd, London, 1928.

———— *Mémoires*, parts I–VI, in *Sochineniya*, q.v.

———— *Memoirs*, ed. D. Maroger, Hamish Hamilton, London, 1955.

———— *Perepiska imperatritsy Yekateriny II s grafom Rumyantsevym Zadunayskim*, Moscow, 1805.

———— 'Perepiska s brat'yami Lyudovika XVI, grafom Provanskim i grafom d'Artua', *RA*, 1890, No. 2, pp. 1–17.

———— 'Perepiska s grafom Brounom', *Osmnadtsatyy vek*, ed. P. Bartenev, I, pp. 367–421.

———— 'Perepiska s knyazem M.N. Volkonskim', ibid., pp. 52–162.

———— *Perepiska s raznymi osobami*, St Petersburg, 1807.

———— *Pis'ma i bumagi imperatritsy Yekateriny II khranyashchiyesya v imperatorskoy publichnoy biblioteke*, ed. A. Bychkov, St Petersburg, 1873.

———— 'Pis'ma imperatritsy Yekateriny II k A.I. Bibikovu no vremya Pugachevskogo bunta', *RA*, 1866, No. 3, pp. 388–98.

———— 'Pis'ma imperatritsy Yekateriny II k grafu Ivanu Grigor'yevichu Chernyshevu, 1764–1773', *RA*, 1871, No. 9, pp. 1313ff.

———— *Pis'ma Yekateriny II k Adamu Vasil'yevichu Olsuf'yevu, 1762–1783*, ed. M.N. Longinov, Moscow, 1863.

———— 'Reskripty G.A. Potemkinu', 1791, *RA*, 1874, No. 2, pp. 246–58.

———— *Sochineniya*, ed. A.N. Pypin, 12 vols, St Petersburg, 1901.

———— 'Yekaterina i Potemkin : podlinnaya ikh perepiska, 1782–1791', *RS*, No. 16, 1876, pp. 33–58, 239–62, 441–78, 571–90 ; No. 17, pp. 21–38, 205–16, 403–26, 635–52.

———— 'Yekaterina II : sobstvennoruchnyyee ee poveleniya, pis'ma izametki, 1770–92', *RS*, No. 3, pp. 310–25, 474–84, 605–27, 689–99 ; No. 8, pp. 60–86, 212–20, 653–90, 853–84 ; No. 9, pp. 37–56, 285–300, 473–504 ; No. 11, pp. 489–96 ; No. 12, 384–90 ; No. 14, pp. 444–54.

———— 'Zapiska o merakh k vosstanovleniyu vo Frantsii korolevskogo pravi tel'stva', *RA*, 1866, No. 3, pp. 399ff.

———— Chappe d'Auteroche, Abbe, *Voyage en Siberie fait par ordre du roi en 1761*, 4 vols, Paris, 1768.

———— Derzhavin, G. Zapiski, *Sochineniya*, ed. Ya. Grot, 7 vols, St Petersburg, 1864–78, vol. 5.

Dmitriyev, I.I., *Vzglyad na moyu zhizn'*, ORP reprint, Cambridge, 1974.

Dokumenty i materialy po istorii Moskovskogo universiteta vo vtoroy polovine XVIII veka, 3 vols, ed. N.A. Penchko, Moscow, 1963.

Dolgoruky, I.M., 'Kapishche moego serdtsa', *RA*, 1890, No. 1, pp. 164ff.

Dubrovin, N. (ed.), *Prisoyedineniye Kryma k Rossii (Reskripty, pis'ma, relyatsii, doneseniya)*, 4 vols, St Petersburg, 1885–89.

Engel'gardt, L.N., *Zapiski, 1766–1836*, Moscow, 1868.

Esterhazy, Comte Valentin, *Lettres du comte Valentin Esterhazy à sa femme, 1784–1794*, ed. E. Daudet, Paris, 1907.

———— *Mémoires du Comte V. Esterhazy*, ed. E. Daudet, Paris, 1905.

654

BIBLIOGRAPHY

Fonvizin, D.I., *Sobraniye Sochineniy*, ed. G.P. Makogonenko, 2 vols, Moscow-Leningrad, 1959.

[Frederick II of Prussia] *Politische Correspondenz*, 46 vols, Berlin, 1879–1939.

Garnovsky, M., 'Zapiski Mikhaila Garnovskogo, 1786–1790', *RS*, No. 15, 1876, pp. 9–38, 237–65, 471–99, 687–720 ; No. 16, 1876, pp. 1–32, 207–38, 399–440.

Glinka, S.N., *Zapiski*, St Petersburg, 1895.

Goertz, J.E. von, *Mémoire sur la Russie*, ed. W. Stribrny, Wiesbaden, 1969.

Golitsyn, F.A., 'Zapiski', *RA*, 1874, No. 1, pp. 1271ff.

Golovina, Grafinya V.N., *Zapiski grafini Goloviny*, ed. S. Shumigorsky, St Petersburg, 1900.

Gribovsky, A.M., *Zapiski o Yekaterine Velikoy*, Moscow, 1847.

———— *Vospominaniya i dnevniki*, ed. P. Bartenev, Moscow, 1899.

Grot, Ya. K., 'Materialy dlya istorii Pugachevskogo bunta. Bumagi Kara i Bibikova', *Zapiski imp. ak. nauk*, Vol. I, prilozheniye No. 4, St Petersburg, 1862, pp. 21–65 ; 'perepiska imperatritsy Yekateriny II s grafom P.I. Paninym', ibid., III, prilozheniye No. 4, 1863, pp. 1–37 ; bumagi otnosyashchiyesya k poslednomu periodu myatezha, ibid., vol. XX, prilozheniye No. 4, 1874, pp. 1–144.

[Haxthausen, G.C.] 'Doneseniya datskogo poslannika Gakstgauzena o tsarstvovanii Petra III i perevorote 1762 goda', *RS*, No. 158, 1914, pp. 539–47 ; No. 160, 1914, pp. 70–80, 262–83, 504–12 ; No. 161, 1915, pp. 274–82, 532–44 ; No. 162, 1915, pp. 33–7, 295–8 ; No. 164, 1915, pp. 359–63.

Helbig, G. von, 'Potemkin der Taurier. Anecdoten zur Geschichte seines Lebens und seiner Zeit', *Minerva*, ein Journal historischen und politischen Inhalts herausgegeben von J.M. von Archenholtz : 1797, vol. 2, pp. 1–21 ; 425–57 ; vol. 3, pp. 105–24 ; 209–37 ; 453–67 ; vol. 4, pp. 110–32 ; 286–309 ; 1798, vol. 1, pp. 12–41 ; 355–73 ; 538–50 ; vol. 2, pp. 160–6 ; 291–319 ; 487–514 ; vol. 3, pp. 154–65 ; 214–33 ; vol. 4, pp. 76–106 ; 300–311 ; 462–84 ; 1799, vol. 1, pp. 145–79 ; 357–76 ; 510–31 ; vol. 2, pp. 67–80 ; 406–31 ; vol. 3, pp. 113–31 ; 427–33 ; 1800, vol. 1, pp. 38–46 ; 433–9 ; vol. 2, pp. 99–108 ; 308–15 ; vol. 3, 514–27 ; vol. 4, pp. 509–47.

[Gelbig, Georg von] *Russkiye izbranniki*, tr. and ed. by V.A. Bil'basov, Berlin, 1900.

Korobkov, N.M., *Fel'dmarshal Rumyanstev. Sbornik Dokumentov i materialov*, Moscow, 1947.

Lopukhin, I.V., *Zapiski I.V. Lopukhina*, London, 1860 ; ORP reprint, 1976.

Lubyanovsky, F.P., 'Vospominaniya,' *RA*, 1872, No. 1, pp. 98–185.

Macartney, G., *The Present State of Russia*, London, 1768.

Maslovsky, D.F., 'Pis'ma i bumagi A.V. Suvorova, G.A. Potemkina i P.A. Rumyantseva 1787–1789gg. Kinburn Ochakovskaya operatsiya', *Sbornik voyenno-istoricheskikh materialov*, vyp. IV, St Petersburg, 1893.

Masson, C.F.P., *Mémoires secrets sur la Russie*, 5 vols, Paris, 1800.

Mertvago, D.B., 'Zapiski Dmitriya Borisovicha Mertvago, 1760—1824'. *RA*, 1867, Supplement.

Minikh, I.E., *Zapiski pisannyye dlya detey*, St Petersburg, 1817.

[Miranda, Francisco de] *Archivo del General Miranda*, vol. II, 1785–7, Caracas, 1929.

Neplyuyev, I.I., *Zapiski (1693–1773)*, St Petersburg, 1893 ; ORP reprint, 1974.

Polnoye Sobraniye Zakonov Rossiyskoy Imperii s 1649 goda, first series, St Petersburg, 1836 *(PSZ)*.

Poniatowski, Stanislas Augustus, *Mémoires*, 2 vols, St Petersburg, 1914.

Poroshin, S.A., *Zapiski*, St Petersburg, 1881.

[Potemkin-Tavricheskiy, Knyaz' G.A.] *Bumagi knyazya Grigoriya Aleksandrovicha Potemkina-Tavricheskogo*, ed. N.F. Dubrovin, Sbornik voyenno-istoricheskikh materialov, vypusk VI, *1774–88*, St Petersburg, 1893 ; vypusk VIII, *1790–93*, St Petersburg, 1895.

———— 'Knyaz' Grigory Aleksandrovich Potemkin-Tavricheskiy, 1739–91. Biograficheskiy ocherk po neizdannym materialam'. *RS*, 1875 ; No. 12, pp. 451–522, 587–700 ; No. 13, pp. 20–40, 159–74 ; No. 14, pp. 217–67.

———— Rasporyazheniya svetleyshogo knyazya Grigorya Aleksandrovicha Potemkina Tavricheskogo kasatel'no ustroyeniyu Tavricheskoy oblasti s 1781 po 1786 gg', *ZIOOID*, 12, Odessa, 1881, pp. 249–329.

BIBLIOGRAPHY

—— 'Sobstvennoruchnyye bumagi knyazya Potemkina', *RA*, 1865, pp. 721ff.

Pronshteyn A.P. (ed.), *Don i Nizhneye Povol'zhe v period krest'yanskoy voyny 1773–1775 godov.* Sbornik dokumentov, Rostov, 1961.

[Pugachev, E.I.] *Dokumenty stavki E.I. Pugacheva, povstancheskikh vlastey i uchrezhdeniy, 1773–1774 gg,* ed. P.V. Ovchinikov et al., Moscow, 1975.

—— *Pugachevshchina,* ed. S.A. Golubtsovyy, S.G. Tomsinsky and G.E. Meyerson, 3 vols, I, 1926, II, 1929, III, 1931.

Richardson, W., *Anecdotes of the Russian Empire,* London, 1784, Frank Cass reprint, London, 1968.

Rulhière, C. de, *Histoire ou Anecdotes sur la Révolution en Russie,* Paris, 1797.

[Rumyantsev, P.A.] *P.A. Rumyantsev,* ed. P.K. Fortunatov, 2 vols, Moscow, 1953.

Senatskiy Arkhiv, 15 vols, St Petersburg, 1888–1913.

Shakhovskoy, Ya. P., *Zapiski 1709–77,* St Petersburg, 1872 ; ORP reprint, 1974.

Shcherbatov, M.M., *On the Corruption of Morals,* tr. and ed. by A. Lentin, Cambridge University Press, 1969.

—— 'Zamechaniya na Bol'shoy Nakaz Yekateriny II', *Neizdannyye Sochineniya,* Moscow, 1935, pp. 16–63.

Shteyngel', Baron, 'Zapiski' in V.I. Semevsky (ed.), *Obshchestvennyye dvizheniya v Rossii v pervuyu polovinu XIX veka,* I, St Petersburg, 1905.

Tuchkov, S.A., *Zapiski 1766–1808,* St Petersburg, 1908.

Vigée Lebrun, Madame E., *Souvenirs,* 2 vols, Paris, 1867.

Vigel', F.F., *Zapiski,* 2 vols, Moscow, 1928 ; ORP reprint, 1973.

Vinsky, G.S., *Moe vremya,* with introduction by I. de Madariaga, ORP reprint, 1974.

'Vokrug Ochakova – 1788 (Dnevnik ochevidtsa)', *RS,* No. 84, September 1895, pp. 147–211.

Yelagin, I.P., 'Povest' o sebe samom', *RA,* No. 1, 1864, pp. 93–110.

Zinov'yev, V.N., *Puteshestvennyye zapiski Vasily Zuyeva ot St Peterburga do Khersona v 1781 i 1782 goda,* St Petersburg, 1787.

Secondary works

Absolyutizm v Rossii (XVII–XVIII vv.) Sbornik statey k semidesyatiletiyu . . . B.B. Kafengauza, ed. N.N. Druzhinin et al, Moscow, 1964.

Adamczyk, T., *Fürst G.A. Potemkin,* Emsdetten, 1936.

Afanas'yeva, T.A. 'Reyestry knig XVIII veka v Moskovskoy Sinodal' noy Tipografii' in Sidorov, A.A. and Luppov, S.P., *Kniga v Rossii do serediny XIX veka,* Leningrad, 1978, pp. 169–76.

Aksakov, S.T., *Detskiye gody Bagrova vnuka,* Moscow, 1954.

Alefirenko, P.K., 'Chumnyy bunt v Moskve v 1771 g', *VI,* 4, 1947, pp. 82ff.

—— 'Pravitel'stvo Yekateriny i frantzuzskaya burzhuaznaya revolyutsiya 1789 goda', *IZ,* No. 22, 1967, pp. 206–51.

—— *Krest'yanskoye dvizheniye i krest'yanskiy vopros v Rossii v 30–50kh godakh XVIII veka,* Moscow, 1958.

—— 'Obshchestvennyye dvizheniya v Moskve vo vtoroy polovine XVIII stoletiya', *Izvestiya ANSSR,* Seriya Istoriya i Filozofiya, t. IV, No. 6, 1947, pp. 521–35.

Aleksandrov, P.A., *Severnaya Sistema,* Moscow, 1914.

Aleksandrov, V.A., 'Sel'skaya obshchina i votchina v Rossi XVII-nachalo XIX v.' in *IZ,* No. 89, 1972, pp. 231–94.

—— *Sel'skaya obshchina v Rossi (XVII – nachalo XIX v.)* Moscow, 1976.

Alexander, J.T., *Emperor of the Cossacks,* Larrami, Kansas, 1973.

—— 'Soviet Historiography on the Pugachev Revolt : A Review Article', *CSS,* IV, Fall 1970, pp. 602–17.

—— *The Politics of Autocracy in a National Crisis : the Imperial Government and Pugachev's Revolt, 1773–1775,* Indiana University Press, Bloomington, Indiana, 1969.

BIBLIOGRAPHY

Alexeiev, N.N., 'Beiträge zur Geschichte des russischen Absolutismus im 18.ten Jahrhundert', *FOG*, Band 6, Berlin, 1958, pp. 7–81.

Allen, W.E.D., *A History of the Georgian People*, Trench, Trubner and Co, London, 1932.

Amburger, E., *Geschichte der Behördenorganisation Russlands von Peter dem Grossen bis 1917*, E.J. Brill, Leyden, 1966.

—— *Geschichte des Protestantismus in Russland*, Evangelisches Verlagswerk, Stuttgart, 1961.

—— *Russland und Schweden, 1762–1772. Die Schwedische Verfassung und die Ruhe des Nordens*, Berlin, 1934.

Anderson, M.S., 'Great Britain and the Growth of the Russian Navy in the Eighteenth Century', *Mariners Mirror*, 42, 1956, pp. 132–78.

—— 'Great Britain and the Russian Fleet, 1769–70', *SEER*, XXXI, 76, December 1952, pp. 148–63.

—— 'Great Britain and the Russo-Turkish War of 1768–74', *EHR*, LXIX, 1954, pp. 39–58.

——'Russia in the Mediterranean, 1788–1791 : A Little-Known Chapter in the History of Naval Warfare and Privateering, *Mariner's Mirror*, 45, No. 1, February 1959, pp. 25–35.

Anderson, R.C., 'British and American Officers in the Russian Navy', *Mariners Mirror*, 33, 1947, pp. 17–27.

—— *Naval Wars in the Baltic during the Sailing Ship Epoch, 1522–1850*, Gilbert Wood, London, 1910.

—— *Naval Wars in the Levant, 1559–1853*, University Press, Liverpool.

Andreescu, C.I., 'La France et la politique orientale de Catherine II d'après les rapports des ambassadeurs français à St Petersbourg', *Mélanges de l'Ecole roumaine en France*, v, Paris, 1927, pp. 3–155.

Andreyev, V.V., *Raskol i ego znacheniye v narodnoy russkoy istorii, Istoricheskiy ocherk*, St Petersburg, 1870.

Andrushchenko, A.I., 'Klassovaya bor'ba yaitskikh kazakov nakanune krest'yanskoy voyny 1773—5,' *Istoriya SSSR*, 1, 1960, pp. 149ff.

—— *Krest'yanskaya voyna*, Moscow, 1969.

—— 'Pugachevskoye vosstaniye i Kyuchuk kaynardzhiyskiy mir' in *Voprosy voyennoy istorii Rossii XVIII i pervaya polovina XIX vekov*, Moscow, 1969, pp. 339–42.

d'Aragon, L.A.C., *Un paladin au XVIIIe siècle. Le Prince Charles de Nassau Siegen*, Paris, 1893.

Arneth, A. von, *Joseph II und Katharina von Russland : Ihr Briefwechsel*, Vienna, 1869.

—— *Maria Theresias letzte Regierungszeit, 1763–1780*, 4 vols, Vienna, 1879.

—— *Maria Theresia und Joseph II, Ihre Correspondenz*, 3 vols, Vienna, 1867.

—— and Flammermont, J., *Correspondance secrète du Comte de Mercy Argenteau avec l'Empereur Joseph II et le Prince de Kaunitz*, 2 vols, Paris, 1889.

Arnold Barton, H., 'Russia and the Problem of Sweden-Finland, 1721–1809', *East European Quarterly*, v, no. 4, pp. 431–55.

Artemev, A., 'Kazanskiye gimnazii v XVIII v.' in *ZHMNP*, 24, July 1874, pp. 20ff.

Askenazy, S., *Die letzte polnische Königswahl*, Göttingen, 1894.

Auerbach, H., *Die Besiedelung der Südukraine in den Jahren 1774–1787*, Wiesbaden, 1965.

Babkin, D.S., *Protsess A.N. Radishcheva*, Moscow-Leningrad, 1952.

Baburin, D., *Ocherki po istorii Manufaktur Kollegii*, Moscow, 1939.

Bacmeister, H.L.C., *Russische Bibiothek zur Kenntniss des gegenwärtiger Zustandes der Litteratur in Russland*, 11 vols, St Petersburg, Riga and Leipzig, 1772–89.

Baehr, S., ' "Fortuna Redux" : The Courtly Spectacle in Eighteenth Century Russia,' *Great Britain and Russia in the Eighteenth Century : Contacts and Comparisons*, ed. A.G. Cross, q.v.

—— 'The Masonic Component in Eighteenth Century Literature', *Russian Literature in the Age of Catherine the Great*, ed. A.G. Cross, q.v.

Bagaley, D., 'Nasledniki Zaporozhskikh zemel' ', *Kievskaya Starina*, 1885, April, pp. 783–90.

Bak, I.S., 'Dmitri Aleksandrovich Golitsyn', *IZ*, No. 26, 1948, pp. 258ff.

Bantych Kamensky, D., *Istoriya Maloy Rossii*, 3 vols, Moscow, 1842.

BIBLIOGRAPHY

Baron, S.W., *The Russian Jew under Tsar and Soviets,* Russian Civilization Series, Macmillan, New York, 1964.

Barskov, P., 'Proekty voyennykh reform tsesarevicha Pavla', *Russkiy istoricheskiy zhurnal,* 1, vol. 3–4, Petrograd, 1917.

Barkov, Ya. L., *Perepiska moskovskikh masonov XVIII veka,* Petrograd, 1915.

Barsukov, A.R., 'Knyaz' Grigoriy Grigorevich Orlov,' *RA,* 1873, No. 1, pp. 1–146.

Barsukov, D.P., *Raszkazy iz russkoy istorii XVIII veka po arkhyvnym dokumentam,* St Petersburg, 1885.

Bartenev, P.B., *Graf A.I. Morkov, Biografiya,* Moscow, 1857.

―――― *Vosemnadtsatyy vek, Istoricheskiy sbornik,* 4 vols, Moscow, 1868–9.

Bartlett, R., *Human Capital, The Settlement of Foreigners in Russia, 1762–1804,* Cambridge University Press, 1979.

Beccaria, C., *Delle delitte e delle pene,* ed. F. Venturi, Einaudi, Turin, 1965.

Beer, A., *Die erste Theilung Polens,* 3 vols., Vienna, 1873.

―――― *Die Orientalische Politik Oesterreichs seit 1774,* Prague, 1883.

―――― *Joseph II, Leopold II und Kaunitz. Ihr Briefwechsel,* Vienna, 1873.

―――― *Leopold II Franz II, und Catharina, Ihre Correspondenz, nebst eine Einleitung zur Geschichte der Politik Leopold's II,* Leipzig, 1874.

Beer, A. and Fiedler, J., *Joseph II und Graf Ludwig Cobenzl : Ihr Briefwechsel,* 2 vols, Fontes Rerum Austriacarum, Vienna, 1873.

Belorussiya v epokhu feodalizma, 3 vols, Academy of Sciences of Belorussia, Minsk, 1961.

Belyavsky, M.T., *Krest'yanskiy vopros v Rossii nakanune vosstaniya Pugacheva,* Moscow, 1965.

―――― *M.V. Lomonosov i osnovaniye Moskovskogo Universiteta,* Moscow, 1955.

―――― 'Novikovskoye Avdot'ino v 1792 g', in *Problemy istorii obshchestvennogo dvizheniya i istoriografii. K 70-letiyu akademika M.V. Nechkinoy,* Moscow, 1971, pp. 49–61.

―――― 'Trebovaniya dvoryan i perestroyka organov upravleniya i suda na mestakh v 1775 g', *Nauchnyye doklady vysshey shkoly istoricheskikh nauk,* No. 4, 1960, pp. 125–43.

―――― 'Vopros o krepostnom prave i polozheniye krest'yan v Nakaze Yekateriny II', *Vestnik Moskovskogo Universiteta,* seriya IX, Istoriya, 1963, No. 6, pp. 44–63.

Bernadsky, V.N. (ed.), *Ocherki po istorii klassovoy bor'by i obshchestvenno-politicheskoy mysli Rossii tret'yey chetverti XVIII v.,* Leningrad, 1962.

Beskrovnyy, L.G., *Khrestomatiya po russkoy voyennoy istorii,* Moscow, 1947.

―――― *Russkaya armiya i flot v XVIII veke (Ocherki),* Moscow, 1958.

Bienemann, F., *Die Statthalterschaftszeit in Liv- und Estland 1783–1796,* Leipzig, 1886.

Bil'basov, V.A., *Didro v Peterburge, 1773–4,* St Petersburg, 1884.

―――― *Istoriya Yekateriny II,* 2 vols, Berlin, 1900.

―――― *Istoricheskiye monografii,* St Petersburg, 1901.

Bill, Valentine, *The Forgotten Class. The Russian Bourgeoisie from the Earliest Beginnings to 1900,* Praeger, New York, 1959.

Billington, J., *The Icon and the Axe, An Interpretive History of Russian Culture,* Alfred A. Knopf, New York, 1966.

Bindoff, S.T., *The Scheldt Question to 1839,* Allen and Unwin, London, 1945.

Black, J.L., *Citizens for the Fatherland. Education, Educators and Pedagogical Ideals in Eighteenth Century Russia,* East European Quarterly, Columbia University Press, New York, 1979.

Blackwell, W., 'The Old Believers and the Rise of Private Industrial Enterprise in Early 19th Century Moscow', *Slavic Review,* 24, No. 3, 1965, pp. 407–24.

Blinov, I., *Gubernatory. Istoriko-yuridicheskiy ocherk,* St Petersburg, 1905.

Blum, J., *Lord and Peasant in Russia from the Ninth to the Nineteenth Century,* Princeton University Press, 1961.

Blum, K.L., *Ein russischer Stattsmann. Des Grafen Jakob Johann Sievers Denkwürdigkeiten zur Geschichte Russlands,* 4 vols, Leipzig and Heidelberg, 1857.

BIBLIOGRAPHY

Bochkarev, V.N., 'Kulturnyye zaprosy russkogo obshchestva nachala tsarastvovaniya Yekateriny II po materialam zakonodatel'noy kommissii 1767 goda', *RS*, No. 161, 1915, pp. 64–72 ; 283–96 ; 545–60 ; No. 162, pp. 38–59, 312–25.

────── *Voprosy politiki v russkom parlamente XVIII goda. Opyt izucheniya politicheskoy ideologii XVIII veka*, Moskow, 1923.

Bogolyubov, V., *N.I. Novikov i ego vremya*, Moscow, 1916.

Bogoslovsky, M.M. 'Dvoryanskiye nakazy v yekaterininskuyu kommissiyu 1767 g.', *Russkoye Bogatstvo*, St Petersburg, June, 1897, pp. 46–83 ; July, pp. 136–52.

Bolkhovitinov, N.N., *Stanovleniye russko-amerikanskikh otnosheniy 1775–1815*, Moscow, 1966.

Borovoy, S. Ya., *Kredit i banki Rossii (seredina XVII v-1861 g.)*, Moscow, 1958.

Brandt, O., *Caspar von Saldern und die nordeuropäische Politik im Zeitalter Katharinas II*, Erlangen and Kiel, 1932.

Brevern de la Gardie, Comtesse de, *Un ambassadeur de Suède à la cour de Catherine II. Feld Maréchal Comte de Stedingk. Choix de dépèches diplomatiques, rapports secrets et lettres particulières de 1790 à 1796*, 2 vols, Stockholm, 1919.

Brown, A.H., 'Adam Smith's First Russian Followers', in Skinner, A. and Wilson, T., (eds), *Adam Smith, Bicentenary Essays*, Oxford, 1974.

────── 'S.E. Desnitsky, Adam Smith and the Nakaz of Catherine II', *Oxford Slavonic Papers*, New Series, Vol. VII, Oxford, 1974, pp. 42–59.

──────'S.E. Desnitsky, i I.A. Tret'yakov v Glazgovskom Universitete, 1761–1767', *Vestnik Moskovskogo Universiteta*, No. 4, 1969, pp. 75–88.

Brownlow, J., *The History and Design of the Foundling Hospital*, London, 1858.

Brückner, A., *Katharina Die Zweite*, Berlin, 1883.

────── *Potemkin*, St Petersburg, 1891.

────── 'Puteshestviye Yekateriny II v poludennyy kray Rossii v 1787 goda', *ZhMNP*, 1872, No. 162, section 2, pp. 1–51.

────── 'Razryv mezhdu Rossiey i Turtsiey v 1787 godu', *ZhMNP*, 1873, No. 168, pp. 128–70.

──────'Schweden und Russland 1788', *HZ*, No. 22, 1869, pp. 314–402.

Buchholtz, A., *Geschichte der Juden in Riga*, Riga, 1899.

Burgess, M., 'Russian Public Theatre Audiences of the 18th and Early 19th Centuries,' *SEER*, 37, No. 88, pp. 160ff.

Burke, E., *Correspondence*, 4 vols, London, 1844.

Butler, W.E., 'The Nakaz of Catherine the Great', *The American Book Collector*, XVI, No. 5, 1966, pp. 19–21.

Cambridge History of Foreign Policy, 1783–1919, I, 1783–1815, by A.W. Ward and G.P. Gooch, Macmillan, New York, 1922.

Chechulin, N.D., 'Ob istochnikakh nakaza', *ZhMNP*, 1902, April, pp. 306–17.

────── *Ocherki po istorii russkikh finansov v tsarstvovaniye Yekateriny II*, St Petersburg, 1906.

────── 'Proekt imperatorskogo soveta v pervyy god tsarstvovaniya Yekateriny II', *ZHMNP*, No. 292, 1894, pp. 68ff.

────── *Russkoye provintsial'noye obshchestvo vo vtoroy polovine XVIII veka*, St Petersburg, 1889.

──────*Vneshnyaya politika Rossii v nachale tsarstvovaniye Yelateriny II, 1762–1774*, St Petersburg, 1896.

────── *Nakaz Imperatritsky Yekateriny II dannyy kommissii po sochineniyu proekta novogo ulozheniya*, Moscow, 1907.

────── *Yekaterina v bor'be za prestol*, Leningrad, 1924.

Chevigny, H., *Russian America. The Great Alaskan Venture, 1741–1867*, Viking Press, New York, 1965.

Chistov, K.V., *Russkiye narodnyye sotsial'no utopicheskiye legendy*, Moscow, 1967.

Chistovich, I., *Istoricheskaya zapiska o sovete v tsarstvovaniye imperatritsy Yekateriny II*, St Petersburg, 1870.

BIBLIOGRAPHY

Christie, I.R., 'Samuel Bentham and the Russian Dnieper Flotilla', *SEER*, L, No. 119, April 1972, pp. 173–97.

———'Samuel Bentham and the Western Colony at Krichev, 1784–87', *SEER*, XLVIII, No. 111, April 1970, pp. 232–47.

Chulkov, N.P., 'Moskovskoye kupechestvo XVIII I XIX vv', *RA*, Vol. 3, No. 12, 1907, pp. 489–502.

Cizova, T., 'Beccaria in Russia,' *SEER*, XL, No. 95, 1962, pp. 384–409.

Colin de Terrail, H., *La Finlande et les Russes depuis les Croisades Suédoises*, Paris/Strasbourg, 1963.

Confino, M., *Domaines et Seigneurs en Russie vers la fin du XVIIIᵉ siècle. Étude de structures agraires et de mentalités économiques*, Collection historique de l'Institut d'Etudes Slaves, XVIII, Paris, 1963.

——— *Systèmes agraires et progrès agricole : L'assolement triennal en Russie aux XVIIIᵉ et XIXᵉ siècles*, Paris/The Hague, 1969.

———'Seigneurs et intendants en Russie au XVIIIᵉ et XIXᵉ siecles', *Revue d'Études Slaves*, Paris, 1962, pp. 61–91.

Conybeare, F.C., *Russian Dissenters*, Harvard Theological Studies, 10, Cambridge, Mass., 1921.

Coquin, F.-X., *La Grande Commission Legislative (1767–1768). Les Cahiers de Doléances urbains*, Louvain and Paris, 1972.

Corberon, Marie Daniel Bourrée de, *Journal Intime: Un Diplomate français à la cour de Catherine II, 1775–1780*, 2 vols, Paris, 1901.

Cotta, S., 'L'illuminisme et la science politique : Montesquieu, Diderot et Catherine II', *Revue internationale d'histoire politique et constitutionelle*, Nouvelle série, No. 16, October–December 1954, pp. 273–87.

Coxe, W., *Travels into Poland, Russia Sweden and Denmark*, 2 vols, London, 1784, Supplementary volume 3, London 1790.

——— *An Account of the Prisons and Hospitals in Russia, Sweden and Denmark*, London, 1781.

Cross, A.G., 'Chaplains to the British Factory in St Petersburg, 1723–1813', *European Studies Review*, Vol. 2, No. 2, April 1972, pp. 125–42.

——— (ed.), *Great Britain and Russia in the Eighteenth Century : Contacts and Comparisons*, Proceedings of an International Conference, 11–15 July 1977, Oriental Research Partners, Newtonville, Mass., 1979.

——— 'Russian Students in Eighteenth Century Oxford (1766–1775) ; *European Studies Review*, Vol. 5, 1975, pp. 91–110.

——— 'Samuel Greig, Catherine the Great's Scottish Admiral', *Mariner's Mirror*, 60, 1976, pp. 251–66.

——— (ed.), *Russian Literature in the Age of Catherine the Great*, Willem A. Meeuws, Oxford, 1976.

——— 'Vasiliy Petrov v Anglii (1772–1776)' in *XVIII vek*, No. 11, Leningrad, 1976.

Czartoryski, Prince Adam, *Memoirs*, 2 vols, London, 1888.

Daniel, W., 'The Merchantry and the Problem of Social Order in the Russian State: Catherine II's Commission of Commerce', *SEER*, Vol. 55, No. 2. April 1977, pp. 185–203.

Danielson, J.R., *Die Nordische Frage in den Jahren 1746–51*, Helsingfors, 1888.

Danske Tractater, 1751–1800, 4 vols, Copenhagen, 1874–82.

Dashkova, Princess E.D., *Memoirs*, ed. K. Fitzlyon, John Calder, London, 1958.

——— 'Delo ob Arsenii Matseyeviche', *ChIOIDR*, 1862, No. 3, pp. 134ff.

Dembinski, B., *Documents relatifs à l'histoire du deuxième et troisième partages de la Pologne*, I, 1788–1791, L'vov, 1902.

Demidova, N.F., 'Byurokratizatsiya gosudarstvennogo apparata absolyutizma v XVII–XVIII vv' in *Absolyutizm v Rossii*, ed. N.M. Druzhinin, q.v.

BIBLIOGRAPHY

Demkov, M.I., *Istoriya russkoy pedagogiki II. Novaya russkaya pedagogika XVIII vek*, Moscow, 1910.

Diderot, D., *Oeuvres Complètes*, ed. J. Assézat and M. Tourneux, 20 vols, Paris, 1875–77.

—— *Mémoires pour Catherine II*, ed. P. Vernière, Garnier, Paris, 1966.

—— *Oeuvres politiques*, ed. P. Vernière, Garnier, Paris, 1963.

Dityatin, I.I., *Ustroistvo i upravleniye gorodov v Rossii*, 2 vols, Moscow, 1875–7.

Dmitrenko, I.I. (ed.), *Sbornik istoricheskikh materialov po istorii kazacheskogo voiska*, I, 1737–1901, St Petersburg, 1896.

Dmitriyev, F., *Istoriya sudebnykh instantsii i grazhdanskogo apellatsionnogo sudoproizvodstva ot sudebnika do uchrezhdeniya o guberniyakh*, Moscow, 1959.

Donnelly, A., *The Russian Conquest of Bashkiria, 1552–1740*, Yale University Press, 1968.

Drage, C.L., *Russian Literature in the Eighteenth Century*, n.p. London, 1978.

Druzhinin, N.M. (ed.), *Absolyutizm v Rossii (XVII–XVIII vv.) Sbornik statey k semidesyatiletiyu . . . B.B. Kafengauza*, Moscow, 1964.

Druzhinina, E.I., *Kyuchuk-Kaynardzhiyskiy mir 1774 goda*, Moscow, 1955.

—— *Severnoye prichernomor'ye v 1775–1780 gg.* Moscow, 1959.

Dubasov, I., 'Tambovskiy kray v koktse XVIII ; nachale XIX st.', *Russiy Vestnik*, 18, 1884 ; pp. 103—38 ; 17, 1884, pp. 313–39, 551–83.

Dubnow, S.M., *History of the Jews in Russia and Poland*, 3 vols, Philadelphia, 1916–20.

Dubrovin, N., *Pugachev i ego soobshchniki*, 3 vols, St Petersburg, 1884.

Dukes, P., *Catherine the Great and the Russian Nobility. A Study based on the materials of the Legislative Commission of 1767*, Cambridge University Press, 1967.

Duran, James A., 'The Reform of Financial Administration in Russia during the Reign of Catherine II', *CSS*, IV, Fall 1970, pp. 483–96.

Dvoryanstvo i krepostnoy stroy v Rossii XVI–XVIII vv. Sbornik posvyyashchennyy pamyati A.A. Novosel'skogo, Moscow, 1975.

Dzhedzhula, K.E., *Rossiya i velikaya frantzuzskaya burzhuaznaya revolyutsiya kontsa XVIII veka*, Kiev University Press, 1972.

Dzhincharadze, V.Z., 'Iz istorii taynoy ekspeditsii pri Senate (1762–1801 gg.)', *Uchenye Zapiski Novgorodskogo gos. ped. instituta*, ist. filolog. fakultet, II, No. 2, 1957, pp. 83–118.

Edgerton, W.B., 'Laying a Legend to Rest. The Poet Kapnist and Ukrainian German Intrigue', *Slavic Review*, September 1971, xxx, No. 3, pp. 551–60.

Eeckaute, Denise, 'Les Brigands en Russie du XVIIᵉ au XIXᵉ Siècle. Mythe et réalité', *Revue d'histoire moderne et contemporaine*, XII, July/September 1965, pp. 161–202.

Efimenko, P.S., 'Kal'nyshevsky, poslednyy koshevoy ataman Zaporozhskoy sechi', *RS*, 1875, No. 14 November, pp. 405–20.

Ehrman, J., *The British Government and Commercial Negotiations with Europe, 1783–1793*, Cambridge University Press, 1963.

—— *The Younger Pitt. The Years of Acclaim*, Constable, London, 1969.

El'yashevich, V.B., *Istoriya prava pozemel'noy sobstvennosti v Rossii*, 2 vols, Paris, 1951.

Emmons, T., *The Emancipation of the Serfs*, Holt Rinehart and Winston, New York, 1970.

Eyngorn, V.O., 'Vospitatel'nyye zavedeniya pri Moskovskom glavnom narodnom uchilishche 1780–1803', in *Sbornik statey v chesti M.K. Lyubavskogo*, Petrograd, 1917, pp. 490–523.

Fateyev, A.M., *Potemkin Tavricheskiy*, Prague, 1945.

Filippov, A.N., 'K voprosu o pervoistochnikakh zhalovannoy gramoty dvoryanstvu', *Izvestiya ANSSR*, 6th series, xx, Nos 5–6, January–May 1926, pp. 430–44.

Firsov, N.I., *Pravitel'stvo i obshchestvo v ikh otnosheniyakh k vneshney torgovle Rossii v tsarstvovaniye imperatritsy Yekateriny II*, Kazan', 1902.

Fisher, A.W., 'Enlightened Despotism and Islam under Catherine II', *Slavic Review*, XXVII, 1968, pp. 542–53.

—— *The Russian Annexation of the Crimea 1772–1783*, Cambridge University Press, 1970.

BIBLIOGRAPHY

Fleischacker, Hedwig, 'Porträt Peters III', *JGOE*, v, Nos 1–2, 1957, pp. 127ff.

Florovsky, A.V., *Iz istorii Yekaterininskoy zakonodatel'noy kommissii 1767 g. Vopros o krepostnom prave*, Odessa, 1910.

—— *Sostav zakonodatel'noy kommissii 1767–74 gg.* Odessa, 1915.

—— 'Un légiste français au service de la Tsarine Catherine II,' *Revue historique du droit français et étranger*, 1924, pp. 515–31.

Foust, C.M., *Muscovite and Mandarin. Russia's Trade with China and Its Setting, 1727–1805*, University of North Carolina Press, 1969.

Freeze, G., 'Social Mobility and the Russian Parish Clergy in the Eighteenth Century', *Slavic Review*, xxxiii, 1974, pp. 641–62.

—— *The Russian Levites. Parish Clergy in the Eighteenth Century*, Harvard University Press, 1977.

Galante Garrone, A., *Gilbert Romme. Storia di un rivoluzionario*, Einaudi, Turin, 1959.

Garrard, J.G. (ed.), *The Eighteenth Century in Russia*, Clarendon Press, Oxford, 1973.

Geffroy, A., *Gustave III et la Cour de France*, Paris, 1867.

Gerhardt, D., *England und der Aufstieg Russlands*, Munich and Berlin, 1933.

German, I.E., *Istoriya russkogo mezhevaniya*, Moscow, 1910.

Gernet, M., *Istoriya tsarskoy tyur'my 1762–1825*, 5 vols, Moscow, 1960–63.

Gessen, Yu., *Istoriya yevreyskogo naroda v Rossii*, 2 vols, Leningrad, 1925–7.

—— *Zakon i zhizn'. Kak sozidalis' ogranichnyye zakony o zhitel'stve v Rossii*, St Petersburg, 1911.

Geyer, D., 'Gesellschaft als Staatliche Veranstaltung', *JGOE*, 14, 1966, pp. 21ff.

—— 'Staatsaufbau und Sozialverfassung. Probleme des russischen Absolutismus am Ende des 18. Jahrhunderts', *CMRS*, vii, No. 3, July–September 1966, pp. 366–77.

Golikova, N.V., 'Organy politicheskogo ssylka i ikh razvitiye v XVII–XVIII vv.' in *Absolyutizm v Rossii*, q.v.

Golobutsky, V.A., *Chernomorskoye kazachestvo*, Kiev, 1956.

—— *Zaporozhskoye kazachestvo*, Kiev, 1957.

—— *Zaporozhskaya Sech v posledniye vremena svoego sushchestvovaniya, 1734–1775*, Kiev, 1961.

Gorodetzky, N., *St. Tikhon Zadonsky, Inspirer of Dostoyevsky*, SPCK, London, 1951.

Got'ye, Yu. V., *Istoriya oblastnogo upravleniya v Rossii ot Petra I do Yekateriny II*, 2 vols, i, Moscow, 1913; ii, 1941.

—— *Ocherki istorii zemlevladeniya v Rossii*, Sergiyev Posad, 1915.

—— 'Otzyvy gubernatorov shestidesyatikh godov XVIII veka ob oblastnom upravlenii' in *Sbornik statey v chesti M.K. Lyubavskogo*, Petrograd, 1917.

—— Review of A.V. Florovsky, *Krepostnoy vopros . . .* (q.v.) in *ZhMNP*, November 1916, pp. 83ff.

Gradovsky, A.D., *Verkhovnoye upravleniye v Rossii i general prokurory*, St Petersburg, 1899.

Green, M., 'Masonry, Kheraskov and Mozart: A Footnote' in Study Group in Eighteenth Century Russia: *Newsletter No 7*, September 1979.

Gribovsky, V.M., *Vysshiy sud i nadzor v Rossii v pervuyu polovinu tsarstvovaniya Yekateriny II*, St Petersburg, 1901.

Griffiths, D.M., 'The Rise and Fall of the Northern System: Court Politics and Foreign Policy in the First Half of Catherine II's Reign', *CSS*, iv, No. 3, Fall 1970, pp. 547–69.

Grigorovich, N., *Kantsler Knyaz' A.A. Bezborodko v svyazi s sobytiyami ego vremeni, SIRIO*, 26 and 29.

Grigor'yev, V., *Reforma mestnogo upravleniya pri Yekaterine*, St Petersburg, 1910.

Gukovsky, G.A., *Ocherki po istorii russkoy literatury XVIII veka. Dvoryanskaya fronda 1750–1760kh godov*, Moscow-Leningrad, 1936.

—— *Ocherki po istorii russkoy literatury i obshchestvennoy mysli XVIII veka*, Leningrad, 1938.

BIBLIOGRAPHY

——— and Orlov, V., 'Podpol'naya poeziya 1778–1800', *Literaturnoye nasledstvo*, Nos 9–10, 1933.

Gulitsky, K.G., *Koliivshchina*, Kiev, 1947.

Guthrie, Maria, *A Tour performed in the years 1795–6 through the Taurida or Crimea*, London, 1802.

Halm, H., *Grundung und erstes Jahrzehnt von Festung und Stadt Cherson, 1778–1788*, Wiesbaden, 1961.

Hamilton, G.H., *The Art and Architecture of Russia*. Pelican History of Art, ed. N. Pevsner, London, 1954.

Hans, N., 'Dumaresq, Brown and Some Early Educational Projects of Catherine II', *SEER*, XL, No. 94, December 1961, pp. 229–35.

——— 'François Pierre Pictet, Secretary to Catherine II', *SEER*, XXVI, No. 87, June 1958, pp. 481–91.

Hassell, J., 'The Implementation of the Russian Table of Ranks during the Eighteenth Century', *Slavic Review*, XXIX, No. 2, June 1970, pp. 283–99.

Haumont, E., *La culture française en Russie*, Paris, 1910.

Haupt, G., 'La Russie et les principautés danubiennes en 1790 – Le Prince Potemkin Tavricheskiy et le *Courier de Moldavie*', *CMRS*, VII, No. 1, January–March 1966, pp. 58–62.

Heier, E., *L.H. Nicolay (1737–1820) and his Contemporaries*, Martinus Nijhoff, The Hague, 1963.

Herrmann, E., *Diplomatische Correspondenz aus der Revolutionszeit, 1791–97*, Gotha, 1867.

——— *Geschichte des russichen Staates*, 7 vols, Gotha, 1860.

Hertzberg, Comte de, *Recueil de déductions, manifestes etc. redigés et publiés par le comte de Hertzberg*, 2 vols : *1756–78* and *1778–9*, Berlin, 1789.

Home, R.W., 'Science as a Career in 18th Century Russia : the Case of F.U.T. Aepinus', *SEER*, LI, No. 122, January 1973, pp. 75–94.

Horn, D.B., *British Public Opinion and the First Partition of Poland*, Oliver and Boyd, Edinburgh and London, 1945.

Hösch, E., 'Das sogenannte "griechische Projekt" Katharinas II', *JGOE*, XII, 1964, pp. 168–206.

Howard, J., *The State of the Prisons in England and Wales with preliminary Observations and an Account of some foreign prisons and hospitals* 4th edn, London, 1792.

Ignatovich, I.I., *Pomeshchishchiye krest'yane nakanune osvobozhdeniya*, Leningrad, 1925.

Ikonnikov, V.S., 'Arseniy Matseyevich, istoriko-biograficheskiy ocherk', *RS*, 1879, No. 24, pp. 731–53 ; 25, pp. 1–34, 577–608 ; 26, pp. 1–34, 177–98.

Indova, E.I., *Dvortsovoye khozyaystvo v Rossii – pervaya polovina XVIII veka*, Moscow, 1964.

——— 'K voprosu o dvoryanskoy sobstvennosti v Rossii v pozdniy feodal'nyy period' in *Dvoryanstvo i krepostnoy stroy*, q.v., pp. 272–93.

——— 'Rol' dvortsovoy derevni pervoy poloviny XVIII veka v formirovaniye russkogo kupechestva', *IZ*, 68, 1961, pp. 189–210.

——— and Preobrazhensky, A.A., Tikhonov, Yu. A., 'Narodnyye dvizheniya v Rossii XVII–XVIII vv.' in *Absolyutizm v Rbssii*, q.v., pp. 50–91.

Istoriya Pravitel'stvuyushchego Senata za dvesti let, 1711–1911, 5 vols, St Petersburg, 1911, Vol. 2, by N.D. Chechulin.

Istoricheskaya zapiska Ryazanskoy muzhskoy gimnazii, Ryazan', 1904.

Jacobs, E.M., 'Soviet Local Elections – What they are and What they are not', *Soviet Studies*, XXII, July 1970, No. 1, pp. 61ff.

Jacobsohn, L., *Russland und Frankreich in den ersten Regierungsjahren der Kaiserin Katharina II, 1762—1772*, Berlin and Koenigsberg, 1929.

Jay Oliva, L., *Misalliance. A Study of French Policy in Russia during the Seven Years' War*, New York University Press, 1974.

Jones, Gareth W., 'Novikov's Naturalized Spectator' in J.G. Garrard (ed.), *The Eighteenth Century in Russia*, q.v.

BIBLIOGRAPHY

—— 'The Closure of Novikov's *Truten'* ', *SEER*, L, No. 118, January 1972, pp. 107–11.

—— 'The Morning Light Charity Schools 1777–80', *SEER*, LVI, No. 1, January 1978, pp. 47–67.

—— 'The Polemics of the 1769 Journals : A Reappraisal', forthcoming.

Jones, R.E., 'Catherine II and the Provincial Reform of 1775 : A Question of Motivation', *CSS*, IV, No. 3, Fall 1970, pp. 497–512.

—— *The Emancipation of the Russian Nobility, 1762–85*, Princeton University Press, 1973.

—— 'Urban Planning and the Development of Provincial Towns in Russia, 1762–1796' in J.G. Garrard (ed.), *The Eighteenth Century in Russia*, q.v.

Kabuzan, V.M., *Izmeneniya v razmeshchenii naseleniya Rossii v XVIII – pervoy polovine XIX v.*, Moscow, 1971.

—— *Narodonaseleniye Rossii v XVIII veke – pervoy polovine XIX v.*, Moscow, 1963.

—— and Troitsky, S.M., 'Izmeneniya v chislennosti, udel'nom vese i razmeshcheniye dvoryanstva v Rossii, 1782–1858 gg.', *Istoriya SSSR*, 1971, No. 4, pp. 153–68.

Kahan, A., 'Continuity in Economic Activity and Policy during the Post-Petrine Period in Russia', *Journal of Economic History*, XXV, 1965, pp. 61–85.

—— 'The Costs of Westernization in Russia : the Gentry and the Economy in XVIIIth Century Russia', *Slavic Review*, XXV, No. 1, March 1966, pp. 42ff.

Kaplan, H., *The First Partition of Poland*, Columbia University Press, New York, 1962.

—— *Russia and the Outbreak of the Seven Years War*, University of California Press, Berkeley and Los Angeles, 1968.

Karasov, A.A., 'Ataman Yefremov', *Istoricheskiy Vestnik*, Vol. 9, 1902, pp. 876ff.

Karnovich, E.P., *Zamechatel'nyye bogatstva chastnykh lits v Rossii*, St Petersburg, 1885.

Karpenko, Z.G., *Gornaya i metallurgicheskaya promyshlennost' zapadnoy Sibiri v 1700–1860kh godakh*, Novosibirsk, 1963.

Kartashov, A., *Ocherki istorii russkoy tserkvi*, 2 vols, Paris, 1959.

Khrapovitsky, A.V., *Dnevnik, 1782–1793*, St Petersburg, 1874.

Kirchner, W., 'Relations économiques entre la France et la Russie au XVIIIe siècle', *Revue d'histoire économique et sociale*, XXXIX, No. 2, 1961, pp. 158–97.

Kizewetter, A.A., *Gorodovoye Polozheniye Yekateriny II 1785 g. Opyt istoricheskogo komentarya*, Moscow, 1909.

—— *Istoricheskiye Ocherki*, Moscow, 1912.

—— *Istoricheskiye Otkliki*, Moscow, 1915.

—— *Istoricheskiye siluety*, Berlin, 1931.

—— *Posadskaya obshchina v Rossii v XVIII stoletii*, Moscow, 1903.

Klier, J.D., 'The Ambiguous Legal Status of Russian Jewry in the Reign of Catherine II' *Slavic Review*, 35, No. 3, 1976, pp. 804–17.

Klochkov, M.V., 'Nakaz imperatritsy Yekateriny II v sudebnoy praktike', *Sbornik statey v chesti M.K. Lyubavskogo*, Petrograd, 1917.

—— *Ocherki pravitel'stvennoy deyatel'nosti vremeni imperatora Pavla I*, Petrograd, 1916.

Klokman, Yu. R., *Fel'dmarshal Rumyantsev v period russko-turetskoy voyny 1768–1774*, Moscow, 1951.

—— 'Gorod v zakonodatel'stve russkogo absolyutizma' in *Absolyutizm v Rossii*, ed. N.M. Druzhinin, q.v.

—— 'Goroda Bel'gorodskoy cherty i gubernskoy reformy 1775 g.', *Voprosy sotsial'no-ekonomicheskoy istorii i istochnikovedeniya, Sbornik statey*, Moscow, 1961.

—— *Ocherki sotsial'no-ekonomicheskoy istorii gorodov severozapadnoy Rossii v seredine XVIII v.*, Moscow, 1960.

—— *Sotsial'no-ekonomicheskaya istoriya russkogo goroda. Vtoraya polovina XVIII veka*, Moscow, 1967.

Knabe, B., *Die Struktur der russischen Posadgemeinden und der Katalog der Beschwerden und Forderungen der Kaufmannschaft, 1762–1767, FOG*, 1975.

BIBLIOGRAPHY

Knorring, N.N., 'Yekaterininskaya zakonodatel'naya kommissiya 1767 goda v osveshcheniye inostrannykh residentov pri russkom dvore', *Sbornik statey posvyashchennykh Pavlu Nikolayevichu Milyukovu*, Prague, 1929, pp. 327–50.

Kobeko, D.I., *Tsesarevich Pavel Petrovich, 1754–1796*, St Petersburg, 1883.

―――― 'Uchenik Vol'tera graf A.P. Shuvalov, 1744–1789', *RA*, 1881, No. 3, pp. 241–90.

Kogan, E.S., *Ocherki istorii krepostnogo prava po materialam votchin Kurakinykh vtoroy poloviny XVIII veka*, Moscow, 1960.

―――― 'Volneniya krest'yan Penzenskoy votchiny A.V. Kurakina vo vremya Pugacheva', *IZ*, No. 37, 1951, pp. 104–24.

Kogan, Yu. Ya., *Prosvetitel' XVIII veka, Ya. P. Kozel'sky*, Moscow, 1958.

Kohut, Z., *The Abolition of Ukrainian Autonomy 1763–86. A Case Study in the Integration of a non-Russian Area into the Empire*, unpublished Ph.D. thesis of the University of Pennsylvania, 1975.

Kokorev, A.V., *Khrestomatiya po russkoy literatury XVIII veka*, Moscow, 1965.

Konopczynski, W., 'England and the First Partition of Poland', *Journal of Central European Affairs*, I, 1948, pp. 1–23.

Korff, Baron A., *Dvoryanstvo i ego soslovnoye upravleniye za stoletiye 1762–1855 godov*, St Petersburg, 1906.

Korkunov, N.M., *Dva proekta preobrazovaniya Senata vtoroy poloviny tsarstvovaniya Yekateriny II (1788 i 1794 godov)*, St Petersburg, 1899.

―――― *Russkoye gosudarstvennoye pravo*, 2 vols, St Petersburg, 1899.

Korsakov, A.N., 'Stepan Ivanovich Sheshkovskiy, 1727–94, Biograficheskiy ocherk', *Istoricheskiy Vestnik*, Vol. 22, 1885, pp. 656–87.

Korsakov, D.A., *Sbornik materialov po istorii kazanskogo kraya v XVIII veke*, Kazan', 1908.

Korsanov, A.I., 'Petr Alekseyev, Protoerey Moskovskogo Arkhangel'skogo sobora, 1727–1801', *RA*, 1880, No. 2, pp. 153ff.

Kostomarov, N., *Sobraniye Sochineniy, Poslednyye gody rechi pospolity*, St Petersburg, 1863–8.

Krummel, W., 'Nikita Ivanovič Panins aussenpolitische Tätigkeit 1747–1758', *JGOE*, 5, Nos 1/2, Breslau 1940, pp. 76–141.

Kudryashev, P., 'Otnosheniye naseleniya k vyboram v Yekaterininskuyu kommissiyu', *Vestnik Yevropy*, November 1909, pp. 79ff ; December 1909, pp. 531ff.

Kulisher, I.M., *Ocherki po istorii russkoy torgovli*, St Petersburg, 1923.

Kulomzin, A., *Gosudarstvennyye dokhody i raskhody v tsarstvovaniye Yekateriny II, SIRIO*, 5, 6.

―――― *Finansovyye dokumenty tsarstvovaniya imperatritsy Yekateriny II, SIRIO*, 28, 45.

―――― 'Pervyy pristup v tsarstvovaniye Yekateriny II k sostavleniyu vysochayshey gramoty dvoryanstvu rossiyskomu', *Materialy dlya istorii russkogo dvoryanstva*, ed. N. Kalashov, St Petersburg, 1885, vyp. II.

Kurmacheva, M.D., 'Krepostnaya intelligentsiya v Rossii XVIII veka', *VI*, 1, 1979, pp. 82–94.

―――― 'Problemy obrazovaniya v ulozhennoy kommissii 1767 g.' in *Dvoryanstvo i krepostnoy stroy*, q.v. pp. 240–64.

Lang, D.M., *A Modern History of Georgia*, Weidenfeld and Nicolson, London, 1962.

―――― *The First Russian Radical*, George Allen and Unwin, London, 1959.

Lappo-Danilevsky, A.S., 'Die russische Handelskommission von 1763–96', in Otto Hötsch (ed.), *Beiträge sur russichen Geschichte*, Berlin, 1907.

―――― *I.I. Betskoy i ego sistema vospitaniya*, St Petersburg, 1904.

―――― 'Sobraniye i svod zakonov imperii rossiyskoy sostavlennyye v tsarstvovaniye Yekateriny II', in *ZhMNP*, No. 309, January 1897, pp. 1–59 ; No. 310, pp. 132–68 ; No. 312, pp. 60–80 ; No. 314, pp. 365–90.

―――― *L'idée de l'état et son évolution en Russie au XVIIIe siècle* in P. Vinogradoff (ed.), *Essays in Legal History*, Oxford, 1913.

―――― *The Serf Question in an Age of Enlightenment*', in *Catherine the Great, A Profile*, ed. M. Raeff, q.v.

BIBLIOGRAPHY

Larivière, C. de, *La France et la Russie au XVIIIe siècle*, Paris, 1909.

Latkin, V.N., *Zakonodatel'nyye kommissii v Rossii v XVIII st.*, St Petersburg, 1887.

Lavrovsky, N., *O pedagogicheskom znachenii sochineniy Yekateriny velikoy*, Khar'kov, 1856.

Lebedev, A., 'Evgeniy Bulgaris, arkhiepiskop slavenskiy i khersonskiy', *Drevnaya i novaya Rossiya*, 1876, No. 31, pp. 209–23.

Lebedev, P.S., *Grafy Nikita i Pyotr Paniny*, St Petersburg, 1863.

Ledieu, P., 'Une oeuvre inédite de Diderot,' *Revue d'histoire économique et sociale*, Nos 3–4, Paris, 1920, pp. 263ff.

LeDonne, J.P., 'Appointments to the Russian Senate', *CMRS*, XVI, No. 1, January–March 1975, pp. 27–56.

————— 'Catherine's Governors and Governors General, 1763–96', *CMRS*, XX, No. 1, January–March 1979, pp. 15ff.

————— 'The Judicial Reform of 1775 in Central Russia', *JGOE*, Vol. 21, 1973, No. 1, pp. 29–45.

————— 'Indirect Taxes in Catherine's Russia, II. The Liquor Monopoly in Catherine's Russia', *JGOE* Vol. 24, 1976, No. 2, pp. 173–207.

————— 'Indirect Taxes in Catherine's Russia, I. The Salt Code of 1781', *JGOE*, Vol. 23, 1975, pp. 161–91.

————— 'The Provincial and Local Police under Catherine the Great, 1775–1796', *CSS*, IV, No. 3, Fall 1970, pp. 513–28.

Lehtonen, U.L., *Die Polnischen Provinzen Russlands unter Katharina in den Jahren 1772–1782*, Berlin, 1907.

Lelewel, J., *Histoire de Pologne*, Paris-Lille, 1844.

LeMaire, J.B.C., Mémoire inédit composé par ordre de G. de Sartine, sur la demande de Marie Thérèse', *Mémoires de la Société de l'histoire de Paris et de L'Ile de France*, ed. A. Gazier, V, 1878, Paris, 1879, pp. 1–131.

Lemercier Quelquejay, C., 'Les Missions Orthodoxes en Pays Musulmans de Moyenne et Basse Volga, 1552–1865', *CMRS*, VIII, No. 3, July–September 1967, pp. 369–403.

Lensen, G.A., *The Russian Push towards Japan, 1697–1875*, Princeton University Press, 1959.

Levin, Yu. D., 'Angliyskaya prosvetitel'skaya zhurnalistika v russkoy literature XVIII veka', in *Epokha prosveshcheniya. Iz istorii mezhdunarodnykh svyazey russkoy literatury*, Leningrad, 1967.

Levitats, I., *The Jewish Community in Russia, 1722–1844*, Studies in history, economics and public law of Columbia University. Octagon Books, New York, 1970.

Ligne, Prince Charles Joseph Emanuel de, *Lettres et penséees du Maréchal Prince de Ligne*, ed. by Baronne de Stael Holstein, 3 vols. London, 1809.

————— *Mémoires et mélanges historiques et littéraires*, 5 vols., Paris, 1827.

Lipinsky, M.A., 'Novvyye dannyye dlya istorii Yekaterininskoy kommissii o sochinenii proekta novogo ulozheniya', *ZHMNP*, 1887, June, pp. 225–93.

Liske, X., 'Beiträge zur Geschichte der Kaniower Zusammenkunft (1787) und ihr Vorlaüfer', *Russiche Revue*, IV, St Petersburg, 1874, pp. 481–508.

————— 'Zur Polnischen Politik Katharina II, 1791', *HZ*, XXX, 1873, pp. 281ff.

Livanova, T., *Russkaya muzykal'naya kul'tura XVIII veka v ee svyazakh s literatury, teatrom i bytom*. 2 vols, Moscow, 1953.

Lodyzhensky, K., *Istoriya russkogo tamozhennogo tarifa*, St Petersburg, 1886.

Łojek, J., 'Catherine II's Armed Intervention in Poland : Origins of the Political Decisions at the Russian Court in 1791 and 1792', *CSS*, IV, No. 3, Fall 1970, pp. 570–93.

————— 'The International Crisis of 1791: Poland between the Triple Alliance and Russia', *East Central Europe*, II, 1, 1975, pp. 1–63.

————— *Upadok konstitucji 3 Maja*, Wrocław, 1976.

Longinov, M.N., *Novikov i Moskovskiye Martynisty, Moscow, 1867.*

Longmire, R.A., *Princess Dashkova and the Intellectual Life of Eighteenth Century Russia*, unpublished M.A. Dissertation, University of London, 1955.

BIBLIOGRAPHY

Longworth, P., *The Art of Victory. The Life and Achievements of Generalissimo Suvorov, 1729–1800*, Constable, London, 1965.

Loone, L.A., 'Krest'yanskiy vopros v obshchesvtvennoy mysli Pribaltiki' in *Materialy po istorii sel'skogo khozyaystva*, v, 1959, pp. 207–23.

Lord, R.H., *The Second Partition of Poland*, Cambridge, Mass., 1915.

—— 'The Third Partition of Poland', *SEER*, III, No. 9, March 1925, pp. 483–98.

Lortholary, A., *Le mirage russe en France au XVIIIe siècle*, Paris, 1951.

Lubimenko, I., 'Un académicien russe à Paris d'áprès ses lettres inédites', *Revue d'histoire moderne*, 10, Nov./Dec. 1935, pp. 415–47.

Lutosłanski, K., *Recueil des actes diplomatiques, traités et documents concernant la Pologne*, I, Lausanne-Paris, 1918.

Lyashchenko, P. I., *History of the National Economy of Russia to the 1917 Revolution*, New York, 1949.

MacArthur, G.H., 'Catherine II and the Masonic Circle of N.I. Novikov', in *CSS*, IV, No. 3, Fall, 1970, pp. 529–46.

MacConnell, A., *A Russian Philosophe, Alexander Radishchev, 1749–1802*, The Hague, 1964.

—— 'Helvetius's Russian Pupils', *Journal of the History of Ideas*, June–September 1963, pp. 373–86.

—— 'The Autocrat and the Open Critic', *Journal of Modern History*, XXXVI, No. 1, March 1964, pp. 14–27.

Madariaga, Isabel de, *Britain, Russia and the Armed Neutrality of 1780*, Yale University Press and Hollis and Carter, London, 1963.

—— 'Catherine II and the Serfs : A Reconsideration of some Problems', *SEER*, LII, No. 126, January 1974, pp. 34–62.

—— 'The Foundation of the Russian Educational System by Catherine II', *SEER*, LVII, No. 3, July 1979, pp. 369–95.

—— 'The Secret Austro-Russian Treaty of 1781', *SEER*, XXXVIII, No. 90, pp. 114–45.

—— 'The Use of British Secret Funds at St Petersburg, 1777–1782', *SEER*, XXXII, No. 79, 1954, pp. 464–74.

Makogonenko, G., *Denis Fonvizin. Tvorcheskiy put'*, Moscow, 1961.

—— *Izbrannyye sochineniya N.I. Novikova*, Moscow-Leningrad, 1951.

—— *Nikolay Novikov i russkoye prosveshcheniye XVIII veka*, Moscow-Leningrad, 1951.

Maksimovich, G.A., *Deyatel'nost' Rumyantseva Zadunayskogo po upravleniyu Malorossii*, Nezhin, 1913.

Malmesbury, James Harris, First Earl of, *Diaries and Correspondence*, 4 vols, London, 1844.

Markova, O.P., 'O neytral'noy sisteme i franko-russkikh otnosheniyakh (vtoraya polovina XVIII v.)', *Istoriya SSSR*, No. 6, 1970, pp. 42–55.

—— 'O proiskhozhdenii tak nazyvayemogo grecheskogo proekta (80e gody XVIII v.)', *Istoriya SSSR*, No. 4, 1958, pp. 52–78.

Markovich, Ya., *Dnevnyye zapiski malorossiyskogo podskarbiya general'nogo Yakova Markovicha*, 2 vols, Moscow, 1859.

Marsden, Ch., *Palmyra of the North*, Faber and Faber, London, 1943.

Martens, G.F. de, *Recueil de traités*, 2nd edn, Göttingen, 1817.

—— *Supplément au Receuil des principaux traités conclus par les puissances d'Europe*, Göttingen, 1807.

Martens, F. de, *Recueil des traités et conventions conclus par la Russie avec les puissances etrangères*, 15 vols, St Petersburg, 1874–1909.

Martynov, I.F., 'Kniga v russkoy provintsii 1760–1790kh gg. Zarozhdeniye provintsial'noy knizhnoy torgovli', in Sidorov, A.A. and Luppov, S.P., q.v., pp. 109–25.

—— 'Notes on V.P. Petrov and His Stay in England (New Materials)', *Study Group on Eighteenth Century Russia, Newsletter* No. 7, 1979.

BIBLIOGRAPHY

Matl', I., 'F. Ya. Yankovich i avstro-serbsko-russkiye svyazi v istorii narodnogo obrazovaniya v Rossii', *XVIII vek*, No. 10, ed. I.Z. Serman, ANSSR, 1975, pp. 76–81.

Mavrodin, V.V., *Krest'yanskaya voyna v Rossii*, 3 vols, Leningrad, 1961, 1966, 1970.

Maykov, P.M., *Ivan Ivanovich Betskoy. Opyt ego biografii*, St Petersburg, 1904.

Metcalf, M.F., *Russia, England, and Swedish Party Politics 1762–1766*, Almqvist and Wiksell International, Stockholm, and Rowman and Littlefield, Totowa, New Jersey, 1977.

Miller, A., *Essai sur l'histoire des institutions agraires de la Russie centrale du XVI au XVIII siècles*, Paris, 1926.

Miller, D., *Ocherki iz istorii yuridicheskogo byta staroy Malorossii. Prevrashcheniye kozatskoy starshiny v dvoryanstvo*, Kiev, 1897.

Milov, L.V., 'O tak nazyvayemykh agrarnykh gorodakh Rossii *XVIII* veka', *VI*, No. 6, June 1968, pp. 54–64.

Moiseyeva, G.N., 'Dopol'nitel'nyye dannyye k obstoyatel'stvam presledovaniya N.I. Novikova', in *XVIII vek*, No. 11, ANSSR, 1976, pp. 149–52.

Montesquieu, Charles Louis de Secondat, Baron de, *De l'Esprit des lois*, ed. Garnier, 2 vols, Paris, 1962.

Mooser, R.-Aloys, *Annales de la musique et des musiciens en Russie au XVIIIe siècle*, 3 vols, Geneva, 1948–51.

—— *Operas, intermezzos, ballets, cantates, oratorios joués en Russie durant le XVIIIe siècle, Essai d'un repertoire alphabétique et chronologique*, Geneva, 1945.

—— *L'opéra comique français en Russie au XVIIIe siècle*, Geneva/Monaco, 1954.

Moroshkin, M., *Iezuity v Rossii s tsarstvovaniya Yekateriny II i do nashego vremeni*, 2 parts, St Petersburg, 1867–70.

Morrison, Kerry, 'Catherine II's Legislative Commission: An Administrative Interpretation', *CSS*, IV, No. 3, Fall 1970, pp. 464–84.

Myakotin, V.A., *Iz istorii russkogo obshchestva. Etyudi i ocherki*, St Petersburg, 1902.

—— *Ocherki sotsial'noy istorii Ukrainy v XVII–XVIII vv.* tom 1. vyp. II, Prague, 1926.

—— 'Prikrepleniye krest'yanstva levoberezhnoy Ukrainy v XVII—XVIII vv.', *Godishnik na Sofiiskiya Universitet*, Sofia, 1932.

Nedosekin, V.I., 'O diskussii po krest'yanskomu voprosu v Rossii nakanune vosstaniya Pugacheva', *Izvestiya Voronezhskogo gosudarstvennogo pedagogicheskogo instituta*, vol. 63, 1967, pp. 326–46.

Neuschäffer, H., *Katharina II und die Baltischen Provinzen. Beiträge zur Baltischen Geschichte*, Hannover Döhren, n.d. (1975).

Nicholas Mikhailovich, Grand Duke, *Russkiye portrety XVIII i XIX stoletii*, St Petersburg, 1905.

Niemcewicz, Julian Ursin, *Notes sur ma captivité à St Petersburg en 1794, 1795, et 1796*, Paris, 1843.

Nolde, B., *La Formation de l'Empire russe. Etudes, Notes et Documents*, Paris, 1953.

Oakley, S., 'Gustavus III's Plans for War with Denmark' in *Studies in Diplomatic History. Essays in Memory of D.B. Horn*, ed. R. Norton and M.S. Anderson, Longmans, London, 1970.

Oberkirch, Baronne H.L., *Mémoires de la baronne d'Oberkirch*, 2 vols, Paris, 1853.

Ocherki po istorii SSSR. XVIII vek. Vtoraya polovina, ed. A.A. Baranovich and B.B. Kafengauz, Moscow, 1956.

Ogarkov, V.V., *Vorontsovy – ikh zhizn' i obshchestvennaya deyatel'nost'*, St Petersburg, 1892.

Ohloblyn, O., 'Ukrainian Autonomists of the 1780s and 1790s and Count P.A. Rumyantsev Zadunaysky', *Annals of the Ukrainian Academy of Arts and Sciences*, Vol. VI, Nos 3–4, 1958, pp. 1313ff.

Okenfuss, M., 'Education and Empire : School Reform in Enlightened Russia', *JGOE*, 27, No. 1, 1979, pp. 41–68.

—— 'The Jesuit Origin of Petrine Education' in J.G. Garrard, ed. *The Eighteenth Century in Russia*, q.v., pp. 106–30.

BIBLIOGRAPHY

Oursel, P., *La Diplomatie française sous Louis XVI. Succession de Bavière et paix de Teschen*, Paris, 1921.

Ouvrard, G., *Lettres d'amour de Catherine II à Potemkin, Correspondance inédite*, Calmann Levy, Paris, 1934.

Ovchinnikov, R.V., 'Sledstviye i sud nad E.I. Pugacheva, *VI*, Nos 3, 4, 5, 7, 9, March–September, 1966.

Page Thaler, R., 'Catherine II's Reaction to Radishchev', *Etudes Slaves et est-européennes*, II, fasc. 3, Autumn, 1957, pp. 154–60.

Paparigopulo, S.V., 'O dvukh Ya. P. Kozel'skikh', *VI*, 1954, No. 8, pp. 109–11.

Papmehl, K., 'The Problem of Civil Liberties in the Records of the Great Commission', *SEER*, XLII, No. 99, 1964, pp. 274–91.

——— *Freedom of Expression in Eighteenth Century Russia*, Martinus Nijhoff, The Hague, 1971.

——— 'The Regimental School established in Siberia by Samuel Bentham', *Canadian Slavonic Papers*, XVIII, 1966.

Parkinson, John, *A Tour of Russia, Siberia, and the Crimea, 1792–1794*, ed. W. Collier, Frank Cass, London 1971.

Pavlenko, N.I., *Istoriya metallurgii v Rossii v XVIII veke*, Moscow, 1962.

——— 'Iz istorii sotsial'no ekonomicheskikh trebovaniy russkoy burzhuazii vo vtoroy polovine XVIII v', *IZ*, No. 59, 1957, pp. 328ff.

——— 'Naemnyy trud v metallurgicheskoy promyshlennosti Rossii vo vtoroy polovine XVIII', *VI*, 1958, No. 6, pp. 41–58.

Pavlova Sil'vanskaya, M.P., 'Sotsial'naya sushchnost' oblastnoy reformy Yekateriny II' in *Absolyutizm v Rossii*, q.v., pp. 460–91.

——— 'Sozdaniye v 1775 godu soslovnykh sudov dlya krest'yan', *Vestnik Moskovskogo Universiteta*, No. 3, 1963, pp. 69ff.

Pekarsky, P., 'Materialy dlya istorii zhurnal'noy i literaturnoy deyatel'nosti Yekateriny II', *Zapiski imperatorskoy akademii nauk*, Vol. 3, 1863, Prilozheniye, pp. 1–90.

——— *Zhizn' i literaturnaya perepiska Petra Ivanovicha Rychkova*, St Petersburg, 1867.

Peters, D., *Politische und gesellschaftliche Vorstellungen in den Aufstandsbewegung unter Pugacev, 1773–1775*, *FOG*, 17, 1973.

Petrov, A., *Voyna Rossii s Turtsiey i pol'skimi konfederatami*, 5 vols, St Petersburg, 1866–74.

——— *Vtoraya turetskaya voyna v tsarstvovaniye Yekateriny II, 1787–1791 gg.*, 2 vols, St Petersburg, 1880.

Petrova, V.A., 'Politicheskaya bor'ba vokrug senatskoy reformy 1763 goda', *Vestnik Leningradskogo Universiteta*, vyp. 2, No. 8, istoriya, yazyk, literatura, 1967, pp. 57ff.

Petrovich, M.B., 'Catherine II and a Fake Peter III in Montenegro', *Slavic Review*, XIV, No. 2, April 1955, pp. 169–94.

Petrushevsky, A., *Generalissimus knyaz' Suvorov*, St Petersburg, 1884.

Pierling, P., *La Russie et le Saint Siege*, 5 vols, Paris, 1912.

Pigarev, K.V., *Tvorchestvo Fonvizina*, Moscow, 1954.

Pingaud, L., *Les français en Russie et les russes en France*, Paris, 1886.

Pintner, W.M., 'The Social Characteristics of the Early Nineteenth Century Russian Bureaucracy', *Slavic Review*, XXIX, No. 3, September 1970, pp. 429–42.

Pipes, R., 'Catherine II and the Jews', *Soviet Jewish Affairs*, Vol. 5, No. 2, pp. 3–20.

——— *Russia under the Old Regime*, Weidenfeld and Nicolson, London, 1974.

Pokrovsky, S.A., *Vneshnyaya torgovlya i vneshnyaya torgovaya politika Rossii*, Moscow, 1947.

——— (ed.), *Yuridicheskiye proizvedeniya progressivnikh russkikh mysliteley*, Moscow, 1959.

Pokrovsky, V. (ed.), *Yekaterina II, ee zhizn' i sochineniya. Sbornik istoriko literaturnykh statey*, Moscow, 1905.

Polonska Vasylenko, N.D., 'Iz istorii yuzhno-Ukrainy v XVIII veke : zaseleniye novorossiyskogo guberniya (1764–1775)', *IZ*, No. 13, 1941, pp. 130ff.

BIBLIOGRAPHY

—— 'The Settlement of the Southern Ukraine 1750–1775', *Annals of the Ukrainian Academy of Arts and Sciences in the US*, Vols IV, V, No. 4(14)-1 (15), Summer-Fall, 1955.

Portal, R., 'Les Bashkirs et le gouvernement russe au XVIIIe siècle', *Revue des études slaves*, 22, 1946, Paris, pp. 82–104.

—— *L'Oural au XVIIIe siècle*, Paris, 1950.

—— 'Manufactures et classes sociales en Russie au XVIIIe siècle', *Revue historique*, 1949, CCI and CCII, pp. 1–23 and 161–85.

'Posobniki i storonniki Pugacheva. Ocherki i razskazy', *RS*, 1, 1876, pp. 476–508 ; 607–26 ; No. 17, 1876, pp. 53ff.

Prokof'yeva, L.S., 'O deystviyakh povstantsev Pravoberezh'ya v krest'yanskom voyne pod prevodi-tel'stvom E.I. Pugecheva', in *Voprosy voyennoy istorii Rossii XVIII i pervaya polovina XIX vekov*, Moscow, 1969, pp. 328–38.

Pronshteyn, A.P., *Zemlya Donskaya v XVIII veke*, Rostov, 1961.

Pushkin, A.S., 'Istoriya Pugacheva,' *Polnoye Sobraniye Sochineniya*, XII, 1949.

Pypin, A.N., *Russkoye masonstvo XVIII i pervaya chetvert' XIX v.*, Petrograd, 1916.

Radishchev, A.N., *Journey from St Petersburg to Moscow*, tr. by L. Wiener, ed. by R. Page Thaler, Cambridge, Mass., 1958.

Raeff, M. (ed.), *Catherine II a Profile*, Hill and Wang, New York, 1972.

—— *Plans for Political Reform in Imperial Russia, 1730–1905*, Russian Civilization Series, Prentice Hall, N.J., 1966.

—— 'Staatsdienst, Aussenpolitik, Ideologien. Die Rolle der Institutionen in der geistigen Ent-wicklung des russischen Adels im 18. Jahrhundert', *JGOE*, Vol. 7, No. 2, 1959, pp. 147–80.

—— 'The Domestic Policies of Peter III and his Overthrow', *AHR*, LXV, No. 5, June 1970, pp. 1289–310.

—— 'The Empress and the Vinerian Professor', *Oxford Slavonic Papers*, VII, 1974, pp. 18–40.

—— 'The Style of Russia's Imperial Policy and Prince G.A. Potemkin', in *Statesmen and State-craft of the Modern West : Essays in Honor of Dwight E. Lee and H. Donaldson Jordan*, ed. G.N. Grob, Barre Publishing Co, Barre, Mass., 1967, pp. 1–51.

—— 'The Well Ordered Police State and the Development of Modernity in Seventeenth and Eigh-teenth Century Europe', *AHR*, LXXX, No. 5, December 1975, pp. 1221ff.

Rahbek Schmidt, K., 'The Treaty between Great Britain and Russia 1776 : A Study in the Develop-ment of Count Panin's Northern System', *Scandoslavica*, I, 1954, pp. 115ff.

—— 'Wie ist Panins Plan zu einem Nordischen System entstanden ?', *Zeitschrift für Slawistik*, II, No. 3, Berlin, 1957, pp. 406–22.

Rambaud, A., *Recueil des Instructions données aux ambassadeurs de France*, 9 : Russie, 1749–1789, Paris, 1890.

Ranke, L. von, *Die deutschen Mächte und der Fürstenbund*, Leipzig, 1875.

Ransel, D., 'An Ambivalent Legacy : The Education of Grand Duke Paul', forthcoming.

—— 'Catherine's Instruction to the Commission on Laws', *SEER*, L, No. 118, January 1972, pp. 10–28.

—— 'Nikita Panin's Imperial Council Project and the Struggle of Hierarchy Groups at the Court of Catherine II', *CSS*, IV, No. 3, Fall 1970, pp. 443–63.

—— 'The Memoirs of Count Munnich', *Slavic Review*, XXX, No. 4, December 1971, pp. 843–52.

—— *The Politics of Catherinian Russia. The Panin Party*, Yale University Press, New Haven and London, 1975.

Rapoarte Consulare Ruse 1770–1796. Documente privind istoria Rominiei, Collectia Eudoxiu de Hurmuzaki, Serie nona, Institute of History of the Academy of the Rumanian People's Republic, I, 1962.

Reading, D.K., *The Anglo-Russian Commercial Treaty of 1734*, Yale Historical Publications, 1938.

Reddaway, W.F. (ed.), *Documents of Catherine the Great. The Correspondence with Voltaire and the Instruction of 1767 in the English text of 1768*, Cambridge University Press, 1931.

BIBLIOGRAPHY

—— 'Great Britain and Poland, 1762–72', *Cambridge Historical Journal*, IV, No. 3, 1934, pp. 221–62.

—— 'Macartney in Russia, 1765–67', *Cambridge Historical Journal*, III, No. 3, 1931, pp. 271ff.

Reimann, E., *Geschichte des Bairischen Erbofolgkrieges*, Leipzig, 1869.

Reychman, J., 'Le commerce polonais en mer noire au XVIIIe siècle par le port de Kherson', *CMRS*, VII, No. 2, April–June 1966, pp. 234–8.

Roberts, M., 'Great Britain and the Swedish Revolution 1772–3'. *The Historical Journal*, VII, No. 1, 1964, pp. 1–46.

—— 'Great Britain, Denmark and Russia, 1763–1770' in *Studies in Diplomatic History. Essays in Memory of David Bayne Horn*, ed. R. Hatton and M.S. Anderson, q.v.

—— *Macartney in Russia*, Supplement 7 to the *EHR*, London, 1974.

—— *Splendid Isolation, 1763–1780*, Reading, 1970.

Roider, K.A., 'Kaunitz, Joseph II, and the Turkish War', *SEER*, LIV, No. 4, October 1976, pp. 538–56.

Romanovich Slavatynsky, A.V., *Dvoryanstvo v Rossii ot nachala* XVIII *veka*, Kiev, 1912.

Rostopchin, F.V., 'Dnevnik', *Devyatnatsatyy vek*, II.

—— 'Poslednyy den' zhizni imperatritsy Yekateriny II', *ChIOIDR*, 1860, otdel V, pp. 155–66.

Rozhdestvensky, S.V., *Ocherki po istorii sistem narodnogo prosveshcheniya v Rossii v* XVIII–XIX *vv.*, St Petersburg, 1912.

Rozman, G., *Urban Networks in Russia, 1750–1800 and Pre-Modern Periodization*, Princeton University Press, 1976.

Rozner, I.G., *Kazachestvo v krest'yanskoy voyny 1773–1775 gg.*, L'vov, 1966.

—— *Yaik pered bur'yey*, Moscow, 1966.

—— 'Yaitskoye kazachestvo nakanune krest'yanskoy voyny 1773–5g.', *VI*, No 10, 1958, pp. 97–112.

Ruban, V.G., *Kratkaya letopis' Malyya Rossii s 1506 po 1776 god*, St Petersburg, 1777.

Rubinshtein, E.I., 'Knigopechataniye v russkoy provintsii XVIII v' in *400 let russkogo knigopechataniya, 1564–1964*, Moscow, 1964.

Rubinshtein, N.L., 'Krest'yanskoye dvizheniye v Rossii vo vtoroy polovine XVIII veka', *VI*, No. 11, 1956, pp. 35–51.

—— *Sel'skoye khozyaystvo Rossii vo vtoroy polovine XVIII v.*, Moscow, 1957.

—— 'Ulozhennaya kommissiya 1754–1766 i ee proekt novogo ulozheniya', *IZ*, 38, 1951, pp. 208–51.

—— 'Vneshnyaya torgovlya Rossii i russkoye kupechestvo vo vtoroy poloviny XVIII v.', *IZ*, 54, 1955, pp. 343–61.

Ryndzyunsky, P.G., *Gorodskoye grazhdanstvo doreformennoy Rossii*, Moscow, 1958.

Sacke, G., 'Adel und Bürgertum in der Gestzgebenden Kommission Katharinas von Russland', *JGOE*, III, 1938, pp. 408–17.

—— 'Adel und Bürgertum in der Regierungszeit Katharinas II von Russland', *Revue belge de philologie et d'histoire*, XVII, 1938, Nos. 3–4, pp. 815–52.

—— *Die Gesetzgebende Kommission Katharinas II. Ein Beitrag zur Geschichte des Absolutismus in Russland*, Breslau, 1940.

—— 'Zur Charakteristik der gesetzgebenden Kommission Katharinas II von Russland', *Archiv für Kulturgeschichte*, XXI, 2, 1931, pp. 161–91.

Safronov, M.M., 'Konstitutsionnyy proekt N.I. Panina – D.I. Fonvizina', *Vspomogatel'nyye istoricheskiye distsipliny*, vol. VI, Leningrad, 1974, pp. 261–80.

Salomon, R., *La Politique orientale de Vergennes*, 1780–84, Paris, 1935.

Samoylov, A.I., 'Zhizn' i deyaniya generala fel'dmarshala knyazya Grigoriya Aleksandrovicha Potemkina-Tavricheskogo', *RA*, 1867, pp. 575–606 ; 993–1027 ; 1203–62 ; 1537–57.

Samoylov, V.V., 'Vozniknoveniye Taynoy Ekspeditsiyi pri Senate', *VI*, 1948, No. 6, pp. 79–81.

Scharf, C., 'Staatsauffassung und Regierungsprogramm eines aufgeklärten Selbstherrschers. Die Instruction des Grossfürsten Paul von 1788' in Ernst Schulin (ed.), *Gedenkschrift Martin Göhring, Studien zur Europäischen Geschichte*, Wiesbaden, 1968, pp. 91–106.

Scherer, E., *Melchior Grimm. L'homme de lettres, le factotum, le diplomate*, Paris, 1887.

Schop Soler, Maria, *Die Spanisch-Russischen Beziehungen im 18. Jahrhundert*, Wiesbaden, 1971.

Schumpeter, E.B., *English Overseas Trade Statistics 1697–1808*, Oxford, 1960.

Scott, H.M., 'Britain, Poland and the Russian Alliance', *The Historical Journal*, XIX, 1, 1976, pp. 53–74.

―――― 'Frederick II, the Ottoman Empire and the Origins of the Russo-Prussian Alliance of April 1764', *European Studies Review*, No. 7, 1977, pp. 153–75.

Scott, James Brown, *The Armed Neutralities of 1780 and 1800*, Oxford University Press, London and New York, 1918.

Seaman, G., 'Folk-Song in Russian Opera of the Eighteenth Century', *SEER*, XLI, No. 96, pp. 144–57.

Ségur, Louis Philippe, Comte de, *Mémoires ou Souvenirs et Anecdotes*, 3 vols, 3rd edn, Paris, 1827.

Semennikov, V., 'Literaturnaya i knigopechatnaya deyatel'nost' v provintsii v kontse XVIII i nachale XIX vv.', *Russkiy Bibliofil.*, 1911, Bk. VI.

Semevsky, V.I., 'Krepostnyye krest'yane pri Yekaterine', *RS*, 17, 1876, pp. 579–618 ; 653–90.

―――― 'Krest'yane dvortsovogo vedomstva', *Vestnik Yevropy*, 1878, No. 5, pp. 44ff. No. 6, pp. 461ff.

―――― *'Krest'yane v tsarstvovaniye Yekateriny* II, 2 vols, St Petersburg, 1901.

―――― *Krest'yanskiy vopros v Rossii*, 2 vols, St Petersburg, 1888.

――――'Razdacha naselennykh imeniy pri Yekaterine', *Otechestvennyye zapiski*, XIII, St. Petersburg, 1877, pp. 204–77.

―――― 'Sel'skiy svyashchennik vo vtoroy poloviny XVIII veka'. *RS*, 19, 1877, pp. 501ff.

――――'Vopros o preobrazovaniya gosudarstvennogo stroya v Rossii v XVIII i pervoy chetverti XIX veka', *Byloye*, No. 1, January 1906, pp. 1–59 ; No. 2, February 1906, pp. 69–117.

Serbina, K.N., *Ocherki iz sotsial'no-ekonomicheskoy istorii russkogo goroda*, Moscow, 1951.

Sergeyevich, V., 'Otkuda neudachi yekaterininskoy zakonodatel' noy kommissii', *Vestnik Yevropy*, 1878, I, January, pp. 188–264.

Shchebalsky, P., *Politicheskaya sistema Petra* III, Moscow, 1870.

―――― 'Yekaterina pisatel'nitsa', *Zarya*, 1869, III, pp. 111ff.

―――― 'Vopros o Kurlyandii pri Petre III', *RA*, 1866, pp. 284–304.

Shchegolev, P.I., *Dekabristy*, Moscow-Leningrad, 1926.

Shchipanov, I. Ya. (ed.), *Iz istorii russkoy filosofiyi* XVII–XIX *vekov, Sbornik statey*, Moscow, 1952.

Shil'der, N.K., *Imperator Aleksandr Pervvy*, 4 vols, St Petersburg, 1897.

―――― *Imperator Pavel Pervyy*, St Petersburg, 1901.

Shtrange, M.M., *Russkoye obshchestvo i frantzuzskaya revolyutsiya*, Moscow, 1956.

―――― 'Istoriya odnogo podlozhnogo ukaza 1763 g.' in *Voprosy sotsial'no ekonomicheskoy istorii i istochnikovedeniya perioda feodalizma v Rossii, Sbornik statey k 70-letiyu A.A. Novosel' skogo*, ANSSR, 1961.

―――― *Demokraticheskaya intelligentsiya v Rossii*, Moscow, 1965.

Shul'ga, I.G., 'K voprosu o razvitii vserossiyskogo rynka v vtoroy polovine XVIII v., *VI*, 1958, No. 10, pp. 35–45.

Sidorov, A.A. and Luppov, S.P., *Kniga v Rossii do serediny* XIX *veka*, Leningrad, 1978.

Simmons, E.J., *English Literature and Culture in Russia, 1553–1840*, Cambridge, Mass., 1935

Sipovič, The Right Rev. C., 'The Diocese of Minsk, its Origin, Extent and Hierarchy', *Journal of Belorussian Studies*, Vol. II, No. 2, London, 1970, pp. 177ff.

Sivkov, K.V., 'Samozvanchestvo v Rossii v posledney treti XVIII veka', *IZ*, No. 31, 1950, pp. 88ff.

―――― 'Taynaya ekspeditsiya ee deyatel'nost' i dokumenty', *Uchenyye zapiski Moskovskogo gos. ped. instituta imeni V.I. Lenina*, Vol. 11, Moscow, 1946, pp. 96–110.

BIBLIOGRAPHY

—— 'Obshchestvennaya mysl' i obshchestvennyye dvizheniya v Rossii v kontse xviii veka', *VI*, 1946, Nos. 5–6, pp. 90–5.

—— 'Podpol'naya politicheskaya literatura v Rossii v posledney treti xviii veka', *IZ*, 1946, No. 19, pp. 63–101.

Smolitsch, I., *Geschichte der russischen Kirche, 1700–1917*, E.J. Brill, Leyden, 1964.

Snegirev, I.M., *Zhizn' Moskovskogo Mitropolita Platona*, Moscow, 1856.

Sobornoye Ulozheniye tsarya Alekseya Mikhaylovicha 1649 goda in *Pamyatniki russkogo prava*, ed. K.A. Sofronenko, Vol. vi, Moscow, 1957.

Soldatov, G.M., *Arseniy Matseyevich, mitropolit Rostovsky, 1706–1772*, St Paul, Minnesota, 1971.

Solov'yev, S.M., *Istoriya padeniya Pol'shi*, Moscow, 1863.

—— *Istoriya Rossii s drevneyshikh vremyon*, reprint ed., 15 vols, Moscow, 1959–66.

Soloveytchik, G., *Potemkin*, Thornton Butterworth, London, 1939.

Storch, H. von, *Annalen der Regierung Katharina der Zweyten, Kaiserin von Russland*, Leipzig, 1798.

—— *Tableau historique et statistique de l'Empire de Russie*, 2 vols, Paris, Basle, 1801.

Stribrny, W., *Die Russlandpolitik Friedrichs des Grossen, 1764–1786*, Würzburg, 1966.

Strube de Piermont, *Lettres russiennes*, n.p. 1760.

Svanström, R. and Palmstierna, C.F., *A Short History of Sweden*, Oxford, 1934.

Svatikov, S.G., *Rossiya i Don 1549–1917. Izsledovaniye po istorii gosudarstvennogo i administrativnogo prava i politicheskikh dvizheniy na Donu*, Belgrade, 1924.

Svetlov, L., 'A.N. Radishchev i politicheskiye protsessy kontsa xviii veka', in *Iz istorii russkoy filosofii xvii–xix vekov*, ed. I.Ya Shchipanov, pp. 38–64.

Svodnyy katalog russkoy knigi grazhdanskoy pechati xviii veka, 1725—1800, 5 vols, Moscow, 1966.

Sychev-Mikhaylov, M.V., *Iz istorii russkoy shkoly i pedagogiki xviii veka*, Moscow, 1960.

Taranovsky, F.V., 'Politicheskaya doktrina v nakaze Yekateriny ii', in *Sbornik statey po istorii russkogo prava posvyashchennyy prof. M.F. Vladimirskomu Budanovu*, Kiev, 1904, pp. 44–86.

Tarle, Ye. V., *Chesmenskiy boy i pervaya russkaya ekspeditsiya v Arkhipelag, 1769–1774*, Moscow, 1945.

Tkhorzhevsky, S.I., *Pugachevshchina v pomeshchichey Rossii*, Moscow, 1930.

Tolstoy, D.A., 'Akademicheskaya gimnaziya v xviii stoletiya', *Sbornik otdeleniya russkogo yazyka i slovesnosti imperatorskoy akademii nauk*, vol. 38, No. 1, St Petersburg, 1866, pp. 1–114.

—— 'Akademicheskiy universitet v xviii stoletiye', op. cit., Vol. 38, No. 6, 1886, pp. 1–67.

—— 'Gorodskiye uchilishcha v tsarstvovaniye Yekateriny ii', *Prilozheniye k LIV tomu zapisok imperatorskoy akademii nauk*, No. 1, St Petersburg, 1886, pp. 1–213.

—— *Rimskiy katolitsizm v Rossii. Istoricheskoye izsledovaniye*, 2 vols, St Petersburg, 1876.

—— 'Vzglyad na uchebnuyu chast' v Rossii v xviii stoletiya do 1782' in *Sbornik otdeleniya russkogo yazyka i slovesnosti imperatorskoy akademii nauk*, St Petersburg, 1886, Vol. 38, No. 4, pp. 1–100.

Torke, H.-J., 'Das russische Beamtentum in der erste Hälfte des 19. Jahrhunderts', *FOG*, 13, 1967, pp. 7–345.

Tourneux, M., *Diderot et Catherine* ii, Paris 1899.

Trachevsky, A., *Soyuz knyazey*, St Petersburg, 1877.

Treaties : *The Consolidated Treaty Series*, ed. Clive Parry, 51 vols, Oceana Publishing Inc., New York, 1969.

Trefoleyev, L., 'Aleksey Petrovich Mel'gunov, general gubernator Yekaterininskikh vremen', *RA*, 1885, pp. 931–78.

Troitsky, S.M., *Finansovaya politika russkogo absolyutizma*, Moscow, 1966.

—— 'Istoriografiya dvortsovykh perevorot v Rossii xviii v.', *VI*, 1966, No. 2, pp. 38–53.

—— 'K probleme konsolidatsii dvoryanstva v Rossii v xviii veke', in *Materialy po istorii sel'skogo khozyaystva i krest'yanstva SSSR, Sbornik* viii, pp. 121–51, Moscow, 1974.

BIBLIOGRAPHY

———— 'Obsuzhdeniye voprosa o krest' yanskoy torgovle v kommissii o kommertsii v seredine 60kh godov', in *Dvoryanstvo i krepostnoy stroy*, q.v.

———— *Russkiy absolyutizm i dvoryanstvo*, Moscow, 1974.

———— 'Sotsial'nyy sostav i chislennost' byurokratii Rossii v seredine XVIII v.', *IZ*, No. 89, 1972, pp. 295–353.

———— 'Zaemnyye knigi krepostnykh kontor kak istochnik po istorii krest'yan v Rossii v seredine XVIII veka' in *Arkheograficheskiy ezhegodnik za 1962*, Moscow, 1963, pp. 269ff.

Tugan Baranovsky, M.I., *Russkaya fabrika*, Moscow-Leningrad, 1934.

Uebersberger, H., *Russlands Orientpolitik in den letzten zwei Jahrhunderten*, Stuttgart, 1913.

Ulyanitsky, V.A., *Dardanelly, Bosfor i Chernoye More v 18 veka*, Moscow, 1883.

———— *Russkiye konsulstva za granitsey v XVIII*, 2 vols, Moscow, 1899.

Unzer, A., *Der Friede von Teschen*, Kiel, 1903.

Vasil'chikov, A.A., *Semeystvo Razumovskikh*, St Petersburg, 1880.

Venturi, F., 'Cesare Beccaria', *Dizionario Biografico degli Italiani*, Rome, 1965.

Veretennikov, V., *K istorii yekaterininskoy general-prokuratory*, Khar'kov, 1914.

Vernadsky, G.V., *Ocherk istorii prava russkogo gosudarstva XVIII–XIX vv.*, Prague, 1924.

———— *Russkoye masonstvo v tsarstvovaniye Yekateriny II*, Petrograd, 1917.

Vladimirsky Budanov, M., *Gosudarstvo i narodnoye obrazovaniye v Rossii XVIII veka*, Yaroslavl', 1874.

———— *Obzor istorii russkogo prava*, St Petersburg, 1900.

Volkov, S.I., *Krest'yane dvortsovykh vladeniy Podmoskov'ya v seredine XVIII*, Moscow, 1959.

Voronov, A.S., *Istoriko-statisticheskoye obozreniye uchebnykh zavedeniy S. Peterburgskogo ucheb-nogo okruga s 1715 po 1828 vklyuchitel'no*, St Petersburg, 1848.

Vosemnadtsatyy vek. Istoricheskiy sbornik izdavayemyy po bumagam famil'nogo arkhiva knyazem Fedorom Alekseyevichem Kurakinym, ed. V.N. Smoly'yaninov, 2 vols, Moscow, 1904–5.

Vsevolodsky Gerngross, V.N., *Russkiy teatr vtoroy poloviny XVIII veka*, Moscow, 1960.

Vyazemsky, P.A., *Zapisnyye knizhki, 1813–1848*, Moscow, 1963.

Waliszewski, K., *Le Roman d'une impératrice*, Paris, 1892.

Welsh, D.J., *Russian Comedy 1765–1823*, Mouton and Co, The Hague, 1966.

Wilson, A.M., *Diderot*, Oxford University Press, 1972.

Woltner, M., *Das Wolgadeutsche Bildungswesen und die russische Schulpolitik*, Teil I, Leipzig, 1937.

Woodham Smith, C., *Queen Victoria, her Life and Times, 1819–1861*, Cardinal, London, 1975.

Yakovtsevsky, V.N., *Kupecheskiy kapital v feodal'no krepostnoy Rossii*, Moscow, 1953.

Yaney, G.L., *The Systematization of Russian Government : Social Evolution in the Domestic Administration of Imperial Russia, 1711–1905*, University of Illinois Press, 1973.

Yaresh, L., 'The "Peasant Wars" in Soviet Historiography', *Slavic Review*, XVI, No. 3, 1957, pp. 241ff.

Yatsunsky, V.K., *Sotsial'no-ekonomicheskaya istoria Rossii XVIII–XIX vv. Izbrannyye trudy*, Moscow, 1973.

Yefremov, E., 'Ya. B. Knyazhnin, Vadim Novgorodskiy', *RS*, No. 3, 1871, pp. 722ff.

Yeroshkin, N.P., *Ocherki istorii gosudarstvennykh uchrezhdeniy dorevolyutsionnoy Rossii*, Moscow, 1960.

Yevreynov, N., *Istoriya telesnykh nakazaniy*, Moscow, 1900.

Zaborov, P.K., *Russkaya literatura i Vol'ter — XVIII pervaya tret' XIX veka*, Leningrad, 1978.

Zagorovsky, E.A., 'Organizatsiya upravleniya Novorossii pri Potemkine', *Zapiski Odesskogo obshchestva istorii i drevnostey*, XXXXI, pp. 52–82.

Zakalinskaya, E.P., *Votchinnoye khozyaystvo Mogilevskoy gubernii vo vtoroy polovine XVIII veka*, Mogilev, 1958.

Zaozerskaya, E.I., 'Le salariat dans les manufactures textiles russes au XVIIIe siècle', *CMRS*, II, Vol. 6, April-June 1965, pp. 189–222.

BIBLIOGRAPHY

Zapadov, V.A., 'K isstorii pravitel'stvennykh presledovaniy N.I. Novikova', xviii *vek,* No. 11, 1976, pp. 38ff.

Zatko, J.J., 'The Organization of the Catholic Church in Russia 1772–84', *SEER,* lxiii, No. 101, June 1965, pp. 303–13.

Zenkovsky, S.A., *Pan-Turkism and Islam in Russia,* Harvard University Press, 1960.

Zheludkov, V.F., 'Krest'yanskaya voyna pod prevoditel'stvom E.I. Pugacheva i podgotovka gubernskoy reformy 1775 goda', *Vestnik Leningradskogo Universiteta,* No. 8, seriya literatury, istorii, yazyka, 1963, No. 2, pp. 56–65.

——— 'Vvedeniye gubernskoy reformy 1775 goda' in Bernadsky, V.N., q.v.

Zhelvakov, N.I., *Khrestomatiya po istorii pedagogiki,* vi, pt. i, Moscow, 1938.

Zhurnal vysochayshego puteshestviya ee Velichestva v poludennyye strany Rossii v 1787 godu, University Press of N.I. Novikov, Moscow, 1787.

Zinkeisen, J.W., *Geschichte des Osmanischen Reiches in Europa,* Gotha, 1859, 7 vols.

[Zubov, P.A.] *Knyaz' Platon Aleksandrovich Zubov,* 1767–1822, *RS,* xvi, pp. 591ff ; xvii, pp. 39ff, 437ff, 691ff.

Zutis, Ya. Ya., *Ostseyskiy vopros v* xviii *veke,* Riga, 1946.

Index